Computer Structures:
Principles and Examples

Computer Structures: Principles and Examples

Daniel P. Siewiorek
Carnegie-Mellon University

C. Gordon Bell
Digital Equipment Corporation

Allen Newell
Carnegie-Mellon University

McGraw-Hill Book Company

New York□St. Louis□San Francisco□Auckland□Bogotá□Hamburg□
Johannesburg□London□Madrid□Mexico□Montreal□New Delhi□
Panama□Paris□São Paulo□Singapore□Sydney□Tokyo□Toronto

This book was set in Caledonia by Black Dot, Inc.
The editors were Charles E. Stewart and James E. Vastyan;
the production supervisor was Joe Campanella.
New drawings were done by Fine Line Illustrations, Inc.
Von Hoffmann Press, Inc., was printer and binder.

Library of Congress Cataloging in Publication Data

Main entry under title:

Computer structures.

   (McGraw-Hill computer science series)
   Bibliography: p.
   Includes index.
   1. Computer architecture—Addresses, essays, lectures.
I. Siewiorek, Daniel P. II. Bell,
C. Gordon. III. Newell, Allen.
QA76.9.Á73C65   621.3819′5   80-27926
ISBN 0-07-057302-6   AACR 1

Computer Structures: Principles and Examples

4 5 6 7 8 9 0 V H V H 8 9 8 7 6 5 4

See Acknowledgments on pages 915–920.
Copyrights included on this page by reference.

**To Brigham, Laura,
Nora, and Paul**

Contents in Brief

Contents[1]

---

[1]This is a "virtual" contents, which means that because many of the computers are relevant to more than one part and section, we have used *italic type* for chapter numbers and titles to indicate a nonsequential mapping for computers placed out of "physical" order. The reader might read (reference) the book according to the virtual order. See the preface for further discussion.

Part 3
COMPUTER CLASSES

Preface

When *Computer Structures: Readings and Examples* was originally published by Gordon Bell and Allen Newell in 1971, the concept of computer structures was just emerging. The book focused on the historical evolution of technology, instruction sets, and uniprocessors. Two new notations were introduced to provide more concise descriptions of instruction sets (ISP, for *instruction-set processor*) and uniprocessor structures (PMS, for *processor-memory-switch*).

In the last decade, the scene has changed dramatically. Technological advances have led to a virtual explosion in the number of computer types and installations. Minicomputers and calculators, still relatively new computer applications in 1971, are the basis of industries today. Entirely new types, such as microprocessors and maxicomputers with vector data-types, now command sizable markets of their own. Techniques such as microprogramming, networks, multiprocessors, and fault tolerance were infrequently applied in 1971; a decade later, these concepts are essential in almost all the new systems.

The 1971 edition of *Computer Structures* introduced the concept of a design space, with each computer structure representing a point in that space. This edition embraces and expands the computer space concept and reflects changes in several dimensions which have since either received common acceptance or been replaced by other dimensions with significantly more impact on the structure's performance.

The number of addresses per instruction is an example of a dimension where common acceptance has developed. Contemporary instruction sets are based on general-register organizations with multiple-byte or -word instructions. The variable-length instruction format enables the computer to assign the largest number of op codes and address bits into a 1-word instruction. Early instruction-set design often meant wasted memory if the instructions were too wide. Too short an instruction could require excess instructions to perform an otherwise simple task. A good instruction-set encoding can increase program density by over 50 percent. With the creation of a large number of instruction sets, designers of new instruction sets have been able to integrate the best features of their predecessors.

Networks are an example of where new dimensions are emerging. Variations in network performance due to instruction-set design are negligible compared to variations in network performance due to operating systems, network topology, network protocol, media bandwidth, etc.

This book emphasizes computer space dimensions with numerous and quantitative subdimensions. Each alternative value for a dimension represents a design alternative. These values and their interactions with other dimensions are illustrated by real machines.

All the machines discussed in this book have actually been constructed and evaluated. The papers, wherever possible, are written by the specific machine architects or people closely associated with the architectures. Several of the machines are presented in elaborate detail, enabling the reader to appreciate the design complexities encountered and design methodologies employed by the architects. Many of these papers have been written specifically for this book. In favoring depth over breadth, the book is not able to discuss all important architectures (nor even all major manufacturers). However, the architectures that are included were carefully selected to uniformly cover the major design principles of computer structures.

The proliferation of computer structures and the emergence of computer families have provided quantitative as well as descriptive data for the book. Wherever possible, data, models, and/or trends are derived from the actual computer structures.

Three notations help to summarize information about the computer structures: ISP, PMS, and Kiviat graphs. An updated version of the original ISP language—ISPS—has been used to formally describe a growing number of major computer architectures. A simulator has been utilized for debugging (e.g., running diagnostic programs written for the hardware implementations of the machines) and data collection (e.g., implementation-independent measures of benchmarks). ISPL, a predecessor of ISPS, was used in the Army-Navy Military Computer Family (MCF) project to evaluate alternative architectures.[1] Several research projects based on formal machine descriptions have also developed, including the generation of microcode, assemblers, diagnostics, and compilers. Since a complete ISPS description of a contemporary machine can be over 50 pages long, we have chosen to provide subsets of the full ISPS descriptions for all but the very simple architectures. These ISPS descriptions are complete except that only a subset of each machine's instruction set is described. All the ISPS descriptions that appear in this book have been compiled and simulated.

The PMS notation for describing the information flow rate of computer structures has been simplified and made more readable. System performance is provided by Kiviat graphs, which display six major system parameters.

It is hoped that this book will serve as an educational resource for three professional groups: the computer engineer, who de-

[1]"Military Computer Architectures: A Look at the Alternatives," special issue of *Computer*, vol. 10, no. 10, October 1977.

signs physical computer systems; the computer scientist, who is concerned primarily with the programming level and with various abstract views of information processing; and the electrical engineer, who sees computer systems as part of a larger technology.

This book presents design choices, structural variations, and systematic analysis, which can be especially useful for the computer engineer charged with designing a new computer system or subsystem. The student of computer engineering who approaches this book with a working knowledge of logic design should find it possible to realize many of the systems described at the next lower levels of logic structure.

For the computer scientist, the levels of computer structure discussed in this book offer significant insight into the physical devices that underlie computer science. Even if the computer scientist does not carry through the design in terms of the lower logic levels, it will still be possible to incorporate the upper levels of computer structure.

The electrical engineer need not study every example in this book. A sampling, plus the overview presented in the first three chapters, is appropriate to give insight into the elaborate growth accompanying the basic digital technology created within electrical engineering.

The book is divided into four parts:

1. Fundamentals
2. Regions of Computer Space
3. Computer Classes
4. Family Range, Compatibility, and Evolution

Part 1 provides an introduction to ISP, PMS, and Kiviat graph notation, sketches the dimensions of the computer space, and provides a discussion of several historically significant machines. Part 2 examines several of the computer space dimensions, contrasting the alternative values for each dimension. Examples of actual computer structures provide a comparative taxonomy of design choices.

Part 3 contains detailed descriptions of computer structures organized by size: monolithic microcomputer, microcomputer, minicomputer, and maxicomputer. Each class has a common set of applications and goals. On the basis of ISP, PMS, and Kiviat graph notations, the structures are compared and contrasted and trends are described.

Part 4 deals with computer families, which comprise several structures implementing a common design goal and frequently employing a common ISP. Extensive data are provided for the comparison of closely related systems, and several alternative analyses are presented, including a discussion of the impact on the system of individual design tradeoffs, such as those presented in Part 2.

This book has both a physical and a "virtual" table of contents. The physical order of the chapters presents the material in a logical progression. If covered in a sequential fashion, the material in this book would span three one-semester courses. Therefore, a "virtual" table of contents, relating chapters by topic, has been provided. The instructor or student can utilize the virtual table of contents to focus on particular subsets of the material and formulate logically independent courses.

This book can be used either as a primary text or as a reference text in a computer architecture course beyond the elementary level. It can also support digital-system design courses ranging from the register-transfer level through the system organization level. Each of the sections of Part 2 given in the virtual table of contents, suitably augmented by selected introductory material from Part 1, would be sufficient for a quarter-length course on individual topics (e.g., microprogramming, memory hierarchies, concurrency, multiple-processors, networks, fault tolerance, language-based computers, and personal computing). Each section also provides sufficient detail to assign programming and/or design projects based on the principles discussed. Semester-length courses can be developed by combining related sections (e.g., multiple-processors and networks, or language-based computers and personal computing systems). A subset of Part 3 on computer classes could form the basis of a course on instruction-set design and evolution. Part 4 provides source material for an advanced course on computer families, including evolution and computer family planning for range and/or compatibility. The family evaluation methodology presented in Part 4 could be extended to other computer families. The January 1978 special issue on computer architecture of the *Communications of the Association for Computing Machinery* is an excellent supplement to Part 4.

This book can be used in both the curriculum for undergraduate programs in computer science prepared by the ACM Committee on Curriculum in Computer Science (C³S) and the IEEE's Curriculum in Computer Science and Engineering (CSE). This book provides material for the hardware portions of the ACM/C³S courses as illustrated in Table 1. [Austing et al. 1979].

For the extensive IEEE/CSE curriculum, with its emphasis on hardware, this book can be used for all computer organization courses, as well as for actual design examples for the digital logic courses. Table 2 on page xvi illustrates how portions of this text support the various topics included in IEEE/CSE courses.

The authors of this book wish to acknowledge a deep debt of gratitude to our many colleagues in the computing profession. Without their contributions and assistance this book could not have been written. We are especially grateful to the authors of papers who shared their design insights with us and to those authors who took time from busy schedules to write chapters specifically for this book. Our thanks also to individuals in various organizations who kindly responded to our numerous requests for information. A special debt is owed Digital Press for providing extensive excerpts from *Computer Engineering: A DEC View of*

Table 1 ACM Committee on Curriculum in Computer Science

Level	Course		Specific topics covered by "Computer Structures"	Example chapters
Elementary level	CS-4	Introduction to Computer Organization	Basic logic design examples	Chap. 2; Chap. 8; Chap. 15
			Hardware implementation of instruction fetch, execute	Chap. 8
			Data flow and block diagram of simple processor	Chap. 8
			Microprogramming	Part 2, Sec. 1
			I/O, interrupts	Part 1, Sec. 2
Intermediate level	CS-6	Operating Systems and Computer Architecture I	I/O, interrupts, addressing, microprograming	Part 1, Sec. 2; Part 2, Sec. 1
			Stacks, displays, reentrant programs	Part 1, Sec. 2; Chap. 16; Chap. 17
			Memory management, paging, segmentation, virtual memory	Part 2, Sec. 2
			Process management	Part 2, Sec. 2
Advanced level	CS-10	Operating Systems and Computer Architecture II	I/O, interrupts, addressing	Part 1, Sec. 2
			Concurrent processes	Part 2, Sec. 2
			Protection	Part 2, Sec. 2
			Pipelining, parallelism	Part 2, Sec. 3
			Networks	Part 2, Sec. 5
			Distributed systems	Part 2, Sec. 4
Special topics		Telecommunications/Networks, Distributed Systems	Networks	Part 2, Sec. 5
			Distributed systems	Part 2, Sec. 4

Hardware Design, by C. G. Bell, J. C. Mudge, and J. E. McNamara.

We are deeply indebted to Gary Leive for his many hours of writing, compiling, simulating, debugging, and formatting the many ISPs in the book. Over 9,400 lines of ISP were produced, of which only about a third appear here. A similar debt is owed Vittal Kini, who assembled the PMS diagrams and checked them for consistency. Jin Kim and Michael Tsao spent many hours assembling the artwork that had to be photographed.

Comments from several reviewers were particularly helpful. Lloyd Dickman provided a comprehensive review of the manuscript. Robert Sproull and John Wakerly offered substantial comments, as did Robert Stanton of IBM on the S/360-S/370 material. A careful editing of Part 1 was done by Eleanor Dickman.

The patience and encouragement of colleagues and students alike—especially Angel Jordan and Joe Traub—were deeply appreciated.

In addition we would like to thank those we worked with at McGraw-Hill, particularly Richard Mickey, the copy editor, who worked long hours carefully preparing the manuscript for production. The patience and diligence of Mrs. Dorothy Josephson, who typed and retyped the many manuscript drafts and letters is worthy of special note. Finally, the support and understanding of our families and wives—Karon, Gwen, and Noel—were an essential ingredient in the completion of this book.

Daniel P. Siewiorek
C. Gordon Bell
Allen Newell

Reference

Austing et al. [1979].

Table 2 A Curriculum in Computer Science and Engineering†
IEEE Computer Society's Model Curriculum Subcommittee

Course	Topics covered by "Computer Structures"	Example chapters
Switching Theory and Digital Logic: DL-1 and DL-2	Programmable controllers; use of PLAs, ROMs	Part 3, Sec. 1
Microprocessor Systems: DL-3	Developments in LSI	Part 3, Secs. 1 and 2; Part 2, Sec. 1
	Microprocessor architecture	
	Common microprocessors:	
	Calculator chips, bit slices,	
	and monolithic microprocessors	
Introduction to Computer Organization: CO-1	Computer units	
	Microprogramming	Part 2, Sec. 1
	Memory hierarchy	Part 2, Sec. 2
	Input/output	Part 1, Sec. 2
	System structure	
	Single-processor	Part 3
	Multiprocessor	Part 2, Sec. 4
	Networks	Part 2, Sec. 5
	Evaluation	Chap. 5
	System examples	
	Intel 8080	Chap. 37
	PDP-8	Chap. 8
	PDP-11	Chap. 38
	IBM S/360 and S/370	Chaps. 40, 41, 51, 52
	CDC-6600	Chap. 43
	Illiac IV	Chap. 20
	Hardware desciption methodologies	
	ISP/PMS	Chaps. 3, 4
I/O and Memory Systems: CO-2	I/O structures	Part 1, Sec. 2
	Memory hierarchies	Part 2, Sec. 2
Computer Architecture: CO-3	Instruction sets	Part 1, Sec. 2
	Main-line computers	Part 3, Sec. 4
	Examples	
	ILLIAC IV	Chap. 20
	TI ASC	Chap. 45
	STARAN	Chap. 21
	Character machines	Part 2, Secs. 7, 8
	Stack	Part 1, Sec. 2
	Parallelism	Part 2, Sec. 3
	Protection	Part 2, Sec. 2
	Multiprocessors	Part 2, Sec. 4
	Networks	Part 2, Sec. 5
Microprogramming: CO-4		Part 2, Sec. 1
Distributed Processing and Networks: CO-5		Part 2, Secs. 4, 5

†"A Curriculum in Computer Science and Engineering Committee Report," IEEE, EH 0119-8, November 1976. Reported on in "Computer Science and Engineering Education," special supplement, *Computer*, vol. 10, no. 12, December 1977, pp. 70–123.

Part 1

Fundamentals

Section 1

Abstraction and Notation

Chapter 1

Computer Classes and Evolution

A computer is a complex system incorporating diverse technologies. Typically, electronic technology is used for computation, magnetic for long-term storage, and electromechanical for input/output. The evolution of computer structures usually correlates with that of the available technology. On occasion sometimes other technologies, such as magnetic core memory and Freon cooling of electronics (see Chap. 44), are developed specifically for use in computer systems. Computer engineers are also adept at applying existing technologies in new ways—for example, cathode-ray tubes as memories (e.g., Williams tubes, ca. 1947), character display terminals, and graphic display terminals; magnetic recording technology for tapes, disks, and drums; and vacuum tubes and transistors for processors.

During the 1960s and 1970s, integrated-circuit semiconductor technology entered a revolutionary phase. The density of individual integrated-circuit chips, measured by the number of logic devices per chip, doubled every 1 or 2 years. In 1972, a single-chip processor was introduced. Prior to that time, a successful computer, such as the first model of the PDP-8 family (the first mass-produced minicomputer), might enjoy a sales volume of 50,000 units over its 5-year life. Contemporary single-chip processors (called microprocessors[1]) may exceed that volume in only 10 days! Computers now come into contact with our everyday lives, in the form of hand calculators, electronic games, computer-controlled appliances, and the like.

Coupled with the vast increase in the numbers of computers is an appreciable increase in the number of computer types. Each type represents a set of design decisions that can be represented as a point in design space. The density of designs in the space allows us to observe commonalities, trends, and the consequence of various design decisions. Over the last three decades, the design of computer structures has evolved from an art to an engineering discipline. The purpose of this book is to discuss these topics through an exploration of the design principles used in contemporary computer structures.

Each system included in this book is a real system that has been implemented. The systems are described by taxonomies, illustrations of existing systems, and comments by the systems' architects. Systems are represented by three consistent sets of

notation: structural (PMS), performance (Kiviat graphs), and behavioral (ISP). Significant details are given so that the reader can understand how the system meets its design goals. Each system has been carefully selected to illustrate a point in the design space as well as to complement the other systems.

This study begins with a presentation of the concepts of computer classes and evolution. Understanding and applying these concepts, which appear frequently throughout the book, will enable the reader to organize the myriad details presented.

Computer Classes

The concept of a computer class attempts to integrate many computer-system details into an overall evaluation, grouping similarly evaluated systems together. Computer systems can be graphically classified according to different metrics, each of which incorporates several complex design details.

One metric of classification is *price*. Figure 1 plots the price (including processor, memory, and input/output) of the computer systems described in this book relative to year of introduction. Four classes have been identified: maxicomputers, minicomputers, microcomputers, and monolithic microcomputers. Each class spans roughly 1½ orders of magnitude in price. Initially, because of the high cost of technology, all systems were maxicomputers. As semiconductor technology increased and costs decreased, new classes of computer systems evolved. Minicomputers appeared around 1965, followed by microcomputers in 1972 and monolithic microcomputers in 1976.

In some cases, a computer system, such as the IBM System/360 or System/370, spans more than one class and actually represents a family of implementations with a wide range in price and performance. Each member of the family is capable of executing programs written for other family members. Thus, while the manufacturer develops software for one machine, the user can move to a compatible higher-performance system whenever it is required. The concept of computer families continues to grow in importance. (See Part 4 for a study of several types of computer families.)

A metric closely related to price is the *size* of the computer system. Maxicomputers typically occupy several large cabinets and require a room to house them. A minicomputer usually occupies one or two cabinets of 10 to 30 ft³ each. Microcomputers—consisting of microprocessor chips, a memory, and input/output interfaces—can be mounted on a single board the size of this book page. Finally, monolithic microcomputers have the entire system (processors, memory, and input/output) integrated into a single chip measuring 2 in × 0.6 in × 0.2 in.

Another general metric is *capacity and functionality*. Section 2 of Part 1 contends that the single most important structural parameter in comparing computer systems is the number of bytes

---

[1]Not to be confused with the term *microprogrammed processor*. In microprocessors *micro-* means physically small and is usually synonymous with a processor-on-a-chip (of silicon), whereas microprogramming is an implementation technique. Note that a microprocessor may or may not be microprogrammed. See Sec. 1 of Part 2 for a detailed discussion of microprogramming.

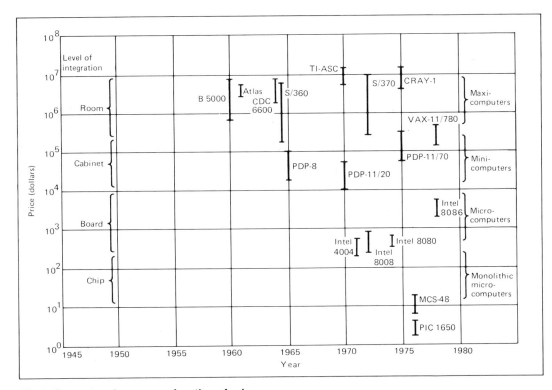

Fig. 1. Computer classes as a function of price.

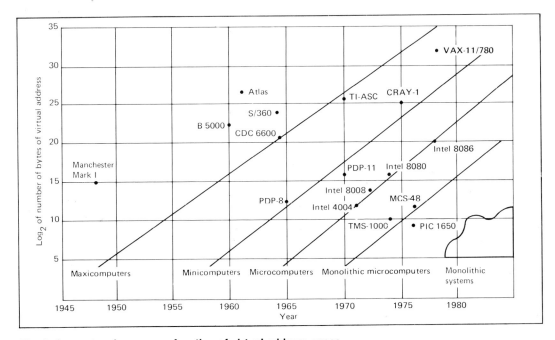

Fig. 2. Computer classes as a function of virtual address space.

of virtual address. *Virtual address* refers to the number of bytes independently addressable by the instruction set of the processor (ISP) (i.e., having unique names). (See Part 2, Sec. 2, for a more detailed discussion of virtual addresses.) Figure 2 plots the computers described in this book by bytes of virtual address according to date of introduction. The same four classes emerge: maxicomputers, minicomputers, microcomputers, and monolithic microcomputers. The number of bytes of virtual address doubles approximately every year (i.e., a byte-addressable ISP increases its address size by 1 bit per year). Thus, as each class evolves, new members of the class are expected to have increased capacity and functionality. Since, according to this metric, classes represent approximately constant price bands, the technology cost reductions serve to increase the capacity and functionality of a class.

On the other hand, technology cost reductions can be used to initiate new, less expensive classes with the same functionality offered by the next higher class several years before. For example, consider the early versions of the minicomputer (PDP-8), the microcomputer (Intel 4004), and the monolithic microcomputer (MCS-48). From Fig. 2 we would expect all three to have roughly similar capacity and functionality, though 5 and 10 years apart in time. It is extremely important to remember that all classes of computers have followed approximately the same evolutionary path as their capacity and functionality have increased. Thus, minicomputers began to include what had been maxicomputer concepts (e.g., caches, pipelining, and floating-point data-types) as soon as the economics of technology allowed (i.e., when the technology could support the added complexity without driving the system cost into another class). Microcomputers and monolithic microcomputers are evolving along similar paths, reflecting a similar time lag.

Not all concepts pass unchanged from one class to the next. For example, timesharing operating systems were developed to provide access to a costly, centralized maxicomputer system for many users, even at diverse locales. Timesharing systems were later applied to minicomputers. Because of their relatively low cost, microcomputers have not yet adopted timesharing facilities, even though several important concepts developed for timesharing, such as online file systems, have already been incorporated into the microcomputer class.

Newer computer classes benefit from the evolutionary process of older classes, adapting to proven concepts quickly where the older classes required a trial-and-error process. Despite the usefulness of understanding computers according to class, it is essential to remember that the principles of computer structures apply to all types of computer systems. Any principle or technique presented in this book can be used to describe any computer class, no matter when it evolved. Part 2 of the book systematically presents the general principles of computer structures, while Part 3 examines detailed variations as functions of constraints of the specific computer classes.

A few anomalies in Fig. 2 are worthy of comment. Several computers of the early maxicomputer class had a large number of addressable bytes. The Atlas and B 5000 heavily utilized less costly secondary storage to give the appearance of a large primary memory. Computers such as the IBM System/360 (a maxicomputer) and the VAX-11/780 (which bridged the gap between high-end minicomputers and low-end maxicomputers) provided an extra large virtual address to allow room for capacity expansion in future family members. The CRAY-1, although considered a maxicomputer, has addressability usually associated with a minicomputer. Thus the CRAY can be regarded either as under addressed for a stand-alone maxicomputer or as a specialized computer (e.g., a vector processor) to be used in conjunction with other, more general-purpose machines.

Another view of capacity and functionality is provided by plotting the number of bytes of physical address by year of introduction, as shown in Fig. 3. This figure illustrates the maximum size of physical memory able to be implemented by the ISP-defined machine. The implemented memory may be substantially less than the virtual memory size on account of physical limitations and/or cost constraints. Figure 3 reinforces the concept of family, showing a slope that approximately doubles every 2 years (½ bit of addressability per year). The maxicomputers and the VAX-11/780 show reasonable alignment with their respective classes. The CRAY-1, however, still falls below the maxicomputer line.

Both Figs. 2 and 3 speculate on the next evolutionary class—monolithic systems. As semiconductor technology densities increase, the contents of a single semiconductor chip will push out onto the nondigital system's functions. Monolithic systems will contain not only the computer and its memory but also input/output devices such as A/D and D/A converters, sensors, actuators, and other specialized analog circuits. The trend towards monolithic systems has already begun with the integration of A/D converters into monolithic microcomputers (e.g., the Intel 8022).

Evolution of Computer Structures

As each computer class evolves, it frequently follows the exact sequence of events found in other computer classes. Part 1, Sec. 2, and Part 3 delineate the evolutionary stages.

The evolutionary process can also occur for subsystems within a single computer class. Myer and Sutherland [1968] recognized the phenomenon for the graphics output function (see Chap. 6). Figure 4 depicts the "wheel of reincarnation" for input/output controllers. The various positions of the wheel can be summarized as:

Position 1   The central processor (P) directly controls the I/O transducer (T) by issuing timed sequences of

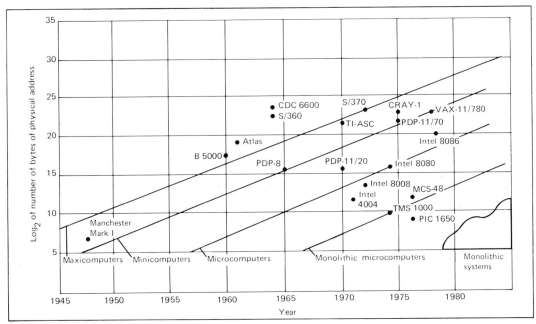

Fig. 3. Computer classes as a function of physical address space.

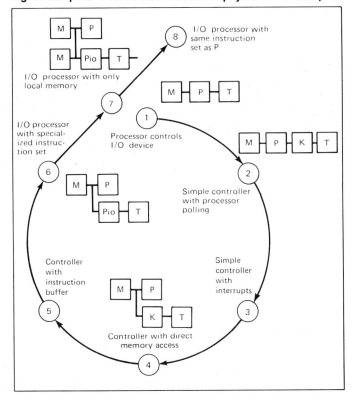

Fig. 4. The wheel of reincarnation for input/output.

control pulses (example: direct I/O control by a microcomputer).

Position 2 A simple controller (K) takes over the generation of the control pulse sequences upon central processor command. The central processor must periodically examine (poll) the controller to see when it has completed a command. The central processor and controller operate in parallel, allowing overlap between computations and I/O (example: Intel 4004).

Position 3 Interrupts are added to the simple controller so that it can signal the central processor upon completion of a command. The central processor need not spend time polling the controller (example: most contemporary minicomputers and microcomputers).

Position 4 Direct memory access (DMA) is added to the controller, so that the controller can move a block of data to or from memory without bothering the central processor. The central processor is interrupted only after the controller has completed the block move, not after each datum, as in position 3 (example: PDP-11).

Position 5 An instruction buffer is added to the controller so that the central processor can set up a sequence of I/O activities. The controller interrupts only after the entire sequence has been executed.

Position 6 The controller is enhanced to contain a complete instruction set, including instructions for program control, looping, and testing. The central processor creates an I/O program in memory that the controller can fetch and execute. The central processor is interrupted only after the entire program of I/O events has been completed (example: IBM System/360 and System/370 channel processors).

Position 7   The I/O processor has a local memory of its own, becoming a computer, and forms a network with the central processor (example: CDC-6600).

Position 8   The I/O processor has a general computer instruction set and may undergo an evolution of its own by being assisted by more and more sophisticated controllers (positions 1 to 7).

A study of the evolutionary chains outlined as parts of the computer space in Part 1, Sec. 2, and Part 2 will enable the reader to recognize the current evolutionary position of a particular computer system and to predict the next phase. The reader is also encouraged to identify wheels of reincarnation (evolutionary chains spiraling around themselves).

Plan of the Book

The book is divided into four parts. The introductory Part 1 is subdivided into three sections. Section 1 presents the hierarchical nature of computer structures as well as the PMS and ISP notations. Section 2 provides a cursory description of the space of computer systems. All computer systems can be viewed as occupying a space whose dimensions are the system's important features. Many features of the actual systems are locked together, as, for example, the relationship between word size and number of instructions in the repertoire: no 12-bit machine has 200 instructions, but several with 32 bits have this capacity. The number of significant variables is much less than the total number of features of computer systems. Such a space provides a basic frame in which to choose representative computer systems for inclusion in the book. Section 3 presents several historically significant computers illustrating the various computer classes. These chapters also serve to familiarize the reader with the notations and abstractions presented in Sec. 1.

Part 2 is a detailed look at eight regions of computer space. Each section in this part illustrates by examples the taxonomy and evolution of design dimensions and contains a series of papers describing computer structures in which these dimensions are prominent. This format enables the reader to focus on variations within a single dimension.

Part 3 organizes computers into classes. The rationale for classes and the properties of each class are explored. Examples of the computer structures allow the reader to observe variations in computer space dimensions for a set of comparable machines. The computers in the smaller classes are described down to the register-transfer level. Larger computers are, by necessity, abstracted to higher levels in the hierarchy. However, the details in the smaller classes should provide the reader with enough experience to extrapolate larger designs through at least the register-transfer level.

Part 4 focuses on series of computers constrained by a common ISP so that they can all execute the same code. These families provide a unique opportunity to study the impact of implementation variations, since several major computer space dimensions are held constant within the family. A simple performance model is used to predict these variations.

A word needs to be said about the "virtual" table of contents. Many of the computer structures are relevant to more than one part and section. Physically, each chapter has to be located at one place in the book. But we have made multiple entries in the Table of Contents, so that, for instance, Chap. 43, on the CDC 6600, physically appears in Part 3, Sec. 4, on maxicomputers, but also forms a significant entry in Part 2, Sec. 3, on concurrency. The book may be read according to the physical table of contents. If it is desired to treat a single topic in depth without reading the entire book, the virtual table of contents should be used as a guide.

References

Myer and Sutherland [1968].

Chapter 2

Levels and Abstractions

The complexity of computer systems is better understood when such systems are organized into different levels. Analysis of each individual level facilitates the orderly understanding of the system's functions. Progression from the most primitive level of the hierarchy to higher levels is accomplished by creating a series of abstractions. By suppressing unnecessary details, each abstraction contains only that information relevant at the higher level. Abstractions provide conceptual paths along which only a small amount of information passes. Abstractions frequently coincide with actual boundaries in the physical systems, since abstractions were initially introduced by the designers as a means of managing the complexity of the system.

Figure 1 illustrates four levels at which a computer can be described. Each system (at any level) is characterized by a set of components and a set of ways to combine those components into structures. The behavior of the systems is formally described according to the behavior of the components and their specific combinations. Elementary circuit theory is an almost prototypic example. The components are R's, L's, C's, and voltage sources. The mode of combination is wiring between the terminals of components, which corresponds to an identification of current and voltage at these terminals. The algebraic and differential equations of circuit theory provide the means whereby the behavior of a circuit can be computed from the properties of its components and the way the circuit is constructed.

There is a recursive feature to most system descriptions. A system, composed of components structured in a given way, may be considered a component in the construction of yet other systems. There are, of course, some primitive components whose properties are not explicable as the resultant of a system of the same type. For example, a resistor is not to be explained by a subcircuit but is taken as a *primitive*. Sometimes there are no absolute primitives, it being a matter of convention what basis is taken. For example, one can build logic design systems from many different sets of primitive logic operations (AND, NOT, NAND, OR, NOT, etc.).

Each system level, as we have used the term in Fig. 1, is characterized by a distinct language for representing the system (i.e., the components, modes of combination, and laws of behavior). These distinct languages reflect special properties of the types of components and of the way they combine. Otherwise, there would be no point in adopting a special representation. Nevertheless, these levels exist in the system analyst's way of describing the same physical system. The fact that the languages are highly distinct makes it possible to be confident about the existence of different system levels. Where we are fuzzy, as in the existence of an additional intermediate level, it is because new representations have not yet congealed into distinct formal languages. As we noted, within each level there exists a whole hierarchy of systems and subsystems. However, as long as these are all described in the same language, e.g., a subroutine hierarchy, all given in machine-assembly language, they do not constitute separate system levels.

With this general view, let us work through the levels of computer systems, starting at the bottom. Each level in Fig. 1 actually has two languages or representations associated with it: an algebraic one and a graphical one. These are isomorphic to each

Level	Sublevel				Description
PMS level				Structures:	Networks, multiple processor systems, computers
				Components:	Processors, memories, switches, controllers, transducers, data operators, links
Program level	High level language sublevel		Application systems	Structures:	Statistical Package for the Social Sciences (SPSS), partial differential equation solver, power system simulator, airline reservation system
				Components:	Mathematical library routines, formatting routines
			Application routines	Structures:	Mathematical functions, plotting packages
				Components:	Subroutines, memory allocation
			Run-time system	Structures:	Memory allocation, input/output, file system
				Components:	Operating system calls
			Operating system	Structures:	Schedulers, allocators, communication
				Components:	Subroutines, coroutines, programs
	ISP sublevel			Structures:	Instruction sets
				Components:	Memory state, processor state, effective address calculation, instruction decode, instruction execution
Logic design level	Register transfer sublevel	Control	Microprogramming	Structures:	Microprograms, microroutines
				Components:	Microsequencer, Microstore
			Hardwired	Structures:	Sequencer
				Components:	Sequential machines
		Data paths		Structures:	Arithmetic units, register files
				Components:	Registers, data operators
	Switching circuit sublevel	Sequential		Structures:	Counters, functional generators, registers
				Components:	Flip-flops, latches, delays
		Combinational		Structures:	Encoders, decoders, data operators
				Components:	Gates
Circuit level				Structures:	Amplifiers, delays, clocks, gates
				Components:	Transistors, relays, resistors, capacitors

Fig. 1. Levels in the digital system hierarchy.

other, the same entities, properties, and relations being given in both.

The lowest level in Fig. 1 is the *circuit level*. Here the components are R's, L's, C's, voltage sources, and nonlinear devices. The behavior of the system is measured in terms of voltage, current, and magnetic flux. These are continuously varying quantities associated with various components, and so there is continuous behavior through time. The components have a discrete number of terminals, whereby they can be connected to other components. Figure 2 shows both an algebraic and a graphical description of an inverter circuit, as well as an algebraic and a graphical description of its behavior. We note that its structure is specified first as a circuit (a directed graph), with symbols for the arcs and nodes. The particular circuit still is an abstraction because the transistor $Q1$, the resistor R, and the stray capacitances C_s are given only token values. The structure can be described symbolically by first writing the relationship describing each of the components (Ohm's law, Faraday's law, etc.) and then the equation which describes the interconnection of the components (i.e., Kirchoff's laws). We observe the behavior of the circuit (probably using an oscilloscope) by applying an input $e_i(t)$ and observing an output $e_o(t)$. Alternatively, if we solve the equations which specify the structure, we obtain expressions which describe the behavior explicitly.

The circuit level is not in fact the lowest level that might be used in describing a computer system. The devices themselves require a different langauge, either that of electromagnetic theory or that of quantum mechanics (for the solid-state devices). It is usually an exercise in a course on Maxwell's equations to show that circuit theory can be derived as a specialization under appropri-

ately restricted boundary conditions. Actually, even at its level of abstraction, circuit theory is not quite adequate to describe computer technology, since there are a number of mechanical devices which must be represented. Magnetic tapes and disks are most likely to come to mind first, but card readers, card punches, line printers, and terminals are other examples. These devices obey laws of motion and are analyzed in units of mass, length, and time.

The next level is the *logic level*. It is unique to digital technology, whereas the circuit level (and below) is what digital technology shares with the rest of electrical engineering. The behavior of a system is now described by discrete variables which take on only two values, called 0 and 1 (or + and −, true and false, high and low). The components perform logic functions: AND, OR, NOT, NAND, etc. Systems are constructed in the same way as at the circuit level, by connecting the terminals of components, which thereby identify their behavioral values. The laws of boolean algebra are used to compute the behavior of a system from the behavior and properties of its components.

The previous paragraph described *combinational circuits* whose outputs are directly related to the inputs at any instant of time. If the circuit has the ability to hold values over time (store information), we get *sequential circuits*. The problem that the combinational-level analysis solves is the production of a set of outputs at time t as a function of a number of inputs at the same time t. As described in textbooks, the analysis abstracts from any transport delays between input and output; however, in engineering practice the analysis of delays is usually considered to be still part of the combinational level. In Fig. 3 we show a combinational network formed from combinational elements which realize three boolean output expressions, O_1, O_2, and O_3, as a function of the input boolean variables A and B. Note that in the symbolic representation of the structure we can write an expression that reflects the structure of the combinational network, but, on reduction, the boolean equations no longer reflect the actual structure of the combinational circuit but become a model to predict its behavior.

The representation of a sequential switching circuit is basically the same as that of a combinational switching circuit, although one needs to add memory components, such as a delay element (which produces as output at time t the input at time $t - \tau$). Thus the equations that specify structure must be difference equations involving time. Again, there is a distinction (even in representation) between *synchronous* circuits and *asynchronous* circuits, namely, whether behavior can be represented by a sequence of values at integral time points ($t = 1, 2, 3, \ldots$) or must deal in continuous time. But this is a minor variation. Figure 4 gives a sequential logic circuit in both an algebraic and a graphical form and shows also the representation of the behavior of the system.

Now it is clear that logic circuits are simply a subspecies of general circuits. Indeed, to design the logic components one

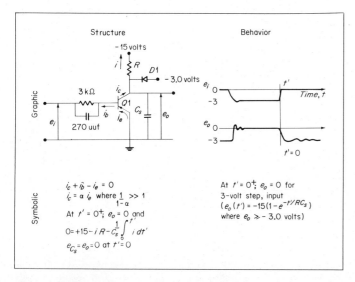

Fig. 2. Electronic-circuit level: inverter circuit.

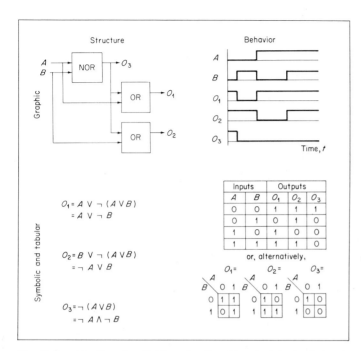

Fig. 3. Combinational-switching-circuit sublevel of the logic level: realization of three logic expressions.

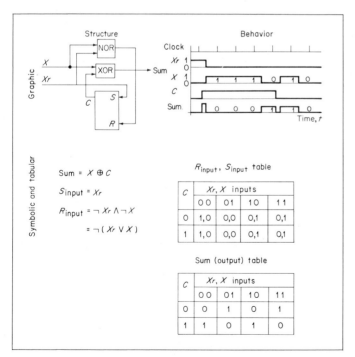

Fig. 4. Sequential-switching-circuit sublevel of the logic level: of x + 1 from serial input string x.

constructs circuit-level descriptions of them. For instance, Fig. 5 shows a circuit for a NAND (or NOR) gate plus a table of its behavior. It is evident that its behavior corresponds to that of the NAND gate only if certain restrictions hold; namely, that one does not look at the voltage (which is identified as the behavior variable in the logic circuit) during certain periods when it is transient ("settling down," to use the common phrase). Thus the logic level is an instance of the circuit level only in the same sense that the circuit level is an instance of Maxwell's equations—as a limiting case in which certain features are deliberately ignored.

One buys a great deal from the specialization to logic circuits, since one can compute the behavior of circuits at the logic level that are extremely complex at the circuit level. The techniques for doing so use an entirely different mathematical apparatus. In general, we cross into another level when the representation at the previous level provides information that is no longer relevant. A lower level is concerned with explaining the behavior of a certain structure, whereas the next higher level takes the lower level as given (a primitive). The higher level is concerned not about internal behavior but only how primitives are combined.

A glance at Fig. 1 shows that we have described only the lower

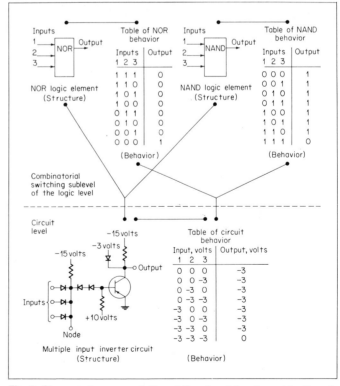

Fig. 5. Change of representation at the circuit level combinational-switching sublevel boundary.

part of the logic level. There is another part, called the *register-transfer level* (or RT level). The components of an RT system are registers and functional transfers between registers. A register is a device that holds a set of bits.[1] The behavior of the system is given by the time course of values of these registers, i.e., their bit sets.

The system undergoes discrete operations, whereby the values of various registers are combined according to some rule and then are stored in another register (thus transferred). The law of combination may be almost anything, from the simple unmodified transfer ($A = B$) to logic combination ($A = B \wedge C$) to arithmetic ($A = B + C$). Thus a specification of the behavior, equivalent to the boolean equations of sequential circuits or the differential equations of the circuit level, is a set of expressions (often called *productions*) which give the conditions under which such transfers will be made. In Fig. 6 we give a picture of an RT system to compute the sum of integers. The figure includes the specification of its behavior and a table that shows the resulting behavior over time. Here the graphical structure of the system includes registers (N, I, S), transfers ($S = S + I$), data operators ($S + I$, $I > N$, etc.). The flowchart shows the behavior of the control with time.

Register-transfer level systems are usually visualized as having two components: data and control. The data part is composed of registers, operators, and data paths. The control part provides the time sequence of signals that evoke activities in the data part. Control parts were initially implemented as hardwired state machines (see Chap. 8 for an example). However, the advent of low-cost read-only memories (ROMs) has made microprogramming the prevalent technique for implementing control sequencers. Figure 7 depicts a typical microprogrammed sequencer. The microprogram sequencer has many of the same properties found in the next higher level, the program level. Microinstructions, contained in the microstore, go through an interpretation cycle: the microinstruction is fetched, the next microaddress calculated, the microinstruction decoded, and signals generated to evoke data-path operations.

There is another representation used at the logic level, the *state-system* representation. The state system is the most general representation of a discrete system available.[2] A system is represented as capable of being in one of n abstract states at any instant of time. (For digital systems, n is finite or enumerable.) Its behavior is specified by a transition function that takes as arguments the current state and the current input and determines

---

[1]This assumes that the elementary state variable of the system holds a bit (i.e., one of two values, such as 0 or 1). This need not be; sometimes the elementary variable holds a decimal digit (one of 10 values) or a character (one of, say, 48 values). For present purposes we can talk in terms of bits without losing anything thereby.

[2]There have been energetic attempts to apply the state-system approach to control systems of a more general nature [Zadeh and Desoer, 1963], although they do not concern us here.

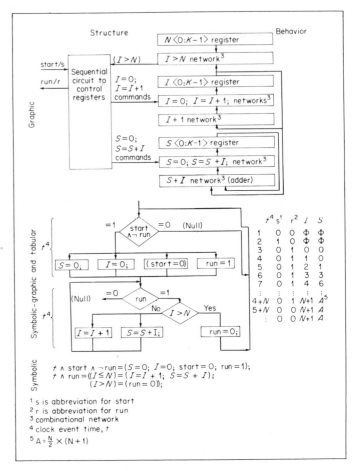

Fig. 6. Register-transfer sublevel of the logic level: computation of the sum of integers.

the next state (and the concomitant output). A digital computer is, in principle, representable as a state system, but the number of states is far too large to make it useful to do so. Instead, the state system becomes a useful representation in dealing with various subparts of the total machine, such as the sequential circuit that controls a magnetic tape. Here the number of states is small enough to be tractable.

In Fig. 8 we give the common representations of the state system. Coincidently, we use the representations of Fig. 8 for the sequential switching circuit of Fig. 4. That is, Fig. 8 may be viewed as an abstraction of the physical system in Fig. 4. To the logic designer the state system is a useful abstraction of a logic design. A design usually passes through the following problem representations:

1   The problem exists in a natural langauge.

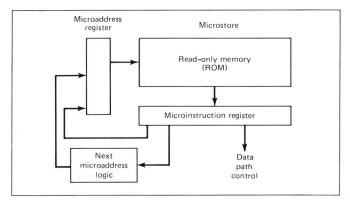

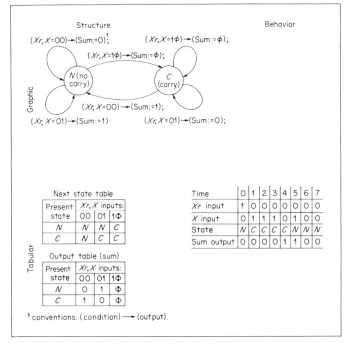

Fig. 7. A typical microprogrammed sequencer.

2 The problem is converted to a state diagram (output as a function of state, and input).

3 The state diagram is represented as a state table and output table.

4 States are assigned (physical memory elements are used).

Fig. 8. State-system representation of the logic level: computation of x + 1 from serial input string x.

5 The excitation table and output tables are formed.

6 The excitation and output logic equations are written (constrained by the actual logic elements).

7 The sequential circuit is drawn.

Let us go to the next higher level, the *program level*. This not only is a unique level of description for digital technology (as was the logic level) but is uniquely associated with computers, namely, with those digital devices that have a central component that interprets a programming language. There are many uses of digital technology, especially in instrumentation and digital controls, that do not require such an interpretation device and hence have a logic level but no program level.

The components of the program level are a set of memories and a set of operations. The memories hold data structures, which represent things both inside and outside the memory, e.g., numbers, payrolls, molecules, and other data structures. The operations take various data structures as inputs and produce new data structures, which again reside in memories. Thus the behavior of the system is the time pattern of data structures held in its memories. The unique feature of the program level is the representation it provides for combining components, that is, for specifying what operations are to be executed on what data structures. This is the program, which consists of a sequence of instructions. Each instruction specifies that a given operation (or operations) be executed on specified data structures. Superimposed on this is a control structure that specifies which instruction is to be interpreted next. Normally this is done in the order in which the instructions are given, with jumps out of sequence specified by branch instructions. Again, Fig. 9 shows a simple program, the data structures, and the behavior.

Two things separate the logic level from the program level. First, computer systems at the logic level are parallel devices, with all components active at the same time. At the program level, computers are represented essentially as serial devices, executing one instruction after another. Second, the program level is essentially linguistic in nature; the logic level is not. At the program level things can be named, abbreviations used, decisions made, instructions interpreted—all concepts that are absent from physical systems. Of course, they are not *really* absent, since a full description of the operation of a program is possible at the logic level. This is done by applying the set of physical behaviors that makes computers show the appropriate linguistic behavior at the program level. Thus, instead of the instruction "go to ALPHA if register zero is negative," there is a logic circuit that transfers the contents of the address field of the instruction register to the program counter, ANDing that transfer with the sign of register zero so that it takes place only if the register is negative. This example reveals the distinct system boundary between the register-transfer level and the program level. The gap between

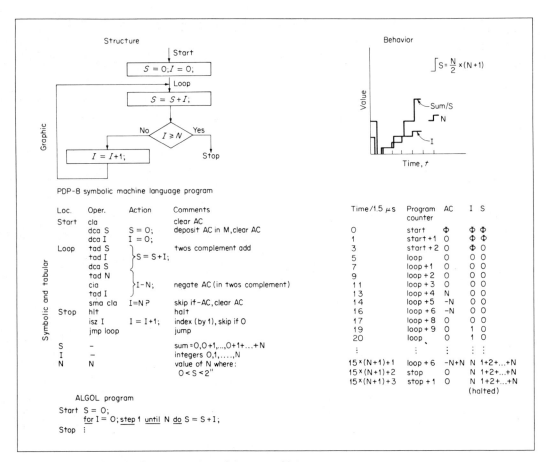

Fig. 9. Programming level: computation of the sum of integers.

these levels is also revealed in the ability of programmers to become expert without knowing anything about representations below the programming level.

The program level constitutes an entire technology in its own right, carrying within it most of the characteristics of computer systems. The ISP (instruction-set processor) sublevel specifies the machine's instruction interpretation cycle: instruction fetch, instruction decode, program counter update, operand address calculation, operand fetch, and instruction execution.

The ISP description system is meant to provide a uniform way of describing instruction sets, i.e., of giving the information contained in a programming manual. It must provide the instruction format, the registers referenced by the instructions, the rules of interpretation of the instructions, and the semantics of each instruction in the processor's repertoire. It must be able to do this for any existing computer and for any anticipated future computer. (See Chap. 4 for a discussion of the ISP notation.)

A number of sophisticated language levels are built upon the ISP sublevel. Operating systems manage system resources (e.g., memory space, CPU time) and provide commonly used functions for use at higher levels. The high-level–language run-time system provides an interface between potentially different operating systems and a high-level language (e.g., FORTRAN, COBOL, ALGOL, or PASCAL). More complex functions, such as a mathematical library, can be performed by routines invoked by user programs. Finally, application systems provide a totally integrated environment where the user need interact only by entering data and reading results. Examples of these integrated environments (e.g., hand-held calculators, personal computers, and video games) are proliferating as computing technology is packaged for less sophisticated users.

We now move to the fourth and last level. In Fig. 1 it is called the processor-memory-switch level, or PMS level for short. It is the view one takes of a computer system when one considers only its most aggregate behavior. It then consists of central processors, core memories, tapes, disks, input/output processors, communication lines, printers, tape controllers, buses, Teletypes, graphics terminals, etc. The system is viewed as processing a medium—information—which can be measured in bits (or digits, characters, words, or the like). Thus the components have capacities and flow rates as their operating characteristics. All details of the program are suppressed, although many gross distinctions of encoding and information type remain, depending on the analysis. Thus one may distinguish program from data, or file space from resident monitor. One may remain concerned with the fact that input data are in alphameric and must be converted into binary, or are bit-serial and must be converted to bit-parallel.

We might characterize this level as the "chemical engineering view of a digital computer," which likens it more to a continuous-process petroleum-distilling plant than to a place where complex FORTRAN programs are applied to matrices of data. Indeed, this system level is more nearly an abstraction from the logic level than from the program level, since it returns to a simultaneously operating flow system. Figure 10 illustrates a PMS diagram for a dual-processor UNIVAC 1108.

The PMS descriptive system is meant to provide a notation for the top level of computer systems. Figure 10 is given in this notation. On the surface it is largely self-explanatory, given the mnemonics of P for processor, M for memory, S for switch, T for transducer (hence also terminal), and K for control (since C is for computer). There is also L for link, but in most computer structures it is unnecessary to distinguish a separate link component, except to show connectivity. (It does become appropriate if communication delays exist.)

There is an issue about whether this small set of components is an appropriate set of primitives, but the issue is not of major proportions. The real issues in the development of the notation come from the stress of two opposite forces. On the one hand, one wants extremely compact notations for expressing computer systems. The systems are large in any event, and if there is much extra notational freight in the way of fixed formats or forced writing of what is already known and assumed, then the notation

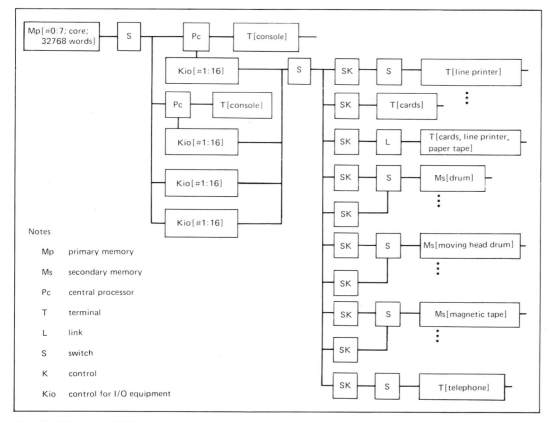

Fig. 10. PMS level: UNIVAC 1108.

will be neither useful nor used. On the other hand, there is a tremendous variety and quantity of information that potentially must be capable of being written into a description: word size, capacity, flow, operation rate, data-types, variations of operation rate for different classes of instructions, parity checking, technology, and on and on. Thus one needs a notation that responds to both these demands—and without being hopelessly complex and difficult to learn. Our attempt at a solution involves a basically simple language with comprehensive (and we think natural) ways of systematic abbreviation and abstraction. The PMS notation will be discussed in Chap. 3.

One advantage to viewing a computer system as a hierarchy of levels is that standard interfaces can be established. If the information flow across the interface is carefully specified, then interchangeable systems can be built on both sides of the interface. One classical standardized interface has been the ISP level. With the machine language precisely defined, hardware implementors have been able to produce machines with a marketable price and performance range while assuring program implementors that their software would execute correctly on any hardware implementation without modification. Thus the software effort can be limited to producing one system. The ISP-level interface also allows hardware designers to incorporate the instruction set in newer, more cost-effective technology without invalidating existing software.

In their paper announcing the IBM System/360 computer, Amdahl, Blaauw, and Brooks [1964] identified three interfaces: architecture, implementation, and realization. They defined *computer architecture* as the attributes of a computer as seen by a machine language programmer. This definition includes the instruction set, instruction format, operation codes, addressing modes, and all registers and memory locations that may be directly manipulated or tested by a machine language program. *Implementation* is defined as the actual hardware structure, logic design, and data-path organization. *Realization* encompasses the logic technologies, packaging, and interconnection.

The terms *architecture* (when used to connote function), *implementation*, and *realization* can also be used at the program level in Fig. 1. Several standard architectures (interfaces) may be enforced at one time. Typical examples include the ISP, operating-system, high-level–language, and application-system levels. As hardware becomes less expensive, it is used to provide more functions. A prime example is the migration of operating-system primitives from software into microcode. Eliminating standard interfaces and bypassing levels of abstraction usually leads to improved system performance by eliminating the intervening levels of interpretation of information. (A decrease in performance may result if the higher-level functionality does not match its application. In such a case, the user has to generate lower-level primitives by applying more costly, functionally complex primitives. Consequently, incorporating new functions into hardware is carefully evaluated and adopted only after a standardized software interface has become stabilized through exposure to many diverse application environments.)

The concepts of hierarchical levels and levels of abstraction will appear repeatedly throughout the book. Chapter 8 illustrates these levels with respect to a simple computer, the PDP-8. Several systems are described at the register-transfer level (e.g., in Part 2, Sec. 1, on microprogrammed processors; Chaps. 18 and 19, on parallelism in the IBM System/360 Model 91; Chap. 33, on the Alto; Chap. 34, on the TMS1000; Chap. 35, on the PIC1650; Chap. 38, on the PDP-11; and Chaps. 48 and 49, on the evolution of HP calculators) in order to give the reader a firm understanding of design at this level. Because of a lack of space, more complex systems cannot be described in as much detail. The ISP and PMS levels are extensively used for these other systems. It is hoped that with the background gained from the register-transfer–level designs the reader can extrapolate such designs for these more complex systems.

References

Amdahl, Blaauw, and Brooks [1964].

Chapter 3

PMS Notation

At the PMS level, a system is described as an interconnected set of components, or individual devices, associated with a set of operations that work on a medium of information measured in bits (or some other base). Such a description is complicated by the amount of detail involved. It takes a whole manual, for instance, to describe the operations of a major computer, such as the IBM System/370. Thus the descriptive system must permit very compressed descriptions. It must also permit description of only those aspects of the components that are of interest, ignoring the rest. And what is of interest at the PMS level? Besides a description of the gross structure of a computer system, it is primarily the analysis of the amounts of information held in various components, the flows of information between components, and the distribution of the control that accomplishes these flows.

Thus a PMS-level description is analogous to the chemical engineer's diagram of a refinery in which the interest is in various kinds of liquid and gas flow. The engineer has to account for matter and energy loss with the system at various stages involving the transduction of materials from one form to another. A specific chemical plant's external performance is measured in terms of its production flow rate for a given cost. With computers, external performance is concerned with the economical accomplishment of discrete tasks, but at the PMS level this translates into operation rates and cost of operations.

For the PMS level we ignore all the fine structure of information processing and consider a system consisting of components that work on a homogeneous medium called *information*. Information comes in packets, called "i-units" (for *information units*), and is measured in bits (or equivalent units, such as characters). I-units have the sort of hierarchical structure indicated by the statement, A record consists of 300 words; a word consists of 4 bytes; a byte consists of 8 bits. A record, then, contains $300 \times 4 \times 8 = 9{,}600$ bits. Each of these numbers—300, 4, 8—is called a *length*, since one often thinks of an i-unit as a spatial sequence of the next lower i-units of which it is composed. For example, one speaks of "word length," and of a record as "300 words long."

Other than being decomposable into a hierarchy of factors, i-units have no other structure at the PMS level. They do have a *referent*, i.e., a *meaning*. Thus it is possible to say of an i-unit that it refers to an employer's payroll, to the pressure of a boiler, or to a prime number satisfying certain conditions. To do so, of course, the i-units *encode* the information necessary to make the refer-ence. At the PMS level we are not concerned with what is referred to, but only with the fact that certain components transform i-units but do not modify their meaning. In fact, these meaning-preserving operations are the most basic information-processing operations of all, and they provide the basic classification of computer components.

PMS Primitives

In PMS there are seven basic component types, each distinguished by the kinds of operations it performs:

Memory, M. A component that holds or stores information (i.e., i-units) over time. Its operations are reading i-units out of the memory and writing i-units into the memory. Each memory that holds more than a single i-unit has associated with it an *addressing system* by means of which particular i-units can be designated or selected. A memory can also be considered as a switch to a number of submemories. The i-units are not changed in any way by being stored in a memory.

Link, L. A component that transfers information (i.e., i-units) from one place to another in a computer system. It has fixed ports. The operation is that of transmitting an i-unit (or a sequence of them) from the component at one port to the component at the other. Again, except for the change in spatial position, there is no change of any sort in the i-units.

Control, K. A component that evokes the operations of other components in the system. All other components are taken to consist of a set of discrete operations, each of which, when evoked, accomplishes some discrete transformation of state. With the exception of a processor, P, all other components are essentially passive and require some other active agent (a K) to set them into small episodes of activity.

Switch, S. A component that constructs a link between other components. Each switch has associated with it a set of possible links, and its operations consist of setting some of these links and breaking others.

Transducer, T. A component that changes the i-unit used to encode a given meaning (i.e., a given referent). The change may involve the medium used to encode the basic bits (e.g., voltage levels to magnetic flux, or voltage levels to holes in a paper card), or it may involve the structure of the i-unit (e.g., bit-serial to bit-parallel). Note that T's are meaning-preserving but not necessarily information-preserving (in number of bits), since the encodings of the (invariant) meaning need not be equally optimal.

Data-operation, D. A component that produces i-units with new meanings. It is this component that accomplishes all the data-operations, e.g., arithmetic, logic, and shifting.

Processor, P. A component that is capable of interpreting a program in order to execute a sequence of operations. It consists of a set of operations of the types already mentioned—M, L, K, S, T, and D—plus the control necessary to obtain instructions from a memory and interpret them as operations to be carried out.

Computer Model (in PMS)

Components of the seven types can be connected to make *stored-program digital computers*, abbreviated by C. For instance, the classical configuration for a computer is

Here Pc indicates a *central processor* and Mp a *primary memory*, namely, one which is directly accessible from a P and holds the program for it. T is a transducer connected to the external environment, represented by X. (The colon-equals (:=) indicates that C is the name of what follows to the right.) Thus a computer is a central processor connected to its primary memory on the one hand and to a transducer on the other, which is what an input/output device is.

Actually the classic diagram had four components, since it decomposed the Pc into a control (K) and an arithmetic unit or data-operation (D):

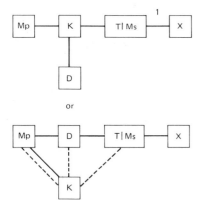

or

where the solid information-carrying lines are for instructions and their data and the dotted lines signify control.

Often logic operations were lumped with control, instead of

[1]The vertical bar expresses mutually exclusive alternatives. Here, a T or Ms exists at the periphery.

with data operations, but this no longer seems to be the appropriate way to decompose the system functionally.

If we associate local control of each component with the appropriate component, we get

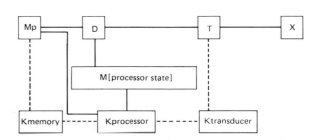

where the solid lines carry the information in which we are interested and the dotted lines carry information about when to evoke operations on the respective components. The solid information-carrying lines between K and Mp are instructions. Now, suppressing the K's, then lumping the processor state memory, the data operators, and the control of the data-operations to form a central processor, we again get

Computer systems can be described in PMS at varying levels of detail. For instance, in the diagrams above we did not write in the links (L's) as separate components. These would be of interest only if the delays in transmission were significant to the discussion at hand or if the i-units transmitted by the L were different from those available at its terminals. Since this is not usually the case in current computers, one indicates simply that two components (e.g., an Mp and a Pc) are connected together. Similarly, often the encoding of information into i-units is unimportant; then there is no reason to show the T's. The same statement holds for K's. Sometimes one wants to show the locus of control, say when there is one control for many components, as in a tape controller, but often this is not of interest. Then there is no reason to show K's in a PMS diagram.

As a somewhat different case, D's never occur in PMS diagrams of computers, since in the present design technology D's occur only as subcomponents of P's. If we were to make PMS-type diagrams of analog computers, D's would show extensively as multipliers, summers, integrators, etc. There would be few memories and variable switches. The rather large patchboard would be represented as a very elaborate, manually fixed switch.

Components are often decomposable into arrangements of other components. Thus, most memories are composed of a switch—the addressing switch—and a number of submemories. Thus a memory is recursively defined. The decomposition stops with the unit memory, which is one that stores only a single i-unit and hence requires no addressing. Likewise, a switch is often composed of a cascade of 1-way to *n*-way switches. For example, the switch that addresses a word on a multiple-headed disk might look like

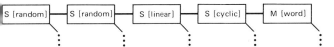

The first S[random] selects a specific Ms.disk.drive.unit; the second S[random] is a switch with random addressing that selects the head (hence the platter and side); S[linear] is a switch with linear accessing that selects the track; and S[cyclic] is a switch with cyclic addressing that finally selects the M[word] along the circular track. Note that the switches are realized by differing technologies. The first two S[random]s are generally electronic (AND-OR gates) with selection times of $10 \sim 100$ μs, or perhaps electromechanical (relays). The S[linear] is the electromechanical action of a stepping motor or a pneumatic-driven, servomechanism-controlled arm that holds the read/write heads; the selection time for a new track is $20 \sim 500$ ms. Finally, the S[cyclic] is determined by the rotation time of the disk and requires from $16 \sim 60$ ms, depending on the speed ($3,600 \sim 1,000$ r/min).

We can write such decompositions of a component into subcomponents either when we actually know the structure of the component or even when we know only the behavior. For example, we could write a memory as random access (M.random) even if it was, in fact, cyclic, as long as its behavior as far as the larger system was concerned took no account of its cyclic character, accepting the average access time as the random-access time.

When people speak of the control element of a computer, they often refer mainly to the processors—not to the control of a disk or magnetic tape, which, however, can often be more complex. When we suppress detail, the control often disappears from a PMS diagram. Similarly, when we agglomerate primitive components (as we did above when combining Mp and Kmemory to be just Mp) into the physically distinct subparts of a computer system, a separate control, K, often occurs. The functionally and physically separate control[1] has evolved. These controls, often as big as a Pc, can be computers with stored control programs. When we decompose a compound control, we find data-operations (D) for calculating addresses or for error-detection and error-

correction data; transducers (T) for changing logic signal levels and information flow widths; memory (M) as it is used in D, T, K, and for buffering; and finally a large control (K) which coordinates the activities of all the other primitives.

It should be clear from the above discussion that components are named according to the function they perform and that they can be composed of many different types of components. Thus, a control (K) may have memory (M) as a subcomponent, and a memory (M) may have a transducer (T) as well as a switch (S) as subcomponents. All these subcomponents exist to accomplish the total function of the component and do not make the component also some other type. For instance, the M that does a transduction (T) from voltages on its input wires to magnetism in its cores and a second transduction from magnetism to voltages on its output wires does not thereby become a transducer as far as the total system functioning is concerned. To the rest of the system all the M can do is to remember i-units, accepting and delivering them in the same form (voltages).

PMS Notation

In the above discussions we used various notations to designate additional specifications for a component, Mp for a functional classification and S[cyclic] for a type of access function. There are many additional specifications one wants to give—so many that it makes no sense to enumerate them all in advance. A fixed position notation, such as standard function notation, F[x, y, z], where the first, second, and third argument places have fixed interpretation, is not suitable. Instead we agree on a single general way of providing additional specifications. If X is a component, we can write

$$X[a_1:v_1;a_2:v_2; \ldots]$$

to indicate that X is further specified by attribute a_1 having value v_1, attribute a_2 having value v_2, etc. Each *parameter* (as we call the pair a:v) is well defined independently of whatever other parameters are given; hence there is no significance to the order in which they are written or the number which have to be written.

According to this notation we should have written M[function:primary] or S[access-function:random] rather than Mp or S[random]. This shows immediately the price paid for the general convention: it requires an excessive amount of writing (which would be even more apparent if a large number of parameters were given), and the extra information seems to be redundant in some cases. We compensate for these disadvantages by several conventions for abbreviating and abstracting parameters. Let us illustrate them by showing some alternative ways of writing Mp:

---

[1]A variety of names for K's are used: controller, adapter, channel, buffer, interface, etc.

M[function:primary]   Complete specification.

M[primary]   Drop the attribute "function," since it can be inferred from the value.

M.primary   Use the value outside the brackets, concatenated with a dot.

M.p   Use an explicitly given abbreviation, namely, primary\p (only if it is not ambiguous).

Mp   Drop the concatenation marker (the dot) if it is not needed to recover the two parts (all components are given by a single capital letter—here M).

Each of these rules corresponds to a natural tendency to abbreviate when redundant information is given; each has as its condition that recovery must be possible.

A PMS Example Using the DEC PDP-8

Let us now describe the PMS structure of an actual, though small, general-purpose computer, the DEC LINC-8, which is a PDP-8 with a LINC processor. Figure 1 gives the detailed PMS diagram. In explaining it, we will concentrate on making the notation clear rather than on discussing substantive features of the system (which are described in Chap. 8). A simplified PMS diagram of the system shows its essential structure:

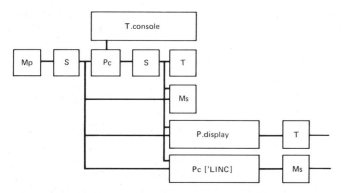

This shows the basic Mp-Pc-T-X structure of a C with the addition of a secondary memory (Ms) and two processors, one of which, Pc['LINC], has its own Ms. Two switches are used: the I/O Bus, which permits access to all the devices, and the Data Break to Mp via Pc, for high–data-rate devices. There are many other switches in the actual system, as one can see from Fig. 1; for example, Mp is really one to eight separate modules connected by a switch S to Pc. Also there are many T's connected to the input/output switch, Sio, which we collapsed as a single T, and similarly for S[' Data Break].

Consider the Mp module. The specifications assert that it is

made with core technology, that its size is 4,096 words; that its operation time is 1.5 µs and that its word size is 13 bits (12 data bits plus one other with a different function). We could have written the same information as

$$M[\text{function:primary; technology:core; operation-time; 1.5 µs;}$$
$$\text{size: 4096 w; word: (12 + 1) b}]$$

In Fig. 1 we wrote only the values, suppressing the attributes, since moderate familiarity with memories permits an immediate inference about what attributes are involved. For example, it is common knowledge that computer memories store information in words; therefore 4,096 w must be the number of words in the memory. As another example, we did not specify the function of the additional bit in the word when we wrote (12 + 1) b. An informed reader will assume this to be a parity bit, since this is the common reason for having an extra bit in a word. If the extra bit had some unusual function, we would have needed to define it. That is, in the absence of additional information, the most common interpretation is to be assumed.

In fact, we could have been even more cryptic and still communicated with most readers:

$$M.\text{core}[1.5 \text{ µs; 4 Kw; 12 b}]$$

This corresponds to the phrase, "a 12-bit, 1.5-µs, 4K core store," which is intelligible to any computer engineer. The 4 Kw stands for $4 \times 1,024 = 4,096$, which again is known to computer engineers; however, if someone less informed took it to be $4 \times 1,000 = 4,000$, no real harm would be done.

Consider the magnetic tapes for Pc. Since there are eight possible tapes that make use of the same controller K through a switch S, we label them #0 through #7. Actually, # is an abbreviation for index, which is an attribute like any other, whose values are integers. Since the attribute is a unique character, we do not have to write #:3 (although we could). The additional parameters give information about the physical attributes of the encoding. These are alternative values, and any tape has only one of them. We use a vertical bar (|) to indicate this (as in BNF notation for grammars). Thus, 45|112 in/s says that one can have a tape with a speed of 45 inches per second or one with 112 inches per second, but not a tape which can be switched dynamically to run at either speed.

For many of the components no further information is given. Thus, knowing that M.magnetic.tape is connected to a control and from there to the Pc tells generally what that K does. It is a *tape controller*, which evokes all the actions of the tape, such as read, write, rewind; therefore these actions do not have to be done by Pc. The fact that there is only one K for many Ms's implies that only one tape can be accessed at a time. Other information could be given, although that just provided is all that

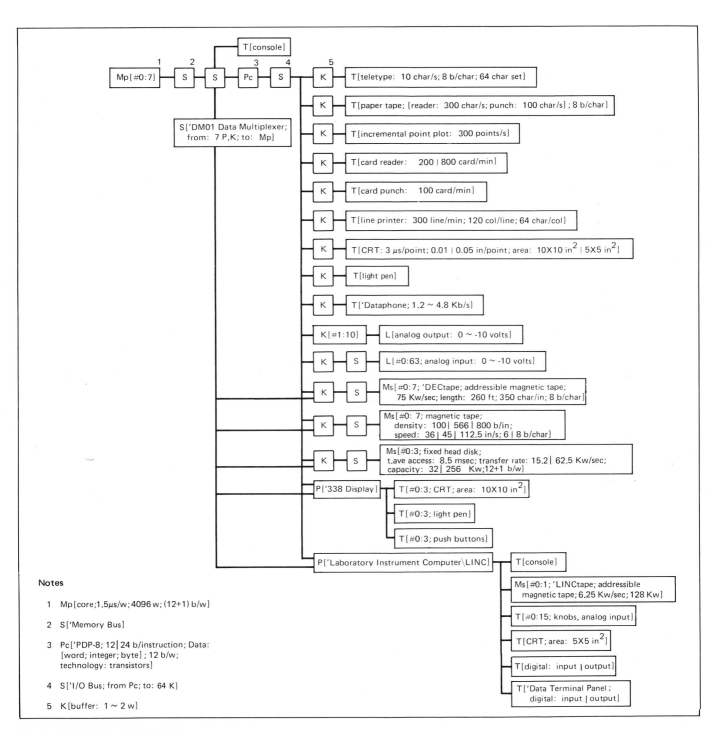

Fig. 1. DEC LINC-8-PDP-8 PMS diagram.

is usual in specifying a controller in an overall description of a system. (The next level of detail goes to the structure of the actual operations and instructions and belongs to the ISP level, not the PMS level.)

As noted earlier, there is significant advantage to defining a PMS diagram at a more detailed level. Thus the notation provides for recursive definition, as in the case of the paper-tape transducer in Fig. 1. There is both a 300 char/s tape reader and a 100 char/s tape punch.

For the Pc in Fig. 1, the manufacturer's name is capitalized and preceded by a single vertical prime or quotation mark: 'PDP-8. By convention, generic names and abbreviations always appear lowercase and proper names always begin uppercase. We have given a few parameters: the data-types, the technology, etc.

We have used several different ways of saying the same thing in Fig. 1 in order to show the range of descriptive notations. Thus the 64 Teletypes are shown by describing a single connection through a switch and putting the number of links in the switch above the connecting line.

Consider, finally, the Pc in Fig. 1. We have given a few parameters: the data-types, the processor state, the word length, etc. These few parameters are easily inferred from the Mp. The basic operation time in a processor is a small multiple of the read time of its Mp. Thus it is predictable that the Pc stores and reads information in 2×1.5 μs (one for instruction fetch, one for data fetch). Again, where this is not the case (as in the CDC 6600) it is necessary to say so. Similarly, the word size in the Pc is the same as the word size of the Mp: 12 data bits. More generally, the Pc must have instructions that take care of evoking all the components of the PMS structure. These instructions do not see the switches and controls as distinct entities; rather, they speak directly to the operation of the M's and T's connected via these switches and controls.

Other summary parameters could have been given for the Pc. None of them would come close to specifying its behavior uniquely, although to those knowledgeable in computers still more can be inferred from the parameters given. For instance, knowing both the data-types available in a Pc and the number of instructions, one can come very close to predicting exactly what the instructions are. Nevertheless, the way to describe a Pc in full detail is not to add larger and larger numbers of summary parameters. It is more direct and more revealing to develop a description at the level of instructions, which is the ISP description.

Because of the evolution of technology, PMS components continue to decrease in physical size. Consider the PDP-5, the immediate predecessor of the PDP-8. When introduced in 1963, the PDP-5 processor logic required 100 boards and occupied 2,100 in² of board space. By 1971, the PDP-8/E required only three boards and 240 in². In 1976 the Intersil 6100 implemented the PDP-8 ISP on a single silicon chip approximately ¼ in on a side. If the PDP-8 ISP were reimplemented today, the processor would occupy a small fraction of the chip area. The next decade will be one of design at the PMS level with many PMS components being integrated into individual semiconductor chips.

Let us end this introduction to the PMS descriptive system by returning to a critical item in its design philosophy. A descriptive scheme for systems as complex and detailed as digital computers must have the ability to range from extremely complete to highly simplified descriptions. It must permit highly compressed descriptions as well as extensive ones and must permit the selective suppression or amplification of whatever aspects of the computer system are of interest to the user. PMS attempts to fulfill these criteria by providing simple conventions for detailed description with additional conventions that permit abbreviation and abstractions, almost without limit. The result is a notation that may seem somewhat fluid, especially on first contact in such a brief introduction as this. But once assimilated, PMS seems to allow some of the flexibility of natural language within enough notational controls to enhance communication considerably.

Chapter 4

An Introduction to ISPS

Mario R. Barbacci

Introduction

This chapter introduces the reader to the ISPS notation. Although some details have been excluded, it covers enough of the language to provide a reading capability. Thus while this chapter in itself might not be sufficient to allow writing ISPS descriptions, it should be detailed enough to permit the reading and study of complex descriptions.

Instruction-Set Processor Descriptions

To describe the instruction-set processor (ISP) of a computer, or any machine, the operations, instructions, data-types, and interpretation rules used in the machine need to be defined. These are introduced gradually as the primary memory state, the processor state, and the interpretation cycle are described. Primary memory is not, in a strict sense, part of the instruction-set processor, but it plays such an important role in its operation that it is typically included in the description. In general, data-types (for example, integers, floating-point numbers, characters, and addresses) are abstractions of the contents of the machine registers and memories. One data-type that requires explicit treatment is the instruction, and the interpretation of instructions is explored in detail.

The PDP-8 ISPS description is a source of examples. In the presentation of the PDP-8 registers and data-types the following conventions will be used: (1) names in uppercase correspond to physical components on the PDP-8 (e.g., program counter and interrupt lines); (2) names in lowercase do not have corresponding physical components (e.g., implementation variables and instruction fields).

Memory State

The description of the PDP-8 begins by specifying the primary memory that is used to store data and instructions:

```
MP\Memory.Primary[0:4095]<0:11>,
```

The primary memory is declared here as an array of 4,096 words, each 12 bits wide. The memory has a name, MP, and an alias,

Memory.Primary. Such aliases are a special form of comment and are useful for indicating the meaning or usage of a register's name. As in most programming languages, ISPS identifiers consist of letters and digits and begin with a letter. A period with no space following is also used to increase readability. The expression [0:4095] describes the structure of the array. It declares the size (4,096 words) and the names of the words (0,1, . . . , 4094,4095). The expression <0:11> describes the structure of each individual word. It declares the size (12 bits) and the names of the bits (0,1, . . . ,10,11).

It should be noted that bit and word *names* are precisely that: identifiers for the subcomponents of a memory structure. These names do not necessarily indicate the absolute position of the subcomponents. Thus, R<7:3> is a valid definition of a 5-bit register. The fact that the five bits are named 7, 6, 5, 4, and 3 should not lead to confusion with the seventh, sixth, etc., positions inside the register. Thus, bit 7 is the leftmost bit, bit 6 is located in the next position to its right, etc., while bit 3 is the rightmost bit.

Memory is divided into 128-word pages. Page zero is used for holding global variables and can be accessed directly by each instruction. Locations 8 through 15 of page zero have the special property called *auto indexing*, whereby when a location is accessed indirectly, the contents of the location are incremented by 1. These regions of memory can be described as part of M as follows:

```
page.zero[0:127]<0:11>   := MP[0:127]<0:11>,
auto.index[0:7]<0:11>    := MP[8:15]<0:11>,
```

The word-naming (and bit-naming) conventions on the left-hand side of a field declaration are independent of the word (bit) names used on the right-hand side: auto. index[0] corresponds to MP[8], auto.index[1] corresponds to MP[9], etc.

Processor State

The processor state is defined by a collection of registers used to store data, instructions, condition codes, etc., during the instruction interpretation cycle.

The PDP-8 has a 1-bit register L, which contains the overflow or carry generated by the arithmetic operations, and a 12-bit register AC, which contains the result of the arithmetic and logic operations. The concatenation of L and AC constitutes an extended accumulator LAC. The structure of the extended accumulator is shown below:

```
LAC<0:12>,
      L\Link<>                := LAC<0>,
      AC\Accumulator<0:11>    := LAC<1:12>,
```

The expression<> indicates a single, unnamed bit (L is only 1 bit long and there is no need to specify a name for it).

The program counter is used to store the address of the instruction currently being executed as the machine steps through a program:

```
PC\Program.Counter<0:11>,
```

Twelve bits are needed in the PC to address all 4,096 locations of MP.

In the PDP-8 I/O devices are allowed to "interrupt" the central processor. When a device requires service from the central processor, it emulates a subroutine call, forcing the processor to execute an appropriate I/O subroutine. The presence of an interrupt request is indicated by setting the interrupt.request flag. The processor can honor these requests or not, depending on the setting of the interrupt.enable bit:

```
interrupt.enable<>,
interrupt.request<>,
```

There are 12 console switches which can be read by the processor. These switches are treated as a 12-bit register by the central processor:

```
switches<0:11>,
```

Instruction Format

Like most data-types and registers on the PDP-8, instructions are 12 bits long:

```
i\instruction<0:11>,
```

An instruction is a special kind of data-type. It is really an aggregate of smaller information units (operation codes, address modes, operand addresses, etc.). The structure of the instructions must be exposed by describing the format. Most PDP-8 instructions contain an operation code and an operand address:

```
op\operation.code<0:2>     := i<0:2>,
ib\indirect.bit<>          := i<3>,
pb\page.bit<>              := i<4>,
pa\page.address<0:6>       := i<5:11>,
```

The abstractions op, ib, pb, and pa allow the treatment of selected fields of the PDP-8 instructions as individual entities.

Partitioning the Description

In ISPS, a description can be divided into sections of the form:

```
**section.name**
<declaration>,
<declaration>,
. . . . . . . . . . . . . . .
**section.name**
<declaration>,
<declaration>,
. . . . . . . . . . . . . .
```

Each section begins with a header, an identifier enclosed between double asterisks. A section consists of a list of declarations separated by commas. Section names are not reserved keywords in the language but are used to convey some information about the entities declared inside the section. The register and memory declarations presented so far can be grouped into sections as shown at the top of page 25.

A few more field declarations have been added. These are used to interpret the I/O and operate instructions. The PDP-8 I/O instruction uses the nine bits of addressing information to specify operations for the I/O devices. These nine bits are divided into a *device selector* field (six bits, io.select<0:5>) and a *device operation* field (three bits, io.pulse<0:2>). Note that several alternate field declarations may be associated with the same portion of a register or data-type, thus adding flexibility to the description. A comment is indicated by an introductory exclamation point, and all characters following the exclamation point to the end of the line are treated as commentary and not as part of the description. The PDP-8 Operate instruction's address field is not interpreted as an address but as a list of suboperations. The DEC PDP-8 processor manuals provide additional details.

Effective Address

The effective address computation is an algorithm which computes addresses of data and instructions:

```
**Effective.Address**

last.pc<0:11>,

MA\effective.memory.address<0:11>:=
     begin
     DECODE pb =>
       begin
       0  := MA ='00000 @ pa,        ! page zero
       1  := MA =last.pc<0:4> @ pa  ! current page
       end next
     IF not ib => LEAVE MA next
     IF MA<0:8> eqv #001 =>
       MP[MA] = MP[MA] + 1 next       ! auto index
     MA = MP[MA]
     end,
```

```
**Memory.State**

MP\Memory.Primary[0:4095]<0:11>,
        page.zero[0:127]<0:11>        := MP[0:127]<0:11>,
        auto.index[0:7]<0:11>         := MP[8:15]<0:11>,


**Processor.State**

LAC<0:12>,
        L\Link<>                      := LAC<0>,
        AC\Accumulator<0:11>       := LAC<1:12>,
PC\Program.Counter<0:11>,
go<>,
interrupt.enable<>,
interrupt.request<>,
switches<0:11>,


**Instruction.Format**

i\instruction<0:11>,
        op\operation.code<0:2>    := i<0:2>,
        ib\indirect.bit<>         := i<3>,
        pb\page.bit<>             := i<4>,
        pa\page.address<0:6>      := i<5:11>,

        io.select<0:5>            := i<3:8>,      ! device select
        io.pulse<0:2>             := i<9:11>,     ! device operation
                io.pulse.1<>          := io.pulse<0>,
                io.pulse.2<>          := io.pulse<1>,
                io.pulse.4<>          := io.pulse<2>,

        group<> := i<3>,                ! microinstruction group
        CLA<>    := i<4>,                ! clear AC
        CLL<>    := i<5>,                ! clear L
        CMA<>    := i<6>,                ! complement AC
        CML<>    := i<7>,                ! complement L
        RAR<>    := i<8>,                ! rotate right
        RAL<>    := i<9>,                ! rotate left
        RT<>     := i<10>,               ! rotate twice
        IAC<>    := i<11>,               ! increment AC
        SMA<>    := i<5>,                ! skip on minus AC
        SPA<>    := i<5>,                ! skip on positive AC
        SZA<>    := i<6>,                ! skip on zero AC
        SNA<>    := i<6>,                ! skip on AC not zero
        SNL<>    := i<7>,                ! skip on L not zero
        SZL<>    := i<7>,                ! skip on L zero
        is<>     := i<8>,                ! invert skip sense
        OSR<>    := i<9>,                ! logical or AC with SWITCHES
        HLT<>    := i<10>,               ! halt the processor
```

Since the memory of the machine is 4,096 words long, addresses have to be 12 bits long. Of the 12 bits in an instruction, 3 bits have been allocated for the operation code (op) and there are only 9 bits (ib, pb, and pa) in the instruction register left for addressing information. These bits, together with some other portions of the processor state, are interpreted by the algorithm to yield the necessary 12 bits of addressing.

Address Computation

Instructions and data tend to be accessed sequentially or within address clusters. This property is called *locality*. The PDP-8 memory is logically divided into 32 pages of 128 words each. The concept of locality of memory references is used to reduce the addressing information by assuming that data are usually in the same page as the instructions that reference them. The pa portion of an instruction is that "address within the current page." The pb portion of an instruction is used as an escape mechanism to indicate when pa is to be used as an address within page 0 (MP[0:127]) instead of the current page.

The address of the current instruction is contained in last.pc and is used to compute the current page number.

The first step of the algorithm,

```
DECODE pb =>
        begin
        0 := MA ='00000 @ pa,
        1 := MA = last.pc<0:4> @ pa
        end next
```

indicates a group of alternative actions, to be selected according to the value of the expression following the DECODE operator. The alternatives appear enclosed between *begin* and *end* and separated by a comma. The expressions 0 := and 1 := are used to label the statements with the corresponding value of pb. The alternative statements can be left unnumbered, in which case they are treated as if they were labeled 0:=, 1:=, 2:=, etc.

The effective address (MA) is built by concatenating a page number with the page address (pa). The @ operator is used to indicate concatenation of operands. If pb is equal to 0, the effective address lies in page 0. If pb is equal to 1, the current page number is used instead.

Constants prefixed with the single quote represent binary numbers. '00000 represents a 5-bit string, which is concatenated with the 7 bits of pa to yield the 12 bits needed.

The transfer operator = modifies the memory or register specified on its left-hand side. If the right-hand side has more bits than the left-hand side, the right-hand side is truncated to the proper size by dropping the leftmost extra bits. If the right-hand side is shorter, enough 0 bits are added on its left until the length of the left-hand side is matched. Thus, the first conditional statement can be written as 0 := MA = pa.

The expression <0:4> is used to select bits 0, . . . ,4 of last.pc. These 5 bits contain the current page number and, together with the 7 bits of pa, yield the necessary 12 bits.

Indirect Addresses

A full 12-bit target address can be stored in a memory location used as a pointer. The instruction needs only to specify the address of this pointer location. Indirect addresses are specified via a bit in the instruction register (ib) which indicates whether we have a direct (ib=0) or an indirect (ib=1) address.

The second step of the algorithm,

```
IF not ib => LEAVE MA
```

is separated from the previous by the operator "next." The statement(s) preceding "next" must be completed before the statement following it can be executed. The first step computes a preliminary effective address. The second step tests the value of ib, and if it is equal to 0, then the preliminary effective address is used as the real effective address. If ib is equal to 1, the preliminary effective address is used to access a memory location containing the real effective address. In the former case, the expression "LEAVE MA" is used to indicate the termination of the procedure (this is similar to a RETURN statement in many programming languages).

Auto Indexing

Constants prefixed with the character # represent octal numbers. Thus #001 is equal to '000000001. The procedure treats indirect addresses as special cases. If a preliminary effective address in the range #0010:#0017 (8 to 15) is used as an indirect address (ib=1), the memory location is first incremented and the new value used as the indirect address:

```
IF MA<0:8> eqv #001 =>
  MP[MA] = MP[MA] + 1 next
MA = MP[MA]
```

By comparing the high-order bits of MA with #001 and ignoring the lower three bits we are in fact specifying a range of addresses (#0010, #0011, #0012, . . . ,#0017). Memory locations #0010:#0017 constitute the autoindexing registers.

Regardless of whether autoindexing has taken place, the last step of the algorithm uses the preliminary effective address (which may have been modified by autoindexing) as the address of a memory location which contains the real effective address:

```
MA=MP[MA]
```

Instruction Interpretation

The instruction interpretation section describes the instruction cycle, i.e., the fetching, decoding, and executing of instructions.

Instruction.Interpretation

```
interpret :=
        begin
        REPEAT begin
                i = MP[PC]; last.pc = PC next
                PC = PC + 1 next
                execute() next
                IF interrupt.enable and
                        interrupt.request =>
                        begin
                        MP[0] = PC next
                        PC = 1
                        end
                end
        end,
```

The instruction cycle is described by a loop. The REPEAT operator precedes a block of statements that are to be continuously executed. The instruction cycle of the machine consists of four steps:

1 A new instruction is fetched (i = MP[PC]).

2 The program counter is incremented (PC = PC + 1). It now points to the next instruction. Under normal circumstances (i.e., unless a Jump takes place) this will be the instruction to be executed next.

3 The instruction is executed (execute()).

4 Interrupt requests, if allowed are honored. The cycle is then repeated.

The semicolon separator is used to indicate concurrency (i.e., two statements separated by a semicolon are executed concurrently):

```
i = MP[PC]; last.pc = PC next
```

Notice how the value of the program counter is saved in last.pc before it is incremented. The effective address procedure relies on the fact that last.pc contains the address of the current instruction.

The execute procedure describes the individual instructions:

```
execute :=
  begin
  DECODE op =>
    begin
    #0\AND := AC = AC and MP[MA()],
    #1\TAD := LAC = LAC + MP[MA()],
    #2\ISZ := begin
                MP[MA] = MP[MA()] + 1 next
                IF MP[MA] eql 0 => PC = PC + 1
              end,
    #3\DCA := begin
                MP[MA()] = AC next
                AC = 0
              end,
    #4\JMS := begin
                MP[MA()] = PC next
                PC = MA + 1
              end,
    #5\JMP := PC = MA(),
    #6\IOT := input.output(),
    #7\OPR := operate()
    end
  end,
```

Instruction mnemonics can be indicated as aliases for the constants used to specify the operation codes:

```
#3\DCA := . . .
```

Operation Code 0\AND:
Logic AND

If the operation code is equal to 0, the contents of the accumulator (excluding the L bit) are replaced by the logical product of the accumulator and a memory location. MA() is used to indicate that the effective address computation must be executed in order to obtain the memory address.

Operation Code 1\TAD:
2's Complement Add

The TAD instruction follows the pattern of the previous instruction. Notice, however, that the complete accumulator (including the L bit) is involved in the operation. L will contain the overflow or carry out of the sign position of AC.

Operation Code 2\ISZ:
Increment and Skip if Zero

This instruction is described in two consecutive steps. The first step indicates that some memory location, specified by the effective address computation, will be incremented by 1. Notice the different uses of MA in the statement:

```
MP[MA] = MP[MA()] + 1
```

The effective address is computed once, MA(), and is used to fetch the memory location, MP[MA()]. The result of the addition must be stored back in the same memory location. This is indicated by using the effective address register, MA, on the left-hand side, MP[MA]. MA already contains the correct address and there is no need to recompute it. In fact, because of the autoindexing operations performed during the effective address computation, the effective address must be computed precisely once.

The second step of the instruction,

```
IF MP[MA] eql 0 => PC = PC + 1
```

tests the result of the addition. If the result is equal to 0 the program counter is incremented by 1, thus, in effect, skipping over the next instruction in sequence. Once again, MA is used instead of MA() to avoid undesirable side effects.

Operation Code 3\DCA:
Deposit and Clear Accumulator

This instruction deposits the accumulator in a memory location and then clears the accumulator (excluding the L bit).

Operation Code 4\JMS:
Jump to Subroutine

This instruction alters the normal sequence of instructions by modifying the program counter so that the next instruction will be not the one following the current instruction, but the one located at a memory location specified by the effective address. The program counter is stored into the location preceding the subroutine code (the result of MA()). The program counter is then modified to point to the first instruction of the subroutine (MA + 1).

Operation Code 5\JMP:
Jump

This instruction also modifies the normal sequence of instructions. It can be used to jump to disjoint pieces of code. If we use ib=1 and specify the address of the location preceding the subroutine, the result of the effective address computation will yield the return address that was stored by the subroutine call.

Operation Code 6\IOT:
Input/Output

The input.output procedure describes two specific cases of I/O instruction, namely those used to control the interrupt mechanism:

```
input.output :=
  begin
  DECODE i<3:11> =>
    begin
    #001\ION :=
      begin
                                ! turn Interrupt ON
      interrupt.enable = 1 next
      RESTART interpret
      end,
    #002\IOF :=
      begin
                                ! turn Interrupt OFF
      interrupt.enable = 0
      end,
                                ! not implemented
    otherwise := no.op()
    end
  end,
```

The "otherwise" operation can be specified in a DECODE operation to indicate a default action to be executed if none of the explicitly named cases (#001 or #002) applies. All other I/O operations default to a predefined ISPS procedure no.op(); this is done simply to keep the examples short.

I/O operation #002 disables interrupts. It typically occurs as the first instruction of an interrupt handling routine. I/O operation #001 enables interrupts. It typically occurs at the end of an interrupt handling subroutine. Its effect is delayed for one instruction (the return from the subroutine) to avoid losing the return address should an interrupt occur immediately. This is achieved by skipping over the last portion of the instruction interpretation cycle:

```
IF interrupt.enable.and.inter-
rupt.request => . . .
```

The "RESTART interpret" operation is used to indicate that the input.output procedure returns, not to the place from which it was invoked (inside execute), but to the beginning of the interpret procedure, thus bypassing interrupt trapping for one instruction.

Operation Code 7\OPR:
Operate

The Operate instruction encodes a large number of primitive "microoperations" in the address bits of an instruction. Some bits (e.g., CLA) represent a microoperation by themselves. Others (e.g., RT and RAL) jointly represent a microoperation. There are several conditional skip microoperations. These are grouped in a separate procedure for readability, as shown on pages 29 and 30.

Several microoperations can appear in the same instruction; however, not all combinations are legal or useful. Microoperations

```
operate :=
        begin
        DECODE group=>
                begin
                0 :=    begin                                       ! Group
                                                                    1 microinstr.
                        IF CLA => AC = 0
                                                ! Clear accumulator
                        IF CLL => L = 0 next
                                                ! Clear link
                        IF CMA => AC = not AC;
                                                ! Complement accumulator
                        IF CML => L = not L next
                                                ! Complement link
                        IF IAC => LAC = LAC + 1 next
                                                ! Increment accumulator
                        DECODE RT =>            ! rotate once or twice
                                begin
                                0 :=    begin           ! once
                                        IF RAL => LAC = LAC slr 1;
                                        IF RAR => LAC = LAC srr 1
                                        end,
                                1 :=    begin           ! twice
                                        IF RAL => LAC = LAC slr 2;
                                        IF RAR => LAC = LAC srr 2
                                        end
                                end
                        end,
                1 :=    begin                                       ! groups 2 and 3.
                        DECODE i<11> =>
                                begin
                                0 :=    begin           ! group 2
                                        skip.group() next
                                        IF CLA => AC = 0 next
                                        IF OSR => AC = AC or switches;
                                        IF HLT => RUN = 0
                                        end,
                                1 :=    begin           ! group 3
                                        IF CLA => AC = 0 next
                                        no.op() ! eae group
                                        end
                                end
                        end
                end
        end
```

(Continued on next page)

```
skip<>,

skip.group :=
        begin
        skip = 0 next
        DECODE is =>                                      ! invert skip condition
                begin
                0 :=    begin
                        IF SNL and (L eql 1) => skip = 1;
                        IF SZA and (AC eql 0) => skip = 1;
                        IF SMA and (AC lss 0) => skip = 1
                        end,
                1 :=    begin
                        IF SZL@SNA@SPA eql 0 => skip = 1;
                        IF SZL and (L eql 0) => skip = 1;
                        IF SNA and (AC neq 0) => skip = 1;
                        IF SPA and (AC geq 0) => skip = 1
                        end
                end next
        IF skip => PC = PC + 1                            ! Skip
        end,
```

are executed at different points in time, thus allowing sequences of transformations to be applied to the accumulator and/or link bit. For instance, in the group 1 microoperations, clearing AC/L is done before complementing them, this is done before incrementing the combined L@AC (LAC) register, and this in turn precedes the rotation of L@AC.

Other Features of ISPS

Not all the features of the notation have been presented in the examples. This section will attempt to provide a list of the missing operations to help readers follow larger descriptions.

Constants

In general, a constant is a sequence of characters drawn from some alphabet determined by the base of the constant. The base of a nondecimal constant is given by a prefix character. The alphabets for the predefined bases in ISPS are:

Base	Prefix	Alphabet
2	'	0,1,?
8	#	0,1,2,3,4,5,6,7,?
10		0,1,2,3,4,5,6,7,8,9,?
16	"	0,1,2,3,4,5,6,7,8,9,A,B,C,D,E,F,?

The question mark can be used to specify a "don't care" digit. Its presence stands for any digit in the corresponding alphabet.

The length of a constant is measured in bits. A decimal constant is one bit longer than the smallest number of bits needed to represent its value to allow representation of negative numbers (don't care decimal digits result in constants of unspecified length). Binary constants have one bit for each digit explicitly written. Octal constants have three bits for each digit explicitly written. Hexadecimal constants have four bits for each digit explicitly written.

Example	Length	Bit pattern
"1000	16	0001000000000000
15	5	01111
#17	6	001111
0	2	00
'0?101	5	0?101
#?2	6	???010

Arithmetic Representation

ISPS allows the user to specify arithmetic operations in four different representations: 2's complement, 1's complement, sign magnitude, and unsigned magnitude (the default is 2's complement). To specify a different representation, the following modifiers can be used.

Modifier	Arithmetic representation
{tc}	2's complement
{oc}	1's complement

{sm}	Sign/magnitude
{us}	Unsigned magnitude

In all the signed representations, the sign bit is the leftmost position of the operand (1 for negative numbers, 0 for positive numbers). The above modifiers can be attached to any arithmetic or relational operator to override a default. They can also be attached to a procedure declaration to set a default throughout the body. When attached to a section name the default applies to all the declarations in the section:

```
test :=
        begin {oc}        ! Default for the body
        . . .
        end,
**Section.l** {tc}        ! Default for the section
        . . .
X = Y + {sm} Z                    ! Instance
```

Arithmetic representation is a property of the operator, not the operand. Thus, the same bit pattern can be treated as a 2's complement or an unsigned integer, depending on the arithmetic context in which it is used.

Sign Extension

All ISPS data operators define results whose length is determined both by the lengths of the operands and the specific operator. Some operations require that their operands be of the same length. This is usually accomplished by "sign-extending" the operands. In the context of unsigned magnitude arithmetic, sign extension is interpreted as zero-extension (i.e., padding with 0s on the left). In 1's and 2's complement arithmetic the expansion is done by replication of the sign bit. In sign magnitude arithmetic the expansion is done by inserting 0s between the sign bit and the most significant bit of the operand.

Data Operators (in Order of Precedence)

Negation and Complement: −, not. Unary − generates the arithmetic complement of the operand (the operation is invalid in unsigned arithmetic.) The result is one bit longer than the operand. The not operator generates the logical complement of the operand. The result has the same length as the operand.

Concatenation: @. The @ operator concatenates the two operands. The length of the result is the sum of the lengths of the operands.

Shift and Rotate: sl0,sll,sld,slr,sr0,sr1,srd,srr. These operators shift or rotate the left operand the number of places specified by the right operand. The result has the same length as the left operand. The operators have the format "sxy," where "x" is either l(eft) or r(ight) to indicate the direction of movement. The "y" is either 0, 1, d(uplicate), or r(otate) to indicate the source of bits to be shifted in. sx1 shifts its left operand, inserting 1s in the vacant positions. sx0 is similar to sx1 but inserting 0s. sxd inserts copies of the bit, leaving the position to be vacated (not the bit being shifted out). sxr inserts copies of the bit being shifted out (i.e., rotates the left operand).

Multiplication, Division, and Remainder: ∗,/,mod. These operators compute the arithmetic product, quotient, and remainder of the two operands, repectively. The lengths of the results are:

Operation	Length of result
∗	Sum of lengths
/	Left operand (dividend)
mod	Right operand (divisor)

Addition and Subtraction: +, −. The + and − operators compute the arithmetic sum and difference of the two operands, respectively. The shortest operand is sign-extended, and the result is one bit longer than the largest operand.

Relational Operations: eql,neq,lss,leq,gtr,geq,tst. These operations perform an arithmetic comparison between the two operands. The shortest operand is sign-extended, and the result is either one or two bits long. The first six operators (i.e., all except tst) produce a one-bit result indicating whether the relation is True (1) or False (0). The tst operator produces a two-bit result indicating whether the relation between the left and right operands is lss (0), eql (1), or gtr (2).

Conjunction and Equivalence: and, eqv. These operators produce the logical product and coincidence operations of the two operands. The shortest operand is zero-extended, and the result is as long as the largest operand.

Disjunction and Nonequivalence: or, xor. These operators produce the logical sum and difference operations of the two operands. The shortest operand is zero-extended, and the result is as long as the largest operand.

Logical and Arithmetic Assignment: =, <=. The logical assignment operator = truncates or zero-extends the source's (right operand's) most significant bits to match the length of the destination (the left operand). The arithmetic assignment operator <= truncates or sign-extends the source to match the length of the destination.

Summary

The foregoing examples should allow the reader to understand all the ISPS descriptions in the book. All the descriptions follow a standard format:

Memory declarations	MP state
	PC state
	External state
	Implementation declarations
Formats and operations	Instruction format
	Address calculation
	Service facilities
Interpreter	Instruction interpretation
	Instruction set

The implementation declarations are required for temporary storage in complex expression evaluations. These variables probably have similar, if not identical, counterparts in the actual machine implementation. However, these variables are invisible to the programmer and hence are not mentioned in the programmer's manual.

The following conventions for capitalization have been adopted. Architectural features, instruction mnemonics, and other names that are capitalized in the manufacturer's literature are in uppercase in the ISPS descriptions to aid recognizability. To aid readability, all ISPS operators that affect control flow are in uppercase. These include: DECODE, IF, RESTART, LEAVE, REPEAT, RESUME, STOP, and WAIT. Everything else is lowercase, including operators (e.g., eql, eqv, leq, lss, mod, neq, no.op, not, or, sl0, sl1, sld, slr, sr0, sr1, srd, srr, tst, and xor), ISPS implementation variable, and the remaining ISPS reserve words (e.g., begin, end, next).

All the ISPS descriptions that appear in this book have been compiled and simulated. The descriptions are complete, except for the instruction-set portion in large machines. In order to keep the size of the descriptions in bounds, we have deleted all but a representative instruction of each op code decoding group for these large machines. Nevertheless, these partial ISPS descriptions have been compiled and simulated.

Section 2

The Computer Space

The preceding chapters have provided a view of a computer system as an organized hierarchy of many levels: physical devices, electronic circuits, logic circuits, register-transfer systems, programs, and PMS systems. We must remember that these are *levels of description* for what, after all, remains the same physical system. Each higher level describes more of the total system, but with a loss of detail. As this is an engineered system, great care is taken that each level represent adequately all the behavior necessary to determine the performance of the system. In natural systems too there are often many levels of description (e.g., in biological systems, from the molecule to the organelle to the cell to the tissue to the organ to the organism).

However, in natural systems we usually depend on statistics to eliminate the details of lower levels and permit aggregation, and they always do so imperfectly. In computer systems, on the other hand, the aggregation is intended to be perfect. It fails, of course, and so both error detection and error correction exist as fundamental activities in computer systems. But these imperfections are ascribed to the system itself and not to our description of it, which is just the opposite from how we treat natural systems. Only the PMS level of description is natural, in the sense of not being the intended result of the design. This is because performance is defined ultimately at the programming level. The aggregations and simplifications that go into a PMS description (e.g., measuring power by bits per second) are approximations, just as they are for any natural system (e.g., measuring the productivity of the economy by gross national product).

We have provided descriptive systems for the top levels of the hierarchy: the PMS level and the ISP level, the latter defining the basic components of the programming level in terms of the RT level just below. These are the two descriptions that are of most concern in the overall design of a computer system. We did not define the lower levels, because they go beyond the focus of this book. Neither did we define the program level, partly because there exists no uniform description (no common programming language) and partly because the computer designer works mostly at the interface, defining the instruction set. This latter is what the ISP provides.[1]

PMS and ISP permit the description of an indefinite number of computer systems—indeed, all that come within the scope of the current design art. (They might even be taken as a definition of what that current art is.) Over 10^7 individual computer systems have in fact come into existence, each of which can be described in PMS and ISP. They are not all radically individual. There are about 10^3 types of computer systems represented, if we define two systems with the same Pc to be of the same type. (By exercising various options, a single computer type could take on 10^5 different forms.)

Of these thousand-odd types, we present in this book about 30. What sort of total population do we have here? What does our minuscule sample look like when compared with the whole? More fundamentally, what are the significant aspects of the computer systems that should be used in a comparison or classification? These are the questions we will try to deal with in this section and subsequently in Part 2.

For any system, either an entire computer C or a component, such as P, M, or S, it is convenient to distinguish its function, its performance, and its structure. The system is designed to operate in some task environment; to accomplish such tasks is its *function*. How well it does these tasks is its *performance*. Evaluation of performance is normally restricted to these tasks. Although it is always noteworthy when a system can perform adequately outside its specified domain (e.g., when a business computer is also a good control computer), it is rarely worth noting when a system cannot perform those tasks it was not built to perform. Thus, function denotes scope, and performance denotes an evaluation within that scope.

Structure denotes those aspects of the system that allow it to perform. This includes descriptions of its subcomponents and how they are organized. Performance of subcomponents often may be considered structure as far as the whole system is concerned, especially if the performance can be taken as given. For example, early digital transmission–oriented telephone lines came in two capacities, ~200 bit/sec and ~2,000 bit/sec. From the viewpoint of the telephone system, these are performance measures; from the viewpoint of a computer system with remote terminals, these are structural parameters. The smaller capacity attaches a single 20-char/terminal to a telephone line, while the larger one requires a structure to multiplex traffic from 10 terminals onto one line.

Typically, design proceeds in a context in which the function of the system to be developed is taken as given and certain structures are available; the problem is to construct a structure that achieves adequate performance.

These terms apply to any designed system. For example, consider automotive vehicles. Function is a classification by use: cars to carry people, trucks to carry goods, racers to win competitions, antiques to satisfy nostalgia and collectors' pride. Performance is those aspects of behavior relevant to function: maximum speed, power-to-weight ratio, cargo capacity, run

---

[1] An increasingly popular view is that the program and RT levels (with ISP in between) are one, thus erasing the difference between hardware and software. The boundary appears to us not quite so invisible. We take the important task to be drawing the boundary in the right place for any specific design.

versus non run for an antique, and so on. Structure is such things as number of wheels, shape of the vehicle, stroke volume, and gear ratios. Structure determines performance, although from the standpoint of design, of course, causality runs the other way: from function to performance to structure. Design also includes an aesthetic component. Just as the shape of a car is not solely determined by function and performance, so, too, the shape of an instruction set reflects aesthetic considerations.

There are, then, three main ways to classify or describe a computer system: according to its function, its performance, or its structure. Each consists in turn of a number of dimensions. It is useful to think of all these dimensions as making up a large space in which any computer system can be located as a point. In such a space all the thousand computer types built to date constitute a sparse scatter, clustering (it is to be hoped) in various regions that make sense functionally and economically. The 30 computer types in this book sample this larger scatter in some way, to give a picture both of the entire space and of the part already explored.

How many dimensions are there in this computer space? Indefinitely many, if one wants to locate a computer with ultimate precision. In fact, if one wants to go all the way, one might as well give the PMS and ISP descriptions (and down through the RT, logic, circuit, and device levels). The virtue of thinking of such a space is to abstract to a small number of dimensions, and to select those that are most relevant. Of the functions, one wants those that most influence the design; of the performance, one wants those that make the largest difference; of structure those that not only affect performance but represent possible design choices by the computer engineer. In addition, one wants dimensions along which there is significant variation. Those aspects of computer systems which are common to all, such as the use of binary devices, though of supreme interest, are not part of the computer space.

No theory of computer systems is sufficiently comprehensive to define completely the dimensions of computer space. Guidelines have sprung from past experience in designing machines, but at some point the architect must simply propose a set of dimensions which are justified later, in performance. Table 1 abstracts a set of dimensions for function and structure. Chapter 5 gives a set for performance. The performance dimensions can be summarized in terms of a Kiviat graph, defined in Chap. 5. Together with ISP and PMS, Kiviat graphs will be used throughout the book to characterize the computer structures under study.

Table 1 gives 2 dimensions for computer system function and 25 for computer structure. However, the dimensions are not all independent. Many of the structure dimensions correlate highly (though not perfectly). Thus, in Table 1 we have put the structure dimensions in seven horizontal groups, with the most relevant at the left in each group. (In the first structure group, we have also added two temporal dimensions, since a strong correlation with time exists.) We have omitted two important dimensions for

which we do not have values: reliability (mean time between failures per operation) and physical size density (e.g., bits per cubic foot), both of which increase with generation.

With each dimension we have indicated the range of possible values. For some (Pc.speed, for example) this is a numerical quantity. However, for most, the range is a discrete set of design choices, which may or may not have a simple ordering. Clearly, these discrete values are selections from a meaningful subspace of design choices, but mostly we do not know how to construct that subspace. The values given are those that have arisen in practice, and they serve to classify the computers in the book. Typically, the discrete sets of design choices are ordered in terms of increasing hardware complexity and increasing system performance. Frequently the set of design choices, having evolved over time, represents a developmental chain, as discussed in Chap. 1. As the structure of a system evolves along a chain, a specialized subsystem may emerge, with the most primitive dimensional values, and then evolve in the same manner as the original system. This phenomenon, illustrated in Chap. 1, has been termed the *wheel of reincarnation* and will be discussed further in Chap. 6.

This section of the book is devoted to a discussion of each of the computer space dimensions. Each dimension will be defined, its basis for selection discussed, and its ordering in Table 1 explained. Chapter 5 presents the computer function and performance dimensions, while Chap. 6 (and Part 2) discusses the structural dimensions. We give the entire set of dimensions here at the beginning, both for later reference and to reinforce the concept of a single computer space in which computer systems can be located. Each dimension in Table 1 has a reference to the part, section, and/or chapters in the book that contain a discussion of that dimension.

A detailed discussion of several structural dimensions has been placed in Part 2, where several real computer systems are used to illustrate the variations across a dimension. The introductions to each section in Part 2 present further refinements to the design choices for the dimension under consideration. Because of the length of these taxonomies, only the major design areas of choice (not the full list of alternative choices) are reproduced in Table 1.

We will refer to the set of dimensions in Table 1 from now on simply as "the computer space."

History

Like all systems subject to variation and selection, computers have evolved through time. So striking and rapid has been this evolution that the concept of "generation" has become firmly embedded in the computer engineering culture (to say nothing of the marketing culture and the view of the lay public). It is at best an ambiguous term, having none of the sharpness of its root term in biological evolution, where it is possible to draw a strict genealogical tree. Nevertheless, the term is useful in stressing that the history of computer systems is not just a story of particular scientists discovering or building particular things, but of a somewhat more impersonal and widespread series of advances that have changed computer systems radically.

The generations are best defined solely in terms of logic technology (see Table 1): the first generation is that of vacuum tubes (1945–1958); the second generation is that of discrete transistors (1958–1966); the third, small- and medium-scale integrated circuits (1966–1972); the fourth, large-scale integration with 100 ~ 10,000 gates per chip (1972–1978); and the fifth, very-large-scale integration (1978–). Chip complexities in the fourth generation were large enough to allow the integration of a processor on a single chip.

It is a measure of American industry's generally ahistorical view of things that the title of "first" generation has been allowed to be attached to a collection of machines that were some generations removed from the beginnings by any reasonable accounting. Mechanical and electromechanical computers existed prior to electronic ones. Furthermore, they were the functional equivalents of electronic computers and were realized to be such. They were also separated by a wide gap in performance and structure, both from each other and from vacuum-tube machines. Thus, by reasonable reckoning, we are currently in the seventh generation of computers, not the fifth. But usage is now too well established to change. The concept of precomputer generation handles this anomaly.

Actually, it was not always viewed thus. Figure 1 reproduces a genealogical tree of the early computers prepared by the National

Fig. 1. The "family tree" of computer design. The remarkable growth of electronic computing systems in the Western world began primarily through government support of research and development in the universities. The need for data-processing facilities of increased capacity inspired further support for their development in both educational instutitions and private industry. The current generation of computers is predominantly the result of development by private industry. The tree lists many of the machines developed in these ways. At the roots are the contributions of many existing technologies to the rapid growth from electromechanical to electronic systems. Some of the milestones are ENIAC (Electronic Numerical Integrator and Computer), the first electronic computer; EDVAC (Electronic Discrete Variable Automatic Computer), the first internally stored-program computer and first acoustic delay-line storage; MADM (Manchester Automatic Digital Machine), the first index registers (B lines) and first cathode-ray-tube electrostatic storage; MTC (Memory Test Computer), the first core-storage computer. (Courtesy of National Science Foundation.)

Table 1   The Computer Space Dimensions

Computer function	
Computer function (Chap. 5)	*Computer class (Chap. 1; Part 3)*
Scientific	Maxicomputer
Commercial	
Manufacturing	Minicomputer
Communications	
Transportation	Microcomputer
Education	Monolithic microcomputer
Home	

Computer structure					
Logic technology (Chap. 6)	*Generation*	*Component complexity*	*Historical date*	*Pc.speed (s)*	*Cost/operation ($/bit/s)*
Mechanical					
Electromechanical			1930	10^{-1}	1000
Vacuum tube	First		1945	10^{-3}	10
Transistor	Second	1 transistor	1958	10^{-5}	1
Hybrid			1964	10^{-6}	
Small- and medium-scale integrated (SSI, MSI)	Third	1 ~ 10 gates, SSI; 10 ~ 100 gates, MSI	1966	10^{-7}	0.1
Large-scale integrated (LSI)	Fourth	100 ~ 10,000 gates	1972	10^{-8}	0.01
Very-large-scale integrated (VLSI)	Fifth	10,000 ~ 100,000 gates	1978	10^{-8}	0.0001
Ultra-large-scale integrated (ULSI)	Sixth	>100,000 gates			

Log bytes of virtual address	*Word size*	*Base*	*Data-types*
1–12	8b	Binary	Word
	12 b	Decimal	Integer|address [integer]
12–20	16 b		Bit|bit vector
	18 b		Instruction
20–24	24 b		Floating point
24–32	32 b		Character
32–48	48 b	Character [6b]	Character string
	64 b	Character [8b]	Word vector
			Vector
			Matrix
			Array
			Lists, stacks

Addresses/instruction (Chap. 6)	*M.processor state (excluding program counter) (Chap. 6)*
0 address [stack]	Stack
1 address	1 accumulator
1 + x [index] address	Accumulator and index registers
1 + g [general register] address	General-register array
2 address	
3 address	No explicit state
n + 1 address	

Table 1 *(Continued)*

PMS structure (Chap. 6; Part 2, Sec. 3, 4, 5)	*Switching (Chap. 6; Part 2, Secs. 4, 5)*	*Processor function (Chap. 6; Part 2, Secs. 1, 6, 7, 8)*
1Pc	1:n[duplex]	P.microprogram
1Pc[interrupt]		Pc
1Pc-nPio	n:m[time-multiplex]	Pc[no io]
1Pc-nPio-P[display]		Pio
2C[duplex]	2:n[dual-duplex]	P.display
nPc[multiprocessing]	n:m[cross-point]	P.language
nPc-P[array|special algorithm]		P.array
nPc[parallel processing]		P.vector move
C[network]		P.algorithm
Network	n/2:n/2[non-hierarchy]	P.fault.tolerant

Accessing algorithm (Chap. 6)	*Mp.size (Chap. 6)*	*Ms.size (Chap. 6)*		*Mp.speed (b/s) (Chap. 6)*	*Ms.speed (b/s) (Chap. 6)*
Linear [stack]					
Linear [queue]					
Bilinear		Tape [large]			$>10^5$
Cyclic-random		Disk [medium]	magnetic card [large]		
Cyclic	Drum [large]	Drum [small]	photostore [large]	$>10^6$	
Random	Core [medium]	Core [smaller]		$>10^7$	$>10^7$
Content	Film [small]			$>10^8$	
Associative	Integrated circuit			$>10^9$	

Multiprocess environment (Part 2, Sec. 2)	*Interprocess communication (Part 2, Sec. 2)*	*Storage hierarchy (Part 2, Sec. 2)*
1 process	Subroutines and traps	
1 process with interrupt-evoked processes	Interrupts from I/O	
1 process with multiple concurrent subprocesses (for example, 1Pc.nPio)	Interprocessor interrupts	
Monitor or fixed process (M) + one-at-a-time (variable) process	Extracodes (programmed operators for monitor calls)	
M + n swapped foreground/background process		Mapping function
M + n processes (multiprogramming) with swapping	Synchronization	Number of maps
No relocation	producer/consumer	Allocation
1 segment	P and V	strategies
2 segments (pure, impure)	Mailboxes	Protection
>2 segments		
Pages		
M + n segments with shared processes	Interprocess communication	
Fixed-length paged segments		
Multiple-length paged segments		
Variable-length segments		

Parallelism (Chap. 6; Part 2, Sec. 3)	*Overlap (Part 2, Sec. 3)*
Serial by bit	Processor-I/O
Serial by character	Processor-memory
Parallel by word	Processor units
Parallel by bit slice	Memory units
Parallel by vector	
Parallel by array	
Multiple control units	
Multiple functional units	
Replication of processors, memory, I/O	

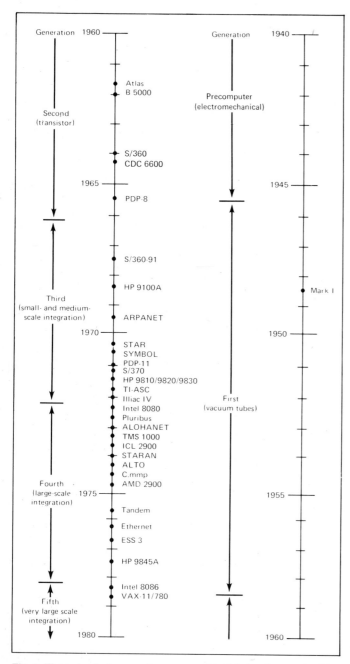

Fig. 2. Time chart of computers covered in this book organized by date of introduction.

Science Foundation in 1959. Notice that the Harvard Mark machines, which were constructed from relays (hence electromechanical) are accorded the place of honor as first-generation (but Babbage is nowhere to be seen).

It is not appropriate to provide here an adequate history of computer technology. The early story has often been told, starting with Babbage and early mechanical calculators, through Hollerith punched cards, on to the relay calculators at Bell Laboratories and Harvard, up to the birth of electronic machines with ENIAC, and finally to the stored-program concept with the von Neumann machine at the Institute for Advanced Studies (IAS), EDSAC at Cambridge University, and EDVAC at the University of Pennsylvania (with the contemporary developments by ZUSE in Germany often left out). The reader is referred to Rosen [1969] and Lavington [1975] for example histories of computers.

Our purpose here is to explore the fundamental principles in computer engineering that have evolved and multiplied. The computer space, for example, has a sufficient population density that significant trends can be noted and illustrated by actual machine example. The population density is also large enough to support several families of related[1] computer structures. These families offer a unique opportunity to observe trends and project models in portions of the computer space where the values for major dimensions are held constant.

Figure 2 lists the computers covered in this book. The computer space in Table 1 and the time chart in Fig. 2 provide an overall framework for the book. We are now ready to consider each of the dimensions individually.

References

Lavington [1975]; Rosen [1969].

[1]Usually via a compatible ISP.

Chapter 5

Function and Performance

Function

The most striking fact about function is the existence of only a single major dimension, and with only a few values. Perhaps we have taken a simplistic view of the functions that computers perform, but we think our computer space represents reality: to wit, there is remarkably little shaping of computer structure to fit the function to be performed.

At the root of this lies the general-purpose nature of computers, in which all the functional specialization occurs at the time of programming and not at the time of design. However, it might seem that specialized environments would not require all the generality, so that functional adaptation would still be possible. But this appears not to be so for two reasons. First, the level of operations of the Pc (as defined in the ISP) is too basic to reflect the kind of specialization offered by the environment (think of information-transfer or conditional-transfer operations). Second, all environments ultimately require a variety of tasks in addition to the main specialized task. These include at least language compilation or assembly, readable formatted output, debugging aids, and other utility routines. By the time these have been added, a substantial requirement for generality has been generated.

However, this is not the whole story. A second part is the difference between the computer type and the specific configuration assembled for a task. The latter is often carefully specialized to the function to be performed. But this is mostly the amount of Mp, the amount and types of Ms, and the number and types of T's. Within limits, these are all items that can be attached to any type of computer (i.e., to any Pc) and are handled in an environment-independent way. Thus there is little specialization of computer types, but great specialization of particular configurations. That this should be the case indicates something about the nature of the functional specialization—that it can be expressed adequately in gross PMS terms, as more bits of storage and more data rate.

There is still more to the story. Some functional specialization exists, as indicated in the dimension. This depends primarily on two kinds of things beyond the reach of the configurational adaptation described above. The first consists of demands for low power consumption, ruggedness, small size, etc. These have strong effects on design, but *below* the ISP and PMS levels. The second consists of demands for large amounts of processing power. One response to this again affects design at the lower levels of logic, devices, and circuitry and has little impact on design at the ISP and PMS level. But response is also possible in terms of the data-types that are built into the ISP. Large machines have data-types that are appropriate to their tasks (with operations to match), and these affect the design. In fact, this effect is the substance of the functional specialization shown in the computer space dimension.

Finally, there is one last part of the story, and it is the most interesting of all. Various groups of computer engineers have felt strongly from time to time that functional specialization should exist, and they have set out to create such machines. These efforts have often produced machines that were different from the existing main line of computers, i.e., were appropriately specialized. But the net effect of almost all such attempts has been that the new idea was seen to be good in general for all computers and was taken back into the main line of computers. Thus, what started out to be a functional separation turned out to be simply a way to produce rapid development of a more universally applicable computer. A classic example is the expansion of input/output facilities in creating a functionally specialized business machine, which simply led to better I/O facilities for all computers. We will have more to say about such examples as we discuss the values along the dimension.

The functional dimensions can be based on the environment of the user's intended application. The following discussion has evolved from Bell and Newell [1971] and Bell, Mudge, and McNamara [1978].

Table 1 elaborates the seven subdimensions by listing typical functions for each. The functionality for each subdimension is arranged in increasing order of complexity. The tabulation illustrates that, for each discipline or environment, functionality evolves to a form of direct, interactive use with multiprogramming.

Scientific

The first machines were clearly designed for scientific calculations. For example, Aberdeen Proving Grounds funded the early work on the ENIAC for the computation of ballistic firing tables. The image used frequently by the early computer designers was the computer as a statistical clerk, the arithmetic unit being the desk calculator, the memory the work sheet, and the program the instructions that the mathematician gave to the clerk.

From a design standpoint, scientific computation has posed two striking requirements. The first is the great accuracy of the numbers, which has led to word lengths of 36 to 64 bits (11 to 19 decimal digits of significance) and arises from the discrete representation of continuous functions, the propagation of round-off error during arithmetic operations, etc. The second is the emphasis on fast arithmetic operations, i.e., on arithmetic power. In the early machines the standard rule for estimating computa-

Table 1   Discipline/Environment-Based Functional Segmentation

Scientific†, engineering, and design
- Numbers, algorithms, symbols, text, graphs: storage and processing
- Traditional batch computation†
- Data acquisition†
- Interactive problem solving†
- Real time (includes calculators and text processing)
- Signal and image processing†
- Data base (notebooks and records)

Commercial environment
- Financial control industry, retail/wholesale, and distribution
- Billing, inventory, payroll, accounts receivable/payable
- Records storage and processing
- Traditional batch data entry
- Transaction processing against data base
- Business analysis (includes calculators)†

Manufacturing control environment
- Records storage and processing
- Batch†
- Data logging and alarm checking
- Continuous real time control
- Discrete real time control
  - Machine-based
  - People/parts flow

Communications, office, and publishing
- Message switching
- Front-end processing
- Store and forward networks
- Speech input/output
- Terminals and systems
- Word processing, including computer conferencing and publishing

Transportation systems
- Network flow control
- On-board control

Education
- Computer-assisted instruction
- Algorithms, symbols, test: storage and processing
- Drill and practice
- Library storage

Home (using TV set)
- Entertainment, record keeping, instruction, data base access

†Implies continuous program development.

Adapted from Bell, Mudge, and McNamara [1978].

tion times was to count the number of multiplications in a program; all else could be neglected. The arithmetic unit has developed to where the floating-point multiply is hardly more expensive than the floating-point add. This requirement for fast arithmetic, however, has really been directed at the logic design level, not at the ISP or PMS level. Thus, the main effect at the ISP is the adoption of long word lengths, floating-point data-types (in addition to integers), and an extensive repertoire of arithmetic operations in the ISP. The main PMS effect is the emphasis on the classic "statistical clerk" PMS design.

The press for increased arithmetic processing has led in recent times to the development of various forms of Pc concurrency, as in the look-ahead of the IBM System/360 Model 91 (Chap. 18) and the n-instruction buffer of the CDC 6600 (Chap. 43). This might be considered a unique functional specialization for scientific computation. Although the needs for scientific computation initiated the exploration of concurrency and parallelism, these functions are applicable in all computers above a certain power, whatever the task domain. Indeed, even microcomputers prefetch instructions. Physical limits on component speed and signal propagation will make these techniques universally attractive.

A better case for permanent specialization can be made in the special-algorithm computers, which compute the fast Fourier transform or do vector operations. Here we finally have systems whose whole design is responsive to a narrow class of problems. This may extend to the very special kinds of Pc parallelism exhibited by the ILLIAC IV (Chap. 20), although there is substantial attempt at generality in such systems.

Whereas early scientific computers dealt mainly with numerical data-types, their use has grown to include text and graphics. In engineering applications, the scientific computer has evolved to a sophisticated notebook for keeping specifications, designs, and scientific records.

Commercial

In the early days of electronic computing it was felt by many that there was a major functional separation between business computing and scientific computing.[1] Scientific problems were "large computing-small input/output"; business problems were "small computing-large input/output." Historically, the IBM 701 scientific computer, for example, used the Pc to control everything dynamically, actually catching the bits from running tapes on the fly (by executing well-timed small loops). These design efforts for business computers resulted in the IBM 702 (and subsequently the IBM 705, 708, and 7080). This machine had two major innovations for IBM: it used characters, and it had a PMS structure that permitted more flexible and voluminous input/output. The latter feature was immediately incorporated into scientific computers, e.g., into the 709, and then into all large

[1]Such feelings are still extant. Whatever the validity of such feelings, the important consideration is their effect on a particular period of computer development.

scientific computers as separate input/output control (either Kio or Pio), for it was realized that there were also demands on input/output for scientific calculation. Thus the bifurcation was temporarily halted.

The specialization to characters as a basic type (as opposed to long words) was already present in the IBM 702 but did not have its effect until 5 years later with the development of the IBM 1401. The latter machine was adapted to business, both in being character-based and in being small enough that small businesses could afford it. It was extremely successful (many thousands were produced) and certainly represents a successful functional specialization for business. However, it is interesting that the specialization has not been maintained, for the IBM System/360 (Chaps. 40, 41, 51, and 52) is again a single machine, although it has in essence two internal ISPs, one centered around characters and the other around floating-point data-types, that is, a business and a scientific specialization residing side by side.[1]

Manufacturing Control

The function of computers in both the manufacturing and the commercial environments has evolved from simple record keeping to direct online human control. Process-control, aerospace, and laboratory instrument–control computers have evolved from their initial use in assisting human operators (controllers) with data logging and alarm condition monitoring to full control of processes with either human or second-computer backup. The structure of the computer and the control task varies widely depending on whether it is a continuous process (e.g., refinery, rolling mill) or a discrete process (e.g., warehouse, automotive, appliance manufacturing). The role of the computer is to act as a sophisticated control (K) in some larger physical process, and thus it plays a subordinate role. The computers' relatively late arrival in this role was due to the high cost and unreliability of early computers, as well as to the lack of necessary interface equipment.

The functional specialization is seen most strongly in the word size, which reflects the appropriate numerical data-type. The numbers used in control processes are generated by physical devices and are rarely better than 0.1 percent accurate. Since elaborate arithmetic calculations are not called for, the numbers, and hence the word size, can be around 12 bits. Most control computers have been 8 to 18 bits per word. A second specialization, again reflecting appropriate data-types, is that all control computers are binary and have boolean operations. This arises because many of the external conditions to be sensed and effected are binary in nature.

About the only other functional specialization of control computers is the interrupt [2] capability to allow them to respond to many potentially concurrent external conditions in real time. This provides overlap of internal and external processing. This is another possible example of functional specialization leading to reunification rather than divergence, for it has again been widely accepted that all general-purpose computers must have good interrupt capabilities. However, in actuality, interrupts, though not existing in early computers, were developed to obtain good input/output facilities, not for control computers.

Communications, Office, and Publication

The functional specialization of communication could be taken as a subfunction of a control computer. The function is mainly to behave as a switch. In a message-switching application the computer transfers messages from terminals (and links) into primary (and sometimes secondary) memories and then transfers them to other terminals (and links). In message switching, messages are first stored and then forwarded. The computer in a telephone exchange functions as a very sophisticated switch control. Here the computer reads the off-the-hook signal, detects the dialed numbers, rings the dialed parties, and finally sets the switches to connect the telephones together. In some instances, when it answers information inquiries about new telephone numbers or reroutes calls to other phones, it functions as a memory. Thus a communications computer is functionally a switch or a control for a switch.

The main distinction between control computers and communications computers is that the task environment of the latter, since it consists of digitally encoded messages (even in the case of the voice telephone exchange), can be handled directly by the communications computer. That is, the communications computer can do the work of transshipment and storage as well as control.

Communications- and message-based computers have evolved from telephone switching control, message switching, and front ends to become dominant parts of communications systems. With these evolving systems, the communications links have changed from analog-based transmission to sampled-data digital transmission. With all-digital transmission, data, voice, and video can ultimately be used in the same system. Voice transducers enable speech communications with the computer.

The Electronic Switching System (ESS) processors of Bell Laboratories (Chap. 28) and BBN's Pluribus (Chap. 23) are two examples of communications computers.

Word processing (i.e., text creation, editing, and reproduction),

---

[1]The story above has been told exclusively in terms of IBM machines. Although this does not distort the picture too strongly in terms of total movements of the field, since IBM dominated the market, concurrent developments were taking place throughout the field. UNIVAC I was the first computer built by a manufacturer and did not have the idiosyncrasies we ascribe to IBM; on the other hand, the marketing effort for it was less.

[2]Apparently introduced in the UNIVAC 1103.

together with long-term storage and retrieval, the transmission to other sites (e.g., electronic mail), has evolved from several systems:

1   Conventional torn-tape message switching (e.g., TWX, Western Union, Telex).

2   Terminals with local storage and editing (e.g., Flexo-writers, Teletype ASRs, magnetic card/magnetic tape automatic typewriters, and the evolving stand-alone word processing terminals).

3   Large, shared text-preparation systems for centralized document preparation, newspaper publication, etc.

4   Large systems with central filing and transmission (distri-bution). These negate the need for substantial hard copy. With these systems, text can be prepared either centrally with the system or with local intelligent word processing systems.

5   Computer conferencing. With this, people can sit at terminals and converse with others without leaving their office.

Transportation

Aircraft and trains (and probably, in the future, automotive vehicles) require real time operation of both discrete and continu-ous control systems. Control is carried out in two parts: on board the vehicle and through the network (airspace, highway) that carries the vehicle. The transportation control function dictates three unique characteristics for the computer structure:

1   Very high reliability to keep to a minimum the likelihood of fatal mishaps

2   Very small size for on-board computers

3   Extreme operating and storage temperature range for on-board computers, especially for automotive vehicles.

Education

The education environment uses systems that are a combination of transaction processing (for the human interaction part), scientific computation to simulate real-world conditions (i.e., physical or natural phenomena), and information retrieval from a data base. These systems are evolving from the drill-and-practice systems—which use a small, simple algorithm—through simulation of particular real-world phenomena, to knowledge-based systems that have a limited, but useful, natural-language–communications capability.

Home

Home computers are beginning to emerge. The dominant use to date is in providing entertainment in the form of games that model simple, real-world phenomena, such as Ping-Pong. Appliances are beginning to have embedded computers that have particular knowledge of their environments. For example, computer-controlled ranges can cook food in standard ways. Alternatively, cooking can be controlled by embedded temperature sensors. Simple calculators to assist checkbook balancing have existed for quite some time. These will soon evolve to provide written transactions for recording and control purposes. Many domestic activities are essentially scaled-down versions of commercial, scientific, education, and message environments.

Another dimension correlated to function is class. (See Table 1 in the introduction to this section.) The class to which a computer system belongs determines its relative capabilities with respect to computers in other classes (see Chap. 1). Thus the computer class roughly determines the price and level of functionality achieved (in Table 1) for hardware/software system tailored to one of the seven application environments.

Performance

Performance is measured in functions per unit of time or, conversely, the time needed to complete a specific function. The concept of performance exists all through the digital design hierarchy (Table 2). At the semiconductor physics level, for example, the time to drain the charge at a PN junction would relate to the transistor turnoff time at the circuit level, which, in turn, would determine gate propagation delay at the switching-circuit level. Gate delays, along with the topological interconnec-tion of the gates, determine the time to execute a register-transfer operation. The sequence of register transfers, along with their execution times, determines the time required to execute an instruction. Finally, the system performance is determined by the mix of instructions required for a particular application.

There are at least two types of performance measures: probabi-listic and deterministic. Probabilistic measures take into account statistical variations in the manufacturing process (e.g., transistors will actually have a range of turnoff times), concurrent activity in the system (e.g., gate propagation delay varies as a function of the number of other gates it must switch, and the states of these other gates vary with their inputs), and the system design (e.g., hardware and software). Deterministic measures attempt to remove the variations by assuming worst-case, average-case, or weighted-average statistics.

For the purposes of this discussion, statistical variations in the first four levels (i.e., semiconductor physics, circuit, gate, and register-transfer) will be ignored. These variations normally stem from the processes of design and manufacturing (e.g., transistors on different semiconductor chips will have slightly different characteristics). Since the hardware must work under all condi-

Table 2 Performance

Level	Typical performance measure	Factors at this level affecting performance
Semiconductor physics	Time to drain charge from PN junction	Junction dimensions Doping concentration Doping profile
Circuit	Transistor turnoff time	Transistor gain Operating point of transistor as determined by its interconnection with other circuit elements (e.g., resistors or voltage supplies) Stray capacitance, inductance
Gate	Gate propagation delay	Gate fan-in/fan-out
Register-transfer	Time to perform a register transfer	Data-path configuration (e.g., number of gates in data path) Control organization
ISP	Time to perform an instruction	Sequence of register-transfer operations
System	Time to perform an application	Instruction mix in application System software System configuration Variations in input to the application

tions, conservative worst-case design practices usually eliminate the statistical variations.[1]

One of the primary uses of performance measures is in the comparison of systems. The performance measure selected then depends on the level of comparison to be used. Table 3 illustrates some of these levels and some of the measures to be discussed in the following subsections.

Hardware Performance Measures

Because they directly reflect the state of technology, hardware performance measures are the easiest to determine or derive. These measures are usually used in individual component selection (e.g., Mp, Ms, T). They can be used to determine whether

increased performance (e.g., transfer rate from a disk) can be absorbed in an existing system or what the most cost-effective component might be.

Occasionally hardware performance parameters are used to predict system performance. Frequently, manufacturers will list a

[1]Note that there are some design practices that can pass these variations up to the ISP level. For example, before the use of crystal clocks became widespread, RC oscillators were widely used. Variations in R and C values could result in a ±10 percent variation in instruction timings. Asynchronous protocols for communication between subsystems also introduce performance variations. Such subsystems respond only upon completion of an activity. This allows the mixing of subsystems with different response times (e.g., mixing of core and semiconductor memory) and thus makes performance dependent on the relative usage of each subsystem type.

Table 3 Various Performance Measures as a Function of Level

Level	Deterministic measures	Probabilistic measures
Hardware	Single parameters • Typical instruction time • Mp size	Average instruction execution time Information rate
	Multiple parameters • Kiviat graph	Weighted average instruction execution time
ISP	CFA absolute and quantitative criteria	Benchmarks
System	Instruction mixes Processor model Knight's model	Synthetic benchmarks Queuing models

series of deterministic parameters to give a "feel" for the system performance. Such a list might include:

Time to execute a register-register ADD instruction, instruction-set size

Mp access time, cycle time, size

Cache access time, cycle time, size

Ms access time, transfer rate, size

Figure 1 gives a PMS diagram of a basic computer that lists a set of six primary parameters that could be used to specify system performance.

Pc. Perhaps the single most important parameter is the performance of the processor. Historically, processor performance has been measured in instructions per second (i/s). The number of instructions per second can be estimated by using the time of a single representative instruction or by the average instruction

execution time (assuming all instructions equally likely). A more accurate measure is a weighted average of instruction execution time using weights derived from a general instruction mix or from the intended application (see the ISP Performance Measures section of this chapter for details).

However, because of variations in instruction semantics, the i/s measure is not always accurate. Consider the following example, which shows three different architectures with two implementations of a stack architecture (one has the stack in the primary memory Mp and the other assumes the stack is implemented in the processor Pc using fast registers). The hardware implementations are held roughly constant (the Pc-Mp data rate), and the architecture is varied in order to compare the effect on performance. Note the difference in the various measures in what should fundamentally be the same performance for a given problem.

A benchmark program will be used to illustrate the various measures. The benchmark program is the simple expression A := B + C, composed of one statement and two operations (:=, +). The statement execution rate (the actual performance) reflects the

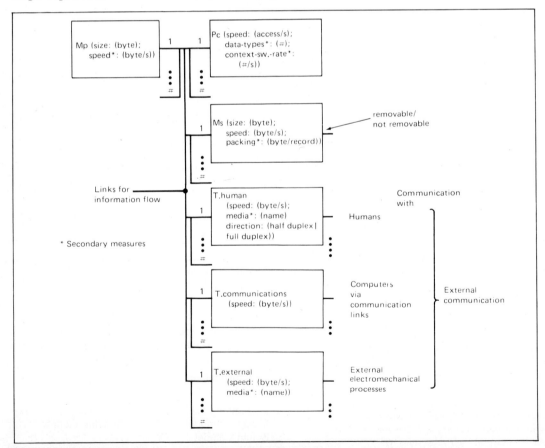

Fig. 1. Basic PMS computer structure model with six relevant performance/structure dimensions.

	Stack (top in Mp)	Stack (top in Pc)	1-address or general-reg.	3-address
Program	push B push C add pop A	push B push C add pop A	load B add C store A	Add B, C, A
No. of instructions	4	4	3	1
Accesses†	4op' + 3a + 6d	4op' + 3a + 3d	3op + 3a + 3d	1op″ + 3a + 3d
Program size bits‡	64	64	72	60
Bits accessed	16 + 48 + 192 = 256	16 + 48 + 96 = 160	24 + 48 + 96 = 168	12 + 48 + 96 = 156
Time to execute (μs)§	0.5 + 1.5 + 6 = 8	0.5 + 1.5 + 3 = 5	0.75 + 1.5 + 3 = 5.25	0.37 + 1.5 + 3 = 4.87
Statement execution rate (actual performance)	1/8 = 0.125 M	1/5 = 0.2 M	1/5.25 = 0.19 M	1/4.87 = 0.21 M
Operand rate	2/8 = 0.25 M	2/5 = 0.4 M	2/5.25 = 0.38 M	2/4.87 = 0.42 M
Instruction rate	4/8 = 0.5 M	4/5 = 0.8 M	3/5.25 = 0.57 M	1/4.87 = 0.21 M
Pc (accesses/s)	1 M	1 M	1 M	1 M

†op = operation, a = address, d = data

‡assumes address/a = 16 b; data/d = 32 b; op = 8 b; op' = 4 b; op″ = 12 b

§Assumes a memory-limited processor which can access 32 b/μs

highest performance for the 3-address machine, whereas the conventional instructions per second measure shows the 3-address machine to have the lowest performance (by a factor of 4 in relation to the fastest machine). A more subtle measure—operation-rate—is correlated with the true benchmark statement execution rate. It should be noted that, except for the first machine, a stack machine with stack in Mp, the information rate (word accesses per second) is a better performance indicator than the conventional instruction rate measure. For more unconventional machines, instructions per second tends to become a significantly poorer measure. For various vector/array machines (e.g., ILLIAC IV, CDC STAR, CRAY-1) which have to operate on at least 64 operands per single instruction, instructions per second would be a poor measure. Hand-held calculators have single, complex instructions, such as sine and polar-to-cartesian coordinate conversion. In this case using anything but a final benchmark problem would be misleading, and accesses per second is best as a Pc performance measure.

The secondary Pc parameters include the number of data-types and the context-switching rate. The number of data-types (e.g., scientific, string, character, lists, vectors) in the Pc gives an indication of performance when it is operated with a particular language. In the case of multiprogramming systems (e.g., real time, transaction, and time sharing), the time to switch from job to job is critical. Thus the process context-switching rate is also an important attribute, since most large computer systems operate with some form of multiprogramming.

Mp, Ms. The memory sizes (in bytes) for both primary and secondary memory give memory capability. The memory transfer rates are needed as secondary measures, especially to compute memory interference when multiple processors are used. The Mp transfer rate also tracks the access rate available to the Pc for secondary memory transfers and external interface transfers. For file systems, which require multiple accesses to secondary memory for single items, the probabilistic measure of file access rate is needed for a more accurate performance estimate. Similarly, for multiprogrammed systems, which use secondary memory to hold programs, the probabilistic measure of program swapping rate is required.

T.human, T.communications, T.external. Communications capabilities with humans, other computers, and other electronically encoded processes are equally important structure and performance attributes. Each channel (e.g., a typewriter) has a certain data rate and direction (half-duplex for two-way communication but in only one direction at a time, full-duplex for simultaneous two-way communication). Collectively, the data rates and the number of channels connected to each of the three different environments (people, computers, other electronically encoded processes) signify quite different styles of computing capability, structure, and function. For example, the absence of any communications connection to other computers implies a stand-alone system. Interconnection only to mechanical processes via electronically encoded links implies a real time structure. Similarly, only human intercommunication with multiple terminals denotes a timesharing or transaction-processing orientation.

Kiviat Graphs

Figure 2 uses a Kiviat graph[1] to display the six main dimensions—processing, primary and secondary memory capaci-

[1]Kiviat graphs were first used to summarize work load–specific performance with dimensions such as Pc, Ms, P_{io} busy, and relative amount of time the Pc or Ms or P_{io} is the only active subsystem [Ferrari, 1978]. The Kiviat graph concept has been adopted and modified in this text as a means for summarizing hardware performance.

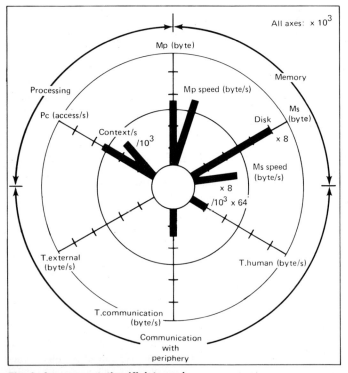

Fig. 2. A representative Kiviat graph.

ty, and the three communication channels—in a single six-dimensional graph, with three secondary dimensions. Each dimension is shown on a logarithmic scale up to a factor of 1 million, with the value 1 denoting the absence of an attribute (e.g., where there is no communication with external systems beyond human interaction). Various secondary measures are also represented. In the case that a dimension takes on values greater than 1 million, all axes are multipled by a scale factor such that the largest value will fit. The scale factor, if other than 1, is noted at the top of each Kiviat graph. When a scale factor is used, the value for some dimensions (e.g., communications with humans) may not be large enough to plot. Rather than erroneously indicate the absence of a dimension, the global scale factor is negated by dividing by a local scale factor denoted by the divide sign (/). All values are for the aggregated system. For example, the Ms dimension represents the total number of bytes on secondary storage (usually assumed to be disk unless otherwise noted). Parameters of individual components can be plotted with a multiplication factor (denoted by ×) indicating the number of identical components in the system. Multiplication factors, usually found on the Ms and T.human dimensions, are applied when there is one dominant component type dictating the value of a dimension. Occasionally dimensions are further specified (e.g., audio, video). The graph conventions include subtleties of showing fixed points (i.e., ROM, or hardwired), averages, and range. The arrangement of the six dimensions allows easy recognition of a structure in terms of the relative mix of the resource and performance attributes. Figure 3 gives a diagram of a computer system in the same order as the graph's dimensions.

While designing the IBM System/360, Gene Amdahl postulated two rules of thumb for a balanced system. The first rule related Pc speed with Mp size, stating that 1 byte of Mp was required to support each instruction per second. The second rule related Pc speed with I/O bandwidth, stating that one bit of I/O was required to support each instruction per second. Note that if the Pc speed is "balanced" with Mp size according to Amdahl's constant (1 byte of Mp per ips), then the value of the two dimensions should be about the same. (In Fig. 2 Pc is accessing 2 million byte/s, corresponding to, say, 600,000 i/s, with Mp of 8 million bytes.)

Thus the Kiviat graph not only summarizes major performance parameters but also graphically depicts the balance of a system. The relative capacity of processor, memory, and I/O is immediately discernible from the Kiviat graphs.

Figure 4 shows how the six-dimensional plot can be used to represent and differentiate various computing structures in which we are interested. The first two structures are keyboard I/O; i.e., they use a single information transducer we know as the typewriter that has half-duplex I/O at 10 characters (or bytes) per second. A 10-char/s teletypewriter is formed by adding a line interface.

The simple, early, fixed-function hand-held calculator, e.g., the HP 35, had a fixed processing/memory structure with about 4 ×

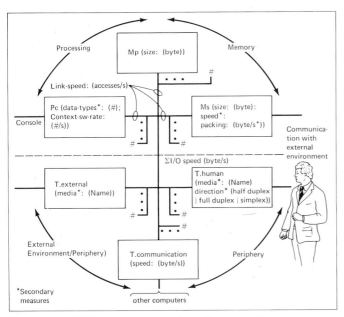

Fig. 3. Basic PMS computer structure diagram redrawn.

10 digits (or 20 bytes, to be more precise) of primary memory and store, limited keyboard input, and a 10-LED (light-emitting diode) output at about 10 char/s. The internal fixed program was stored in about 2,000 ROM bytes; hence there is a single, fixed point on the graph, and the operation rate of the unit is fixed at about 100 accesses/s of the HP 35's powerful data-types. The HP 65 programmable calculator is shown next, with various fixed functions being replaced by programs; Mp and Ms are each 500 bytes. The functions in ROM, though still present, are not apparent to the user and are therefore absent from the graph.

Figures 4e and f give graphs of various terminal structures, beginning with a fixed-function terminal operating at 10,000 accesses/s (or 100 μs/access), with about 1,000 bytes of local memory and 2,400 bit/s, or 300 byte/s, access to a computer. The intelligent terminal shown is programmable, with 20,000 Pc accesses/s operating on a 4,000-byte primary memory. Mass storage, here a floppy disk, is also provided. Communication to the external world is at 2,400 baud, or 300 byte/s. Output to the terminal screen is at 2,400 byte/s, or 19,200 bit/s, with input at 10 char/s.

The next two systems (Fig. 4g and h) are remote job entry stations, the first fixed-function and the second programmable. The fixed-function station has two I/O channels, one of 2,400 baud (i.e., three hundred 8-bit bytes per second) for the card reader and one of 4,800 baud (or 300 lines/min or 5 lines/s at 120 bytes per line = 600 byte/s) for the line printer. The second RJE (remote job entry) terminal includes a Pc at 50,000 accesses/s and an Mp of 16 Kbyte. A tape unit of 50 Kbyte/s holds 300 Mbyte.

Figure 4i is a programmable store-and-forward system with 16 Kbyte of Mp, a rate of 100,000 accesses/s Pc, and a context-switching time of 1 ms. There are 32 lines of 10 to 150 byte/s. The four communication links to other computers operate at 600 or 1,200 byte/s (or 4,800 or 9,600 baud).

Figure 4j is a fixed-function remote full-duplex analog multiplexor with 16 channels operating at 16 × 100 byte/s and multiplexed into a 1,200-byte/s (9,600-baud) line; hence the line limits the maximum sampling rate.

Figure 4k is a programmable remote stand-alone process-control system. Note the absence of any lines to communicate with other machines. A secondary memory system of 10 Mbyte is used for communication with other computers. Net Pc (2,000 accesses/s) and Mp (2,000 bytes) resources are given. Net capabilities are those left after the other resources are managed. One hundred transducers are sampled each 10 ms with three transducers connected to humans at a data rate of 30 byte/s.

The last series of systems (Fig. 4l, m, and n) are general-purpose, multiprogrammed computers. The first is a batch system with card and line printer. The next is a PDP-11/70 with 100 real time inputs, 60 terminals, and 2 connections to other computers. Finally, the PDP-10/KL10 is a large, multiuser (100) timesharing system.

Kiviat graphs will be used in conjunction with PMS diagrams and ISP descriptions to characterize the computer systems presented in Part 3.

ISP Performance Measures

We are more often concerned with characterizing the performance of an ISP than a particular implementation of that ISP. With rapid changes in the performance of circuit technology, a computer user may wish to estimate performance over a range of implementations. Furthermore, the introduction of implementations at different times can reflect sufficiently different underlying technologies, causing performance measures to be biased toward the newer system. Thus, performance measures independent of technology are helpful in making a long-term commitment to an ISP with the intention of upgrading to new implementations.

An example of a performance measure depending solely on the ISP is the number of bits per instruction. A larger bits per instruction rating requires a higher memory-to-processor bandwidth to support a given instructions per second rate. On the other hand, a smaller number of bits per instruction may imply a weak semantic content per instruction, thus requiring more instructions to accomplish a given task. Clearly a number of metrics are required, as well as methodology for establishing their relative importance.

The following subsection describes the initial screening phase of the Army-Navy Computer Family Architecture (CFA) Project [Fuller, Stone, and Burr, 1977]. In addition to several absolute

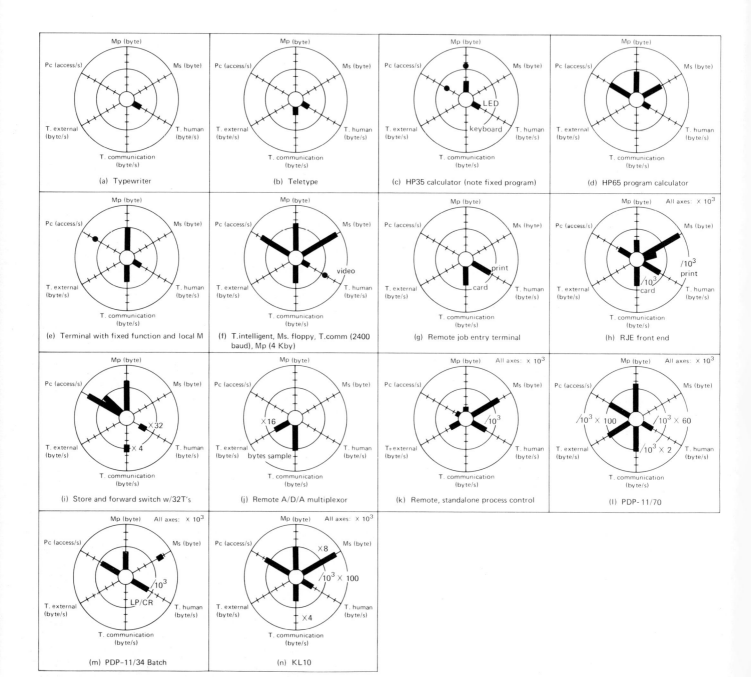

Fig. 4. Examples of Kiviat graphs for various computing systems.

criteria representing the minimum state of the art in ISP design, 17 quantitative criteria were selected to differentiate between ISPs. In order to reduce these measures to a single metric for comparison, a weighting scheme was utilized. Potential users weighted each parameter according to their subjective estimate of the importance of the parameter to their application. These quantitative measures (with their relative weights given in parentheses) fell into four general areas:

- Measures of ISP growth or stretch potential. Examples include virtual and physical address space size and op code density (weight .273).

- Measures of responsiveness to I/O. Examples include size of Pc state, I/O initiation, and maximum interrupt latency (weight .404).

- Measures of ease of programmability, including subroutine linkage, virtualizability, and direct addressability (weight .269).

- Measures of software capture, including estimates of the usage base (weight .057).

It is interesting to note that the weighting factors were relatively constant, with a slight skew toward I/O responsiveness (e.g., average weight was .059, while I/O initiation had a weight of .1238 and maximum interrupt latency had a weight of .0917).

Ultimately, the accuracy of the quantitative criteria depends on the accuracy of the weights assigned to the parameters and, to some extent, on the machines involved in the sample. The derivation of the weighted, normalized averages approximates a point-accumulation game. A certain number of points are collected per parameter. Several computers with similar values for a given parameter divide the points for that parameter among them. If an unusual ISP excels in one attribute, it might gather the vast majority of points for that parameter.[1] For example, when the PDP-8 was added to the list of nine computers in the CFA study, the PDP-8 finished a strong second to the Interdata 8/32. The PDP-8, with a 12-bit word, accumulated many points in the I/O area while losing only a little ground in areas where the other nine computers were competing with each other.

Thus, before using the CFA quantitative criteria, the user should test the limitations of the weighting mechanism by trying different weights and different mixes of computers. Easy to gather data for and easy to apply, the quantitative criterion is a good exercise for the student.

[1]Consider nine ISPs. Eight require 16 bits to initiate I/O, one requires 12 bits. Assuming that smaller is better, the normalized weights become .972 for each 16-bit machine and 1.296 for the 12-bit machine. The 12-bit machine will garner 33 percent more points in this category.

Initial Screening[2]

Absolute Criteria. The CFA selection committee specified nine *absolute criteria* that it felt a candidate computer architecture needs to satsify if it is going to meet the requirements of future military computer systems. All the absolute criteria (with the exception of the subsetability criterion) had to be satisfied by an implementation of the architecture which was operational by 1 January 1976. This eliminated speculative decisions based on promises or potential solutions that looked inviting, but might not come to fruition. Failure to satisfy any absolute criterion resulted in the elimination of the architecture from further consideration. The nine absolute criteria are given below.

Virtual memory support   The architecture must support a virtual to physical address translation mechanism.

Protection   The architecture must have the capability to add new, experimental (i.e., not fully debugged) programs that may include I/O without endangering reliable operation of existing programs.

Floating-point support   The architecture must explicitly support one or more floating-point data types with at least one of the formats yielding more than 10 decimal digits of significance in the mantissa.

Interrupts and traps   It must be possible to write a trap handler that is capable of executing a procedure to respond to any trap condition and then resume operation of the program. The architecture must be defined such that it is capable of resuming execution following any interrupt (e.g., power failure, disk read error, console halt).

Subsetability   At least the following components of an architecture must be able to be factored out of the full architecture:

- a. *Virtual-to-Physical Address Translation Mechanism*
- b. *Floating Point Instructions and Registers (if separate from general purpose registers)*
- c. *Decimal Instructions Set (if present in full architecture)*
- d. *Protection Mechanism*

In order to retain program compatibility across the implementations of the architecture, this criterion was extended to include the following requirement: *The trap mechanism of the architec-*

[2]Abstracted from S. H. Fuller, H. S. Stone, and W. E. Burr, "Initial Selection and Screening of the CFA Candidate Computer Architectures," *AFIPS Conf. Proc.*, vol. 46, June 1977, pp. 139–146.

ture must be defined such that instructions in the full architecture, but not implemented in the subset machine, trap on the subset machine and that it be possible to write trap routines for the subset machine that allow it to interpretively execute those instructions not implemented directly in hardware (or firmware) and then resume execution. (This is an elaboration of the interrupt/traps absolute criterion.)

Multiprocessor support   The architecture must support some form of "test-and-set" instruction to allow for the communication and synchronization of multiple processors.

Input/output controllability   A processor must be able to exercise absolute control over any I/O processor and/or I/O controller.

Extensibility   The architecture must have some method for adding instructions to the architecture consistent with existing formats. There must be at least one undefined code point in the existing opcode space of the instruction formats.

Read-only code   It must be possible to execute programs from read-only storage.

Table 4 shows the score of each candidate architecture on each of the absolute criteria. Note that none of the nine architectures failed to meet the last five criteria: subsetability, multiprocessor support, I/O controllability, extensibility, and read-only code. This is in part the case because we limited our evaluation to

reasonably successful architectures, but is partly the result of not defining these criteria precisely enough prior to applying them to the candidate architectures. For example, by not clearly defining how to test for the practical subsetability of an architecture, we made it virtually impossible for an architecture to fail this criterion. Subsequent studies would be well advised to consider more precise definitions of these (and any additional) absolute criteria before evaluating alternative architectures against them.

Quantitative Criteria.   In addition to the absolute criteria, the CFA committee specified seventeen quantitative criteria that it felt would be helpful in the initial screening process. A number of these quantitative criteria measure attributes of a computer architecture better measured by benchmarks, or test programs [Fuller et al., 1977b]. However, the CFA committee recognized that it did not have the resources to run benchmarks on all nine candidate architectures and therefore proceeded with the use of these quantitative criteria to help select three or four candidate architectures, out of the original nine candidate architectures, for more intensive study via test programs.

The quantitative criteria are described below and the score of each architecture on the quantitative criteria is given in Table 5.

Virtual address space

V_1:   *The size of the virtual address space in bits.*
V_2:   *Number of addressable units in the virtual address space.*

Table 4   Candidate Architecture Value for Absolute Criteria

					Candidate computer architectures					
Absolute criterion	*IBM S/370*	*Inter-Data 8/32*	*Rolm AN/UY K-28†*	*DEC. PDP-11*	*Univac AN/UY K-7*	*SEL 32*	*Burroughs B6700*	*Univac AN/UY K-20*	*Litton AN/GY K-12*
1 Virtual memory	Y	Y	N	Y	Y	N	Y	N	Y
2 Protection	Y	Y	Y	Y	Y	Y?	N	N	Y?
3 Floating point	Y	Y	Y	Y	N	Y	Y	Y	N
4 Interrupts/traps	Y	?	Y	Y	Y	Y	Y	Y	Y
5 Subsetability	Y	Y	Y	Y	Y?	Y	Y?	Y	Y?
6 Multi processor	Y	Y	Y	Y	Y	Y	Y	Y	Y
7 I/O controllability	Y	Y	Y	Y	Y	Y	Y	Y	Y
8 Extensibility	Y	Y	Y	Y	Y	Y	Y	Y	Y
9 Read-only code	Y	Y	Y	Y	Y	Y	Y	Y	Y
summary	Y	?	N	Y	N	N	N	N	N

Y   Yes, meets criteria

N   No, fails criteria

Y?   Yes (but with some reservations)

?   Unresolved

†The AN/UYK-28 is instruction-set upward-compatible with the Data General NOVA computer architecture. Other ROLM computers that are also compatible with the NOVA architecture are the AN/UYK-19 and AN/UYK-27. The AN/UYK-28 is incompatible with the Data General ECLIPSE computer architecture, Data General's upward-compatible extension of the NOVA.

Table 5 Candidate CFA Values for Quantitative Criteria

#	Quantitative criteria	IBM S/370	Inter-Data 8/32	Rolm AN/UY K-28	DEC PDP-11	Univac AN/UY K-7	SEL 32	Burroughs B6700	Univac AN/UY K-20	Litton AN/GY K-12
						Candidate CFA's				
1	V_1†	27	27	20	20	24	22	24	20	20
2	V_2†	27	27	20	19	24	22	20	17	20
3	P_1†	27	27	22‡	25	23	26‡	24	20	29
4	P_2†	27	27	22†	24	23	26‡	20	17	29
5	U	.371	.355	.039	.043	.15	.450	.019	.125	.219
6	C_{s_1}	1344	1632	1008	1168	992	304	306	1328	1008
7	C_{s_2}	576	576	112	144	448	288	204	336	752
8	C_{m_1}	3168	1120	1882	736	1472	768	408	2256	1344
9	C_{m_2}	1312	32	544	430	1472	704	408	720	1088
10	K	1	0	0	1	0	0	0	0	0
11	B_1	17,300	185	13,800§	14,700	346	75	90	400	30
12	B_2¶	16,000	14	169	311	147	23	207	8	6
13	I	64	16	48	16	128	64	169	80	32
14	D	15	27	20	19	18	22	18	20	20
15	L	6192	560	114	112	2112	288	255	—	1376
16	J_1	1904	2368	1360	1040	1280	960	459	1408	1344
17	J_2	1136	1280	320	400	1280	960	459	640	1088

†These values are of the form 2^x where x = indicated data except for B6700 which is of the form $3(2^x)$.

‡With memory bank switching.

§Includes Novas.

¶Millions of dollars.

Physical address space

P_1: The size of the physical address space in bits.

P_2: The number of addressable units in the physical address space.

Fraction of instruction space unassigned Let it be defined as the fraction of the instruction space in the architecture that is unassigned. Specifically:

$$U = \sum_{1 \le i < \infty} u_i 2^{-i}$$

where u_i is the number of unassigned instructions of length i.

Size of central processor state

C_{s_1}: The number of bits in the processor state of the full architecture.

C_{s_2}: The number of bits in the processor state of the minimum subset of the architecture (i.e., without Floating Point, Decimal, Protection, or Address Translation Registers).

C_{m_1}: The number of bits that must be transferred between the processor and primary memory to first save the processor state of the full architecture upon interruption and then restore the processor state prior to resumption. This measure differs from C_{s_1}, above in that "register bank switching," where provided for in the candidate architectures, may eliminate the need to save some registers in primary memory, while the instruction fetches required to save the state are included in C_{m_1} but not in C_{s_1}.

C_{m_2}: The measure analogous to C_{m_1} for the minimum subset of the architecture.

Usage base

B_1: Number of computers delivered as of the latest date for which data exist prior to 1 June 1976.

B_2: Total dollar value of the installed computer base as of the latest date for which data exist prior to 1 June 1976.

I/O initiation

I: The minimum number of bits which must be transferred between main memory and any processor (central, or I/O) in order to output one 8-bit byte to a standard peripheral device.

Virtualizability

K: is unity if the architecture is virtualizable as defined in Popek and Goldberg [1974]; otherwise, K is zero.

Direct instruction addressability

D: The maximum number of bits of primary memory which one instruction can directly address given a single base register, which may be used but not modified.

Maximum interrupt latency Let L be the maximum number of bits which may need to be transferred between memory and any processor (central processor, I/O controller, etc.) between the time an interrupt is requested and the time that the computer starts processing that interrupt (given that interrupts are enabled).

Subroutine linkage

J_1: The number of bits which must be transferred between the processor and memory to save the user state, transfer to the called routine, restore the user state, and return to the calling routine, for the full architecture. No parameters are passed.

J_2: The analogous measure to J_1 above for the minimum architecture (e.g., without Floating Point registers).

Composite Score of the Quantitative Criteria. After applying the quantitative criteria just discussed, the CFA committee had to determine how the performance of the candidate architectures on these criteria would be used to screen out all but three or four of the architectures for further consideration in the test program and software evaluation phases of the study. Clearly, the candidate architectures should be ordered relative to each of the seventeen quantitative criteria and these independent orderings studied to detect weaknesses and strengths of the competing architectures. However, some summary measure was ultimately needed to assist the committee in its selection of the final architectures to undergo more intensive study. A variety of thresholding and weighing schemes were proposed, but the particular scheme that follows was the scheme chosen by the CFA committee.

Relative weighing of criteria Each voting organization of the CFA committee was given 100 points to distribute among the various measures to indicate their relative importance to the organization. The weight for criterion x, W[x], was defined as the total number of points given criterion x by all the voting CFA organizations, divided by the total number of points handed out. The weights for the quantitative criteria based on responses from 24 voting CFA committee members is given in Table 6.

Table 6   Quantitative Criteria Composite Weights

Criterion	Army weights	Navy weights	Full CFA Committee weights
V_1	.0412	.0444	.0433
V_2	.0438	.0575	.0529
P_1	.0425	.0706	.0612
P_2	.0387	.0637	.0554
U	.0513	.0644	.0600
C_{s_1}	.0587	.0375	.0466
C_{s_2}	.0675	.0219	.0371
C_{m_1}	.0700	.0544	.0596
C_{m_2}	.0713	.0319	.0450
K	.0500	.0587	.0558
B_1	.0450	.0244	.0313
B_2	.0200	.0281	.0254
I	.0875	.1419	.1238
D	.0912	.1081	.1025
L	.0812	.0969	.0917
J_1	.0637	.0626	.0629
J_2	.0762	.0331	.0475

Normalization When attempting to combine these quantitative measures into a composite measure we faced two problems:

a   The measures are defined such that good computer architectures maximize some measures and minimize others. Specifically, the measures that a computer architecture should maximize are: V_1, V_2, P_1, P_2, U, K, B_1, B_2, and D; while the measures that should be minimized are: C_{s1}, C_{s2}, C_{m1}, C_{m2}, I, L, J_1, and J_2.

Let our composite measure be a maximal measure and transform all minimal measures to maximal measures by taking the reciprocal: $X' = 1/X$.

b   Measures that inherently involve large magnitudes are not necessarily more important than smaller measures. For example, V_1 is on the order of 10^4 to 10^9 while K is either 0 or 1.

To resolve this problem of differing scale, the values for the quantitative criteria were normalized by dividing each value by the average value of the criterion over the set of nine architectures. For example, the nine measures for criteria I are (64, 16, 48, 16, 128, 64, 169, 80, 32), the average value is 68.6, and the normalized measures are (0.93, 0.23, 0.70, 0.23, 1.87, 0.93, 2.47, 1.17, 0.47).

Normalized measures have the attractive properties that they all lie in the range (0,M); have a mean across the set of M architectures of unity; and the standard deviation of the set of normalized measures is in the interval (0, $M^{0.5}$). We could have taken the normalization process a step further and adjusted the spread of each measure so that the measure gave a standard deviation of unity (or some other constant) across the set of architectures being evaluated. We did not do this for all measures. Some measures were better "discrimination functions" than others and we did not want in general to lose this information by further normalization. However, the committee agreed that it is important to normalize the standard deviation of some of the measures; specifically, V_1, V_2, P_1, P_2, and D were normalized to have a mean *and* standard deviation of unity. These measures may differ by several orders of magnitude between candidate architectures, but the CFA Committee did not feel that the utilities, as expressed by the measures, differ by orders of magnitude.

Scaling and composition of the quantitative measures In order to combine the individual measures the committee used a simple, linear sum of each normalized measure X scaled by its corresponding weighing coefficient W[X]. The weighing coefficients have been defined so that they sum to unity and hence the composite measure A is in fact a normalized measure with a mean of 1. Using the weights given in Table 6 and the values of the quantitative criteria given in Table 5 we get the composite measures for the candidate architectures shown in Table 7.

System Performance Measures

In order to measure the performance of a specific computer (e.g., a PDP-11) it is necessary to know the ISP, the hardware performance, and the frequency of use for the various instructions. The execution time T is the dot product of the fractional utilization of each instruction Ui and the time Ti to execute each instruction.

There are three ways to estimate the instruction utilization U and hence obtain T; each provides increasingly better answers. The first simply defines either a typical or average instruction. The second uses "standard" benchmarks to characterize precisely

Table 7   Ranking Based on the Quantitative Criteria

Architecture	Score
Interdata 8/32	1.68
PDP-11	1.43
IBM S/370	1.36
AN/GYK-12	0.94
ROLM	0.92
B6700	0.91
SEL-32	0.86
AN/UYK-7	0.46
AN/UYK-20	0.44

a machine's performance. In this way machines can be compared according to an absolute measure. The third would be the use of a specific, unique benchmark when the actual use has not been characterized in terms of the standard benchmark (and may even not be easily characterized in terms of it). This last alternative is needed for real time and transaction processing, where computer selection and installation is predicated on doing the job exactly.

Typical Instructions

The simplest single parameter of performance—instruction time for a simple operation (e.g., ADD)—was used in the first two computer generations, especially since high-level languages were less frequently used. Such a metric is an approximation of the average instruction time. It assumes (1) that all machines have about the same ISP (hence there is little difference among instructions); or (2) that a specific data-type will be used more heavily than another; or (3) that a typical add time will be given (e.g., the operand is in a random location in primary memory cell rather than being cached or in a fast register).

It is possible to determine the average instruction time by executing one of every possible instruction. However, since the instruction use depends so much on the program data they interpret, this metric is poor. A better measure is to keep statistics about the use of all programs and to give the average instruction time based on use of all programs. The usefulness of such a measure is for the comparison of two different implementations of the same architecture. It is inadequate when applied to specific usage.

Early attempts to make more accurate characterizations were based on weighting the instruction use (i.e., forming a typical U) according to task (e.g., floating-point versus indexing and character handling) to give a better performance measure. Instruction mixes were developed which better evaluated performance (see Table 8).

Studies of frequency counts of instruction executions have been described by several authors. The best known is the Gibson mix, developed by Jack C. Gibson at IBM in 1959. Gibson divided the instructions of the IBM 704 and 650 into 13 classes and counted how many instructions of each class were executed. His sample size was 17 programs, approximately 9 million instructions. The results are described in Gibson [1970]; we tabulate them in Table 8.

Gonter [1969] has compared the Gibson mix and the University of Massachusetts mix, using essentially the same classification and tracing 15 million instructions on the CDC 3600. His results correlate well with Gibson's; they are tabulated in Table 8.

The Carnegie-Mellon data are based on a dynamic trace of 5.3 million instructions on a PDP-10 over six programs written in five languages (ALGOL, BASIC, BLISS, and two variations of FORTRAN), one algorithm written by four different programmers, the five compilers, and a large scientific program [Lunde, 1977].

Table 8   Percentage of Executed Instructions

	Machine					
Class	*IBM 650/704, Gibson's results*	*CDC 3600, U. Mass.† results*	*PDP-10, CMU‡ results*	*PDP-11, DEC results*	*S/360, U. of Toronto results*	*HP 3000, HP results*
Load, store	31.2	30.0	42.4	22.4	48.1	34.0
Branches	16.6	38.3	28.2	33.7	17.7	16.0
Fixpoint add, subtract	6.1	1.2	12.4	19.0	10.2	⎫
Compares	3.8	1.2	....	12.5	7.0	⎪
Floating add, subtract	6.9	0.5	4.9	0.0	0.0	⎪
Floating multiply	3.8	0.5	2.6	0.0	0.0	⎬ 33.0
Floating divide	1.5	0.2	1.1	0.0	0.0	⎪
Fixpoint multiply	0.6	0.1	1.1	0.0	0.0	⎪
Fixpoint divide	0.2	0.1	0.5	0.0	0.3	⎭
Shifting	4.4	2.2	3.9	4.6	4.4	1.0
Logical	1.6	0.5	1.0	4.3	4.9	5.0
Miscellaneous	5.3	0.0	1.5	3.3	7.0	11.0
Indexing	18.0	13.4	....	0.0	....	
Fullword	....	6.9	....	0.0	....	
I/O control	....	0.0	0.1	....	0.0	
Interregister transfer	....	5.0	....	0.0	0.0	
Monitor communication	....	....	0.0	0.2	0.0	
User UUOs	....	....	0.3	0.0	....	

The classes are not equally applicable to all ISPs, as indicated by leaders. This applies in particular to index register instructions.

In Gibson's original classification, use of indexing was counted as an extra instruction in the "Indexing" class; the "Compare" class consisted of the 3-way skips in the 704.

In the U. Mass. version of the Gibson classification, the "Compares" class consists of all the vector search operations, "Indexing" is all the index-register instructions, "Fullword" is all the 48-bit instructions. The "Interregister transfer" class also includes other instructions that manipulate only the processor state.

Gibson's results were obained by using mostly scientific programs, but also some business data processing programs, coded in unspecified languages.

The U. Mass. results were obtained by using assembly- and FORTRAN-coded programs, including the FORTRAN compiler and the assembler.

†U. Mass. = University of Massachusetts.

‡CMU = Carnegie-Mellon University.

The DEC results were obtained from tracing 7.6 million instructions of an assembler, editor, various compilers (DIBOL, FORTRAN, BASIC, PASCAL), and four application programs [Strecker, 1976a].

The University of Toronto mix [Alexander, Gregg, and Wortman, 1975] traced almost 9 million instructions from 19 XPL programs consisting of student-written compilers and the XPL system. The RX (register-indexed storage) instruction load (L) represented over 27 percent of the instructions executed. BRANCH ON CONDITION and STORE added a further 14 percent and 10 percent respectively.

The HP 3000 is a stack-based machine supporting a block-structured system programming language (SPL). The benchmark included 14 interactive sessions of making inquiries to a data base [Blake, 1977]. The inquiry programs were written in COBOL and used the HP 3000's Image data base facility. Three other sessions engaged the BASIC interpreter in interactive program development. There were five more sessions using the Editor to manipulate COBOL source statements. In addition, three jobs were running in batch. One was a COBOL compilation, another an RPG COMPILE AND GO, and the third an SPL COMPILE AND GO, including a SORT. Blake does not give sufficient detail to break down the stack and immediate operations into the individual categories in Table 8 (e.g., compares and fixpoint add and subtract). However, Blake indicates that LOAD TO TOP OF STACK (18 percent), BRANCH ON CONDITION (10 percent), and STORE FROM TOP OF STACK (7 percent) are the most frequently executed instructions.

Other, similar mixes and experiments are reported by Arbuckle [1966], Connors, Mercer, and Sorlini [1970], Raichelson and Collins [1966], and the early study done by Herbst, Metropolis, and Wells [1955].

Typical Instruction Models

It is possible to predict performance on the basis of a small number of fundamental deterministic measures. Such a model is illustrated in Table 9. Performance is related to terms for the processor and memory. Each parameter is affected by various implementation techniques as well as by basic technology. Several of the techniques that appear in Part 2 of this book are listed in the table. This model will be illustrated on actual systems in Chap. 39 and in Sec. 5 of Part 4. Table 9 represents yet another organization of the computer space dimensions.

Knight [1966] (Fig. 5) extends the concept of a typical instruction model to the system level by introducing I/O. Rather than an absolute measure of performance, Knight's model is the product of three factors: processing time, memory size (in words), and word length.

The formula was derived (roughly) to measure power so that technological change could be modeled. Applying the formula is like measuring automotive vehicle power as a product of speed, weight, and the number of wheels. (Such an indicator is roughly proportional to a car's momentum.) Thus, although it is a reasonable single-number indication for power, a computer buyer could not use it directly.

Table 9   A Simple Model of Processor Performance

$$\frac{1}{\text{Performance}} = \underset{\substack{\text{processor} \\ \text{logic}}}{K_1 t_1} + \underset{\text{memory read pause}}{K_2 t_2}$$

Number of microcycles per machine instruction:	Memory used per operation:
K_1 (microcycles/operation)	**K_2 (bits/operation)**
Ways to decrease K_1:	Ways to decrease K_2:
Multiple registers or register sets	Increase operand bits/instruction
Multiple data paths	(e.g., scalar vs. serial data-
Multiple function units	types, vector vs. scalar data-
Processor/memory overlap	types)
Fewer microsteps (microinstruction	More efficient ISP
decoding, more parallelism, etc.)	
Multiplexing processor logic (e.g.,	
CDC 6600 barrel)	
More efficient ISP	
Tailor microcode flow according to macro-	
instruction usage frequency	
Data-path cycle time:	**Memory access time:**
t_1 (seconds/microcycle)	**t_2 (seconds/bit)**
Ways to decrease t_1:	Ways to decrease t_2:
Faster technology (e.g., for whole	Faster technology
data path or only critical	Apparent speedup (e.g., I/O
components)	spaces, caches)
Shorter microcycles (e.g., multiple-	Widening word access (e.g., mak-
length microcycles)	ing data path wider, multiple
More efficient microinstruction fetch	fetches on a multiplexed bus)
(microcoded machines only) (e.g.,	More efficient utilization of
interleaved control stores, multiple	bandwidth (e.g., instruction
microword fetch, pipeline microword	prefetch, processor/memory
fetch/execution)	overlap)

$$P = \frac{\frac{[(L \cdot 7)(T)(WF)]^i}{10^{12}[32,000(36 \cdot 7)]^i}}{t_c + t_{I/O}}$$

$$t_c = 10^4[C_1 A_{FI} + C_2 A_{FL} + C_3 M + C_4 D + C_5 L]$$

$$t_{I/O} = P \times OL_1 [10^6 (W_{I1} \times B \times 1/K_{I1}) + (W_{O1} \times B \times 1/K_{O1})$$
$$+ N(S_1 + H_1)] R_1$$
$$+ (1\text{-}P) OL_2 [10^6 (W_{I2} \times B \times 1/K_{I2}) + (W_{O2} \times B \times 1/K_{O2})$$
$$+ N(S_2 + H_2)]$$

Variables—attributes of each computing system

P = the computing power of the nth computing system
L = the word lengths (in bits)
T = the total number of words in memory
t_c = the time for the Central Processing Unit to perform 1 million operations
$t_{I/O}$ = the time the Central Processing Unit stands idle waiting for I/O to take place
A_{FI} = the time for the Central Processing Unit to perform 1 fixed point addition
A_{FL} = the time for the Central Processing Unit to perform 1 floating point addition
M = the time for the Central Processing Unit to perform 1 multiply
D = the time for the Central Processing Unit to perform 1 divide
L = the time for the Central Processing Unit to perform 1 logic operation
B = the number of characters of I/O in each word
K_{I1} = the Input transfer rate (characters per second) of the primary I/O system
K_{O1} = the Output transfer rate (characters per second) of the primary I/O system
K_{I2} = the Input transfer rate (characters per second) of the secondary I/O system
K_{O2} = the Output transfer rate (characters per second) of the secondary I/O system
S_1 = the start time of the primary I/O system not overlapped with compute
H_1 = the stop time of the primary I/O system not overlapped with compute
S_2 = tne start time of the secondary I/O system not overlapped with compute
H_2 = the stop time of the secondary I/O system not overlapped with compute
R_1 = 1 + the fraction of the useful primary I/O time that is required for non-overlap rewind time

Semi-constant factors		Values	
Symbol	Description	Scientific computation	Commercial computation
WF	the word factor		
	a. fixed word length memory	1	1
	b. variable word length memory	2	2
C_1	weighting factor representing the percentage of the fixed add operations		
	a. computers without index registers or indirect addressing	10	25
	b. computers with index registers or indirect addressing	25	45
C_2	weighting factor that indicates the percentage of floating additions	10	0
C_3	weighting factor that indicates the percentage of multiply operations	6	1
C_4	weighting factor that indicates the percentage of divide operations	2	0
C_5	weighting factor that indicates the percentage of logic operations	72	74
P	percentage of the I/O that uses the primary I/O system		
	a. systems with only a primary I/O system	1.0	1.0
	b. systems with a primary and secondary I/O system	variable	variable
W_{I1}	number of input words per million internal operations using the primary I/O system		
	a. magnetic tape I/O system	20,000	100,000
	b. other I/O systems	2,000	10,000
W_{O1}	number of output words per million internal operations using the primary I/O system	the values are the same as those given above for W_{I1}	
W_{I2} W_{O2}	number of input/output words per million internal operations using the secondary I/O system	the values are the same as those given above for W_{I1}	
N	number of times separate data is read into or out of the computer per million operations	4	20
OL_1	overlap factor 1—the fraction of the primary I/O system's time not overlapped with compute		
	a. no overlap—no buffer	1	1
	b. read or write with compute—single buffer	.85	.85
	c. read, write and compute—single buffer	.7	.7
	d. multiple read, write and compute—several buffers	.60	.60
	e. multiple read, write and compute with program interrupt—several buffers	.25	.55
OL_2	overlap factor 2—the fraction of the secondary I/O system's time not overlapped with compute	values are the same as those given above for OL_1, a through e	
i	the exponential memory weighting factor	.5	.333

Fig. 5. Knight's functional model algorithm to calculate P for any computer system. *(Courtesy of* Datamation, *vol. 12, no. 9, September 1966, p. 42.)*

Benchmarks

A carefully designed standard benchmark gives the best estimate of real use, because the benchmark is totally understood and can be run on several different machines. Several organizations, especially those that purchase or use many machines extensively, have one or more programs characteristic of their own particular work load. Whether a standard benchmark is of value in characterizing performance depends on the degree to which it is typical of the actual computer's use. A further advantage of standard benchmarks is that they are written in the higher-level language to be used by the computer; hence they reflect the application as well as characterizing the language machine architecture.

The strongest advantage of the benchmark scheme is that it can handle a total problem and integrate all features of the computer. But there is a difficulty. The result depends not only on the type of computer (e.g., an IBM System/370 Model 165), but on the exact configuration (e.g., the number of words of Mp), and even on the operating system and the software (e.g., the specific version of FORTRAN). Thus, although the benchmark performance number perhaps comes closest to serving as an adequate single performance figure, it is weaker as a parameter characterizing the structure of the computer than one characterizing a contingent total system.

Two scientific benchmarks of the National Physical Laboratory in the United Kingdom are useful because of the extensive effort in designing them to be typical (e.g., frequencies of the trigonometric functions, subroutine calls, and I/O were considered). Although these benchmarks characterize a scientific mix by using FORTRAN, they can be used when comparing various languages.

Similar benchmarks for commercial processing generally use the COBOL language. The U.S. Steel COBOL data [U.S. Steel, 1978], Table 10, consist of timings from a common synthetic benchmark run on 125 different hardware/software environments representing 13 major manufacturers. The tests are run voluntarily by users. Each test is executed 100,000 times. These timings allow relative comparisons between hardware/compiler/operating system environments on a uniform, compute-bound task.

The CFA [*Computer*, October 1977] study attempted to modify the traditional benchmarking methodology in order to eliminate contributions due to technology, system configuration, and system software. The following subsection summarizes the approach and results. The test program methodology as described is very labor-intensive in that several programmers have to write several benchmarks for several computers. The programmers are assigned programs on specific machines according to a statistically designed experiment. The statistical design attempts to minimize the variation due to different programmers and maximize variation due to the ISP. Substantial data collection on the dynamics of test program execution was made possible by an ISP simulator instrumented with counters. The results of the study are not expandable to other architectures, since the statistical design depends on the assignment of programmers to test programs and computers. To evaluate another set of ISPs (or even add one to the set used in CFA) would require designing another statistical experiment from scratch.

Evaluation of Computer Architectures via Test Programs[1]

The concept of writing benchmarks, or test programs, is not a new idea in the field of computer performance evaluation and is generally considered the best test of a computer system [Lucas, 1971; Bernwell, 1975; Wichmann, 1973]. For the purpose of the CFA committee, we define a *test program* to be a relatively small program (100 to 500 machine instructions) that was selected as representative of a class of programs. The CFA committee's test program evaluation study described here had to address the central problems facing conventional benchmarking studies:

a   How is a representative set of test programs selected?

b   Given limited manpower, how are programmers assigned to writing test programs in order to maximize the information that can be gained?

We faced an additional problem because we evaluated computer architectures, independent of any of their specific implementations. In other words, when evaluating particular computers, time is the natural measure of how fast a test program can be executed. However, a computer architecture does not specify the execution time of any instructions and so an alternative to time must be chosen as a metric of execution speed.

Guidelines for Test Programs Specification.   The Test Program Subcommittee attempted to establish a strategy for defining and coding the test programs that would minimize the variability due to differences in programmer skill. The strategy devised was as follows:

a   The test programs would be small "kernel" type programs, of not more than 200 machine instructions. (In the end, a few test programs required more than 200 instructions.) It was felt that only small programs could be specified and controlled with sufficient precision to minimize the effects of programmer variability. Moreover, resources were not available to define, code, test, and measure a significant set of larger programs.

b   The programs were defined as structured programs, using

---

[1]Abstracted from S. H. Fuller, P. Shaman, D. Lamb, and W. Burr, "Evaluation of Computer Architectures via Test Programs," *AFIPS Conf. Proc.* vol. 46, June 1977, pp. 147–160.

Table 10   U.S. Steel COBOL Benchmarks as of 1978

	Total time (s)	Speed relative to IBM 1460		Total time (s)	Speed relative to IBM 1460
Burroughs Corporation			**IBM**		
B 1700	563	372	IBM 1460	209,176	1
B 2500	4,785	44	IBM 7010	11,524	18
B 3500	2,408	87	S/360 Model 50 emulating IBM 7010	12,187	17
B 3700	1,596	131	IBM 7074	4,618	45
B 4700	1,032	203	S/360 Model 65 emulating IBM 7074	3,069	68
B 4800	572	366	IBM 7094	5,423	39
B 5500	9,295	23			
B 6700	901	232	S/360 Model 30	6,064	34
B 7700	316	662	S/360 Model 40	2,999	70
			S/360 Model 50	1,344	156
Control Data Corporation			S/360 Model 65	529	395
CDC 3300	4,550	46	S/360 Model 75	313	668
CDC 6500	1,434	146	S/360 Model 195	151	1,385
Cyber 72	1,093	191			
Cyber 73	836	250	S/370 Model 125	4,462	47
			S/370 Model 135	3,426	61
Data General Corporation			S/370 Model 145	1,490	140
C/300 Eclipse	3,497	60	S/370 Model 155	601	348
			S/370 Model 158	256	817
Digital Equipment Corporation			S/370 Model 158 (multiprocessor)	284	737
PDP-11/45	70,172	3	S/370 Model 165	191	1,095
			S/370 Model 168-3	120	1,743
General Electric Corporation			S/370 Model 168-3 (multiprocessor)	107	1,955
GE-415	5,163	41	**NCR**		
GE-425	3,691	57	Century 100	15,382	14
GE-435	2,903	62	Century 200	3,880	54
GE-615	5,642	37	**RCA**		
GE-635	2,006	104	Spectra 70/35	6,576	32
			Spectra 70/45	3,494	60
Hewlett-Packard			Spectra 70/55	1,309	160
HP 3000-II	4,298	19	**Sperry-Univac**		
			UNIVAC 1108	481	435
Honeywell Information Systems			**Texas Instruments**		
H-110	17,371	12	TI 960A	44,407	5
H-120	13,007	16	**Xerox Data Systems**		
H-125	10,718	20	Sigma 7	3,101	67
H-2200	18,740	11			
H-6060	1,179	177			
H-6080	756	277			

a PL/I-like Program Definition Language (PDL) and then "hand translated" into the assembly languages of the respective architectures.

c   Programmers were not permitted to make *algorithmic* improvements or modifications, but rather were required to translate the PDL descriptions into assembly language. Programmers were free to optimize their test programs to the extent possible with highly optimizing compilers. This "hand translation" of strictly defined algorithms was expected to reduce variations due to programmer skill.

d   All test programs except the I/O Interrupt test programs were coded as reentrant, position-independent (or self-relocating) subroutines. This was believed to be consistent with the best contemporary programming practice and provides a good test of an architecture's subroutine and addressing capabilities.

Selection of the Twelve Test Programs.   The CFA committee appointed a subcommittee responsible for developing a set of test program specifications consistent with the guidelines just discussed. This subcommittee defined a set of 21 test programs that were intended to be broadly representative of the basic types of operations performed by military computer systems. The CFA committee reviewed these 21 test programs, committee members were asked to rank the relevance of these test programs to the applications of their particular organization, and it was agreed that the top 12 programs would be the basis of the test program study. The full specification of the 12 selected test programs is given in Fuller et al. [1976a] and a brief description of these test programs is given below.

A. *I/O kernel four priority levels* requires the processor to field interrupts from four devices, each of which has its own priority level. While one device is being processed, interrupts from higher priority devices are allowed.

B. *I/O kernel, FIFO processing,* also fields interrupts from four devices, but without consideration of priority level. Instead, each interrupt causes a request for processing to be queued; requests are processed in FIFO order. While a request is being processed, interrupts from other devices are allowed.

C. *I/O device handler* processes application programs' requests for I/O block transfers on a typical tape drive, and returns the status of the transfer upon completion.

D. *Large FFT* computes the fast Fourier transform of a large vector of 32-bit floating point complex numbers. This benchmark does exercise the machine's floating point instructions, but principally tests its ability to manage a large address space. (Up to one-half of a million bytes may be required for the vector.)

E. *Character search* searches a long character string for the first occurrence of a potentially large argument string. It exercises the ability to move through character strings sequentially.

F. *Bit test, set, or reset* tests the initial value of a bit within a bit string, then optionally sets or resets the bit. It tests one kind of bit manipulation.

G. *Runge-Kutta integration* numerically integrates a simple differential equation using third-order Runge-Kutta integration. It is primarily a test of floating-point arithmetic and iteration mechanisms.

H. *Linked list insertion* inserts a new entry in a doubly linked list. It tests pointer manipulation.

I. *Quicksort* sorts a potentially large vector of fixed-length strings using the Quicksort algorithm. Like FFT, it tests the ability to manipulate a large address space, but it also tests the ability of the machine to support recursive routines.

J. *ASCII to floating point* converts an ASCII string to a floating point number. It exercises character-to-numeric conversion.

K. *Boolean matrix transpose* transposes a square, tightly-packed bit matrix. It tests the ability to sequence through bit vectors by arbitrary increments.

L. *Virtual memory space exchange* changes the virtual memory mapping context of the processor.

S, M and R: Measures of an Architecture's Performance

Very little has been done in the past to quantify the relative (or absolute) performance of computer architectures, independent of specific implementations. Hence, like it or not, we had little choice but to define measures of architecture performance for ourselves.

Fundamentally, performance of computers is measured in units of space and time. The measures that were used by the CFA Committee to measure a computer architecture's performance on the test programs were:

Measure of Space

S: Number of bytes used to represent a test program.

Measure of Execution Time

M: Number of bytes transferred between primary memory and the processor during the execution of the test program.

R: Number of bytes transferred among internal registers of the processor during execution of the test program.

All of the measures described in this section are measured in units of 8-bit bytes. A more fundamental unit of measure might be bits, but we faced a number of annoying problems with respect to carry propagation and field alignment that make the measurement of S, M, and R in bits unduly complex. Fortunately, all the computer architectures under consideration by this committee are based on 8-bit bytes (rather than 6, 7, or 9-bit bytes) and hence the byte unit of measurement can be conveniently applied to all these machines.

Summary

The test programs were assigned to programmers based on a statistical design involving three phases, denoted as I, II, and III. In Phase I eight programmers were assigned two test programs to implement on each of the three machines. Phase III was a smaller version of Phase I, involving only four programmers. Phase II was a somewhat more complex design that involved each of three programmers writing nine different test programs, three on each machine. Phase II was intended to give some information on the interaction between particular test programs and machines that was not available with much precision from Phases I and III.

The principal result of the test program study that were passed along to the life-cycle cost models [Cornyn et al., 1977] was the composite performance of the candidate architectures for Phases I and III on the set of 12 test programs. An analysis of Variance (ANOVA) procedure was used to determine the overall relative performance of the three candidate machines (Table 11). Unity indicates average performance and the lower the score on any of the measures, the better the machine handled the set of test programs.

In other words, the test program results indicate that the IBM S/370 needs 46 percent more memory than the Interdata 8/32 to represent the set of test programs (or 21 percent more than the average of the three architectures) and the PDP-11 is essentially average in its use of memory.

Considering the test program results in a little more detail, in Phase I the data revealed the IBM S/370 to be significantly worse than the other two machines on S, M, and R measures at a significance level of 0.05 (i.e., the 95 percent confidence intervals all failed to include the point where the IBM S/370 equals the performance of the other machines). Moreover, the overall performance of the PDP-11 was virtually identical to that of the Interdata 8/32. Some part of the poor performance of the IBM S/370 can be traced to test program A (the priority I/O kernel). In Phase III alone, none of the comparisons among the three machines was significant at the 0.05 level because of the small number of data points (24). However, the PDP-11 was noticeably the worst of the three machines on all three measures. The IBM S/370 dominated the Interdata 8/32 with regard to the M measure, the Interdata was better for the S measure, and there was little difference between the two for the R measure. The relatively poor performance of the PDP-11 appeared to be due to the quicksort test program, test program I, which worked with a list much larger than the 64K byte virtual address space of the PDP-11.

Statistical results from Phases I and III were combined. In this analysis the ranking of the three machines from best to worst on the three measures was: Interdata 8/32, PDP-11, and IBM S/370. The average performance of the three architectures in Phases I and III is given in Table 11.

The outcome of Phase II largely corroborates the results of the other two experiments. The ranking of the three machines, from best to worst, is: PDP-11, Interdata 8/32, IBM S/370. This ranking prevails for all three measures, S, M, and R. It is important to recall that Phase II included test program A, for which the IBM

Table 11   Average Performance of the Architectures on the 12 Test Programs

Architecture	S	M	R
PDP-11	1.00	0.93	0.94
IBM S/370	1.21	1.27	1.29
Interdata 8/32	0.83	0.85	0.83

S/370 performs relatively poorly, and does not include test programs D and I, which are relatively difficult to implement on the PDP-11, because they have large data structures. Because of the magnitude of the experimental error in these test programs and the relatively small number of data points in Phase II (27), we were not able to detect any test program/architecture interactions that were statistically significant.

Queuing Models

System performance is also a function of configuration (e.g., amount of Mp or Ms; data transfer rates; latency; seek time). A large body of work exists in applying queuing models to total systems (hardware, OS, I/O, and configuration) in order to predict system performance bottlenecks and to suggest remedies. A discussion of queuing models is beyond the scope of this text. The reader is referred to the September 1978 issue of the ACM's *Computer Surveys*, or to the numerous performance evaluation textbooks, for an introduction to queuing models.

Economies of Scale

To evaluate the performance of machines, it is necessary to consider economies of scale. For nearly all manufactured objects (e.g., transportation vehicles, electricity generators, buildings) some economy of scale exists because of high fixed costs that do not increase as rapidly as the output increases.

Factors leading to economies of scale for computers often include several dimensions. The same software can be used on many models. Sales and maintenance personnel can service a wide range of equipment. Manufacturing facilities can be adapted to produce different models.

Grosch [1953] suggested that there was an economy of scale for computers according to the performance/price relationship:

$$\text{Performance} = \text{constant} \times \text{price}^2$$

Several studies [Sec. 5 of Part 4; Knight, 1966; Solomon, 1966; Phister, 1979; Sharpe, 1969; Turn, 1974] have examined the validity of this formula for various machines. On the other hand, it is possible to price machines using this relationship. Clearly, performance must increase more rapidly than price for improved operating economy.

Because the studies do not cover wide price ranges, there is some doubt that the square law holds. Indeed, over a narrow range (a factor of 4), a linear approximation to the data would appear to fit as well as the square law does.[1] See Fig. 6.

One computer component that could be predicated on a square-law relationship is core memory. There is an overhead cost

[1] In Chap. 52 the exponent is found to range from 1.0 for the S/360 family to 1.6 for the S/370 family.

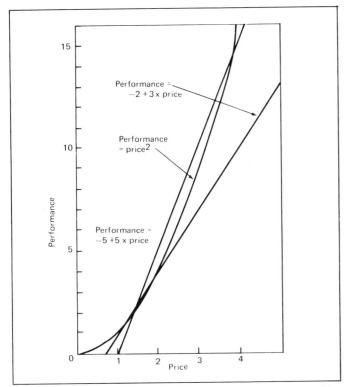

Fig. 6. A comparison of linear and square law relationships between price and performance.

associated with the base packaging, power, and interface. The electronic selection follows a square law; a doubling of the selection circuitry provides access to a core stack that is 4 times larger. All other costs are roughly linear, although the manufacturing cost for larger stacks would probably follow some economy of scale due to the high setup cost of threading core memories.

Another point is that Grosch's law, derived from the definition of performance, is itself a definition. Consider Knight's model:

Performance = processing rate × memory size × word length

If we ignore word length (assuming word length is constant for members of a computer class or family), then performance does increase as the square of memory price, since the factors of rate and size are each a function of memory price. To derive this result we proceed as follows.

Let P equal the price of the memory on the system. Assume the use of a $2^k \times 1$ memory chip and a memory system n bits wide, and further assume that the processor can use 100 percent of the memory data rate. To supply concrete cost and performance parameters we will use a 4-kilobit chip, which in 1978 cost about $25 and had a cycle time (at the processor) of about 500 ns. Then,

Processing rate = memory data rate

$$= 2 \times 10^6 (n + m)$$

where m = number of chips in the processor

$$= 2 \times 10^6 (n + kn)$$

since m is linearly related to n

$$= 2 \times 10^6 K_1 n$$

$$= \frac{K_2 P}{25}$$

since n is proportional to $P/($price per chip$)$, and

Memory size $= \dfrac{P}{\text{price per bit}}$

$$= \frac{4{,}096}{25} P$$

since the price per bit is 25/4,096. Substituting in Knight's model, we get

$$\text{Performance} = \frac{4{,}096}{25} P \times K_2 \frac{P}{25}$$

$$= K_3 P^2$$

Thus, according to this performance model, Grosch's law holds by definition because

1   Memory price and processor price are linearly related (predictably, since they use the same semiconductor technology).

2   Processor performance is usually matched to memory size, as suggested by Amdahl (see page 46).

References

Alexander, Gregg, and Wortman [1975]; Arbuckle [1966]; Bell, Mudge, and McNamara [1978]; Bell and Newell [1971]; Bernwell [1975]; Blake [1977]; Connors, Mercer, and Sorlini [1970]; Cornyn, Smith, Svirsky, and Coleman [1977]; Ferrari [1978]; Fuller, Burr, Shaman, and Lamb [1976]; Fuller, Burr, Shaman, and Lamb [1977]; Fuller, Stone, and Burr [1977]; Gibson [1970]; GML [1977]; Gonter [1969]; Grosch [1953]; Herbst, Metropolis, and Wells [1955]; Knight [1966]; Lucas [1971]; Phister [1979]; Popek and Goldberg, [1974]; Raichelson and Collins [1966]; Sharpe [1969]; Smith, Cornyn, Coleman, Estell, and Sabin [1977]; Solomon [1966]; Strecker [1976a]; Turn [1974]; U.S. Steel [1978]; Wagner, Lieblein, Rodriguez, and Sabin [1977]; Wichmann [1973].

Chapter 6

Structure

We now turn from function and performance, which provide design constraints and objectives, to the dimensions of structure, which provide the space in which the design is actually cast. A structural dimension is one in which the designer can attain any of the values along the dimension by relatively direct means. Thus a machine is completely specified by listing all its values along the structural dimensions. From this, the system's function and its performance within that function can be determined.

What dimensions should be selected for structure? The viewpoint is distinctly different from that of performance, where one averages and combines many features to summarize effective output. This tends to obscure structure. For structure, one wants maximally independent aspects which are easily obtained if selected as a design choice. For example, a computer designer who had only a single dimension to describe a computer would undoubtedly select the logic technology used in the Pc and K's; this tells a good deal about many aspects of the computer's structure. In fact, the technology and the average number of bits processed per second by the Pc are correlated, and so each can be used to predict the other, though only imperfectly. If one is interested in performance, the effective number of bits per second is preferred; if one is interested in design, technology is preferred.

The computer space in Table 1 in the introduction to this section presents our choice of the major structure dimensions. There are fewer rationales to validate the choice of dimensions here than there are for performance. Nevertheless, there are a few hallmarks. Perhaps the most important is redundancy (the opposite side of the coin from independence, mentioned above). Several dimensions of structure may covary, so that giving any one of them is tantamount to giving the others. This covariation need not come from physical dependence; it may arise from the nature of an appropriate design and good engineering practice. Such a cluster of covarying dimensions is likely to indicate an important dimension (which one among the correlates is to be used is a secondary matter.) Table 1 in the introduction to this section is organized in terms of such clusters, with one of each selected as the main representative and placed at the left. The following subsections discuss each of the seven clusters of covarying dimensions in turn.

Technology

Among the technology dimensions are generation, component complexity, and date. These dimensions, which were briefly mentioned in the introduction to Sec. 2, will be explored in more detail below. Also listed are Pc speed (operations per second) and cost (dollars per million operations), both of which vary directly (or inversely) with logic technology. The Pc operation rate is strongly correlated with logic technology, as we have indicated in the computer space. Our discussion about technology and generations is also about operation rate. The principal reason for the higher operation rate is faster logic technology. Technology also has a secondary effect on increasing speed. More reliable devices allow large computers to be built. Smaller devices allow higher device densities, thus decreasing stray capacitance and inductance and shortening transmission delays. Smaller components also allow increased interconnection density.

Operation rate is relatively highly correlated with total performance. If we hold the structure and parallelism constant, the simplest way to increase performance is by increasing the clock rate. The increase in the performance/cost ratio over the past three decades of computers' evolution has made their primary gains through higher operation rates.

We have indicated only a few of the dimensions that are correlated with technology. In fact, the only dimensions in Table 1 of the section introduction that are independent of technology are the word length and the Pc addresses per instruction. All the rest show dependence on technology. For some, such as memory speed and size, there is a direct correlation. For others, such as PMS structure and parallelism, the development of more complex versions—the leading edge, so to speak—depends on technology, but there is free use of all versions that are in existence at any given time. There are still other dimensions of importance, not shown in Table 1 of the section introduction, that have also changed with technology, e.g., electric power consumption.

A comparison of the machines in a common computer family will reveal both variations and factors independent of technology. The simple two-parameter model involving Pc microcycle time (a function of technology) and Mp memory pause time (a function both of technology and system design) in Chap. 5 is applied to the System/360, System 370 (see Chap. 52), and PDP-11 (see Chap. 39) computer families. The model is able to explain most of the variation between the family members. And in the case of the System/360 and PDP-11 families, the dominant term is Pc microcycle time, which is almost wholly determined by technology.

Throughout this section we have referred to technology as the dominant factor in the computer. Does this mean that computer development waits upon new fundamental windfalls? We have been lucky in getting the transistor and, to a lesser degree, the integrated circuit from external efforts. However, core memories were invented for the computer and resulted because of need. Read-only memories have also resulted both from development at the circuit level and from pressure above, requiring the memories to be developed. All the electromechanical secondary memories (e.g. magnetic tape, drums, disks, and photostores) have resulted from the computer's needs. Special packaging (e.g., the dual inline package, or DIP) and interconnect (e.g., printed circuit boards, chip carriers) technologies were also developed for computers. Thus, despite the dominant technology, the computer often shapes development.

The transistor and integrated circuit have had a profound impact on the structure of computers. Further, the proliferation of computer structures built from these technologies has provided enough data points that several interesting trends can be seen.

Figure 1 shows a family tree (taxonomy) of the most common digital integrated circuits.[1] The least complex functions are in the upper portion of the figure, and the most complex are at the bottom. In addition, the circuits are ordered by generation, starting with the second generation on the left side of the figure and progressing to the fifth generation on the right side. The circuits are clustered roughly by the regularity of the function and whether memory is associated with the function. Circuit regularity is important in large-scale integrated circuits because it is desirable to implement regular structures to minimize area-consuming interconnections and, thus, to simplify layout and understanding and to aid testing.

As indicated in Fig. 1, the branching of the integrated circuit family tree began in earnest at the beginning of the third generation. At that time, advances in integrated-circuit technology permitted collections of basic logic primitives (AND, NAND, etc.) and sequential circuit components (flip-flops, registers, etc.) to occupy a single integrated circuit rather than an entire module. This had the benefit of providing a drastic reduction in size between the second and third generation computer designs. But it also had the drawback that modules contained a wide variety of functions and were thus specialized.

As the densities began to approach 100 gates, the construction of complete arithmetic units on a single chip became possible. The earliest and most famous chip, the 74181 arithmetic logic unit (ALU), provided up to 32 functions of two 4-bit variables. By the fourth generation, it became possible to construct on a single chip very large combinational circuits, such as a complete 16- by 16-bit multiplication circuit (e.g., the TRW Corp. multiplier) requiring about 5,000 gates.

Progress during the fourth and fifth generations has not been without its problems, however. Without well defined functions such as addition and multiplication, semiconductor suppliers

[1]Figure 1 and the discussion surrounding it are adapted from Bell, Mudge, and McNamara [1978].

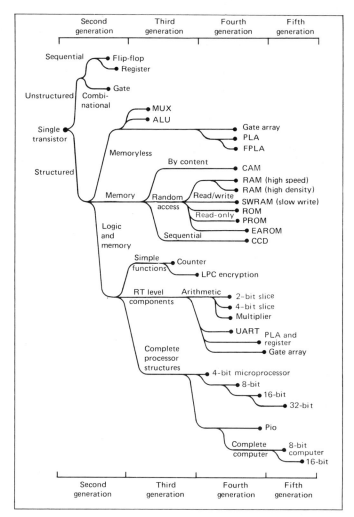

Fig. 1. Family tree of digital integrated circuit functions. (From G. G. Bell, J. C. Mudge, and J. E. McNamara, *Computer Engineering: A DEC View of Hardware Systems Design,* Digital Press, 1978, p. 29.)

cannot provide high density products in high volume because there are few large-scale, general purpose universal functions.

To address these problems, two methods of effectively customizing large-scale integrated circuit logic are included in Fig. 1. These are the programmable logic array (PLA) and the gate array (also called master slice.) The programmable logic array (PLA) is an array of AND-OR gates that can be interconnected to form the sum-of-products terms in a combinational logic design. Gate arrays are simply a large number of gates placed on the chip in fixed locations where they can be interconnected during the final metalization stages of semiconductor manufacture.

There is a special branch of the tree shown in Fig. 1 purely for memory functions. Memory is used in the processor as conventional memory, but it can also be used as an alternative to conventional logic for performing combinational logic functions. For example, the inputs to a combinational function can be used as an address, and the output can be obtained by reading the contents of that address. Memory can also be used to implement sequential logic functions. For example, it can be used to hold state information for a microprogram. (See Sec. 1 of Part 2.)

There is a special branch for bit-slice components that can be combined to form data paths of arbitrary widths. These are being used to construct most of today's high-speed digital systems, mid-range computers, and computer peripherals. Although there have been several bit-slice families, the AMD Corp. 2900-series has become the most widely used (see Chaps. 13, 14, and 15).

The final branch of the tree in Fig. 1 is the most complex and is used to mark the fourth (microprocessor-on-a-chip) generation of technology and the beginning of the fifth (computer-on-a-chip) generation. The fourth generation is marked by the packaging of a complete processor on a single silicon die. Using this standard, the fifth generation has already begun, since a complete computer (processor with memory), called a *monolithic microcomputer* in our computer classification of Chap. 1, now occupies a single die. The evolution in complexity during each generation simply permits larger–word-length processors or computers to be placed on one chip. At the beginning of the fourth generation, a 4-bit processor was the benchmark; toward the end of the fourth generation, a complete 16-bit processor could be placed on a single chip.

Figure 2 plots the increase in IC complexity as a function of time, a graph known as the *Moore plot*. In 1964, Gorden E. Moore, then director of research at Fairchild Semiconductor, predicted that the component count per IC chip would double every year. Indeed, since the introduction of the planar transistor (1959), with a component density of 1, this essential doubling has occurred each year up to the present. According to the Moore plot, integrated-circuit chips composed of 1 million components are predicted for the early 1980s. As pointed out by Moore, three factors must be considered to contribute equally to the doubling of component count per year: (1) an increase in chip area, (2) a decrease in minimum physical dimensions of components, and (3) the contributions made by the invention of new structures and/or circuit cleverness.

The result given in Fig. 2 is exponential and indicates that the number of bits per chip for a metal oxide semiconductor (MOS) memory doubles every two years according to the relationship:

Number of bits per chip $= 2^{t-1962}$

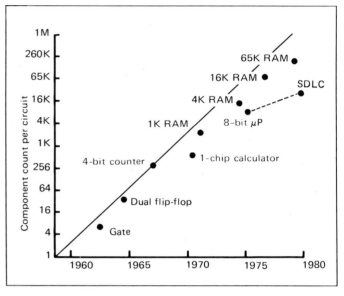

Fig. 2. The increase in an integrated circuit density as a function of calendar year.

There are separate curves, each following this relationship, for bipolar read-write memories, bipolar read-only memories, and MOS read-only memories. Thus products lead or lag behind the above state-of-the art time line by one to three years according to the following rules:

- Bipolar read-write memories lag by two to three years.
- Bipolar-read-only memories lag by about one year.
- MOS read-only memories lead by one year

Random logic, as represented by the 8-bit microprocessor and SDLC chip in Fig. 2, actually lies on a different exponential curve. Chapter 36 discusses the trends in microprocessor densities.

After density, the most important characteristic of integrated circuits is price. The price of integrated circuits is probably the hardest of all the parameters to identify and predict because it is set by a complex marketplace.

The price/history of integrated circuits is reflected very dramatically in the price history of a special class of integrated circuits, semiconductor memory. The semiconductor memory price curves, given in Fig. 3, are also interesting because of the important role of memory in past and future computer structures.[1]

[1]Discussion of Fig. 3 adapted from Bell, Mudge, and McNamara [1978].

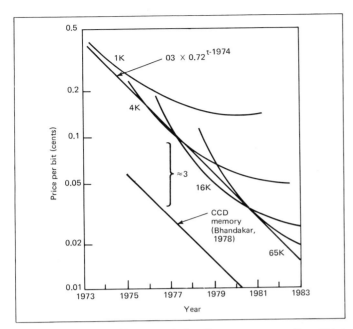

Fig. 3. Price per bit of integrated circuit memory versus time. Price per bit of computer memory has declined and should continue to decline as is shown here for successive generations of random-access memory circuits capable of handling from 1,024 (1K) to 65,536 (65K) bits of memory. Increasing complexity of successive circuits is primarily responsible for price reduction but less complex circuits also continue to decline in price. (Adapted from Noyce [1977:69]; courtesy of *Scientific American*.)

As shown in the figure, the 1978 price per bit was roughly 0.08¢ and 0.07¢ per bit for the 4-K bit and 16-K bit integrated circuit chips, respectively, giving prices of \$3.30 and \$11.50.

Two factors influence the price of integrated circuits: density in bits per integrated circuit and price per bit. The two factors have not had equal influence in reducing costs because, while chip density has improved by a factor of 2 each year (Fig. 2), the price per bit (at the integrated circuit level) has not declined by a factor of 2 every two years. The equation for the line drawn in Fig. 3 is:

$$\text{Price/bit (¢)} = 0.3 \times 0.72^{t-1974}$$

Large-scale integration (LSI) has two strong advantages: both the cost per function and the failure rate per function decrease exponentially. As semiconductor components get larger they also become more reliable per function. Figure 4 depicts the failure rate per million hours per gate for bipolar technology as a function of the number of gates on a chip. The curve marked "Mil 217A"

was derived from data from about 1965 [Mil 217A, 1965]. The curve marked "Mil Model 217B (1974)" was generated from a reliability predictive model ca. 1974 [Mil 217B, 1974]. In order to calibrate the Mil Model 217B, actual failure data are also plotted. The curve marked "Field Data" was derived from a reliability study of a population of video terminals over a period of a year [Harrahy, 1977]. The curve marked "Life Cycle Data" was derived from elevated-temperature testing of chips followed by translation by a mathematical model from failure rates at elevated temperature to rates at ambient temperature [Siewiorek, 1978b]. Finally, the improvement in the 3,000-gate Motorola Mc 6800 was plotted [Queyssac, 1979].

It has been demonstrated that the failure rate per function has decreased by more than an order of magnitude. Plots of failure per bit of bipolar random-access memory (RAM) indicate that the failure rate per gate and per bit are comparable for comparable levels of integration. Obviously the chip failure rate is a function of chip complexity (i.e., failure rate per function decreases by an order of magnitude over two orders of gate complexity and two to three orders of memory complexity) and is not a constant (i.e., failure rate would decrease by the same order of magnitude as complexity increased.) The Mil Model 217B predicted an upturn in reliability per function beyond a complexity of about 200 gates, presumably because of the immaturity of the fabrication process at that scale of integration. It is more likely to assume a decreasing function as long as the complexity is within the state of the art, as illustrated by the Mc 6800 curve.

Another assumption deals with the relative position of the curves with respect to the axis. One study (curve 1965*a*) showed that a failure rate of 0.4 failures per 10^6 hours was a good approximation for state-of-the-art ICs at that time (one to four gates per IC). Another study examined small functional units composed of discrete components and ICs. Various 10-element units showed failure rates of 0.83 to 1.8 per 10^6 hours (curve 1965*b*). While the data are incomplete (having been based on a study in 1965, when integrated circuits had just been introduced), it is reasonable to assume that reliability per function for a given chip complexity improves with time, as illustrated by the Mc 6800 curve.

Bytes of Virtual Address and Information Structure: Information Base, Word Length, and Data-Types

All computers structure their information in a hierarchy of units, which we defined as an i-unit. For example, the IBM System/360 starts with the bit; then the byte, which is 8 bits; then the word, which is 4 bytes; then the record, which is a variable number of

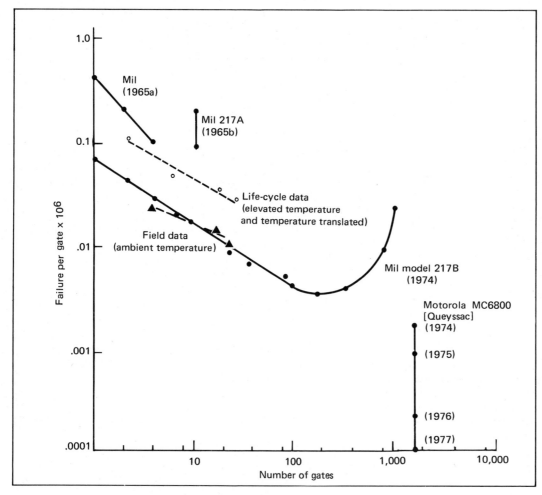

Fig. 4. Failure rate per gate as a function of chip complexity for bipolar technology.

words. In between, playing minor roles, are decimal digits (4 bits), the halfword, and the double word. The single most important structural dimension after technology is bytes of virtual address, from which, at a given point in time, the class to which the computer belongs can be inferred (see Chap. 1). Subsequently, the attributes of the information organization can be inferred from the computer class.

A number of features of the design are related to this hierarchical organization of data. Before considering them, however, it is important to characterize the organization itself, beginning at the bottom of the information hierarchy.

At the bottom there is the bit, encoded in two-state devices. Although other numbers of states are possible, and ternary

(three-state) machines have been proposed occasionally, digital technology has developed exclusively to handle binary information. There are several reasons for this. The first is the requirement for high reliability and high signal-to-noise ratios in the basic devices. Generally a basic n-state device (i.e., one not built up from other k-state devices) is realized by breaking a continuous physical dimension, such as voltage, current, or magnetic flux, into n discrete levels of regions. Reliability and signal-to-noise ratio then depend on keeping adequate separation. This is easiest to do with two states (in their limiting form they are on-off devices) and becomes progressively more difficult as n increases. The second reason is the simplicity of the logic design for binary representations. A basic device for combining two ternary digits must deal with $3 \times 3 = 9$ configurations, rather than $2 \times 2 = 4$ configurations for the binary case. This also gets worse as n increases.

A final reason—the coup de grace, so to speak—is that no one has ever found striking advantages for the resulting processing structure in having more than two states. Thus there are no compelling reasons to suffer the first two disadvantages. In short, what might have been an important dimension on which to distinguish computers, namely, the number of states in the basic encoding, turns out instead to be one of the great uniformities in digital technology.

Information Base

That the physical devices deal ultimately in bits does not imply that the information processing must be organized in terms of bits. It is possible to select an arbitrary *base* (one with any number of states) and construct the entire ISP in its terms. A base unit is represented physically, of course, as a set of bits. If one wanted a base 13 machine, for example, one would have to use at least 4 bits (with 16 states) to encode it. But no operations at the ISP level would refer to anything but base units and data structures built up from sets of base units, and there would be no way to manipulate directly the bits that represented the base. Thus, using a base other than binary obtains whatever advantages might accrue to n-state units, without any of the disadvantages at the device level.

Computers have been built with a variety of different bases, the main ones being binary, decimal, and character. The character has shifted between a 6-bit character and an 8-bit character (byte).[1] The arguments for bases other than binary (which represents the natural base of the computer) all hinge on the alphabets used externally by human beings and the desire to avoid conversions into a different representation inside the computer. With universal acceptance of higher languages, such as FORTRAN and ALGOL, this argument has also lost much of its force. In fact, all third-generation machines are binary. Nevertheless, in the fifties there was much controversy over which base to use. Third- and fourth-generation machines provide at least partial support for decimal and character data-types. Support for these alternate bases can even be found in single-chip processors (see Chap. 37)

There is little difference between binary and decimal computers in their ISP organization. However, there is a great difference between these two and character machines. The latter are designed for handling text and are constructed to deal with variable-length strings of characters. Correspondingly, they de-emphasize numerical computation. Both these decisions affect the

ISP considerably. Thus, in the computer space we indicate the base dimension along with the word-length dimension. The two together make up a single dimension.

Word Length

Let us now examine the role of word length. The word is the first major information unit above the base. It is defined as n bits for a binary computer or n digits for a decimal computer (character machines being excluded as not having a fixed word length). Sometimes there are intermediate units, but they always play a minor role and we can disregard them at this stage. As we noted earlier, the main determinant of word length has been the function of the total system: large word lengths for arithmetic systems, small word lengths for control systems (and character strings for business). Thus, only within narrow limits is the word length a free design choice.

However, the interesting thing about word length is not so much its determinant as the way it affects other aspects of the total system design. This starts with a design decision that the unit of information transfer between components will be a word. As soon as this becomes the case, then registers in various components must hold a word, since that is what arrives or is to be transmitted. Thus the word becomes the information unit of the Mp, and most of the registers of the Pc hold one word. The instruction is designed to fit into a submultiple or multiple of one word, since that is the number of bits that is obtained "at once" and hence can be used to effect the next time increment of processing.

Once these basic features are set, others follow. An integral number of any smaller units, such as characters, should fit into a word, since otherwise a set of words will not provide a homogeneous sequence of subunits. (That is, only five 6-bit characters fit into 32 bits, so that a set of 32-bit words filled with 6-bit characters has a number of 2-bit holes in it. This can complicate algorithms that deal with long character strings.) The constraint of compatibility is not so strong with Ms, since speeds are slow enough to permit conversion algorithms (either hardware or software). Still, the system is simpler (and therefore usually will work better) if incommensurabilities of information units do not exist. Thus, to pick an example, the number of parallel tracks on magnetic tapes tends to divide evenly into the word length. IBM tapes for the 700 series of 36-bit machines have six data tracks; for the System/360, which has a 32-bit word, the tapes have eight data tracks.

There is an interesting correlation between the word length of a computer and the number of data-types that it makes available. The operations in a computer can be classified according to the type of data they operate upon. Each data-type tends to have a certain set of operations appropriate to it (for example, $+$, $-$, $\times$, and $/$ for numbers), and the decision to include a data-type carries

---

[1] Seven bits have been used for communication purposes but have never been made the basis of a machine, as far as we know.

with it the decision to include its operations. Thus the number of operations tends to grow with the number of data-types. The total amount of hardware in a computer grows as the word size (because data paths are word-parallel[1]) and also as the number of operations. Thus machines with large word size tend to be large machines (i.e., in a larger computer class) and have many data-types and many operations.

There are three additional, somewhat independent features that support the relationship between word size, number of data-types, and size of computer. First, with a large system there will already be available many of the pieces necessary to add additional operations. That is, the marginal cost of a new operation goes down as the system grows. Therefore, given a large system, there is a tendency to add more operations. The number of operations per data-type is not easy to increase; rather, one adds new data-types.

Second, with small word lengths, one cannot define many worthwhile data-types that will fit into a word, and multiple-word data-types are left to the programmer to define with software. With large word lengths there are many different worthwhile data-types that fit into the word, for instance, decompositions of the word into partial words or into character strings. Each of these requires additional operations, since the initial data-types involve the entire word or some large part of it (i.e., the word, address, and integer operations).

Third, since memory addresses are usually 1 word in length, the word size determines the size of the immediately addressable memory space. The most serious mistake that a computer architect can make is not providing enough address bits in the instruction (see Chap. 47). With semiconductor memory densities doubling every 1 to 2 years, the address size needs enough room to support a ½- to 1-bit growth in memory size per year over the life of the architecture.[2] Short addresses can be expanded into larger, virtual addresses by linking the contents of a register to the processor-produced address or by adding the contents of a larger base register (see Sec. 2 of Part 2). However, the program will still have only a small immediately accessible address space and will have to manipulate the address expansion registers explicitly (potentially through operating-system calls). This explicit address management both complicates program writing and degrades program performance (see Chap. 22). Wide word sizes are good for providing wide addresses; however, they are a source of substantial overhead in instructions that do not reference memory. Hence instruction sets have shifted either from 1-word

instructions to multiple words per instruction (as in the PDP-11), or to composing instructions of a variable number of bytes, as in the VAX-11/780 and Intel 8086.

In sum, the word length stands as an indicator of many aspects of the machine. It not only tells something about the basic organization of many components but also indicates how big the computer is (i.e., the computer class), both in number of data-types and number of operations.

The one design choice that makes word lengths have few of the consequences just described is making a computer bit-serial rather than bit-parallel. In many machines information transfers are conducted on a single bit stream (especially Pc-Mp transfers). Coincident with this is the construction of operations on a bit-by-bit basis. This works well for arithmetic and logic operations. Time is traded for hardware. The cost of the system becomes independent of word length, but the processing rates go down correspondingly. This design decision was an extremely important one when logic was expensive and unreliable. It has become less so in the current era, where processors and transfer paths are relatively few in number while both the cost and the reliability of components have improved. However, as large parallel processors are considered ($\sim 10^3$ P's), bit-serial processors again become a serious design alternative. (See Chap. 21.)

In summary, word length is an important dimension, and we find many characteristics either proportional to or inversely proportional to it. To be sure, these relations hold only for current design practice, as we have seen with the bit-serial designs.

Data-Types

We have presented the number of data-types as being correlated with word length and also with computer size through the effect on number of operations. In essence, a data-type is made up recursively of a concatenation of subparts, which themselves are data-types. This concatenation may be an iteration of a data-type to form an array. Fig. 5 shows the structure of various data-types and how each is built from more primitive data-types.

If required, an operation can be defined in terms of other (presumably more primitive) operations. It is necessary first to define the data format explicitly (including perhaps some additional memory).

Three additional aspects need to be noted with respect to data-types: two substantive and one notational. First, not everything one does with an item of data makes use of all the properties of its data-type. For example, numbers have to be moved from place to place. This operation is not a numerical operation and does not depend on the item's being a number. In fact, for the purpose of data transmission, the item is only a word (assuming it fits into a single word) and can be treated as such. Second, one can often embed one kind of operation in another, so as to coalesce

---

[1]The issue of bit-serial versus bit-parallel is discussed subsequently.
[2]Indeed, Chap. 1 indicated that the number of bytes of virtual address is growing, over all ISPs in the book, at 1 bit per year, while the number of bytes of physical address is growing at ½ bit per year.

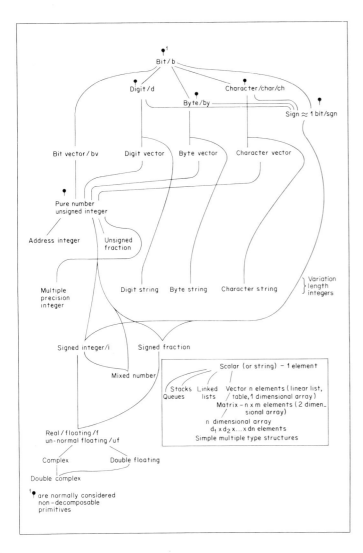

Fig. 5. Common data-types recognized by processor hardware.

Data-Types Embedded in Other Data-Types for Common Operations

word
  integer
    fraction
    mixed
    unsigned integer
    address integer
  boolean vector
    boolean (single bit)
    integer sign (divide or multiply by two operations)
    field
  single-precision floating
    single-precision unnormalized floating
double word
  double-precision integer
    fraction
    mixed
  double-precision floating-point
    double-precision unnormalized floating-point
character string
  digit string

data-types. An example is encoding the Mp addresses into the same integer data-type as is used for regular arithmetic. Then there need be no separate data-type for addresses.[1] The upshot of both these aspects can be seen in the following table, where we present an outline structure of data-types that shows how one data-type can be embedded in another for various purposes.

[1]However logical a course may seem, it is not always done this way. For example, the IBM 7090 (and other members of that family) have a 15-bit address data-type and a 36-bit integer data-type, with separate operations for each.

The notational aspect is the use in PMS of a mnemonic abbreviation scheme for data-types. Table 1 shows how an abbreviation is made up of a letter giving the precision, a letter giving the name, and a letter giving the length.

The simple naming convention does not take into account all that is known about a data-type. The information carrier for the data is only partially included in the length characteristic. Thus the carrier should also include the data base and the sign convention for representing negative numbers. The common sign conventions are sign magnitude (sm), true complement (i.e., tc, 2's complement for base 2), and radix-1 complement (i.e., oc, 1's complement for base 2).

For each of the data-types the processor must have the implied operators. In fact, being able to represent a particular entity is useful only if particular transformations can be carried out on the entity. The most primitive operation is data movement (i.e., transmission.) Data movement can be thought of as a complex operation consisting of accessing (locating), reading, and writing. Data-types which represent numbers require the ability to perform the arithmetic operations +, −, ×, /, ABS ( ), SQRT, MAX, MIN, etc. The address integer is a special case of an arithmetic quantity, and often only addictive arithmetic operations (+ and −) are available for it. Boolean scalars (or vectors) require some subset of the 16 logic operations (sufficient subsets are NOT, AND/NOT, OR). When character strings are represented, the concatenation, deletion, and transmission operations are

Table 1   Abbreviations Used to Name Data-Types

Precision	Data-type name	Length-type
fractional/f	boolean/b	scalar†
quarter/q	sign	vector/v
half/h	decimal digit/digit/d	matrix
single/s	octal digit/octal/o	array
double/d	character/char/ch/c‡	string/st
triple/t	byte/by	
quadruple/q	syllable	
multiple/m	word/w	
integer/i	signed integer/i	
	unsigned integer/ui	
	fraction/fr	
	fixed/mixed/mx	
	floating/real/f	
	unnormalized floating/uf	
	complex real/complex/cx	

Examples:

w	word
bv	boolean vector
i	integer
sfr	single-precision fraction
mx	mixed
di	double integer
10d	10 decimal digit (scalar)
ch.st	character string
sf	single-precision floating
suf	single-precision unnormalized floating
df	double-precision floating
duf	double-precision unnormalized floating

†May be optionally omitted from name.

‡The most common character size is 8 bits and is called a *byte*. Hence byte ≡ 8-bit character.

required. Alternatively, we can look to string-processing languages like SNOBOL to see the operations they require. If the strings also represent numeric quantities, then the arithmetic operations are necessary. Almost all arithmetic and symbolic data require relational operations between two quantities, yielding a boolean result (true or false). These relational operators are eql and neq, but for arithmetic quantities include gtr, geq, lss, leq. The more complex structured data-types (e.g., vectors and arrays) also have a range of certain primitive operations such as scalar accessing and transmission. Typical operations of vectors are search and element-by-element compare operations.

Although far from perfect, there is a rough order in which specific data-types are included in a computer (see Fig. 5). To be located at a point on the data-type dimension of the computer space (say at floating point) means to have all the data-types below on the dimension (i.e., integer, address, bit vector). Occasionally machines which violate this rule have arisen. Decimal machines

do not generally have boolean data-types, and there has been some attempt at machines with only floating point, i.e., without a separate integer type (see Chap. 9).

The reason behind this cumulation of data-types in a fixed order is that certain general tasks must be performed by any computer. It must transmit data between the Pc and Mp, and this transmission has nothing to do with the meaning or content of the data; thus there is always the "unit of transmission," which is the word (except on character machines). Next, all computers manipulate addresses to achieve generality (e.g., to compile), providing for a second data-type. Next come integers—since almost all algorithms make use of arithmetic—and on up to floating-point numbers, multiple-precision, and vector and string operations. At each stage the uses are more specialized so that lower ones cannot be eliminated, except for a few cases such as handling addresses as regular integers.

Bytes of Virtual Address

As we saw in Chap. 1, the number of bytes of virtual address strongly correlates with computer class. From the computer class we can infer (at a given point in time) computer size, data-types, and word length. Thus the number of bytes of virtual address follows technology as the most important structural dimension of computer space.

The virtual address is the address produced by the processor and presented to the memory subsystem. This address is the result of an effective address calculation that may involve address displacements from the instruction and base/index/memory management registers from the processor state. The latter registers frequently expand the length of the address beyond the address displacement contained in the instruction. It is not surprising that the number of bytes of virtual address correlates with word length and data-types.

Since the Pc must manipulate virtual addresses as the most fundamental data-type, path width and word width are highly correlated with the number of bytes of virtual address. Internal Pc data-path width can be reduced either by time-multiplexing portions of the virtual address through the Pc data paths or by providing separate hardware, with wider data paths, for virtual address calculations. The first approach suffers a costly performance penalty, while the second approach is costly in terms of duplicate hardware functionality. Note, however, that the second approach has been used to retrofit an existing ISP with a larger virtual address in order to extend the useful life of the ISP (e.g., see Chap. 47).

Addresses per Instruction and Processor State

The number of addresses in an instruction has been a traditional way of describing processors (i.e., their ISPs) and hence the computer systems containing these processors.[1] This dimension has become less significant with the increased complexity of computer systems and the generally wide acceptance of the general-register structure.

Originally the dimension was simple: 1-, 2-, 3-, and 4-address machines were constructed. It has become somewhat more complex. A "one plus one" machine has one address for data and one for determining the next instruction and is to be distinguished from a 2-address machine, which uses both addresses for data. Index registers and so-called general registers provide instruction schemes that lie somewhere between 1- and 2-address organizations. When processors admit several instruction formats or variable-length instructions, matters become even more complicated.

A correlated dimension in the computer space is the amount of processor state, that is, the number of bits that exist in the processor, as described in the ISP (i.e., PC state described in Chap. 4). This is the amount of information that can be held at the end of one instruction to provide the processing context for the next instruction. It consists of a number of status and mode bits (in modern machines packaged into registers, but in earlier machines simply scattered around in the processor), the next instruction address, the accumulator and other arithmetic registers, the index registers, and other general registers making up a "scratchpad" memory. It is a simpler descriptor of the ISP than addresses per instruction, since it is independent of the number and variety of instruction formats. It is easy to define processor state generally for any ISP, but difficult to define addresses per instruction.

The processor state is not the total number of bits in the processor, since there may be registers in the physical system that are used within the interpretation of one instruction but which carry no information between instructions. Address registers for obtaining operands from Mp are the most common such "underground" or "temporary" registers, but there can be others. We implied this distinction by defining processor state in terms of the ISP rather than the physical processor (i.e., Implementation Declarations described in Chap. 4).

The correlation between the processor state and the number of addresses per instruction is not simple, since it rests on two separate issues. For the first, note that larger programs perform transformations on the state of Mp (or even Ms or Tio's) and are not concerned with the state of the processor. Processor state enters only because, in decomposing the total algorithm into a series of small steps, it is not possible (or efficient) to make each step a transformation from Mp to Mp. Basically, this happens because the instruction does not hold enough information to specify the Mp-to-Mp transformations. For example, if one wants to add two numbers, two operands are required, and an instruction must

contain at least two addresses; if it does not, then an intermediate state (i.e., processor state) must be created to hold the information while the additional instructions are fetched. Thus, 1-address organizations require the most processor state, with less for 2- and 3-address organizations. This consideration stops at 3 (two operands and a result) because only a few elementary operations are more than binary. The processor state cannot be eliminated entirely, however, since there must be at least an instruction address (a Program Counter\PC register) to maintain continuity of the program.

The second source of correlation between processor state and instructions per address comes from differential access time to processor registers and to Mp. As long as there is an appreciable differential, substantial gains in processing power can be obtained from increasing processor state. This derives, again, from the structure of algorithms that generate intermediate results that are used almost immediately afterward and then are of no further interest. Rapid temporary storage and retrieval are beneficial under these conditions. Thus, working against higher address organization is the extra time to store in Mp results that need only temporary storage. Thus, also, index registers and general registers almost always imply increased processor state, although they need not do so logically (that is, the registers could exist in Mp and still have their effect on the instruction format).

With interrupts and multiprogramming the processor state gains additional significance, since it is the amount of information that has to be saved and restored in switching programs. For example, in the Honeywell H-800, an early 3-address computer, the processor state per program consisted only of the program counter and index registers, and when I/O halts occurred during processing, the Pc was switched immediately to another program. Eight programs could run concurrently (by having a total processor state of 64 program registers). In present computers with general-register state, often $25 \sim 100$ words must be stored, which implies an appreciable time for switching contexts.[1]

We can now consider briefly the different organizations according to addresses per instruction. To show the common similarities, we give in Fig. 6 a state diagram that can be used for all processors. In common is the basic idea of the stored program: fetch an instruction, determine what the instruction is to do, then execute it (the fetch-execute cycle). Other than this, only a part of the state diagram will be applicable to a given processor type.

As shown in the computer space, the addresses-per-instruction dimension starts with zero addresses, then one address, then one plus indexing, one plus general registers, and on up to two, three, and variable addresses. However, from an expository viewpoint

---

[1]Although used mostly to describe Pc's, the description applies to any processor.

[1]Members of the microcomputer class (or larger) frequently have several sets of Pc state registers for use by users and operating systems. Context-switching time then becomes only the time to specify the new register set to use.

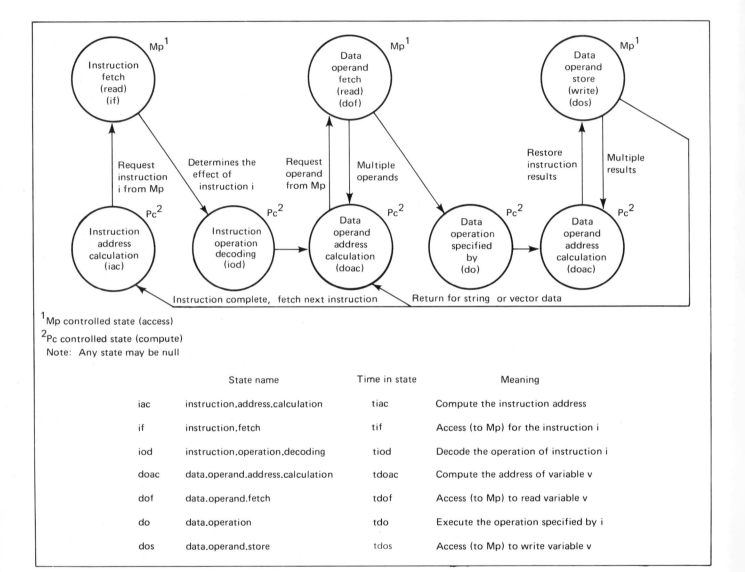

^{1}Mp controlled state (access)
^{2}Pc controlled state (compute)
Note: Any state may be null

	State name	Time in state	Meaning
iac	instruction.address.calculation	tiac	Compute the instruction address
if	instruction.fetch	tif	Access (to Mp) for the instruction i
iod	instruction.operation.decoding	tiod	Decode the operation of instruction i
doac	data.operand.address.calculation	tdoac	Compute the address of variable v
dof	data.operand.fetch	tdof	Access (to Mp) to read variable v
do	data.operation	tdo	Execute the operation specified by i
dos	data.operand.store	tdos	Access (to Mp) to write variable v

Fig. 6. ISP interpretation state diagram.

one should follow a different course, starting with single-address machines, then indexing, then 2- and 3-address machines, then general registers, and finally the zero-address and variable-address organizations. This not only puts the more common organizations first but makes it easy to relate the organizations to each other.

P(1 address) and P(1 + index address)

These Pc's constitute most first-, second-, and simple third-generation computers.

A significant change to the 1-address machine was the addition of the index register (called B-tubes) in the Manchester University machine in the early 1950s. Index registers are motivated by the frequent occurrence, in 1-address systems, of circuitous address calculations that involve first computing the address (e.g., the index of an array in Mp) and then planting it just ahead in the instruction stream in order to make use of it as an address. Providing a set of index registers introduces a second address into the instruction, even though of extremely limited function. Thus we classify processors with indexing as having $(1 + x)$ addresses per instruction.[1] An alternative view of index registers suggests that they double the number of data-types by allowing operations on vector data elements rather than just scalars.

For the 1-address processor, the processor state (Mps) typically consists of the program counter (instruction location counter), an accumulator AC, a multiplier-quotient register MQ (the extension of AC), and one or more index registers X or XR.

With only one address in the instruction, the one arithmetic register, AC, must be used for temporary results. Thus an effective-address integer (z) is computed as a function of the address part (part a) of the instruction i and the index registers. This process is typically

$$z := a + X[j]$$

where X[j] is the jth index register as specified in the instruction.

There are several forms for the transmission operators between AC and Mp.

AC = z	load immediate
AC = Mp[z]	load direct
AC = Mp[Mp[z]]	load indirect
Mp[z] = AC	store direct
Mp[Mp[z]] = AC	store indirect

In indirect operations a convention may be required to determine what address in Mp[z] is to be used.

Similarly, the binary operations (+, −, *, /, AND, OR, XOR, @, etc.) are generally of the form[2]

$$AC = AC \ b \ Mp[z]$$

Rarely do we find the symmetrical operation form

$$Mp[z] = AC \ b \ Mp[z]$$

For unary operations (NOT, −, etc.), the most common forms are

$$AC = u \ AC$$
$$AC = u \ Mp[z]$$

Rarely do we find

$$Mp[z] = u \ Mp[z]$$
$$Mp[z] = u \ AC$$

[1]Indirect addressing, on the other hand, does not add to the addresses per instruction; rather, it introduces a second operation per instruction.
[2]Any of the addressing modes suggested above can be used for an operand: that is, z immediate, Mp[z] direct, and Mp[Mp[z]] indirect.

In both the above cases, the operations that place results in Mp[z] are excluded because of the added cost of including the symmetrical function and the marginal utility of such a function, since u is no longer available for further processing.

The transmission, unary, and binary operators account for almost all operations in P(1 address) computers (see Chap. 8). If we allow AC to stand for any part of the M.processor.state\Mps, rather than just the accumulator, then additional instructions would involve input/output data transmission, e.g.,

$$Mp = T \quad \text{and} \quad T = Mp$$

and conditional execution

$$\text{branch.if .zero.AC} := IF(AC \ eql \ 0) \Rightarrow (PC = z),$$

Having index registers requires operations to process them. At a minimum they must be loaded and stored (usually from and to Mp); i.e.,

Mp[z] = X	store index
X = Mp[z]	load index register

But simple operations on an X are also desirable; for example,

$$X = X + 1$$

Here X is used to point to (access) the next element in a vector. More complex operations can be carried out by placing X in the AC register, via the program steps:

AC = X	load AC with X
AC = f(AC)	manipulate AC
X = AC	load X with AC

An operation to add k to X would then be

AC = X	next
AC = AC + k	next
X = AC	

instead of

Mp[z] = X	next
AC = Mp[z]	next
AC = AC + k	next
Mp[z] = AC	next
X = Mp[z]	

which assumes no transmission paths between X and AC.

Ideally we would like to perform any operation directly on X as simply

$$X = X + k$$

From this begins the idea that X should look like the main arithmetic register AC. This is, no doubt, one evolutionary path to general-register processors.

P(2 address) and P(3 address)

The addresses (a) specify operands in Mp (Fig. 6). The Mps decreases as the number of addresses per instruction increases, since the operands need not be held temporarily between instructions (i.e., each instruction performs a complete operation).

The instruction form for the 3-address computer is

$$Mp[a_3] = Mp[a_1] \text{ b } Mp[a_2]$$

where b is a binary operator and a_1, a_2, and a_3 are the addresses specifying the operands. In the case of unary operations (u), a_2 is usually blank. In the case of a binary operation and a 3-address computer, the states are iac, if, iod, doac, dof, doac, dof, do, doac, das (Fig. 6).

A 2-address computer does not necessarily require more processor state than a 3-address computer, since the operations can correspond to

$$Mp[a_2] = Mp[a_2] \text{ b } Mp[a_{a1}]$$

and

$$Mp[a_2] = u \text{ } Mp[a_1]$$

However, sometimes extra Mps is useful. The BRANCH ON ACCUMULATOR instruction allows results to be checked directly without referring to Mp. An especially useful instruction in 2-address computers is the transmission instruction (a special-case unary operation): $Mp[a_2] = Mp[a_1]$.

The IBM 1401 has two registers, A.address and B.address, which hold a_1 and a_2 and can be loaded by the a_1 and a_2 parts of the instruction. These registers point to (address) operands and do not contain data. The remaining processor state is the Instruction.address. The 1401 has instructions with no address parts, and these instructions take as operand addresses the values of A.address and B.address as of the previous instruction. The state-diagram specialization (Fig. 6) is roughly

iac, if, iod[doac₁,dof₁doac₂,dof₂,do,doac₂,dos₂] . . .
        [doac₁,dof₁,doac₂,dof₂,do,doac₂,dos₂]

where the sequence delimited by the brackets is the operation on a character; because the 1401 operates on variable-length strings, it is repeated until the end of the string.

P(n + 1 address)

Processors with $n + 1$ addresses deviate only slightly from the n-address processors above. The final, or +1, address explicitly specifies the address of the next instruction. Therefore, it can be used with any instruction set. There are two reasons why +1 addressing is used. First, freedom is provided in the placement of each instruction within the program address space. Second, the next instruction address can be calculated in parallel with the execution of the current instruction.

For computers with cyclic memories, the +1 address allows both data and the next instruction to be specified independently, providing the opportunity to arrange the program and data in an optimum fashion. Since each instruction completion time depends on the location of data, it is desirable that the next instruction location be variable rather than the implicit next address used for most processors. This is almost universal practice in computers with Mp.cyclic.

Microprogrammed processors may use the +1 address to locate the next instruction, and there may be several such next addresses (see Sec. 1 in Part 2). Microprogram subroutines tend to be short (intrinsic to interpreting an instruction set), and there are many jump addresses. The increased speed from not having to compute the next instruction address is worth the added space cost. The IBM System/360 Model 30 (Chap. 12) shows the use of multiple +1 addresses and if classified according to our scheme would be at least a P(micro-program; 3 + 1 address).

P(general register)

The general-register processor has a small array of registers that can be used for multiple functions. These have fast access compared with the Mp, so that it pays to do as much processing as possible within them. Since the general register array is small, it requires only a small address (3 to 8 bits). Thus the instruction format contains fields for one (or more) general registers. There must still exist addressing for Mp, though this never exceeds a single address. Thus we classify general-register machines as (1 + g) addresses per instruction.

The organization of a (1 + g) system can vary from something very close to a (1 + x) organization, in which essentially every instruction involves some Mp information, to an organization in which the only Mp instructions are transfers between Mp and Mps (the processor state holding the general registers) and there is a 2- or 3-address instruction set involving only Mps (see the CDC 6600 in Chap. 43 and the CRAY-1 in Chap. 44). That is, from a data point of view the Mps acts like a directly addressable Mp.

The processor state of a general-register processor is invariably held entirely within the general-register array (rather than having additional independent registers). This is due in part to an already available mechanism (the array) and in part to the need for program switching, which is somewhat simplified by having all the Mps held in a single homogeneous memory.

The general registers typically perform a variety of functions:

1 Arithmetic registers (accumulator and the accumulator extension for the multiplier-quotient).

2 Index registers.

3 A second index register or base register. If the program addresses (a) are short, a base register is needed to address any area of Mp.

4 Subroutine linkage registers.

5 Program flag (sense) registers for boolean variables.

6 Stack pointer (P may have multiple simultaneously active stacks).

7 Address pointers to data arrays and lists.

8 Temporary data storage for intermediate results.

9 Temporary program storage for short program loops.

The power of a general-register processor is obtained because the registers can serve many functions. Thus the operations on these registers can be extensive, because the operations need not be duplicated in other parts of the structure. For example, special operations for index registers are not necessary, because the operations for integers apply universally to both the accumulator and index registers. Of course, such generality requires compromises. The stack computer is faster for problems that can utilize stacks, whereas the general-register Pc must utilize Mp for the stack(s) and does not have the encoding efficiency of a pure stack processor (see below). In addition, the assignment (and reassignment) of general registers is most crucial, since they are a scarce resource with many uses. A general-register organization allows processors with a high degree of parallelism to be constructed, since several instruction subsequences can be executed concurrently.

The actual number of registers is rather critical and depends not only on the algorithms of tasks coded but also on the technology. In multiprogramming and interrupt computers, the program switching time increases with the number of registers.[1] Thus the

[1]With decreased hardware costs, many Pc's are implemented with several different register sets. A portion of Mps determines which register set is part of the currently executing Mps. At program-switching time, only the portion of the Mps needs to be changed to point to an unused or previously specified register set. Thus context-switching time can be made essentially independent of Mps size.

upper bound on the number of registers is both cost and program switching time.

We would expect to find instructions that produce the following effects:

Format	Addresses/instruction
$G[g] = u\ G[g]$	1g
$G[g_1] = u\ G[g_2]$	2g
$Mp[a] = u\ Mp[a]$	1
$Mp[a_1] = u\ Mp[a_2]$	2
$G[g] = u\ Mp[a]$	1 + g
$Mp[a] = u\ G[g]$	1 + g
$G[g] = G[g]\ b\ Mp[a]$	1 + g
$G[g_1] = G[g_1]\ b\ G[g_2]$	2g
$G[g_1] = G[g_2]\ b\ G[g_3]$	3g
$Mp[a] = G[g]\ b\ Mp[a]$	1 + g
$Mp[a_1] = Mp[a_2]\ b\ Mp[a_3]$	3

where

u are unary operators |NOT|−| etc.

b are binary operators (+|−|/|*|AND|OR|XOR| etc.)

G is the general-register array

g, g_1, g_2, g_3 are instruction parts specifying a general register, G

a, a_1, a_2, a_3 are Mp addresses specified as a function of instruction general registers (for example, a := (address + G[g]) or a := (address + G[g_1] + G[g_2]) in the IBM System/360)

General registers can be thought of as an outgrowth (generalization) of the (1 + x) processors, as we have already suggested. Alternatively, they can be thought of as evolving from a 2- or 3-address structure. The UNIVAC 1103A, a 2-address processor, was no doubt a forerunner of the general-register UNIVAC 1107 and 1108.

P.stack (0 addresses per instruction)

From a PMS viewpoint the P.stack is built around having a first-in-last-out memory (M.stack) as part of the processor state. Conceptually, it is built around the fact that computations can often be sequenced so that no explicit names (i.e., addresses) are required for temporary results. All operations are performed on the top of the stack. As each partial result is computed, it is pushed down in the stack and appears again to participate as an operand at exactly the appropriate point in later calculation. Thus the stack operates as an implicit memory for all intermediate products, and not only are transfers between P and Mp avoided but space in the instruction for Mp addresses is also eliminated.

Instructions in such a system consist only of operations, since all their operands are in the stack. Thus the instruction format is that of zero addresses per instruction. There must, of course, be some addressing of Mp (just as in a general-register organization). The addresses for Mp may themselves sit in the stack so that the instruction contains only the transfer (load or store) operation, not the address. It is necessary to have some way of getting fresh data into the stack, and all P.stacks have at least one operation that loads an address written in the program stream onto the top of the stack. On the other hand, there may be load/store instructions with explicit Mp addressing information.

Why there should be this happy correspondence between calculations and memory to be performed and stack memories requires a little explication. It rests fundamentally on the phrase structuring of calculation in which each partial result is required at one and only one point, so that each subcomputation can be nested in the program (and hence its result nested in the stack) in the same order in which it will occur as operand to the one operation that uses it.

There are several arguments against a P.stack. Multiple stacks are often required. Part of the power of a P.stack is derived from having higher-speed Mps for the stack. Yet only the top few (2 ~

8) registers of the stack can be in Mps. When M.stack overflows into Mp, the speed of operations can become much slower than if there were no stack at all. A simpler implementation, for example, P.general.registers, is as fast and perhaps more flexible. Temporary results that may be used frequently, such as common subexpressions, can be stored in a general register. Another difficulty with the stack is the difficulty in accessing other than the top. If full addressing is provided, then the organization has become almost general-register. Yet another difficulty arises from inhomogeneity of data-types, especially if several of them are packed into a single word (the width of the stack). Thus, for instance, in one stack machine (the Burroughs B 5000 in Chap. 9) there is a completely separate nonstack ISP for string manipulation.

A simple numerical computation is given in Table 2 as a comparison of the P.stack, P.1.address, and P.general.register. Here, the P.stack is probably shown at its best, as there are no array-index calculations or program-flow manipulations involving

Table 2   Comparison of Stack, General-Register, and Accumulator Pc for Evaluating the Expression:
$$f = (a - b)/(c - d \times e)$$

	Pc.stack [stack contents]	Pc. general. register	Pc.1address
	Push a [a]	Load G[1], a	Load d
	Push b [a, b]	Subtract G[1], b	Multiply e
	Subtract [a − b]	Load G[2], d	Inverse subtract c†
	Push c [a − b, c]	Multiply G[2], e	Store temporary
	Push d [a − b, c, d]	Inverse subtract G[2], c†	Load a
	Push e [a − b, c, d, e]	Divide G[1], G[2]	Subtract b
	Multiply [a − b, c, d × e]	Store G[1], f	Divide temporary
	Subtract [a − b, c − d × e]		Store f
	Divide [(a − b)/(c − d × e)]		
	Pop f [ ] − stores stack at location, f		
Program size:			
Address integer/ai	6 ai	6 ai + 8 ai (gr)	8 ai
Pcodes/o	4 o‡	7 o	8 o
Program size for hypothetical example machines	6 × (10 + 2) + 4 × 6 ——— 96	6 × (10 + 6 + 4)§ + 1 × (6 + 2 + 4)§ ——— 134	8 × (10 + 6) ——— 128
Program size in bits for real C's	B 5000: 144	IBM S/360: 208 (above)† : 224 (actual) plus base register overhead (0 ~ 192)¶	PDP-8: 96 (above)† : 180 (actual)
Number of Mp references for data	6	6	8

†Not an instruction in the specific example machines

‡Assumes a special short form encoding for pushes and pops.

§Assumes 16 general registers.

¶Not completely true, since System/360 has only a 12-bit address and uses base registers. Some overhead should be assumed. Worst case (but not unreasonable) is 6 × 32 or 192-bit overhead.

testing, etc. The criteria we measure are the algorithm encoding space and the problem running time. The hypothetical machines are all assumed to have 10-bit addresses and 6-bit opcodes. The stack machine is further assumed to have a special 2-bit opcode for specifying push and pop instructions.

The typical kinds of instructions interpreted by a P.stack are:

Operation	Interpreter state sequence	Example
Load	iac, if, iod, doac, dos	M.stack.top = Mp[v]
Store	iac, if, iod, doac, dos	Mp[v] = M.stack.top
Unary operation	iac, if, iod, do	M.stack.top = u M.stack.top
Binary operation	iac, if, iod, do	M.stack.top = M.stack.top b M.stack.top-1

The comparison of a stack and a general-register machine has to be done on the basis of a total environment. Table 2 indicates the superiority of stacks in program density (as measured in number of bits) for numeric computation. Generally, stack computers are designed to execute efficiently block-structured higher-level languages. The nesting of temporary variables on block entry and their subsequent release on block exit matches the last-in–first-out discipline provided by a stack. Likewise subroutines and interrupts also exhibit a last-in–first-out execution order. Machines such as the Burroughs B 5000 and Hewlett-Packard HP 3000 effectively have two stack pointers (see Sec. 2 in Part 2). The first points to global variables accessible from all blocks; the second identifies temporary variables used in the currently executing block. All variable accesses occur with relative offset to the current values of the stack pointers. The value of the temporary stack pointer is automatically adjusted by hardware upon block entry and exit. Variables at other block levels (so-called lexical levels) must be set up in software by remembering their positions relative to software stack (or frame) pointers. To make these other variables more accessible, sufficient hardware stack pointers must be added to accommodate each block level. (See the B 6700 discussion in Part 2, Sec. 2. The B 6700 has stack pointers called *display registers*.) These extra stack pointers are akin to the special-purpose index registers in P(1 + x) machines.

One method of comparing stack and general-register organizations is via a technology-independent benchmark. Wichmann [1976] compared some 40 hardware/software systems on the recursively defined Ackermann's function. Measuring the calling performance of a recursively defined function is important for two reasons:

- Procedure calls are significant resource consumers. Lunde [1977] showed that, on average, a procedure call occurs every 40 assembly language instructions.

- Recursion is the most general form of procedure call.

Table 3 depicts a subset of the data presented in Wichmann [1976]. The last line was supplied [Blake, 1977]. Although there are many sources for variations (including language, compiler, and hardware), Table 3 indicates that minimal variation exists between stack machines (e.g., B 5500, B 6700, and HP 3000) and general-register machines (e.g., PDP-10, PDP-11) in the number of instructions executed per call or the number of words of storage used per call.

Two other interesting points of comparison can be made between stacks and general-register machines. Blake [1977] indicates that the average number of memory references per HP 3000 instruction was 2.2 for the data processing benchmark described in Chap. 5. The number of memory references per PDP-11 instruction for the DEC benchmarks in Chap. 5 was 2.16. The PDP-11 and the HP 3000 are contemporary 16-bit minicomputers. Second, Blake indicated that the four top-of-stack registers in the HP 3000 were sufficient for the vast majority of computations. Extra memory traffic generated by insufficient stack registers was only 0.085 memory references per instruction, or 4 percent of Pc-Mp traffic. Lunde [1977] indicated that eight general registers were sufficient for the benchmarks he measured.

Thus, there seems to be little difference in performance between stack and general-purpose computers. Software, particularly compilers, may be easier to write for stack machines because of the hardware support for block-structured higher-level languages. Whether stack machines would be applicable to other computing environments that do not use block-structured languages is still an open question. Table 4 summarizes the stack and general-register comparison.

Table 3   Ackermann's Function

Language/computer	Time per call (μs)	Instruction per call	Words per call
ALGOL 60			
B 5500	135	19.5	7
B 6700	41.2	16	13
BLISS 10			
PDP-10	53.15	1.5	5
PASCAL			
IBM S/370 Model 158	39	42.5	30
PALGOL			
PDP-11/20	46	1.3	3
BLISS 11			
PDP-11/20	31	8	2
SPL			
HP 3000	24	?	?

Table 4   Comparison of Stack and General-Register Architectures

	Stack	*General-Register*
Number of registers	Approximately the same	
Register use	Dedicated	Arbitrary
Control of registers	Hardwired	Explicit in program when used as stack
Access to local variables	Top of stack	Full set in general registers
Compiler	Easy	Resource allocation problem
Program encoding	Fewer bits	Bits for register specification

Variable Numbers of Addresses per Instruction

Although there are a few operations that require the specification of three or more addresses, these are of such low frequency that only a few machines have been built (e.g., the VAX-11/780) that have more than three data addresses and one next-instruction address. (Some of the microprogrammed processors have more than one next-instruction address, and they often do several operations in parallel in one instruction.)

However, processors that can have a variable number of operands have been developed. Most of these involve the use of an instruction that is larger than a single Mp word. Thus, bringing in the first word of an instruction, which contains the operation code, determines how many additional operands are needed and hence how many additional operands are needed and hence how many additional words to obtain from Mp. (In a character-based system this may require several reads per operand; in a word-based system this may be one or two operands per read.) The gain in such a system is the higher average density of operations per instruction, bought at the price of extra Mp accesses.

Most such variable-address processors have a mixture of one, two, and three addresses per instruction—simply a mix of the types already considered. Chapter 42 on the DEC VAX-11 shows the architecture of such a system with instructions encoded into a byte string. Each instruction can have any number of addresses, and each address can be calculated in a variety of ways: address memory, a general register, or a stack. Some instructions that operate on strings do, in fact, require more than three addresses per instruction.

The fundamental limit to such variability is the processor state (plus the additional within-instruction temporary state). This, of physical necessity, must be finite, and the number of addresses must yield an amount of information that is less than this total state. Otherwise the processor cannot hold on to it to process it.[1]

---

[1]If it processes a large amount of information, but in pieces (i.e., sequentially in real time), it is not really executing a single instruction based on all the addresses but has decomposed the total computation, just as a single-address organization has.

Thus the various processors that claim to operate from a higher language (see the P.languages of Part 2, Sec. 7) must in fact either translate into another, simpler programming language, as does the SYMBOL (Chap. 30), or become an interpreter that processes a small amount of a language statement before the rest.

PMS Structure

Spurred by cheaper components with higher density and greater reliability, the PMS structure of computers has become the most rapidly evolving dimension in the computer space. Historically computers were modeled as an arithmetic section, input/output devices, a memory for holding instructions and data, and a single control to force the other components to interact. (Fig. 7). Figure 8 depicts the addition of Ms.

If we separate each component according to its function, assign control (K) to each element, and then introduce the processor (P), we get the structure depicted in Fig. 9. Of course, a large part of P is a data operator (D). The processor has the behavioral properties attributed to the structure of Fig. 7. If we include the control within each component, we get Fig. 10 from Fig. 9.

For a consideration of larger structures, consisting of several Mp's, P's, Ms's, and T's, it would seem logical to expand the system as shown in Fig. 11, in which everything is connected through a single switch. If the central S has sufficient power for multiple conversations, this indeed provides maximum generality. However, although designs have been proposed for such

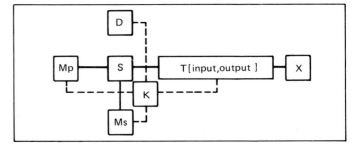

Fig. 7. Early model of a stored program digital computer PMS diagram.

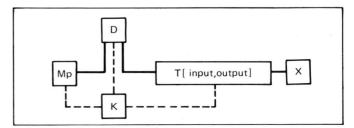

Fig. 8. Early computer model (with Ms and S) PMS diagram.

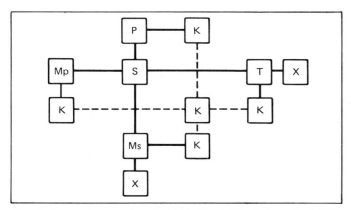

Fig. 9. General computer model (with distributed control) PMS diagram.

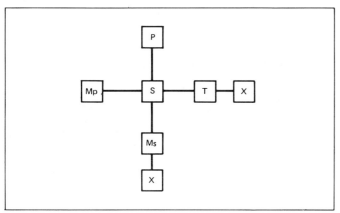

Fig. 10. General computer model (without K) PMS diagram.

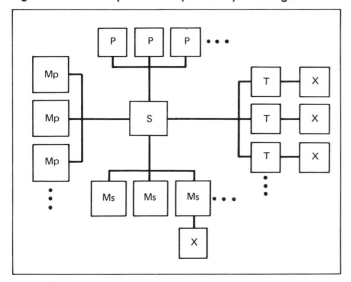

Fig. 11. General computer model (with multiple components) PMS diagram.

systems, technology and economics have so far prohibited their actual realization. Instead, there has developed the general latticelike structure shown in Fig. 12. Each switch in this structure connects components on one side with components on the opposite side (the S interconnecting the P's being the exception).

The lattice structure of Fig. 12 is hierarchical in the sense that the Mp's form the inner core and one travels out toward the periphery in moving from left to right. With this movement there is a general decrease in data rate, it being highest through the Mp-P switch and lower as one moves to the right.

The model has five switches (S). One switch connects the computer's peripheral devices with the external environment (human beings, other processes, etc.). Three switches appear alike in the way they interconnect Mp with P, P with K, and K with (T|Ms), respectively. However, they are usually quite different. We would expect any P to connect with any Mp. We probably would expect to have only one or two Pio's connected to a given set of K's. Most certainly one or two K's would manage a given set of Ms's or T's. Thus the structure nearest the periphery becomes more like a tree than a lattice (examples are provided in Figs. 13 and 14). The last switch in Fig. 12, unlike the above four, provides intercommunication among the processors. In any multiple-processor structure (even 1Pc-nPio) there must be communication among the processors. A switch of this type is organized as a nonhierarchy and appears like a conventional telephone exchange, since any P can call any other. On the other hand, the amount of communication (measured in bits) is rather low.

The P's and (usually) Mp's have their controls associated with them, and we have not bothered to show such K's in the diagram. The K's that are shown provide control for the T's and Ms's. These are separated in the figure because they are separated in current computer systems and made into identifiable physical components. Under current technology they are expensive devices, so that one K per T or Ms is not always economical.[1] Therefore, each K needs to be shared among a set of T's and Ms's. (That is, one purchases a single magnetic-tape controller for, say, four magnetic tapes.) The shared K also explains why only one of a given class of devices (e.g., magnetic tapes) can operate at a time. As technology changes (especially costs), these separate K's are disappearing.

Nearly all the computers discussed in this book fit the lattice model of Fig. 12. However, it is not unlikely that structures will be or have been built that do not conveniently fit it.

The values along the PMS structure dimension of the computer space have been generated from the general model and laid out in the order of their evolution. This evolution is strictly from less

---

[1]This situation is changing as inexpensive microcomputers are dedicated to the controller task.

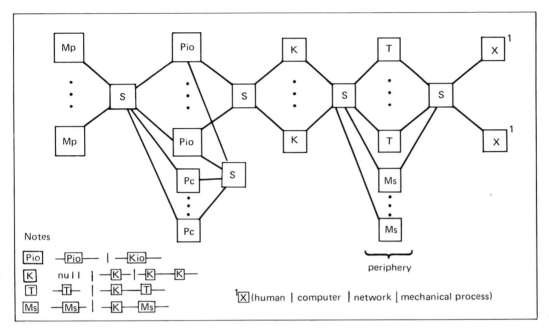

Fig. 12. General computer model (multiprocessors) PMS diagram.

complex to more. The seemingly more complex network structures, such as the duplexed computers, are not necessarily as complex as a single-multiprocessor computer. Duplex computers have been used for some time.

The evolution of multiple-computer structures has been

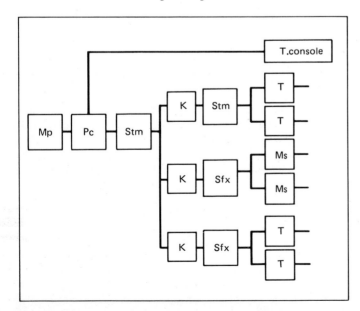

Fig. 13. Tree-structured computer (1-Pc) PMS diagram.

spurred by the availability of cheap miniprocessors and microprocessors. The subdimensions of the nPc and nC (network) space have become sufficiently rich to warrant a more detailed discussion in Secs. 4 and 5 of Part 2. The proponents of multiple-processor systems believe that the addition of several large processors to a structure will always increase the performance of a one-processor structure. The cost/performance debate of a single processor versus a multiprocessor has generally been resolved in favor of the single, large processor. However, advances in multiprogramming software and the demand for attributes other than cost/performance (e.g., availability, reliability, and significant applications requiring raw performance beyond that of a uniprocessor) have led to a proliferation of multiple Pc and C structures.

The simple l-Pc structure shown in Fig. 13 is a tree. Although there are no values on the information rates, the nature of the fixed[1] and time-multiplexed switches indicates that perhaps the top two T's, one Ms, and one of the bottom T's can *all* be active at a given time. In Fig. 14 a 1-Pc, 2-Pio computer is given. Here we note that the control of one secondary memory is by a Kio rather than the Pio. (The Kio cannot fetch its next instruction from Mp and must rely on Pc for control.) Note that there is necessarily a lattice connection between the 2 Mp and the Pc, 2 Pio, and Kio.

[1]A relative value for the attribute that denotes the time a switch is closed. *Fixed* usually denotes a time duration such that more than 1 i-unit is transmitted.

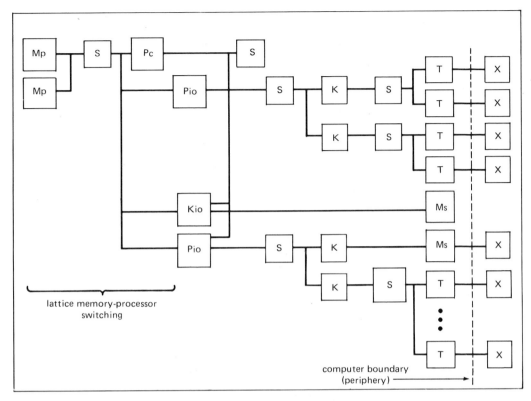

Fig. 14. Tree-structured computer (1Pc-2Pio and lattice Mp-P switch) PMS diagram.

The special cases of P.displays, multiprocessors, P(array|wired algorithm), and parallel processing are all realized from the general model of Fig. 12.

As was pointed out in Chap. 1, evolutionary chains in the computer space which wrap back upon themselves follow a pattern called the *wheel of reincarnation* [Myer and Sutherland, 1968]. Figure 15 depicts another evolution, this time for the graphics output function. The trajectory around the wheel follows:

Position 1: Point plotting. The computer includes a single-instruction display controller that can plot a picture on a point-by-point basis under command of the central processor. For most displays, except storage scopes, the processor can barely calculate the next point fast enough to keep the display refreshed. Hence, the system is processor-bound, and the display may be idle.

Position 2: Vector plotting. By adding the ability to plot lines (i.e., vectors), a single instruction to the display processor will free some of the processor and begin to keep all but the fastest display busy.

Position 3: Character plotting and alphanumeric plotting. With the realization that characters are a major part of what is displayed, commands to display a character are added, further freeing the processor. Many of the point-plotting displays were extended to have character-generation capability.

Position 4: General figure and character display. In reality, a picture does not consist of just characters and vectors; each element of the picture is actually a string of characters and a set of closed or open polygons to be displayed starting at a particular point. By providing the control display with a direct memory access channel, the display can fetch each string of text and generate polygons without involving the central processor.

Position 5: Display processors. With the ability to put up subpictures with no processor intervention, it is easy for the whole picture to be displayed by linking the elements together in some fashion. This merely requires JUMP and SUBROU-TINE call instructions so that common picture elements do not have to be redefined.

Position 6: Integrated display and central processor. Now, all

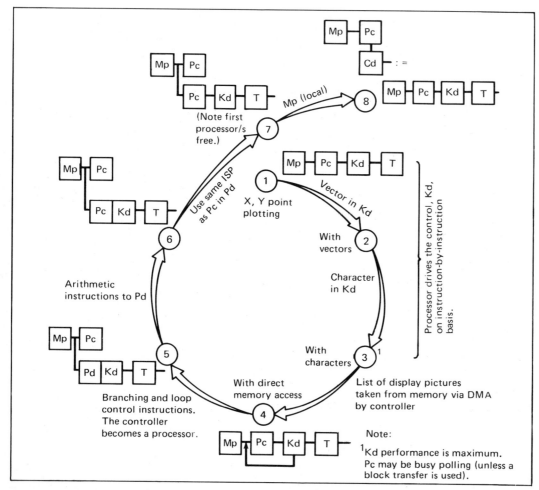

Fig. 15. The wheel of reincarnation. (From C. G. Bell, J. C. Mudge, and J. E. McNamara, *Computer Engineering: A DEC View of Hardware Systems Design*, Digital Press, 1978, p. 202.)

the data paths and states are present for a fully general-purpose processor so that the central processor need never be called on again. This requires a slightly more general-purpose interpreter. By minor perturbations, the processor design can be refined in such a way as to execute the same instruction set as the original host computer because the cost of incompatibility is too great. Two processors require two compilers, diagnostics, manuals, and support for use. This state provides the same capability as that shown in position 1. The original processor is completely free, and there is a display processor with the capability of executing both the original instruction set and the display instruction set.

Position 7: Two computer structures. Alternatively, the processor can be isolated as a separate computer and reconnected in some fashion to the central processor–primary memory pair in

position 1. Such a structure is just a basic computer with the addition of a general figure and character display (position 4).

Position 8: A separate computer. A separate computer is formed solely for display, and the options available for picture processing can be decided again from the wheel of reincarnation.

Wheels of reincarnation usually occur when enhanced functionality causes a specialized function to evolve. The specialized function evolves through the following stages:

- Simple, dedicated hardware executes primitive commands under control of a Pc.

- More complex hardware becomes able to execute several

primitive commands for each Pc command. Thus, a specialized instruction set is developing.

- The specialized hardware can fetch and sequence through command lists in a shared memory. The K is now a P.

- The special P becomes more general in order to offload housekeeping functions from Pc. At this point P.special is a primitive Pc, and subject to all the evolutionary pressures of Pc's that are members of a given computer class.

Other examples of systems on the wheel of reincarnation include:

- Ms controllers for disks and tapes

- Terminal controllers, multiplexers, and concentrators

- Communication-line controllers

- Processors to support a particular high-level language (e.g., ALGOL, LISP, PASCAL)

Switching

A principal issue of computer design at the PMS level is switching. The switching dimension of the computer space is correlated with PMS structure, as we have just seen. To have a more complex structure, more complex intercommunication (switching) is required.

Figure 16 illustrates the eight forms of communication between the major PMS component types. The various switches[1] in Fig. 12 implement one or more of these communication functions. Each form of communication, with its impact on the switching structure, will be discussed in turn.

Pc-Mp Communication. Pc-Mp communication is the primary performance determiner of a computer structure. The Pc fetches instructions from and manipulates data in Mp. Thus the Pc-Mp bandwidth (e.g., in words per second) potentially limits the Pc's execution rate. Various techniques have been developed to reduce the Pc's request rate to memory (e.g., caches, as described in Part 2, Sec. 2).

Pc-K Communication. The Pc initializes and issues commands to the K's. The K performs the requested action.

K-Pc Communication. The K informs the Pc (i.e., ONLINE, READY) of its status and the status of the I/O command (i.e., DONE, ERROR, etc.). The availability of new status information can be signified to the Pc by means of a special signal called an *interrupt* (see Part 2, Sec. 2).

Ks-Pc Communication. Simple controllers return data to or

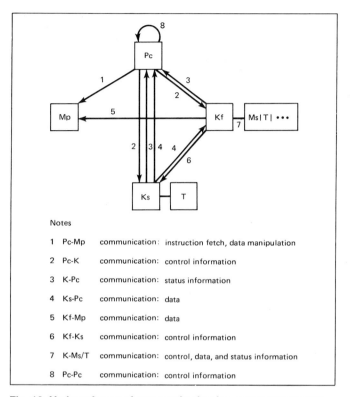

Fig. 16. Various forms of communication in a computer system.

Notes

1	Pc-Mp	communication:	instruction fetch, data manipulation
2	Pc-K	communication:	control information
3	K-Pc	communication:	status information
4	Ks-Pc	communication:	data
5	Kf-Mp	communication:	data
6	Kf-Ks	communication:	control information
7	K-Ms/T	communication:	control, data, and status information
8	Pc-Pc	communication:	control information

take data from the Pc. Usually Ks is an inexpensive controller for low–data-rate devices.

Kf-Mp Communication. Sophisticated controllers do not require the Pc to intervene in fetching or storing data to Mp. Rather, these controllers of high–data-rate devices access Mp directly.

Kf-Ks Communication. A sophisticated controller (e.g., a Pio) may issue commands to a simple controller, which returns data directly to the Kf.

K-Ms|T Communication. Controllers issue commands to and|receive data or status information from individual Ms's and T's. Depending on the data transfer rate of the devices, this communication may require high-speed communication techniques as used in Pc-Mp communication.

Pc-Pc Communication. Multiple Pc's in the computer structure have to exchange information in order to cooperate. The various types of Pc-Pc communication are listed in Part 2, Sec. 2.

The switching problem then is to provide a physical structure that supports various forms of communication. One technique would be to set up a switching structure for each separate type of

---

[1]A *bus* is a special form of a switch. Buses are actually the dominant way of realizing switches in contemporary computer structures. For the current discussion we will use the more general term *switch.*

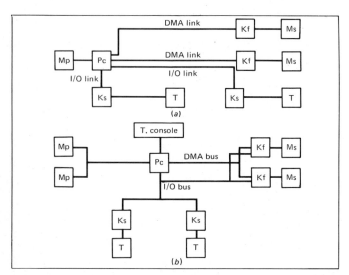

Fig. 17. Examples of a radial bus structure. (a) A radial link structure. (b) PMS structure of the PDP-8.

communication and derive a PMS structure similar to Fig. 16. Such PMS structures, common in the early days of computers, are termed *radial buses* (see Fig. 17), since their communication paths diverge radially from the Pc. Figure 17(*b*) illustrates the PMS structure of the early members of the PDP-8 family. The PDP-8 put control/status/data information for similar devices into three major buses: memory (Pc-Mp), I/O (Pc-K, K-Pc, Ks-Pc), and DMA (Pc-K, K-Pc, with some processor logic to handle the Kf-Pc-Mp communication). Kf could also be controlled via the I/O bus. With multiple devices on a bus, each bus also needs arbitration logic to determine successive control of the bus (e.g., to initiate a conversation), as well as addressing information to determine the receptor of the information.

In contrast to the specialized link bus for each communication type is a single bus for all communications. Figure 18 depicts the

PDP-11 Unibus. While the Unibus is more economical than radial bus structures, the single bus limits the overall bandwidth available to the system, thus limiting the system processing rate. For a further evaluation of the evolution of the PDP-8 and PDP-11 bus structure, see Chaps. 46 and 47.

Figure 19 illustrates the hierarchical nature of switches: more complex switches are formed by cascading (connecting) the primitive switches together. Figure 19 divides switches into two groups and ten categories:

Group I.   Connecting dissimilar components
1   Simple. Communication between (connection to) one component of type *a* and one component of type *b*.
2   Duplex. Communication between one component of type *a* and several components of type *b*. This is the bus structure found in most computers where the *a* component is a processor and the *b* components are Mp|Ms|T. See Chap. 8 and Chap. 38 for a discussion of typical bus structures.
3   Dual-duplex. Communication between two components of type *a* and several (*n*) components of type *b*. Up to min(2,n) conversations at a time. This switch is often found in dual-processor systems.
4   Time-multiplexed cross-point, concurrency 1. Any component of type *a* can communicate with any component of type *b* with only one conversation at a time. This is a generalization of switch 2, the duplex switch.
5   Cross-point, concurrency, min(m,n). Any component of type *a* can communicate with any component of type *b* with up to min(m,n) conversations at a time. This is a generalization of switch 3, the dual-duplex. This switch is used in the C.mmp multiprocessor (Chap. 22) and the Burroughs multiprocessors (Chap. 9).

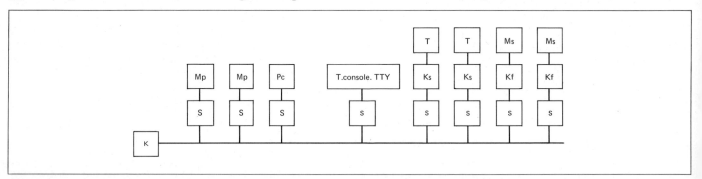

Fig. 18. The PDP-11 unibus.

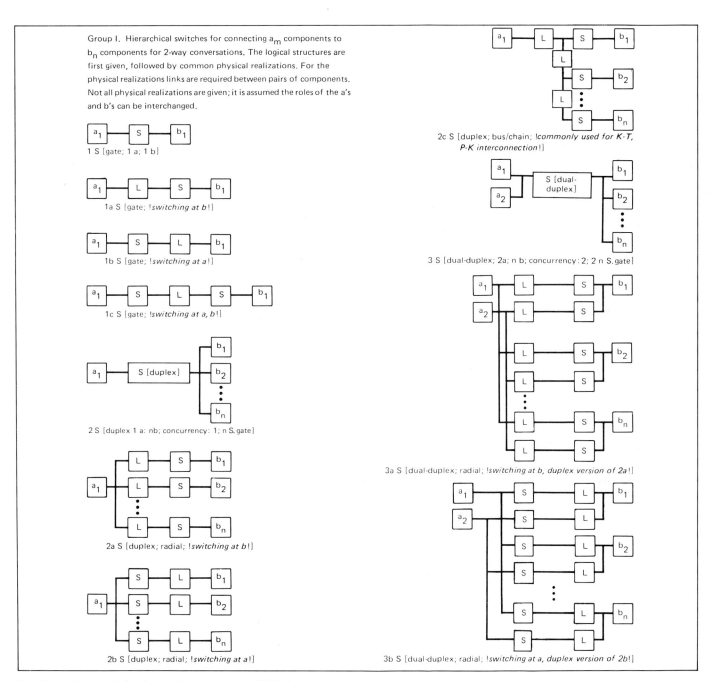

Fig. 19. Logical and physical switch structures PMS diagrams.

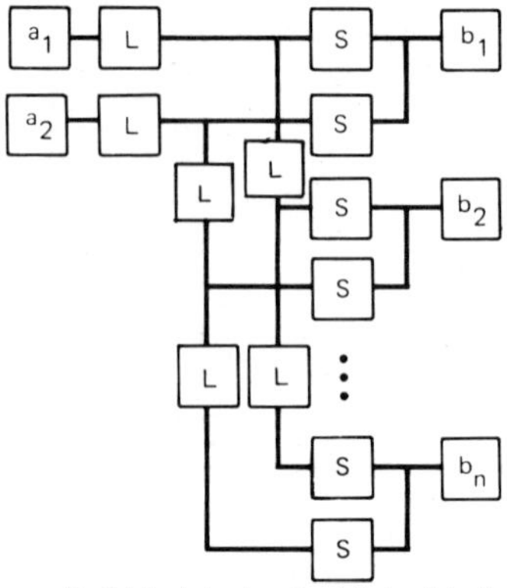

3c S [dual-duplex; bus/chain; !*duplex version of 2c*!]

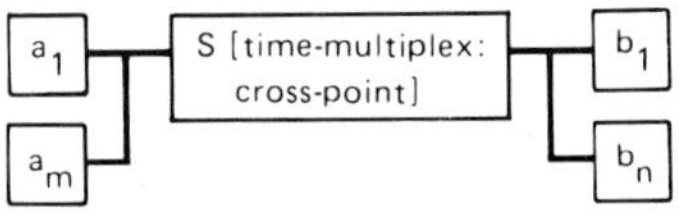

4 S [time-multiplex; cross-point; m a: n b: concurrency: 1; m + n S.gate; !*cascade of a duplex*!]

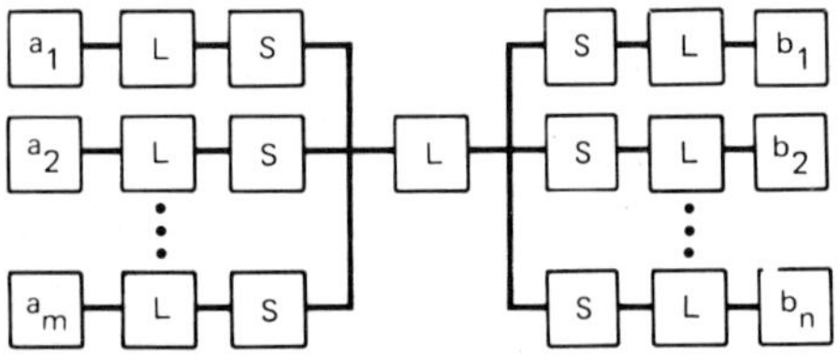

4a S [time-multiplex; cross-point; radial; central; concurrency: 1]

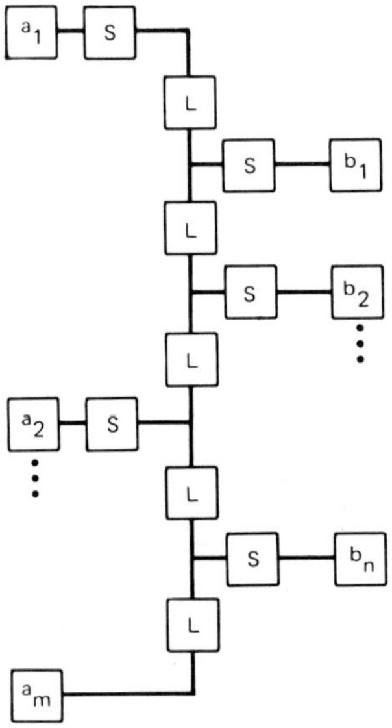

4b S [time-multiplex; cross-point: bus/chain]

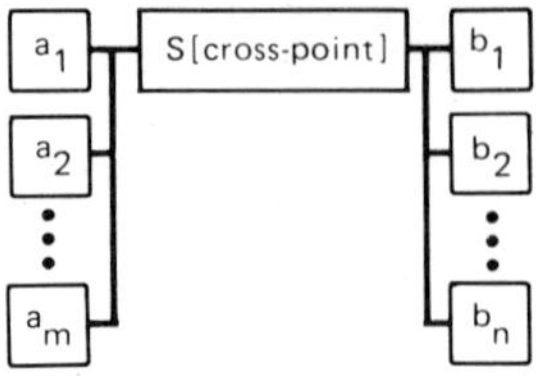

5 S [cross-point; m a; n b: concurrency: min (m,n); mxn S.gate]

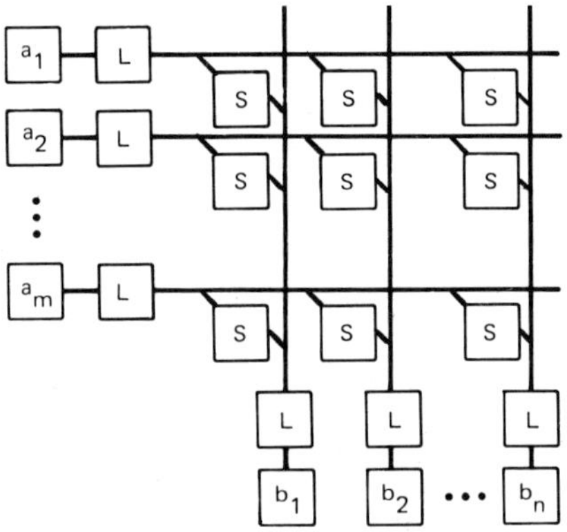

5a S [cross-point: radial: !*Links to a or b may be null*!]

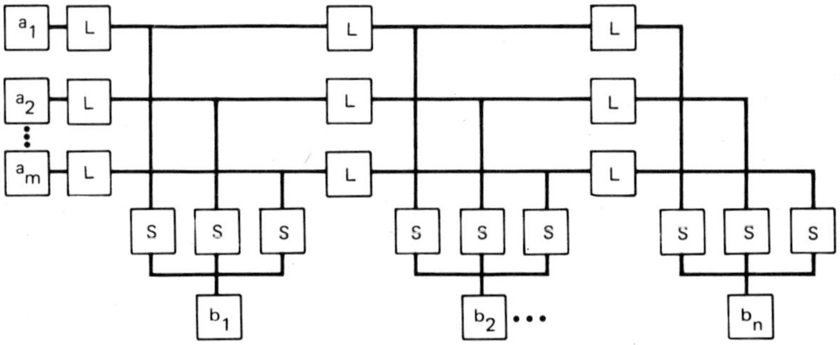

5b S [cross-point: bus/chain! *used for M_p-P interconnection*!]

Fig. 19. (Continued)

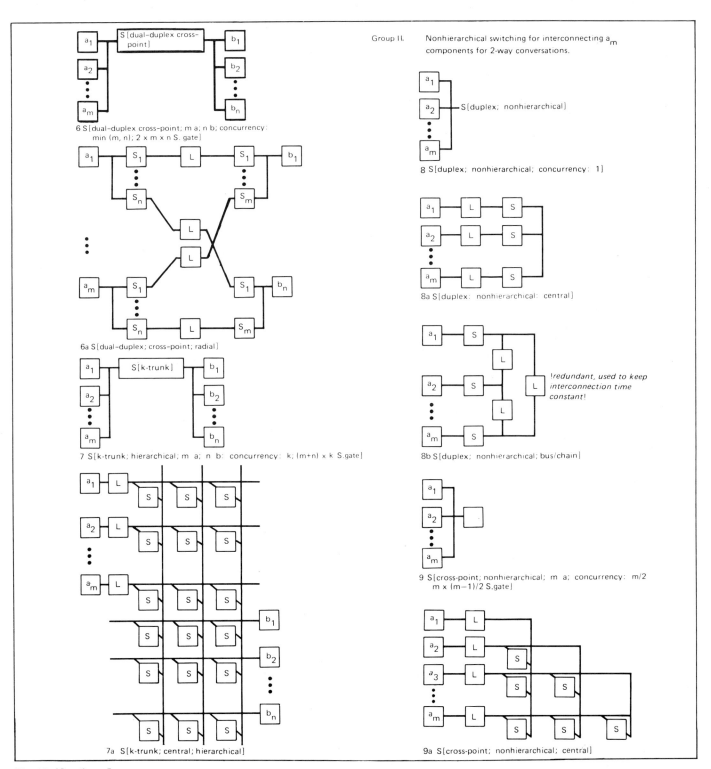

6 S[dual-duplex cross-point; m a; n b; concurrency: min (m, n); 2 x m x n S. gate]

6a S[dual-duplex; cross-point; radial]

7 S[k-trunk; hierarchical; m a; n b; concurrency: k; (m+n) x k S.gate]

7a S[k-trunk; central; hierarchical]

Group II.   Nonhierarchical switching for interconnecting a_m components for 2-way conversations.

8 S[duplex; nonhierarchical; concurrency: 1]

8a S[duplex; nonhierarchical; central]

!redundant, used to keep interconnection time constant!

8b S[duplex; nonhierarchical; bus/chain]

9 S[cross-point; nonhierarchical; m a; concurrency: m/2 m x (m−1)/2 S.gate]

9a S[cross-point; nonhierarchical; central]

Fig. 19. (Continued)

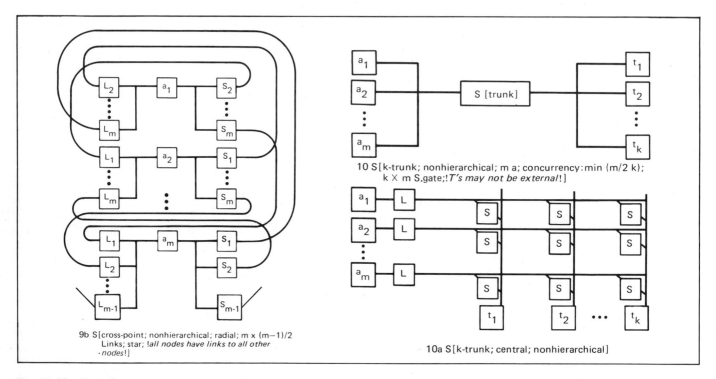

9b S[cross-point; nonhierarchical; radial; m x (m—1)/2
Links; star; !all nodes have links to all other
·nodes!]

10 S[k-trunk; nonhierarchical; m a; concurrency:min (m/2 k);
k X m S.gate;!T's may not be external!]

10a S[k-trunk; central; nonhierarchical]

Fig. 19. (Continued)

6   Dual-duplex cross-point, concurrency min (m,n). This structure can be regarded either as a generalization of switch 3 or a distributed form of switch 5. The dual-duplex cross-point was used in the Pluribus multiprocessor (Chap. 23) for improved reliability over a centralized cross-point switch.

7   K-trunk, concurrency K. The trunk structure can be viewed as a higher-concurrency version of switch 4 or a reduced-cost version of switch 5. A noncomputer example of a trunk switch is the telephone exchange.

Group II.   Connecting similar components

8   Duplex. This corresponds to switch 2. Any component can communicate with any other component, one conversation at a time. The Cm* multiprocessor cluster uses this form of switch (see Part 2, Sec. 4).

9   Cross-point. Analogous to switch 5.

10   K-trunk. Analogous to switch 7.

With this preliminary introduction to the switching problem, it is now possible to trace the evolution of switching structures in the major areas of Pc-Mp, Pc-K, and K-Ms communications. A more

detailed discussion and taxonomy of switching structures can be found in Sec. 4 of Part 2.

Processor-Memory Switching

With the advent of multiple processors, memory-processor switching became an important problem. The Mp-P switch is what makes multiple processors possible, and it is a determining factor in both performance and reliability.

The structure of the processor-memory switch for computers that have multiple memories and multiple processors is a lattice if simultaneous memory-processor dialogues are allowed. A cross-point switch provides redundancy and is used to form the lattice structure. To vary from the full-duplex/duplex switch (for m memories and one processor, or p processors and one memory) requires more components to be devoted to the switching, to buffering, and to arbitration control (see Chap. 22). Hence duplex switches are used on most multiprocessor computers. The processor-memory switching possibilities can be seen nicely in Fig. 19. The important switch parameters are the number of memories, the number of processors, and the number of simultaneous processor-memory dialogues. In current designs P always originates the dialogue, which is generally taken to mean the reading or writing of a given word in Mp. The range of complexity is roughly

$$S[null; 1M; 1P; concurrency: 1]|$$
$$S[simplex^1|half-duplex^2|full-duplex^3;$$
$$(mM; 1P) | (1M; pP); concurrency: 1]$$
$$S[time-multiplex cross-point; mM; pP; concurrency:1] |$$
$$S[cross-point; mM; pP; concurrency: min(m,p)]$$

An S.duplex can be used to increase the number of processors that can be connected to the memory system while not having to provide additional switch points on each memory. For example, in the CDC 3600 [Casale, 1962] a basic S[8M; 4P; concurrency:4] is expanded by placing another S[1M; 6P; concurrency: 1] in series to give a possible overall S[8M; 24P; concurrency: 4]. This scheme was used to provide multiple processor accesses to the memories.

Processor-Control Swiching

The first switching problem developed with the need to communicate with several input/output devices. This switching is hierarchical in nature; one (or two) processors maintain control of many K's by issuing K a primitive task. At the completion of the task the K signals the processor that the task has been completed.

The switch provides a link between processor and controls for the secondary memory or the terminals and is parameterized by the number of processors, the number of controls, the number of simultaneous conversations, and the component that originates the dialogue. In these switches the control of information transmission is always by the processor. The evolution has been approximately as follows:

1   S[null; 1P, 1K; concurrency: 1; initiator: P]
    P and K are connected during data transfers.

2   S[simplex|half-duplex|full-duplex/duplex: 1P; 1K; concurrency: 1; initiator: P,K]
    Each K operates independently because it can return or request communication with P when the control task is completed.

3   S[dual-duplex; 2P; 1K; concurrency: 2; initiator: P, K]
    Duplex paths from dual P's to each K for reliability.

4   S[cross-point; pP; kK; concurrency: min (p,k) initiator: P,K]
    General case of multiple P's and K's with communication among the components.

[1]A switch that allows communication in one direction between two ports.
[2]A switch that allows communication in either direction but only one direction at a time.
[3]A switch that allows concurrent communication between two ports.

The early machines used the first structure, and concurrent operation of controls was possible only by starting several controls and by very carefully programming the timing for the data transfers. Two conditions occurred to cause this: The buffering for a T or an Ms was associated with the processor, and the control could not signal the processor. Although rather trivial to implement, the idea of allowing a K to signal the processor (item 2 above) did not occur until after the idea of arithmetic processor traps was incorporated into processors. The interrupt was used as the method by which a K communicated its desire to converse with a P. The early IBM 709 provided a separate, independent processor for handling the communication with input/output equipment. Simultaneous processor-to-input/output or secondary-memory dialogues could take place (provided the devices were connected to the right processor). In most of the early computers, part of the control function (data buffering) was associated with the Pc, and thus only one device could operate at a time. This stemmed from the comparatively high cost of registers, so that links were established for a fixed period of time during a complete block transfer of data.

In some of the military computers a duplicate set of K's is provided for reliability. The more elaborate switching structures (types 3 and 4 above) are rarely used between Pio's and K's; thus to work on a peripheral requires the use of the rest of the computer. The S.dual-duplex is becoming more common; it provides a method of offline operation for maintaining better component utilization and a more reliable structure.

Control-Terminal and Control-Secondary-Memory Switching

The switches that link a control with a particular terminal or secondary memory are generally fairly straightforward. Normally, a fixed-duplex switch is used. However, a dual-duplex switch is used if multiple access paths to the component are required. The switch links a secondary memory to a control during the transmission of relatively long information units (e.g., records). A typical example of such a switch is the bus structure used when magnetic tape units connect to a common control. Only one of the units operates at a time (although all can be rewinding simultaneously). The switches are far less interesting than those above. Because they are nearer the periphery, failure in them does not imply a failure in the complete system.

Processor Function

The emergence of complex PMS structures is coincident with the development of functionally specialized processors. In the simple computers of Figs. 7 to 11 there is place only for Pc. In the general lattice there can be a Pc specialized to perform no input/output operations; one or more Pio's specialized to communicate with the

T's, and Ms's and even to organize information in Mp for transshipment; additional Pio's specialized to handle graphic displays (hence P.display); a Pc specialized to tolerate failure; and even P's specialized to work on specific data-types (for example, P.array) or specific algorithms (e.g., the fast Fourier transform). In addition, any of these processors may be realized by microprogramming which is to say, by having its ISP interpreted by a specialized P.microprogram.

Although the existence of various functionally specialized processors is coupled most closely with the PMS structure dimension, the processors themselves are defined primarily by the data-types they can process. On the other hand, the inclusion of microprogrammed processors really extends the PMS structure dimension to where a P can be seen as a cascade of two P's.

The processor-function dimension in the computer space is laid out in an evolutionary way, so that its correspondence with PMS structure is clear. P.microprogram is put at the beginning of the dimension ahead of Pc, not because it occurs earlier in evolutionary development, but because it extends the PMS dimension down into the processor. Any of the P's along the dimension can be attained by a P.microprogram.

As an actual dimension characterizing a total computer it must be viewed cumulatively (similarly to the data-type dimension). Thus, if a computer has a Pio, it also has a Pc, and if it has a P.array it also has the prior ones. There are numerous exceptions to this, such as small Pc's with P.displays (hence with no Pio's). This evolutionary ordering does not correspond to complexity or number of data-types in the P. Pc and P.array are the most complex; Pio and P.vector.move are least.

We will make a few brief comments on each functional type, taking them in the order of the dimension.

Microprogram Processor (P.microprogram)

The term *microprogramming* was introduced initially in "The Best Way to Design an Automatic Calculating Machine" [Wilkes, 1951]. We use *microprogrammed* to mean that an ISP is defined by an interpreter program residing in an internal Mp, processed by an internal processor (the P.microprogram). Thus the structure is really an external processor (ISP) being defined by the computer formed as

$$\boxed{\text{P}} := \boxed{\text{Mp(internal; read-only)}^1} - \boxed{\text{P.microprogram}}$$

The operations that microprogram processors perform are primitive in comparison with other processors. The task of the microprocessor is to interpret the instructions of the ISP it is realizing. This involves mostly data transfers among the registers of the processor state (Mps) plus simple boolean tests. Although it

must handle all the data-types of the larger ISP, it does so only as bit fields to be extracted and transferred from one register to another. The complex data operations (e.g., multiplication) are carried out by other units (D's). In fact, if a complex instruction set were to be used for the P.microprogram, the external processor might as well be implemented directly in hardware. In very minimal P's, for example, C(PDP-8) in Chap. 8, the ISP is essentially already at the level of a microprogram ISP, as shown by the inclusion of instructions that can be microcoded.

The long lag between the idea of microprogramming and its more widespread adoption is due to several reasons. Early ISPs were comparatively straightforward, so that a microprogram approach was not economically justified. The interpretation overhead time is higher than with the hardwired approach, and unless complex functions are realized this time becomes objectionable. In addition, suitable read-only memories were not developed until the mid-1960s (though it is unclear whether this is cause or effect). An additional feature of using a P.microprogram is the ability to realize several ISPs within a single physical processor. IBM has exploited this feature extensively in the System/360 and System/370 (Chap. 40, 41, and 51), by far the most ambitious use of microprogramming. One can argue that without the additional payoff, which was used to ease the transition to a new, incompatible computer system by providing emulation of the old system, the microprogramming would be marginal.

Microprogramming is now so popular that all but the very largest or very smallest machines are being microprogrammed. The microprogramming dimension is explored in detail in Sec. 1 of Part 2.

Central Processors (Pc)

Central processors interpret an instruction set for manipulating arithmetic, logic, and symbolic data-types. In all simple systems it is the only processor and thus does all tasks. The growth of processor specialization can be described in terms of relieving the Pc of simpler functions that require substantial processing time but do not make full use of the devices within the Pc, such as the arithmetic units. Crucial to this issue is the time it takes the Pc to switch from one task to another (recall the discussion on Mps, the processor state), since many of the jobs that are removed to specialized processors are demand jobs, such as input/output.

With the removal of tasks from the Pc, it becomes more specialized. A very pure example of this is the Pc of the CDC 6600 (Chap. 43), which has no input/output instructions of any kind in the Pc. That is, not only has the control and management of communication and transmission with the T's and Ms's been removed from the Pc, but the act of initiation has been removed as well and placed in the Pio's. Thus, the 6600 Pc is just an engine for working on the arithmetic, logic, and symbolic (address) data-types.

---

[1]Many contemporary microprogrammed processors have read/write memory to allow changes in the microprogram.

The mixture of operations to be performed in most complex algorithms prevents specialization of the Pc from going very far, e.g., from there being a P.arithmetic, for with every switch between capabilities distributed in distinct P's there must be intercommunication of the components, which introduces communication delays.

Input/Output Processors (Pio)

The Pio specializes in the management of peripherals (secondary memories and terminals). It is also called a *peripheral processor, a data channel,* and a *channel.*[1] The tasks a Pio and its subordinate peripherals perform are the transmission of information between Ms and Mp; the transmission of information between the computer and some real time system outside the computer (e.g., human); and the transmission of information outside the C, via a T to other information media (e.g., a card reader, a card punch, or a line printer). All these tasks are similar and often are considered the same, though in principle they can be quite different. A task in this environment is the management of some quantum of information, whether it be one bit or character, a voice message, or a record or file from magnetic disk or magnetic tape. Thus a Pio does not usually change any information; it is merely an interpreter for moving information. There are three exceptions: computation is required for error correction and/or detection; computation is required if recoding and reformatting are done; and computation is required when search operations are carried out on Ms without Pc intervention.

These computing tasks require only a fairly simple instruction set. Typically it contains jumping (branching); data transmission with Mp to initialize process variables; simple counting ability, e.g., to control error retries; subroutine calling; interrupt process handling; initializing KMs or KT; testing the state of KMs or KT; and sometimes code conversion (data in one code format are converted to another code). Thus substantial arithmetic and logic facility is not needed.

Display Processors (P.display)

The P.display is a complex Pio that processes information for display terminals. The data-type is a representation of a complex graphic object, usually made up of curves, and spatially localized text. The representations vary considerably from system to system, using various list pointers and vector encodings. The operations on the data-types include refreshing the display (due to the short-term persistence of the CRT); the selective modification of the representation under commands from the T.display or the

Pc, such as adding or deleting a line, or inserting text; the control of T.inputs such as keyboards, light pens, or joysticks; and the performance of more complex geometric transformations, such as translation, rotation, scale change, and determination of hidden lines.

Language Processors (P.language)

Language P's interpret a high-level language that has been designed to some external criterion, such as a procedure-oriented language (ALGOL or FORTRAN) or a list language (LISP). Thus complexity takes the form of a complex data-type for the instruction, rather than a complex data-type for processing (e.g., floating complex numbers). When such processors are extended to do all the things a Pc also does, they become more complex than a Pc.

Language-based machines are discussed in greater depth in Sec. 7 of Part 2.

Array Processors (P.array)

The array processor might be considered a more general Pc. It has been proposed or discussed in the literature for some time. The information unit processed is an array of one (vector) or two (matrix) dimensions. Instructions are provided to operate on these data. The specification of algorithms for a P.array is based on the assumption that an operation can be carried out in parallel for all array elements. Actually, both serial (sequential) and parallel (concurrent) execution can be implemented. Both structures have the same logical characteristics, from an ISP viewpoint, and may differ only in execution rate.

Section 3 of Part 2 categorizes array processors and presents several examples, including STARAN, TI ASC, and Illiac IV.

Vector-Move Processors

The vector-move processor is a special-case P.array. It is capable only of moving a vector of words at some location in Mp to some other location within Mp. Because of its limited instruction set, such a P is found only in computers that require constant Mp shuffling. This condition arises either because of a hierarchy of Mp speeds or because the programs must have a particular structure before they can be interpreted by the processor. A time-shared computer might require such a processor for multiprogram memory management. It is therefore common to find block (vector) transmission instructions in a Pc. The IBM System/360 has Pio[Storage channel] for this function.

Special Algorithm Processors (P.algorithm)

Only a small number of special algorithm processors have been specified or implemented. High performance is almost guaranteed by hardwiring and specialization. The time to fetch the

---

[1]These terms are usually used without distinguishing between a Pio and a Kio, that is, whether the device interprets a sequential program (and thus is capable of sustained independent activity) or only decodes a single instruction.

algorithm (instruction fetch time) and many of the references to Mp for temporary data are eliminated by hardwiring. A hardwired algorithm can easily outperform a stored program by a factor of 10 ~ 100. The lack of these processors in systems stems mainly from lack of market demand.

It is not clear that the special algorithm processors meet our criteria for being a processor, because of the rather limited functions they perform. In fact, some so-called processors are just K's, or D's, since they have no instruction location counter and interpret only a single instruction at a time, requesting each new instruction from a superior component.

Algorithms that have been hardwired (or proposed) include the fast Fourier transform using the Cooley-Tukey algorithm; cross-correlation, autocorrelation, and convolution processing; polynomial and power-series evaluation; floating-point array processing; and neural network simulation.[1] Programmable processors with specialized data paths to support these algorithms have also been constructed (e.g., Floating Point Systems' AP-120B Array Processor with pipelined 38-bit floating-point add, and floating-point multiply units that can produce a result every 167 ns).

Fault-Tolerant Processors

Gaining wide acceptance are processors constructed primarily to tolerate failures. Initially these processors were devoted to special-purpose aerospace control (e.g., the JPL Self-Test and Repair Computer, Chap. 27). Fault tolerance is now being applied to such commercial activities as communications (e.g., telephone switching, Chap. 28, data switching, Chap. 23) and transaction processing (Chap. 29). The PMS structure, ISP, and implementation details of these processors depend strongly on such specifications as assumed fault type, assumed fault extent (e.g., local or global), and specified system goal (e.g., availability, reliability, or data integrity). The basic concepts of fault tolerance as well as several example systems are presented in Sec. 6 of Part 2.

Memory Access

The most useful classification of memories is according to their accessing algorithm.[2] These are queue (access according to first-in-first-out discipline); stack (access according to first-in-last-out discipline); linear (e.g., a tape with forward read and rewind); bilinear (e.g., a tape with forward and backward read); cyclic (e.g.,

---

[1]*Chasm: A Macromodular Computer for Analog Neuron Models* [Molnar, 1967].

[2]Access for writing should be distinguished from access for reading. Memories are conceivable with arbitrarily different read and write access algorithms (e.g., random read and cyclic write.) However, in general, the two access algorithms are tightly coupled, and normally only the read access algorithm is given.

a drum); random (e.g., core); and content and associative. All these memories are explicitly addressed except the stack and queue, which deliver an implicitly specified i-unit on each read.

Memory size and basic operation times (i.e., the time constants in the access algorithm) are important too, of course. But once a distinction is made between Mp and Ms, then for any given technological era there have existed characteristic sizes and speeds for memories of a specified access algorithm. Where there has been variation, either it has been linear with size (e.g., buying two boxes of magnetic core Mp versus buying one) or there has been a narrow range of cost/performance tradeoff (as in data rate for magnetic tapes, in which modest increases in density and tape speed can be bought for substantially increased price). Table 5 shows the relative price, size, and performance of various memories. The memory-size versus information-rate plot (Fig. 20) shows the clustering of memories and their suitability for a particular function.

From a technology standpoint, Mp's have been constrained to either cyclic- or random-access memories (although one can easily construct any type from random-access memories). Similarly, Ms's have been constrained to be cyclic or linear, although quasi-random access has been achieved with some disks and magnetic-card memories (random by block and linear or cyclic within a block). Any Ms's can be part of almost any computer structure. Thus there is no large effect of Ms structure on the main design features of computer systems, and they are not discussed to any extent in the remainder of the book. Our discussion of memory type here deals exclusively with Mp and Mps.

Stack and Queue Memories (M.stack, M.queue)

Data elements in a stack and queue are not accessed explicitly, as we have noted. The stack has some unique properties that aid in the compilation and evaluation of nested arithmetic expressions. Although there are no machines employing stacks exclusively for primary memory, there are stacks in some arithmetic processors. Chapter 9 presents a processor with a stack memory (i.e., with stacks in the processor state). Several other processors provide support for stacks through stack manipulation instructions (e.g., the PDP-11 and VAX-11).

Cyclic-Access Memories (Mp.cyclic)

Nearly all the first-generation (vacuum-tube) computers had Mp.cyclic. The Mp.cyclic acoustic, magnetostrictive delay line, and magnetic drum provided an inexpensive, simple, producible memory. By the second generation the cost of Mp.random (though still more expensive than an Mp.cyclic) was about equal to the processor logic. The incremental cost for an Mp.random in a large system was then small, whereas the performance gain could be a factor of up to 3,000 (access time of 10 μs versus 30 ~ 30,000 μs). Some of the first-generation machines were reimplemented

Table 5 Memory Characteristics

Memory module	Function	Access method	Memory size		Memory performance		Cost/bit ($)†
			Module size (bits)	Modules/ computer	Access time (s)	Data rate (bits/s)	
Punched paper card	Permanent, archival	Random + linear	(500 ~ 1,000)/ card; ~ 1,000 card/unit	1 ~ 2	$10^0 ~ 10^3$	10^4	2×10^{-6} + 2×10^{-1}
Magnetic card	Secondary, archival	Linear + constant + cyclic	3×10^9	1 ~ 4	$10^{-1} ~ 10^0$	0.4×10^6	1.5×10^{-8} + 5×10^{-5}
Magnetic tape	Secondary, archival	Linear	7×10^8	1 ~ 16	$10^0 ~ 10^2$	$0.4 ~ 4 \times 10^6$	2×10^{-8} + 4×10^{-5}
Moving-head, floppy disk	Secondary	Cyclic	$10^6 ~ 10^7$	1 ~ 2	$10^{-1} ~ 10^1$	10^5	$10^{-5} + 10^{-3}$
Moving-head disk pack	Secondary, files swapping	Linear + cyclic	4×10^9	1 ~ 16	$10^{-2} ~ 10^0$	$10^6 ~ 10^7$	3×10^{-6} + 3×10^{-5}
Fixed-head disk	Secondary, files swapping	Cyclic	$10^7 ~ 10^8$	1 ~ 40	$10^{-3} ~ 10^{-2}$	$10^6 ~ 10^7$	$10^{-3} ~ 10^{-4}$
Drum	Secondary, swapping	Cyclic	$(1 ~ 5) \times 10^7$	1 ~ 10	$10^{-1} ~ 10^{-3}$	$10^6 ~ 10^7$	10^{-3}
Magnetic bubbles	Secondary, swapping	Cyclic	$(1 ~ 5) \times 10^6$	1 ~ 10	$10^{-2} ~ 10^{-3}$	$10^5 ~ 10^6$	$10^2 ~ 10^{-4}$
Charge-coupled devices	Secondary, swapping	Cyclic	$10^6 ~ 10^7$	1 ~ 10	$10^{-3} ~ 10^{-4}$	$10^6 ~ 10^7$	$10^{-2} ~ 10^{-4}$
Video disk (write once)	Secondary	Cyclic	$10^{10} ~ 10^{12}$	1 ~ 10	$10^{-1} ~ 10^0$	$10^6 ~ 10^7$	5×10^{-8} + 5×10^{-7}
Bulk core memory	Primary and/or secondary, swapping	Random	10^7	1 ~ 8	$(2 ~ 10) \times 10^{-6}$	$10^6 ~ 10^8$	$0.02 ~ 0.05$
High-speed core or thin-film memory	Primary	Random	$10^5 ~ 10^6$	1 ~ 16	$(0.2 ~ 2) \times 10^{-6}$	$10^7 ~ 10^8$	$10^{-2} ~ 10^{-1}$
Integrated circuit (MOS memory)	Primary	Random	$10^4 ~ 10^6$	1 ~ 20	$10^{-7} ~ 10^{-6}$	$10^8 ~ 10^9$	$10 ~ 10^{-3}$
Integrated circuit (bipolar memory)	Primary, processor state	Random	$10^4 ~ 10^6$	1 ~ 20	$10^{-8} ~ 10^{-7}$	$10^{10} ~ 10^9$	$10^{-3} ~ 10^{-2}$
Integrated circuit (content addressable)	Primary, cache	Content, random	2×10^5	1 ~ 2	$~10^{-7}$	10^9	1 ~ 3
Read only	Processor instruction-set definition	Random	$(1 ~ 5) \times 10^5$	1	10^{-7}	10^9	10^{-2}

†The first component is the memory medium (e.g., a disk pack), and the second component is the transducer (e.g., a disk drive).

using transistors. Only a few new cyclic-access machines were introduced in the second generation. Most notable was the low-cost Packard-Bell PB-250 using transistor logic and magnetostrictive delay lines.

Nearly all these computers used some form of $n + 1$ addressing. The memory is organized on a digit-by-digit serial basis for a word. Hence, the arithmetic or logic function hardware is implemented for only a single digit. An operation is done for the entire word by iterating over all digits in time; thus the cost of a serial computer is nearly independent of its word length.

Because of the cyclic and synchronous nature of these Mp's, it is difficult to synchronize them with secondary memories and terminals (which are also synchronous). The very early machines had no large secondary memories. In some cases, where magnetic tape was used, it was added at very low performance (low density, low speed, and, therefore, low data rates) so that synchronization

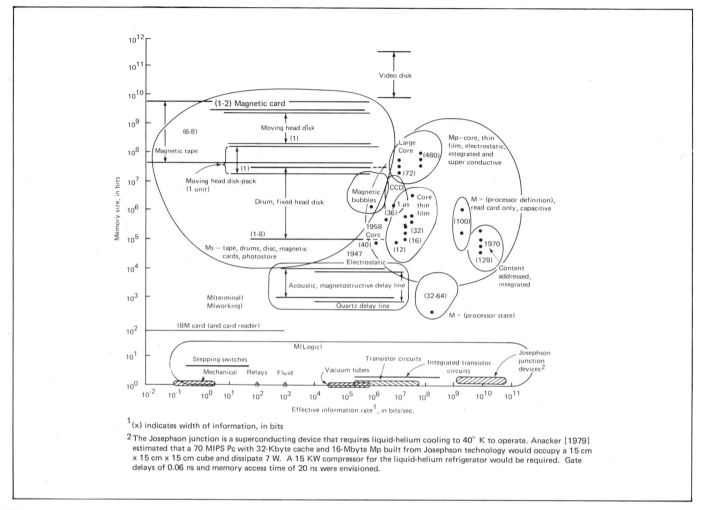

Fig. 20. Memory size versus effective information rate.

was not a problem. In other cases a small random-access core memory was added to provide synchronization between the two memories.

The major application of M.cyclic is now for Ms, where the price per bit of disk memory has been decreasing at a rate of 22 percent per year and the price per bit of magnetic tape has been decreasing at 10 percent per year over the last 25 years.

Random-Access Memories (Mp. random)

Random-access memories were used late in the first generation, and they have remained the predominant memory during the second, third, and fourth generations. It is unlikely that their popularity will decline unless content-addressable memories can

be constructed sufficiently cheaply (if then). The earliest first-generation random-access memories were electrostatic and depended on maintaining a charge on plates of an array of capacitors. The most common was the Williams tube (invented by F. H. Williams at the University of Manchester), which works in essence like a CRT, with the beam used to charge a capacitor array at the tube face [Williams and Kilburn, 1949]. Other schemes included an array of capacitors that could be selected by digital logic.

Late in the first generation Forrester [1951] invented the core memory, which rapidly became the predominant primary-memory component. In the fourth generation (1972) semiconductor memory (bipolar for speed, MOS for bulk) has become the dominant memory technology.

The random-access memory seems nearly perfect for the Mp's of present computers. Of course, enthusiasm for this memory may be based on not knowing how computers would have developed if we had not had it. However, with little or no effort an M.random can be a stack, a queue, a linear, a cyclic, and even (within limits) a content or associative memory. It is an organization very hard to beat.

Content-Addressable and Associative Memories

It is possible to conceive of many exotic accessing capabilities, and numerous proposals have been made involving either theoretical structures or experimental prototypes. Since no particular varieties have become widespread, terminology is still variable. Content-addressable memories are usually taken to mean a collection of cells of predetermined size (i.e., a fixed i-unit) such that if one presents as the address the contents of a predetermined part of the cell (the tag or content address) then the contents of the entire cell will be retrieved. An associative memory is usually taken to mean a system that, when presented with an item of information, delivers one or more "associated" items of information. The principle of association is variable, yielding different kinds of associative memories. Content-addressable memories provide a form of association, as do all memories, in fact. Thus the term *associative memory* tends to denote forms of association different from familiar ones—forms that presumably have less sharp constraints imposed by the structure of memory (as opposed to the structure of the information in the memory).

STARAN implements an associative memory from random-access memories under the control of special bit-serial processors. Variations of associative memories have been used to increase performance in the form of caches and instruction buffers (see Secs. 2 and 3 in Part 2). In the latter two cases there is a large but slower Mp.random behind the content-addressable memory. The purpose of the fast, small content-addressable memory is to hold local, current data so that an access will not have to be made to the random-access memory.

There are immediate uses for content-addressable memories with a large information-content address. For example, the read-only memories for microprogram processors use long words principally because content-addressable memories are not available. Ideally a microprogrammed processor would like to look at a fairly large processor state to determine what action is to be taken in the microprogram.

It is interesting to speculate about the evolution of computers if a content-addressable memory had been developed in place of the random-access memory.

Multiprocess Environment and Storage Hierarchies

The multiprocess environment region of computer space has become so important that even single-chip microprocessors (e.g., Zilog Z8000, Intel 8086) have added memory management units. Memory management allows multiple processes to be resident in Mp, all in various stages of execution, and for these processes to intercommunicate. A closely related topic is storage hierarchy, whereby several different types of memory technology (from small, fast, and expensive to large, slow, and low-cost) are integrated into the system to appear as one large, fast, and economical memory. The purpose of multiprocess environment and storage hierarchies is to improve not only individual program performance but also system throughput. Section 2 in Part 2 is devoted to these important, interlaced dimensions.

Parallelism and Overlap

Several techniques have evolved to increase system performance via overlap and parallelism. Section 3 of Part 2 presents a detailed discussion of these various techniques.

References

Anacker [1979]; Bell, Mudge, and McNamara [1978]; Bhandarkar and Juliussen [1978]; Blake [1977]; Bloch and Galage [1978]; Casale [1962]; Forrester [1951]; Harrahy [1977]; Hoagland [1979]; Kenney, Lou, McFarlane, Chan, Nadan, Kohler, Wagner, and Zernike [1979]; Lunde [1977]; Military Handbook 217A [1965]; Military Handbook 217B [1974]; Molnar [1967];Myer and Sutherland [1968]; Noyce [1977]; Queyssac [1979]; Siewiorek, Kini, Mashburn, and Joobbani [1978]; Wichmann [1976]; Wilkes [1951]; Williams and Kilburn [1949].

Section 3

Computers of Historical Significance

This section features a discussion of four computers whose impact on computer structures is still being felt today: the Manchester Mark 1, the PDP-8, the B 5000, and the Atlas. It also provides detailed examples of the concepts already introduced, including ISP, PMS, and Kiviat graph notations and the concepts of digital system hierarchy and computer classes.

The four computers are arranged in order of size. The Mark 1, if constructed with contemporary technology, would be a monolithic microcomputer. The PDP-8, fabricated on a single CMOS chip (Intersil 6100), is a contemporary microcomputer. The B 5000 would be considered a contemporary minicomputer. (The discussion of the B 5000, supported by PMS diagrams and Kiviat graphs, traces the evolution of a computer family. Computer families will be discussed more extensively in Part 4.) Finally, the Atlas pioneered many of the concepts implemented in maxicomputers.

This section encapsulates Parts 3 and 4 of the book. As is the convention throughout Parts 3 and 4, it begins with critiques of each computer.

The Manchester Mark 1

The Mark 1 was the world's first stored-program computer. It executed its first program on June 21, 1948, ushering in a new technological revolution of major impact for the next three decades. Chapter 7 describes the organization and ISP of the Mark 1, the simplest ISP in this book.

The PDP-8

The 12-bit PDP-8 was the first mass-produced minicomputer, setting the standard for its class. The PDP-8 is considered in depth because:

1 It has a simple but nontrivial ISP, whose influence still affects such contemporary architectures as the Hewlett-Packard HP 2100 series and the Data General NOVA series. Study of this ISP will help the reader understand the general ISP concept. The same is true for its simple but nontrivial PMS structure.

2 The implementation is simple enough to illustrate clearly the complete set of levels in the digital design hierarchy: PMS, programming, logic, and circuit. Only a few other single examples in this book will be able to illustrate several levels in the hierarchy (e.g., the HP 9845, Chap. 31; the

TMS1000, Chap. 34; the PIC1650, Chap. 35; the PDP-11, Chap. 38; and the HP 9810/20/30, Chap. 49).

A discussion of the entire PDP-8 family can be found in Chap. 46. Figure 1 is the Kiviat graph for the PDP-8.

The B 5000, a Stack Machine

The B 5000 is an outstanding example of stack organization and memory segmentation. (The following comments concern the P.stack computers manufactured by both English Electric and Burroughs; a discussion of memory segmentation is postponed until Part 2.) There are four basic P.stack computer families: B 5000 → B 5500 → B 6500/B 7500; D825 → D830 → B 8500; KDF 9; and B 6700/B 7700. Root members of the first three families were made available at about the same time by Burroughs of Pasadena, California, Burroughs of Paoli, Pennsylvania, and English Electric. The IBM Corporation later responded with a proposed Pc.stack, but the machine never entered the production phase. The Hewlett-Packard HP 3000 is a stack-based minicomputer.

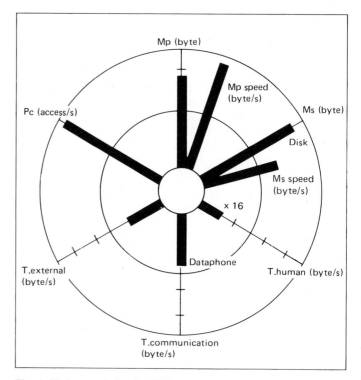

Fig. 1. Kiviat graph for the PDP-8.

The Pc.stack is a major alternative to the main-line organization of 1 address per instruction (augmented with index registers or general registers). It tries to capitalize on the hierarchical character of computation to avoid having to give memory shuffling instructions explicitly. In Chap. 6, we gave a comparison of a trivial computation using a stack and a general-register organization, in order to make clear the case for stacks. However, we did not there attempt any definitive analysis. It has been asserted [Amdahl et al., 1964a] that the Pc.stack derives its power only from its having some fast-working memory in the Pc, thus that it is dominated by the general-register organization. Our own feeling is that the compile and compiled program execution times for the Pc.stack are indeed impressive. However, no definitive analysis has been published, as far as we know. Pc.stack is certainly an organization that rates serious study by any computer designer.

B 5000, B 6500/B 7500, D825, and KDF 9

The PMS structure diagram of the B 5000 and B 6500/B 7500 (Figs 2 to 6) should be compared with Burroughs' own structure representation. The D825 structure is similar. All the Burroughs computers in Table 1 have the multiprocessor structure.

Burroughs was probably the first computer company to take matters of the structure and organization seriously. The D825 hardware and software were designed for military command and control applications, which demand very high uptime and availability. As various computer components in the structures fail,

continuous operation is possible at a reduced level through the fail-soft design. However, to our knowledge, no published account exists on how well this design works in practice from a performance and reliability viewpoint.

The structures in the B 6500, especially, allow Kio's to be freely assigned to any T or Ms, thereby achieving better equipment utilization. The S(16 Mp; 16P) is probably overdesigned in the Burroughs B 6500 computers. These structures generally have a maximum 4(P + Kio), although the design is based on 16(P + Kio). The Kio's (Chap. 9) may be overdesigned, as well, since a K capable of controlling a simple T.card.reader can also control a complex Ms.disk or Ms.magnetic.tape. The comparison of Pc.stack, Pc.1.address, and Pc.general.register makes the assumption that an unlimited hardware stack resides in Pc. The B 5500 has a local M.stack in Pc of 4 words. The size and number of stacks, and their use by software, are most important. The KDF9 has two independent stacks: one for arithmetic expression evaluation and one for holding subroutine return addresses.

Multiprocessing in the B 6500 is facilitated by the hardware stack features of the architecture. The stack mechanism allows efficient implementation of temporary storage and reentrant software, such as block-structured languages similar to ALGOL. The Segment Dictionary, or Program Reference Table, which was the basis for the Burroughs descriptor method of segmenting in the B 5000, has been moved to the bottom of the tree-structured hardware stack. This allows processes and instantiations of the same program (using different branches of the stack tree) to share

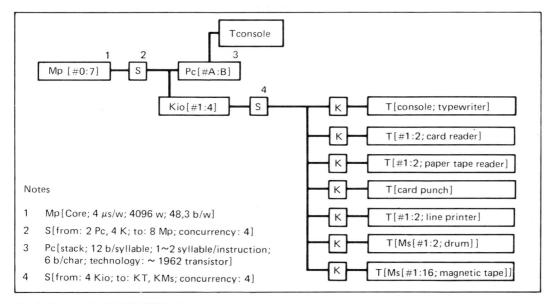

Notes

1   Mp[Core; 4 μs/w; 4096 w; 48,3 b/w]

2   S[from: 2 Pc, 4 K; to: 8 Mp; concurrency: 4]

3   Pc[stack; 12 b/syllable; 1~2 syllable/instruction; 6 b/char; technology: ~ 1962 transistor]

4   S[from: 4 Kio; to: KT, KMs; concurrency: 4]

Fig. 2. Burroughs B 5000 PMS diagram.

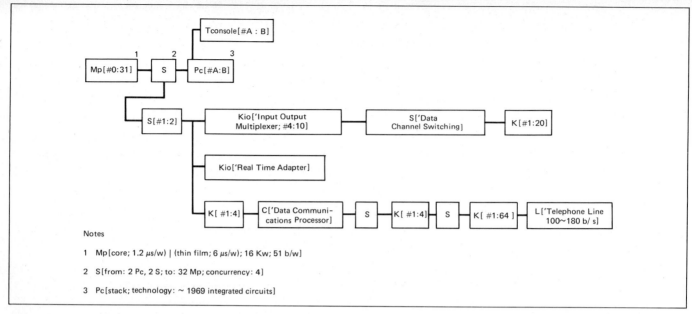

Notes

1 Mp[core; 1.2 μs/w] | (thin film; 6 μs/w); 16 Kw; 51 b/w]

2 S[from: 2 Pc, 2 S; to: 32 Mp; concurrency: 4]

3 Pc[stack; technology: ~ 1969 integrated circuits]

Fig. 3. B 6500, B 7500 PMS diagram.

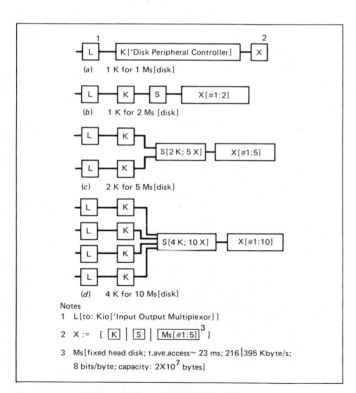

Notes

1 L[to: Kio['Input Output Multiplexor]]

2 X := [K | S | Ms[#1:5]]³

3 Ms[fixed head disk; t.ave.access~ 23 ms; 216|395 Kbyte/s; 8 bits/byte; capacity: 2X10⁷ bytes]

Fig. 4. Burroughs B 6500, B 7500 Ms[disk] PMS diagrams.

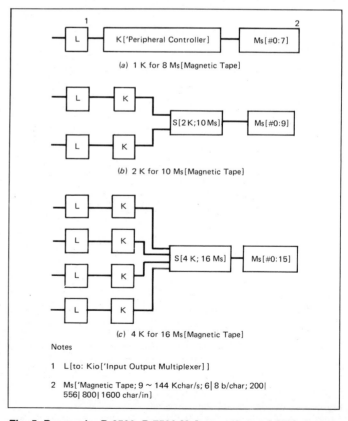

Notes

1 L[to: Kio['Input Output Multiplexer]]

2 Ms['Magnetic Tape; 9 ~ 144 Kchar/s; 6|8 b/char; 200| 556| 800| 1600 char/in]

Fig. 5. Burroughs B 6500, B 7500 Ms[magnetic tape] PMS diagrams.

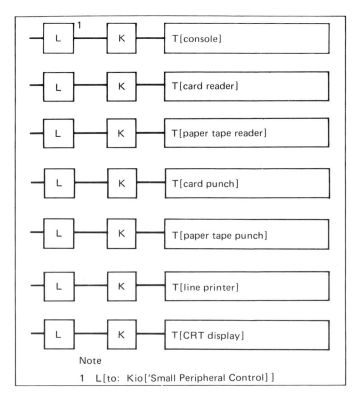

Fig. 6. Burroughs B 6500, B 7500 peripheral transducer PMS diagrams.

reentrant code through a shared Segment Dictionary. The operating-system global information that resides at the base of the trunk of the tree may also be similarly shared. This flexible, tree-structured hardware stack mechanism (the "cactus stack") is discussed in Chap. 16.

The D825 ISP differs from other Pc.stack computers in that the data, d, for operations can be in either of two places—the stack or Mp. Consider the unary or binary operations:

$$d_2 = u\ d_1$$
$$d_3 = d_1\ b\ d_2$$

In either of these cases d_1, d_2, or d_3 can be the top of Stack/S; or Mp[Address + Base Address + [Σindex registers [A,B,C]]]. This flexibility allows the Pc to behave as a 0-, 1-, 2-, or 3-addresses per instruction processor.

The B 5000 is more conventional than the D825 in its use of stacks (see references in Table 1). There are only load and store (that is, push and pop instructions) to transfer data between Mp

and one stack. Actually, the B 5000 has several important features that make it worthy of study:

1 The stacks.

2 Data-type specification. A data-type is declared by placing a type identifier with the data. Thus, for example, there is one add operation for both fixed and floating-point, the data telling which addition is to take place.

3 Multiprogram mapping. Descriptors are used to access variables (scalars, vectors, and arrays). This indirect addressing technique allows multiprogramming; however, the reader should note that the data are not protected against other accesses (corrected in the B 6500).

4 Failure of the Pc.stack for character processing. The B 5000 has a character mode to allow processing of string data, and the stack is not used in this mode. In effect, a separate string-processing ISP is incorporated in the Pc.

5 Multiprocessing. A B 5000 can have two Pc's.

B 6700/B 7700

The B 6700 and B 7700 series extended the concepts of the B 5000 and B 6500/7500 series. Like the latter, they are zero-address (stack) machines with enhanced versions of the Burroughs descriptor method of segmentation to achieve virtual memory (see Sec. 2 of Part 2 for a comparison of the B 5000 and B 6700 segmentation schemes). The hardware and the operating-system software, known as the *Master Control Program* (MCP), likewise exhibit a strong interdependence as a result of a conscious effort to develop a unified hardware-software system. The B 7700 system is strictly upward-compatible with the B 6700 but uses more sophisticated hardware techniques to achieve greater speed and flexibility.

The B 6700 was issued ca. 1969 and is a direct descendant of the B 6500. Designed as a medium to large high-speed information processing system, it is capable of addressing a core memory of up to 1 Mw with a cycle time of 500 ns, 1.2 μs, or 1.5 μs (options are shown in Table 2). Its configuration of peripherals is expandable to a maximum of 256 units. These may be controlled by up to three Pio's sharing access to Mp with the Pc's through a cross-point switch. Since as many as three Pc's may be configured into a B 6700 system, multiprocessing is possible. To aid in multiprocessing, each Pc has two interrupt networks: one to respond to interrupts generated within the processor (exception conditions, etc.) and the other to respond to externally generated interrupts (I/O interrupts, interprocessor interrupts, etc.). The processors share in the handling of external interrupts on an equal basis and under control of the MCP.

The B 6700 uses a 51-bit word plus an additional 52nd bit for

Table 1   Pc.stack Computers

Company or basis computer name	Disclosure date[a]	Delivery date	Ancestry	Relative power	References
English Electric KDF 9	/60	4/63	George[c]	. . .	Allmark and Lucking [1962], Davis [1960], Hamblin [1962]
Burroughs (Paoli, Pa.)					
D825[d]	/61				Anderson et al. [1962]
D830[d]			Extended-performance D825		
B 8500[e]	4/66[b]	1/67[f]	Developed at laboratory producing D825, D830	20–30	
Burroughs (Pasadena, Calif.)					
B 5000	/62	2/63		1/2	Allmark and Lucking [1962], Barton [1961], Bock [1963], Carlson [1963]
B 5500		11/64	Successor to B 5000	1–1.7[g]–1.9[g]	Lonergan and King [1961] Hauck and Dent [1968]
B 6500		1/68[f]	B 5500 based with improved multi- and shared-programmed mapping	5–6	
B 7500			Extended-performance B 6500	10	
B 6700	/69		B 6500	25	
B 7700			Extended-performance B 6700	80	
Theory or language-based:					
IPL-VI	/58		Language:IPL-IV, V		Shaw et al. [1958]
EULER	/67	/67	Language:EULER(ALGOL⁺)		Weber [1967], Wirth and Weber [1966a, b]
ALGOL			Language:ALGOL		Anderson [1961]
Argonne Laboratory					
IPL-VC			Language:IPL-V		Hodges [1964]

[a]First edition of manual, or a paper, or the appearance in *Adams Computing Characteristics Quarterly*.
[b]Still evolving. B 8501 was discontinued in 1968.
[c]George, University of New South Wales, interpreter using Polish notation and a stack. Circa 1957 [Hamblin, 1962].
[d]Produced for command and control (military) applications.
[e]B 8500 is a system name; the Pc is a B 8501.
[f]Reported. Actual delivery unknown.
[g]Dual processor.

word parity that is generated and checked during processor-memory transfers. Of the 51 bits, three are control or tag bits inaccessible to programs running in user state. The control bits allow division of labor between hardware and software to make efficient use of both. These tag bits are also used as part of the memory-protection scheme to provide read-only access to individual words. The remaining 48 bits in the word form a single precision operand or a sequence of 8-bit, 6-bit, or 4-bit characters. A machine language program consists of a sequence of "syllables" each of 8-bit length and occurring 6 to a word. An operation may be defined by from 1 to 7 syllables. The 51-bit words may also contain segment descriptors of various kinds. Such descriptors

Table 2   B 6700 Central Units Chart

Style no.	Description	Processor speed (MHz)	No. of input/output processors	Additional input/output processors	Notes
B 6711	One processor	2.5/2.5	1	0	Used only with 65K memory modules
B 6721	One processor (can have a B6721-1 second processor)	2.5/2.5	1	1	Used only with 65K memory modules
B 6712	One processor	2.5/5.0	1	1 or 2	Used with any of the available memory modules
B 6722	Two processors	2.5/5.0	1	1 or 2	Used with any of the available memory modules
B 6714	One processor	5.0/5.0	1	1 or 2	Used with any of the available memory modules
B 6724	Two processors	5.0/5.0	1	1 or 2	Used with any of the available memory modules
B 6734	Three processors	5.0/5.0	2	1	Used with any of the available memory modules
B 6780	Input/output processor				
B 6780-1	Data switching channel, up to 12 per input/output processor	. . . .	. . . .	. . . .	Optional
B 6790	Maintenance-diagnostic-logic processor for B 6722, B 6724, & B 6734 systems (second input/output processor required)	. . . .	. . . .	. . . .	Optional
B 6004-1	98,304-byte (16,384-word) 1.2-μs memory module	. . . .	. . . .	. . . .	
B 6005-1	393,216-byte (65,536-word) 1.5-μs memory module	. . . .	. . . .	. . . .	
B 6006-1	98,304-byte (16,384-word) 500-ns memory module	. . . .	. . . .	. . . .	

have fields that hold the memory or disk address of the base of a segment, the length of the segment, a bit to indicate whether the segment is resident or nonresident, etc. The length field of the descriptor is used by the hardware to establish whether an access is being made to a forbidden area of memory, thus providing further memory protection.

The machine language operations are divided into three classes: Primary, Variant, and Edit. The Primary operators, which use 1 syllable, are the most frequently executed and include the Arithmetic, String, and Logic operations. The Variant class of operators uses 2 syllables to extend the operation-code space. These include such less often executed operations as I/O instructions. The third set of operators allows extensive editing of strings. In one instance, the TABLE ENTER EDIT instruction allows the editing of strings to be driven by a table of microoperations on strings residing in memory. These Edit class instructions may consume up to 7 syllables, with the first of these indicating how many syllables make up the instruction.

The I/O in the B 6700 is handled totally asynchronously by Pio's

known as I/O modules (IOMs, see Fig. 7). Under control of the MCP the Pc constructs list instructions to be performed by the IOMs in shared memory. It then inserts a processing request in a predefined I/O request queue buffer area in shared memory. The request may be handled by any of the IOMs and is routed to the relevant I/O controller and its device. When the request is processed, an exception condition occurs, and the IOM inserts a reply in a predefined queue, which is scanned by the Pc's for evidence either of I/O completion or of error. By means of "exchanges" (i.e., cross-point switches) the peripherals may be multiported to more than one Kio and Pio to provide redundant paths of access for higher availability. Separate Pdcp's (Data Communication Processors) are used to provide control over terminals and data communication networks.

The B 7700, which is a successor to the B 6700, is strictly upward-compatible with the latter to the extent that the B 6700's programs need not be recompiled to run on the B 7700. The ISP was extended to include vector data-types by adding vector mode operations to the Primary mode operator class. However, the

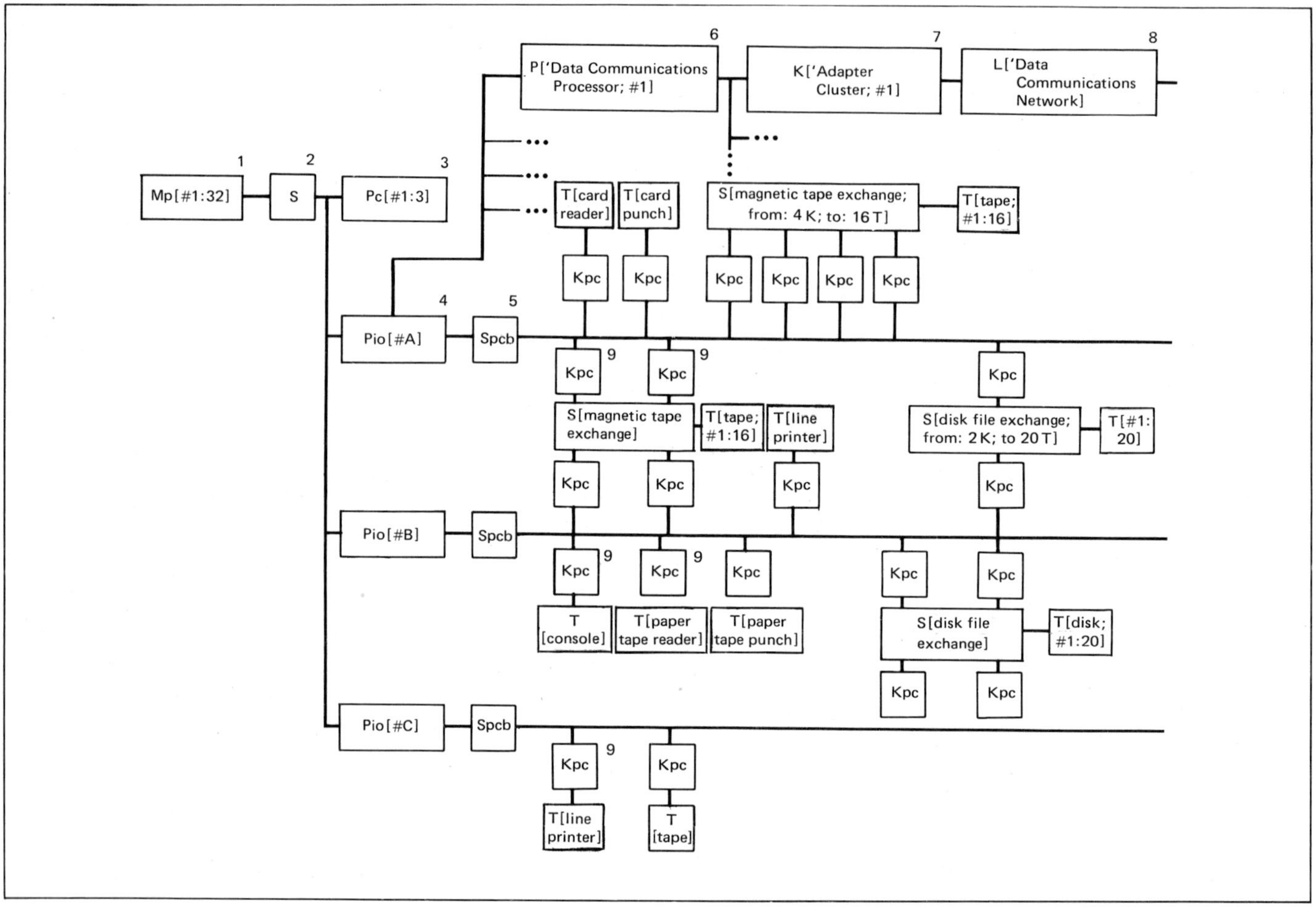

Fig. 7. Burroughs B 6700/7700 system PMS diagram.

B 7700 implementation allows greater processing speeds and flexibility (see Table 3). The maturing of integrated-circuit technology is reflected in the B 7700 hardware design by the exclusive use of semiconductor memory with 88 ns/byte read-access time. The standard memory module has evolved from the B 6700 to contain 1.5 Mbyte. In addition, the cross-point switch allowing sharing of Mp by the Pc's has expanded to allow a total of eight requesters of memory (Pc's and IOMs). The maximum transfer rate of an IOM has increased from 1.6 Mbyte/s to 6.75 Mbyte/s. The Pc speed has also risen from the 2.5- and 5-MHz options in the B 6700 to 16 MHz in the B 7700.

Internal parallelism, as well as faster logic, allows the B 7700 to achieve high operating speeds. The instruction-execution unit has a pipeline organization, and instructions are prefetched in the processor. Thirty-two words of fast local memory (Program Buffer) in the processor allow tight inner loops of program instruction syllables to reside in the processor, thus speeding up execution. In addition to the Program Buffer, another 32-word fast Stack Buffer is provided for the 32 locations immediately below the top of the stack for faster access to the stack. Finally, a fast Associative Memory (ASM, i.e., a *cache*), is implemented to provide fast access to general data and descriptors residing outside the stack. The Pc consists of three main sections: the Program Section, the Storage Section, and the Execution Section. A simplified block diagram of the Pc is shown in Fig. 8.

The hardware implementation of the B 7700 shows an increased

Notes

1. Mp[48b data + 3b control + 1b odd parity)/w; address: 20-bit;
     Max size: 1 Mw;
     system options:
        ('B 6700:
            [32 modules max.; module options: ([65 Kw;
                tc = 1.5 μs]|
                [16 Kw; tc = 1.2 μs] |
                [16 Kw; tc = 500 ns])]
)|
        ('B 7700:
            [8 modules max.; module options: [1.5 Mbyte; t[read] = 88 ns]
            ]
)
     ]

2. S[crosspoint; system options =
        ('B 6700 = [from: [3 Pc; 3 Pio] ;
                     to: 32 M;
                     concurrency: 6
                     ]
)|
        ('B 7700: [from: 8 'Requestors total;
                     to: 8M;
                     concurrency: 8
        ! 'Requestors are either Pc or Pio!
)
     ]

3. P$_c$[clock frequency: (2.5 MHz|5 MHz); 3 Pc max/system ('B 6700 only); modes: (word|vector (B 7700 only)|string:
     [4-bit; 6-bit; 8-bit characters]); states: ('Master Control Program ('MCP)| 'Normal (user)); stack architecture; addressing
     methods: ('Data Descriptor \DD| 'Segment Descriptor\SD| 'Indirect Reference Word\IRW| 'Stuffed Indirect Reference
     Word\SIRW)]
     ]

4. P$_{io}$[controlled by Pc; 3 Pio max/system ('B 6700 only) systems; functions: [data switching (20 channels max.); Data
     Communication Processor interface (4dcp.Max.); Real Time Adapter Interface; maintain peripheral system
     |configuration table for software use]]

5. S$_{pcb}$['Peripheral Control Bus; from: Pio; to: 20 Kpc; transfer rate:
     [('B 6700: (1|2) by/1,2μs) ('B 7700: 6.75 Mbytes/s)]]

6. P$_{dcp}$['Data Communications Processor; max 4 Pdcp/Pio; functions: data communication for (real-time operation|remote
     computing| remote inquiry | on-line programming); !In a three-Pio B 6700 system a Maintenance Diagnostic Logic
     Processor (Pmdl) preempts Pdcp's from one Pio-Pdcp interface!
     ]

7. Kac['Adapter Cluster; (#1:16) 'Data Communications Adapter \'DCA; 'DCA options:
        (
        ['B 6650-1; asynchronous; (direct| modem); 600 b/s max; (2-wire |'100 series) modem; bit-serial transmission;
        half-duplex]|

        ['B 6650-2; asynchronous; (direct | modem); 1800 b/s max; (2-wire |'202 series) data set; bit-serial transmission;
        half-duplex]|

        ['B 6650-3; modem; synchronous; 2400 b/s max; '201 series data set; bit-serial transmission; half-duplex]

        ['B 6650-4; same as '6650-3 except 4800 b/s max]|

        ['B 6650-5; same as '6650-3 except 9600 b/s max]|

        ['B 6650-6; 'Touch Tone® telephone input]|

        ['B 6650-7; 'audio response]|

        ['B 6650-8; 'automatic dial out]
        );
     16 Kac max/Pio]

8. Ldcn['Data Communications Network; 16 Ldcn max/Kac]

9. Kpc['Peripheral Controller; options: ('Large controller| 'Small controller);
     Functions: ('Large controller: [high speed devices; (T.mag.tape | T.disk.file|
                                          Tdisplay)]
                   'Small controller: [low speed devices; (Tprinter | T.card.reader|
                                          T.card.punch |– – –)]
     (5 'large controller + 5 'small controller) max./cabinet; 2 cabinets max/Pio; !A small controller may occupy a large
     controller slot!
     ]

Fig. 7. (Continued)

Table 3　Central Components of the B 7700 System

Style no.	Description
B 7750	System includes one central processor (16 MHz with vectors), one input/output processor with 24 data-switching channels, one maintenance diagnostic unit, one operator console with dual displays and control.
B 7760	System includes two central processors (16 MHz with vectors), two input/output processors with 24 data-switching channels each, one maintenance diagnostic unit, one operator console with dual displays and control.
B 7770	System includes three central processors (16 MHz with vectors), two input/output processors with 24 data switching channels each, one maintenance diagnostic unit, one operator console with dual displays and control.
B 7780	System includes four central processors (16 MHz with vectors), two input/output processors with 24 data-switching channels each, one maintenance diagnostic unit, one operator console with dual displays and control.
B 7001-4	Basic memory module—1.5 megabytes of 88 ns/byte read access, error-correcting memory, four-way interleaving that permits four-word transfers to and from memory.
B 7702	Additional central processor.
B 7785	Additional input/output processor.

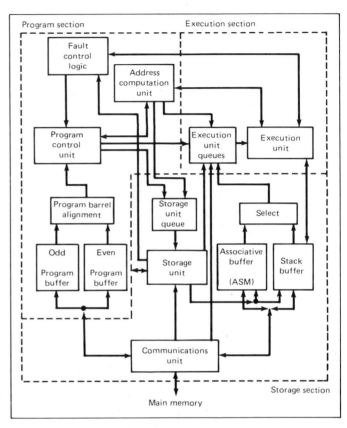

Fig. 8. Simplified block diagram of central processor module. (Copyright © 1976 Burroughs Corporation. Reproduced with permission.)

concern for high reliability, high availability, and fault tolerance. We see the incorporation of high-reliability components, error-detection circuits on data paths throughout the machine, instruction retry procedures, single-bit error correction in memory, and modular design. In addition, separate power supplies, redundant regulators for each module, and redundant buses are used. The MCP dynamically reconfigures system modules to exclude failed modules temporarily. A special-purpose Maintenance and Diagnostic Processor (MDP) is used to locate faults to the single clock period and flip-flop, thus indentifying the faulty IC chip. Disk files may be physically allocated in specific disk areas to facilitate maintenance and reconstruction in the event of failure. Protected and duplicated disk files are additional features allowing users to perform their own data recovery. Finally, some degree of control with respect to dynamic error recovery is provided to the user in the form of fault-conditional statements in high-level languages.

Figures 9 to 11 depict the relative performance of the B 5000, B 6500/B 7500, and B 6700/B 7700 families.

The Atlas

The Atlas is one of the most important machines described in this book. The prototype was originally designed and constructed at Manchester University. The Atlas 1 and Atlas 2 were produced by Ferranti Corp. (prior to its becoming part of I.C.T.[1]). Atlas 1 is the most interesting; it incorporates most of the features of the Atlas prototype. The Lincoln Laboratory TX-2 [Clark, 1957] influenced some Atlas features: multiple index registers and interrupt processing of input/output devices. Atlas' detailed internal structure is described in Sumner et al. [1962].

[1]International Computers and Tabulators, U. K.

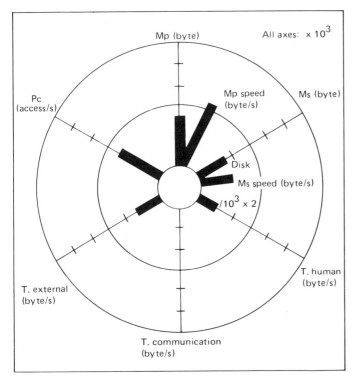

Fig. 9. Kiviat graph for the B 5000.

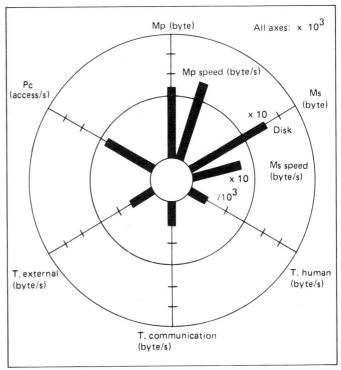

Fig. 10. Kiviat graph for the B 6500/B 7500.

Two original features, one-level storage and extracodes, have been copied in many other machines. A one-level store is common to most new time-shared or multiprogrammed computers.

The extracode feature allows ordinary machine operation codes to be used to call subroutines. Commonly used complex instructions (such as sin, cos, and monitor calls) can be written in a common operating system accessible to all users. Initially these subroutines were stored in a read-only memory.

The ISP is straightforward and extremely nice. The extracode idea appears in the SDS 900 series and was used in the SDS 940 system for defining common-user instructions. The IBM System/360 SVC (supervisor call) instruction is an adaptation of the extracode.

Atlas was about the earliest computer to be designed with a software operating system and the idea of user machine in mind. The operating system has been nicely described [Kilburn et al., 1961] and evaluated [Morris et al., 1967].

In a letter to the authors of this book, F. H. Sumner makes the following comments on Atlas.

The initial ideas and the preliminary research on the Atlas computer

system started in the Department of Computer Science of the University of Manchester in 1956. The team, under the direction of Professor T. Kilburn, was later supplemented by several members of the I.C.T. Computer Research Department, and the prototype machine was working in the department by the Autumn of 1961. The first production model became operational in January 1963.

The significant features of the system can be summarised as:

1 The provision of a virtual address field greater than the real address space.

2 The implementation of a "one-level" store using a mixture of core store and drum store.

3 The interrupt system and the method of peripheral control.

4 The realisation at the design stage that there would be a complex operating system and the provision in the hardware of specific features to assist such an operating system.

The method of peripheral control permitted the attachment of a large number of on-line peripherals with rapid responses and entry into the operating system for a peripheral requiring attention. This, together with the multiprogramming features, makes the design ideal for the attachment of keyboards for the provision of multi-

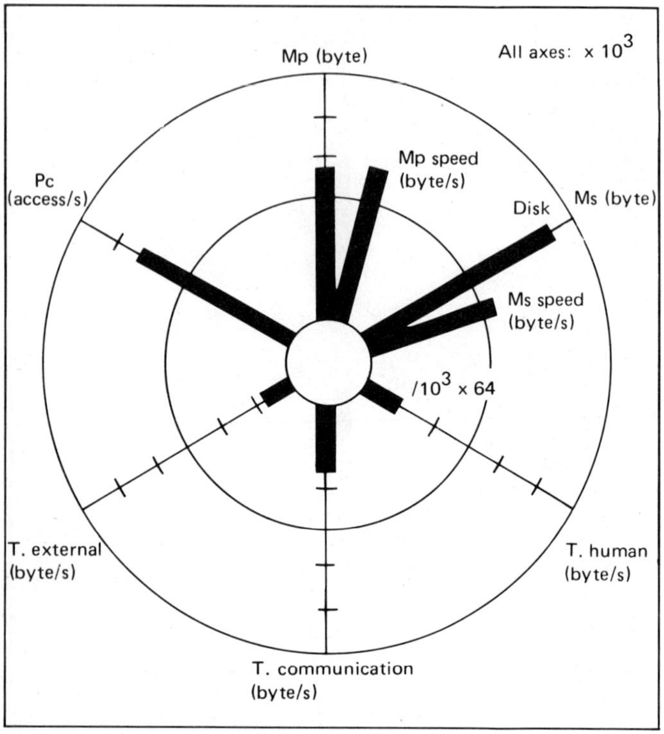

Fig. 11. Kiviat graph for the B 6700/B 7700.

access operation. In the original design, provision for several such on-line typewriters was made, but at the production stage it was decided to remove these as an economy measure. In view of the subsequent development of on-line operation, this was rather an unfortunate decision.

The Atlas computer at the University has now been in continuous operation for four years and it is expected to provide for the major part of the University's computing needs until 1971.

During the period of its operation the provision of extensive monitoring and logging information has permitted the behaviour of the system to be studied in detail. The results of these studies have been extremely valuable in the design of a successor to the Atlas.

References

Allmark and Lucking [1962]; Amdahl et al. [1964a]; Anderson [1961]; Anderson, Hoffman, Shifman, and Williams [1962]; Barton [1961]; Bock [1963]; Carlson [1963]; Clark [1957]; Davis [1960]; Hamblin [1962]; Hauck and Dent [1968]; Hodges [1964]; Kilburn, Howarth, Payne, and Sumner [1961]; Lonergan and King [1961]; Morris, Sumner, and Wyld [1967]; Shaw [1958]; Sumner, Haley, and Chen [1962]; Weber [1967]; Wirth and Weber [1966a].

Chapter 7

The Manchester Mark 1[1]

S. H. Lavington

Upon arrival at Manchester in December 1946, Williams and Kilburn set about perfecting a digital store, at first using the commercially available type CV1131 12-inch diameter cathode ray tubes [Kilburn, 1948; Williams and Kilburn, 1949]. The principle of a two-state electrostatic store can be visualised from the following simple experiment. Start with a focussed CRT beam and turn the beam current on (thus producing a charged "dot") and off again repeatedly. *Negative* voltage pulses will be induced by capacitive coupling in a pick-up plate placed close to the outer surface of the CRT screen. Now move the beam whilst it is on so as to write a "dash" on the screen, then move the beam back whilst the current is off, and then switch on the current again. This time a *positive* voltage pulse is induced. With dots and dashes representing logical 0's and 1's, readable as negative and positive voltage signals, a binary storage system is available. Other representations such as a "focus/defocus" system were also used. Now although the electrostatic charge leaks away in about 0.2 seconds, automatic refreshing (re-writing) of the information in less than 0.2 seconds is a simple matter electronically. (cf a modern MOS solid-state store.) Since the refresh rate is rapid, long term drifts in electrode supply voltage, etc are not critical and a robust store can be made from standard components. In contrast, the mercury acoustic delay-line stores chosen by other workers had to be constructed to close physical tolerences. The biggest advantage of the CRT store was that it allowed random access whereas other contemporary systems were sequential.

By the Autumn of 1947 the Manchester group had successfully stored 2048 digits for a period of hours [Kilburn, 1948] and the way was clear for the construction of a prototype computer "to subject the system to the most searching tests possible" [Williams et al., 1951]. Kilburn took the initiative with the logical design. The "baby machine," as it was called, had a specification which may be expressed in modern terminology as follows:

32-bit word length

Serial binary arithmetic using two's complement integers

Single-address format order code

Main store: 32 words, extendable to 8192 words, random access

Computing speed: 1.2 milliseconds per instruction.

The instruction format had three bits assigned to the function field, 13 bits to the address field and the remaining 16 bits were unused. The main store consisted of a single CV 1131 Williams Tube, with each 32-digit line occupying about 10 cms on the screen and being scanned in 272 microseconds. A complete "beat" of 306 microseconds consisted of 32×8.5 microsecond digit periods plus a four digit fly-back time. The rhythm of the whole processor was synchronised to this store beat. There was notional provision for extending up to 256 Williams tubes to yield a total storage capacity of 8192 words. The arithmetic unit was based on a serial subtractor and the logic employed EF50 pentode tubes, used widely for wartime applications. Using this technology, flip-flops (bistable circuits) were extremely costly and temporary storage throughout the central machine was implemented with Williams Tubes wherever possible. Thus the accumulator and control register (instruction counter) were Williams Tubes. One incidental advantage of the use of CRT's was that the contents of main store, accumulator and control register could be viewed on a monitor CRT during or after a computation—so providing a simple output mechanism. Input for the prototype was via a 32-position keyboard and operators control switches.

The machine first ran a program in June 1948 [Williams and Kilburn, 1948] and as far as can be ascertained it was therefore the world's first stored-program computer. A complete diagram of the prototype Mark 1 is given in Williams et al. [1951] and Fig. 1 is a simplified version showing the main flow of information. The Williams Tube which implemented the control register was also used to hold the present instruction (PI) itself subsequent to its being read out of main store. Either the value of control or the value of this PI could be fed from the "control" Williams Tube to

[1]Excerpted from S. H. Lavington, *A History of Manchester Computers*, NCC Publications, Manchester, England, 1975, pp. 7–10.
Editor's note: Further discussion of the Mark 1 can be found in the above publication.

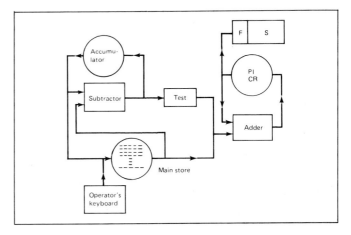

Fig. 1. A simplified diagram of the prototype Mark 1 showing the main information paths.

Table 1

Decimal value of function bits	An early notation	Modern mnemonic	Explanation of operation
0	s, C	JMP S	Absolute indirect unconditional jump: set the control register equal to the contents of address S.†
1	c+s, C	JRP S	Relative indirect unconditional jump: add the contents of address S to the control register.†
2	−s, A	LDN S	Load negative: set the accumulator equal to the negated contents of address S.
3	a, S	STO S	Store: copy the contents of the accumulator to address S.
4 or 5‡	a−s, A	SUB S	Subtract: set the new value of the accumulator equal to the former contents minus the contents of address S.
6	Test	CMP	Compare against zero: the value in the accumulator is tested. If it is less than zero, one is added to the control register thus causing the next sequential instruction to be skipped.
7	Stop	STP	Stop: cease automatic mode, and await manual commands from the operator's keyboard.

†Note that +1 was always added to the control register at the end of every order, so the programmer used JMP and JRP to point to an instruction one before the line he intended to jump to.
‡To economise on logic elements only partial decoding of the function bits was carried out.

an 8-bit (extendable to 16-bit) flip-flop register known as the staticisor. This staticised function bits (F) and operand addresses (S) during the execution of an order, and then staticised the address of the next order during the instruction-fetch phase. An interesting anomaly was that numbers were stored with the least significant digit on the left–a system which makes sense to engineers if not to mathematicians!

As has been noted, two's complement was used to represent negative numbers, though the now familiar rules for addition/subtraction and the formation of the complement of a number were not implemented in the usual way. The main emphasis of the project at this time was to prove the practicability of the Williams Tube for realising the stored-program concept and so the arithmetic logic was kept as simple as possible. The subtractor was the *only* arithmetic facility provided, it being preferred to an adder because a subtractor can be used without alteration to form complements and to perform additions whereas the converse is not true. As may be seen from Fig. 1 an operand entered the accumulator by being fed through the subtractor; this "subtract from zero" thus complemented the operand before it reached the accumulator. The effect of a positive load could be programmed in two orders by performing a negative load and then subtracting the contents of the accumulator from a zero operand. An addition of two quantities p, q was programmed by a four-order sequence as follows:

load negative p

subtract q

store the resulting (−p −q)

load negative to achieve (+p +q)

The order code of the the prototype had provision for eight functions, specified as in Table 1.

Three demonstration programs were run on the prototype machine, the first one involving determination of the highest factor of an integer by a method which would give a long run, the result of which could be easily checked. To quote [Williams and Kilburn 1948], "the highest proper factor of 2^{18} was found by trying in a single routine every integer from $2^{18}−1$ downward, the necessary divisions being done not by long division, but by the primitive process of repeated subtraction of the divisor. Thus about 130,000 numbers were tested, involving some 3.5 million operations. The correct answer was obtained in a 52-minute run. The instruction table in the machine contained 17 entries."

The original program was written by Tom Kilburn. G C Tootill, an engineer on loan to Manchester from TRE from mid-1947 to mid-1949, also wrote programs for the prototype and a notebook kept by him over the period 4th June to 28th November 1948 has survived. From entries in this notebook it seems that Kilburn's program was first run on Monday 21st June.

References

Kilburn [1948]; Williams and Kilburn [1948]; Williams and Kilburn [1949]; Williams, Kilburn, and Tootill [1951].

APPENDIX 1 MARK 1 1SP DESCRIPTION

```
MARK1 :=
    begin

! The Manchester Mark-I architecture is described.

! The Mark-I was an early (circa 1948) computer.

**MP.State**

    M[0:8191]<0:31>,

**PC.State**

    PI\Present.Instruction<0:15>,
        f\function<0:2> := PI<0:2>,
        s<0:12> := PI<3:15>,
    CR\Control.Register<0:12>,
    ACC\Accumulator<0:31>,

**Instruction.Execution**{tc}

    icycle\instruction.cycle{main} :=
        begin
        REPEAT
            begin
            PI ← M[CR]<0:15> next
            DECODE f =>
                begin
                #0  := CR ← M[s],
                #1  := CR ← CR + M[s],
                #2  := ACC ← - M[s],
                #3  := M[s] ← ACC,
              #4:#5 := ACC ← ACC - M[s],
                #6  := IF ACC lss 0 => CR ← CR + 1,
                #7  := STOP()
                end next
            CR ← CR + 1
            end
        end
    end
```

Chapter 8

Structural Levels of the PDP-8[1]

C. Gordon Bell / Allen Newell /
Daniel P. Siewiorek

A map of the PDP-8 design hierarchy, based on the Structural Levels View of Chap. 2, is given in Fig. 1, starting from the PMS structure, to the ISP, and down through logic design to circuit electronics. These description levels are subdivided to provide more organizational details such as registers, data operators, and functional units at the register transfer level.

The relationship of the various description levels constitutes a tree structure, where the organizationally complex computer is the top node and each descending description level represents increasing detail (or smaller component size) until the final circuit element level is reached. For simplicity, only a few of the many possible paths through the structural description tree are illustrat-

[1]Originally printed in C. G. Bell, J. C. Mudge, and J. E. McNamara, *Computer Engineering: A DEC View of Hardware System Design*, Digital Press, 1978, pp. 209–228.

ed. For example, the path showing mechanical parts is missing. The descriptive path shown proceeds from the PDP-8 computer to the processor and from there to the arithmetic unit, or more specifically, to the Accumulator (AC) register of the arithmetic unit. Next, the logic implementing the register transfer operations and functions for the *j*th bit of the Accumulator is given, followed by the flip-flops and gates needed for this particular implementation. Finally, on the last segment of the path, there are the electronic circuits and components from which flip-flops and gates are constructed.

Abstract Representations

Figure 1 also lists some of the methods used to represent the physical computer abstractly at the different description levels. As mentioned previously, only a small part of the PDP-8 description tree is represented here. The many documents which constitute the complete representation of even this small computer include logic diagrams, wiring lists, circuit schematics, printed circuit board photo etching masks, production description diagrams, production parts lists, testing specifications, programs for testing and diagnosing faults, and manuals for modification, production, maintenance, and use. As the discussion continues down the abstract description tree, the reader will observe that the tree

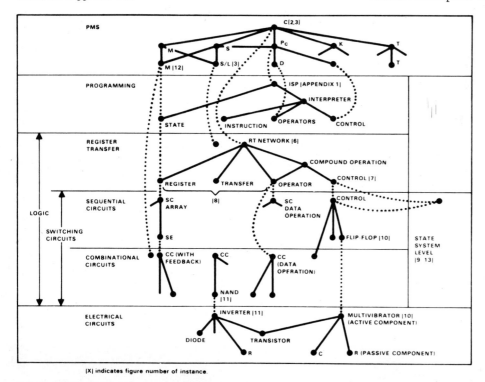

|X| indicates figure number of instance.

Fig. 1. PDP-8 hierarchy of descriptions.

110

conveniently represents the constituent objects of each level and their interconnection at the next highest level.

The PMS Level

The PDP - 8 computer in PMS notation is:

C[PDP-8 technology:transistors: 12 b/w:
   descendants:' PDP-8/S, ' PDP-8/I, ' PDP-8/L,
   ' 8/E, ' 8/F, ' 8/M, ' 8/A, ' CMOS-8;
   antecedents: ' PDP-5;
   Mp[core; #0:7; 4096 words; tc:1.5 μs/word];]
   Pc(Mps(2 to 4 words);
     instruction length:1|2 words;
     address/instruction:1;
     operations on data:(=, +, Not, And, Minus
     (negate), Srr 1(/2), Slr 1 (×2), +)
     optional operations:(×,/,normalize);
     data-types:word, integer, Boolean vector;
     operations for data access:4);
   P(display; '338);
   P(c; ' LINC);
   S(' I/O Bus; 1 Pc; 64 K);
   Ms(disk, ' DECtape, magnetic tape);'
   T(paper tape, card, analog, cathode-ray tube)

As an example of PMS structure, the LINC-8-338 is shown in Fig. 2; it consists of three processors (designated P): Pc(' LINC), Pc(' PDP-8), and P.display('338). The LINC processor is a very capable processor with more instructions than the PDP-8 and is available in the structure to interpret programs written for the LINC. Because of the rather limited instruction set being interpreted, one would hardly expect to find all the components present in Fig. 2 in an actual configuration.

The switches (S) between the memory and the processor allow eight primary memories (Mp) to be connected. This switch, in PMS called S(' memory Bus; 8 Mp; 1 Pc; time-multiplexed; 1.5 μs/word), is actually a bus with a transfer rate of 1.5 microseconds per word. The switch makes the eight memory modules logically equivalent to a single 32,768-word memory module. There are two other connections (a switch and a link) to the processor excluding the console. They are the S(' I/O Bus) and L(' Data Break; Direct Memory Access) for interconnection with peripheral devices. Associated with each device is a switch, and the I/O Bus links all the devices. A simplified PMS diagram (Fig. 3) shows the structure and the logical-physical transformation for the I/O Bus, Memory Bus, and Direct Memory Access link. Thus, the I/O Bus is:

S(' I/O Bus duplex; time-multiplexed; 1 Pc; 64K;*Pc controlled,*
K requests; t:4.5 μs/w)

The I/O Bus is nearly the same for the PDP-5, 8, 8/S, 8/I, and 8/L. Hence, any controller can be used on any of the above computers provided there is an appropriate logic level converter (PDP-5, 8, and 8/S use negative polarity logic; the 8/I and 8/L, positive logic). The I/O Bus is the link to the controllers for processor-controlled data transfers. Each word transferred is designated by a processor in-out transfer (IOT) instruction. Due to the high cost of hardware in 1965, the PDP-8 I/O Bus protocol was designed to minimize the amount of hardware to interface a peripheral device. As a result, only a minimal number of control signals were defined with the largest portion of I/O control performed by software.

A detailed structure of the processor and memory (Fig. 4) shows the I/O Bus and Data Break connections to the registers and control in the notation used in the initial PDP-8 reference manual. This diagram is essentially a functional block diagram. The corresponding logic for a controller is given in Fig. 3 in terms of logic design elements (ANDs and ORs). The operation of the I/O Bus starts when the processor sends a control signal and sets the six I/O selection lines (IO.SELECT <0:5>) to specify a particular controller. Each controller is hardwired to respond to its unique 6-bit code. The local control, K[k], select signal is then used to form three local commands when ANDed with the three IOT command lines from the processor. These command lines are called IO.PULSE.1, IO.PULSE.2, and IO.PULSE.4. Twelve data bits are transmitted either to or from the processor, indirectly under the controller's control. This is accomplished by using the AND/OR gates in the controller for data input to the processor, and the AND gate for data input to the controller. A single skip input is used so that the processor can test a status bit in the controller. A controller communicates back to the processor via the interrupt request line. Any controller wanting attention simply ORs its request signal into the interrupt request signal. Normally, the controller signal causing an interrupt is also connected to the skip input, and skip instructions are used in the software polling that determines the specific interrupting device.

The Data Break input for Direct Memory Access provides a direct access path for a processor or a controller to memory via the processor. The number of access ports to memory can be expanded to eight by using the DM01 Data Multiplexer, a switch. The DM01 port is requested from a processor (e.g., LINC or Model 338 Display Processor) or a controller (e.g., magnetic tape). A processor or controller supplies a memory address, a read or write access request, and then accepts or supplies data for the accessed word. In the configuration (Fig. 1), Pc[' LINC] and P[' 338] are connected to the multiplexer and make requests to memory for both their instructions and data in the same way as the PDP-8 processor. The global control of these processor programs is via the processor over the I/O Bus. The processor issues start and stop commands, initializes their state, and examines their

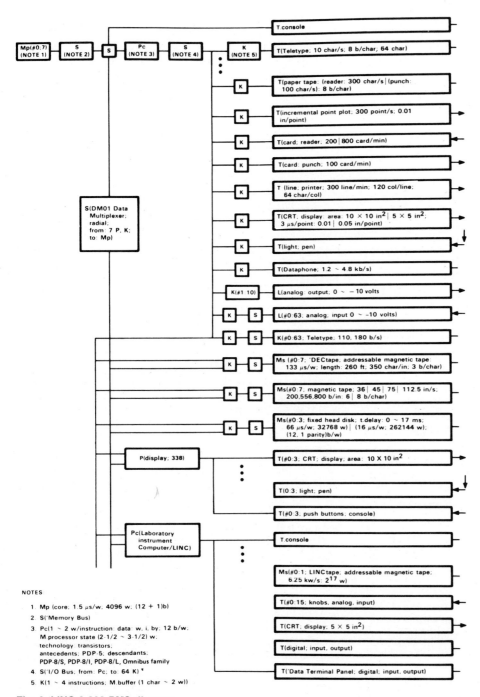

Fig. 2. LINC-8-338 PMS diagram.

NOTES

1. Mp (core; 1.5 μs/w; 4096 w; (12 + 1)b)

2. S('Memory Bus)

3. Pc(1 ~ 2 w/instruction; data: w. i. by; 12 b/w.
   M.processor state (2·1/2 ~ 3·1/2) w;
   technology: transistors;
   antecedents: PDP-5; descendants:
   PDP-8/S, PDP-8/I, PDP-8/L, Omnibus family

4. S('I/O Bus; from: Pc; to: 64 K)

5. K(1 ~ 4 instructions; M.buffer (1 char ~ 2 w))

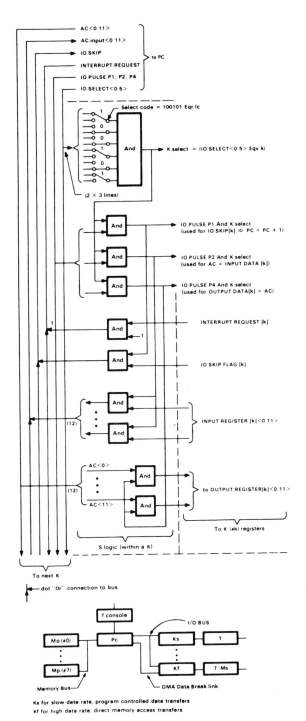

To next K

◄── dot "Or" connection to bus.

Ks for slow-data-rate, program-controlled data transfers
Kf for high-data-rate, direct-memory-access transfers

Fig. 3. PDP-8 S('I/O Bus) logic and PMS diagrams.

final state when a program in the other processor halts or requires assistance.

When a controller is connected to the Data Break or to the DM01 Data Multiplexer, it only accesses memory for data. The most complex function these controllers carry out is the transfer of a complete block of data between the memory and a high speed transducer or a secondary memory (e.g., DECtape or disk). A special mode, the Three Cycle Data Break, allows a controller to request the next word from a block in memory.

The DECtape was derived from M.I.T.'s Lincoln Laboratory LINCtape unit. Data were explicitly addressed by blocks (variable but by convention 128 words). Thus, information in a block could be replaced or rewritten at random. This operation was unlike the early standard IBM format magnetic tape in which data could be appended only to the end of a file.

Programming Level (ISP)

The ISP of the PDP-8 processor is probably the simplest for a general purpose stored program computer. It operates on 12-bit words, 12-bit integers, and 12-bit Boolean vectors. It has only a few data operators, namely, =, +, minus (negative of), not, and slr 1 (rotate bits left), srr 1 (rotate bits right), (optional) ×, /, and normalize. However, there are microcoded instructions, which allow compound instructions to be formed in a single instruction.

The ISP of the basic PDP-8 is presented in Appendix 1. The 2^{12}-word memory (declared MP[0:4095]<0:11>) is divided into 32 fixed-length pages of 128 words each (not shown in the ISPS description). Address calculation is based on references to the first page, page.zero, or to the current page of the Program Counter (PC\Program.Counter). The effective address calculation procedure, called MA in Appendix 1, provides for both direct and indirect reference to either the current page or the first page. This scheme allows a 7-bit address to specify a local page address.

A 2^{15}-word memory is available on the PDP-8, but addressing more than 2^{12} words is comparatively inefficient. In the extended range, two 3-bit registers, the Program Field and Data Field registers, select which of the eight 2^{12}-word blocks are being actively addressed as program and data. These are not given in the ISPS description.

There is an array of eight 12-bit registers, called the auto.index registers, which resides in page.zero. This array (auto.index [0:7]<0:11>:=MP[#10: #17]<0:11>) possesses a useful property: whenever an indirect reference is made to it, a 1 is first added to its contents. (That is, there is a side effect to referencing.) Thus, address integers in the register can select the next member of a vector or string for accessing.

The processor state is minimal, consisting of a 12-bit accumulator (AC\Accumulator<0:11>), an accumulator extension bit called the Link (L\Link), the 12-bit Program Counter, the GO flip-flop,

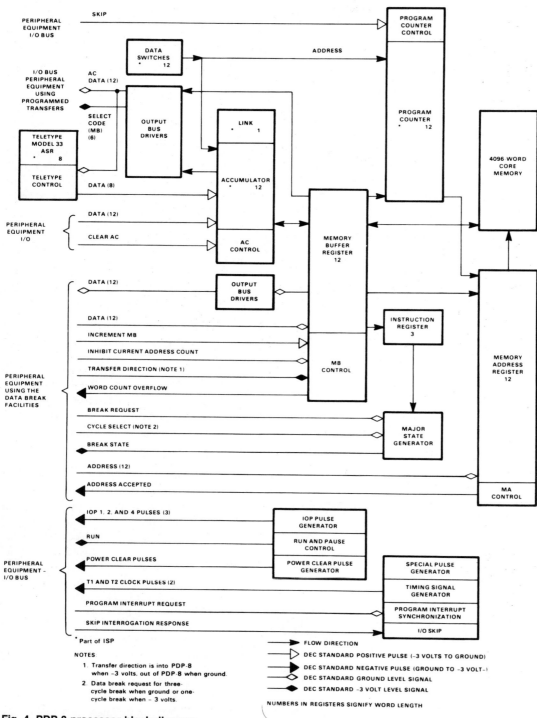

Fig. 4. PDP-8 processor block diagram.

and the INTERRUPT.ENABLE bit. The external processor state is composed of console switches and an interrupt request.

The instruction format can also be presented as a decoding diagram or tree (Fig. 5). Here, each block represents an encoding of bits in the instruction word. A decoding diagram allows one more descriptive dimension than the conventional, linear ISPS description, revealing the assignment of bits to the instruction. Figure 5 still requires ISPS descriptions for the memory, the processor state, the effective address calculation, the instruction interpreter, and the execution for each instruction. Diagrams such as Fig. 5 are useful in the ISP design to determine which instruction operation codes are to be assigned to names and operations, and which instructions are free to be assigned (or encoded).

There are eight basic instructions encoded by 3 opcode bits of the instruction.register, that is, IR<0:2>. Each of the first memory reference six instructions, where the opcode is less than or equal to 5, has four addressing modes (direct page.zero, direct current.page, indirect page.zero, and indirect current.page). The first six instructions in the following four categories are:

1 *Data transmission*
   "deposit and clear Accumulator" (DCA). (Note that the add instruction, TAD, is used for both data transmission and arithmetic.)

2 *Binary arithmetic*
   "two's complement add to the Accumulator" (TAD).

3 *Binary Boolean*
   "and to the Accumulator" (AND).

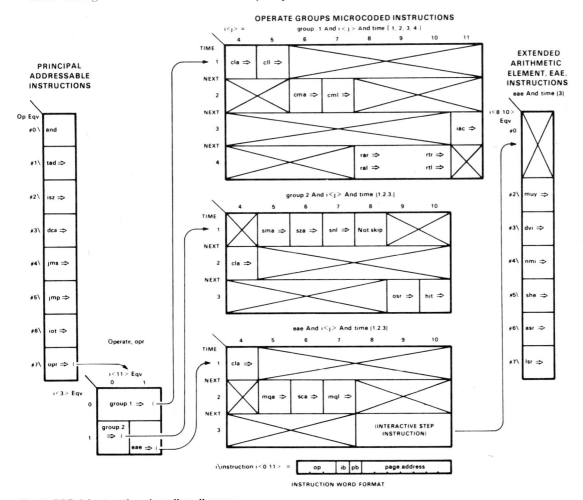

Fig. 5. PDP-8 instruction decoding diagram.

4 *Program control*
   "jump/set Program Counter" (JMP); "jump to subroutine" (JMS); "index memory and skip if results are zero" (ISZ).

The subroutine calling instruction, JMS, provides a method for transferring a link to the beginning (or head) of the subroutine. In this way arguments can be accessed indirectly, and a return is executed by a "jump indirect" instruction to the location storing the returned address. This straightforward subroutine call mechanism, although inexpensive to implement, requires reentrant and recursive subroutine calls to be interpreted by software rather than by hardware. A stack for subroutine linkage, as in the PDP-11, would allow the use of read-only memory program segments consisting of pure code. This scheme was adopted in the CMOS-8.

The "in-out transfer" instruction, opcode 6, IOT uses the remaining nine bits of the instruction to specify instructions to input/output devices. The six io.select bits select 1 of 64 devices. Three conditional pulse commands to the selected device, io.pulse.1, io.pulse.2, and io.pulse.4, are controlled by the IOT, io.control<0:2> operation code bits. The instructions to a typical I/O device are:

1 Testing a Boolean Condition of an IO device.
   IF io.pulse.1$\Rightarrow$
   (IF io.skip.flag[io.select]$\Rightarrow$
   PC = PC + 1)

2 Output data to a device from Accumulator.
   IF io.pulse.4$\Rightarrow$
   (output.register[io.select] =
   AC)

3 Input data from a device to Accumulator.
   IF io.pulse.2$\Rightarrow$
   (AC = input.register[io.select])

There are three microcoded instruction groups selected by (IR<0:2> eqv #7), called the operate instructions. The instruction decoding diagram (Fig. 5) and the ISP description show the microinstructions which can be combined in a single instruction. These instructions are: operate group 1 ((IR<0:2> eqv #7) and not ib) for operating on the processor state; operate group 2 ((IR<0:2> eqv #7) and not ib<> and MB<11>) for testing the processor state; and the Extended Arithmetic Element group (not included in the ISP description) (IR<0:2> eqv #7 and ib<> and MB<11>) for multiply, divide, etc. Within each instruction the remaining bits, <4:10> or <4:11>, are extended instruction (or opcode) bits: that is, the bits are microcoded to select additional instructions. In this way, an instruction is actually programmed (or microcoded, as it was originally named before "microprogramming" was used extensively). For example, the instruction, "set

link to 1," is formed by coding the two microinstructions, "clear link" following by "complement link."

If (IR <0:2> eqv #7) and (group eqv 0)) $\Rightarrow$
   If MB<5> $\Rightarrow$ L = 0; next
   If MB<7> $\Rightarrow$ L = not L)

Thus, in operate group 1, the instructions "clear link, complement link, and set link" are formed by coding MB<5,7> = 10,01, and 11, respectively. The operate group 2 instructions are used for testing the condition of the processor state. These instructions use bits 5, 6, and 8 to code tests for the Accumulator. The AC skip conditions are coded as never, always, AC eql 0, AC neg 0, AC lss 0, AC leq 0, AC geq 0 and AC gtr 0. The optional Extended Arithmetic Element (EAE) includes additional Multiplier Quo-

Table 1   PDP-8 Register Transfer Control Signals and Data Break Interface

```
AC/Accumulator, L/Link and combined L, AC LAC
  AC = 0; AC = #7777; AC = not AC; LAC = LAC + 1;
  L = 0; L = 1; L = not L;
  LAC = LAC srr 1; LAC = LAC srr 2;  !rotates right
  LAC = LAC slr 1; LAC = LAC slr 2;  !rotates left
  AC = AC or SWITCHES; AC = AC and MB; AC = IO.BUS
  AC = AC xor MB; LAC = carry (AC.MB);
  (note that previous two commands form: LAC = AC + MB).
MB/Memory.Buffer
  MB = MB + 1;                               !Increment
  MB = PC; MB = AC; MB = M[MA]; MB = DB.DATA.   !Set
  MB = 0;
MA/Memory.Address
  MA<0:4> = 0; MA = PC; MA = MB; MA<5:11> = MA<5:11>;
  MA = DB.ADDRESS.
PC/Program.Counter
  PC = 0; PC<0:4> = 0;                        !Clear
  PC = MB; PC<5:11> = MB<5:11>;              !Set
  PC = PC + 1                                !Increment
IR/Instruction.Register
  IR = 0;                                    !Clear
  IR = M[MA]<0:2>                            !Load
M/Memory[0:4095]<0:11>
  M[MA] = MB;                                !write
  MB = M[MA]                                 !read
DB/DATA.BREAK interface
  DB.DATA<0:11>                              ! Input to MB
  DB.ADDRESS<0:11>                           ! Input to MA
  MB<0:11>
  DB.REQUEST                                 ! Control inputs to Pc
  DB.DIRECTION
  DB.CYCLE.SELECT<0:11>
  ADDRESS.ACCEPTED                           ! Control outputs from Pc
  WORD.COUNT.OK
  BREAK.STATE
```

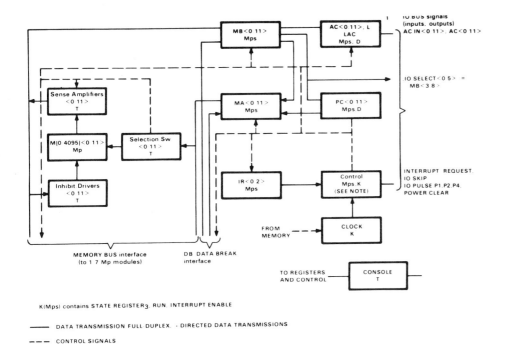

Fig. 6. PDP-8 register transfer level PMS diagram.

tient (MQ) and Shift Counter (SC) registers and provides the hardwired operations, "multiply," "divide," "logical shift left," "arithmetic shift," and "normalize." If all the nonredundant and useful variations in the two operate groups were available as separate instructions in the manner of the first seven (DCA, TAD, etc.), there would be approximately 7 + 12 (group 1) + 10 (group 2) + 6 (EAE) = 35 instructions in the PDP-8.

The Interrupt Scheme

External conditions in the input/output devices can request that the processor be interrupted. Interrupts are allowed if the processor's interrupt enable flip-flop is set (if INTERRUPT. ENABLE eqv 1). A request to interrupt (i.e., INTERRUPT. REQUEST = 1) clears the interrupt enable bit (INTERRUPT. ENABLE = 0), and the processor behaves as though a "jump to subroutine" 0 instruction (JMS 0) has been executed. A special IOT instruction (MB<0:11> eql #6001) followed by a "jump to subroutine indirect" to 0, and instruction (MB<0:11> eql #5220) returns to the processor to the interruptable state with INTER-RUPT.ENABLE a 1. The program time to save the processor state is six memory accesses (9 microseconds), and the time to restore the state is nine memory accesses (13.5 microseconds).

Only one interrupt level is provided in the hardware. If multiple priority levels are desired, programmed polling is

required. Most I/O devices have to interrupt because they do not have a program-controlled device interrupt-enable switch. For multiple devices, approximately three cycles (4.5 microseconds) are required to poll each interrupter.

Register Transfer Level

More detail is required than is provided by either the PMS or ISP levels to describe the internal structure and behavior of the processor and memory. Figure 4 shows the registers and controllers at a block diagram level, and Fig. 6 gives a more detailed version using PMS notation. Table 1 gives the permissible register transfer operations that the processor's sequential control circuit can give to the PDP-8 registers.

Although electrical pulse voltages and polarities are not shown in Table 1, the operations are presented in considerably more detail than shown in Fig. 4. As Fig. 6 shows, the registers in the processor cannot be uniquely assigned to a single function. In a minimal machine such as the PDP-8, functional separation is not economical. Thus, there are not completely distinct registers and transfer paths for memory, arithmetic, program, and instruction flow. (This sharing complicates understanding of the machine.) However, Fig. 6 clarifies the structure considerably by defining all the registers in the processor (including temporaries and controls). For example, the Memory Buffer (MB\Memory.Buffer<0:11>)

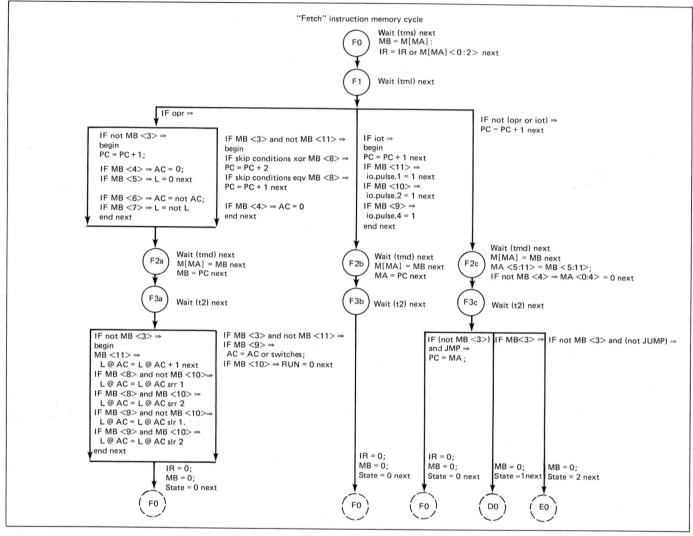

Fig. 7. PDP-8 Pc state diagram.

is used to hold the word being read from or written to memory. The Memory Buffer also holds one of the operands for binary operations (for example, AC = AC and MB). The Memory Buffer is also used as an extension of the Instruction.Register during the instruction interpretation. The additional physical registers, not part of the ISP, are:

MB\Memory.Buffer<0:11>
   Holds memory data, instruction, and operands.
MA\Memory.Address<0:11>
   Holds address of word in memory being accessed.
IR\Instruction.Register<0:2>

Holds the value of current instruction being performed.
state.register<0:1>
   A ternary state register holding the major state of memory cycle being performed—declared as 2 bits.
F\Fetch:=(IF state.register eqv 0)
   Memory cycle to fetch instruction.
D\Deferred:=(IF state.register eqv 1)
   Memory cycle to get address of operand.
E\Execute:=(IF state.register eqv 2)
   Memory cycle to fetch (store) operand and execute the instruction.

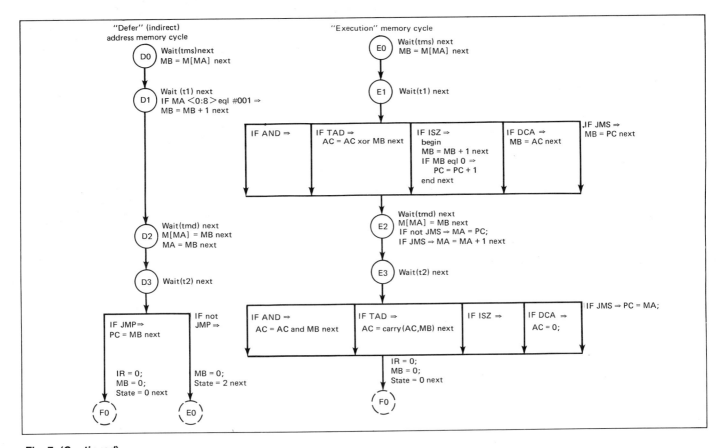

Fig. 7. (Continued)

The emphasis in Fig. 6 is on the static definition (or declaration) of the information paths, the operations, and state. The ISP interpretation (Appendix 1) is the specification for the machine's behavior as seen by a program.

As the temporary hardware registers are added, a more detailed ISPS definition must be given in terms of time and in terms of temporary and control registers. Instead, a state diagram (Fig. 7) is given to define the actual processor which is constrained by both the ISP registers, the temporary registers implied by the implementation, and time. The relationship among the state diagram, the ISP description, and the logic is shown in the hierarchy of Fig. 1. In the relationships shown in the figures, one can observe that the ISP definition does not have all the necessary detail for fully defining a physical processor. The physical processor is constrained by actual hardware logic and lower level details even at the circuit level. For example, a core memory is read by a destructive process and requires a temporary register (MB) to hold the value being rewritten. This is not represented

within a single ISPS language statement because ISPS defines only the nondestructive transfer; however, it can be considered as the two parallel operations MB = MP[MA]; MP[MA] = 0. The explanation of the physical machine, including the rewriting of core using ISPS, is somewhat more tedious than the highest level description shown in Appendix 1. For this reason, the state diagram is used (Fig. 7), and the description of the physical machine (in ISPS) is left as an exercise for the reader.

The state diagram (Fig. 7) is fundamentally driven by minor clock cycles as seen from both the state diagram and the times when the four clock signals are generated. Thus, there are 3 (state.register eqv #0,#1,#2) × 4 (clock) or 12 major states in the implementation. The Instruction.Register is used to obtain two more F2b and F3b, for the description. The state.register values 0, 1, and 2 correspond to fetching, deferred or indirect addressing (i.e., fetching an operand address), and executing. The state diagram does not describe the Extended Arithmetic Element operation, the interrupt state, or the data break states

(which add 12 more states). The initialization procedure, including the console state diagram, is also not given. One should
observe that, at the beginning of the memory cycle, a new
state.register value is selected. The state.register value is
always held for the remainder of the cycle; i.e., only the
sequences F0, F1, F2, F3, or D0, D1, D2, D3, or E0, E1, E2, E3
are permitted.

Logic Design Level (Registers and Data Operations)

Proceeding from the register transfer and ISP descriptions, the
next level of detail is the logic module. Typical of the level is the
1-bit logic module for an accumulator bit, AC <j>, illustrated in
Fig. 8. The horizontal data inputs in the figure are to the logic
module from AC<j>, MB<j>, AC<j> input from the IO.Bus.
In, and switches <j>. The control signal inputs whose names are
identified using the vertical bar (e.g., | AC =0 |) command the
register operations (i.e., the transfers). They are labeled by their
respective ISP operations (for example, AC = AC and MB, AC =

AC slr 1, for rotate once left). The sequential state machine, for
the processor Pc(K), generates these control signal inputs using a
combinational circuit as the one shown in Fig. 9.

Logic Design Level (Pc Control, Pc(K) Sequential State Machine Network)

The output signals from the processor sequential machine (Fig. 9)
can be generated in a straightforward fashion by formulating the
Boolean expressions directly from the state diagram in Fig. 7. For
example, the AC = 0 control signal is expressed algebraically and
with a combinational network in Fig. 9. Obviously, these Boolean
output control signals are functions which include the clock, the
state.register, and the states of the arithmetic registers (for
example, AC = 0, L = 0, etc.). The expressions should be factored
and minimized so as to reduce the hardware cost of the control for
the interpreter. Although the sequential controller for the
processor is mentioned here only briefly, it constitutes about half
the logic within the processor.

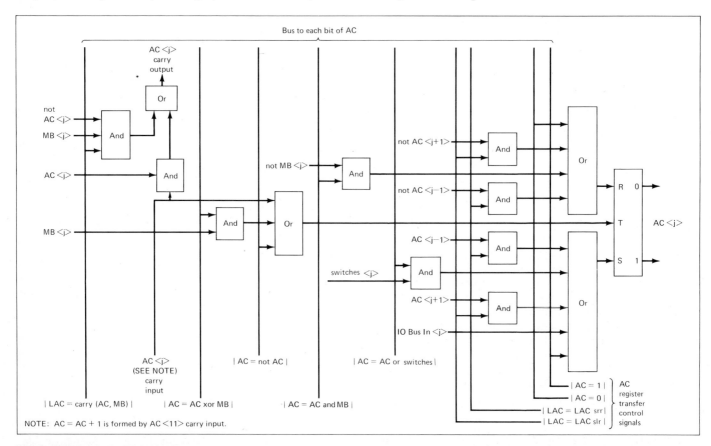

Fig. 8. PDP-8 AC<j> bit logic diagram.

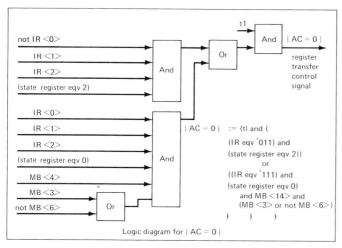

Fig. 9. PDP-8 Pc(K) AC=O signal logic equation and diagram.

Circuit Level

The final level of description is the circuits that form the logic functions of storage (flip-flops) and gating (NAND gates). Figures 10 and 11 illustrate some of these logic devices in detail. In Fig. 10 a direct set/direct clear flip-flop (a sequential logic element) is described in terms of circuit implementation, combinational logic equivalent, a state table, and its algebraic behavior. Note that this is not a conventional textbook circuit because it has no output delay and responds directly and immediately to an input. Some conventional sequential logic elements are used in the PDP-8, including RS(Reset-Set), T(Trigger), D(Delay), and JK. A delay in the flip-flops makes them behave in the same way as the "textbook" primitives in sequential circuit theory. The outputs require a series delay, Δt, such that, if the inputs change at time, t, the outputs will not change until $t + \Delta t$. In actuality, the PDP-8 uses capacitor-diode gates at the flip-flop inputs so that input

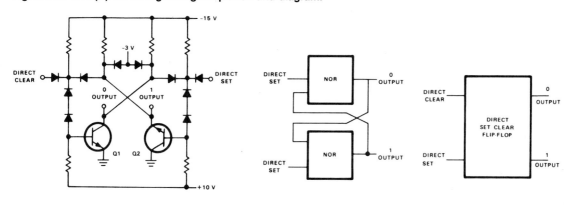

(a) Flip-flop circuit.

(b) Combinational logic equivalent of flip-flop.

(c) Direct set-clear flip-flop sequential logic element.

Table of Circuit Input-Output

Outputs (At t)		Inputs		Outputs (At t+) (See Note)	
1	0	Direct Set	Direct Clear	1	0
0	-3	-3	-3	0	-3
-3	0	-3	-3	-3	0
-3	0	-3	0	-3	0
0	-3	-3	0	-3	0
-3	0	0	-3	0	-3
0	-3	0	-3	0	-3

Table of Flip-Flop Input-Output

Outputs (At t)		Inputs		Outputs (at t+) (See Note)	
1	0	Direct Set	Direct Clear	1	0
1	0	0	0	1	0
0	1	0	0	0	1
0	1	0	1	0	1
1	0	0	1	0	1
0	1	1	0	1	0
1	0	1	0	1	0

Note this is not an "ideal" sequential circuit element because there is no delay in the output.

Fig. 10. PDP-8 direct-coupled flip-flop and logic diagram.

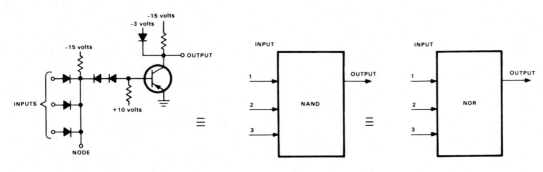

(a)   Multiple input inverter circuit.

(b)   NAND logic element.

(c)   NOR logic element.

Table of Circuit Behavior			
Input			
1	2	3	Output
0	0	0	−3
0	0	−3	−3
0	−3	0	−3
0	−3	−3	−3
−3	0	0	−3
−3	0	−3	−3
−3	−3	0	−3
−3	−3	−3	0

Table of NAND Behavior			
Input			
1	2	3	Output
0	0	0	1
0	0	1	1
0	1	0	1
0	1	1	1
1	0	0	1
1	0	1	1
1	1	0	1
1	1	1	0

Table of NOR Behavior			
Input			
1	2	3	Output
1	1	1	0
1	1	0	0
1	0	1	0
1	0	0	0
0	1	1	0
0	1	0	0
0	0	1	0
0	0	0	1

Fig. 11. PDP-8 combinational circuit and logic diagram.

changes will not be noticed until after the clock passes. This achieves the same effect.

Figure 11 illustrates the combinational logic elements used in the PDP-8. The circuit selection is limited to the inverter circuit with single or multiple inputs. These are more familiarly called NAND gates or NOR gates, depending on whether one uses positive and/or negative logic level definitions.

The core memory structure is given in Fig. 6. A more detailed block diagram showing the core stack with its twelve 64×64 1-bit core planes is needed. Such a diagram, though still a functional block diagram, takes on some of the aspects of a circuit diagram because a core memory is largely circuit level details. The memory (Fig. 12) consists of the component units: the two address decoders (which select 1 each of 64 outputs in the X and Y axis directions of the coincident current memory); selection switches (which transform a coincident logic address into a high current path to switch the magnetic cores); the 12 inhibit drivers (which switch a high current or no current into a plane when either a 1 or 0 is rewritten); 12 sense amplifiers (which take the induced low sense voltage from a selected core from a plane being switched or not switched and transform it into a 1 or 0); and the core stack, an array $M[\#0{:}\#7777]{<}0{:}11{>}$. Figure 12 also includes the associated circuit level hardware needed in the core memory operation (e.g., power supplies, timing, and logic signal level conversion amplifiers).

The timing signals are generated within the control portion of the processor and are shown together with processor clock in Fig. 13. The process of reading a word from memory is:

1 A 12-bit selection address is established on the MA$<0{:}11>$ address lines, which is 1 of #10000 (or 4096) unique

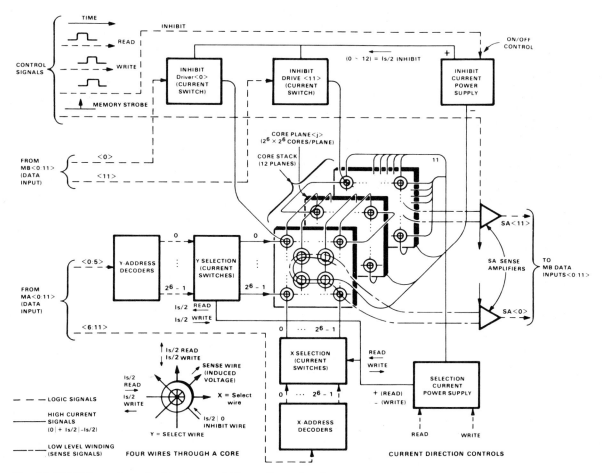

Fig. 12. PDP-8 four-wire coincident current (three dimensions) core memory logic diagram.

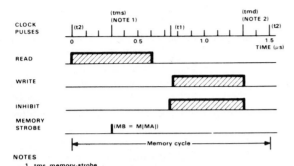

Fig. 13. PDP-8 clock and memory timing diagram.

numbers. The upper 6 bits <0:5> select 1 of 64 groups of Y addresses, and the lower 6 bits <6:11> select 1 of 64 groups of X addresses.

2 The read logic signal is made a 1 at time t2.

3 A high current path flows via the X and Y selection switches. In each of the X and Y directions, 64 × 12 cores have selection current (Ix and Iy). Only one core in each plane is selected since Ix = Iy = Iswitching/2, and the current at the selected intersection = Ix + Iy = Iswitching.

4 If a core is switched to 0 (by having Iswitching amperes through it), then a 1 is present and is read at the output of the plane bit sense amplifiers. A sense amplifier receives an input from a winding that threads every core of every bit within a core plane [#0:#7777]. All 12 cores of the selected word are reset to 0. The time at which the sense amplifier is observed is tms (the memory strobe), which also causes the transfer MB = M[MA].

5 The read current is turned off by timing in the memory module.

6 The inhibit and write (slightly delayed) logic signals are turned on at time t1. The bit inhibit signal is present or not, depending on whether a 0 or 1, respectively, is written into a bit.

7 A high current path flows via the X and Y selection switches, but in an opposite direction to the read case (see item 2). If a 1 is written, no inhibit current is present and the net current in the selected core is −Iswitching. If a 0 is written, the current is −Iswitching +(Iswitching/2) and the core remains reset.

8 The inhibit and write logic signals are turned off at time tmd specified by timing in the memory module, and the memory cycle is completed.

Device Level

For a discussion of the behavior of the transistor as it is used in these switching circuit primitives, the reader should consult semiconductor electronics and physics textbooks. It is hoped that the reader has gained a sense of how to think about the hierarchical decomposition of computers into particular levels of analysis (and synthesis) and that the hierarchical approach will be of aid in the reading of Parts 2, 3, and 4.

References

Bell, Mudge, and McNamara [1978].

APPENDIX 1   PDP-8 ISP DESCRIPTION

```
PDP8 :=
    begin

! The basic PDP-8 instruction set (without extended arithmetic element)
! is implemented.  No I/O devices are included in the description.
! I/O instruction execution is limited to the instructions that
! deal with the internal interrupt enable flags and status.

! Reference: "The DIGITAL Small Computer Handbook", 1967 Edition,
!            Digital Equipment Corporation.

**MP.State**

    MP[#0:#7777]<0:11>,                   ! Main memory (4k words)
        page.zero[#0:#177]<0:11> := MP[#0:#177]<0:11>,
        auto.index[#0:#7]<0:11>  := MP[#10:#17]<0:11>,

    MB<0:11>                              ! Memory buffer

**PC.State**

    L<>,                                 ! Link bit
    AC<0:11>,                            ! Accumulator

    PC<0:11>                             ! Program counter

**External.State**

    switches<0:11>,                      ! Console data switches
    interrupt.request<>                  ! Any device requesting interrupt

**Implementation.Declarations**

    go<>,                                ! 1 when running
    interrupt.enable<>,                  ! 1 when Pc can be interrupted
    last.pc<0:11>,
    skip<>                               ! Skip flag

**Instruction.Format**

    IR\instruction.register<0:2>,        ! Operation code
    ib\indirect.bit<>       := MB<3>,    ! Memory reference:
                                         ! 0 = direct; 1 = indirect
    pb\page.bit<>           := MB<4>,    ! 0 = zero page; 1 = current page
    pa\page.address<0:6> := MB<5:11>,
    io.select<0:5>          := MB<3:8>,  ! I/O device select
    io.pulse<0:2>           := MB<9:11>, ! I/O pulse control bits
        io.pulse.1<>          := io.pulse<0>,
        io.pulse.2<>          := io.pulse<1>,
        io.pulse.4<>          := io.pulse<2>,
```

APPENDIX 1 (*Cont'd.*)

```
! Instruction format (continued)

    group<>              := MB<3>,        ! Microinstruction group
    CLA<>                := MB<4>,        ! Clear AC
    CLL<>                := MB<5>,        ! Clear Link
    CMA<>                := MB<6>,        ! Complement AC
    CML<>                := MB<7>,        ! Complement Link
    RAR<>                := MB<8>,        ! Rotate right
    RAL<>                := MB<9>,        ! Rotate left
    RTx<>                := MB<10>,       ! Rotate twice
    IAC<>                := MB<11>,       ! Increment AC
    SMA<>                := MB<5>,        ! Skip on minus AC
    SPA<>                := MB<5>,        ! Skip on positive AC
    SZA<>                := MB<6>,        ! Skip on zero AC
    SNA<>                := MB<6>,        ! Skip on AC not zero
    SNL<>                := MB<7>,        ! Skip on Link not zero
    SZL<>                := MB<7>,        ! Skip on Link zero
    is<>                 := MB<8>,        ! Invert skip sense
    OSR<>                := MB<9>,        ! Logical or AC with switches
    HLT<>                := MB<10>        ! Halt the processor

**Address.Calculation**

    MA\effective.memory.address<0:11> :=
        begin
        MA = '00000 @ pa next                    ! Zero page
        IF pb => MA<0:4> = last.pc<0:4> next     ! Current page
        IF ib =>                                 ! Indirect bit
            begin
            IF MA<0:8> eql #001 =>               ! Auto index
                MP[MA] = MP[MA] + 1 next
            MA = MP[MA]                          ! Indirect address
            end
        end

**Instruction.Interpretation**

    start{main} :=
        begin
        go = 1 next
        run()
        end,

    run\instruction.interpretation :=
        begin
        IF go =>
            begin
            MB = MP[PC]; last.pc = PC next
            PC = PC + 1 next
            exec() next
            IF interrupt.enable and interrupt.request =>
                begin
                MP[0] = PC next
                PC = 1
                end next
            RESTART run
            end
        end
```

APPENDIX 1 (Cont'd.)

```
**Instruction.Execution**{us}

    exec\instruction.execution :=
        begin
        IR = MB<0:2> next
        IF (IR geq #3) and (IR leq #5) => MA() next
        IF IR leq #2 => MB = MP[MA()] next
        DECODE IR =>
            begin
            #0 := AND.:= AC = AC and MB,                ! And
            #1 := TAD := L@AC = L@AC + MB,               ! Two's complement add
            #2 := ISZ := begin                          ! Increment and
                                                        ! skip if zero
                            MB = MB + 1 next
                            IF MB eql 0 => PC = PC + 1
                            end,
            #3 := DCA := begin                          ! Deposit and
                            MB = AC next                ! clear accumulator
                            AC = 0
                            end,
            #4 := JMS := begin                          ! Jump to subroutine
                            MB = PC next
                            PC = MA + 1
                            end,
            #5 := JMP := PC = MA,                        ! Jump
            #6 := IOT(),                                 ! I/O execution
            #7 := OPR()                                  ! Operate
                                                        ! microinstructions

            end next
        IF (IR geq #2) and (IR leq #4) => MP[MA] = MB
        end,

    IOT :=                                              ! I/O Transmission
        begin
        DECODE MB<3:11> =>
            begin
            #001 := ION := begin                        ! Turn interrupt on
                            interrupt.enable = 1 next
                            RESTART run
                            end,
            #002 := IOF := interrupt.enable = 0,         ! Turn interrupt off
            otherwise :=  no.op()                        ! Not implemented
            end
        end,
```

APPENDIX 1 (Cont'd.)

```
skip.group :=
    begin
    skip = 0 next
    DECODE is =>
        begin
        0 := begin
                IF SNL and (L  eqv 1) => skip = 1;
                IF SZA and (AC eql 0) => skip = 1;
                IF SMA and (AC LSS 0) => skip = 1
            end,
        1 := begin
                IF SZL@SNA@SPA eqv 0  => skip = 1;
                IF SZL and (L  eqv 0) => skip = 1;
                IF SNA and (AC neq 0) => skip = 1;
                IF SPA and (AC geq 0) => skip = 1
            end
        end next
    IF skip => PC = PC + 1                    ! Skip
    end,

opr :=                                        ! Operate Instructions
    begin
    DECODE group =>
        begin
        0 := begin                            ! Group 1 microinstructions
            IF CLA => AC = 0;                 ! Clear accumulator
            IF CLL => L = 0 next              ! Clear link
            IF CMA => AC = not AC;            ! Complement accumulator
            IF CML => L = not L next          ! Complement link
            IF IAC => L@AC = L@AC + 1 next    ! Increment accumulator
            DECODE RTx =>
                begin
                0 := begin                    ! Rotate
                    IF RAL => L@AC = AC@L;
                    IF RAR => AC@L = L@AC
                    end,
                1 := begin                    ! Rotate two places
                    IF RAL => L@AC = L@AC slr 2;
                    IF RAR => L@AC = L@AC srr 2
                    end
                end
            end,
        1 := DECODE MB<11> =>                  ! Group 2 and 3
                begin
                0 := begin                    ! Group 2 microinstructions
                    IF HLT => go = 0;
                    skip.group() next
                    IF CLA => AC = 0 next
                    IF OSR => AC = AC or switches
                    end,
                1 := no.op()                  ! EAE group
                end
        end
    end
end            ! End of description
```

Chapter 9

Design of the B 5000 System[1]

William Lonergan / Paul King

Computing systems have conventionally been designed via the "hardware" route. Subsequent to design, these systems have been handed over to programming systems people for the development of a programming package to facilitate the use of the hardware. In contrast to this, the B 5000 system was designed from the start as a total hardware-software system. The assumption was made that higher level programming languages, such as ALGOL, should be used to the virtual exclusion of machine language programming, and that the system should largely be used to control its own operation. A hardware-free notation was utilized to design a processor with the desired word and symbol manipulative capabilities. Subsequently this model was translated into hardware specifications at which time cost constraints were considered.

Design Objectives

The fundamental design objective of the B 5000 system was the reduction of total problem through-put time. A second major objective was facilitation of changes both in programs and system configurations. Toward these objectives the following aspects of the total computer utilization problem were considered:

Statement of problems in higher-level machine-independent languages; efficiency of compilation of machine language; speed of compilation of machine language; program debugging in higher-level languages; problem set-up and load time; efficiency of system operation; ease of maintaining and making changes in existing programs, and ease of reprogramming when changes are made in a system configuration.

Design Criteria

Early in the design phase of the B 5000 system the following principles were established and adopted:

Program should be independent of its location and unmodified as stored at object time; data should be independent of its location; addressing of memory within a program should take advantage of contextual addressing schemes to reduce redundancy; provisions should be made for the generalized handling of

[1]*Datamation*, vol. 7, no. 5, May 1961, pp. 28–32.

indexing and subroutines; a full complement of logical, relational and control operators should be provided to enable efficient translation of higher-level source languages such as ALGOL and COBOL; program syntax should permit an almost mechanical translation from source languages into efficient machine code; facilities should be provided to permit the system to largely control its own operation; input-output operations should be divorced from processing and should be handled by an operating system; multi-programming and true parallel processing (requires multiple processors) should be facilitated, and changes in system configuration (within certain broad limitations) should not require reprogramming.

System Organization

The B 5000 system achieves its unique physical and operational modularity through the use of electronic switches which function logically like telephone crossbar switches. Figure 1 depicts the basic organization of the system as well as showing a maximum system.

Master Control Program

A master control program will be provided with the B 5000 system. It will be stored on a portion of the magnetic drum. During normal operations, a small portion of the MCP will be contained in core memory. This portion will handle a large percentage of recurrent system operations. Other segments of the MCP will be called in from the magnetic drum, from time to time, as they are required to handle less frequently-occurring events, or system situations. Whenever the system is executing the master control program, it is said to be in the Control State. All entries to the Control State are made via "interrupts." A special operation is provided, which can only be executed when the system is in the Control State, to permit control to return to the object program it was executing at the time the "interrupt" occurred.

The following are a few typical occurrences which cause an automatic "interrupt" in the system: An input-output channel is available, an input-output operation has been completed or an indexing operation was attempted which violated the storage protection features built into the system.

In addition to processing interrupt conditions, the master control program handles fundamental parts of the total system operation such as the initiation of all input-output operations, linking of input-output areas when required, file control, allocation of memory, scheduling of jobs (priority ratings, system requirements of each object program, and the present system configuration are considered), maintenance of an operations log and maintenance of a system description.

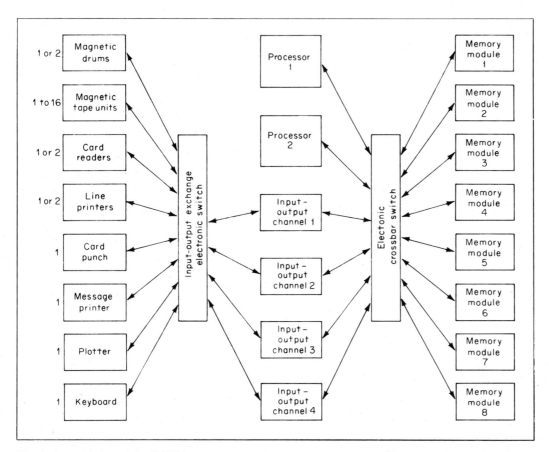

Fig. 1. Organization of the B 5000 system.

Operating Modes

The B 5000 can either operate with fixed-length words or with variable-length fields. These two modes of operation are called the word mode and the character mode. For certain operations, a processor operating on words is most desirable, and for other operations, a variable field length mode of operation is most desirable. By combining both abilities in one processor, a processor can operate in the mode most desirable for the operation at hand. In a B 5000 system, it is even possible for one processor to be operating in the word mode and the other in the character mode.

When operating in the word mode, a standard format for the data word is used as illustrated in Fig. 2.

Note that the standard word is an octal floating point word. However, the mantissa is treated as an integer rather than as a fraction (heretofore the reverse has been common practice). This provides two benefits: first, an integer has the same internal representation as its unnormalized floating point correspondent; and, second, the range of numbers that can be expressed, rather than being from 8^{+64} to 8^{-63}, is 8^{+76} to 8^{-51}. The first feature eliminates the need for fixed-to-floating point conversion; integers and floating point numbers can be mixed in arithmetic calculations. The second expands the range where trouble with range is most often encountered, namely, in numbers with extremely large magnitude.

The flag serves a dual purpose. The function of the flag depends

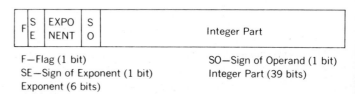

F	S E	EXPO NENT	S O	Integer Part

F—Flag (1 bit)
SE—Sign of Exponent (1 bit)
Exponent (6 bits)

SO—Sign of Operand (1 bit)
Integer Part (39 bits)

Fig. 2. Data word—word mode.

on how the program references the data word. If the data word is a single variable and not an element of an array, the flag identifies the word as being operand, that is, a data word. If the word is an element of an array, the flag may be used to identify this particular element as an element of data which is not to be processed by the normal program (for example, a boundary point in mesh calculations).

When operating in the character mode, each data word consists of eight alphanumeric characters as illustrated in Fig. 3. Programs in the character mode can address any character in a word. Fields can start at any position in a word. A processor in a single operation can operate on fields of any length up to 63 characters long; operations on fields of greater length can easily be programmed. For example, two 57 character fields could be compared in a single operation.

There are two instances when the character mode operates with words of the type used in the word mode. Operations are provided in the character mode for converting numeric information in the alphanumeric representation to the standard word type of the word mode and vice versa. In both of these instances, the length of the alphanumeric fields being converted to or from the word mode type of word can be no greater than eight characters long. Again, conversion of fields of greater length can easily be programmed.

The purpose of the word mode is to provide the advantages of high-speed parallel operations, floating-point abilities and the inherent information density possible in a binary machine. In the first case, it is economically feasible to provide parallel operations in a word machine; the cost of parallel operations on variable length fields would be prohibitive. In the last case, a given size memory can contain over twenty percent more numeric information if that information is expressed in binary rather than binary-coded decimal, and over eighty percent more information than can be expressed in six-bit alphanumeric representation.

The purpose of the character mode is to provide editing, scanning, comparison and data manipulative abilities (although addition and subtraction are also provided). The type of editing facilities provided obviate the need for the artificial "add-shift-extract-store" type of editing. For example, operations are provided for generalized insertion of editing symbols (such as blanks, decimal points, floating dollar signs, etc.) and for the substitution or suppression of any unwanted characters. For those interested in the new area of Information Processing Languages, the character mode is particularly well suited to list structures.

First Character	Second Character	Third Character	Fourth Character	Fifth Character	Sixth Character	Seventh Character	Eighth Character

Fig. 3. Data word—character mode.

Program Organization

Programs in the B 5000 are composed of strings of syllables. A syllable is the basic unit of the program and is twelve bits in length. The term "syllable" is used rather than instruction to distinguish it from conventional single-address or multi-address instructions. Each program word contains four syllables and they are executed sequentially in a left-to-right order within the program word, and sequentially by word. Branching is allowed to any syllable within a word. Before delving into some of the details of the internal operation of the B 5000 processor, it is necessary to discuss stacks, Polish notation, and the Program Reference Table.

The Stack

The internal organization of single-address computers forces the wasting of both programming and running time for the storage and recall of the intermediate results in the sequence of computation. The data must be placed into the proper registers and memory cells before the operation can be executed, and their contents must often be completely rearranged before the next operation can be performed. Multi-address computers are constructed to make the execution of a few selected operations more efficient, but at the expense of building inefficiencies into all the rest. Automatic programming aids attack this problem indirectly: they relieve the programmer of the need to laboriously code his way around machine design, but they still must provide object coding to accomplish the storage and recall functions. In brief, conventionally designed computers, with or without automatic programming aids, require the wasteful expenditure of programming effort, memory capacity, and running time to overcome the limitations of their internal organization.

The problem is attacked directly in the B 5000 by incorporation of a "pushdown" stack, which completely eliminates the need for instructions (coded or compiled) to store or recall intermediate results.

In a B 5000 processor, the stack is composed of a pair of registers, the A and B registers, and a memory area. As operands are picked up by the programs, they are placed in the A register. If the A register already contains a word of information, that word is transferred to the B register prior to loading the operand into the A register. If the B register is also occupied by information, then the word in B is stored in a memory area defined by an address register S. Then the word A can be transferred to B and the operand brought into the A register. The new word coming into the stack has pushed down the information previously held in the registers. As each pushdown occurs, the address in the S register is automatically increased by one. The information contained in the registers is the last information entered into the stack; the stack operates on a "last in–first out" principle. As information is operated on in the stack, operands are eliminated from the stack and results of operations are returned to the stack. As information in the stack is used up by operations being performed, it is possible to cause "pushups," i.e., a word is brought from the memory area addressed by the S register, and the address in the S register is decreased by one.

To eliminate unnecessary pushdowns and pushups, the A and B registers both have indicators used for remembering whether the registers contain information or are empty. When an operand is to be placed in the stack and either of the registers is empty, no pushdown into memory occurs. Also, when an operation leaves one or both of the registers empty, no automatic pushup occurs.

Polish Notation

The Polish logician, J. Lukasiewicz, developed a notation which allows the writing of algebraic or logical expressions which do not require grouping symbols and operator precedence conventions. For example, parentheses are necessary as grouping symbols in the expression A(B + C) to convey the desired interpretation of the expression. In the expression A + B/C, the normal interpretation is A+(B/C), rather than (A+B)/C, because of the convention that the / operator is of higher precedence than the + operator. The right-hand Polish notation used in the B 5000 is based on placing the operators to the right of their operands: A + B becomes AB + in Polish notation. A+B+C can be written either as AB+C+, or as ABC++. In the expression ABC+ +, the first + operator says to add the operands B and C. The second + operator says to add A to the sum of B and C. Returning to the first examples above, A(B+C) can be written as BC+A× or ABC+× in Polish. The second example is written as BC/A+ or ABC/+. The extension of Polish notation to handle equations is shown in the following example:

Conventional notation Z=A(B−C)/(D+E)
Polish notation ABC−×DE+/Z=

The Stack in Use

To illustrate the functioning of the stack, two simple examples are shown in Figs. 4 and 5. In the examples, the letters P, Q, and R represent syllables in the program that cause the operands P, Q, and R to be picked up and placed in the stack. The symbols + and × represent syllables that cause the add and multiply operations to occur. The two examples represent different ways of writing P(Q+R) in Polish notation. The first example in Fig. 4 does not require pushdowns or pushups. The second example, shown in Fig. 5, requires a pushdown in the execution of the syllable R, and a pushup in the execution of the syllable ×. The columns in the

Polish Notation QR + P×

Syllable Executed	Contents of	
	Register A	Register B
Q	Q	Empty
R	R	Q
+	Empty	R+Q
P	P	R+Q
×	Empty	P(R+Q)

Fig. 4

table represent the contents of the various registers after execution of the syllable listed in the first column.

Independence of Addressing

One of the goals set in the design of the B 5000 was to make the programs independent of the actual memory locations of both the program itself and the data, in order to provide really automatic program segmentation. Through automatic program segmentation, it is possible to have program size practically independent of the size of core memory. The systems analyst or programmer intending to do multi-processing is then no longer faced with the difficult task of planning what jobs are to be run together in order that system storage capacities are not exceeded.

In achieving independence of addressing, a solution requiring large contiguous areas of memory was not deemed satisfactory. Each segment of the program and each data area should be completely relocatable without modification to the program. It is

Polish Notation PQR + ×

Syllable Executed		Contents of			
		Register A	Register B	Register S	Cell 101
P		P	Empty	100	—
Q		Q	P	100	—
R	Pushdown	Empty	Q	101	P
	Execute	R	Q	101	P
+		Empty	Q−R	101	P
×	Pushup	Q−R	P	100	—
	Execute	Empty	P(Q−R)	100	—

Fig. 5

then possible to load all the segments of a program or programs onto the drum at load time and call in the segments to any available space in core memory as needed during run time. If some segment of a program is overlaid by a subsequent segment of a program, the segment of the program destroyed in core memory is still available on the drum to be called in again if needed.

Due to the very high program densities in the B 5000, the availability of high capacity drum storage on every system and automatic segmentation, a minimum B 5000 system has the capacity for a program or programs equivalent to approximately 40,000 to 60,000 single address instructions. Of course, if an installation normally ran such large programs, the system would very likely not be a minimum system. However, the installation having an occasional need to run very large programs is not prevented from doing so by storage capacity.

Processing speed now becomes a function of the size of core memory. If large programs are run in a system with small core memory, time will be consumed in recalling program segments from drum to core. If the core memory is expanded, less time will be spent in such activity and the program or programs will be speeded up, and no reprogramming is required.

Program Reference Table

The means of achieving independence of addressing in the B 5000 is called a Program Reference Table (PRT). The PRT is a 1,024 word relocatable area in memory used primarily for storing control words that locate data areas or program segments. There are also control words for describing input-output operations. These control words, called descriptors, contain the base address and size of data areas, program segments and input-output operation areas. A descriptor specifying an input-output operation also contains the designation of the unit to be used and the type of operation to be performed. Operands may also be stored in the PRT, providing direct access to single values such as indices, counts, control totals, etc.

In the word mode of the B 5000, every item of data is considered to be either a single value or an element of an array of data. If it is a single value, it will be obtained directly by indexing a descriptor contained in the PRT.

Program segments are described by program descriptors. In addition to core base address, the program descriptor contains the location in drum storage of the program segment and an indication if the program segment is currently in core memory starting at the address specified in the descriptor. Entry to a program segment is made via its program descriptor contained in the PRT. If the program segment is in core memory, entry will be made to the program segment. However, when entry is attempted to a program segment whose descriptor indicates that the segment is not in core memory, automatic entry to the Master Control Program will occur and the desired segment will then be brought in from the drum. Notice that in moving from one segment to another, it is not necessary to know whether the segment to be entered is currently in core memory. Branching within a program segment is self-relative, i.e., the distance to jump either forward or backward is specified, not the address to be jumped to.

As a result of keeping all actual addresses of data and program in the PRT, the program itself does not contain any addresses, but only references to the PRT. To specify one of the 1,024 positions in the PRT requires only 10 bits which contributes greatly to the high program density achieved in the B 5000. Since the PRT is relocatable, references to the PRT contained in the program are to relative locations, thus completely freeing the program from any dependence whatsoever on actual memory locations.

The Word Mode Program

The word mode of the B 5000 processor has four types of syllables. The syllable type is distinguished by the two high-order bits of each 12-bit syllable. The types of syllable and the identification bits are:

00—Operator Syllable
01—Literal Syllable
10—Operand Call Syllable
11—Descriptor Call Syllable

The first of these, the operator syllable, causes operations to be performed. The remaining ten bits of the operator syllable are the operation codes. There are approximately sixty different operations in the word mode. For those operations requiring an operand or operands, the processor checks for sufficient operands in the registers; if they are not there, pushups from the stack in memory occur automatically.

The literal syllable is used for placing constants in the stack to be used as operands. The ten bits of the literal syllable are transferred to the stack. This allows the program to contain integers less than 1,024 as constants.

The operand call syllable, and the descriptor call syllable address locations in the program reference table. The purpose of the operand call syllable is to place an operand in the stack; the purpose of the descriptor call syllable is to place the address of an operand, a descriptor, in the stack. There are four situations that arise, depending on the word read from the program reference table.

1 The word is an operand.
2 The word is a descriptor containing the address of the operand.

3   The word is a descriptor containing the base address of the data area in which the operand resides.

4   The word is a program descriptor containing the base address of a subroutine.

For (1), the operand call syllable has completed its action by placing an operand in the stack. The descriptor call syllable will cause the construction of a descriptor of the operand, replacing the operand by the constructed descriptor.

For (2), the operand call syllable then reads the operand from the cell addressed. The descriptor call syllable has completed its action.

For (3), indexing of the descriptor by the item that is now the second item in the stack occurs. For an operand call syllable, the operand is obtained from the indexed address; for the descriptor call syllable, action is complete after the indexing.

In the case of (4), subroutine entry occurs to the subroutine addressed. A word of the three previous types may be left in the registers upon return from the subroutine, in which instance the actions described above will take place, depending upon the type of syllable which initiated the subroutine.

Essentially, the four types of action that occur for an operand call syllable are obtaining an operand directly, indirectly, from an array, or by computation. Sometimes in the use of the call syllables, it is not known which type of action will occur for a particular syllable when the program is created. This is particularly true for call syllables in subroutines.

Programs in the word mode consist of strings of syllables which follow the rules of Polish notation. Variable length strings of call syllables and literal syllables, which place items of information in the stack, are followed by operator syllables which perform their operations on information in the stack.

The indexing features of the B 5000 allow generalized indexing and at the same time provide complete storage protection. Data areas and program segments of different programs may be intermingled, but a program is prevented from storing outside of its data areas. The method of indexing allows any of the 1,024 words of the program reference table to be considered index registers. Multilevel indexing is provided, i.e., indices of arrays can themselves be elements of arrays.

The subroutine control provided in the B 5000 allows nesting of subroutines—even recursive nesting (a subroutine is a subroutine of itself) arbitrarily deep. Dynamic allocation of storage for parameter lists and temporary working storage simplify the use of subroutines. Storage is automatically allocated and deallocated as required.

Character Mode Program

In the character mode of the B 5000 Processor, there is only one type of syllable, called the operator syllable. Program segments in the character mode are constructed of strings of these syllables. The character mode is designed to provide editing, formatting, comparison, and other forms of data manipulation. In doing so, the processor uses two areas of memory—the source and destination areas. When a program switches from word mode to character mode, two descriptors containing the base addresses of these areas are supplied. The source area or destination area may be changed at any time during character mode so that the program may act on several areas.

The character mode operator syllable is split into two 6-bit parts; the last part specifies the operation to be performed and the first part specifies the number of times the operation is to be performed. Operations are provided for the transferring, deletion, comparison, and insertion of characters or bits. Also, there are operations which allow the repetition of syllable strings. This is quite useful for complex table look-up operations and for editing information which contains repeated patterns.

Conclusion

The Burroughs B 5000 system has been designed as an integrated hardware-software package which offers such benefits as savings in the memory space required to store equivalent object programs; multi-processing and parallel processing; and running identical programs on systems with different size memories and different system configurations with no loss in individual system efficiency.

References

Lonergan and King [1961]; Barton [1961]; Bock [1963]; Carlson [1963]; Maher [1961].

Chapter 10

One-Level Storage System[1]

T. Kilburn / D. B. G. Edwards / M. J. Lanigan /
F. H. Sumner

Summary After a brief survey of the basic Atlas machine, the paper describes an automatic system which in principle can be applied to any combination of two storage systems so that the combination can be regarded by the machine user as a single level. The actual system described relates to a fast core store-drum combination. The effect of the system on instruction times is illustrated, and the tape transfer system is also introduced since it fits basically in through the same hardware. The scheme incorporates a "learning" program, a technique which can be of greater importance in future computers.

1. Introduction

In a universal high-speed digital computer it is necessary to have a large-capacity fast-access main store. While more efficient operation of the computer can be achieved by making this store all of one type, this step is scarcely practical for the storage capacities now being considered. For example, on Atlas it is possible to address 10^6 words in the main store. In practice on the first installation at Manchester University a total of 10^5 words are provided, but though it is just technically feasible to make this in one level it is much more economical to provide a core store (16,000 words) and drum (96,000 words) combination.

Atlas is a machine which operates its peripheral equipment on a time division basis, the equipment "interrupting" the normal main program when it requires attention. Organization of the peripheral equipment is also done by program so that many programs can be contained in the store of the machine at the same time. This technique can also be extended to include several main programs as well as the smaller subroutines used for controlling peripherals. For these reasons as well as the fact that some orders take a variable time depending on the exact numbers involved, it is not really feasible to "optimum" program transfers of information between the two levels of store, i.e., core store and drum, in order to eliminate the long drum access time of 6 msec. Hence a system has been devised to make the core drum store combination appear to the programmer as a single level of storage, the requisite transfers of information taking place automatically. There are a number of additional benefits derived from the scheme adopted, which include relative addressing so that

routines can operate anywhere in the store, and a "lock out" facility to prevent interference between different programs simultaneously held in the store.

2. The Basic Machine

The arrangement of the basic machine is shown in Fig. 1. The available storage space is split into three sections; the private store which is used solely for internal machine organization, the central store which includes both core and drum store, in which all words are addressed and is the store available to the normal user, and finally the tape store, which is the conventional backing-up large capacity store of the machine. Both the private store and the main core store are linked with the main accumulator, the *B*-store, and the *B*-arithmetic unit. However the drum and tape stores only have access to these latter sections of the machine via the main core store.

The machine order code is of the single address type, and a comprehensive range of basic functions are provided by normal engineering methods. Also available to the programmer are a number of extra functions termed "extracodes" which give automatic access to and subsequent return from a large number of built-in subroutines. These routines provide

1   A number of orders which would be expensive to provide in the machine both in terms of equipment and also time because of the extra loading on certain circuits. An example of this is the order:
    Shift accumulator contents $\pm n$ places where n is an integer.

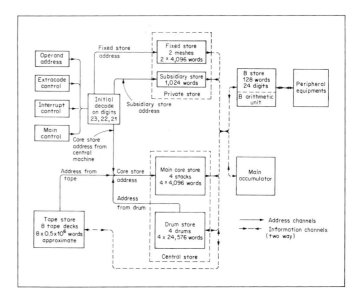

Fig. 1. Layout of basic machine.

[1]*IRE Trans.*, *EC-11*, vol. 2, April 1962, pp. 223–235

2   The more complex mathematical operations, e.g., sin x, log x, etc.

3   Control orders for peripheral equipments, card readers, parallel printers, etc.

4   Input-output conversion routines.

5   Special programs concerned with storage allocation to different programs being run simultaneously, monitoring routines for fault finding and costing purposes, and the detailed organization of drum and tape transfers.

All this information is permanently required and hence is kept in part of the private store termed the "fixed store" [Kilburn and Grimsdale, 1960] which operates on a "read only" basis. This store consists of a woven wire mesh into which a pattern of small "linear" ferrite slugs are inserted to represent digital information. The information content can only be changed manually and will tend to differ only in detail between the different versions of the Atlas computer. In Muse this store is arranged in two units each of 4096 words, a unit consisting of 16 columns of 256 words, each word being 50 bits. The access time to a word in any one column is about 0.4 μsec. If a change of column address is required, this figure increases by about 1 μsec due to switching transients in the read amplifiers. Subsequent accesses in the new column revert to 0.9 μsec. The store operates in conjunction with a subsidiary core store of 1024 words which provides working space for the fixed store programs, and has a cycle time of about 1.8 μsec. There are certain safeguards against a normal machine user gaining access to addresses in either part of the private store, though in effect he makes use of this store through the extracode facility.

The central store of the machine consists of a drum and core store combination, which has a maximum addressable capacity of about 10^6 words. In Muse the central store capacity is about 96,000 words contained on 4 drums. Any part of this store can be transferred in blocks of 512 words to/from the main core store, which consists of four separate stacks, each stack having a capacity of 4096 words.

The tape system provides a very large capacity backing store for the machine. The user can effect transfers of variable amounts of information between this store and the central store. In actual fact such transfers are organized by a fixed store program which initiates automatic transfers of blocks of 512 words between the tape store and the main core store. The system can handle eight tape decks running simultaneously, each producing or demanding a word on average every 88 μsec.

The main core store address can thus be provided from either the central machine, the drum, or the tape system. Since there is no synchronization between these addresses, there has to be a priority system to allocate addresses to the core store. The drum has top priority since it delivers a word every 4 μsec, the tape next

priority since words can arise every 11 μsec from 8 decks and the machine uses the core store for the rest of the available time. A priority system necessarily takes time to establish its priority, and so it has been arranged that it comes into effect only at each drum or tape request. Thus the machine is not slowed down in any way when no drum or tape transfers take place. The effect of drum and tape transfers on machine speed is given in Appendix 1.

To simplify the control commands given to the drum, tape, and peripheral equipment in the machine, the orders all take the form $b \rightarrow S$ or $s \rightarrow B$ and the identification of the required command register is provided by the address S. This type of storage is clearly widely scattered in the machine but is termed collectively the V-store.

In the central machine the main accumulator contains a fast adder [Kilburn, et al., 1960b] and has built-in multiplication and division facilities. It can deal with fixed or floating point numbers and its operation is completely independent of the B-store and B-arithmetic unit. The B-store is a fast core store (cycle time 0.7 μsec) of 120 twenty-four bit words operating in a word selected partial flux switching mode [Edwards et al., 1960]. Eight "fast" B lines are also provided in the form of flip-flop registers. Of these, three are used as control lines, termed main, extracode, and interrupt controls respectively. The arrangement has the advantage that the control numbers can be manipulated by the normal B-type orders, and the existence of three controls permits the machine to switch rapidly from one to another without having to transfer control numbers to the core store. Main control is used when the central machine is obeying the current program, while the extracode control is concerned with the fixed store subroutines. The interrupt control provides the means for handling numerous peripheral equipments which "interrupt" the machine when they either require or are providing information. The remaining "fast" B lines are mainly used for organizational procedures, though $B124$ is the floating point accumulator exponent.

The operating speed of the machine is of the order of 0.5×10^6 instructions per second. This is achieved by the use of fast transistor logic circuitry, rapid access to storage locations, and an extensive overlapping technique. The latter procedure is made possible by the provision of a number of intermediate buffer storage registers, separate access mechanisms to the individual units of core store and parallel operation of the main accumulator and B-arithmetic units. The word length throughout the machine is 48 bits which may be considered as two half-words of 24 bits each. All store transfers between the central machine, the drum and tape stores are parity checked, there being a parity digit associated with each half-word. In the case of transfers within the central store (*i.e.*, between main core store and drum) the parity digits associated with a given word are retained throughout the system. Tape transfers are parity checked when information is transferred to and from the main core store, and on the tape itself a check sum technique involving the use of two closely spaced heads is used.

The form of the instruction, which allows for two B-modifications, and the allocation of the address digits is shown in Fig. 2a. Half of the addressable store locations are allocated to the central store which is identified by a zero in the most significant digit of the address. (See Fig. 2b.) This address can be further subdivided into block address and line address in a block of 512 words. The least significant digits, 0 and 1, make it possible to address 6 bit characters in a half word and digit 2 specifies the half word.

The function number is split into several sections, each section relating to a particular set of operations, and these are listed in Fig. 2c. The machine orders fall into two broad classes, and these are:

1　B *codes*: These involve operations between a B line specified by the B_A digits in the instruction and a core store line whose address can be modified by the contents of a B line determined by the B_m digits. There are a total of 128 B lines, one of which, B_0, always contains zero. Of the other lines 90 are available to the machine user, 7 are special registers previously mentioned, and a further 30 are used by extracode orders.

2　A *Codes*: These involve operations between the Accumulator and a core store line whose address can now be doubly modified first by contents of B_m and then by the contents of B_A. Both fixed and floating point orders are provided, and in the latter case numbers take the form of $X8^Y$, the digit allocation of X and Y being shown in Fig. 2d. When fixed point working occurs, use is made only of the X digits.

3.　One-Level Store Concept

The choice of system for the fast access store in a large scale computer is governed by a number of conflicting factors which include speed and size requirements, economic and technical difficulties. Previously the problem has been resolved in two extreme cases either by the provision of a very large core store, e.g., the 2.5 megabit [Papian, 1957] store at M.I.T., or by the use of a small core store (40,000 bits) expanded to 640,000 bits by a drum store as in the Ferranti Mercury [Lonsdale and Warburton, 1956; Kilburn et al., 1956] computer. Each of these methods has its disadvantages, in the first case, that of expense, and in the second case, that of inconvenience to the user, who is obliged to program transfers of information between the two types of store and this can be time consuming. In some instances it is possible for an expert machine user to arrange his program so that the amount of time lost by the transfers in the two-level storage

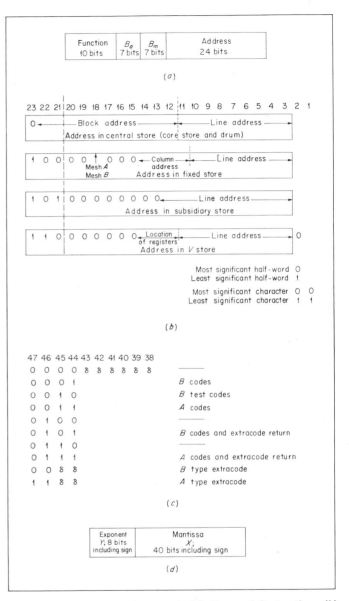

Fig. 2. Interpretation of a word. (a) Form of Instruction. (b) Allocation of address digits. (c) Function of decoding. (d) Floating-point number X8^y.

arrangement is not significant, but this sort of "optimum" programming is not very desirable. Suitable interpretative coding [Brooker, 1960] can permit the two-level system to appear as one level. The effect is, however, accompanied by an effective loss of machine speed which, in some programs and depending on details of machine design, can be quite severe, varying typically, for example, between one and three.

The two-level storage scheme has obvious economic advantages, and inconvenience to the machine user can be eliminated by making the transfer arrangements completely automatic. In Atlas a completely automatic system has been provided with techniques for minimizing the transfer times. In this way the core and drum are merged into an apparent single level of storage with good performance and at moderate cost. Some details of this arrangement on the Muse are now provided.

The central store is subdivided into blocks of 512 words as shown by the address arrangements in Fig. 2b. The main core store is also partitioned into blocks of this size which for identification purposes are called pages. Associated with each of these core store page positions is a "page address register" (P.A.R.) which contains the address of the block of information at present occupying that page position. When access to any word in the central store is required, the digits of the demanded block address are compared with the contents of all the page address registers. If an "equivalence" indication is obtained, then access to that particular page position is permitted. Since a block can occupy any one of the 32 page positions in the core store, it is necessary to modify some digits of the demanded block address to conform with the page positions in which an equivalence was obtained.

These processes are necessarily time consuming but by providing a by-pass of this procedure for instruction accesses (since, in general, instruction loops are all contained in the same block) then most of this time can be overlapped with a useful portion of the machine or core store rhythm. In this way information in the core store is available to the machine at the full speed of the core store and only rarely is the over-all machine speed affected by delays in the equivalence circuitry.

If a "not equivalence" indication is obtained when the demanded block address is compared with the contents of the P.A.R.'s, then that address, which may have been B-modified, is first stored in a register which can be accessed as a line of the V-store. This permits the central machine easy access to this address. An "interrupt" also occurs which switches operation of the machine over to the interrupt control, which first determines the cause of the interrupt and then, in this instance, enters a fixed store routine to organize the necessary transfers of information between drum and core store.

A. Drum Transfers

On each drum, one track is used to identify absolute block positions around the drum periphery. The records on these tracks are read into the θ registers which can be accessed as lines of the V-store and this permits the present angular drum position to be determined, though only in units of one block. In this way the time needed to transfer any block while reading from the drums

can be assessed. This time varies between 2 and 14 msec since the drum revolution time is 12 msec and the actual transfer time 2 msec.

The time of a writing transfer to the drums has been reduced by writing the block of information to the first available empty block position on any drum. Thus the access time of the drum can be eliminated provided there are a reasonable number of empty blocks on the drum. This means, however, that transfers to/from the drum have to be carried out by reference to a directory and this is stored in the subsidiary store and up-dated whenever a transfer occurs.

When the drum transfer routine is entered the first action is to determine the absolute position on a drum of the required block. The order is then given to carry out the transfer to an empty page position in the core store. The transfer occurs automatically as soon as the drum reaches the correct angular position. The page address register in the vacant position in the core store is set to a specific block number for drum transfers. This technique simplifies the engineering with regard to the provision of this number from the drum and also provides a safeguard against transferring to the wrong block.

As soon as the order asking for a read transfer from the drum has been given, the machine continues with the drum transfer program. It is now concerned with determining a block to be transferred back from the core store to the drum. This is necessary to ensure an empty core store page position when the next read transfer is required. The block in the core store to be transferred has to be carefully chosen to minimize the number of transfers in the program and this optimization process is carried out by a learning program, details of which are given in Sec. 5. The operation of this program is assisted by the provision of the "use" digits which are associated with each page position of the core store.

To interchange information between the core store and drums, two transfers, a read from and a write to the drum, are necessary. These have to be done sequentially but could occur in either order. The technique of having a vacant page position in the core store permits a read transfer to occur first and thus allows the time for the learning program to be overlapped either into the waiting period for the read transfer or into the transfer time itself. In the time remaining after completion of the learning program an entry is made into the over-all supervisor program for the machine, and a decision is taken concerning what the machine is to do until the drum transfer is completed. This might involve a change to a different main program.

A program could ask for access to information in a page position while a drum or tape transfer is taking place to that page. This is prevented in Atlas by the use of a "lock out" (L.O.) digit which is provided with each Page Address Register. When a lock out digit is set at 1, access to that page is permitted only when the address has been provided either by the drum system, the tape system, or the interrupt control. The last case permits all transfers from paper tape, punched card, and other peripheral equipments, to be handled without interference from the main program. When the transfer of a block has been completed, the organizing program resets the L.O. digit to zero and access to that page position can then be made from the central machine. It is clear that the L.O. digit can also be used to prevent interference between programs when several different ones are being held in the machine at the same time.

In Sec. 3 it was stated that addresses demanding access to the core store could arise from three distinct sources, the central machine, the drum, and the tape. These accesses are complicated because of (1) the equivalence technique, and (2) the lock out digit. The various cases and the action that takes place are summarized in Table 1.

The provision of the Page Address Registers, the equivalence circuitry, and the learning program have permitted the core store and drum to be regarded by the ordinary machine user as a one-level store, and the system has the additional feature of "floating address" operation, i.e., any block of information can be stored in any absolute position in either core or drum store. The minimum access time to information in this store is obviously limited by the core store and its arrangement, and this is now discussed.

B. Core Store Arrangement

The core store is split into four stacks, each with individual address decoding and read and write mechanisms. The stacks are then combined in such a way that common channels into the machine for the address, read and write digits, are time shared between the various stacks. Sequential address positions occur in two stacks alternately and a page position which contains a block of 512 sequential addresses is thus arranged across two stacks. In this way it is possible to read a pair of instructions from consecutive addresses in parallel by increasing the size of the read channel. This permits two instructions to be completely obeyed in three store "accesses." The choice of this particular storage arrangement is discussed in Appendix 2.

The coordination of these four stacks is done by the "core stack coordinator" and some features of this are now discussed, starting with the operation of a single stack.

C. Operation of a Single Stack of Core Store

The storage system employed is a coincident current M.I.T. system arranged to give parallel read out of 50 digits. The reading operation is destructive and each read phase of the stack cycle is followed by a write phase during which the information read out may be rewritten. This is achieved by a set of digit staticizors which are loaded during the read phase and are used to control the inhibit current drivers during the write phase. When new information is to be written into the store, a similar sequence is followed, except that the digit staticizors are loaded with the new information during the read phase. A diagram indicating the different types of stack cycle is shown in Fig. 3.

There is a small delay W_D ($\simeq$100 nsec) between the "stack request" signal, SR, and the start of the read phase to allow for setting of the address state and the address decoding. The output information from the store appears in the read strobe period, which is towards the end of the read phase. In general, the write phase starts as soon as the read phase ends. However, the start of the write phase may be held up until the new information is available from the central machine. This delay is shown as W_w in Fig. 3c. The interval T_A between the stack request and the read strobe is termed the stack access time, and in practice this is approximately one-third of the cycle time T_C. Both T_A and T_C are functions of the storage system and assuming that W_w is zero have typical values of 0.7 μsec and 1.9 μsec respectively. A holdup gate in the request channel prevents the next stack request occurring before the end of the preceding write phase.

D. Operation of the Main Core Store with the Central Machine

A schematic diagram of the essentials of the main core store control system is shown in Fig. 4. The control signals SA_1 and SA_2 indicate whether the address presented is that of a single word or a pair of sequentially addressed instructions. Assuming that the flip-flop F is in the reset condition, either of these signals results in the loading of the buffer address register (B.A.R.). This loading is done by the signal B.A.B.A. which also indicates that the buffer register in the central machine has become free.

In dealing with the first request the block address digits in the B.A.R. are compared with the contents of all the page address registers. Then one of the indications summarized in Table 1 and

Table 1   Comparison of Demanded Block Address with Contents of the P.A.R.'s Resultant State of Equivalence and Lock Out Circuits

Source of address	{*Equivalence* } {*Lock out = 0* } [*E.Q.*]	*Not equivalence* [*N.E.Q.*]	{*Equivalence* } {*Lock out = 1*} [*E.Q. & L.O.*]
1. Central Machine	Access to required page position	Enter drum transfer routine	Not available to this program
2. Drum System	Access to required page position	Fault condition indicated	Fault condition indicated
3. Tape System	Access to required page position	Fault condition indicated	Fault condition indicated

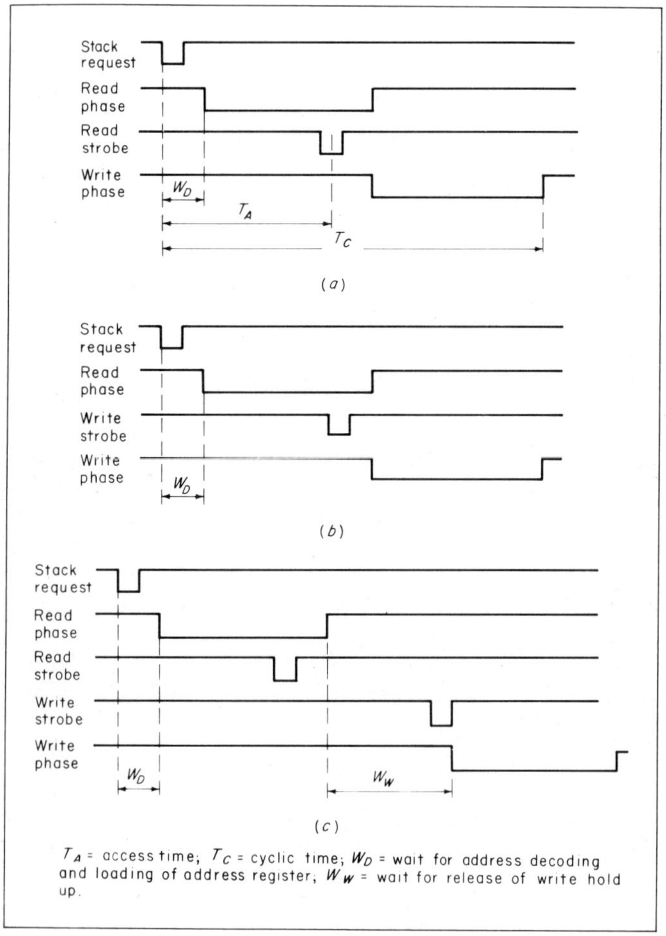

T_A = access time; T_C = cyclic time; W_D = wait for address decoding and loading of address register, W_W = wait for release of write hold up.

Fig. 3. Basic types of stack cycle (*a*) Read order (s→A). (*b*) Write order (a→s). (*c*) Read-write order (b + s→S).

indicated in Fig. 4 is obtained. Assuming access to the required store stack is permitted, then a set C.S.F. signal is given which resets the flip-flop *F*. If this occurs before the next access request arises, then the speed of the system is not store-limited. In most cases SET CSF is generated when the equivalence operation on the demanded block address is complete, and the read phase of the appropriate stack (or stacks) has started. Until this time the information held in the B.A.R. must not be allowed to change. In Fig. 5 a flow diagram is shown for the various cases which can arise in practice.

When a single address request is accepted, it is necessary to obtain an "equivalence" indication and form the page location digits before the stack request can be generated. The SET CSF signal then occurs as soon as the read phase starts. If a "not equivalent" or "equivalent and locked out" indication is obtained, a

stack request is not generated and the contents of the B.A.R. are copied in to a line of the *V*-store before SET CSF is generated.

When access to a pair of addresses is requested (i.e., an instruction pair), the stack requests are generated on the assumption that these instructions are located in the same page position as the last pair requested, i.e., the page position digits are taken from the page digit register. (See Fig. 4.) In this way the time required to obtain the equivalent indication and form the page location digits is not included in the over-all access time of the

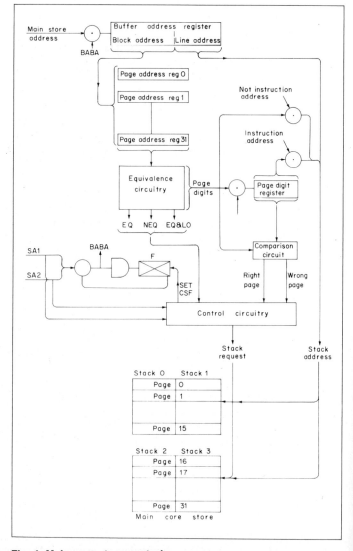

Fig. 4. Main core store control.

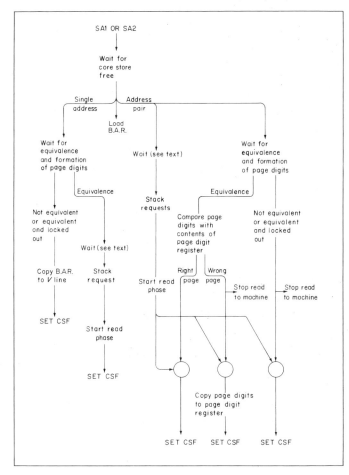

Fig. 5. Flow diagram of main core store control.

system. The assumption will normally be true, except when crossing block boundaries. The latter cases are detected and corrected by comparing the true position page digits obtained as a result of the equivalence operation with the contents of the page digit register, and a "right page" or "wrong page" indication is obtained. (See Fig. 4.) If a wrong page is accessed this is indicated to the central machine and the read out is inhibited. The true page location digits are copied into the page digit register, so that the required instruction pair will be obtained when next requested. The read out to the central machine is also inhibited for "not equivalent" or "equivalent and locked out" indications.

In Fig. 5 the waiting time indicated immediately before the stack request is generated can arise for a number of reasons:

1 The preceding write phase of that stack has not yet finished.

2 The central machine is not yet ready either to accept information from the store or to supply information to it.

3 It is necessary to ensure a certain minimum time between successive read strobes from the core stacks to allow satisfactory operation of the parity circuits, which take about 0.4 μsec to check the information. This time could be reduced, but as it is only possible to get such a condition for a small part of the normal instruction timing cycle it was not thought to be an economical proposition.

The basic machine timing is now discussed.

4. Instruction Times

In high-speed computers, one of the main factors limiting speed of operation is the store cycle time. Here a number of techniques, e.g., splitting the core store into four separate stacks and extracting two instructions in a single cycle, have been adopted despite a fast basic cycle time of 2 μsec in order to alleviate this situation. The time taken to complete an instruction is dependent upon

1 The type of instruction (which is defined by the function digits)

2 The exact location of the instruction and operand in the core or fixed store since this can affect the access time

3 Whether or not the operand address is to be modified

4 In the case of floating point accumulator orders, the actual numbers themselves

5 Whether drum and/or tape transfers are taking place

The approximate times for various instructions are given in Table 2. These figures relate to the times between completing instructions when a long sequence of the same type of instruction is obeyed. While this method is not ideal, it is necessary because in practice obeying one instruction is overlapped in time with some part of three other instructions. This makes the detailed timing complicated, and so the timing sequence is developed slowly by first considering instructions obeyed one after another. It is convenient to make these instructions a sequence of floating point additions with both instruction and operand in the core store and with the operand address single B-modified.

To obey this instruction the central machine makes two requests to the core store, one for the instruction and the second for the operand. After the instruction is received in the machine the function part has to be decoded and the operand address modified by the contents of one of the B registers before the operand request can be made. Finally, after the operand has been obtained the actual accumulator addition takes place to complete

Table 2   Approximate Instruction Times

Type of instruction	Number of modifications of address	Instruction in core store. Operands in core store. Time (μsec)	Instructions in fixed store. Operands in core store. Time (μsec)	Instructions in fixed store. Operands in fixed store. Time (μsec)
Floating Point Addition	0	1.4	1.65	1.2
	1	1.6	1.65	1.2
	2	2.03	1.9	1.9
Floating Point Multiplication	0, 1 or 2	4.7	4.7	4.7
Floating Point Division	0, 1 or 2	13.6	13.6	13.6
Add Store Line to an Index Register	0	1.53	1.65	1.15
	1	1.85	1.85	1.85
Add Index Register to Store Line and Rewrite to Store Line	0	1.63	1.65	
	1	1.8	1.7	

the instruction. The time from beginning to end of one instruction is 6.05 μsec and an approximate timing schedule is as follows in Table 3.

If no other action is permitted in the time required to complete the instruction (steps 1 to 8 in Table 3), then the different sections of the machine are being used very inefficiently, e.g., the accumulator adder is used only for less than 1.1 μsec. However, the organization of the computer is such that the different sections,

Table 3†   Timing Sequence for Floating Point Addition (Instructions and Operands in the Core Store)

Sequence	Time interval between steps (μsec)	Total time (μsec)
1. Add 1 to Main Control		0
(Addition time)	0.3	
2. Make Instruction Request		0.3
(Transfer times, equivalence time and stack access time)	1.75	
3. Receive Instruction in Central Machine		2.05
(Load register and decode)	0.2	
4. Function decoding complete		2.25
(Single address modification)	0.85	
5. Request Operand		3.10
(Transfer times, equivalence time and stack access time)	1.75	
6. Receive Operand in Central Machine		4.85
(Load register)	0.1	
7. Start Addition in Accumulator		4.95
(Average floating point addition, including shift round and standardise)	1.1	
8. Instruction complete		6.05

†In step 4, time is for single address modification. Times for no modification and two modifications are 0.25 μsec and 1.55 μsec respectively.

such as store stacks, accumulator and *B*-arithmetic unit, can operate at the same time. In this way several instructions can be started before the first has finished, and then the effective instruction time is considerably reduced. There have, of course, to be certain safeguards when, for example, an instruction is dependent in any way on the completion of a preceding instruction.

In the time sequence previously tabulated, by far the longest time was that between a request in the central machine for the core store and the receipt in the central machine of the information from that store. This effective access time of 1.75 μsec is made up as shown in Table 4. It has been reduced in practice by the provision of two buffer registers, one in the central machine and the other in the core stack coordinator. These allow the equivalence and transfer times to be overlapped with the organization of requests in the central machine.

In this way, provided the machine can arrange to make requests fast enough, then the effective access time is reduced to 0.8 μsec. Further, since three accesses are needed to complete two instructions (one for an instruction pair and one for each of the two operands) the theoretical minimum time of an instruction is 1.2 μsec $3 \times 0.8/2$ and it then becomes store limited. Reference to Table 3 shows that the arithmetic operation takes 1.2 μsec to

Table 4   Effective Store Access Time

Sequence	Total time (μsec)
1. Request in Central Machine	0
2. Request in Core Stack Coordinator	0.25
3. Equivalence complete and request made to selected stack	0.95
4. Information in Core Stack Coordinator	1.65
5. Information in Central Machine	1.75

complete so that, on the average, the capabilities of the store and the accumulator are well matched.

Another technique for reducing store access time for instructions has also been adopted. This permits the read cycles of the two stacks to start assuming that the same page will be referred to as in the previous instruction pair. This, of course, will normally be true and there is sufficient time to take corrective procedures should the page have been changed. The limit of 1.2 μsec per instruction is not reduced by this technique, but the possibility of reaching this limit under other conditions is enhanced.

A schematic diagram of the practical timing of a sequence of floating point addition orders is shown in Fig. 6. The overlapping is not perfect and in the time between successive instruction pairs the computer is obeying four instructions for 25 per cent of the time, three for 56 per cent and two for 19 per cent. It is therefore to be expected that the practical time for the complete order is greater than the theoretical minimum time; it is in fact approximately 1.6 μsec.

For certain types of functions the reading of the next pair of instructions before completing both instructions of the first pair would be incorrect, e.g., functions causing transfer of control. Such situations are recognized during the function decoding, and the request for the next instruction pair is held up until a suitable time.

In a sequence of floating point addition orders with the operand addresses unmodified the limit is again 1.2 μsec while the time obtained is 1.4 μsec. For accumulator orders in which the actual accumulator operation imposes a limit in excess of 2 μsec then the actual time is equal to this limit.

Perhaps a more realistic way of defining the speed of the computer is to give the time for a typical inner loop of instructions. A frequently occurring operation in matrix work in the formation of the scalar product of two vectors, this requires a loop of five instructions:

1   Element of first vector into accumulator. (Operand *B*-modified.)

2   Multiply accumulator by element of second vector. (Operand *B*-modified.)

3   Add partial product to accumulator.

4   Copy accumulator to store line containing partial product.

5   Alter count to select next elements and repeat.

The time for this loop with instructions and operands on the core store is 12.2 μsec. The value of the overlapping technique is shown by the fact that the time from starting the first instruction to finishing the second is approximately 10 μsec.

When the drum or tape systems are transferring information to or from the core store, then the rate of obeying instructions which also use the core store will be affected. The affect is discussed in more detail in Appendix 1. The degree of slowing down is dependent upon the time at which a drum or tape request occurs relative to machine requests. It also depends on the stacks used by the drum or tape and those being used by the central machine. The approximate slowing down is by a factor of 25 per cent during a drum transfer and by 2 per cent for each active tape channel. (See Appendix 1.)

5.   The Drum Transfer Learning Program

The organization of drum transfers has been described in Sec. 2A. After the transfer of the required block from the drum to the core

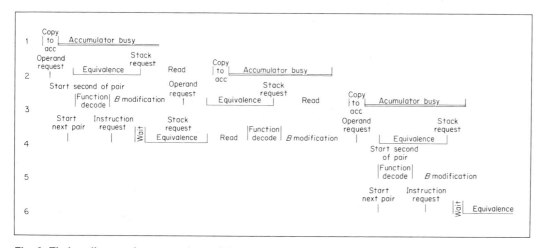

Fig. 6. Timing diagram for a sequence of floating point addition orders. (Single-address modification.)

store has been initiated, the organizing program examines the state of the core store, and if empty pages still exist, no further action is taken. However, if the core store is full, it is necessary to arrange for an empty page to be made available for use at the next nonequivalence. The selection of the page to be transferred could be made at random; this could easily result in many additional transfers occuring, as the page selected could be one of those in current use or one required in the near future. The ideal selection, which would minimize the total number of transfers, could only be made by the programmer. To make this ideal selection the programmer would have to know (1) precisely how his program operated, which is not always the case, and (2) the precise amount of core store available to his program at any instant. This latter information is not generally available as the core store could be shared by other central machine programs, and almost certainly by some fixed store program organizing the input and output of information from slow peripheral equipments. The amount of core store required by this fixed store program is continuously varying [Kilburn et al., 1961]. The only way the ideal pattern of transfers can be approached is for the transfer program to monitor the behavior of the main program and in so doing attempt to select the correct pages to be transferred to the drum. The techniques used for monitoring are subject to the condition that they must not slow down the operation of the program to such an extent that they offset any reduction in the number of transfers required. The method described occupies less than 1 percent of the operating time, and the reduction in the number of transfers is more than sufficient to cover this.

That part of the transfer program which organizes the selection of the page to be transferred has been called the "learning" program. In order for this program to have some data on which to operate, the machine has been designed to supply information about the use made of the different pages of the core store by the program being monitored.

With each page of the core store there is associated a "use" digit which is set to "1" whenever any line in that page is accessed. The 32 "use" digits exist in two lines of the V-store and can be read by the learning program, the reading automatically resetting them to zero. The frequency with which these digits are read is governed by a clock which measures not real time but the number of instructions obeyed in the operation of the main program. This clock causes the learning program to copy the "use" digits to a list in the subsidiary store every 1024 instructions. The use of an instruction counter rather than a normal clock to measure "time" for the learning program is due to the fact that the operations of the main program may be interrupted at random for random lengths of time by the operation of peripheral equipments. With an instruction counter the temporal pattern of the blocks used will be the same on successive runs through the same part of the program. This is essential if the learning program is to make use of this pattern to minimize the number of transfers.

When a nonequivalence occurs and after the transfer of the required block has been arranged, the learning program again adds the current values of the "use" digits to the list and then uses this list to bring up to date two sets of times also kept in the subsidiary store. These sets consist of 32 values of t and T, one of each for each page of the core store. The value of t is the length of time since the block in that page has been used. The value of T is the length of the last period of inactivity of this block. The accuracy of the values of t and T is governed by the frequency with which the "use" digits are inspected.

The page to be written to the drum is selected by the application in turn of three simple tests to the values of t and T:

1   Any page for which $t > T + 1$, or

2   That page with $t \neq 0$ and $(T - t)$ max, or

3   That page with T_{max} (all $t = 0$).

The first rule selects any page which has been currently out of use for longer than its last period of inactivity. Such a page has probably ceased to be used by the program and is therefore an ideal one to be transferred to the drum. The second rule ignores all pages with $t = 0$ as they are in current use, and then selects the one which, if the pattern of use is maintained, will not be required by the program for the longest time. If the first two rules fail to select a page, the third ensures that if the page finally selected is wrong, in that it is immediately required again; then, as in this case, T will become zero and the same mistake will not be repeated.

For all the blocks on the drum a list of values of τ is kept. The values of τ are set when the block is transferred to the drum:

τ = time of transfer − value of t for transferred page

When a block is transferred to the core store, the value of τ is used to set the value of T.

T = time of transfer − value of τ for this block
= length of last period of inactivity

for the block transferred from the drum t is set to 0.

In order to make its decision the learning program has only to update two short lists and apply at the most three simple rules; this can easily be done during the 2 msec transfer time of the block required as a result of the nonequivalence. As the learning program uses only fixed and subsidiary store addresses, it is not slowed down during the period of the drum transfer.

The over-all efficiency of the learning program cannot be known until the complete Atlas system is working. However, the value of the method used has been investigated by simulating the behavior of the one-level store and learning program on the Mercury computer at Manchester University. This has been done for several problems using varying amounts of store in excess of the core store available. One of these was the problem of forming the product A of two 80th order matrices B and C. The three matrices were stored row by row, each one extending over 14 blocks; only 14 pages of core store were assumed to be available. The method of multiplication was

b_{11} × 1st row of C = partial answer to 1st row of A

b_{12} × 2nd row of C + partial answer = second partial answer, etc.

Thus matrix B was scanned once, matrix C 80 times and each row of matrix A 80 times.

Several machine users were asked to spend a short time writing a program to organize the transfers for a general matrix multiplication problem. In no case when the method was applied to the above problem were fewer than 357 transfers required. A program written specifically for this problem which paid great attention to the distribution of the rows of the matrices relative to block divisions required 234 transfers. The learning program required 274 transfers; the gain over the human programmer was chiefly due to the fact that the learning program could take full advantage of the occasions when the rows of A existed entirely within one block.

Many other problems involving cyclic running of single or multiple sets of data were simulated, and in no case did the learning program require more transfers than an experienced human programmer.

A. Prediction of Drum Transfers

Although the learning program tends to reduce the number of transfers required to a minimum, the transfers which do occur still interrupt the operation of the program for from 2 to 14 msec as they are initiated by nonequivalence interrupts. Some or all of this time loss could be avoided by organizing the transfers in advance. A very experienced programmer having sole use of the core store could arrange his own transfers in such a way that no unnecessary ones ever occurred and no time was ever wasted waiting for transfers to be completed. This would require a great deal of effort and would only be worthwhile for a program that was going to occupy the machine for a long time. By using the data accumulated by the learning program it is possible to recognize simple patterns in the use made by a program of the various blocks of the one-level store. In this way a prediction program could forecast the blocks required in the near future and organize the transfers. By recording the success or failure of these forecasts the program could be made self-improving. For the matrix multiplication problem discussed above the pattern of use of the blocks containing matrix C is repeated 80 times, and a considerable degree of success could be obtained with a simple prediction program.

6. Conclusions

A specific system for making a core-drum store combination appear as a single level store has been described. While this is the actual system being built for the Atlas machine the principles involved are applicable to combinations of other types of store, for example, a tunnel diode–fast core store combination for an even faster machine. An alternative which was considered for Atlas, but which was not as attractive economically, was a fast core–slow core store combination. The system too can be extended to three levels of storage, and indeed if 10^6 words of total storage had to be provided then it would be most economical to provide it on a third level of store such as a file drum.

The automatic system does require additional equipment and introduces some complexity, since it is necessary to overlap the time taken for address comparison into the store and machine operating time if it is not to introduce any extra time delays. Simulated tests have shown that the organization of drum transfers are reasonably efficient and other advantages which accrue, such as efficient allocation of core storage between different programs and store lock out facilities, are also invaluable. No matter how intelligent a programmer may be, he can never know how many programs or peripheral equipments are in operation when his program is running. The advantage of the automatic system is that it takes into account the state of the machine as it exists at any particular time. Furthermore if as in normal use there is some sort of regular machine rhythm even through several programs, there is the possibility of making some sort of prediction with regard to the transfers necessary. This involves no more hardware and will be done by program. However, this stage will probably be left until results on the actual system are obtained.

It can be seen that the system is both useful and flexible in that it can be modified or extended in the manner previously indicated. Thus despite the increase in equipment, the advantages which are derived completely justify the building of this automatic system.

APPENDIX 1   ORGANIZATION OF THE ACCESS REQUESTS TO THE CORE STORE

There are three sources of access requests to the core store, namely the central machine, the drum, and the tape systems. In deciding how the sequence of requests from all three sources are to be serialized and placed in some sort of order, a number of facts have to be considered. These are

1   All three sources are asynchronous in nature.

2   The drum and tape systems can make requests at a fairly high rate compared with the store cycle time of approxi-

mately 2 μsec. For example, the drum provides a request every 4 μsec and the tape system every 11 μsec when all 8 channels are operative.

3   The drum and tape systems can be stopped only in multiples of a block length, i.e., 512 words. This means that any system devised for accessing the core store must deal with both the average rates of drum and tape requests specified in 2. Only the central machine can tolerate requests being stopped at any time and for any length of time. From these facts a request priority can be stated which is

a   Drum request.

b   Tape request.

c   Central machine request.

4   A machine request can be accepted by the core store, but because there is no place available to accept the core store information, its cycle is inhibited and further requests held up. In the case of successive division orders this time can be as long as 20 μsec, in which case 5 drum requests could be made. To avoid having an excessive amount of buffer storage for the drum two techniques are possible:

a   When drums or tapes are operative do not permit machine requests to be accepted until there is a place available to put the information.

b   Store the machine request and then permit a drum or tape request.
    The latter scheme has been adopted because it can be accommodated more conveniently and it saves a small amount of time.

5   If the central machine is using the private store then it is desirable for drum and tape transfers to the core store not to interfere with or slow down the central machine in any way.

6   When the central machine, drum and tape are sharing the core store, then the loss of central machine speed should be roughly proportional to the activity of the drum or tape systems. This means that drum or tape requests must "break" into the normal machine request channel as and when required.

The system which accommodates all these points is now discussed. Whenever a drum or tape request occurs, inhibit signals are applied to request channel into the core stack coordinator. This results in a "freezing" of the state of flip-flop F (Fig. 5) and this state is then inspected (Fig. 7, point X). If the state is "busy" this means that a machine order has been stopped somewhere between the loading of the buffer address register (B.A.R.) and the stack request. Normally this time interval can vary from about 0.5 μsec if there are no stack request holdups to 20 μsec in the case of certain accumulator holdups. In either case

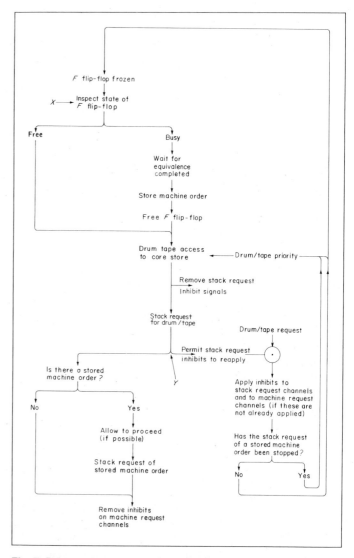

Fig. 7. Drum and tape break in systems.

sufficient time is allowed after the inspection to ensure that the equivalence operation has been completed. If an equivalence indication is obtained, all the information relevant to this machine order (i.e., the line address, page digits, stack(s) required and type of stack order) are stored for future reference. Use is made here of the page digit register provided to allow the by-pass on the equivalence circuitry for instruction accesses. The core store is then made free for access by the drum or the tape. If the core store is found to be free on inspection, the above procedure is omitted.

A drum or tape access (as decided by the priority circuit) to the core store then occurs, which removes the inhibits on the stack request channels. When the stack request for the drum or tape cycle is initiated, these inhibits are allowed to reapply. At this stage (Fig. 7, point *Y*), if there is a stored machine order it is allowed to proceed if possible. The inhibits on the machine request channels are removed when the stack request for the stored machine order occurs. If there is no stored machine order, this is done immediately, and the central machine is again allowed access to the core store. However, another drum or tape request can arise before the stack request of the stored machine order occurs, in particular because this latter order may still be held up by the central machine. If this is the case the drum or tape is allowed immediate access and a further attempt is made to complete the stored machine order when this drum or tape stack request occurs.

If the stored machine order is for an operand, the content of the page digit register will correspond to the location of this operand. The next machine request for an instruction pair will then almost certainly result in a "wrong page" indication. This is prevented by arranging that the next instruction pair access does not by-pass the equivalence circuitry.

The effect on the machine speed when the drum or tapes are transferring information to or from the core store is dependent upon two factors. First, upon the proportion of time during which the buffer register in the core coordinator is busy dealing with machine requests, and second, upon the particular stacks being used by the central machine and the drum or tape. If the computer is obeying a program with instructions and operands on the fixed or subsidiary store, then the rate of obeying instructions is unaffected by drum or tape transfers. A drum or tape interrupt occurring when the B.A.R. is free prevents any machine address being accepted onto this buffer for 1.0 μsec. However, if the B.A.R. is busy then the next machine request to the core store is delayed until 1.8 μsec after the interrupt if different stacks are being used, or until 3.4 μsec after the interrupt if the stacks are the same.

When the machine is obeying a program with instructions and operands on the core store, the slowing down during drum transfers can be by a factor of two if instructions, operands, and drum requests use the same stacks. It is also possible for the machine to be unaffected. The effect on a particular sequence of orders can be seen by considering the one discussed in Sec. 4 and illustrated in Fig. 6. In this sequence the instructions are on stacks 0 and 1 while the operands are on stacks 2 and 3. If the drum or tape is transferring alternately to stacks 0 and 1 then the effect of any interrupt within the 3.2 μsec of an instruction pair is to increase this time by between 0.5 and 3.4 μsec depending upon where the interrupt occurred. The average increase is 1.8 μsec and for a tape transfer with interrupts every 88 μsec the computer can obey instructions at 98 percent of the normal rate. During drum transfers the interrupts occur every 4 μsec, which would

suggest a slowing down to 60 per cent of normal. However, for any regular sequence of orders the requests to the core store by the machine and by the drum rapidly become synchronized with the result in this particular case that the machine can still operate at 80 percent of its normal speed.

APPENDIX 2   METHODS OF DIVISION OF THE MAIN CORE STORE

The maximum frequency with which requests can be dealt by a single stack core store is governed by the cycle time of the store. If the store is divided into several stacks which can be cycled independently, then the limit imposed on the speed of the machine by the core store is reduced. The degree of division which is chosen is dependent upon the ratio of core store cycle time to other machine operations and also upon the cost of the multiple selection mechanisms required.

Considering a sequence of orders in which both the instruction and operand are in the core store, then for a single stack store the limit imposed on the operating speed by the store is two cycle times per order, i.e., 4 μsec is Atlas. This is significantly larger than the limits imposed by other sections of the computer (Sec. 4). If the store is divided into two stacks and instructions and operands are separated, then the limit is reduced to 2 μsec which is still rather high. The provision of two stacks permits the addressing of the store to be arranged so that successive addresses are in alternate stacks. It is therefore possible by making requests to both stacks at the same time to read two instructions together, so reducing the number of access times to three per instruction pair. Unfortunately such an arrangement of the store means that operands are always on the same stacks as instruction pairs, and the limit imposed by the cycle time is still 2 μsec per order even if the two operand requests in the instruction pair are to different stacks and occur at the same time.

Division into any number of stacks with the addressing system working through each stack in turn cannot reduce the limit below 2 μsec since successive instructions normally occur in successive addresses and are therefore in the same stack. However, four stacks arranged in two pairs reduces the limit to 1 μsec as the operands can always be arranged to be on different stacks from the instruction pairs. In order to reduce the limit to 0.5 μsec it is necessary to have eight stacks arranged in two sets of four and to read four instructions at once, which would increase the complexity of the central machine.

The limit of 1 μsec is quite sufficient and further division with the stacks arranged in pairs only enables the limit to be more easily obtained by suitable location of the instructions and operands.

The location of instructions and operands within the core store is under the control of the drum transfer program, thus when

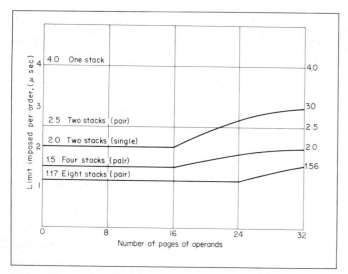

Fig. 8. Limit imposed by cycle time on operating speed for different divisions of the core store.

there are several stacks instructions and operands are separated wherever possible. Under these conditions it is possible to calculate the limit imposed on the operating speed by the cycle time for different divisions of the core store. The results are shown

in Fig. 8; for stacks arranged in pairs instructions are read in pairs and in all cases both instructions and operands are assumed to be on the core store. Operands are assumed to be selected at random from the operand space; for instance, in the case of two stacks arranged as a pair, successive operand requests have equal probability of belonging to the same stack or to alternate stacks.

The limit imposed by a four stack store is never severe compared with other limitations; for example, the sequence of floating point addition orders discussed in Sec. 4 required 1.6 μsec per order with ideal distribution of instructions and operands. Division into eight stacks, although it reduces the limit, will not have an equivalent effect on the over-all operating speed, and such a division was not considered to be justified.

References

Kilburn, Edwards, Lanigan, and Sumner [1962]; Brooker [1960]; Edwards, Lanigan, and Kilburn [1960]; Kilburn, Edwards, and Thomas [1956]; Kilburn, Edwards, and Aspinall [1960]; Kilburn and Grimsdale [1960]; Kilburn, Howarth, Payne, and Sumner [1961]; Lonsdale and Warburton [1956]; Papian [1957]; Fotheringham [1961]; Hartley [1968]; Howarth [1963]; Howarth, Jones, and Wyld [1962]; Howarth, Payne, and Sumner [1961]; Morris, Sumner, and Wyld [1967]; Sumner, Haley, and Chen [1962].

Part 2

Regions of Computer Space

Part 2 continues the development of the computer space by delving into details in eight regions of the computer space. Each section opens with a tabulation and discussion of the major subdimensions. The subdimension values are illustrated by actual computer systems, many of which are described in this book. The sections conclude with a series of chapters meant to illustrate various values of the subdimensions and how they correlate with values for other computer space dimensions in actual machines.

The chapters in Part 2 have been selected for their primary emphasis on a single region of computer space. Subsequently, Parts 3 and 4 will examine complete computer systems and treat all computer space dimensions equally.

Section 1 discusses the current major computer implementation technique: microprogramming. While this computer space region should properly be labeled "Implementation Techniques," microprogramming's popularity and richness deserve a separate treatment.

Section 2 examines the region of memory hierarchies and support of multiple processes. The concern for effective utilization of memory has impacted even the smallest microcomputers.

Concurrency to achieve high performance in single-processor systems is the subject of Sec. 3.

The advent of low-cost microcomputers has ignited substantial interest in multiple-processor systems. Section 4 discusses the various ways multiple processors can be interconnected and the important parameters for evaluating the effectiveness of the PMS structure. Three major categories of multiple-processor structures are identified and illustrated: tightly coupled multiprocessors communicating via address space; loosely coupled distributed multiprocessors communicating via messages, all Pc's working on one task; and networks communicating via messages, each Pc working on different tasks. Section 4 gives examples of the first two types of multiple-processor systems.

Network technology has advanced so significantly in the last decade that one section, Sec. 5, is devoted solely to the network region of the computer space.

The concern for reliable computing has been with us from the earliest days. The need for reliable computers continues as our dependency on computers grows. Now all but the smallest computers have introduced redundancy to improve system reliability and/or maintainability. The fault-tolerant region of computer space in Sec. 6 is one of the least well-formed of any treated in the book. However, this will change as more fault-tolerant systems are built and experience accumulates.

The final two sections of Part 2 discuss related regions of computer space. Section 7 examines computers intended to execute a single higher-level programming language. Since the programming environment is completely specified (in contrast with the open-ended environments found in general-purpose systems), design decisions can be made to favor specialization. Section 8 looks at another constrained environment, that of personal computers. Personal computing systems are dedicated to providing a rich, responsive programming environment to a single user.

Section 1

Microprogram-Based Processors

Microprogramming

Microprogramming is a form of emulation wherein one ISP is used to interpret a target ISP. The microprogramming ISP is usually kept more primitive than the target ISP in order to maintain an acceptable level of performance. Microprogramming can also be viewed as a technique that imposes an interpreter between the hardware and the target ISP. Since a microprogrammed ISP is similar to a conventional ISP that interprets macro-level programs, all the principles and techniques of ISP design apply. Increased performance, for example, is brought about by adding to the number of data-types (via hardwiring).

Conceptually, a computer can be divided into a data part and a control part. The data part is composed of registers, functional units, and interconnecting paths. The control part translates machine language instructions into an ordered sequence of control signals that manipulate the data part in order to realize the machine language instruction. A microprogrammed control part uses a stored program to generate the necessary control signals.

Figure 1 depicts a canonical microsequencer. Microinstructions are fetched from a microstore. Each microinstruction contains a set of bits for controlling the data path as well as information about where the next microinstruction is stored, which may vary according to the status of a portion of the data part. This sequencing of microinstructions provides the required sequencing of data-path functions. Microprogramming has many of the essential ingredients of programming, including branching, loops, and subroutines. However, microprogramming makes several concessions to hardware in order to achieve high performance. These concessions tie the microcode very closely to the hardware, thus increasing the complexity of microcoding over regular programming.

There are several advantages to using microprogramming to implement an ISP.

- Regularity. Microprogramming permits an orderly approach to control design. The microprogram is easy to debug and maintain. It makes the control easy to check via coding techniques (e.g., parity and Hamming code).

- Flexibility and tailorability. Microprogramming makes it possible to postpone detailed design decisions. New features can be added easily.

- Emulation. It allows interpreting other ISPs.

- Extensibility. An implementation can have its useful life

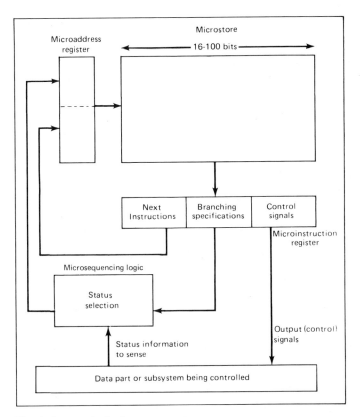

Fig. 1. A canonical microsequencer.

extended by the addition of new features (e.g., new instructions to increase functionality, portions of operating-system code to increase performance).

- Cost-effectiveness. Microprogramming can implement complex ISPs.

All these advantages do not come free. There are some disadvantages:

- Cost. There is a fixed overhead for microcoded control, which consists of the microsequencer and minimum microstore. Very simple ISPs are best implemented directly in hardware, since their complexity does not warrant the cost overhead of a microsequencer. The actual breakpoint between hardwired and microprogrammed control depends on the semantic content of the ISP and the relative technology cost of the two implementation approaches.

- Performance. A hardwired design will be faster than a microprogrammed design built from the same technology, since the former does not have the overhead of fetching and decoding of microinstructions.

With the current state of technology providing dense (i.e., with small package count) and low-cost ROM and RAM, the advantages of microprogramming far outweigh the disadvantages. Microprogramming is found in several significant computer families (IBM System/360 and System/370, Chaps. 40, 41, 51, and 52; PDP-11, Chap. 47), as well as in other diverse areas (e.g., hand calculators, Chap. 34; personal computers, Part 4, Sec. 3, and Chap. 33; and telephone switching computers, Chap. 28). It is interesting to note that the IBM System/360 family was planned around microprogramming at a time when ROM technology was not a cost-effective competitor with hardwired logic. But given the rate of technological change and the projected life of the System/360 family, the decision to use microprogramming was the correct one and acted as a pull to develop cost-effective read-only memory technology.

Dimensions of Microprogram Space

Table 1 depicts the dimensions of the microprogram space. Each dimension will be briefly discussed.

Microword Format. The single most important dimension is the form of the microword. If the word is fully encoded, so that each possible bit pattern specifies a single sequence of data-path operations (instructions), the microword format is called *vertical*. Vertical microwords tend to be short (i.e., 16 to 40 bits). Vertical microprogramming is very similar to regular programming because of its sequential nature.

Horizontal microwords are wide (i.e., 40 to 100 or more bits). Each subfield controls a data function directly, and all the operations specified by the various subfields can be executed in parallel. Horizontal microword subfields require little (if partially encoded) or no decoding, thus saving the time required by a decoding circuit. Note that even a 10-ns decoding circuit represents a significant overhead for a machine that executes microwords in 100 ns. Since horizontal microwords can also trigger several concurrent actions (if the data part supports concurrency), high-performance implementations almost always use a horizontal microword format.

Whereas vertical microprograms are characterized by long sequences of narrow microwords, horizontal microprograms are characterized by short, intertwined sequences of wide microwords. In either case, designers attempt to decrease the length of sequences (i.e., by the use of microsubroutines) and/or the width of microwords (i.e., by encoding mutually exclusive operations) in order to minimize the microstore size. There is some evidence that, for a given ISP, the microstore size measured in bits, regardless of implementation, is relatively constant when compared to variations in microstore size between different ISPs.[1]

---

[1]The S/370 microstore sizes range from 380 to 560 Kbit for implementations without operating-system support (Chap. 52). PDP-11 microstore sizes range from 10 to 23 Kbit (Chap. 39).

Table 1　Dimensions of the Microprogram Space

Microword format
  Vertical
    Completely encoded
  Horizontal
    Partially encoded
    No encoding
Microword decoding
  Static
  Dynamic
    Escape modes
    Residual control
Microword sequencing
  Microprogram counter
  Next microinstruction address field
Microword sequence alteration
  Microaddress alteration
    OR
    Add (relative branch offset)
  Jump
  Repeat until condition
  Return from subroutine
Microword constants
  ROM
  Emit field
Data-path concurrency
  Pipelining
  Multiple functional elements
  Multiple data paths
  Explicit bus control
Clocks
  One
  Multiple
Target instruction decoding
  Programmed
  Op code used as microroutine address
  ROM/PLA Branch Table
Modifications in microinstruction semantics
  Fields from instruction register modify data-path functions
    and/or choose general register.

Microword Decoding. In static decoding the subfields in a microword have only one meaning for each decoding. *Dynamic decoding*, in which a single subfield has multiple meanings, is one way to shrink the length of a microword. The different meanings can be triggered by the escape mode, a special decoding of some other field, or in residual control they can be determined by state in the micromachine set by the execution of a previous instruction.

Microword Sequencing. Microword sequencing can be provided by a microprogram counter that is analogous to the program counter at the programming level. Higher-performance machines, however, usually embed the address of the next microinstruction in the current microinstruction. This increases the size of the microword but also increases performance, since fetching of the next microinstruction does not have to wait for the update of a counter.[1]

Microword Sequence Alteration. Fast changes in microword sequencing are an absolute necessity, since they happen so frequently. The most prevalent method is to alter the next microinstruction address field by ORing in status bits left as the result of a previous operation. Other possibilities include adding, repeating a microword until a condition is met, jumping or branching, and fetching a previously stored address (e.g., return from microsubroutine).

Any conditioned sequence changes will introduce some programming complexity, as depicted in Fig. 2. In order to execute microinstructions as fast as possible, the fetch of the next microinstruction is overlapped with the execution of the current microinstruction (see Part 2, Sec. 3). Thus the condition code–setting information from the ALU operation of microinstruction 1 is available only after the fetch of microinstruction 2 has begun. Thus the first time the operation of microinstruction sequencing can be altered is in the fetch of microinstruction 3. Microprogram-

ming could be simplified (at the cost of performance) if microinstruction 2 were a null operation. Rather than lose the performance, microprogrammers attempt to set up the branch status at least one full microinstruction before the conditional branch.

Microword Constants. Another tradeoff between flexibility, speed, and microword width is the provision for constants. When emulating a target ISP, there will be key constants (e.g., the address of the program counter in a register file, masks for decoding, the number of a special memory location, and increments to a program counter) that have to be provided. These constants can be stored in a ROM addressed by a microword subfield (thereby incurring the delay of a ROM access) or by an immediate operand in a microword subfield called *emit*. The emit subfield is as wide as the widest desired constant and hence requires many more bits than are required to encode the number of different constants. If infrequently used, the emit field is a prime candidate for multiple-subfield definition via dynamic decoding.

Data-Path Concurrency. Performance can be increased via increased concurrency. In general the techniques discussed in Sec. 3, while targeted for the ISP level, can also be used at the microprogramming level. Figure 2 has already illustrated the overlap (pipelining) of microinstruction fetch and execution. Multiple operations can be triggered by the same microinstruction (e.g., an ALU function and program-counter update) if there are sufficient functional elements and data paths to support the concurrency. Overlap is also possible between the microprogrammed processor and Mp if the processor is given sufficient control over the bus (as opposed to the IBM System/360 Model 30, Chap.

[1]There are mechanisms of combinatorially implementing a counter so that the extra performance degradation is only that of a 6 to 10-gate delay rather than a ripple carry delay of 70 to 100 gates. It is also possible to overlap microprogram-counter update with microword fetch if the microprogram counter is double-buffered. In this case the only performance degradation is the execution of a branch instruction for nonsequential flow. Microcode sequences tend to be short; hence one out of every three or four instructions could be a branch, still severely impacting performance.

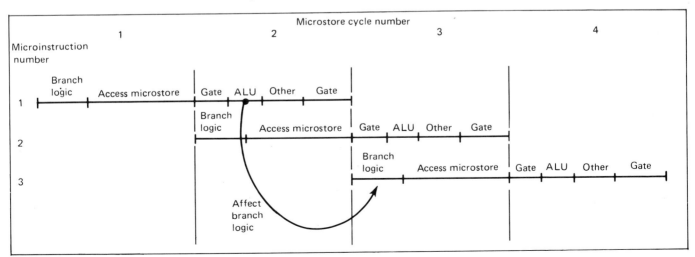

Fig. 2. Timing of a typical microsequence.

12, for example, which has only the primitives READ and WRITE).

Clocks. In the case of complex data paths there will be microoperations that do not require the worst-case time (usually defined by the time to transit the data-path loop completely) to execute. By having multiple-microcycle clocks selectable by the microinstruction, each microinstruction needs only specify the minimum time required to complete rather than the worst-case time. (See Chap. 39 for an example of the use of multiple clocks.)

Target-Instruction Decoding. The primary use of microprogramming is to emulate a target ISP. One of the most important aspects of emulation is quickly arriving at the unique microcode sequence required to emulate the target instruction. The sequence can be arrived at by sequentially testing bits of the op code (see Chap. 12), by using the op code as a unique microroutine address, or by using the op code to index a ROM or PLA containing the microroutine address (see Chapter 39).

Modification of Microinstruction Semantics. In order to minimize the number of microinstructions it is desirable to have the same microsequence perform operations parameterized by fields in the macroinstruction word. Prime macroinstruction candidates would be fields that specify an ALU function and fields that specify a register (see Sec. 3 in Part 3).

Examples of Microprogrammed Processors in This Book

Microprogramming and the Design of the Control Circuits in an Electronic Computer

Chapter 11 is an extension of an earlier paper by Wilkes. It includes an example of a microprogrammed processor. In the earlier paper, "The Best Way to Design an Automatic Computing Machine" [Wilkes, 1951], the essential ideas of microprogramming were first outlined.

The observation that an instruction set, or ISP, should be looked at as a program to be interpreted is the basis of microprogramming. The idea of an ISP is our acknowledgment that we, too, view a processor as a program.

There is little to say about this chapter; it is historical, yet timely and well written. Microprogramming, like others of Wilkes' ideas, is present in many of our computers.

IBM System/360 Model 30

Chapter 12 presents an example of an early microprogrammed implementation and should be contrasted with some of the later designs.

Bit-Sliced Microprogrammable Chip Sets

Bit-slice families usually have two major chip types: those dealing with data and those with control. Data chips contain ALUs, register files, and condition sensing. Control chips are usually microprogram sequencers that manipulate addresses (i.e., increment, select alternate source, and stack) rather than data. Bit slices are aimed at replacement of MSI implementations of existing ISPs and at application areas requiring large computational power (e.g., signal processing). Bit slices have some advantages over single-chip processors:

- *Flexibility.* Bit-sliced chips are cascadable, allowing the user to select the length of data and/or control fields. Bit slices may take n chips to realize the data-path width of a single processor. Thus there are n times as many pins available as in a single-chip processor (assuming the same packaging technology). These extra pins can be translated into more user visibility and control of the inside of each chip.
- *Speed.* Chip slices usually have smaller logic density per chip, which allows more power dissipation (hence speed) per function than a single-chip processor. Of course, the extra delay of off-chip signals and their frequency of use may negate some of this advantage.

Table 2 sketches the characteristics of some bit-slice processors.

Chapters 13 and 14 discuss the Am2900 bit-sliced processor family. The first-generation data (Am2901) and control (Am2909) chips can be contrasted against the second-generation chips (Am2903 and Am2910). The chips may be studied as computer structures in their own right. However, these chips are frequently used to emulate other ISPs. An example implementation of a PDP-8 using the Am2903/2910 is given in Chap. 15.

Am2901/2909. Although bit-sliced processors predated the Am2901/2909 series (Intel 3000; see Adams [1978]), the AMD chips have quickly become the industrial standard for medium-performance computers. Figure 3 illustrates how bit slices might be interconnected to emulate another ISP.

Chapter 13 gives a thorough introduction to the Am2901 microprocessor slice and the Am2909 bit-sliced microprogram sequencer. The information is sufficiently detailed that the chip data paths can be studied as an implementation of a computer. Also, the reader is encouraged to attempt a design of ISPs in this book using the bit slices.

Am2903/2910. The 2 years between the introduction of the 2901/2909 and the 2903/2910 produced significant advances in bit-sliced architecture. The reader is encouraged to compare and contrast the chips while asking, Why was this feature added?

Table 2   Bit Slices

	Intel 3002/3001	Am2901/2909	Am2903/2910	TI SN74S481/482	Motorola Mc 10800/10801
Technology	Schottky TTL	Schottky TTL	Schottky TTL	Schottky TTL	ECL
Number of pins per package:					
Data part	28	40	48	48	48
Controller	40	28	40	20	48
Cycle time (μs)	0.1–0.2	0.1–0.2	0.1–0.2	0.1–0.14	0.01–0.05
Slice width (bits)	2	4	4	4	4
Maximum microstore size	512	Address expand-able in 4-bit slices	4K	Address expand-able in 4-bit slices	Address expand-able in 4-bit slices
Register file size	11	16	16	external	external
Stack size	· · · · · · · · · · · ·	4	5	4 (in controller)	4
Basic instruction-set size	50	168	265	93	78
Year introduced	1975	1976	1977	1976	1977

Inevitably the answer will be, To speed up the emulation of a particular function found in another ISP. By studying these added features, the reader should develop an awareness of the level of complexity required in contemporary computer design. Table 3 summarizes the major differences between the 2901/2909 and 2903/2910 chip sets. Some points to observe are listed below.

- The 2901 comes in a 40-pin package, whereas the 2903 employs a 48-pin package. The extra pins are used for a second direct ALU input, increased ALU destination and functions, and chip programmability. In addition, some pins on the 2903 have time-multiplexed functions, thus increasing the functionality of the pins in common between the 2901 and 2903.

- The 2901 has a 9-bit microinstruction field: 3 bits for ALU source, 3 bits for ALU destination, and 3 bits for ALU function. The 2903 uses 9 bits plus 2 special bits for an 11-bit microinstruction field: 3 bits for ALU source, 4 bits for ALU destination, and 4 bits for ALU function (more extensive logic operations, arithmetic operations involving the carry bit, and 3-address microinstructions).

- Pins are set aside on the 2903 for chip position programmability. Whereas the 2901 deals primarily with boolean and 2's complement data-types, the position of the bit slice in a data word is immaterial. The added functions on the 2903 such as NORMALIZE and SIGNED MULTIPLY require that a bit slice be identified as a least significant, middle-significant, or most significant slice. The function performed in a single operation may differ according to the slice's relative position. (Note that the 2901 can perform all the functions of the 2903 by utilizing more microcode and/or more external hardware. For example, the 2's complement multiplication in Chap. 13 takes five 2901 microinstructions, whereas only three microinstructions are required for the 2903 in Chap. 14.)

- There are additional functions on the 2903 to handle more extended data-types and operators. In particular, normalization (for floating-point mantissa operation), data-representation conversion between 2's complement and sign/magnitude (again for floating-point mantissa manipulation), unsigned/2's complement multiplication, 2's complement division, byte swapping, parity generation, and incrementation by 1 or 2 are functions more representative

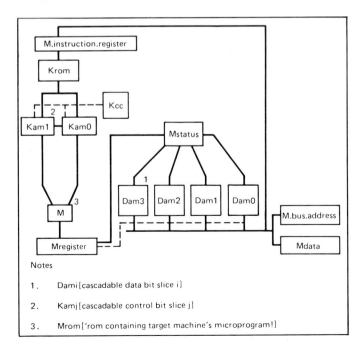

Notes

1. Dami [cascadable data bit slice i]

2. Kamj [cascadable control bit slice j]

3. Mrom ['rom containing target machine's microprogram!]

Fig. 3. PMS figure of a typical Pc constructed from bit slices.

Table 3   Comparison of Am2901/Am2901 and Am2909/Am2910 Chips

	Data/Memory	
	Am2901	*Am2903*
Technology	Low-power Schottky	Low-power Schottky
Minimum clock period	105 ns	80 ns
Organization	4-bit cascadable slice	4-bit cascadable slice
Pins	40	48
Microinstruction field length	9	11
Number of working registers	16	16
		Expandable
Data-types supported	Boolean	Boolean
	2's complement integer	2's complement integer
		Unsigned integer
		Sign/magnitude
Operators	3 arithmetic	7 arithmetic
	Add	Add
	Subtract (2)	Add carry (4)
		Subtract (2)
	5 logic	9 logic
	OR	OR
	AND (2)	AND (2)
	XOR	XOR
	XNOR	XNOR
		NOR
		NAND
		Constant (2)
	Logic shifts	Logic shifts
		Arithmetic shifts
		Sign extend
		Special functions
		Increment by 1 or 2
		Unsigned multiply
		2's complement multiply
		2's complement divide
		Single/double-length normalize
		Sign/magnitude conversion to/from 2's complement
Status	Overflow	Overflow
	Zero	Zero
	Carry-out	Carry-out
		Sign
	Control	
	Am2909	*Am2910*
Technology	Low-power Schottky	Low-power Schottky
Typical delay	55 ns	35 ns
Organization	4-bit cascadable slice	12-bit, noncascadable
Pins	28	40
Address sources	External	External
	4-deep stack	5-deep stack
	Microprogram counter	Microprogram counter
	Register	Register
Number of instructions	24	16

of minicomputer/maxicomputer ISPs (e.g., the System/370 and the PDP-11). The 2901 data-types are sufficient for microcoded controller applications and emulation of simple ISPs (e.g., the PDP-8 and the HP-2116).

- The 2903 allows for expansion of the number of working registers beyond 16. Thus the hardware register-bank switching (used in fast-context swap situations such as interrupt processing and operating-system calls) defined in contemporary ISPs can be implemented with 2903s but not 2901s.

- The 2909 microsequencer is bit-sliced so that the user can choose microaddresses whose lengths are a multiple of 4. The 2910 is a single, noncascadable chip with a fixed microaddress width of 12 bits.

- The microsequencers deal with one data-type: addresses (or unsigned integers). Thus only simple-integer operations are supported (e.g., increment, stack PUSH/POP, and external ORing for microbranches). The 40-pin 2910 offers a more extensive set of operations than the 28-pin 2909. The 2910 has a loop counter that can be used in microinstruction loops (e.g., multiplication or division routines and block-transfer control). In addition, the 2910 has 16 sequence-control instructions, most conditioned by external inputs, including a three-way BRANCH.

Am2903/2910 ISP.   The ISPs of the 2903 and 2910 are provided as an appendix to Chap. 14. The reader is encouraged to use the ISP in implementation exercises, such as the one in Chap. 15.

PDP-8 Implementation with the Am2903/2910.   Chapter 15 provides the Am2903/2910 microcode for a basic PDP-8. This design should be contrasted to the SSI PDP-8 implementation in Chap. 8.

Other Microprogramming Examples in This Book

PDP-11.   Chapter 39 traces the microcoded implementation of an entire minicomputer family that encompasses both vertical and horizontal microword formats.

TMS 1000.   Chapter 34 discusses a single-chip micropro-grammed implementation extensively used in hand-held calculators.

The Hewlett-Packard HP 9100A Computing Calculator.   The microprogrammed implementation of an early calculator is given in Chap. 48.

The Hewlett-Packard HP 9810/20/30 Calculators.   The evolution from horizontally encoded to vertically encoded micropro-gram instruction format based on a minicomputer ISP is evident in the second-generation HP calculators in Chap. 49.

The Hewlett-Packard HP 9845 Desk-Top Computer.   The third generation of desk-top computers is also vertically micropro-grammed, as detailed in Chap. 31.

The three chapters on HP calculators illustrate the evolution of a concept and its microprogrammed implementation.

References

Adams [1978]; Davies [1972]; Tucker [1967]; Wilkes [1951].

Chapter 11

Microprogramming and the Design of the Control Circuits in an Electronic Digital Computer[1]

M. V. Wilkes / J. B. Stringer

1. Introduction

Experience has shown that the sections of an electronic digital computer which are easiest to maintain are those which have a simple logical structure. Not only can this structure be readily borne in mind by a maintenance engineer when looking for a fault, but it makes it possible to use fault-locating programmes and to test the equipment without the use of elaborate test gear. It is in the control section of electronic computers that the greatest degree of complexity generally arises. This is particularly so if the machine has a comprehensive order code designed to make it simple and fast in operation. In general, for each different order in the code some special equipment must be provided, and the more complicated the function of the order the more complex this equipment. In the past, fear of complicating unduly the control circuits of the machines has prevented the designers of electronic machines from providing such facilities as orders for floating-point operations, although experience with relay machines and with interpretive subroutines has shown how valuable such orders are. This paper describes a method of designing the control circuits of a machine which is wholly logical and which enables alterations or additions to the order code to be made without *ad hoc* alterations to the circuits. An outline of this method was given by one of us [Wilkes, 1951] at the Conference on Automatic Calculating Machines at the University of Manchester in July 1951.

The operation called for by a single machine order can be broken down into a sequence of more elementary operations; for example, shifting a number in the accumulator one place to the right may involve, first, a transfer of the number to an auxiliary shifting register, and secondly, the transfer of the number back to the accumulator along an oblique path. These elementary operations will be referred to as *micro-operations*. Basic machine operations, such as addition, subtraction, multiplication, etc., are thought of as being made up of a *micro-programme* of micro-operations, each micro-operation being called for by a *micro-order*. The process of writing a micro-programme for a machine order is very similar to that of writing a programme for the whole calculation in terms of machine orders.

[1]*Proc. Cambridge Phil. Soc.*, pt. 2, vol. 49, April 1953, pp. 230–238.

For the method to be applicable it is necessary that the machine should contain a suitable permanent rapid-access storage device in which the micro-programme can be held—a diode matrix is proposed in the case of the machine discussed as an example below—and that means should be provided for executing the micro-orders one after the other. It is also necessary that provision should be made for conditional micro-orders which play a role in micro-programming similar to that played by conditional orders in ordinary programming.

Since the only feature of the machine which has to be designed specially for any particular set of machine orders is the configuration of diodes in the matrix, or the corresponding configuration in whatever equivalent device is used, there is no difficulty in making changes to the order code of the machine if experience shows them to be desirable; in fact, the design of the machine in the first place can be carried out completely without a firm decision on the details of the order code being taken, as long as care is taken to provide accommodation for the greatest number of micro-orders that are likely to be required. It would even be possible to have a number of interchangeable matrices providing for different order codes, so that the user could choose the one most suited to his particular requirements.

2. Description of the Proposed System

The system will be described in relation to a parallel machine having an arithmetical unit designed along conventional lines. This will contain a set of registers and an adder together with a switching system which enables the micro-operations in the various machine orders to be performed. Some of the micro-operations will be simple transfers of a number from one register to another with or without shifting of the number one place to the left or the right, while others will also involve the use of the adder. Any particular micro-operation can be performed by applying pulses simultaneously to the appropriate gates of the switching system. In certain cases it may be possible for two or more micro-operations to take place at the same time.

It will be convenient to regard the control system as consisting of two parts. A register is needed to hold the address of the next order due to be executed, and another to hold the current order while it is being executed, or at any rate during part of that time. Some means of counting the number of steps in a shifting operation or a multiplication must also be provided. One method of meeting these requirements is to provide a group of registers and an adder together with a switching system which enables transfers of numbers, with or without addition, to be made. This part of the control system will be called the *control register unit*. In any case the operations which need to be performed on the numbers standing in the control register unit during the execution of an order are, like the operations performed in the arithmetical unit, regarded as being made up of a sequence of micro-operations, each of which is performed by the application of pulses to appropriate gates.

The other part of the control system is concerned with control of the sequence of micro-orders required to carry out each machine order, and with the operation of the gates required for the execution of each micro-order. This will be called the *micro-control unit*; it consists of a decoding tree, two rectifier matrices and two registers (additional to those of the control register unit) connected as indicated in Fig. 1, which shows how the pulses used to operate the gates in the arithmetical unit and control register unit are generated. A series of control pulses from a pulse generator are applied to the input of the decoding tree. Each pulse is routed to one of the output lines of the tree, according to the number standing in register I. The output lines all pass into a rectifier matrix A and the outputs of this matrix are the pulses which operate the various gates associated with micro-operations. Thus one input line of the matrix corresponds to one micro-order. The *address* of the micro-order is the number which must be placed in register I to cause the control pulse to be routed to the corresponding line. The output lines from the tree also pass into a second matrix B, which has its outputs connected to register II. This matrix has wired on it the address of the micro-order to be performed next in time so that the address of this micro-order is placed in register II. Just before the next control pulse is applied

to the input of the tree a connexion is established between register II and register I, and the address of the micro-order due to be executed next is transferred into register I. In this way the decoding tree is prepared to route the next incoming control pulse to the correct output line. Thus application of pulses alternately to the input of the tree and to the gate connecting registers I and II causes a predetermined sequence of micro-orders to be executed.

It is necessary to have means whereby the course of the micro-programme can be made conditional on whether a given digit in one of the registers of the arithmetical unit or control register unit is a 1 or a 0. The means of doing this is shown at X in Fig. 1. A two-way switch, controlled by a special flip-flop called a *conditional flip-flop*, is inserted between matrix A and matrix B. The conditional flip-flop can be set by an earlier micro-order with any digit from any one of the registers. Two separate addresses are wired into matrix B, and the one which passes into register I, and thus becomes the address of the next micro-order, is determined by the setting of the conditional flip-flop.

Conditional micro-orders play the same part in the construction of micro-programmes as conditional orders play in the construction of ordinary programmes; apart from their obvious uses in micro-programmes for such operations as multiplication and division, they enable repetitive loops of micro-orders to be used.

If desired, two branchings may be inserted in the connexions between matrix A and matrix B, so that any one of four alternative addresses for the next micro-order may be selected according to the settings of two conditional flip-flops. Another possibility is to make the output from the decoding tree branch before it enters matrix A so that the nature of the micro-operation that is performed depends on the setting of the conditional flip-flop.

The micro-programme wired on to the matrices contains sections for performing the operations required by each order in the basic order code of the machine. To initiate the operation it is only necessary that control in the micro-programme should be sent to the correct entry point. This is done by placing the function digits of the order in the least significant part of register II, the other digits in this register being made zero. The micro-programme is constructed so that when this number passes into register I, control in the micro-programme is sent to the correct entry point.

The switching system in the arithmetical unit may either be designed to permit a large variety of micro-operations to be performed, or it may be restricted so as to allow only a small number of such operations. In a machine with a comprehensive order code there is much to be said for having the more flexible switching system since this will enable an economy to be made in the number of micro-orders needed in the micro-programme.

A similar remark applies in connexion with the degree of flexibility to be provided when designing the switching system for the control register unit. If the specification of the machine allows the same number of registers to be used in the arithmetical and

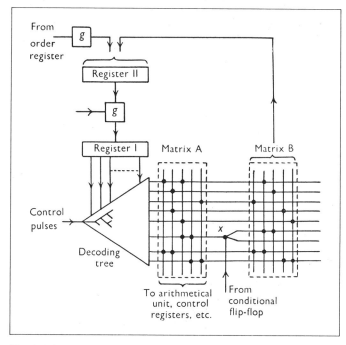

Fig. 1. Micro-control unit.

control sections, the construction of these two sections may be identical except as far as the number of digits is concerned. In a new machine under construction in the Mathematical Laboratory, Cambridge, the registers are being constructed in basic units each containing five registers and an adder-subtractor together with the associated switching system. It is hoped that it will be possible to use identical units in the arithmetical unit and in the control register unit.

3. Example

An example will now be given to show the way in which a micro-programme can be drawn up for a machine with a single-address order code covering the usual operations. It is supposed that the arithmetical unit contains the following registers:

A   Multiplicand register.

B   Accumulator (least significant half).

C   Accumulator (most significant half).

D   Shift register.

The registers in the control register unit are as follows:

E   Register connected to the access circuits of the store; the address of a storage location to which access is required is placed here.

F   Sequence control register; contains address of next order due to be executed.

G   Register used for counting.

It was assumed when drawing up the micro-programme that there was an adder-subtractor in the arithmetical unit with one input permanently connected to register D, and a similar adder-subtractor in the control register unit with one input permanently connected to register G. For convenience it was assumed that the switching systems in each case were comprehensive enough to provide any micro-operation required. It was further supposed that the arithmetical unit provided for 20 digits and that the numbers 0, 1 and 18 could be introduced at will into one of the registers or the adder of the control register unit. Two conditional flip-flops are used. All micro-operations including those involving access to the store are supposed to take the same amount of time. Reference will be made to this point in §4.

Table 1 gives the order code of the machine, and Table 2 the micro-programme. Each line of Table 2 refers to one micro-order; the first column gives the address of the micro-order, the second

Table 1

Notation:	Acc = accumulator
	Acc_1 = most significant half of accumulator
	Acc_2 = most significant half of accumulator
	n = storage location n
	$C(X)$ = contents of X (X = register or storage location)

Order	Effect of order
A n	$C(Acc) + C(n)$ to Acc
S n	$C(Acc) - C(n)$ to Acc
H n	$C(n)$ to Acc_2
V n	$C(Acc_2) \cdot C(n)$ to Acc, where $C(n) \geq 0$
T n	$C(Acc_1)$ to n, 0 to Acc
U n	$C(Acc_1)$ to n
R n	$C(Acc) \cdot 2^{-(n+1)}$ to Acc
L n	$C(Acc) \cdot 2^{n+1}$ to Acc
G n	If $C(Acc) < 0$, transfer control to n; if $C(Acc) \geq 0$, ignore (i.e., proceed serially)
I n	Read next character on input mechanism into n
O n	Send $C(n)$ to output mechanism

column specifies the micro-operations called for in the arithmetical unit of the machine, and the third column specifies the micro-operations called for in the control register unit. The fourth column shows which conditional flip-flop, if any, is to be set and the digit which is to be used to set it; for example, $(1)C_s$ means that flip-flop number 1 is set by the sign digit of the number in register C, while $(2)G_l$ means that flip-flop number 2 is set by the least significant digit of the number in register G. In the case of unconditional micro-orders columns 5 and 7 are blank and column 6 contains the address of the next micro-order to be executed. In the case of conditional micro-orders column 5 shows which flip-flop is used to operate the conditional switch and columns 6 and 7 give the alternative addresses to which control is to be sent when the conditional flip-flop contains a 0 or a 1 respectively.

Micro-orders 0 to 4 are concerned with the extraction of orders from the store. They serve to bring about the transfer of the order from the store to register E and then cause the five most significant digits of the order to be placed in register II with the result that control is transferred to one of the micro-orders 5 to 15, each of which corresponds to a distinct order in the machine order code. In this way the sequence of micro-orders needed to perform the particular operation called for is begun.

The way in which the various operations are performed can be followed from Table 2. In the section dealing with multiplication, it is assumed that numbers lie in the range $-1 \leq x < 1$ and that negative numbers are represented in the machine by their complements with respect to 2. It will be noted that the process of drawing up a micro-programme is very similar to that of drawing

Table 2

Notation: A, B, C, ... stand for the various registers in the arithmetical and control register units (see §3 of the text). "C to D" indicates that the switching circuits connect the output of register C to the input of register D; "$(D + A)$ to C" indicates that the output of register A is connected to the one input of the adding unit (the output of D is permanently connected to the other input), and the output of the adder to register C.

A numerical symbol n in quotes (e.g., "n") stands for the source whose output is the number n in units of the least significant digit.

		Arithmetical unit	Control register unit	Conditional flip-flop Set	Use	Next micro-order 0	1
	0		F to G and E			1	
	1		$(G+$"1"$)$ to F			2	
	2		Store to G			3	
	3		G to E			4	
	4		E to decoder			...	
A	5	C to D				16	
S	6	C to D				17	
H	7	Store to B				0	
V	8	Store to A				27	
T	9	C to Store				25	
U	10	C to Store				0	
R	11	B to D	E to G			19	
L	12	C to D	E to G			22	
G	13		E to G	$(1)C_s$		18	
I	14	Input to Store				0	
O	15	Store to Output				0	
	16	$(D+$Store$)$ to C				0	
	17	$(D-$Store$)$ to C				0	
	18				1	0	1
	19	D to B (R)†	$(G-$"1"$)$ to E			20	
	20	C to D		$(1)E_s$		21	
	21	D to C (R)			1	11	0
	22	D to C (L)‡	$(G-$"1"$)$ to E			23	
	23	B to D		$(1)E_s$		24	
	24	D to B (L)			1	12	0
	25	"0" to B				26	
	26	B to C				0	
	27	"0" to C	"18" to E			28	
	28	B to D	E to G	$(1)B_I$		29	
	29	D to B (R)	$(G-$"1"$)$ to E			30	
	30	C to D (R)		$(2)E_s$	1	31	32
	31	D to C			2	28	33
	32	$(D+A)$ to C			2	28	33
	33	B to D		$(1)B_I$		34	
	34	D to B (R)				35	
	35	C to D (R)			1	36	37
	36	D to C				0	
	37	$(D-A)$ to C				0	

†Right shift. The switching circuits in the arithmetic unit are arranged so that the least significant digit of register C is placed in the most significant place of register B during right shift micro-operations, and the most significant digit of register C (sign digit) is repeated (thus making the correction for negative numbers).

‡Left shift. The switching circuits are similarly arranged to pass the most significant digit of register B to the least significant place of register C during left shift micro-operations.

up an ordinary programme for an automatic computing machine and the problems involved are very much alike.

4.   The Timing of Micro-Operations

The assumption that all micro-operations take the same length of time to perform is not likely to be borne out in practice. In particular in a parallel machine it may not be possible to design an adder in which the carry propagation time is sufficiently short to enable an addition to be performed in substantially the same length of time as that taken for a simple transfer. It will be necessary, therefore, to arrange that the wave-form generator feeding the decoding tree should, when suitably stimulated by a pulse from one of the outputs from matrix A, supply a somewhat longer pulse than that normally required. Other operations may take many times as long to perform as an ordinary micro-order; for example, access to and from the store (particularly if a delay store is used) and operation of the input and output devices of the machine. The sequence of operations in the micro-programme must therefore be interrupted. One way of doing this is to prevent pulses from the wave-form generator reaching the decoding tree during the waiting period. This method, although quite feasible, appears to involve just the kind of complication which the present system is designed to avoid. A more attractive system is to make the machine wait on a conditional micro-order which transfers control back to itself unless the associated conditional flip-flop is set. Setting of this flip-flop takes place when the operation is completed, and control then goes to the next micro-order in the sequence. The machine is thus in a condition of "dynamic stop" while waiting for the operation to be completed. This system has the advantage that no complication is introduced into the units supplying the wave-forms to the decoding tree and that the control equipment required is similar to that already provided for other purposes.

5.   Discussion

It will be seen that the equipment needed to execute a complicated order in the machine order code is of the same form as that required for a simple one, namely outlets from the decoding tree and diodes in the matrices. Quite complicated orders can, therefore, be built into the machine without difficulty. In particular, arithmetical operations on numbers expressed in floating binary form and other similar operations can be micro-programmed and it is found that they do not involve very large numbers of micro-orders. For example, a micro-programme providing for the floating-point operations of addition, subtrac-

tion, and multiplication needs about 70 micro-orders. The switching system in the arithmetical unit must, of course, be designed with these operations in view. The decoding tree and matrices of a parallel machine with 40 digits in the arithmetical unit and provision for 256 micro-orders would only amount to about 15% of the total equipment in the machine, so that it appears that such a machine can well be provided with built-in facilities of considerable complexity.

The number of micro-orders needed in a complicated micro-programme can sometimes be reduced by making use of what might be called *micro-subroutines*. For example, when two numbers have to be added together in a floating binary machine, some shifting of one of them is usually necessary before the addition can take place. By making the micro-orders for this shifting operation serve also when a multiplication is called for, considerable saving is effected.

Four registers is the bare minimum needed in the arithmetical unit in order to enable the basic arithmetical operations to be performed. If any extension or refinement of the facilities provided is required, it may be necessary to increase the number of registers. For example, four registers are not sufficient to enable a succession of products to be accumulated without the transfer of intermediate results to the store, since the accumulator must be clear at the beginning of a multiplication. The addition of one register enables the accumulation of products to be provided for in the micro-programme. If this register is associated with the outlet from the store, it also enables some of the waiting time for storage access to be eliminated. To do this the micro-programme is arranged to call for a number from the store as soon as it is known that the number will be required and to continue with other necessary micro-operations before finally proceeding to use the number. The "dynamic stop" would occur just before the number is required for use. Another way of saving time is to arrange, in the case of those orders which permit it, for the next order to be extracted from the store before the operation currently being performed has been completed.

The minimum number of registers required in the control register unit of the machine for the simplest mode of operation is three. If extra registers are provided facilities similar to those provided by the B-lines in the machine at Manchester University could be included in the micro-programme.

6.   Microprogramming Applied to Serial Machines

All the discussion so far as been with reference to parallel machines because the technique described in this paper is most adapted to that type of machine. It is, however, possible to design a serial machine along the same lines. In a parallel computer with an asynchronous arithmetical unit every gate requires only one kind of wave-form to operate it and the timing of that wave-form is not critical. In a serial machine, on the other hand, different gates require different wave-forms and the same gate may require different wave-forms at different times; further, all these wave-forms must be critically timed. These complications may be handled by including in the micro-control unit a third matrix, C, for selecting the appropriate wave-form for each micro-order. The main wave-form, routed by the decoding tree and matrix A, opens a gate which is fed by a wave-form selected by matrix C. This enables a wave-form of correct duration to be applied to any selected gate in the arithmetical or control sections of the machine.

References

Wilkes and Stringer [1953]; Boutwell and Hoskinson [1963]; Flynn and MacLaren [1967]; Green [1966]; Greene, Dean, and Updike [1964]; Mercer [1957]; Patzer and Vandling [1967]; Rosin [1969]; Tucker [1967]; Weber [1967]; Wilkes [1951]; Wilkes [1958].

Chapter 12

Microprogramming the IBM System/360 Model 30[1]

Helmut Weber

Microprograms are sequences of microprogram words. A microprogram word is composed of 60 bits and contains various fields which control the basic functions in the IBM System/360 Model 30 CPU. These basic functions are storage control, control of the data flow registers and the Arithmetic-Logic-Unit (ALU), microprogram sequencing and branching control, and status bit-setting control. Microprogram words are stored in a Card Capacitor Read-Only Storage (CCROS). Fetching one microprogram word and executing it takes 750 nsec, the basic machine cycle.

Figure 1 shows in simplified form the data flow of the IBM System/360 (IBM 2030 CPU). It consists of a core storage with up to 65,536 8-bit bytes and a local storage (accessible by the microprogrammer but not explicitly by the 360 language programmer), a 16-bit storage address register (M, N), a set of ten 8-bit data registers (I, J, . . . , R), an arithmetic-logic-unit (ALU), connecting 8-bit wide buses (Z, A, B, M, N-bus), temporary registers (A, B), switches and gates.

Figure 2 shows the more important fields of a microprogram word. Only 47 bits are shown. Other fields contain various parity bits and special control bits. The field interpretation given in Fig. 2 is as for microprogram words in the second Read-Only Storage unit (Compatibility ROS) if the machine is equipped with the 1620 Compatibility Feature. The meaning of the microprogram word fields is explained in connection with Fig. 3 which shows the symbolic representation of a microprogram word together with an example as it appears on a microprogram documentation sheet.

The fields of the microprogram word can be grouped in five categories:

1 ALU control fields: CA, CF, CB, CG, CV, CD, CC

2 Storage control fields: CM, CU

3 Microprogram sequencing and branching fields: CN, CH, CL

4 Status bit setting field: CS

5 Constant field: CK

ALU control fields. On the line designated "ALU" in Fig. 3 an

[1]Abstracted from Helmut Weber, "A Microprogrammed Implementation of EULER on IBM System/360 Model 30," *Comm. ACM*, vol. 10, no. 9, September 1967, pp. 549–558; material based on Fagg et al. [1964], pp. 205–231. Figure 4 and related text by Siewiorek, Bell, and Newell.

ALU statement can appear. It will specify an A-source and a B-source, possibly an A-source modifier and a B-source modifier, an operator, a destination, and possibly a carry-in control and a carry-out control.

CA is the A-source field. It controls which one of the 10 8-bit data registers is connected to the transient A-register and therefore to the A-input of the ALU.

CB is the B-source field. It controls whether the R, L, or D-register or the CK-field is connected to the transient B-register and therefore to the B-input of the ALU. If "K" (CB = 3) is specified in this field, the 4-bit constant field CK is doubled up; i.e., the same four bits are used as the high digit and the low digit.

Between the A-register and the ALU input is a straight/cross switch and a high/low gate. Its function is controlled by the CF-field. Depending on the value of this field, no input is gated into the ALU (Ø) or only the low (L) or high digit (H) is admitted. CF = 3 gates all eight bits straight through, whereas the codes CF = 5, 6, and 7 cross over the two digits of the byte before admitting the low (XL) or high digit (XH) or both digits (X).

Between the B-register and the ALU input is a high/low gate and a true/complement control. The high/low gate is controlled by the CG-field in the same manner as the high/low gate in the A-input. The true/complement control is operated by the CV-field. It admits the true byte to the ALU (+) of the inverted byte (−) or controls a six-correct mechanism for decimal addition (@).

The operator and carry controls are given by the CC-field. This field specifies binary addition without carry handling (+0), addition with injection of a 1 (+1) (for instance, to stimulate subtraction in connection with the B-input inverter), addition with saving the carry in bit 3 of register S (+0,Save C, and +1,Save C), and addition using an old carry stored in bit 3 of register S and saving the new carry in this same bit (+C,Save C). Other codes specify logical operations (AND, OR, XOR).

The CD-field specifies into which register the result of the ALU operation is gated. Any one of the 10 data registers can be specified. Z means that the ALU output is gated nowhere and will be lost.

Storage control fields. On the line designated "storage" in Figure 3, a storage statement can appear. It will specify whether this microcycle is a ready cycle, a write cycle, a store cycle or a no-storage access cycle, and from where the storage address is supplied (CM-field) and whether storage access is to main storage or local storage (CU-field). Note that a full storage cycle (1.5 μsec) corresponds to two read-only storage cycles (750 nsec).

The codes CM = 3, 4, or 5 specify read cycles. The addresses are supplied from the register pairs IJ, UV, and LT, respectively. A read cycle reads 1 byte of data from core storage into the storage data register R.

A write cycle regenerates the data from the storage data register R at the address supplied in the last read cycle.

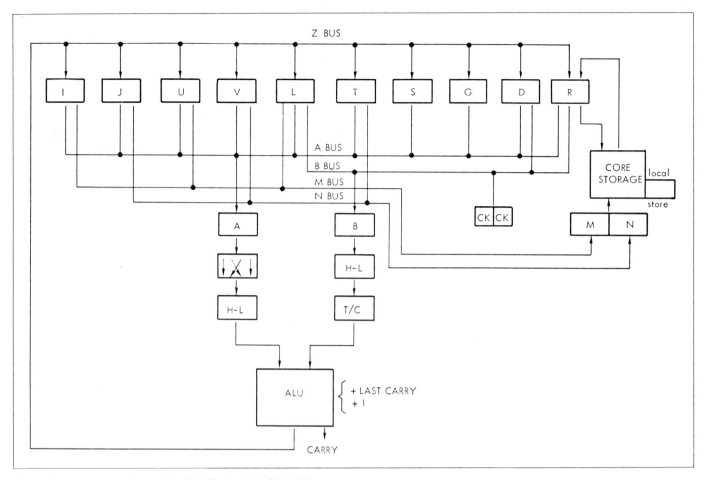

Fig. 1. Simplified data flow of the IBM System/360 Model 30.

CN	CH	CL	CM	CU	CA	CB	CK	CD	CF	CG	CV	CC	CS
0000	O	O	Write	MS	*	R	0	Z̄	O	O	+	+O	No status setting
0001	⊥	⊥	No access	LS	*	L	1	*	H	H	−	+⊥	LZ̄→S5
0010	RO	*	Store	*	*	D	2	*	Through	Thr.	*	And	HZ̄→S4
0011	S⊥	*	IJ→MN	*	*	K	3	*			@	Or	HZ̄→S4,LZ̄→S5
0100	*	G⊥	UV→MN		S		4	*	*			+0,save C	0→S4,0→S5
0101	*	R=Valid dec	LT→MN		*		5	*	XL			+⊥,sdve C	⊥→S⊥
0110	ALU carry	R⊥	*		*		6	S	XH			+C,save C	0→SO
0111	SO	Z̄=0	*		R		7	R	X			XOR	⊥→SO
1000	R2	G7			D		8	D					0→S2
1001	S2	S3			L		9	L					ANSNZ̄→S2
1010	S4	S5			G		X'A'†	G					0→S6
1011	S6	S7			T		X'B'	T					⊥→S6
1100	G0	R3			V		X'C'	V					0→S7
1101	G2	G3			U		X'D'	U					⊥→S7
1110	G4	G5			J		X'E'	J					*
1111	G6	Interrupt			I		X'F'	I					0→S⊥

†X'A' means hexadecimal digit A=1010

Fig. 2. IBM System/360 Model 30 microprogram word. (Detailed explanation is provided in text.) The field interpretation is given for microprogram words in compatability ROS if the machine is equipped with the 1620 compatibility feature. Fields marked "*" contain designators not explained here in order not to confuse the basic principles.

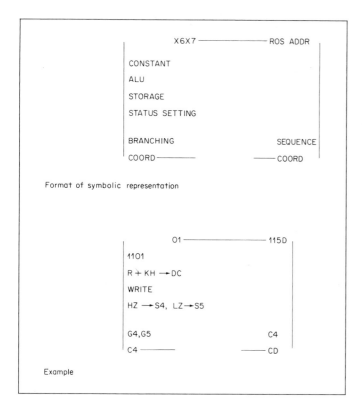

Fig. 3. Symbolic representation of a System/360 Model 30 microprogram word.

A store cycle acts exactly as a write cycle except that it inhibits in the read cycle immediately preceding it the insertion of the data byte from storage into the R-register.

The CU-field specifies whether storage access should be to main storage (MS) or to a local storage of 256 bytes not explicitly addressable by the 360 language programmer.

Microprogram sequencing and branching. Each microprogram word is stored at a unique address in ROS. A 13-bit ROS address register (W3 . . . W7, XO . . . X7) holds the address of the word being executed. For the symbolic representation of a microprogram (Fig. 3) the ROS address is given in hexadecimal in the upper right corner, and the last two bits of this address are repeated in binary on the upper margin.

After execution of a microprogram step, the next sequential word will not be executed. Instead the address of the next word to be executed is derived as follows. The high five bits (W) remain the same, unless they are changed by a special command in the microword, not explained here (so-called module switching). The next six bits (XO . . . X5) are supplied from the CN-field (written in hexadecimal in the symbolic representation of Fig. 3). The low

two bits are set according to conditions specified in the CH and CL fields. X6 is set according to the condition specified by CH. For instance, if CH = 8, then the bit R2 is transferred to X6; if CH = 6, then X6 is set to one if in the last ALU operation a carry had occurred. It is set to zero if no carry had occurred. X7 is controlled by CL. If, for instance, CL = 0, then X7 is set to zero; if X7 = 5, then X7 is set to one if both digits in R are valid decimal digits (i.e., RO . . . R3 ≤ 9 and R4 . . . R7 ≤ 9), X7 is set to zero if either digit in R is not a valid decimal digit (i.e., RO . . . R3 > 9 or R4 . . . R7 > 9). This microprogram sequencing scheme allows a four-way branch after the execution of each microprogram word.

Status bit setting. The CS-field allows the unconditional or conditional setting of certain status bits to be specified, combined in register S. If, for instance, CS = 3, then S4 is set to one if the result of the ALU operations performed in this microprogram cycle shows a zero in the high digit (i.e., Z0 = Z1 = Z2 = Z3 = 0); S4 is set to zero otherwise. At the same time, S5 is set to one if the result of the ALU operation shows a zero in the low digit (i.e., Z4 = Z5 = Z6 = Z7 = 0); S5 is set to zero otherwise. If CS = 9, then S2 is set to one if the result of the ALU operation is not zero (i.e., at least one of the bits Z0 . . . Z7 is equal to 1). If the result of the ALU operation is zero, then S2 is not changed.

Constant field. The 4-bit CK-field is used for various purposes. One instance explained in the ALU statement is to supply a constant B-source for an ALU operation. Other examples not explained here any further are the addressing of a few specific scratchpad local storage locations, module switching (replacement of the high part W of the ROS address), and the control of certain special functions.

Symbolic representation of microprograms. Microprograms are symbolically represented as a network of boxes (Fig. 3) each representing a microword, connected by nets indicating the possible branching ways. Figure 4 gives an example of a microprogram (to be explained in the next section). There exist programming systems to aid in the development of microprograms. They contain symbolic translators to translate the contents of a box according to Fig. 3 into the contents of the actual fields of the microprogram word according to Fig. 2. A drawing program generates documentation. These systems usually also contain programs for simulation and generation of the actual ROS cards.

Example Microprogram

Figure 4 contains a possible microprogram for decoding and executing the S/360 logic OR instruction: OR R1,R5, which is encoded as ''1615. (The accompanying table annotates the OR instruction microprogram depicted in Fig. 4.) The associated

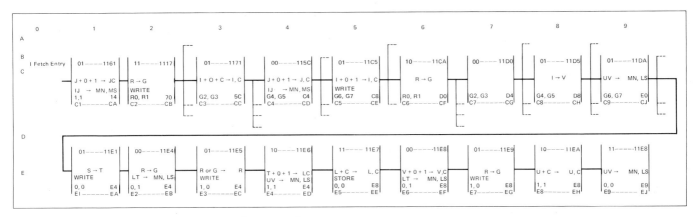

Fig. 4. A sample microprogram for the S/360 OR instruction.

register pair I and J is assumed to hold the program counter. The register pairs UV and LT are used to formulate the storage addresses of the two operands. In this case the operands are registers assumed to be in local memory.

References

Weber [1967]; Fagg, Brown, Hipp, Doody, Fairclough, and Greene [1964]; Green [1966].

Address	Location in figure	Description
''1161	C1	The program counter IJ addresses main storage. The addressed byte in main storage is read out into the storage data register R. The program counter is updated by adding 1 to register J. A possible carry is saved to be added to I.
''1117	C2	The op code has been read from main storage into R. It is also transferred (through the ALU) to register G. A four-way branch occurs on the two highest bits R0 and R1 of the op code. For the RR op codes (i.e., Branch, Status Setting, Fixed- Point Fullword, Logical, Floating-Point Long, and Floating-Point Short), this branch goes to ROS word ''1171. Other instruction formats branch to ''1170, ''1172, or ''1173, indicated by the three lines not continued.
''1171	C3	To complete the updating of the program counter, the carry from ''1117 is added into I. Op code decoding continues on the next two bits of the op code. RR format Fixed-Point Fullword and Logical instructions branch to ROS address ''115C.
''115C	C4	The second byte of the instruction is read from main store into register R. The program counter IJ is again incremented. Decoding of the op code continues. The RR format instructions AND, Compare Logical, OR, and XOR branch to ROS address ''11C5.
''11C5	C5	Update of the program counter is completed. The RR format instruction OR branches to ROS address ''11CA.
''11CA, ''11D0	C6, C7	Decoding of register operand R1.
''11D5, ''11DA	C8, C9	Fetch of the first byte of R1 from Local Store; decoding of register operand R2.
''11E1, ''11E4	E1, E2	Fetch of the first byte of R2 from Local Store.
''11E5	E3	The OR of the first bytes of R1 and R2 is formed.
''11E6, ''11E7	E4, E5	The results of the first byte are stored back into R1. The pointer to R2 is incremented in preparation for fetching the second byte of R2.
''11E8, ''11E9, ''11EA, ''11EB	E6, E7 E8, E9	The second byte of R2 is fetch from Local Store, the pointer to R1 is incremented, and the second byte of R2 is fetched from Local Store. To complete the OR instruction, the cycle from ROS address ''11E5 through ''11E8 would have to be repeated until all four bytes of the final operand were computed.

Chapter 13

Bit-Sliced Microprocessor of the Am2900 Family: The Am2901/2909[1]

Introduction

The Am2900 Family

The Am2900 Family consists of a series of LSI building blocks designed for use in microprogrammed computers and controllers. Each device is designed to be expandable and sufficiently flexible to be suitable for emulation of many existing machines.

Figure 1 illustrates a typical system architecture. There are two "sides" to the system. At the left is the control circuitry and on the right is the data manipulation circuitry. The block labeled "2901 array" consists of the ALU, scratchpad registers, and data steering logic (all internal to the Am2901's), plus left/right shift control and carry lookahead circuit. Data is processed by moving it from main memory (not shown) into the 2901 registers, performing the required operations on it, and returning the result to main memory. Memory addresses may also be generated in the 2901's and sent out to the memory address register (MAR). The four status bits from the 2901's ALU are captured in the status register after each operation.

The logic on the left side is the control section of the computer. This is where the Am2909 is used. The entire system is controlled by a memory, usually PROM, which contains long words called microinstructions. Each microinstruction contains bits to control each of the data manipulation elements in the system. There are, for example, 9 bits for the 2901 instruction lines, 8 bits for the A and B register addresses, 2 or 3 bits to control the shifting multiplexers at the ends of the 2901 array, and bits to control the register enables on the MAR, instruction register, and various bus transceivers. When the bits in a microinstruction are applied to all the data elements and everything is clocked, then one small operation (such as a data transfer or a register-to-register add) will occur.

Each microinstruction contains not only bits to control the data hardware, but also bits to define the location in PROM of the next microinstruction to be executed. The fields are labeled in Fig. 1 as I, CC, and BA. The I field controls the sequencer. It indicates where the next address is located—the μPC, the stack, or the direct inputs—and whether the stack is to be pushed or popped.

[1]Abstracted from *The Am2900 Family Data Book*, Advanced Micro Devices, Inc., 1976.

The CC field contains bits indicating the conditions under which the I field applies. These are compared with the condition codes in the status register and may cause modification to the I field. The comparing and modification occurs in the block labeled "control logic." Frequently this is just a PROM. The BA field is a branch address or the address of a subroutine.

Pipelining

The address for the microinstructions is generated by the sequencer, starting from a clock edge. The address goes from the sequencer to the ROM, and an access time later, the microinstruction is at the ROM outputs.

A pipeline register is a register placed on the output of the microprogram memory to essentially split the system in two. The pipeline register contains the microinstruction currently being executed ①. (Refer to the circled numbers in Fig. 1.) The data manipulation control bits go out to the system elements and a portion of the microinstruction is returned to the sequencer ② to determine the address of the next microinstruction to be executed. That address ③ is sent to the ROM, and the next microinstruction ④ sits at the input of the pipeline register. So while the 2901's are executing one instruction, the next instruction is being fetched from ROM. Note that there is no sequential logic in the sequencer between the select lines and the output. This is important because the loop ① to ② to ③ to ④ must occur during a single clock cycle. During the same time, the loop from ① to ⑤ must occur in the 2901's. These two paths are roughly the same (around 200 ns worst case for a 16-bit system). The presence of the pipeline register allows the microinstruction fetch to occur in parallel with the data operation rather than serially, allowing the clock frequency to be doubled.

The emulation of an existing machine by Fig. 1 works as follows. A sequence of microinstructions in the PROM is executed to fetch an instruction from main memory. This requires that the program counter, often in a 2901 working register, be sent to the memory address register and incremented. The data returned from memory is loaded into the instruction register. The contents of the instruction register are passed through a PROM or PLA to generate the address of the first microinstruction which must be executed to perform the required function. A branch to this address occurs through the sequencer. Several microinstructions may be executed to fetch data from memory, perform ALU operations, test for overflow, and so forth. Then a branch will be made back to the instruction fetch cycle. At this point, there may be branches to other sections of microcode. For example, the machine might test for an interrupt here and obtain an interrupt service routine address from another mapping ROM rather than start on the next machine instruction.

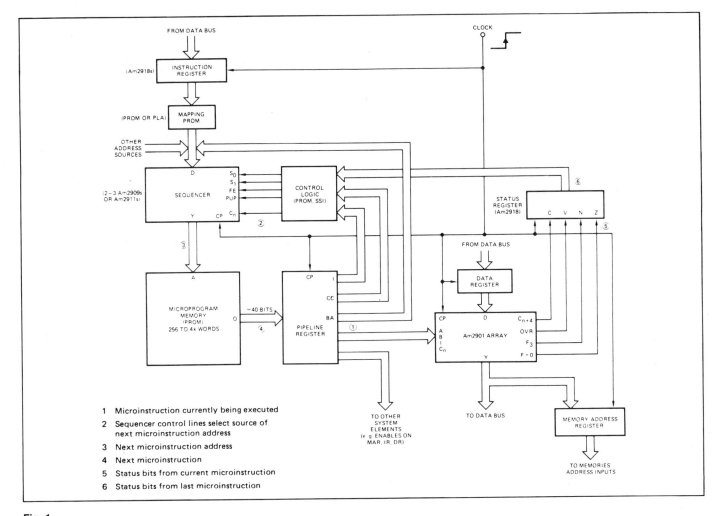

Fig. 1

Am2901: Four-Bit Bipolar Microprocessor Slice

The device, as shown in Fig. 2, consists of a 16-word by 4-bit two-port RAM, a high-speed ALU, and the associated shifting, decoding, and multiplexing circuitry. The 9-bit microinstruction word is organized into three groups of 3 bits each and selects the ALU source operands, the ALU function, and the ALU destination register. The microprocessor is cascadable with full lookahead or with ripple carry, has three-state outputs, and provides various status flag outputs from the ALU. Advanced low-power Schottky processing is used to fabricate this 40-lead LSI chip.

Architecture

A detailed block diagram of the bipolar microprogrammable microprocessor structure is shown in Fig. 3. The circuit is a 4-bit slice cascadable to any number of bits. Therefore, all data paths within the circuit are 4 bits wide. The two key elements in the Fig. 3 block diagram are the 16-word by 4-bit two-port RAM and the high-speed ALU.

Data in any of the 16 words of the random-access memory (RAM) can be read from the A port of the RAM as controlled by the 4-bit A address field input. Likewise, data in any of the 16 words of the RAM as defined by the B address field input can be

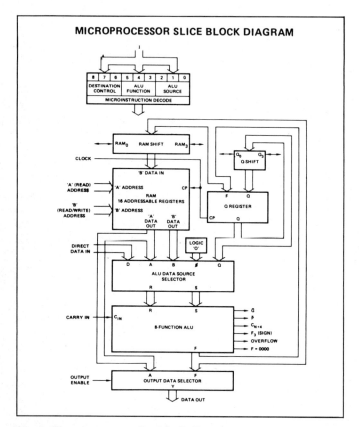

MICROPROCESSOR SLICE BLOCK DIAGRAM

Fig. 2. Microprocessor slice block diagram.

simultaneously read from the B port of the RAM. The same code can be applied to the A select field and B select field, in which case the identical file data will appear at both the RAM A port and B port outputs simultaneously.

When enabled by the RAM write enable (RAM EN), new data is always written into the field (word) defined by the B address field of the RAM. The RAM data-input field is driven by a three-input multiplexer. This configuration is used to shift the ALU output data (F) if desired. This three-input multiplexer scheme allows the data to be shifted up one bit position, shifted down one bit position, or not shifted in either direction.

The RAM A port data outputs and RAM B port data outputs drive separate 4-bit latches. These latches hold the RAM data while the clock input is LOW. This eliminates any possible race conditions that could occur while new data is being written into the RAM.

The high-speed Arithmetic Logic Unit (ALU) can perform three binary arithmetic and five logic operations on the two 4-bit words R and S. The R input field is driven from a two-input multiplexer,

while the S input field is driven from a three-input multiplexer. Both multiplexers also have an inhibit capability; that is, no data is passed. This is equivalent to a zero source operand.

In Fig. 3, the ALU R-input multiplexer has the RAM A port and the direct data inputs (D) connected as inputs. Likewise, the ALU S-input multiplexer has the RAM A port, the RAM B port, and the Q register connected as inputs.

The two source operands not fully described as yet are the D input and Q input. The D input is the 4-bit-wide direct data-field input. This port is used to insert all data into the working registers inside the device. Likewise, this input can be used in the ALU to modify any of the internal data files. The Q register is a separate 4-bit file intended primarily for multiplication and division routines, but it can also be used as an accumulator or holding register for some applications.

This multiplexer scheme gives the capability of selecting various pairs of the A, B, D, Q, and O inputs as source operands to the ALU. These five inputs, when taken two at a time, result in ten possible combinations of source operand pairs. These combinations include AB, AD, AQ, AO, BD, BQ, BO, DQ, DO, and QO. It is apparent that AD, AQ, and AO are somewhat redundant with BD, BQ, and BO in that if the A address and B address are the same, the identical function results. Thus, there are only seven completely non-redundant source operand pairs for the ALU. The Am2901 microprocessor implements eight of these pairs. The microinstruction inputs used to select the ALU source operands are the I_0, I_1, and I_2 inputs. The definitions of I_0, I_1, and I_2 for the eight source operand combinations are as shown in Table 1. Also shown is the octal code for each selection.

The I_3, I_4, and I_5 microinstruction inputs are used to select the ALU function. The definition of these inputs is shown in Table 2. The octal code is also shown for reference. The normal technique for cascading the ALU of several devices is in a lookahead carry mode. Carry generate, $\overline{G}$, and carry propagate, $\overline{P}$, are outputs of the device for use with a carry-lookahead generator such as the

Table 1   ALU Source Operand Control

	Microcode			ALU source operands	
I_2	I_1	I_0	Octal code	R	S
L	L	L	0	A	Q
L	L	H	1	A	B
L	H	L	2	O	Q
L	H	H	3	O	B
H	L	L	4	O	A
H	L	H	5	D	A
H	H	L	6	D	Q
H	H	H	7	D	O

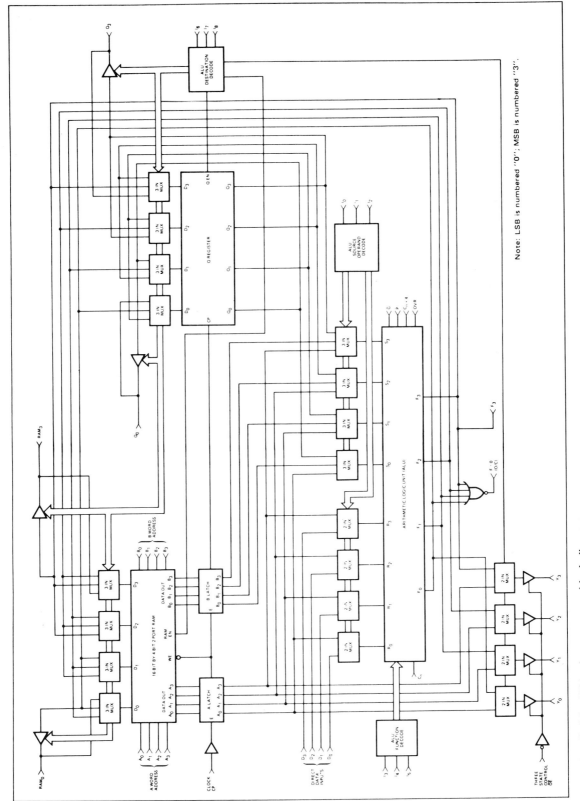

Note: LSB is numbered "0"; MSB is numbered "3".

Fig. 3. Detailed Am2901 microprocessor block diagram.

171

Table 2   ALU Function Control

Microcode			Octal code	ALU function	Symbol
I_5	I_4	I_3			
L	L	L	0	R plus S	R + S
L	L	H	1	S minus R	S − R
L	H	L	2	R minus S	R − S
L	H	H	3	R OR S	R ∨ S
H	L	L	4	R AND S	R ∧ S
H	L	H	5	R̄ AND S	R̄ ∧ S
H	H	L	6	R EX-OR S	R ⊻ S
H	H	H	7	R EX-NOR S	R̄ ⊻ S

Am2902 ('182). A carry-out, C_{n+4}, is also generated and is available as an output for use as the carry flag in a status register. Both carry-in (C_n) and carry-out (C_{n+4}) are active HIGH.

The ALU has three other status-oriented outputs. These are F_3, F = 0, and overflow (OVR). The F_3 output is the most significant (sign) bit of the ALU and can be used to determine positive or negative results without enabling the three-state data outputs. F_3 is non-inverted with respect to the sign bit output Y_3. The F = 0 output is used for zero detect. It is an open-collector output and can be wire ORed between microprocessor slices. F = 0 is HIGH when all F outputs are LOW. The overflow output

(OVR) is used to flag arithmetic operations that exceed the available 2's complement number range. The overflow output (OVR) is HIGH when overflow exists; that is, when C_{n+3} and C_{n+4} are not the same polarity.

The ALU data output is routed to several destinations. It can be a data output of the device and it can also be stored in the RAM or the Q register. Eight possible combinations of ALU destination functions are available as defined by the I_6, I_7, and I_8 microinstruction inputs. These combinations are shown in Table 3.

The 4-bit data output field (Y) features three-state outputs and can be directly bus-organized. An output control ($\overline{OE}$) is used to enable the three-state outputs. When $\overline{OE}$ is HIGH, the Y outputs are in the high-impedance state.

A two-input multiplexer is also used at the data output such that either the A port of the RAM or the ALU outputs (F) are selected at the device Y outputs. This selection is controlled by the I_6, I_7, and I_8 microinstruction inputs. Refer to Table 3 for the selected output for each microinstruction code combination.

As was discussed previously, the RAM inputs are driven from a three-input multiplexer. This allows the ALU outputs to be entered non-shifted, shifted up one position (multiplied by 2), or shifted down one position (divided by 2). The shifter has two ports; one is labeled RAM_0 and the other is labeled RAM_3. Both of these ports consist of a buffer-driver with a three-state output and an input to the multiplexer. Thus, in the shift-up mode, the RAM_3 buffer is enabled and the RAM_0 multiplexer input is

Table 3   ALU Destination Control

Microcode			Octal Code	RAM function		Q-register function		Y output	RAM shifter		Q shifter	
I_8	I_7	I_6		Shift	Load	Shift	Load		RAM_0	RAM_3	Q_0	Q_3
L	L	L	0	X	None	None	F → Q	F	X	X	X	X
L	L	H	1	X	None	X	None	F	X	X	X	X
L	H	L	2	None	F → B	X	None	A	X	X	X	X
L	H	H	3	None	F → B	X	None	F	X	X	X	X
H	L	L	4	Down	F/2 → B	Down	Q/2 → Q	F	F_0	IN_3	Q_0	IN_3
H	L	H	5	Down	F/2 → B	X	None	F	F_0	IN_3	Q_0	X
H	H	L	6	Up	2F → B	Up	2Q → Q	F	IN_0	F_3	IN_0	Q_3
H	H	H	7	Up	2F → B	X	None	F	IN_0	F_3	X	Q_3

X—Don't care. Electrically, the shift pin is a TTL input internally connected to a three-state output which is in the high impedance state.

B—Register Addressed by B inputs.

Up is toward MSB. Down is toward LSB.

enabled. Likewise, in the shift-down mode, the RAM_0 buffer and RAM_3 input are enabled. In the no-shift mode, both buffers are in the high-impedance state and the multiplexer inputs are not selected. This shifter is controlled from the I_6, I_7, and I_8 microinstruction inputs as defined in Table 3.

Similarly, the Q register is driven from a three-input multiplexer. In the no-shift mode, the multiplexer enters the ALU data into the Q register. In either the shift-up or shift-down mode, the multiplexer selects the Q register data appropriately shifted up or down. The Q shifter also has two ports; one is labeled Q_0 and the other is Q_3. The operation of these two ports is similar to the RAM shifter and is also controlled from I_6, I_7, and I_8 as shown in Table 3.

The clock input to the Am2901 controls the RAM, the Q register, and the A and B data latches. When enabled, data is clocked into the Q register on the LOW-to-HIGH transition of the clock. When the clock input is HIGH, the A and B latches are open and will pass whatever data is present at the RAM outputs. When the clock input is LOW, the latches are closed and will retain the last data entered. If the RAM EN is enabled, new data will be written into the RAM file (word) defined by the B address field when the clock input is LOW.

There are eight source operand pairs available to the ALU as selected by the I_0, I_1, and I_2 instruction inputs. The ALU can perform eight functions—five logic and three arithmetic. The I_3, I_4, and I_5 instruction inputs control this function selection. The carry input, C_n, also affects the ALU results when in the arithmetic mode. The C_n input has no effect in the logic mode. When I_0 through I_5 and C_n are viewed together, the matrix of Table 4 results. This matrix fully defines the ALU/source operand function for each state.

The ALU functions can also be examined on a "task" basis, i.e., add, subtract, AND, OR, etc. In the arithmetic mode, the carry will affect the function performed; while in the logic mode, the carry will have no bearing on the ALU output. Table 5 defines the various logic operations that the Am2901 can perform, and Table 6 shows the arithmetic functions of the device. Both carry-in LOW ($C_n = 0$) and carry-in HIGH ($C_n = 1$) are defined in these operations.

Logic Functions for G, P, C_{n+4}, and OVR

The four signals, G, P, C_{n+4}, and OVR are designed to indicate carry and overflow conditions when the Am2901 is in the add or subtract mode. Table 7 indicates the logic equations for these four signals for each of the eight ALU functions. The R and S inputs are the two inputs selected according to Table 1.

Table 4 Source Operand and ALU Function Matrix

Octal $I_{5,4,3}$	ALU function	Octal $I_{2,1,0}$ ALU source							
		0 A, Q	1 A, B	2 O, Q	3 O, B	4 O, A	5 D, A	6 D, Q	7 D, O
0	$C_n = L$ R plus S $C_n = H$	A + Q A + Q + 1	A + B A + B + 1	Q Q + 1	B B + 1	A A + 1	D + A D + A + 1	D + Q D + Q + 1	D D + 1
1	$C_n = L$ S minus R $C_n = H$	Q − A − 1 Q − A	B − A − 1 B − A	Q − 1 Q	B − 1 B	A − 1 A	A − D − 1 A − D	Q − D − 1 Q − D	−D − 1 −D
2	$C_n = L$ R minus S $C_n = H$	A − Q − 1 A − Q	A − B − 1 A − B	−Q − 1 −Q	−B − 1 −B	−A − 1 −A	D − A − 1 D − A	D − Q − 1 D − Q	D − 1 D
3	R OR S	A $\vee$ Q	A $\vee$ B	Q	B	A	D $\vee$ A	D $\vee$ Q	D
4	R AND S	A $\wedge$ Q	A $\wedge$ B	0	0	0	D $\wedge$ A	D $\wedge$ Q	0
5	$\overline{R}$ AND S	$\overline{A} \wedge$ Q	$\overline{A} \wedge$ B	Q	B	A	$\overline{D} \wedge$ A	$\overline{D} \wedge$ Q	0
6	R EX-OR S	A $\veebar$ Q	A $\veebar$ B	Q	B	A	D $\veebar$ A	D $\veebar$ Q	D
7	R EX-NOR S	$\overline{A \veebar Q}$	$\overline{A \veebar B}$	$\overline{Q}$	$\overline{B}$	$\overline{A}$	$\overline{D \veebar A}$	$\overline{D \veebar Q}$	$\overline{D}$

+ = Plus; − = Minus; $\vee$ = OR; $\wedge$ = AND; $\veebar$ − EX-OR

Table 5 ALU Logic Mode Functions (C_n Irrelevant)

Octal $I_{5,4,3}$ $I_{2,1,0}$		Group	Function
4	0		$A \wedge Q$
4	1	AND	$A \wedge B$
4	5		$D \wedge A$
4	6		$D \wedge Q$
3	0		$A \vee Q$
3	1	OR	$A \vee B$
3	5		$D \vee A$
3	6		$D \vee Q$
6	0		$A \veebar Q$
6	1	EX-OR	$A \veebar B$
6	5		$D \veebar A$
6	6		$D \veebar Q$
7	0		$\overline{A \veebar Q}$
7	1	EX-NOR	$\overline{A \veebar B}$
7	5		$\overline{D \veebar A}$
7	6		$\overline{D \veebar Q}$
7	2		$\overline{Q}$
7	3	INVERT	$\overline{B}$
7	4		$\overline{A}$
7	7		$\overline{D}$
6	2		Q
6	3	PASS	B
6	4		A
6	7		D
3	2		Q
3	3	PASS	B
3	4		A
3	7		D
4	2		0
4	3	"ZERO"	0
4	4		0
4	7		0
5	0		$\overline{A} \wedge Q$
5	1	MASK	$\overline{A} \wedge B$
5	5		$\overline{D} \wedge A$
5	6		$\overline{D} \wedge Q$

Pin Definitions

A_{0-3} The four address inputs to the register stack used to select one register whose contents are displayed through the A port.

B_{0-3} The four address inputs to the register stack used to select one register whose contents are displayed through the B port and into which new data can be written when the clock goes LOW.

I_{0-8} The nine instruction control lines to the Am2901, used to determine what data sources will be applied to the ALU ($I_{0,1,2}$), what functions the ALU will perform ($I_{3,4,5}$), and what data is to be deposited in the Q register or the register stack ($I_{6,7,8}$).

O_3, RAM_3 A shift line at the MSB of the Q register (Q_3) and the register stack (RAM_3). Electrically these lines are three-state outputs connected to TTL inputs internal to the Am2901. When the destination code on $I_{6,7,8}$ indicates an up shift (octal 6 or 7), the three-state outputs are enabled and the MSB of the Q register is available on the Q_3 pin and the MSB of the ALU output is available on the RAM_3 pin. Otherwise, the three-state outputs are OFF (high-impedance) and the pins are electrically LS-TTL inputs. When the destination code calls for a down shift, the pins are used as the data inputs to the MSB of the Q register (octal 4) and RAM (octal 4 or 5).

O_0, RAM_0 Shift lines like Q_3 and RAM_3, but at the LSB of the Q register and RAM. These pins are tied to the Q_3 and RAM_3 pins of the adjacent device to transfer data between devices for up and down shifts of the Q register and ALU data.

D_{0-3} Direct data inputs. A 4-bit data field which may be selected as one of the ALU data sources for entering data into the Am2901. D_0 is the LSB.

Y_{0-3} The four data outputs of the Am2901. These are three-state output lines. When enabled, they display either the four outputs of the ALU or the data on the A port of the register stack, as determined by the destination code $I_{6,7,8}$.

$\overline{OE}$ Output enable. When $\overline{OE}$ is HIGH, the Y outputs are OFF; when $\overline{OE}$ is LOW, the Y outputs are active (HIGH or LOW).

$\overline{P}$, $\overline{G}$ The carry generate and propagate outputs of the Am2901's ALU. These signals are used with the Am2902 for carry-lookahead. See Table 7 for the logic equations.

OVR Overflow. This pin is logically the Exclusive-OR of the carry-in and carry-out of the MSB of the ALU. At the most significant end of the word, this pin indicates that the result of an arithmetic 2's complement operation has overflowed into the sign bit. See Table 7 for logic equation.

$F = 0$ This is an open-collector output which goes HIGH (OFF) if the four ALU outputs F_{0-3} are all LOW. In positive logic, it indicates the result of an ALU operation is 0.

C_n The carry-in to the Am2901's ALU.

C_{n+4} The carry-out of the Am2901's ALU. See Table 7 for equations.

CP The clock to the Am2901. The Q register and register stack outputs change on the clock LOW-to-

Table 6 ALU Arithmetic Mode Functions

Octal $I_{5,4,3}$ $I_{2,1,0}$		$C_n = 0$ (LOW) Group	$C_n = 0$ (LOW) Function	$C_n = 1$ (HIGH) Group	$C_n = 1$ (HIGH) Function
0	0	ADD	A + Q	ADD plus one	A + Q + 1
0	1	ADD	A + B	ADD plus one	A + B + 1
0	5	ADD	D + A	ADD plus one	D + A + 1
0	6	ADD	D + Q	ADD plus one	D + Q + 1
0	2	PASS	Q	Increment	Q + 1
0	3	PASS	B	Increment	B + 1
0	4	PASS	A	Increment	A + 1
0	7	PASS	D	Increment	D + 1
1	2	Decrement	Q − 1	PASS	Q
1	3	Decrement	B − 1	PASS	B
1	4	Decrement	A − 1	PASS	A
2	7	Decrement	D − 1	PASS	D
2	2	1's complement	−Q − 1	2's complement (negate)	−Q
2	3	1's complement	−B − 1	2's complement (negate)	−B
2	4	1's complement	−A − 1	2's complement (negate)	−A
1	7	1's complement	−D − 1	2's complement (negate)	−D
1	0	Subtract (1's complement)	Q − A − 1	Subtract (2's complement)	Q − A
1	1	Subtract (1's complement)	B − A − 1	Subtract (2's complement)	B − A
1	5	Subtract (1's complement)	A − D − 1	Subtract (2's complement)	A − D
1	6	Subtract (1's complement)	Q − D − 1	Subtract (2's complement)	Q − D
2	0	Subtract (1's complement)	A − Q − 1	Subtract (2's complement)	A − Q
2	1	Subtract (1's complement)	A − B − 1	Subtract (2's complement)	A − B
2	5	Subtract (1's complement)	D − A − 1	Subtract (2's complement)	D − A
2	6	Subtract (1's complement)	D − Q − 1	Subtract (2's complement)	D − Q

Table 7

Definitions (+ = OR)

$$P_0 = R_0 + S_0 \qquad G_0 = R_0 S_0 \qquad C_4 = G_3 + P_3 G_2 + P_3 P_2 G_1 + P_3 P_2 P_1 G_0 + P_3 P_2 P_1 P_0 C_n$$
$$P_1 = R_1 + S_1 \qquad G_1 = R_1 S_1 \qquad C_3 = G_2 + P_2 G_1 + P_2 P_1 G_0 + P_2 P_1 P_0 C_n$$
$$P_2 = R_2 + S_2 \qquad G_2 = R_2 S_2$$
$$P_3 = R_3 + S_3 \qquad G_3 = R_3 S_3$$

$I_{5,4,3}$	Function	$\overline{P}$	$\overline{G}$	C_{n+4}	OVR
0	R + S	$\overline{P_3 P_2 P_1 P_0}$	$\overline{G_3 + P_3 G_2 + P_3 P_2 G_1 + P_3 P_2 P_1 G_0}$	C_4	$C_3 \vee C_4$
1	S − R	← Same as R + S equations, but substitute $\overline{R_i}$ for R_i in definitions →			
2	R − S	← Same as R + S equations, but substitute $\overline{S_i}$ for S_i in definitions →			
3	R ∨ S	LOW	$P_3 P_2 P_1 P_0$	$\overline{P_3 P_2 P_1 P_0} + C_n$	$\overline{P_3 P_2 P_1 P_0} + C_n$
4	R ∧ S	LOW	$\overline{G_3 + G_2 + G_1 + G_0}$	$G_3 + G_2 + G_1 + G_0 + C_n$	$G_3 + G_2 + G_1 + G_0 + C_n$
5	$\overline{R} \wedge S$	LOW	← Same as R ∧ S equations, but substitute $\overline{R_i}$ for R_i in definitions →		
6	R ⊻ S	← Same as $\overline{R \vee S}$, but substitute $\overline{R_i}$ for R_i in definitions →			
7	$\overline{R \veebar S}$	$G_3 + G_2 + G_1 + G_0$	$\overline{G_3 + P_3 G_2 + P_3 P_2 G_1 + P_3 P_2 P_1 G_0}$	$\dfrac{\overline{G_3 + P_3 G_2 + P_3 P_2 G_1}}{+ P_3 P_2 P_1 P_0 (G_0 + \overline{C_n})}$	See note

Note: $[\overline{P_2} + \overline{G_2}\overline{P_1} + \overline{G_2}\overline{G_1}\overline{P_0} + \overline{G_2}\overline{G_1}\overline{G_0}C_n] \veebar [\overline{P_3} + \overline{G_3}\overline{P_2} + \overline{G_3}\overline{G_2}\overline{P_1} + \overline{G_3}\overline{G_2}\overline{G_1}\overline{P_0} + \overline{G_3}\overline{G_2}\overline{G_1}\overline{G_0}C_n]$

HIGH transition. The clock LOW time is internally the write enable to the 16×4 RAM which comprises the "master" latches of the register stack. While the clock is LOW, the "slave" latches on the RAM outputs are closed, storing the data previously on the RAM outputs. This allows synchronous master-slave operation of the register stack.

Expansion of the Am2901

Any number of Am2901's can be interconnected to form CPU's of 12, 16, 24, 36, or more bits, in 4-bit increments. Figure 4 illustrates the interconnection of three Am2901's to form a 12-bit CPU, using ripple carry. Figure 5 illustrates a 16-bit CPU using carry lookahead, and Fig. 6 is the general carry lookahead scheme for long words.

With the exception of the carry interconnection, all expansion schemes are the same. The Q_3 and RAM_3 pins are bidirectional left/right shift lines at the MSB of the device. For all devices except the most significant, these lines are connected to the Q_0 and RAM_0 pins of the adjacent more significant device. These connections allow the Q registers of all Am2901's to be shifted left or right as a contiguous n-bit register, and also allow the ALU output data to be shifted left or right as a contiguous n-bit word prior to storage in the RAM. At the LSB and MSB of the CPU, the shift pins should be connected to three-state multiplexers which can be controlled by the microcode to select the appropriate input signals to the shift inputs. (See Fig. 7.)

The open-collector $F = 0$ outputs of all the Am2901's are connected together and to a pull-up resistor. This line will go HIGH if and only if the output of the ALU contains all zeros. Most systems will use this line as the Z (zero) bit of the processor status word.

The overflow and F_3 pins are generally used only at the most significant end of the array, and are meaningful only when 2's complement signed arithmetic is used. The overflow pin is the Exclusive-OR of the carry-in and carry-out of the sign bit (MSB). It will go HIGH when the result of an arithmetic operation is a number requiring more bits than are available, causing the sign bit to be erroneous. This is the overflow (V) bit of the processor status word. The F_3 pin is the MSB of the ALU output. It is the sign of the result in 2's complement notation, and should be used as the negative (N) bit of the processor status word.

The carry-out from the most significant Am2901 (C_{n+4} pin) is the carry-out from the array, and is used as the carry (C) bit of the processor status word.

Carry interconnections between devices may use either ripple carry or carry lookahead. For ripple carry, the carry-out (C_{n+4}) of each device is connected to the carry-in (C_n) of the next more significant device. Carry lookahead uses the Am2901 lookahead carry generator. The scheme is identical with that used with the 74181/74182. Figures 5 and 6 illustrate single- and multiple-level lookahead.

Shift I/O Lines at the End of the Array

The Q-register and RAM left/right shift data transfers occur between devices over bidirectional lines. At the ends of the array, three-state multiplexers are used to select what the new inputs to the registers should be during shifting. Figure 7 shows two Am25LS253 dual four-input multiplexers connected to provide four shift modes. Instruction bit I_7 (from the Am2901) is used to select whether the left-shift multiplexer or the right-shift multiplexer is active. (See Table 8.) The four shift modes in this example are:

Zero — A LOW is shifted into the MSB of the RAM on a down shift. If the Q register is also shifted, then a LOW is deposited in the Q-register MSB. If the RAM or both registers are shifted up, LOWs are placed in the LSBs.

One — Same as zero, but a HIGH level is deposited in the LSB or MSB.

Rotate — A single-precision rotate. The RAM MSB shifts into the LSB on a right shift and the LSB shifts into the MSB on a left shift. The Q register, if shifted, will rotate in the same manner.

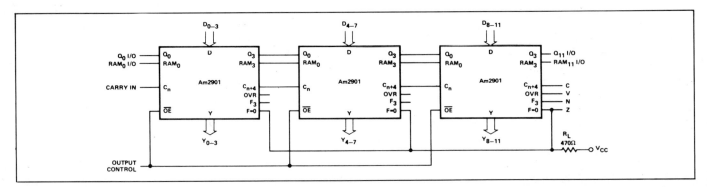

Fig. 4. Three Am2901's used to construct 12-bit CPU with ripple carry. Corresponding A, B, and 1 pins on all devices are connected together.

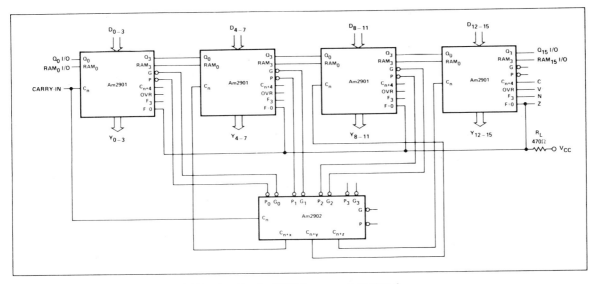

Fig. 5. Four Am2901's in a 16-bit CPU using the Am2902 for carry lookahead.

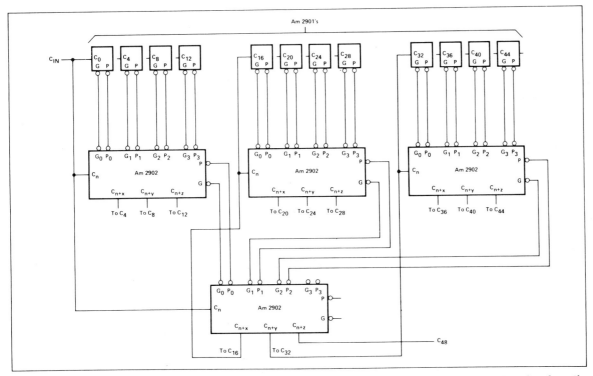

Fig. 6. Carry lookahead scheme for 48-bit CPU using 12 Am2901's. The carry-out flag (C48) should be taken from the lower Am2902 rather than the right-most Am2901 for higher speed.

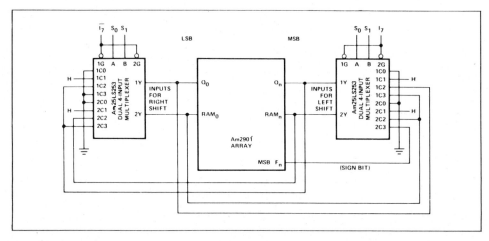

Fig. 7. Three-state multiplexers used on shift I/O lines.

Arithmetic   A double-length arithmetic shift if Q is also shifted. On an up shift a zero is loaded into the Q-register LSB and the Q-register MSB is loaded into the RAM LSB. On a down shift, the RAM LSB is loaded into the Q-register MSB and the ALU output MSB (F_n, the sign bit) is loaded into the RAM MSB. (This same bit will also be in the next less significant RAM bit.)

Hardware Multiplication

Figure 8 illustrates the interconnections for a hardware multiplication using the Am2901. The system shown uses two devices for 8×8 multiplication, but the expansion to more bits is simple—the significant connections are at the LSB and MSB only.

The basic technique used is the "add and shift" algorithm. One clock cycle is required for each bit of the multiplier. On each cycle, the LSB of the multiplier is examined; if it is a 1, then the multiplicand is added to the partial product to generate a new partial product. The partial product is then shifted one place toward the LSB, and the multiplier is also shifted one place toward the LSB. The old LSB of the multiplier is discarded. The

cycle is then repeated on the new LSB of the multiplier available at Q_0.

The multiplier is in the Am2901 Q register. The multiplicand is in one of the registers in the register stack, R_a. The product will be developed in another of the registers in the stack, R_b.

The A address inputs are used to address the multiplicand in R_a, and the B address inputs are used to address the partial product in R_b. On each cycle, R_a is conditionally added to R_b, depending on the LSB of Q as read from the Q_0 output, and both the Q and the ALU output are shifted left one place. The instruction lines to the Am2901 on every cycle will be:

$I_{8,7,6} = 4$ (shift register stack input and Q register left)
$I_{5,4,3} = 0$ (Add)
$I_{2,1,0} = 1$ or 3   (select A, B or O, B as ALU sources)

Figure 8 shows the connections for multiplication. The circled numbers refer to the paragraphs below.

1   The adjacent pins of the Q register and RAM shifters are connected together so that the Q registers of both (or all) Am2901's shift left or right as a unit. Similarly, the entire

Table 8

Code			Source of new data				Shift	Type
I_7	S_1	S_0	Q_0	Q_n	RAM_0	RAM_n		
H	L	L	0	Q_{n-1}	0	F_{n-1}	Up	Zero
H	L	H	1	Q_{n-1}	1	F_{n-1}	(Right)	One
H	H	L	Q_n	Q_{n-1}	F_n	F_{n-1}		Rotate
H	H	H	0	Q_{n-1}	Q_n	F_{n-1}		Arithmetic
L	L	L	Q_1	0	F_1	0	Down	Zero
L	L	H	Q_1	1	F_1	1	(Left)	One
L	H	L	Q_1	Q_0	F_1	F_0		Rotate
L	H	H	Q_1	F_0	F_1	$RAM_n = RAM_{n-1} = F_n$		Arithmetic

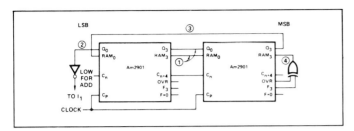

Fig. 8. Interconnection for dedicated multiplication (8 by 8 bit) (corresponding A, B, and I connected together).

8-bit (or more) ALU output can be shifted as a unit prior to storage in the register stack.

2 The shift output at the LSB of the Q register determines whether the ALU source operands will be A and B (add multiplicand to partial product) or O and B (add nothing to partial product). Instruction bit I_1 can select between A, B or O, B as the source operands; it can be driven directly from the complement of the LSB of the multiplier.

3 As the new partial product appears at the input to the register stack, it is shifted left by the RAM shifter. The new LSB of the partial product, which is complete and will not be affected by future operations, is available on the RAM_0 pin. This signal is returned to the MSB of the Q register. On each cycle then, the just-completed LSB of the product is deposited in the MSB of the Q register; the Q register fills with the least significant half of the product.

4 As the ALU output is shifted down on each cycle, the sign bit of the new partial product should be inserted in the RAM MSB shift input. The F_3 flag will be the correct sign of the partial product unless overflow has occurred. If over-

flow occurs during an addition or subtraction, the OVR flag will go HIGH and F_3 is not the sign of the result. The sign of the result must then be the complement of F_3. The correct sign bit to shift into the MSB of the partial product is therefore $\overline{F_3} \oplus OVR$; that is, F_3 if overflow has not occurred and $\overline{F_3}$ if overflow has occurred. On the last cycle, when the MSB of the multiplier is examined, a conditional subtraction rather than addition should be performed, because the sign bit of the multiplier carries negative rather than positive arithmetic weight.

$$Y = -Y_i 2^i + Y_{i-1} 2^{i-1} + \cdots + Y_0 2^0$$

This scheme will produce a correct 2's complement product for all multiplicands and multipliers in 2's complement notation.

Figure 9 is a table showing the input states of the Am2901's for each step of a signed 2's complement multiplication.

Am2909 Microprogram Sequencer

General Description

The Am2909 is a 4-bit-wide address controller intended for sequencing through a series of microinstructions contained in a ROM or PROM. Two Am2909's may be interconnected to generate an 8-bit address (256 words), and three may be used to generate a 12-bit address (4096 words). Figure 10 is a block diagram of the Am2909.

The Am2909 can select an address from any of four sources. They are: (1) a set of external direct inputs (D); (2) external data from the R inputs, stored in an internal register; (3) a 4-word-deep

Initial Register States

R	
0	Multiplier
1	Multiplicand
2	X
3	X

Am2901 Microcode

Program _____ 2's Comp. Multiply _____

Date _____ 8/5/75 _____ By _____ J. S. _____

Final Register States

R	
0	Multiplier
1	Multiplicand
2	LSH Product
3	MSH Product

S, F →	D	Description	Repeat	A	B	I_{876}	I_{543}	I_{210}	C_n	Q_0	Q_3	RAM_0	RAM_3	Jump To	If
O ∨ A	Q	Move Multiplier to Q	—	0	X	0	3	4	X	X	X	X	X		
O ∧ B	B	Clear R_3	—	X	3	2	4	3	X	X	X	X	X		
(O+B)/2 / (A+B)/2	B	Cond. Add & Shift	n−1	1	3	4	0	1 or 3 / $I_1 = Q_0 LO$	0	—	RAM_0	—	$F_3 \veebar OVR$		
(B−O)/2 / (B−A)/2	B	Cond. Subt. & Shift	—	1	3	4	1	1 or 3 / $I_1 = Q_0 LO$	1	—	RAM_0	—	$F_3 \veebar OVR$		
O ∨ Q	B	Move LSH Prod. to R_2	—	X	2	2	3	2	X	X	X	X	X		

X = Don't Care   S = Source   F = Function   D = Destination

Fig. 9

push/pop stack; or (4) a program counter register (which usually contains the last address plus one). The push/pop stack includes certain control lines so that it can efficiently execute nested subroutine linkages. Each of the four outputs can be ORed with an external input for conditional skip or branch instructions, and a separate line forces the outputs to all zeros. The outputs are three-state.

Architecture of the Am2909

A detailed logic diagram is shown in Fig. 11. The device contains a four-input multiplexer that is used to select either the address register, direct inputs, microprogram counter, or file as the source of the next microinstruction address. This multiplexer is controlled by the S_0 and S_1 inputs.

The address register consists of four D-type, edge-triggered flip-flops with a common clock enable. When the address register enable is LOW, new data is entered into the register on the clock LOW-to-HIGH transition. The address register is available at the multiplexer as a source for the next microinstruction address. The direct input is a 4-bit field of inputs to the multiplexer and can be selected as the next microinstruction address.

The Am2909 contains a microprogram counter (μPC) that is composed of a 4-bit incrementer followed by a 4-bit register. The

incrementer has carry-in (C_n) and carry-out (C_{n+4}) such that cascading to larger word lengths is straightforward. The μPC can be used in either of two ways. When the least significant carry-in to the increment is HIGH, the microprogram register is loaded on the next clock cycle with the current Y output word plus one (Y + 1 $\rightarrow$ μPC). Thus sequential microinstructions can be executed. If this least significant C_0 is LOW, the incrementer passes the Y output word unmodified and the microprogram register is loaded with the same Y word on the next cycle (Y $\rightarrow$ μPC). Thus, the same microinstruction can be executed any number of times by using the least significant C_n as the control.

The last source available at the multiplexer input is the 4×4 file (stack). The file is used to provide return address linkage when executing microsubroutines. The file contains a built-in stack pointer (SP) which always points to the last file word written. This allows stack reference operations (looping) to be performed without a push or pop.

The stack pointer operates as an up/down counter with separate push/pop and file enable inputs. When the file enable input is LOW and the push/pop input is HIGH, the PUSH operation is enabled. This causes the stack pointer to increment and the file to be written with the required return linkage—the next microinstruction address following the subroutine jump which initiated the PUSH.

If the file enable input is LOW and the push/pop control is LOW, a POP operation occurs. This implies the usage of the return linkage during this cycle and thus a return from subroutine. The next LOW-to-HIGH clock transition causes the stack pointer to decrement. If the file enable is HIGH, no action is taken by the stack pointer regardless of any other input.

The stack pointer linkage is such that any combination of pushes, pops, and stack references can be achieved. One microinstruction subroutines can be performed. Since the stack is 4 words deep, up to four microsubroutines can be nested.

The ZERO input is used to force the four outputs to the binary zero state. When the ZERO input is LOW, all Y outputs are LOW regardless of any other inputs (except $\overline{OE}$). Each Y output bit also has a separate OR input such that a conditional logic 1 can be forced at each Y output. This allows jumping to different microinstructions on programmed conditions.

The Am2909 features three-state Y outputs. These can be particularly useful in military designs requiring external ground support equipment (GSE) to provide automatic checkout of the microprocessor. The internal control can be placed in the high-impedance state, and preprogrammed sequences of microinstructions can be executed via external access to the control ROM/PROM.

Definition of Terms

A set of symbols is used to represent various internal and external registers and signals used with the Am2909. Since its principal

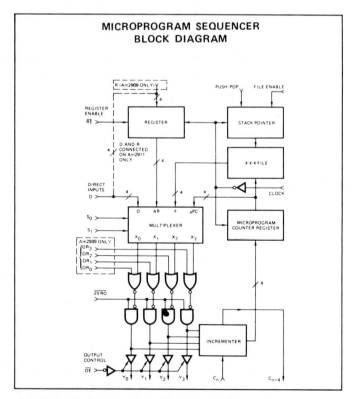

Fig. 10. Microprogram sequencer block diagram.

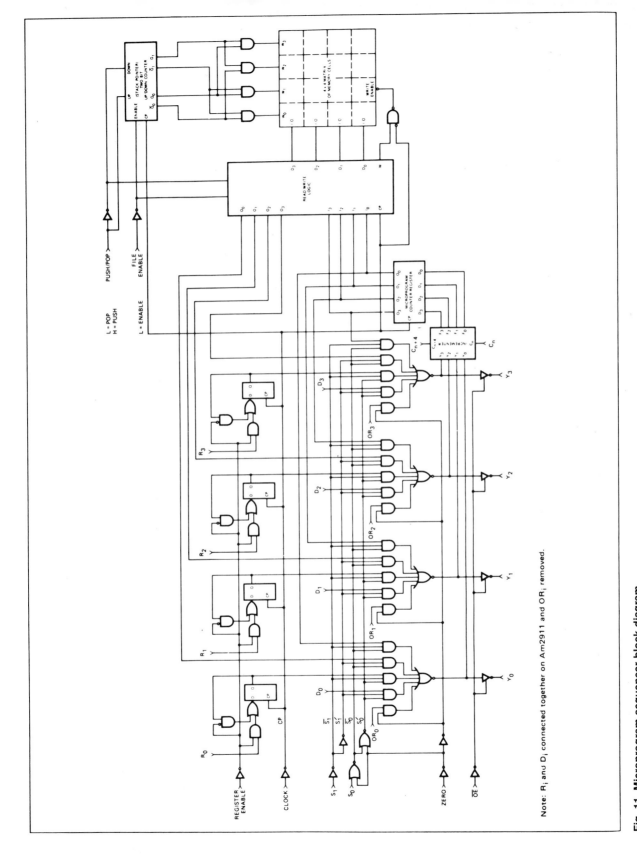

Note: R_i and D_i connected together on Am2911 and OR_i removed.

Fig. 11. Microprogram sequencer block diagram.

181

application is as a controller for a microprogram store, it is necessary to define some signals associated with the microcode itself. Figure 12 illustrates the basic interconnection of Am2909, memory, and microinstruction register. The definitions here apply to this architecture.

Inputs to Am2909

S_1, S_0	Control lines for address source selection.
$\overline{FE}$, PUP	Control lines for push/pop stack.
$\overline{RE}$	Enable line for internal address register.
OR_i	Logic OR inputs on each address output line.
$\overline{ZERO}$	Logic AND input on the output lines.
$\overline{OE}$	Output enable. When $\overline{OE}$ is HIGH, the Y outputs are OFF (high impedance).
C_n	Carry-in to the incrementer.
R_i	Inputs to the internal address register.
D_i	Direct inputs to the multiplexer.
CP	Clock input to the AR and μPC register and push-pop stack.

Outputs from the Am2909

Y_i	Address outputs from Am2909 (address inputs to control memory).
C_{n+4}	Carry-out from the incrementer.

Internal Signals

μPC	Contents of the microprogram counter.
REG	Contents of the register.
STK0–STK3	Contents of the push/pop stack. By definition, the word in the 4×4 file addressed by the stack pointer is STK0. Conceptually data is pushed into the stack at STK0; a subsequent push moves STK0 to STK1; a pop implies STK3 → STK2 → STK1 → STK0. Physically, only the stack pointer changes when a push or pop is performed. The data does not move. I/O occurs at STK0.
SP	Contents of the stack pointer.

External to the Am2909

A	Address to the control memory.
I(A)	Instruction in control memory at address A.
μWR	Contents of the microword register (at output of control memory). The microword register contains the instruction currently being executed.
T_n	Time period (cycle) n.

Operation of the Am2909

Figure 13 lists the select codes for the multiplexer. The two bits applied from the microword register (and additional combinational logic for branching) determine which data source contains the

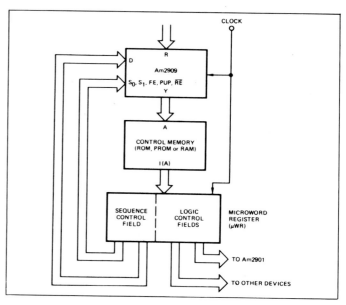

Fig. 12. Microprogram sequencer control.

address for the next microinstruction. The contents of the selected source will appear on the Y outputs. Figure 13 also shows the truth table for the output control and for the control of the push/pop stack. Table 9 shows in detail the effect of S_0, S_1, $\overline{FE}$, and PUP on the Am2909. These four signals define what address appears on the Y outputs and what the state of all the internal registers will be following the clock LOW-to-HIGH edge. In this illustration, the microprogram counter is assumed to contain initially some word J, the address register some word K, and the four words in the push/pop stack R_a through R_d.

Figure 14 illustrates the execution of a subroutine using the Am2909. The configuration of Fig. 11 is assumed. The instruction being executed at any given time is the one contained in the microword register (μWR). The contents of the μWR also control (indirectly, perhaps) the four signals S_0, S_1, $\overline{FE}$, and PUP. The starting address of the subroutine is applied to the D inputs of the Am2909 at the appropriate time.

In the columns on the left is the sequence of microinstructions to be executed. At address J + 2, the sequence control portion of the microinstruction contains the command "Jump to subroutine at A." At the time T_2, this is in the μWR, and the Am2909 inputs are set up to execute the jump and save the return address. The subroutine address A is applied to the D inputs from the μWR and appears on the Y outputs. The first instruction of the subroutine, I(A), is accessed and is at the inputs of the μWR. On the next clock transition, I(A) is loaded into the μWR for execution, and the return address J + 3 is pushed onto the stack. The return instruction is executed at T_5.

Address Selection

OCTAL	S_1	S_0	SOURCE FOR Y OUTPUTS	SYMBOL
0	L	L	Microprogram Counter	μPC
1	L	H	Register	REG
2	H	L	Push-Pop stack	STK0
3	H	H	Direct inputs	D_i

Output Control

OR_i	$\overline{ZERO}$	$\overline{OE}$	Y_i
X	X	H	Z
X	L	L	L
H	H	L	H
L	H	L	Source selected by S_0 S_1

Z = High Impedance

Synchronous Stack Control

$\overline{FE}$	PUP	PUSH-POP STACK CHANGE
H	X	No change
L	H	Increment stack pointer, then push current PC onto STK0
L	L	Pop stack (decrement stack pointer)

H = High
L = Low
X = Don't Care

Fig. 13 Am 2909 multiplexer selection codes.

Table 9 Output and Internal Next-Cycle Register States for Am2909

Cycle	$S_1, S_0, \overline{FE}, PUP$	μPC	REG	ST K0	ST K1	ST K2	ST K3	Y_{OUT}	Comment	Principal use
N	0 0 0 0	J	K	Ra	Rb	Rc	Rd	J	Pop stack	End loop
N + 1	....	J + 1	K	Rb	Rc	Rd	Ra	...		
N	0 0 0 1	J	K	Ra	Rb	Rc	Rd	J	Push μPC	Set up loop
N + 1	....	J + 1	K	J	Ra	Rb	Rc	...		
N	0 0 1 X	J	K	Ra	Rb	Rc	Rd	J	Continue	Continue
N + 1	....	J + 1	K	Ra	Rb	Rc	Rd	...		
N	0 1 0 0	J	K	Ra	Rb	Rc	Rd	K	Pop stack; Use AR for address	End loop
N + 1	....	K + 1	K	Rb	Rc	Rd	Ra	...		
N	0 1 0 1	J	K	Ra	Rb	Rc	Rd	K	Push μPC; Jump to address in AR	JSR AR
N + 1	....	K + 1	K	J	Ra	Rb	Rc	...		
N	0 1 1 X	J	K	Ra	Rb	Rc	Rd	K	Jump to address in AR	JMP AR
N + 1	....	K + 1	K	Ra	Rb	Rc	Rd	...		
N	1 0 0 0	J	K	Ra	Rb	Rc	Rd	Ra	Jump to address in STK0; Pop stack	RTS
N + 1	....	Ra + 1	K	Rb	Rc	Rd	Ra	...		
N	1 0 0 1	J	K	Ra	Rb	Rc	Rd	Ra	Jump to address in STK0; Push μPC	
N + 1	....	Ra + 1	K	J	Ra	Rb	Rc	...		
N	1 0 1 X	J	K	Ra	Rb	Rc	Rd	Ra	Jump to address in STK0	Stack ref (loop)
N + 1	....	Ra + 1	K	Ra	Rb	Rc	Rd	...		
N	1 1 0 0	J	K	Ra	Rb	Rc	Rd	D	Pop stack; Jump to address on D	End loop
N + 1	....	D + 1	K	Rb	Rc	Rd	Ra	...		
N	1 1 0 1	J	K	Ra	Rb	Rc	Rd	D	Jump to address on D; Push μPC	JSR D
N + 1	....	D + 1	K	J	Ra	Rb	Rc	...		
N	1 1 1 X	J	K	Ra	Rb	Rc	Rd	D	Jump to address on D	JMP D
N + 1	....	D + 1	K	Ra	Rb	Rc	Rd	...		

X = Don't care, 0 = LOW, 1 = HIGH, Assume C_n = HIGH

Note: STK0 is the location addressed by the stack pointer.

CONTROL MEMORY

Execute Cycle	Microprogram	
	Address	Sequencer Instruction
	J−1	—
T0	J	—
T1	J+1	—
T2	J+2	JSR A
T6	J+3	—
T7	J+4	—
—	—	—
—	—	—
—	—	—
T3	A	I(A)
T4	A+1	—
T5	A+2	RTS
—	—	—
—	—	—
—	—	—
—	—	—

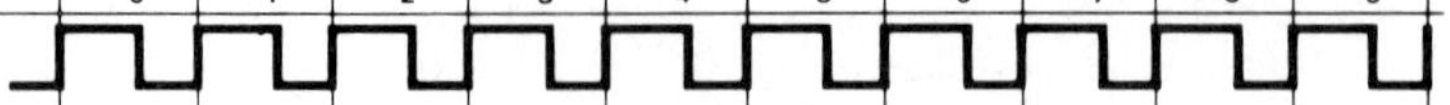

Execute Cycle			T_0	T_1	T_2	T_3	T_4	T_5	T_6	T_7	T_8	T_9
Clock Signals			⎍	⎍	⎍	⎍	⎍	⎍	⎍	⎍	⎍	⎍
Am2909 Inputs (from µWR)		S_1, S_0	0	0	3	0	0	2	0	0		
		$\overline{FE}$	H	H	L	H	H	L	H	H		
		PUP	X	X	H	X	X	L	X	X		
		D	X	X	A	X	X	X	X	X		
Internal Registers		µPC	J+1	J+2	J+3	A+1	A+2	A+3	J+4	J+5		
		STK0	—	—	—	J+3	J+3	J+3	—	—		
		STK1	—	—	—	—	—	—	—	—		
		STK2	—	—	—	—	—	—	—	—		
		STK3	—	—	—	—	—	—	—	—		
Am2909 Output		Y	J+1	J+2	A	A+1	A+2	J+3	J+4	J+5		
ROM Output		(Y)	I(J+1)	JSR A	I(A)	I(A+1)	RTS	I(J+3)	I(J+4)	I(J+5)		
Contents of µWR (Instruction being executed)		µWR	I(J)	I(J+1)	JSR A	I(A)	I(A+1)	RTS	I(J+3)	I(J+4)		

C_n = HIGH

Fig. 14. Subroutine execution.

APPENDIX 1   AM2909 ISP DESCRIPTION

```
AM2909 :=
   begin

! ISPS description of AMD AM2909 bit slice microprogram sequencer.

! The AM2909 is a 4 bit slice (expandable to 4*n bits) address controller.
! The controller is designed to be used with the AM2901 microprocessor
! slice and external memory.

! Simulation of the AM2909 alone is possible, but emulation of any
! computer systems requires that this description be joined with
! the AM2901 description.

**PC.State**

   uPC<3:0>    := incr<3:0>,       ! Microprogram counter
   REG<3:0>,                       ! Address register
   SP<1:0>,                        ! Stack pointer
   STACK[0:3]<3:0>,                ! Stack register file

**External.State**

   Cn<>,                           ! Carry in
   Cn4<>       := incr<4>,         ! Carry out
   D<3:0>,                         ! Direct inputs
   FE<>,                           ! Stack register file enable
   OE<>,                           ! Output enable control line
   OR.<3:0>,                       ! Logical OR inputs
   PUP<>,                          ! Push/pop control line
   R<3:0>,                         ! Address register inputs
   RE<>,                           ! Register enable control line
   S<1:0>,                         ! Address select control lines
   ZERO<>,                         ! Zero out control line

**Implementation.Variables**

   incr<4:0>,                      ! Incrementer

   macro z := |'1111|,             ! High impedence constant


**Operation.Cycle**{us}

start{main} :=                              ! Initialization
   begin
   OE = FE = 0;
   RE = ZERO = 1 next

   run :=                                   ! Basic operation loop
      begin
      Y() next                              ! Put out selected address
      IF not FE =>                          ! Perform any stack operation
         begin
         DECODE PUP =>
            begin
            '0\pop   := (SP = SP - 1),
            '1\push  := (SP = SP + 1 next
                         STACK[SP] = uPC)
            end
         end next
      IF not RE => REG <- R;                ! Load register if enabled
      incr = uPC + Cn next     ! Increment pc
      RESTART run
      end
   end,

**Address.Source.Selection**{us}

   Y()<3:0> :=
      begin
      DECODE ZERO @ OE =>
         begin
         '00      := Y = uPC = '0000,
         ['01,'11]:= Y = z,
         '10      := DECODE S =>
            begin
            '00 := Y = uPC = uPC or OR.,
            '01 := Y = uPC = REG or OR.,
            '10 := Y = uPC = STACK[SP] or OR.,
            '11 := Y = uPC = D or OR.
            end
         end
      end,

end    ! End of AM2909 description
```

APPENDIX 2   AM2901 ISP DESCRIPTION

```
AM2901 :=
    begin

! ISPS description of the AMD 2901 4 bit slice microprocessor.

! Page 1 contains the declaration of all actual and implementation
!        variables.
! Page 2 describes the basic instruction cycle and the source and
!        destination access computations.
! Page 3 defines the actual instruction execution process.
! Page 4 contains routines that aid in computation of the carry generate
!        (G), overflow (OVR), and carry propagate (P).
!        outputs.

**PC.State**

    R<3:0>,                             ! R inputs to ALU
    S<3:0>,                             ! S inputs to ALU
    F<3:0> := ALU<3:0>,                 ! Output from ALU
    Q<3:0>,                             ! Output from Q register

**MP.State**

    RAM[0:15]<3:0>,                     ! 16 X 4 bit 2 port RAM
    A.LATCH<3:0>,                       ! A RAM port latch
    B.LATCH<3:0>,                       ! B RAM port latch

**External.State**

    A<3:0>,                             ! A RAM port input address
    B<3:0>,                             ! B RAM port input address
    D<3:0>,                             ! Direct data inputs
    Y<3:0>,                             ! Data outputs
    OE<>,                               ! Output enable (tristate control)
    P<>,                                ! Carry propogate
    G<>,                                ! Carry generate
    OVR<>,                              ! Overflow
    FEQLO<>,                            ! High if ALU output = 0
    Cn<>,                               ! Carry in
    Cn4<> := ALU<4>,                    ! Carry out
    RAM0<>,                             ! Low order shift input/output
    RAM3<>,                             ! High order shift input/output
    Q0<>,                               ! Low order Q shift input/output
    Q3<>,                               ! High order Q shift input/output

**Instruction.Format**

    I<8:0>,                             ! Instruction inputs
       src<2:0>   := I<2:0>,            ! Source operand field
       op<2:0>    := I<5:3>,            ! Operation field
       dest<2:0>  := I<8:6>,            ! Destination operand field

**Implementation.Variables**

    ALU<4:0>,                           ! ALU + carry output

    ctemp<3:0>,                         ! Temporary for generating carry

    macro z := |'1111|,                 ! Tristate constant

**Instruction.Cycle**{us}

start{main} :=                          ! Initialization
    begin
    OE = OVR = FEQLO = Cn4 = 0;
    P = G = 1 next

    run :=                              ! Main instruction cycle
        begin
        source() next
        exec() next
        destination() next
        RESTART run
        end
    end,

**Access.Computation**{us}

    source :=                           ! Source calculation
        begin
        A.LATCH = RAM[A];
        B.LATCH = RAM[B] next
        DECODE src =>
            begin
            #0 := (R = A.LATCH; S = Q      ),
            #1 := (R = A.LATCH; S = B.LATCH),
            #2 := (R = 0      ; S = Q      ),
            #3 := (R = 0      ; S = B.LATCH),
            #4 := (R = 0      ; S = A.LATCH),
            #5 := (R = D      ; S = A.LATCH),
            #6 := (R = D      ; S = Q      ),
            #7 := (R = D      ; S = 0      )
            end
        end,
```

```
    destination :=                      ! Destination calculation
        begin
        DECODE dest =>
            begin
            #0 := (Q = F; Y = F),
            #1 := (Y = F),
            #2 := (Y = RAM[A]; RAM[B] = F),
            #3 := (Y = F; RAM[B] = F),
            #4 := (Y = F; RAM[B] @ RAM0 = RAM3 @ F; Q @ Q0 = Q3 @ Q),
            #5 := (Y = F; RAM[B] @ RAM0 = RAM3 @ F),
            #6 := (Y = F; RAM3 @ RAM[B] = F @ RAM0; Q3 @ Q = Q @ Q0),
            #7 := (Y = F; RAM3 @ RAM[B] = F @ RAM0)
            end
        end,

**Instruction.Execution**{us}

    exec :=
        begin
        DECODE op =>
            begin
            #0 := (ALU = R + S;                     ! R + S
                   P   = ((R or S) neq{us} '1111);
                   G   = g.compute(R, S);
                   OVR = ALU<4> xor ALU<3>),
            #1 := (ALU = S - R;                     ! S - R
                   P   = (((not R) or S) neq{us} '1111);
                   G   = g.compute((not R), S);
                   OVR = ALU<4> xor ALU<3>),
            #2 := (ALU = R - S;                     ! R - S
                   P   = (R or (not S)) neq{us} '1111);
                   G   = g.compute(R, (not S));
                   OVR = ALU<4> xor ALU<3>),
            #3 := (ALU = R or S;                    ! R or S
                   P   = 0;
                   G   = ((R or S) eql{us} '1111) next
                   Cn4 = OVR = (not G) or Cn),
            #4 := (ALU = R and S;                   ! R and S
                   P   = 0;
                   G   = ((R and S) eql{us} '0000) next
                   Cn4 = OVR = (not G) or Cn),
            #5 := (ALU = ((not R) and S;            ! R and S
                   P   = 0;
                   G   = (((not R) and S) eql{us} '0000) next
                   Cn4 = OVR = (not G) or Cn),
            #6 := (ALU = R xor S;                   ! R xor S
                   P   = (((not R) and s) neq{us} '0000);
                   G   = not g.compute((not R), S);
                   Cn4 = c67(not R, S);
                   OVR = ovr67(not R, S)),
            #7 := (ALU = R eqv S;                   ! R eqv S
                   P   = ((R and S) neq{us} '0000);
                   G   = not g.compute(R, S);
                   Cn4 = c67(R, S);
                   OVR = ovr67(R, S))
            end next
        FEQLO = (F eqv '0000)
        end,

** Service.Facilities **{us}

    g.compute(r.<3:0>, s.<3:0>)<> :=
        begin
        g.compute = (((r. and s.) and ('1@(r. OR s.)<3:1>)
                    and ('11@(r. or s.)<3:2>)
                    and ('111@(r. or s.)<3>))
                    eql{us} '0000)
        end,

    c67(r.<3:0>, s.<3:0>)<> :=                      ! Carry for OP 6 and 7
        begin
        c67 = not(((r. or s.) eql{us} '1111) and ((r. and s.)<3:1> neq{us} '000)
                and ((r. and s.)<0> or (not Cn)))
        end,

    ovr67(r.<3:0>, s.<3:0>)<> :=                    ! Overflow for OP 6 and 7
        begin
        ctemp = (r. or s.) and (r. and s.) or ('000 @ Cn)
                and ('11 @ (r. or s.)<2:1>) and ('111 @ (r. or s.)<2>) next
        ovr67 = (((ctemp<2:0> eql{us} '000) and ctemp<3>)
                or (not((r. or s.)<3> or (ctemp<2:0> eql '000))))
        end,

end    ! End of AM2901 description
```

Chapter 14

The Am2903/2910[1]

General Description of the Am2903

The Am2903 is a 4-bit expandable bipolar microprocessor slice. The Am2903 performs all functions performed by the industry standard Am2901A and, in addition, provides a number of significant enhancements that are especially useful in arithmetic-oriented processors. Infinitely expandable memory and three-port, three-address architecture are provided by the Am2903. In addition to its complete arithmetic and logic instruction set, the Am2903 provides a special set of instructions which facilitate the implementation of multiplication, division, normalization, and other previously time-consuming operations. The Am2903 is supplied in a 48-pin dual in-line package.

Architecture of the Am2903

The Am2903 is a high-performance cascadable 4-bit bipolar microprocessor slice designed for use in CPU's, peripheral controllers, microprogrammable machines, and numerous other applications. The 9-bit microinstruction selects the ALU sources, function, and destination. The Am2903 is cascadable with full lookahead or ripple carry, has three-state outputs, and provides various ALU status flag outputs. Advanced low-power Schottky processing is used to fabricate this 48-pin LSI circuit.

All data paths within the device are 4 bits wide. As shown in Fig. 1, the device consists of a 16-word by 4-bit two-port RAM with latches on both output ports, a high-performance ALU and shifter, a multi-purpose Q register with shifter input, and a 9-bit instruction decoder.

Two-Port RAM

Any two RAM words addressed at the A and B address ports can be read simultaneously at the respective RAM A and B output ports. Identical data appears at the two output ports when the same address is applied to both address ports. The latches at the RAM output ports are transparent when the clock input, CP, is HIGH, and they hold the RAM output data when CP is LOW. Under control of the $\overline{OE}_B$ three-state output enable, RAM data can be read directly at the Am2903 DB I/O port.

External data at the Am2903 Y I/O port can be written directly into the RAM, or ALU shifter output data can be enabled onto the Y I/O port and entered into the RAM. Data is written into the RAM at the B address when the write enable input, $\overline{WE}$, is LOW and the clock input, CP, is LOW.

Arithmetic Logic Unit

The Am2903 high-performance ALU can perform seven arithmetic and nine logic operations on two 4-bit operands. Multiplexers at the ALU inputs provide the capability to select various pairs of ALU source operands. The $\overline{E}_A$ input selects either the DA external data input or RAM output port A for use as one ALU operand, and the $\overline{OE}_B$ and I_0 inputs select RAM output port B, DB external data input, or the Q-register content for use as the second ALU operand. Also, during some ALU operations, zeros are forced at the ALU operand inputs. Thus, the Am2903 ALU can operate on data from two external sources, from an internal and external source, or from two internal sources. Table 1 shows all possible pairs of ALU source operands as a function of the $\overline{E}_A$, $\overline{OE}_B$, and I_0 inputs.

When instruction bits I_4, I_3, I_2, I_1, and I_0 are LOW, the Am2903 executes special functions. Table 4 defines these special functions and the operation which the ALU performs for each. When the 2903 executes instructions other than the nine special functions, the ALU operation is determined by instruction bits I_4, I_3, I_2, and I_1. Table 2 defines the ALU operation as a function of these four instruction bits.

Am2903's may be cascaded in either a ripple carry or lookahead carry fashion. When a number of Am2903's are cascaded, each slice must be programmed to be a most significant slice (MSS), intermediate slice (IS), or least significant slice (LSS) of the array. The carry generate, $\overline{G}$, and carry propagate, $\overline{P}$, signals required for a lookahead carry scheme are generated by the Am2903 and are available as outputs of the least significant and intermediate slices.

The Am2903 also generates a carry-out signal, C_{n+4}, which is generally available as an output of each slice. Both the carry-in, C_n, and carry-out, C_{n+4}, signals are active HIGH. The ALU generates two other status outputs. These are negative, N, and overflow, OVR. The N output is generally the most significant (sign) bit of the ALU output and can be used to determine positive or negative results. The OVR output indicates that the arithmetic operation being performed exceeds the available 2's complement number range. The N and OVR signals are available as outputs of the most significant slice. Thus the multi-purpose $\overline{G}$ /N and $\overline{P}$ /OVR outputs indicate $\overline{G}$ and $\overline{P}$ at the least significant and intermediate slices, and sign and overflow at the most significant slice. To some extent, the meanings of the C_{n+4}, $\overline{P}$ /OVR, and $\overline{G}$ /N signals vary with the ALU function being performed. Refer to Table 5 for an exact definition of these four signals as a function of the Am2903 instruction.

[1]Abstracted from "Am2903, The Superslice" and "Am2910 Microprogram Controller" specification sheets, Advanced Micro Devices, Inc., 1978.

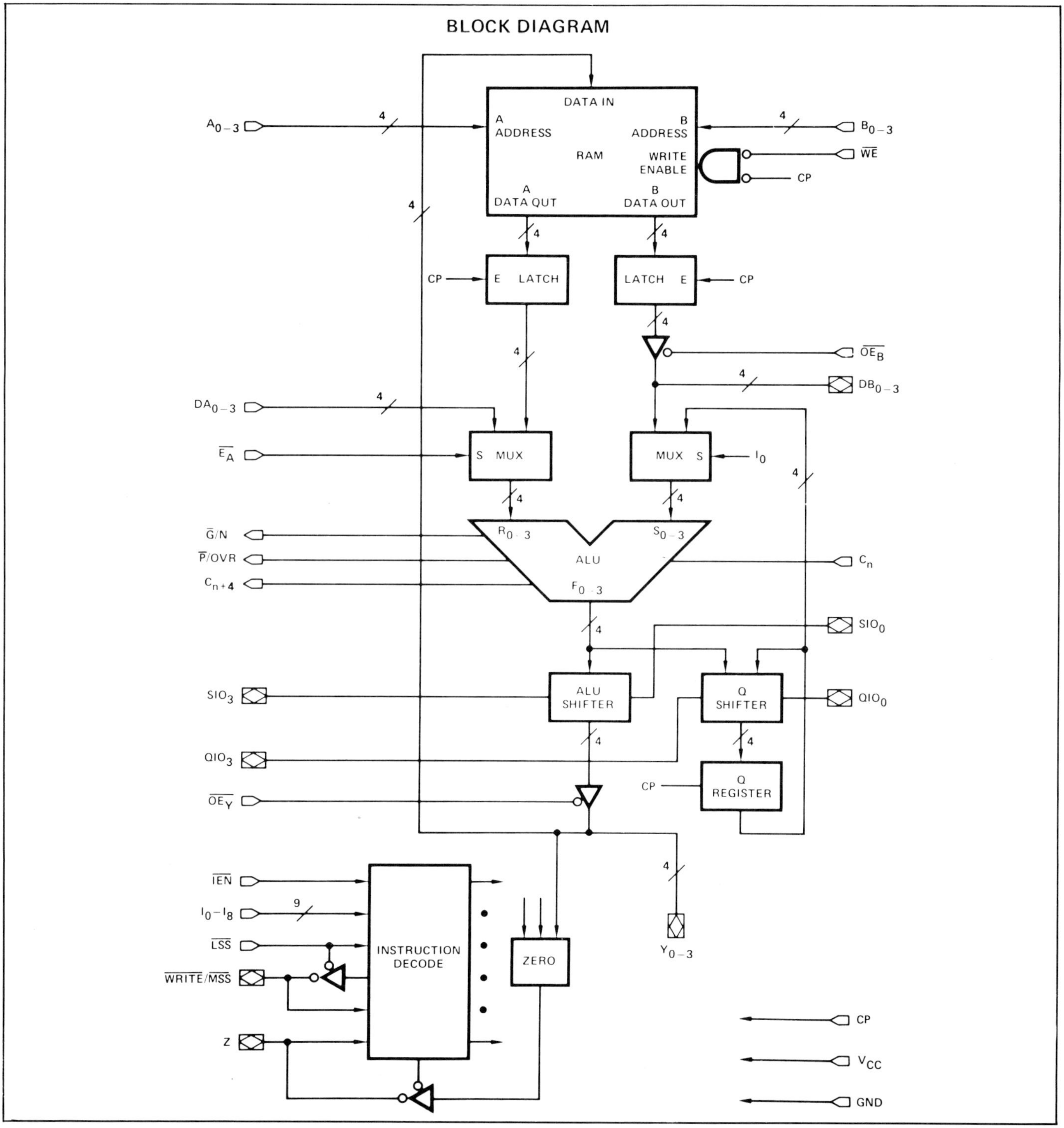

BLOCK DIAGRAM

Fig. 1. Block diagram.

Table 1   ALU Operand Sources

$\overline{E}_A$	I_0	$\overline{OE}_B$	ALU operand R	ALU operand S
L	L	L	RAM output A	RAM output B
L	L	H	RAM output A	DB_{0-3}
L	H	X	RAM output A	Q Register
H	L	L	DA_{0-3}	RAM output B
H	L	H	DA_{0-3}	DB_{0-3}
H	H	X	DA_{0-3}	Q Register

L = LOW   H = HIGH   X = don't care

ALU Shifter

Under instruction control, the ALU shifter passes the ALU output (F) non-shifted, shifts it up one bit position (2F), or shifts it down one bit position (F/2). Both arithmetic and logical shift operations are possible. An arithmetic shift operation shifts data around the most significant (sign) bit position of the most significant slice, and a logical shift operation shifts data through this bit position (see Fig. 2). SIO_0 and SIO_3 are bidirectional serial shift inputs/outputs. During a shift-up operation, SIO_0 is generally a serial shift input

Table 2   ALU Functions

I_4	I_3	I_2	I_1	Hex code	ALU functions
L	L	L	L	0	I_0 = L Special functions
					I_0 = H F_i = HIGH
L	L	L	H	1	F = S Minus R Minus 1 Plus C_n
L	L	H	L	2	F = R Minus S Minus 1 Plus C_n
L	L	H	H	3	F = R Plus S Plus C_n
L	H	L	L	4	F = S Plus C_n
L	H	L	H	5	F = $\overline{S}$ Plus C_n
L	H	H	L	6	F = R Plus C_n
L	H	H	H	7	F = $\overline{R}$ Plus C_n
H	L	L	L	8	F_i = LOW
H	L	L	H	9	$F_i = \overline{R}_i$ AND S_i
H	L	H	L	A	$F_i = R_i$ Exclusive - NOR S_i
H	L	H	H	B	$F_i = R_i$ Exclusive - OR S_i
H	H	L	L	C	$F_i = R_i$ AND S_i
H	H	L	H	D	$F_i = R_i$ NOR S_i
H	H	H	L	E	$F_i = R_i$ NAND S_i
H	H	H	H	F	$F_i = R_i$ OR S_i

L = LOW   H = HIGH   i = 0 to 3

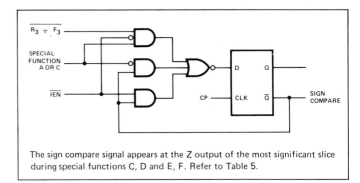

The sign compare signal appears at the Z output of the most significant slice during special functions C, D and E, F. Refer to Table 5.

Fig. 2

and SIO_3 a serial shift output. During a shift down operation, SIO_3 is generally a serial shift input and SIO_0 a serial shift output.

To some extent, the meaning of the SIO_0 and SIO_3 signals is instruction-dependent. Refer to Tables 3 and 4 for an exact definition of these pins.

The ALU shifter also provides the capability to sign-extend at slice boundaries. Under instruction control, the SIO_0 (sign) input can be extended through Y_0, Y_1, Y_2, and Y_3 and propagated to the SIO_3 output.

A cascadable 5-bit parity generator/checker is designed into the Am2903 ALU shifter and provides ALU error detection capability. Parity for the F_0, F_1, F_2, and F_3 ALU outputs and SIO_3 input is generated and, under instruction control, is made available at the SIO_0 output.

The instruction inputs determine the ALU shifter operation. Table 4 defines the special functions and the operation the ALU shifter performs for each. When the Am2903 executes instructions other than the nine special functions, the ALU shifter operation is determined by instruction bits $I_8I_7I_6I_5$. Table 3 defines the ALU shifter operation as a function of these four bits.

Q Register

The Q register is an auxiliary 4-bit register. It is intended primarily for use in multiplication and division operations; however, it can also be used as an accumulator or holding register for some applications. The ALU output, F, can be loaded into the Q register, and/or the Q register can be selected as the source for the ALU S operand. The shifter at the input to the Q register provides the capability to shift the Q-register contents up one bit position (2Q) or down one bit position (Q/2). Only logical shifts are performed. QIO_0 and QIO_3 are bidirectional shift serial inputs/outputs. During a Q-register shift-up operation, QIO_0 is a serial shift input and QIO_3 is a serial shift output. During a shift-down operation, QIO_3 is a serial shift input and QIO_0 is a serial shift output.

Double-length arithmetic and logical shifting capability is provided by the Am2903. The double-length shift is performed by connection QIO_3 of the most significant slice to SIO_0 of the least significant slice, and executing an instruction which shifts both the ALU output and the Q register.

The Q register and shifter are controlled by the instruction inputs. Table 4 defines the Am2903 special functions and the operations which the Q register and shifter perform for each. When the Am2903 executes instructions other than the nine special functions, the Q register and shifter operation is controlled by instruction bits $I_8I_7I_6I_5$. Table 3 defines the Q register and shifter operation as a function of these four bits.

Output Buffers

The DB and Y ports are bidirectional I/O ports driven by three-state output buffers with external output enable controls. The Y output buffers are enabled when the $\overline{OE}_Y$ input is LOW and are in the high-impedance state when $\overline{OE}_Y$ is HIGH. Likewise, the DB output buffers are enabled when the $\overline{OE}_B$ is LOW and in the high-impedance state when $\overline{OE}_B$ is HIGH.

The zero, Z, pin is an open-collector input/output that can be wired ORed between slices. As an output it can be used as a zero detect status flag and generally indicates that the Y_{0-3} pins are all LOW, whether they are driven from the Y output buffers or from an external source connected to the Y_{0-3} pins. To some extent the meaning of this signal varies with the instruction being performed. Refer to Table 5 for an exact definition of this signal as a function of the Am2903 instruction.

Instruction Decoder

The Instruction Decoder generates required internal control signals as a function of the nine instruction inputs, I_{0-8}; the Instruction Enable input, $\overline{IEN}$: the $\overline{LSS}$ input; and the $\overline{WRITE}/\overline{MSS}$ input/output.

The $\overline{WRITE}$ output is LOW when an instruction which writes data into the RAM is being executed. Refer to Tables 3 and 4 for a definition of the $\overline{WRITE}$ output as a function of the Am2903 instruction inputs.

When $\overline{IEN}$ is HIGH, the $\overline{WRITE}$ output is forced HIGH and the Q register and Sign Compare Flip-Flop contents are preserved.

When $\overline{IEN}$ is LOW, the $\overline{WRITE}$ output is enabled and the Q register and Sign Compare Flip-Flop can be written according to the Am2903 instruction. The Sign Compare Flip-Flop is an on-chip flip-flop which is used during an Am2903 divide operation (see Fig. 3).

Programming the Am2903 Slice Position

Tying the $\overline{LSS}$ input LOW programs the slice to operate as a least significant slice (LSS) and enables the $\overline{WRITE}$ output signal onto the $\overline{WRITE}/\overline{MSS}$ bidirectional I/O pin. When $\overline{LSS}$ is tied HIGH, the $\overline{WRITE}/\overline{MSS}$ pin becomes an input pin. Tying the $\overline{WRITE}/\overline{MSS}$ pin HIGH programs the slice to operate as an intermediate slice (IS), and tying it LOW programs the slice to operate as a most significant slice (MSS).

Am2903 Special Functions

The Am2903 provides nine special functions which facilitate the implementation of the following operations:

- Single- and double-length normalization
- 2's complement division
- Conversion between 2's complement and sign magnitude representation
- Incrementation by 1 or 2

Table 4 defines these special functions.

The single-length and double-length normalization functions can be used to adjust a single-precision or double-precision floating-point number in order to bring its mantissa within a specified range.

Three special functions which can be used to perform a 2's complement, non-restoring divide operation are provided by the Am2903. These functions provide both single- and double-precision divide operations and can be performed in n clock cycles, where n is the number of bits in the quotient.

The unsigned multiply special function and the two 2's complement multiply special functions can be used to multiply two n-bit unsigned or 2's complement numbers in n clock cycles. These functions utilize the conditional add and shift algorithm. During the last cycle of the 2's complement multiplication, a conditional subtraction, rather than addition, is performed because the sign bit of the multiplier carries negative weight.

The sign/magnitude–2's complement special function can be used to convert number representation systems. A number expressed in sign/magnitude representation can be converted to the 2's complement representation, and vice-versa, in one clock cycle.

The increment by 1 and increment by 2 special functions can be used to increment an unsigned or 2's complement number by 1 or 2. This is useful in 16-bit-word, byte-addressable machines, where the word addresses are multiples of 2.

Pin Definitions

A_{0-3} Four RAM address inputs which contain the address of the RAM word appearing at the RAM A output port.

B_{0-3} Four RAM address inputs which contain the address of the RAM word appearing at the RAM B

Table 3   ALU Destination Control for I_0 OR I_1 OR I_2 OR I_3 OR I_4 = HIGH, $\overline{IEN}$ = LOW

I_8	I_7	I_6	I_5	Hex code	ALU shifter function	SIO_3 Most sig. slice	SIO_3 Other slices	Y_3 Most sig. slice	Y_3 Other slices
L	L	L	L	0	Arith. F/2 → Y	Input	Input	F_3	SIO_3
L	L	L	H	1	Log. F/2 → Y	Input	Input	SIO_3	SIO_3
L	L	H	L	2	Arith. F/2 → Y	Input	Input	F_3	SIO_3
L	L	H	H	3	Log. F/2 → Y	Input	Input	SIO_3	SIO_3
L	H	L	L	4	F → Y	Input	Input	F_3	F_3
L	H	L	H	5	F → Y	Input	Input	F_3	F_3
L	H	H	L	6	F → Y	Input	Input	F_3	F_3
L	H	H	H	7	F → Y	Input	Input	F_3	F_3
H	L	L	L	8	Arith. 2F → Y	F_2	F_3	F_3	F_2
H	L	L	H	9	Log. 2F → Y	F_3	F_3	F_2	F_2
H	L	H	L	A	Arith. 2F → Y	F_2	F_3	F_3	F_2
H	L	H	H	B	Log. 2F → Y	F_3	F_3	F_2	F_2
H	H	L	L	C	F → Y	F_3	F_3	F_3	F_3
H	H	L	H	D	F →Y	F_3	F_3	F_3	F_3
H	H	H	L	E	SIO_0 → Y_0, Y_1, Y_2, Y_3	SIO_0	SIO_0	SIO_0	SIO_0
H	H	H	H	F	F → Y	F_3	F_3	F_3	F_3

Parity = $F_3 \veebar F_2 \veebar F_1 \veebar F_0 \veebar SIO_3$

$\veebar$ = Exclusive OR

$\overline{WE}$ output port and into which new data is written when the $\overline{WE}$ input and the CP input are LOW. The RAM write enable input. If $\overline{WE}$ is LOW, data at the Y I/O port is written into the RAM when the CP input is LOW. When $\overline{WE}$ is HIGH, writing data into the RAM is inhibited.

DA_{0-8} A 4 bit external data input which can be selected as one of the Am2903 ALU operand sources; DA_0 is the least significant bit.

$\overline{EA}$ A control input which, when HIGH, selects DA_{0-8} and, when LOW, selects RAM output A as the ALU R operand.

DB_{0-3} A 4-bit external data input/output. Under control of the $\overline{OE}_B$ input, RAM output port B can be directly read on these lines, or input data on these lines can be selected as the ALU S operand.

$\overline{OE}_B$ A control input which, when LOW, enables RAM output B onto the DB_{0-3} lines and, when HIGH, disables the RAM output B tri-state buffers.

C_n The carry-in input to the Am2903 ALU.

I_{0-8} The nine instruction inputs used to select the Am2903 operation to be performed.

$\overline{IEN}$ The Instruction enable input which, when LOW, enables the $\overline{WRITE}$ output and allows the Q register and the Sign Compare Flip-Flop to be written. When $\overline{IEN}$ is HIGH, the $\overline{WRITE}$ output is forced HIGH and the Q register and Sign Compare Flip-Flop are in the hold mode.

C_{n+4} This output generally indicates the carry-out of the Am2903 ALU. Refer to Table 5 for an exact definition of this pin.

$\overline{G}$ /N   A multi-purpose pin which indicates the carry generate, $\overline{G}$, function at the least significant and intermediate slices, and generally indicates the sign, N, of the ALU result at the most significant slice. Refer to Table 5 for an exact definition of this pin.

$\overline{P}$ /OVR   A multi-purpose pin which indicates the carry

| Y_2 | | Y_1 | Y_0 | SIO_0 | $\overline{Write}$ | Q Reg. & shifter function | QIO_3 | QIO_0 |
Most sig. slice	Other slices							
SIO_3	F_3	F_2	F_1	F_0	L	Hold	Hi-Z	Hi-Z
F_3	F_3	F_2	F_1	F_0	L	Hold	Hi-Z	Hi-Z
SIO_3	F_3	F_2	F_1	F_0	L	Log. Q/2 → Q	Input	Q_0
F_3	F_3	F_2	F_1	F_0	L	Log. Q/2 → Q	Input	Q_0
F_2	F_2	F_1	F_0	Parity	L	Hold	Hi-Z	Hi-Z
F_2	F_2	F_1	F_0	Parity	H	Log. Q/2 → Q	Input	Q_0
F_2	F_2	F_1	F_0	Parity	H	F → Q	Hi-Z	Hi-Z
F_2	F_2	F_1	F_0	Parity	L	F → Q	Hi-Z	Hi-Z
F_1	F_1	F_0	SIO_0	Input	L	Hold	Hi-Z	Hi-Z
F_1	F_1	F_0	SIO_0	Input	L	Hold	Hi-Z	Hi-Z
F_1	F_1	F_0	SIO_0	Input	L	Log. 2Q → Q	Q_3	Input
F_1	F_1	F_0	SIO_0	Input	L	Log. 2Q → Q	Q_3	Input
F_2	F_2	F_1	F_0	Hi-Z	H	Hold	Hi-Z	Hi-Z
F_2	F_2	F_1	F_0	Hi-Z	H	Log. 2Q → Q	Q_3	Input
SIO_0	SIO_0	SIO_0	SIO_0	Input	L	Hold	Hi-Z	Hi-Z
F_2	F_2	F_1	F_0	Hi-Z	L	Hold	Hi-Z	Hi-Z

L = LOW

H = HIGH

Hi-Z = high-impedance

propagate, $\overline{P}$, function at the least significant and intermediate slices, and indicates the conventional 2's complement overflow, OVR, signal at the most significant slice. Refer to Table 5 for an exact definition of this pin.

Z An open-collector input/output pin which, when HIGH, generally indicates the Y_{0-3} outputs are all LOW. For some special functions, Z is used as an input pin. Refer to Table 5 for an exact definition of this pin.

SIO_0, SIO_3 Bidirectional serial shift inputs/outputs for the ALU shifter. During a shift-up operation, SIO_0 is an input and SIO_3 an output. During a shift-down operation, SIO_3 is an input and SIO_0 is an output. Refer to Tables 3 and 4 for an exact definition of these pins.

QIO_0, QIO_3 Bidirectional serial shift inputs/outputs for the Q shifter which operate like SIO_0 and SIO_3. Refer to Tables 3 and 4 for an exact definition of these pins.

$\overline{LSS}$ An input pin which, when tied LOW, programs the chip to act as the least significant slice (LSS) of an Am2903 array and enables the $\overline{WRITE}$ output onto the $\overline{WRITE}/\overline{MSS}$ pin. When $\overline{LSS}$ is tied HIGH, the chip is programmed to operate as either an intermediate or most significant slice and the $\overline{WRITE}$ output buffer is disabled.

$\overline{WRITE}/$ $\overline{MSS}$ When LSS is tied LOW, the WRITE output signal appears at this pin; the $\overline{WRITE}$ signal is LOW when an instruction which writes data into the RAM is being executed. When $\overline{LSS}$ is tied HIGH, $\overline{WRITE}/\overline{MSS}$ is an input pin; tying it HIGH programs the chip to operate as an intermediate slice (IS) and tying it LOW programs the chip to operate as the most significant slice (MSS).

Y_{0-3} Four data inputs/outputs of the Am2903. Under control of the $\overline{OE}_Y$ input, the ALU shifter output data can be enabled onto these lines, or these lines can be used as data inputs when external data is written directly into the RAM.

Table 4

I_8	I_7	I_6	I_5	Hex code	Special function	ALU function	ALU shifter function	SIO$_3$ Most sig. slice	SIO$_3$ Other slices	SIO$_0$	Q Reg. & shifter function	QIO$_3$	QIO$_0$	$\overline{WRITE}$
L	L	L	X	0, 1	Unsigned Multiply	$F = S + C_n$ if $Z = L$ $F = R + S + C_n$ if $Z = H$	Log. $F/2 \rightarrow Y$ (Note 1)	Hi-Z	Input	F_0	Log. $Q/2 \rightarrow Q$	Input	Q_0	L
L	L	H	X	2, 3	Two's Complement Multiply	$F = S + C_n$ if $Z = L$ $F = R + S + C_n$ if $Z = H$	Log. $F/2 \rightarrow Y$ (Note 2)	Hi-Z	Input	F_0	Log. $Q/2 \rightarrow Q$	Input	Q_0	L
L	H	L	L	4	Increment by One or Two	$F = S + 1 + C_n$	$F \rightarrow Y$	Input	Input	Parity	Hold	Hi-Z	Hi-Z	L
L	H	L	H	5	Sign/Magnitude-Two's Complement	$F = S + C_n$ if $Z = L$ $F = \overline{S} + C_n$ if $Z = H$	$F \rightarrow Y$ (Note 3)	Input	Input	Parity	Hold	Hi-Z	Hi-Z	L
L	H	H	X	6, 7	Two's Complement Multiply, Correction	$F = S + C_n$ if $Z = L$ $F = S - R - 1 + C_n$ if $Z = H$	Log. $F/2 \rightarrow Y$ (Note 2)	Hi-Z	Input	F_0	Log. $Q/2 \rightarrow Q$	Input	Q_0	L
H	L	L	X	8, 9	Single Length Normalize	$F = S + C_n$	$F \rightarrow Y$	F_3	F_3	Hi-Z	Log. $2Q \rightarrow Q$	Q_3	Input	L
H	L	H	X	A, B	Double Length Normalize and First Divide Op.	$F = S + C_n$	Log. $2F \rightarrow Y$	$R_3 \veebar F_3$	F_3	Input	Log. $2Q \rightarrow Q$	Q_3	Input	L
H	H	L	X	C, D	Two's Complement Divide	$F = S + R + C_n$ if $Z = L$ $F = S - R - 1 + C_n$ if $Z = H$	Log. $2F \rightarrow Y$	$\overline{R_3 \veebar F_3}$	F_3	Input	Log. $2Q \rightarrow Q$	Q_3	Input	L
H	H	H	X	E, F	Two's Complement Divide, Correction and Remainder	$F = S + R + C_n$ if $Z = L$ $F = S - R - 1 + C_n$ if $Z = H$	$F \rightarrow Y$	F_3	F_3	Hi-Z	Log. $2Q \rightarrow Q$	Q_3	Input	L

NOTES 1. At the most significant slice only, the C_{n+4} signal is internally gated to the Y_3 output.
2. At the most significant slice only, $F_3 \veebar OVR$ is internally gated to the Y_3 output.
3. At the most significant slice only, $S_3 \veebar F_3$ is generated at the Y_3 output.

L = LOW
H = HIGH
X = don't care

Hi-Z = high impedance
$\veebar$ = Exclusive OR
Parity = $SIO_3 \veebar F_3 \veebar F_2 \veebar F_1 \veebar F_0$

Table 5

(Hex) $I_8I_7I_6I_5$	(Hex) $I_4I_3I_2I_1$	I_0	GI (I = 0 to 3)	PI (I = 0 to 3)	C_{n+4}	$\overline{P}/OVR$		$\overline{G}/N$		Z		
						Most sig. slice	Other slices	Most sig. slice	Other slices	Most sig. slice	Intermediate slice	Least sig. slice
X	0	H	0	1	0	0	0	F_3	$\overline{G}$	$\overline{Y}_0\overline{Y}_1\overline{Y}_2\overline{Y}_3$	$\overline{Y}_0\overline{Y}_1\overline{Y}_2\overline{Y}_3$	$\overline{Y}_0\overline{Y}_1\overline{Y}_2\overline{Y}_3$
X	1	X	$\overline{R}_i \wedge S_i$	$\overline{R}_i \vee S_i$	$G \vee PC_n$	$C_{n+3} \veebar C_{n+4}$	$\overline{P}$	F_3	$\overline{G}$	$\overline{Y}_0\overline{Y}_1\overline{Y}_2\overline{Y}_3$	$\overline{Y}_0\overline{Y}_1\overline{Y}_2\overline{Y}_3$	$\overline{Y}_0\overline{Y}_1\overline{Y}_2\overline{Y}_3$
X	2	X	$R_i \wedge \overline{S}_i$	$R_i \vee \overline{S}_i$	$G \vee PC_n$	$C_{n+3} \veebar C_{n+4}$	$\overline{P}$	F_3	$\overline{G}$	$\overline{Y}_0\overline{Y}_1\overline{Y}_2\overline{Y}_3$	$\overline{Y}_0\overline{Y}_1\overline{Y}_2\overline{Y}_3$	$\overline{Y}_0\overline{Y}_1\overline{Y}_2\overline{Y}_3$
X	3	X	$R_i \wedge S_i$	$R_i \vee S_i$	$G \vee PC_n$	$C_{n+3} \veebar C_{n+4}$	$\overline{P}$	F_3	$\overline{G}$	$\overline{Y}_0\overline{Y}_1\overline{Y}_2\overline{Y}_3$	$\overline{Y}_0\overline{Y}_1\overline{Y}_2\overline{Y}_3$	$\overline{Y}_0\overline{Y}_1\overline{Y}_2\overline{Y}_3$
X	4	X	0	S_i	$G \vee PC_n$	$C_{n+3} \veebar C_{n+4}$	$\overline{P}$	F_3	$\overline{G}$	$\overline{Y}_0\overline{Y}_1\overline{Y}_2\overline{Y}_3$	$\overline{Y}_0\overline{Y}_1\overline{Y}_2\overline{Y}_3$	$\overline{Y}_0\overline{Y}_1\overline{Y}_2\overline{Y}_3$
X	5	X	0	$\overline{S}_i$	$G \vee PC_n$	$C_{n+3} \veebar C_{n+4}$	$\overline{P}$	F_3	$\overline{G}$	$\overline{Y}_0\overline{Y}_1\overline{Y}_2\overline{Y}_3$	$\overline{Y}_0\overline{Y}_1\overline{Y}_2\overline{Y}_3$	$\overline{Y}_0\overline{Y}_1\overline{Y}_2\overline{Y}_3$
X	6	X	0	R_i	$G \vee PC_n$	$C_{n+3} \veebar C_{n+4}$	$\overline{P}$	F_3	$\overline{G}$	$\overline{Y}_0\overline{Y}_1\overline{Y}_2\overline{Y}_3$	$\overline{Y}_0\overline{Y}_1\overline{Y}_2\overline{Y}_3$	$\overline{Y}_0\overline{Y}_1\overline{Y}_2\overline{Y}_3$
X	7	X	0	$\overline{R}_i$	$G \vee PC_n$	$C_{n+3} \veebar C_{n+4}$	$\overline{P}$	F_3	$\overline{G}$	$\overline{Y}_0\overline{Y}_1\overline{Y}_2\overline{Y}_3$	$\overline{Y}_0\overline{Y}_1\overline{Y}_2\overline{Y}_3$	$\overline{Y}_0\overline{Y}_1\overline{Y}_2\overline{Y}_3$
X	8	X	0	1	0	0	0	F_3	$\overline{G}$	$\overline{Y}_0\overline{Y}_1\overline{Y}_2\overline{Y}_3$	$\overline{Y}_0\overline{Y}_1\overline{Y}_2\overline{Y}_3$	$\overline{Y}_0\overline{Y}_1\overline{Y}_2\overline{Y}_3$
X	9	X	$\overline{R}_i \wedge S_i$	1	0	0	0	F_3	$\overline{G}$	$\overline{Y}_0\overline{Y}_1\overline{Y}_2\overline{Y}_3$	$\overline{Y}_0\overline{Y}_1\overline{Y}_2\overline{Y}_3$	$\overline{Y}_0\overline{Y}_1\overline{Y}_2\overline{Y}_3$
X	A	X	$R_i \wedge S_i$	1	0	0	0	F_3	$\overline{G}$	$\overline{Y}_0\overline{Y}_1\overline{Y}_2\overline{Y}_3$	$\overline{Y}_0\overline{Y}_1\overline{Y}_2\overline{Y}_3$	$\overline{Y}_0\overline{Y}_1\overline{Y}_2\overline{Y}_3$
X	B	X	$\overline{R}_i \wedge S_i$	$\overline{R}_i \vee S_i$	0	0	0	F_3	$\overline{G}$	$\overline{Y}_0\overline{Y}_1\overline{Y}_2\overline{Y}_3$	$\overline{Y}_0\overline{Y}_1\overline{Y}_2\overline{Y}_3$	$\overline{Y}_0\overline{Y}_1\overline{Y}_2\overline{Y}_3$
X	C	X	$R_i \wedge S_i$	1	0	0	0	F_3	$\overline{G}$	$\overline{Y}_0\overline{Y}_1\overline{Y}_2\overline{Y}_3$	$\overline{Y}_0\overline{Y}_1\overline{Y}_2\overline{Y}_3$	$\overline{Y}_0\overline{Y}_1\overline{Y}_2\overline{Y}_3$
X	D	X	$\overline{R}_i \wedge \overline{S}_i$	1	0	0	0	F_3	$\overline{G}$	$\overline{Y}_0\overline{Y}_1\overline{Y}_2\overline{Y}_3$	$\overline{Y}_0\overline{Y}_1\overline{Y}_2\overline{Y}_3$	$\overline{Y}_0\overline{Y}_1\overline{Y}_2\overline{Y}_3$
X	E	X	$R_i \wedge S_i$	1	0	0	0	F_3	$\overline{G}$	$\overline{Y}_0\overline{Y}_1\overline{Y}_2\overline{Y}_3$	$\overline{Y}_0\overline{Y}_1\overline{Y}_2\overline{Y}_3$	$\overline{Y}_0\overline{Y}_1\overline{Y}_2\overline{Y}_3$
X	F	X	$\overline{R}_i \wedge \overline{S}_i$	1	0	0	0	F_3	$\overline{G}$	$\overline{Y}_0\overline{Y}_1\overline{Y}_2\overline{Y}_3$	$\overline{Y}_0\overline{Y}_1\overline{Y}_2\overline{Y}_3$	$\overline{Y}_0\overline{Y}_1\overline{Y}_2\overline{Y}_3$
0	0, 1	L	0 if Z = L, $R_i \wedge S_i$ if Z = H	S_i if Z = L, $R_i \vee S_i$ if Z = H	$G \vee PC_n$	$C_{n+3} \veebar C_{n+4}$	$\overline{P}$	F_3	$\overline{G}$	Input	Input	Q_0
0	2, 3	L	0 if Z = L, $R_i \wedge S_i$ if Z = H	S_i if Z = L, $R_i \vee S_i$ if Z = H	$G \vee PC_n$	$C_{n+3} \veebar C_{n+4}$	$\overline{P}$	F_3	$\overline{G}$	Input	Input	Q_0
0	4	L	See Note 1	See Note 2	$G \vee PC_n$	$C_{n+3} \veebar C_{n+4}$	$\overline{P}$	F_3	$\overline{G}$	$\overline{Y}_0\overline{Y}_1\overline{Y}_2\overline{Y}_3$	Input	$\overline{Y}_0\overline{Y}_1\overline{Y}_2\overline{Y}_3$
0	5	L	0	S_i if Z = L, $\overline{S}_i$ if Z = H	$G \vee PC_n$	$C_{n+3} \veebar C_{n+4}$	$\overline{P}$	F_3 if Z = L, $F_3 \veebar S_3$ if Z = H	$\overline{G}$	S_3	Input	Input
0	6, 7	L	0 if Z = L, $R_i \wedge S_i$ if Z = H	S_i if Z = L, $\overline{R}_i \wedge S_i$ if Z = H	$G \vee PC_n$	$C_{n+3} \veebar C_{n+4}$	$\overline{P}$	F_3	$\overline{G}$	Input	$\overline{Y}_0\overline{Y}_1Y_2\overline{Y}_3$	Q_0
0	8, 9	L	0	S_i	See Note 3	$Q_2 \veebar Q_1$	$\overline{P}$	Q_3	$\overline{G}$	$\overline{Q}_0\overline{Q}_1\overline{Q}_2\overline{Q}_3$	$\overline{Q}_0\overline{Q}_1\overline{Q}_2\overline{Q}_3$	$\overline{Q}_0\overline{Q}_1\overline{Q}_2\overline{Q}_3$
0	A, B	L	0	S_i	See Note 4	$F_2 \veebar F_1$	$\overline{P}$	F_3	$\overline{G}$	See Note 5	See Note 5	See Note 5
0	C, D	L	$R_i \wedge S_i$ if Z = L, $\overline{R}_i \wedge S_i$ if Z = H	$R_i \vee S_i$ if Z = L, $\overline{R}_i \wedge S_i$ if Z = H	$G \vee PC_n$	$C_{n+3} \veebar C_{n+4}$	$\overline{P}$	F_3	$\overline{G}$	Sign Compare FF Output	Input	Input
0	E, F	L	$R_i \wedge S_i$ if Z = L, $\overline{R}_i \wedge S_i$ if Z = H	$R_i \vee S_i$ if Z = L, $\overline{R}_i \wedge S_i$ if Z = H	$G \vee PC_n$	$C_{n+3} \veebar C_{n+4}$	$\overline{P}$	F_3	$\overline{G}$	Sign Compare FF Output	Input	Input

Notes
1. If $\overline{LSS}$ is LOW, $G_0 = S_0$ and $G_{1,2,3} = 0$
2. If $\overline{LSS}$ is LOW, $P_0 = 1$ and $P_{1,2,3} = S_{1,2,3}$
   If $\overline{LSS}$ is HIGH, $P_i = S_i$
3. At the most significant slice, $C_{n+4} = Q_3 \veebar Q_2$
   At other slices, $C_{n+4} = G \vee PC_n$
4. At other slices, $C_{n+4} = G \vee PC_n$
   At the most significant slice, $C_{n+4} = F_3 \veebar F_2$
   At other slices, $C_{n+4} = G \vee PC_n$
5. $Z = \overline{Q_0 \wedge \overline{Q}_3 \overline{F}_0 \overline{F}_1 \overline{F}_2 \overline{F}_3}$

L = LOW = 0
H = HIGH = 1
$\wedge$ = OR
$\wedge$ = AND
$\veebar$ = EXCLUSIVE OR
$P = P_3 P_2 P_1 P_0$
$G = G_3 \vee G_3 P_3 \vee G_2 P_3 \vee G_1 P_2 P_3 \vee G_0 P_1 P_2 P_3$
$C_{n+3} = G_2 \vee G_1 P_2 \vee G_0 P_1 P_2 \vee C_n P_0 P_1 P_2$

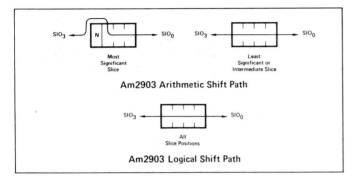

Fig. 3. Sign compare flip-flop.

OE$_Y$ A control input which, when LOW, enables the ALU shifter output data onto the Y$_{0-3}$ lines and, when HIGH, disables the Y$_{0-3}$ three-state output buffers.

SP   The clock input to the Am2903. The Q Register and Sign Compare Flip-Flop are clocked on the LOW-to-HIGH transition of the CP signal. When enabled by $\overline{\text{WE}}$, data is written in the RAM when CP is LOW.

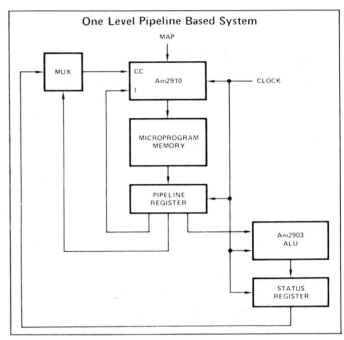

Fig. 4. Typical microprogram architecture.

Using the Am2903

Am2903 Applications

The Am2903 is designed to be used in microprogrammed systems. Figure 4 illustrates a recommended architecture. The control and data inputs to the Am2903 normally will all come from registers clocked at the same time as the Am2903. The register inputs come from a ROM or PROM—the "microprogram store." This memory contains sequences of microinstructions which apply the proper control signals to the Am2903's and other circuits to execute the desired operation.

The address lines of the microprogram store are driven from the Am2910 Microprogram Sequencer. This device has facilities for storing an address, incrementing an address, jumping to any address, and linking subroutines. The Am2910 is controlled by some of the bits coming from the microprogram store. Essentially, these bits are the "next instruction" control.

Note that with the microprogram register in between the microprogram memory store and the Am2903's, a microinstruction accessed on one cycle is executed on the next cycle. As one microinstruction is executed, the next microinstruction is being read from microprogram memory. In this configuration, system speed is improved because the execution time in the Am2903's occurs in parallel with the access time of the microprogram store. Without the "pipeline register," these two functions must occur serially.

Expansion of the Am2903

The Am2903 is a 4-bit CPU slice. Any number of Am2903's can be interconnected to form CPU's of 8, 16, 32, or more bits, in 4-bit increments. Figure 5 illustrates the interconnection of four Am2903's to form a 16-bit CPU, using ripple carry.

With the exception of the carry interconnection, all expansion schemes are the same. The QIO$_3$ and SIO$_3$ pins are bidirectional left/right shift lines at the MSB of the device. For all devices except the most significant, these lines are connected to the QIO$_0$ and SIO$_0$ pins of the adjacent more significant device. These connections allow the Q registers of all Am2903's to be shifted left or right as a contiguous n-bit register, and also allow the ALU output data to be shifted left or right as a contiguous n-bit word prior to storage in the RAM. At the LSB and MSB of the CPU, the shift pins should be connected to a shift multiplexer which can be controlled by the microcode to select the appropriate input signals to the shift inputs.

Device 1 has been defined as the least significant slice (LSS) and its $\overline{\text{LSS}}$ pin has accordingly been grounded. The Write/Most Significant Slice ($\overline{\text{WRITE/MSS}}$) pin of device 1 is now defined as being the Write output, which may now be used to drive the write enable ($\overline{\text{WE}}$) signal common to the four devices. Devices 2 and 3 are designated as intermediate slices and hence the $\overline{\text{LSS}}$ and $\overline{\text{WRITE/MSS}}$ pins are tied HIGH. Device 4 is designated the

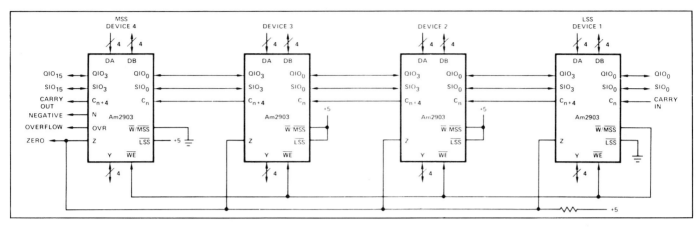

Fig. 5. 16-bit CPU with ripple carry.

most significant slice ($\overline{\text{MSS}}$) with the $\overline{\text{LSS}}$ pin tied HIGH and the $\overline{\text{WRITE}}/\overline{\text{MSS}}$ pin held LOW. The open-collector, bidirectional Z pins are tied together for detecting zero or for inter-chip communication for some special instruction. The carry-out (C_{n+4}) is connected to the carry-in (C_n) of the next chip in the case of ripple carry. For a faster carry scheme, an AM2902 may be employed (as shown in Fig. 6) so that the $\overline{G}$ and $\overline{P}$ outputs of the Am2903 are connected to the appropriate $\overline{G}$ and $\overline{P}$ inputs of the Am2902, while the C_{n+x}, C_{n+y}, and C_{n+z} outputs of the Am2902 are connected to the C_n input of the appropriate Am2903. Note that $\overline{G}$ /N and $\overline{P}$ /OVR pin functions are device-dependent. The most

significant slice outputs N and OVR while all other slices output $\overline{G}$ and $\overline{P}$.

The $\overline{\text{IEN}}$ pin of the Am2903 allows the option of conditional instruction execution. If $\overline{\text{IEN}}$ is LOW, all internal clocking is enabled, allowing the latches, RAM, and Q register to function, if $\overline{\text{IEN}}$ is HIGH, the RAM and Q register are disabled. The RAM is controlled by $\overline{\text{IEN}}$ if $\overline{\text{WE}}$ is connected to the $\overline{\text{WRITE}}$ output.

It would be appropriate at this point to mention that the Am2903 may be microcoded to work in either two- or three-address architecture modes. The two-address modes allow A + B → B while the three-address mode makes possible A + B → C.

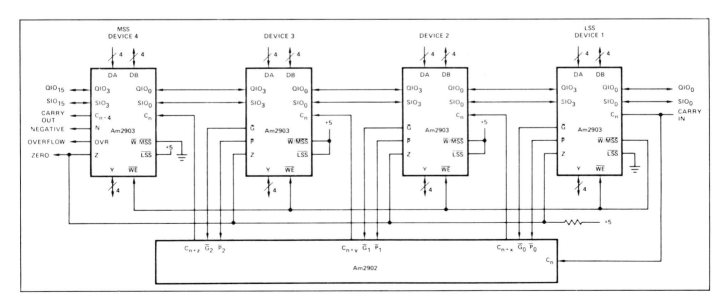

Fig. 6. 16-bit CPU with carry look ahead.

Implementation of a three-address architecture is made possible by varying the timing of $\overline{\text{IEN}}$ in relationship to the external clock and changing the B address. This technique is discussed in more detail under Memory Expansion.

Parity

The Am2903 computes parity on a chosen word when the instruction bits I_{5-8} have the values of 4_{16} to 7_{16} as shown in Table 3. The computed parity is the result of the Exclusive-OR of the individual ALU outputs and SIO_3. Parity output is found on SIO_0. Parity between devices may be cascaded by the interconnection of the SIO_0 and SIO_3 ports of the devices as shown in Fig. 6. The equation for the parity output at the SIO_0 port of device 1 is given by $SIO_0 = F_{15} \veebar F_{14} \veebar F_{13} \veebar \cdots \veebar F_1 \veebar F_0 \veebar SIO_{15}$.

Sign Extend

Sign extend across any number of Am2903 devices can be done in one microcycle. Referring again to the table of instructions (Table 3), the sign extend instruction (Hex instruction E) on I_{5-8} causes the sign present at the SIO_0 port of a device to be extended across the device and appear at the SIO_3 port and at the Y outputs. If the least significant bit of the instruction (bit I_5) is HIGH, Hex instruction F is present on I_{5-8}, commanding a shifter pass instruction. At this time, F_3 of the ALU is present on the SIO_3 output pin. It is then possible to control the extension of the sign across chip boundaries by controlling the state of I_5 when I_{6-8} are HIGH. Figure 7 outlines the Am2903 in sign extend mode. With I_{6-8} held HIGH, the individual chip sign extend is controlled by I_{5A-D}. If, for example, I_{5A} and I_{5B} are HIGH while I_{5C} and I_{5D} are LOW, the signal present at the boundaries of devices 2 and 3 (F_3 of device 2) will be extended across devices 3 and 4 at the SIO_3 pin of device 4. The outputs of the four devices will be available at

their respective Y data ports. The next positive edge of the clock will load the Y outputs into the address selected by the B port. Hence, the results of the sign extension are stored in the RAM.

Special Functions

When $I_{0-4} = 0$, the Am2903 is in the special function mode. In this mode, both the source and destination are controlled by I_{5-8}. The special functions are in essence special microinstructions that are used to reduce the number of microcycles needed to execute certain functions in the Am2903.

Normalization, Single- and Double-Length

Normalization is used as a means of referencing a number to a fixed radix point. Normalization strips out all leading sign bits such that the two bits immediately adjacent to the radix point are of opposite polarity.

Normalization is commonly used in such operations as fixed-to-floating point conversion and division. The Am2903 provides for normalization by using the Single-Length and Double-Length Normalize commands. Figure 8a represents the Q register of a 16-bit processor which contains a positive number. When the Single-Length Normalize command is applied, each positive edge of the clock will cause the bits to shift toward the most significant bit (bit 15) of the Q register. Zeros are shifted in via the QIO_0 port. When the bits on either side of the radix point (bits 14 and 15) are of opposite value, the number is considered to be normalized, as shown in Fig. 8b. The event of normalization is externally indicated by a HIGH level on the C_{n+4} pin of the most significant slice (C_{n+4} MSS $= Q_3$ MSS $\veebar Q_2$ MSS).

There are also provisions made for a normalization indication via the OVR pin one microcycle before the same indication is

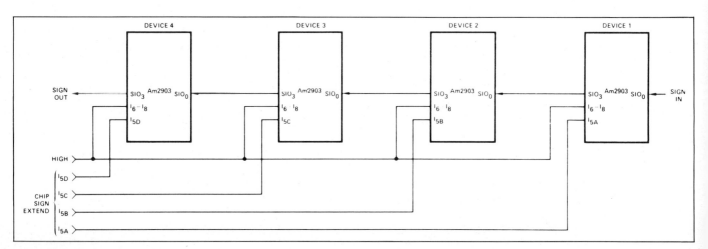

Fig. 7. Sign extend.

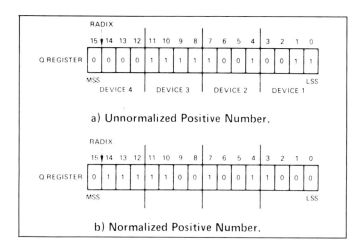

a) Unnormalized Positive Number.

b) Normalized Positive Number.

Fig. 8

available on the C_{n+4} pin (OVR = Q_2 MSS $\veebar$ Q_1 MSS). This is for use in applications that require a stage of register buffering of the normalization indication.

Since a number consisting of all zeros is not considered for normalization, the Am2903 indicates when such a condition arises. If the Q register is zero and the Single-Length Normalization command is given, a HIGH level will be present on the Z line. The sign output, N, indicates the sign of the number stored in the Q register, Q_3 MSS. An unnormalized negative number (Fig. 9a) is normalized in the same manner as a positive number. The results of single-length normalization are shown in Fig. 9b. The device interconnection for single-length normalization is outlined in Fig. 10. During single-length normalization, the number of shifts performed to achieve normalization can be counted and stored in one of the working registers. This can be achieved by forcing a HIGH at the C_n input of the least significant slice, since during this special function the ALU performs the function $[B] + C_n$ and the result is stored in B.

Normalizing a double-length word can be done with the Double-Length Normalize command, which assumes that a user-selected RAM register contains the most significant portion of the word to be normalized while the Q register holds the least significant half (Fig. 11). The device interconnection for double-length normalization is shown in Fig. 12. The C_{n+4}, OVR, N, and Z outputs of the most significant slice perform the same functions in double-length normalization as they did in single-length normalization except that C_{n+4}, OVR, and N are derived from the output of the ALU of the most significant slice in the case of double-length normalization, instead of the Q register of the most significant slice as in single-length normalization. A high-level Z line in double-length normalization reveals that the outputs of the ALU and Q register are both zero, hence indicating that the double-length word is zero.

When double-length normalization is being performed, shift counting is done either with an extra microcycle or with an external counter.

Sign/Magnitude–2's Complement Conversion

As part of the special instruction set, the Am2903 can convert between 2's complement and sign/magnitude representations. Figure 13 illustrates the interconnection needed for sign/mag-

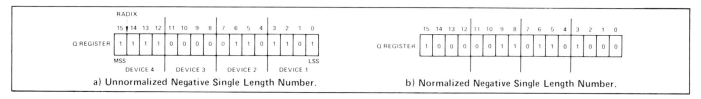

a) Unnormalized Negative Single Length Number.

b) Normalized Negative Single Length Number.

Fig. 9

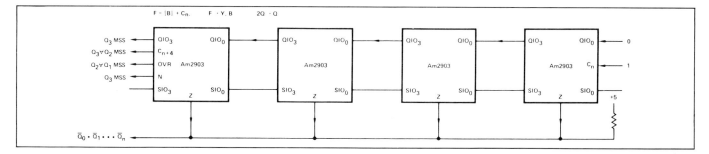

Fig. 10. Single-length normalize.

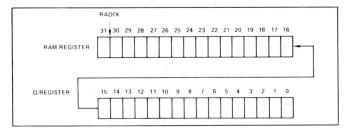

Fig. 11. Double-length word.

nitude–2's complement conversion. The C_n input of device 1 is connected to the Z pin. The sign bit (S_3 MSS) is brought out on the Z line and informs the other ALU's whether the conversion is being performed on a negative or a positive number. If the number attempted to be converted is the most negative number in 2's complement [i.e., 100 . . . 00(-2^n)], an overflow indication will occur. This is because -2^n is 1 greater than any number that can be represented in sign magnitude notation and hence an attempted conversion to sign magnitude from -2^n will cause an

overflow. When minus zero in sign/magnitude notation (100 . . . 0) is converted to 2's complement notation, the correct result is obtained (0 . . . 0).

Increment by 1 or 2

Incrementation by 1 or 2 is made possible by the special function of the same name. This command is quite useful in the case of byte-addressable words. A word may be incremented by 1 if C_n is LOW or incremented by 2 if C_n is HIGH.

Unsigned Multiply

This special function allows for easy implementation of unsigned multiplication. Figure 14 is the multiply flow chart. The algorithm dictates that initially the RAM word addressed by address port B be zero, the multiplier be in the Q register, and the multiplicand be in the register addressed by address port A. The initial conditions for the execution of the algorithm are that (1) register R_0 be reset to zero; (2) the multiplicand be in R_1; and (3) the multiplier be in R_2. The first operation transfers the multiplier R_2 to the Q register. The Unsigned Multiply (2's complement

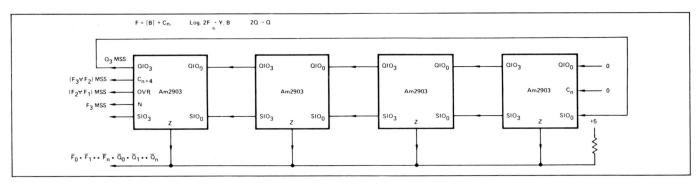

Fig. 12. Double-length normalize.

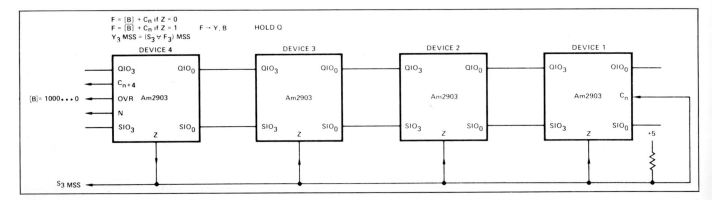

Fig. 13. 2's complement↔sign/magnitude.

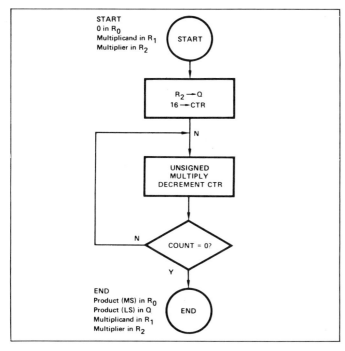

Fig. 14. 16x16 multiply flowchart.

multiply) instruction is then executed 16 (15) times. During the Multiply instruction, R_0 is addressed by RAM address port B and the multiplicand is addressed by RAM address port A.

When the Unsigned Multiply command is given, the Z pin of device 1 becomes an output while the Z pins of the remaining devices are specified as inputs as shown in Fig. 15. The Z output of device 1 is the same state as the least significant bit of the Q register during the Unsigned Multiply instruction; therefore, the

Z output of device 1 informs the ALU's of all the slices, via their Z pins, to output the sum of the partial product (referenced by the B address port) plus the multiplicand (referenced by the A address port) if Z = 1. If Z = 0, the output of the ALU is simply the partial product (referenced by the B address port). Since C_n is held LOW, it is not a factor in the computation. Each positive-going edge of the clock will internally shift the ALU outputs toward the least significant bit and simultaneously store the shifted results in the register selected by the B address port, thus becoming the new partial sum. During the down-shifting process, the C_{n+4} generated in device 4 is internally shifted into the Y_3 position of device 4. At this time, one bit of the multiplier will down-shift out of the QIO_0 ports of each device into the QIO_3 port of the next least significant slice. The partial product is shifted down between chips in a like manner, between the SIO_0 and SIO_3 ports, with SIO_0 of device 1 being connected to QIO_3 of device 4 for purposes of constructing a 32-bit-long register to hold the 32-bit product. At the finish of the 16×16 multiply, the most significant 16 bits of the product will be found in the registers referenced by the B address lines while the least significant 16 bits are stored in the Q register. Using a typical computer control unit (CCU), as shown in Fig. 16, the unsigned multiply operation requires only two lines of microcode, as shown in Fig. 17, and is executed in 17 microcycles.

2's Complement Multiplication

The algorithm for 2's complement multiplication is illustrated by Fig. 14. The initial conditions for 2's complement multiplication are the same as for the unsigned multiply operation. The 2's Complement Multiply command is applied for 15 clock cycles in the case of 16×16 multiply. During the down-shifting process the term N-OVR generated in device 4 is internally shifted into the Y_3 position of device 4. The data flow shown in Fig. 16 is

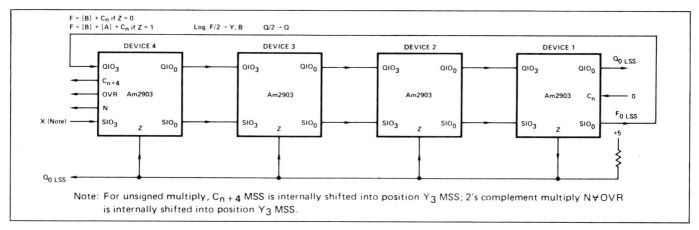

Note: For unsigned multiply, C_{n+4} MSS is internally shifted into position Y_3 MSS; 2's complement multiply N⩝OVR is internally shifted into position Y_3 MSS.

Fig. 15. Multiply.

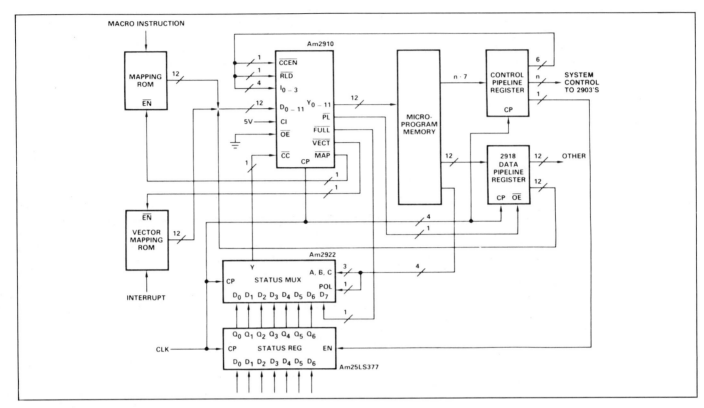

Fig. 16. Typical computer control unit (CCU).

still valid. After 15 cycles, the sign bit of the multiplier is present at the Z output of device 1. At this time, the user must place the 2's Complement Multiply Last Cycle command on the instruction lines. The interconnection for this instruction is shown in Fig. 18. On the next positive edge of the clock, the Am2903 will adjust the partial product, if the sign of the multiplier is negative, by subtracting out the 2's complement representation of the multiplicand. If the sign bit is positive, the partial product is not adjusted. At this point, 2's complement multiplication is complete. Using a typical CCU, the 2's complement multiply operation requires only three lines of microcode, as shown in Fig. 19, and is executed in 17 microcycles.

2's Complement Division

The division process is accomplished by using a four-quadrant non-restoring algorithm which yields an algebraically correct answer such that the divisor times the quotient plus the remainder equals the dividend. The algorithm works for both single-precision and multi-precision divide operations. The only condi-

Micro Memory Address	Am2910 Inst	Data Pipeline Reg.	I_0	$I_4 - I_1$	$I_8 - I_5$	$\overline{OEB}$	$\overline{OEY}$	$A_3 - A_0$	$B_3 - B_0$	C_n	Comment
n	LDCT	$00F_{16}$	X	6	6	X	X	R_2	X	0	Load Counter & $R_2 \rightarrow Q$
n+1	RPCT	n+1	0	0	0	0	0	R_1	R_0	0	Unsigned Multiply

Fig. 17. Microcode for unsigned 16x16 multiply.

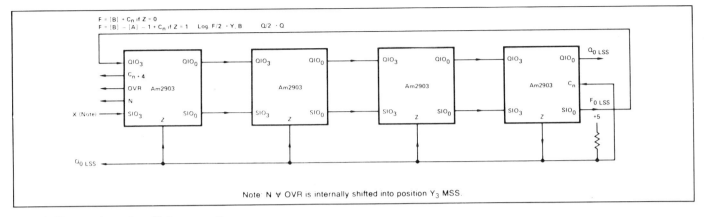

Fig. 18. 2's complement multiply, correction.

Memory Address	Am2910 Inst	Data Pipeline Reg.	I_0	$I_4 - I_1$	$I_8 - I_5$	$\overline{OEB}$	$\overline{OEY}$	$A_3 - A_0$	$B_3 - B_0$	C_n	Comment
n	LDCT	$00E_{16}$	X	6	6	X	X	R_2	X	0	Load Counter & $R_2 \rightarrow Q$
n+1	RPCT	n+1	0	0	2	0	0	R_1	R_0	0	2's Complement Multiply
n+2	X	X	0	0	6	0	0	R_1	R_0	Z	2's Complement Multiply (Last Cycle)

Fig. 19. Microcode for 2's complement 16x16 multiply.

tion that needs to be met is that the absolute magnitude of the divisor be greater than the absolute magnitude of the dividend. For multi-precision divide operations the least significant bit of the dividend is truncated. This is necessary if the answer is to be algebraically correct. Bias correction is automatically provided by forcing the least significant bit of the quotient to a 1, yet an algebraically correct answer is still maintained. Once the algorithm is completed, the answer may be modified to meet the user's formal requirements, such as rounding off or converting the remainder so that its sign is the same as the dividend's. These format modifications are accomplished using the standard Am2903 instructions.

The true value of the remainder is equal to the value stored in the working register 2^{n-1} when n is the number of quotient digits.

The following paragraphs describe a double-precision divide operation. The double-precision flow chart is based upon the use of the architecture detailed in Fig. 18.

Referring to the flow chart outlined in Fig. 20, we begin the algorithm with the assumption that the divisor is contained in R_0, while the most significant and least significant halves of the dividend reside in R_1 and R_4, respectively. The first step is to duplicate the divisor by copying the contents of R_0 into R_3. Next

the most significant half of the dividend is copied by transferring the contents of R_1 into R_2 while simultaneously checking to ascertain if the divisor (R_0) is zero. If the divisor is zero then division is aborted. If the divisor is not zero, the copy of the most significant half of the dividend in R_2 is converted from its 2's complement to its sign/magnitude representation. The divisor in R_3 is converted in like manner in the next step, while a test is done to see if the results of the dividend conversion yielded an indication on the overflow pin of the Am2903. If the output of the overflow pin is a 1 then the dividend is -2^n and hence is the largest possible number, meaning that it cannot be less than the divisor. What must be done in this case is to scale the dividend by down-shifting the upper and lower halves stored in R_1 and R_4 respectively. After scaling, the routine requires that the algorithm be reinitiated at the beginning.

Conversely, if the output of the overflow pin is not a 1, the sign magnitude representation of the divisor (R_3) is shifted up in the Am2903, removing the sign while at the same time testing the results of 2's complement to sign/magnitude conversion of the divisor in the Am2910. If the results of the test indicate that the divisor is -2^n, i.e., overflow equals 1, then the lower half of the dividend is placed in the Q register and division may proceed.

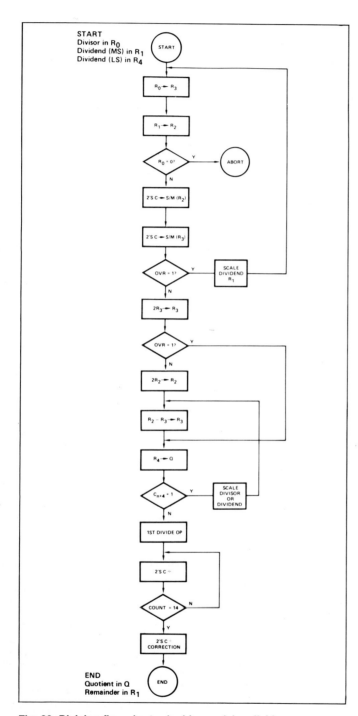

Fig. 20. Division flow chart—double precision divide.

This is possible because the divisor is now guaranteed to be greater than the dividend. If overflow is not a 1 then we must proceed by shifting out the sign of the sign/magnitude representation of the dividend stored in R_2. At this point we are able to check whether the divisor is greater than the dividend by subtracting the absolute value of the divisor (R_3) from the absolute value of the upper half of the dividend (R_2) and storing the results in R_3. Next, the least significant half of the dividend is transferred from R_4 to the Q register while simultaneously the carry from the result of the divisor-dividend subtraction is tested. If the carry (C_{n+4}) is 1, indicating the divisor is not greater than the dividend, then a scaling operation must occur. This involves either shifting up the divisor or shifting down the dividend. If the carry is not 1 then the divisor is greater than the dividend and division may now begin.

The first divide operation is used to ascertain the sign bit of the quotient. The 2's Complement Divide instruction is then executed 14 times in the case of a 16-bit divisor and a 32-bit dividend. The final step is the 2's Complement Correction command, which adjusts the quotient by allowing the least significant bit of the quotient to be set to a 1. At the end of the division algorithm the 16-bit quotient is found in the Q register while the remainder now replaces the most significant half of the dividend in R_1. It should be noted that the remainder must be shifted down 15 places to represent its true value. The interconnections for these instructions are shown in Figs. 21, 22, 23. Using a typical CCU as shown in Fig. 15, the double-precision divide operation requires only 11 lines of microcode, as shown in Fig. 24.

For those applications that require truncation instead of bias correction, the same algorithm as above should be implemented except one additional 2's Complement Divide instruction should be used in lieu of the 2's Complement Divide Correction and Remainder instruction. However, this technique results in an invalid remainder.

It is possible to do multiple-precision divide operations beyond the double-precision divide shown above. For example, to do a triple-precision divide for a 16-bit CPU, the upper two-thirds of the dividend are stored in R_1 and Q as in the case for double-precision divide. The lower third of the dividend is stored in a scratch register, R_5. After checking that the magnitude of the divisor is greater than the magnitude of the dividend, using the same tests as defined in Fig. 20, the procedure is as follows:

1   Execute a Double-Length Normalize/First Divide Operation instruction.

2   Execute the 2's Complement Divide instruction 15 times.

3   Transfer the contents of Q, the most significant half of the quotient, to R_2.

4   Transfer R_5 to Q.

5   Execute the 2's Complement Divide instruction 15 times.

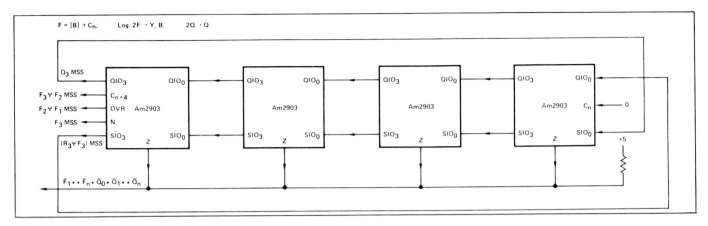

Fig. 21. Double-length normalize/first divide operation.

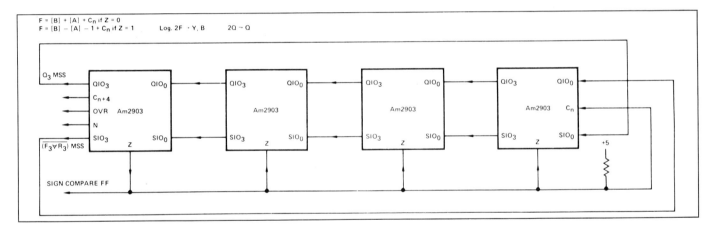

Fig. 22. 2's complement divide.

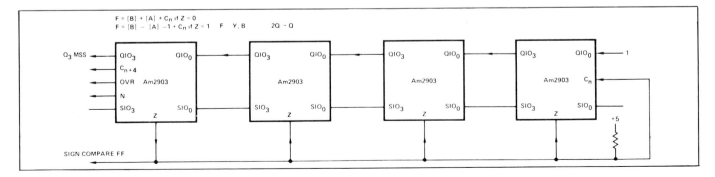

Fig. 23. 2's complement divide correction.

Micro Memory Address	Am2910 Inst.	Data Pipeline Reg.	I_0	I_4-I_1	I_8-I_5	$\overline{EA}$	A_3-A_0	B_3-B_0	C_n	Am2922 SEL	POL	Am29LS18 $\overline{E}$	Comment
n	CONT	X	0	6	4	0	R_0	R_3	0	X	X	0	$R_0 \rightarrow R_3$
n+1	CJP	Abort	0	6	4	0	R_1	R_2	0	Z	1	X	$R_1 \rightarrow R_2$, if $R_0 = 0$ Abort
n+2	CONT	X	0	0	5	X	X	R_2	0	X	X	0	2's C to S/M (R_2)
n+3	CJP	Scale Dividend	0	0	5	X	X	R_3	0	OVR	1	0	2's C to S/M (R_3), if OVR ≥ 1, scale
n+4	CJP	n+7	0	4	9	X	X	R_2	0	OVR	1	X	Shift out sign of divisor
n+5	CONT	X	0	4	9	X	X	R_3	0	X	X	X	Shift out sign of divisor
n+6	CONT	X	0	2	F	0	R_2	R_3	1	X	X	0	Dividend – Divisor $\rightarrow R_3$
n+7	CJP	Scale Dividend or Divisor	0	6	6	0	R_4	X	0	C_{n+4}	0	X	$R_4 \rightarrow Q$, if Carry = 1, scale
n+8	PUSH	$00D_{16}$	0	0	A	0	R_0	R_1	0	0	1	X	Loop set up & First Divide Operation
n+9	RFCT	X	0	0	C	0	R_0	R_1	Z	X	X	X	Test Loop Count & 2's C Divide
n+A	CONT	X	0	0	E	0	R_0	R_1	Z	X	X	X	2's C Divide Correction

Fig. 24. Microcode for double precision divide.

6 Execute the 2's Complement Divide Correction and Remainder instruction.

The upper half of the quotient is then in R_2, the lower half of the quotient is in Q, and the remainder is in R_1. This technique can be expanded for any precision which is required.

Byte Swap

The multi-port architecture of the Am2903 allows for easy implementation of high- and low-order byte swapping. Figure 25 outlines a byte-swap implementation utilizing two data ports. Initially, the lower-order 8-bit byte is stored in devices 1 and 2 while the high-order byte is in devices 3 and 4. When the user wishes to exchange the two bytes, the register location of the desired word is placed on the B address port. When the byte-swap line is brought LOW, the bytes to be swapped will be flowing from the DB ports of the Am2903 through the Am25LS240/244 three-state buffers. The outputs of the three-state buffers are permuted so that the byte swap is achieved. The resultant permuted data is presented to the DA ports of the Am2903, where it is reloaded into the memories of the Am2903 on the next positive edge of CP using the permuted data source and function

commands of $F = \overline{A}$ plus $C_n(C_n = 0)$ for the Am25LS240 or $F = A$ plus $C_n(C_n = 0)$ for the Am25LS244 and the destination command $F \rightarrow Y, B$.

A higher-speed technique for achieving the byte-swap operation uses the Y input/output ports with $\overline{OE}_Y$ held HIGH rather than the DA port inputs. This technique bypasses the ALU, thus allowing faster operation. The Am2903 destination command $F \rightarrow Y, B$ should be used.

Memory Expansion

The Am2903 allows for a theoretically infinite memory expansion. Figure 26 pictures a 4-bit slice of a system which has 48 words of RAM and 16 words of ROM. RAM storage is provided by the Am2903 and the Am29705's. The 29705 RAM is functionally identical to the Am2903 RAM. The Am29751 is used to store constants and masks and is addressable from address port A only. The system is organized around five data buses. Inter-bus communication may be done through the Am29705's or the Am2903. The memory addressing scheme specifies the data source for the R input of the ALU emanating from the register locations specified by address field A. A_{0-3} address 16 memory locations in each chip while address bits A_{4-6} are decoded and used

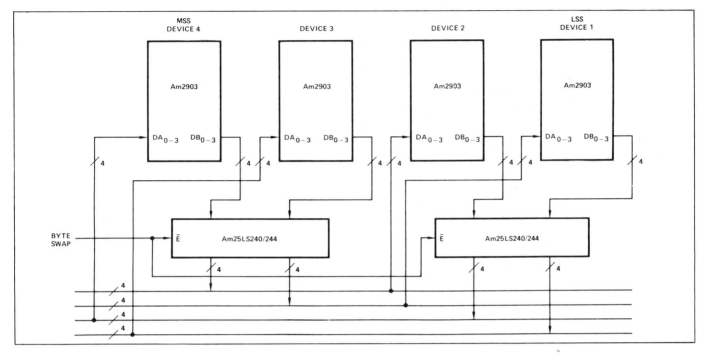

Fig. 25. Byte swap.

for the output enable for the desired chip. The B address field is used both to select the S input of the ALU and to specify the register location where the result of the ALU operation is to be stored.

Bits B_{0-3} are for source register addressing in each chip. Bits B_4 and B_5 are used for chip output enable selection. B_{6-9} access the 16 destination addresses on each chip, while bits B_{10} and B_{11} control the Write Enable of the desired chip. The source and destination register address are multplexed so that when the clock is HIGH, the source register address is presented to the B address ports of the RAM's. The Instruction Enable ($\overline{IEN}$) is HIGH at this time. The data flows from the Y port or the internal B port, as selected by the decoder whose inputs are B_4 and B_5. When the clock goes LOW, the data emanating from the selected Y outputs of the Am29705's and the RAM outputs of the Am2903 are latched and the destination address is now selected for use by the RAM address lines. When the destination address stabilizes on the address lines, the $\overline{IEN}$ pin is brought LOW. The $\overline{WRITE}$ output of the Am2903 will now go LOW, enabling the decoder sourced by address bits B_{10} and B_{11}. The selected decoder line will go LOW, allowing the desired memory location to be written into. To switch between two- and three-address architecture, the user simply makes the source and destination addresses the same, i.e., $B_{0-3} = B_{6-9}$. For two-address architecture, the MUX is removed from the circuit.

General Description of the Am2910

The Am2910 microprogram controller is an address sequencer intended for controlling the sequence of execution of microinstructions stored in microprogram memory. Besides the capability of sequential access, it provides conditional branching to any microinstruction within its 4096-microword range. A last-in, first-out stack provides microsubroutine return linkage and looping capability; there are five levels of nesting of microsubroutines. Microinstruction loop-count control is provided with a count capacity of 4096.

During each microinstruction, the microprogram controller provides a 12-bit address from one of four sources: (1) the microprogram address register (μPC), which usually contains an address 1 greater than the previous address; (2) an external (direct) input (D); (3) a register/counter (R) retaining data loaded during a previous microinstruction; or (4) a five-deep last-in, first-out stack (F).

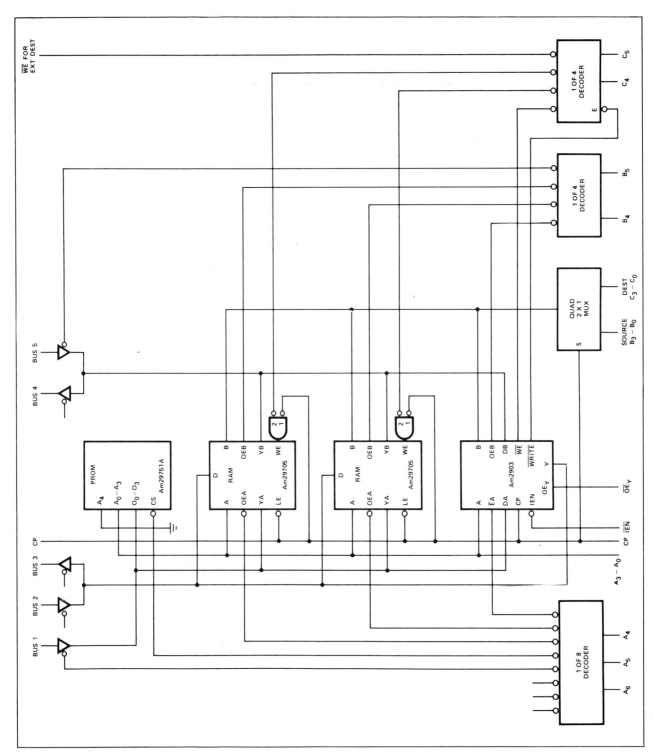

Fig. 26. Expanded memory.

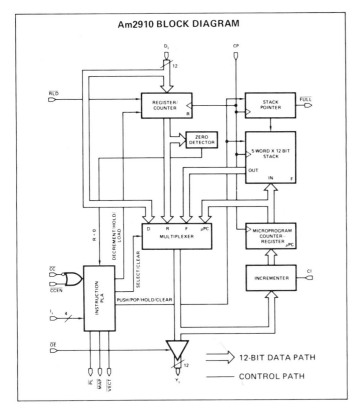

Fig. 27. Am2910 block diagram.

Architecture of the Am2910

The Am2910 is a bipolar microprogram controller intended for use in high-speed microprocessor applications. It allows addressing of up to 4096 words of microprogram. A block diagram of the Am2910 is shown in Fig. 27, and its application in a microcomputer is depicted in Fig. 28.

The controller contains a four-input multiplexer that is used to select either the register/counter, direct input, microprogram counter, or stack as the source of the next microinstruction address.

The register/counter consists of 12 D-type, edge-triggered flip-flops, with a common clock enable. When its load control, $\overline{RLD}$, is LOW, new data is loaded on a positive clock transition. A few instructions include load; in most systems, these instructions will be sufficient, simplifying the microcode. The output of the register/counter is available to the multiplexer as a source for the next microinstruction address. The direct input furnishes a source of data for loading the register/counter.

The Am2910 contains a microprogram counter (μPC) that is

composed of a 12-bit incrementer followed by a 12-bit register. The μPC can be used in either of two ways: When the carry-in to the incrementer is HIGH, the microprogram register is loaded on the next clock cycle with the current Y output word plus one ($Y + 1 \rightarrow \mu PC$). Sequential microinstructions are thus executed. When the carry-in is LOW, the incrementer passes the Y output word unmodified so that μPC is reloaded with the same Y word on the next clock cycle ($Y \rightarrow \mu PC$). The same microinstruction is thus executed any number of times.

The third source for the multiplexer is the direct (D) input. This source is used for branching.

The fourth source available at the multiplexer input is a 5-word by 12-bit stack (file). The stack is used to provide return address linkage when executing microsubroutines or loops. The stack contains a built-in stack pointer (SP) which always points to the last file word written. This allows stack reference operations (looping) to be performed without a pop.

The stack pointer operates as an up/down counter. During microinstructions 1, 4, and 5, the PUSH operation is performed. This causes the stack pointer to increment and the file to be written with the required return linkage. On the cycle following the PUSH, the return data is at the new location pointed to by the stack pointer.

During five microinstructions, a POP operation may occur. The stack pointer decrements at the next rising clock edge following a POP, effectively removing old information from the top of the stack.

The stack pointer linkage is such that any sequence of pushes, pops, or stack references can be achieved. At RESET (instruction 0), the depth of nesting becomes 0. For each PUSH, the nesting depth increases by 1; for each POP, the depth increases by 1. The depth can grow to 5. After a depth of 5 is reached, $\overline{FULL}$ goes LOW. Any further PUSHes onto a full stack overwrite information at the top of the stack but leave the stack pointer unchanged. This operation will usually destroy useful information and is normally avoided. A POP from an empty stack may place non-meaningful data on the Y outputs but is otherwise safe. The stack pointer remains at 0 whenever a POP is attempted from a stack already empty.

The register/counter is operated during three microinstructions (8, 9, and 15) as a 12-bit down-counter, with result = zero available as a microinstruction branch test criterion. This provides efficient iteration of microinstructions. The register/counter is arranged so that if it is preloaded with a number n and then used as a loop termination counter, the sequence will be executed exactly $n + 1$ times. During instruction 15, a three-way branch under combined control of the loop counter and the condition code is available.

The device provides three-state Y outputs. These can be particularly useful in designs requiring automatic checkout of the

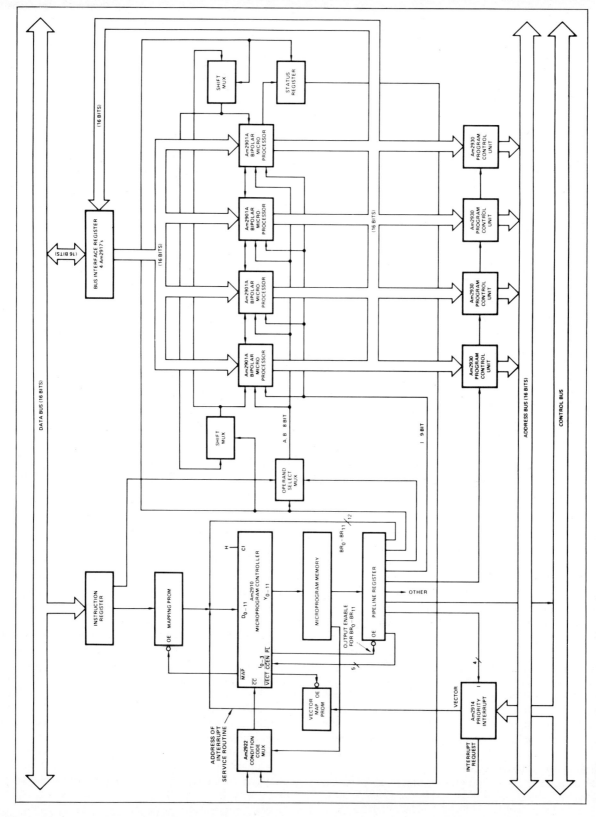

Fig. 28. Typical bipolar microcomputer using Am2910.

208

processor. The microprogram controller outputs can be forced into the high-impedance state, and pre-programmed sequences of microinstructions can be executed via external access to the address lines.

Operation

Table 6 shows the result of each instruction in controlling the multiplexer which determines the Y outputs, and in controlling the three enable signals $\overline{PL}$, $\overline{MAP}$, and $\overline{VECT}$. The effect on the register/counter and the stack after the next positive-going clock edge is also shown. The multiplexer determines which internal source drives the Y outputs. The value loaded into μPC is either identical to the Y output or else 1 greater, as determined by CI. For each instruction, one and only one of the three outputs PL, MAP, and VECT is LOW. If these outputs control three-state enables for the primary source of microprogram jumps (usually part of a pipeline register), a PROM which maps the instruction to a microinstruction starting location, and an optional third source (often a vector from a DMA or interrupt source), respectively, the three-state sources can drive the D inputs without further logic.

Several inputs, as shown in Table 7, can modify instruction execution. The combination CC HIGH and $\overline{CCEN}$ LOW is used as a test in 10 of the 16 instructions. $\overline{RLD}$, when LOW, causes the D input to be loaded into the register/counter, overriding any HOLD or DEC operation specified in the instruction. OE, normally LOW, may be forced HIGH to remove the Am2910 Y outputs from a three-state bus.

The Am2910 Instruction Set

The Am2910 provides 16 instructions which select the address of the next microinstruction to be executed. Four of the instructions are unconditional—their effect depends only on the instruction. Ten of the instructions have an effect which is partially controlled by an external, data-dependent condition. Three of the instructions have an effect which is partially controlled by the contents of the internal register/counter. The instruction set is shown in Table 6. In this discussion it is assumed that C_n is tied HIGH.

In the 10 conditional instructions, the result of the data-dependent test is applied to $\overline{CC}$. If the $\overline{CC}$ input is LOW, the test is considered to have been passed, and the action specified in the name occurs; otherwise, the test has failed and an alternate (often simply the execution of the next sequential microinstruction) occurs. Testing of $\overline{CC}$ may be disabled for a specific microinstruction by setting $\overline{CCEN}$ HIGH, which unconditionally forces the action specified in the name; that is, it forces a pass. Other ways of using $\overline{CCEN}$ include (1) tying it HIGH, which is useful if no microinstruction is data-dependent; (2) tying it LOW if data-

dependent instructions are never forced unconditionally; or (3) tying it to the source of Am2910 instruction bit I_0, which leaves instructions 4, 6, and 10 as data-dependent but makes others unconditional. All of these tricks save one bit of microcode width.

The effect of three instructions depends on the contents of the register/counter. Unless the counter holds a value of zero, it is decremented; if it does hold zero, it is held and a different microprogram next address is selected. These instructions are useful for executing a microinstruction loop a known number of times. Instruction 15 is affected both by the external condition code and the internal register/counter.

Perhaps the best technique for understanding the Am2910 is to simply take each instruction and review its operation. In order to provide some feel for the actual execution of these instructions, Fig. 29 is included and depicts examples of all 16 instructions.

The examples given in Fig. 29 should be interpreted in the following manner: The intent is to show microprogram flow as various microprogram memory words are executed. For example, the CONTINUE instruction, instruction 14, as shown in Fig. 29, simply means that the contents of microprogram memory word 50 are executed and then the contents of word 51 are executed. This is followed by the contents of microprogram memory word 52 and the contents of microprogram memory word 53. The microprogram addresses used in the examples were arbitrarily chosen and have no meaning other than to show instruction flow. The exception to this is the first example, JUMP ZERO, which forces the microprogram location counter to address ZERO. Each dot refers to the time that the contents of the microprogram memory word is in the pipeline register. While no special symbology is used for the conditional instructions, the test to follow will explain what the conditional choices are in each example.

It might be appropriate at this time to mention that AMD has a microprogram assembler called AMDASM, which has the capability of using the Am2910 instructions in symbolic representation. AMDASM's Am2910 instruction symbolics (or mnemonics) are given in Fig. 29 for each instruction and are also shown in Table 6.

Instruction 0. JZ (JUMP and ZERO, or RESET) unconditionally specifies that the address of the next microinstruction is zero. Many designs use this feature for power-up sequences and provide the power-up firmware beginning at microprogram memory word location 0.

Instruction 1 is a CONDITIONAL JUMP-TO-SUBROUTINE via the address provided in the pipeline register. As shown in Fig. 29, the machine might have executed words at addresses 50, 51, and 52. When the contents of address 52 are in the pipeline register, the next address control function is the CONDITIONAL JUMP-TO-SUBROUTINE. Here, if the test is passed, the next instruction executed will be the contents of microprogram memory location 90. If the test has failed, the JUMP-TO-

Table 6 Instructions

Hex I_3-I_0	Mnemonic	Name	Reg/cntr contents	Fail $\overline{CCEN} \neq LOW$ and $\overline{CC} \neq HIGH$		PASS $\overline{CCEN} = High$ or $\overline{CC} = low$		Reg/cntr	Enable
				Y	STACK	Y	STACK		
0	JZ	JUMP ZERO	X	0	CLEAR	0	CLEAR	HOLD	PL
1	CJS	COND JSB PL	X	PC	HOLD	D	PUSH	HOLD	PL
2	JMAP	JUMP MAP	X	D	HOLD	D	HOLD	HOLD	MAP
3	CJP	COND JUMP PL	X	PC	HOLD	D	HOLD	HOLD	PL
4	PUSH	PUSH COND LD CNTR	X	PC	PUSH	PC	PUSH	†	PL
5	JSRP	COND JSB R/PL	X	R	PUSH	D	PUSH	HOLD	PL
6	CJV	COND JUMP VECTOR	X	PC	HOLD	D	HOLD	HOLD	VECT
7	JRP	COND JUMP R/PL	X	R	HOLD	D	HOLD	HOLD	PL
8	RFCT	REPEAT LOOP, CNTR $\neq 0$	$\neq 0$	F	HOLD	F	HOLD	DEC	PL
			$= 0$	PC	POP	PC	POP	HOLD	PL
9	RPCT	REPEAT LOOP, CNTR $\neq 0$	$\neq 0$	D	HOLD	D	HOLD	DEC	PL
			$= 0$	PC	HOLD	PC	HOLD	HOLD	PL
A	CRTN	COND RTN	X	PC	HOLD	F	POP	HOLD	PL
B	CJPP	COND JUMP PL & POP	X	PC	HOLD	D	POP	HOLD	PL
C	LDCT	LD CNTR & CONTINUE	X	PC	HOLD	PC	HOLD	LOAD	PL
D	LOOP	TEST END LOOP	X	F	HOLD	PC	POP	HOLD	PL
E	CONT	CONTINUE	X	PC	HOLD	PC	HOLD	HOLD	PL
F	TWB	THREE-WAY BRANCH	$\neq 0$	F	HOLD	PC	POP	DEC	PL
			$= 0$	D	POP	PC	POP	HOLD	PL

†If $\overline{CCEN}$ = LOW and $\overline{CC}$ = HIGH, hcld; else load.   X = Don't Care

Table 7   Pin Functions

Abbreviation	Name	Function
D_i	Direct Input Bit i	Direct input to register/counter and multiplexer. D_0 is LSB.
I_i	Instruction Bit i	Selects one-of-sixteen instructions for the AM 2910.
$\overline{CC}$	Condition Code	Used as test criterion. Pass test is a LOW on $\overline{CC}$.
$\overline{CCEN}$	Condition Code Enable	Whenever the signal is HIGH, $\overline{CC}$ is ignored and the part operates as though $\overline{CC}$ were true (LOW).
CI	Carry-In	Low order carry input to incrementer for microprogram counter.
$\overline{RLD}$	Register Load	When LOW forces loading of register/counter regardless of instruction or condition.
$\overline{OE}$	Output Enable	Three-state control of Y_i outputs.
CP	Clock Pulse	Triggers all internal state changes at LOW-to-HIGH edge.
V_{CC}	+5 Volts	
GND	Ground	
Y_i	Microprogram Address Bit i	Address to microprogram memory. Y_0 is LSB, Y_{11} is MSB.
$\overline{FULL}$	FULL	Indicates that five items are on the stack.
$\overline{PL}$	Pipeline Address Enable	Can select #1 source (usually Pipeline Register) as direct input source.
$\overline{MAP}$	Map Address Enable	Can select #2 source (usually Mapping PROM or PLA) as direct input source.
$\overline{VECT}$	Vector Address Enable	Can select #3 source (for example, Interrupt Starting Address) as direct input source.

SUBROUTINE will not be executed; the contents of microprogram memory location 53 will be executed instead. Thus, the CONDITIONAL JUMP-TO-SUBROUTINE instruction at location 52 will cause the instruction either in location 90 or in location 53 to be executed next. If the TEST input is such that location 90 is selected, value 53 will be pushed onto the internal stack. This provides the return linkage for the machine when the subroutine beginning at location 90 is completed. In this example, the subroutine was completed at location 93 and a RETURN-FROM-SUBROUTINE was found at location 93.

Instruction 2 is the JUMP MAP instruction. This is an unconditional instruction which causes the $\overline{MAP}$ output to be enabled so that the next microinstruction location is determined by the address supplied via the mapping PROMs. Normally, the JUMP MAP instruction is used at the end of the instruction fetch sequence for the machine. In the example of Fig. 29, microinstructions at locations 50, 51, 52, and 53 might have been the fetch sequence, and at its completion at location 53, the jump map function would be contained in the pipeline register. This example shows the mapping PROM outputs to be 90; therefore, an unconditional jump to microprogram memory address 90 is performed.

Instruction 3, CONDITIONAL JUMP PIPELINE, derives its branch address from the pipeline register branch address value (BR_0–BR_{11} in Fig. 28). This instruction provides a technique for branching to various microprogram sequences depending upon the test condition inputs. Quite often, state machines are designed which simply execute tests on various inputs waiting for the condition to come true. When the true condition is reached, the machine then branches and executes a set of microinstructions to perform some function. This usually has the effect of resetting the input being tested until some point in the future. Figure 29 shows the conditional jump via the pipeline register address at location 52. When the contents of microprogram memory word 52 are in the pipeline register, the next address will be either location 53 or location 30 in this example. If the test is passed, the value currently in the pipeline register (3) will be selected. If the test fails, the next address selected will be contained in the microprogram counter, which in this example is 53.

Instruction 4 is the PUSH/CONDITIONAL LOAD COUNTER instruction and is used primarily for setting up loops in microprogram firmware. In Figure 29, when instruction 52 is in the pipeline register, a PUSH will be made onto the stack and the counter will be loaded on the basis of the condition. When a PUSH occurs, the value pushed is always the next sequential instruction address. In this case, the address is 53. If the test fails, the counter is not loaded; if it is passed, the counter is loaded with the value contained in the pipeline register branch address field. Thus, a single microinstruction can be used to set up a loop to be executed a specific number of times. Instruction 8 will describe how to use the pushed value and the register/counter for looping.

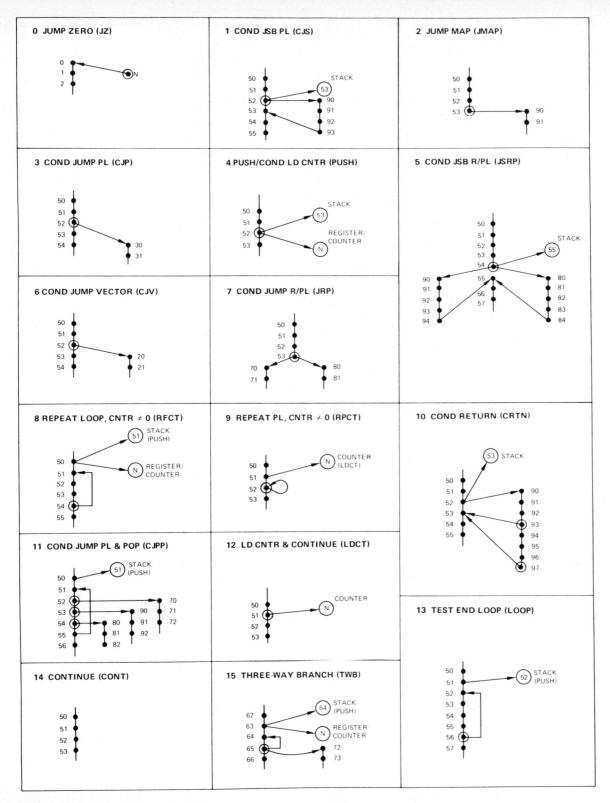

Fig. 29. Am2910 execution examples.

Instruction 5 is a CONDITIONAL JUMP-TO-SUBROUTINE via the register/counter or the contents of the Pipeline register. As shown in Fig. 29, a PUSH is always performed and one of two subroutines executed. In this example, either the subroutine beginning at address 80 or the subroutine beginning at address 90 will be performed. A return-from subroutine (instruction 10) returns the microprogram flow to address 55. In order for this microinstruction control sequence to operate correctly, both the next-address fields of instruction 53 and the next-address fields of instruction 54 have to contain the proper value. Let us assume that the branch address fields of instruction 53 contain the value 90 so that it will be in the Am2910 register/counter when the contents of address 54 are in the pipeline register. This requires that the instruction at address 53 load the register/counter. Now, during the execution of instruction 5 (at address 54), if the test fails, the contents of the register (value = 90) will select the address of the next microinstruction. If the test input passes, the pipeline register contents (value = 80) will determine the address of the next microinstruction. Therefore, this instruction provides the ability to select one of two subroutines to be executed based on a test condition.

Instruction 6 is a CONDITIONAL JUMP VECTOR instruction which provides the capability to take the branch address from a third source heretofore not discussed. In order for this instruction to be useful, the Am2910 output, $\overline{VECT}$, is used to control a three-state control input of a register, buffer, or PROM containing the next microprogram address. This instruction provides one technique for performing interrupt-type branching at the microprogram level. Since this instruction is conditional, a pass causes the next address to be taken from the vector source, while failure causes the next address to be taken from the microprogram counter. In the example of Fig. 29, if the CONDITIONAL JUMP VECTOR instruction is contained at location 52, execution will continue at vector address 20 if the TEST input is HIGH and the microinstruction at address 53 will be executed if the TEST input is LOW.

Instruction 7 is a CONDITIONAL JUMP via the contents of the Am2910 register/counter or the contents of the pipeline register. This instruction is very similar to instruction 5, the CONDITIONAL JUMP-TO-SUBROUTINE via R or PL. The major difference between instruction 5 and instruction 7 is that no push onto the stack is performed with 7. Figure 29 depicts this instruction as a branch to one of two locations depending on the test condition. The example assumes the pipeline register contains the value 70 when the contents of address 52 are being executed. As the contents of address 53 are clocked into the pipeline register, the value 70 is loaded into the register/counter in the Am2910. The value 80 is available when the contents of address 53 are in

the pipeline register. Thus, control is transferred to either address 70 or address 80, depending on the test condition.

Instruction 8 is the REPEAT LOOP, COUNTER ≠ ZERO instruction. This microinstruction makes use of the decrementing capability of the register/counter. To be useful, some previous instruction, such as 4, must have loaded a count value into the register/counter. This instruction checks to see whether the register/counter contains a non-zero value. If so, the register/counter is decremented, and the address of the next microinstruction is taken from the top of the stack. If the register/counter contains zero, the loop exit condition is occurring; control falls through to the next sequential microinstruction by selecting μPC; the stack is POPped by decrementing the stack pointer, but the contents of the top of the stack are thrown away.

An example of the REPEAT LOOP, COUNTER ≠ ZERO instruction is shown in Fig. 29. In this example, location 50 most likely would contain a PUSH/CONDITIONAL LOAD COUNTER instruction which would have caused address 51 to be PUSHed onto the stack and the counter to be loaded with the proper value for looping the desired number of times.

In this example, since the loop test is made at the end of the instructions to be repeated (microaddress 54), the proper value to be loaded by the instructions at address 50 is one less than the desired number of passes through the loop. This method allows a loop to be executed 1 to 4096 times. If it is desired to execute the loop from 0 to 4095 times, the firmware should be written to make the loop exit test immediately after loop entry.

Single-microinstruction loops provide a highly efficient capability for executing a specific microinstruction a fixed number of times. Examples include fixed rotates, byte swap, fixed-point multiply, and fixed-point divide.

Instruction 9 is the REPEAT PIPELINE REGISTER, COUNTER ≠ ZERO instruction. This instruction is similar to instruction 8 except that the branch address now comes from the pipeline register rather than the file. In some cases, this instruction may be thought of as a one-word file extension; that is, by using this instruction, a loop with the counter can still be performed when subroutines are nested five deep. This instruction's operation is very similar to that of instruction 8. The differences are that on this instruction, a failed test condition causes the source of the next microinstruction address to be the D inputs; and, when the test condition is passed, this instruction does not perform a POP because the stack is not being used.

In the example of Fig. 29, the REPEAT PIPELINE, COUNTER ≠ ZERO instruction is instruction 52 and is shown as a single microinstruction loop. The address in the pipeline register would be 52. Instruction 51 in this example could be the LOAD COUNTER AND CONTINUE instruction (instruction 12). While the example shows a single microinstruction loop, by simply changing the address in a pipeline register, multi-instruction loops can be performed in this manner for a fixed number of times as determined by the counter.

Instruction 10 is the conditional RETURN-FROM-SUBROUTINE instruction. As the name implies, this instruction is used to branch from the subroutine back to the next microinstruction address following the subroutine call. Since this instruction is conditional, the return is performed only if the test is passed. If the test is failed, the next sequential microinstruction is performed. The example in Fig. 29 depicts the use of the conditional RETURN-FROM-SUBROUTINE instruction in both the conditional and the unconditional modes. This example first shows a JUMP-TO-SUBROUTINE at instruction location 52, where control is transferred to location 90. At location 93, a conditional RETURN-FROM-SUBROUTINE instruction is performed. If the test is passed, the stack is accessed and the program will transfer to the next instruction at address 53. If the test is failed, the next microinstruction at address 94 will be executed. The program will continue to address 97, where the subroutine is complete. To perform an unconditional RETURN-FROM-SUBROUTINE, the conditional RETURN-FROM-SUBROUTINE instruction is executed unconditionally; the microinstruction at address 97 is programmed to force $\overline{CCEN}$ HIGH, disabling the test, and the forced PASS causes an unconditional return.

Instruction 11 is the CONDITIONAL JUMP PIPELINE register address and POP stack instruction. This instruction provides another technique for loop termination and stack maintenance. The example in Fig. 29 shows a loop being performed from address 55 back to address 51. The instructions at locations 52, 53, and 54 are all conditional JUMP and POP instructions. At address 52, if the TEST input is passed, a branch will be made to address 70 and the stack will be properly maintained via a POP. Should the test fail, the instruction at location 53 (the next sequential instruction) will be executed. Likewise, at address 53, either the instruction at 90 or 54 will be subsequently executed, depending on whether the test has been passed or failed. The instruction at 54 follows the same rules, going to either 80 or 55. An instruction sequence as described here, using the CONDITIONAL JUMP PIPELINE and POP instruction, is very useful when several inputs are being tested and the microprogram is looping waiting for any of the inputs being tested to occur before proceeding to another sequence of instructions. This provides the powerful jump-table programming technique at the firmware level.

Instruction 12 is the LOAD COUNTER AND CONTINUE instruction, which simply enables the counter to be loaded with the value at its parallel inputs. These inputs are normally connected to the pipeline branch address field which (in the architecture being described here) serves to supply either a branch address or a counter value, depending upon whether the microinstruction has been executed. There are altogether three ways of loading the counter: the explicit load by this instruction 12, the conditional load included as part of instruction 4, and the use of the $\overline{RLD}$ input along with any instruction. The use of $\overline{RLD}$ with any instruction overrides any counting or decrementation specified in the instruction, calling for a load instead. Its use provides additional microinstruction power, at the expense of one bit of microinstruction width. This instruction 12 is exactly equivalent to the combination of instruction 14 and $\overline{RLD}$ LOW. Its purpose is to provide a simple capability to load the register/counter in those implementations which do not provide microprogrammed control for $\overline{RLD}$.

Instruction 13 is the TEST END-OF-LOOP instruction, which provides the capability of conditionally exiting a loop at the bottom; that is, this is a conditional instruction that will cause the microprogram to loop, via the file, if the test is failed or else to continue to the next sequential instruction. The example in Fig. 29 shows the TEST END-OF-LOOP microinstruction at address 56. If the test fails, the microprogram will branch to address 52. Address 52 is on the stack because a PUSH instruction has been executed at address 51. If the test is passed at instruction 56, the loop is terminated and the next sequential microinstruction at address 57 is executed, which also causes the stack to be POPped, thus accomplishing the required stack maintenance.

Instruction 14 is the CONTINUE instruction, which simply causes the microprogram counter to increment so that the next sequential microinstruction is executed. This is the simplest microinstruction of all and should be the default instruction which the firmware requests whenever there is nothing better to do.

Instruction 15, THREE-WAY BRANCH, is the most complex. It provides for testing of both a data-dependent condition and the counter during one microinstruction and provides for selecting among one of three microinstruction addresses as the next microinstruction to be performed. Like instruction 8, a previous instruction will have loaded a count into the register/counter while pushing a microbranch address onto the stack. Instruction 15 performs a decrement-and-branch-until-zero function similar to instruction 8. The next address is taken from the top of the stack until the count reaches zero; then the next address comes from the pipeline register. The above action continues as long as the test condition fails. If at any execution of instruction 15 the test condition is passed, no branch is taken; the microprogram counter register furnishes the next address. When the loop is ended, either because the count has become zero or because the conditional test has been passed, the stack is POPped by decrementing the stack pointer, since interest in the value contained at the top of the stack is then complete.

The application of instruction 15 can enhance performance of a variety of machine-level instructions, for instance: (1) a memory search instruction to be terminated either by finding a desired memory content or by reaching the search limit, (2) variable-field-length arithmetic terminated early upon finding that the content of the portion of the field still unprocessed is all zeros, (3) key search in a disc controller processing variable-length records, and (4) normalization of a floating-point number.

As one example, consider the case of a memory search instruction. As shown in Fig. 29, the instruction at microprogram address 63 can be instruction 4 (PUSH), which will push the value 64 onto the microprogram stack and load the number n, which is one less than the number of memory locations to be searched before giving up. Location 64 contains a microinstruction which fetches the next operand from the memory area to be searched and compares it with the search key. Location 65 contains a microinstruction which tests the result of the comparison and also is a THREE-WAY BRANCH for microprogram control. If no match is found, the test fails and the microprogram goes back to location 64 for the next operand address. When the count becomes zero, the microprogram branches to location 72, which does whatever is necessary if no match is found. If a match occurs on any execution of the THREE-WAY BRANCH at location 65, control falls through to location 66, which handles this case. Whether the instruction ends by finding a match or not, the stack will have been POPped once, removing the value 64 from the top of the stack.

APPENDIX 1 AM2903 ISP DESCRIPTION

```
AM2903 :=
    begin

! ISPS description of the AM2903 4 bit slice microprocessor.

! Page 1 of the description contains declarations of simple carriers
!       **PC.State** and **MP.STATE** sections describe the actual
!       carriers contained within the AM2903 chip.
!       **External.State** describes the simple carriers that
!       terminate in pins.
!       **Implementation.Declarations** describe carriers necesary
!       for the ISP description.

! Page 2 describes the access computations used to source and sink
!       computation data.

! Page 3 contains descriptions of the basic operation cycle and
!       the actual instruction execution.

! Page 5 - 9 contain descriptions of computations for the Z, G.N,
!       P.OVR, and Cn4 output pins plus the "gi" and "pi"
!       intermediate carry generate and carry propogate computations.

**PC.State**

    ASHFT<3:0>,                         ! ALU shifter
    R<3:0>,                             ! R inputs to ALU
    S<3:0>,                             ! S inputs to ALU

**MP.State**

    RAM[0:15]<3:0>,                     ! 16 X 4 bit 2 port RAM

**External.State**

    A<3:0>,                             ! A RAM port input address
    B<3:0>,                             ! B RAM port input address
    Cn<>,                               ! Carry in
    DA<3:0>,                            ! Direct data input (R input)
    DB<3:0>,                            ! Direct data input (S input)
    EA<>,                               ! HIGH => R = DA, LOW => R = A
    F<3:0>,                             ! Sign of ALU (MSS)
                                        ! Output from ALU
    IEN<>,                              ! Instruction enable (LOW true)
    LSSL<>,                             ! LOW => Least Significant Slice
    OEB<>,                              ! LOW enables RAM port B
    OEY<>,                              ! LOW enables ALU shift to Y
    Q<3:0>,                             ! Output from Q register
    QIO3<>,                             ! Q register shift MSB
    QIO0<>,                             ! Q register shift LSB
    SIO3<>,                             ! ALU shift MSB
    SIO0<>,                             ! ALU shift LSB
    W.MSS<>,                            ! LSS=LOW  => NOT WRITE output
                                        ! LSS=HIGH => input pin:
                                        !     HIGH => IS, LOW => MSS
    WE<>,                               ! Write Enable: LOW => RAM = Y
    Y<3:0>,                             ! Data input/output

    I<8:0>,                             ! Instruction inputs

**Implementation.Declarations**

    p<>,                                ! Accumulator for computed P
    g<>,                                ! Accumulator for computed G
    cn3<>,                              ! Accumulator for computed Cn+3
    write<>,                            ! Internal write flag

    dest<3:0> := I<8:5>,                ! Destination select
    op<3:0>   := I<4:1>,                ! Function OP code
    i0<>      := I<0>,                  ! I<0> (part of source select)

    macro hiz    := |'1111|,           ! Tristate constant
    macro parity := |F<3> xor F<2> xor F<1> xor F<0> xor SIO3|,
    macro mss    := |LSSL and (not W.MSS)|,

**Access.Computation**{us}

    source :=                           ! Source calculation
        begin
        DECODE EA @ I<0> @ OEB =>
            begin
            #0 := (R = RAM[A]; S = RAM[B]),
            #1 := (r = ram[a]; s = db    ),
            #2:#3 := (R = RAM[A]; S = Q   ),
            #4 := (R = DA    ; S = RAM[B]),
            #5 := (R = DA    ; S = DB    ),
            #6:#7 := (R = DA    ; S = Q    )
            end
        end,

    destination :=                      ! Destination calculation
        begin
        DECODE I<8:7> =>
            begin
            0 := begin
                                        ! ASHFT= F/2
                0 := begin
```

```
                ASHFT @ SIO0 = SIO3 @ F next
                IF mss and (not I<5>) => ASHFT<3>@ASHFT<2> = ASHFT<2>@ASHFT<3>;
                WRITE = 0;
                DECODE I<6> =>
                    begin
                    0 := qio3 = qio0 = hiz,
                    1 := q @ qio0 = qio3 @ q
                    end
                end,
            1 := begin                  ! ASHFT= F
                ASHFT = F; SIO0 = parity; WRITE = I<6> xor I<5>;
                DECODE I<6:5> =>
                    begin
                    0 := QIO3 = QIO0 = hiz,
                    1 := Q @ QIO0 = QIO3 @ Q,
                    2:3 := (QIO3 = QIO0 = hiz; Q = F)
                    end
                end,
            2 := begin                  ! ASHFT= 2F
                SIO3 @ ASHFT = F @ SIO0 next
                IF mss and (not I<5>) => SIO3 @ ASHFT<3> = ASHFT<3> @ SIO3;
                WRITE = 0;
                DECODE I<6> =>
                    begin
                    0 := QIO3 = QIO0 = hiz,
                    1 := QIO3 @ Q = Q @ QIO0
                    end
                end,
            3 := begin                  ! ASHFT= <F>, <SIO0>
                DECODE I<6:5> eql '10 =>
                    begin
                    0 := (ASHFT = F; SIO3 = F<3>; SIO0 = hiz),
                    1 :=  ASHFT <= SIO0
                    end;
                WRITE = not I<6>;
                DECODE I<6:5> eql '01 =>
                    begin
                    0 := QIO3 = QIO0 = hiz,
                    1 := QIO3 @ Q = Q @ QIO0
                    end
                end
            end
        end,

**Instruction.Cycle**

    run :=                              ! Main instruction cycle
        begin
        WRITE = 1 next
        DECODE IEN =>
            begin
            0 := begin
                source() next
                exec() next
                IF I<4:0> NEQ 0 => destination() next
                IF not LSSL => W.MSS = WRITE next
                IF not OEY => Y = ASHFT next
                IF not WE => RAM[B] = Y next
                Z() next
                gi(); pi() next
                CN4(); P.OVR(); G.N()
                end,
            1 := WRITE = 1
            end next
        RESTART run
        end.

**Instruction.Execution**{us}

    exec :=
        begin
        DECODE I<4:1> =>
            begin
            "0 := (DECODE I<0> =>
                        begin
                        0 := (special.functions()),
                        1 := F = '1111
                        end),
            "1 := F = ((S - R) - 1) + Cn,
            "2 := F = ((R - S) - 1) + Cn,
            "3 := F = (R + S) + Cn,
            "4 := F = S + Cn,
            "5 := F = (not S) + Cn,
            "6 := F = R + Cn,
            "7 := F = (not R) + Cn,
            "8 := F = 0,
            "9 := F = (not R) and S,
            "A := F = R eqv S,
            "B := F = R xor S,
            "C := F = R and S,
            "D := F = not (R or S),
            "E := F = not (R and S),
            "F := F = R or S.
            end
        end.
```

```
! Special functions are decoded from I<8:5> when I<4:0> equal zero.
! These are the built-in multiplication, division, and normalization
! functions.

    special.functions :=
        begin
        DECODE I<8:5> =>
            begin
            "0:"3 := begin                          ! Multiply
                DECODE Z =>                         ! Unsigned and TC F
                    begin                           !   outputs are identical.
                    0 := F = S + Cn,
                    1 := F = (S + R) + Cn
                    end next
                DECODE mss =>
                    begin
                    0 := (ASHFT @ SIO0 = SIO3 @ F; WRITE = 0),
                    1 := (SIO3 = hiz;               ! MSS
                        DECODE I<6> =>              ! I<6> = 0 => US
                        begin                       ! I<6> = 1 => TC
                        0 := ASHFT @ SIO0 = Cn4 @ F,
                        1 := ASHFT @ SIO0 = (F<3> xor P.OVR()) @ F
                        end)
                    end.
            "4:"5 := begin                          ! Increment by one or two
                DECODE I<5> =>                      ! SM-Two's Complement
                    begin
                    0 :=  ASHFT = F = (S + 1) + Cn,
                    1 := (DECODE Z =>
                        begin
                        0 := ASHFT = F = S + Cn,
                        1 := ASHFT = F = (not S) + Cn
                        end next
                        IF mss => ASHFT<3> = S<3> xor F<3>)
                    end;
                    SIO0 = parity; QIO3 = QIO0 = hiz; WRITE = 0
                end.
            "6:"7 := begin                          ! Two's Complement
                DECODE Z =>                         ! Multiply Correction
                    begin
                    0 := F = S + Cn,
                    1 := F = (not S) + Cn
                    end next
                DECODE mss =>
                    begin
                    0 := ASHFT @ SIO0 = SIO3 @ F,
                    1 := (SIO3 = hiz;
                        ASHFT @ SIO0 = (F<3> xor P.OVR()) @ F)
                    end;
                Q @ QIO0 = QIO3 @ Q; WRITE = 0
                end.
            "8:"B := begin                          ! Normalize
                F = S + Cn next
                DECODE I<6> =>
                    begin
                    0 := (ASHFT = F; SIO3 = F<3>; SIO0 = hiz),
                    1 := (DECODE mss =>
                        begin
                        0 := SIO3 @ ASHFT = F @ SIO0,
                        1 := SIO3 @ ASHFT
                            = (R<3> xor F<3>) @ F<2:0> @ SIO0
                        end)
                    end;
                QIO3 @ Q = Q @ QIO0; WRITE = 0
                end.
            "C:"F := begin                          ! Two's Complement divide
                DECODE Z =>
                    begin
                    0 := F = (S + R) + Cn,
                    1 := F = ((S - R) - 1) + Cn
                    end next
                DECODE I<6> =>
                    begin
                    0 := DECODE mss =>
                        begin
                        0 := SIO3 @ ASHFT = F @ SIO0,
                        1 := SIO3 @ ASHFT
                            = (R<3> xor F<3>) @ F<2:0> @ SIO0
                        end,
                    1 := (ASHFT = F; SIO3 = F<3>; SIO0 = hiz)
                    end;
                QIO3 @ Q = Q @ QIO0; WRITE = 0
                end
            end
        end.
```

```
    Z()<> :=                             ! Compute Zero output
        begin
        DECODE I<4:1> =>
            begin
            "0 := DECODE I<0> =>
                begin
                0 := DECODE I<8:5> =>
                    begin
                    ["0:"3,"6:"7]:= IF not LSSL => Z = Q<0>,
                    "4 := Z = ASHFT eql 0,
                    "5 := IF mss => Z = S<3>,
                    "8:"9 := Z = Q eql 0,
                    "A:"B := Z = (Q eql 0) and (F eql 0),
                    "C:"F := IF mss => Z = R<3> eqv F<3>
                    end,
                1 := Z = ASHFT eql 0
                end,
            "1:"F := Z = ASHFT eql 0
            end
        end.
    gi()<3:0> :=                         ! Intermediate Carry Generate
        begin                            !   computation.
        DECODE I<4:1> =>
            begin
            "0 := begin
                DECODE I<0> =>
                    begin
                    0 := DECODE I<8:5> =>
                        begin
                        "0:"3 := DECODE Z =>
                            begin
                            0 := gi = 0,
                            1 := gi = R and S
                            end,
                        "4 := DECODE LSSL =>
                            begin
                            0 := gi = '000 @ S<0>,
                            1 := gi = 0
                            end,
                        ["5,"8:"B]:= gi = 0,
                        "6:"7 := DECODE Z =>
                            begin
                            0 := gi = 0,
                            1 := gi = (not R) and S
                            end,
                        "C:"F := DECODE Z =>
                            begin
                            0 := gi = R and S,
                            1 := gi = (not R) and S
                            end
                        end,
                    1 := gi = 0
                    end
                end,
            ["1,"9,"B]:= gi = (not R) and S,
            "2 := gi = R and (not S),
            ["3,"A,"C,"E]:= gi = R and S,
            "4:"8 := gi = 0,
            ["D,"F]:= gi = (not R) and (not S)
            end
        end.
    pi()<3:0> :=                         ! Intermediate Carry Propogate
        begin                            !   computation.
        DECODE I<4:1> =>
            begin
            "0 := DECODE I<0> =>
                begin
                0 := DECODE I<8:5> =>
                    begin
                    "0:"3 := DECODE Z =>
                        begin
                        0 := pi = S,
                        1 := pi = R or S
                        end,
                    "4 := DECODE LSSL =>
                        begin
                        0 := pi = S<3:1> @ 1,
                        1 := pi = S
                        end,
                    "5 := DECODE Z =>
                        begin
                        0 := pi = S,
                        1 := pi = not S
                        end,
                    "6:"7 := DECODE Z =>
                        begin
                        0 := pi = S,
                        1 := pi = (not R) or S
                        end,
                    "8:"B := pi = S,
                    "C:"F := DECODE Z =>
                        begin
                        0 := pi = R or S,
                        1 := pi = (not R) or S
                        end
```

```
                                          end,
                          1 := pi = '1111
                        end,
              ["1,"B]:= pi = (not R) or S,
               "2  := pi = R or (not S),
              ["3,"A]:= pi = R or S,
               "4  := pi = S,
               "5  := pi = not S,
               "6  := pi = R,
               "7  := pi = not R,
              ["8:"9,"C:"F]:= pi = '1111
                end,
              end,
Cn4()<> :=                          ! Carry Out
  begin
  DECODE I<4.1> ->
          begin
          "0 := DECODE I<0> =>
                  begin
                  0 := DECODE I<8:5> =>
                      begin
                      ["0:"7,"C:"F]:= Cn4 = g or (p and Cn),
                       "8:"9 := DECODE mss =>
                                  begin
                                  0 := Cn4 = g or (p and Cn),
                                  1 := Cn4 = Q<3> xor Q<2>
                                  end,
                       "A:"B := DECODE mss =>
                                  begin
                                  0 := Cn4 = g or (p and Cn),
                                  1 := Cn4 = F<3> xor F<2>
                                  end
                      end,
                  1 := Cn4 = 0
                  end,
          "1:"7 := Cn4 = g or (p and Cn),
          "8:"F := Cn4 = 0
          end
  end,

P.OVR()<> :=                         ! (not P)/OVR pin
  begin
  p = pi() eqv '1111 next
  DECODE mss =>
          begin
          0 := DECODE I<4:1> =>
                  begin
                  "0 := P.OVR = (not p) and (not I<0>),
                  "1:"7 := P.OVR = not p,
                  "8:"F := P.OVR = 0
                  end,
          1 := DECODE I<4:1> =>
                  begin
                  "0 := DECODE I<0> =>
                          begin
                          0 := DECODE I<8:5> =>
                              begin
                              ["0:"7,"C:"F]:= P.OVR = Cn3 xor Cn4,
                               "8:"9 := P.OVR = Q<2> xor Q<3>,
                               "A:"B := P.OVR = F<2> xor F<1>
                              end,
                          1 := P.OVR = 0
                          end,
                  "1:"7 := P.OVR = Cn3 xor Cn4,
                  "8:"F := P.OVR = 0
                  end
          end
  end,
G.N()<> :=                          ! (not G)/N pin
  begin
  DECODE mss =>
          begin
          0 := G.N = not g,
          1 := DECODE I<4:1> =>
                  begin
                  "0 := DECODE I<0> =>
                          begin
                          0 := DECODE I<8:5> =>
                              begin
                              ["0:"4,"6:"7,"A:"F]:= G.N = F<3>,
                               "5 := DECODE Z =>
                                      begin
                                      0 := G.N = F<3>,
                                      1 := G.N = F<3> xor s<3>
                                      end,
                              "8:"9 := G.N = Q<3>
                              end,
                          1 := G.N = F<3>
                          end,
                  "1:"F := G.N = F<3>
                  end
          end
  end,

end     ! End of AM2903 description
```

APPENDIX 2 (right)   AM2910 ISP DESCRIPTION

```
AM2910 :=
  begin

! ISPS description of AMD AM2910 microprogram sequencer.

! The AM2910 is a 12 bit microprogram address controller.
! The controller is designed to be used with the AM2901 or the AM2903
! microprocessor slice and external memory.

! Simulation of the AM2910 alone is possible, but emulation of any
! computer systems requires that this description be joined with
! the AM2901 or AM2903 description.

**PC.State**

    uPC<11:0>,                          ! Microprogram counter
    R<11:0>,                            ! Address register
    SP<2:0>,                            ! Stack pointer
    STACK[0:5]<11:0>,                   ! Stack register file

**External.State**

    macro pl.   := |'011|,              ! Pipeline address enable
    macro map.  := |'101|,              ! Map address enable
    macro vect. := |'110|,              ! Vector address enable

    CI<>,                               ! Carry in
    CC<>,                               ! Condition code input bit
    CCEN<>,                             ! Condition code enable input bit
    D<11:0>,                            ! Direct inputs
    FULL<>,                             ! Stack full flag
    ir<8:0>,                            ! Instruction register
       i<3:0> := ir<3:0>,               ! Instruction vector affecting 2910
    OE<>,                               ! Output enable control line
    RLD<>,                              ! Register load
    MAP<>  := enable<1>,                ! Map address enable flag
    PL<>   := enable<2>,                ! Pipeline address enable flag
    VECT<> := enable<0>,                ! Vector address enable flag

**Implementation.Variables**

    enable<2:0>,                        ! Enable conditions
    fail<>,                             ! CC fail flag
    pass<>,                             ! CC pass flag
    macro hiz := |"FFFF|,               ! High impedence constant

**Operation.Cycle**{us}

    run{main} :=                        ! Basic operation loop
            begin
            IF not RLD => R = D next    ! Forced (external) load of reg.
            Y() next                    ! Put out selected address
            uPC = Y + CI next           ! Increment pc
            RESTART run
            end,

**Address.Source.Selection**{us}

    Y()<11:0> :=
        begin
        IF i eql "2 => enable = map.;
        IF i eql "6 => enable = vect.;
        If (i neq "2) and (i neq "6) => enable = pl.;
        fail = (not CCEN) and CC next
        pass = not fail next
        DECODE i =>
            begin
            "0 := JZ   := (Y = SP = 0; FULL = 1),
            "1 := CJS  := (IF fail => (Y = uPC);
                           IF pass => (Y = D; push.())),
            "2 := JMAP := (Y = D),
            "3 := CJP  := (IF fail => (Y = uPC);
                           IF pass => (Y = D)),
            "4 := PUSH := (Y = uPC; push.(); IF pass => R = D),
            "5 := JSRP := (IF fail => (Y = R);
                           IF pass => (Y = D); push.()),
            "6 := CJV  := (IF fail => (Y = uPC);
                           IF pass => (Y = D)),
            "7 := JRP  := (IF fail => (Y = R);
                           IF pass => (Y = D)),
            "8 := RFCT := (IF R eql 0 => (Y = uPC; pop()) next
                           IF R neq 0 => (Y = STACK[SP]; R = R - 1)),
            "9 := RPCT := (IF R eql 0 => (Y = uPC) next
                           IF R neq 0 => (Y = D; R = R - 1)),
            "A := CRTN := (IF fail => (Y = uPC);
                           IF pass => (Y = STACK[SP] next pop())),
            "B := CJPP := (IF fail => (Y = uPC);
                           IF pass => (Y = D; pop())),
            "C := LDCT := (Y = uPC; R = D),
            "D := LOOP := (IF fail => (Y = STACK[SP]);
                           IF pass => (Y = uPC; pop())),
            "E := CONT := (Y = uPC),
            "F := TWB  := (DECODE R eql 0 =>
                              begin
                              0 := (IF fail => (Y = STACK[SP]);
                                    IF pass => (Y = uPC; pop()); R = R - 1),
                              1 := (IF fail => (Y = D);
                                    IF pass => (Y = uPC); pop())
                              end)
            end next
        IF OE => Y = hiz
        end,

    pop  := (IF SP neq 0 => SP = SP - 1; FULL = 1),

    push. :=
        begin
        DECODE SP eql #4 =>
            begin
            0 := (FULL = 1; SP = SP + 1),
            1 := (FULL = 0)
            end next
        STACK[SP] = uPC
        end

end     ! End of AM2910 description
```

Chapter 15

A PDP-8 Implemented from AMD Bit-Sliced Microprocessors

Michael Tsao

An example of a microprogrammable system based on the Am2910 sequencer and the Am2901 ALU will illustrate design with bit slices. The target machine is the PDP-8 ISP (see Appendix 1 of Chap. 8). This register-transfer (RT) level design of the micromachine is thus optimized toward the basic PDP-8. However, the general principles involved in microprogramming bit slices are illustrated by this example. A major goal of this design is the clarity of implementation, rather than the economy of design.

Overview

The basic implementation is a *one-stage pipeline* as shown in Fig. 1 in Chap. 13. In this micromachine, the pipeline register stores the current microinstruction, which is being executed by the Am2910 Sequencer and the Am2901 ALU. The status information (zero, overflow, etc.) of the ALU operations is stored in the Status Register. In a one-stage pipeline design, conditional branches can be executed only by the microinstruction following the microcycle that has generated the branching status. The Am2910 sequencer is used instead of the Am2909 to simplify the design and to aid understandability. A more cost-effective design might actually result from using the Am2909 sequencer, since the number of microinstruction types used to emulate the PDP-8 is small. The Am2901 ALU is used because it more closely reflects the ISP of the PDP-8.

A timing diagram for a typical microcycle is shown in Fig. 1. The indicated delays are typical values, illustrating the timing requirements rather than actual component performances. On the rising edge of the system clock, the Pipeline Register latches the microinstruction to be executed during this microcycle. The output of the Pipeline Register is valid 15 ns later. After another 15-ns delay, the Condition Code input to the Am2910 is valid. The microsequencer generates the next microaddress based on the current microinstruction and the Condition Code input. When the microprogram memory output is valid (approximately 130 ns after the rising clock edge), the microcycle can be restarted. Concurrently with the sequencer operation and microword fetch, the Am2901 ALU executes the operations specified by the microword in the Pipeline Register. The output of the ALU is

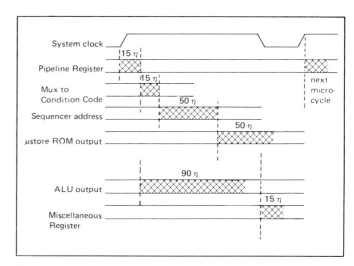

Fig. 1. One-stage pipeline microcycle timing waveform.

valid prior to the falling edge of the system clock. External registers, such as the Memory Address Register (MAR) and the Status Register, use the falling clock edge to latch results from the ALU output port. In this design, the duty cycle of the system clock does not need to be symmetrical at 50 percent.

RT-Level Implementation and the Microword Format

The RT-level implementation of the Am2900/PDP-8 is shown in Fig. 2 for the control part, and in Fig. 3 for the data part. The design can best be explained in conjunction with the microword format shown in Table 1. The ISPS description of the RT-level design is listed in Appendix 2. The following subsections discuss the meaning of each microword field and the associated RT-level components. For each microword field, there are three possible bit sizes: the number of bits *normally* required for the associated components, the *minimum* required for this PDP-8 application, and the *actual* field size used. The position of each field in the microword is defined in the ISPS description. The reason for inserting extra bits is to align the fields on octal boundaries, thus aiding the reading of the encoded microprogram.

Sequencer Instruction and Address Field

The Am2910 sequencer normally requires a 4-bit-wide instruction and a 12-bit-wide "next address" direct input. The microprogram occupies less than 128 words, requiring only 7 bits of address. Two extra instruction bits and two extra address bits are inserted as 0s in this design example for octal boundary alignment.

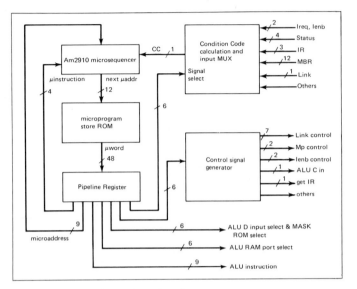

Fig. 2. Micromachine—control and sequencer.

Out of sixteen Am2910 instructions, only 4 are used in this example: Conditional Jump Subroutine (CJS, #01), Conditional Jump (CJP, #03), Conditional Return from Subroutine (CRTN, #12), and Continue (CONT, #16). Therefore, it is theoretically possible to use only 2 bits of information to specify these four actions.

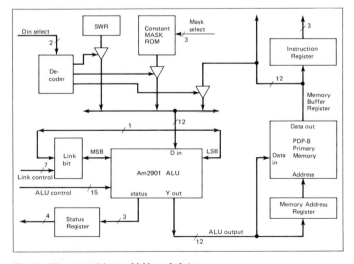

Fig. 3. Micromachine—ALU and data.

Table 1   The Microword Format and Required Bits per Field

Bits per field	Normal	Minimum	Actual (ISP)
Micro sequencer control			
Microinstruction	4	2	6
Next microaddress	12	7	9
Condition code select	(6)	6	6
ALU control			
ALU instruction			
Source	3	3	3
Function	3	3	3
Destination	3	3	3
RAM A port select	4	3	3
RAM B port select	4	3	3
Direct input select	(2)	2	3
Constant mask select	(3)	3	3
Miscellaneous control signals			
Control signal select	(4)	4	6
Total	48	39	48

Condition Code Input Selection

There is only one condition code (CC) input for the Am2910. The status conditions have to be multiplexed into this input. The assignments for the multiplexer input lines can be found in the ISP description in Appendix 1 (ISPS procedure Condition.Code). Five bits are used to select one out of 32 different input signals. The sixth bit in this field is used to select between the original signal and the complement of the signal. In this manner, the micromachine can branch when the signal is either high or low. When an unconditional microprogram branch is required, a logic 0 can be selected for the CC input.

Each bit from the Instruction Register (IR, 5 bits) or from the Memory Buffer Register (MBR, 12 bits) can be selected individually. This capability is used for the basic PDP-8 instruction decode, effective address calculation, and the Group 7 microinstruction decode. Random combinational logic is used to generate a single skip.enable signal for the portion of the microprogram that decodes the PDP-8 skip conditions. Interrupt requests are also handled by using combinational logic in a similar manner.

ALU Operations and the Link Bit

Three Am2901 ALU chips are cascaded to form the PDP-8 ALU section. The ALU requires a 9-bit opcode: source, function, and destination. Six bits are used to encode the A port (3 bits) and B port (3 bits) select, since only a subset of the sixteen ALU RAM registers is used in this implementation.

The PDP-8 Link bit is constructed from random logic controlled by a set of signals. For economic reasons, random logic is used rather than adding another Am2901 chip. The Link bit does not correspond to any Am2901 function, and its control would have to be separately microprogrammed. Another alternative for the PDP-8 Link bit is to use one of the Am2901 RAM registers for storing the value. In this case, additional Link-handling microcode would have to be inserted after each PDP-8 ALU operation, increasing the target instruction execution time.

Data Input to the ALU

There is only one method of writing external data into the Am2901 ALU. It is through the Direct (D) input. In this PDP-8 design, three sources are connected to share the D input: data from the main memory (MBR), constants for ALU operations (the Mask ROM), and data in the switch register (SWITCHES). These three sources are connected by an input bus to the D input port on the ALU. The microword selects which one of the three will be the source during any given microcycle.

The use of a separate ROM to store the constants can be debated. An alternative is to store the constants in the microword. It is wasteful to dedicate a microword bit field to this purpose, since the width of this field must be the same as the ALU width and constants are used infrequently. If the microword fields are multiplexed, we violate the design goal of clarity. Hence, a constant ROM is a good compromise between the two conflicting objectives. One need only store the address of the constant in the microprogram.

Miscellaneous Control Signals

The data part of this design requires many miscellaneous control signals. For example, the Link bit uses seven different signals to control its operation. Analysis indicates that only one of these signals needs to be asserted during any given microcycle. The Miscellaneous Control Select field in the microword selects one and only one signal during each microcycle. The selection code is decoded and directed to the associated destinations. The assignments of the signals can be found in the ISPS description.

The PDP-8 Primary Memory

The primary memory (MP) for the PDP-8 target machine is assumed to be constructed from "static" semiconductor memory chips. In this type of memory, the output constantly displays the content of the location selected by the address input, unless a write operation is in progress. In this PDP-8 design, the ALU output is connected with the Memory Address Register (MAR) and with the data input port of the MP. When the write enable line of the MP is asserted, the content of the ALU output port is latched into the location selected by the MAR. The Memory Buffer Register (MBR), an ISP implementation pseudoregister, is constantly displaying the content of the location selected by the MAR. For the ISPS simulation, the memory access speed is assumed to be less than one microcycle. One can read the value of

MBR (containing data from MP) two microcycles after a "write" into the MAR.

The Microprogram

The encoded microprogram that emulates the PDP-8 basic instruction set is listed in Appendix 2. This program listing is extracted from an ISPS simulator command file used to simulate this microprogrammable machine. The content of the constant ROM (Mask) is defined using the ISPS simulator "set" command, e.g., "set Mask[4]=#0177." The content of the microprogram store is also defined in this manner. As an example, the instruction fetch cycle is now described. (For readability, the encoded microword is broken into seven fields separated by dashes.)

set uMP[000] = #03–010–10–403–12–00–10
!RUN: MAR ← LastPC←PC, IF PDP8.go = 0 goto HALT:

If the PDP-8.go bit is off (Condition code select 10), the microprogram jumps to Halt: (location 010). The content of PC (ALU RAM[1]) is pushed to the ALU output. The value is also latched into LastPC (ALU RAM[2]). Concurrently, the value is latched into the Memory Address Register (MAR) using the control code 10.

set uMP[001] = # 16–000–00–503–11–21–00 !PC←PC+1

The value #0001 is selected from the constant Mask ROM (21). The PC value is selected at the ALU A port, added to the constant, and then latched back into PC.

set uMP[002] = #03–040–41–703–05–10–15
!IR←ALU.Mb←MBR, goto Exec:

The content of the Memory Buffer Register (obtained by the MP[MAR] operation) is latched into the ALU.Mb (ALU RAM[5]). In this cycle, the MBR is also latched into the Instruction Register (IR) by the control signal 15. The microprogram jumps to the instruction execution section (location 040, Exec:) by forcing a pass-test condition (41) into the Am2910 sequencer Condition Code input.

set uMP[004] = #03–000–03–741–00–20–10
!ENDex: MAR ← 0, IF no interrupt goto RUN:

When the instruction execution is finished, the microprogram returns to this point. The MAR is set to zero in anticipation of interrupt servicing. The MAR will be reset to the correct PC value by microinstruction uMP[001] later on. If the interrupt request is not granted (condition code 03), the microprogram jumps back to RUN: (location 000). Otherwise, the program continues to location uMP[005] to handle the interrupt.

Implementation and Simulation Results

The micromachine and the microcode were simulated and tested by the ISPS simulator. The results are presented here.

Chip Count

Since the micromachine was not actually built, the chip count is an estimate of the required hardware parts. The goal of this exercise is to identify the inefficient area in terms of the parts count, and to suggest alternative IC chip types that may reduce the parts count. (See Table 2.)

The parts count for this microprogrammed PDP-8 implementation is 35 chips. Of these IC parts, over two-thirds (25 chips) are SSI or MSI types. If IC custom-made parts are available for the Link bit, the Skip-condition generate, and the Pipeline Register, the design can be reduced to 22 chips.

Target-Machine Instruction Execution Speed

Two methods of comparing this microprogrammed PDP-8 and a basic PDP-8 are discussed here. By counting the average number of microinstructions executed for a target instruction, one can estimate the execution speed of the emulated PDP-8. Or one can compare the execution speed of the two ISPS simulators.

For each target PDP-8 instruction, the microprogram must execute the following number of microinstructions (Table 3).

On the average, 18 microwords (4 + 3 + 6 + 5 or 4 + 3 + 11) are needed to do one PDP-8 target instruction. At the manufacturer-recommended microcycle time of 150 ns, and not counting the PDP-8 Mp access time, the microprogram execution speed is 2.7 μs per target instruction (150 ns $\times$ 18). The Mp access time is usually quoted at 1.3 μs for PDP-8/E and /M [Bell, Mudge, and McNamara, 1978]. For an average instruction (i.e., indirect memory reference), three memory accesses are required: instruction fetch, pointer to data (one level of indirection), and the actual data fetch. When these are added to the 2.7-μs microprogram execution time, the projected maximum average instruction time is 6.6 μs.

Another method of comparison involves the ISPS simulator. Several PDP-8 benchmark and diagnostic programs were simulated. The CPU times used by each simulator were compared. The microcoded PDP-8 uses approximately 20 times the CPU time used by the basic PDP-8 ISP. Translated into simulation CPU time, the ISP simulator of the micromachine executes approximately 1.5 PDP-8 target instructions for every CPU second on a DEC KL-10 processor.

Table 2   Chip Count for a Microprogrammed PDP-8

Chip count	Description
6	Microstore. The microword width is between 39 bits and 48 bits (see Table 1). In using 8-bit-wide ROM or EPROM parts, six such chips are required. Since the microprogram is less than 128 words (7 address bits), many commercially available memory chips can be used here.
6	Pipeline Register (Pipe). Eight-bit-wide D flip-flops are assumed here. This register is very expansive in terms of chip count. An alternative would be having a special ROM type that can latch the data in the output buffer. Another alternative is to latch the microaddress instead of the microword. In this second design, the microword fetch and ALU-Sequencer operations are in series rather then in parallel as in the original design. This is a classical cost-performance tradeoff.
1	Am2910 microsequencer. The advantage of using the Am2910 instead of the Am2909 Sequencer is evident here. The Am2909 requires two chips instead of one Am2910 for this example.
3	Am2901 ALU bit slices. Three slices are used to provide the 12-bit-wide PDP-8 data path.
5 (estimated)	Link bit and associated hardware. The link bit in this design is constructed of a D flip-flop, some tristate drivers, and input multiplexers. SSI implementation of the Link bit requires 14 percent (5 out of 35) of the total chip count. An alternative is to use a custom-made MSI chip for the Link bit. A second alternative is to implement the Link bit in the ALU RAM registers. In this second design, additional microcode will have to be inserted to handle the special cases, degrading the overall performance.
3	Condition Code input multiplexer. Two 16-to-1 MUXs and two 2-to-1 MUXs.
4	PDP-8 Skip condition generate. The argument for a custom MSI chip can also be made here.
3	Constant Mask ROM and associated ALU D input selection control. The Constant Mask uses two ROM chips. The D input control uses one 2-to-4 decoder. The source registers for the ALU D input bus are assumed to have build-in tristate drivers.
4 (estimated)	Other miscellaneous parts.

Table 3   Average Number of Microinstructions Executed for a Target Instruction

Words	Description
4	PDP-8 instruction fetch cycle. Check PDP-8.go, fetch target instruction, increment PC, check interrupt conditions.
3	Instruction decodes. A straightforward binary decision decode tree is implemented in microcode. An alternative is to use the Instruction Decode Mapping ROM capability of the Am2910. The advantage of this alternative is not clear in view of the simple PDP-8 ISP.

6	Effective Address Calculation. Depending on the addressing mode, there are five possibilities
	    2 words PDP-8 Page 0 address
	    4 words current page
	    6 words indirect address, Page 0
	    8 words indirect address, current page
	    9 words auto index
	On the average, approximately six microinstructions are needed to calculate the PDP-8 effective address (equivalent to the Page 0 indirect address).

5	Memory Reference Instructions. For each target instruction, the microcode fetches data from primary memory, executes the operation, and deposits the result in memory. Depending on the particular target instruction, anywhere between two microinstructions (JMP) and eight microinstructions (ISZ) are needed. On the average, five microinstructions are assumed.
(11)	PDP-8 OPR group microinstructions. The decoding and execution of the PDP-8 OPR instructions are highly sequential in nature. Therefore, 11 microinstructions executed is taken as the average.

Summary

In this chapter, the design of a microprogrammed PDP-8 was presented. The central component of this micromachine was the AMD bit-sliced microprocessor. Although the design was optimized toward the basic PDP-8 configuration, many issues common to all microprogramming and RT-level hardware designs were illustrated. In simulating the micromachine, the usefulness of the ISP descriptive language as a design tool was also demonstrated.

References

Bell, Mudge, and McNamara [1978].

```
AMD8 :=
    begin

! ISP of a PDP8 emulator using the AM2901 and AM2910 bit slice uPc chips

! The AM2901 description is expanded to fit the 12 bits wide PDP8 data path.
! The AM2910 sequencer uses 7 address bits to address 128 microwords.

! This AMD8 description contains the following major sections.
! (1) declarations for the PDP8 target machine, the sequencer, and the ALU.
! (2) implemantation pseudo registers for the ISPS description.
! (3) the main microcycle execution loop.
! (4) the sequencer Condition Code (CC) input mutiplexer.
! (5) the generator for the PDP8 skip condition and miscellaneous control signals.

**PDP8.State**

    MP[0:4095]<11:0>,                     ! Basic PDP8 4k memory
    switches<11:0>,                       ! Switch Register
    L<>,                                  ! Link Register
    interrupt.enable<>,                   ! Interrupt Enable
    PDP8.go<>,                            ! RUN bit for the PDP8 target machine

    IR<0:4>,                              ! Instruction register & pb & ib
    pb<> := IR<4>,                        ! Page bit
    ib<> := IR<3>,                        ! indirect bit
    MAR<11:0>,                            ! Memory Address Register

**Sequencer.State**

    uMP[0:127]<47:0>,                     ! Microprogram memory
    PIPE<47:0>,                           ! Pipeline Register
    ! sequencer controls
    uIR<5:0>         := PIPE<47:42>,      ! AM2910 instruction, padded to 6 bits
    nxtAddr<8:0>     := PIPE<41:33>,      ! next micro-address field
    CCsel<5:0>       := PIPE<32:27>,      ! select condition code input

    ! ALU controls
    ALUir<8:0>    := PIPE<26:18>,         ! ALU Instruction
      src<2:0> := ALUir<8:6>,            !    Source
      fnc<2:0> := ALUir<5:3>,            !    function
      dst<2:0> := ALUir<2:0>,            !    destination
    ALUport<5:0> := PIPE<17:12>,          ! ALU RAM port select
    DircSel<2:0> := PIPE <11:9>,          ! ALU direct input Select
    MaskSel<2:0> := PIPE <8:6>,           ! constant mask select

    MisCntr<5:0> := PIPE <5:0>,           ! Miscellaneous Control signals

**ALU.State**

    mask[0:15] <11:0>,                    ! constant mask ROM
    status<3:0>,                          ! ALU result status
      SEQ.ovr<> = status<3>,             ! SEQ stack overflow
      ALU.ovr<> = status<2>,             ! ALU result overflow
      ALU.n<>   = status<1>,             ! ALU result is negative
      ALU.z<>   = status<0>,             ! ALU result is zero

**Implementation.Registers**

    AMD8.go<>,                            ! go bit for the micro machine

    interrupt.request<>,                  ! Interrupt request
    MBR<11:0>,                            ! Memory Buffer Register, output of MP[MAR]
    MB<0:11>     := MBR<11:0>,            ! PDP8 bit assignments
    group<>      := MB<3>,                ! Microinstruction group
    CLA<>        := MB<4>,                ! Clear AC
    CLL<>        := MB<5>,                ! Clear Link
    CMA<>        := MB<6>,                ! Complement AC
    CML<>        := MB<7>,                ! Complement Link
    RAR<>        := MB<8>,                ! Rotate right
    RAL<>        := MB<9>,                ! Rotate left
    RTx<>        := MB<10>,               ! Rotate twice
    IAC<>        := MB<11>,               ! Increment AC
    SMA<>        := MB<5>,                ! Skip on minus AC
    SPA<>        := MB<5>,                ! Skip on positive AC
    SZA<>        := MB<6>,                ! Skip on zero AC
    SNA<>        := MB<6>,                ! Skip on AC not zero
    SNL<>        := MB<7>,                ! Skip on Link not zero
    SZL<>        := MB<7>,                ! Skip on Link zero
    is<>         := MB<8>,                ! Invert skip sense
    OSR<>        := MB<9>,                ! Logical or AC with switches
    HLT<>        := MB<10>,               ! Halt the processor

    uMP.out <47:0>,                       ! uStore output
    CCode<>,                              ! condition code input

    Din<11:0>,                            ! direct input to ALU
    ALU.Cin<>,                            ! ALU carry in

    Temp.AM2910<15:0>,
    uMP.addr<6:0> := Temp.AM2910<6:0>,    ! effective uStore address

    Temp.AM2901<17:0>,
    ALU.out<11:0> := Temp.AM2901<11:0>,   ! ALU result Y output
    ALU.Cout<>    := Temp.AM2901<15>,     ! ALU carry out
    ALU.lsb<>     := Temp.AM2901<16>,     ! ALU LSB output from RAM shifter
    ALU.msb<>     := Temp.AM2901<17>,     ! ALU MSB output from RAM shifter
```

```
**AMD8.Execution**

start.AMD8 {main} :=
    begin

    ! initialize the micro machine
    AMD8.go = 1;                          ! get the uMachine going
    uMP.out = uMP[0];                     ! start at uAddr 0

    ! initialize the target machine
    ! force interrupt handling which begins at PDP8 PC=1
    PDP8.go = 1;                          ! get the target-machine going
    interrupt.enable = 1;                 ! enable interrupt
    interrupt.request = 1 next            ! request interrupt

    run.AMD8 :=                           ! one uCycle
        begin

        ! First half of the cycle
        PIPE = uMP.out next               ! latch uWord

        uALU.opr :=                       ! ALU operations
            begin
            DECODE DircSel =>             ! select Direct input to ALU
                begin
                #0 := Din = 0,
                #1 := Din = MBR,
                #2 := Din = mask[MaskSel],
                #3 := Din = switches
                end;
            DECODE MisCntr =>             ! set ALU carry in bit
                begin
                #14 := ALU.Cin = 1,
                OTHERWISE := ALU.Cin = 0
                end next

            ! Do ALU computation, input instruction, Aport, Bport,
            ! Direct input, carry in, MSB, LSB, and enable output
            Temp.Am2901 = AM2901(ALUir, ('0 @ ALUport<5:3>),
                                  ('0 @ ALUport<2:0>), Din, ALU.Cin, L, L, '0)
            end;                          ! end of uALU.opr

        uSeq.opr :=                       ! sequencer operation
            begin
            Condition.Code() next

            ! Do sequncer computation, input instrcution, next address,
            ! condition code, etc.
            Temp.AM2910 = AM2910(uIR<3:0>, ('000 @ nxtAddr<8:0>),
                                  CCode, '0110) next
            uMP.out = uMP[uMP.addr]       ! uStore ROM access
            end next                      ! end of uSEQ.opr

        ! Second half of the cycle
        status<3:0> = Temp.Am2910<15> @ Temp.Am2901<14>
                        @ Temp.Am2901<13> @ Temp.Am2901<12>;
        Do.Control() next

        IF AMD8.go => RESTART run.AMD8    ! end of run.AMD8
        end                               ! end of start.AMD8

    end,                                  ! end of start.AMD8

**Condition.Code**

    Condition.Code :=                     ! calculate condition code
        begin
        Decode ('0 @ CCsel<4:0>) =>       ! look at lower 5 bits
            begin
            #00 := CCode = 0,             ! #00 => always pass test
                                          ! #40 => always fail test
            #01 := CCode = 1,             ! #01 => always fail test
                                          ! #41 => always fail test
            #02 := CCode = Skip.Cond(),   ! calculate Skip condition
            #03 := CCode = interrupt.request AND interrupt.enable,
                                          ! check for interrupt handling

            #04 := CCode = status<0>,     ! ALU.z, ALU output eql 0
            #05 := CCode = status<1>,     ! ALU.n, ALU MSB
            #06 := CCode = status<2>,     ! ALU.ovr, ALU operation overflow
            #07 := CCode = status<3>,     ! SEQ.ovr, sequncer stack overflow

            #10 := CCode = PDP8.go,       ! target machine RUN bit
            #11 := CCode = IR<2>,         ! LSB of the 3 bits IR
            #12 := CCode = IR<1>,
            #13 := CCode = IR<0>,         ! MSB of the 3 bits IR
            #14 := CCode = pb,            ! page bit
            #15 := CCode = ib,            ! indirect bit
```

```
            #20 := CCode = MB<11>,           ! IAC, MBR<0>, LSB
            #21 := CCode = MB<10>,           ! RTx,  HLT
            #22 := CCode = MB<09>,           ! RAL,  OSR
            #23 := CCode = MB<08>,           ! RAR,  is
            #24 := CCode = MB<07>,           ! CML, SNL, SZL
            #25 := CCode = MB<06>,           ! CMA, SZA, SNA
            #26 := CCode = MB<05>,           ! CLL, SMA, SPA
            #27 := CCode = MB<04>,           ! CLA
            #30 := CCode = MB<03>,           ! group
            #31 := CCode = MB<02>,
            #32 := CCode = MB<01>,
            #33 := CCode = MB<00>,           ! MBR<11>, MSB
            #34 := CCode = L,                ! Link bit

            OTHERWISE := CCode = 0
        end next                             ! end of decode

    ! when CCsel<5>=0 will pass test if the selected signal is low, "0"
    ! when CCsel<5>=1 will pass test if the selected signal is high, "1"
    IF CCsel<5> => CCode = not CCode

    end,                             ! end of Condition.Code


**Skip.Conditions.for.PDP8**

    Skip.Cond<> :=                   ! calculate PDP8 skip condition
        begin
        DECODE is =>
            begin
            '0 := Skip.Cond =        ! normal skip sense
                     (SNL and L) or
                     (SZA and ALU.z) or
                     (SMA and ALU.n),
            '1 := Skip.Cond =        ! invert skip sense
                     (NOT (SZL or SNA or SPA)) or
                     (SZL and NOT L) or
                     (SNA and NOT ALU.z) or
                     (SPA and NOT ALU.n)
            end
        end,                         ! end of Skip.Cond


**Miscellaneous.Controls**

    Do.Control :=                    ! do the miscellaneous control functions
        begin
        DECODE MisCntr =>            ! 6 bits
            begin
            #00 := NO.OP(),          ! no op
            #01 := IF ALU.Cout =>    ! IF carry.out THEN complement Link
                      L = not L,

            #02 := L = ALU.lsb,      ! L = old LSB
            #03 := L = ALU.msb,      ! L = old MSB

            #04 := L = 0,            ! clear Link
            #05 := IF CLL => L = 0,  ! conditional clear

            #06 := L = not L,        ! negate Link
            #07 := IF CML => L = not L,   ! conditional negate

            #10 := (MAR = ALU.out next    ! set MAR
                      MBR = MP[MAR]),      ! read PDP8 main memory
            #11 := (MP[MAR] = ALU.out next ! write into PDP8 MP
                      MBR = MP[MAR]),

            #12 := interrupt.enable = 0,! clear Intrupt enable
            #13 := interrupt.enable = 1,! set Interrupt enable

            #14 := ALU.Cin = 1,      ! set ALU carry in
            #15 := IR = MB<0:4>,     ! get instruction

            #16 := PDP8.go = 0,      ! stop the target machine
            #17 := AMD8.go = 0,      ! stop the micro machine


            OTHERWISE := NO.OP()
            end
        end,                         ! end of Do.Control

! logical end of the AMD8 description
```

```
! ISPS of the AM2910 and AM2901 descriptions.
! Only the key parts of the description are listed here.
! The intension is to show the necessary modifications
! on the original ISP, making the description callable
! from the AMD8 description.
!
! ***************************************************************
!! AMD 2910 microsequencer description in procedureal form
!
!AM2910 (i<3:0>, D<11:0>, CC<>, Misc.in<3:0>) <15:0> :=
!    begin
!
!**AM2910.External.State**
!
!    CCEN<>      := Misc.in<3>,       ! enable CC input
!    CI<>        := Misc.in<2>,       ! carry in to increament uPC
!    RLD<>       := Misc.in<1>,       ! load R register with D input
!    OE<>        := Misc.in<0>,       ! enable output
!
!    FULL<>,                          ! Stack full flag
!    MAP<>   := enable<1>,            ! Map address enable flag
!    PL<>    := enable<2>,            ! Pipeline address enable flag
!    VECT<>  := enable<0>,            ! Vector address enable flag
!
!
!**AM2910.Operation.Cycle**(us)
!
!    run.AM2910 (main) :=             ! Basic operation loop
!       begin
!       If not RLD => R = D next      ! Forced (external) load of reg.
!       Y() next                      ! Put out selected address
!       AM2910 = Full @ enable<2:0> @ Y next
!       uPC = Y + CI                  ! Increment pc
!       end,                          ! end of run.AM2910
!
!       ...                           ! description of Y()
!
!    end,                             ! end of AM2901 description
!
!
!
! ***************************************************************
!! AM2901 ALU description in procedural form
!
!AM2901 (I<8:0>, A<3:0>, B<3:0>, D<11:0>, Cn<>, R3in<>, R0in<>, OE<>) <17:0> :=
!    begin
!
!**AM2901.External.State**
!
!    out<17:0>,                       ! Output carrier
!      R3out<>  := out<17>,           ! RAM3 output
!      R0out<>  := out<16>,           ! RAM0 output
!      Cn4<>    := out<15>,           ! Carry out
!      OVR<>    := out<14>,           ! Overflow
!      F3<>     := out<13>,           ! Sign bit out
!      FEQL0<>  := out<12>,           ! High if ALU output = 0
!      Y<11:0>  := out<11:0>,         ! Data outputs
!    c.out<>  := alu<12>,             ! Carry out
!
!**AM2901.Instruction.Cycle**
!
!    run.AM2901(main) :=              ! Initialization
!       begin
!       OVR = feql0 = c.out = 0 next  ! init flags
!       source() next
!       exec() next
!       destination() next
!       F3 = f<11>; Cn4 = c.out next  ! set final flags
!       AM2901 = out                  ! push out ALU result
!       end,
!
!       ...                           ! description of source(), etc..
!
!    end                              ! end of AM2901 description
!
!
!    end                              ! end of AMD8 description
```

225

```
!
!
! Simulator command file for the AM2900 implementation of the PDP8
!
radix octal
!
! constant Mask ROM, used as input to the ALU Direct input port
s Mask[0]=#0000
s Mask[1]=#0001
s Mask[2]=#0002
s Mask[3]=#0010
s Mask[4]=#0177
s Mask[5]=#7600
s Mask[6]=#7770
s Mask[7]=#0777
!
! the micro program
!      micro word format
!     #||   Sequencer instruction
!      |       01   CJS,   conditional jump to subroutine
!      |       03   CJP,   conditional jump to program
!      |       12   CRTN,  conditional return from subroutine
!      |       16   CONT,  continue
!
!    #|||     next micro address
!
!    #||      select conditional input signals
!     |       (see ISPS.Cond.Code for signal assignments)
!
!         #|||  ALU instructions (see AM2901 descriptions)
!                 431  used as NO.OP
!
!            #||   Aport, Bport (ALU RAM register assignments)
!             |      0     AC
!             |      1     PC
!             |      2     Last.PC
!             |      4     ALU.ma, for effective addr calc.
!             |      5     ALU.mb, copy of Mp output
!             |      others - not used
!
!               #||   Dinput source select, constant Mask select
!
!                  #||   Miscellaneous controls
!                        (See ISP description Do.Control for detail)
!
! instruction fetch and interrupt handling cycle
!         # # ## ####
s uMP[000]=#0301010403120010   !RUN:     MAR+LastPC+PC, IF PDP8.go=0 goto HALT:
s uMP[001]=#1600000503112100   !         PC+PC+1
s uMP[002]=#0304041703051015   !         IR+Mb+MBR, goto Exec:
!
s uMP[004]=#0300003741002010   !ENDex:   MAR+0, IF no-Intr goto RUN:
s uMP[005]=#1600000301010011   !         MP[0]+PC
s uMP[006]=#0300041703012100   !         PC+1, goto RUN:
!
s uMP[010]=#0301041231000017   !HALT:    stop uMachine, goto to Halt:
!
!
!
! effective address calculation
! use ALU.mb, and Last.PC, return ALU.ma
!         # # ## ####
s uMP[020]=#0302314543542410   !subMA:   MAR+ma+#0177 & mb, IF pb=0 goto MAa:
s uMP[021]=#1600000540202500   !         Q+LastPC & #7600 ! get current page #
s uMP[022]=#1600000033440010   !         MAR+ma+Q or ma ! form 12bits addr
s uMP[023]=#1200015540402600   !MAa:     crtn, Q+ma & #7770, IF Ib=0 RETURN
s uMP[024]=#1600000660002300   !         Q ← Q xor #0010 ! check auto index
s uMP[025]=#0302704703041000   !         ma+MP[MAR], IF no-Auto-Index goto MAb:
s uMP[026]=#1600000503442111   !         MP[MAR]+ma+ma+1 ! incr. Auto-index Reg
!
s uMP[027]=#1600000401400000   !MAb:     MAR+ma ! latch new addr
s uMP[030]=#1200041403000000   !         crtn, RETURN ! extra cycle for Mp access
!
!
! do MB=MP[ma()], fetch data in Mp pointed by ALU.ma
!         # # ## ####
s uMP[032]=#0102041431000000   !MpMa:    cjs, call SUBMa:
s uMP[033]=#1200041703051000   !         crtn, ALU.mb+MP[MAR], RETURN
!
! do MP[ma]=MB, depposit ALU.mb in PDP8 Mp
s uMP[034]=#1600000401400010   !MpMaMb:  MAR+ALU.ma
s uMP[035]=#0300441401500011   !         MP[ma]+mb, goto ENDex:
!
!
! instruction execution
!         # # ## ####
s uMP[040]=#0306653431000000   !Exec:    IF IR<0>=1 goto IR4567:
s uMP[041]=#0305052431000000   !         IF IR<1>=1 goto IR23:
s uMP[042]=#0103241431000000   !         cjs, call MpMa:
s uMP[043]=#0304551431000000   !         IF IR<2>=1 goto TAD:
s uMP[044]=#0300441143500000   !AND:     AC+AC & ALU.mb, goto ENDex:
s uMP[045]=#0300441103500001   !TAD:     LAC+LAC+ALU.mb, goto ENDex:


! ISZ and DCA
!         # # ## ####
s uMP[050]=#0305551431000000   !IR23:    IF IR<2>=1 goto DCA:
s uMP[051]=#0103241431000000   !ISZ:     cjs, call MpMa:
s uMP[052]=#1600000503552100   !         ALU.mb ← ALU.mb+1
s uMP[053]=#0303404431000000   !         IF ALU.Z=0 goto MpMaMb:
s uMP[054]=#0303441503112100   !         PC+PC+1, goto MpMaMb:
!
s uMP[055]=#0102041431000000   !DCA:     cjs, call subMa:
s uMP[056]=#1600000403050000   !         ALU.mb ← AC
s uMP[057]=#0303441443000000   !         AC+0, goto MpMaMb:
!
! the other 4 instructions
!         # # ## ####
s uMP[066]=#0307752431000000   !IR4567:  IF IR<1>=1 goto IR67:
s uMP[067]=#0102041431000000   !         cjs, call subMa:
s uMP[070]=#0307351431000000   !         IF IR<2>=1 goto JMP:
s uMP[071]=#1600000403150000   !JMS:     ALU.mb+PC
s uMP[072]=#0303441502412100   !         PC+ALU.ma+1, goto MpMaMb:
s uMP[073]=#0300441403410000   !JMP:     PC ← ALU.ma, goto ENDex:
!
! group 6 instruction, IOTs
! turn on and turn off interrupt enable
!         # # ## ####
s uMP[077]=#0312051431000000   !IR67:    IF IR<2>=1 goto OPR:
s uMP[100]=#1600000540502700   !IOT:     Q+ALU.mb & #0777
s uMP[101]=#1600000661002100   !         ALU.out+Q xor #0001
s uMP[102]=#0310404431000000   !         skip IF ALU.z=0
s uMP[103]=#0300041431000013   !!        enable interrupt, goto RUN:
s uMP[104]=#1600000661002200   !         ALU.out+Q xor #0002
s uMP[105]=#0300404431000000   !         IF ALU.z=0 goto ENDex:
s uMP[106]=#0300441431000012   !         disable interr, goto ENDex:
!
! Group 7 operating instructions
!         # # ## ####
s uMP[120]=#0314070431000000   !OPR:     IF GRP=1 goto mGRP2:
s uMP[121]=#0312327231000005   !mGRP1:   skip IF CLA=0, cond clear Link
s uMP[122]=#1600000443000000   !         AC+0
s uMP[123]=#0312525770002007   !         skip IF CMA=0, Q+#7777,cond comp Link
s uMP[124]=#1600000053000000   !         AC+ not AC
s uMP[125]=#0312720431000000   !         skip IF IAC=0
s uMP[126]=#1600000503002101   !         LAC+LAC+1, carry-out cond comp Link
!
! do rotates
!         # # ## ####
s uMP[127]=#0313363431000000   !         IF RAR=1 goto Right:
s uMP[130]=#0300422431000000   !         IF RAL=0 goto ENDex:
s uMP[131]=#0300421407000003   !Left:    LAC+LAC*2, IF rt=0 goto ENDex:
s uMP[132]=#0300441407000003   !         LAC+LAC*2, goto ENDex:
s uMP[133]=#0300421405000002   !Right:   LAC+LAC/2, IF rt=0 goto ENDex:
s uMP[134]=#0300441405000002   !         LAC+LAC/2, goto ENDex:
!
! group 2 micro instructions
!         # # ## ####
s uMP[140]=#0300460431000000   !mGRP2:   IF Mb<11>=1 goto ENDex:
s uMP[141]=#0314321401000000   !         skip IF halt=0
s uMP[142]=#1600000401000016   !         PDP8.go=0, Y+AC
s uMP[143]=#0314502431000000   !         skip IF Skip.cond=0
s uMP[144]=#1600000503112100   !         PC+PC+1
s uMP[145]=#0314727431000000   !         skip IF cla=0
s uMP[146]=#1600000443000000   !         ac+0
s uMP[147]=#0300422431000000   !         IF osr=0 goto ENDex:
s uMP[150]=#0300441533003000   !         AC+AC or SWR, goto ENDex:
!
! end of microcode
!
```

Section 2

Memory Hierarchies and Multiple Processes

During the 1950s, computers were used primarily in a single-user, stand-alone environment. Starting in the late 1950s, a number of parallel developments in computer architecture and software evolved, all seeking to make more efficient use of expensive hardware installations. These developments sought not only to increase the number of tasks completed per unit of time but also to increase the efficiency of hardware usage on single tasks. An equally significant motivation for these developments was to make computers easier to use.

At least four major system-level concepts served as a focal point for these developments: multiprogramming, timesharing, virtual memory, and virtual machines.

Multiprogramming

In multiprogramming, portions of different programs concurrently reside in memory. A program is run either to completion or to a natural breakpoint, such as a request for I/O. A software monitor then switches control to another program. Switching to another program instead of idling the Pc while waiting for an I/O request allows for concurrent operation of Pc and I/O hardware, thus increasing the efficiency of the Pc. The software monitor, however, represents a source of overhead, since it requires Pc and Mp resources to execute.

Timesharing

Timesharing systems allow multiple users to simultaneously interact with the hardware. In addition to the capabilities of a multiprogramming system, other functionalities must be added to the software for sharing programs, sharing facilities, and protecting users from each other, including command language interpreters for terminal inputs, editors for program preparation, and a scheduler that assures each user of periodically receiving the attention of the Pc.

Virtual Memory

Early computer users had to explicitly handle storage allocation if their program was larger than Mp. The user had to divide the program into modules, specify what modules were to be initially loaded, and dynamically specify what module was to replace (or overlay) which Mp resident module. Virtual memory provides the user with a memory that can be larger than physical Mp. The virtual memory system handles overlays in a user-transparent manner by deferring the binding between user and physical addresses until instruction execution time.

Virtual Machines

Multiprogramming and timesharing systems provide an "abstract" machine to the user. This "machine" has to be different from the actual hardware, since certain shared activities, such as I/O, and certain functions, such as execution of a Halt instruction, can affect other users. Thus the concept of a virtual machine was evolved (see Buzen and Gagliardi [1973] for a historical treatment of virtual machines). A virtual machine is an abstract machine that responds exactly as does the physical machine (see Fig. 1). Hence each user has what appears to be a separate "copy" of the physical machine. Protection is provided by a virtual machine monitor. With a virtual machine, users can coexist running under different operating systems. Programs executing under different run-time systems interfaced to different operating systems can co-operate. Functions that previously required a *dedicated* machine (e.g., operating system modification, I/O, and diagnostics) can execute on their own virtual machine.

Rather than attempt to trace the intertwined development of each of these four concepts, we will discuss the regions of memory

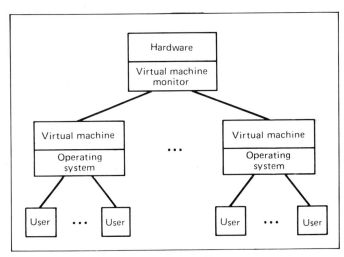

Fig. 1. Implementation of a virtual machine.

hierarchy management and multiprocessing in separate subsections and then illustrate their combination and interaction via examples from existing computers.

Memory Hierarchy Management

Because of the variations in cost and performance of various memory technologies, contemporary memory systems are composed of a number of memory technologies. Figure 2 depicts the physical structure of contemporary memory systems. Usually the fastest, and most expensive, technology is used in the registers in the Pc. Ideally one would like to execute programs as if all data existed in Pc registers. When more data are required, slower, larger, and lower-cost storage, such as Mp, is added. Larger program and data storage and medium-term storage can be provided by Ms. Finally, Mt provides archival or long-term storage. Other forms of memory, such as caches and extended bulk storage, have been added between the previously discussed levels in the storage hierarchy in an attempt to bridge the gap between larger, slower storage at higher levels and smaller, faster storage at the next lower level. Typical access time, transfer time, size, and technology for each level in the hierarchy are also shown in Fig. 2. It should be noted that random-access memories are usually employed through the M.extended level, thus making access and transfer time identical. At the Ms and Mt levels there is an access delay, usually due to physical motion that is several orders of magnitude larger than the information transfer time. Hence these devices tend to be block-oriented so that multiple data are transferred for each access.

An important breakpoint in the memory hierarchy occurs when the number of available addressable units exceeds the number of unique addresses producible by the processor. Prior to that

point there are automatic techniques that can be used to make the multiple levels in the hierarchy appear as one, the so-called one-level store. Beyond that point the meaning of an address has to be changed and the programmer has to modify the address space in an overt action such as a call to an operating system.

Table 1 lists the dimensions of the memory hierarchy region of computer space. The first dimension is that of mapping functions. Figure 3 graphically depicts the translation from processor-generated addresses (usually called the *address space* or *name space*) to physical memory (usually called the *memory space* or *physical space*). Consider a particular program, PROGRAM-1, one of many that might wish to reside in the Mp. PROGRAM-1 assumes a set of addresses, some explicitly and some implicitly, in the addressing algorithm it uses. PROGRAM-1 requires a memory space that has addresses that satisfy all these requirements, the implicit and explicit ones (explicit addresses present in the program and data and implicit relations between addresses due to addressing algorithms—e.g., that programs are laid sequentially in Mp, or that the elements of an array are to be accessed by indexing and hence must occupy consecutive addresses). Once the address requirements are met, the program does not "care" how these addresses are realized. Let us call this address space required by PROGRAM-1 its *virtual memory*, Mv. Thus, each program has its own virtual memory. (You might say each program has its own Mp, except, as we shall see, this Mp may be many times bigger than any actual Mp and still be entirely feasible.)

Actually, to run PROGRAM-1 requires that it be placed in the real Mp in such a way that the real addresses of Mp containing it satisfy all the requirements, that is, that it be a faithful image of the virtual memory. Thus there must be some *memory mapping* that maps the actual addresses into the actual memory. Once PROGRAM-1 is placed in Mp there must be some process that takes each virtual address (as it occurs to be processed in an instruction) and finds the actual address in Mp, so that the correct contents can be obtained.

This might seem simply a complicated and abstract way to view matters, but it becomes essential as soon as we realize that the computer can have hardware memory mappings other than the familiar direct-addressing structure of Mp. What we have really done is to divorce the addressing required by the programs from that provided by the physical computer, so that we can redesign the addressing (via the memory mapping) to meet new design requirements that were not apparent when the original random-addressing schemes were created.

Let us make the notion of memory mapping more precise. The program contains virtual addresses, z (that is, symbols in the program that denote addresses are taken to denote addresses in Mv). During the execution of the program, whenever there is a reference to an address z (either explicitly via an address calculation or implicitly via, say, getting the next instruction), a

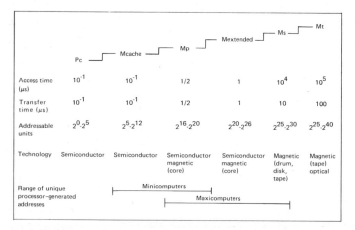

	Pc	Mcache	Mp	Mextended	Ms	Mt
Access time (μs)	10^{-1}	10^{-1}	$1/2$	1	10^4	10^5
Transfer time (μs)	10^{-1}	10^{-1}	$1/2$	1	10	100
Addressable units	2^0-2^5	2^5-2^{12}	2^{16}-2^{20}	2^{20}-2^{26}	2^{25}-2^{30}	2^{25}-2^{40}
Technology	Semiconductor	Semiconductor	Semiconductor magnetic (core)	Semiconductor magnetic (core)	Magnetic (drum, disk, tape)	Magnetic (tape) optical
Range of unique processor-generated addresses			Minicomputers	Maxicomputers		

Fig. 2. Characteristics of levels in the memory hierarchy.

Table 1   Storage Hierarchy Dimensions

Mapping function
  Identity
  Linear
    Concatenation
    Addition
  Segmented
    Linear
    Symbolic
Number of maps
  1
  2
  n
Mapping function implementation
  Table lookup
  Associative lookup
  Set-associative
Size of allocated unit
  Uniform
  Set of uniform
  Variable
    Static
    Dynamic
Allocation strategies
  Fetch
    Demand
    Prefetch
  Placement (variable-size allocation unit only)
    First fit
    Best fit
  Replacement
    Optimal
    FIFO
    Least recently used
    Random
    Periodic
Usage data
  Modified
  Used
  Reference count
Protection
  Basis
    Word
    Page/segment
    Page lock
    Capability
  Number of objects
    1
    2
    n
  Access control (mapping only)
    No restrictions
    Read only as data
    Read only as program
    Nonexisting memory
    Nonresident

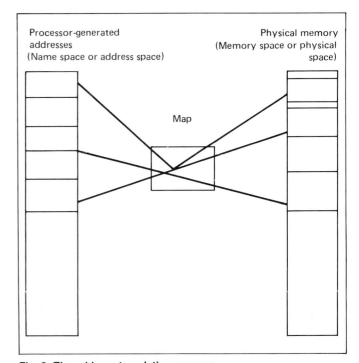

Fig. 3. The address translation process.

computation occurs on z to obtain the actual address in Mp. This computation is part of the Pc, just as is an automatic indexing or indirect-addressing calculation. It takes as input not just the virtual address z but information on where the program is located in Mp. The latter information is called the *map*, and a program's map information is determined when it is placed into Mp on a given run. Thus, using ISP notation, and calling the address calculation f, we get

$$Mv[z] := Mp[f(z, map)]$$

That is, the information in virtual memory at virtual address z is the same as the information in actual memory at address f(z, map).

This whole scheme is built to permit programs to be placed in Mp's in various ways, e.g., relocated or scattered around, and still make it possible to run the program. Any such scheme brings a solution to the protection problem, namely, that for some values of z the above calculation cannot take place or is invalid (i.e., there is no mapping for z). This can correspond to a violation of protection, which can then be prevented. All calculations may even be permissible, but f is usually arranged so that it never produces an address in anyone else's part of Mp.

The memory map is part of each user's program. With many

users, it must reside in Mp, since there will not be enough space in Mps (processor state) to hold a large amount of mapping information. However, when a program is being executed, some part of the mapping information becomes part of the Mps (i.e., at least the Mp address of the rest of the map).

Random-access memories for Mp constrain the mapping by requiring linear addresses of the form Mp[0:p], since the mapping calculation must be economical (as it is performed with very high frequency). We would not consider a map structure which provides every word in Mv to be mapped into an arbitrary word in Mp, for this would require a map exactly the same size as Mv. With many programs in Mp, there would be little room for anything but maps. Similarly, the amount of processing in the calculation must be minimal. These two aspects highly constrain the mapping scheme.

Three major types of mapping functions have been used. In the first, the identity function, there is no map. The processor virtual address space is identical to the physical memory space. This mapping function is used primarily on stand-alone, dedicated computers.

The second type is frequently referred to as *paging* and is depicted in Fig. 4. In paging, the processor-generated address is divided into two fields, a page number and a displacement within page. The page number is used to index into a *page table*, from which the physical page number is retrieved. The physical page number can be either concatenated or added to the displacement to create the final physical address. This form of address map is called a *linear map*, since manipulation of the virtual address, such as adding an index, can cause the page number in the virtual address to increase, thus accessing a different physical page potentially without warning to the user. Note that p′ may contain more than, fewer than, or exactly as many bits as p.

The third type of mapping function is two-dimensional and is termed *segmentation*. Two major forms of segmentation have been used: linear and symbolic. Figure 5 illustrates the linear mapping. The processor-generated virtual address is composed of three fields: the segment number, the page number, and the

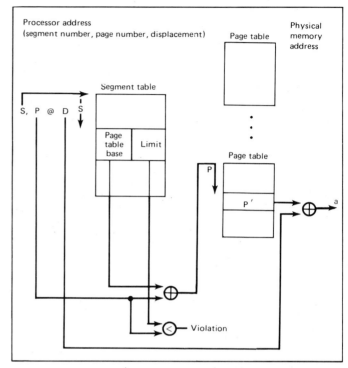

Fig. 5. The address translation process for linear segmentation.

displacement. The segment number is used to index into a segment table. The starting address (base) of the page table is coupled with the virtual page number as an index to retrieve the physical page number. The physical page number is then concatenated or added to the displacement to generate the final physical address. The virtual page number is compared to a limit field in the selected segment table entry as a check on whether the page number is within bounds for this segment. This provides some measure of protection so that virtual address manipulations do not cross segment boundaries without warning the user. (Note that a similar bounds check could have been made on the displacement field in the paging function outlined in Fig. 4.)

However, it is still possible in linear segmentation to inadvertently cross a segment boundary if the proper value is added to the virtual address. Symbolic segmentation prevents segmentation boundary crossing by computations on the virtual address. Figure 6 depicts symbolic segmentation. The virtual address is a duple: a segment number and a displacement. The main difference between symbolic segmentation and the prior schemes is that the hardware enforces a boundary between the segment and displacement virtual address fields. Adding a number to the displacement in a virtual address calculation cannot modify the segment field.

Figure 7 illustrates one implementation of symbolic segmentation used on the Burroughs B5000. The instruction pointer

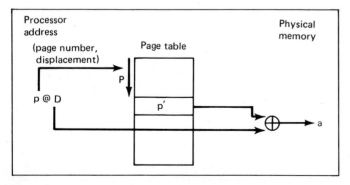

Fig. 4. The address translation process for paging.

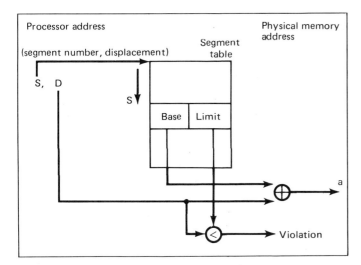

Fig. 6. The address translation process for symbolic segmentation.

consists of a duple: instruction word pointer and syllable within word. The instruction consists of operations or data fetches to the stack. All data fetches are indirect through a user-unique Program Reference Table (PRT). The PRT can contain the operand, the address of an operand, or a descriptor. The descriptor is used to address arrays of data. The array base is contained in the descriptor and the index is contained in the machine stack. Thus there is no way a user, by modifying the operand index on the stack, can access a different array (e.g., a different segment). The segment base and displacement are physically disjoint.

It is interesting to observe that the symbolic segmentation is carried even further in more recent Burroughs machines. Figure 8 illustrates the segmentation used in the B 6700. The instruction pointer now consists of a triple: stack number, displacement, and instruction in segment. Each user has a different stack number. The displacement in stack specifies which code segment is currently executing, while the instruction within segment specifies the actual instruction. The PRT is replaced by a set of program stacks. The currently active program stack is pointed to by the Environment Pointer.

The second major dimension in Table 1 is the number of maps. If there is only one map, then the map's contents have to be changed when program execution is switched. Since operating-system calls occur frequently, there usually are two maps, one for the supervisor and one for users. A generalization would be to have *n* maps split among programs with different privileges. These maps can provide for sharing a block of Mp among several users. This block of Mp would not have to be duplicated, so that operating-system software, including compilers, assemblers, loaders, and editors, could be usefully shared.

The third dimension deals with the implementation of the

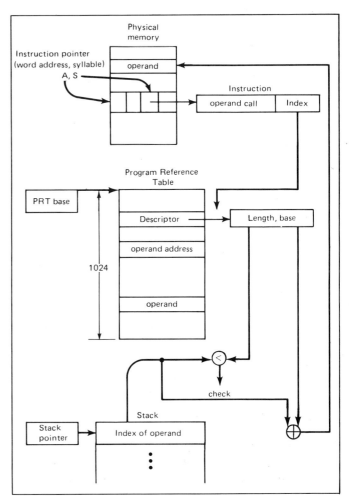

Fig. 7. Symbolic segmentation on the B5000.

mapping function. The simplest form is table lookup, using a portion of the address to index into a table. The table can reside in fast registers or in memory. If the sum of map entries is larger than the set of available fast registers, an associative lookup scheme can be used. In an associative memory, each entry is stored along with an identifying key. The key, in this case, is the page or segment number. Thus, when presented with the address, the associative memory simultaneously searches all locations for a match on the key. If a match is found, the address-mapping data are made available from the high-speed associative memory. If the key is not found, the required mapping information must be retrieved from memory. Associative memories are costly to implement and hence small.

A scheme which combines the ease of table lookup with the power of associativity is depicted in Fig. 9. Set-associative

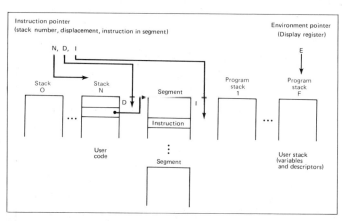

Fig. 8. Symbolic segmentation in the B6700.

addressing divides an address into three fields: tag, index, and displacement. The index field is used to simultaneously access n sets of tables. Each of the n tables simultaneously compares its tag field contents with the tag field specified by the address. If there is

a match, a hit occurs and the displacement is used to index into the data block to select the address-mapping information. If there is no match, the address-mapping information must be retrieved from memory. Note that both the associative Lookup and the set-associative implementations for mapping functions larger than fast storage can also be used for buffering instructions and data from a larger memory. In the latter case the memory is referred to as a *cache* (because frequently used data are cached away) or a look-aside memory (because there is an auxiliary memory that can be "looked" into) [Liptay, 1968; Katzan, 1971]. More will be said about data caches later.

The fourth major dimension is the size of the allocated unit. We have observed that the mapping function has to refer to blocks of virtual addresses rather than individual addresses to keep the map size manageable. The units most frequently are of one size. This not only makes for simpler address-mapping hardware, but it also makes it easier to overlay one unit with another when information has to be brought in from higher up in the hierarchy. A potential problem with uniform size is that large, logically connected information (e.g., a large array or matrix) will require many units if

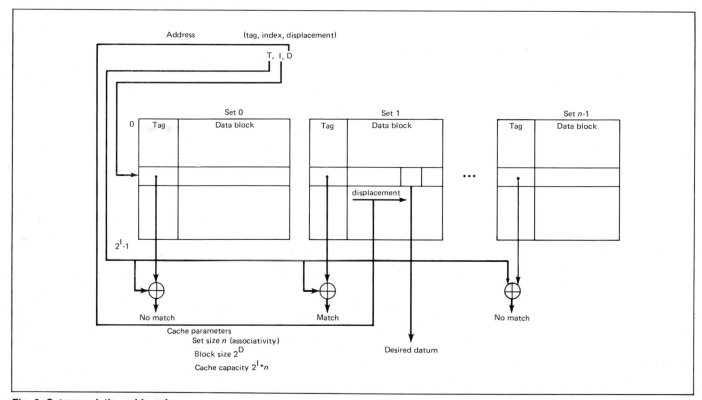

Fig. 9. Set associative addressing.

the units are too small. On the other hand, if the units are too large, a significant amount of memory may be wasted, since not all the locations in a unit are being utilized (i.e., there is *internal fragmentation*). One way to relieve the multiple-unit or fragmentation problem is to have a small number of uniform sizes. The MULTICS system has two different page sizes (64 and 1,024 words). The actual size of pages is a strong function of the ratio of access time to transfer time of block-oriented storage. See Denning [1970] for a detailed discussion.

The approaches of one or a small set of uniform allocation sizes apply to linear (e.g., paged) mapping functions. Segmented mapping functions can have variable-sized units selected at program load (e.g., static) or program run (e.g., dynamic) time. Variable-size allocation units face the problem of *external fragmentation*, wherein the total amount of unused memory, called *holes*, is substantially larger than the size requested for a new segment yet no hole is large enough to wholly contain the segment. At this point the allocated segments in memory have to be consolidated and the holes compacted. See Denning [1970] for an extensive comparison of paging and segmentation schemes.

When the virtual address space is larger than physical memory at any stage in the memory hierarchy, allocation strategies have to be used in order to manage the current content of physical memory. Typically storage devices are organized into blocks. The first reference to a particular block requires that the entire block be fetched from the next higher level in the memory hierarchy. Subsequent accesses to the block require only that fast storage be accessed. The faster storage is capable of storing several blocks, which are replaced on a dynamic basis. This allocation strategy includes fetch, placement, and replacement. These strategies have been extensively surveyed in the literature [Belady, 1966; Randell and Kuehner, 1968; Denning, 1970; Katzan, 1971; Kuck, 1978] and will be only briefly discussed here.

The first strategy is deciding when to fetch a new unit. Demand fetching (e.g., demand paging) fetches a new unit only when it is referenced. Prefetch is an anticipatory scheme whereby units are fetched prior to their actual reference. Prefetching is used primarily in association with instructions, since there is a high probability that the next instruction to be executed is the next one in sequence. See Part 2, Sec. 3, for a more complete discussion of instruction prefetching.

The second strategy applies only to variable-sized allocation units. In what hole should the new segment be placed—the first one found, or the one nearest in size?

Finally, when storage on the existing memory level is exhausted and new information is referenced, some old information must be replaced. If the total reference pattern is known beforehand, it will be possible to find an optimal sequence which replaces the smallest number of units [Belady, 1966]. In a multiprogramming environment it is not possible to predetermine usage patterns.

Hence replacement algorithms are sought that attempt to approximate usage patterns. FIFO (first in, first out), LRU (least recently used), random, and periodic (see Chap. 10) have all been used.

Given that there is a mapping function, other functions can be performed during the address translation. One function is unit usage data concerned with such questions as: Has the unit been modified or written into? (if not, the unit can be replaced without copying to a higher level in the memory hierarchy); Has the unit been used? (if not, it should not be replaced, since some program segment is waiting for it); and, How many times has the unit been referenced since the last unit was replaced? (Less frequently referenced or nonreferenced units may not be referenced for a long time in the future). These usage data are often used in deciding which unit should be replaced.

Another important function that goes along with address mapping is protection. The requirement for protection in a multiprogramming environment is obvious. If two independent programs are to be resident in Mp at the same time, they must not have access to each other's physical memory space. Not only would such access (especially for writing) have disastrous consequences when the programs were running, but they would also be entirely unpredictable and undebuggable from the viewpoint of the individual programmers. Protection can be on the basis of individual words (i.e., tags), or it can be on the basis of a whole page or segment. Protection can also be provided if each page has a lock which the user program must match. These three protection bases are "object-oriented" in that they deal with physical portions of memory. *Capability addressing*, an alternative mechanism based on the access path to an object, has been used. It offers more flexibility than object-based protection, since different users can be given different privileges instead of being given the same identical privilege as in object-based protection.

Another important aspect of protection is the number of objects that the hardware can concurrently provide protection checks on at run time. If only one or two objects are supported by hardware, substantial software overhead must be expended for dynamically managing the hardware.

Finally, the type of access to objects can be limited to (1) no restrictions, (2) read-only as data, (3) read-only as program, and (4) no access. One final bit of information is that the object is addressable but not currently resident in this level of the memory hierarchy.

Let us return to Fig. 2 and consider each level in the memory hierarchy. The Pc generates virtual addresses that are mapped. Mcache is a high-speed register file that automatically attempts to capture the locality of the program. It is well known that executing programs exhibit locality, i.e., the next address generated is, with a high probability, the next sequential address, an address recently referenced, or an address very near a recently referenced address. If the cache fetch and replacement algorithm is efficient, then there is a high probability that the next referenced address will be in the cache (ie., there is a high *hit ratio*), and the performance of the memory system will asymptotically approach the performance of the cache. Note that caches can also be used to store address-mapping information for complex mapping functions (see Chap. 42).

The next level in the hierarchy is Mp, which is followed by Mextended. In cases where the virtual address space is larger than Mp, Mextended is lower-performance memory that can be used for less frequently accessed units. In STARAN (Chap. 21) the user explicitly manages the placement of pages into Mp and Mextended to maximize performance. In the case where the virtual address space is smaller than Mp or Mp plus Mextended (e.g., minicomputers), the extra memory is used either for anticipatory prefetching or as a fast paging device (new pages are made resident by a change of the memory-mapping tables rather than after the lengthy wait for Ms to access a block).

Finally, both Ms and Mt are characterized by a high t.access/ t.transfer ratio and hence are block-oriented; i.e., a block of information is transferred for each access in order to cut down the accessing overhead per unit.

At each level in the memory hierarchy we could have a mapping function with associated values for all of the parameters in Table 1. Generally there is only one map, associated with Mp. However, the cheap yet effective cache has become more and more common. It usually appears between the Pc and Mp, but it can appear between any two levels in the memory hierarchy. Caches, and their cousins, instruction prefetch buffers, usually employ an identity mapping function. Caches have nontrivial values for the other dimensions in Table 1 that usually are not as well known as those for the Mp map, since the cache algorithms are locked in hardware and are invisible even to systems programs.

Multiprocess Environment

Table 2 lists the range of software structures built upon the dimensions in Table 1 and the range of interprocess communications. At the simplest level there is only a single program and there is no need for interprocess communication. Variables of the program are completely accessible to the whole program, and the address space is essentially uniform. The single program can be extended with subroutine calling, which produces a hierarchy of communication contexts. There is not a fixed number of levels to the hierarchy, since each subroutine may call others ad nauseum. When subroutines are present, address names and values within the subroutine become addresses which are local to that part of the subprogram. Such a structuring is apparent when we look at the higher-level languages, such as FORTRAN, ALGOL, PASCAL, and PL/I, where there are explicit statements for controlling the names (addresses) that are available to each of the parts of the

Table 2 Mp Concurrency

Multiprocess environment	Interprocess communication
1 process	Subroutines and traps
1 process with interrupt-evoked processes	Interrupts from I/O
1 process with multiple concurrent subprocesses (for example, 1Pc.nPio)	Interprocessor interrupts
Monitor or fixed process (M) + one-at-a-time (variable) process	Extracodes (programmed operators for monitor calls)
M + n swapped foreground/ background process	
M + n processes (multiprogramming) with swapping	
No relocation	Synchronization
1 segment	Producer/consumer
2 segments (pure, impure)	P and V
>2 segments	mailboxes
Pages	
M + n segments with shared processes	Interprocess communication
Fixed-length paged segments	
Multiple-length paged segments	
Variable-length segments	

program. The concept of subroutine structure has been with us almost from the first programs.

The trap is a hardware subroutine call when conditions occurring within a single process cause another part of the program to be called. Typical conditions which cause traps are arithmetic results outside expected range and erroneous program conditions (e.g., trying to call someone else's program). The trap causes a change in context that is synchronized with the process causing it. Trapping is a form of program interruption; a trap is an intraprocess interrupt, as distinct from interprocess interrupts.

The next level of multiprocess environment is one program with interrupts. Intercommunication between two independent processes (processes carried out by two independent components) is usually accomplished by using the program interrupt. The interrupting process requests that a program interrupt occur in a component (the interruptee). The interrupter's request is acknowledged by the interruptee, and a change of process state occurs in the interruptee; a new process is then run in the interruptee on behalf of the interrupter. A Kio uses the program-interrupt request to communicate with its superior Pio or Pc. The program interrupt can also be used among processors in a multiprocessor system and between one Pc and *n* Pio's.

Usually the interruptee is equipped with certain logic which is capable of arranging the priorities of requesting interrupters. The typical kinds of interrupt requests are component faults (e.g., parity error), the running out of a timer, and various task completions (e.g., when a program has been completed, a tape unit has rewound, a disk arm has stopped moving, a certain record has been found on tape, a buffer is full).

State diagrams would show how all of the communication methods above are similar to one another. A typical interrupt state diagram is shown in Fig. 10. There are four states: normal process interpretation, process state saving, interrupt process interpretation, and process state restoration. The sequence is as follows:

1 Normal instruction interpretation is occurring in the interruptee.

2 The interrupter requests an interrupt.

3 After some delay, t.acknowledgment, a state is reached in which part of the interruptee's process state is saved.

4 After t.acknowledgment + t.save, a program is running in the interruptee in response to the interrupter.

5 The interrupt program is run for t.interrupt.

6 At the completion of the interrupt program, the original process state is restored in the interrupter.

7 After t.restore, normal processing resumes in the interrupter.

The significant attributes of the system are the various times required to move from state to state. These times are directly related to the amount of process state which must be saved (and restored) when context is switched. Most interrupt systems allow several independent classes and/or sources of interrupters. The classes are arranged in priority so that lower-level interrupters are ignored until higher-level interrupt programs are run to completion. The design problems associated with intercommunication are not those of implementation but of knowing what should be implemented. The PMS structure part and the corresponding register-transfer implementations for intercommunication are, by comparison, straightforward.

The next level of multiprocess environment is the monitor process plus user processes. The monitor program provides the user with a set of utilities that greatly simplifies the user's programming effort. These utilities usually include I/O, memory hierarchy management, and program loading, among others. A mechanism is required for evoking the monitor process from the user process. The usual mechanism is to provide special instructions which are akin to subroutine calls. These are called *extracodes* and were perhaps first suggested for the Atlas (Chap. 10). Each extracode can be looked at as just a call to a specific subroutine. The variables of the user's (caller's) process are made available to the called (extracode-defined) process. The calling usually is accompanied by a context shift, in which the monitor process takes command to interpret the instruction. When a function such as the input or output of a file is required, the main process issues a call to the monitor to make the transfer. (In theory, the monitor knows about conditions in the system and has the capability to perform the complex function.) A central monitor control can then begin to run another process if the request is one which would normally halt the computer. This form of communication is useful in supplying extra facilities to users and in providing a method of knowing what the users are doing (e.g., so that equipment will be better utilized).

The final levels in multiprocess environment are monitor plus multiple processes where the multiple processes are swapped (e.g., run to completion), multiprogrammed (e.g., run to a natural breakpoint), and shared programs (e.g., with interactive time-sharing users). In these latter levels, intercommunication complexity increases.

In a multiple-process system there are shared resources to which access can be granted only on a one-at-a-time basis until access is completed. Various methods of process synchronization are listed in Table 2 and described briefly below. (See Presser [1975] for a more extensive discussion of process synchronization.) In the case of dedicated applications the form of interprocess communication is completely known and some simple synchronizing schemes may be adequate. For example, two processes might be in a producer-consumer relationship communicating via a flag. The producer checks the flag to see if it is 0 before placing data in a buffer and setting the flag to 1. If the flag is nonzero, the producer must wait. The consumer checks the flag for opposite conditions. If the flag is 1, the consumer picks up the data and clears the flag to 0. If the flag is 0, the consumer is ahead of the producer and the consumer must wait. Synchronization in this producer-consumer situation requires only memory and/or flag sharing between processors. This form of synchronization has been used in the Datasaab FCPU [Lawson and Magenhagen, 1975].

For more complex synchronization the binary semaphore

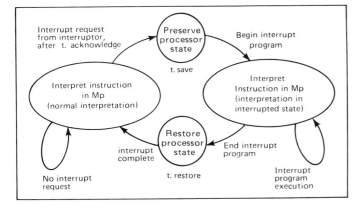

Fig. 10. State diagram for the interrupt process.

primitives P and V can be used [Dijkstra, 1968a]. Processes coordinate by a special flag called a *mutex semaphore*. Consider Fig. 11, where processes P1 and P2 share a table. In order to ensure that one process is not operating on table data that the other process is changing (a critical section of the program, according to Dijsktra), the two processes must synchronize their use of the table. A semaphore S is provided for this coordination.

The value of S (initially 0) indicates whether the table is being used by a process (S = 1) or not (S = 0). P(S) samples the value of S. When P(S) finds S = 0 it sets S = 1 and allows the process to continue. V(S) relinquishes control of the table by setting S to 0. Semaphores are easily generalized to the case of n processes rather than just two. Unlike the producer-consumer synchronization, the testing and setting of S by P must be an indivisible action; otherwise the following sequence could occur, in which both process P1 and process P2 gain access to the table:

P in P1 tests S and finds it 0.

P in P2 tests S and finds it 0.

P in P1 sets S to 1.

P in P2 sets S to 1.

P1 uses the table.

P2 uses the table.

Most contemporary computers provide mechanisms for implementing P's using read-modify-write memory cycles (Chap. 38). Read-modify-write instructions maintain control of the memory between the read and write phases to allow a modification of the memory cell by that process. No other process can use the memory until that instruction is completed. Figure 12 depicts an implementation of the P,V synchronization primitives using the IBM System/360-System/370 "test and set" (code TS) instruction. TS reads a value from memory, sets condition codes, modifies the value to all 1s, and writes the value into memory.

The implementation in Fig. 12 is a form of "busy waiting." It is desirable to put processes to sleep if they are not successful in their first attempt to gain a resource, so that the hardware can execute other processes. Sleeping processes do not consume any

P:	TS	S	Test semaphore and set to all ones.
	BM	P	Branch if the old contents were not zero.
V:	SR	0,0	Form zero by subtract register R0 from itself.
	ST	0,S	Clear semaphore.

Fig. 12. An implementation of P,V in the IBM System/360.

system resources (other than the overhead involved in making the process dormant or active). Some form of queuing is also necessary to ensure that no process is permanently blocked.

Let us turn to the nPc (multiple-processor) case and consider two processes, executing on different Pc's and sharing the same resource. Assume that process synchronization occurs through shared memory. An Exchange Register with Memory instruction can be used for nonbusy semaphore communication. When P1 wants to use the shared resource it places its identity in a register and executes an Exchange instruction. If the new value in the register is 0, then the resource is available for use. If it is nonzero, then some other process is using the resource and the requesting process puts itself to sleep (turns off its run flip-flop or awaits an interrupt). When the process finishes with the resource it awakens the process identified by the semaphore variable (unless that process is itself). Figure 13 depicts an implementation of P,V using the Exchange instruction. A survey and comparison of other high-level synchronizing primitives can be found in Lipton [1973].

Some means of notifying other processes is required. One mechanism, used on the multiminiprocessor C.mmp (16 PDP-11's communicating with 16 memories through a cross-point switch; see Chap. 22), is to provide an interrupt register addressable by all processors. Writing a 1 into bit i causes an interrupt in processor i.

The Exchange instruction mechanism breaks down when more

P1:	P(S);	P2:	P(S);
	use table;		use table;
	V(S);		V(S);
	compute;		compute;
	go to P1;		go to P2;

Fig. 11. Process synchronization through semaphores.

P:	Move myidentity to R
	Exchange R,S
	If R ≠ 0 then wait
V:	Clear R
	Exchange R,S
	If R ≠ myidentity then awake process identified by R

Fig. 13. Implementation of P,V using the exchange instruction.

than two processes need to utilize a resource. An alternative scheme, employed on C.mmp, uses the Interrupt register and two semaphores. Processes test the primary semaphore in the normal manner. If it is nonzero, they OR a bit corresponding to their processor number into a word (called *processes pending*) in memory. When the process wants to give up the resource by doing a V, it places the processes pending word in the Interrupt register and clears the primary semaphore. Processes reawakened by the interrupt attempt to do a P on a secondary semaphore, recording their identity if they lose. The process that wins then performs a P on the primary semaphore. In this manner the semaphores are tested only when the resource is known to be free.

Processors can even be efficiently multiprogrammed with the assistance of some special hardware features. When a process is put to sleep its context (contents of registers, condition codes, program counter, etc.) can be saved and another process initiated. Saving and restoring registers can be extremely time-consuming. A single instruction which saves context in memory (Chap. 43) on several selectable sets of processor registers can substantially cut register-saving overhead. In the latter case a single instruction selects which complete set of processor registers to use as context for the currently running process and saves the many memory cycles that may be necessary in the former case. The identity of the next process to run can be selected from a priority queue. Rather than interrupt a processor when a process it owns can be awakened, the identity of the process is placed in the processor's hardware priority queue. This is similar in concept to the pseudointerrupt device (PID) used on the BBN multiprocessor (Chap. 23).

One drawback of the semaphores is that if a processor dies while its process is holding on to a semaphore, the entire system may block while waiting for the single semaphore. In order to keep the system operating and assist recovery from hardware failures, each semaphore, or block of semaphores, can have a time out associated with it. If the semaphore is not set to 0 within a specified time, it should clear itself (busy waiting) or awaken the next (sleeping) process waiting for the semaphore. In the double-lock case described above the primary semaphore time is turned on when the semaphore becomes nonzero, while on the secondary semaphore the timer is turned on immediately, since the process to be awakened may also have died.

Another form of interprocess communication, which can be used in both single- and multiple-processor systems, is the mailbox. A process can send information to another process by placing a message in a queue called a mailbox. Each process examines (either periodically or upon an interrupt generated by a deposit into the mailbox) its mailbox in order to respond to a request. The producer-consumer synchronization discussed earlier is a limited form of mailbox communication, since only 1 bit of information (buffer full/empty) is exchanged.

Examples

Now we will turn to examining some system examples that employ different solutions to the multiprocess environment and memory hierarchy problems. Other examples can be found throughout the book in conjunction with various computer descriptions. The reader is encouraged to note how the multiprocess environment and memory hierarchy parameter choices fit in with the system objectives and other design parameters.

Table 3 lists several existing systems and focuses on the attributes of one of the memory maps. The generic type of system represented by each example will now be discussed.

No Special Mapping Hardware (Intel 8080)

If no hardware exists in the Pc to accomplish a memory address mapping, then when the address z is encountered in the program, the information at Mp[z] will be obtained. There are still, however, two different ways to obtain the effect of a virtual memory.

First, one can operate interpretively, with a software system taking the place of hardware. That is, the programs of all the users are in a nonmachine language (e.g., a higher, procedure-oriented language), and each access in the language is processed by the software interpreter before an accesss is made to Mp. It is clear that all the logical power of a memory mapping is available with this scheme. The only drawback is the loss of efficiency from the interpretation, which may range over a factor from 5 to 100. Consequently this scheme is used only in special circumstances, such as multiuser timeshared conversational algebraic languages.

The second scheme is to modify the code at the time it is placed in Mp for a given run, so that all addresses in the code correspond to the actual Mp addresses used. That is, an assembly or translation operation is performed each time the program is placed in Mp. The advantage of this scheme is that no further address calculations are necessary. There are three disadvantages. Assembly operations are expensive, so that, although the scheme is tolerable if the program is brought in once and run to completion, it is not tolerable if programs are continually being swapped in and out of Mp. In addition, the program must be laid into continuous intervals of Mp corresponding to predetermined segments of the program, for assembly occurs on a static representation of the program and cannot unravel the potential effect of address algorithms. Finally, the size of Mv (i.e., the addresses used externally) must be no greater than Mp.

Relative to these software schemes—one interpretive and very expensive and one involving assembly (i.e., compilation) and loading—the hardware schemes to be described appear as address interpreters, where the cost of continuous interpretation has been made tolerable.

Table 3   Storage Hierarchy Examples

Machine	Type	Mapping function	Size of allocated unit	Allocation strategies	Protection	Comments on method of memory allocation among multiple users
Intel 8080	Mp	Identity	. . . .	. . . .	. . . .	No special hardware. Completely done by interpretive programming.
IBM 1800	Mp	Identity	Word	. . . .	Bit/word	A protection bit per memory cell. Bit specifies whether cell can be written or accessed. One special user plus one other user. The time to change bits if a user job is changed makes the method nearly useless. No memory allocation hardware.
SDS Sigma 2	Mp	Identity	Page	. . . .	Bit/page	Protection bit per page (see above). No memory allocation hardware.
IBM S/360	Mp	Identity	Page	. . . .	Storage key/page	Each block of memory has a user number which must coincide with the currently active user number. Memory relocation must be done by conventions or relocation software. A fixed, small number of users are permitted by the hardware (there are a limited number of keys). No memory allocation by hardware. A program cannot be moved until it is run to completion.
IBM 7040	Mp	Linear with concatenation	Variable	. . . .	Single segment	One protection count and one field register (addresses formed and checked by logic operations). All programs are written as though their origin were location 0. The count register determines the number of high-order bits to be examined. The field register is then compared for identity with the requested address. Memory allocation blocks must be in powers of 2. Unless blocks are the same size, the memory utilization can be poor. Although faster than the following scheme (which requires a hardware adder), the inflexibility of location and size makes it restrictive.
CDC 6600	Mp	Linear with concatenation	Variable	. . . .	Single segment	One set of protection and relocation registers (base address and limit registers). Also called boundary registers. All programs written as though their origin were location 0. The relocation register specifies the actual loca-

Table 3   (Continued)

Machine	Type	Mapping function	Size of allocated unit	Allocation strategies	Protection	Comments on method of memory allocation among multiple users
						tion of the user, and the protection register specifies the number of words allowed. As users enter and leave, primary-memory holes form, requiring the moving of users. Pure prodecures can be implemented only by moving the impure part adjacent to the pure part.
UNIVAC 1108	Mp	Linear with concatenation	Variable	. . . .	Two segments	Two sets of protection and relocation registers. Similar to above. Simple, pure procedures with one data array area can be implemented.
Intel 8086	Mp	Linear with addition	16 words	. . . .	Four segments	Segment used is a function of the instruction interpretation cycle (e.g., code, data, stack, extra). Protection provided by software allocation ensuring that 16-word segments do not overlap.
Atlas	Mp	Linear with concatenation implemented with 32-entry associative tables	512 words	Demand fetch Periodic replacement	. . . .	First virtual memory. For each page (2^6 to 2^{12} words) in a user's virtual memory, corresponding information is kept concerning the actual physical location in primary or secondary memory. A hardware map may be placed between the processor and memory to transform processor virtual addresses into physical addresses. If the map is in primary memory, it may be desirable to have "associative registers" at the processor-memory interface to remember previous reference to virtual pages, and their actual locations.
B 5500	Mp	Symbolic segmented	Variable <1024 words	Demand fetch Best fit Cyclic replacement	Base/limit in descriptors	All data are considered part of a descriptor array which is referred to by a number. A descriptor table indexed by a descriptor number is used to locate the array in Mp and give its size.
IBM S/360-91	Instruction prefetch	Identity	8 bytes	Prefetch FIFO replacement	. . . .	Instruction buffer has eight 8-byte locations for sequential addresses and two 8-byte locations for branch target instructions in anticipation of successful branches.
PDP-11/70	Cache	Identity	4 bytes	Demand fetch Random replacement	. . . .	Cache implemented as a set-associative lookup with two sets, 4 bytes per block, and 256 blocks per set.

Protection Hardware for Words or Pages
(IBM 1800, SDS Sigma 2, IBM System/360)

There are three schemes in Table 3 that provide means of protecting one part of Mp against references from other programs. The rationale for these designs is that there will be only two users (or user classes), one user being superior and assumed perfect (its program debugged). References to Mp via the imperfect program to a perfected and superior part of Mp are forbidden. These schemes provide no method of hardware mapping, and physical addresses are the same as virtual addresses. In the simplest scheme, as in the IBM 1800, a protect bit is added to every word in Mp. Any reference to a word with a protect bit causes an error. The other two schemes protect on the basis of blocks of words.

Protection and Relocation Register Hardware
(IBM 7040, CDC 6600, UNIVAC 1108)

A protection and relocation mechanism is used in three schemes in Table 3. These provide one or two linearly mapped segments via a relocation register and bounds register pair. Generally, these schemes restrict $Mv \leq Mp$.

An additive protection and relocation register pair is shown in Fig. 14, in which four users are occupying an Mp[0:7999]. Each user program is written to occupy a continuous address space in virtual Mv. Thus in ISP, when Pc is running a user, the Relocation and Protection Registers are loaded and initialized by the monitor to the values in the User Location Information Table. Then the hardware performs the following check:

$$Mv(z) <0:3> := \text{begin}$$
$$\quad \text{DECODE } (z \text{ gtr } R.\text{protection}) \Rightarrow$$
$$\quad 0\backslash\ Mv \leftarrow Mp[z + R.\text{relocation}],$$
$$\quad 1\backslash\ \text{Protection.violation} \leftarrow 1$$
$$\quad \text{end}$$

Protection and Relocation are the two registers that specify mapping. The implementation of this scheme generally takes the form of adding the contents of the relocation register after all address calculations have taken place. Thus, in PMS we might think of the structure

Page-Map Hardware (Intel 8086, Atlas)

This scheme is essentially a generalization of n protect/relocate registers but includes more control bits and restricts each block to

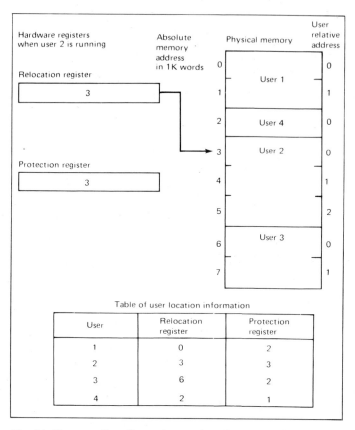

Fig. 14. Memory allocation using a relocation, protection register pair.

User	Relocation register	Protection register
1	0	2
2	3	3
3	6	2
4	2	1

be the same size. Note that Mv can be greater than Mp. In addition, parts of the virtual memory may remain unused.

As indicated in the discussion of map implementation, there are two general ways the map may be implemented:

1 A complete map is first considered as a conventional, explicitly addressed M whose addresses correspond to the virtual address pages. At a given page-memory address the contents of the map specify the address in Mp. The map is similar to an indirect reference. However, the map is usually about 10 times faster and about 1/1,000 the size, since it keeps track only of pages, not words. The PMS structure is

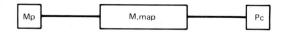

2 The map is retained in Mp and referenced by a protection and a relocation register set for the particular active user.

In order to avoid making references to Mp for each word reference to Mv by a Pc, a small, fast M(associative) or M(set.associative) is placed between Pc and Mp. The PMS structure is

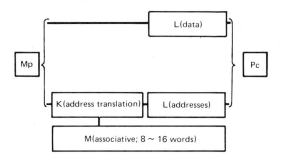

Segment Hardware (B5500)

The hardware required to support segmentation is illustrated in Figs. 6, 7, and 8. The discussion of this hardware can be found in the discussion of Table 1.

Instruction Prefetch (IBM System/360 Model 91)

Instruction prefetch buffers are used in high-performance Pc systems in an attempt to minimize the imbalance between Pc execution rate and Mp instruction supply rate. Instruction prefetch buffers attempt to take advantage of instruction locality by fetching blocks of instructions prior to their use. These buffers are invisible to the programmer but are nonetheless important in the implementation of an ISP. Even several microprocessors employ a one-instruction prefetch (in which the next instruction in sequence is fetched while the current instruction is being decoded and executed). See Part 2, Sec. 3, for a more detailed discussion of instruction prefetch buffers.

Cache (PDP-11/70)

Like instruction prefetch buffers, caches dynamically attempt to capture locality. Caches can be used for instruction and data buffering or mapped address buffering. They are transparent to the programmer and can appear between any two levels in the memory hierarchy. Most contemporary data/instruction caches are implemented as set-associative rather than pure associative because of the latter's cost.

Figure 9 illustrates the major parameters in cache design: cache capacity, block size, and set size. The cache capacity is the maximum number of memory words that can be resident in the cache. The block size is the number of words fetched from memory at the same time. The set size (associativity) is the number of blocks in the cache that can have the same index.

	Set Size (associativity)	Block Size (Bytes)	Cache Capacity (Bytes)
PDP-11/60	1	2	2048
PDP-11/70	2	4	2048
IBM S/370-165	4	32	8192

Fig. 15. Examples of parameters for set associative caches.

Figure 15 depicts the values of these parameters for some contemporary caches.

The selection of the appropriate cache parameters can have a dramatic impact on computer system performance. Consider the following simple model. Let h be the cache "hit ratio," that is, the probability that an addressed word is in the cache. If t.inst is the average instruction time, t.proc is the average time between processor requests for memory, t.cache is the cache access time, and t.mem is the memory access time, then:

$$t._{inst} = t._{proc} + ht._{cache} + (1 - h)t._{mem}$$

and

$$Performance = \frac{1}{t._{inst}}$$

If $h = 1$, then all memory requests are in cache and the memory system responds to all accesses at cache speed. At the other extreme, if $h = 0$, the cache has no impact on system performance. Figure 16 illustrates the impact of the cache hit ratio on performance for various ratios of t.proc to t.mem with t.proc= 1 μs and t.cache= 200 ns.

The cache hit ratio h is a complex function of the cache parameters and application program behavior. Economics dictates that the cache capacity be as small as it can be while remaining compatible with the selected performance goal. There is a classical engineering tradeoff over block size (the larger the block, the less frequently memory has to be accessed, but too large a block size for fixed cache capacity decreases the number of blocks resident in cache and hence the probability of finding a data or nonsequentially referred instruction in the cache). A similar tradeoff exists over set size. Historically, cache hit ratios have been determined experimentally by simulating address traces produced by application programs with various cache organizations. Figure 17 illustrates the results of such a study used in the PDP-11/60 cache design [Mudge, 1977]. Similar studies have been reported for other cache implementations [Strecker, 1976b; Meade, 1970].

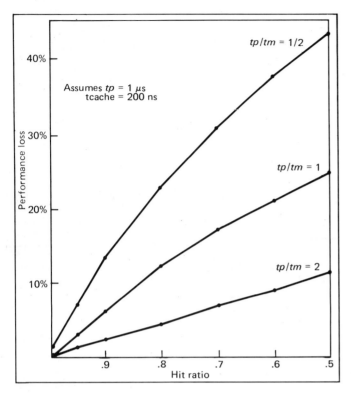

Fig. 16. Impact of cache hit ratio on system performance.

PDP-11	Set Size	Block Size (Bytes)	Cache Capacity (Bytes)	Hit Ratio
	1	2	512	.7
	1	2	1024	.75
	1	2	2048	.87
	2	2	1024	.82
	2	2	2048	.93
	2	2	4096	.93

Fig. 17. The effect of cache organization on the cache hit ratio.

Example Machines

Several papers in this book trace the development of virtual machine concepts from their roots in virtual memory systems.

Atlas

The Atlas has been described in Chap. 10. Atlas pioneered the concept of virtual memory with its one-level store. The Atlas extracodes were a forerunner of the standard user–operating-system interface commonly used today. By executing these special instructions, complete firmware or software functions can be evoked.

B5000

The B5000, introduced in Chap. 9, had several interesting innovations even though it is most often remembered as a stack machine. However, a common theme in Burroughs machines has been the integration of hardware and software design with the consequence of hardware support for software primitives. The B5000 provides extensive hardware support for block-structured languages. Virtual memory is supported by segmentation and indirect referencing through descriptors stored in the Program Reference Table.

B6500/7500

An evolution to the basic B5000, the B6500/7500, offers even more hardware assistance to dynamic memory control. Chapter 16 gives a detailed discussion of the tagged memory (tags identify memory words as data, descriptors, and control words), descriptor formats, the concept of lexical levels in programs, and the corresponding hardware development of display registers. Multiprogramming as supported by a stack environment is also discussed.

Cleary [1969] illustrates how the hardware defined by Hauck and Dent in Chap. 16 can be used by software to support multiple processes, process activation and deactivation, locking (synchronization), software interrupts, and event signaling. Feustel [1973] provides a detailed discussion of the advantages of tagged architectures.

ICL 2900

Based on many of the ideas developed by Manchester University's MU-5 [Ibbett and Capon, 1978], the ICL 2900 series has bloodlines traceable to the Atlas machine. ICL's design goals are very similar to Burroughs' and provide extensive hardware support to the software. But unlike Burroughs, ICL has not implemented a pure segmented virtual memory, but rather a paged-segmented virtual memory.

Keedy (Chap. 17) presents the fundamentals of virtual memory and traces the ICL rationale that ended up in a paged-segmented design. While logically tracing the design process, Keedy outlines a series of virtual memory designs, one of which is the basis for the virtual memory design for almost all contemporary computer manufacturers. The advantages and disadvantages of each virtual memory system should prove of interest to students and designers alike. Keedy concludes with discussions of memory protection, the instruction set, and multiprogramming on the ICL 2900 series.

VAX-11/780

Chapter 42 describes the multiprocess environment and virtual memory for a computer with 32-bit virtual address space. A translation buffer (a cache for translated addresses) was added to the VAX implementation to lessen the performance impact of the complex address translation and protection checking algorithms.

References

Belady [1966]; Buzen and Gagliardi [1973]; Cleary [1969]; Denning [1970]; Dijkstra [1968b]; Feustel [1973]; Ibbett and Capon [1978]; Katzan [1971]; Kuck [1978]; Lawson and Magenhagen [1975]; Liptay [1968]; Lipton [1973]; Meade [1970]; Mudge [1977]; Presser [1975]; Randell and Kuehner [1968]; Strecker [1976b].

Chapter 16

Burroughs' B6500/B7500 Stack Mechanism[1]

E. A. Hauck / B. A. Dent

Introduction

Burroughs' B6500/B7500 system structure and philosophy are an extention of the concepts employed in the development of the B5500 system. The unique features, common to both hardware systems, are that they have been designed to operate under the control of an executive program (MCP) and are to be programmed in only higher level languages (e.g., ALGOL, COBOL, and FORTRAN). Through a close integration of the software and hardware disciplines, a machine organization has been developed which permits the compilation of efficient machine code and which is addressed to the solution of problems associated with multiprogramming, multiprocessing and time sharing.

Some of the important features provided by the B6500/B7500 system are dynamic storage allocation, re-entrant programming, recursive procedure facilities, a tree structured stack organization, memory protection and an efficient interrupt system. A comprehensive stack mechanism is the basic ingredient of the B6500/B7500 system for providing these features.

B6500/B7500 Processor

The command structure of the B6500/B7500 Processor is Polish string, which allows for the separation of program code and data addresses. The basic machine instruction is called an operator syllable. This operator syllable is variable in length, from a minimum of 8 bits to a maximum of 96 bits. In the interest of code compactness, more frequently used operator syllables are encoded in the 8 bit form.

The Processor is provided with a hardware implemented stack in which to manipulate data and store dynamic program history. Also, data may be located in arrays outside the stack and may be brought to the stack temporarily for processing. Program parameters, local variables, references to program procedures and data arrays are normally stored within the stack.

The data word of the B6500/B7500 Processor is 51 bits long. Data are transferred between memory and within the Processor in 51 bit words. The first 3 bits of the word are used as tag bits, which

serve to identify the various word types as illustrated in Fig. 1. The remaining 48 bits are data. Tag bits, in addition to identifying word type, provide the B6500/B7500 Processor with two unique features: (1) data may be referenced as an operand, with the processor worrying about whether the operand consists of one or two words, and (2) system integrity and memory protection are extended to the level of the basic machine data words. If a job attempts to execute data as program code, or to modify program code, the system is interrupted.

The Stack

The stack consists of an area of memory assigned to a job. This stack area serves to provide storage for basic program and data references associated with the job. In addition, it provides a facility for the temporary storage of data and job history. When the job is activated, four high speed registers (A, X, B and Y) are linked to the job's stack area (Fig. 2). This linkage is established by the stack pointer register (S), which contains the memory address of the last word placed in the stack memory area. The four top-of-stack registers (A, X, B and Y) function to extend the job's stack into a quick access environment for data manipulation.

Data are brought into the stack through the top-of-stack registers. The stack's operating characteristic is such that the last operand placed into the stack is the first to be extracted. The top-of-stack registers become saturated after having been filled with two operands. Loading a third operand into the top-of-stack

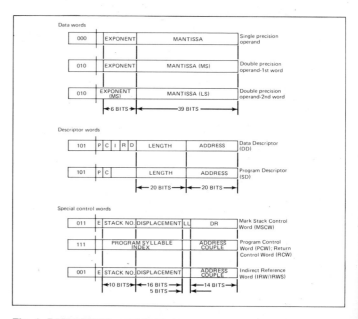

Fig. 1. B6500/B7500 word formats.

[1]*SJCC*, 1968, pp. 245–251.

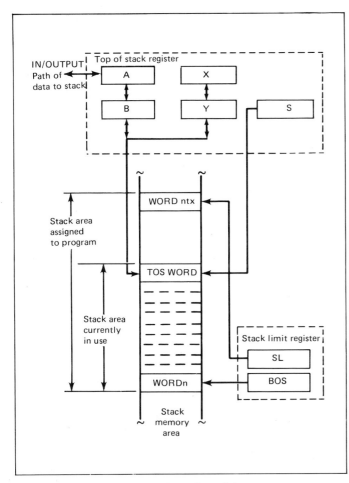

Fig. 2. Top of stack and stack bounds registers.

In the figure:

IN/OUTPUT Path of data to stack

Top of stack register

A   X

B   Y   S

WORD ntx

TOS WORD

Stack area assigned to program

Stack area currently in use

Stack limit register

SL

WORDn   BOS

Stack memory area

registers causes an operand to be pushed from the top-of-stack registers into the stack memory area. The stack pointer register (S) is incremented by one as each additional word is placed into the stack memory area; and is, of course, decremented by one as a word is withdrawn from the stack memory area and placed in the top-of-stack registers. As a result, the S register continually points to the last word placed into the job's stack memory area.

A job's stack memory area is bound, for memory protection, by two registers, the Base of Stack (BOS) register, and the Stack Limit (SL) register. The contents of the BOS register defines the base of the stack area, and the SL register defines the upper limit of the stack area. The job is interrupted if the S register is set to the value contained in either SL or BOS.

The contents of the top-of-stack registers are maintained automatically by the processor hardware in accordance with the environmental demands of the current operator syllable. If the

current operator syllable demands that data be brought into the stack, then the top-of-stack registers are adjusted to accommodate the incoming data, and the surplus contents of the top-of-stack registers if any, are pushed into the job's stack memory area. Words are brought out of the job's stack memory area and pushed into the top-of-stack register for operator syllables which require the presence of data in the top-of-stack registers, but do not explicitly move data into the stack.

Top-of-stack registers operate in an operand oriented fashion as opposed to being word oriented. Calling a double precision operand into the top-of-stack registers implies the loading of two memory words into the top-of-stack registers. The first word is always loaded into the A register where its tag bits are checked. If the word has a double precision tag, a second word is loaded into X. The A and X registers are then concatenated to form a double precision operand image. The B and Y registers concatenate when a double precision operand is moved to the B register. The double precision operand splits back to single words as it is pushed from the B and Y registers into the stack memory area. The reverse process is repeated when the double precision operand is eventually popped up from the stack memory area back into the top-of-stack registers.

Data Addressing

Three mechanisms exist within the B6500/B7500 Processor for addressing data or program code: (1) Data Descriptor (DD)/ Segment Descriptor (SD), (2) Indirect Reference Word (IRW), and (3) Stuffed Indirect Reference Word (IRWS). The Data Descriptor (DD) and Segment Descriptor (SD) are B5500 carry-overs and provide the basic mechanism for addressing data or program segments which are located outside of the job's stack area. The basic addressing component of the descriptor is an absolute machine address. The Indirect Reference Word (IRW) and the Stuffed Indirect Reference Word (IRWS) are B6500/B7500 mechanisms for addressing data located within the job's stack memory area. The addressing component of both the IRW and IRWS is a relative address. The IRW is used to address within the immediate environment of the job's stack, and addresses relative to a display register (described later in Non-Local Addressing). The IRWS is used to address beyond the immediate environment of the current procedure, and the addresses relative to the base of the job's stack. Addressing across stacks is accomplished with an IRWS.

The Descriptor

In general, the descriptor functions to describe and locate data or program code associated with a given job. The Data Descriptor

(DD) is used to fetch data to the stack or store data from the stack into an array which resides outside the job's stack area. The format of Data and Segment Descriptors are illustrated in Fig. 1. The ADDRESS field of both descriptors is 20 bits in length and contains the absolute address of an array in either main system memory or in the back-up disk store. The Presence bit (P) indicates whether the referenced data are present in main system memory or in the back-up disk store, and is set equal to ONE when the referenced data are present in main system memory.

A Presence Bit Interrupt is incurred when the job makes reference to data via a descriptor which has a P bit equal to ZERO. The Presence Bit Interrupt stimulates the operating system (called the Master Control Program, or MCP) to move the data from disk to main memory. The data location on disk is contained in the ADDRESS field of the DD when the P bit is equal to ZERO. After transferring the data array into the main memory, the operating system (MCP) marks the descriptor present by setting the P bit equal to ONE, and places the current memory address into the ADDRESS field of the descriptor. The interrupted job is then reactivated.

A Data Descriptor may describe either an entire array of data words, or a particular element within an array of data words. If the descriptor describes an entire array, the Indexed bit (I-bit) in the descriptor is ZERO, indicating that the descriptor has not yet been indexed. The LENGTH field of the descriptor defines the length of the data array.

A particular element of an array may be described by indexing an array descriptor. Memory protection is insured during indexing operations by performing a comparison between the LENGTH field of the descriptor and the index being applied to it. An Invalid Index Interrupt is incurred if the index value exceeds the length of the memory area defined by the descriptor.

If the value being used to index the descriptor is valid, the LENGTH field of the descriptor is replaced by the index value. At this time the I-bit in the descriptor is set to ONE to indicate that indexing has taken place. The ADDRESS and LENGTH fields are added together to generate an absolute machine address whenever a present, indexed Data Descriptor is used to fetch or store data.

The Double Precision bit (D) is used to identify the referenced data as being either single or double precision and, as a result, is also associated with the indexing operation. The D bit being equal to ONE signifies double precision and implies that the index value be multiplied by two before indexing.

The Read-Only bit (R) specifies that the memory area described by the Data Descriptor is a read-only area. An interrupt is incurred upon referencing an area through a descriptor with the intention to write if the R bit is equal to ONE.

The Copy bit (C) identifies a descriptor as being a copy of a master descriptor and is related to the present bit action. The intent of the copy action is to keep multiple copies of an absent descriptor linked back to one master descriptor. Copy action is incurred when a job attempts to pass by name an absent Data Descriptor. When this occurs, the hardware manufactures a copy of the master descriptor, forces the C bit equal to ONE and inserts into the ADDRESS field the address of the master descriptor. Thus, multiple copies of absent descriptors are all linked back to the master descriptor.

Non-Local Addressing

The most important single aspect of the B6500/B7500 stack is its facility for storing the dynamic history of a program under execution. Two lists of program information are saved in the B6500/B7500 stack, the stack history list and the addressing environment list. The stack history list is dynamic in nature, varying as the job is driven through different program paths with changing sets of data. Both lists are generated and maintained by the B6500/B7500 hardware system.

The stack history list is formed from a list of Mark Stack Control Words (MSCW) which are linked together by their DF fields (Fig. 3). A MSCW is inserted into the stack as a procedure is entered, and is extracted as that procedure is exited. Therefore, the stack

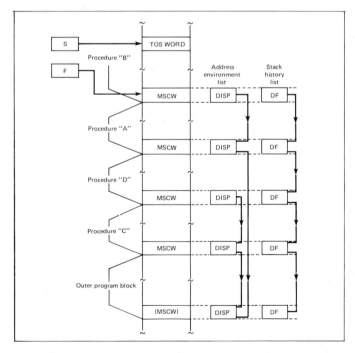

Fig. 3. Stack history and addressing environment list.

history list grows and contracts in accordance with the procedural depth of the program. Mark Stack Control Words serve to identify the portion of the stack related to each procedure. When the procedure is entered, its parameters and local variables are entered in the stack following the MSCW. When executing the procedure, its parameters and local variables are referenced by addressing relative to the location of the related MSCW.

Each MSCW is linked back to the prior MSCW through the contents of its DF field to identify the point in the stack where the prior procedure began. When a procedure is exited, its related portion of the stack is discarded. This action is achieved by setting the stack pointer register (S) to point to the memory cell preceding the most recent MSCW (Fig. 4). This top-most MSCW, pointed to by another register (F), is in effect deleted from the stack history list by causing F to point back at the prior MSCW, thereby placing it at the head of the stack history list.

This concept is implemented in the Burroughs' B5500 system, and it provides a convenient means to handle subroutine entry and exit. But this mechanism alone also gives rise to one of the most serious limitations of the ALGOL implementation on the B5500. In the B5500 stack, local variables are addressed relative to the first Mark Stack Control Word (which corresponds to the outer-most block), or relative to the most recent Mark Stack Control Word (which corresponds to the current procedure). All intervening Mark Stack Control Words, however, are invisible to the current procedure. This means that the variables declared global to the current procedure, but local to some other procedure, cannot be addressed at all! This inability to reference

variables declared non-local to the current procedure but local to some other procedure is termed the non-local addressing problem.

The manner in which these variables are addressed in the B6500/B7500 stack can best be understood by analyzing the structure of an ALGOL program. The addressing environment of an ALGOL procedure is established when the program is structured by the programmer, and is referred to as the lexicographical ordering of the procedural blocks (Fig. 6a). At compile time, this lexicographical ordering is used to form address couples. An address couple consists of two items: 1) the lexicographical level (ll) of the variable, and 2) an index value (δ) used to locate the specific variable within a given lexicographical level. The lexicographical ordering of the program remains static as the program is executed, thereby allowing variables to be referenced via address couples as the program is executed.

The B6500/B7500 contains a network of Display Registers (D0 through D31) which are caused to point at the appropriate MSCW (Fig. 5). The local variables of all procedures global to the current procedure are addressed in the B6500/B7500 relative to the Display Registers.

The address couple is converted into an absolute memory address when the variable is referenced. The lexicographical level

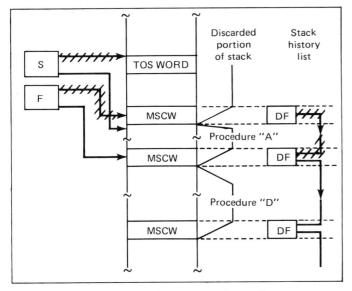

Fig. 4. Stack cut-back operation on procedure exit.

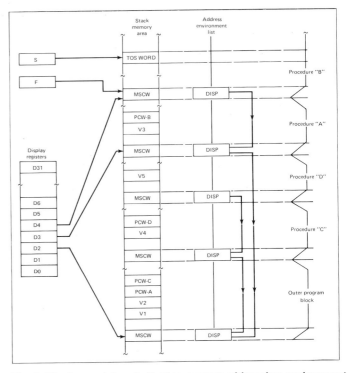

Fig. 5. Display registers indicating current addressing environment.

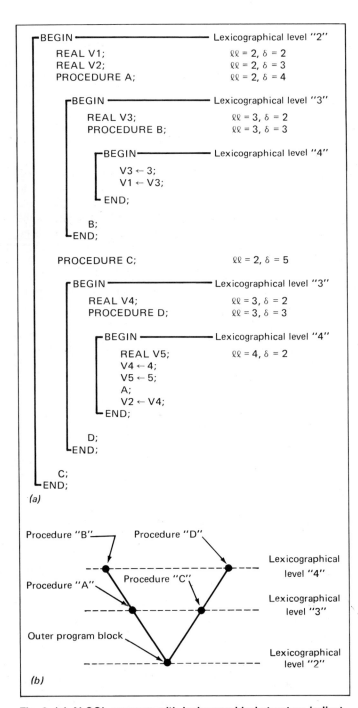

(a)

(b)

Fig. 6. (a) ALGOL program with lexicographical structure indicated. (b) Addressing environment tree of ALGOL program in (a).

portion of the address couple functions to select the Display Register which contains an absolute memory address pointing at the MSCW related to the procedural block (environment) where the referenced variable is located. The index value of the address couple is then added to the contents of the Display Register to generate an absolute memory address to locate the variable.

It should be recognized that the address couples assigned to the variables in a program are not unique. This is true because of the ALGOL scope of definition rules, which imply that two variables may have identical address couples only if there is no procedure within which both of the variables can be addressed. So this addressing scheme works because, whereas two variables may have the same address couples, there is never any doubt as to which variable is being referenced within any particular procedure.

What this does imply, however, is that there is a unique place (a MSCW) to which each Display Register must point during the execution of any particular procedure, and that the settings of the Display Registers might have to be changed, upon procedure entry or exit, to point to the correct MSCW. This list of MSCWs to which the Display Registers must point is called the addressing environment of the procedure.

The addressing environment of the program is maintained by the hardware. It is formed by linking the MSCW's together in accordance with the lexicographical structure of the program. This linkage information is contained with the Stack Number (Stack No.) and Displacement (DISP) fields of the MSCW, and is inserted into the MSCW whenever a procedure is entered. The contents of the DISP field indicate the environment in which the entered procedure was declared. Thus the addressing environment list is formed by linking each procedure entry Mark Stack Control Word back to the MSCW appearing immediately below the declaration for that procedure. This forms a tree structured list which indicates the legitimate addressing environment of each procedure under dynamic conditions (Figs. 5 and 6b). This list is searched by the hardware to update the Display Registers' contents whenever a procedure entry or exit occurs.

The entry and exit mechanism of the Processor hardware automatically maintains both stack lists to reflect the current status of the program. Therefore, the system is able to respond to, and return from, interrupts conveniently. Interrupt response is handled as a procedure entry. Upon recognition of an interrupt condition, the hardware causes the stack to be marked, inserts into the stack an indirect reference word (address couple) pointing to the interrupt handling procedure, inserts a literal constant to identify the interrupt condition, and then causes an entry into the operating system interrupt-handling procedure. The Display Registers will track with the entry into the interrupt-handling procedure to make all legitimate variables visible. Also upon return, the Display Registers track back to the environment of the former procedure, making all of its variables visible again.

Multiple Stacks and Re-Entrant Code

The B6500/B7500 stack mechanism provides a facility to handle several active stacks. These stacks are organized into a single tree structure. The trunk of this tree structure is a stack which contains certain operating system global variables, and contains all of the Segment Descriptors describing the various procedures within the operating system.

Let us make a distinction between a program, which is a set of executable instructions, and a job, which is single execution of a program for a particular set of data. As the operating system is requested to run a job, a level-1 branch of the basic stack is created. This level-1 branch is a stack which contains only the Segment Descriptors describing the executable code for the named program. Emerging from this level-1 branch is a level-2 branch, a stack to contain the variables and data for this job. Thus, starting from the job's stack and tracing downward through the tree structure, one would find first the stack containing the variables and data for the job (at level 2), the program code to be executed (at level 1), and finally the operating system's stack at the trunk (level 0).

A subsequent request to run another execution of an already-running program would require that only a level-2 branch be established. This level-2 stack branch would sprout from the level-1 stack that describes the already running program. Thus two jobs which are different executions of the same program will have a common node, at level 1, which describes the executable code. It is in this way that program code, which is not modifiable, is re-entrant and shared. It comes about simply from the proper tree-structured organization of the various stacks within the machine. Thus all programs within the system are re-entrant, including all user programs as well as the compilers and the operating system itself.

The B6500/B7500 stack mechanism also provides the facility for a single job to split itself into two independent jobs. It is anticipated that the most common use of this facility will occur when there is a point in a job where two relatively large independent processes must be performed. This kind of splitting could be used to make full use of a multiprocessor configuration, or simply to reduce elapsed time by multiprogramming the independent processes.

This kind of program splitting becomes almost literally "reproduction by budding" in the B6500/B7500 system. A split of this type is handled by establishing a new limb of the tree structured stack, with the two independent jobs sharing that part of the stack which was created before the budding was requested. The process is recursively defined, and can happen repeatedly at any level. An implementation restriction limits the total number of separate stacks to 1024.

This tree-structure organization for handling multiple stacks is referred to as the Saguaro Stack System.

Linkage of stack branches is achieved through a single array of data descriptors, the stack vector array (Fig. 7). A data descriptor is entered into the array for every stack branch as it is set up by the operating system. This data descriptor, the stack descriptor, serves to describe the length of the memory area assigned to a stack branch, and its location in either main memory or on disk.

A stack number is assigned to each stack branch to indicate the position of its stack descriptor within the stack vector array. The stack number is used as an index value to locate the related stack descriptor from the stack vector array for subsequent reference.

The stack vector array's size and location in memory is described by the stack vector descriptor. This descriptor is located in a reserved position of the stack's trunk (Fig. 7). All references to stack branches are made through the stack vector descriptor which is indexed by the value of the stack number to select the stack descriptor for the referenced stack.

A Presence Bit Interrupt is incurred upon making reference to a stack which is not present in memory. This Presence Bit Interrupt facility provides the means to permit stack overlays and recalls under dynamic conditions. Idle or inactive stacks may be moved from main memory to disk as the need arises, and when subsequently referenced will cause a Presence Bit Interrupt which triggers the operating system to recall the non-present stack from disk.

Referencing a variable within the current addressing environment of an active procedure is accomplished through the use of the address couples contained in the IRW and the address couple field of the Program Control Word (PCW) as shown in Fig. 1. Both references are made relative to the Display Registers specified by the address couple. The address couple and Display Registers are

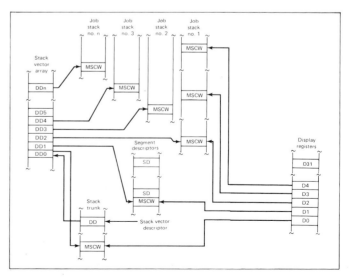

Fig. 7. Multiple linked stacks.

usable only for addressing variables within the scope of the current addressing environment. Reference to variables beyond the scope of the current environment is accomplished by a stuffed IRWS. This causes the addressing to be accomplished by addressing relative to the base of the stack (BOS) in which the variable is located.

The IRWS contains information specifying the stack number (Stack No.), the location (DISP) of the related MSCW, and the displacement (δ) of the parameter relative to the MSCW. The absolute memory location of the sought parameter is formed by adding the contents of DISP and δ to the base address of the referenced stack. The base address of the stack is determined by accessing the stack descriptor as described previously. The information contents of the stuffed IRWS with the exception of δ, is dynamic in nature and must therefore be accumulated as the program is executed. The contents of the stack number (Stack No.) and DISP fields are entered into the IRWS by a special hardware operator which is invoked by the software whenever the program attempts to pass a parameter by name.

References

Burroughs [1964]; Burroughs [1965]; Randall and Russell [1964].

Chapter 17

An Outline of the ICL 2900 Series System Architecture

J. L. Keedy[1]

Summary The system architecture of the ICL 2900 Series is outlined informally. Its central feature, the virtual machine concept, is described and related to virtual storage, segmentation and paging. The procedural approach is then discussed and its implementation by a stack mechanism is described. Further sections outline the protection mechanisms, and the instruction set and related features. Finally the virtual machine approach is related to global system activities.

The paper has been written such that it may be of interest to readers without a specialist knowledge of computer architecture.

Shortly after its announcement in October, 1974, the ICL 2900 Series[2] was described in the popular computing press [Dorn, 1974] as little more than a copy of the B6700/7700 systems. It is easy to see how this happened, when one discovers that it is a stack oriented machine with a segmented virtual memory which makes extensive use of descriptors. In reality the implementation of these techniques is very different in the two computer families, and although a more serious attempt has been made to evaluate these differences [Doran, 1975] this is to some extent unsatisfactory since the author has, I believe, fallen into the same trap, albeit more subtly, of viewing the ICL 2900 through the eyes of someone thoroughly steeped in B6700 ideas. In fact, although the ICL 2900 has features in common with the B6700, radical differences exist, and some of the ICL 2900 features have more affinity to other systems, such as MULTICS [Organick, 1972]. Before the similarities and differences between such systems and the ICL 2900 Series can be fully appreciated, it is highly desirable that the ICL 2900 system architecture should first be understood in its own right. The real novelty of the architecture lies in the way in which its designers returned to first principles, and in the simplicity and elegance of the result. In this paper I shall therefore describe its architecture in a manner which attempts to reflect the thoughts of its designers, aiming at a level of description similar to Organick's description of the B6700 [Organick, 1973]. No attempt will be made to compare and contrast it with other systems, and it is hoped that the paper will provide an intelligible overview to readers without specialist knowledge of computer architecture.

1. The Virtual Machine

Faced with a problem to be solved using the computer, the user formulates a solution in a high level computer language such as COBOL or FORTRAN, and having satisfied himself of its correctness he will regard the resultant program as "complete." This is in one sense correct. His encoded algorithm will, if he has done his job well, be logically complete. However, even after it has been compiled, the user's program (or in more complex cases, his sequence of programs which comprise a job) must co-operate with other programmed subsystems (operating system, data management software, library routines, etc.) to solve the user's problem. The efficiency with which the problem is solved depends to a considerable extent on how the whole aggregate of necessary subsystems co-operates, and not merely on any one subsystem. It follows that it will be advantageous for a computer architecture to provide facilities for the efficient construction and execution of such aggregates. The 2900 Series explicitly recognises these aggregates, calling the environment in which each one operates a "virtual machine."[3] An aggregate itself is called a "process image," its execution by a processor is a "process," and its state of execution as characterised by processor registers is its "process state."

In the following sections we shall develop the idea of the virtual machine by considering its mainstore requirements, the dynamic relationship between its components, its protection requirements and its instruction set. But before we embark on this a few further remarks are necessary.

The fundamental concept, that each job runs in its own virtual machine containing all the code and data required to solve the application problem, allows the programmer to suppose that he is the sole user of the computer. But economic reality dictates that the real machine must be capable of solving several problems simultaneously, and this necessity for multiprogramming raises a set of problems which could threaten to destroy the advantages of the virtual machine approach. For example, how are the independent virtual machines co-ordinated, synchronised and scheduled? How, in view of high main storage costs, can separate process-images be permitted to have a private copy of common subsystems (e.g., the operating system)? How can virtual machines communicate with each other? Such questions will be borne in mind as we develop the concept of the virtual machine, and subsequently we shall consider them more directly, in an attempt

---

[1]*Australian Computer Journal*, vol. 9, no. 2, July 1977, pp. 53–62.
[2]References to the ICL 2900 Series in this paper are to the larger members of the new ICL range, which should not be confused with the ICL 2903 or the ICL 2904 computers.

[3]The term "virtual machine" has a wide variety of meanings in computer jargon. In this paper it is used consistently in the special ICL sense described here.

to show that the benefits and principles of the virtual machine are not compromised by the secondary modifications which are introduced to facilitate the efficient multiprogramming of several processes in separate virtual machines.

2.   The Segmented Virtual Store

The relatively high cost of main store when compared with other storage devices, such as drums and discs, forces the computer architect to consider how this essential system component can be utilised with greatest efficiency. Amongst the more pressing problems in this area are:

a   The process-image, and possibly even the user program alone, may exceed the size of available main store.

b   Competition for main store by a number of programs may exist (e.g. in a time sharing system).

c   Efficient use of main store for variable length tables, etc.

The most promising technique for solving such problems is the virtual storage concept, first used on the Atlas machines. In order to ensure that the user's needs are satisfied we shall look at this solution in the light of program structures.

The output of a compiler consists mainly of a series of logical regions comprising an object program. Most third generation architectures treat the object program as a single logical unit (e.g. for protection purposes), but certain advantages accrue if the logically separate regions, such as code sections and data areas, which we shall for the moment call program segments, are recognised as separate entities. For example, the separation of code segments from data segments considerably simplifies the production of "pure" reentrant code; this in principle allows separate virtual machines to use a single real copy of common code (e.g. operating system procedures) whilst allowing us to retain the concept of a process image containing all the code necessary to solve the user's problem. We shall see other advantages of the architectural recognition of segmentation in due course.

A characteristic feature of segments within a process-image is their need to cross-reference each other, the obvious technique for implementing this being to form an address consisting of segment number plus displacement within segment. If we now form for each virtual machine a "segment table" consisting of a list of entries (one per segment in the process-image), which map the segments onto main store addresses, and make this available to the hardware, then the hardware can calculate the exact main store location of any item cross-referenced by a "segment number plus displacement" address. If a segment table entry also contains a marker indicating whether the segment is present in main store, or is temporarily held on a secondary storage device (e.g. a drum), and a record of the length of each segment (see Fig. 1),

then we have the rudiments of a segmented virtual store. This concept allows part or all of a process-image to reside temporarily outside main store on some secondary storage device, and thus in principle solves our problems of (a) a process-image which exceeds the size of main store, and (b) competition for main store usage in a time-sharing environment. Our remaining problem (c) of variable length segments can in principle be solved by allowing the recorded segment length to be changed.

The hardware procedure for translating a "segment number plus displacement" address (i.e. a virtual address) into a main store address is as follows. If P_i indicates that segment i is not in main store, the hardware causes an interrupt to allow the software to read the segment into main store; otherwise the virtual address i (segment number), j (displacement) is calculated as $R_i + j$. A further advantage of this scheme is that the test $j > L_i$ reveals erroneous attempts to jump to non-existent code or to access non-existent data beyond the upper bound of any segment.

Although this segmentation scheme is conceptually complete, the practicalities of multiprogramming require the introduction of certain modifications for the sake of efficiency. The existence of a separate entry in each virtual machine's segment table for those segments required in all virtual machines (e.g. operating systems

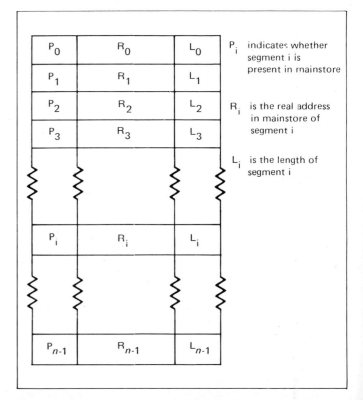

Fig. 1. A segment table for a process-image consisting of n segmen

code) would not only be wasteful of space—it would also add significant overheads when moving such a segment around in the virtual store, since each segment table in the system would have to be updated. The solution adopted in the 2900 Series is to recognise a second category of segment table, the "public" segment table, containing an entry for each common or "public" segment. Since only one copy of this table need exist (thus saving space and allowing efficient movement of public segments) the process-image of a job is defined by a combination of its local segment table plus the one public segment table, and the hardware tests the most significant bit of a segment number to select the appropriate table (local segments are numbered 0-8191, public segments 8191-16383).

A third class of segment is shared locally between certain but not all virtual machines. Such segments, which are rather misleadingly called "global segments" are particularly useful for implementing real-time transaction processing on the 2900 Series. To implement such global segments as public segments has the undesirable side-effect that they would become accessible to virtual machines not privileged to access them, by virtue of their appearance in the public segment table. Since in practice global segments are relatively rare, to include them in each appropriate local segment table is unlikely to lead to a serious misuse of storage space, but the updating of multiple entries when the segment is moved, or when its length is changed, remains a difficulty (especially as each virtual machine sharing the segment may allocate to it a different segment number). The 2900 Series therefore permits a third class of segment table, the "global" segment table, which contains entries similar to other segment table entries. However, the global tables are not ordered by segment number, but are referenced via the local segment tables, which for global entries contain an indirection marker and in place of a segment's main store address the address of the appropriate global segment table entry (see Fig. 2). In this way movements of a global segment require that only the global segment table entry be updated, whilst rapid access is achieved via the local segment table.

We now have an addressing structure capable of mapping virtual machines efficiently onto the storage hierarchy, but there remains the practical question of economic main store management. Since we have followed the most natural path by allowing variable length segments (with the additional potential space saving benefit of allowing the length of a segment to vary at execution time), we are forced to come to terms with the well-known problem of the "external" fragmentation of main store. This is illustrated in Fig. 3, which shows a map of a main store containing segments and holes left by segments no longer in main store; there is clearly enough free space for the new segment, but it cannot be loaded because the holes are not contiguous.

The 2900 Series designers examined the various solutions to

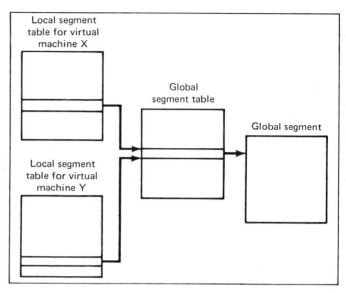

Fig. 2. Two virtual machines sharing a segment addressed via a Global Segment Table.

this problem and decided to adopt the paging technique, whereby variable length segments are divided into fixed length pages, thus allowing main store allocation to be effected in fixed length blocks as is shown in Fig. 4.

This solution, which always allows a paged segment to be loaded provided that sufficient store blocks are free, requires the introduction of page tables, and the interpretation of a virtual address as "segment number plus page number plus page displacement." The actual 2900 Series virtual address structure is shown in Fig. 5, from which it can be seen that a virtual machine may contain up to 2^{14} segments each consisting of 2^{18} bytes divided into pages of length 2^{10} bytes.

The segment table entry is now modified to point to a page table (one per paged segment), which is indexed by the page number part of the virtual address and contains the main store addresses of

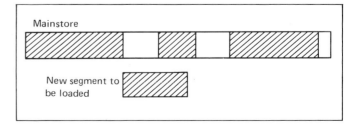

Fig. 3. An example of the external fragmentation of a main store.

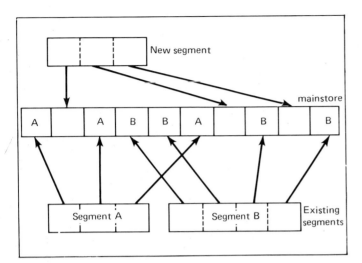

Fig. 4. Paged allocation of segments in main store.

all resident pages. Two of the advantageous side-effects of the paging solution are (a) that a segment can be brought into main store in stages, and (b) the length of segments can be extended without having to find a new block of store large enough to hold the whole segment.

The main drawback with paging is that it can lead to "internal fragmentation," the loss of main store space at the end of a segment caused by the necessity of rounding the segment length up to an integral number of pages. The average proportional loss of storage, assuming that the average segment size s is large in relation to the page size p, will be $p/2s$ (i.e. half a page per segment). It is intuitively obvious that this loss can be minimised in two possible ways: by keeping the page size small in relation to the average segment size and/or by attempting to produce segments whose lengths are as close as possible to an integral number of pages. But the page size must not become too small (otherwise the overheads of page tables and secondary store transfers become too great) and the segment size as previously defined is of an arbitrary length, dependent upon the logical

program structure (and therefore not normally a multiple of page size). The 2900 Series therefore compromises by treating a physical segment as consisting of one or more logical regions, called areas, produced by a compiler. This gives the user the flexibility to create longer segments in relation to page size, and also to attempt to create segments whose length is as near as possible a multiple of the page size, and thereby to help reduce storage loss through internal fragmentation. For reasons which will become clear when we discuss protection the areas comprising a segment should share the same properties (e.g. read only data); and for obvious reasons only one variable length area can be included in a segment.

Since there are some segments for which paging is irrelevant (e.g. main store resident segments of the operating system) the architecture allows for both paged and non-paged segments. Figure 6 shows the logical structure of the segment and page tables for a particular virtual machine.

3. Subroutines, Procedures and the Stack

We now return to the concept that the efficient execution of a user's task depends not merely on his own program but upon the

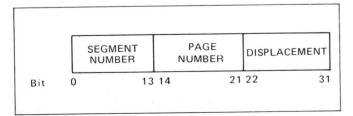

Fig. 5. The 2900 series virtual address.

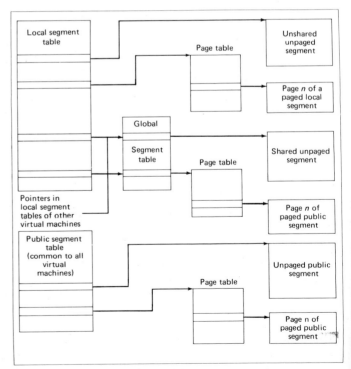

Fig. 6. The structure of the page and segment tables for a virtual machine.

totality of code and data required to solve his problem. It is essential that the virtual machine, the environment for executing such a process-image, provides mechanisms enabling efficient dynamic co-operation between the various subsystems comprising the process image.

Inter-subsystem calls are really only a special case of calls between code routines within the process-image, the more general case being the subroutine or procedure call, which appears in one form or another in all the major high level languages. The question may now be restated as: how can subroutine/procedure calls be flexibly and efficiently incorporated into the architectural model?

A relatively complex subroutine needs its own variables and work areas. If it is to be used recursively such work areas must be created on each entry to the subroutine. It also needs a mechanism for linkage with the calling code, which may also supply it with parameters. Such a subroutine is called in 2900 terminology a "procedure," and is implemented with the aid of a last-in first-out hardware assisted stack.

Each stack is held as a separate segment[1] and is controlled by four registers (see Fig. 7):

a   Stack Segment Numbers (SSN)—the base address of the stack.

b   Stack Front (SF)—the address of the next free location in the stack.

c   Local Name Base (LNB)—the start address of the name-space for the current procedure or lexical level.

d   Extra Name Base (XNB)—can be used for example to

[1]Thus a virtual machine may support several stacks, and therefore several (co-operating) processes.

address the start of a previous lexical level in the stack or as an off-stack pointer.

A procedure call takes place in two stages—a software pre-call sequence and a hardware call instruction. The software stores the current LNB value at the address held in SF, raises SF to leave space free for linkage data, stores the parameters at the new top of stack, and raises LNB to point to the next lexical level. The hardware call instruction then inserts the linkage data and in the normal case begins executing the new procedure (see Fig. 8). This procedure now has access to its parameters via LNB and to a new workspace starting at SF. It is free to call further procedures (or itself recursively) or to call the hardware exit instruction, which causes the stack to be collapsed back to the previous local name space, and the calling procedure will then be resumed at the instruction following the call instruction.[2]

4.   Main Store Protection

One of the main functions of a computer architecture is to provide mechanisms which ensure that procedures have appropriate access to the data and code segments necessary for the execution of their task, but are not permitted to interfere with other segments in an unauthorised way. Such a requirement appears at two levels, within a virtual machine and between virtual machines.

Let us consider first the avoidance of interference within a single virtual machine. The most obvious example of the need for this is to prevent an untested user program from corrupting the other subsystems in its virtual machine.

The inadequacies of the traditional solution to this problem—the recognition of two classes of program (privileged software and unprivileged programs)—become obvious if we consider a "compile and go" system such as BASIC with the compiler itself

[2]There is, of course, a simple "jump and link" instruction (which stores a return address at the top of the stack) for use in implementing more trivial subroutines.

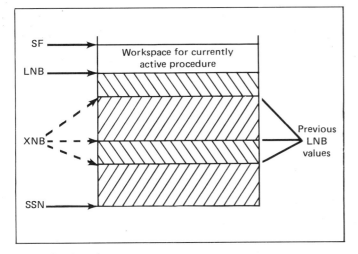

Fig. 7. Stack registers.

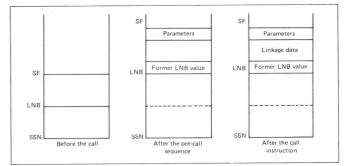

Fig. 8. The stages of a procedure call.

running as an unprivileged program: in this situation the compiler is unnecessarily endangered by the executing program. At the other extreme one could envisage a totally safe system in which each procedure has its own data class, and is only permitted to access data areas of this class; but the overheads in such a system would be high.

The intermediate solution selected for the 2900 Series architecture provides protection at the segment level (since this type of object is already known to the hardware) and associates with a process a 4 bit Access Control Register (ACR), allowing a range 0-15 of protection classes. Each segment table entry has an associated "read access key" (RAK) and "write access key" (WAK). Only if RAK ⩾ ACR is the procedure permitted to read a segment, or if WAK ⩾ ACR to write a segment. Likewise a segment can only be executed if a further marker in the segment table entry, the "execute permission bit" (EPB) is set.

The access control register is contained within the "program status register"(PSR), as is also a one-bit register known as PRIV, which in fact controls access to the PSR (and therefore to ACR). Under normal circumstances PRIV is reset, thus prohibiting changes to ACR (which reflects the protection level of the current procedure).

However if the procedure attempts to call another procedure which executes with a different ACR value, reference is made (either by hardware, or by a software interrupt routine running with PRIV on) to a software-created system call table to validate whether the call is permitted. If so ACR is assigned the value associated with the called procedure, PRIV is reset and the procedure is entered. Since PSR is stored on procedure entry as part of the linkage data, the hardware exit instruction can normally reload ACR with the appropriate value on returning to the calling procedure.[1]

By limiting the privilege of changing ACR to the lowest level of interrupt software access to segments within the same process image is properly controlled within sixteen levels of privilege—this being sufficient to provide a highly structured operating system with several levels remaining for user programs. The one apparent loophole in the scheme, the possibility that a less privileged level passes as a parameter to a more privileged level a manufactured but valid address to which it is not permitted access, is overcome by the provision of a special hardware "validate" instruction, which the called routine uses to find out

what type of access (if any) the ACR level of the calling routine has to data at the address supplied. This is possible because the linkage information in the stack contains the ACR value of the calling routine, which can be checked against the WAK and RAK values in the segment table entry for the address to be validated.

For obvious reasons the architecture must also provide a mechanism to ensure that certain instructions (e.g. instructions controlling input-output devices) are not misused, and this is also achieved by testing the PRIV bit in the PSR.

Finally, the question of store protection between virtual machines (i.e. prohibiting interference between user jobs) is automatically solved by the addressing structure. Any address used within a virtual machine is transformed into a real address by means of the virtual machine's own segment tables. It is simply impossible to access a location not contained in these segment tables.

5. The Instruction Set

The instruction set for the 2900 Series was designed specifically with the needs of high-level languages in mind, and its objectives include efficiency of compilation and execution, reliability of execution, and compactness of object code. In order to achieve these objectives the 2900 Series instruction set interlocks closely with descriptors, registers and the stack in manipulating the basic data formats.[2]

Although the segmentation protection scheme provides a fair degree of execution reliability (e.g. by ensuring that data is not "executed" as code, that code and read-only data cannot be corrupted, etc.), this is oriented to ensuring non-interference between different subsystems and programs. In order to provide a means of detecting execution errors within a single high-level language program or subsystem (e.g. an attempt to access an array element beyond the array boundaries, or to perform an indexed jump beyond the boundaries of a specific code module) the 2900 Series employs "descriptors," which associate with a virtual address a description of the object addressed.[3] Descriptors, which provide other facilities in addition to run-time error checking, are in four standard formats each consisting of 32 bits for the description plus 32 bits for the address:

---

[1]This description refers to calls which reduce ACR value (i.e. increase privilege), and to the corresponding returns. Calls which increase ACR value (i.e. reduce privilege) and corresponding returns involve the creation of an additional stack to ensure that on-stack data is not available to non-privileged code; such calls are generally avoided, because of the overheads involved in creating a new stack.

[2]Bits; 8-bit bytes in EBCDIC and packed decimal formats; 32 or 64 bit words containing logical or fixed-point numerical values; 32, 64 or 128 bit words for floating-point numbers; 32, 64 or 128 bit words containing 7, 15, or 31 digit signed decimal integers.

[3]Unlike MULTICS or B6700 descriptors, the ICL 2900 descriptor mechanism is internal to an address space, rather than a means of defining the address space.

Vector Descriptors contain a size field indicating whether a data element is 1, 8, 32, 64 or 128 bits in length; a bound field containing a count of elements; a bound-check inhibit indicator; and a scale bit-which indicates whether address modifiers are to be scaled in accordance with the size field. The vector descriptor can be used to address individual primitive data items (such as an integer variable) or single dimension arrays of primitive elements. Provision for multi-dimensional arrays is in the form of dope-vectors consisting of triplets, each describing a dimension.

String Descriptors describes rows of bytes, e.g. character strings, and hold an indication of the string length.

Descriptor Descriptors point to other descriptors and thus provide an indirect addressing facility.

Code Descriptors consist of normal code descriptors, system call descriptors, and escape descriptors. Normal code descriptors serve as operands for procedure call instructions not requiring a change of privilege, and for exit instructions not requiring an increase in privilege. System call descriptors contain instead of an address a pair of indices which reference a System Call Table entry (see Sec. 4); they are used as operands for procedure calls requiring a change of privilege and for exits requiring an increase of privilege. Escape descriptors, however, may be interchanged with any other descriptor as an exceptional means of by-passing normal code sequencing rules. On detection of an escape descriptor as an instruction operand the hardware causes entry to the code routine whose address is held in the escape descriptor, without executing the instruction for which it serves as an operand. The escape routine might typically monitor the use of a particular table or procedure, or instigate the loading into virtual store of some exception procedure not normally required (e.g. an error routine). A special mechanism is available to allow an escape routine, having placed the "correct" descriptor in a register, to cause the original instruction to be executed "correctly," and thence return to the normal code sequence.

In considering what form the register set should take, it was evident almost from the beginning that special purpose registers with dedicated functions would be more suitable than interchangeable general purpose registers for a "high level language machine" such as the 2900 Series. The problem with the latter is that compiler-writers, not being in a position to predict in advance the dynamic execution of programs to be compiled, are forced into following a set of conventions, which may be wasteful but which certainly distorts any theoretical advantages of having general purpose registers. On the other hand dedicated registers, if carefully designed, provide an appropriate tool for the compiler writer. At the same time they allow the hardware designer to

optimise his implementation on the basis of the known purposes of the registers.

The 2900 Series provides the compiler-writer with both a dedicated set of registers and a virtually infinite number of on-stack locations which in practice serve as registers.[1] In addition to the four stack registers already described (SSN, SF, LNB, XNB) the following registers are "visible" to each process-image in unprivileged mode: a variable length accumulator (ACC) whose size (32, 64 or 128 bits) is controlled by a 2-bit register ACS; an index modifier (B) used mainly for address modification; a descriptor register (DR) used for addressing operands; a program counter (PC); a real-time clock (RTC); an overflow indicator (OV); a condition code (CC); and a program mask (PM) used to inhibit specific program interrupts.[2]

There are 113 functions in the instruction set, providing facilities for arithmetic, character manipulation, logical operations, instruction sequencing, etc. Most instructions operate on two operands, one of which (normally a register holding data or a descriptor) is usually implied by the function. The other operand may be a string whose descriptor is held in DR or may be specified in the operand field of the instruction (e.g. as a literal, a displacement from a stack register, etc.). The size of an instruction is 16 or 32 bits, depending on the method of specifying the operand rather than on the function code. Similarly function codes are not dependent on the length of the accumulator, so that the same functions are used, for example, in single precision and double precision floating point operations. To illustrate how the interplay of descriptors, registers and the stack results in efficient and compact object code which can be efficiently compiled from high level languages, we take three brief examples: arithmetic, array handling and character spring manipulation.

The stack is of course particularly well suited to the evaluation of arithmetic expressions by means of "reverse Polish" notation, and typical sequences such as "store accumulator value at top of stack, raise top of stack pointer, load new value into accumulator," or "add (multiply etc.) accumulator value and top of stack value, lower top of stack pointer" are efficiently compacted into single instructions.

Array handling will typically consist of a logical subscript value

---

[1] Since the more powerful machines have a slave-store dedicated to the stack, this statement is true not only logically but also in terms of physical speed.

[2] In reality ACS, OV, CC and PM are visible parts of the invisible (privileged) register PSR (program status register) which also contains ACR and PRIV. Other invisible registers include SSR (system status), LSTB and PSTB (base registers for the local and public segment tables), an interval timer (IT) and an instruction counter (IC). The totality of registers is called the "image store."

held in the B register operating on an array addressed by a vector descriptor. A single hardware instruction is able to check that the subscript does not exceed the bound of the array, and to find the start address of the logical element required by scaling the subscript (using the size field in the descriptor). Special functions also exist for performing efficient index arithmetic on multi-dimensional arrays.

Since the 24-bit length field of a string descriptor (rather than the instruction itself) can determine the length of store-to-store operations for character manipulation, long operations can always be performed as single instructions[1], and need not be broken down into sequences of shorter operations (say 256 bytes in length), as on some machines.

These examples not only illustrate the tendency in the 2900 Series instruction set to efficiency and compactness of the object code produced, but point also to simplifications in the compilation phase by reducing the necessity for performing arbitrary tasks such as top of stack pointer manipulation, subscript scaling and character string length checkup.

6. The System as a Collection of Virtual Machines

Whilst not ignoring the problems raised by multiprogramming, the previous discussion has looked at the architecture largely from the view point of a single virtual machine. The emphasis now changes as we consider such questions as: How is the allocation of real resources (e.g. processor time, mainstore) to virtual machines controlled? How are external interrupts (e.g. peripheral interrupts) handled? How is the use of shared data segments synchronised? In other words, how can virtual machines be forced to co-operate with each other?

The answer must be: these tasks are carried out by one or more subsystems. We shall call them collectively the "Kernel." But how can the Kernel be integrated into the architectural model described above without distorting it beyond recognition?

One possibility would be to provide the Kernel with its own special virtual machine—an apparently attractive solution if we take external interrupts into account. But since the data necessary for handling interrupts (e.g. a peripheral request table) originates from procedure calls in other virtual machines, the solution in fact implies radical modifications to the architecture.

The alternative solution, to consider the Kernel as a component part of every virtual machine, also requires modifications but these are more in the spirit of our fundamental principles. The

Kernel will itself be held in public code segments in order that it can operate in any virtual machine, and will make use of public data segments to store information relating to such functions as scheduling. Some mechanism for synchronising the use of these shared data areas will of course be required to maintain the integrity of the data, and since the model has not placed restrictions on the use of public and global data segments this synchronisation problem can in fact arise in subsystems outside the Kernel. For this reason and because it does not solve the problem for a system with multiple processors, the use of non-interruptible code execution does not adequately solve the problem of synchronisation. The 2900 Series designers therefore included a variant of the semaphore solution [Dijkstra, 1968a].

The semaphore is an integer associated with a resource to ensure that it is allocated exclusively to one process at a time, and takes the values:

-1	Resource free
0	Resource in use—no waiting processes
1	Resource in use—one waiting process
$n(>0)$	Resource in use—n waiting processes

Assuming that processes co-operate by accessing shared tables, etc. via a semaphore (it is to their advantage to do so), then the mutual exclusion problem is limited to testing and updating the semaphore itself; this is solved by providing two non-interruptible hardware instructions—"increment and test" (which adds one to the semaphore and sets a condition code indicating its new status)—and "test and decrement" (which sets a condition code showing the status of the semaphore then decrements it by one).

"Increment and test" allows a process to request use of the semaphored resource and test whether the request was successful (condition code zero) or whether the process was merely added to the count of waiting processes (condition code positive).

"Test and decrement" allows a process to relinquish a semaphored resource which has been allocated to it, and to test whether the other processes are waiting (condition code positive). The missing link in this scheme, the ability of a process relinquishing the resource to advise a waiting process, is supplied by an event system which permits waiting processes to suspend on an "event" and relinquishing processes to cause the event.

Control of the event system is of course a function of the Kernel, and the scheme can be used independently of semaphores, to provide a general purpose synchronising facility. For example a user program can associate an event with a peripheral access request, and so be informed by event of the request termination. A process may cause an event, test for occurrence of an event, suspend on events, or nominate an interrupt routine to be entered on the occurrence of an event. The flexibility of the

---

[1]Such operations can be interrupted by hardware and subsequently resumed, thus ensuring that time critical interrupts are not delayed, and that virtual store interrupts arising from non-presence in main memory of (part of) one or both operands, can be serviced in mid-instruction.

event system is further improved by the provision of a primitive message passing facility (e.g. an indication of the success or failure of the peripheral request), thus creating a powerful mechanism for virtual machine synchronisation and communication.

There remains now the question of interrupt handling by the Kernel. Since we have defined the Kernel as a component of all process-images, it is evident that external interrupts will be accepted, and the initial decoding performed, in the currently active virtual machine. An attractive implementation of this is to treat interrupts as forced procedure calls, thus automatically storing the interrupted process state in the stack and at the same time creating a new working space for the interrupt routine. Unfortunately this solution runs into difficulties with interrupts whose purpose is to signify that there is no more space in main store at the top of the stack. Thus virtual store interrupts (and all interrupts of higher priority) are directed to a special stack known to the hardware, which, however, operates in all other respects like a normal stack.

Conclusion

The features of the 2900 Series system architecture described in this article are not peculiar to a particular model within the 2900 Series, but provide the basis at an architectural level for a compatible range of models, varying considerably in power and cost. This is achieved by means of two interfaces—the "Kernel Interface" which embodies the general architectural model, and the "Primitive Level Interface" which defines the instruction set and associated features. Neither of these interfaces can be regarded as a purely hardware interface, since the cost and power objectives of a particular model in the range will determine what is economic to implement as hardware, what as microprograms, what as software, etc.

The Kernel cannot be regarded as an operating system—it does not even provide a logical facility for communication between the operator and either the system or user programs—but is rather a primitive layer of software which provides further levels of software (operating systems, data management systems, etc.) with a consistent abstraction of the architectural model, regardless of the implementation details of individual computers in the range. Thus the Kernel Interface guarantees to the higher levels of software that resources (whether hardware resources such as peripheral channels or software resources such as events) are handled in a uniform manner and within the virtual machine framework provided by the lower level.

The Primitive Level Interface corresponds approximately to a hardware instruction set, but like the Kernel Interface, its description does not imply its mode of implementation. Thus it is to be expected that for smaller models in the range some functions (e.g. floating point operations) might be implemented in the Kernel software. Similarly whilst the larger models will use special rapid storage locations to implement registers, at the lower end registers might be implemented in ordinary main store locations. The importance of these two interfaces is that taken together they create an abstract machine which provides an efficient and reliable environment for the compilation and execution of user programs written in high level languages.

References

Dijsktra [1968a]; Doran [1975]; Dorn [1974]; Keedy [1976]; Organick [1972]; Organick [1973].

Section 3

Concurrency: Single-Processor Systems

At any given time, technology determines the major time constants (e.g., memory access time, microprocessor cycle time) that dictate the performance of an implementation. The simple two-parameter model involving microcycle time and memory pause time presented in Chap. 5 has been applied to three computer families and shown to be a good predictor of performance of minicomputers and maxicomputers (see Chaps. 39 and 52).

Computer implementations can exceed the performance available through technology alone by introducing concurrency into the organization. The degree of concurrency is the number of operations that are happening simultaneously. The concurrency in a structure is also a measure of its complexity; to have a highly concurrent structure implies control structure together with multiple data paths (and operations) that can be simultaneously active.

The impact of concurrency on software varies from none to need for totally new programming styles. Instruction prefetch and interleaved memory are two examples of hardware concurrency that are totally transparent to the software. Some concurrency techniques impact only the operating system (e.g., processor-I/O overlap) or impact user software in minor ways (e.g., in the imprecise interrupts in the IBM System S/360 Model 91). At the extreme, concurrency structures may not only require dedicated programming but also require entirely new algorithms (as do associative and multiple processors, for example). In general, only the first two levels of software impact are acceptable for general-purpose computing. The extreme level is usually acceptable only for solving special-purpose problems where the computer is actually a support processor to a general-purpose computer.

Table 1 lists the dimensions of the concurrency space. There are two major approaches to achieving concurrency: overlap of heterogeneous functional units and parallelism of homogeneous functional units.

Overlap

Processor-I/O

Consider the traditional view of a computer with processor, memory, and I/O. The earliest computers employed the processor to control I/O. Since the speed differential between electronic and mechanical technologies was two orders of magnitude, the processor was inefficiently utilized. When a small amount of logic was moved into the I/O device, the processor only had to start the

Table 1   Concurrency Dimensions

Overlap (heterogeneous functional units)
  Processor-I/O
    Polling
    Interrupts
  Processor-memory
    Instruction prefetch
      1
      n
    Cache
      Instruction
      Data
      Instruction/data
  Processor
    Pipeline
    Multiple function units
  Memory
    Memory interleaving
    Bus-memory overlap
    Multiword access
Parallelism (homogeneous functional units)
  Serial by bit
  Serial by character
  Parallel by word
  Parallel by bit slice of many words, serial by bit
    Associative processors
  Parallel by vector
  Parallel by array
  Multiple control units
  Multiple function units
    Asynchronous
    Lockstep
Replication of processors, memory, I/O
  1Pc
  1Pc-nPio
  1Pc-nPio-rP(display)
  mPc-nPio-rP(display)
  mPc-nP(array)
  Network

I/O operation and then continue non-I/O processing. Periodic polling of the state of I/O devices was used to determine I/O completion.

So that time would not have to be spent periodically polling I/O devices, the concept of an interrupt was introduced, whereby the I/O device signals the processor upon completion by forcing a change in the processor state. The processor state change involves the initialization of an interrupt-handling program. Interrupt schemes can be categorized by priority and number of levels:

- Single-priority, single-level. Interrupts are either totally enabled or disabled. When any interrupt is honored, the processor starts executing a program from a designated point in memory. Resolution of the identity of the interrupting I/O device is through polling.

- Single-priority, multiple-level. Interrupts are either totally enabled or disabled. When an interrupt is honored, the processor starts executing a program unique to the I/O device in which the interrupt has originated. No resolution of device identity is required.

- Multiple-priority, single-level. I/O devices are assigned prioritites and may interrupt only if their priority is higher than that of the currently executing program in the processor. All honored interrupts switch processor execution to a single interrupt program.

- Multiple-priority, multiple-level. I/O devices are assigned priorities, and when an interrupt is honored, an interrupt program unique to the device is evoked.

A critical measure of performance is interrupt response time, the time between an I/O device's requesting the attention of the Pc by posting an interrupt and the Pc's executing the first instruction of a program to service that I/O device. The selection of the interrupt scheme to employ in a computer is a function of a cost/response-time tradeoff. If response time is critical, computer implementations contain several register sets selectable by the interrupt scheme. Thus the time to switch the context (i.e., the state of the interrupted program) under program control is significantly reduced.

Processor-Memory

Another area of overlap in the traditional machine is between the processor and memory. For any given technology, memory speed is less than that of processor speed. This is partly due to the delays in accessing a word from a large memory array and partly to delays imposed by the processor-memory bus protocol. Thus ways have been developed to cut down memory-to-processor delays. Many of these schemes are based on using a memory that is of multiple word width (e.g., 2 words or 4).

One mechanism is to prefetch instructions so that the next instruction is available as soon as the processor is ready. Prefetching is implemented by fetching a block of instructions and storing them in an instruction buffer. The block can be transferred simultaneously (see the subsection Memory below) or sequentially (the next sequential instruction is fetched during the execution of the current instruction). In an n-instruction buffer, a block of instructions is kept in the local instruction buffer. Table 2 depicts

Table 2   Concurrency in Machines Treated in This Book

	Processor-I/O	Processor-memory	Processor	Memory	Parallelism
			Overlap		
IBM S/360-91	Interrupts	Instruction prefetch: eight 64-bit words	10-or more-stage pipe 3 arithmetic units	16-way interleaving 64-bit word access	Parallel by word Asynchronous multiple function units
CDC 6600	Interrupts in peripheral processing units	Instruction prefetch: eight 60-bit words	10 arithmetic units	32-way interleaving 60-bit word access	Parallel by word Multiple control units Asynchronous multiple function units
STARAN	Interrupts	User-controlled page loading: 512–4096 32-bit words	3-stage pipe	Separate data and instruction memories 5-way interleaving 32-bit word access	Serial by bit Parallel by bit slice
TI ASC	Interrupts	Instruction prefetch: eight 32-bit words Operand prefetch: eight 32-bit words	4-stage pipe for instructions 8-stage pipes for arithmetic units	8-way interleaving 256-bit word access	Parallel by word Multiple control units
Illiac IV	Interrupts	Instruction prefetch: eight 64-bit words	2-stage fetch/execute pipe	Separate data and instruction memories 8-way interleaving 512-bit word access	Parallel by word 64 lockstep functional units
CRAY-1	Interrupts	Instruction prefetch: 64 16-bit words	12 arithmetic units	16-way interleaving 64-bit word access	Parallel by word Multiple control units

the number of instructions at a time prefetched by machines in this book. These machines also represent a variety of techniques of when to update the instruction buffers as a function of the location of the program counter.

One problem with the instruction buffer technique is that it assumes the next instruction to be executed is the next one in sequence. This may not be true in the case of a branch instruction. Branch instructions not only occur frequently (measurements indicate that 25 to 30 percent of the dynamic instruction count consists of branches [Strecker, 1976a; and Lunde, 1977]) but may also impose a delay if the target instruction for the branch is not in the instruction buffer. At least two schemes have evolved to minimize the impact of branches:

- Make the instruction buffer large enough to hold program loops.

Machine	Number of instructions in instruction buffer
Illiac IV	128
CDC 6600	32 in FIFO stack
TI ASC	2 sets of 32
CRAY-1	4 sets of 64
IBM S/360-91	16 plus 4 branch target

- Also prefetch instructions from the branch target address in case it does not reside in the instruction buffer.

Chapter 18 contains a detailed discussion of the considerations in instruction prefetching and branching.

A generalization of the prefetch of sequential blocks of instructions is to provide for multiple segments of frequently used code to be in the instruction buffer. The CRAY-1 has four sets of instruction buffers that can be considered an instruction cache. Caches can be provided for instructions and operands. There may be separate caches, or instructions and operands may share the same cache. Caches are described in more detail in Sec. 2 of Part 2. Caches are included in processor-memory overlap because of their similarity to instruction buffers and because caches usually replace multiple words (e.g., set size) at the same time, with subsequent word replacement overlapped with processor execution.

Processor

Overlap is also possible among the various parts composing the processor. There are several distinct phases to the execution of an instruction: instruction fetch, instruction decode, effective-address calculation, operand fetching, execution, and storage of results. Normally these operations are carried on sequentially in time on the same set of hardware (in temporal sequencing) as

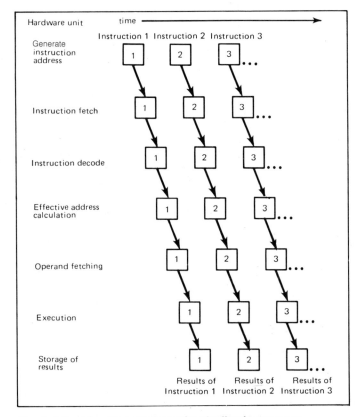

Fig. 1. A time-function diagram of a pipelined processor.

shown in the state diagram, Fig. 1. However, if specialized hardware is provided for each phase, instructions can move between phases (in spatial sequencing) and several instructions can be in various phases of completion at the same time.[1] Figure 1 illustrates the pipeline, sometimes referred to as an assembly-line, process. Each hardware unit starts on the next instruction as soon as it has completed an instruction. This pipeline has seven hardware units, hence seven stages. Thus up to seven instructions can be in execution at the same time. The pipeline is limited by, and lockstepped to, the slowest hardware unit. A completed instruction is produced every cycle of the slowest unit, or once every t time units.

Several factors complicate this simplistic view of pipelining. First, there are several aspects of program behavior that prevent the pipeline from realizing its maximum performance:

- Bubbles in the pipeline. Not all instructions will require every stage of the pipeline. In strict pipelines, such as in

[1]An elaboration of pipelining is to extend the ISP to include vector data-types so that the execution phase can also be pipelined.

the TI ASC (Chap. 45), instructions cannot bypass other partially executed instructions even if they do not need the hardware unit currently occupied and can use a different hardware unit that is currently unoccupied. If the pipeline is not organized so that the vast majority of the instructions require every stage in the pipeline, the effective speedup over nonpipelined processors will be substantially less than T_{total}/T_{slow} where T_{total} is the total time an instruction spends in the pipeline, and T_{slow} is the time spent in the slowest stage.

- Branches. Branches that change the sequence of program flow (so that the next instruction to be executed is not the next instruction in sequence) force the aborting of those instructions partially executed and a refilling of the pipeline. If such branches occur very frequently they can negate the performance gain of the pipeline. For example, if the fraction p of the instructions are branches that change the sequencing, then the limit value[1] of performance improvement over a nonpipelined processor is $1/p$. Various schemes have been developed for branch direction prediction in attempts to keep pipeline-emptying branch operations to a minimum. (See Chap. 18.) Another approach is to limit branches either by having compilers which pipeline or "vectorize" user code (see Chap. 45) or by providing vector data-types in the user-level language so that each instruction manipulates more data (see Chaps. 44 and 45).

- Large T_{slow}. Some instructions take much longer to execute than others (e.g., a floating-point divide takes longer than an integer add). Thus many instructions are held up by the slower operations. To alleviate this problem, multiple function units were introduced. In principle, any of the units in a pipeline can be replicated, or indeed the whole pipeline, as in the TI ASC with up to four pipes. However, the use of multiple function units has been applied mostly in the area of arithmetic operations: integer add, multiply, and divide; shift and logical; and floating add, multiply, and divide. Since the arithmetic functional units have differing completion times, instructions may actually finish out of sequence. This poses problems with respect to register usage, condition codes, and result storage. See Chaps. 18 and 19 for a detailed discussion of these problems.

Table 2 shows the use of pipelining and multiple function units in machines described in this book. A detailed survey of issues in pipelining can be found in Ramamoorthy and Li [1977].

Memory

A simple form of overlap in memory is the division of the memory array into modules. Figure 2 illustrates two forms of address

[1]For an n-stage pipeline, the expected throughput is $\sum_{i=0}^{n-1} (1-p)^i = [1-(1-p)^n]/p$. If it is assumed that n is large, the limiting throughput is $1/p$.

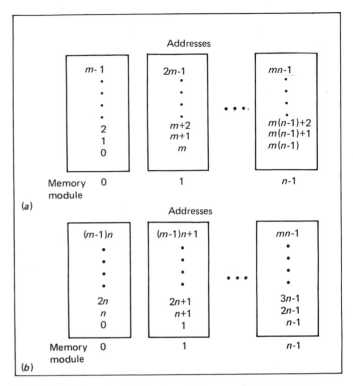

Fig. 2. (a) High-order interleaving. (b) Low-order interleaving.

assignment for a block of n·m memory words arranged m words per module. In low-performance systems, or systems where reliability is a major concern, high-order interleaving is used. High-order interleaving means that a memory module responds to only one pattern of high-order address bits (memory module 0 responds to 0 . . . 0, memory module 1 responds to 0 . . . 1, etc.) corresponding to blocks of m words with consecutive addresses in each memory module. The amount of memory in the system can be increased by simply adding more memory modules. And if a memory module fails, its only impact on the system is to make a contiguous block of memory inaccessible.

High-performance machines often employ low-order interleaving (Fig. 2b), where consecutive words are stored in different memory modules. Low-order interleaving can contribute to higher performance in two ways:

- Single-word requests. In the implementation of memories, it is often the case that the memory can provide the stored information (in what is known as access time, or t.access) faster than it can accept a new request (in what is called cycle time, or t.cycle). The ratio t.cycle/t.access is often in the range of 2 to 5. If references are staggered to enough different memory modules, the apparent memory response time can become arbitrarily close to t.access. Each memory module will have an apparent response time of t.access so long as it is not selected again within (t.cycle − t.access). Thus the (t.cycle − t.access) is overlapped with requests to other memory modules. The actual memory performance will be a function of the degree of interleaving (the number of memory modules), the ratio t.cycle/t.access, and the actual memory-reference pattern (see Chap. 10).

- Multiple-word requests. Blocks of adjacent memory words can be provided in t.access. Thus the apparent access time per word is reduced. (See Chap. 43.)

Another aspect of memory performance improvement is the overlap of processor-memory bus operations with the memory modules. Figure 3 illustrates a processor-memory bus cycle with a select time, a wait for memory to respond, a data transmission time, and the closing portion of the bus cycle. If memory is fast enough (as is memory 1), either through technology or interleaving, the recovery portion of the memory cycle can be overlapped with the remainder of the bus cycle. However, if the memory is slow (as is memory 2), then the bus cycle will incur an additional delay.

A way to minimize bus overhead is to transfer multiple memory words per cycle. This can be done either by a wider, multiword bus data path or by a bus subprotocol which sequentially sends multiple data words each bus cycle. Both techniques require either multiword-wide memory modules or memory interleaving to be effective. Table 2 lists the interleaving and number of bits accessed per memory cycle for machines described in this book.

Parallelism

Recall that parallelism is the concurrent operation by homogeneous functional units. The simplest form of parallelism deals with data-types and with how many bits are simultaneously involved in an operation.

Serial by Bit

At the most elementary level, only one bit of an n-bit word is operated on at a given time. There is no concurrency, and even the most trivial operations on n bits require a time proportional to n. The bit-serial processor was used in the first generation because the cyclic primary memories to which it connected were fundamentally bit-serial. Some bit- and byte-serial processors were implemented during the dawn of LSI technology in order to squeeze a processor onto a single chip. Bit-serial processors have also been used when either a large number of cheap processors were interconnected into a high-performance machine or the machine's word width was extremely large (see Chap. 21, where 256 serial processors are used on 256 bit/word data).

Serial by Character

ISPs that support variable-length character-string (e.g., business machines, such as the IBM 1401) or decimal-string (e.g., scientific calculators, such as the TMS1000, Chap. 34) data-types frequently are implemented to operate on a character or a digit at a time. Long or variable-length data strings are processed by iteration. Serial-by-character implementations (e.g., 4- or 8-bit data paths) of wide data-type ISPs (e.g., 16 or 32 bits) have been used for low-cost (e.g., IBM System/360 Model 30, Chap. 12) or technology-constrained (e.g., Intel 8080 and 8086, Chap. 37) implementations.

Parallel by Word

The simple parallel-by-word processor is the most common processor type. This has come about in part because main memories have become parallel by word. Within the processor almost every internal register-transfer operation requires one or more clock times. Most of these processors do only one operation at a time. As a rule, the simple processor is locked to the primary memory cycle time and approximately 2 to 10 events (clock times) are available within the processor per memory cycle.

Parallel by Bit Slice

Figure 4b contrasts the memory-processor organization of parallel-by-word and parallel-by-bit-slice machines. The parallel-by-bit-slice memory is sometimes referred to as a *look-aside memory*. Since one bit of all memory words is available on one access, it is possible to search all of memory simultaneously for specified contents by iteration on bit slices. This processor-memory organization is sometimes used to implement a content-addressable memory (e.g., a memory word can be selected by its contents or some attribute or a subfield of its contents rather than by address) or an associative processor.

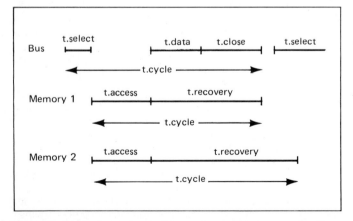

Fig. 3. Overlap of processor—memory bus with memory operation.

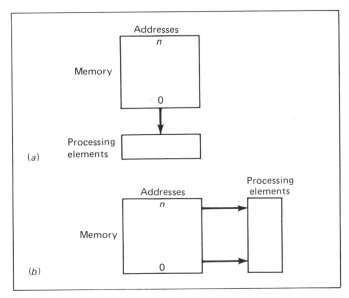

Fig. 4. (a) Parallel by word. (b) Parallel by bit slice.

Associative processors are particularly well suited to applications involving searching or matrix manipulation. Example applications are data base inquiry systems, image processing, seismic processing, and weather prediction. Chapter 21 describes one commercially available bit-sliced processor. Yau and Fung [1977] and Thurber and Wald [1975] provide a more extensive survey of associative processors.

Parallel by Vector

A conceptual extension to the parallel-by-bit-slice processor is the parallel by vector (a one-dimensional array of words) processor. Several machines have been called vector machines (see Chaps. 44 and 45). However, these machines do not operate on all elements of the vector at the same time, but rather employ pipeline techniques to operate on several elements concurrently.

Parallel by Array

Machines called *array processors* have been built (see Chaps. 20 and 21) which can actually operate on the elements of a vector simultaneously but which must execute a sequence of actions to perform an operation on an entire array.

Flynn [1966] categorized high-speed processors according to whether there are single (SI) or multiple (MI) instruction streams (i.e., one or more processors) and whether each stream has single (SD) or multiple (MD) data streams (i.e., vectors or arrays). The next three categories roughly correspond to Flynn's taxonomy.

Multiple Control Units. The concept of time-multiplexing a high-performance data-path unit among several control units has been employed in several machines. Each control unit maintains the Pc state of separate instruction streams. The data-path unit may be cyclically multiplexed among up to 10 control units with each control unit–data-path time slice appearing as an independent virtual machine. The relatively slower preformance of the control units is usually due to performance limits of low-cost memory, wherein the memory can supply data only at a fraction of the data-path unit's processing rate. Hence data-path utilization is driven up by parallel memory operation.

The cost of an *n*-control unit, time-multiplexed data-path unit should be contrasted to the cost of *n* separate computers each complete with control and data paths. The multiple control unit approach is cheaper when the computer is constructed from discrete or SSI logic. However, the advent of LSI with integral control and data on the same chip makes the separate computer approach more attractive. (See Part 2, Sec. 4, for details.)

Several of the computers that are described in this book have employed the multiple control unit approach to providing multiple peripheral processors (Pio's) for a high-performance Pc. Part 3, Sec. 4, outlines the evolution of the concept from the CDC 6600 (Chap. 43) to the TI ASC (Chap. 45) and the CRAY-1 (Chap. 44).

Multiple Function Units. In contrast to the multiple control unit approach, where the control unit, in fetching the data from Mp, is slow compared with the data-path unit, the multiple function unit approach is used when performance is limited by the data-path units. In such systems, there is considerable processor-memory overlap (e.g., through instruction prefetch, caching, memory interleaving, and multiword access) so that the access of data (instructions and operands) from memory is essentially at the speed of internal processor registers. Hence the bottleneck is the data operators, particularly the complex data operators (such as multiply and divide) or operators for complex data-types (i.e., floating-point).

Multiple functional units may operate asynchronously or in lockstep. Asynchronous functional units are usually heterogeneous, with the number of each unit type chosen in an attempt to balance the expected incidence of operators in the instruction stream and the execution time of the operator. Table 3 lists the type and number of units used in machines described in this book. Asynchronous functional units usually operate on one instruction stream. However, because of the parallelism and the unequal execution time, instructions may finish out of sequence. Hence, a complex control unit is required to ensure that instructions whose operands depend on the results of other instructions are not executed before the results are available. Resource allocation of the functional units must also be performed. This control resides

Table 3   Multiple Function Units

Machine	Multiple function units
IBM S/360 Model 91	Fixed Arithmetic Unit Floating Add Floating Multiply/Divide
CDC 6600	Increment (2) Fixed Add Fixed Multiply (2) Divide Shift Logical Branch Floating Add
CRAY-1	Fixed Add (3) Fixed Multiply Shift (2) Logical (2) Floating Add Floating Multiply Reciprocal Approximation Population Count

in the "scoreboard" for the CDC 6600. Chapter 19 describes in detail one possible control algorithm.

If the multiple function units operate in lockstep, performing the same operation on different data, an array organization called an *array processor* results. Chapter 20[1] describes a system with one central control unit and 64 processing elements (PEs). The control unit broadcasts an instruction to be executed by all PEs on local data. Each PE can make minor modifications of the broadcast instruction (usually of the form of operand address modification) or be programmed to ignore the instruction (via a centrally stored PE disable mask). Such array processors are suitable to a class of very structured problems, usually involving a large proportion of array data-types. To achieve the potential parallelism of an array processor, the programmer must pay particular attention to algorithm design and data placement. Hence array processors are usually treated as special-purpose machines that are attached to a general-purpose processor which provides program development support. See Kuck [1977] for a discussion of parallel programming considerations.

Replication of Processors, Memory, I/O. Another method to enhance performance is by replication of entire PMS components. The earliest form of replication was the attachment of specialized-function processors (e.g., I/O, display, and array processors) to

[1]STARAN also allows similar behavior.

offload a central processor. With the advent of LSI and the availability of low-cost processors, multiple processor systems have become popular. The number of dimensions in the multiple processor design space is so large that a detailed discussion of these systems requires two complete sections (see Part 2, Secs. 4 and 5).

Examples of Systems with Concurrency

This section contains details of three computers that span a wide range of concurrency techniques: the IBM System/360 Model 91, intended for general-purpose computing; the Illiac IV, intended for special-purpose array processing; and STARAN, intended for special-purpose associative processing. Each of these systems employs several concurrency techniques, and it is appropriate to study how these techniques are integrated into a single system. The available technology will dictate physical sizes (such as the bit-slice size of an associative processor) and time ratios (such as the relative ratio of memory fetch time to floating-point add). These parameters have a major impact on the final system implementation. As technology evolves, these sizes and ratios change, so that the optimal implementation architecture also changes. Nevertheless, it is entirely appropriate for the student to study these designs in detail, all the while searching for these key sizes and ratios. An interesting exercise would be to redesign these architectures using contemporary technology. (The student will have a chance to observe a design evolution through time in Part 3, Sec. 4, which traces the evolution from the CDC 6600 to the TI ASC and the CRAY-1).

The IBM System/360 Model 91

The goal of the Model 91 was to attain a performance increase of one to two orders of magnitude over the prior-generation machine, the IBM 7090. Since logic technology provided a speedup of only a factor of 4, the remaining factor was sought through organizational concurrency. Two papers from the January 1967 *IBM Journal* (Chaps. 18 and 19) provide a detailed discussion of the design parameters selected for the Model 91 implementation.

Chapter 18 describes the various concurrency techniques:

- Memory interleaving
- Multiword memory access
- Instruction pipeline
- Multiple arithmetic units
- Buffers to smooth data flow to and from memory, including instruction prefetch, operand prefetch, and operand storage

- Instruction interlocks
- Branch prefetch and loops
- Interrupt handling

Chapter 19 presents a general scheme for handling multiple arithmetic units. The various forms of System 360 instructions (i.e., register-register, register-storage, and storage-storage) are dynamically converted to a pseudoregister form. Precedence relations are maintained through a scheme of operand tagging and reservation stations (buffers) on operator inputs. Instruction prefetching plus 4-bit tags allows local optimization of programs dynamically to the point that storage into memory of intermediate results called for by the program may be used without waiting for the memory to be read on a subsequent instruction, since the intermediate results may be available to flow directly to its next usage point. Keller [1975] presents a generalization of operand tagging as well as discussions of other high-performance techniques.

Taken as a pair, Chaps. 18 and 19 lay out many of the design issues that must be resolved in such high-concurrency machines as the CDC 6600, the TI ASC, and the CRAY-1.

The Illiac IV

The Illiac IV project was initiated at the University of Illinois in 1966. Design goals called for 1,000 megaflop (millions of floating-point operations per second) achieved through both organizational and technological advances.

The organization of Illiac IV evolved from earlier SOLOMON design studies [Slotnick et al., 1962; Gregory and McReynolds, 1963]. These machines were designed for special-purpose problems with matrix data-types and a potential for a high degree of parallelism. This problem class includes differential equations, matrix manipulations, weather data processing, and linear algebra [Thurber and Wald, 1975].

As originally envisioned, the Illiac IV was to contain 256 processing elements (PEs) arranged in four quadrants of 64 PEs. In each quadrant, the PEs were to be arranged in an 8 by 8 array with each PE connected to its four nearest neighbors (north, south, east, and west). The interconnection pattern allows for high speed data sharing[1] between PEs. The PEs had 2048 words of local memory and executed instructions broadcast from a central control unit.

The Illiac IV project also chose to push the state of the art in technology. Emitter-coupled logic (ECL) was selected with 2- to 3-ns gate delays packaged 20 gates per chip. A 25-MHz clock rate

[1]For example, a two-dimensional differential equation can be solved by the "relaxation method," whereby each data point is iteratively replaced by the average of its north, south, east, and west neighbors until the change from one iteration to the next is below a preset error threshold.

and a 140-ns memory cycle time were also specified. Problems with crosstalk and noise margins in the ECL chips caused a reduction in chip size to seven gates per package. The decreased density lead to larger board area, increasing cabling, and increased delays. After more effort, Texas Instruments was able to commercially offer 20-gate ECL chips as a direct result of its work on the Illiac IV project. These chips were used in the TI ASC (Chap. 45).

Thin-film technology was initially selected for PE memories. However, the decreased ECL density consumed so much more space that the thin-film memory could not fit in the space that remained. Thus thin film was dropped in favor of 256-bit–bipolar-semiconductor memory chips produced by Fairchild.

Several technological firsts have been claimed for the Illiac IV [Feierbach and Stevenson, 1979] including:

- First large-scale use of ECL integrated circuits
- Earliest successful large-scale use of a design automation system, ouside of IBM, to design circuit cards
- First large-scale use of bipolar-semiconductor memory chips in a large computer's Mp
- First successful use of large, multilayer laminated circuit boards (12 layers)

Illiac IV was delivered to NASA's Ames Research Center in California in the spring of 1972 with Burroughs serving as the overall system contractor. Escalation of the total project cost (estimated at $31 million in 1972) forced cutting the architecture back to one quadrant with 64 PEs. Nagging technology problems prevented full operational status until 1975. In early 1979 the machine was available about 50 percent of the time for user jobs, with 20 to 40 hours per week going to actual repairs.

Illiac IV runs with stand-alone, single-user software [Falk, 1976]. General-purpose machines provide multiple-user software development aids. Applications include solution of two-dimensional aerodynamic flow equations, weather and climate prediction models, signal processing (e.g., beam forming, convolution, and fast Fourier transform), radiation modeling, linear programming, and finite-difference seismic simulations. In 1979, Illiac IV ran with a 13-MHz clock with practical operation of up to 15 million floating-point operations per second (megaflops). This contrasts with 5 megaflops for a CDC 7600 observed by Ames users and 138 sustained megaflops for a CRAY-1. At a logic complexity of a million gates, Illiac IV was the most complex operational computer structure of its day.

Figure 5 depicts the Illiac IV system as of early 1979. The 64 processing elements (PEs), their associated local memory, and the control unit are located at the bottom of the figure. The control unit can broadcast operands to all PEs and can fetch any word from the PE memory. Peak execution rate for hand-coded loops is about ½ million 64-bit floating-point operations per second.

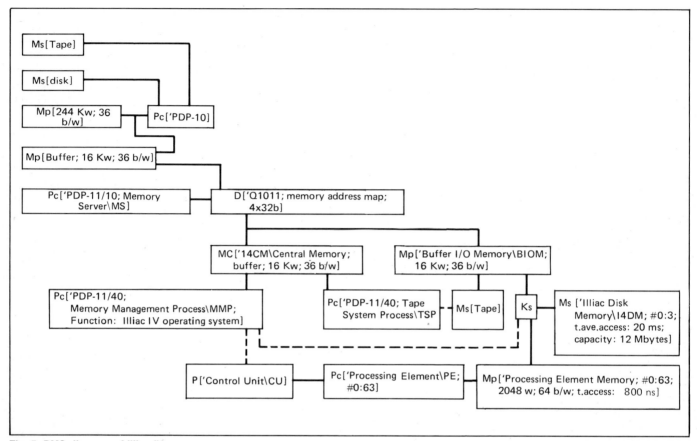

Fig. 5. PMS diagram of Illiac IV.

The backing store for Illiac IV is the 12 Mbyte, 500 Mbit/s fixed-head disk called I4DM (Illiac IV Disk Memory). Online mass storage is provided by PDP-10 Ms. When a data set is to be processed by Illiac IV, it is moved from PDP-10 files or tape into the PE's local memory and I4DM. Data between devices are moved via the Central Memory (I4CM). The Memory Management Process (MMP) implements Illiac IV file-transfer requests.

Figure 6 summarizes the maximum I/O rates and capacities of the Illiac IV memory hierarchy. As with many high-performance processors, the processor consumes data faster than the I/O system can provide them, forming an I/O bottleneck. Using Amdahl's rule of thumb of 1 bit of I/O per instruction per second (see Chap. 5 on performance), Illiac IV requires about 2^{25} bit/s of I/O. The I4DM/PE data path can supply 2^{29} bit/s, but the I4DM capacity is only 2^{29} bits or 16 s worth of data. Further data would have to come from magnetic tape at 2^{20} bit/s, a mismatch of a factor of 2^5. Thus one would expect that Illiac IV would perform well on problems requiring small amounts of data or data-intensive

problems of short duration. Even these classes of problems face an I/O bottleneck due to the latency in accessing data. The I4DM latency of 20 ms corresponds to 300 K to 800 K operations of the PEs.

Table 4 [Feierbach and Stevenson, 1979] summarizes the main applications using Illiac IV in early 1979. They were:

- **Aircraft/SAR.** Processing airborne Synthetic Aperture Radar (SAR) video data.
- **GISS.** Weather model.
- **I4TRES.** Seismic simulation.
- **LANDSAT.** Classification and color assignment of LAND-SAT images.
- **SHUTTLE.** Space shuttle reentry simulation.
- **2D-STRATO.** Model of chemical effects on stratosphere.
- **2D-TRANSONIC.** Simulation of transonic flow over two-dimensional airfoils.

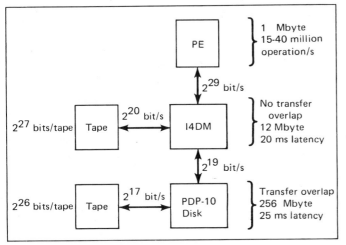

Fig. 6. Illiac IV data rates.

- 3D-Compress. Computing the velocity field for turbulent compressible flows.
- 3D-Galaxy. Simulating the formation and evolution of galactic structure due to gravitation.
- 3D-Incompress. Computing the velocity field for turbulent incompressible flow.

Table 4 illustrates the impact of latency and transfer time from I4DM. Latency varies from 1 to 125 percent of compute time, while latency plus transfer varies from 1 to 250 percent of compute time. Initial problem/data load time varies from less than 1 percent to 1,396 percent of compute time. Thus one of the major lessons to be learned from Illiac IV is that it is not sufficient just to

design a high-speed Pc, since low I/O data rates and/or long I/O latency can negate a significant portion of the Pc's performance.

STARAN[1]

In the spring of 1972 Goodyear Aerospace introduced the STARAN associative processor. Figure 7 depicts the overall organization of the STARAN B. STARAN was designed to operate either stand-alone or in conjunction with a host computer. The basic building block is an associative Array Module (AM). Each AM consists of a 256- by 256-bit memory array, 256 bit-serial processing elements (PEs), and a routing network that allows diverse forms of memory array accessing. A STARAN can consist of from 1 to 32 AMs. Because of their large number the PEs are serial processors with only elementary logic capability. Even common functions, such as add (see Chap. 21) have to be programmed from ANDs and EXCLUSIVE-ORs. However, this bit-serial nature allows for a high degree of variability in data-types and partitioning the memory arrays into subfields. In the follow-on STARAN E the user can specify floating-point numbers with 2 to 100 bits of mantissa and 7 to 11 bits of exponent. Fixed-point numbers can have 3 or more bits of representation.

A unique feature of the AMs is the variety of accessing modes available for the 256 by 256 memory array. Access may be to words, subfields of words, bit slices, every ith bit, etc. Control of the access mode is via an 8-bit code. Each accessing mode acts as a stencil to select a unique pattern of 256 bits from the AM. Some general rules for determining the access mode are:

- If the mode value contains n ones and $8 - n$ zeros, the stencil selects 2^n bits from each of $2^{(8-n)}$ memory words.

[1]TM Goodyear Aerospace Corporation, Akron, Ohio 44315.

Table 4   Characteristics of Some Major Illiac Programs

Applications	Compute time	I4DM latency time	PEM-I4DM transfer time	Total run time	System-I4DM transfer time
Aircraft/SAR	28	22 (79)	2 (7)	52 (186)	768 (1,396)
GISS	10,800	930 (8)	60 (0)	10,900 (101)	150 (1)
I4TRES	10,800	10,800 (100)	500 (5)	22,100 (204)	900 (8)
LANDSAT	210	3 (1)	3 (1)	216 (103)	540 (257)
SHUTTLE	790	300 (37)	10 (1)	800 (101)	60 (5)
2D-STRATO	950	480 (51)	15 (1)	965 (101)	700 (74)
2D-Transonic	1,110	640 (57)	250 (22)	2,000 (180)	40 (6)
3D-Compress	3,630	1,630 (45)	370 (10)	4,000 (110)	25 (0)
3D-Galaxy	2,000	740 (37)	45 (2)	2,045 (102)	360 (18)
3D-Incompress	400	500 (125)	100 (25)	10,000 (250)	20 (2)

Notes: Time in seconds; parenthetical numbers are percentage with respect to compute time.

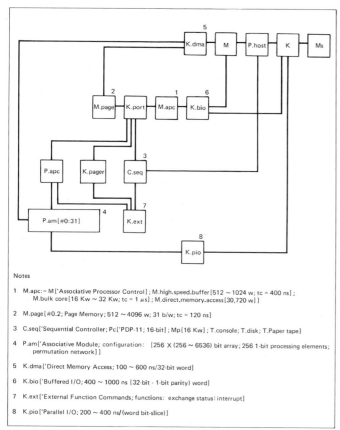

Notes

1 M.apc:= M ['Associative Processor Control] ; M.high.speed.buffer [512 ~ 1024 w; tc = 400 ns] ; M.bulk core [16 Kw ~ 32 Kw; tc = 1 μs] ; M.direct.memory.access [30,720 w]]

2 M.page [#0.2; Page Memory; 512 ~ 4096 w; 31 b/w; tc = 120 ns]

3 C.seq ['Sequential Controller; Pc ['PDP-11; 16-bit] ; Mp [16 Kw] ; T.console; T.disk; T.Paper tape]

4 P.am ['Associative Module; configuration: [256 X (256 ~ 6536) bit array; 256 1-bit processing elements; permutation network]]

5 K.dma ['Direct Memory Access; 100 ~ 600 ns/32-bit word]

6 K.bio ['Buffered I/O; 400 ~ 1000 ns [32-bit · 1-bit parity] word]

7 K.ext ['External Function Commands; functions: exchange status | interrupt]

8 K.pio ['Parallel I/O; 200 ~ 400 ns/ (word bit-slice)]

Fig. 7. PMS diagram of STARAN.

- If the leftmost n bits of the mode are 1s and the rightmost $8-n$ bits are 0s, then $2^{(8-n)}$ consecutive memory words (with the leftmost n bits assumed 0), and the leftmost n bits indicate the bit-sliced addresses (with the rightmost $8-n$ bits assumed 0).

If the rightmost n bits of the mode are 1s and the leftmost $8-n$ bits are 0s, then the $2^{(8-n)}$ memory words will be spaced 2^n apart. The 2^n accessed bits will be consecutive. The leftmost $8-n$ bits indicate the address of accessed words (with the rightmost n bits assumed 0), and the rightmost n bits indicate the bit-sliced address accessed (with the leftmost $8-n$ bits 0).

The most commonly used access modes are mode 0 and its complement, mode 255. Mode 0 is the bit-slice mode where 1 bit of each array word is accessed. Mode 255 is word mode and accesses 256 bits of one array word. Some useful accessing modes are listed in the following table.

STARAN Addressing Modes

Mode (base 2)	Number of selected words	Number of accessed bits
00000000	256 words spaced 1 apart	1 bit-slice mode
00000011	64 words spaced 4 apart	4 consecutive bits addressed 0–3
00001111	16 words spaced 16 apart	16 consecutive bits addressed 0–15
00111111	4 words spaced 64 apart	64 consecutive bits addressed 0–63
11111111	1	256 consecutive bits, word mode
11111100	4 consecutive words addressed 0–3	64 bits spaced 4 apart
11110000	16 consecutive words addressed 0–15	16 bits spaced 16 apart
11000000	64 consecutive words addressed 0–63	4 bits spaced 64 apart

The stencil can be positioned anywhere in the array memory by adding the displacement field from the accessing instruction to the starting address of the consecutive block of words or bits.

Once accessed, the data can be rearranged by a $2n$ flip-permutation and shift network [Batcher, 1977; Batcher, 1976]. The flip permutation takes an input bit of an input line I and assigns it to an output line

$$I \oplus G = (i_{n-1} \oplus f_{n-1},\ i_{n-2} \oplus f_{n-2}, \cdots,\ i_1 \oplus f_1,\ i_0 \oplus f_0)$$

where f is an n-bit flip-control vector and i_j, f_j are the n-bit binary representation of the input line position and F, respectively. For example, $F = 0$ represents the identity permutation. For $F = 2^j$, the flip permutation interchanges each group of 2^j lines. For $F = 2^n - 1$, data are completely reversed from end to end (this is the mirror permutation). The shift permutation is a shift of 2^m places modulo 2^p where m and p are integers such that $0 \le m < p \le n$. A shift of 2^m modulo 2^p divides the 2^n data items into groups of 2^p items each and shifts the items within each group right-end around 2^m places. Many diverse permutations can be developed by selection of flip/shift permutations or by successive passes of data through the flip network. For example, a left shift of data can be accomplished by a mirror flip, a positive shift, and a remirror flip. The flip network permutes data on memory-to-PE transfers, PE-to-PE transfers, and PE-to-memory transfers.

A single Associative Processor Control (APC) fetches instructions from control memory and broadcasts them to the PEs. The PEs may choose whether or not to execute the instruction according to a program-settable mask bit in each PE. The APC has 18 registers: a common register for AM input/output, an array register that specifies which AMs are to take part in an operation, a block length counter for block transfers, a data pointer for base addressing, four field-pointer registers for indexing, two field-length counters for specifying operand lengths, and eight branch and link registers for subroutine linkage and base addressing.

The APC allows overlap in instruction fetching and execution. Most STARAN instructions use only 31 bits. The 32d is a speedup bit that enables fetching of future instructions. The speedup bit is set to 1 if both the current instruction and the following instruction are not branches. If the speedup bit of instruction n is 1, the control unit starts fetching instruction $n + 1$ (if it has not already been started) and $n + 2$. The control unit fetch mechanism uses the following algorithm:

Speed-up bit of instruction

$n - 1$	n	*Fetch operation*
0	0	Wait until the address of the next instruction is determined and then fetch it.
0	1	Start fetching $n + 1$ and $n + 2$.
1	1	Start fetching $n + 2$ ($n + 1$ is already being fetched).
1	0	Do nothing ($n + 1$ is already being fetched).

Thus, there may be up to three instructions and instruction-addresses in the pipe at one time. The assembler sets the speedup bit whenever possible by examining the following statement before completing the assembly of an instruction.

The control memory is multiported and provides storage for application programs as well as buffer space for communication with a host computer. A variety of memory speeds are provided for each of the control memory functions, high-speed buffer and bulk core storage. Up to 30 K words of control memory is externally accessible via DMA.

The page memory is used for program storage. The first page is for the subroutine library, while pages 1 and 2 are for application code. The three pages are large enough to hold all instructions of most program loops (each page memory holds 512 words in STARAN B and 4,096 words in STARAN E). The APC reads instructions from one page while the other page is being loaded by the program pager. Thus the instruction pages act as a high-speed (120-ns) cache that must be explicitly managed by the user issuing page-memory load commands.

There are some advantages to user-controlled page loading:

- Blocks can be of any size.
- Blocks can be prefetched far in advance of their execution.
- Both sides of branches may be prefetched.

- Blocks may be left in the buffer if it is known they will be needed again in the near future.

Presumably, the programmer can take a global look at the program and do a better job of loading instruction buffers than hardware can. Unfortunately the task of deciding when and where to load the page memories is not easy and is done only to fine-tune a program for maximum speed. Most STARAN programs use static page loading. At load time, some of the program is loaded into pages whose contents are fixed during execution. If the program is short enough, all of it is loaded into the page memories. The larger page size of STARAN E makes this possible in many cases.

All the various STARAN controllers intercommunicate via the External Function (EXF) logic. Controllers issue 19-bit commands to the EXF and receive 1-bit sense signals in return.

STARAN provides a variety of channels for I/O:

- Direct Memory Access from the host processor up to 20 Mbytes/s for control memory or AM transfers
- Buffered I/O for block transfers up to 10 Mbytes/s/AM
- Parallel I/O directly into AMs up to 160 Mbyte/s/AM

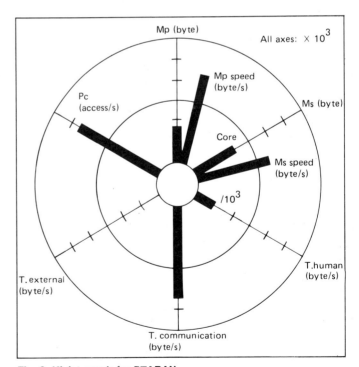

Fig. 8. Kiviat graph for STARAN.

Table 5   Performance Comparison of STARAN B versus Conventional Computer Systems

Project	STARAN time (t_S)	Conventional computer time (t_C)	Ratio (t_C/t_S)
LACIE			
Classification	8.0 min[a]	(360/75) 210 min[a]	26
Clustering	0.62 min[a]	(360/75) 35 min[a]	56
427 SPACE COMPUTATION COMPLEX			
SPG4 algorithm			
Worst case (512 objects)	451 ms[b]	(H6080) 1280 ms[b]	2.8
Best case (1536 objects)	180 ms[b]	(H6080) 7680 ms[b]	42.7
Digital photogrammetry			
Map production	3.4 min	(CDC 6400) 75 min	22.1
Stereo correlation	1.47 h[c]	(CDC 6600) 12.0 h[c]	8.1
SACWARDANS (data mgt.)			
Minimum load	9.54 min[d]	(H6080) 227.4 min[d]	23.8
Maximum load	1.32 h[d]	(H6080) 83.19 h[d]	63.0
Image averaging process	0.17 s	(360/195) 8.04 s[e]	47.3
	0.17 s	(360/65) 60.0 s[e]	353

[a] NASA data (Large Area Crop Inventory Experiment)

[b] Mitre data

[c] Army ETL data

[d] AF and PRC data (based on H6080 enhancement with STARAN, STARAN also results in 3 to 1 file reduction)

[e] U.S. government data

STARAN B has been programmed for two general types of application [Boulis, 1977]: bit-manipulation tasks (e.g., data base management, text searching, command and control, and air traffic control) and bit-group–manipulation tasks (e.g., image process-ing, signal processing, weather forecasting, reactor design, and fluid dynamics applications). STARAN B applications have been measured at 20 MOPs (million operations per second) using two arrays in an image-processing application [Vocar, 1977]. Table 5 illustrates the type of performance encountered over a range of applications.

The advent of larger memory chips provided the reason for reimplementation of the architecture as STARAN E. At the same time, some of the architectural shortcomings of the STARAN B were corrected. These modifications included longer word length (up to 65 kilobits), higher transfer rate between array and control memory (via an eight-port crossbar switch that allows for cycle-steal memory access among the AMs and between AMs and external devices), and larger page-memory sizes. Table 6 high-lights the major differences between the STARAN B and the STARAN E. Whereas STARAN B could execute a 1,024-point 16-bit real FFT in 3 ms, STARAN E requires only 0.6 ms.

Software primarily consists of a macro assembler, a linker, a loader, and debugging aids. Macros are provided for the common vector operations (e.g., FMPF, multiply array field by array field) so that the applications programmer does not deal with the bit-serial level of detail. Table 7 lists the STARAN instruction and macro instruction sets.

Table 6   Comparison of Staran Models B and E

Feature	STARAN B	STARAN E
Memory		
Page memory		
Size	512–1024 words	4096–8192 words
Speed	200 ns	100ns
High-speed data buffers		
Size	512–1024 words	512–8192 words
Associative modules		
Number of modules	1:32	1:8
Number of PEs	256:8192	256:2048
Memory array	256 by 256	256 by 256
Number of arrays per module	1	9:256
Instruction execution speed	120 ns	100 ns

Table 7   STARAN Macro-Apple Instruction Set [1]

I. Macro directives

LCLA	DECLARE LOCAL ARITHMETIC STRING
LCLC	DECLARE LOCAL CHARACTER STRING
GBLA	DECLARE GLOBAL ARITHMETIC STRING
GBLC	DECLARE GLOBAL CHARACTER STRING
MACRO	BEGIN MACRO DEFINITION
MEND	END MACRO DEFINITION
MGO	BRANCH CONDITIONALLY
MLMT	SET LIMIT ON NUMBER OF MGO STATEMENTS
MSET	ASSIGN VALUE TO MACRO VARIABLE SYMBOL
MDCL	DECLARE ARGUMENT FIELD SYMBOLS TO BE MACROS
MNOP	INSERT SEQUENCE SYMBOL
MNOTE	ISSUE MACRO ERROR MESSAGE
MEXIT	TERMINATE MACRO DEFINITION

II. Assembler directives

START	START APPLE SOURCE PROGRAM
END	END APPLE SOURCE PROGRAM
ORG	INITIALIZE LOCATION COUNTER
EQU	EQUATE VALUE TO SYMBOL
DF	DEFINE COMMON REGISTER OR ARRAY FIELD
DS	DEFINE STORAGE IN AP CONTROL MEMORY
TOF	ADVANCE TO TOP OF FORM
DC	DEFINE CONSTANT VALUE IN AP CONTROL MEMORY
GEN	GENERATE MACHINE INSTRUCTION
NOP	PERFORM NO OPERATION
DA	GENERATE CHARACTER STRING
EXTRN	REFERENCE EXTERNALLY DEFINED SYMBOLS
ENTRY	DEFINE EXTERNALLY REFERENCED SYMBOLS
AIF	CONDITIONALLY ALTER ASSEMBLY SEQUENCE
AGO	UNCONDITIONALLY ALTER ASSEMBLY SEQUENCE
ANOP	ASSIGN EXECUTION LOCATION COUNTER TO SYMBOL
AERR	INCREMENT ASSEMBLER ERROR COUNTER
NLIST	OPTIONALLY DISABLE ASSEMBLY LISTING
LIST	ENABLE ASSEMBLY LISTING

III. Branch instructions

B	BRANCH UNCONDITIONALLY
BZ	BRANCH IF REGISTER IS ZERO
BNZ	BRANCH IF REGISTER IS NOT ZERO
BBS	BRANCH IF COMMON REGISTER BIT IS SET
BBZ	BRANCH IF COMMON REGISTER BIT IS ZERO
BRS	BRANCH IF ANY Y RESPONSE STORE BIT IS SET
BNR	BRANCH IF ALL Y RESPONSE STORE BITS ARE ZERO
BOV	BRANCH IF ANY ARITHMETIC OVERFLOW
BNOV	BRANCH IF NO ARITHMETIC OVERFLOW
BAL	BRANCH AND LINK TO SUBROUTINE

RPT	REPEAT NEXT INSTRUCTION
LOOP	LOOP THROUGH AN ADDRESS

IV. Load and Store register instructions

LRR	LOAD REGISTER(S) FROM REGISTER(S)
LI	LOAD REGISTER(S) WITH IMMEDIATE VALUE
LR	LOAD REGISTER(S) FROM AP CONTROL MEMORY
SR	STORE REGISTER(S) IN AP CONTROL MEMORY
INCR	INCREMENT REGISTER(S)
DECR	DECREMENT REGISTER(S)
LPSW	LOAD PROGRAM STATUS WORD FROM AP CONTROL MEMORY
SPSW	SWAP PROGRAM STATUS WORD

V. Associative array instructions

A. Load Response Store (RS) Register

L	LOAD RS FROM SOURCE
LN	COMPLEMENT SOURCE, THEN LOAD RS
LOR	INCLUSIVE-OR SOURCE WITH RS
LORN	COMPLEMENT SOURCE, THEN INCLUSIVE-OR SOURCE WITH RS
LAND	AND SOURCE WITH RS
LANDN	COMPLEMENT SOURCE, THEN AND SOURCE WITH RS
LXOR	EXCLUSIVE-OR SOURCE WITH RS
LXORN	COMPLEMENT SOURCE, THEN EXCLUSIVE-OR SOURCE WITH RS
LC	LOAD COMMON REGISTER FROM FIELD IN ARRAY WORD
LCM	LOAD COMMON REGISTER FIELD FROM FIELD IN ARRAY WORD
LCW	LOAD COMMON REGISTER FROM RESPONSE STORE REGISTER FIELD
SET	SET RESPONSE STORE REGISTER
CLR	CLEAR RESPONSE STORE REGISTER
ROT	ROTATE RESPONSE STORE OR COMMON REGISTER

B. Store Response Store (RS) Register

S	STORE RS INTO ASSOCIATIVE ARRAY
SM	STORE MASKED RS INTO ARRAY
SN	COMPLEMENT RS, THEN STORE RS INTO ARRAY
SNM	COMPLEMENT RS, THEN STORE MASKED RS INTO ARRAY
SOR	INCLUSIVE-OR RS WITH ARRAY
SORM	INCLUSIVE-OR MASKED RS WITH ARRAY
SORN	COMPLEMENT RS, THEN INCLUSIVE-OR RS WITH ARRAY
SORNM	COMPLEMENT RS, THEN INCLUSIVE-OR MASKED RS WITH ARRAY
SAND	AND RS WITH ARRAY
SANDM	AND MASKED RS WITH ARRAY

[1]Goodyear Aerospace Corp.

SANDN	COMPLEMENT RS, THEN AND RS WITH ARRAY
SANDNM	COMPLEMENT RS, THEN AND MASKED RS WITH ARRAY
SC	STORE COMMON REGISTER INTO FIELD IN ARRAY OR RS
SCW	STORE COMMON REGISTER INTO FIELD IN SINGLE RS OR ARRAY WORD

C. Parallel array field searches †

EQC	ARRAY FIELDS EQUAL TO COMMON REGISTER FIELD
EQF	EQUAL ARRAY FIELDS
NEC	ARRAY FIELDS NOT EQUAL TO COMMON REGISTER FIELD
NEF	NOT EQUAL ARRAY FIELDS
GTC	ARRAY FIELDS GREATER THAN COMMON REGISTER FIELD
GTF	GREATER THAN ARRAY FIELDS
GEC	ARRAY FIELDS GREATER THAN OR EQUAL TO COMMON REGISTER FIELD
GEF	GREATER THAN OR EQUAL ARRAY FIELDS
LTC	ARRAY FIELDS LESS THAN COMMON REGISTER FIELD
LTF	LESS THAN ARRAY FIELD
LEC	ARRAY FIELDS LESS THAN OR EQUAL TO COMMON REGISTER FIELD
LEF	LESS THAN OR EQUAL ARRAY FIELDS
MAXF	MAXIMUM (HIGHEST) ARRAY FIELD(S)
MINF	MINIMUM (LOWEST) ARRAY FIELD(S)
NHI	ARRAY FIELDS NEXT HIGHER THAN COMMON REGISTER FIELD
NLO	ARRAY FIELDS NEXT LOWER THAN COMMON REGISTER FIELD
BLC	ARRAY FIELDS GREATER THAN COMMON REGISTER AND LESS THAN BLOCK LENGTH COUNTER/DATA POINTER
ZF	ARRAY FIELDS EQUAL TO ZERO
NZF	ARRAY FIELDS NOT EQUAL TO ZERO

D. Parallel array field moves †

MVF	MOVE ARRAY FIELD INTO ARRAY FIELD
MVCF	MOVE ONE'S COMPLEMENT OF ARRAY FIELD INTO ARRAY FIELD
MVNF	MOVE NEGATIVE OF ARRAY FIELD INTO ARRAY FIELD
MVAF	MOVE ABSOLUTE VALUE OF ARRAY FIELD INTO ARRAY FIELD
INCF	MOVE ARRAY FIELD WITH INCREMENT INTO ARRAY FIELD
DECF	MOVE ARRAY FIELD WITH DECREMENT INTO ARRAY FIELD

E. Parallel array field logical operations †

ORC	INCLUSIVE-OR COMMON REGISTER FIELD WITH ARRAY FIELD
ORF	INCLUSIVE-OR ARRAY FIELD WITH ARRAY FIELD
ANDC	AND COMMON REGISTER FIELD WITH ARRAY FIELD
ANDF	AND ARRAY FIELD WITH ARRAY FIELD
XORC	EXCLUSIVE-OR COMMON REGISTER FIELD WITH ARRAY FIELD
XORF	EXCLUSIVE-OR ARRAY FIELD WITH ARRAY FIELD
CMPC	COMPLEMENT COMMON REGISTER FIELD INTO ARRAY FIELD
SETF	SET ARRAY FIELD
CLRF	CLEAR ARRAY FIELD

F. Parallel array field arithmetic operations †

1. Fixed point

ADC	ADD COMMON REGISTER FIELD TO ARRAY FIELD
ADF	ADD ARRAY FIELD TO ARRAY FIELD
SBC	SUBTRACT COMMON REGISTER FIELD FROM ARRAY FIELD
SBF	SUBTRACT ARRAY FIELD FROM ARRAY FIELD
ISBC	SUBTRACT ARRAY FIELD FROM COMMON REGISTER FIELD
MPC	MULTIPLY ARRAY FIELD BY COMMON REGISTER FIELD
MPE	MULTIPLY ARRAY FIELD BY ARRAY FIELD
DVC	DIVIDE ARRAY FIELD BY COMMON REGISTER FIELD
DVF	DIVIDE ARRAY FIELD BY ARRAY FIELD
SQRTF	CALCULATE SQUARE ROOT OF ARRAY FIELD

2. Floating point

(a) Single precision (8 bit exponent; 24 bit mantissa)

FADC	ADD COMMON REGISTER FIELD TO ARRAY FIELD
FADF	ADD ARRAY FIELD TO ARRAY FIELD
FSBC	SUBTRACT COMMON REGISTER FIELD FROM ARRAY FIELD
FSBF	SUBTRACT ARRAY FIELD FROM ARRAY FIELD
FISBC	SUBTRACT ARRAY FIELD FROM COMMON REGISTER FIELD
FMPC	MULTIPLY ARRAY FIELD BY COMMON REGISTER FIELD
FMPF	MULTIPLY ARRAY FIELD BY ARRAY FIELD
FDVC	DIVIDE ARRAY FIELD BY COMMON REGISTER FIELD
FDVF	DIVIDE ARRAY FIELD BY ARRAY FIELD
FSQRTF	CALCULATE SQUARE ROOT OF ARRAY FIELD

†All instructions in these groups are understood to be applied to masked words.

(b) Double precision (8 bit exponent; 56 bit mantissa)

DADF	ADD ARRAY FIELD TO ARRAY FIELD
DSBF	SUBTRACT ARRAY FIELD FROM ARRAY FIELD
DMPF	MULTIPLY ARRAY FIELD BY ARRAY FIELD
DDVF	DIVIDE ARRAY FIELD BY ARRAY FIELD
DSQRTF	CALCULATE SQUARE ROOT OF ARRAY FIELD

G. Miscellaneous parallel array instructions

FIND	FIND FIRST RESPONDER(Y RESPONSE STORE BITS SET)
STEP	STEP TO FIRST RESPONDER AND CLEAR IT
RESVFST	STEP TO FIRST RESPONDER AND CLEAR ALL OTHERS
COUNTRS	COUNT RESPONDERS
SHIFTY	SHIFT Y END-OFF (OPTIONAL Pio REQUIRED)
ROTATY	ROTATE Y END-AROUND (OPTIONAL Pio REQUIRED)

VI. Control and Test instructions

INT	CONTROL AND TEST INTERRUPT
ILOCK	CONTROL AND TEST INTERLOCK
WAIT	DEACTIVATE AP
RUN	START LOADING OVERLAY MODULE
RUNBF	IDENTIFY OVERLAY MODULE
IOWAIT	WAIT OR BRANCH IF I/O IS BUSY
INSTP	INTERRUPT SEQUENTIAL PROCESSOR PROGRAM
EXIT	TRANSFER CONTROL TO BATCH OPERATING SYSTEM (BOS)

VII. Input/Output (I/O) instructions

A. Standard I/O instructions

OPEN	INITIALIZE DATASET
OBUFF	DEFINE I/O DATASET
READ	START READING
RBUFF	DEFINE INPUT BUFFER
WRITE	START WRITING
WBUFF	DEFINE OUTPUT BUFFER
CLOSE	RELEASE DATASET

B. Optional parallel I/O (Pio) instructions

TPIO	CONTROL AND TEST Pio CONTROL
MAM	MOVE DATA FROM ARRAY TO ARRAY
SAM	STORE DATA FROM ARRAY INTO AP CONTROL MEMORY
LAM	LOAD DATA IN ARRAY FROM AP CONTROL MEMORY
DPIO	DEFINE Pio MOVE, STORE, OR LOAD

VIII. Program pager instructions

STRTSG	START PAGE SEGMENT
ENDSG	END PAGE SEGMENT
MVSG	MOVE PAGE SEGMENT
MVSGI	MOVE PAGE SEGMENT IMMEDIATELY
PAGER	CONTROL AND TEST PROGRAM PAGER

As of January 1979, five STARANs have been built. A listing of the configuration of existing STARAN systems is given in Table 8. All STARAN systems include one AP array, AP control, control memory, program pager, sequential controller, disk, line printer, card reader, and control terminal.

Table 8   STARAN Configuration

System	Series	Arrays†	Pio	Comments
1	B	4	Yes	
2	B	4	Yes	Parallel-head disk
3	B	2	No	
4	B	2	No	Multiple tape units
5	E	4	No	Cross bar I/0 to array

†B arrays are 256 PEs by 256 bits.

  E arrays are 256 PEs by 9,216 bits.

References

Barnes, Brown, Kato, Kuck, Slotnick, and Stokes [1968]; Batcher [1976]; Batcher [1977]; Boulis and Faiss [1977]; Falk [1976]; Feierbach and Stevenson [1979]; Flynn [1966], Gregory and McReynolds [1963]; Keller [1975]; Kuck [1968]; Lunde [1977]; Ramamoorthy and Li [1977]; Ruben, Faiss, Lyon, and Quinn [1976]; Slotnick et al. [1962]; Thurber and Wald [1975]; Vocar and Faiss [1977]; Yau and Fung [1977].

Chapter 18

The IBM System/360 Model 91: Machine Philosophy and Instruction-Handling[1]

D. W. Anderson / F. J. Sparacio / F. M. Tomasulo

Abstract The System/360 Model 91 central processing unit provides internal computational performance one to two orders of magnitude greater than that of the IBM 7090 Data Processing System through a combination of advancements in machine organization, circuit design, and hardware packaging. The circuits employed will switch at speeds of less than 3 nsec, and the circuit environment is such that delay is approximately 5 nsec per circuit level. Organizationally, primary emphasis is placed on (1) alleviating the disparity between storage time and circuit speed, and (2) the development of high speed floating-point arithmetic algorithms.

This paper deals mainly with item (1) of the organization. A design is described which improves the ratio of storage bandwidth and access time to cycle time through the use of storage interleaving and CPU buffer registers. It is shown that history recording (the retention of complete instruction loops in the CPU) reduces the need to exercise storage, and that sophisticated employment of buffering techniques has reduced the effective access time. The system is organized so that execution hardware is separated from the instruction unit; the resulting smaller, semiautonomous "packages" improve intra-area communication.

Introduction

This paper presents the organizational philosophy utilized in IBM's highest performance computer, the System/360 [Amdahl, Blaauw, and Brooks, 1964] Model 91. The first section of the paper deals with the development of the assembly-line processing approach adopted for the Model 91. The organizational techniques of storage interleaving, buffering, and arithmetic execution concurrency required to support the approach are discussed. The final topic of this section deals with design refinements which have been added to the basic organization. Special attention is given to minimizing the time lost due to conditional branches, and the basic interrupt problem is covered.

The second section is comprised of a treatment of the instruction unit of the Model 91. It is in this unit that the basic control is exercised which leads to attainment of the performance objectives. The first topic is the fetching of instructions from storage. Branching and interrupting are discussed next. Special handling

[1]*IBM Journal*, vol. 11, January 1967, pp. 8–24.

of branching, such that storage accessing by instructions is sometimes eliminated, is also treated. The final section discusses the interlocks required among instructions as they are issued to the execution units, the initiation of operand fetches from storage, status switching operations, and I/O handling.

CPU Organization

The objective of the Model 91 is to attain a performance greater by one to two orders of magnitude than that of the IBM 7090. Technology (that is, circuitry and hardware) advances[2] alone provide only a four-fold performance increase, so it is necessary to turn to organizational techniques for the remaining improvement. The appropriate selection of existing techniques and the development of new organizational approaches were the objectives of the Model 91 CPU design.

The primary organizational objective for a high performance CPU is concurrency—the parallel execution of different instructions. A consideration of the sequence of functions involved in handling a typical processor instruction makes the need for this approach evident. This sequence—instruction fetching, instruction decoding, operand address generating, operand fetching, and instruction execution—is illustrated in Fig. 1. Clearly, a primary goal of the organization must be to avoid the conventional concatenation of the illustrated functions for successive instructions. Parallelism accomplishes this, and, short of simultaneously performing identical tasks for adjacent instructions, it is desired to "overlay" the separate instruction functions to the greatest possible degree. Doing this requires separation of the CPU into loosely coupled sets of hardware, much like an assembly line, so that each hardware set, similar to its assembly line station counterpart, performs a single specific task. It then becomes

[2]Circuits employed are from the IBM ASLT family and provide an in-environment switching time in the 5 nsec range.

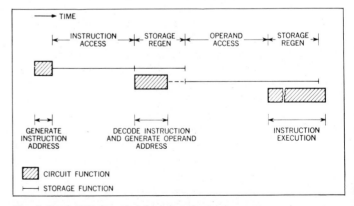

Fig. 1. Typical instruction function time sequence.

possible to enter instructions into the hardware sets at shortly spaced time intervals. Then, following the delay caused by the initial filling of the line, the execution results will begin emerging at a rate of one for each time interval. Figure 2 illustrates the objective of the technique.

Defining the time interval (basic CPU clock rate) around which the hardware sets will be designed requires the resolution of a number of conflicting requirements. At first glance it might appear that the shorter the time interval (i.e., the time allocated to successive assembly line stations), the faster the execution rate will be for a series of instructions. Upon investigation, however, several parameters become apparent which frustrate this seemingly simple pattern for high performance design. The parameters of most importance are:

1 An assembly-line station platform (hardware "trigger") is necessary within each time interval, and it generally adds a circuit level to the time interval. The platform "overhead" can add appreciably to the total execution time of any one instruction since a shorter interval implies more stations for any pre-specified function. A longer instruction time is significant when sequential instructions are logically dependent. That is, instruction n cannot proceed until instruction $n + 1$ is completed. The dependency factor, therefore, indicates that the execution time of any individual instruction should not be penalized unnecessarily by overhead time delay.

2 The amount of control hardware—and control complexity—required to handle architectural and machine organization interlocks increases enormously as the number of assembly line stations is increased. This can lead to a situation for which the control paths determining the gating between stations contain more circuit levels than the data paths being controlled.

Parameters of less importance which influence the determination of the basic clock rate include:

1 The number of levels needed to implement certain basic data paths, e.g., address adders, instruction decoders, etc.

2 Effective storage access time, especially when this time is relatively short. Unless the station-to-station time interval of the CPU is a sub-multiple of storage access time the synchronization of storage and CPU functions will involve overhead time.

Judgment, rather than algorithms, gave the method by which the relative weights of the above parameters were evaluated to determine the basic station-to-station time interval.[1] The interval selected led to a splitting of the instruction handling functions as illustrated in Fig. 3.[2]

It can be seen in Fig. 3 that the basic time interval accommodates the assembly line handling of most of the basic hardware functions. However, the storage and many execution operations

[1] The design objective calls for a 60 nsec basic machine clock interval. The judgment exercised in this selection was tempered by a careful analysis of the number of circuit levels, fan in, fan out, and wiring lengths required to perform some of the basic data path and control functions. The analysis indicated that 11 or 12 circuit levels of 5–6 nsec delay per level were required for the worst-case situations.

[2] Figure 3 also illustrates that the hardware sets are grouped into larger units—instruction unit, main storage control element, fixed-point execution unit, floating-point execution unit. The grouping is primarily caused by packaging restrictions, but a secondary objective is to provide separately designable entities having minimum interfacing. The total hardware required to implement the required CPU functions demands three physical frames, each having dimensions 66″ L × 15 ″ D × 78″ H. The units are allocated to the frames in such a way as to minimize the effects of interframe transmission delays.

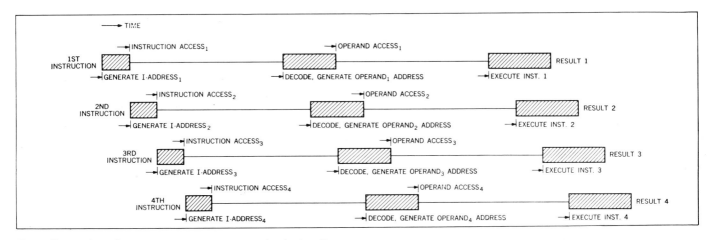

Fig. 2. Illustration of concurrency among successive instructions.

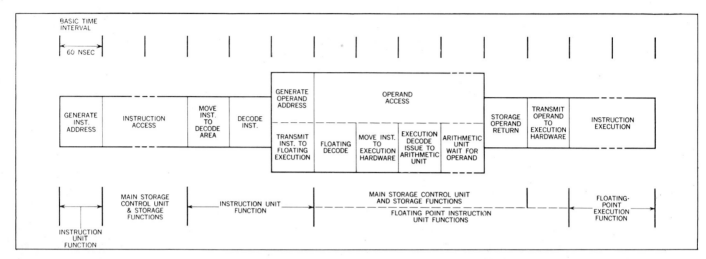

Fig. 3. CPU assembly-line stations required to accommodate a typical floating-point storage-to-register instruction.

require a number of basic intervals. In order to exploit the assembly line processing approach despite these time disparities, the organizational techiques of storage interleaving [Buchholz, 1962], arithmetic execution concurrency, and buffering are utilized.

Storage interleaving increases the storage bandwidth by enabling multiple accesses to proceed concurrently, which in turn enhances the assembly line handling of the storage function. Briefly, interleaving involves the splitting of storage into independent modules (each containing address decoding, core driving, data read-out sense hardware, and a data register) and arranging the address structure so that adjacent words—or small groups of adjacent words—reside in different modules. Figure 4 illustrates the technique.

The depth of interleaving required to support a desired concurrency level is a function of the storage cycle time, the CPU storage request rate, and the desired effective access time. The

effective access time is defined as the sum of the actual storage access time, the average time spent waiting for an available storage, and the communication time between the processor and storage.[1]

Execution concurrency is facilitated first by the division of this function into separate units for fixed-point execution and floating-point execution. This permits instructions of the two classes to be executed in parallel; in fact, as long as no cross-unit dependencies exist, the execution does not necessarily follow the sequence in which the instructions are programmed.

Within the fixed-point unit, processing proceeds serially, one instruction at a time. However, many of the operations required only one basic time interval to execute, and special emphasis is placed on the storage-to-storage instructions to speed up their execution. These instructions (storage-to-storage) enable the Model 91 to achieve a performance rate of up to 7 times that of the System/360 Model 75 for the "translate-and-test" instruction. A number of new concepts and sequences [Litwiller and Adler] were developed to achieve this performance for normally storage access-dependent instructions.

The floating-point unit is given particular emphasis to provide additional concurrency. Multiple arithmetic execution units, employing fast algorithms for the multiply and divide operations and carry look-ahead adders, are utilized [Anderson, Earle, Goldschmidt, and Powers, 1967]. An internal bus has been designed [Tomasulo, 1967] to link the multiple floating-point execution units. The bus control correctly sequences dependent

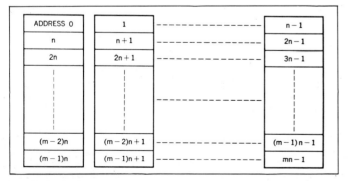

Fig. 4. Arrangement of addresses in *n* storage modules of *m* words per module.

[1]Effective access times ranging from 180–600 nsec are anticipated, although the design of the Model 91 is optimized around 360 nsec. Interleaving 400 nsec/cycle storage modules to a depth of 16 satisfies the 360 nsec effective access design point.

"strings" of instructions, but permits those which are independent to be executed out of order.

The organizational techniques described above provide balance between the number of instructions that can be prepared for arithmetic execution and those that can actually be executed in a given period, thereby preventing the arithmetic execution function from creating a "bottleneck" in the assembly line process.

Buffering of various types plays a major role in the Model 91 organization. Some types are required to implement the assembly line concept, while others are, in light of the performance objectives, architecturally imposed. In all cases the buffers provide queueing which smooths the total instruction flow by allowing the initiating assembly line stations to proceed despite unpredictable delays down the line. Instruction fetch, operand fetch, operand store, operation, and address buffering are utilized among the major CPU units as illustrated in Fig. 5.[1]

Instruction fetch buffering provides return data "sinks" for

previously initiated instruction storage requests. This prefetching hides the instruction access time for straight-line (no branching) programs, thereby providing a steady flow of instructions to the decoding hardware. The buffering is expanded beyond this need to provide the capacity to hold program loops of meaningful size. Upon encountering a loop which fits, the buffer locks onto the loop and subsequent branching requires less time, since it is to the buffers rather than to storage. The discussion of branching given later in this paper gives a detailed treatment of the loop action.

Operand fetch buffers effectively provide a queue into which storage can "dump" operands and from which execution units can obtain operands. The queue allows the isolation of operand fetching from operand usage for the storage-to-register and storage-to-storage instruction types. The required depth[2] of the queue is a function of the number of basic time intervals required for storage accessing, the instruction "mix" of the operating program, and the relative time and frequency of execution bottlenecks. Operand store buffering provides the same function as fetch buffering, except that the roles of storage and execution

---

[1]Eight 64-bit double words comprise the array of instruction buffers. Six 32-bit operand buffers are provided in the fixed-point execution unit, while six 64-bit buffers reside in the floating-point execution unit. Three 64-bit store operand buffers along with three store address and four conflict address buffers are provided in the main storage control element. Also, there are six fixed-point and eight floating-point operand buffers.

[2]To show precise algorithms defining these and other buffering requirements is impractical, since different program environments have different needs. The factors considered in selecting specific numbers are cited instead.

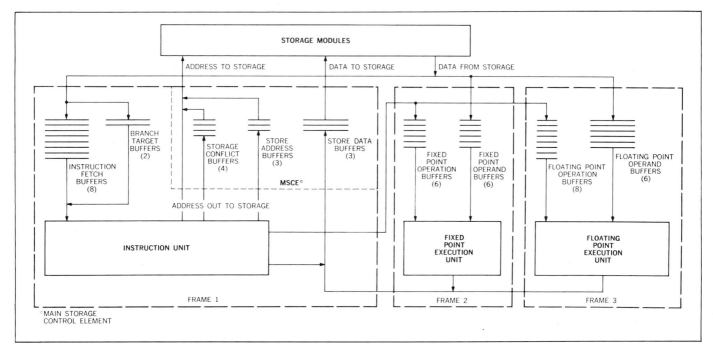

Fig. 5. Buffer allocation and function separation.

are reversed. The number of store buffers required is a function of the average waiting time encountered when the desired storage module is busy and the time required for the storage, when available, to utilize the operand.

Operation buffers in the fixed-point and floating-point execution units allow the instruction unit to proceed with its decoding and storage-initiating functions while the execution units wait for storage operands or execution hardware. The depth of the operation buffering is related to the amount of operand buffering provided and the "mix" of register-to-register and storage-to-register instruction types.

Address buffering is used to queue addresses to busy storage modules and to contain store addresses during the interval between decoding and execution of store instructions. The instruction unit is thereby allowed to proceed to subsequent instructions despite storage conflicts or the encountering of store operations. These buffers have comparators associated with them to establish logical precedence when conflicting program references arise. The number of necessary store address buffers is a function of the average delay between decode and execution, while the depth of the queue caused by storage conflicts is related to the probable length of time a request will be held up by a busy storage module [Boland, Granito, Marcotte, Messina, and Smith, 1967].

Concurrency Limitations

The assembly line processing approach, using the techniques of storage interleaving, arithmetic concurrency, and buffering, provides a solid high-performance base. The orientation is toward smooth-flowing instruction streams for which the assembly line can be kept full. That is, as long as station n need only communicate with station $n + 1$ of the line, highest performance is achieved. For example, floating-point problems which fit this criterion can be executed internally on the Model 91 at up to 100 times the internal speed of the 7090 [Flynn and Low, 1967].

There are, however, cases where simple communication between adjacent assembly line stations is inadequate, e.g., list processing applications, branching, and interrupts. The storage access time and the execution time are necessarily sequential between adjacent instructions. The organization cannot completely circumvent component delay in such instances, and the internal performance gain diminishes to about one order of magnitude greater than that of the 7090.

The list processing application is exemplified by sequentialism in addressing, which produces a major interlock situation in the Model 91. The architecturally specified usage of the general purpose registers (GPR's) for both address quantities and fixed-point data, coupled with the assembly line delay between address generation and fixed-point execution, leads to the performance slowdown. Figure 6 illustrates the interlock and the resulting delay. Instructions n and $n + 1$ set up the interlock on GPR X since they will alter the contents of X. The decode of $n + 3$ finds that the contents of X are to be used as an address parameter, and since the proper contents are not available $n + 3$ must wait until $n + 1$ is executed. The interlock technique involves assigning the decode area a status count for each GPR. A zero status count indicates availability. As fixed-point instructions pass through the decode, they increment the appropriate counter(s). A decode

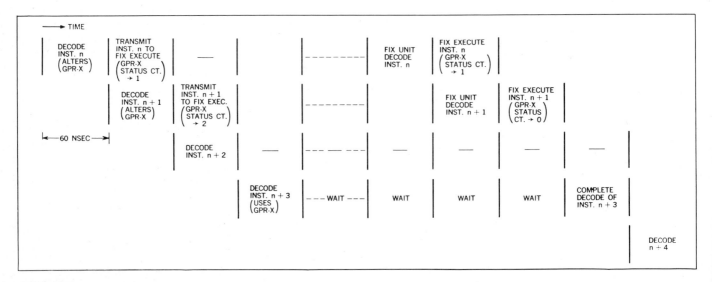

Fig. 6. GPR address interlock.

requiring an unavailable (non-zero status count) GPR cannot be completed. As the fixed-point execution unit completes instructions it decrements the appropriate counter(s), thus eventually freeing the register.

Branching leads to another sequential situation, since a disruption in the instruction supply is created. (Techniques employed to minimize or circumvent the storage access delay involved in obtaining the new instructions are discussed under *Instruction Supplying* in the following section of this paper.) Conditional branching poses an additional delay in that the branch decision depends on the outcome of arithmetic operations in the execution units. The Model 91 has a relatively lower performance in cases for which a large percentage of conditional branch instructions lead to the branch being taken. The discontinuity is minimized, when the branch is not taken, through special handling of the condition code (CC) and the conditional branch instruction (BC). The condition code is a two-bit indicator, set according to the outcome of a variety of instructions, and can subsequently be interrogated for branching through the BC instruction. Since the code is to represent the outcome of the last decoded CC-affecting instruction, and since execution can be out of sequence, interlocks must be established to ensure this. This is accomplished, as illustrated in Fig. 7, by tagging each instruction at decode time if it is to set the CC. Simultaneously, a signal is communicated throughout the CPU to remove all tags from previously decoded but not executed instructions. Allowing only the execution of the tagged instruction to alter the code ensures that the correct CC will be set. The decode hardware monitors the CPU for outstanding tags; only when none exists is the condition code considered valid for interrogation.

The organization assumes that, for a conditional branch, the CC will not be valid when the "branch-on-condition" (BC) is decoded (a most likely situation, considering that most arithmetic and logical operations set the code). Rather than wait for a valid CC, fetches are initiated for two instruction double-words as a hedge against a successful branch. Following this, it is assumed that the branch will fall, and a "conditional mode" is established. In conditional mode, shown in Fig. 8, instructions are decoded and conditionally forwarded to the execution units, and concomitant operand fetches are initiated. The execution units are inhibited from completing conditional instructions. When a valid condition code appears, the appropriate branching action is detected and activates or cancels the conditional instructions. Should the no-branch guess prove correct, a substantial head start is provided by activating the conditionally issued and initiated operand fetches for a number of instructions. If the branch is successful, the previously fetched target words are activated and provide work while the instruction fetching is diverted to the new stream. (Additional optimizing techniques are covered under the discussion of branching in a subsequent section of this paper.)

Interrupts, as architecturally constrained, are a major bottleneck to performance in the assembly line organization. Strict adherence to a specification which states that an interrupt on instruction n should logically precede and inhibit any action from being taken on instruction $n + 1$ leaves two alternatives. The first would be to force sequentialism between instructions which may lead to an interrupt. In view of the variety of interrupt possibilities defined, this course would totally thwart high performance and is necessarily discarded. The second is to set aside sufficient information to permit recovery from any interrupt which might arise. In view of the pipeline and execution concurrency which allows the Model 91 to advance many instructions beyond n prior to its execution, and to execute independent instructions out of sequence ($n + m$ before n), the recovery problem becomes

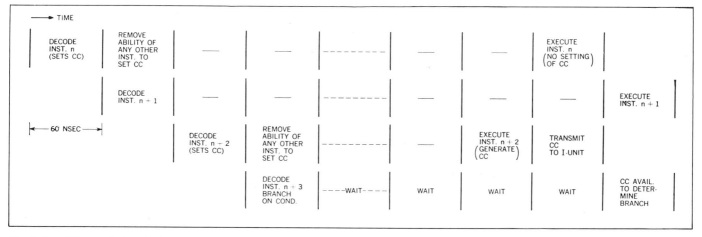

Fig. 7. Condition code interlock.

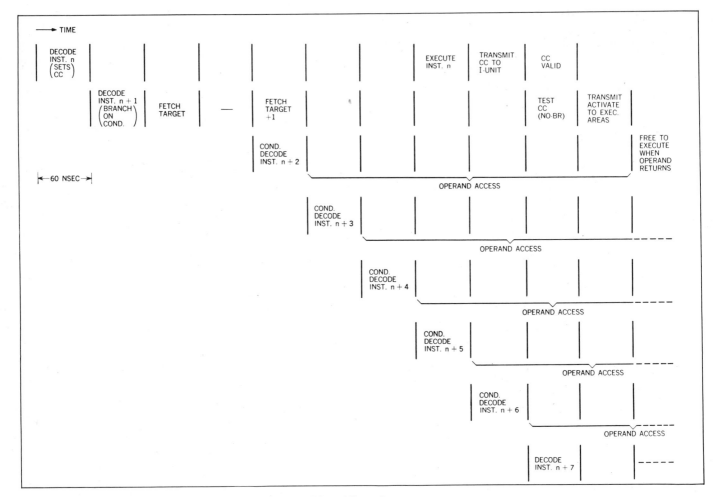

Fig. 8. Conditional instruction issuing: the branch-on-condition philosophy.

extremely complex and costly. Taking this approach would entail hardware additions to the extent that it would severely degrade the performance one is seeking to enhance. The impracticality of both alternatives by which the interrupt specifications could be met made it mandatory that the specifications themselves be altered. The architecture was compromised by removing the above-mentioned "precedence" and "inhibit" requirements. The specification change led to what is termed the "imprecise interrupt" philosophy of the Model 91 and reduced the interrupt bottleneck to an instruction supply discontinuity. The imprecise interrupt, and the manner in which the instruction discontinuity is minimized, are covered in the next section of the paper.

The bottlenecks discussed above gave rise to the major interlocks among the separate CPU areas. Within each of the areas, however, additional considerations hold. These are discussed as appropriate in the next section or in following papers.

Instruction Unit

The central control functions for the Model 91 CPU are performed in the instruction unit. The objective here is to discuss these functions in terms of how they are performed and to include the reasons for selecting the present design. However, before proceeding with this discussion it will be useful to examine some over-all design considerations and decisions which directly affect the instruction unit functions. In approaching the design of the instruction unit, many program situations were examined, and it was found that while many short instruction sequences are nicely ordered, the trend is toward frequent branching. Such things as performing short work loops, taking new action based on data results, and calling subroutines are the bases upon which programs are built and, in many instances, these factors play a larger role in the use of available time than does execution. Consequently, emphasis on branch sequencing is required. A second finding was that, even with sophisticated execution algorithms, very few programs can cause answers actually to flow from the assembly line at an average rate in excess of one every two cycles. Inherent inter-instruction dependencies, storage and other hardware conflicts, and the frequency of operations requiring multi-cycle execution all combine to prevent it.

Consideration of branching and execution times indicates that, for overall balance, the instruction unit should be able to surge ahead of the execution units by issuing instructions at a faster-than-execution rate. Then, when a branch is encountered, a significant part of the instruction unit slowdown will be overlapped with execution catch-up. With this objective in mind it becomes necessary to consider what constitutes a fast issue rate and what "trade-offs" would be required to achieve it. It is easily shown that issuing at a rate in excess of one instruction per cycle leads to a rapid expansion of hardware and complexity. (Variable-length instructions, adjacent instruction interdependencies, and storage requirements are prime factors involved.) A one-cycle maximum rate is thereby established, but it too presents difficulties. The assembly line process requires that both instruction fetching and instruction issuing proceed concurrently in order to hide storage delays. It is found through program analysis that slightly more than two instructions will be obtained per 64-bit instruction fetch[1] and that approximately 80% of all instructions require an operand reference to storage. From this it is concluded that issuing the average instruction entails approximately 1.25 storage accesses: 0.45 (instruction fetches) + 0.80 (operand fetches). This figure, with the one-per-cycle issue rate goal, clearly indicates a need for either two address paths to storage and associated return capabilities, or for multiple words returned per fetch. In considering these options, the initial tendency is to separate instruction and operand storage access paths. However, multiple paths to storage give rise to substantial hardware

additions and lead to severe control problems, particularly in establishing storage priorities and interlocks due to address dependencies. With a one-at-a-time approach these can be established on each new address as it appears, whereas simultaneous requests involve doing considerably more testing in a shorter time interval. Multiple address paths to storage were considered impractical because of the unfavorable compromise between hardware and performance.

The multiple-words-returned-per-fetch option was considered in conjunction with instruction fetching since the instruction stream is comprised of sequential words. To prevent excessive storage "busying" this approach requires a multiple word readout at the storage unit along with a wider data return path. Also, the interleaving factor is altered from *sequential* to *multi-sequential*, i.e., rather than having sequential double words in different storage modules, groups of sequential words reside in the same module. The interlock problems created by this technique are modest, the change in interleaving technique has little performance effect,[2] and storage can be (is, in some cases) organized to read out multiple words, all of which make this approach feasible. However, packaging density (more hardware required for wide data paths), storage organization constraints, and scheduling were such that this approach was also discarded. As a consequence, the single-port storage bus, which allows sequential accessing of double words, was adopted. This fact, in conjunction with the 1.25 storage accesses required per instruction, leads to a lowering of the average maximum issue rate to 0.8 instructions per machine cycle. The instruction unit achieves the issue rate through an organization which allows concurrency by separating the instruction supplying from the instruction issuing function.

Instruction Supplying

Instruction supplying includes the provision of an instruction stream which will support the desired issue rate in a sequential (non-branch) environment, and the ability to switch readily to a new instruction stream when required because of branching or interrupts.

---

[1]Storage-to-storage (SS) instructions are not considered here. They can be viewed as macro-operations and are treated as such by the hardware. The macro-operations are equivalent to basic instructions, and the number of micro-instructions involved in performing an SS function indicates that many instruction fetches would be required to perform the same function using other System/360 instructions.

[2]This is more intuitive than analytical. Certainly for strictly random addressing, the interleave technique is irrelevant. However, in real applications, programs are generally localized with (1) the instructions sequential and (2) branches jumping tens or hundreds rather than thousands of words. Data is more random because, even though it is often ordered in arrays, quite frequently many arrays are utilized concurrently. Also, various data constants are used which tend to randomize the total use. A proper analysis must consider all these factors and so becomes complex. In any event, as long as the interleave factor remains fixed the interference appears little affected by small changes in the interleaving pattern.

Sequential Instruction Fetching.   Provision of a sequential string of instructions has two fundamental aspects, an initiation or start-up transient, and a steady-state function. The initial transient entails filling the assembly line ahead of the decode station with instructions. In hardware terms, this means initiating sufficient instruction fetches so that, following a wait of one access time, a continuous flow of instruction words will return from storage. Three double-word fetches are the minimum required to fill the assembly line, since approximately two instructions are contained within a double word, and the design point access time is six machine cycles. The actual design exceeds the minimum for several reasons, the first being that during start-up no operand requests are being generated (there are no instructions), and consequently the single address port to storage is totally available for instruction fetching. Second, the start-up delay provides otherwise idle time during which to initiate more fetches, and the eight double words of instruction buffering provide space into which the words can return. A third point is that, should storage requiring more than six cycles of access time be utilized, more fetching-ahead will be required. Finally, establishing an excess queue of instructions during the transient time will allow temporary maintenance of a full assembly line without any further instruction fetching. The significance of this action is that it allows the issuing of a short burst of instructions at a one-per-cycle rate. This follows from the fact that the single, normally shared storage address port becomes exclusively available to the issue function. A start-up fetching burst of five double instruction words was the design point which resulted when all of these factors had been considered.[1]

Steady-state instruction supplying serves the function of maintaining a full assembly line by initiating instruction fetches at appropriate intervals. The address port to storage is multiplexed between instruction fetches and operand fetches, with instructions receiving priority in conflict situations. An additional optimization technique allows the instruction fetching to re-advance to the start-up level of five double words ahead if storage address time "slots" become available. A flow chart of the basic instruction fetch control algorithm is shown in Fig. 9,[2] while Fig. 10 is a schematic of the data paths provided for the total instruction supplying function. Some of the decision blocks

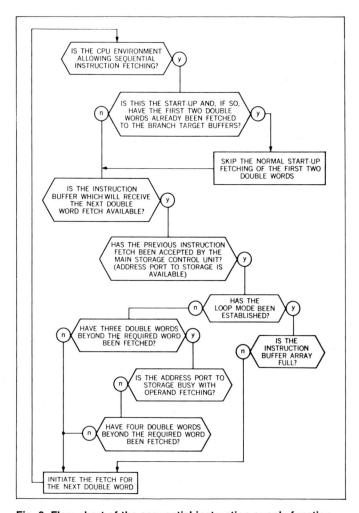

Fig. 9. Flow chart of the sequential instruction-supply function.

contained in the flow chart result from the effects of branch instructions; their function will be clarified in the subsequent discussion of branching. There are two fundamental reasons for checking buffer availability in the algorithm. First, the instruction buffer array is a modulo-eight map of storage that is interleaved by sixteen. Second, fetches can return out of order because storage may be busy or of varying performance. For example, when a branch is encountered, point one above implies that the target may overlay a fetch which has not yet returned from storage. In view of the second point, it is necessary to ensure that the unreturned fetch is ignored, as it would be possible for a new fetch to return ahead of it. Proper sequencing is accomplished by "tagging" the buffers assigned to outstanding fetches, and preventing the initiation of a new fetch to a buffer so tagged.

---

[1]The one disadvantage to over-fetching instructions is that the extra fetches may lead to storage conflicts, delaying the subsequently initiated operand fetches. This is a second-order effect, however, first because it is desirable for the instruction fetches to win conflicts unless these fetches are rendered unnecessary by an intervening branch instruction, and second because the sixteen-deep interleaving of storage significantly lowers the probability of the conflict situation.

[2]In this flow chart, unlabeled exits from decision blocks imply that a "wait" state will exist until the required condition has been satisfied.

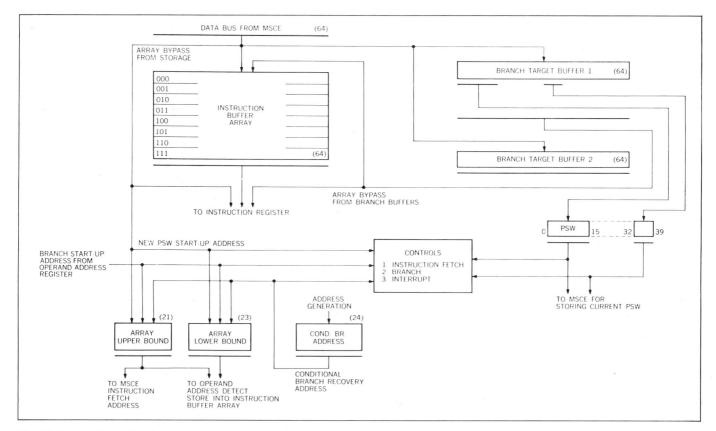

Fig. 10. Data paths for the basic instruction supply.

Branch Handling. Branching adds to the complexity of the instruction supplying function because attempts are made to minimize discontinuities caused by the branching and the consequent adverse effects on the issue rate. The discontinuities result because for each branch the supply of instructions is disrupted for a time roughly equivalent to the greater of the storage access period (start-up transient previously mentioned), or the internal testing and "housekeeping" time required to make and carry out the branch decision. This time can severely limit the total CPU performance in short program loops. It has a somewhat less pronounced effect in longer loops because the branch time becomes a smaller percentage of the total problem loop time and, more important, the instruction unit has greater opportunity to run ahead of the execution units (see Fig. 11). This last makes more time available in which to overlap the branch time with execution catch-up.

The detrimental performance effect which stems from short loops led to a dual branch philosophy. The first aspect deals with

branches which are either forward into the instruction stream,[1] beyond the prefetched instructions, or if backward from the branch instruction, greater than eight double-words back. In these situations, the branch storage-delay is unavoidable. As a hedge against such a branch being taken, the branch sequencing (Fig. 12) initiates fetches for the first two double words down the target path. Two branch buffers are provided (Fig. 10—the instruction supply data flow) to receive these words, in order that the instruction buffer array will be unaffected if the result is a no-branch decision. The branch housekeeping and decision making are carried on in parallel with the access time of the target fetches. If a branch decision is reached before the access has been completed, additional optimizing hardware routes the target fetch around the buffer and directly to the instruction register, from which it will be decoded. Minor disadvantages of the technique

[1]In the actual program the branch instruction would precede the target for this case.

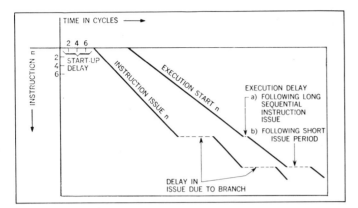

Fig. 11. Schematic representation of execution delays caused by (branch) discontinuities in the instruction issuing rate, for the case in which the issuing rate is faster than the execution rate.

are that the "hedge" fetching results in a delay of the no-branch decision and may lead to storage conflicts. Consequently, a small amount of time is lost for a branch which "falls through."

The second aspect of the branch philosophy treats the case for which the target is backward within eight double words of the branch instruction. A separation of eight double words or less defines a "short" loop—this number being chosen as a hardware/performance compromise. Part of the housekeeping required in the branch sequencing is a "back eight" test. If this test is satisfied the instruction unit enters what is termed "loop mode." Two beneficial results derive from loop mode. First, the complete loop is fetched into the instruction buffer array, after which instruction fetching ceases. Consequently, the address port to storage is totally available for operand fetching and a one instruction per cycle issue rate is possible. The second advantage gained by loop mode is a reduction by a factor of two to three in the time required to sequence the loop-establishing branch instruction. (For example, the "branch on index" instruction normally requires eight cycles for a successful branch, while in loop mode three cycles are sufficient.) In many significant programs it is estimated that the CPU will be in loop mode up to 30% of the time.

Loop mode may be established by all branch instructions except "branch and link." It was judged highly improbable that this instruction would be used to establish the type of short repetitious program loops to which loop mode is oriented. A conditional branch instruction, because it is data dependent and therefore less predictable in its outcome than other branch instructions, requires special consideration in setting up loop mode. Initial planning was to prevent looping with this instruction, but consultation with programmers has indicated that loops are frequently closed conditionally, since this allows a convenient means for loop breaking when exception conditions arise.

Furthermore, in these situations the most likely outcome is often known and can be utilized to bias the branch decision whichever way is desirable. For such reasons, the "back eight" test is made during the sequencing of a conditional branch instruction, and the status is saved through conditional mode. Should it subsequently be determined that the branch is to be taken, and the "saved" status indicates "back eight," loop mode is established. Thereafter the role of conditional mode is reversed, i.e., when the conditional branch is next encountered, it will be assumed that the branch will be taken. The conditionally issued instructions are from the target path rather than from the no-branch path as is the case when not in loop mode. A cancel requires recovery from the branch guess. Figure 12 is a flow chart of this action. In retrospect, the conditional philosophy and its effects on loop mode, although significant to the performance of the CPU and conceptually simple, were found to require numerous interlocks throughout the CPU. The complications of conditional mode, coupled with the fact that it is primarily aimed at circumventing storage access delays, indicate that a careful re-examination of its usefulness will be called for as the access time decreases.

Interrupts.   Interrupts, like branching, are another disruption to a smooth instruction supply. In the interrupt situation the instruction discontinuity is worsened because, following the recognition of the interrupt, two sequential storage access delays are encountered prior to receiving the next instruction.[1] Fortunately, and this is unlike branches, interrupts are relatively infrequent. In defining the interrupt function it was decided that architectural "imprecise" compromise mentioned in the previous section would be invoked only where necessary to achieve the required performance. In terms of the assembly line concept, this means that interrupts associated with an instruction unit decode time interval will conform with the specifications. Consequently, only interrupts which result from address, storage, and execution functions are imprecise.

One advantage of this dual treatment is that System/360 compatibility is retained to a useful degree. For example, a programming strategy sometimes employed to call special subroutines involves using a selected invalid instruction code. The ensuing interrupt provides a convenient subroutine entry technique. Retaining the compatible interrupt philosophy through the decoding time interval in the Model 91 allows it to operate

---

[1]This arises from the architectural technique of indirectly entering the interrupt subroutines. In System/360 the interrupts are divided into classes. Each class is assigned a different, fixed low storage address which contains the status to which the CPU shall be set should an interrupt of the associated class occur. Part of this status is a new program address. Consequently, interrupting requires obtaining a new supply of instructions from storage indirectly, through the new status word.

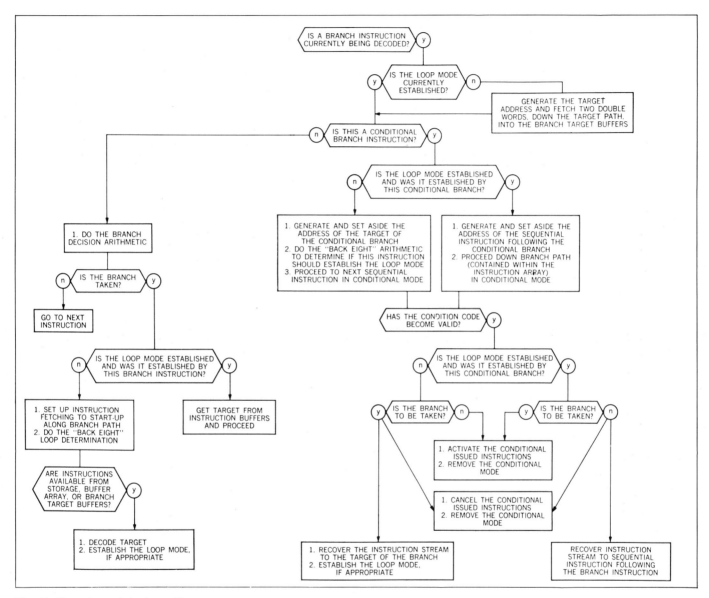

Fig. 12. Flow chart of the branching sequence.

programs employing such techniques. The manifestation of this approach is illustrated in the flow chart of Fig. 13. In accordance with System/360 specifications, no further decoding is allowed once either a precise or an imprecise interrupt has been signalled. With the assembly line organization, it is highly probable that at the time of the interrupt there will be instructions still in the pipeline which should be executed prior to changing the CPU status to that of the interrupt routine. However, it is also desirable

to minimize the effect of the interrupt on the instruction supply, so the new status word is fetched to the existing branch target buffer in parallel with the execution completion. After the return from storage of the new status word, if execution is still incomplete, further optimizing allows the fetching of instructions for the interrupt routine. Before proceeding, it becomes necessary to consider an implication resulting from the dual interrupt philosophy. Should a precise interrupt have initiated the action, it is

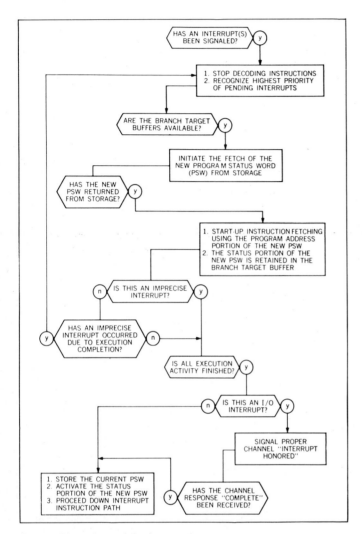

Fig. 13. Flow chart of the interrupt sequence.

completion. However, the relative infrequency of I/O interrupts renders negligible the degradation caused by this.

Instruction Issuing

The instruction-issuing hardware initiates and controls orderly concurrency in the assembly line process leading to instruction execution. It accomplishes this by scanning each instruction, in the order presented by the program, and clearing all necessary interlocks before releasing the instruction. In addition, should a storage reference be required by the operation, the issuing mechanism performs the necessary address calculations, initiates the storage action, and establishes the routing by which the operand and operation will ultimately be merged for execution. In addition, certain essential inter-instruction dependencies are maintained while the issue functions proceed concurrently.

In terms of the assembly line of Fig. 3, the moving of instructions to the decode area, the decode, and the operand address generation comprise the issue stations. The moving of instructions to the decode area entails the taking of 64-bit double-words, as provided by the instruction supply, and extracting from them the proper instruction half-words, one instruction at a time. The instruction register is the area through which this is accomplished (Fig. 14). The register efficiently handles variable-length instructions and provides a stable platform from which to decode. All available space in this 64-bit register is kept full of instructions yet to be decoded, provided only that the required new instruction information has returned from storage. The decoder scans across the instruction register, starting at any half-word (16-bit) boundary, with new instructions refilling any space vacated by instruction issuing. The register is treated conceptually as a cylinder; i.e., the end of the register is concatenated with the beginning, since the decode scan must accommodate instructions which cross double-word boundaries.

The decoding station is the time interval during which instruction scanning and interlock clearing take place. Instruction-independent functions (interval timer update, wait state, certain interrupts and manual intervention) are subject to entry interlocks during this interval. Instruction-associated functions also have interlocks which check for such things as the validity of the scanned portion of the instruction register, whether or not the instruction starts on a half-word boundary, whether the instruction is a valid operation, whether an address is to be generated for the instruction (and if so, whether the address adder is available), and where the instruction is to be executed. In conjunction with this last point, should the fixed- or floating-point execution units be involved, availability of operation buffering is checked. Inter-instruction dependencies are the final class of interlocks which can occur during the decoding interval. These arise because of decision predictions which, if proven wrong, require that decod-

possible that the execution "cleanup" will lead to an imprecise condition. In this event, and in view of the desire to maintain compatibility for precise cases, the logically preceding imprecise signal should cancel all previous precise action. The flow chart (Fig. 13) illustrates this cancel-recovery action. Should no cancel action occur (the more likely situation), the completion of all execution functions results, with one exception, in the release of the new status word and instruction supply. The I/O interrupts require special consideration because of certain peculiarities in the channel hardware (the System 360/Model 60–75 channel hardware is used). Because of them, the CPU-channel communication cannot be carried out in parallel with the execution

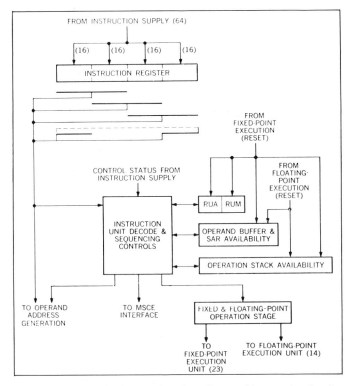

Fig. 14. Data flow for instruction decoding and instruction issuing.

ing cease immediately so that recovery can be initiated with a minimum of backup facilities.

Such occurrences as the discovery of a branch wrong guess or a store instruction which may alter the prefetched instruction stream generate these inter-instruction interlocks. Figure 15 illustrates the interlock function. The placement of a store instruction in the instruction stream, in particular, warrants further discussion because it presents a serious time problem in the instruction unit. The dilemma stems both from the concurrency philosophy and from the architectural specification that a store operation may alter the subsequent instruction. Recall that, through the pipeline concept, decoding can occur on successive cycles, with one instruction being decoded at the same time the address for the previous instruction is being generated. Therefore, for a decode which follows a store instruction, a test between the instruction counter and the storage address is required to detect whether or not the subsequent decode is affected by the store. Unless rather extensive recovery hardware is used, the decode, if affected, must be suppressed. However, the assembly line basic time interval is too short to both complete the detection and block the decode. The simplest solution would require a null decode time following each store issue. However, the frequency

of store instructions is high enough that the performance degradation would be objectionable. The compromise solution which was adopted reduces the number of decoding delays by utilizing a truncated-address compare. The time requirements prohibit anything more than a compare of the low-order six bits of the storage address currently being generated, using the algorithm illustrated in Fig. 16.

The algorithm attaches relatively little significance to the low-order three adder bits (dealing with byte, half-word and full-word addresses) since the primary performance concern is with stores of double-words. It is seen, for example, that for the full-word case the probability of a carry into the double-word address is approximately 1/4, while for double-word handling it is negligible. The double-word address three-bit compare will occur with 1/8 probability while the word boundary crossover term has a probability of 1/16 (probability that instruction can cross boundary, 1/2, × probability that the crossover is into the store-affected word, 1/8). The two cases thus have the probabilities:

$$\text{Full word} \quad 1/4 + 1/8 + 1/6 = 7/16 \quad \text{and}$$
$$\text{Double-word} \; 1/8 + 1/16 = 3/16.$$

These figures indicate the likelihood of a decode time-interval delay following the issue of a store instruction. When such a decode delay is encountered, the following cycle is used to complete the test, that is, to check the total address to determine whether an instruction word has in fact been altered. To this effect, the generated storage address is compared with the upper and lower bounds of the instruction array (Fig. 16). A between-the-bounds indication results in a decode halt, a re-fetch of the affected instruction double-word, then resumption of normal processing. This second portion of the interlock is only slightly less critical in timing than the first. Figure 17 illustrates the pre-fetch timing sequence. One difficulty with the store interlock is that in blocking the decode, it must inhibit action over a significant portion of the instruction unit. This implies both heavy loading and lengthy wire, each of which seriously hampers circuit performance. It was therefore important that the unit be as small as possible and that the layout of the hardware constantly consider the interlock.

For each instruction, following the clearing of all interlocks, the decode decision determines whether to issue the instruction to an execution unit and initiate address generation, or to retain the instruction for sequencing within the instruction unit. The issuing to an execution unit and the operand fetching for storage-to-register (RX) instructions constitutes a controlled splitting operation; sufficient information is forwarded along both paths to effect a proper execution unit merge. For example, buffer assignment is carried in both paths so that the main storage control element will return the operand to the buffer which will be accessed by the

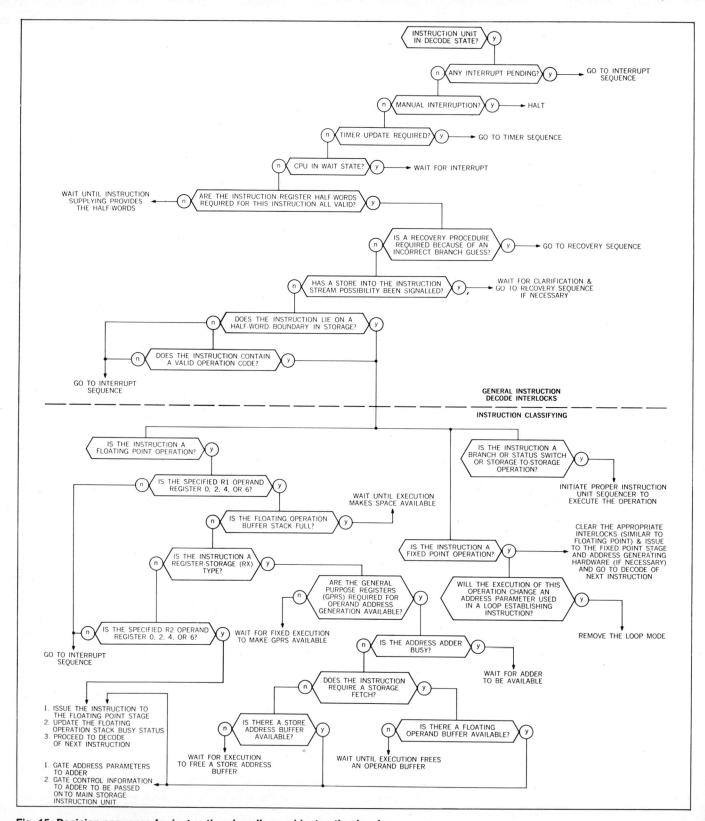

Fig. 15. Decision sequence for instruction decoding and instruction issuing.

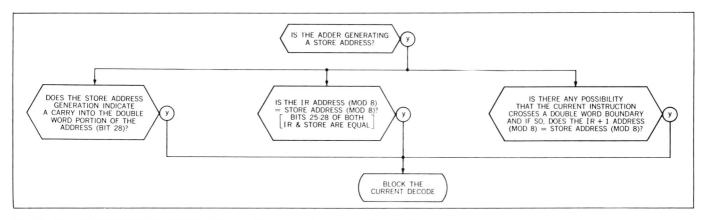

Fig. 16. Decode interlock (established following the issue of a store instruction).

execution unit when it prepares to execute the instruction. With this technique the execution units are isolated from storage and can be designed to treat all operations as involving only registers.

A final decoding function is mentioned here, to exemplify the sort of design considerations and hardware additions that are caused by performance-optimizing techniques. The branch sequencing is optimized so that no address generation is required when a branch which established the loop mode is re-encountered. This is done by saving the location, within the instruction array, of the target. It is possible, even if unlikely, that one of the instructions contained in a loop may alter the parameter originally used to generate the target address which is now being assumed. This possibility, although rare, does require hardware to detect the occurrence and terminate the loop mode. This hardware includes two 4-bit registers, required to preserve the address of the general purpose registers (X and B) utilized in the target address generation, and comparators which check these

addresses against the sink address (R1) of the fixed-point instructions. Detection of a compare and termination of loop mode are necessary during the decoding interval to ensure that subsequent branch sequencing will be correct.

The address-generating time interval provides for the combining of proper address parameters and for the forwarding of the associated operation (fetch or store) control to the main storage control element through an interface register. A major concern, associated with the address parameters, was to decide where the physical location of the general purpose registers should be. This concern arises since the fixed-point execution unit, as well as the instruction unit, makes demands on the GPR's, while the packaging split will cause the registers to be relatively far from one of the units. It was decided to place them in the execution unit since, first, execution tends to change the registers while address generation merely examines their contents, and second, it was desired that a fixed-point execution unit be able to iteratively use any particular register on successive time intervals. In order to circumvent the resulting time delay (long wire separation) between the general purpose registers and the address adder, each register is fed via "hot" lines to the instruction unit. The gating of a particular GPR to the adder can thereby be implemented locally within the instruction unit, and no transmission delay is incurred unless the register contents have just been changed.

Placing the GPR's outside the instruction unit creates a delay of two basic time intervals before a change initiated by the instruction unit is reflected at the address parameter inputs from the GPRs. This delay is particularly evident when it is realized that the address generated immediately following such a GPR change generally requires the contents of the affected register as a parameter. For example, branch on index, branch on count, branch and link, and load address are instruction unit operations

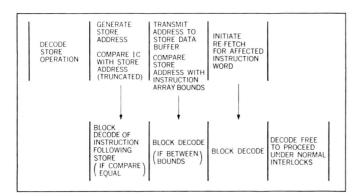

Fig. 17. Effect of the decode interlock on pre-fetched instructions.

which change the contents of a GPR. Further, in loop situations the target of the branch frequently uses the changed register as an index quantity in its address. Performance demands led to the incorporating of controls which recognize the above situation and effect a by-pass of the GPR. This entails substituting the content of the adder output register (which contains the new GPR data) for the content of the affected GPR. One performance cycle was saved by this technique.

In addition to address generation, the address adder serves to accomplish branch decision arithmetic, loop mode testing, and instruction counter value generation for various situations. In order to perform all of these functions, it was required that the adder have two 32-bit inputs and one input of 12 bits. One of the 32-bit inputs is complementable and a variety of fixed, single-bit inputs is provided for miscellaneous sequences. The data path is illustrated in Fig. 18.

Status Switching and Input/Output. The philosophy associated with status switching instructions is primarily one of design expediency. Basic existing hardware paths are exercised wherever possible, and an attempt is made to adhere to the architectural interrupt specifications. When status switching instructions are encountered in conditional mode the instruction unit is halted and no action is taken until the condition is cleared.

The supervisor call (SVC) instruction is treated by the interrupt hardware as a precise interrupt. The same new status word pre-fetch philosophy is utilized in the load program status word (LPSW) operation.

One difficulty encountered in conjunction with the start-up fetching of instructions following a status switch (or interrupt) is that a new storage protect key[1] is likely to obtain. Consequently, a period exists during which two protect keys are active, the first for previously delayed, still outstanding accesses associated with the current execution clean-up, and the second for the fetching of instructions. This situation is handled by sending both keys to the main storage control element and attaching proper control information to the instruction fetches.

The set program mask (SPM) implementation has a minor optimization: Whenever the new mask equals the current mask, the instruction completes immediately. Otherwise an execution clean-up is effected before setting the new mask to make certain that outstanding operations are executed in the proper mask environment.

I/O instructions, and I/O interrupts, require a wait for channel communications. The independent channel and CPU paths to storage demand that the CPU be finished setting up the I/O controls in storage before the channel can be notified to proceed. Once notified, the channel must interrogate the instruction-addressed device prior to setting the condition code in the CPU. This is accomplished by lower-speed circuitry and involves units some distances away; consequently, I/O initiation times are of the order of 5–10 microseconds.

References

Anderson, Sparacio, and Tomasulo [1967]; Amdahl, Blaauw, and Brooks [1964]; Anderson, Earle, Goldschmidt, and Powers [1967]; Boland, Granito, Marcotte, Messina, and Smith [1967]; Buchholz et al. [1962]; Flynn and Low [1967]; Litwiller and Adler [private communication]; Tomasulo [1967].

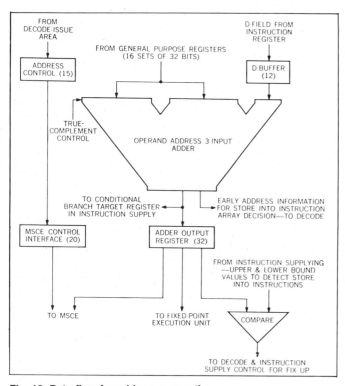

Fig. 18. Data flow for address generation.

[1]The storage protect key is contained in the program status word (PSW). It is a tag which accompanies all storage requests, and from it the storage can determine when a protect violation occurs.

Chapter 19

An Efficient Algorithm for Exploiting Multiple Arithmetic Units[1]

R. M. Tomasulo

Abstract This paper describes the methods employed in the floating-point area of the System/360 Model 91 to exploit the existence of multiple execution units. Basic to these techniques is a simple common data busing and register tagging scheme which permits simultaneous execution of the independent instructions while preserving the essential precedences inherent in the instruction stream. The common data bus improves performance by efficiently utilizing the execution units without requiring specially optimized code. Instead, the hardware, by "looking ahead" about eight instructions, automatically optimizes the program execution on a local basis.

The application of these techniques is not limited to floating-point arithmetic or System/360 architecture. It may be used in almost any computer having multiple execution units and one or more "accumulators." Both of the execution units, as well as the associated storage buffers, multiple accumulators and input/output buses, are extensively checked.

Introduction

After storage access time has been satisfactorily reduced through the use of buffering and overlap techniques, even after the instruction unit has been pipelined to operate at a rate approaching one instruction per cycle [Anderson, Sparacio, and Tomasulo, 1967], there remains the need to optimize the actual performance of arithmetic operations, especially floating-point. Two familiar problems confront the designer in his attempt to balance execution with issuing. First, individual operations are not fast enough[2] to allow simple serial execution. Second, it is difficult to achieve the fastest execution times in a universal execution unit. In other words, circuitry designed to do both multiply and add will do neither as fast as two units each limited to one kind of instruction.

The first step toward surmounting these obstacles has been presented in Anderson, Earle, Goldschmidt, and Powers [1967], i.e., the division of the execution function into two independent parts, a fixed-point execution area and a floating-point execution area. While this relieves the physical constraint and makes concurrent execution possible, there is another consideration. In order to secure a performance increase the program must contain an intimate mixture of fixed-point and floating-point instructions. Obviously, it is not always feasible for the programmer to arrange this and, indeed, many of the programs of greatest interest to the user consist almost wholly of floating-point instructions. The subject of this paper, then, is the method used to achieve concurrent execution of floating-point instructions in the IBM System/360 Model 91. Obviously, one begins with multiple execution units, in this case an adder and a multiplier/divider [Anderson, Sparacio, and Tomasulo, 1967].

It might appear that achieving the concurrent operation of these two units does not differ substantially from the attainment of fixed-floating overlap. However, in the latter case the architecture limits each of the instruction classes to its own set of accumulators and this guarantees independence.[3] In the former case there is only one set of accumulators, which implies program-specified sequences of dependent operations. Now it is no longer simply a matter of classifying each instruction as fixed-point or floating-point, a classification which is independent of previous instructions. Rather, it is a question of determining each instruction's relationship with all previous, incompleted instructions. Simply stated, the objective must be to preserve essential precedences while allowing the greatest possible overlap of independent operations.

This objective is achieved in the Model 91 through a scheme called the common data bus (CDB). It makes possible maximum concurrency with minimal effort (usually none) by the programmer or, more importantly, by the compiler. At the same time, the hardware required is small and logically simple. The CDB can function with any number of accumulators and any number of execution units. In short, it provides a hardware algorithm for the automatic, efficient exploitation of multiple execution units.

The next section of this paper will discuss the physical framework of registers, data paths and execution circuitry which is implied by the architecture and the overall CPU structure presented in Anderson, Sparacio, and Tomasulo [1967]. Within this framework one can subsequently discuss the problem of precedence, some possible solutions, and the selected solution, the CDB. In conclusion will be a summary of the results obtained.

Definitions and Data Paths

While the reader is assumed to be familiar with System/360 architecture and mnemonics, the terminology as modified by the

---

[1] *IBM Journal*, vol. 11, January 1967, pp. 25–33.
[2] During the planning phase, floating-point multiply was taken to be six cycles, divide as eighteen cycles and add as two cycles. Anderson, Earle, Goldschmidt, and Powers [1967] explains how times of 3, 12, and 2 were actually achieved. This permitted the use of only one, instead of two, multipliers and one adder, pipelined to start an add cycle.

[3] Such dependencies as exist are handled by the store-fetch sequencing of the storage bus and the condition code control described in Anderson, Earle, Goldschmidt, and Powers [1967].

context of the Model 91 organization will be reviewed here. The instruction unit, in preparing instructions for the floating-point operation stack (FLOS), maps both storage-to-register and register-to-register instructions into a pseudo-register-to-register format. In this format R1 is always one of the four floating-point registers (FLR) defined by the architecture. It is usually the *sink* of the instruction, i.e., it is the FLR whose contents are set equal to the result of the operation. Store operations are the sole exception[1] wherein R1 specifies the *source* of the operand to be placed in storage. A word in storage is really the sink of a store. (R1 and R2 refer to fields as defined by System/360 architecture.)

In the pseudo-register-to-register format "seen" by the FLOS the R2 field can have three different meanings. It can be an FLR as in a normal register-to-register instruction. If the program contains a storage-to-register instruction, the R2 field designates the floating-point buffer (FLB) assigned by the instruction unit to receive the storage operand. Finally, R2 can designate a store data buffer (SDB) assigned by the instruction unit to store instructions. In the first two cases R2 is the *source* of an operand; in the last case it is a sink. Thus, the instruction unit maps all of storage into the 6 floating-point buffers and 3 store data buffers so that the FLOS sees only pseudo-register-to-register operations.

The distinction between source and sink will become quite important during the discussion of precedence and should be fixed firmly in mind. All of the instructions (except store and compare) have the following form:

R1   op   R2⎯⎯⎯→ R1
Register   Register   Register

            or

            buffer
source   source   sink

For example, the instruction AD 0, 2 means "place the double-precision sum of registers 0 and 2 in register 0," i.e., R0 + R2 → R0. Note that R1 is really both a source and a sink.[2] Nevertheless, it will be called the sink and R2 the source in all subsequent discussion.

This definition of operations and the machine organization taken together imply a set of data registers with transfer paths among them. These are shown in Fig. 1. The major sets of registers (FLR's, FLB's, FLOS and SDB's) have already been discussed, both above and in Anderson, Sparacio, and Tomasulo [1967]. Two additional registers, one sink and one source, are shown feeding each execution circuit. Initially these registers were considered to be the internal working registers required by the execution circuits and put to multiple use in a way to be described below. Later, their function was generalized under the

reservation station concept and they were dissociated from their "working" function.

In actually designing a machine the data paths evolve as the design progresses. Here, however, a complete, first-pass data path will be shown to facilitate discussion. To illustrate the operation let us consider, in turn, four kinds of instructions—load of a register from storage, storage-to-register arithmetic, register-to-register arithmetic, and store. Let us first see how each can be accomplished *in vacuo*; then what difficulties arise when each is embedded in the context of a program. For simplicity double-precision (64-bit operands) will be used throughout.

Figure 2 shows the timing relationship between the instruction unit's handling of an instruction and its processing by the FLOS decode. When the FLOS decodes a load, the buffer which will receive the operand has not yet been loaded from storage.[3] Rather than holding the decode until the operand arrives, the FLOS sets control bits associated with the buffer which cause its content to be transmitted to the adder when it "goes full." The adder receives control information which causes it to send data to floating-point register R1, when its source register is set full by the buffer.

If the instruction is a storage-to-register arithmetic function, the storage operand is handled as in load (control bits cause it to be forwarded to the proper unit) but the floating-point register, along with the operation, is sent by the decoder to the appropriate unit. After receiving the buffer the unit will execute the operation and send the result to register R1.

In register-to-register arithmetic instructions two floating point registers are transmitted on successive cycles to the appropriate execution unit.

Stores are handled like storage-to-register arithmetic functions, except that the content of the floating-point register is sent to a store data buffer rather than to an execution unit.

Thus far, the handling of one instruction at a time has proven rather straightforward. Now consider the following "program":

Example 1

LD   F0   FLB1   LOAD register F0 from buffer 1

MD   F0   FLB2   MULTIPLY   register F0 by buffer 2

The load can be handled as before, but what about the multiply? Certainly F0 and FLB2 cannot be sent to the multiplier as in the case of the isolated multiply, since FLB1 has not yet been set into F0.[4] This sequence illustrates the cardinal precedence principle:

---

[1]Compares do not, of course, alter the contents of R1.
[2]This economy of specification compounds the difficulties of achieving concurrency while preserving precedence, as will be seen later.

[3]A FULL/EMPTY control bit indicates this. The bit is set FULL by the Main Storage Control Element and EMPTY when the buffer is used. LOAD uses the adder in order to minimize the buffer outgates and the FLR ingates.
[4]Note that the program calls for the product of FLB1 and FLB2 to be placed in F0. This hints at the CDB concept.

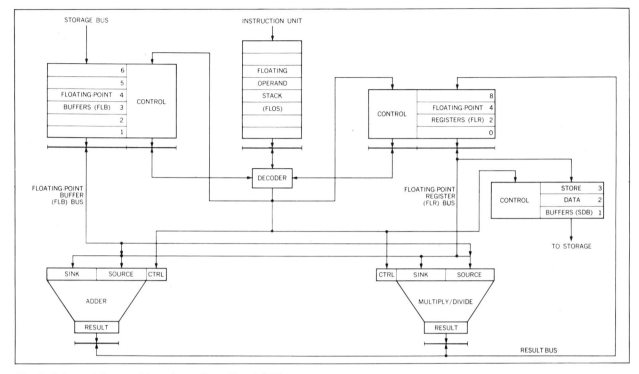

Fig. 1. Data registers and transfer paths without CDB.

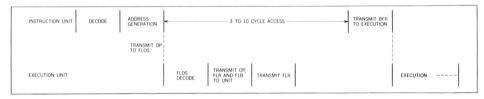

Fig. 2. Timing relationship between instruction unit and FLOS decode for the processing of one instruction.

No floating-point register may participate in an operation if it is the sink of another, incompleted instruction. That is, a register cannot be used until its contents reflect the result of the most recent operation to use that register as its sink.

The design presented thus far has not incorporated any mechanism for dealing with this situation. Three functions must be required of any such mechanism:

1 It must recognize the existence of dependency.

2 It must cause the correct sequencing of the dependent instructions.

3 It must distinguish between the given sequence and such sequences as

```
LD   F0,   FLB1
MD   F2,   FLB2
```

Here it must allow the independent MD to proceed regardless of the disposition of the LD.

The first two requirements are necessary to preserve the logical integrity of the program; the third is necessary to meet the performance goal. The next section will present several alternatives for accomplishing these objectives.

Preservation of Precedence

Perhaps the simplest scheme for preserving precedence is as follows. A "busy" bit is associated with each of the four floating-point registers. This bit is set when the FLOS decode issues an instruction designating the register as a sink; it is reset when the executing unit returns the result to the register. No instruction can be issued by the FLOS if the busy bit of its sink is on. If the source of a register-to-register instruction has its busy bit on, the FLOS sets control bits associated with the source register. When a result is entered into the register, these control bits cause the register to be sent via the FLR bus to the unit waiting for it as a source.

This scheme easily meets the first two requirements. The third is met with the help of the programmer; he must use different registers to achieve overlap. For example, the expression A + B + C + D * E can be programmed as follows:

Example 2

LD	F0,	D	F0 = D
LD	F2,	C	F2 = C
LD	F4,	B	F4 = B
MD	F0,	E	F0 = D * E
AD	F2,	F0	F2 = C + D * E
AD	F4,	A	F4 = A+ B
AD	F2,	F4	F2 = A + B + C + D * E

The busy bit scheme should allow the second add and the multiply to be executed simultaneously (really, in any order) since they use different sinks. Unfortunately, the timing chart of Fig. 3a shows not only that the expected overlap does not occur but also that many cycles are lost to transmission time. The overlap fails to materialize because the first add uses the result of the multiply, and the adder must wait for that result. Cycles are lost to control because so many of the instructions use the adder. The FLOS cannot decode an instruction unless a unit is available to execute it. When an assigned unit finishes execution, it takes one cycle to transmit the fact to the FLOS so that it can decode a waiting instruction. Similarly, when the FLOS is held up because of a busy sink register, it cannot begin to decode until the result has been entered into the register.

One solution that could be considered is the addition of one or more adders. If this were done and some programs timed, however, it would become apparent that the execution circuitry would be in use only a small part of the time. Most of the lost time would occur while the adder waited for operands which are the result of previous instructions. What is required is a device to collect operands (and control information) and then engage the execution circuitry when all conditions are satisfied. But this is precisely the function of the sink and source registers in Fig. 1. Therefore, the better solution is to associate more than one set of registers (control, sink, source) with each execution unit. Each such set is called a *reservation station*.[1] Now instruction issuing depends on the availability of the appropriate kind of reservation

station. In the Model 91 there are three add and two multiply/ divide reservation stations. For simplicity they are treated as if they were actual units. Thus, in the future, we will speak of Adder 1(A1), Adder 2 (A2), etc., and M/D 1 and M/D 2.

Figure 3b shows the effect of the addition of reservation stations on the problem running time: five cycles have been eliminated. Note that the second AD now overlaps the MD and actually executes before the first AD. While the speed increase is gratifying and the busy bit method easy to implement, there remains a dependence on the programmer. Note that the expression could have been coded this way:

Example 3a

LD	F0,	E
MD	F0,	D
AD	F0,	C
AD	F0,	B
AD	F0,	A

Now overlap is impossible and the program will run six cycles longer despite having two fewer instructions. Suppose however, that this program is part of a loop, as below:

Example 3b

LOOP 1	LD	F0,	Ei
	MD	F0,	Di
	AD	F0,	Ci
	AD	F0,	Bi
	AD	F0,	Ai
	STD	F0,	Fi
	BXH i, −1, 0, LOOP 1 (decrease i by 1, branch if i > 0)		
LOOP 2	LD	F0,	Ei
	LD	F2,	Ei + 1
	MD	F0,	Di
	MD	F2,	Di + 1
	AD	F0,	Ci
	AD	F2,	Ci + 1
	AD	F0,	Bi
	AD	F2,	Bi + 1
	AD	F0,	Ai
	AD	F2,	Ai + 1
	STD	F0,	Fi
	STD	F2,	Fi + 1
	BXH i, −2, 0, LOOP 2		

[1]The fetch and store buffers can be considered as specialized, one-operand reservation stations. Previous systems, such as the IBM 7030, have in effect employed one "reservation station" ahead of each execution unit. The extension to several reservation stations adds to the effectiveness of the execution hardware.

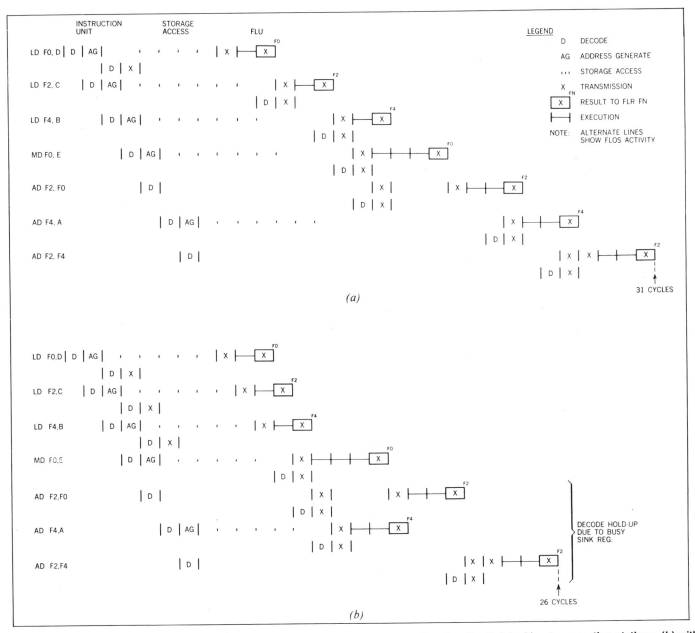

Fig. 3. Timing for the instruction sequence required to perform the function A + B + C + D ∗ E: (a) without reservation stations, (b) with reservation stations included in the register set.

Iteration $n + 1$ of LOOP 1 will appear to the FLOS to depend on iteration n, since the instructions in both iterations have the same sink. But it is clear that the two iterations are, in fact, independent. This example illustrates a second way in which two instruction sequences can be independent. The first way, of course, is for the two strings to have different sink registers. The second way is for the second string to begin with a load. By its definition a load launches a new, independent string because it instructs the computer to destroy the previous contents of the specified register. Unfortunately, the busy bit scheme does not recognize this possibility. If overlap is to be achieved with this scheme, the programmer must write LOOP 2. (This technique is called *doubling* or *unravelling*. It requires twice as much storage but it runs faster by enabling two iterations to be executed simultaneously.)

Attempts were made to improve the busy bit scheme so as to handle this case. The most tempting approach is the expansion of the bit into a counter. This would appear to allow more than one instruction with a given sink to be issued. As each is issued, the FLOS increments the counter; as each is executed the counter is decremented. However, major difficulty is caused by the fact that storage operands do not return in sequence. This can cause the result of instruction $n + 1$ to be placed in a register before that of n. When n completes, it erroneously destroys the register contents.

Some of the other proposals considered would, if implemented, have been of such logical complexity as to jeopardize the achievement of a fast cycle.

The Common Data Bus

The preceding sections were intended to portray the difficulties of achieving concurrency among floating-point instructions and to show some of the steps in the evolution of a design to overcome them. It is clear, in retrospect, that the previous algorithms failed for lack of a way to uniquely identify each instruction and to use this information to sequence execution and set results into the floating-point registers. As far as action by the FLOS is concerned, the only thing unique to a particular instruction is the unit which will execute it. This, then, must form the basis of the common data bus (CDB).

Figure 4 shows the data paths required for operation of the CDB.[1] When Fig. 4 is compared with Fig. 1 the following changes, in addition to the reservation stations, are evident: Another output port has been added to the buffers. This port has

been combined with the results from the adder and multiplier/divider; the combination is the CDB. The CDB now goes not only to the registers but also to the sink and source registers of all reservation stations, including the store data buffers but excluding the floating-point buffers. This data path will enable loads to be executed without the adder and will make the result of any operation available to all units without first going through a floating-point register.

Note that the CDB is fed by all units that can alter a register and that it feeds all units which can have a register as an operand. The control part of the CDB enumerates the units which feed the CDB. Thus the floating-point buffers 1 through 6 are assigned the numbers 1 through 6; the three adders (actually reservation stations) are numbered 10 through 12; the two multiplier/dividers are 8 and 9. Since there are eleven contributors to the CDB, a four-bit binary number suffices to enumerate them. This number is called a *tag*. A tag is associated with each of the four floating-point registers (in addition to the busy bit[2]), with both the source and sink registers of each of the five reservation stations and with each of the three Store Data Buffers. Thus a total of 17 four-bit tag registers has been added, as shown in Fig. 4.

Tags also appear in another context. A tag is generated by the CDB priority controls to identify the unit whose result will next appear on the CDB. Its use will be made clear shortly.

Operation of this complex is as follows. In decoding each instruction the FLOS checks the busy bit of each of the specified floating-point registers. If that bit is zero, the content of the register(s) may be sent to the selected unit via the FLR bus, just as before. Upon issuing the instruction, which requires only that a unit be available to execute it, the FLOS not only sets the busy bit of the sink register but also sets its tag to the designation of the selected unit. The source register control bits remain unchanged. As an example, take the instruction, AD F0, FLB1. After issuing this instruction to Adder 1 the control bits of F0 would be:

BB   TAG
1   1010 (A1)

So far the only change from previous methods is the setting of the tag. The significant difference occurs when the FLOS finds the busy bit on at decode time. Previously, this caused a suspension of decoding until the bit went off. Now the FLOS will issue the instruction and update the tag. In so doing it will not transmit the register contents to the selected unit but it will transmit the "old" tag. For example, suppose the previous AD was

---

[1] The FLB and FLR busses are retained for performance reasons. Everything could be done by a slight extension of the CDB but time would be lost due to conflicts over the common facility.

[2] The busy bit is no longer necessary since its function can be performed by use of an unassigned tag number. However, it is convenient to retain it.

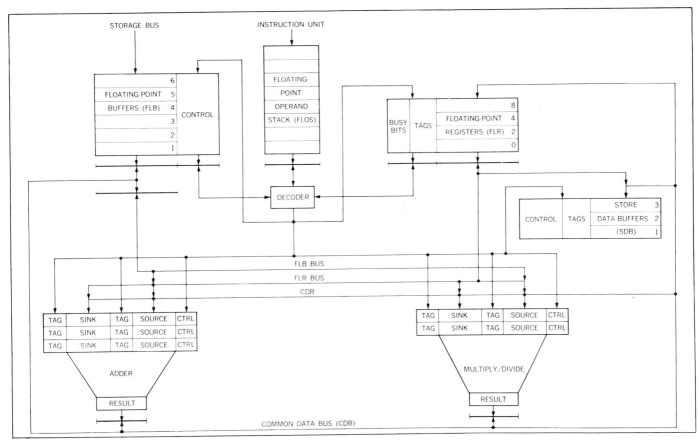

Fig. 4. Data registers and transfer paths, including CDB and reservation stations.

followed by a second AD. At the end of the decode of this second AD, F0's control bits would be:

BB	TAG
1	1011 (A2)

One cycle later the sink tag of the A2 reservation station would be 1010, i.e., the same as A1, the unit whose result will be required by A2.

Let us look ahead temporarily to the execution of the first AD. Some time after the start of execution but before the end,[1] A1 will request the CDB. Since the CDB is fed by many sources, its time-sharing is controlled by a central priority circuit. If the CDB is free, the priority control signals the requesting adder, A1, to

outgate its result *and* it broadcasts the tag of the requestor (1010 in this case) to all reservation stations. Each active reservation station (selected but awaiting a register operand) compares its sink and source tags to the CDB tag. If they match, the reservation station ingates the data from the CDB. In a similar manner, the CDB tag is compared with the tag of each *busy* floating-point register. All busy registers with matching tags ingate from the CDB and reset their busy bits.

Two steps toward the goal of preserving precedence have been accomplished by the foregoing. First, the second AD cannot start until the first AD finishes because it cannot receive both its operands until the result of the first AD appears on the CDB. Second, the result of the first AD cannot change register F0 once the second AD is issued, since the tag in F0 will not match A1. These are precisely the desired effects.

Before proceeding with more detailed considerations let us recapitulate the essence of the method. The floating-point register

---

[1]Since the required lead time is two cycles, the request is made at the start of execution for an add-type instruction.

tag identifies the last unit whose result is destined for the register. When an instruction is issued that requires a busy register, the tag is sent to the selected unit in place of the register contents. The unit continuously compares this tag with that generated by the CDB priority control. When a match is detected, the unit ingates from the CDB. The unit begins executing as soon as it has both operands. It may receive one or both operands from either the CDB or the FLR bus; the source operand for storage-to-register instructions is transmitted via the FLB bus.

As each instruction is issued the existing tag(s) is (are) transmitted to the selected unit and then the sink tag is updated. By passing tags around in this fashion, all operations having the same sink are correctly sequenced while other operations are allowed to proceed independently. Finally, the floating-point register tag controls the changing of the register itself, thereby ensuring that only the most recent instruction will change the register. This has the interesting consequence that a loop of the following kind:

Example 4

```
LOOP    LD     F0,   Ai
        AD     F0,   Bi
        STD    F0,   Ci STORE
        BXH    i,    −1, 0, LOOP
```

may execute indefinitely without any change in the contents of F0. Under normal conditions only the final iteration will place its result in F0.

As mentioned previously, there are two ways of starting an independent instruction string. The first is to specify a different sink register and the second is to load a register. The CDB handles the former in essentially the same way as the busy bit scheme. The load, which had been a difficult problem previously, is now very simple. Regardless of the register tag or busy bit, a load turns the busy bit on and sets the tag equal to the floating-point buffer which the instruction unit had assigned to the load. This causes subsequent instructions to sequence on the buffer rather than on whatever unit may have identified the register as its sink prior to the load. The buffer controls are set to request the CDB when the storage operand arrives. The following example and Fig. 5 show this clearly.

Example 5

```
LD      F0,   FLB1
DD      F0,   FLB2    DIVIDE
STD     F0,   A
LD      F0,   FLB3
AD      F0,   FLB4
```

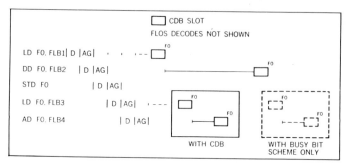

Fig. 5. Timing sequence for Example 5, showing effect of CDB.

Note that the add finishes before the divide. The dashed line portion of Fig. 5 shows what would happen if the busy bit scheme alone were used. Figure 6 displays the sequences followed under the two schemes. This figure graphically illustrates the bottleneck caused by using a single sink register with a busy bit scheme. Because all data must pass through this register, the program is reduced to strictly sequential execution, steps 1 through 7. With the CDB, on the other hand, the sink register hardly appears and

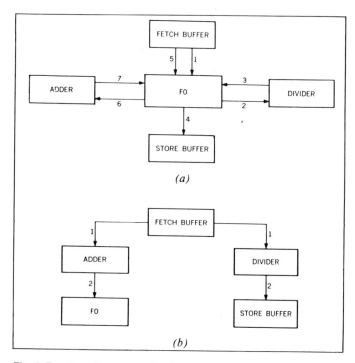

Fig. 6. Functional sequence for Example 5 (a) with busy bit controls only, (b) with CDB.

the program is broken into two independent, concurrent sequences. This facility of the CDB obviates the need for loop doubling.

The CDB makes it possible to execute some instructions in, effectively, no time at all. In the above example, the store took place during the CDB cycle following the divide. In a similar fashion a register-to-register load of a busy register is accomplished by moving the tag of the source floating-point register to the tag of the sink floating-point register. For example, in the sequence

```
AD      F0,    FLB1
LDR     F2,    F0          move F0 to F2
```

the tag of F0 will be 1010 (A1) at the time the LDR is decoded. The decoder simply sets F2's tag to 1010. Now, when the result of the AD appears on the CDB both F0 and F2 will ingate since the CDB tag of 1010 will match the tag of each register. Thus, no unit or extra time was required for the execution of the LDR.

A number of details have been omitted from this discussion in order to clarify the concept, but really only two are of operational significance. First, every unit must request the CDB two cycles before it finishes execution. (These two cycles are required for propagation of the request to the CDB controls, the establishment of priority among competing units, and propagation of a "select" signal to the chosen unit.) This limits the execution time of any instruction to a two-cycle minimum. (Of course, the faster the execution the less the need for, or gain from, concurrency.) It also adds one[1] cycle to the access time for loads. Because of buffering and overlap, this does not usually cause an increase in problem running time.

The second point is concerned with mixed precision. Because the architectural definition causes the low-order part of an FLR to be preserved during single-precision operation, an error can occur in the following kind of program:

```
LD      F0,    FLB1
AD      F0,    FLB2
AE      F0,    FLB3
```

Since only the last instruction, which is single-precision, will change F0, the low order result of the double-precision AD will be lost. This is handled by associating a bit with each register to indicate whether a particular register is the sink of an outstanding single- or double-precision instruction. If this bit does not match

the "length" of the instruction being decoded, the decode is suspended until the busy bit goes off. While this stratagem[2] solves the logic problem, it does so at the expense of performance. Unfortunately, no way has been found to avoid this. Note, however, that all-single- or all-double-precision programs run at the maximum possible speed. It is only the interface between single- and double-precision to the *same* sink register that suffers delay.

Conclusions

Two concepts of some significance to the design of high-performance computers have been presented. The first, reservation stations, is simply an expeditious method of buffering, in an environment where the transmission time between units is of consequence. Because of the disparity between storage access and circuit speeds and because of dependencies between successive operations, it is observed (given multiple execution units) that each unit spends much of its time waiting for operands. In effect, the reservation stations do the waiting for operands while the execution circuitry is free to be engaged by whichever reservation station fills first.

The second, and more important, innovation, the CDB, utilizes the reservation stations and a simple tagging scheme to preserve precedence while encouraging concurrency. In conjunction with the various kinds of buffering in the CPU, the CDB helps render the Model 91 less sensitive to programming. It should be evident, however, that the programmer still exercises substantial control over how much concurrency will occur. The two different programs for doing A + B + C + D * E illustrate this clearly.

It might appear that the CDB adds one cycle to the execution time of each operation, but in fact it does not. In practice only 30 nsec of the 60-nsec CDB interval are required to perform all of the CDB functions. The remaining time could, in this case, be used by the execution unit to achieve a shorter effective cycle. For example, if an add requires 120 nsec, then add plus the CDB time required is 150 nsec. Therefore, as far as the add is concerned, the machine cycle could be 50 nsec. Besides, even without the CDB, a similar amount of time would be required to transmit results both to the floating-point registers and back as an input to the unit generating the result.

The following program, a typical partial differential equation inner loop, illustrates the possible performance increase.

---

[1] It does not add two cycles since storage gives one cycle prenotification of the arrival of data.

[2] Further complications arise from the fact that single-precision multiply produces a double-precision product. This is handled separately but with the same time penalty as above.

```
LOOP    MD      F0,   Ai
        AD      F0,   Bi
        LD      F2,   Ci
        SDR     F2,   F0
        MDR     F2,   F6
        AD2     F2,   Ci
        STD     F2,   Ci
        BXH     i,   −1, 0  LOOP
```

Without the CDB one iteration of the loop would use 17 cycles, allowing 4 per MD, 3 per AD and nothing for LD or STD. With the CDB one iteration requires 11 cycles. For this kind of code the CDB improves performance by about one third.

References

Tomasulo [1967]; Anderson, Earle, Goldschmidt, and Powers [1967]; Anderson, Sparacio, and Tomasulo [1967].

```
S360.MODEL.91.MFU :=
    begin

! ISPS description of the 360/91 Floating-Point Execution Unit (FLEU).

! Reference: (1) R.M.Tomasulo, "An Efficient Algorithm for Expoiting
!               Multiple Arithmetic Units", IBM Journal, January 1967,
!               Pages 25-33.

!            (2) S.F.Anderson, et.al.., "The IBM System/360 Model 91:
!               Floating-Point Execution Unit", IBM Journal, January 1967,
!               Pages 34-53.

! ISP Implementation notes:

!      Actual execution of floating point instructions is not
!      described.

!      Reference (2) indicates that FLRs and FLBs are 72 bits long.
!      All other indications (ref(1)) lead to the conclusion that
!      they are 69 bits long.

!      Reference (2) shows the FLOS registers to be 14 bits long.
!      If the floating point instruction opcodes are mapped from the
!      standard eight bits to six bits, the FLOS will contain
!      14 bit registers.  The mapping was accomplished by eliminating
!      bits <0> and <2> which are identical in all instructions.
!      Register arrays that contain TAGS and other control bits
!      are implemented with separate TAG and BUSY arrays.
!      This implementation is a restriction of the ISPS simulator,
!      not of the ISPS language.

!      This description does not provide any of the functions of the
!      360/91 Instruction Unit or main memory access.  For simulation,
!      it is necessary to load the FLOS with instructions folded
!      to 14 bits as noted above.  It is also necessary to preset all
!      initial tags an busy bits and load the FLBs prior to simulation.

**FLEU.State**

    FLB[1:6]<0:63>    := bufs[1:6]<0:63>,! Floating Point Buffers (FLB)
    FLB.BUSY[1:6]<>   := busys[1:6]<>,   ! Floating Point Buffer Busy
                                         ! Communication with external storage

    FLR[1:4]<0:63> := bufs[7:10]<0:63>,  ! Floating Point registers
    FLR.TAG[1:4]<0:3>:=tags[7:10]<0:3>,  ! Register tag field
    FLR.BUSY[1:4]<>:= busys[7:10]<>,     ! Register busy field

    SDB[1:3]<0:63>:= bufs[11:13]<0:63>,  ! Store Data Buffer
    SDB.TAG[1:3]<0:3>:=tags[11:13]<0:3>,! Store Data Buffer tag field
    SDB.BUSY[1:3]<>   := busys[11:13]<>, ! Store Data Buffer busy field
                                         ! Communication with external storage

    FLOS[1:8]<0:13>,                     ! Floating Point Operation Stack

    flosio<0:2>,                         ! Counter for number of instructions
                                         ! in FLOS.

    ir<0:13>,                            ! Instruction register
        opcode<0:5> := ir<0:5>,          ! Operation code
        R1<0:3>     := ir<6:9>,          ! Sink register
        R2<0:3>     := ir<10:13>,        ! Source register

    pc<0:2>,                             ! "Program counter" for FLOS

**MD.Unit.State**

    MRS.SINK[8:9]<0:63> :=               ! Multiplier reserve (sink) stations
          bufs[14:15]<0:63>,
    MRS.SINK.TAG[8:9]<0:3> :=            ! Multiplier reserve (sink) tag
          tags[14:15]<0:3>,
    MRS.SINK.BUSY[8:9]<> :=              ! Multiplier reserve (sink) busy
          busys[14:15]<>,

    MRS.SOURCE[8:9]<0:63> :=             ! Multiplier reserve (source) stations
          bufs[16:17]<0:63>,
    MRS.SOURCE.TAG[8:9]<0:3> :=          ! Multiplier reserve (source) tag
          tags[16:17]<0:3>,
    MRS.SOURCE.BUSY[8:9]<> :=            ! Multiplier reserve (source) busy
          busys[16:17]<>,

    mrs.busy[8:9]<>,                     ! Station free (0) or busy (1).

    MRS.CONTROL[8:9]<0:5>,               ! Multiply reservation station
                                         ! control bits - actual size
                                         ! and use in 360/91 is unknown

    MPY.RESULT<0:63>,                    ! Multiplier result buffer

    mrs<5:0>,                            ! Address of current reservation station
**Add.Unit.State**

    ARS.SINK[10:12]<0:63> :=             ! Adder reserve (sink) stations
          bufs[18:20]<0:63>,
    ARS.SINK.TAG[10:12]<0:3> :=          ! Adder reserve (sink) tag
          tags[18:20]<0:3>,
    ARS.SINK.BUSY[10:12]<> :=            ! Adder reserve (sink) busy
          busys[18:20]<>,

    ARS.SOURCE[10:12]<0:63> :=           ! Adder reserve (source) stations
          bufs[21:23]<0:63>,
```

```
    ARS.SOURCE.TAG[10:12]<0:3> :=        ! Adder reserve (source) tag
          tags[21:23]<0:3>,
    ARS.SOURCE.BUSY[10:12]<> :=          ! Adder reserve (source) busy
          busys[21:23]<>,

    ars.busy[10:12]<>,                   ! Station free (0) or busy (1).

    ARS.CONTROL[10:12]<0:5>,             ! Add reservation station control
                                         ! bits - actual number and use
                                         ! in 360/91 is unknown

    add.result<0:63>,                    ! Adder result

    ars<5:0>,                            ! Address of current reservation station

**Implementation.Declarations**

    bufs[1:23]<0:63>,
    tags [1:23]<0:3>,
    busys[1:23]<>,

    newflb<>,

    macro not.defined := |no.op()|,

**FLEU.Execution**

    start(main) :=
        begin
        mrs = 8;
        pc = 0;
        newflb = 1;
        ars = 10 next
        FLR.BUS(); FLB.BUS(); MD.UNIT(); ADD.UNIT();
        flos.decode()
        end,

    flos.decode :=
        begin
        WAIT (flosio neq '0000) next
        ir = FLOS[pc + 1] next
        begin{us}
        DECODE opcode<0>@opcode<2:5> =>         ! Decode into groups according
            begin                               ! to execution unit.
[#10,#30,
 #02,#20] := DECODE opcode =>                   ! Loads and stores
            begin
            [#40, #60] := begin                 ! Store operations
                SDB.BUSY[R2] = 1;
                DECODE FLR.BUSY[map(R1)] =>
                    begin
                    0 := SDB.TAG[R2] = map(R1) + 6,
                    1 := SDB.TAG[R2] = FLR.TAG[map(R1)]
                    end
                end,
            otherwise   := begin                ! Load operations
                FLR.BUSY[map(R1)] = 1;
                FLR.TAG[map(R1)]  = R2
                end
            end,
[#14,#34,
 #15,#35] := (IF (free.md() eql 0) => RESTART flos.decode next md()),
 otherwise := (IF (free.add() eql 0) => RESTART flos.decode next add())
            end
        end next
        pc = (pc + 1) mod 8 next
        flosio = flosio - 1 next
        RESTART flos.decode
        end,

    md :=                                ! Instruction to multiply/divide
        begin
        MRS.CONTROL[free.md] = opcode next
        DECODE FLR.BUSY[map(R1)] =>                    ! Sink busy?
            begin
            0 := (MRS.SINK[free.md] = FLR[map(R1)] next
                FLR.BUSY[map(R1)] = 1; FLR.TAG[map(R1)] = free.md;
                MRS.SINK.BUSY[free.md] = 0),
            1 := (MRS.SINK.TAG[free.md] = FLR.TAG[map(R1)];
                MRS.SINK.BUSY[free.md] = 1 next
                FLR.TAG[map(R1)] = free.md)
            end next
        DECODE opcode<0> =>                            ! Source decode
            begin
            0 := DECODE FLR.BUSY[map(R2)] =>           ! RR format
                begin
                0 := (MRS.SOURCE[free.md] = FLR[map(R2)];
                    MRS.SOURCE.BUSY[free.md] = 0),
                1 := (MRS.SOURCE.TAG[free.md] = FLR.TAG[map(R2)];
                    MRS.SOURCE.BUSY[free.md] = 1)
                end,
            1 := DECODE FLB.BUSY[R2] =>                ! RX format
                begin
                0 := (MRS.SOURCE.TAG[free.md] = FLB[R2];
                    MRS.SOURCE.BUSY[free.md] = 0),
                1 := (MRS.SOURCE.TAG[free.md] = R2;
                    MRS.SOURCE.BUSY[free.md] = 1)
                end
            end
        end,
```

APPENDIX (cont'd)

```
    free.md()<0:3> :=              ! See if a multiply unit is free
      begin
      free.md = 0 next
      IF not mrs.busy[9] => free.md = 9 next
      IF not mrs.busy[8] => free.md = 8 next
      IF free.md neq 0 => mrs.busy[free.md] = 1
      end,

    add :=                         ! Instruction to Add unit
      begin
      ARS.CONTROL[free.add] = opcode next
      DECODE FLR.BUSY[map(R1)] =>
        begin
        0 := (ARS.SINK[free.add] = FLR[map(R1)] next
             FLR.BUSY[map(R1)] = 1; FLR.TAG[map(R1)] = free.add;
             ARS.SINK.BUSY[free.add] = 0),
        1 := (ARS.SINK.TAG[free.add] = FLR.TAG[map(R1)];
             ARS.SINK.BUSY[free.add] = 1 next
             FLR.TAG[map(R1)] = free.add)
        end next
      DECODE opcode<0> =>                         ! Source decode
        begin
        0 := DECODE FLR.BUSY[map(R2)] =>          ! RR format
             begin
             0 := (ARS.SOURCE[free.add] = FLR[map(R2)];
                  ARS.SOURCE.BUSY[free.add] = 0),
             1 := (ARS.SOURCE.TAG[free.add] = FLR.TAG[map(R2)];
                  ARS.SOURCE.BUSY[free.add] = 1)
             end,
        1 := DECODE FLB.BUSY[R2] =>               ! RX format
             begin
             0 := (ARS.SOURCE[free.add] = FLB[R2];
                  ARS.SOURCE.TAG[free.add] = 0),
             1 := (ARS.SOURCE.TAG[free.add] = R2;
                  ARS.SOURCE.BUSY[free.add] = 1)
             end
        end
      end,

    free.add()<0:3> :=             ! See if an Adder is free
      begin
      free.add = 0 next
      IF not ars.busy[12] => free.add = 12 next
      IF not ars.busy[11] => free.add = 11 next
      IF not ars.busy[10] => free.add = 10 next
      IF free.add neq 0 => ars.busy[free.add] = 1
      end,

**MD.Execution**

    MD.UNIT{process; us} :=
      begin
      IF not.mrs.busy[mrs] or
         (MRS.SOURCE.BUSY[mrs] or MRS.SINK.BUSY[mrs]) =>
         begin
         mrs<0> = not mrs<0> next        ! Look at other station
         RESTART MD.UNIT
         end next
      DECODE MRS.CONTROL[mrs] =>
         begin
         '00 := mult.long    := not.defined, ! Instruction executions
         '01 := mult.short   := not.defined, !  are not implemented
         '10 := divide.long  := not.defined,
         '11 := divide.short := not.defined
         end next
      CDB(mpy.result, mrs) next
      WAIT (CDB eql mrs) next
      mrs.busy[mrs] = 0;
      MRS.SOURCE.BUSY[mrs] = MRS.SINK.BUSY[mrs] = 0 next
      RESTART MD.UNIT
      end,

**Adder.Execution**

    ADD.UNIT{process; us} :=
      begin
      IF not ars.busy[ars] or
         (ARS.SINK.BUSY[ars] or ARS.SOURCE.BUSY[ars]) =>
         begin
         ars = ars + 1 next
         IF ars gtr 12 => ars = 10 next
         RESTART ADD.UNIT
         end next
      DECODE ars.control[ars] =>      ! Actual Instruction executions
         begin                        !  are not described.
         #00 := LPDR := not.defined, ! RR: Load positive-long
         #01 := LNDR := not.defined, ! RR: Load negative-long
         #03 := LCDR := not.defined, ! RR: Load complement-long
         #04 := HDR  := not.defined, ! RR: Halve-long
         #11 := CDR  := not.defined, ! RR: Compare-long
         #12 := ADR  := not.defined, ! RR: Add normalized-long
         #13 := SDR  := not.defined, ! RR: Subtract normalized-long
         #16 := AWR  := not.defined, ! RR: Add unnormalized-long
         #17 := SWR  := not.defined, ! RR: Subtract unnormalized-long) -RR
         #20 := LPER := not.defined, ! RR: Load positive-short
         #21 := LNER := not.defined, ! RR: Load negative-short
         #23 := LCER := not.defined, ! RR: Load complement-short
         #24 := HER  := not.defined, ! RR: Halve-short
         #31 := CER  := not.defined, ! RR: Compare-short
         #32 := AER  := not.defined, ! RR: Add normalized-short
         #33 := SER  := not.defined, ! RR: Subtract normalized-short
         #36 := AUR  := not.defined, ! RR: Add unnormalized-short
```

```
         #37 := SUR  := not.defined, ! RR: Subtract unnormalized-short
         #51 := CD   := not.defined, ! RX: Compare-long
         #52 := AD   := not.defined, ! RX: Add normalized-long
         #53 := SD   := not.defined, ! RX: Subtract normalized-long
         #56 := AW   := not.defined, ! RX: Add unnormalized-long
         #57 := SW   := not.defined, ! RX: Subtract unnormalized-long
         #71 := CE   := not.defined, ! RX: Compare-short
         #72 := AE   := not.defined, ! RX: Add normalized-short
         #73 := SE   := not.defined, ! RX: Subtract normalized-short
         #76 := AU   := not.defined, ! RX: Add unnormalized-short
         #77 := SU   := not.defined, ! RX: Subtract unnormalized-short
         otherwise := no.op()
         end next
      CDB(add.result, ars) next
      WAIT (CDB eql ars) next
      ars.busy[ars] = 0;
      ARS.SOURCE.BUSY[ars] = ARS.SINK.BUSY[ars] = 0 next
      RESTART ADD.UNIT
      end,

    map(r<3:0>)<3:0>{us} :=     ! Routine to map FLR numbers 0,2,4,8 to
      begin                     !  the ISPS required numbers: 1,2,3,4.
      DECODE  r =>
         begin
         0 := map = 1,
         2 := map = 2,
         4 := map = 3,
         8 := map = 4,
      otherwise := map = r
         end
      end,

CDB(cdb.data<0:63>, cdb.tag<0:3>)<5:0>{process; critical} :=
    begin

! The Common Data Bus has the outputs of the Add Unit, the
! Multiply Unit, and the Floating Buffers as sources.
! Destinations are the Add and Multiply reservation stations,
! the registers, and the store data buffers.

**CDB.Control**

    ctr<5:0>,                   ! Counter

    **CDB.Execution**

    cdbus{main; us} :=
      begin
      CDB = 0;
      ctr = 7 next
      cdb.run :=
         begin
         IF (tags[ctr] eql cdb.tag) and (busys[ctr]) =>
            (bufs[ctr] = cdb.data; busys[ctr] = 0) next
         ctr = ctr + 1 next
         IF ctr lss 23 => RESTART cdb.run
         end next
      CDB = cdb.tag
      end
    end,

FLR.BUS{process} :=
    begin

! The FLR bus has the floating registers as the source and
! The reservation stations of both the Multiply and Add units
! as destinations.

**FLR.Bus.Control**

    ctr<5:0>,                   ! Counter

    **FLR.Execution**

    flrbus{main; us} :=
      begin
      IF not FLR.BUSY[1] => FLR.CHK(FLR[1], 7) next
      IF not FLR.BUSY[2] => FLR.CHK(FLR[2], 8) next
      IF not FLR.BUSY[3] => FLR.CHK(FLR[3], 9) next
      IF not FLR.BUSY[4] => FLR.CHK(FLR[4], 10) next
      RESTART flrbus
      end,

    FLR.CHK(flr.data<0:63>, flrtag<0:3>)<0:3> :=
      begin
      ctr = 11 next
      flr.run :=
         begin
         IF (tags[ctr] eql flrtag) and (busys[ctr]) =>
            (bufs[ctr] = flr.data; busys[ctr] = 0) next
         ctr = ctr + 1 next
         IF ctr lss 23 => RESTART flr.run
         end
      end,
```

APPENDIX (cont'd)

```
FLB.BUS(process) :=
    begin

! The floating point buffers are the source.  The destinations are:
! the Add Reservation Station Source buffers and the Multiply
! Reversation Station Source buffers.

**FLB.Bus.Control**

    ctr<5:0>,                    ! Counter

    **FLB.Execution**

    flbbus{main; us} :=
        begin
        WAIT(newflb) next
        IF not FLB.BUSY[1] => FLB.CHK(FLB[1], 1) next
        IF not FLB.BUSY[2] => FLB.CHK(FLB[2], 2) next
        IF not FLB.BUSY[3] => FLB.CHK(FLB[3], 3) next
        IF not FLB.BUSY[4] => FLB.CHK(FLB[4], 4) next
        IF not FLB.BUSY[5] => FLB.CHK(FLB[5], 5) next
        IF not FLB.BUSY[6] => FLB.CHK(FLB[6], 6) next
        newflb = 0 next
        RESTART flbbus
        end,

    FLB.CHK(flb.data<0:63>, flbtag<0:3>)<0:3> :=
        begin
        ctr = 16 next
        flb.run :=
            begin
            IF (tags[ctr] eql flbtag) and (busys[ctr]) =>

                (bufs[ctr] = flb.data; busys[ctr] = 0) next
            ctr = ctr + 1 next
            IF ctr eql 18 => ctr = 21 next
            IF ctr lss 23 => RESTART flb.run
            end
        end
    end

end     ! End of 360/91 MFU
```

Chapter 20

The Illiac IV System[1]

W. J. Bouknight / *Stewart A. Denenberg*
David E. McIntyre / *J. M. Randall*
Amed H. Sameh / *Daniel L. Slotnick*

Abstract The reasons for the creation of Illiac IV are described and the history of the Illiac IV project is recounted. The architecture or hardware structure of the Illiac IV is discussed—the Illiac IV array is an array processor with a specialized control unit (CU) that can be viewed as a small stand-alone computer. The Illiac IV software strategy is described in terms of current user habits and needs. Brief descriptions are given of the systems software itself, its history, and the major lessons learned during its development. Some ideas for future development are suggested. Applications of Illiac IV are discussed in terms of evaluating the function $f(x)$ simultaneously on up to 64 distinct argument sets x_i. Many of the time-consuming problems in scientific computation involve repeated evaluation of the same function on different argument sets. The argument sets which compose the problem data base must be structured in such a fashion that they can be distributed among 64 separate memories. Two matrix applications: Jacobi's algorithm for finding the eigenvalues and eigenvectors of real symmetric matrices, and reducing a real nonsymmetric matrix to the upper-Hessenberg form using Householder's transformations are discussed in detail. The ARPA network, a highly sophisticated and wide ranging experiment in the remote access and sharing of computer resources, is briefly described and its current status discussed. Many researchers located about the country who will use Illiac IV in solving problems will do so via the network. The various systems, hardware, and procedures they will use is discussed.

Introduction

It all began in the early 1950's shortly after EDVAC ["Electronic Computers," 1969] became operational. Hundreds, then thousands of computers were manufactured, and they were generally organized on Von Neumann's concepts, as shown and described in Fig. 1. In the decade between 1950 and 1960, memories became cheaper and faster, and the concept of archival storage was evolved; control-and-arithmetic and logic units became more sophisticated: I/O devices expanded from typewriter to magnetic tape units, disks, drums, and remote terminals. But the four basic components of a conventional computer (control unit (CU), arithmetic-and-logic unit (ALU), memory, and I/O) were all present in one form or another.

The turning away from the conventional organization came in

[1]Subsetted from *Proc. IEEE*, April 1972, pp. 369–388.

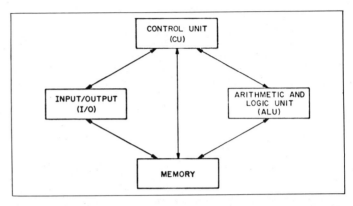

Fig. 1. Functional relations within a conventional computer. The CU has the function of fetching instructions which are stored in memory, decoding or interpreting these instructions, and finally generating the microsequences of electronic pulses which cause the instruction to be performed. The performance of the instruction may entail the use or "driving" of one of the three other components. The CU may also contain a small amount of memory called registers that can be accessed faster than the main memory. The ALU contains the electronic circuitry necessary to perform arithmetic and logical operations. The ALU may also contain register storage. Memory is the medium by which information (instructions or data) is stored. The I/O accepts information which is input to or output from Memory. The I/O hardware may also take care of converting the information from one coding scheme to another. The CU and ALU taken together are sometimes called a CPU.

the middle 1960's, when the law of diminishing returns began to take effect in the effort to increase the operational speed of a computer. Up until this point the approach was simply to speed up the operation of the electronic circuitry which comprised the four major functional components. (See Fig. 1.)

Electronic circuits are ultimately limited in their speed of operation by the speed of light (light travels about one foot in a nanosecond) and many of the circuits were already operating in the nanosecond time range. So, although faster circuits could be made, the amount of money necessary to produce these faster circuits was not justifiable in terms of the small percentage increase of speed.

At this stage of the problem two new approaches evolved.

1 *Overlap:* The hardware structure of the conventional organization was modified so that two or more of the major functional components (or subcomponents within a major component) could overlap their operations. Overlap means that more than one operation is occurring during the same time interval, and thus total operation time is decreased.

Before operations could be overlapped, control sequences between the components had to be decoupled. Certainly the CU could at least be fetching the next instruction while the ALU was executing the present one.

2 *Replication:* One of the four major components (or subcomponents within a major component) could be duplicated many times. (Ten black boxes can produce the result of one black box in one-tenth of the time if the conditions are right.) The replication of I/O devices, for example, was a step taken very early in the evolution of digital computers—large installations had more than one tape drive, more than one card reader, more than one printer.

Since the above two philosophies do not mutually exclude each other, a third approach exists which consists of both of them in a continuously variable range of proportions.

The overlapping philosophy was implemented largely through the buffer and pipeline mechanisms. The pipeline mechanism (see Fig. 2) breaks down an operation into suboperations, or stages, and decouples these stages from each other. After the stages are decoupled they can be performed simultaneously or, equivalently, in parallel. The buffer mechanism allows an operation to be decoupled into parallel operation by providing a place to store information.

The replication philosophy is exemplified by the general multiprocessor which replicates three of the four major components (all but the I/O) many times. The cost of a general multiprocessor is, however, very high and further design options

were considered which would decrease the cost without seriously degrading the power or efficiency of the system. The options consist merely of recentralizing one of the three major components which had been previously replicated in the general multiprocessor—the memory, the ALU, or the CU. Centralizing the CU gives rise to the basic organization of a vector or array processor such as Illac IV. This particular option was chosen for two main reasons.

1 *Cost:* A very high percentage of the cost within a digital computer is associated with CU circuitry. Replication of this component is particularly expensive, and therefore centralizing the CU saves more money than can be saved by centralizing either of the other two components.

2 *Structure:* There is a large class of both scientific and business problems that can be solved by a computer with one CU (one instruction stream) and many ALUs. The same algorithm is performed repetitively on many sets of different data: the data are structured as a vector, and the vector processor of Illac IV operates on the vector data. All of the components of data structured as a vector are processed simultaneously or in parallel.

The Illac IV project was started in the Computer Science Department at the University of Illinois with the objective of developing a digital system employing the principle of parallel operation to achieve a computational rate of 10^9 instructions/s. In order to achieve this rate, the system was to employ 256

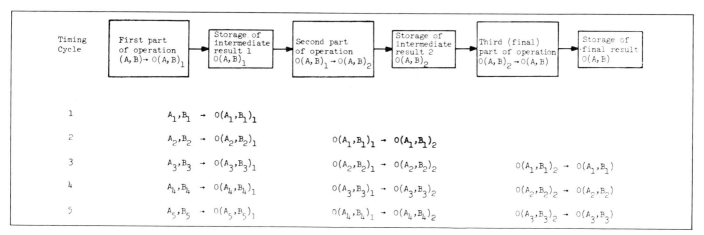

Fig. 2. Pipelined operation. The large boxes represent the circuits required to transform the operands A and B into the Quantity $O(A, B)$ (some function of A and B, say, the sum of A and B). The smaller boxes represent storage stages for the intermediate results $O(A, B)_1$ and $O(A, B)_2$ and the desired result $O(A, B)$. The operation O has been broken down into three stages, each of which accepts as input the output of the previous stage, and all of which perform a stage of the operation at the same time. At each step of the timing cycle, the pipeline accepts a new pair of operands (A, B) and the previous pair moves to the next stage. This mode of operation causes results (the sum in this example) to appear at the end of the pipeline at time intervals equal to the time of operation of the slowest stage of the pipeline.

processors operating simultaneously under a central control divided into four subassembly quadrants of 64 processors each. Due primarily to subcontractor problems several basic technological changes were necessitated during the course of the program, principally, reduction in individual logic-circuit complexity and memory technology. These resulted in cost escalation and schedule delays, ultimately limiting the system to one quadrant with an overall speed of approximately 200 million instructions/s. It is this one-quadrant system that will be discussed for the remainder of this paper.

The approach taken in Illiac IV surmounts fundamental limitations in ultimate computer speed by allowing—at least in principle—an unlimited number of computational events to take place simultaneously. The logical design of Illiac IV is patterned after that of the Solomon [Slotnick, Borck, and McReynolds, 1962; Slotnick, 1967] computers, prototypes of which were built by the Westinghouse Electric Corporation in the early 1960's. In this design a single master CU sends instructions to a sizable number of independent processing elements (PEs) and transmits addresses to individual memory units associated with these PEs ("PE memories," PEMs). Thus, while a single sequence of instructions (the program) still does the controlling, it controls a number of PEs that execute the same instruction simultaneously on data that can be, and usually are, different in the memory of each PE.

Each of the 64 PEs of Illiac IV is a powerful computing unit in its own right. It can perform a wide range of arithmetical operations on numbers that are 64 binary digits long. These numbers can be in any of the six possible formats: the number can be processed as a single number 64 bits long in either a fixed or a "floating" point representation, or the 64 bits can be broken up into smaller numbers of equal length. Each of the memory units has a capacity of 2048 64-bit numbers. The time required to extract a number from memory (the access time) is 188 ns, but because additional logic circuitry is needed to resolve conflicts when two or more sections of Illiac IV call on the memory simultaneously, the minimum time between successive operations of memory is increased to 350 ns.

Each PE has more than 100,000 distinct electronic components assembled into some 12,000 switching circuits. A PE together with its memory unit and associated logic is called a processing unit (PU). In a system containing more than six million components one can expect a component or a connection to fail once every few hours. For this reason much attention has been devoted to testing and diagnostic procedures. Each of the 64 processing units will be subjected regularly to an extensive library of automatic tests. If a unit should fail one of these tests, it can be quickly unplugged and replaced by a spare, with only a brief loss of operating time. When the defective unit has been taken out of service, the precise cause of the failure will be determined by a separate diagnostic computer. Once the fault has been found and repaired, the unit will be returned to the inventory of spares.

Illiac IV could not have been designed at all without much help from other computers. Two medium-sized Burroughs 5500 computers worked almost full time for two years preparing the artwork for the system's printed circuit boards and developing diagnostic and testing programs for the system's logic and hardware. These formidable design, programming, and operating efforts were under the direction of Arthur B. Carroll, who, during this period, was the project's deputy principal investigator.

The Illiac IV system is scheduled for completion by the end of this calendar year; the fabrication phase is essentially complete with some final assembly and considerable debugging yet to be completed.[1]

Hardware Structure

Illiac IV in Brief

As stated in the Introduction, the original design of Illiac IV contained four CUs, each of which controlled a 64-ALU array processor. The version being built by the Burroughs Corporation will have only one CU which drives 64 ALUs as shown in Fig. 3. It is for this reason that Illiac IV is sometimes referred to as a quadrant (one-fourth of the original machine) and it is this abbreviated version of Illiac IV that will be discussed for the remainder of this paper. For a more complete description of the Illiac IV architecture see Slotnick [1971]; Denenberg [1971]; and Barnes et al. [1968].

One difference between Illiac IV and a general array processor is that the CU has been decoupled from the rest of the array processor so that certain instructions can be executed completely

[1]All of this work was sponsored under a Grant (Contract USAF 30(602)4144) from the Advanced Research Projects Agency.

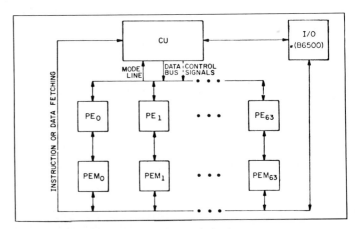

Fig. 3. Functional block diagram of Illiac IV.

within the resources of the CU at the same time that the ALU is performing its vector operations. In this way another degree of parallelism is exploited in addition to the inherent parallelism of 64 ALUs being driven simultaneously. What we have is 2 computers inside Illiac IV: one that operates on scalars, and one that operates on vectors. All of the instructions, however, emanate from the computer that operates on scalars—the CU.

Each element of the ALU array is not called by its generic name (ALU) but is called a PE. There are 64 PEs, and they are numbered from 0 to 63. Each PE responds to appropriate instructions if the PE is in an active *mode*. (There exist instructions in the repertoire which can activate or deactivate a PE.) Each PE performs the same operation under command from the CU in the lock-stepped manner of an array processor. That is, since there is only one CU, there is only one instruction stream and all of the ALUs respond together or are lock-stepped to the current instruction. If the current instruction is ADD for example, then all the ALUs will add—there can be no instruction which will cause some of the ALUs to be adding while others are multiplying. Every ALU in the array performs the instruction operation in this lock-stepped fashion, but the operands are vectors whose components can be, and usually are, different.

Each PE has a full complement of arithmetic and logical circuitry, and under command from the CU will perform an instruction "at-a-crack" as an array processor. Each PE has its own 2048 word 64-bit memory called a PE memory (PEM) which can be accessed in no longer than 350 ns. Special routing instructions can be used to move data from PEM to PEM. Additionally, operands can be sent to the PEs from the CU via a full-word (64-bit) one-way communication line, and the CU has eight-word one-way communication with the PEM array (for instruction and data fetching).

An Illiac IV word is 64 bits, and data numbers can be represented in either 64-bit floating point, 64-bit logical, 48-bit fixed point, 32-bit floating point, 24-bit fixed point, or 8-bit fixed point (character) mode. By utilizing the 64-bit, 32-bit, and 8-bit data formats, the 64 PEs can hold a vector of operands with either 64, 128, or 512 components. Since Illiac IV can add 512 operands in the 8-bit integer mode in about 66 ns, it is capable of performing almost 10^{10} of these "short" additions/s. Illiac IV can perform approximately 150 million 64-bit rounded normalized floating-point additions/s.

The I/O is handled by a B6500 computer system. The operating system, including the assemblers and compilers, also resides in the B6500.

The Illiac IV System

The Illiac IV system can be organized as in Fig. 4. The Illiac IV system consists of the Illiac IV array plus the Illiac IV I/O system. The Illiac IV array consists of the array processor and the CU. In

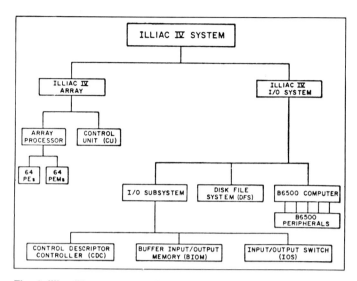

Fig. 4. Illiac IV system organization.

turn, the array processor is made up of 64 PEs and their 64 associated memories—PEMs. The Illiac IV I/O system comprises the I/O subsystem, the disk file system (DFS), and the B6500 control computer. The I/O subsystem is broken down further to the CDC, BIOM, and IOS. The B6500 is actually a medium-scale computer system by itself.

The Illiac IV array will be discussed first, in a general manner, followed by two illustrative problems which indicate some of the similarities and differences in approach to problem solving using sequential and parallel computers. The problems also serve to illustrate how the hardware components are tied together. Finally, the Illiac IV I/O system is discussed briefly.

The Illiac IV Array. Fig. 5 represents the Illiac IV array—the CU plus the array processor.

CU. The CU is not just the CU that we are used to thinking of on a conventional computer, but can be viewed as a small unsophisticated computer in its own right. Not only does it cause the 64 PEs to respond to instructions, but there is a repertoire of instructions that can be completely executed within the resources of the CU, and the execution of these instructions is overlapped with the execution of the instructions which drive the PE array. Again, it is worthwhile to view Illiac IV as being two computers, one which operates on scalars and one which operates on vectors.

The CU contains 64 integrated-circuit registers called the ADVAST data buffer (ADB), which can be used as a high-speed scratch-pad memory. ADVAST is an acronym for advanced station and is one of the five functional sections of the CU. Each register of the ADB (D0 through D63) is 64 bits long. The CU also has 4

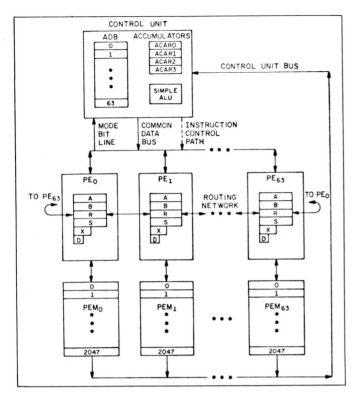

Fig. 5. Illiac IV array.

accumulator registers called ACAR0, ACAR1, ACAR2, and ACAR3, each of which is also 64 bits long. The ACARs can be used as accumulators for integer addition, shifting, Boolean operations, and holding loop-control information—such as the lower limit, increment, and upper limit. In addition the ACARs can be used as index registers to modify storage references within the memory section (PEM).

PE. Each PE is a sophisticated ALU capable of a wide range of arithmetic and logical operations. There are 64 PEs numbered 0 through 63. Each PE in the array has 6 programmable registers: the A register (RGA) or accumulator, the B register (RGB), which holds the second operand in a binary operation (such as ADD, SUBTRACT, MULTIPLY, or DIVIDE), the R or routing register (RGR), which transmits information from one PE to another, the S register (RGS) which can be used as temporary storage by the programmer, the X register (RGX) or index register to modify the address field of an instruction, and the D or mode register (RGD), which controls the active or nonactive status of each PE independently. The RGD determines whether a PE will be active or passive during instruction execution. Since this register is under the programmer's control, individual PEs within the array of 64

PEs may be set to enabled (active) or disabled (passive) status based on the contents of one of the other PE registers. For example, there are instructions which disable all PEs whose RGR contents are greater than their RGA contents. Only those PEs in an enabled state are able to execute the current instruction. All registers are 64 bits except RGX which is 16 bits, and RGD which is 8 bits.

PEM. Each PE has its own 2048-word 64-bits per word random-access memory. Each memory is called a PEM, and they are numbered 0 through 63 also. PE and PEM taken together are called a *processing unit* or PU. PE_i may only access PEM_i so that one PU cannot modify the memory of another PU. Information can, however, be passed from one PU to another via the routing network, which is one of the 4 paths by which data flow through the Illiac IV array.

Data paths. There are four paths by which data flow through the Illiac IV array. These paths are called the CU bus, the common-data bus (CDB), the routing network, and the mode-bit line.

1 *CU bus:* Instructions or data from the PEMs in blocks of eight words can be sent to the CU via the CU bus. The instructions to be executed are distributed throughout the PEMs and are fetched in blocks of eight words to the CU via the CU bus as necessary. Although the operating system takes care of fetching and executing instructions, data can also be fetched in blocks of eight words under program control using the CU bus.

2 *CDB:* Information stored in the CU can be "broadcast" to the entire 64 PE array simultaneously via the CDB. A value such as a constant to be used as a multiplier need not be stored 64 times in each PEM; instead this value can be stored within a CU register and then broadcast to each enabled PE in the array. In addition the operand or address portion of an instruction is sent to the PE array via the CDB.

3 *Routing network:* Information in one PE register can be sent to another PE register by special routing instructions. (Information can be transferred from PE register to PEM by standard LOAD or STORE instructions.) High-speed routing lines run between every RGR of every PE and its nearest left and right neighbor (distances of −1 and +1, respectively) and its neighbor 8 positions to the left and 8 positions to the right (−8 and +8, respectively). Other routing distances are effected by combinations of routing −1, +1, −8, or +8 PEMs; that is, if a route of 5 to the right is desired, the software will figure out that the fastest way to do this is by a right route of 8 followed by three left routes of 1. Fig. 6 shows one way to view the connectivity which exists between PEs. As can be seen from the figure, PE_0 is connected to PE_{56}, PE_1, PE_8, and PE_{63}.

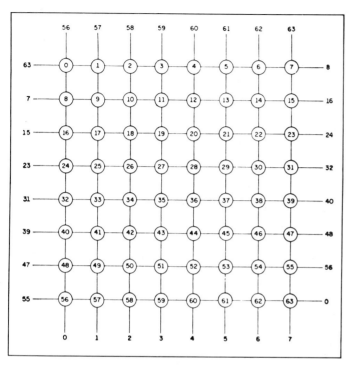

Fig. 6. PE routing connections.

4 *Mode-bit line:* The mode-bit line consists of one line coming from the RGD of each PE in the array. The mode-bit line can transmit one of the eight mode bits of each RGD in the array up to an ACAR in the CU. If this bit is the bit which indicates whether or not a PE is on or off, we can transmit a "mode pattern" to an ACAR. This mode pattern reflects the status or on-offness of each PE in the array; then there are instructions which are executed completely within the CU that can test this mode pattern and branch on a zero or nonzero condition. In this way branching in the instruction stream can occur based on the mode pattern of the entire 64-PE array.

Some Illustrative Problems

Adding two aligned arrays. Let us first consider the problem of adding two arrays of numbers together. The Fortran statements for a conventional computer might look like:

DO 10 I = 1, N

10 $A(I) = B(I) + C(I)$.

The two Fortran instructions are compiled to a set of machine-language instructions which include initialization of the loop,

looping instructions, and the addition of each element of the B array to the proper element in the C array, and storage to the A array. Except for the initialization instructions, the set of machine-language instructions is executed N times. Therefore, if it takes M μs to pass once through the loop, it will take about N times M μs to perform the above Fortran code.

Now suppose the same operations are to be performed on Illac IV. Arrangement of the data in memory becomes a primary consideration—the data must be arranged to exploit the parallelism of operation of the PEs as effectively as possible. The worst way to use the PEs would be to allocate storage for the A, B, and C arrays in just one PEM. Then instructions would have to be written just as they were in a conventional machine to loop through an instruction set N times.

Let us consider the problem as consisting of three cases: $N = 64$, $N < 64$, and $N > 64$, and then see what each case entails in terms of programming for Illac IV.

1   $N = 64$: To reflect the case where $N = 64$, we have arranged the data as shown in Fig. 7. In order to execute the two lines of Fortran code, only the three basic Illac IV machine-language instructions are necessary: 1) LOAD all PE Accumulators (RGA) from location $\alpha + 2$ in all PEMs. 2) ADD to the PE Accumulators (RGA) the contents of location $\alpha + 1$ in all PEMs. 3) STORE result of all PE Accumulators to location α in all PEMs.

Since every PE will execute each instruction *at the same time* or in parallel, accessing its own PEM when necessary, the 64-loads, additions, and stores will be performed while just three instructions are executed. This is a speedup of 64 times for this case, in execution time.

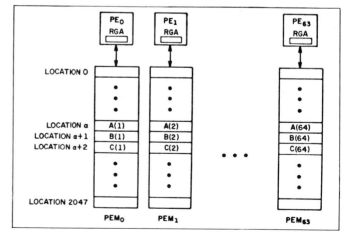

**Fig. 7. Arrangement of data in PEM to accomplish
DO 10 I = 1, 64
10 $A(I) = B(I) + C(I)$.**

The three instructions to perform the 64 additions in Illiac IV assembly language (Ask) would actually look like:

    LDA   ALPHA + 2;
    ADRN   ALPHA + 1;
    STA   ALPHA;

(note that since each instruction operates on a vector; a memory location can be considered a *row* of words rather than a single word).

2   $N<64$: Since there are exactly 64 PEs to perform calculations, a proper question is: what happens if the upper limit of the loop is not exactly equal to 64? If the upper limit is less than 64, there is no problem other than that the total PE array will not be utilized.

   The tradeoff the potential user of Illiac IV must consider here is how much (or how often) is Illiac IV underutilized? If the under-utilization is "too much" then the problem should be considered for running on a conventional computer. However, the user should keep in mind that he usually does not feel too guilty if he underutilizes the resources of a conventional system—he does not use every tape drive, every bit of available core, every printer, and every byte of disk space for most of his conventional programs.

3   $N>64$: When the upper limit of the loop is greater than 64, the programmer is faced with a storage allocation problem. That is, he has various options for storing the A, B, and C arrays, and the program he writes to perform the 2 Fortran statements will vary considerably with the storage allocation scheme chosen. To illustrate this let us consider the special case where $N=66$ with the A, B, and C arrays stored as shown in Fig. 8.

   To perform the 66 additions on the data stored as shown in Fig. 8, *six* Illiac IV machine-language instructions are now necessary:

   LOAD   RGA from location $\alpha + 4$.
   ADD to RGA contents of location $\alpha + 2$.
   STORE result to location α.
   LOAD RGA from location $\alpha + 5$.
   ADD to RGA contents of location $\alpha + 3$.
   STORE result to location $\alpha + 1$.

The addition of two more data items to the A, B, and C arrays not only necessitates extra Illiac IV instructions but complicates the data storage scheme. In this instance, the programmer might as well DIMENSION the A, B, and C arrays to 128 as 66. Note that the particular storage scheme shown in Fig. 8 wastes almost 3 rows of storage (186 words). The storage could have been packed much closer so that $B(1)$ followed $A(66)$ in PE_2 of row $\alpha + 1$, *but* the program to add the arrays together would have to do much more

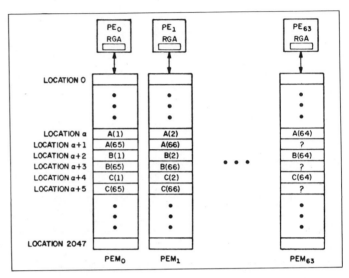

Fig. 8. Arrangement of data in PEM to accomplish
   DO 10 I = 1, 66
10 $A(I) = B(I) + C(I)$.

shuffling to properly align the arrays before adding. An Illiac IV program is highly dependent on the storage scheme chosen.

Uncoupling sequential code. Finally let us consider the Fortran code:

    DO 10 I = 2, 64
    10 $A(I) = B(I) + A(I - 1)$.

How would we do the above instructions on a parallel computer such as Illiac IV? At first, it appears we cannot perform the above algorithm on Illiac IV because it is inherently sequential. If we recognize that the 2 Fortran statements above are only a shorthand for 63 Fortran statements:

    $A(2) = B(2) + A(1)$
    $A(3) = B(3) + A(2)$

    .

    .
    $A(63) = B(63) + A(62)$
    $A(64) = B(64) + A(63)$

and that each of the 63 statements is executed sequentially, we see that each statement in the sequence relies on the result computed from the previous statement. That is, $A(3)$ cannot be computed until the statement above it has computed $A(2)$. Therefore, the 63 additions cannot be done in parallel if we literally try to apply the 2 Fortran statements as they stand. However, using mathematical subscript notation:

$$A_2 = B_2 + A_1$$
$$A_3 = B_3 + A_2 = B_3 + B_2 + A_1$$
$$A_4 = B_4 + A_3 = B_4 + B_3 + B_2 + A_1$$

.

.

.

$$A_N = B_N + B_{N-1} \cdots B_2 + A_1.$$

We see that the elements of the A array can be computed independently using the formula

$$A_N = A_1 + \sum_{i=2}^{N} B_i, \quad \text{for } 2 \leq N \leq 64.$$

The Fortran code to perform the above formula would be:

```
    S = A(1)
    DO 10 N = 2,64
    S = S + B(N)
10  A(N) = S.
```

The above Fortran code is equivalent to the original code (its end

results are the same) but now the computation of the A array has been *decoupled* so that each value of A in the array can be computed *independently*.

An arrangement of data to effect this program is shown in Fig. 9 and the program might be as follows.

1 Enable all PEs. (Turn on all PEs.)

2 All PEs LOAD RGA from location α.

3 $i \leftarrow 0$.

4 All PEs LOAD RGR from their RGA. [This instruction is performed by *all* PEs, whether they are ON (enabled) or OFF (disabled).]

5 All PEs ROUTE their RGR contents a distance of 2^i to the right. (This instruction is also performed by all PEs, regardless of whether they are ON or OFF.)

6 $j \leftarrow 2^i - 1$.

7 Disable PEs number 0 through j. (Turn them OFF.)

8 All enabled PEs ADD to RGA, the contents of RGR. (Fig. 9 shows the state of RGR, RGA, and RGD (the mode status)—which PEs are ON and which are OFF—after this step has been executed when $i = 2$.)

9 $i \leftarrow i + 1$.

10 If $i < 6$ go back to step 4, otherwise to step 11.

11 Enable all PEs.

12 All PEs STORE the contents of RGA to location $\alpha + 1$.

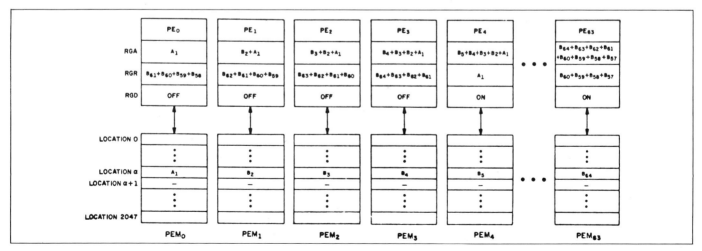

Fig. 9. Status of data in PEM, RGA, RGR, and mode status (RGD) while executing
DO 10 I = 2, 64
10 $A(I) = B(I) + A(I - 1)$.
The mode status (RGD) and the contents of PEM, RGA, and RGR are shown after step 8 (i = 2) of the program.

Note that this same algorithm can be applied to the solution of problems where the recurrence is of the form: $F_i = C_i * F_{i-1}$ which decouples to $F_N = (\prod_{i=2}^{N} C_i)F_1$. All that need be done is that step 8 be changed to MULTIPLY rather than ADD. Note also that if $C_i = i$ $(i = 1,2,\ldots,64)$ and $F_1 = 1$ we have an algorithm for computing $N!$ on Illiac IV; that is, when the algorithm is complete PE_N will contain $(N + 1)!$

This example tries to illustrate that it is not always immediately clear if an algorithm can be decoupled so that it can operate in parallel, or is so dependent on what happened before that it can only be executed sequentially. In this example, it appears that the algorithm is sequential, but upon closer inspection, the parallelism appears. Potential Illiac IV users will probably need much practice in analyzing problems using a parallel viewpoint, especially if they have already been conditioned to viewing their problems only in terms of solving them on a sequential conventional computer. The tool, for better or for worse, shapes the uses it is put to.

Illiac IV I/O System. The Illiac IV array is an extremely powerful information processor, but it has of itself no I/O capability. The I/O capability, along with the supervisory system (including compilers and utilities), resides within the Illiac IV I/O system. The Illiac IV I/O system (see Fig. 10) consists of the I/O subsystem, a DFS, and a B6500 control computer (which in turn supervises a large laser memory and the ARPA network link). The total Illiac IV system consisting of the Illiac IV I/O system and the Illiac IV array is shown in Fig. 11. All system configurations shown are transitory, and more than likely will have changed several times in the next year or so.

I/O subsystem. The I/O subsystem consists of the control descriptor controller (CDC), the buffer I/O memory (BIOM), and the I/O switch (IOS).

1 *CDC:* The CDC monitors a section of the CU waiting for an I/O request to appear. The CDC can then interrupt the B6500 control computer which can, in turn, try to honor the request and place a response code back in that section of the CU via the CDC. This response code indicates the status of the I/O request to the program in the Illiac IV array.

The CDC causes the B6500 to initiate the loading of the PEM array with programs and data from the Illiac IV disk (also called the DFS). After PEM has been loaded, the CDC can then pass control to the CU to begin execution of the Illiac IV program.

2 *BIOM:* The B6500 control computer can transfer information from its memory through its CPU at the rate of 80×10^6 bits/s. The Illiac IV DFS accepts information at the rate of 500×10^6 bits/s. This factor of over six in information transfer rates between the two systems necessitates the placing of a rate-smoothing buffer between them. The BIOM is that buffer. A buffer is also necessary for the conversion of 48-bit B6500 words to 64-bit Illiac IV words which can come out of the BIOM two at a time via the 128-bit wide path to the DFS. The BIOM is actually four PE memories providing 8192 words of 64-bit storage.

3 *IOS:* The IOS performs two functions. As its name implies, it is a switch and is responsible for switching information from either the DFS or from a port which can accept input from a real-time device. All bulk data transfers to and from the PEM array are via IOS. As a switch it must ensure that only one input is sending to the array at a given time. In addition, the IOS acts as a buffer between the DFS and the array, since each channel from the Illiac IV disk to the IOS is 256 bits wide and the bus from the IOS to the PEM array is 1024 bits wide.

DFS. The DFS consists of two storage units, two electronics units, and two disk file controllers. The DFS is also called the Illiac IV disk or simply, the Disk. The Disk is of 10^9-bit capacity, having 128 heads, with one head per track. The DFS has two channels, each of which can transmit or receive data at a rate of 0.5×10^9 bits/s over a path 256 bits wide; however, if both channels are sending or receiving simultaneously the transfer rate is 10^9 bits/s.

B6500 control computer. The 6500 control computer consists of a central processing unit (CPU), a memory, a multiplexor, and a set of peripheral devices (card reader, card punch, line printer, 4 magnetic tape units, 2 disk files and a console printer, and a keyboard). It is the function of the B6500 to manage all programmers' requests for system resources. This means that the operating system will reside on the B6500. All compiling and assembling of programs is also performed on the B6500. Utilities, such as card-to-disk, card-to-tape, etc., are also executed on the B6500. From a total system standpoint, the Illiac IV array can be considered as a special-purpose peripheral device of the B6500

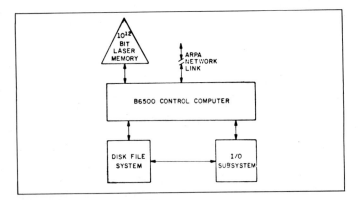

Fig. 10. Illiac IV I/O system.

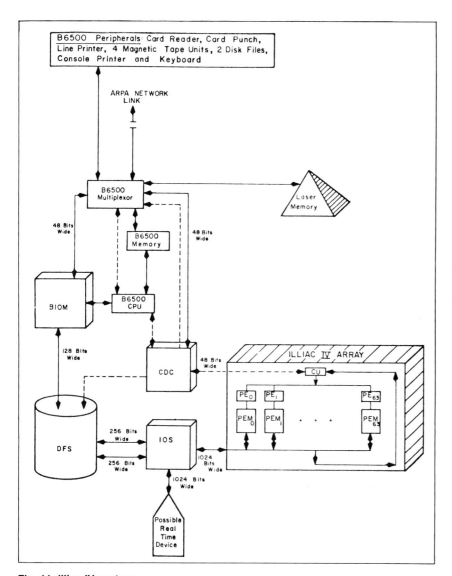

Fig. 11. Illiac IV system.

capable of solving certain classes of problems with extremely high speed.

1 *Laser memory:* The B6500 supervises a 10^{12}-bit write-once read-only laser memory developed by the Precision Instrument Company. The beam from an argon laser records binary data by burning microscopic holes in a thin film of metal coated on a strip of polyester sheet, which is carried by a rotating drum. Each data strip can store some 2.9 billion bits. A "strip file" provides storage for 400 data strips containing more than a trillion bits. The time to locate data

stored on any one of the 400 strips is 5 s. Within the same strip data can be located in 200 ms. The read and record rate is four million bits per second on each of two channels. A projected use of this memory will allow the user to "dump" large quantities of programs and data into this storage medium for leisurely review at a later time; hard copy output can optionally be made from files within the laser memory.

2 *ARPA network link:* The ARPA network is a group of computer installations separated geographically but connected by high-speed (50 000 bits/s) data communication

lines. On these lines, the members of the "net" can transmit information—usually in the form of programs, data, or messages. The link performs an information switching function and is handled by an interface message processor (IMP) and a network control program stored within each member installation's "host" computer. Each IMP operates in a "store and forward mode," that is, information in one IMP is not lost until the receiving IMP has signalled complete reception and retention of the message. The IMP interfaces with each member's computer system and converts information into standard format for transmission to the rest of the net. Conversely, the IMP accepts information in a standard format and converts it to the particular data format of the member installation. In this way, the ARPA network is a form of a computer utility with each contributing member offering its unique resources to all of the other members. The Illiac IV system then is an ARPA network resource that will be shared by the members of the ARPA network; even the host site of the Illiac IV, Ames Research Center at Moffett Field, Calif., will be constrained to access Illiac IV via the ARPA network.

References

Bouknight, Denenberg, McIntyre, Randall, Sameh, and Slotnick [1972]; Barnes, Brown, Kato, Kuck, Slotnick, and Stokes [1968]; Denenberg [1971]; "Electronic Computers" [1969]; Slotnick [1967]; Slotnick [1971]; Slotnick, Borck, and McReynolds [1962].

Chapter 21

A Productive Implementation of an Associative Array Processor: STARAN[1]

Jack A. Rudolph / Kenneth E. Batcher

Introduction [Rudolph]

The associative or content-addressed memory has been an attractive concept to computer designers ever since Slade and McMahon [1957] described a "catalog" memory. Associative memories offered relief from the continuing problem presented by the typical coordinate-addressed memory which requires that an "address" be obtained or calculated before data stored at that address may be retrieved. The associative memory could acquire in a single memory access any data from memoy without pre-knowledge of its location. Ordered files and sorting operations could be eliminated. Unfortunately, early associative memories were expensive, hence none found their way as the "main frame" memory into any commercial computer design.

The organization of an associative memory (AM) requires that each n-bit physical word of the memory be connected to a dedicated processing element (PE) which performs the compare function between a bit read non-destructively from the word and a corresponding input bit from a query word. The PE's for all words are driven by a central controller, thus a single query bit is simultaneously compared with the corresponding stored bit in every word of the AM. With the ability to simultaneously write back the state of each PE into a specified bit position of each word it became possible to perform bit-serial arithmetic between fields of bits within each physical memory word. An array of associative memory words could then be viewed as an array of simple computers—an associative array processor (AP)—with all the simple computers in the array simultaneously executing the same instruction obtained from a common control unit as is done in the more complex ILLIAC-IV design.

An alternative AP design provides a PE at each bit of each physical memory word. This design, though complex in terms of logic and interconnection requirements, permits a simultaneous compare of all bits in a query word with all bits of the memory word rather than the serial-by-bit operation described earlier.

Due to the early high cost of semi-conductor memory and logic

elements none of the many associative processor designs described in the literature were attractive enough to warrant development. However, it has now become commercially feasible to construct a computing system embodying "main frame" memory content addressability coupled with array arithmetic capability operating under a more or less conventional stored program control system.

Several proprietary versions of the associative processor (AP) are being developed. The first working engineering model known to the author, built for USAF by Goodyear Aerospace Corporation, was demonstrated during a Tri-Service contract review in June, 1969 at Akron, Ohio [Fulmer and Meilander, 1970]. The same machine, modified to include a larger instruction memory, was loaned by USAF in 1971 to the FAA for conflict detection tests in a live air traffic control terminal environment at Knoxville, Tennessee operating in a multi-computer configuration with a Univac 1230 conventional computer [Rudolph, Fulmer and Meilander, 1971]. The original test objectives were achieved by December, 1971 and additional experiments involving terrain avoidance processing were completed successfully in June, 1971.

The lessons learned in programming and testing the USAF AP model resulted in a new design called STARAN S which was committed to production in 1971. This first commercial AP was publicly introduced in a series of live demonstrations in May, 1972 at the TRANSPO exhibit in Washington, D.C. and in June, 1972 at Boston, Mass.

This paper describes STARAN S and its programming language, provides examples of its applications, and discusses measures of AP cost-effectiveness.

STARAN Description

A configuration diagram of STARAN S is shown in Fig. 1. Studies have shown that initial uses of AP's would be weighted toward real-time applications involving interface with a wide variety of sensors, conventional computers, signal processors, interactive displays, and mass storage devices. To accommodate all such interfaces the STARAN system was divided into a standardized main frame design and a custom interface unit. A variety of I/O options implemented in the custom interface unit includes conventional direct memory access (DMA), buffered I/O (BIO) channels, external function channels (EXF) and a unique interface called parallel I/O (PIO).

A top-cut diagram of the STARAN main frame is shown in Fig. 2. It consists of a conventionally addressed control memory for program storage and data buffering, a control logic unit for sequencing and decoding instructions from control memory and from one to thirty-two modular AP arrays. A typical AP array is shown in Fig. 2.

To accommodate both bit-slice accesses for associative process-

[1]This chapter is compiled from Rudolph [1972], *Proc. FJCC*, 1972, pp. 229–241; and Batcher [1974], *Proc. NCC*, 1974, pp. 405–410.

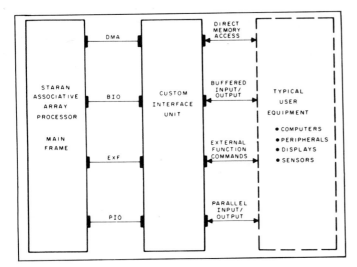

Fig. 1. STARAN system configuration.

ing and word-slice accesses for STARAN input/output (I/O), the data are stored in a multi-dimensional access (MDA) memory (Fig. 2).[1] It has wide read and write busses for parallel access to a large number (256) of memory bits. The write mask bus allows selective writing of memory bits. Memory accesses (both read and write accesses) are controlled by the address and access mode control inputs; the access mode selects a stencil pattern of 256 bits, while the address positions the stencil in memory.

[1]The passage beginning with this paragraph is from Batcher [1974].

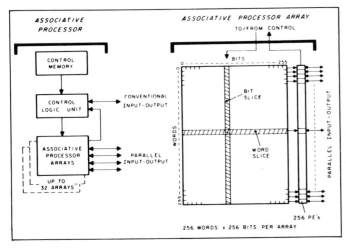

Fig. 2. Associative processor diagrams.

For many applications, the MDA memory is treated as a square array of bits, 256 words with 256 bits in each word. The bit-slice access mode (Fig. 2) is used in the associative operations to access one bit of all words in parallel, while the word access mode (Fig. 2) is used in the I/O operations to access several or all bits of one word in parallel.

The MDA memory structure is not limited to a square array of 256 by 256. For example, the data may be formatted as records with 256 8-bit bytes in each record. Thirty-two such records can be stored in an MDA memory and accessed several ways. To input and output records, one can access 32 consecutive bytes of a record in parallel (Fig. 3a). To search key fields of the data, one can access the corresponding bytes of all records in parallel (Fig. 3b). To search a whole record for the presence of a particular byte, one can access a bit from each byte in parallel (Fig. 3c).

The MDA memories in the STARAN array modules are bipolar. They exhibit read cycle times of less than 150 nsec and write cycle times of less than 250 nsec.

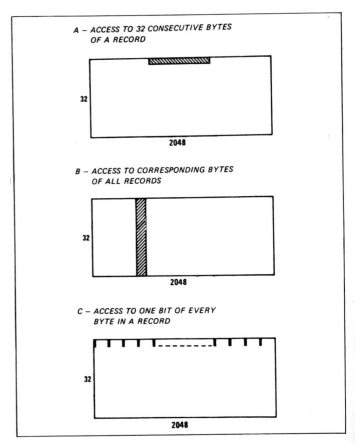

Fig. 3. Accessing 256-byte records.

STARAN Array Modules

A STARAN array module (Fig. 4) contains an MDA memory communicating with three 256-bit registers (M, X, and Y) through a flip (permutation) network. One may think of an array module as having 256 small processing elements (PE's), where a PE contains one bit of the M register, one bit of the X register, and one bit of the Y register.

The M register drives the write mask bus of the MDA memory to select which of the MDA memory bits are modified in a masked-write operation. The MDA memory also has an unmasked-write operation that ignores M and modifies all 256 accessed bits. The M register can be loaded from the other components of the array module.

In general, the logic associated with the X register can perform any of the 16 Boolean functions of two variables; that is, if x_i, is the state of the ith X-register bit, and f_i is the state of the ith flip network output, then:

$$x_i \leftarrow \phi(x_i, f_i) \ (i = 0, 1, \ldots , 255)$$

where ϕ is any Boolean function of two variables. Similarly, the logic associated with the Y-register can perform any Boolean function:

$$y_i \leftarrow \phi(y_i, f_i) \ (i = 0, 1, \ldots , 255)$$

where y_i is the state of the ith Y-register bit. The programmer is given the choice of operating X alone, Y alone, or X and Y together.

If X and Y are operated together, the same Boolean function, ϕ, is applied to both registers:

$$x_i \leftarrow \phi(x_i, f_i)$$
$$y_i \leftarrow \phi(y_i, f_i)$$

The programmer also can choose to operate on X selectively, using Y as a mask:

$$x_i \leftarrow \phi(x_i, f_i) \quad \text{(where } y_i = 1)$$
$$x_i \leftarrow x_i \quad \text{(where } y_i = 0)$$

Another choice is to operate on X selectively while operating on Y:

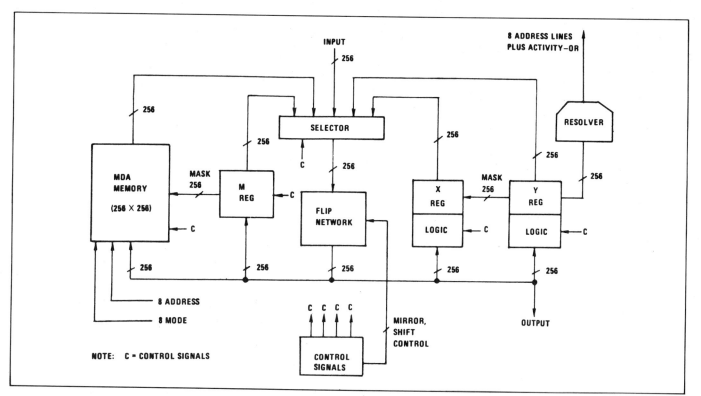

Fig. 4. STARAN array module.

$$x_i \leftarrow \phi \ (x_i, f_i) \qquad \text{(where } y_i = 1)$$
$$x_i \leftarrow x_i \qquad\qquad \text{(where } y_i = 0)$$
$$y_i \leftarrow \phi \ (y_i, f_i)$$

In this case, the old state of Y (before modification by ϕ) is used as the mask for the X operation.

For a programming example, the basic loop of an unmasked add fields operation is selected. This operation adds the contents of a Field A of all memory words to the contents of a Field B of the words and stores the sum in a Field S of the words. For n-bit fields, the operation executes the basic loop n times. During each execution of the loop, a bit-slice (a) of Field A is read from memory, a bit-slice (b) of Field B is read, and a bit-slice (s) of Field S is written into memory. The operation starts at the least significant bits of the fields and steps through the fields to the most significant bits. At the beginning of each loop execution, the carry (c) from the previous bits is stored in Y, and X contains zeroes:

$$x_i = 0$$
$$y_i = c_i$$

The loop has four steps:

Step 1: Read Bit-slice a and exclusive-or ($\oplus$) it to X selectively and also to Y:

$$x_i \leftarrow x_i \oplus y_i a_i$$
$$y_i \leftarrow y_i \oplus a_i$$

The states of X and Y are now:

$$x_i = a_i c_i$$
$$y_i = a_i \oplus c_i$$

Step 2: Read Bit-slice b and exclusive-or it to X selectively and also to Y:

$$x_i \leftarrow x_i \oplus y_i b_i$$
$$y_i \leftarrow y_i \oplus b_i$$

Registers X and Y now contain the carry and sum bits:

$$x_i = a_i c_i \oplus a_i b_i \oplus b_i c_i = c'_i$$
$$y_i = a_i \oplus b_i \oplus c_i = s_i$$

Step 3: Write the sum bit from Y into Bit-slice s and also complement X selectively:

$$s_i \leftarrow y_i$$
$$x_i \leftarrow x_i \oplus y_i$$

The states of X and Y are now:

$$x_i = c'_i \oplus s_i$$
$$y_i = s_i$$

Step 4: Read the X-register and exclusive-or it into both X and Y:

$$x_i \leftarrow x_i \oplus x_i$$
$$y_i \leftarrow y_i \oplus x_i$$

This clears X and stores the carry bit into Y to prepare the registers for the next execution of the loop:

$$x_i = 0$$
$$y_i = c'_i$$

Step 3 takes less than 250 nsec, while Steps 1, 2, and 4 each take less than 150 nsec. Hence, the time to execute the basic loop once is less than 700 nsec. If the field length is 32 bits, the add operation takes less than 22.4 microsec plus a small amount of setup time. The operation performs 256 additions in each array module. This amounts to 1024 additions, if four array modules are enabled, to achieve a processing power of approximately 40 MIPS (million-instructions-per-second).

The array module components communicate through a network called the flip network. A selector chooses a 256-bit source item from the MDA memory read bus, the M register, the X register, the Y register, or an outside source. The bits of the source item travel through the flip network, which may shift and permute the bits in various ways. The permuted source item is presented to the MDA memory write bus, M register, X register, Y register, and an outside destination.

The permutations of the flip network allow inter-PE communication, A PE can read data from another PE either directly from its registers or indirectly from the MDA memory. One can permute the 256-bit data item as a whole or divide it into groups of 2, 4, 8, 16, 32, 64, or 128 bits and permute within groups.

The permutations allowed include shifts of 1, 2, 4, 8, 16, 32, 64, or 128 places. One also can mirror the bits of a group (invert the left-right order) while shifting it. A positive shift of mirrored data is equivalent to a negative shift of the unmirrored data. To shift data a number of places, multiple passes through the flip network may be required. Mirroring can be used to reduce the number of passes. For example, a shift of 31 places can be done in two passes: mirror and shift 1 place on the first pass, and then remirror and shift 32 places on the second pass.

The flip network permutations are particularly useful for Fast Fourier transforms (FFT's). A 2^n point FFT requires n steps, where each step pairs the 2^n points in a certain way and operates on the two points of each pair arithmetically to form two new points. The flip network can be used to rearrange the pairings between steps. Bitonic sorting [Batcher, 1968] and other algorithms [Stone, 1971] also find the permutations of the flip network useful.

Each array module contains a resolver reading the state of the Y register. One output of the resolver (activity-or) indicates if any Y bit is set. If some Y bits are set, the other output of the resolver indicates the index (address) of the first such bit. Since the result of an associative search is marked in the Y register, the resolver indicates which if any words respond to the search.

Other STARAN Elements

Figure 5 is a block diagram of a typical STARAN system with four array modules. Each array module contains an assignment switch that connects its control inputs and data inputs and outputs to AP (associative processor) control or the PIO (parallel input/output) module.

The AP control unit contains the registers and logic necessary to exercise control over the array modules assigned to it. It receives instructions from the control memory and can transfer 32-bit data items to and from the control memory. Data busses communicate with the assigned array modules. The busses connect only to 32-bits of the 256-bit-wide input and output ports of the array modules (Fig. 4), but the permutations of the array module flip networks allow communication with any part of the array. The AP control sends control signals and MDA memory addresses and access modes to the array modules and receives the resolver outputs from the array modules.

Registers in the AP control include:

1 An instruction register to hold the 32-bit instruction being executed.

2 A program status word to hold the control memory address of the next instruction to be executed and the program priority level.

3 A common register to hold a 32-bit search comparand, an operand to be broadcast to the array modules, or an operand output from an array module.

4 An array select register to select a subset of the assigned array modules to be operated on.

5 Four field pointers to hold MDA memory addresses and allow them to be incremented or decremented for stepping through the bit-slices of a field, the words of a group, etc.

6 Three counters to keep track of the number of executions of loops, etc.

7 A data pointer to allow stepping through a set of operands in control memory.

8 Two access mode registers to hold the MDA memory access modes.

The parallel input/output (PIO) module contains a PIO flip network and PIO control unit (Fig. 5). It is used for high bandwidth I/O and inter-array transfers.

The PIO flip network permutes data between eight 256-bit ports. Ports 0 through 3 connect to the four array modules through buffer registers. Port 7 connects to a 32-bit data bus in the PIO control through a fan-in, fan-out switch. Ports 4, 5, and 6 are spare ports for connections to high bandwidth peripherals, such as parallel-head disk stores, sophisticated displays, and radar video channels. The spare ports also could be used to handle additional array modules. High bandwidth inter-array data transfers up to 1024 bits in parallel are handled by permuting data between Ports 0, 1, 2 and 3. Array I/O is handled by permuting data between an array module port and an I/O port. The PIO flip network is controlled by the PIO control unit.

The PIO control unit controls the PIO flip network and the array modules assigned to it. While AP control is processing data in some array modules the PIO control can input and output data in the other array modules. Since most of the registers in the AP control program are duplicated in PIO control; it can address the array modules associatively.

The control memory holds AP control programs, PIO control programs, and microprogram subroutines. To satisfy the high instruction fetch rate of the control units (up to 7.7 million instructions per second), the control memory has five banks of bipolar memory with 512 32-bit words in each bank. Each bank is expandable to 1024 words. To allow for storage of large programs, the control memory also has a 16K-word core memory with a cycle

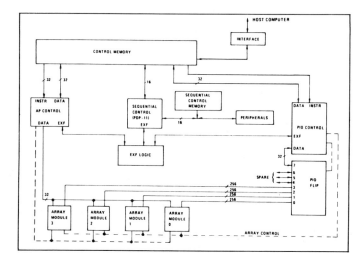

Fig. 5. Typical STARAN block diagram.

time of 1 microsec. The core memory can be expanded to 32K words. Usually the main program resides in the core memory, and the system microprogram subroutines reside in bipolar storage. For flexibility, users are given the option of changing the storage allocation and dynamically paging parts of the program into bipolar storage.

A Digital Equipment Corporation (DEC) PDP-11 minicomputer is included to handle the peripherals, control the system from console commands, and perform diagnostic functions. It is called sequential control to differentiate it from the STARAN parallel processing control units. The sequential control memory of 16K 16-bit words is augmented by a 8K×16-bit "window" into the main control memory. By moving the window, sequential control can access any part of control memory. The window is moved by changing the contents of an addressable register.

The STARAN peripherals include a disk, card reader, line printer, paper-tape reader/punch, console typewriter, and a graphics console.

Synchronization of the three control units (AP control, sequential control, and PIO control) is maintained by the external function (EXF) logic. Control units issue commands to the EXF logic to cause system actions and read system states. Some of the system actions are: AP control start/stop/reset, PIO control start/stop/reset, AP control interrupts, sequential control interrupts, and array module assignment.

The design of STARAN allows it to be connected to other computers (host computers) as a special-purpose peripheral. The interface can take many different forms. One could connect to an I/O channel of the host. Alternately, one could connect to the memory bus of the host so that it can address STARAN memory directly and/or allow STARAN to address its memory directly. For example, the STARAN at Rome Air Development Center [Feldman] is connected to an I/O channel of a Honeywell HIS-645 computer. At Goodyear Aerospace, another STARAN is interfaced to the direct memory access port of an SDS Σ 5 computer.

Associative Processor Software [Rudolph]

The STARAN software system consists of a symbolic assembler called APPLE (for *Associative Processor Programming LanguagE*), and a set of supervisor, utility, debug, diagnostic, and subroutine library program packages. An associative compiler has not yet been developed for STARAN. Early applications of STARAN must therefore be accomplished by assembly language programmers. Programmers find APPLE a convenient language to use, however, and write significantly fewer instructions to program a suitable application on STARAN than would have to be written for a conventional machine since APPLE's command structure reflects the content addressability and processing characteristics of the associative arrays the language controls. For example, although

the programmer must explicitly define his record formats via field definition statements, he usually need not be concerned with physical record location in the arrays. Also, he need not order data tables by key, since any desired datum may be located in one parallel search operation. A third example of APPLE convenience is the elimination of the conventional programming loop which requires advancing a list pointer, examination of an exit criterion, and making a decision for each pass over different data sets. The APPLE array instruction processes all pertinent data sets simultaneously and does not require initialization of an index register with the count of data sets to be processed.

Internally, all software packages with the exception of array diagnostics and the subroutine library operate on the SC. In the minimum STARAN configuration the software packages are furnished on paper tape for input via the SC tape reader. Where STARAN is installed with interface to a conventional computer system in a multicomputer configuration, APPLE and supporting software can be input to STARAN using the existing peripherals of the conventional computer.

The usual load, store, test, branch, and control instructions required for sequential execution of an application program are present in APPLE. Where APPLE departs most from conventional assemblers is in the search and arithmetic array instructions. A representative set of fixed point standard instructions is shown in Table 1 with the approximate timing formulas. Hardware floating point is available on special order.

Associative search and arithmetic instructions are of two types, "argument register" and "field." In the first an operand (32 bits max) stored in the argument register of AP control is used as the search or arithmetic argument against a specified field in all array words simultaneously. Instructions of the field type perform similar operations but between specified fields within each array word.

Instruction execution times are dependent upon n, the number of bits in the operands (fields) involved in the instruction executions, but are not functions of the number of operands being processed, which relationship is exactly the opposite of that existing in the conventional computer. This characteristics dependence of execution time on operand or field length is a consequence of the word-parallel bit-serial design of the associative arrays discussed earlier.

From the programmer's point of view, Table 1 has interesting connotations, some of which are:

1   In real-time applications the programmer can easily time out his initial flow diagram since programming loops in the conventional sense are eliminated. This single consequence of associative processing can save much of the reprogramming effort invariably found necessary during the testing phase of conventional attacks on real-time problems.

2   He can conserve on execution time (and array memory

Table 1 Typical APPLE Associative Fixed Point Instructions

Mnemonic	Instruction	Approx. execution time (μs)*			MIPS† per array for $n = 32$
		Formula	$n = 16$	$n = 32$	
	Argument register instructions				
EQC	EXACT MATCH COMPARAND	$0.6 + 0.15n$	3.0	5.4	47
GTC	GREATER THAN COMPARAND	$0.7 + 0.15n$	3.1	5.5	47
LTC	LESS THAN COMPARAND	$0.7 + 0.15n$	3.1	5.5	47
ADC	ADD AR TO FIELD	$2.8 + 0.85n$	16	30	8.5
	Field instructions				
EQF	EXACT MATCH FIELDS	$0.6 + 0.43n$	7.4	14	18
GTF	GREATER THAN FIELDS	$2.3 + 0.43n$	9.1	16	16
LTF	LESS THAN FIELDS	$2.3 + 0.43n$	9.1	16	16
MAXF	MAX FIELDS	$0.6 + 0.68n$	11	23	11
MINF	MIN FIELDS	$0.6 + 0.68n$	11	23	11
ADF	ADD FIELD TO FIELD	$2.8 + 0.85n$	16	30	8.5
MPF	MULTIPLY FIELD BY FIELD	$5.8 + 2.9m + 0.85mn + 0.4$	277	980	0.26

*n or m equal number of bits in operand.

†Max execution rate of specified instructions for single array with all 256 PE's active.

space) by defining fields to use only as many bits as are required by the application.

3 He has no need for overhead-generating techniques such as indexed file constructions, linked lists, or sort and merge operations usually needed in a conventional computer. This capability results in a significant reduction both in the number of instructions which must be written and executed and the amount of memory required.

Array Storage Allocation

The concept of a file of related records as used in associative processing requires some discussion. In conventional approaches to file generation one thinks of the distinction between a logical file and a corresponding physical file; that is, a logical collection of records, usually ordered by some key, is placed as a block of contiguous addresses in a physical file. The conventional operating system keeps track of the beginning address and the block length for the file whether stored in core or on external stores. Thus in most cases logically different files are stored in physically separate areas of store.

The associative approach differs from the conventional approach in several ways: the records within the logical file need not and usually are not ordered by any key; records within a logical file usually are not stored in contiguous locations in an area of the array or on external devices; and the operating system generally is not required to keep track of individual file beginning addresses and block lengths.

In STARAN, records belonging to different logical files may be physically intermixed in the array as well as being logically unordered. Within each record format, in addition to defining the item fields, the programmer defines a set of control tag fields. How these tags are used is described below.

When new records are added to a logical file the update program writes the new, properly formatted record into the first available empty array location. Since empty array locations usually are not contiguously located within the array, records belonging to a specific file are scattered throughout the array in random locations. This characteristic is illustrated in the array map example of Fig. 6.

Empty array memory locations are identified by executing an EQC on a one-bit activity tag field using a "0" as the search criterion. The execution time for this search (see Table 1) is less than one microsecond at the end of which time all processing elements for physical memory words containing a 0 in the activity field will be in the "ON" state. At the conclusion of the search a hardware pointer automatically points to the PE having the lowest physical address in the array (or arrays). The new record, with its activity field set to a "1," is written into this first empty location. The hardware pointer then moves to the next available empty memory location for writing another record if a batch of new entries must be loaded. If no empty locations are found the program will exit to whatever routine the programmer has chosen for handling this type of error—for example, if appropriate to a specific application, the program may select an age test of all records in a particular file, purging the oldest to make room for

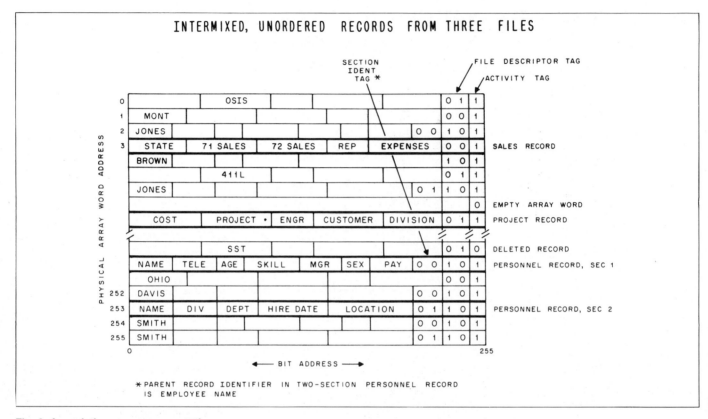

Fig. 6. Associative array map example.

the newest. A record once located may be deleted from a file by merely setting the activity bit to a "0."

When a specific file is to be processed in some manner, the scattered locations containing the file's records are activated by performing EQC's on both the activity field and an n-bit "file descriptor" tag field. If, as in the example of Fig. 6, the file descriptor field is two bits long, the entire selected file will be ready for processing in less than 2 microseconds (<1 μs for the activity bit search, <1 μs for the file descriptor field search).

Where record lengths are greater than the 256-bit length of the associative array word, several non-contiguous associative array words may be used to store the single record in sections, one section per array word. The format for each record section must contain the same activity and file descriptor fields as are used in all record formats, and in addition it must contain a parent record identifier and an n-bit "section identifier" tag field. The scattered locations containing the desired section of all records in the specific file may be activated by performing EQC's on the activity,

file descriptor, and section identifier fields. All three searches can be completed in approximately 2 or 3 microseconds.

These two or three tag search operations in the AP permit random placement of records in the physical file and eliminate the bookkeeping associated with file structuring and control required in conventional systems. The same approach is used for files which exceed the capacity of the associative arrays—the records of such files are stored in a similar manner on external mass storage devices and are paged into the arrays as required.

The strategy used to allocate array storage space can have a significant effect on program execution time. An example is shown in Fig. 7, where the products of three operand pairs are required. In A, the operands are stored in a single array word. For 20-bit fixed point operands the three MPF instructions would execute in a total of 1175 microseconds. All similar data sets stored in other array words would be processed during the same instruction execution. However, an alternative storage scheme (B) which utilizes three PE's per data set requires only one MPF execution

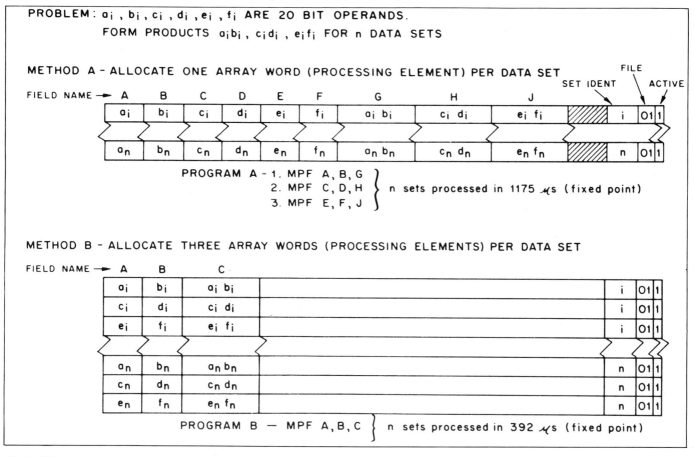

PROBLEM: a_i, b_i, c_i, d_i, e_i, f_i ARE 20 BIT OPERANDS.

FORM PRODUCTS $a_i b_i$, $c_i d_i$, $e_i f_i$ FOR n DATA SETS

METHOD A - ALLOCATE ONE ARRAY WORD (PROCESSING ELEMENT) PER DATA SET

PROGRAM A - 1. MPF A, B, G
2. MPF C, D, H } n sets processed in 1175 μs (fixed point)
3. MPF E, F, J

METHOD B - ALLOCATE THREE ARRAY WORDS (PROCESSING ELEMENTS) PER DATA SET

PROGRAM B — MPF A, B, C } n sets processed in 392 μs (fixed point)

Fig. 7. Effect of array memory allocation on execution time.

to produce the three products in 392 microseconds. If one thousand data sets were involved in each case the average multiply times per product would be 392 and 131 nanoseconds, respectively, but at the expense, in B, of using 3000 processing elements. Unused bits in B may be assigned to other functions.

A last example of how array storage allocation can affect program execution time is shown in Fig. 8, where the columns represent fields. Here the sum e_1, of 16 numbers is required. If the 16 numbers are directly or as a result of a previous computation stored in the same field of 16 physically contiguous array words, the near-neighbor relationships between the processing elements can be used to reduce the number of ADF executions to four. All similar 16 number sets would be processed at the same time.

STARAN Applications

While many papers have appeared (see Minker [1971] for a comprehensive bibliography) which discuss the application of AM's and AP's in information retrieval, text editing, matrix computations, management information systems and sensor data processing systems, there are none yet published which describe actual results with operating AP equipment in any application. (But see Stillman [1972] for a recent AM application result.)

Recent actual applications of the AP have been in real-time sensor related surveillance and control systems. These initial applications share several common characteristics:

1 A highly active data base.

2 Operations upon the data base involve multiple key

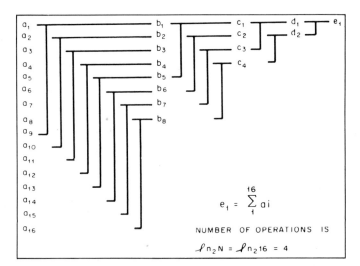

Fig. 8. Tree-sum example.

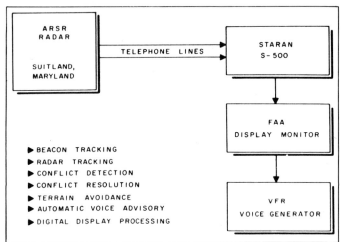

Fig. 9. Air traffic control application.

searches in complex combinations of equal, greater, between-limits, etc., operations.

3 Identical processing algorithms may be performed on sets of records which satisfy a complex search criterion.

4 One or more streams of input data must be processed in real time.

5 There is a requirement for real-time data output in accordance with individual selection criteria for multiple output devices.

A portion of the processing inherent in these applications is parallel-oriented and well suited to the array processing capability of the AP. On the other hand these same applications also involve a significant amount of sequentially-oriented computation which would be inefficient to perform upon any array processor, a simple example being coordinate conversion of serially occurring sensor reports.

Air Traffic Control

An example of an actual AP application in an air traffic control environment is shown in Fig. 9. In this application a two array (512 processing elements) STARAN S-500 model was interfaced via leased telephone lines with the output of the FAA ARSR long range radar at Suitland, Maryland. Digitized radar and beacon reports for all air traffic within a 55 mile radius of Philadelphia were transmitted to STARAN in real time. An FAA air traffic controller's display of the type used in the new ARTS-III terminal ATC system and a Metrolab Digitalk-400 digital voice generator were interfaced with STARAN to provide real-time data output.

The controller's keyboard was used to enter commands, call up various control programs and select display options.

Although a conventional computer is not shown explicitly in Fig. 9 the sequentially oriented portions of the overall data processing load were programmed for and executed in the STARAN sequential controller as shown in Fig. 10. Sequential and associative programs and instruction counts for STARAN are shown in Table 2. In a larger system involving multiple sensors and displays, and more ATC functions such as metering and spacing, flight plan processing, and digital communications, the sequential and parallel workloads would increase to the point where a separate conventional computer system interfaced with the AP would be required.

The STARAN system was sized to process 400 tracks. Since the instantaneous airborne count in the 55 mile radius of Philadelphia was not expected to exceed 144 aircraft, a simulation program was developed to simultaneously generate 256 simulated aircraft tracks. Display options permitted display of mixed live and simulated aircraft. The 400 aircraft capacity is representative of the density expected as North-South traffic loads increase through the late '70s. Conflict prediction and resolution programs based upon computed track data were demonstrated and used to display conflict warning options. Automatic voice services were provided for operator-designated aircraft, thus simulating warning advisories for VFR pilots requesting the service. The voice messages, which in an operational system would be automatically radioed to the pilot, were generated by the Metrolab unit from digital formats produced by the associative processor and broadcast in the demonstration area via a public address system. A typical message would be read out in voice as, "ABLE BAKER CHAR-

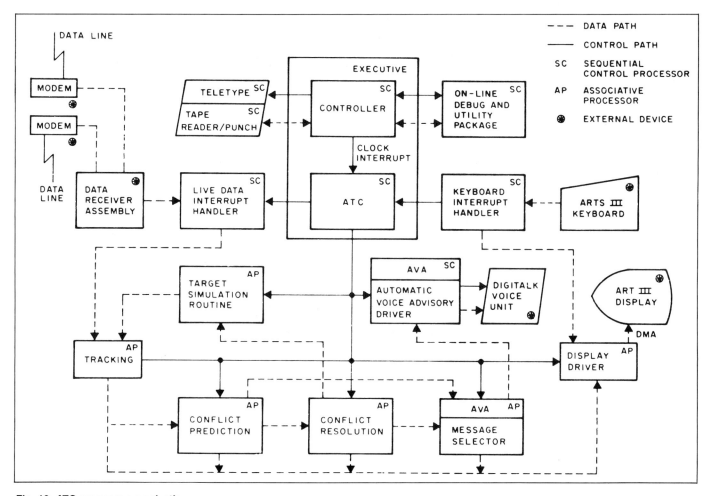

Fig. 10. ATC program organization.

Table 2   STARAN Air Traffic Control Programs

Sequential programs		Associative programs	
Name	Instruction count	Name	Instruction count
Executive		Tracking system	881
Keyboard interrupt		Track simulation system	415
Real time interrupt	1600	Turn detection	88
Live data input		Conflict prediction	488
Automatic voice output		Conflict resolution	296
		Automatic voice advisory	709
		Display processing	1140
		Total	4017
		Field definition statements included	514
Net operating instructions	1600	Net operating instructions	3493

LIE, FAST TRAFFIC SEVEN O'CLOCK, 4 MILES, ALTITUDE 123 HUNDRED, NORTHEAST BOUND."

Top level flow charts for four of the associative programs, used in the demonstration are shown in Figs. 11, 12, 13, and 14. A detailed report is in preparation describing all of the ATC programs used in this demonstration, but some comments on the four flow charts shown may be of interest.

Live target tracking (Fig. 11) is performed in two dimensions (mode C altitude data was not available) using both radar and beacon target reports to track all aircraft. Incoming reports are correlated against the entire track file using five correlation box sizes, three of which vary in size with range. Any incoming report which does not correlate with an existing track is used to automatically initiate a new tentative track. An aircraft track must correlate on two successive scans and have a velocity exceeding 21 knots to qualify as an established track and must correlate on three successive scans to achieve a track firmness level high enough to be displayed to a controller as a live target. There are provisions for 15 levels of track firmness including 7 "coast" levels.

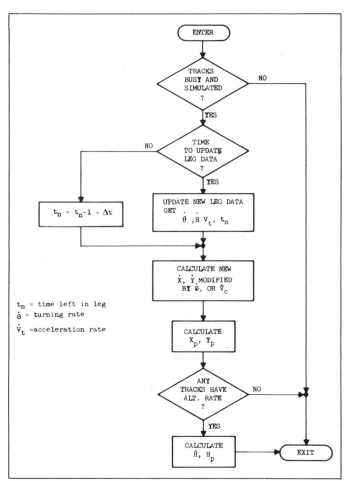

Fig. 12. Tracking simulation.

If a report correlates with more than one track, special processing (second pass resolve) resolves the ambiguity. Correlated new reports in all tracks are used for position and velocity smoothing once per scan via an alpha-beta tracking filter where for each track one of nine sets of alpha-beta values is selected as a function of track history and the correlation box size required for the latest report correlation. If both beacon and radar reports correlate with a track, the radar report is used for position updating. Smoothed velocity and position values are used to predict the position of the aircraft for the next scan of the radar and for the look-ahead period involved in conflict prediction.

Track simulation processing (Fig. 12) produces 256 tracks in three dimensions with up to four programmable legs for each track. Each leg can be of 0 to 5 minute duration and have a turn rate, acceleration, or altitude rate change. A leg change can be

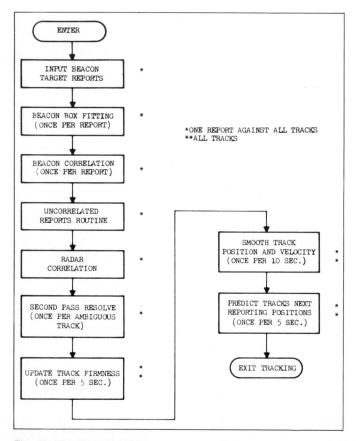

Fig. 11. Live target tracking.

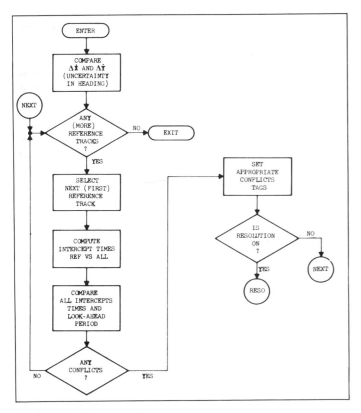

Fig. 13. Conflict prediction.

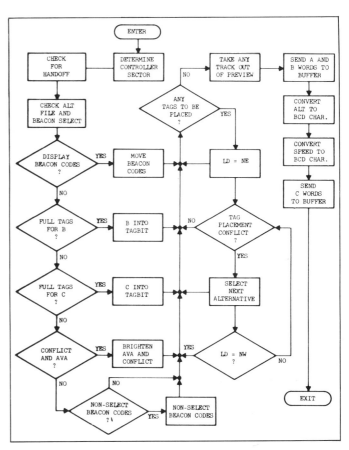

Fig. 14. Display processing.

forced by the conflict resolution program to simulate pilot response to a ground controller's collision avoidance maneuver command. Targets may have velocities between 0 and 600 knots, altitudes between 100 and 52,000 feet, and altitude rates between 0 and 3000 feet per minute.

The conflict prediction program sequentially selects up to 100 operator-designated "controlled" or "AVA" aircraft, called reference tracks in Fig. 13, and compares the future position of each during the look-ahead period with the future positions of all live and simulated aircraft and also to the static position of all terrain obstacles. Any detected conflicts cause conflict tags in the track word format to be set, making the tracks available for conflict display processing. A turn detection program not shown opens up the heading uncertainty for turning tracks.

Display processing (Fig. 14) is a complex associative program which provides a variety of manage-by-exception display options and automatically moves operator-assigned alphanumeric identification display data blocks associated with displayed aircraft so as to prevent overlap of data blocks for aircraft in close proximity to one another on the display screen. Sector control, hand off, and quick-look processing is provided.

All programs listed in Table 2 were successfully demonstrated at three different locations in three successive weeks, using live radar data from the Suitland radar at each location. The associative programs were operated directly out of the bulk core and page 0 portions of control memory since there was no requirement, in view of the low 400 aircraft density involved, for the higher speed instruction accesses available from the page memories. At intervals during the demonstration all programs were demonstrated at a speed-up of 20 times real time with the exception of the live data and AVA programs which, being real-time, cannot be speeded up. Timing data for the individual program segments will be available in the final report. The entire program executed in less than 200 milliseconds per 2 second radar sector scan or in less than 10 percent of real time. All programming effort was completed in 4½ months with approximately 3 man-years of effort. This was the first and as of this writing the only actual demonstration of a production associative processor in a live signal environment known to the author. It was completed in June, 1972. Other actual applications currently in the programming process at Goodyear involve sonar, electronic warfare and large scale data management systems. These will be reported as results are achieved.

Fast Fourier Transform[1]

The Fast Fourier Transform (FFT) is a basic operation in digital signal processing which is being widely used in the real-time processing of radar and sonar signals. The structure of the FFT algorithm is such that it can be segmented into many similar concurrent operations. Parallel implementation of the FFT can provide orders of magnitude speed increases over sequential computer execution times. The organization of STARAN lends itself to efficient manipulation of data in the FFT.

The Air Force supplied real radar data (on tapes) to GAC to be transformed by the STARAN system. A 512-point, 16-bit FFT was performed on this real data in 2.7 milliseconds using only two MDA arrays. A 1024-point transform on real input data could be performed in about 3.0 milliseconds using all four arrays available at GAC's STARAN evaluation and training facility. For comparison purposes, the following is a list of reported execution times for a 1024-point, real input, FFT:

Sequential computers	
XDS Sigma 5	660 msec
IBM 360/67	446 msec
UNIVAC 1108	190 msec (complex)
UNIVAC 1108 (with array processor attachment)	29.2 msec (complex)

Special purpose FFT systems	
Time/Data 90 System	28 msec
ELSYTEC 306/HFFT	18 msec
SPECTRA SYSTEM '900'	9.2 msec

Sonar Post-Processing

Sensor data processing can be split into two major categories— signal processing and post-processing. Signal processing is the area of the system where operations such as the FFT are performed; post-processing involves the sorting and editing of the signal processor output data to determine tactical information such as whether a real target is in the coverage area and where the target is.

The job of sorting the spectral lines that result from the FFT operations is a formidable task, especially in a multi-sensor case. The trend has been for increasing the sensitivity of signal processing systems. The acoustic signal line sorting task that accompanies any increased sensitivity can be staggering. For

[1]The passage beginning here is from Batcher.

instance, a 6 dB improvement in sensitivity, in a classified Navy sonar system, would result in increasing the target load by a factor of 16 and the computer processing load by a factor of 250 or more.

A digital sonar signal processing system, under development at the Naval Air Development Center (NADC), requires that subroutines operate on the target spectral lines (outputs from an FFT) and other input data to form outputs suitable for later use in classification algorithms. Since the system is a multi-sensor system, these subroutines must process a very large volume of data in real time. The content addressability feature of STARAN provides the potential for significant performance gains due to the requirement for many searches in these post-processing subroutines.

As a consequence of this potential improvement, NADC issued a contract to GAC to assess the comparative run times for the STARAN versus a large-scale conventional computer (the CDC-6600). NADC-developed algorithms for the most time consuming operations in the post-processor system were programmed on the STARAN computer. Real data was then processed on both the STARAN and, by NADC, on a CDC-6600.

The STARAN executed the programs, using the real data, 200 times faster than the CDC-6600.

String Search

A processing function used by several agencies for locating specific character strings (such as place names) in textual information, was developed for STARAN and tested on a sample data base. The same function was executed on a conventional computer (Sigma 5) for a timing comparison. The STARAN solution ran 100 times faster. This function is also applicable to nondefense applications such as patent, legal, and chemical information searches where cost of search may be a limiting parameter.

Summary [Rudolph]

Although several manufacturers are developing associative processor equipment, the first version to be produced in a production configuration was introduced in May of 1972 by Goodyear Aerospace Corporation following FAA on-site tests in 1971 at Knoxville, Tennessee of a USAF-owned engineering model built and demonstrated by Goodyear in 1969.

The processor provides full content addressability and array arithmetic capability within "main frame" memory coupled with a unique capability for wide bandwidth (over 3000 megabits/sec for a 4-array STARAN) input-output data transfers to mass data stores. The associative programming language, APPLE, provides a flexible and convenient assembler for programming array arithmetic and search algorithms without the complex and costly indexing, nested loop and data manipulation constructions required in conventional computer programming.

The associative processor may be viewed as a software-programmable super-peripheral, or special purpose subsidiary processor, for attachment to any general purpose conventional computer system via standard channel attachment. In this role the super-peripheral is assigned parallel oriented problem segments and data bases which would otherwise, through excess operating system software overhead, tend to choke the conventional machine.

Although first applications of the associative processor are of the real time, dedicated, command and control type, the extension to large scale data base management, on-line management information systems with immediate response to complex multiple-key queries, and large scale matrix computations await only user decision and ingenuity to accomplish now that production hardware and software has become available at the 370/145 price level.

The cost effectiveness of associative processing has yet to be proven in operational systems, but test results from initial users should accumulate rapidly now that associative processing is no longer only an interesting concept in the literature.

References

Batcher [1974]; Rudolph [1972]; Batcher [1968]; Feldman; Fulmer and Meilander [1970]; Minker [1971]; Rudolph, Fulmer, and Meilander [1971]; Slade and McMahon [1957]; Stillman [1972]; Stone [1971].

Section 4

Multiple-Processor Systems[1]

Introduction

With the advent of larger-scale integrated circuits, it is possible to construct highly complex system building blocks. Indeed, design with mass-produced processors and memories as primitive components is now a viable, if not the only, approach to providing the advanced functionality that increasingly sophisticated users require. We are entering an era where multiple-processor systems are not only an everyday occurrence but also a necessity.

For the purposes of this discussion we will consider a multiple-processor system to be composed of two or more processors that are capable of independent instruction execution and able to exchange information through some interconnection mechanism. Thus array processors (such as the Illiac IV) and associative processors (such as STARAN) are excluded from the present discussion.

The purpose of this section is threefold. First, the reasons motivating multiple-processor PMS structures are explored. Second, the issues in interconnecting multiple processors are illustrated. This represents a continuation of the interconnect-bus-switching discussion in Chap. 6 on computer space structure. This discussion of interconnection demonstrates that there is a continuum from processors sharing a common memory (those termed *tightly coupled multiprocessors*) to processors communicating via messages but cooperating on one task (termed *loosely coupled, distributed multiple processors*) and on to independent computer systems interconnected to share information (termed *networks*). The third, and last, purpose of this section is to provide examples of tightly coupled multiprocessors. Networks, a very mature interconnection technology, are described in Sec. 5.

Motivations for Developing Multiple-Processor Systems

The earliest form of multiple-processor systems was local computer networks designed to make efficient use of large uniprocessors by segmenting particular functions among particular machines. As an example, front-end processors would be dedicated to batch input and terminal control. Other processors might handle I/O spooling, as did the IBM attached support processors (Chap 52). Subsequently, geographically distributed networks evolved.

[1]Parts of this section introduction are based on an unpublished research paper, "The Multiple-Processor Design Space," by Daniel P. Siewiorek.

There are several reasons for justifying a particularly network. The following list is adapted from Roberts [1967]:

Load sharing. A problem (program and data) initiated at one computer that is temporarily overloaded is sent to another for processing. The cost of transshipment must clearly be less than the costs of delay in getting the problem processed. Load sharing implies highly similar facilities at the nodes of the network.

Data sharing. A program is run at a node that has access to a large, specialized data base, such as a specialized automated library. It is less costly to bring the program to the data than to bring the data to the program.

Program sharing. Data are sent to a computer that has a specialized program. This might happen because of the size of the program (hence, fundamentally the same reason as data sharing), but it might also happen because the knowledge (i.e., initialization and error rituals) to run the program is available at one computer but not at another.

Specialized facilities. Within the network there need exist only one of various rarely used facilities, such as large random-access memories, special display devices, or special-purpose array processors.

Message switching. There may be a communication task of such magnitude that sophisticated switching and control are worthwhile.

Reliability. If some components fail, others can be used in their place, thus permitting the total system to degrade gracefully. (At the present state of the art, peripheral computers are needed to isolate the periphery from the unreliability of the network, and vice versa.)

Peak computer power. Large parts of the total system can be devoted for short periods to a single task, if there are important real time constraints to be met. This depends on being able to fractionate the task into independent subtasks.

Communication multiplexing. Efficient use of communication facilities is obtained by multiplexing a number of low–data-rate users. This may not be a reason for a network per se but may justify a larger network, provided that there is some reason for having one in the first place.

Better communication. A community of users (e.g., a scientific or engineering community) that could mutually use the same programs and data bases and converse about these directly (i.e., not by writing about them but in the context of mutual use) might become a much more productive community, with less duplication of work and faster communication of results.

Better load distribution through preprocessing. Some tasks require very high–data-rate communication with a computer. By doing preprocessing in a smaller computer, a reduced information rate can be sent to the more general system.

Meanwhile, multiprocessor systems were evolving. A multiprocessor system is distinguished from a network in that in the former, processors share memory, whereas in the latter, processors intercommunicate by a preestablished message protocol. As with networks, there are many reasons for justifying individual multiprocessor structures. A partial list might include:

Peak computing power. The entire system can be devoted to a single problem. A multiprocessor system can solve problems with higher or more frequent interprocessor communication than a network, since interprocessor communications are more efficient.

Performance/cost. Advanced technology produces low-cost processors whose instruction/second/dollar ratio is 10 to 100 times better than that of large, high-speed processors. Even though these low-cost processors have minimal functionality (simple instruction set, limited data types), there are special applications for which this functionality is adequate.

Availability and graceful degradation. Multiprocessor systems can be designed with no central, critical component. Thus failures can be configured out of a system for only an incremental loss in computing power. Multiprocessors are more cost-effective than uniprocessors with respect to the relative cost of redundancy. A uniprocessor system requires redundant hardware for failure detection, diagnosis, and recovery. A multiprocessor need only have hardware for failure detection while relying on the nonaffected processors to perform the diagnosis and recovery in software.

Modular growth. Systems can be designed so that processors, memories, and I/O subsystems can be added incrementally. Thus systems can be tailored to individual applications or grow incrementally to meet demand.

Functional specialization. Functionally specialized processors can be added to improve performance for a particular application.

The next section examines some generic processor interconnection schemes and illustrates the continuum of computer structures between networks and multiprocessors. Subsequently, parameters of this design space are presented and the space illustrated by examples of existing multiple-processor systems.

General Multiple-Processor Structures: A Continuum

The computer structure space ranging from networks to multiprocessors can be viewed as a near continuum where cost and performance increase as more functions are built into hardware (Figs. 1–3). Table 1 depicts the generic interconnection mechanisms for a two-processor system. The mechanisms can be contrasted along several dimensions:

Data-transfer protocol. The effort required to transfer a single item of information. This may vary from complete coordination of software running on both processors for each individual item (e.g., serial line) to requests resolved automatically by hardware (e.g., multiported memory).

Performance. Maximum number of bits transferred per second.

Interpretation. Whether the information items can be used directly by the other processor (as in shared memory), or whether the total or partial information has to be interpreted (as in messages).

Initialization protocol. The effort to establish an information transfer.

Table 1   Generic Processor Interconnection Mechanisms

System type	Interconnection	Data transfer rate, bit/s	Cost, $	Cost/bit/s, $	Overhead
Multicomputer systems (networks)	Serial line	7×10^3	800	0.115	Software data transfer Software initialization
	Serial bus	1×10^6	1,700	0.0017	Hardware data transfer Software initialization
	Bus link	8×10^6	4,500	0.00056	Hardware data transfer Software initialization
Multiprocessor systems	Bus switch	18×10^6	8,500	0.00047	Hardware initialization
	Bus window	19×10^6	10,000	0.00053	Hardware initialization and transfer Software-initialized mapping
	Multiported (shared) memory	25×10^6	7,000	0.00028	Hardware initialization and transfer

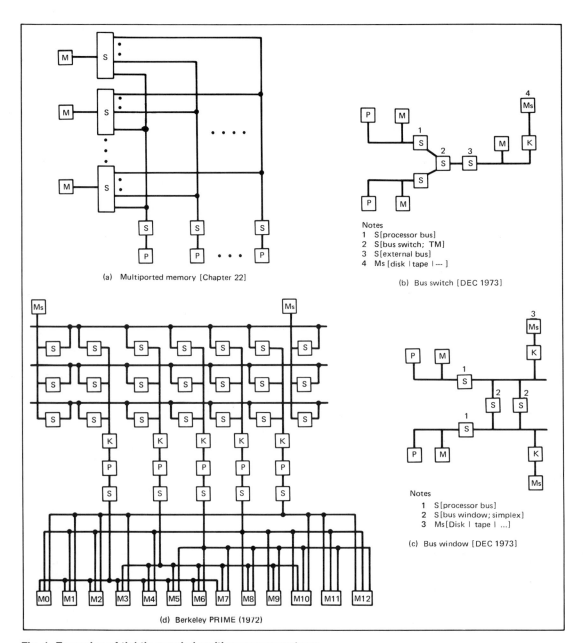

(a) Multiported memory [Chapter 22]

Notes
1 S[processor bus]
2 S[bus switch; TM]
3 S[external bus]
4 Ms [disk | tape | ---]

(b) Bus switch [DEC 1973]

Notes
1 S[processor bus]
2 S[bus window; simplex]
3 Ms[Disk | tape | ...]

(c) Bus window [DEC 1973]

(d) Berkeley PRIME (1972)

Fig. 1. Examples of tightly coupled multiprocessor systems.

Granularity of access. In principle, any interconnection mechanism can handle single-item transfers. However, the overhead associated with a complete transfer may dictate that several items be blocked together for efficiency. The size of this block is the granularity of access, and it may range from several thousand words to one word.

The generic multiple-processor interconnection mechanism will be discussed with respect to each of these dimensions.

First, consider multiple-computer systems or networks where communication is typically by large blocks. In order to compare the effective performance of the generic multiple-processor structures, models will be developed for the time to set up

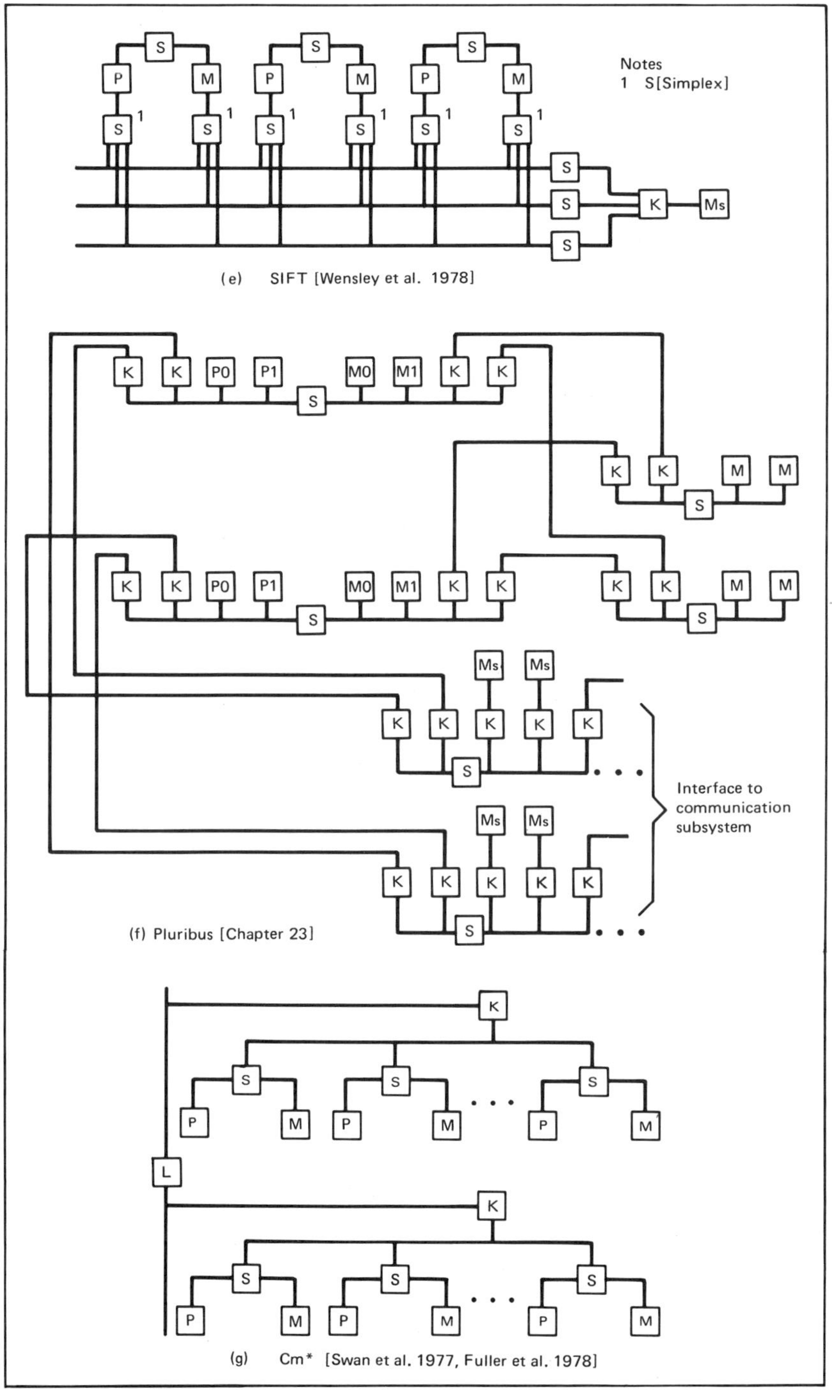

Notes
1 S[Simplex]

(e)   SIFT [Wensley et al. 1978]

(f) Pluribus [Chapter 23]

Interface to
communication
subsystem

(g)   Cm* [Swan et al. 1977, Fuller et al. 1978]

Fig. 1. (cont.).

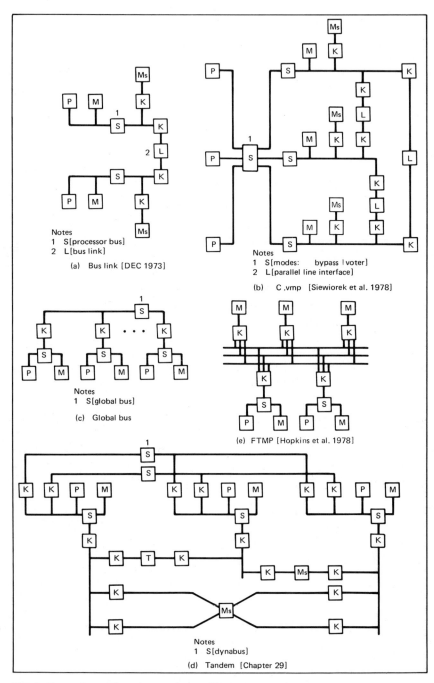

Fig. 2. Examples of loosely coupled multiprocessor systems.

(initialize) and the time to perform a block (data) transfer. A summary table will then be constructed to compare the initialization overhead, the block transfer overhead, and the minimum response time (granularity of access). In order to have a common basis of comparison for the various structures, it will be assumed that all the decisions have been made about the data transfer and all parameters have been calculated.

- *Serial line.* The serial line is the earliest and simplest form of interconnection. A hardware interface is provided for character (8-bit) or word transfers (see Figs. 3*a* and 4). The hardware serializes the datum and sends it to the other interface, which causes a condition the software can sense on completion of the transfer (e.g., setting a flag or posting an interrupt). Speed is usually in the 110- to 9,600-baud range. Software in each computer has to establish a conversation (usually via the serial line), pick a transfer direction, and agree upon the format and length of the data to be transferred (see data transfer protocol in Fig. 4). Since the initialization overhead is so large, only block transfers of data are economically feasible.

  Figure 5 depicts the timing for a single item data transfer for a serial line. A datum is placed in the serial line register, and at a time equal to T_8 later it is assembled in the receiver and an interrupt generated. The receiver calculates for b before issuing an acknowledge character. At a time equal to T_8 later, the sender is interrupted and spends a time units processing the acknowledgment. The initialization process requires several such character transmissions and acknowledgments to pass the block transfer parameters (characters from sender might consist of a SEND command and block identification; characters from the receiver might consist of a START OF TRANSFER command and a length). Each item of the block is also sent by a transmission-acknowledgment pair. Table 2 symbolically lists the initialization time (assuming one word for each of the four initialization parameters), data transfer time (assuming D_b bytes of data), and minimum response time (time to transfer 1 byte of data).

- *Serial bus.* The serial bus is a high-speed serial interconnection between serial bus interfaces (the loop in Figs. 3*c* and 6). Typically the interface is given a pointer to a software formatted memory block containing transmission information (e.g., destination and block length) and data (e.g., software-interpreted commands or data). The interface generates message-header, source, and error-detection code fields. The interface also inserts the software-generated destination, length, and data fields. The resultant message is placed on the serial bus during the next bus idle period. When transmission has been completed, a flag is set or an interrupt is posted. The receiving portion of the interface scans messages for a match between processor number and destination field. When a match occurs, the source, length, and data fields are assembled at a specified location in memory (via direct memory access after each

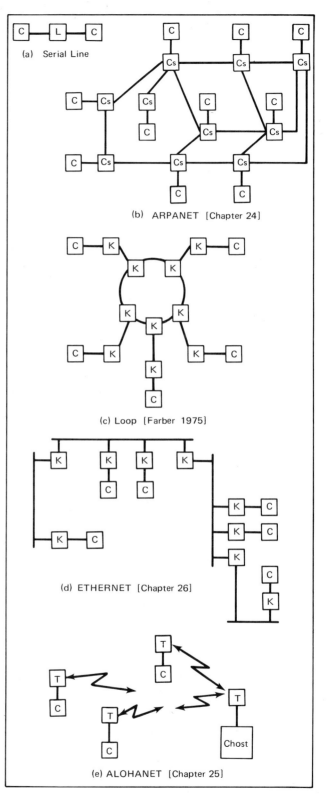

(a) Serial Line

(b) ARPANET [Chapter 24]

(c) Loop [Farber 1975]

(d) ETHERNET [Chapter 26]

(e) ALOHANET [Chapter 25]

Fig. 3. Examples of networks.

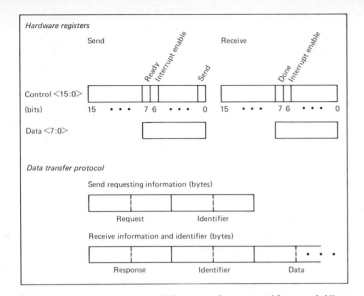

Fig. 4. Hardware registers and data transfer protocol for a serial line unit.

Serial-line unit

initialization and data transfer

a = sender processing time
b = receiver processing time
T_8 = transmission time for 8-bit character
n = number of characters
time = $n(a + b + 2T_8)$

Fig. 5. Timing for a single item data transfer over a serial line.

Table 2 Summary of Generic Processor Interconnection Performance

Interconnection technique	Performance, bit/s	Initialization	Data transfer	Minimum response time (granularity)
1. Serial-line unit	7×10^3	$8(a + b + 2T_8)$	$D_b(a + b + 2T_8)$	$2(a + b + 2T_8)$
2. Serial bus	1×10^6	$8T_b(O_b + R_b) + b$	$8T_b(O_b + D_b) + a + b$	$8T_b(20_b + R_b + 1) + a + b$
3. Bus link	8×10^6	$3(a + b + 2T_p)$	$a + (1/2)T_{DMA}D_b$	$2(a + b + 2T_p)$
4. Bus switch	18×10^6	$a + b$	0–50% degradation on each access	$a + b$
5. Bus window	19×10^6	$a + b + T_p$	0–50% degradation on each access	$a + b + T_p$
6. Multiported memory	25×10^6	1 instruction	0–20% degradation	2 instructions

For $a = b = 100T_p$ $T_8 = 573T_p$ $D_b = 1{,}024$
 $T_b = (1/2)T_p$ $O_b = 6$ instruction time = 4 μs
 $T_{DMA} = T_p$ $R_b = 4$ $T_p = 2\mu$s

Interconnection technique	Initialization	Data transfer	Minimum response time
1. Serial-line unit	$10{,}768T_p$ / 21.5 ms	$D_b(1{,}346T_p)$ / 2,756 ms	$2(1{,}346T_p)$ / 5.4 ms
2. Serial bus	$140T_p$ / 0.28 ms	$8T_p(6 + D_b) + 200T_p$ / 16.9 ms	$336T_p$ / 0.67 ms
3. Bus link	$606T_p$ / 1.2 ms	$100T_p + (1/2)T_pD_b$ / 1.2 ms	$404T_p$ / 0.8 ms
4. Bus switch	$200T_p$ / 0.4 ms	....	$200T_p$ / 0.4 ms
5. Bus window	$201T_p$ / 0.4 ms	....	$201T_p$ / 0.4 ms
6. Multiported memory	$2T_p$ / 0.004 ms	....	$4T_p$ / 0.008 ms

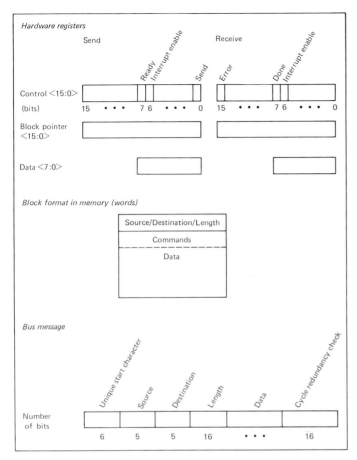

Fig. 6. Hardware registers and bus transfer protocol for a serial bus.

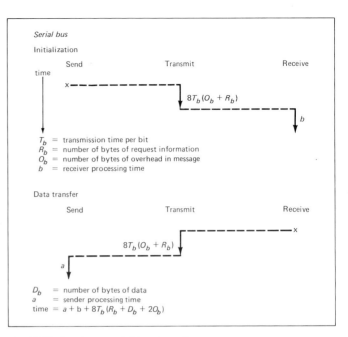

Fig. 7. Timing for a serial bus transfer.

serial word is received). Finally the interface checks the error-detection code field, posts an error flag if an error is detected, and either sets a flag or posts an interrupt to notify the processor of a received message.

The nondata information in a message (header, source, destination, length, and error code) may require 40 to 180 bits and represents overhead that cuts down the effective data transfer rate. Serial bus speeds range from 1 to 3 million bits per second.

Figure 7 depicts the initialization and data transfer timings. Table 2 lists the initialization, data transfer, and minimum response times.

- *Bus link*. The bus link is a half-duplex parallel interconnection between two buses (Figs. 2a and 8). Both single-word transfers and block transfers may be supported. The word-transfer mode can be used to exchange initializing information (e.g., word count and starting address) for block

transfers. Control information—e.g., direction of transfer, mode of transfer (word or block), and interrupt request—is passed between the buses by special hardware status bits, thus further simplifying the communications software. Once the bus link is initialized (with word count, starting address, transfer direction, and mode), the block transfer can begin. The source bus uses its address for a direct memory access (DMA) to pick up the first item in the block. The word count is decremented, the address incremented, and the item passed to the other bus. The second bus starts a DMA cycle using its address for storing the item. The transmission is completed by decrementing word count and incrementing the address on the second bus. When a word count reaches zero, an interrupt is generated on the appropriate bus.

Due to the initialization protocol, interprocess communications tend to have a large granularity. Speed of the block transfer is usually one-third to one-half memory speed because of the memory-bus protocol overhead for DMA. Figure 9 and Table 2 depict the various timings for the bus link.

In multiprocessor systems the various processors can alternately access the same memory on a word-by-word basis. The generic mechanisms are:

- *Bus switch*. The bus switch electronically connects a shared bus to one of two processor buses (see Figs. 1b and 10). The

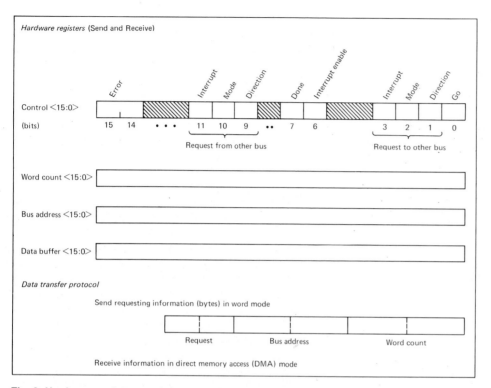

Fig. 8. Hardware registers and data transfer protocol for a bus link.

shared bus may consist of both shared peripherals and memory. Software on one processor bus can request the switch to attach the shared bus. If the shared bus is not currently assigned, the switch connects the shared bus and notifies the requesting processor by raising a control signal or generating an interrupt.

If the shared bus is being used, the currently connected processor is notified. The currently connected processor must remove its request for connection within a specified time, or else the switch automatically cancels the request. In either case, upon request cancellation, the shared bus is connected to the new processor and the new processor is notified.

The shared bus may appear to be slower than the processor bus because of delays imposed by the switch. Processors frequently perform some internal computations after asserting a bus request. If the memory access time plus the switch delay is less than the time of this internal computation, no degradation of the shared bus performance is seen by the processor. Figure 11, and Table 2 show the different timings for the bus switch.

- *Bus window.* The bus window provides full-duplexed address-space sharing between two buses (Figs. 1c and 12).

The window intercepts memory access requests for a range of addresses on one bus and translates them to a program-settable range on the target bus. Target-bus accesses are performed by a DMA bus cycle. The window may be enabled for bidirectional or unidirectional read/write or read-only accesses. In addition, the window can be totally disabled for independent processing.

As in the bus link, the window has control bits wired between the buses for exchange of initialization and cooperation information. When disabled, the window can be used for single-word transfers in order to exchange more extensive information (e.g., identity of memory block to share). If peripheral devices have control registers in the memory address space, the window can be used for both memory and peripheral sharing.

Figure 13 and Table 2 illustrate the various times associated with the bus window. As with the bus switch, delays imposed by the bus window may or may not be seen as degradation by the processor. Additional information on bus-link, bus-switch, and bus-window-like mechanisms can be found in DEC [1973].

- *Multiported memory.* A general multiported memory is shown in Fig. 1a. Processors make requests to memory, which the individual memories arbitrate and grant. Arbitra-

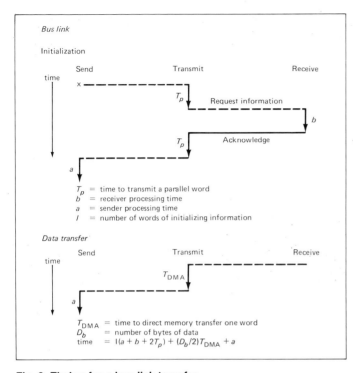

Fig. 9. Timing for a bus-link transfer.

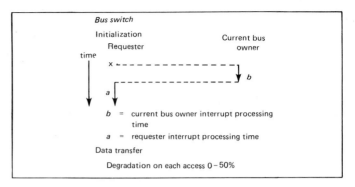

Fig. 11. Timing for a bus-switch transfer.

Multiple-Processor Space

Multiple-processor structures represent points in the design-space continuum. In this section we will present parameters of that design space. A structure is more accurately described when more parameters are given, until, in the limit, there is a unique specification of the structure. In order for structural comparisons to be useful, the number of parameters should be limited. Further, each parameter should allow inferences about other system attributes.

Table 3 presents some parameters that may be used to categorize multiple-processor systems. The parameters are arranged in decreasing order of generality. The first parameter, node type, allows inferences to be made about the expected range of interconnections, performance, and implementation. However, subsequent parameters are required for a more complete understanding of the structure. The reader is invited to suggest other parameters (such as concurrency and deadlock control) or to rearrange the given parameters so that the most information is transmitted by the fewest parameters. The parameters in Table 3 are discussed beginning on the next page.

tion is usually round robin and access is granted for only a single-word transfer.

As with the bus window, addresses may be translated to allow a larger physical address space to be accessed by a smaller processor address space. Thus initialization consists simply of loading an address translation register.

Figure 14 and Table 2 depict the multiported memory timings. The memory arbitration logic may or may not constitute a performance degradation. (See the foregoing description of the bus switch.)

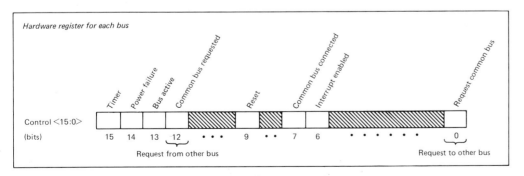

Fig. 10. Hardware register for a bus switch.

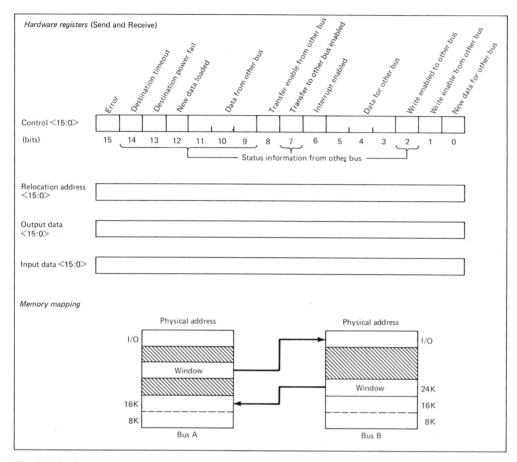

Fig. 12. Hardware registers and memory mapping for a bus window.

• *Node types.* Nodes in the multiple-processor structure may be identical PMS components (homogeneous) or different PMS components (nonhomogeneous). Nonhomogeneous structures are usually composed of memory- and processor-type nodes. Thus a nonhomogeneous system implies a shared memory system.

Homogeneous structures are mostly multicomputer in nature (there are notable exceptions). This implies a computer network with local, unshared memories and communication via messages through a coupled I/O subsystem.

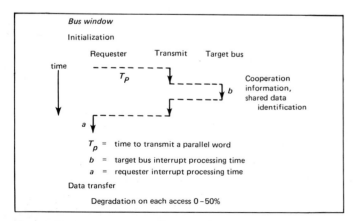

Fig. 13. Timing for a bus-window transfer.

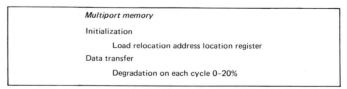

Fig. 14. Timing for a multiported memory transfer.

Table 3   Multiple-Processor Design-Space Parameters

Dimensions

Node types
Nonhomogeneous
Homogeneous
Memory system
Logical structure of address space
  Local
  Shared
    1
    n
    n(m)
Protection
  None
  Object
  Capability
Physical structure of memory
  Size
    Immediate
    System
  Redundancy
    Replication (*r)
    Coding
      Parity (*p)
      Hamming (*h)
Memory switch
Logical structure
  Accessibility
    All
    Partial
      Overlapped
      Multiple disjoint
  Access time
    Uniform
    Hierarchical
Physical structure
  Interconnection
    Direct (circuit-switched)
    Logical paths
      (message-switched)
  Growth rate
    Linear
    Polynomial
  Concurrency

Processor-memory data paths
Width of data path
Sharing
  Simplex
  Half-duplex
  Full-duplex
  Half-multiplexed
  Full-multiplexed
  Broadcast
Data rate
Delay
I/O system
Logical structure
  I/O initialization
    Uniform from all processors
    Partial
  I/O data transmission
    Uniform to all processors/memory
    Partial
  Access Time
    Uniform
    Hierarchical
Physical structure
  Size
  Data rate
  Interconnection
    Direct (circuit-switched)
    Logical paths (message-switched)
  Growth rate
    Linear
    Polynomial
  Concurrency
  Sharing
    Simplex
    Half-duplex
    Full-duplex
    Half-multiplexed
    Full-multiplexed
    Broadcast
Ratios
Memory bandwidth/processor bandwidth
I/O bandwidth/memory bandwidth
Interprocessor communication
Interprocessor interrupt
Pseudointerrupt device
Segment typing
Mailboxes

The relationship of processors to memories is the single most important attribute for distinguishing between various multiple-processor systems. The dimensions have been divided into three areas: memory system, memory switch, and processor-memory data paths.

- *Memory system.* The logic structure of the address space is the virtual memory the programmer must manipulate (Fig. 15). The address space may be shared or local. Local address spaces are associated with a processor. Any data

Fig. 15. The logical structure of the shared address space.

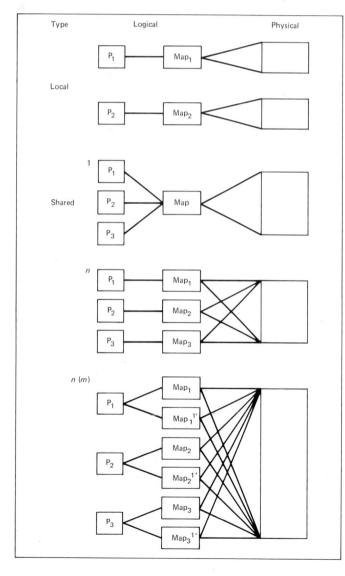

sharing would have to be under program control, thus implying easy enforcement of data protection but a large granularity for data access. An integer in parentheses indicates the number of local address spaces.

Shared memory may consist of one large address space or n address spaces mapped into a large physical address space. A number in parentheses indicates the number of distinct sets of address maps for each address space. Data sharing is efficient, but some form of protection mechanism must be provided. Access may be restricted on an object basis (i.e., a processor has no authority to write, read, execute, etc., from the shared memory segment) or on a capability basis (i.e., software processes have no capability to write, read, execute, etc., a shared memory segment or request another software process to perform the operation for it).

The physical structure of memory includes the size immediately accessible to a processor and the total system size. The memory may also include redundancy for reliability purposes. The redundancy can take the form of full replication (represented by an integer r), parity (p), or Hamming code (h).

- *Memory switch.* The memory switch provides access to shared memory (Fig. 16). It is not present in systems with only local memories whose communication is through the I/O system (see below).

The logic structure of the memory switch includes those attributes that impact a system's programmer. The accessibility of shared memory impacts problem decomposition, interprocess communication, and the form of data structures. All of shared memory may be accessible from all processors, only a portion of shared memory may be accessible to each processor with suitable overlap to provide shared access, or subsets of processors may share portions of memory disjointed from the rest of memory.

The system's programmer is also interested in whether the access time to shared memory is uniform or hierarchial, i.e., whether access time varies as a function of the physical structure of memory.

An important aspect of the physical structure of the memory switch is the interconnection discipline.

- *Path discipline.* One of the key problems in multiple-processor systems (or any system with multiple, shared resources) is the prevention of deadlocks. The path discipline suggests the approach taken to deadlock resolution on the interconnecting data paths.

A set of activities is defined to be deadlocked when no activity can proceed without acquiring a resource already held by another activity [Habermann, 1972]. The necessary conditions for deadlock are: (1) resources must not be sharable or preemptable, (2) resources must be retained while an activity is acquiring further resources, and (3) there must be a circularity in the resource requirements of

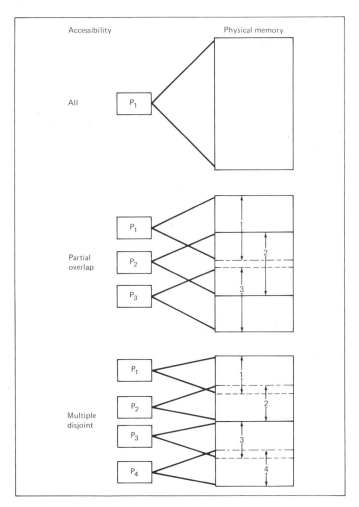

Fig. 16. Memory switch logical structure.

deadlock prevention affords because of the dynamic nature of the allocation. Deadlock detection and recovery is used in systems where deadlocks are allowed to occur; resource utilization may increase, but the recovery mechanism is often costly.

Generally either deadlock prevention or detection and recovery is used for the data paths. Potential for deadlocks exists only in systems where multiple paths are required for one information exchange. In circuit switching, each path is obtained in a sequential manner until the information path is completed. Deadlock prevention is usually employed for performance considerations, since a deadlock detection mechanism would be quite complex in order to recognize deadlocks from general system congestion and would also represent a single point of system failure.

In message switching, each physical path is held only long enough to pass a message from one buffer to another. Messages proceed in an incremental fashion to their destination. Buffers are thus the resources which may deadlock. Rather than restrict the interconnection patterns, message-switched systems frequently provide more buffers than required in a worst-case situation (as does Cm*) or a sufficiently large number of buffers so that the probability of deadlock is arbitrarily small (as does the ARPANET).

Finally, the growth rate of the switch complexity is important, since it affects cost, while switch concurrency (i.e., the number of accesses that can be in progress simultaneously) affects both cost and performance.

- *Processor-memory data paths.* There are several subdimensions required to specify the data-path dimension. *Width of data* is the number of data bits transmitted simultaneously. *Data rate* is the number of bits transferred per second. *Delay* is the amount of time from the initialization of a transfer at the source to its reception at the destination. Thus delay is a measure of physical proximity of sources and destinations. Finally, *sharing* indicates the control discipline used on the data paths. On a simplex line, information is passed in only one direction and no arbitration is required. A half-duplex line allows information to flow from one point to another in one direction at a time. However, arbitration must be used in order to turn the line around for information flow in the other direction. Full-duplex allows simultaneous, bidirectional information flow between points. Half-multiplexed allows information to flow in one directon either from one point to one of many points or from one of many to one. Such a scheme can be used in multiported memories, and because of the unidirectional information flow, very efficient arbitration techniques exist. Full-multiplexed allows bidirectional information flow between many sources and destinations in a one-at-a-time manner (a common example is a bus). Arbitration overhead for data-path usage can be high. Finally, broadcast allows information to flow from one source to many destinations.

the activities. There are at least three ways of dealing with deadlocks: deadlock prevention, deadlock avoidance, and deadlock detection and recovery. In deadlock prevention a static analysis is made of a system with known interconnection demands and the system is constructed so that no deadlock can ever occur. Since the analysis is made on the static system, there is no overhead during system operation. A major disadvantage of deadlock prevention is that it is geared to worst-case assumptions about the dynamic state of the system. Consequently system resources may be poorly utilized. Deadlock avoidance employs the current state of the system to determine whether a request for resources can lead to potential deadlock. A possible increase in resource utilization may thus occur over what

Table 4 Example Points in the Multiple-Processor Design Space

| System | Node types | Memory system | | | Memory switch | | | |
| | | Logical structure | Physical structure | | Logical structure | | Physical structure | |
			Immediate size	System size	Accessibility	Access time	Inter-connection	Growth rate
C.mmp	Non-hom	16(4)*p	64 Kbyte	16 Mbyte	All	Uniform	Circuit	Polynomial
Plessey 250	Non-hom	1	?	?	?	?	Circuit	Polynomial
Prime	Non-hom	5	?	?	Overlapped	Uniform	Circuit	Polynomial
Bus switch	Non-hom	local(2)+1	64 Kbyte	256 Kbyte	All	Uniform	Circuit	Polynomial
Pluribus	Non-hom	local(14)+14	64 Kbyte	1 Mbyte	All	Uniform	Circuit	Polynomial
Bus window	Hom	local(2)+2	64 Kbyte	128 Kbyte	All	Hierarchical	Circuit	Polynomial
Cm*	Hom	n(2)*p	64 Kbyte	2684 Mbyte	All	Hierarchical	Message	Linear
SIFT	Hom	n*3	?	?	All	Hierarchical	Circuit	Polynomial
C.vmp	Hom	1 * 3 or local	64 Kbyte	64 Kbyte	All	Uniform	Circuit	Polynomial
Bus link	Hom	local	64 Kbyte	....	....	....	....	....
Global bus	Hom	local	....	....	....	....	....	....
Tandem	Hom	local	64 Kbyte	....	....	....	....	....
FTMP	Hom	1 * 3	....	....	....	....	....	....
Serial line	Hom	local	....	....	....	....	....	....
ARPANET	Hom	local	....	....	....	....	....	....
Loops	Hom	local	....	....	....	....	....	....
ETHERNET	Hom	local	....	....	....	....	....	....
ALOHANET	Non-hom	local	....	....	....	....	....	....

The destinations must make an active decision on whether the data are meaningful for them.

- *I/O system.* The I/O system dimensions parallel those of the memory system. In multiprocessors with shared memory, the I/O system may or may not be analogous to the logical structure and physical structure used for the memory system. In multiple-processor systems with local memory, the I/O system is used for interprocessor communication and thus becomes the major differentiating feature of different architectures. The I/O system dimensions should be self-explanatory, considering the foregoing discussion of the memory system dimensions.

- *Ratios.* Ratios between processor, memory, and I/O bandwidth are important in determining whether the system is balanced or even usable. It is a common pitfall to focus on processor-memory bandwidth and neglect I/O-memory bandwidth. Thus new problems and/or data cannot be brought into the system fast enough to utilize the high processor-memory bandwidth, and the system fails to achieve its performance goals on a sustained basis.

- *Interprocessor communication.* The form of interprocessor communication determines the responsiveness of the system to I/O, exceptional conditions, and even requests from other processors cooperating on the same task. Notification can be sent via interprocessor interrupts (as in C.mmp), via a prioritized queue that processors periodically examine (as in the Pluribus), via building communication segment types on top of existing mapping and sharing (as in the Cm*), or via mailboxes.

System Examples

Table 4 depicts a number of multiple-processor systems arranged by their values of the design-space parameters. Systems closer to each other in the table are also closer to each other in concepts. Figures 1, 2, and 3 illustrate the various systems.

The first eight systems share an address space and are considered multiprocessors. The next five systems can be considered distributed multiple-processor systems or local networks in that communication is via the I/O system with more or less hardware support for information transfer. These five systems are

Concurrency	Processor-memory data paths				Processor-I/O data paths			
	Width	Sharing	Data rate	Delay	Width	Sharing	Data rate	Delay
16	16	h.m	$16 \times 25 \times 10^6$	2×10^{-7}				
?	24	h.m	$m \times 25 \times 10^6$	?				
5	16	h.m	?	?				
1	16	h.d	18×10^6	3×10^{-7}				
1	16	h.d	25×10^6	2×10^{-7}				
2	16	f.d	19×10^6	5×10^{-7}				
1	16	f.m	16×10^6	10^{-5}				
3	16	h.m	10^6	?				
1					16	h.d	13×10^6	10^{-7}
....					16	h.d	10^7	5×10^{-7}
....					16	f.m	?	?
....					16	f.m	10^8	?
....					1	f.m	10^6	?
....					1	h.d.	10^4	?
....					1	s	5×10^4	10^{-1}
....					1	s	10^6	?
....					1	b	?	?
....					1	b	?	?

frequently dedicated to one task at a time, although the task might be one of a wide variety of general tasks. The last five systems are networks of processors communicating through the I/O system primarily for the purpose of sharing data.

C.mmp

C.mmp is the classical multiprocessor, with 16 processors sharing 16 memory modules through a cross-point switch. Chapter 22 presents the architecture, software structure, reliability experience, and performance of C.mmp. The multiple applications implemented on C.mmp indicate that there are several classes of important applications that can utilize process-level parallelism to the point of achieving speedup in a linear relationship to the number of processors utilized. An important aspect of the software organization of these applications is that the code on all processors is identical. Communications and scheduling are via message queues. Thus an application can be debugged on a uniprocessor. When the code is run in production mode it can utilize all available processors (i.e., it does not have to be rewritten or modified if processors are not available because of other users' demands or hardware failure). The hardware performance param-

eters of C.mmp are summarized in Fig. 17. C.mmp was retired on March 5, 1980.

Pluribus

The Pluribus was conceived in 1972 by Bolt Beranek and Newman (BBN), the implementors of the ARPANET, as a modular, high-performance IMP. Since traffic volumes at ARPANET sites varied widely, an architecture was sought that would span a 10 to 1 performance range. Modularity plus high availability requirements favored a multiprocessor architecture.

The Pluribus PMS structure is depicted in Fig. 1f. Processors share an address space implemented by a distributed cross-point switch. The processors, Lockheed SUEs, have a unified memory and I/O address space as in the PDP-11. The 64-Kbyte address space is divided into local and shared. Shared memory access is provided by bus couplers, which recognize four 8-Kbyte address windows. Shared memory addresses are mapped by the bus coupler from 16 bits to a 20-bit, systemwide shared address space. A processor bus can be connected to multiple shared memory buses.

Two processors share the same processor bus, since the

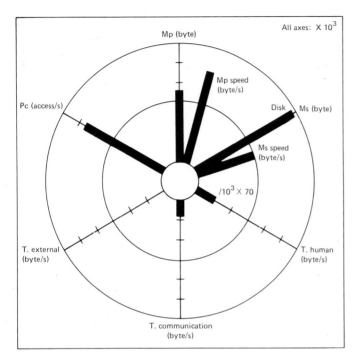

Fig. 17. Sixteen processor configuration of C.mmp.

processor bus cycle (which is 100 ns) and local memory access time (which is 450 ns) are fast enough to support the Pc-Mp bandwidth of both processors without degradation (a processor memory request approximately every 2 μs). Each processor executes out of its own Mp, thus eliminating Mp contention. The local Mp's act as code and temporary data caches. The application code is small enough (less than 16 Kwords) to remain resident in the local Mp's. The shared memory is used only for shared system data, interprocess communications, redundant copies of local code, and less frequently used system code.

Any number of processor, shared memory, and I/O buses can be interconnected via bus couplers. Bus couplers need only be provided for those communication paths that will actually be used. However, the normal structure will be symmetric and require $P \times (M + I)$ bus couplers, where P, M, and I are the number of processor, memory, and I/O buses, respectively.

Interprocessor control is via a special set of registers in the I/O address space. A processor accesses these registers on another processor's bus by establishing a path via an I/O bus consisting of a forward path through an I/O bus coupler and a backward path through the target processor's I/O bus coupler. Since the bus coupler access is circuit-switched, this organization is prone to

deadlock if two processors are simultaneously attempting to use the same two I/O coupler paths in different directions. This deadlock potential is considered acceptable, since the interprocessor control is attempted very infrequently (i.e., only in reconfiguration attempts after a failure).

The major form of interprocess communication is via the pseudointerrupt device (PID). The PID is a hardware priority queue that exists on the I/O bus. When polled by a processor, the PID returns the highest priority number in the queue and deletes the number. The PIDs are typically used to schedule processes. Each number corresponds to a process that can be run on any Pc. I/O devices (upon completion of an operation) or processes can enter numbers into the PID. Thus, in a dedicated, special-purpose application, the PID eliminates the overhead in context swapping and scheduling associated with interrupts and system monitor calls. In order to work in a real time application, however, the system's programmer has to ensure that the PID is polled frequently enough that no I/O information is lost. In the IMP application the highest-speed device has to be serviced within 400 μs of its request. Since the worst case would be when all processors simultaneously started executing a new task, the code is divided into strips. Each strip represents a task that, once started, runs to completion. There is no temporary context between tasks. Each strip requires at most 300 μs to execute, ensuring the necessary frequency of PID interrogation.

Division of an application into strips places a significant burden on the application programmer. The interprocessor communication mechanisms would have to be rethought if the Pluribus were to be used in a general-purpose environment.

By the last quarter of 1978, twenty Pluribus systems had been delivered, each dedicated to one of the following applications:

- ARPANET IMP, two- and three-processor systems
- Private Line Interface (PLI), allowing secure data to pass through a nonsecure network
- Very Distant Adapter (VDA), allowing remote computers to access an ARPANET IMP with an error-checking protocol called Very Distant Host (VDH) protocol

A fourth application, a terminal communications controller, was under development.

Chapter 23 presents the Pluribus architecture, as well as fault-tolerant features. Comments on the Pluribus as a fault-tolerant architecture are found in Part 2, Sec. 6.

Other Systems

Other multiple-processor systems are described elsewhere in the book. Chapter 29 describes a loosely coupled system designed for high data integrity. Part 2, Sec. 5, discusses the ARPANET, ALOHANET, and ETHERNET. Part 3, Sec. 4, presents the CDC 6600 and TI ASC, which utilize high-speed hardware to implement several virtual peripheral processes that can communicate through shared memory. Part 2, Sec. 3, contains Illiac IV and STARAN, so-called single–instruction-multiple–data-stream machines (SIMD), wherein multiple processors execute the same program on different data in lockstep. Part 4, Sec. 5, discusses the multiprocessor systems produced for the IBM System/360 and System/370 families.

References

DEC [1973]; Dijkstra [1968a]; Fuller, Ousterhout, Raskin, Rubinfeld, Sindhu, and Swan [1978]; Habermann [1972]; Heart, Ornstein, Crowther, and Barker [1973]; Hopkins, Smith, and Lala [1978]; Katsuki, Elsan, Mann, Roberts, Robinson, Skowronski, and Wolf [1978]; Lawson and Megenhagen [1975]; Lipton [1973]; Roberts [1967]; Siewiorek, Kini, Mashburn, McConnel, and Tsao [1978]; Swan, Fuller, and Siewiorek [1977]; Wensley, Lamport, Goldberg, Green, Levitt, Melliar-Smith, Shotak, and Weinstock [1978]; Wulf and Bell [1972].

Chapter 22

The C.mmp/Hydra Project: An Architectural Overview

Henry H. Mashburn

Summary This article describes the C.mmp/Hydra project at Carnegie-Mellon University. Included are detailed descriptions of the PMS structure of C.mmp (a multiprocessor built from minicomputers) and its major components. An overview of its operating system, Hydra, is provided with emphasis on those sections most concerned with and influenced by the architecture. The project is also discussed in terms of performance, reliability, programming methodologies, and problems encountered.

In 1971 the Computer Science Department at Carnegie-Mellon University (CMU) undertook a project to construct C.mmp (Computer.multi-mini-processor), a relatively large-scale multiprocessor, from minicomputers. A number of project goals and criteria influenced the design:

- Minicomputers would be used as the processing elements of a multiprocessor that would support a general-purpose, time-shared environment.

- The machine would be symmetric: there would be no master-slave relation among the processors.

- A large address space would be provided.

- As much as possible, commercially available hardware would be used.

To provide the necessary programming environment, a novel operating system was proposed, its principal component being its kernel, Hydra [Wulf, Cohen, Corwin, Jones, Levin, Pierson, and Pollack, 1974; Wulf, Levin, and Pierson, 1975]. The following criteria were used in designing the operating system:

- Separation of policy and mechanism: a kernel of mechanisms of "universal applicability" would be created from which varying policies could be implemented.

- A capability-based protection system and an object-oriented virtual memory would provide support for data abstraction; it would be extensible to user-defined data-types.

- The software would exploit the existence of multiple copies of many hardware elements for reliability.

- The structure of the system would be nonhierarchical.

- The system would be able to run for extended periods with no human operator.

The resulting C.mmp/Hydra-system has been completed and has met these goals. It has been running as a general departmental resource since mid-1975, supporting a time-shared user community as well as large-scale computing tasks, such as speech-understanding systems.

Table 1 summarizes the basic hardware and performance of C.mmp.

The Hardware: C.mmp

C.mmp is an asynchronous, multiple–instruction stream, multiple–data stream (MIMD) multiprocessor. To achieve the goal of symmetry, the processors and primary memory (Mp) are connect-

Fig. 1. The C.mmp multiprocessor.

Table 1   C.mmp Hardware Summary

Structure	Symmetric, central cross-point–connected MIMD multiprocessor allowing up to 16 Pc's and 16 memories.
Processors	PDP-11 models 11/20 or 11/40, in any mix. A 16-Pc configuration of 11/20's and 11/40's was built. Eleven 11/40 models are currently in use.
Shared memory	32-Mbyte total shared address space. 2.7 Mbyte implemented using both core and MOS.
Secondary storage	700 Mbyte total moving-head disks. 6 Mbyte total fixed-head paging disks.
Performance	4.3 MIPS for 11/40 configuration, 3.0 MIPS for current 11/40 configuration. 26.3×10^6 references/s total memory bandwidth.

ed by a central cross-point switch. Before detailed design began, this structure was extensively studied by simulation and analytic models [Bhandarkar, 1972; Strecker, 1971], and it was determined that a 16 × 16 cross-point switch could be optimal, given the available technology. The TTL and Schottky TTL logic families were used for the switch and the relocation hardware because only they offered a fair range of MSI components. MSI components in the faster ECL logic were not available at the time. Essentially all of C.mmp is built with 1971–1972 technology, although some of the more recent additions use MOS LSI.

The Digital Equipment Corporation PDP-11 was chosen for the processors (Pc's) primarily because of its Unibus architecture. The Unibus allowed easy interfacing to the shared memory and kept the Pc modifications minimal. A further advantage of the Unibus was that it allowed DMA transfers to use relative, rather than physical, addresses because all addresses on the Unibus can be mapped in a uniform way by the relocation scheme, which will be described in detail. Therefore, the peripheral devices would need no modification to access the 25-bit shared memory address, even though they generate only the standard 18-bit Unibus address.

The following descriptions are primarily architectural, although some internal algorithms are described. For implementation detail, consult Fuller and Harbison [1978].

1.1 The PMS Structure

Figure 2 shows the PMS structure as of early 1979.[1] There are 16 processor ports and 16 memory ports in the cross-point switch (Smultiport, or Smp). The Pc's are slightly modified PDP-11/20 and PDP-11/40 processors, each connected to all the memories by Smp via the relocation unit (Dmap). The Pc's are further interconnected by an *interprocessor bus* (IP-bus), which provides basic control functions such as *start*, *halt*, and three levels of *interprocessor* interrupt (IPI), as well as the broadcasting of a 60-bit nonrepeating clock value used for interval timing and unique name generation. Note that this clock does *not* synchronize the internal operation of the processors.

C.mmp was constructed in several major stages: four prototype switches (1 × 1, 1 × 2, 2 × 2, 4 × 4), the full 16 × 16 switch with five 11/20's as processors, and finally the 16 × 16 Smp with a full processor complement of sixteen Pc's: five 11/20's and eleven 11/40's. The 16 memory ports were initially configured with 1.4 Mbyte of core memory, and a similar amount of MOS memory was added later.

In early 1977 the Pc modifications for the 11/40 were completed, and by June 1977, C.mmp itself was completed by adding

eleven 11/40's to the existing five 11/20's. Any mix of these two Pc models is possible. The desire to exploit a writable control store included in the 11/40 modifications, and performance measurements indicating that symmetry in processor speed is desirable,[2] led to exclusion of the 11/20's in early 1978, leaving the eleven 11/40's as the total Pc complement.

In the original PMS design [Wulf and Bell, 1972], a second cross-point switch was included to connect peripheral devices to any Pc's Unibus. For reasons of economy, this switch was never built and peripherals were assigned to specific Unibuses. I/O requests are mapped from requesting processors to the processor controlling the device via an IPI and a simple per-Pc queuing system in the operating-system kernel. The lack of the second cross-point switch has not been detrimental to the system.

1.2 Shared Memory Access

Access to shared primary memory (Mp) is performed in two stages: relocation of the 18-bit processor-generated address into a 25-bit address space, and resolution of contention in accessing that memory location. These jobs are performed by the *relocation unit* Dmap and the cross-point switch Smp, respectively.

1.2.1 The Relocation Mechanism: Dmap Dmap resides on the Unibus of each Pc and generally appears as a peripheral device, intercepting and mapping most addresses as they are placed on the Unibus. The planned, but not implemented, 2 Kbyte processor cache memory (Mcache) would interface to the Pc through Dmap.

Dmap divides the 32-Mbyte address space into thirty-two 8-Kbyte directly addressable pages that may be physically placed anywhere in shared memory. There are four address spaces, specified by 2 bits in the *processor status word* (PS). Therefore, four sets of eight address-mapping registers are provided in each relocation unit. To allow communication between address spaces without explicit addressing changes, the stack page is common to all four spaces.

The four address spaces are the heart of the memory protection mechanism: in only one space (1,1 in the PS space bits) are the relocation registers and the PS directly addressable. Since this page is used exclusively by the Hydra kernel [Wulf, Cohen, Corwin, Jones, Levin, Pierson, and Pollack, 1974], protecting the PS from indirect changes (see Sec. 1.5 of this chapter) guarantees

---

[1]Although shown in Fig. 2 to indicate its place in the architecture, only a prototype of Mcache was implemented.

[2]Many parallel decompositions of algorithms require that all processes synchronize between steps of computation. If some processes are running on slower Pc's, the processes executing on faster Pc's waste time waiting for the slower Pc's processes to report completion. The effect is like a convoy: all ships move at the speed of the slowest. See Sec. 3.1.2 of this chapter and Fig. 7 for a measurement of this effect.

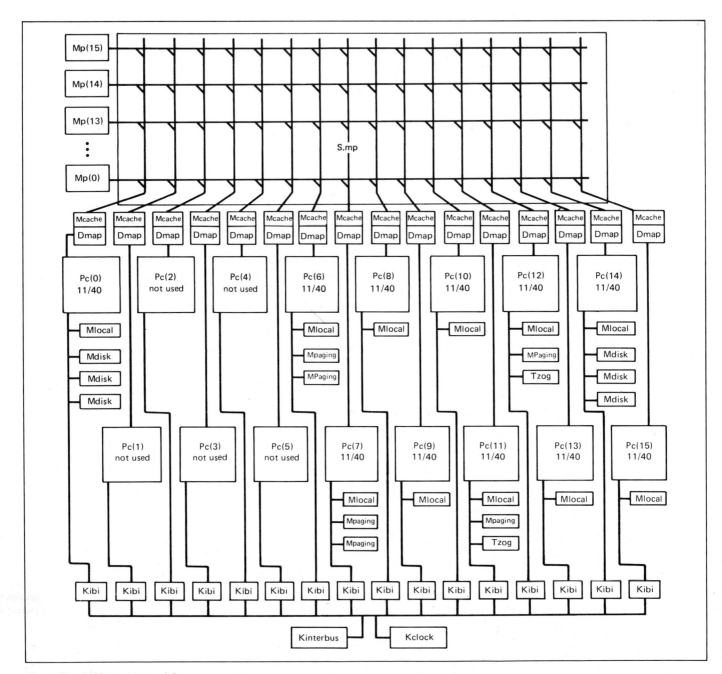

Fig. 2. The PMS structure of C.mmp.

that no addressability changes may be made without the approval of the operating system. All entries to the kernel, whether by interrupt or user request, force the assertion of both space bits.

To allow direct addressability, two of the relocation registers in (1,1) space are disabled, one each for the Mlocal page and the peripheral device control-register page. With these registers disabled, addresses that would normally be mapped are passed along the Unibus unchanged to be received by the addressed memory or register location. Since the registers of Dmap are given addresses in the control-register page, they are always addressable by Hydra.

As illustrated in Fig. 3, the Dmap intercepts the 18-bit UNIBUS addresses (16-bit words plus the two space bits) and converts them in the following manner: the three high-order bits of the 16-bit word select a register from the bank specified by the space bits. The contents of the register provide a 12-bit page-frame number; the remaining 13 bits from the address word are the displacement within that page. The two are concatenated to form the 25-bit shared memory address. The 13-bit displacement gives an 8-Kbyte page size. This transparent mapping is performed for all shared memory accesses. In addition to the 12 page-frame bits, there are 4 bits in each relocation register used for control. The first three are designated *no page loaded*, *write-protected*, and *written-into*, and the fourth bit controls whether values from the page may be stored in Mcache.

After the 25-bit address is generated, Mcache is checked to see if the data are already available. If the access is a read cycle and the datum is in Mcache, the datum is immediately returned, bypassing shared memory. Although Mcache is a write-through design, only read-only data are cached, because the cache/Pc PMS structure allows multiple, and possibly different, copies of a datum. However, since approximately 70 percent of the memory accesses are to code rather than data, the read-only requirement is expected to produce a high "hit" rate for pure code programs [Fuller and Harbison, 1978].

The internal characteristics of Mcache are:

Capacity	2 Kbyte
Block size	2 bytes (one word stored or returned per access)
Set size	1

Although only a single prototype of Mcache was built, it is estimated that it would save 50 percent of the time for a read cycle if the data were in the cache. However, it is important to realize that the motivation for including a cache on each processor was to reduce memory contention rather than directly provide fast memory. The effects of not having the caches will be discussed in Sec. 3.1.4 of this chapter.

Parity for both data and the 25-bit address is generated by the Dmap interface to the bus from the switch. The address parity is checked at the switch interface. If the check fails, the request is aborted and the processor interrupted. Data parity is not checked until the data are read from memory and returned to a Dmap. The fact that data parity is checked only by Dmap and not at any other point either in the cross-point switch or in the memory modules themselves has probably contributed to the reliability problems due to parity errors (see Sec. 3.3.1). Separate parity bits are maintained for both bytes of the word: one byte is given odd parity, the other, even. This detects words of all 1s or all 0s, both of which are common results of transient timing errors.

1.2.2 The Cross-Point Switch: Smp Smp routes the 25-bit address request to the memory port specified by the high-order four bits of the address. A port is requested by setting the bit corresponding to the requesting Pc in the port's *request register*. Contention for the port is resolved by periodically gating the request register into a second register, the *queue register*, which is left-shifted as the port becomes available. The shifting creates a priority-ordered queue: as a 1 bit is shifted out, the corresponding Pc is granted access to the port. Processor 15 is assigned the high-order bit and processor 0 the low-order bit, defining the priority. When the queue register is 0, all requests have been satisfied. The request register is again gated into the queue register and cleared, and a new cycle begins. A second request for the same port by a processor must enter via the request register; hence equality of service among the Pc's is maintained. The two-level request mechanism obscures the internal queue's priority ordering to the point that it is of virtually no importance outside the switch, preserving the symmetry of Smp.[1] The switch's maximum concurrency (16 independent paths) is achieved if all Pc's request different ports.

---

[1]In the worst case, in which all Pc's repeatedly access the same port, the lowest-priority Pc suffers a 50 percent memory access time degradation, but since this situation is extremely rare in practice, the effect is negligible [McGehearty, 1980].

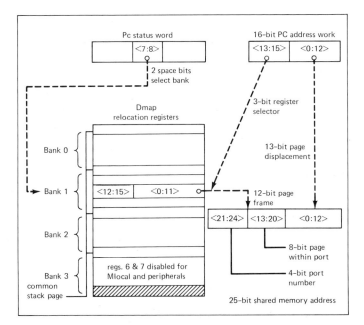

Fig. 3. C.mmp address relocation.

The centralized and symmetric design of Smp makes the cost of memory access equal for all Pc's. Including address translation, switch overhead (no contention), and round-trip cable delay, the cost is about 1 µs. Although high by today's standards, more than equal to the access time of the memory, it has not proved prohibitive, or even annoying. The memory connected to Smp permits a maximum total bandwidth of 26.3×10^6 memory references per second, a value well matched to the speed of the 1971-vintage processors (see Table 2).

Smp was designed to allow partitioning of the system into smaller units. Each of the 256 cross-points has a switch that may be used to manually enable or disable it. These switches, plus a global cross-point set switch, set the flip-flops that control the individual cross-points. Now disconnected for reliability and software security, there was a program interface that allowed setting of the cross-point configuration from Pc 0.

The ability to partition the system was originally intended to allow multiple versions of the operating system to coexist. However, funds were not available to provide sufficient primary and secondary store to allow simultaneous execution of multiple copies of Hydra. Currently, the principal use of the manual cross-point enable switches is to disconnect faulty hardware elements. A Pc and a single memory port are sometimes partitioned out of the system to allow maintenance to proceed concurrently with normal operations.

1.3 Primary Memory

The current complement of primary memory is 2.7 megabytes of mixed technology: eleven ports containing 1.4 megabytes of core memory and five ports with 1.3 megabytes of MOS memory. Technologies are not mixed within a memory port.

The memory port control of Smp permits each port to be interleaved in as many ways as there are independently driven memory modules. Interleaving is specified by the page number, bits 13 to 20 of the 25-bit address (see Fig. 3). C.mmp's core memories are 16-Kbyte modules, and there are eight independently driven modules per port, allowing eight-way interleaving.

Table 2 Shared Memory Characteristics

Core memory	250-ns access, 650-ns cycle time 16-Kbyte module size, 8 modules per port 8-way interleaved within a port 1.71×10^6 references/s per port maximum bandwidth
MOS memory	330-ns access, 450-ns cycle time 65-Kbyte module size, 4 modules per port No interleaving 1.49×10^6 references/s per port maximum bandwidth

(a)

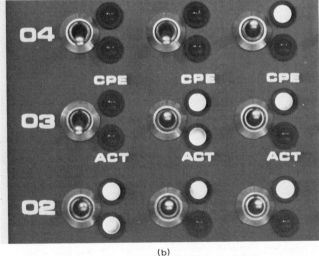

(b)

Fig. 4. The crosspoint switch. (*a*) The crosspoint display panel with the system partitioned into two disjoint 8 x 8 machines. (*b*) A detail of the display panel. Three Pc's are selectively permitted access to ports 2, 3, and 4 as shown by the crosspoint enable (CPE) lights. Two of the Pc's are actively accessing memory (ACT lights).

The MOS memory has four 65-Kbyte modules per port. However, they are not independent, having only one refresh control board, and so are not interleaved. Ports can have up to 256 pages, or 2 megabytes, of memory. Table 2 provides specifications and measurements of the memories.

Each Pc also has 8 Kbyte of local (nonshared) core memory (Mlocal).

1.4 The Interprocessor Bus

The IP-bus provides a common clock as well as interprocessor control. These two logically and functionally separate features use separate data paths, although they share a common control (Kinterbus). Each processor has an *interbus interface* (Kibi) that defines the processor's bus address and makes available the bus functions to the software.

The first function is to continuously broadcast the 60-bit, 250-KHz Kclock. This is done by multiplexing the clock value onto a 16-bit-wide data path in four time periods, low-order bits first. Any Kibi requesting a Kclock read waits for the initial time period and then buffers the four transmissions in four local holding registers available to the software. Clock values are often used for unique names [Wulf, Cohen, Corwin, Jones, Levin, Pierson, and Pollack, 1974; Wulf, Levin, and Pierson, 1975], and so the otherwise unused high-order four bits of the fourth local register are set to the reader's Pc number to ensure uniqueness when any number of Kibi's read the bus simultaneously.

Each Kibi has a countdown register for interval timing. It may be initialized to a nonzero value by the program, and it is decremented by 1 every 16 μs (timing supplied by Kclock). The Pc is interrupted when the register reaches zero.

The second bus function is the interprocessor interrupt and control mechanism. Each Pc may interrupt, halt, continue, or start any other Pc, including itself. Each Kibi has a 16-bit register for each of the control operations. The operations are invoked by setting the bit(s) corresponding to the processor(s) to be controlled in the appropriate register. Setting the ith bit invokes the operation on Pc(i). A second 16-bit-wide data path is eight-way–time-multiplexed, each control operation being assigned a time period. As the appropriate period arrives, each Kibi ORs its control operation register onto the bus and clears the register. Synchronization of bus access, as well as operation specification, is accomplished by the multiplexed time periods. The Kibi also inspects the bus to see if the specified operation is being invoked on its processor; if so, the requested action is performed. Although eight time periods are available, only six are used: three priority levels of IPI, halt, continue, and start; the remaining two are ignored.

Each Kibi provides a manual switch register that defines the set of Pc's that the host Pc may interrupt or control. As with the control operation registers, setting switch i permits the Pc to invoke IP-bus functions on Pc(i). These registers, one per processor, are used with the manual cross-point enable switches

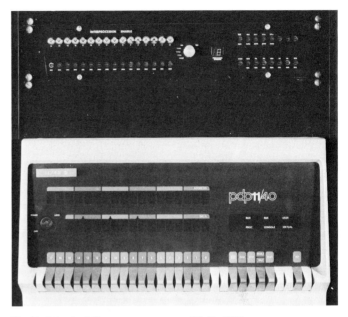

Fig. 5. A typical C.mmp processor with its Kibi.

to partition the system. A 16-bit LED display register is also provided to selectively display the four words of Kclock or the interval-timing counter and its control register.

1.5 Pc Modifications

The PDP-11's used on C.mmp were slightly modified to provide software protection and make the Pc's compatible with a multiprogramming environment. Also, a writable microstore was added to the 11/40's. The actual modifications were similar for both PDP-11 models; however, their implementations were quite different because of the differing internal implementations of the two models. In neither case were the changes extensive. Certain instructions were made privileged to ensure the integrity of the system software. In particular, HALT, WAIT, and RESET were prohibited from user programs. Since the processor status word (PS) controls the relocation address space of the executing program (and hence memory protection), two instructions which may modify it from user space were also prohibited: RTI (return from interrupt) and RTT (return from trap). Both of these instructions load the PS from the stack. Since they are sometimes used in subroutine calling sequences, they are trapped and emulated by the kernel for user executions—after an appropriate checking of the new PS to be loaded.

Because the operating system must leave some context information on the stack during protected procedure calls [Cohen and Jefferson, 1975; Wulf, Cohen, Corwin, Jones, Levin, Pierson, and Pollack, 1974], address bounds checking was added to the *stack pointer register,* R6. Stack overflow protection existed, but it was necessary to augment it with underflow checking. The *stack underflow register* (SUR) prohibits all accesses to the stack page at addresses higher than its contents.[1] This protection extends to all accesses, whether by stack operations or direct addressing, thus protecting the previous context information. Additionally, R6 is constrained so that its contents always lie in the stack page (page 0) of Dmap.

Because of the difficulty of modifying a processor, the stack underflow register and the comparison circuitry were physically placed on one of the relocation unit boards. This remote placement compounded the timing difficulties of adding stack-limit checking to the processors. Having to protect the PS by disallowing user execution of RTI and RTT increased the perturbation of stack-operation timing. Unfortunately both of these modifications were necessary to ensure safe operation of a multiprocessing, multiuser operating system.

1.6 Writable Microstore

The PDP-11/40 is implemented via a horizontal microprocessor [DEC, 1972] with provision for extended control store to implement various instruction-set options. At CMU, a writable control store was developed in place of the standard extensions [Fuller, Almes, Broadley, Forgy, Karlton, Lesser, and Teter, 1976]. The writable store contains 1,024 eighty-bit words, a general mask-shift unit used for field extraction and data manipulation at the microprogram level, and a microprogram subroutine facility.

No such extension was possible for the 11/20, since it is not a microprogrammed processor. This asymmetry in the configuration was a major reason for the removal of the 11/20's.

1.7 Peripheral Devices

Peripheral devices on C.mmp are standard PDP-11 Unibus-interface devices; no modifications are required. Two of the device types are unique: the zero-latency paging disks and the graphic displays. The paging disks have 8 Kbyte per track, which exactly matches C.mmp's page size. Their controllers achieve zero latency by continuously monitoring the position of the disk under the fixed heads and, for full track transfers, can start the transfer at any 16-word sector boundary, calculating the proper displacement into the page. As the disk turns, the memory address is "wrapped around" when the start of track is reached.

The graphic displays are a CMU-designed and -built vector display [Rubin, Guggenheim, and Bihary, 1978]. The two on C.mmp are equipped with a transparent touch screen in front of the CRT display for specialized man-machine interaction studies

[1]In the PDP-11 instruction set, stacks grow from higher to lower addresses.

in the ZOG data base management project [Robertson and Ramakrishna, 1977].

Table 3 summarizes the major devices and is an indication of the capabilities of the machine.

2.   The Software: Hydra

A discussion of C.mmp would not be complete without an introduction to its unique operating system, Hydra. Hydra provides two basic mechanisms: (1) process creation and scheduling and (2) a capability-protected, object-oriented virtual memory system for date abstraction. In this section, emphasis will be placed on those features of the Hydra kernel most related to the multiprocessor architecture.

2.1 Processes, Scheduling, and Control

The features of Hydra most directly influenced by the architecture are process scheduling and control. The heart of Hydra's multiprocess, multiprocessor scheduler is the Kernel Multiprogramming System (KMPS). This system also implements several of the process control functions, including the synchronization primitives.

2.1.1 Processes and Scheduling: KMPS   In Hydra, the unit of scheduling is the *process*. Process scheduling is done in two phases: long-term (job selection) and short-term (context-swap frequency). Perhaps nowhere else in the kernel is the notion of policy-mechanism separation so clearly employed as in this two-level scheduler [Levin, Cohen, Corwin, Pollack, and Wulf, 1975].

KMPS provides the basic process creation and scheduling mechanisms as a parameterized short-term scheduler. It is driven, in turn, by one or more long-term schedulers. These schedulers, known as *policy modules* (PMs), are implemented as user-level programs and provide independent scheduling policies for different job streams, such as timesharing and batch.

Table 3   Major Devices on C.mmp

Quantity	Device type
3	200-Mbyte moving-head disks, 3330-type
2	40-Mbyte moving-head disks, 2314-type
2	20-Mbyte moving-head disks, 2314-type
6	1-Mbyte fixed-head, zero-latency paging disks
2	Vector graphic display terminals with touch screens
1	600 l/min line printer
1	9-track magnetic tape drive
1	Interface to ARPANET
n	Assorted local terminal interfaces

On account of the symmetry of the architecture, processes usually need not be bound to specific processors. KMPS schedules among processors as though the Pc's were merely a resource pool. The PMs need not be concerned with the multiprocessor aspects of scheduling. A PM simply supplies KMPS with a stream of processes to be run; KMPS will make the necessary multiprocessor scheduling considerations.

KMPS schedules according to four basic parameters supplied by the PMs for each process:

Process priority	The process's relative priority among the set of processes controlled by KMPS
Time quantum	Maximum execution duration, composed of a time-slice length and number of slices
Processor mask	A bit mask of permissible Pc's for the process; normally set to indicate any Pc
Maximum page set size	The maximum number of pages that the process may have resident in Mp at any given time

When a process is started, the four parameters are set and KMPS places it on the *feasible* list, a list of runnable processes. When selected from this list, a process may execute until it blocks, completes its time quantum, or is preempted by a higher-priority process. If preempted, the process is returned to the feasible list and waits until resources are again available at its priority. KMPS reconsiders its scheduling at the end of each time slice on any Pc; all Pc's execute KMPS asynchronously. When a process consumes its time quantum, it is returned to its controlling PM for reconsideration of long-term scheduling.

The basic KMPS mechanisms for scheduling and multiplexing the processes onto Pc's are quite straightforward: First, the highest-priority is chosen from the feasible list. Then, according to the process's processor mask, the highest-priority Pc is chosen, and the process is enqueued for that Pc. The Pc is then sent an IPI instructing it to reconsider its scheduling. If the incoming process is of higher priority than the one currently running, a context swap to the new process takes place and the previous process is returned to the feasible list. If the incoming process is not of higher priority, it is returned to the feasible list and no rescheduling takes place. Allowing the selected processor to make the scheduling decision at a time of its choice (controlled by Pc interrupt priority) helps to eliminate race conditions that would otherwise be rampant because of the asynchronous nature of C.mmp.

The scheduling mechanisms are quite efficient, since only half the mechanism need be invoked for most operations. Usually either the process or the Pc is known. For example, at the end of a time slice the Pc is known to be free and all that is needed is to identify the highest-priority process that it may execute. Similarly, a blocked process that is awakened only requires that a processor be assigned. The full mechanism is needed only when a new process is introduced into KMPS control. An additional mechanism allows Pc's with heavy DMA or interrupt traffic to be shielded from computational burdens by assigning them a lower priority. High-priority Pc's that have become idle can "steal" processes from lower-priority Pc's, freeing them for I/O duties. This mechanism is important in reducing overrun errors (see 3.3.1).

With these mechanisms, KMPS is capable of controlling a large number of processes; the system routinely runs with more than 100 processes without inordinate overhead.

2.1.2 Synchronization One of the most crucial functions of an asynchronous multiprocessor is its ability to synchronize independent instruction streams when required. Hydra uses, and provides at user level, a number of synchronization mechanisms. Most basic of these is the spin lock, implemented by continuous polling of a shared memory location. Because of the memory contention generated, spin locks are generally undesirable and are avoided within the kernel. However, because the fast mechanisms of the kernel are not available at user level, spin locks are sometimes useful for brief critical sections in user programs.

The most important synchronization mechanisms are the KMPS lock and the two forms of semaphore [Dijkstra, 1968a] implemented by Hydra. Another mechanism, based on message passing, is discussed in the next section. While these mechanisms are semantically equivalent, they differ widely in implementation and timing characteristics. The choice of mechanisms is dictated by both synchronization context and performance considerations.

The KMPS lock is a low-level, mutual-exclusion primitive operating below the process level. It is the logical equivalent of a spin lock, but its implementation uses interprocessor interrupts to avoid the memory contention inherent in continuous polling. The use of KMPS locks is restricted to places where context swap is not allowed, such as in interrupt routines.

A KMPS lock is implemented with two counters and a bit mask of waiting Pc's. When a lock request is made, the lock counter is indivisibly decremented (from 1) and tested. If the result is 0, the requesting Pc has control of the critical section. Otherwise, the Pc must wait. In this case, the Pc places its bit in the waiting processor mask and executes a WAIT FOR INTERRUPT instruction, idling the Pc. When a Pc unlocks a lock, it increments the lock counter, sets the second counter (sublock) to 1, and sends the highest-level IPI to all Pc's in the wait mask.

The blocked Pc's, upon receipt of the interrupt, resume execution and contend for the sublock. One, randomly determined, will see that its decrement of the sublock field has resulted in 0 and will remove its bit from the mask and assume control of the critical section. The others resume waiting. By allowing the sublock to be reset on each unlock operation, the lock counter contains the number of processors blocked (negated) while the lock is locked. This information is used in consistency checks that detect either incorrect lock addresses or damaged locks.

The advantages of this apparently complex system are twofold: it is extremely cheap in the nonblocking case (most frequent), and there are no memory cycles consumed in blocking, although the Pc is unavailable. The performance of this mechanism is excellent and will be discussed in a following section.

Semaphores differ from locks in two ways: their counters may have large values, and since they are process-level primitives, blocked processes are rescheduled. Each semaphore maintains a queue of blocked processes that will be rescheduled in the order that they have blocked.

Two forms are supported: one internal to Hydra (kernel semaphore) and one for user-level programs (PM semaphore). The difference is (conceptually) in their behavior when blocking. If a process must block on a kernel semaphore, a token for the process is appended to a queue within the semaphore and the Pc selects a new process from the KMPS feasible list. In particular, the pages of the blocked process remain core-resident.

Blocking on a PM semaphore is more complex. Not only is a token for the process enqueued, but a scheduling decision to swap the pages of the process must also be made. This decision is delayed for a period (currently 500 ms, a parameter controlled by the PM), so that if the critical section is freed during this time, the process may possibly continue. In this case, the behavior is much like the faster kernel semaphore and averts considerable paging overhead. If during the delay the process cannot continue, it is returned to the PM for the duration of its blocked period and its pages become eligible for swapping. Although this mechanism pays a penalty of potential paging overhead, it ensures that a deadlock in user code does not result in a kernel deadlock. Upon receipt of the signal that the process may enter the critical section, the PM will again consider it for long-term scheduling and order it restarted by KMPS.

2.1.3 Interprocess Communication   A variety of hardware and software communication mechanisms are available within C.mmp/Hydra. The hardware provides two: First, and most basic, is sharing memory, used extensively by both kernel and user-level programs. Second is the IP-bus control functions, which are used strictly within the kernel. The three IPI levels are used for scheduling, interprocessor I/O request queuing, and synchronization. The IP bus HALT and START functions are used during system initialization and by a monitoring Pc to regain control of a Pc lost through serious error.

Hydra provides two software mechanisms: an interprocess interrupt (analogous to the IP-bus interrupt for Pc's) and a message facility. The KMPS *control* function allows one process to

interrupt another. Control interrupt entries are made at specified points associated with each process. Each process also has a control mask associated with it; the process sending a control function supplies a similar mask. A nonzero intersection of the masks causes the interrupt to be taken.[1] Depending on the interrupt, additional data may be available in certain predefined stack addresses [Newcomer, Cohen, Jefferson, Lane, Levin, Pollack, and Wulf, 1976]. A similar function, *desynch*, can be used to free a process blocked on a PM semaphore or while waiting for a message. In this case, an exception return is made from the blocking kernel call.

The Hydra Port System provides a general message facility that can be used for user-level interprocess communications and synchronization [Newcomer, Cohen, Jefferson, Lane, Levin, Pollack, and Wulf, 1976]. Messages are sent to and received by *ports*,[2] which may be interconnected via unidirectional links between an output channel of one port and an input channel of another. The messages are typed and may contain both data and a single capability (discussed in the next section). The basic port operations are SEND, RECEIVE, and an RSVP function that requests a reply to the message sent. Because the memory protection system provides protection only on a per-page basis, messages, which are always smaller than a page, must be created within the kernel and therefore are not directly addressable by user programs. Additional mechanisms, necessary only because of the memory protection limitations, are provided for creation of messages and copying of their contents.

The RECEIVE operation may block until a message is received by a port. Since ports, not processes, are connected, blocking provides a way to synchronize a dynamically changing set of cooperating processes in a producer-consumer relationship. No process requires knowledge of the number, role, or memory of the other processes: it knows only of its connection to a shared port and the operation it is to perform.

The Port System also provides a uniform user-level interface to the I/O system. Devices appear as ports, and requests are entered by sending an appropriately formatted message to the device. The fact that devices are physically connected to specific Pc's is completely obscured, and the common interface allows easy interchange of similar devices.

2.2 Protection and Data Abstraction

Although the protection and data abstraction mechanisms of Hydra are not dependent upon the architecture, the following

---

[1] Interrupting a user program must be simulated by Hydra to protect the PS. Exception interrupts, such as attempting to access nonexistent memory, have entry points associated with each process similar to the entry for control interrupts. When entry is made, the stack is loaded by Hydra with the (PC,PS) pair to simulate an interrupt to the entry point.
[2] Not to be confused with Smp memory ports.

brief introduction to these mechanisms is presented, since they were among the principal design criteria for the operating system. Detailed discussions may be found in the Hydra monograph Wulf, Levin, and Harbison [1980] and also in Cohen and Jefferson [1975], Wulf, Cohen, Corwin, Jones, Levin, Pierson, and Pollack [1974], and Newcomer, Cohen, Jefferson, Lane, Levin, Pollack, and Wulf [1976].

In Hydra, all data are encapsulated in *objects*, which may only be accessed via *capabilities*. The set of all objects is known as the Global Symbol Table (GST, pronounced *ghost*). Capabilities have a varying set of access and operation *rights* that are automatically checked whenever a capability is used to name an object. If a capability has insufficient rights for the requested access or operation, a signal is returned to the caller pointing out the protection violation. Hydra provides a set of 16 generic rights that are interpreted uniformly for all object types. An additional eight rights, the auxiliary rights, are available for each object type, and their interpretation is dependent on their type. Sharing of objects is permitted by copying capabilities for the object, possibly with the access rights restricted to limit authority.

Objects have a unique name (generated from the 60-bit clock), a type, and optionally a *data part* and list of capabilities (*C-list*). The data part allows storage of a limited amount of data (4,000 bytes). The C-list allows an object to contain up to 250 references to other objects. General graph structures may be built via these capability references. The protection mechanism is not hierarchical and may be used to protect structures with arbitrary interconnections. Objects may be referenced via a *path* of capabilities in the C-lists of other objects (if all capabilities along the path have sufficient rights).

The representations of both capabilities and objects are never directly manipulated by user-level programs; all representation knowledge is the domain of the kernel.

Nearly everything is represented as an object: processes, pages, semaphores, I/O devices, ports, and a great variety of other types. Every executing program has a basic list of capabilities known as its *Local Name Space* (LNS). The LNS and all objects reachable by paths rooted in the LNS are the instantaneous protection domain of the program. To prevent forgeries, objects may be referenced only by such paths; they are never directly referenced by name. An LNS typically contains capabilities for its code and data pages plus capabilities for any other objects that the program must manipulate.

Protected procedure calls switch protection domains. All programs are represented by *procedure objects*, which have C-lists containing capabilities for code pages, data pages, and *parameter templates*, as well as any other objects required. A procedure may have capability parameters in the same sense that a subroutine has address reference parameters. When called, the procedure's C-list and the actual parameters are merged into an LNS for the new protection domain. Procedure calls stack LNS's,

so that calls may be nested or recursive. The templates specify the parameter's position in the LNS and the necessary *check rights* and type of the actual capability. If the check rights or type doesn't match, a protection violation is signaled and the call aborted. A parameter template may also specify *rights amplification* to add certain rights to a parameter capability. The amplified capabilities exist only in the LNS of the called procedure and are rarely, if ever, returned to the caller.

Two other forms of template are used. *Creation templates*, which specify the initial form and type of an object, are used by a common object creation routine to create an instance of a particular type. *Amplification templates* provide rights amplification outside the procedure call mechanism. These are not made generally available.

The kernel provides a small number of basic object types and a mechanism for creation of user-defined types. A new type is represented by a *TYPE object* that embodies the abstractions of a class of objects. The TYPE object specifies the representation of data in the new class and also the operations that may be performed on the object. Auxiliary rights may be defined to protect these operations. The code defining the representation manipulations of an operation is encapsulated as a procedure object and is stored in the C-list of the TYPE object. Generally, only these procedures may use rights amplification, either by template or in the procedure call, to gain sufficient rights to directly access the representation of the new type. To allow use of the new type, a creation template, made from the TYPE object, is made available as needed.

To invoke an operation on an instance of the new object type, Hydra provides a *typecall* mechanism similar to the protected procedure call. Performing a typecall on an object of the new type actually specifies a call on one of the procedures in the C-list of the TYPE object. A capability for an object of the specific type is passed, possibly with rights amplification, to the procedure implementing the desired operation. A different typecall is provided for each operation on an abstract data-type, and the index of the procedure in the type object is typically hidden in a macro or routine in the source language.

The typecall mechanism is used to implement all user-level subsystems in the Hydra operating system. For example, PMs create PM process objects to encapsulate PM scheduling data. For a detailed example of how typecall was used to create an extensible file system, see Almes and Robertson [1978].

3. The Hardware-Software Interaction: Performance, Programming Methods, Problems, and Reliability

Developing the operating system and implementing several large application programs has resulted in a considerable body of knowledge about how the architecture has interacted with the software. Some expected problems, such as multiprocessor scheduling and synchronization, have been solved efficiently and effectively. Others, mostly unanticipated, have been difficult to solve or minimize, although in one case—reliability—the software methods developed are considered one of the project's major successes [Wulf and Harbison, 1978].

3.1 System Performance

The following sections present an overview of the performance of the C.mmp/Hydra system. Again, the emphasis is on the architecture and its effects. The data presented have been collected over a period of years and represent a number of different system configurations, since measurements were taken in parallel with hardware development. The concurrent measurement and construction unfortunately prevented simultaneous measurement of more than a subset of the potential 16 Pc's. To offset this, modeling results extending the measured data are presented where available.

To measure the system, a number of specialized tools were created. Two software tools were created to measure the system behavior in parallel execution. A *software tracer*, partially implemented in microcode, was built to selectively trace events such as kernel calls and object accesses on the entire set of executing Pc's. A *script driver* [McGehearty, 1980] provided a mechanism to impose a variable and repeatable synthetic load on the system and make timing measurements at the user level. A special *hardware monitor* [Swan, 1976] with its own host computer was developed to measure performance at the memory-access and instruction level on individual Pc's. The monitor's high-impedance probes, which were attached to the measured Pc's Unibus, allowed fine-grained measurements to be taken with insignificant perturbation of the Pc. Memory traffic in Smp was measured with an access counter that integrated accesses to all 16 memory ports.

3.1.1 An Application Example
An artificial intelligence application, the Harpy Speech Understanding System [Lowerre, 1976], was implemented on C.mmp, among other machines. The system was extensively studied as an indicator of the performance and problems associated with large, complex tasks in the C.mmp/Hydra environment.

The following brief description of Harpy and its implementation on C.mmp is presented to aid understanding of the application and its measurements. The system recognizes speech from many speakers, although the recognizable utterances are restricted to a finite, task-constrained vocabulary. Knowledge about the task, grammar, and vocabulary is represented in a finite-state graph structure, one word of the vocabulary per node. Paths along interconnections between nodes represent acceptable sentences in the grammar. When an utterance is to be processed, the word nodes are replaced by networks containing representations of the phonemes (units of speech) for all pronunciations of the words.

After digitization, an utterance is examined by a probability-based heuristic search that compares each phoneme of the utterance to those in the nodes of the knowledge graph. As the search proceeds, a recognition tree of the most probable transitions in the graph is built. At the end, the utterance is identified by backtracking along the path of highest probability in the recognition tree.

The search was implemented in two phases, each executed by a set of cooperating processes. In the first phase, the possible transitions in the knowledge graph were calculated for the current phoneme of the utterance. The second phase performed a probability calculation for each transition identified in the first phase and discarded those of low probability. Steps of high probability were retained as the next level of the recognition tree. The processes were synchronized so that all performed the first phase, then all performed the second phase. This sequence was iterated until all phonemes of the utterance were processed. No process was allowed to continue to the next phase until all processes had completed the current phase.

To ensure that the measurements were indicative of the architecture, the number of processes was limited to the number of Pc's available at the time of measurement and the code and data were always resident in Mp. These precautions eliminated the effects of scheduling and paging. The measurements in Fig. 6a [Oleinick, 1979] were made with a 1,000-word vocabulary, representing a large search space and heavy compute load. The same 15 utterances were processed for each measurement.

Since versions of Harpy also exist for the PDP-10 (the KL10 model, a medium- to large-scale uniprocessor with 1.8 MIPS, and also an older KA10 model with 0.4 MIPS) and an 11/40 Unix system, some performance comparisons can be made with these systems. As Fig. 6a shows, C.mmp achieved better performance than KL10 with four Pc's on the 1,000-word vocabulary task. In comparison with the single 11/40 Unix system, shown in Fig. 6b, a single process on C.mmp required only slightly greater time to execute the task than did the uniprocessor, indicating that overhead is low in the parallel environment [Wulf and Harbison, 1978]. For the Unix and KA10 measurements, a small (37-word) vocabulary was used. For reference, measurements of the KL10's performance on the 37-word vocabulary task are also included in Fig. 6b.

The speedup gained by adding a Pc to Harpy was less than linear on account of underutilization of the processes [Oleinick, 1979]. Because of unequal allocation of work, the processes lost time waiting for the working processes to complete a phase of the search so that the next phase could begin. Considerable effort was invested in optimizing the allocation of work, and process utilization reached 64 percent, limited by the overhead necessary in partitioning the heuristic search. The partitioning overhead is

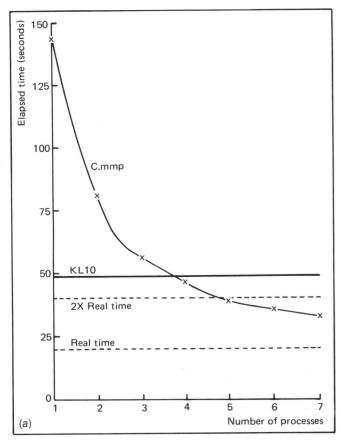

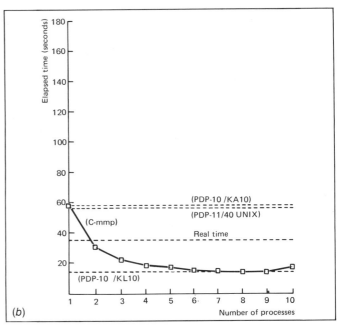

(b) **C.mmp compared with a 11/40 Unix System, a KA10, and a KL10 with a 37-word vocabulary task.**

Fig. 6. Comparative performance of C.mmp with other machines on the Harpy Speech Understanding System. (a) C.mmp versus KL10 with a 1000-word vocabulary task.

also responsible for the fact that C.mmp required seven Pc's to match KL10 performance on the 37-word vocabulary task but only four on the more computation-intensive 1,000-word task. Although this problem is seen to be in the decomposition of Harpy rather than specific to C.mmp/Hydra, it demonstrates a problem with multiprocessors and parallel decompositions: if a Pc must wait for all other processors to complete their task before proceeding to the next computational step, then speedup will be limited by the balance of work among the Pc's. This is similar to the problem of unequal execution speeds mentioned in 3.1.2.

3.1.2. Synchronization and Its Effects Studies of the synchronization mechanisms in Hydra indicated that the mechanisms themselves did not cause much overhead, although the methodology of use was critical. In a study of the KMPS lock, several benchmark programs each created 16 cooperating processes

designed to cause varying frequencies of synchronization within the kernel [Marathe, 1977]. For these experiments, a 14-Pc configuration (including the 11/20's) was used so that scheduling 16 processes would ensure full Pc utilization. The measurements, taken with the hardware monitor to avoid any perturbation of the system, indicate that in the worst cases:

- Fewer than 10 percent of locking requests blocked.

- Less than 1 percent of execution time was lost in blocking.

- The duration of an average KMPS lock-protected critical section was less than 700 μs.

A model, verified by the hardware monitor measurements, predicted that if the KMPS lock mechanism were extended to a 48-Pc system, the time lost in blocking would be less than 4 percent [Marathe, 1977].

Although the lock-unlock code is highly efficient, the fact that so little time is lost in blocking is due primarily to the methodology of synchronization. The critical factors are association of locks with data structures rather than code segments, and choosing synchronization primitives on the basis of the duration of the critical section to be protected. By associating synchronization primitives with data structures, several processes may execute the code for a critical section without mutual interference, since they each lock different locks. Contention is limited to the degree of sharing of a specific instance of a data structure. In Hydra, nearly every shared data structure has its own locking primitive. For example, each of the tens of thousands of objects in the GST has a KMPS semaphore for mutual exclusion. Also, some highly shared structures, e.g., the KMPS feasible list, are segmented to allow multiple locks and a higher degree of parallel access without contention.

Another advantage of associating the synchronization with data structures is that both the primitives and data structures may be dynamically created and destroyed as the load or growth of the system may dictate. The code remains unchanged during the lifetimes of the dynamically created data structures. Binding locks to code results in static structures that require programmer intervention for alteration.

The importance of choosing the appropriate primitive was shown by a study of a parallel root-finding algorithm [Oleinick and Fuller, 1978]. Figure 7 illustrates the difference between spin locks and PM semaphores. Because the average blocking time is short compared with the overhead of PM semaphores (at least 5 ms), the spin lock produced better performance by a factor of 2. For the PM semaphore curves, the *e* parameter is the delay time in milleseconds before a blocked process was returned to the PM. Note that zero delay (*e*=0, in PM0, an early PM) causes poor performance due to paging overhead (see Sec. 2.1.2). The degradation of performance caused by adding the ninth Pc is not due to the synchronization primitives, but is caused by the system configuration: eight 11/40's and three 11/20's. As soon as one 11/20 was used, the entire task force of processes slowed down, since all were forced to wait for the slowest to report completion.

The choice of primitive is equally important in Hydra. If the estimated average blocked period was greater than context-swap time, a KMPS semaphore was used; otherwise a KMPS lock was best. Measurements indicate that the average KMPS semaphore blocked period ran as high as 300 ms [Jain, 1978] because semaphores were used for signaling I/O event completion. Clearly, if locks, which do not release the Pc, had been used, the impact on performance would have been severe.

3.1.3 Scheduling

The script driver was used to measure the combined performance of KMPS and the PM as it would be perceived by a terminal user, especially with respect to variation in response time [McGehearty, 1980]. The load placed on the system was controlled by both the number of jobs (terminal users) and the compute time required by each job. To minimize effects other than scheduling, several restrictions were placed on the synthetic job stream:

- All jobs were independent.
- All jobs executed at the same KMPS priority.
- Jobs made no accesses to the GST (which might cause I/O or contention for an object).

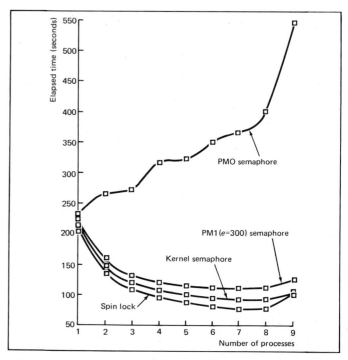

Fig. 7. Effect of different synchronization primitives on the root-finder program.

- All codes and data simultaneously fitted into Mp.

Timings were measured by the script process using the global time base, Kclock. For this experiment, a configuration of ten 11/40's was used. Nine Pc's executed the synthetic job stream and the tenth ran the script driver process (which was locked onto that Pc to prevent interference with the measurements).

To create a synthetic user load, the script driver jobs were assigned compute times in exponential distributions with mean times of 1, 5, and 10 corresponding to light, medium, and heavy loads. Each job waited 10 s between compute requests to simulate user response time. A total of 400 compute/wait cycles were executed for each set of jobs. Because of the varying compute time requests, the variation in response time was normalized for all processes by calculating a *stretch factor*, the response time divided by the requested compute time.

The variation of the stretch factor measures equality of service and, to the user, the predictability of response time for a request. The measurements indicate that the scheduling system was able to maintain reasonably equal service even when the machine was saturated. As shown in Fig. *8a, b,* and *c,* only one job in 20 experienced a stretch factor as much as twice the mean. The greatest variation occurred in the lightest load (Fig. *8a*), where

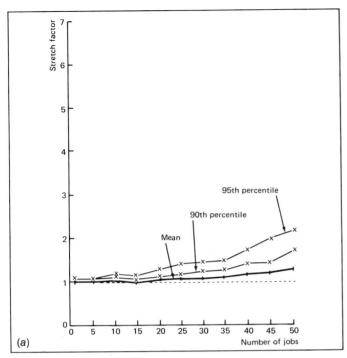

(a)

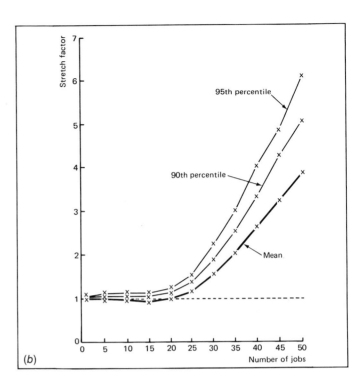

(b)

Fig. 8. Variation in normalized response times for job streams of varying computational requirements. (a) Low computing load, mean = 1 s compute time per interaction. (b) Medium computing load, mean = 5 s compute time per interaction. (c) Heavy computing load, mean = 10 s compute time per interaction.

the effects of scheduling were least dominated by computation. The sharp rise in Fig. 8b and c indicates the load at which the machine was saturated. The mean stretch factor dips below 1 in Fig. 8a and b because of statistical variations caused by slight differences in relative Pc and memory speeds.

3.1.4 Memory Contention Although a predictable result of not having implemented Mcache, memory contention has been a problem for high-performance multiprocess application programs on C.mmp. If three Pc's access the same memory port, that port becomes saturated. This limited access resulted in poor performance of multiprocess programs with shared code pages. The solution was to distribute copies of the code pages in different ports to each process. The critical code pages were few, and so the copies did not make excessive demands on memory. Accesses to data were less frequent and sufficiently evenly distributed through the data base not to cause significant contention. Although the code for the operating system is widely shared, its execution is sufficiently asynchronous that memory contention has not been a noticeable problem. Figure 9 illustrates the contention due to shared code pages for the root-finder program.

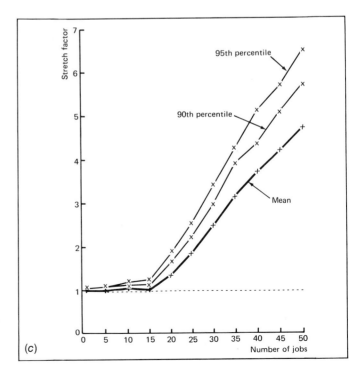

(c)

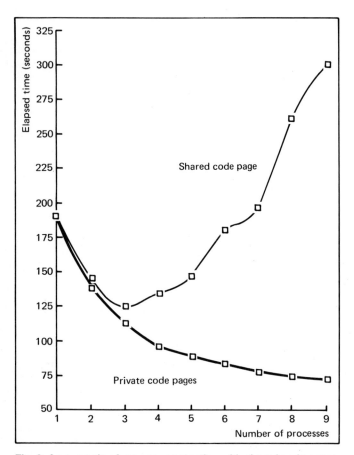

Fig. 9. An example of memory contention with shared code pages.

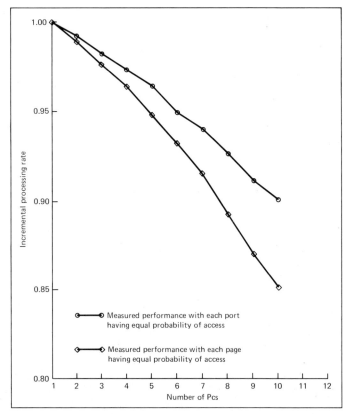

Fig. 10. Processing power for each additional processor.

As illustrated in Fig. 10, detailed stand-alone (without Hydra) measurements of memory contention taken with a synthetic job stream indicate that the incremental value of a Pc is 99 percent for the second Pc and decreases uniformly to 86 percent for the ninth Pc, with a measurement error of about 3 percent [McGehearty, 1980]. The synthetic jobs executed 25 repetitions of a 100-instruction sequence that was chosen as representative of typical instruction mixes for PDP-11's [Marathe, 1977; McGehearty, 1980]. Each processor executed the same instruction sequence, although neither code nor data were shared. After each 25 executions of the 100-instruction sequence, different memory ports for both code and data were independently chosen. The choice of port was either uniform for the 16 ports or weighted by the number of pages available in each port. The selection of different memory ports was repeated 4,096 times, each time including the 25 executions of the synthetic instruction sequence. Since there was no sharing, the results are representative of the

general-purpose, time-shared environment envisioned for the machine.

3.2 The Effects of Using Minicomputers

While C.mmp has shown that small processors can be effectively harnessed into a large-scale system, the decision to use minicomputers has not been without problems. Two characteristics of most minicomputers available in 1971 and 1972 have had considerable impact on the project: first, they were not designed for reliability; second, the small word size affects both data representation and addressing. The small address size has proved to be a serious problem.

3.2.1 The Small-Address Problem   The small-address problem (SAP) [Wulf and Harbison, 1978] stems directly from the use of minicomputers as the processing elements of C.mmp. The PDP-11, being a 16-bit machine, can address only a 64-Kbyte space. This is much too small for large-scale applications, although it is often sufficient for individual subsystems of the operating system.

The problem typically appears in addressing an application's data base. Large problems tend to have large data bases, and the 16-bit address allows access only through a 65-Kbyte window. The problem hasn't been as severe for code, because the size of the code has usually been relatively small. In cases where code size was important (e.g., Hydra), subroutine-calling sequences were developed that automatically made the called routine addressable before entry and restored addressability of the caller upon return.

The real cost of SAP is the all-pervasive concern for the addressability of the data during the design and coding of a program. Demand paging was precluded by the 16-bit address and limitations in the relation mechanism. Dmap does not retain sufficient information to identify the address causing a nonexistent memory fault [Levin, Cohen, Corwin, Pollack, and Wulf, 1975]. Therefore the Hydra paging system was forced to require that working-set and addressability changes be written into the program. While the mechanisms the paging system provides are clean and efficient, the necessity of having to explicitly juggle the working set and its addressability results in design and coding burdens. Performance problems, although secondary to programming problems, stem from the frequency of addressing changes. The cost of addressing changes is minimized by a microcoded relocation-register loading function available to user-level programs, and by the fact that the relocation registers are always addressable in the kernel.

In the Hydra kernel, the performance cost of SAP has been measured at 5.5 percent, or an addressing change every 16 instructions [Marathe, 1977]. This is higher than the cost incurred by moderately optimized user programs for two reasons. First is size: Hydra is, by a considerable margin, the largest program executing on C.mmp. It has nearly 50 code pages and from 10 to 100 data pages, depending on load. The order-of-magnitude variation of the data space needed contributes to the frequency of addressing changes by forcing nearly all data structures to be dynamically addressed. Dynamic addressing, in turn, is made more expensive in the kernel by the second reason: the necessity of disabling two relocation registers in the (1,1) addressing space (see Fig. 3). Perhaps if Dmap supported more relocation registers and a smaller page size, the problem (performance, at least) would be somewhat alleviated [Wulf and Harbison, 1978].

Figure 11 illustrates a case study of the effects of the SAP [Wulf and Harbison, 1978]. The task is the Harpy speech understanding system with the 37-word vocabulary. Two versions of the same task are compared: one with dynamic mapping and one with static mapping. In the dynamic mapping version, Harpy checks each data access for addressability; in the static case, the program assumes the data are addressable. Note that a factor of 3 in performance was gained by simplifying the code even though in

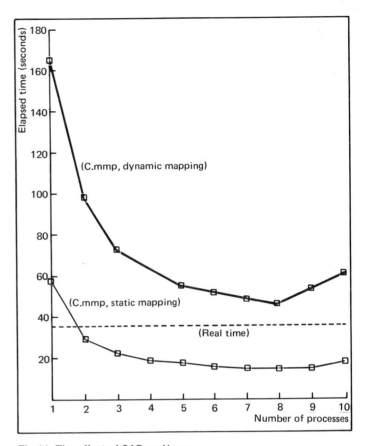

Fig 11. The effect of SAP on Harpy.

actuality no addressing changes were ever necessary—the cost was incurred by *checking* for addressability.

Another example is in the coding of the operating system's Command Language (CL). The CL provides a small ALGOL-like programming language (similar to BLISS-11, the implementation language used for Hydra [Wulf, Russell, and Habermann, 1971]), complete with variable declarations and macro facilities. Static data structures were used to implement the CL, with the result that although the code is simple, the size of the symbol table is quite restricted. This has limited the utility of its macro processor in tailoring the user's interactive environment.

3.2.2 The Effect on the Capability Protection System Hydra represents capabilities in 16 bytes, or 8 words. Eleven bytes are required: 8 for the global name and 3 for the rights field. The remaining 5 bytes are allocated to reliability checks and other implementation details. Having to move 8 words per capability is a significant source of overhead in the protected procedure call.

Recent measurements of typical Hydra typecalls, the most frequently executed version of the protected procedure call, indicate that an overhead of about 30 ms is to be expected. Detailed software traces of the calls indicate at least 50 percent of the time was spent in merging the capabilities into the new LNS. While creating the new LNS is the major function of the call, several factors are responsible for its being so expensive: making the capabilities addressable at both source and destination, the locking required for the capability copies, and simply moving the 8-word representation. Since this move cannot be done indivisibly, the locking is required. The typecalls studied were catalog lookups and had fewer than 15 capabilities per LNS. That fraction of the overhead devoted to building the LNS is proportional to LNS length.

The result of the high overhead has been that although the capability-based protection system is highly effective, its efficiency has often limited its use. In particular, protected procedure calls are used on a considerably larger grain than was anticipated. It should be noted that this is not considered a problem inherent in capability systems, but an artifact of implementation with small words and on hardware not specifically intended to support capability addressing.

3.2.3 Indivisible Operations   The implementation of locks in a multiprocessor is dependent on having at least one indivisible operation on shared memory. Although not specified in the PDP-11 ISP, the 11/20 and 11/40 both perform indivisible read-modify-write cycles. Smp maintains the indivisibility, making any instruction using this access mode indivisible. Increment, decrement, and shift instructions are used in the construction of the various forms of lock in Hydra. The fact that the bit manipulation instructions are made indivisible automated the synchronization of the bit mask operations so critical in using the IP-bus functions. The richness of the indivisible instruction set has been of great value to C.mmp and should not be underestimated.

3.2.4 Lack of Error Checking   The necessity of constructing C.mmp from available minicomputers greatly restricted the possible-fault-tolerant mechanisms that could be incorporated. For example, neither of the two PDP-11 models used, nor the Unibus, has error-checking abilities; one must assume that their results are correct. Experience has shown that this is frequently not the case. Therefore elaborate error checking and correcting of the shared memory and its access path were not justified, because of the possibility of data corruption on the Unibus.

The lack of checking by the hardware forced the burden onto the software, with a resultant penalty in performance. Software checking generally consists of checksums and type and consistency checks. Because data integrity is considered highly important, the error-checking burden falls most heavily on the GST.

3.3 Reliability

In spite of the difficulties, the machine has been reasonably reliable, considering its highly experimental and unique nature. Recent statistics indicate that the total system *mean time to crash* (MTTC) from all causes is, with one exception, fluctuating between 6 and 15 h, averaged on a monthly basis. This is more than enough to be a useful research tool, especially since the average downtime after a crash is only about five minutes and the machine automatically reloads itself (operator intervention is virtually never required). In a research environment, availability has proved to be more important than absolute reliability. Figure 12 illustrates the distribution of crashes during the end of construction and the beginning of an intensive maintenance period. Completion of the machine allowed engineering efforts to be directed to reliability, and the error rate improved accordingly.

3.3.1 Reliability Experience   The reliability experience has been quite varied: many failures that were once common are now rare or nonexistent, others are still apparent, and some reappear from time to time. The failure rate has been significantly improved through a program of intensive maintenance, which has been in progress since completion of the basic machine.

Memory parity failures have, with rare exception, been the most common failure mode. Most are transient, but hard errors happen with regularity. Often the memory failure rate has largely determined the MTTC. For example, the sharp peak in Fig. 12 was caused by memory-related errors when the last of the MOS

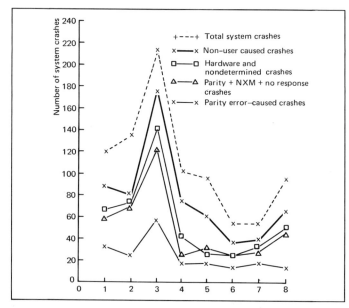

Fig. 12. Distribution of crashes on C.mmp. Eight months data: 1 July 1977 to 8 February 1978.

memory was installed. A methodology for recovering from transient memory failures in the shared memory of the operating system is now being developed, and a marked improvement in reliability is expected from this one recovery effort, since most memory parity failures happen in the operating-system kernel. Memory failures in user-allocated pages present a lesser problem.

Transient failures, while it is always difficult to isolate their source, have been an especially large problem on C.mmp, since there are few, if any, trace points in most data paths. Not including powerful debugging aids in the logical design has continuously hampered development. There was little that could be done for the processors, but aids could have been incorporated into all the CMU-built logic. When this weakness was realized, one tracking register (for the program counter) was added to Dmap; another (for operand addresses) is being developed. A similar weakness became evident in the software: often information about a failure was lost by the operating system, making recording of the conditions for transients unreliable. Robust crash-logging procedures have alleviated this to a great extent.

A transient failure that has eluded solution is the problem of "false NXM's." The processor reports a nonexistent memory (NXM) exception, but upon analysis it is found that the memory is responding and the instruction, registers, and index word(s) are well formed; no exception should have resulted. Because of the lack of checkpoints in the memory data paths, there is insufficient information available to isolate what may be failing.

Another long-standing transient problem deals with stack operations. This usually appears as misexecution of subroutine call/ return instructions or as interrupt entry/exit mistakes. The most common form of the error is one word too many (few) pushed (popped) onto (from) the stack. No cause has ever been isolated, and no method of recovering from this failure has been developed, but, fortunately, it is relatively rare.

A pleasant surprise has been the reliability of Smp. Although it is the most complex component of the multiprocessor hardware, it is now among the most reliable. No doubt the relatively simple design, conservative implementation, and careful construction have paid off. The complexity of Smp is indicated in the chip counts in Table 4, which also includes the expected chip failure rates as calculated by Autofail, a CMU-developed hard-failure model based on the Military Standardization Handbook 217B

model [Siewiorek, Kini, Jobbani, and Bellis, 1978; Bellis, 1978]. Figure 13 illustrates the relative simplicity of the four types of PC boards used in Smp.

An early problem with Smp required considerable effort to fix: Certain conditions, characterized by a memory access not completed by the Unibus master, could cause Smp to deadlock on account of the lack of a time-out circuit in the memory port control logic. Any other Pc attempting to access the deadlocked port will block until manually cleared. This situation was often caused by poorly designed I/O controllers that recovered from errors by simply aborting the current access with no regard for proper termination of Unibus or switch protocols.

While the known cases that deadlocked memory ports were isolated and individually remedied, the most important result was an appreciation of the design principle of mutual suspicion [Schroeder, 1972]. The switch should never trust that an operation started will necessarily be completed; it must be prepared to time-out, clear itself, and report a failure condition to the requesting processor.

The IP-bus is as unreliable as the switch is trustworthy. Having no error checking whatsoever, its reliability is so poor that if a cheap and highly effective method of software recovery had not been found, the bus would be nearly unusable. The mode of failure is transient loss of interprocessor interrupts and changing interrupt levels—usually from level 7 to level 6. Although no cause has been isolated, a simple system of pending interrupt masks allows an interrupted Pc to determine the validity of the interrupt. The same masks allow automatic repetition of lost interrupts, likely by a different Pc.

Two remaining long-term reliability artifacts of the architecture are:

1 Overrun errors on I/O-device DMA transfers caused by memory port contention. This is a predictable result of not having the planned cache memories and is effectively recovered from in software.

2 Having I/O devices associated with specific processors causes undesirable dependency on that processor. A partial solution has been developed in software to recover from transient failures, but frequent or hard failures force a shutdown for repair or reconfiguration. Fortunately, shutdown is very rare.

3.3.2 Software Recovery Methods within Hydra As the above description of the failures encountered indicates, fault tolerance is the result of a highly cooperative effort between hardware and software. Some failures, such as losing interprocessor interrupts, produce no damage and require so little effort in software recovery that little motivation exists to correct the hardware. Others (deadlocked memory ports) are impossible to recover from with software; much effort has been devoted to eliminating the

Table 4   Chip Complexity and Theoretical Failure Rate for Smp

Logic unit	Chips	Gates	Failures per 10^6 h
Cross-point logic	1,656	29,808	328.9
Priority contention resolution	864	7,344	121.7
Processor interfaces	384	3,552	57.1
Crosspoint enable/disable	544	4,448	77.7
Totals	3,448	45,152	585.4

Fig. 13. PC boards used in the crosspoint switch. (*a*) Crosspoint logic (72 boards). (*b*) Priority contention resolution (16 boards). (*c*) Pc interface (16 boards). (*d*) Memory interface (16 boards).

sources of failure. The software recovery methods, developed by design and evolution, may be grouped by similarity: methods for recovery from frequent failures that have little probability of nonlocal damage, and methods for treating relatively rare, but serious, failures that may imply systemwide damage.

The first class of failures is typically transient, though frequent, and does not involve shared data structures. Examples are IPI failures, DMA overruns, and memory parity failures in user-allocated pages. Although simple recovery methods of retrying and reporting failure are used to handle these errors, a consistent effort is made to reflect the error report back to a level where there is sufficient information for proper action [Parnas, 1972].

For the second class of errors, those serious enough to imply nonlocal damage, two major techniques have been developed, both of which exploit the parallel environment of C.mmp. In the Hydra kernel, the availability of multiple Pc's is used to create a robust recovery and logging system, and at user level, multiple processes are used in an analogous manner.

Important system elements of Hydra, such as job scheduling

and file systems, are implemented as user-level programs. Their response to errors is critical to system reliability, and several multiprocessing techniques are used. The processes may be multiple incarnations of the subsystem's server processes, or they may be free-running *daemon* processes created specifically to play a watchdog role in ensuring the correct and reliable operation of the subsystem. The multiple-incarnations approach accepts the loss of a server and the processes dependent upon it as a method of limiting damage and also tends to improve response. The daemon approach is specifically creating redundancy for reliability.

Within the kernel, serious errors are handled by a formal mechanism, *the suspect/monitor* model, which causes the whole system to pause so that a known state is reached before a sequence of error logging and analysis is performed. This procedure allows a wide range of options, from continuing execution, possibly with configuration changes, to reloading (again, possibly reconfigured). Developed in response to the low reliability of the developing hardware and software, suspect/monitor was retrofitted to the existing software.

Invocation of the suspect monitor sequence may occur in two ways: First, a Pc may detect an error condition either by hardware trap or software check. It then becomes the *suspect*, and a *monitor* Pc is randomly chosen from the remaining processors. Second, a Pc executing the *watchdog* routine detects that some other processor has apparently not been executing. The watchdog processor becomes the monitor and declares the apparently nonexecuting Pc to be the suspect. The watchdog routine is executed by all processors as part of several frequently used interrupt service routines and sets a bit (corresponding to the executing processor) in a mask maintained by the watchdog. Periodically this mask is compared with a mask of Pc's known to have completed initialization (upmask) and then cleared. Any processors in the upmask but not in the watchdog mask are declared suspects.

Once the monitor is chosen, it and the suspect achieve synchronization by means of a shared-state variable. Each advances the variable to the next state upon entry. Both examine the state, and if it is not in the synchronized state, each waits for the other to advance it to that state. The monitor times all waits for the suspect to reach a desired state, and if synchronization is not achieved quickly, the monitor attempts to force the suspect Pc to execute the recovery code with a sequence of IP-bus operations. Continued failure to synchronize causes the monitor to abort the sequence and force a reload. Multiple suspects are processed one at a time by the same monitor.

The suspect's sequence is: record all Pc state at the time of failure, including which pages were addressable; copy its local memory; execute a short-diagnostic; and, assuming correct execution of the diagnostic, attempt analysis of the failure. Completion of these actions is communicated to the monitor via the state variable. Because of the sensitive nature of the suspect's execu-

tion, several coding restrictions were employed in its implementation. For reliability, no stack operations are performed, the Pc state–logging code is straight-line, and a flag is set upon entry to the suspect routine to force an immediate halt upon repeated entry for any reason. Halting causes a monitor time-out, forcing a reload and preventing the previously logged data from being overwritten.

Once synchronized, the monitor follows the suspect through its sequence and, after successful completion, has the following options:

- Continue with no changes.
- Halt the suspect and continue.
- "Quiesce" the suspect and continue.
- Reload.
- Reload and delete suspect from configuration.
- Reload and quiesce the suspect.

Quiescing a processor allows it to service I/O device interrupts but not to execute any other functions (notably user programs). This way, the duty cycle is kept low, and it is hoped, so is the probability of a failure. This mode is required to keep processors with critical I/O devices in the configuration. Since most data structures lack the redundancy and associated verification routines to guarantee repair of damage, all paths through suspect/ monitor currently lead to one of the system reload options.

The analysis that the suspect may perform is highly failure-dependent. Because of the problems of installing any recovery scheme in an existing large program, the problems of analysis are only beginning to be examined. Recovery from memory parity failures during kernel execution is being considered as the first candidate for analytical recovery. These parity failures are considered serious enough to invoke suspect/monitor because of the requirement to maintain the integrity of the GST. Also, a page may hold segments of many objects, and so a failure may imply future trouble if not caught promptly. For parity failures, the analysis must ascertain three things: whether the failure is repeatable, whether it happened during interrupt service, and whether any critical data structures were locked. If any of these is true, recovery is not possible. There is no way to report the failure to the process while servicing an interrupt. If locked, a data structure may be in an inconsistent state. In these cases, the suspect notifies the monitor to reload the system. Otherwise, the failure has occurred during a kernel call and may be aborted with a parity failure report. The caller may then decide whether to retry the call. No claim is made that this particular method is optimal; it is intended to illustrate the role of analysis in the suspect/monitor. However, it does promise a high probability of recovering from the majority of parity failures with an acceptably small risk of undetected damage.

The auto-restart mechanism is responsible for reloading the system and is invoked by the suspect/monitor mechanism. Three basic steps are involved: adjusting the configuration masks for any deleted or quiesced processors, constructing a free memory list (deleting pages that have been marked errant), and loading a fresh copy of the kernel from disk. The new system is entered and initialization begins. This sequence is normally accomplished without human intervention and is so reliable that C.mmp runs without an operator.

The last mechanism associated with failure recovery is the automatic diagnostic driver, which initiates and monitors the deleted processors' execution of a diagnostic. The driver maintains a history of the failures found by each processor as well as the processor's successful executions of the diagnostic. The histories may be printed on command and are also accessible from Hydra. If a processor is able to successfully run the diagnostic for a period of time determined by its failure history over the previous few days, the driver automatically returns it to the system. Automatic return is accomplished by executing the standard per-processor initialization and does not require pausing or reloading the system.

4. Conclusion

The successful implementation of systems such as Harpy, ZOG, several language compilers, several file and directory systems, ARPANET support, and measurement tools such as the script driver has shown that C.mmp and Hydra provide a useful, general-purpose computing environment on a multiprocessor. The symmetric design of C.mmp has proved to be valuable in error-recovery techniques and in simplifying process scheduling. Also, the kernel approach to operating-system design, the protection system, and the mechanisms for data abstraction have effectively allowed construction of much of the operating system as user-level programs.

The problems, such as reliability, memory contention, and the small-address problem, have been effectively managed, if not solved entirely. These problems were challenging and the reliability problems, especially, motivated a profitable research effort.

References

Almes and Robertson [1978]; Bellis [1978]; Bhandarkar [1972]; Cohen and Jefferson [1975]; DEC [1972]; Dijkstra [1968a]; Fuller, Almes, Broadley, Forgy, Karlton, Lesser, and Teter [1976]; Fuller and Harbison [1978]; Jain [1978]; Levin, Cohen, Corwin, Pollack, and Wulf [1975]; Lowerre [1976]; Marathe [1977]; McGehearty [1980]; Newcomer, Cohen, Jefferson, Lane, Levin, Pollack, and Wulf [1976]; Oleinick [1979]; Oleinick and Fuller [1978]; Parnas [1972]; Robertson and Ramakrishna [1977]; Rubin, Guggenheim, and Bihary [1978]; Schroeder [1972]; Siewiroek, Kini, Joobbani, and Bellis [1978]; Strecker [1971]; Swan [1976]; Wulf and Bell [1972]; Wulf, Cohen, Corwin, Jones, Levin, Pierson, and Pollack [1974]; Wulf and Harbison [1978]; Wulf, Levin, and Harbison [1980]; Wulf, Levin, and Pierson [1975]; Wulf, Russell, and Habermann [1971].

Chapter 23

Pluribus—An Operational Fault-Tolerant Multiprocessor[1]

David Katsuki / Eric S. Elsam / William F. Mann
Eric S. Roberts / John G. Robinson
F. Stanley Skowronski / Eric W. Wolf

Summary The authors describe the Pluribus multiprocessor system, outline several techniques used to achieve fault-tolerance, describe their field experience to date, and mention some potential applications. The Pluribus system places the major responsibility for recovery from failures on the software. Failing hardware modules are removed from the system, spare modules are substituted where available, and appropriate initialization is performed. In applications where the goal is maximum availability rather than totally fault-free operation, this approach represents a considerable savings in complexity and cost over traditional implementations. The software-based reliability approach has been extended to provide error-handling and recovery mechanisms for the system software structures as well. A number of Pluribus systems have been built and are currently in operation. Experience with these systems has given us confidence in their performance and mantainability, and leads us to suggest other applications that might benefit from this approach.

I. Introduction

The multiprocessor discussed in this paper had its beginnings in 1972 when the need for a second-generation interface message processor (IMP) [Heart et al., 1970] for the ARPA network (ARPANET) [Roberts and Wessler, 1970; Heart, 1975; Wolf, 1973] became apparent. At that time, the IMP's Bolt Beranek and Newman (BBN) had already installed at more than thirty-five ARPANET sites were Honeywell 316 and 516 minicomputers. The network was growing rapidly in several dimensions: number of nodes, hosts, and terminals; volume of traffic; and geographic coverage (including plans, now realized, for satellite extensions to Europe and Hawaii). A goal was established to design a modular machine which, at its lower end, would be smaller and less expensive than the 316's and 516's while being expandable in capacity to provide ten times the bandwidth of, and capable of servicing five times as many input–output (I/O) devices as, the 516 [Heart et al., 1973]. Related goals included greater memory addressing capability and increased reliability.

We decided on a multiprocessor approach because of its promising potential for modularity, for cost per performance

[1]*Proc. IEEE*, vol. 66, no. 10, October 1978, pp. 1,146–1,159.

advantages, for reliability, and because the IMP algorithm was clearly suitable for parallel processing by independent processors.

The IMP's communicate with host computers and with asynchronous terminals (IMP's with terminals attached are called TIP's [Ornstein et al., 1972]). Hosts use the network of IMP's and lines to communicate data messages of up to about 8000 bits; the IMP's divide these messages into packets up to about 1000 bits long. The functions performed by the IMP are those of a communications processor; they include storing and forwarding packets, generating headers, routing, retransmission, error checking, packet and message acknowledgment, message assembly and sequencing, flow control, line error detection, host and line status monitoring, and related housekeeping functions. The IMP's also send status and performance data to a network control center (NCC) which monitors and controls network operations [McKenzie et al., 1972; Ornstein and Walden, 1975]. The ARPANET IMP's operate 24 hours a day, often in unattended locations.

In applications of this sort, reliability requirements differ from those commonly found in other real-time systems. The IMP network forms only a part of a larger system; even a perfectly operating network is not sufficient to guarantee perfect overall system performance. Failures in the host, or in the interface between the host and IMP, may still introduce errors. What this means is that some sort of host-process to host-process error control is required for critical applications; the best that the IMP network can provide is a good environment for host-level error recovery processes. These processes need a network which rarely makes errors and which, when such errors do occur, can effectively process host-to-host retransmissions. In other words, occasional dropped messages and brief outages are acceptable; outages of more than a few minutes are undesirable even if scheduled in advance.

Once we realized that what was needed was not so much reliability as the ability to recover gracefully from failures, we began to see ways to provide a much more robust network by coding this type of fault-tolerance into our operating system and application algorithms, and by including special modular hardware designs. The machine that emerged [Heart et al., 1973; Ornstein and Walden, 1975; Bressler, Kraley, and Michel, 1975; Ornstein et al., 1975; Heart et al., 1976] we call the Pluribus (Fig. 1 shows a typical Pluribus installation). It provides simple checking procedures such as parity, amputation features which allow failing equipment to be isolated and, optionally, redundant components. The software uses these features to detect, report, and isolate hardware failures. Since the symptoms of many subtle software failures are similar to those of intermittent hardware errors, fault-tolerant procedures which adequately recover from one can also recover from the other.

There is a spectrum of fault-tolerant approaches which are appropriate in various applications [Avizienis, 1976; Avizienis, 1975]; our approach opts for a relatively inexpensive system which

Fig. 1. The Pluribus front-end processor at Bolt Beranek and Newman's Research Computer Center.

can quickly reinitialize itself, omitting troublesome components. This approach is especially suitable for applications in which brief outages can be tolerated and where overall correctness can be ensured by other techniques.

II. Pluribus System Architecture

The Pluribus may be characterized as a symmetric, tighlty coupled multiprocessor, designed to be flexible and highly modular. Modules are physically isolated to protect against common failures, and a form of distributed switch is employed for intermodule communications. In this section, we discuss these characteristics and describe the hardware architecture of the Pluribus.

A. Major Design Decisions

In order to make the basic operation of the Pluribus clearer, it is useful to examine some of the major design decisions that have directed its development, and to consider those decisions in the context of other options for multiprocessor system design. We have identified three areas which we believe are key aspects of the Pluribus approach to multiprocessing, each of which is considered in greater detail below.

Processor Symmetry One dimension of multiprocessing involves the degree of inter-processor symmetry within the system [Enslow, 1974, p. 83]. In this dimension, one extreme might be a typical general purpose computer system, including a central

processor, a front-end processor, and perhaps one or more channel processors. Such an asymmetric system is relatively inflexible in power since increasing its central processing capacity requires the introduction of a more powerful central processor. Building redundancy into an asymmetric system can be expensive, since replication of all critical resources involves duplicating virtually the whole machine.

At the other extreme are systems like the Pluribus in which all processors are identical. In such systems, the advantages of redundancy and flexibility are much easier to achieve since they include only one type of processing unit. Even without explicit redundancy, a symmetric system can provide graceful degradation of throughput when a processing element fails. Pluribus systems which are sized for fully redundant operation include just one extra processing module; thus the degradation which results from failure of any processing module consists only of a loss of excess throughput capacity.

Processor Coupling Another multiprocessing dimension is the level at which processors cooperate to accomplish overall system requirements. At one extreme the processors might run totally separate programs under the direction of a supervisor program, communicating only at arm's length. Such processors may be described as "loosely coupled" [Enslow, 1974, p. 15]. At the other extreme, which is characterized by array processors such as ILLIAC IV [Barnes et al., 1968], the processors run in lockstep, with a single program operating simultaneously on a number of data streams. The Pluribus lies between these extremes. Its processors are tightly coupled in the sense that all processors can access all system resources and perform all parts of the operational program; they operate independently except for necessary software interlocks on specific I/O devices and data structures.

Flexibility Although one of the goals in the creation of the Pluribus was to develop a machine with high throughput, this goal was complemented by the need for a smaller, cheaper machine with relatively low throughput. Similarly, although the Pluribus was conceived as having at least two of every resource to permit recovery after failures, it was also clear that not all applications required or could afford a fully redundant system. Thus it was desirable for the architecture to be flexible in at least two ways: The size-flexibility goal was to smooth large incremental steps in the cost-performance curve by utilizing a highly modular design, which could provide processing capacity well beyond our anticipated needs. Flexibility in the area of fault-tolerance and fault-recovery was a related goal, since the need for fault-tolerance involves primarily economic considerations and we wanted to allow our customers to select fault-tolerance features independent of their throughput requirements. Also implied in each of these goals was the requirement for easy expansion to meet changing requirements.

B. System Overview

A central requirement in any multiprocessor is that processing elements be able to communicate both among themselves and with shared resources such as memories and I/O equipment. Ease of communication is always desirable and is vital in tightly coupled systems, since any delays or unwieldiness would immediately impact system operation and reduce programmability. These considerations, together with a natural desire for symmetry and simplicity, led us to adopt a unified addressing structure in which all common memory and I/O devices share the same address space. The Pluribus development was strongly influenced by previous unified-bus architectures in which processing, memory, and I/O units share not only a common address structure but also a single, time-multiplexed bus (the DEC PDP-11 is perhaps the most familiar example of this). Although multiprocessors based on the unified bus are both easily extensible and conceptually simple structures, they are vulnerable to single failures anywhere along the bus. In addition, the maximum throughput of such multiprocessors is limited both by the design bandwidth of the bus as well as by contention for common resources. To avoid these problems we used a unified bus to create the functional modules which make up the system, but not to form the main connection structure. We defined three basic functional modules which share a common address space but have separate intermodule communications paths: processor *buses*, memory *buses*, and I/O *buses*. A simplified system diagram is shown in Fig. 2.

(In the following sections we will often use the term *bus* to mean a logical and physical module, as in "processor *bus*," rather than just an interconnection system. All such usages will be italicized for clarity.)

The system for interconnecting these modules had several major requirements. It had to be easily extensible to support as many as eight memory or I/O *buses* (common *buses*) and eight or more processor *buses*. It had to permit the operating software to remove malfunctioning modules from the system and incorporate newly acquired or repaired modules. In addition, it had to impose minimal cost penalties for smaller systems, while scaling up smoothly to produce large systems. Finally, it had to have no common point of failure which could lead to total system failure.

The approach we finally adopted is similar in function to a central crossbar switch although it differs greatly in implementation. The crossbar switch approach allows an extremely high-bandwidth interconnection scheme and has been used to advantage in several multiprocessors [Wulf and Bell, 1972]. However, the usual implementation techniques are vulnerable to single-point failures. To avoid these problems, we distributed the components of the switch among the various system modules in such a way that no single failure points remain. Switch elements are called bus couplers and consist of two circuit boards connected by a cable.

The bus couplers function by recognizing a range of addresses on processor or I/O *buses*, and initiating an access request on the appropriate common *bus* as a result. Since memory and I/O *buses* share a 20-bit address space, bus couplers must map 16-bit processor addresses into 20-bit system addresses under program control (see Fig. 3). In addition to handling inter-*bus* communications, bus couplers perform several other functions which will be described later.

Modularity Since the basic Pluribus was modular at several levels, an unusual degree of flexibility was available when we set out to define standard structures within the system. The three basic system modules described above have clear logical functions within the system, but their actual implementation depended on various tradeoffs between cost, throughput, and available physical components.

It was decided early that the goals of flexibility and symmetry could be achieved by segmenting the operational tasks into strips of code (task distribution routines, task-oriented application routines, timers, etc.) which could be run by any available processor. The concept was that the code should be both reentrant and accessible to all processors at all times. The primary function of the common memory modules is to provide space for data buffers, program work areas, and inter-processor communications areas. Code storage is divided into two parts: lightly used code is stored on common memory *buses* and is shared between processors; heavily used code is replicated in local memory on each processor *bus*. This strategy minimizes contention for access to common memory while holding down costs, especially since, in

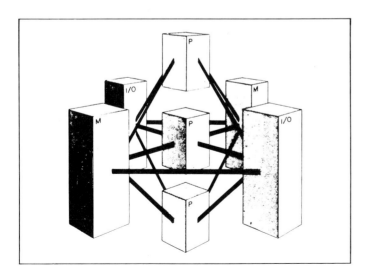

Fig. 2. A simplified view of the functional modules in a typical Pluribus system showing their interconnectivity. No physical relationships are implied.

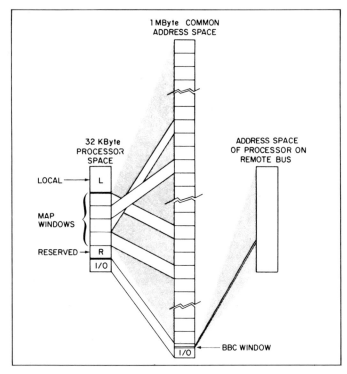

Fig. 3. Pluribus system address space, showing the mapping of processor "local" address space into the system space. "Backwards bus coupling" path from one processor *bus* through an I/O *bus* to another processor *bus* is shown on the right.

most applications, only a small part of the code is heavily used. The I/O modules were intended to support both polled low-speed I/O devices and high-speed interfaces capable of direct memory transfers. Couplers provide direct paths both from processor *buses* to I/O *buses* for control and polling, and from I/O *buses* to memory *buses* for direct memory transfers.

All normal processor-to-processor communication occurs through locations in common memory. However, to initialize the system, it must be possible for one processor to access the local memory and control registers of a processor on a different *bus*. To allow this, the bus couplers provide a limited reverse path through any common I/O *bus*.

In the following sections, we describe the physical implementation of these system modules and detail several support functions required by the architecture.

C. Physical System Structure

As mentioned in previous papers [Heart et al., 1973; Ornstein and Walden, 1975], we chose the Lockheed SUE minicomputer as the

point of departure for our system. It is a 16-bit machine, generally similar to the DEC PDP-11, which incorporates a unified address structure and an asynchronous, time-multiplexed bus. It also permits the attachment of a flexible combination of processors, memory, and I/O units. In contrast to the PDP-11, the SUE has its bus arbitration logic physically separated from the processor. This feature permits a bus to have one or several processors, or none at all. The Pluribus uses the bus, arbitration logic, processors, memories, and several minor I/O units of the SUE.

The basic Pluribus building block is the *bus* module. This module contains a modified SUE bus and card cage for up to twenty-four cards, together with completely self-contained cooling fans and power supply. Two *bus* modules can be connected to form an extended *bus*. A Pluribus system rack contains up to five *bus* modules, and each rack is typically supplied with a separate source of ac power. Systems sized to be fully redundant allow any *bus* module or any rack to be powered down for maintenance without affecting system availability (see Fig. 4).

Bus Structure (See Fig. 5)   A processor *bus* contains one or two processors and their associated local memory, a bus arbiter, and one bus coupler per logical path. Our current applications require 8 to 12K words of local memory for each processor. The flexibility

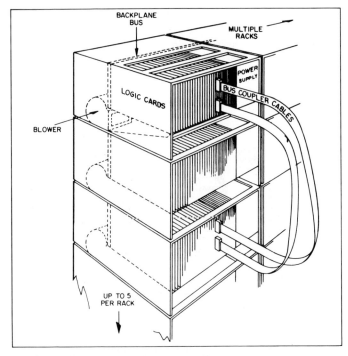

Fig. 4. Physical organization of bus modules. Modules are independently supplied with power and cooling.

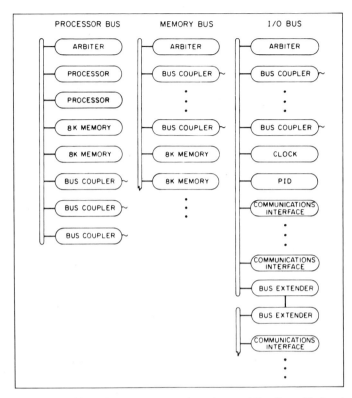

Fig. 5. Local bussing structure and contents of the three kinds of bus modules.

of the processor *bus* allows us to easily vary this parameter as memory prices or the requirements of the application change.

The common memory *bus* contains an arbiter, bus coupler cards for all the connected paths, and enough memory modules to support the application. Up to 512K words of common memory can be supported in a system, although that amount of memory would probably not be concentrated on one memory *bus*. Typical Pluribus systems have from 32K to 80K words of memory on each *bus*, depending on the application.

In addition to the bus arbiter and bus coupler cards, an I/O *bus* also contains cards for each of the various types of I/O interfaces that are required, including interfaces for modems, terminals, host computers, etc., as well as interfaces for standard peripherals. The I/O *bus* also houses a number of special units including (1) a real-time clock (RTC) which is used by the system for timing processes and communications links (2) a special hardware task disbursing unit known as the pseudo-interrupt device (PID) discussed further below and (3) a reload card which monitors up to eight communication lines, watching for (and processing) specially formatted reload messages from the outside world.

Inter-Bus Connection System   Since all processors in our system must be able to perform any system task, *buses* are connected so that all processors can access all shared memory and control the operation and sense the status of any I/O unit (see Figs. 2 and 6).

To connect processors and common memory, one card of a bus coupler is installed on a common memory *bus*, and the other on a processor *bus*. Similar connections are made from every processor *bus* to every common I/O *bus*. Coupler cards are connected by cables which may be up to 30 ft long, although most systems require a maximum of 10 ft.

The memory or I/O end of a bus coupler contains address-recognition circuitry and may be strapped to recognize and pass on to the memories or I/O devices any desired address range. When a processor makes a reference to common memory or I/O *buses*, the bus coupler cards on the processor *bus* all map the 16-bit address on the processor *bus* into a 20-bit system address and pass it to bus couplers at the other ends of the connecting cables. If the address is within the recognition range of a memory or I/O end bus coupler, it will request a service cycle on its *bus*. Data from the selected memory cell or device register are then passed back along the coupler path to the processor. This feature differentiates the system address space so that requests for memory or I/O *bus* access only cause service cycles on appropriate *buses*, thereby avoiding unnecessary contention.

Given a bus coupler connecting each processor *bus* to each common memory *bus*, all processors can access all common memory; I/O devices which do direct memory transfers must also access the common memories. These I/O devices are attached to as many I/O *buses* as are required to physically accommodate the number of devices and allow redundancy if necessary. Couplers connect each I/O *bus* to each memory *bus*. This coupler path is much like the processor-to-memory coupler path except that no address mapping needs to be done. I/O devices must respond to processor requests for action or information and in this respect the I/O devices act like memories. Bus couplers are also used to connect each processor *bus* to each I/O *bus*. Here also, a mapping must be done between the 16-bit processor address space and the 20-bit system space (see Fig. 3).

Processor *buses* need to access each other in order to start and stop each other and reload local memories. We provide this low bandwidth interconnection by allowing a processor to access another processor *bus* via its processor-to-I/O bus coupler. The coupler provides a small (4-word) mapping window from I/O space to each processor's space. A processor accesses another processor on a different *bus* by setting up and referencing this "backwards bus-coupling" window in system I/O space.

The coupler paths that connect processor *buses* into memory and I/O *buses* have program-settable enabling switches at their far (memory and I/O) ends, thus permitting processors to be cut into and out of ("amputated" from) the system. The reverse paths in the processor-to-I/O couplers also have enabling switches; nor-

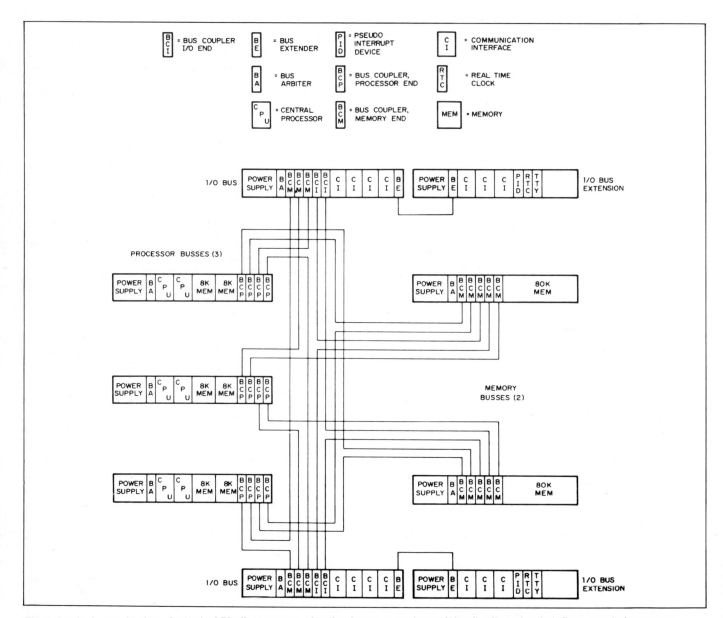

Fig. 6. Logical organization of a typical Pluribus system, showing interconnections of the distributed switch (bus coupler) structure.

mally the forward paths are turned on and the backwards paths are shut off. Since these paths represent a hazard whereby a "sick" processor or device could damage the system, we have arranged that only by storing a password at the proper address can a switch be changed. A processor can neither enable or disable its own access paths but one processor, deciding that another is sick and should be eliminated from the system, can amputate the *bus* of the offending processor. Reinstatement of an amputated *bus* happens in a similar manner.

Parity   To aid in detecting faulty bus couplers or defective memory, we compute and check parity across all bus coupler paths using a parity computation based on both data and address [U.S. Pat., 1977]. The scheme detects both "all zeros" and "all ones" failures. For writes to common memory, parity is computed at the processor or I/O end of the bus coupler and stored in the memory cell with the data. When the memory cell is read, the stored parity is checked at the processor or I/O end of the bus coupler. For accesses from processors to units on the I/O *buses* we use "feedback" parity; for writes to I/O the parity is computed by a special card on the I/O *bus*. The parity is then sent back up the coupler to the processor *bus* where it is compared with parity computed on that *bus*. For reads from I/O the special I/O parity card computes parity and compares it with recomputed parity on the processor *bus*.

Pseudo-Interrupt Device   Real-time systems or, more generally, systems requiring fast response, employ priority interrupt mechanisms to direct the attention of the processor to the most urgent tasks. Reliability and load sharing requirements make it desirable that any processor be able to service any I/O device, but also raise such questions as which processor to interrupt for servicing. We have opted for a simple yet flexible method: each "interrupt event" (DMA completion, RTC tick, software events, etc.), instead of actually interrupting a processor, writes a value associated with its priority to a hardware queuing device called the PID. The software is designed to allow each processor to put aside the context of its present computation periodically and check the PID. The PID, upon being read, will produce the highest value that has been stored in it and simultaneously delete that value from its internal queue. The processor can then use that value as an index to a table of tasks to be performed. The software uses the PID in a similar manner: each time a "strip" of code completes, it writes the number of the next strip in that task to the PID. When that becomes the highest number in the PID, the next available processor will execute the associated strip.

Our system does have two traditional interrupts, however. One is a 60-Hz clock interrupt. Each bus has its own 60-Hz clock, but conceptually this is an interrupt going to all processors; its main function is to time out locked data structures. The other classical interrupt is the power-fail/power-restore interrupt; each processor handles a power-fail interrupt from its own *bus* in the traditional way. Furthermore, bus couplers connected to processor *buses* will pass on any power-fail interrupt detected at their memory or I/O ends. A restoration of power causes first a *bus* master-reset and then a processor interrupt. We have adapted this interrupt mechanism to serve also as a *bus* activity watchdog timer. If any *bus* fails to show access activity for one second, a hardware timer fires, causing an artificial power-restore reset and interrupt. This provides recovery from some illegal hardware and software states.

D. Redundancy

To assure that a particular machine has enough redundant resources to allow survival in the face of component failures, we include at least one extra *bus* of each type so that a failure of any one resource, or the *bus* holding that resource, will not result in system failure. This approach also permits the system to survive many combinations of multiple failures. Thus if a system requires four processors to function at minimum acceptable throughput, six processors would be provided for reliability since the failure of any processor *bus* would disable two processors. Similarly, if a machine required at least 60K of memory to function, we would provide two *buses* each containing 60K of memory, or three *buses* each containing 30K of memory. It is important to note that redundant resources configured into a given machine are not idly standing by since they are used by the running machine to produce performance greater than the acceptable minimum.

I/O ports pose a special problem, since the devices and lines to which they are connected are frequently not doubled. For reliability, I/O interfaces can be doubled on separate I/O *buses*, but both interfaces must usually drive a single cable leaving the machine. We allow this by constructing all of our I/O port drivers with circuits that present a high impedance while unpowered. In addition, each I/O interface has a watchdog timer which, if not held off by repeated processor accesses, will disconnect the driver circuits within a second. Thus the likelihood that malfunctioning or unpowered I/O interfaces will interfere with the signals put on the external cable by the backup I/O interface is kept to a minimum.

III. The Pluribus Operating System[1]

Unlike most conventional systems, the principal responsibility for maintaining reliability in the Pluribus is placed on the system software rather than in the hardware structure. The Pluribus hardware was designed to provide an appropriate vehicle for software reliability mechanisms. Besides normal error checking and reporting in the hardware itself, programmed tests, using known data patterns are run at intervals. When hardware errors are detected, system software exploits the redundancy of the hardware by forming a new logical system configuration which excludes the failing resource, using redundant counterparts in its place.

Pluribus systems also check the validity of their software structures. Redundant information is intentionally introduced into the data structures at various points and checked by processes operating upon those structures. An example of this technique applied to buffer structures is described in Sec. IV. In addition, periodic background processes are used to recompute certain

[1]Portions of Secs. IV, V, and VII of this paper have appeared in "Software Fault-Tolerance in the Pluribus," J. G. Robinson and E. S. Roberts, *AFIPS Conference Proceedings*, vol. 47, copyright AFIPS Press, Montvale, NJ. Reproduced with permission.

variables which are maintained by the operational system. If the recomputation uncovers a discrepancy, the variables are fixed directly or a more drastic recovery procedure is initiated.

In many cases, a failure is not detected at the exact time of occurrence but later when the software encounters some failure-induced discrepancy. By this time, the effects of the failure may be more widespread and the actual cause of the failure may be difficult to determine. In such cases, the system is not able to perform instantaneous recovery and seeks instead to restore normal operation as quickly as possible.

The remainder of this section discusses the organization of the Pluribus operating system and some of the techniques used for achieving coordination of multiple processors. These techniques are further explored below where two examples of Pluribus fault-tolerant software strategies are presented. One of these examines the Pluribus IMP buffer system in detail, and the other covers strategies for understanding failures when they occur and effecting necessary repairs.

A. General Responsibility of the Operating System

The software reliability mechanisms for a Pluribus system are coordinated by a small operating system (called STAGE) which performs the management of the system configuration and the recovery functions. The overall goal of the operating system is to maintain a reliable, current map of the available hardware and software resources. The map must include accurate information not only about the hardware structure of the machine, but also about variables and data structures associated with the processes that use that hardware. Moreover, the operating system must function correctly even after parts of the system hardware have ceased to be operational. New resources, as they are discovered (e.g., because hardware has been added or repaired), should be incorporated as part of the ongoing operation of the application system.

Since any component of the system may fail at any time, the operating system must monitor its own behavior as well as that of the application system. It may not assume that any element of hardware or software is working properly—each must be tested before it is used and retested periodically to ensure that it continues to function correctly. The operating system must be skeptical of its current picture of the system configuration and continually check to see if the environment has changed.

Based on these considerations, the Pluribus operating system builds the map of its environment step by step. Each step tests and certifies the proper operation of some aspect of the environment, relying on those resources certified by previous steps as primitives. Early steps examine the operation of the local processor and its associated private resources. Subsequent steps look outward and begin to discover and test more global resources of the system, giving the checking process a layered appearance.

In the Pluribus operating system, each processor begins by checking its own operation and by finding a clock for use as a time base. Once these resources have been verified, the processor can begin to coordinate with the other active processors to develop an accurate picture of the system.

At the same time, the system must balance the need for reliable primitives with the need to accomplish normal operation efficiently. When all the environment has been certified, the system should spend most of its processing power on advancing the operational algorithms and return only occasionally to the task of reverifying its primitives. When failures of the environment have been detected, however, the power of the system must be brought to bear on the task of reconfiguring to isolate the failure.

B. Hierarchical Structure of the STAGE System

The Pluribus operating system is organized as a sequence of stages which are polled by a central dispatcher. A processor starts with only the first stage enabled. As each stage succeeds in establishing a proper map of its segment of the system state, it enables the next stage to run. Each stage may use information guaranteed by earlier stages and thus may run only if the previous stage has successfully completed its checks. Once enabled, a stage will be polled periodically to verify that the conditions for successful completion of that stage continue to apply. The system applies most of its processing power to the last stage that is enabled but returns periodically to poll each earlier stage. The application system is the final stage in the sequence and may run only after the earlier stages have verified all the configuration information of the application and the validity of the data structures.

Table 1 lists each stage of the Pluribus operating system, together with the aspects of the environment it guarantees. Many of the functions listed will not be discussed further but are provided to illustrate the layering of stages.

Since processors continue to perform each of the stages periodically, changes in the environment will eventually be noted. Any stage detecting a discrepancy in the configuration map will disable all later stages until the discrepancy is repaired. Then, all the later stages, which might depend on data verified by the disabling stage, will be forced to run all their checks, guaranteeing that they will make any further modifications to the configuration map necessitated by the first change. A serious failure, such as a nonexistent-memory interrupt, disables all but the first stage. In these cases, some reconfiguration might be needed, and all stages should perform all their checks before the application system is resumed.

C. Establishing Communication

So far, we have described the progress of one processor through the staged checking procedures of the operating system. All processors in the Pluribus perform the same checks, since it is

Table 1   Pluribus Operating System Stages

Stage	Function
0	Checksum local memory code (for stages 0, 1, 2). Initialize local interrupt vectors, and enable interrupts. Discover Processor bus I/O. Find some real-time clock for system timing.
1	Discover all usable common memory pages. Establish page for communication between processors.
2	Find and checksum common memory code (for stages 3, 4, 5). Checksum whole page ("reliability page").
3	Discover all common busses, PIDS, and real-time clocks.
4	Discover all processor bus couplers and processors.
5	Verify checksum (from stage 2) of reliability page code (for rest of stages plus perhaps some application routines). External reloading of missing code pages is possible once this stage is running.
6	Checksum all of local code.
7	Checksum common memory code. Maintain page allocation map.
8	Discover common I/O interfaces.
9	Poll application-dependent reliability and initialization routines. Periodically trigger restarts of halted processors.
10	Application system.

important that they agree about the state of the system resources. Coordination of multiple processors with potentially different views of the hardware configuration requires two mechanisms: the processors must agree on an area of common memory in which to record the machine configuration map, and they must cooperate in their decisions to modify the map.

The first step in coordinating the multiple processors of a Pluribus is to agree on a page of memory through which to communicate. The procedure for initially establishing the page for communication is clearly delicate. Prior to establishing the page, the processors have no way to communicate about where it will be. The procedure must operate correctly in the face of failures which might leave some of the processors seeing a different set of common memory pages from the rest. Processors which are unable to see the communication area will attempt to use another memory page and must be prevented from interfering with the unaffected processors.

Any processor that is first starting up (or restarting after some massive failure) can assume nothing about the location of the communication page. Any page may be used, and therefore a small area for communication control variables is reserved on each page of common memory. Part of this area is used for a brief memory test, which must succeed before the page may be used at all. Every processor attempts to establish the lowest numbered (lowest address in memory space) page that it sees as the page

through which to communicate. To be valid, any page must have a pointer to the current communication page, and the communication page must point to itself.

Each processor looks at the pointer on the lowest numbered page it can see. There are three possible states for the pointer. First, if it points to the page itself, the processor has found the communication page and may now proceed to interact with other processors about the common environment. If it points to a higher numbered page, the processor may just fix the pointer, as the requirement that the communication page be lowest makes this case inconsistent. If it points to a lower numbered page, the processor must attempt to check if the indicated communication page is active. It must assume that the data might simply be old or invalid and must time it out using a dedicated entry in a special array of timers which is allocated on each page. The processor increments the timer and, if it ever reaches a certain threshold, unilaterally fixes the communication pointer and starts to use this page for communication. The processor is prevented from doing this by any other processor which is successfully using the lower numbered communication page; all such processors periodically zero all the timers on all memory pages in the system.

Consider what happens during various possible hardware failures. If the memory *bus* containing the communication page is lost, all processors will attempt to establish a new communication page on the other *bus*. Using their timers on the new lowest page (which initially points to the old one after the failure), they await the threshold. No one is holding the timers to zero, so the new page becomes the communication page when some processor's timer first runs out.

A processor blinded to the communication page by a *bus* or coupler failure will try to establish a higher numbered page for communication. From the point of view of the failing processor, this case is indistinguishable from the previous case, where the common *bus* failed. Since the rest of the processors are satisfied with the communication pointer, they will hold all timers to zero, and the failed processor will never be able to change the communication page pointer. If the processor sees a set of pages disjoint from the rest of the system, it behaves as if no other processors are running, but there is no memory where it may interfere and now we have two systems operating independently. In this case it is likely that the two systems will interfere over other resources; since multiple failures are required for this situation to occur in a Pluribus, we choose not to attempt recovery here.

D. The Consensus Mechanism

When configuration data must be updated, it is crucial to coordinate the Pluribus processors before making the modification. The mechanism to accomplish this goal we call consensus. Each stage has a consensus which is maintained as part of its environment. The first step in forming a consensus is to determine the set of processors that is executing the corresponding stage. This set has certified the primitives necessary to maintain successfully this stage's portion of the configuration map. In order for the system to respond to failures, the consensus must be kept current—new processors must be able to join it rapidly and processors that may have halted or ceased to run the stage must be erased from the set.

Each processor, based on its hardware address in the Pluribus, is assigned a bit in three consensus arrays, called "next," "smoothed," and "fix-it." As part of running the corresponding stage, every processor periodically sets its bit in the next consensus array to show that it wishes to participate in the consensus. After enough time has elasped for each properly running processor to set its bit, this array is copied into the smoothed consensus and cleared. The set of processors in the smoothed array will then be used as a basis for decisions to reconfigure some portion of the resource map.

Any processor which wishes to modify some configuration information sets its bit in the appropriate fix-it array. Processors that agree with the configuration map clear their bits, and bits corresponding to processors not in the smoothed array are also cleared.

In effect, the bits in the fix-it array represent the votes of the individual processors in favor of a potential modification. In most cases, it is desirable that all processors agree before making the change. All processors wait until the fix-it array matches the smoothed array before implementing the fix. Other modifications might require only majority or two-thirds agreement. The choice of policy often depends on some tradeoff between resources (e.g., should we use more memory or more processors?). The Pluribus approach allows us to make this choice independently at each stage.

Since each processor in the Pluribus performs each stage of the checking code, the consensus mechanism provides the coordination needed to change the configuration map gracefully. When a stage detects a failure, the processor sets the appropriate fix-it bit and disables the following stages. When enough processors detect the failure they implement the fix to the configuration map. Now these processors can complete the later stages, devoting their attention to any further changes required by the failure. A processor which sees a different picture of the resources and cannot reach agreement with the rest of the system hangs forever at the point of detecting the discrepancy. This technique effectively prevents the processor from damaging the system.

E. Application-Dependent Checking

In general, it is desirable for the application system to perform its own checks before initiating or resuming normal operation. The last stage provides a mechanism which polls application-oriented processes to perform consensus-driven checks and repairs of their own data structures. This stage uses the results of the hardware (application-independent) discovery stages to certify its own data structures. For example, it could allocate or deallocate device parameter blocks as the I/O devices are discovered or disappear and initialize spare memory pages for use as data buffers as they become available. User-written reliability checks can be performed on any of the application data structures, and the appropriate reinitialization invoked to remedy failures.

Occasionally, it is possible for a processor checking application data structures to implement minor repairs to the data structures unilaterally. For major reconfigurations of the data structures, such as complete application system reinitialization, the checking routines must signal to the stage dispatcher that consensus is needed. The last concurring processor is then permitted to perform the reinitialization routine. Just as the early stages guarantee the hardware map, the application-dependent routines have the consensus mechanism at their disposal to validate the system data structures before entering the system. In addition, the application system data structures are rechecked periodically during normal system operation.

IV.   An Example of Application Reliability

We use two general techniques to ensure the validity of data structures in the Pluribus. First, redundant information, where it exists, is checked for discrepancies, and appropriate action taken if they exist. Second, since detailed examination of all data for inconsistency is deemed impossible for any system of nontrivial complexity, we use watchdog timers to ensure the correct operation of the application system at various levels. As an example, we will discuss the buffer management strategy for the Pluribus IMP system.

Buffers in the Pluribus IMP circulate through the system from queue to queue; in some cases, they may be shared between two or more processes. Since a compromised queue structure may, in general, rapidly degrade the performance of the system, elaborate checking methods are built into the IMP program at various levels. In particular, we must be able to detect queues that are crossed or looped and buffers that have been lost (are on no queue at all).

Associated with each buffer in the system is a set of use bits corresponding to various processes that consume buffers. Any process that enqueues a buffer for some other process first sets the use bit for that process. When a process dequeues a buffer, the appropriate use bit must be on or the buffer will not be processed. As a special case, buffers on the system free list must have all their bits turned off. The buffer-freeing routine only returns a buffer to the free list if the last remaining use bit is that of the freeing process.

This technique intentionally generates redundant information and continually validates it as a buffer circulates through the system. In other words, the existence of a buffer on a queue informs the system that some processing is desired for that buffer. In principle, the use bit signals the same thing. Each buffer-processing routine could scan all the buffers in the system for those with its use bit set, but such a strategy would clearly be inefficient. The redundancy check gives preference to neither the queue nor the use bit as an indication of need for service, but rather requires agreement between the two indicators. When they disagree, the system assumes that a failure has indeed occurred and attempts to correct it by forcing the queue to be empty, so that the effects of the failure can be contained as much as possible.

The use bits allow the prompt detection of looped and crossed queues. In addition, an improper buffer pointer will often lead to a failure of the use bit check.

We must also consider the case of a buffer which has been lost from all queues. This condition could arise due to a program bug or as a result of a queue being emptied after a use bit failure. We could employ a classical garbage-collection scheme for this purpose; unfortunately, the demand for buffers is often great in a high-speed communication system, and the requisite locking of the buffer resources during such a garbage collection would likely result in lost inputs.

The recovery scheme we have chosen is a watchdog timer mechanism. Each buffer has associated with it a flag set by normal activity of the buffer which, in this case, is defined to be the periodic appearance of that buffer on the free list. Whenever a buffer is freed, its flag is set. In addition, flags for all the buffers on the free list are set periodically. In the high-speed communications environment, where data passes through a network node very rapidly, each buffer must appear on the free list at least once every two minutes. Therefore, each buffer flag is checked every two minutes to be sure it is set, and then cleared. A zero flag indicates that the buffer has dropped out of normal activity, and the buffer is unilaterally freed and its use bits cleared. In this way, any lost buffer is detected within at most four minutes and returned to normal usage.

V. Advantages of the Pluribus Approach to Fault-Tolerance

Two factors help to make our approach a cost-effective one. First, fault-tolerance is implemented primarily in software. This not only allows us to use unspecialized off-the-shelf hardware for much of our system, but also gives us considerable flexibility by allowing us to try new ideas as the product develops. When the time comes to upgrade machines in the field, a new software release is infinitely preferable to hardware modification. Implementing most fault detection in software also allows more complete error reporting than is characteristic of static-redundancy approaches.

The second factor is the modular nature of the Pluribus. Initially, the modular approach was chosen to permit easy expansion of the capabilities of a system to fit an application without being hampered by system-size boundaries. Our system expands by adding the same hardware modules as those which are duplicated to create a dynamic fault-tolerant system. Thus any system with more than the minimum number of processors for a given application both performs well and is fault-tolerant. A processor failure in such a system merely causes it to run a little slower. Since individual processors are relatively inexpensive, the percentage increase in system cost for processor redundancy is usually small, especially in large systems.

Sometimes the system requirements justify only limited fault-tolerance. An example is the large front-end processor which services the BBN Research Computer Center [Mann, Ornstein, and Kraley, 1976]. Here the bulk of the machine is fully redundant, but several of the host interfaces are used only occasionally for experimental systems, and their users can tolerate an occasional outage. Therefore, these interfaces are not duplicated, with a resultant savings in cost.

An additional factor contributing to cost-effectiveness is the relatively low percentage of processing power spent in explicit error detection (about 1 percent for current systems). We depend to a large extent on checks embedded in the operating program (such as code checksums) to detect errors, since the program is able to recover from failures whose effects are detected well after the fact. It is common practice for large software systems to include checks for some "impossible" software states and bad data structures. We have expanded these checks to be comprehensive, including checks which catch many types of hardware errors as well as lingering software problems.

One interesting effect of our approach is to make even a minimal, nonredundant machine significantly more resilient to transient failures caused by either hardware or software. All of the fault-tolerant mechanisms which run in the large systems run also in the small ones, and there are many transient failures which cause only momentary confusion which is usually solved by some level of reset or reinitialization. Obviously, a solid failure of some critical component or destruction of the program cannot be resolved without redundant resources, but these are by no means the only possible failures.

One result of our modular approach is that in contrast to the usual state of affairs, we expect larger systems to be more reliable than smaller ones, since more resources are available to be redistributed in case of trouble.

VI. Recent Field Experience

During the past year, we have had the opportunity to observe eight Pluribus IMP systems both under general operational conditions and in controlled field tests; the availability of these machines has been above 99.7 percent (by availability we mean uptime divided by scheduled uptime, excluding power and air-conditioning failures). Almost all the downtime was caused by program bugs which have been corrected since. Most recently, availability has been above 99.9 percent and we expect it to improve further as the machines reach maturity.

In evaluating this experience in terms of fault-tolerant perform-ance, we feel that it is important to go beyond overall availability numbers and discuss the kinds of faults that the Pluribus system can report, the kinds we observed in the field, and the effects these faults had on system behavior.

The concepts of availability and fault-tolerance are complex when applied to a Pluribus since failure of a component generally results in a reduction in, rather than a complete loss of, performance. In many applications this is an advantage since extra capacity is useful during periods of peak load and reduced service is tolerable while repairing faults. For example, if an I/O interface or an entire I/O *bus* fails, the machine automatically substitutes a spare element with only a momentary (often unnoticeable) interruption of service and with no loss in performance. In the case of processors and memory, however, all resources are normally in use (none are in a standby mode) and the loss of any one (or several) of them forces a reduction in performance, but does not keep the system from running.

When used as an IMP, the principal measure of Pluribus performance is throughput. In the tests described below, the presence of program bugs (since corrected) resulted in somewhat lower availability than we had expected, but the three machines easily exceeded their contractual requirements and were able to deliver better than 92 percent of their rated throughput capacity 99.76 percent of the time and better than 50 percent of capacity 99.83 percent of the time.

Under normal operating conditions, it is possible to observe an IMP only by means of its reports to the NCC or by the reports of its neighbors in the network. Since IMP's often operate unattend-ed, emphasis has been placed on the ability of each Pluribus to evaluate and report its internal hardware and software health. Three varieties of trouble-report messages are sent to the NCC.

Since the Pluribus continually evaluates the state of its hard-ware (see the discussion of the STAGE system), one type reports trouble in the hardware area. Examples of this are I/O errors, memory parity errors, power failures, and changes in configura-tion. The second type reflects the results of numerous interlocks and consistency checks which are made regarding tables, queues, variables, and other software entities. The third category concerns the Pluribus' role as part of the network. These reports monitor normal throughput statistics and temporary discontinuities in IMP-IMP message handling protocols, and are normally not directly pertinent to the fault-tolerance of the Pluribus itself. In a few cases the reports are received some time after a fault has been detected and dealt with by the Pluribus, but most fault messages appear within a few seconds.

In the normal course of building and operating Pluribus systems during the past year, we observed a number of unexpected hardware and software faults, but to verify our ideas and procedures we also wanted to observe a number of failure modes which would be expected to occur infrequently under normal operating conditions. To this end, we conducted an extensive series of tests over a three-month period using three four-processor Pluribus IMP's with redundant I/O interfaces, intercon-nected by high-speed terrestrial and satellite links. These tests demonstrated how the Pluribus handles many of the possible faults that might be encountered during the life of the equipment. We believe that the combination of the unexpected and planned faults we experienced constitutes a valid sample of the wide variety of intermittent failures in either hardware or software which such systems are likely to encounter. Examples of the types of fault recovery which were provoked or observed during these tests are discussed in the following.

1 *Failures on the processor bus.* We powered off various combinations of processor *buses* to demonstrate that the system would continue with traffic processing. We also tried placing bad instructions in various processors' local memories. In power failure situations, the remaining processors continued to operate without reinitialization. Data handled by the failed processor(s) was recovered by network protocols and a number of trouble-reports indicat-ed this fact. Data structures which were "locked" by the failed processors were "unlocked" by a software watchdog timer. When power was restored, the processors were smoothly readmitted to the system. Processors with bad local memory either halted or looped, and were quickly reloaded by other processors and brought back into operation automatically.

2 *Errors in or loss of common memory.* We created situations whereby the system suddenly saw common memory disappear. In some cases we powered off the memory *bus*; in others we "removed" memory from usability tables. We also observed some spontaneous parity errors. Since common memory pages are assigned specific roles at initialization time, loss of one or more pages caused a variety of reactions, depending on the role of the lost memory and the amount remaining. At one extreme, loss of all common memory prevented the system from continu-ing. At the other, loss of one of several pages of message buffers caused only a brief adjustment of memory assign-ments by the Stage program. Most Pluribus systems are organized for fully redundant operation and have spare

code and variable pages. Loss of a primary code or variables area caused a short transient in operations while the spare was initialized. As an example, loss of one-half of physical common memory (several pages of code, variables, and buffers) caused a reconfiguration lasting 15 s or less. During this period, all processors agreed on the reallocation of the remaining memory and reevaluated its usability. As a further test, we destroyed the integrity of various pages of common memory by storing random data in the check-summed areas. The system reacted by restoring the contents of the affected page from the backup copy. This process required about 10–12 s. We also created test conditions in which the system found that all copies of critical programs in common memory were unusable (their checksum was bad). At this time the system automatically requested that it be reloaded (from another of the Pluribus IMP's or the NCC). It should also be emphasized that the integrity of message buffers is also protected by software checksums; data harmed in any way is reported to the NCC, and the originator is notified so that retransmission can take place.

3   *Loss of I/O device.* We both created and observed several situations wherein I/O devices were either removed or experienced errors. In these cases, the I/O device was eliminated from usability tables by all processors and a backup device substituted. The system continued to operate, although in some cases, depending on the configuration being used, reinitialization was required. Loss of an entire I/O *bus* was handled in much the same way.

4   *Loss of critical hardware.* We observed that redundantly configured Pluribus systems would survive the loss of the RTC and the PID by swapping to the backup. Very little time was lost before the system continued. Errors in PID and RTC operation also are checked for and reported.

5   *Internal software errors.* As previously mentioned, the STAGE system and the IMP code are designed to check on the internal consistency of various software structures. In addition, the system ensures that none of the asynchronous processes is allowed to remain in a waiting state or in a loop. On a very infrequent basis, we observed that a Pluribus will report that such a condition was detected and corrected. We also forced many of these situations to occur by destroying key data structures or by causing queues to be looped or crossed. The system detected these, reported the problem, and continued normally, reinitializing if necessary.

6   *Artificial pathological conditions.* We did not attempt to cause pathological behavior of Pluribus hardware components which would, for example, write zeros to portions of memory or amputate *buses* at random, although we simulated these conditions with the software. Our observations of pathological behavior in the field, although infrequent, convince us that many of these cases can be withstood by the fault-tolerant software. For example,

during field tests we observed that some extraneous data appear occasionally in certain critical tables causing the Pluribus to reinitialize quickly or to suspend activity on a communications link briefly. The problem was traced to a special reloading device which was being improperly activated. This situation was eliminated by a minor program change.

We have now gained enough experience with the Pluribus fault-tolerant mechanisms to have confidence in their ability to detect and cope with failures. In the field, spontaneous failures have been of a relatively minor nature and have been successfully dealt with. Under test conditions, all the major and minor failures which occurred or which we created were well tolerated and the systems continued to function within their rated capacities.

VII.   Pluribus System Maintainability

Most fault-tolerant systems are designed to be repaired, sooner or later, by humans. Maintainability thus becomes a significant factor in long-term system performance. Since many systems are designed to recover from any single failure, but not from all multiple failures, the mean time to repair (MTTR) directly influences on-line spares requirements and hence the system cost for any given performance goal. To minimize MTTR, the system must provide accurate and unambiguous information about the nature of the detected fault and the automatic recovery process initiated. The environment in which the system operates is also important since the maintaining authority must be notified and must initiate the repair process as soon as possible.

The actual repair process may be carried out at several levels depending on the accuracy of the diagnostics and the obscurity of the failure symptoms. At the lowest level, the repair is accurately defined by the diagnostic and involves only the replacement of a faulty component. At the highest level, the failure may be caused by a design bug in either hardware or software. For the latter, the system must provide sufficient tools to permit overriding the operational recovery procedures. They must permit the repair personnel to reconfigure the system and run any required diagnostic procedures. The more powerful repair tools must be guarded to avoid operator-induced errors. Ideally this "fool-tolerance" [Goldberg, 1975, p. 32] should extend into all phases of repair. In practice we use only a two-level protection scheme that relies on experienced personnel not to make catastrophic errors.

Although we tend to think of hardware malfunctions as separate from software malfunctions, the symptoms of failure and the recovery procedures are frequently similar. In the Pluribus, the first detection of a fault is usually through failure of an embedded check in the main program, and frequently that is all that is required to initiate a correct recovery procedure. When the diagnostic value of an embedded check is insufficient to define a recovery procedure, various modular diagnostics may be run on the system. Thus in the case of a memory whose checksum is discovered to be wrong, the recovery action is to run a brief memory diagnostic and, if the memory appears usable, to restore the code from a spare copy.

Including a spare copy of some resource helps system recovery only if that spare resource works. Although it is traditional to run modular diagnostics on spare resources, our strategy has been to force the system to rotate use of resources from time to time. In some cases we use manual procedures, but the tendency has been to include automatic rotation procedures in the operational system software. This technique is clearly more appropriate to our application than it would be to a more traditional fault-tolerant requirement, since rotating faulty hardware into the operational system could cause a transient malfunction. On the other hand, it provides a better test of the hardware than modular diagnostics would provide.

One advantage of our reliance on embedded checks for failure detection is that we can detect that class of failure which is rarely caught by diagnostics. It is axiomatic that the operational program is the best program for certifying the hardware, but our operational program has also become the most comprehensive diagnostic for the hardware. In our experience, some of the most subtle hardware failures occur during operation of the application system, even though hardware diagnostic programs detect no errors. By augmenting the operational system with diagnostic capabilities, we have often been able to isolate even obscure or intermittent failures without interrupting normal operation.

A. Reporting Facilities

In the Pluribus IMP, the mechanism for reporting errors, recovery operations, and change-of-status information is the system trap (i.e., a supervisor call). Traps are reported locally on the system terminal and are also sent via trouble-reports to the network log at the NCC, where they serve a variety of diagnostic purposes. Understanding the nature of a failure in the running system requires fairly accurate knowledge of the state of the machine at the instant of the failure. The initial implementation of the trap mechanism recorded only the code number of the trap, which set of processors had encountered it, and a total occurrence count. This proved inadequate for accurate diagnosis and we have augmented the original trap mechanism to allow for saving a large snapshot of the instantaneous state of the processor, including such information as the contents of general registers, the global system time, map register settings, the last value read from the PID, and other important local data. These snapshots allow us to examine diagnostic information about the failure after the recovery code has taken effect and normal operation of the system has resumed. In an operational IMP, the snapshot information is sent to a data collection program at the NCC, where it is both stored for future reference and printed out on a log terminal. The snapshot facility is usually only enabled for that set of traps which indicate system malfunctions of some kind, since there are many normal traps which indicate such things as network topology changes. The same data collection program also keeps track of the current configuration of each machine and reports any changes on the log terminal. Thus the reconfiguration resulting from some module failure is immediately apparent. Correlating a reconfiguration with preceding snapshot error messages is usually sufficient to isolate solid failures.

B. Remote Diagnosis and Repair

Where the failure is intermittent, or error indications are ambiguous, we can make further diagnosis from the NCC using the remote connection capabilities of the network. This allows personnel at the NCC to interact with a system at a remote site exactly as if they were using the system control terminal at the site. We have provided a command structure in the system which allows us to make either "soft" or "firm" overrides of the configuration control structure, loop communications links, and run a variety of special diagnostics, monitors, and traffic generators. This enables us to diagnose many problems from the NCC even before dispatching repair personnel to the site (this can be especially appropriate for diagnosing program bugs). The current software is best at diagnosing the solid failures typical of mature hardware and treats most long-term intermittents as unrelated transients. Although we plan to implement heuristics which can deal with this type of problem, the diagnosis of long-term intermittents currently requires human intervention. Fully redundant Pluribus systems may be thought of as networks of paths and *buses*, so by causing the system not to use a particular path or *bus* and watching the trap log, we are usually able to localize the source of a hardware intermittent. Partitioning the *bus* and using some subset of the modules on the *bus* further localizes an intermittent traced to a particular *bus*, and repairs can then proceed. The same tools for reconfiguration are, of course, also available to maintenance personnel on site through the system control terminal, and trap reports sent to the NCC are duplicated also.

C. Partitioning

In extreme cases, when all normal diagnostic approaches have been exhausted, it is also possible to partition a fully redundant machine into two separate machines and run the operational system in one half while running stand-alone diagnostics or another copy of the system in the other half. We originally expected to use this approach quite frequently, but experience has shown the technique to be less useful than we expected.

Splitting a system is a combination of many "firm" overrides of the configuration control which are not currently protected against operator error (i.e., deleting the last copy of a resource from the use tables, or overlapping system resources across the partition). There is also the problem of identifying fault-free components to include in the operational system half. In general, being able to identify a faulty module which is to be excluded from the operational system implies that we can fix the fault by replacing the module, which usually obviates the need for partitioning into two machines. And finally, once a machine has been split, any new failures are likely to cause fatal problems that the machine might have been able to cope with had it not been split. Our current feeling is that the risks of splitting an operational system usually outweigh the advantages.

D. Reloading and Down-Line Loading

An important facility provided by the Pluribus hardware allows us to load and start the machine with no onsite personnel. This is accomplished by special-format messages which trigger a simple reload device when received over the network. This device is used to load a software package capable of dumping or reloading the operating system and application code. The source of reload code may be either some other Pluribus IMP on the network, or a disk file at the network control center. These reloading facilities are also used for distributing software updates to the machines in the field. A Pluribus IMP which discovers all copies of some application code page to be compromised will attempt to get a down-line reload from a neighbor IMP. This request is reported to the NCC where an operator then sets up the reload source for the transfer. Its use enables an IMP without duplicated resources to recover quickly from transient failures caused by hardware or software.

E. Maintenance Experience

The prototype Pluribus systems performed their error recovery functions well in many cases. Minor problems were often bypassed so effectively that the users and maintenance personnel were never aware of the problem. Even following drastic failures, such as the loss of a common memory bus, normal system operation was restored within seconds. From our experience with these early systems, however, certain deficiencies in our original strategies have become clear.

In some failure cases, one repair would lead to another, until eventually a fairly major reinitialization would be performed, with obvious effects on the users of the system. Unfortunately, the massive recovery often destroyed evidence of the original failure, or masked evidence necessary for effective diagnosis. While the goal of restoring the system to normal operation was achieved, we were left without any idea of why the reinitialization was required. This was particularly frustrating when the frequency of occurrence was on the order of hours or days.

In other cases, normal operation seemed to continue while some hardware failure occurred undetected. Either the failure was covered by effective recovery at a fairly low level in the system or it occurred in a redundant portion of the hardware which was not being exercised. A second failure in conjunction with the first would remove the last copy of some critical resource, causing the system to fail.

These initial experiences led through several intermediate steps to the current set of maintenance tools and diagnostics. In the prototype systems, we were forced to remove the system software and run stand-alone diagnostics when trouble arose. Development of the original recovery algorithms into early versions of the current STAGE system allowed diagnosis and repair while running the operational system; however, system programmers were required to interpret the traps and wrestle the system into different configurations during repair. The usual repair team during this period included a system programmer (usually at the NCC) watching and interpreting the traps, with a maintenance technician on site replacing components.

At present, the tools and diagnostics are well enough defined and documented so that usually only maintenance personnel are required for a repair. Hardware and software staff at the NCC may offer suggestions when maintenance personnel are dispatched to a site and may still direct occasional repair efforts if a difficult problem or inexperienced personnel require it, but this is the exception rather than the rule.

VIII. Other Applications and Extensions

Since the Pluribus has evolved from a communications application where overall system availability rather than total fault-coverage is the goal, our approach is most obviously suitable for similar applications. We have opted for an approach which depends heavily upon reconfiguration and reinitialization when faults are detected, and which requires very little special hardware beyond that needed to implement our multiprocessor architecture. Our approach would not be suitable for applications where absolutely no downtime can be tolerated, where total computational context must be preserved over failures, or where overall correctness must be ensured. In these cases, traditional approaches involving some form of static redundancy or execution redundancy are indicated [Avizienis, 1975; Avizienis, 1976]. Techniques somewhat similar to ours, but for a redundant uniprocessor, are in use in the Bell System's latest Electronic Switching System [Myers et al., 1977]. Although we have not closely investigated applications outside the communications area, we believe our approach is suitable for many other tasks, and we discuss several of these briefly below.

A. Message Systems

We have made an extensive study of the possibility of using the Pluribus computer as the basis for a message system. By message system we mean not only traditional message-switching such as is done in the Telex system, but also a system of mailboxes and files by which users can exchange and file messages without recourse to the U.S. Postal System, secretaries, or filing cabinets, and which will permit complicated searches and sorts of message files. Such a system must have high availability but could easily tolerate brief outages after a failure.

B. Real-Time Signal Processing

We have already built one system which is the front-end and control processor for a seismic data collection network, and which performs some preprocessing of seismic data [Gudz, 1977]. We believe this application can be extended to other areas of real-time signal processing with requirements for high overall system availability. Since many signal processing tasks can be broken into parallel components, the multiprocessor architecture would be especially appropriate.

C. General-Purpose Timesharing Systems

It seems to us that explicit use of fault-tolerant techniques could benefit general purpose timesharing systems and large operating systems. These systems operate continuously and are subject to minor hardware errors and subtle software bugs, but do not require totally uninterrupted operation. Although most large systems include some self-checking in the software, software fault-tolerance, to be truly effective, must be well integrated into the overall system design, and into the special hardware features which are usually required.

One of the primary purposes of most large operating systems is to provide disk and tape handling features. In this context, reinitialization in response to faults is a much more serious problem than, for example, in the IMP. Various checkpointing procedures may be required to restore the overall system state to a point where restart is possible [Yourden, 1972, pp. 340–353]. Large operating systems often support a variety of checkpointing services since the best techniques to use under these circumstances depend in part on the applications being serviced; in cases involving on-line database updates, the application programs themselves must be designed around their fault-tolerance requirements.

D. Reservations Systems

Airline, hotel, and car rental reservation systems provide good examples of on-line database systems which could benefit from well-designed software fault-tolerance systems. Once a reservation has been accepted, it must not be lost. Backup techniques such as dual updating of two copies of the database, perhaps located in different cities with independent central processors and telecommunications systems, may be worthwhile. On the other hand, minor problems (hardware or software) may be tolerated, especially if the problems can be resolved by reentering on-line transactions which were affected by the fault. Even with dual machines in remote locations, using a machine like the Pluribus would increase the reliability of each site separately, and provide substantial computing power in an expandable package. Further research will be required to understand fully the implications to the Pluribus of database integrity requirements for reservation systems.

E. Process Control

Our approach is clearly more appropriate to some areas of process control than to others. We envision a typical application in the area of overall supervisory systems coordinating a number of subsidiary systems or controllers, and incorporating tasks such as inventory control and job scheduling. Processes that could afford to stop momentarily would be controlled directly. End-to-end error correction and fault-masking hardware would be used in the machine interface for applications needing overall fault-tolerance. As with the previous applications, some form of checkpointing would be built in to preserve context over restarts.

References

Avizienis [1975]; Avizienis [1976]; Barnes et al. [1968]; Bressler, Kraley, and Michel [1975]; Enslow [1974]; Goldberg [1975]; Gudz [1977]; Heart [1975b]; Heart, Kahn, Ornstein, Crowther, and Walden [1970]; Heart, Ornstein, Crowther, and Barker [1973]; Heart, Ornstein, Crowther, Barker, Kraley, Bressler, and Michel [1976]; Mann, Ornstein, and Kraley [1976]; McKenzie, Cosell, McQuillan, and Thrope [1972]; Myers et al. [1977]; Ornstein, Crowther, Kraley, Bressler, Michel, and Heart [1975]; Ornstein, Heart, Crowther, Rusell, Rising and Michel [1972]; Ornstein and Walden [1975]; Roberts and Wessler [1970]; U.S. Pat. 4,035,766 [1977]; Wolf [1973]; Wulf and Bell [1972]; Yourden [1972].

Section 5

Networks

Introduction

Table 1 lists the basic dimensions of a computer network design space. Real networks can be represented as a point in design space by specifying the values of each dimension. Frequently real networks incorporate more than one alternative value (intercon-

nections or different capacities, varying physical separation, etc.). This multiplicity and range of values for a single dimension is encouraged by:

- Varying cost functions. The functions change over time and locality, fostering local optimization.

- Technology evolution. As the network evolves and expands over time, new technology (or new cost functions) becomes available and is factored into the expansion plans.

- User evolution. As network usage evolves, the network will adapt to the new patterns.

Thus it is extremely rare that a network can be described by selecting one parameter from each of the dimensions in Table 1. However, we offer the taxonomy as an orderly way of discussing the various decisions that make up a network's design. During our discussion of the various dimensions, the reader will note that some of the dimensions are interrelated, i.e., the selection of a value for one dimension may dictate, or at least bias, the selection of a value for another dimension. This phenomenon is characteristic of complex system design. It is not sufficient to use one dimension to optimize, because of its impact on other dimensions. Hence the would-be designer must first understand the available alternatives and then seek a harmonious blend of the design parameters in order to optimize against cost-, performance-, and reliability-based objective functions. It is essential that the designer identify constraints, design variables, and objective functions. Moreover, a network changes with time as the objective functions of machines, links, and user costs dynamically change. The next section will present a brief discussion of the design parameters. The following section will examine actual networks; the student is encouraged to analyze them to see the interdependence of the design parameters.

Network Design-Space Parameters

Components Interconnected

As in most system designs, the intended application is the primary shaper of the eventual structure. The network may only exist to tie remote *terminals* to a centralized computer. Historically, terminals had relative low data rates limited by available voice-grade phone lines (e.g., 100–300 bit/s), but the advent of interactive graphics, intelligent terminals, better links, and modulator-demodulators (modems) will cause this attribute to be upgraded.

Computer-to-*computer* communication involves higher data rates and larger blocks of data than terminal-to-computer communications. The type of information transmitted (e.g., data files, facsimile, real time voice, or real time video) significantly impacts

Table 1 The Network Design Space

Components interconnected	Host access
Terminal-computer	Direct
Computer-computer	Subnet
Homogeneous-heterogeneous	**Protocols**
Topology	Host
Logical	Subnet
Centralized	Line
Distributed	Character
Hierarchical	**Routing**
Physical proximity	Deterministic
>1 km (global)	Flooding
100–1,000 m (building)	Fixed
<100 m (room)	Split traffic
Physical structure	Ideal observer
Interconnection	Stochastic
Point-to-point	Random
Simplex	Isolated
Half-duplex	Local delay estimate
Full-duplex	Shortest queue
Multiplexed	Distributed
Broadcast	Periodic update
Interconnection capacity	Asynchronous update
Serial	**Flow control**
0–300 bit/s	Isarithmic
300–2,400 bit/s	Buffer storage allocation
2.4–19.2 Kbit/s	Special route assignment
56–230.4 Kbit/s	**Reliability**
Parallel	Error rate
1 ≥ Mbit/s	Assumed perfect
Switching	Probability per bit
Circuit	Survivability
Message	Redundancy
Packet	Error codes
Access connection	**Performance**
Direct	Capacity
Multiplexed	Individual components
Broadcast	Total network
Concentrators	Response time
	Time to connect

not only the communication data rate but also the allowable transmission delay.

Whether the interconnected components are identical (forming a *homogeneous* network, shown in Fig. 1*a*) or different (forming a *heterogeneous* network, Fig. 1*b*)—and for whatever reason, whether dictated by the application or by economics—can have a major impact on design decisions in other dimensions (e.g., host access and access connection)

Topology

The individual functions of a network (e.g., routing and switching) may be either *centralized* or *distributed*. Networks of the earliest form had all logical and physical functions centralized. These networks were called *star networks* (Fig. 2*a*), since everything was connected to a centralized node, usually the host computer. Centralized networks are conceptually easier to design but are limited by the capacity and reliability of the central resource. Alternatively, a network function can be distributed over several nodes in the network (as in the packet routing of the ARPANET, Fig. 2*b*).

Hierarchical networks are interconnections of several networks and may be carried out to any number of levels. Figure 2*c* illustrates the simple case of a hierarchical star network, while Fig. 2*d* depicts local distributed networks interconnected via a backbone network.

The *physical proximity* of the interconnected components determines the feasibility of several other parameters, including interconnection capacities and routing strategies. A geographically distributed network where nodes are more than a kilometer apart will be significantly different from a local network whose nodes are separated by a few meters.

These topology subdimensions are an attempt to abstract properties that might be shared by several networks. But the flexibility and evolution of networks, particularly of those where geographical distribution impacts the topology through local, autonomous decisions (i.e., those in which physical distance is greater than 1 km), means that it is very unlikely that two networks will be exactly the same. Thus the definitive method of

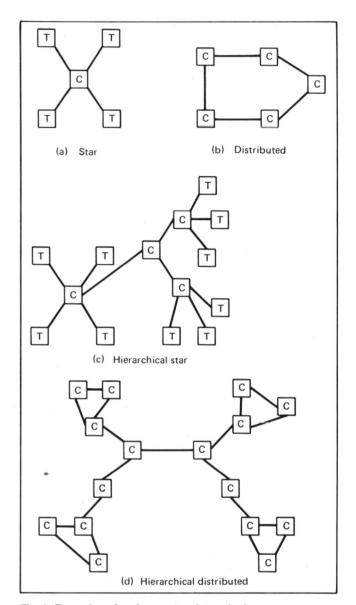

Fig. 2. Examples of various network topologies.

describing the topology is to give the complete *physical structure* including node types, link types, and geometry.

Interconnection

Following the specification of the components to be interconnected and their topology, the next most important dimension is the means of interconnection. Historically, the majority of networks have had *point-to-point* links. Communications across the links

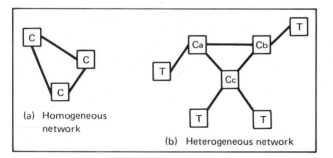

Fig. 1. Homogeneous and heterogeneous networks.

could be unidirectional (*simplex*), bidirectional but only in one direction at a time (*half-duplex*), bidirectional and in both directions at the same time (*full-duplex*), or combined with other communications (*multiplexed*).

The availability of high-bandwidth channels by ground and/or satellite-based radio has spurred interest in interconnecting nodes via *broadcasting*. Whenever a node wishes to communicate it broadcasts over a common channel. The channel protocol (see below) resolves any contention for the channel.

Interconnection Capacity

The information-rate capacity of the interconnections determines the best-case performance of the network. The capacity may be allocated hierarchically, with lower capacity at the periphery (or access points) to the network and higher capacities where multiple communications may be multiplexed onto a single interconnection.

Most interconnections are serial because of cost. The cost of communications can be a significant fraction of the cost of the overall network. Thus ways to reduce communications cost may influence the values of subsequent dimensions (e.g., switching, access, and protocols). For a given information flow, a single high-capacity interconnection is cheaper than a set of lower-capacity interconnections (although the former is less tolerant of failures). During the design study for the ARPANET [Roberts and Wessler, 1970] it was shown that a 25-fold increase in line capacity (from 2 to 50 Kbit/s) cost only a factor of 10 more.

Serial interconnections spanned ranges dictated either by device characteristics (e.g., hard-copy terminals are usually less than 300 bit/s) or telephone network characteristics (e.g., voice-grade phone lines can carry up to 2.4 Kbit/s).

Parallel interconnections are only economically feasible for short distances, less than 100 m.

Switching

In *circuit* switching, a dedicated path is established by connecting a succession of point-to-point links between the source and destination. A prime example of a circuit-switched network is the telephone system.

Network traffic by nature moves in bursts. In the telephone network, a phone call averages only 3 min in duration. The overhead for establishing the circuit is only a few seconds and is acceptable, given the duration of a call. TYMNET [Schwartz, 1977] is an example of a circuit-switched terminal network. However, terminal-to-computer communication is of much shorter duration than telephone calls and occurs more frequently (as in a character-by-character transmission from a 30 char/s terminal to a computer). Setting up a circuit for the duration of a session would lead to underutilization of the interconnection's capacity. On the other hand, establishing a circuit for each transmission

(e.g., for each character or file) would add exceedingly large delays. Thus alternatives to circuit switching are sought.

The first alternative is *message* switching. Each piece of information is bundled into a message with source and destination information. The message is multiplexed with other messages on the interconnections between nodes. The message is routed from node to node until the destination is reached. Message switching is often called *store and forward*, since the messages are stored at intermediate nodes and then forwarded. Several new dimensions are introduced by message switching, including routing, protocols, and flow control. Messages must contain extra bits so that the correct destination can be found. Longer messages may be subdivided into blocks of fixed size (see Fig. 3a) to ease the task of message multiplexing. Each block contains such information as the message identity and block number, as well as error-checking information. Only the first block has information about the number of blocks in the message as well as the source and destination. When all the blocks are received at the destination, the message is reassembled into its original form and an acknowledgment sent back. All blocks travel the same route, and intermediary nodes must hold the complete message before forwarding until it is all received. AUTODIN is an example of a message-switched network.

A variation of message switching, termed *packet switching*, was introduced to decrease the response time of the network by dividing the message into packets (Fig. 3b), each of which carries complete routing information. Thus the packets can be independently routed through the network, perhaps over different paths. Packets can be retransmitted as soon as they are received. Both the MERIT network [Aupperle, 1973] and the ARPA network [Chap. 24] are examples of packet-switching networks.

Access Connection

Access to the network can take several forms: a *direct*, dedicated interconnection; a multiplexed interconnection; a broadcast interconnection (as in the ETHERNET); or a concentrator. A concentrator multiplexes diverse traffic onto a high-capacity interconnection in order to save the cost of multiple long-distance interconnections.

Host Access

Computers that provide the computational cycles for a network are called *hosts*. The hosts may be tied together directly or via a communication subnet. The subnet logically separates data processing from data communications. Although the subnet approach may be less efficient than direct host-to-host interconnection, it has several advantages:

- Modularity. The subnet can be brought up independently. It can be incrementally expanded. And host computer

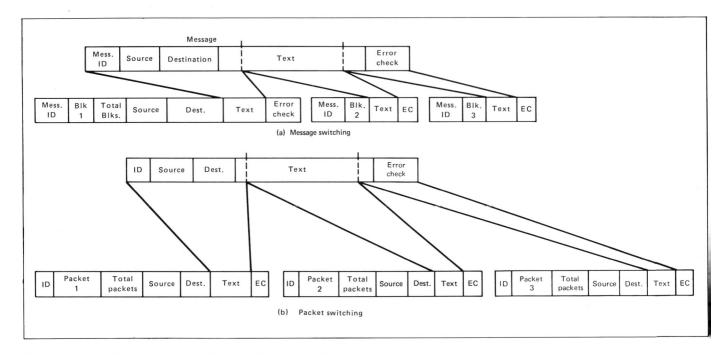

Fig. 3. Example of (a) message switching and (b) packet switching.

software, especially complex operating systems, needs very little modification, since only a new type of I/O device is being added to the system. In direct host-to-host interconnection, each different type of host may require separate software; for N host types in the system, there would be potentially N^2 software additions.

- Adaptability. Changes can be made in the subnet, including changes in protocols, message formats, and routing, without affecting host-computer software.

- Reliability. The subnet can be made of highly reliable processors, perhaps specially built. Also, since these processors have no I/O devices other than network interconnections, the subnet processors can be many times more reliable than the hosts, with the result that the subnet approach is more reliable than the direct approach.

- Maintainability. Since the subnet is autonomous, special error-detection and recovery procedures can be evoked, such as down-line loading of code form adjacent subnet processors. See Chap. 24 for a more detailed discussion.

Protocols

A network can be viewed as a hierarchy of levels. Each lower level provides a reliable, but transparent, communications system for the next higher level. Each level has a protocol that consists of

message format, routing control, and error handling. Figure 4 illustrates this hierarchy. At each level (for example, at the subnet level) messages from the next higher level (in this instance, the host) are broken into a series of packets. A header (routing information) and an error check are appended. The header–error check combination represents a "bit bucket" that envelops the text from the next higher level (which includes its own header and error check) and delivers the text reliably to its destination. Interconnections themselves may have a line protocol (as in SDLC [IBM, 1974] or ETHERNET [Chap. 26]). All this information (e.g., protocol and message text) consists of characters which have their own formats when placed on a line (perhaps including start and stop bits, parity bits, and 7-bit ASCII code).

Of course, the more levels a message must be transformed through, the more bits (headers and error checks) that must be appended. If the number of overhead bits becomes too large, most of the network resources will be devoted to transmitting overhead. Some early measurements on the ARPANET [Kleinrock and Naylor, 1974] indicated that the average packet was 218 bits long, of which 168 bits were overhead!

Routing

In message- and packet-switched networks, a mechanism must be provided for determining the routing of messages or packets

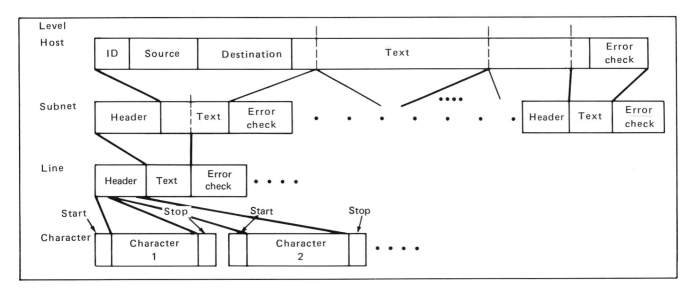

Fig. 4. Levels of protocol in a typical network.

from source to destination. Routing mechanisms must also ensure that messages[1] do not enter into a routing loop, thus never exiting the network. Routing mechanisms take two general forms: *deterministic* (i.e., predetermined and fixed) and *stochastic* (i.e., dynamically variable). Several variations of these two basic mechanisms have been proposed or implemented [Greene and Pooch, 1977].

One of the simplest deterministic routing algorithms is *flooding*, wherein a node retransmits a received message over all its links except the link over which the message has been received. Eventually the message permeates the network. The source is notified of completion upon receiving a copy of its transmitted message.

Conceptually, flooding has several advantages, including simple implementation, insensitivity to network topological changes, and the ability to ensure minimal delay in message delivery. However, flooding contributes to network congestion and hence is not cost-effective.

In *fixed* routing, network topology and traffic patterns are assumed static. Optimal routings can be computed and stored in each node. Obviously fixed routings do not adapt to varying network configuration, fluctuations in traffic patterns, or network outages. Fixed routing is often used in centralized networks or distributed networks with a single routing node (e.g., TYMNET) [Schwartz, 1977].

Split routing provides multiple routing paths with the actual path selected via a predetermined probability. Each node routes messages according to the specified probability.

If complete instantaneous knowledge of the network is known, optimal routing of each message is possible. Since complete knowledge is not feasible, on account of network delays, this *ideal observer* routing is used as a theoretical limit to compare other routing mechanisms with.

Stochastic routing mechanisms combine network topology with an estimate of the current network state. The simplest is *random* routing, which transmits the received message out over a link selected at random. The message arrives at its destination after a random "walk."

Isolated routing mechanisms determine routing of messages on the basis of local information only. Network state may be estimated by keeping track of message acknowledgment delays as a function of the destination and the link transmitted over (this method is known as the *local delay estimate*) or by retransmitting the message as soon as possible (the *shortest queue* or "hot potato" method).

Distributed routing mechanisms exchange observed delay information between nodes, thus allowing nodes farther from sources of congestion to "learn" about dynamic network variations. Usually nodes exchange information only with their nearest neighbors.

Flow Control

The purpose of flow control is to relieve (or at least to limit) network congestion (either locally or globally) and to prevent or

[1]For the remainder of this section we will use the word *message* to mean either message or packet.

minimize deadlocks (situations in message-switching networks in which all resources, such as message buffers, are allocated and yet no message is able to be delivered, thus freeing up resources for new messages).

In *isarithmic* control, the total number of packets in the system is held constant. Dummy (nil) packets are added to the number of real information packets to keep the total constant. New messages may enter the system only by replacing dummy packets. Outgoing messages are replaced by dummy packets. Dummy packets are circulated through the network by being passed on to nearest neighbors.

In *buffer storage allocation*, space must be reserved at the destination for message reassembly before the message can be introduced into the network. This flow-control mechanism is used in the ARPA network.

Special route assignment attempts to control congestion by altering the routing on the basis of long-term traffic patterns to minimize delay or by avoiding congested nodes. Periodic updating of estimated network conditions is required, as in the distributed routing mechanisms described above.

Reliability

Networks are composed of many interconnected components and are therefore subject to outside disturbances which may cause garbling of message transmissions or even the loss of several network components.

Networks are usually designed to ensure correct operation within an assumed transmission *error rate* and *survivability* in spite of component (link or mode) failures. Errors in transmissions can be caused by external electromagnetic radiation or by congested network operation (for an example, see the contention channels in the ALOHANET and ETHERNET, which use networkwide error detection as a means of managing congestion). These transient errors are usually tolerated by a detection and retransmission mechanism.

Error detection is accomplished by appending an error-check code to each message. The error check works on a principle of redundancy and can be designed to guarantee detection of a specified number of random bit changes and/or a specified length (a burst) of consecutive bits, any or all of which can be in error. Most error-check codes also have a high probability of detecting errors in excess of those guaranteed to be caught. An effective network transmission error rate (i.e., rate of undetected faulty messages) is usually a dominant network design parameter. The cost, in terms of the encoding and decoding complexity and the number of error-check bits, is directly related to the specified number of random-bit or burst errors to be detected.

Retransmission of a message is usually triggered by failure to receive a positive acknowledgment within a specified period of time. Each level of network protocol has extensive provision for

transient-error survival [e.g., see ETHERNET (Chap. 26) for both line and host levels, ARPANET (Chap. 24) for subnet and host levels].

Since networks are composed of a multitude of interconnected components, the network must be able to survive component failures, or else it will be available only when all its components are properly operating. Network survival is usually accomplished by (1) designing network interfaces so that a component failure cannot cause other components to fail (the "domino effect" occasionally exhibited by power networks) and (2) providing redundancy via alternate paths between nodes and by other means.

Performance

The other primary metric by which the quality of a network design can be judged is performance. A crude measure of performance is the *capacity* of individual components or of the total network. More meaningful measures are those perceived by the user, such as *response time* and time to establish a two-way dialogue (*time to connect*).

Network Examples

The previous section presented a taxonomy of the network design space. In this section we will briefly present some actual points in that space. We will conclude by discussing the three networks presented in detail by Chaps. 24, 25, and 26.

Historically there have been many examples of networks. Roads, pipelines, railroads, and shipping are all commodity-based networks. But communication networks are the ones that have the most direct impact on computer networks. Communication networks have evolved from telegraphic to telephone to radio.

Computer-related networks were first constructed to provide remote access to a centralized facility. The first such facilities serviced a small geographical area. Remote terminal access to a central site evolved until distances spanned thousands of miles. SABRE I [Knight, 1972] was the first online airlines reservation system; it was jointly developed by IBM and American Airlines in the early 1960s. SABRE consisted of a central computer with 2,000 nationwide terminals.

With the availability of low-cost processors and the increasing dominant cost of communications, terminal concentrators were evolved to multiplex many terminals onto a single communications line, such as in the Dartmouth Time Sharing System (DTSS) [Hargraves, 1974]. Commercial timesharing systems, such as the GE Informations System (Fig. 6) [McCalley and Barrett, 1978] and TYMNET (Fig. 8) [Schwartz, 1977], also use terminal concentrators. The ALOHANET provides central computer access via radio packet switching rather than the more traditional leased land lines.

The concept of computers dedicated to I/O (for example, the CDC 6600, Chap. 43) perhaps even predated terminal concentrators. The concept arose to functionally specialize computers in a computer network. A special-purpose network for air defense, SAGE (Semiautomatic Ground Environment) [Everett, Zraket, and Benington, 1957], received sensor data from several sources (e.g., radar and visual) and transmitted information to various weapons systems. Each computer was duplicated for reliability.

General computer-computer networks became common after the construction of the ARPANET, which pioneered packet-switching technology.

LLL Octopus

One of the oldest and most extensive local computer networks is the OCTOPUS network at the Lawrence Livermore Laboratory, Livermore, California. LLL is a major research laboratory run under contract with the Department of Energy by the University of California. Large computing facilities were required for nuclear research performed by the laboratory, and security dictated that the facilities be provided locally.

The OCTOPUS network is actually separated into six functionally independent subnetworks tied to a collection of six worker computers. The pool of worker computers continually evolves so that the laboratory always has the most advanced computation engines available. In 1966, the worker computers consisted of two CDC 6600s, a CDC 3600, a UNIVAC LARC, an IBM Stretch, and two IMB 7094s. In 1978 the worker-computer pool had evolved to four CDC 7600s and two CDC Stars. To allow the smooth introduction of worker-computer types without disrupting network availability, LLL defined several high-speed data channels (36-bit, 10^7 bit/s and 4×10^7 bit/s; 12-bit, 1.5×10^6 bit/s) to which all OCTOPUS subnetworks interface and to which all new worker computers must interface.

Figure 5 illustrates the OCTOPUS network configuration as of the beginning of 1979. Each of the six subnetworks will be described below.

File Transport Subnetwork One of the original motivations for the OCTOPUS network was to provide a large central data base. There are two advantages of such a centralized data base:

1. Economies of scale. Online secondary storage is cheapest with very large storage devices.
2. Flexibility. Files can be created on one worker computer and subsequently accessed on another, increasing availability and allowing load balancing.

A dual-processor PDP-10 with a shared 256-Kword buffer memory serves as the memory hierarchy controller and buffer for moving files from one secondary storage medium to another. In 1979 there were twelve 100-megabyte disks. An IBM photostore provides 10^{12} bits of online storage capacity via a photographic process to store archival data. Since the photographic process is irreversible, the photostore is a write-once, then read-only storage. File updates require copying the data to buffer memory or disk and subsequent rewriting to a fresh cell of the photostore.

Terminal Subnetwork Four PDP-8 minicomputers provide access to the worker computers for 512 teletypewriters. The PDP-8's provide concentration of teletypewriter characters into lines, routing of completed lines (messages) to the appropriate worker computer, and character-by-character disassembly of lines from the worker computer to the terminal. Three PDP-11's provide similar capabilities for 768 advanced terminals.

The File Transport Subnetwork uses the Terminal Subnetwork to send control messages between the PDP-10's and the worker computers. Control messages are usually short and do not mix well with the large files transported over the File Transport Subnetwork.

Remote Job Entry Terminal Subnetwork Three PDP-11's provide access to the worker computers from 40 remote stations, each equipped with card readers and line printers.

Television Monitor Display System (TMDS) Subnetwork Two PDP-11/45's provide 96 channels of output to 1,024 television monitor users. Pictures measuring 512 bits by 512 bits stored on disk can be routed through the File Transport PDP-10's to the TMDS subnetwork.

Computer Hardcopy Output Recording System (CHORS) Subnetwork Two Mod Comp computers provide access to hard-copy output on three microfilm or two nonimpact printers. CHORS worker channels simulate tape operation of a CDC 7600 peripheral processing unit (PPU).

Multi-Access Storage System (MASS) Subnetwork. Two TI 980 minicomputers provide access to a 10^{12} bit CDC 385 MSF tape library. High-speed MASS channels provide access to CDC 7600 819 disks via PPUs at 4×10^7 bit/s.

GE Information Services

The General Electric MARK III Service computer network provides remote computational capabilities (timesharing and batch) to cover 600 cities in 21 countries. The network can support a peak load of approximately 1,800 simultaneous users accessing three data processing centers. Access to the data processing centers is provided by over 200 minicomputer concentrators interconnected by 300,000 miles of telephone lines [McCalley and Barrett, 1978].

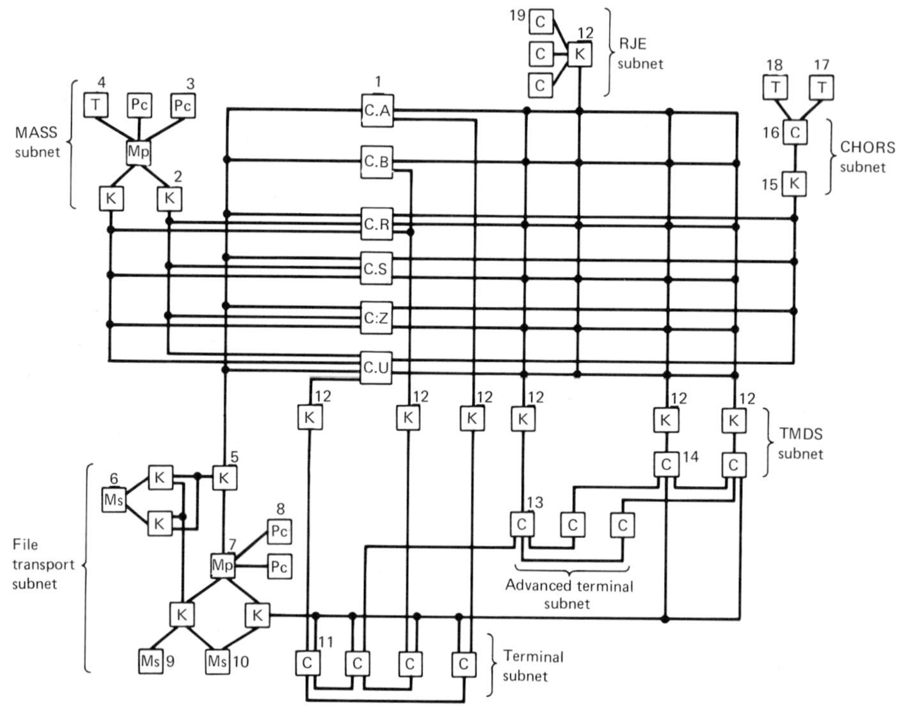

Fig. 5. LLL's OCTOPUS network.

Notes

1 C ['Worker Computers; #A, B: CDC STAR; #R, S, Z, U: CDC 7600]
2 K ['Multi-Access Storage System/MASS; 40 Mbit/s]
3 Pc['TI 980A]
4 T ['CDC Mass Storage Facility/MSF; 64 Mbit/cartridge; 16K cartridges; read/write; 4.5 Mbit/s; cartridge.access: 9s]
5 K ['LLL Data Channel; 36 b; 10^7 bit/s]
6 Ms[Disk; #0-11; 800 Mbytes]
7 Mp[Core; 36 b/w; 256 Kw; 1 μsec]
8 Pc['File Transport; PDP-10]
9 Ms[IBM 1360 Photostore; 10^{12} bits; record: 250 Kbit/s; read: 10^6 bit/s; t.access: 5 sec]
10 Ms[IBM 2321 Data Cell; #0-4; 2×10^{10} bits]
11 C ['PDP-8; interconnected by: 9.6K ~ 500K bps serial line; attached to 128 terminals; 10 cps]
12 K ['Octopus Channel; 1.5×10^6 bps]
13 C ['PDP-11/34; interconnected by: 9.6K ~ 500K bit/serial line; attached to 256 terminals; 30 ~ 960 cps]
14 C ['PDP-11/45; Television Monitor Display System/TMDS; interconnected by: 9.6K ~ 500K serial line; 96 channels; 1024 monitors]
15 K ['Computer Hardcopy Output Recording System/CHORS bus; 10 Mbit/s]
16 C ['Mod Comp II]
17 T ['Honeywell Nonimpact Printer]
18 T ['FR-80 Film Recorder]
19 C ['Remote Job Entry/RJE; PDP-11/10; card reader; line printer]

The network is a hierarchical star composed of three levels (Fig. 6): remote concentrators, central concentrators, and central switches. User access is provided by dialing the nearest remote concentrator. The remote concentrators are minicomputers that multiplex terminal information into messages for shipment to central concentrators. There are four types of remote concentrators that vary with respect to the number of dial-up ports and line speeds. The remote concentrators are located at 20 network distribution points. The MiniRemote Concentrator (MRC) is intended to operate in unattended locations. Programs stored in read-only memories ask the central concentrators to load MRC software down-line in case of initialization or software corruption. The remote concentrators sense dial-up terminal characteristics (e.g., baud rate and character set) and convert all transmissions to

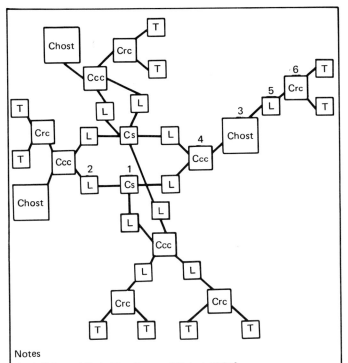

Fig. 6. General Electric Mark III service network.

Notes

1 Cs['Central Switching Center; 'Diginet 1600]

2 L[56 Kbit/s; full-duplex]

3 Chost [Host cluster; foreground: 'Honeywell 6088; background: 'IBM S/370| 'Honeywell DN355; !See Fig. 7!]

4 Ccc ['Central Concentrator: 'GPAC 4000 with 12 ports]

5 L[9.6|14.4|19.2 Kbit/s ; full-duplex]

6 Crc['Remote concentrator; 'Honeywell H416 with 48 ports to 300 bit/s | 'GE Diginet 1600 with 96 ports to 1200 bit/s |'GE Diginet 1600 with 14 ports to 9600 bit/s |'MRC mini remote concentrator with 32 asynchronous ports to 2400 bit/s or 12 synchronous ports to 56 Kbit/s]

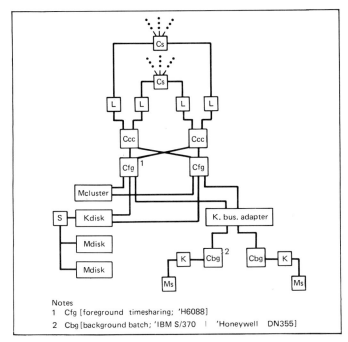

Notes

1 Cfg [foreground timesharing; 'H6088]

2 Cbg [background batch; 'IBM S/370 | 'Honeywell DN355]

Fig. 7. General Electric Mark III host cluster.

central concentrator attached to the desired host center. Further load balancing occurs at the host center, since the user can run on either host on account of the sharing of job information and files. Central concentrators intercommunicate via messages composed of a 10-byte header, up to 168 characters of text, an end-of-text character, and an error-check character.

There are two switching centers that interconnect all central concentrators. The switching center redundancy prevents single failures from crippling the network. Average yearly availability has exceeded 99.7 percent on account of hardware redundancy at the switching-center, central-concentrator, and host-center levels (see Fig. 7).

A network monitoring system gathers data on network configuration, network activity, and exceptional conditions. Network response is periodically checked by sending out dummy messages.

TYMNET

TYMNET (Fig. 8) is a terminal-oriented network that provides interterminal communication as well as access to timesharing hosts. The network has evolved to where user hosts can interface to share the network's intercommunication and user resources. The network supports three message types: control, short text (up to 56 characters), and long text (up to 168 characters). Message routing is via virtual circuits determined by central routing control. When a user logs on, the virtual circuit is established for

a single virtual-terminal format. The virtual-terminal format allows for the independent development of remote and central concentrator software. Communication to central concentrators is via messages composed of a 7-byte header, up to 56 characters of text, an end-of-text character, and an error-check character that is the EXCLUSIVE OR of all previous characters. There are 16 central concentrators, each of which can support up to 12 remote devices, 2 switching centers, and up to 5 host computers. The central concentrators either provide access to the host (Fig. 7) or routing to an appropriate central concentrator via the central switches. Each host center has more than one central concentrator for reliability reasons. The source central concentrator helps balance network load by assigning the user to the least loaded

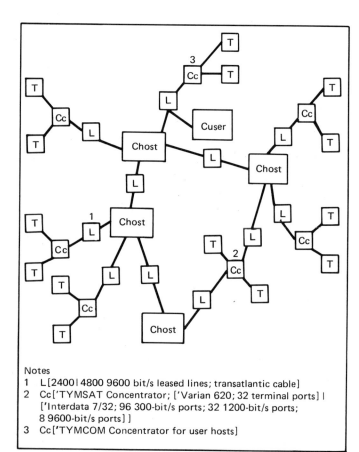

Notes
1   L [2400 l 4800 9600 bit/s leased lines; transatlantic cable]
2   Cc ['TYMSAT Concentrator; ['Varian 620; 32 terminal ports] l
     ['Interdata 7/32; 96 300-bit/s ports; 32 1200-bit/s ports;
     8 9600-bit/s ports]]
3   Cc ['TYMCOM Concentrator for user hosts]

Fig. 8. TYMNET network.

the duration of the session. The TYMSAT concentrators combine user messages, identified by their virtual-channel numbers, into the larger-format messages for efficiency. Round-trip message delays average 400 ms in the United States and 800 ms for overseas connections [Schwartz, 1977].

The MERIT Computer Network

The MERIT computer network (Fig. 9) is an experiment in interconnecting university computation centers for the purpose of expanding the facilities available to any user. MERIT became fully operational in October 1972 and interconnects three Michigan universities (Michigan State University, University of Michigan, and Wayne State University) within 80 miles of each other.

A subnetwork of Communications Computers (CC) interconnects the host machines. A subnetwork approach was selected to minimize the impact on the diverse host operating systems, to isolate the network communications function, and to simplify the network interfacing.

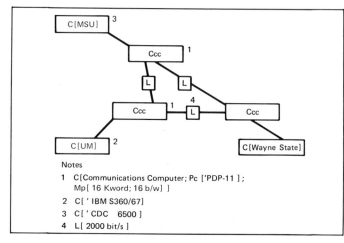

Notes
1   C [Communications Computer; Pc ['PDP-11];
     Mp[16 Kword; 16 b/w]]
2   C[' IBM S360/67]
3   C[' CDC 6500]
4   L[2000 bit/s]

Fig. 9. The MERIT computer network as of 1973.

The ARPA Network

Perhaps the best-known and most widely copied computer network is the ARPA Network. The ARPANET has been extensively studied and documented in the literature. The Advanced Research Projects Agency (ARPA) of the Department of Defense started development in late 1968 of a new type of computer network. The network was intended to interconnect, via common-carrier lines, dissimilar computers at geographically distributed ARPA-sponsored research sites. The primary purpose of this interconnection was to allow resource sharing among the research sites so that researchers might share data and interactively use programs existing at other sites. The network was also intended to stimulate research in packet-switching and protocol technology. Roberts and Wessler [1970] outline the ARPA Network goals.

The ARPA Network has been operational for over 10 years and has become a national facility. The network has grown from 4 sites to about 60 sites interconnecting over 100 independent computer systems via a subnet constructed of Interface Message Processors (IMPs). (See Table 2.) The network is in a constant state of evolution. Provision for terminal access to the network for sites without independent host computers was added via special IMPs

Table 2   ARPANET Growth

Year	Number of nodes	Year	Number of nodes
Late 1969	4	Early 1973	40
Mid-1970	10	Mid-1974	46
Early 1971	15	Mid-1975	56
Mid-1971	26	Mid-1977	58
Late 1972	34	Mid-1978	61

cailed Terminal Interface Processors (TIPs). A multiprocessor IMP, called Pluribus, was developed for the twin goals of orderly, modular growth and enhanced reliability of the subnet (see Chap. 23). Satellite channels have been added to allow Europe (via Norway) and Hawaii access to the network.

A schematic map of the ARPA Network as of mid-1978 is shown in Fig. 10, while a geographical distribution is shown in Fig. 11. As can be seen from the map, each site consists of up to eight (four real, four fake) independent computer systems (hosts) and one IMP, TIP, or Pluribus. Each IMP may be connected to as many as

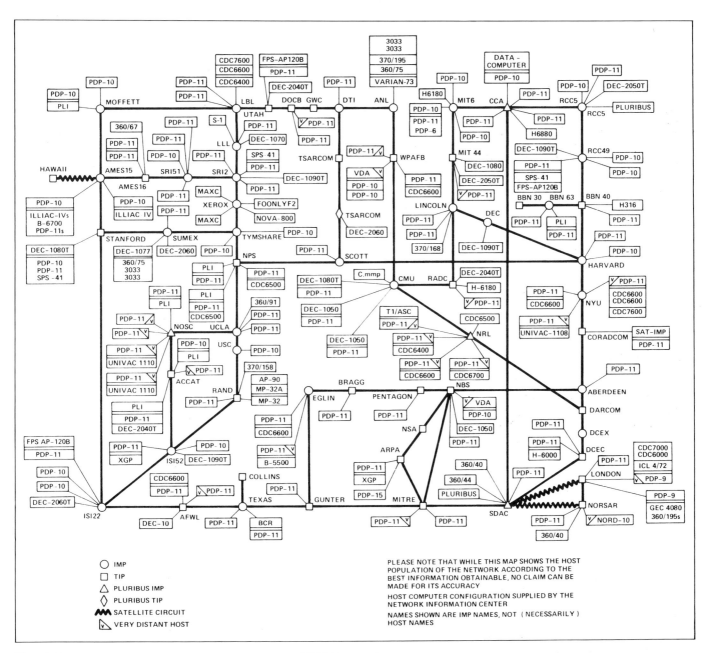

Fig. 10. ARPANET logical map, June 1979 (from the ARPANET Directory).

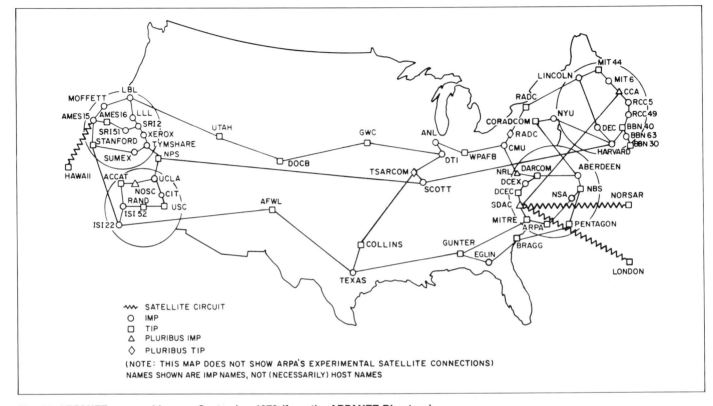

Fig. 11. ARPANET geographic map, September 1979 (from the ARPANET Directory).

five other IMPs using telephone lines of from 9.6 to 230.4 Kbit/s. The typical bandwidth is 50 Kbit/s.

Chapter 24 describes the design of the IMP subnet, including message format and protocol, packet format and protocol, routing, reliability, hardware design, software design, and projected performance. Chapter 23 describes a multiprocessor explicitly designed for the IMP application while giving a good insight into multiprocessor design trade-offs and parallel decomposition of an application. Chapter 23 also illustrates how reliability techniques can be used in a multiprocessor dedicated to the communications task.

Some of the IMP algorithms described in Chap. 24 have been altered to improve network performance [McQuillan, Crowther, Cosell, Walden, and Heart, 1972]:

- Deadlocks. Under heavy traffic conditions, it was possible for the subnet to deadlock. The condition, termed *reassembly lockup* (Fig. 12), occurs when all of an IMP's buffers are allocated to reassembly of multiple packet messages (messages A and B in IMP 3) and cannot accept packets for other messages. Deadlock occurs if all the adjacent IMPs (IMP 2) have filled buffers for the IMP in question but none of the packets (of messages C, D, and E for this example) are those required to complete a message and thus to release buffer space. A request for reassembly space before accepting a message from a host was added to the subnet protocol.

- Sequence Control. Since the deadlock prevention mechanism described above provided flow control and since the original flow control mechanism (in which each IMP could originate at most 63 messages) required large tables in the IMPs, the link mechanism was dropped. Sequence control was handled by sequence numbers between each source and destination IMP.

- Acknowledgments. Separate acknowledgment packets for successfully received packets generated extra network traffic. A 10 to 20 percent networkwide improvement was achieved by "piggybacking" acknowledgments on top of normal data packets.

Models presented in McQuillan, Crowther, Cosell, Walden, and Heart [1972] indicated that the above changes lead to:

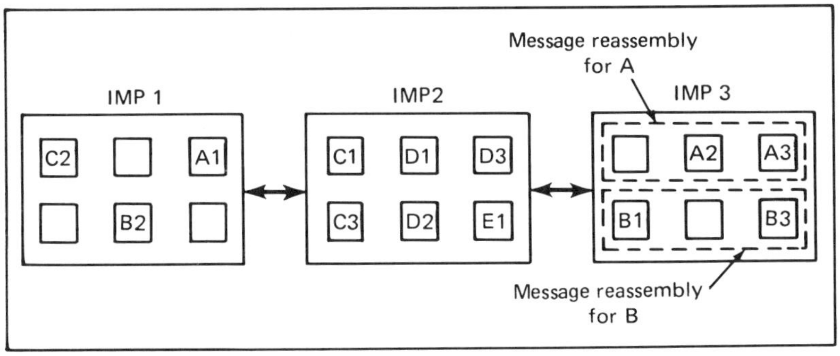

Fig. 12. Reassembly lockup in the ARPANET.

- Program processing time per packet decreased by 20 percent.

- Line throughput increased by 4 to 7 percent.

- IMP throughput increased by 17 to 21 percent.

- Line overhead on a full-length packet decreased from 29 percent to 16 percent. A 50-Kbit/s line can handle 43 full packets per second instead of the previous 38 full packets per second.

The following provisions were made in the original IMP definition to allow for gathering of statistics on network behavior [Kleinrock and Naylor, 1974]:

- A trace bit in each individual packet. Each traced packet was to create a message to the network measurement center (NMC) at UCLA containing the following time stamps: the arrival of the last bit of the packet, the placing of the packet on a queue, the start of transmission of the packet, and the receipt of an ACK.

- For a more macroscopic view of network behavior, accumulated statistics can be collected, including a histogram of message lengths, the number of messages from each host, the number of control messages, and channel statistics (e.g., the number of words sent, number of errors, and the number of times the free buffer list is empty).

- Snapshots of multiple IMPs at nearly the same time, including queue lengths and routing table information.

- Status reports sent to the Network Control Center (NCC) at BBN. These reports are sent each minute and include the up or down status of the host, the number of ACKS received, the number of packets entering from the host, the number of "I'm OK, you're OK" messages that failed to arrive, etc.

In August 1973 an experiment was conducted to collect data on the ARPANET. Table 3 summarizes the data reported in Klein-

Table 3 ARPANET Experiment
Week of Aug. 1–7, 1973

Total number of bits	6.3×10^9
Total number of messages	26×10^6
Average number of messages per second entering network	47
Messages	
Average number of packets per message	1.12
Average number of bits per message	243
Average packet length in bits	218
Overhead per packet in bits	168
Efficiency of buffer storage	18.4%
Average round-trip delay	93 ms
Average number of IMP hops per packet	3.31
Average path length between ARPA Network nodes	5.32

Packet traffic vs. path length

Hops	%
0	22
1	16
2	8
3	12
4	8
5	9
6–11	25

Site dependencies
  80% of traffic generated by the busiest $\frac{1}{3}$ of nodes
  90% of traffic between 12.6% of possible site pairs
  44% of traffic to a single favorite site (note: favorite site varies from node to node)

Average line utilization	
With overhead	.071
Without overhead	.0077
Maximum line utilization	.134

Error rate
  Average 1 per 12,880 packets
  Worst case 1 per 340 packets

Table 4   Network Reliability Summary

Month	Line outage	IMP down					Average host traffic		
		All causes*	Percent	Hardware/software		No. of nodes	Packets/day		
				MTBF, h	MTTR, h:min		Internode	Intranode	
September '77	0.12%	0.41%	0.11	805	0:52	58	6,978,967	2,254,913	
October	0.43%	0.63%	0.16	1,116	1:46	58	7,555,457	2,899,477	
November	0.49%	0.41%	0.06	1,368	0:50	58	7,926,677	3,379,314	
December	0.59%	0.38%	0.04	1,484	0:37	·59	7,485,728	3,712,888	
January'78	0.35%	0.43%	0.13	814	1:02	59	7,435,571	3,291,647	
February	0.21%	0.30%	0.09	1,053	0:59	59	7,619,331	3,277,811	
March	0.31%	0.37%	0.03	1,438	0:25	59	8,116,198	2,589,444	
April	0.19%	0.43%	0.18	773	1:25	60	8,315,295	1,903,111	
May	0.54%	0.51%	0.10	811	0:50	60	8,655,575	1,976,583	
June	0.17%	0.30%	0.10	1,062	1:06	60	8,297,662	1,815,891	

*Includes P.M., site environmental problems, retrofits, and other causes.

rock and Naylor [1974]. Up until that experiment, traffic on the ARPA Network had been growing exponentially from 10^5 packets a day in October 1971 to 4×10^6 packets a day in August 1973. Table 4 summarizes more recent network traffic.

Another experimental study of the ARPANET was conducted in May 1974 [Kleinrock, Naylor, and Opderbeck, 1976], focusing on determining network overhead. This second study also confirmed the gross network behavior of the August 1973 experiment.

Figure 13 indicates the number of bits added to each message for protocol and control at each level in the ARPA Network. The efficiency of the network (i.e., the number of data bits transmitted divided by the total number of bits transmitted) is a function of user traffic characteristics (whether it consists of a small number of large data files or a large number of small data files). Figure 14 depicts the measured data, indicating only 8.8 percent data and 91.2 percent overhead distributed among the various levels. Since the line utilization was low (6.73 percent), causing the background tasks to dominate the transmission, Kleinrock, Naylor, and Opderbeck projected the capacity distribution assuming a saturated network with the same traffic characteristics. The projection indicates that data increase to 23.4 percent and overhead decreases to 76.6 percent. Even though network protocols are

constantly evolving, the network designer should realize that a large portion of the network capacity will be devoted to network protocol and control.

Control of the ARPA Network was turned over to the Defense Communications Agency (DCA) in 1977.

The ALOHA Network

A development concurrent with the ARPA Network was the ALOHA Network, which became operative in 1970 at the University of Hawaii. Initially, the ALOHA Network was designed

Level	Function	Number of bits
Level — 2 Host	protocol	40
	control	93.5
Level — 1 Subnet	protocol	80
	control	64
Level — 0 Line	protocol	88
	control	16

Fig. 13. Number of bits required for protocol and control overhead in the ARPA Network.

Measured	(May 1974) [Kleinrock 1976]	Bits/sec/line	% of traffic	% of line capacity
	Level — 0 Line	444.08	13.2	0.89
	Level — 1 Subnet	308.00	9.1	0.62
	Level — 2 Host	158.72	4.7	0.32
	Background (routing, status reports, etc.)	2160.96	64.2	4.32
	Data	295.56	8.8	0.59
		3367.32	100.00	6.74
Projected				
	Level — 0 Line	17610.3		35.2
	Level — 1 Subnet	12213.95		24.4
	Level — 2 Host	6294.15		12.6
	Background (routing, status reports, etc.)	2160.96		4.3
	Data	11720.64		23.4
		50000.00		99.9

Fig. 14. Measured and projected overhead in the ARPA Network.

to provide remote terminal access to a centralized computing facility. Because of the local economics of leased common-carrier lines (telephone calls between different islands were charged at long-distance rates), an alternative interconnection approach was sought. The technology selected was packet switching via radio broadcast channels.

Two radio channels—a random-access channel for user-to-computer communication and a broadcast channel for computer-to-user communication—tie the remote terminals to the central site. A "Menehune" (Hawaiian for imp, hence Interface Message Processor, or IMP) receives the random-access channel packets for assembly for the Host. Packets are one-half (40 characters) or a whole (80 characters) terminal line in length. Individual terminals broadcast on the random-access channel whenever a line-terminating character is typed by the user. The error-check character in the packet is used not only to detect random-bit errors but also to detect errors in multiple simultaneous transmissions, which, with a high probability, will not produce a legal packet whose bits and error-check character match. If a terminal does not receive a positive ACK within a specified time, the terminal will retransmit the packet. Since the packet may not be acknowledged because of contention on the random-access channel, the terminals wait a randomly selected period before retransmitting to avoid endless contention for the random-access channel. The ALOHA Network is thus a contention network.

The Host returns information via the broadcast channel, to which all terminals are listening. Chapter 25 summarizes the design decisions and experiences with the ALOHA Network. Suggestions for improving the efficiency of the random-access channel are also considered. The random-access channel becomes clogged in high-traffic situations, since all packets are garbled due to contention and no packets are received intact. It has been calculated that the channel capacity (maximum throughput) of useful information is $1/2e$, or 0.184, for a pure ALOHA technique. A slotted ALOHA technique for satellite channels has been proposed in which transmission can be started only at discrete intervals. The channel capacity then rises to $1/e$, or 0.368.

Chapter 25 also suggests that the random-access and broadcast channels be combined. This not only saves radio hardware but also allows terminals to listen to the random-access channel and postpone transmission if the channel is busy. This may increase throughput by a factor of 3 to 5. This single-broadcast channel concept is employed in the ETHERNET.

ETHERNET

With the advent of cheap minicomputers, terminals, and intelligent terminals, there are more and more situations where a local network is required for intercommunication, resource sharing, and so forth. Further, because of the mobility of individuals and organizations, such a network has to be very flexible and easily modifiable.

The ETHERNET was evolved to solve these problems. It consists of stations interconnected with a passive broadcast medium, the ether. Based on the ALOHA Network packet-switching technology, computer network stations broadcast into the ether. All stations listen and the desired destination picks off the packet by recognizing its unique address. If the channel is in use, stations do not broadcast. Contention is detected by comparing what was placed on the ether to what the station hears from the ether. (Hence the ETHERNET is also a contention network.) If there is a mismatch, the station can abort the packet and try again later. This prevents the ALOHA Network's lengthy time out for lack of positive acknowledgment. Further, contentions are limited to a small window following the completion of the previous packet. Thus, in the limit for small packets, the channel capacity is that of the slotted ALOHA technique. For longer packets, channel capacity approaches 1.0, since contentions are so short.

In the case of high network load, the random retransmission time is lengthened to automatically adapt to congestion. It should be noted that the ETHERNET is only a line protocol, in that packets have only a high probability of successful delivery. Subnet- and Host-level protocols can be built on top of the ETHERNET protocol by the use of concepts such as positive acknowledgment on receipt of a packet. However, the ETHERNET does provide routing and flow-control functions which traditionally have appeared only at the higher levels of protocols.

Conclusions

As our dependency on computers grows, network technology will be even more important than it is today. Indeed, with the advent of the cheap microprocessor, structures that were once designed as a single logical entity (e.g., the disk controller) are actually a network of several microprocessors.

References

Aupperle [1973]; Doll [1974]; Everett, Zracket, and Benington [1957]; Falk and McQuillan [1977]; Greene and Pooch [1977]; Hargraves [1974]; IBM [1974]; Kleinrock and Naylor [1974]; Kleinrock, Naylor, and Opderbeck [1976]; Knight [1972]; McCalley and Barrett [1978]; McQuillan, Crowther, Cosell, Walden, and Heart [1972]; Roberts and Wessler [1970]; Schwartz [1977].

Chapter 24

The Interface Message Processor for the ARPA Computer Network[1]

F. E. Heart / R. E. Kahn / S. M. Ornstein /
W. R. Crowther / D. C. Walden

Introduction

For many years, small groups of computers have been interconnected in various ways. Only recently, however, has the interaction of computers and communications become an important topic in its own right.[2] In 1968, after considerable preliminary investigation and discussion, the Advanced Research Projects Agency of the Department of Defense (ARPA) embarked on the implementation of a new kind of nationwide computer interconnection known as the ARPA Network. This network will initially interconnect many dissimilar computers at ten ARPA-supported research centers with 50-kilobit common-carrier circuits. The network may be extended to include many other locations and circuits of higher bandwidth.

The primary goal of the ARPA project is to permit persons and programs at one research center to access data and use interactively programs that exist and run in other computers of the network. This goal may represent a major step down the path taken by computer time-sharing in the sense that the computer resources of the various research centers are thus pooled and directly accessible to the entire community of network participants.

Study of the technology and tariffs of available communications facilities showed that use of conventional *line switching* facilities would be economically and technically inefficient. The traditional method of routing information through the common-carrier switched network establishes a dedicated path for each conversation. With present technology, the time required for this task is on the order of seconds. For voice communication, that overhead time is negligible, but in the case of many short transmissions, such as may occur between computers, that time is excessive. Therefore, ARPA decided to build a new kind of digital communication system employing wideband leased lines and *message switching*, wherein a path is not established in advance and each

message carries an address. In this domain the project portends a possible major change in the character of data communication services in the United States.

In a nationwide computer network, economic considerations also mitigate against a wideband leased line configuration that is topologically fully connected. In a non-fully connected network, messages must normally traverse several network nodes in going from source to destination. The ARPA Network is designed on this principle and, at each node, a copy of the message is stored until it is safely received at the following node. The network is thus a store and forward system and as such must deal with problems of routing, buffering, synchronization, error control, reliability, and other related issues. To insulate the computer centers from these problems, and to insulate the network from the problems of the computer centers, ARPA decided to place identical small processors at each network node, to interconnect these small processors with leased common-carrier circuits to form a *subnet*, and to connect each research computer center into the net via the local small processor. In this arrangement the research computer centers are called *Hosts* and the small processors are called *Interface Message Processors*, or *IMPs*. (See Fig. 1.) This approach divides the genesis of the ARPA Network into two parts: (1) design and implementation of the IMP subnet, and (2) design

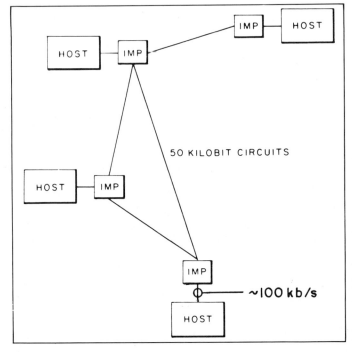

Fig. 1. Hosts and IMPs.

[1]*Proc. AFIPS SJCC*, 1970, pp. 551–567.
[2]A bibliography of relevant references is included at the end of this paper; a more extensive list may be found in Cuadra [1968].

and implementation of protocols and techniques for the sensible utilization of the network by the Hosts.

Implementation of the subnet involves two major technical activities: providing 50-kilobit common-carrier circuits and the associated modems; and providing IMPs, along with software and interfaces to modems and Host computers. For reasons of economic and political convenience, ARPA obtained common-carrier circuits directly through government purchasing channels; AT&T (Long Lines) is the central coordinator, although the General Telephone Company is participating at some sites and other common carriers may eventually become involved. In January 1969, Bolt Beranek and Newman Inc. (BBN) began work on the design and implementation of IMPs; a four-node test network was scheduled for completion by the end of 1969 and plans were formulated to include a total of ten sites by mid-1970. This paper discusses the design of the subnet and describes the hardware, the software, and the predicted performance of the IMP. The issues of Host-to-Host protocol and network utilization are barely touched upon; these problems are currently being considered by the participating Hosts and may be expected to be a subject of technical interest for many years to come.

At this time, in late 1969, the test network has become an operating reality. IMPs have already been installed at four sites, and implementation of IMPs for six additional sites is proceeding. The common carriers have installed 50-kilobit leased service connecting the first four sites and are preparing to install circuits at six additional sites.

The design of the network allows for the connection of additional Host sites. A map of a projected eleven-node network is shown in Fig. 2. The connections between the first four sites are indicated by solid lines. Dotted lines indicate planned connections.

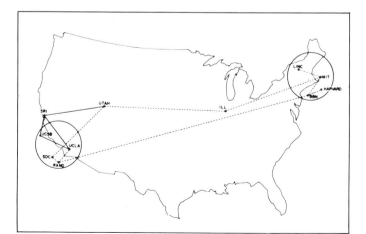

Fig. 2. Network map (from the ARPANET Directory).

Network Design

The design of the network is discussed in two parts. The first part concerns the relations between the Hosts and the subnet, and the second part concerns the design of the subnet itself.

Host-Subnet Considerations

The basic notion of a subnet leads directly to a series of questions about the relationship between the Hosts and the subnet: What tasks shall be performed by each? What constraints shall each place on the other? What dependence shall the subnet have on the Hosts? In considering these questions, we were guided by the following principles: (1) The subnet should function as a *communications system* whose essential task is to transfer bits reliably from a source location to a specified destination. Bit transmission should be sufficiently reliable and error free to obviate the need for special precautions (such as storage for retransmission) on the part of the Hosts; (2) The average transit time through the subnet should be under a half second to provide for convenient interactive use of remote computers; (3) The subnet operation should be completely autonomous. Since the subnet must function as a store and forward system, an IMP must not be dependent upon its local Host. The IMP must continue to operate whether the Host is functioning properly or not and must not depend upon a Host for buffer storage or other logical assistance such as program reloading. The Host computer must not in any way be able to change the logical characteristics of the subnet; this restriction avoids the mischievous or inadvertent modification of the communication system by an individual Host user; (4) Establishment of Host-to-Host protocol and the enormous problem of planning to communicate between different computers should be an issue separated from the subnet design.

Messages, Links, and RFNMs   In principle, a single transmission from one Host to another may range from a few bits, as with a single teletype character, up to arbitrarily many bits, as in a very long file. Because of buffering limitations in the subnet, an upper limit was placed on the size of an individual Host transmission; 8095 bits was chosen for the maximum transmission size. This Host unit of transmission is called a *message*. The subnet does not impose any pattern restrictions on messages; binary text may be transmitted. Messages may be of variable length; thus, a source Host must indicate the end of a message to the subnet.

A major hazard in a message switched network is congestion, which can arise either due to system failures or to peak traffic flow. Congestion typically occurs when a destination IMP becomes flooded with incoming messages for its Host. If the flow of messages to this destination is not regulated, the congestion will back up into the network, affecting other IMPs and degrading or even completely clogging the communication service. To solve this problem we developed a quenching scheme that limits the flow of messages to a given destination when congestion begins to occur or, more generally, when messages are simply not getting through.

The subnet transmits messages over unidirectional logical paths between Hosts known as *links*. (A link is a conceptual path that has no physical reality; the term merely identifies a message sequence.) The subnet accepts only one message at a time on a given link. Ensuing messages on that link will be blocked from entering the subnet until the source IMP learns that the previous message has arrived at the destination Host. When a link becomes unblocked, the subnet notifies the source Host by sending it a special control message known as *Ready for Next Message* (or RFNM), which identifies the newly unblocked link. The source Host may utilize its connection into the subnet to transmit messages over other links, while waiting to send messages on the blocked links. Up to 63 separate outgoing links may exist at any Host site. When giving the subnet a message, the Host specifies the destination Host and a link number in the first 32 bits of the message (known as the *leader*). The IMPs then attend to route selection, delivery, and notification of receipt. This use of links and RFNMs also provides for IMP-to-Host delivery of sequences of messages in proper order. Because the subnet allows only one message at a time on a given link, Hosts never receive messages out of sequence.

Host-IMP Interfacing   Each IMP will initially service a single Host. However, we have made provision (both in the hardware and software) for the IMP to service up to four Hosts, with a corresponding reduction in the number of permitted phone line connections. Connecting an IMP to a wide variety of different Hosts requires a hardware interface, some part of which must be custom tailored to each Host. We decided, therefore, to partition the interface such that a standard portion would be built into the IMP, and would be identical for all Hosts, while a special portion of the interface would be unique to each Host. The interface is designed to allow messages to flow in both directions at once. A bit serial interface was designed partly because it required fewer lines for electrical interfacing and was, therefore, less expensive, and partly to accommodate conveniently the variety of word lengths in the different Host computers. The bit rate requirement on the Host line is sufficiently low that parallel transfers are not necessary.

The Host interface operates asynchronously, each data bit being passed across the interface via a *Ready For Next Bit/There's Your Bit* handshake procedure. This technique permits the bit rate to adjust to the rate of the slower member of the pair and allows necessary interruptions, when words must be stored into or retrieved from memory. The IMP introduces between bits a (manually) adjustable delay that limits the maximum data rate; at

present, this delay is set to 10 μsec. Any delay introduced by the Host in the handshake procedure further slows the rate.

System Failure   Considerable attention has been given to the possible effects on a Host of system failures in the subnet. Minor system failures (e.g., temporary line failures) will appear to the Hosts only in the form of reduced rate of service. Catastrophic failures may, however, result in the loss of messages or even in the loss of subnet communication. IMPs inform a Host of all relevant system failures. Additionally, should a Host computer go down, the information is propagated throughout the subnet to all IMPs so they may notify their local Host if it attempts to send a message to that Host.

Specific Subnet Design

The overriding consideration that guided the subnet design was reliability. Each IMP must operate unattended and reliably over long periods with minimal down time for maintenance and repair. We were convinced that it was important for each IMP in the subnet to operate autonomously, not only independently of Hosts, but insofar as possible from other IMPs as well; any dependency between one IMP and another would merely broaden the area jeopardized by one IMP's failure. The need for reliability and autonomy bears directly upon the form of subnet communication. This section describes the process of message communication within the subnet.

Message Handling   Hosts communicate with each other via a sequence of messages. An IMP takes in a message from its Host computer in segments, forms these segments into *packets* (whose maximum size is approximately 1000 bits), and ships the packets separately into the network. The destination IMP reassembles the packets and delivers them in sequence to the receiving Host, who obtains them as a single unit. This segmentation of a message during transmission is completely invisible to the Host computers. Figures 3, 4, and 5 illustrate aspects of message handling.

The transmitting Host attaches an identifying leader to the beginning of each message. The IMP forms a *header* by adding further information for network use and attaches this header to each packet of the message.

Each packet is individually routed from IMP-to-IMP through the network toward the destination. At each IMP along the way, the transmitting hardware generates initial and terminal framing characters and parity check digits that are shipped with the packet and are used for error detection by the receiving hardware of the next IMP.

Errors in transmission can affect a packet by destroying the framing and/or by modifying the data content. If the framing is disturbed in any way, the packet either will not be recognized or will be rejected by the receiver. In addition, the check digits

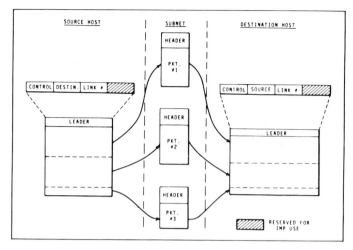

Fig. 3. Messages and packets.

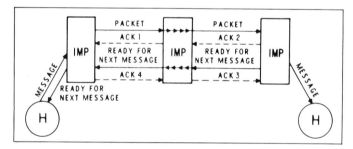

Fig. 4. RFNMs and acknowledgments.

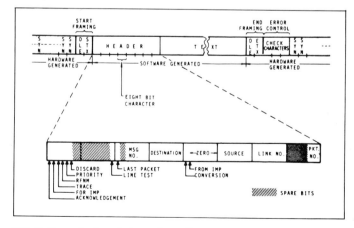

Fig. 5. Format of packet on phone line.

provide protection against errors that affect only the data. The check digits can detect all patterns of four or fewer errors occurring within a packet, and any single error burst of a length less than twenty-four bits. An overwhelming majority of all other possible errors (all but about one in 2^{24}) are also detected. Thus, the mean time between undetected errors in the subnet should be on the order of years.

As a packet moves through the subnet, each IMP stores the packet until a positive acknowledgment is returned from the succeeding IMP. This acknowledgment indicates that the message was received without error and was accepted. Once an IMP has accepted a packet and returned a positive acknowledgment, it holds onto that packet tenaciously until it in turn receives an acknowledgment from the succeeding IMP. Under no circumstances (except for Host or IMP malfunction) will an IMP discard a packet after it has generated a positive acknowledgment. However, an IMP is always free to refuse a packet by simply not returning a positive acknowledgment. It may do this for any of several reasons: the packet may have been received in error, the IMP may be busy, the IMP buffer storage may be temporarily full, etc.

At the transmitting IMP, such discard of a packet is readily detected by the absence of a returned acknowledgment within a reasonable time interval (e.g., 100 msec). Such packets are retransmitted, perhaps along a different route. Acknowledgments themselves are not acknowledged, although they are error checked in the usual fashion. Loss of an acknowledgment results in the eventual retransmission of the packet; the destination IMP sorts out the resulting duplication by using a message number and a packet number in the header.

The packets of a message arrive at the destination IMP, possibly out of order, where they are reassembled. The header is then stripped off each packet and a leader, identifying the source Host and the link, followed by the reassembled message is then delivered to the destination Host as a single unit. See Fig. 3.

Routing Algorithm   The routing algorithm directs each packet to its destination along a path for which the total estimated transit time is smallest. This path is not determined in advance. Instead, each IMP individually decides onto which of its output lines to transmit a packet addressed to another destination. This selection is made by a fast and simple table lookup procedure. For each possible destination, an entry in the table designates the appropriate next leg. These entries reflect line or IMP trouble, traffic congestion, and current subnet connectivity. This routing table is updated every half second as follows:

Each IMP estimates the delay it expects a packet to encounter in reaching every possible destination over each of its output lines. It selects the minimum delay estimate for each destination and periodically (about twice a second) passes these estimates to its immediate neighbors. Each IMP then constructs its own routing table by combining its neighbors' estimates with its own estimates of the delay to that neighbor. The estimated delay to each neighbor is based upon both queue lengths and the recent performance of the connecting communication circuit. For each destination, the table is then made to specify that selected output line for which the sum of the estimated delay to the neighbor plus the neighbor's delay to the destination is smallest.

The routing table is consistently and dynamically updated to adjust for changing conditions in the network. The system is adaptive to the ups and downs of lines, IMPs, and congestion; *it does not require the IMP to know the topology of the network*. In particular, an IMP need not even know the identity of its immediate neighbors. Thus, the leased circuits could be reconfigured to a new topology without requiring any changes to the IMPs.

Subnet Failures   The network is designed to be largely invulnerable to circuit or IMP failure as well as to outages for maintenance. Special status and test messages are employed to help cope with various failures. In the absence of regular packets for transmission over a line, the IMP program transmits special *hello* packets at half-second intervals. The acknowledgment for a hello packet is an *I heard you* packet.

A *dead line* is defined by the sustained absence (approximately 2.5 seconds) on that line of either received regular packets or acknowledgments; no regular packets will be routed into a dead line, and any packets awaiting transmission will be rerouted. Routing tables in the network are adjusted automatically to reflect the loss. We require acknowledgment of thirty consecutive *hello* packets (an event which consumes at least 15 seconds), before a dead line is defined to be alive once again.

A dead line may reflect trouble either in the communication facilities or in the neighboring IMP itself. Normal line errors caused by dropouts, impulse noise, or other conditions should not result in a dead line, because such errors typically last only a few miliseconds, and only occasionally as long as a few tenths of a second. Therefore, we expect that a line will be defined as dead only when serious trouble conditions occur. If dead lines eliminate all routes between two IMPs, the IMPs are said to be *disconnected* and each of these IMPs will discard messages destined for the other. Disconnected IMPs cannot be rapidly detected from the delay estimates that arrive from neighboring IMPs. Consequently, additional information is transmitted between neighboring IMPs to help detect this condition. Each IMP transmits to its neighbors the length of the shortest existing path (i.e., number of IMPs) from itself to each destination. To the smallest such received number per destination, the IMP adds one. This incremented number is the length of the shortest path from that IMP to the destination. If the length ever exceeds the number of network nodes, the destination IMP is assumed to be unreachable and therefore disconnected.

Messages intended for dead Hosts (which are not the same as dead IMPs) cannot be delivered; therefore, these messages require special handling to avoid indefinite circulation in the network and spurious arrival at a later time. Such messages are purged from the network either at the source IMP or at the destination IMP. Dead Host information is regularly transmitted with the routing information. A Host computer is notified about another dead Host only when attempting to send a message to that Host.

An IMP may detect a major failure in one of three ways: (1) A packet expected for reassembly of a multiple packet message does not arrive. If a message is not fully reassembled in 15 minutes, the system presumes a failure. The message is discarded by the destination IMP and both the source IMP and the source Host are notified via a special RFNM. (2) The Host does not take a message from its IMP. If the Host has not taken a message after 15 minutes, the system presumes that it will never take the message. Therefore, as in the previous case, the message is discarded and a special RFNM is returned to the source Host. (3) A link is never unblocked. If a link remains blocked for longer than 20 minutes, the system again presumes a failure; the link is then unblocked and an error message is sent to the source Host. (This last time interval is slightly longer than the others so that the failure mechanisms for the first two situations will have a chance to operate and unblock the link.)

Reliability and Recovery Procedures   For higher system reliability, special attention was placed on intrinsic reliability, hardware test capabilities, hardware/software failure recovery techniques, and proper administrative mechanisms for failure management.

To improve intrinsic reliability, we decided to ruggedize the IMP hardware, thus incurring an approximately ten percent hardware cost penalty. For ease in maintenance, debugging, program revision, and analysis of performance, all IMPs are as similar as possible; the operational program and the hardware are nearly identical in all IMPs.

To improve hardware test capabilities, we built special *cross-patching* features into the IMP's interface hardware; these features allow program-controlled connection of output lines to corresponding input lines. These crosspatching features have been invaluable in testing IMPs before and during field installation, and they should continue to be very useful when troubles occur in the operating network. These hardware test features are employed by a special hardware test program and may also be employed by the operational program when a line difficulty occurs.

The IMP includes a 512-word block of protected memory that secures special recovery programs. An IMP can recover from an IMP failure in two ways: (1) In the event of power failure, a power-fail interrupt permits the IMP to reach a clean stop before the program is destroyed. When power returns, a special automatic restart feature turns the IMP back on and restarts the program. (We considered several possibilities for handling the packets found in an IMP during a power failure and concluded that no plan to salvage the packets was both practical and foolproof. For example, we cannot know whether the packet in transmission at the time of failure successfully left the machine before the power failed. Therefore, we decided simply to discard all the packets and restart the program.) (2) The second recovery mechanism is a "watchdog timer," which transfers control to protected memory whenever the program neglects this timer for about one minute. In the event of such transfer, the program in unprotected memory is presumed to be destroyed (either through a hardware transient or a software failure). The program in protected memory sends a reload request down a phone line *selected at random*. The neighboring IMP responds by sending a copy of its whole program back on the phone line. A normal IMP would discard this message because it is too long, but the recovering IMP can use it to reload its program.

Everything unique to a particular IMP must thus reside in its protected memory. Only one register (containing the IMP number) currently differs from IMP-to-IMP. The process of reloading, which requires a few seconds, can be tried repeatedly until successful; however, if after several minutes the program has not resumed operation, a later phase of the watchdog timer shuts off all power to the IMP.

In addition to providing recovery mechanisms for both network and IMP failures, we have incorporated into the subnet a *control center* that monitors network status and handles trouble reports. The control center, located at a network node, initiates and follows up any corrective actions necessary for proper subnet functioning. Furthermore, this center controls and schedules any modifications to the subnet.

Introspection Because the network is experimental in nature, considerable effort has been allocated to developing tools whereby the network can supply measures of its own performance. The operational IMP program is capable of taking statistics on its own performance on a regular basis; this function may be turned on and off remotely. The various kinds of resulting statistics, which are sent via the network to a selected Host for analysis, include "snapshots," ten-second summaries and packet arrival times. Snapshots are summaries of the internal status of queue lengths and routing information. A synchronization procedure allows these snapshots, which are taken every half second, to occur at roughly the same time in all network IMPs; a Host receiving such snapshot messages could presumably build up an instantaneous picture of overall network status. Ten-second summaries include such IMP-generated statistics as the number of processed messages of each kind, the number of retransmissions, the traffic to and from the local Host, and so forth; this statistical data is sent to a

selected Host every ten seconds. In addition, a record of actual packet arrival times on modem lines allows for the modeling of line traffic. (As part of its research activity, the group at UCLA is acting as a network measurement center; thus, statistics for analysis will normally be routed to the UCLA Host.)

Perhaps the most powerful capability for network introspection is *tracing*. Any Host message sent into the network may have a "trace bit" set in the leader. Whenever it processes a packet from such a message, the IMP keeps special records of what happens to that packet—e.g., how long the packet is on various queues, when it comes in and leaves, etc. Each IMP that handles the traced packet generates special trace report messages that are sent to a specified Host; thus, a complete analysis of what has happened to that message can be made. When used in an orderly way, this tracing facility will aid in understanding at a very detailed level the behavior of routing algorithms and the behavior of the network under changing load conditions.

Flexibility Flexibility for modifications in IMP usage has been provided by several built-in arrangements: (1) provision within the existing cabinet for an additional 4K core bank; (2) modularity of the hardware interfaces; (3) provision for operation with data circuits of widely different rates; (4) a program organization involving many nearly self-contained subprograms in the IMP program structure.

This last aspect of flexibility presents a somewhat controversial design choice. There are many advantages to keeping all IMP software nearly identical. Because of the experimental nature of the network, however, we do not yet know whether this luxury of identical programs will be an optimal arrangement. Several potential applications of "Host-unique" IMP software have been considered—e.g., using ASCII conversion routines in each IMP to establish a "Network ASCII" and possibly to simplify the protocol problems of each Host. As of now, the operational IMP program includes a *structure* that permits unique software plug-in packages at each Host site, but no plug-ins have yet been constructed.

The Hardware

We selected a Honeywell DDP-516 for the IMP processor because we wanted a machine that could easily handle currently anticipated maximum traffic and that had already been proven in the field. We considered only economic machines with fast cycle times and good instruction sets. Furthermore, we needed a machine with a particularly good I/O capability and that was available in a ruggedized version. The geographical proximity of the supplier to BBN was also a consideration.

The basic machine has a 16-bit word length and a 0.96-μsec memory cycle. The IMP version is packaged in a single cabinet, and includes a 12K memory, a set of 16 multiplexed channels (which implement a 4-cycle data break), a set of 16 priority interrupts, a 100-μsec clock, and a set of programmable status lights. Also packaged within this cabinet are special modular interfaces for connecting the IMP to phone line modems and to Host computers; these interfaces use the same kind of 1 MHz and 5 MHz DTL packs from which the main machine is constructed. In addition, a number of features that have been incorporated make the IMP somewhat resilient to a variety of failures.

Teletypes and high-speed paper tape readers which are attached to the IMPs are used only for maintenance, debugging, and system modification; in normal operation, the IMP runs without any moving parts except fans. Within the cabinet, space has been reserved for an additional 4K memory. Figure 6 is a picture of an IMP, and Figure 7 shows its configuration.

Ruggedization of computer hardware for use in friendly environments is somewhat unusual; however, we felt that the considerable difficulty that IMP failures can cause the network justified this step. Although the ruggedized unit is not fully "qualified" to MIL specs, it does have greater resistance to temperature variance, mechanical shock and vibration, radio frequency inter-

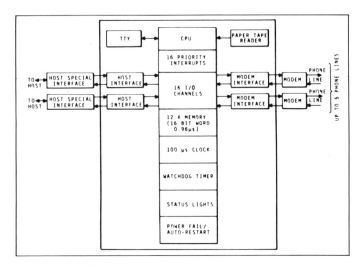

Fig. 7. IMP configuration.

ference, and power line noise. We are confident that this ruggedization will increase the mean time to failure.

Modular Host and modem interfaces allow an IMP to be individually configured for each network node. The modularity, however, does not take the form of pluggable units and, except for the possibility of adding interfaces into reserved frame space, reconfiguration is impractical. Various configurations allow for up to two Hosts and five modems, three Hosts and four modems, etc. Each modem interface requires approximately one-fourth the amount of logic used in the C.P.U. The Host interface is somewhat smaller (about one-sixth of the C.P.U.).

Interfaces to the Host and to the modems have certain common characteristics. Both are full duplex, both may be crosspatched under program control to test their operation, and both function in the same general manner. To send a packet, the IMP program sets up memory pointers to the packet and then activates the interface via a programmable control pulse. The interface takes successive words from the memory using its assigned output data channel and transmits them bit-serially (to the Host or to the modem). When the memory buffer has thus been emptied, the interface notifies the program via an interrupt that the job has been completed. To receive information, the program first sets pointers to the allocated space in the memory into which the information is to flow. Using a control pulse it then readies the interface to receive. When information starts to arrive (here again bit-serially), it is assembled into 10-bit words and stored into the IMP memory. When either the allocated memory space is full or the end of the data train is detected, the interface notifies the program via an interrupt.

The modem interfaces deal with the phone lines in terms of 8-bit characters; the interfaces idle by sending and receiving a

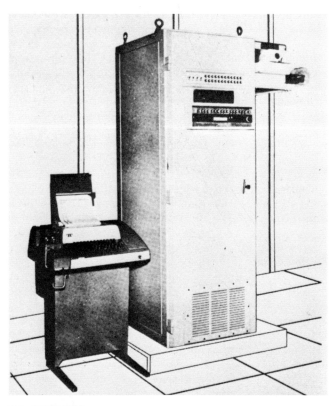

Fig. 6. The IMP.

sync pattern that keeps them in character sync. Bit sync is maintained by the modems themselves, which provide both transmit and receive clocking signals to the interfaces. When the program initiates transmission, the hardware first transmits a pair of initial framing characters (DLE, STX). Next, the text of the packet is taken word by word from the memory and shifted serially onto the phone line. At the end of the data, the hardware generates a pair of terminal framing characters (DLE, ETX) and shifts them onto the phone line. After the terminal framing characters, the hardware generates and transmits 24 check bits. Finally, the interface returns to idle (sync) mode.

The hardware doubles any DLE characters within the binary data train (that is, transmits them twice), thereby permitting the receiving interface hardware to distinguish them from the terminal framing characters and to remove the duplicate. Transmitted packets are of a known maximum size; therefore, any overflow of input buffer length is evidence of erroneous transmission. Format errors in the framing also register as errors. Check bits are computed from the received data and compared with the received check bits to detect errors in the text. Any of these errors set a flag and cause a program interrupt. Before processing a packet, the program checks the error flag to determine whether the packet was received correctly.

IMP Software

Implementation of the IMPs required the development of a sophisticated operational computer program and the development of several auxiliary programs for hardware tests, program construction, and debugging. This section discusses in detail the design of the operational program and briefly describes the auxiliary software.

Operational Program

The principal function of the operational program is the processing of packets. This processing includes segmentation of Host messages into packets for routing and transmission, building of headers, receiving, routing and transmitting of store and forward packets, retransmitting of unacknowledged packets, reassembling received packets into messages for transmission to the Host, and generating of RFNMs and acknowledgments. The program also monitors network status, gathers statistics, and performs on-line testing. This real-time program is an efficient, interrupt-driven, involute machine language program that occupies about 6000 words of memory. It was designed, constructed, and debugged over a period of about a year by three programmers.

The entire program is composed of twelve functionally distinct pieces; each piece occupies no more than one or two pages of core

(512 words per page). These programs communicate primarily through common registers that reside in page zero of the machine and that are directly addressable from all pages of memory. A map of core storage is shown in Fig. 8. Seven of the twelve programs are directly involved in the flow of packets through the IMP: the *task* program performs the major portion of the packet processing, including the reassembly of Host messages; the *modem* programs (IMP-to-Modem and Modem-to-IMP) handle interrupts and resetting of buffers for the modem channels; the *Host* programs (IMP-to-Host and Host-to-IMP) handle interrupts and resetting of buffers for the Host channels, build packet headers during input, and construct RFNMs that are returned to the source Host during output; the *time-out* program maintains a software clock, times out unacknowledged packets for retransmission, and attends to infrequent events; the *link* program assigns and verifies message numbers and keeps track of links. A background loop contains the remaining five programs and deals with initialization, debugging,

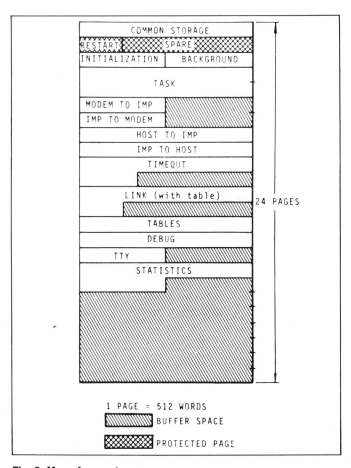

Fig. 8. Map of core storage.

testing, statistics gathering and tracing. After a brief description of data structures, we will discuss packet processing in some detail.

Buffer Allocation, Queues, and Tables   The major system data structures (see Table 1) consist of buffers and tables. The buffer-storage space is partitioned into about 70 fixed length buffers, each of which is used for storing a single packet. An unused buffer is chained onto a free buffer list and is removed from this list when it is needed to store an incoming packet. A packet, once stored in a buffer, is never moved. After a packet has been successfully passed along to its Host or to another IMP, its buffer is returned to the free list. The buffer space is partitioned in such a way that each process (store and forward traffic, Host traffic, etc.) is always guaranteed some buffers. For the sake of program speed and simplicity, no attempt is made to retrieve the space wasted by partially filled buffers.

In handling store and forward traffic, all processing is on a per packet basis. Further, although traffic to and from Hosts is composed of *messages*, the IMP rapidly converts to dealing with packets; the Host transmits a message as a single unit but the IMP takes it one buffer at a time. As each buffer is filled, the program selects another buffer for input until the entire message has been provided for. These successive buffers will, in general, be scattered throughout the memory. An equivalent inverse process occurs on output to the Host after all packets of the message have arrived at the destination IMP. No attempt is ever made to collect the packets of a message into a contiguous portion of the memory.

Buffers currently in use are either dedicated to an incoming or an outgoing packet, chained on a queue awaiting processing by the program, or being processed. Occasionally, a buffer may be simultaneously found on two queues; this situation can occur when a packet is waiting on one queue to be forwarded and on another to be acknowledged.

There are four principal types of queues:

Task: Packets received on Host channels are placed on the Host task queue. All received acknowledgments, dead Host and routing information, *I heard you* and *hello* packets are placed on the system task queue; all other packets from the modems are placed on the modem task queue. The program services the system task queue first, then the Host task queue, and finally the modem task queue.

Table 1   Program Data Structures

5000 words—message buffer storage
120 words—queue pointers
300 words—trace blocks
100 words—reassembly blocks
150 words—routing tables
400 words—link tables
300 words—statistics tables

Output: A separate output queue is constructed for each modem channel and each Host channel. Each modem output queue is subdivided into an acknowledgment queue, a priority queue, a RFNM queue, and a regular message queue, which are serviced in that order. Each Host output queue is subdivided into a control message queue, a priority queue, and a regular message queue, which are also serviced in the indicated order.

Sent: A separate queue for each modem channel contains packets that have already been transmitted on that line but for which no acknowledgment has yet been received.

Reassembly: The reassembly queue contains those packets that are being reassembled into messages for the Host.

Tables in core are allocated for the storage of queue pointers, for trace blocks, for reassembly information, for statistics, and for links. Most noteworthy of these is the link table, which is used at the source IMP for assignment of message numbers and for blocking and unblocking links, and at the destination IMP to verify message numbers for sequence control.

Packet Flow and Program Structure   Figure 9 is a schematic drawing of packet processing; the processing programs are described below.

The *Host-to-IMP* routine (H → I) handles messages being transmitted from the local site. The routine uses the leader to construct a header that is prefixed to each packet of the message. It also creates a link for the message if necessary, blocks the link, puts the packets of the message on the Host task queue for further processing by the task routine, and triggers the programmable task interrupt. The routine then acquires a free buffer and sets up a new input. The routine tests a hardware trouble indicator,

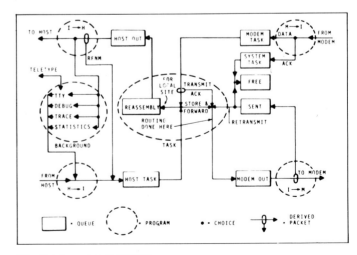

Fig. 9. Internal packet flow.

verifies the message format, and checks whether or not the destination is dead, the link table is full, or the link blocked. The routine is serially reentrant and services all Hosts connected to the IMP.

The *Modem-to-IMP* routine (M → I) handles inputs from the modems. This routine consists of several identical routines, one for each modem channel. (Such duplication is useful to obtain higher speed.) This routine sets up an input buffer (normally obtained from the free list), places the received packet on the appropriate task queue, and triggers the programmable task interrupt. Should no free buffers be available for input, the buffer at the head of the modem task queue is preempted. If the modem task queue is also empty, the received packet is discarded by setting up its buffer for input. However, a sufficient number of free buffers are specifically reserved to assure that received acknowledgments, routing packets, and the like are rarely discarded.

The *task routine* uses the header information to direct packets to their proper destination. The task routine is driven by the task interrupt, which is set whenever a packet is put on a task queue. The task routine routes packets from the Host task queue onto an output queue determined from the routing algorithm.

For each packet on the modem task queue, the task routine first determines whether sufficient buffer space is available. If the IMP has a shortage of store and forward buffers, the buffers on the modem task queue are simply returned to the free list without further processing. Normally, however, an acknowledgment packet is constructed and put near the front of the appropriate modem output queue. The destination of the packet is then inspected. If the packet is not for the local site, the routing algorithm selects a modem output queue for the packet. If a packet for the local site is a RFNM, the corresponding link is unblocked and the RFNM is put on a queue to the Host. If the packet is not a RFNM, it is joined with others of the same message on the reassembly queue. Whenver a message is completely reassembled, the packets of the message are put on an output queue to the Host for processing by the IMP-to-Host routine.

In processing the system task queue, the task routine returns to the free list those buffers from the sent queue that have been referenced by acknowledgments. Any packets skipped over by an acknowledgment are designated for retransmission. Routing, *I heard you*, and *hello* packets are processed in a straightforward fashion.

The *IMP-to-Modem* routine (I → M) transmits successful packets from the Modem output queue. After completing the output, this routine places any packet requiring acknowledgment on the sent queue.

The *IMP-to-Host* routine (I → H) sets up successive outputs of packets on the Host output queues and constructs a RFNM for each non-control message delivered to a Host. RFNM packets are returned to the system via the Host task queue.

The *time-out* routine is started every 25.6 msec (called the time-out period) by a clock interrupt. The routine has three sections: the fast time-out routine, which "wakes up" any Host or modem interrupt routine that has languished (for example, when the Host input could not immediately start a new input because of a shortage in buffer space); the middle time-out routine, which retransmits any packets that have been too long on a modem sent queue; and the slow time-out routine, which marks lines as alive or dead, updates the routing tables and does long term garbage collection of queues and other data structures. (For example, it protects the system from the cumulative effect of such failures as a lost packet of a multiple packet message, where buffers are tied up in message reassembly.) It also deletes links automatically after 15 seconds of disuse, after 20 minutes of blocking, or when an IMP goes down.

These three routines are executed in the following pattern:

$$\text{FFFF} \quad \text{FFFF} \quad \text{FFFF} \quad \text{FFFF} \quad \text{FFFF} \quad \text{FFFF} \quad \dots$$
$$\quad \text{M} \qquad \text{M} \qquad \text{M} \qquad \text{M} \qquad \quad \text{M}$$
$$\qquad \qquad \qquad \qquad \qquad \quad \text{S}$$

and, although they run off a common interrupt, are constructed to allow faster routines to interrupt slower ones should a slower routine not complete execution before the next time-out period.

The *link* routine enters, examines, and deletes entries from the link table. A table containing a separate message number entry for many links to every possible Host would be prohibitively large. Therefore, the table contains entries only for each of 63 total outgoing links at any Host site. Hashing is used to speed accessing of this table, but the link program is still quite costly; it uses about ten percent of both speed and space in a conceptually trivial task.

Initialization and Background Loop   The IMP program starts in an initialization section that builds the initial data structures, prepares for inputs from modem and Host channels, and resets all program switches to their nominal state. The program then falls into the background loop, which is an endlessly repeated series of low-priority subroutines that are interrupted to handle normal traffic.

The programs in the IMP background loop perform a variety of functions: TTY is used to handle the IMP Teletype traffic; DEBUG, to inspect or change IMP core memory; TRACE, to transmit collected information about traced packets; STATISTICS, to take and transmit network and IMP statistics; PARAMETER-CHANGE, to alter the values of selected IMP parameters; and DISCARD, to throw away packets. Selected Hosts and IMPs, particularly the Network Measurement Center and the Network Control Center, will find it necessary or useful to communicate with one or more of these background loop programs. So that these programs may send and receive messages from the network, they are treated as "fake Hosts." Rather than duplicating portions of the large IMP-to-Host and Host-to-IMP routines, the background loop programs are treated as if they were Hosts, and they can thereby utilize existing programs. The "For IMP" bit or the "From IMP" bit in the leader indicates that a given message is for or from a fake Host program in the IMP. Almost all of the background loop is devoted to running these programs.

The TTY program assembles characters from the Teletype into network messages and decodes network messages into characters for the Teletype; TTY's normal message destination is the DEBUG program at its own IMP; however, TTY can be made to communicate with any other IMP Teletype, any other IMP DEBUG program or any Host program with compatible format.

The DEBUG program permits the operational program to be inspected and changed. Although its normal message source is the TTY program at its own IMP, DEBUG will respond to a message of the correct format from any source. This program is normally inhibited from changing the operational IMP program; local operator intervention is required to activate the program's full power.

The STATISTICS program collects measurements about network operation and periodically transmits them to the Network Measurement Center. This program sends but does not receive messages. STATISTICS has a mechanism for collecting measurements over 10-second intervals and for taking half-second snapshots of IMP queue lengths and routing tables. It can also generate artificial traffic to load the network. When turned on, STATISTICS uses 10 to 20 percent of the machine capacity and generates a noticeable amount of phone line traffic.

Other programs in the background loop drive local status lights and operate the parameter change routine. A thirty-two word parameter table controls the operation of the TRACE and STATISTICS programs and includes spares for expansion; the PARAMETER-CHANGE program accepts messages that change these parameters.

Control Organization.   It is characteristic of the IMP system that many of the main programs are entered both as subroutine calls from other programs and as interrupt calls from the hardware. The resulting control structure is shown in Fig. 10. The programs are arranged in a priority order; control passes upward in the chain whenever a hardware interrupt occurs or the current program decides that the time has come to run a higher priority program, and control passes downward only when the higher priority programs are finished. No program may execute either itself or a lower priority program; however, a program may freely execute a higher priority program. This rule is similar to the usual rules concerning priority interrupt routines.

In one important case, however, control must pass from a higher priority program to a lower priority program—namely, from the several input routines to the TASK routine. For this special case, the computer hardware was modified to include a low-priority hardware interrupt that *can be set by the program.* When this interrupt has been honored (i.e., when all other

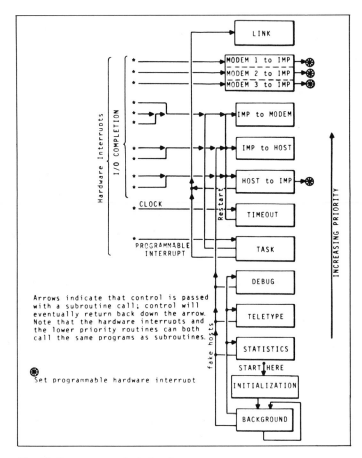

Fig. 10. Program control structure.

interrupts have been serviced), the TASK routine is executed. Thus, control is directed where needed without violating the priority rules.

Some routines must occasionally wait for long intervals of time, for example, when the Host-to-IMP routine must wait for a link to unblock. Stopping the whole system would be intolerable; therefore, should the need arise, such a routine is dismissed, and the TIMEOUT routine will later transfer control to the waiting routine.

The control structure and the partition of responsibility among various programs achieve the following timing goals:

1   No program stops or delays the system while waiting for an event.

2   The program gracefully adjusts to the situation where the machine becomes compute-bound.

3   The Modem-to-IMP routine can deliver its current packet

to the TASK routine before the next packet arrives and can always prepare for successive packet inputs on each line. This timing is critical because a slight delay here might require retransmission of the entire packet. To achieve this result, separate routines (one per phone line) interrupt each other freely after new buffers have been set up.

4 The program will almost always deliver packets waiting to be sent as fast as they can be accepted by the phone line.

5 Necessary periodic processes (in the time-out routine) are always permitted to run, and do not interfere with input-output processes.

Support-Software

Designing a real-time program for a small computer with many high rate I/O channels is a specialized kind of software problem. The operational program requires not only unusual techniques but also extra software tools; often the importance of such extra tools is not recognized. Further, even when these issues are recognized, the effort needed to construct such tools may be seriously underestimated. The development of the IMP system required the following kinds of supporting software:

1 Programs to test the hardware.

2 Tools to help debug the system.

3 A Host simulator.

4 An efficient assembly process.

So far, three hardware test programs have been developed. The first and largest is a complete program for testing all the special hardware features in the IMP. This program permits running any or all of the modem interfaces in a crosspatched mode; it even permits operating together *several* IMPs in a test mode. The second hardware test program runs a detailed phone line test that provides statistics on phone line errors. The final program simulates the modem interface check register whose complex behavior is otherwise difficult to predict.

The software debugging tools exist in two forms. Initially we designed a simple stand-alone debugging program with the capability to do little more than examine and change individual core registers from the console Teletype. Subsequently, we embedded a version of the stand-alone debugging program into the operational program. This operational debugging program not only provides debugging assistance at a single location but also may be used in *network testing* and *network debugging*.

The initial implementation of the IMP software took place without connecting to a true Host. To permit checkout of the Host-related portions of the operational program, we built a "Host Simulator" that takes input from the console Teletype and feeds the Host routines exactly as though the input had originated in a real Host. Similarly, output messages for a destination Host are received by the simulator and typed out on the console Teletype.

Without recourse to expensive additional peripherals, the assembly facilities on the DDP-516 are inadequate for a large program. (For example, a listing of the IMP program would require approximately 20 hours of Teletype output.) We therefore used other locally available facilities to assist in the assembly process. Specifically, we used a PDP-1 text editor to compose and edit the programs, assembled on the DDP-516, and listed the program on the SDS 940 line printer. Use of this assembly process required minor modification of existing PDP-1 and SDS 940 support software.

Projected IMP Performance

At this writing, the subnet has not yet been subjected to realistic load conditions; consequently, very little experimental data is available. However, we have made some estimates of projected performance of the IMP program and we describe these estimates below.

Host Traffic and Message Delays

In the subnet, the Host-to-Host transit time and the round-trip time (for RFNM receipt) depend upon routing and message length. Since only one message at a time may be present on a given link, the reciprocal of the round-trip delay is the maximum message rate on a link. The primary factors affecting subnet delays are:

- Propagation delay: Electrical propagation time in the Bell system is estimated to be about 10 μsec per mile. Cross country propagation delay is therefore about 30 msec.

- Modem transmission delay: Because bits enter and leave an IMP at a predetermined modem bit rate, a packet requires a modem transmission time proportional to its length (20 μsec per bit on a 50-kilobit line).

- Queueing delay: Time spent waiting in the IMP for transmission of previous packets on a queue. Such waiting may occur either at an intermediate IMP or in connection with terminal IMP transmissions into the destination Host.

- IMP processing delay: The time required for the IMP program to process a packet is about 0.35 msec for a store-and-forward packet.

Because the queueing delay depends heavily upon the detailed traffic load in the network, an estimate of queueing delay will not be available until we gain considerable experience with network operation. In Table 2, we show an estimate of the one-way and round-trip transit times and the corresponding maximum message

Table 2   Transit Times and Message Rates

	Minimum	Maximum
Single word message		
Transit time	5 msec	50 msec
Round-trip	10 msec	100 msec
Max. message rate/link	100/sec	10/sec
Single full packet message		
Transit time	45 msec	140 msec
Round-trip	50 msec	190 msec
Max. message rate/link	20/sec	5/sec
8-packet message		
Transit time	265 msec	360 msec
Round-trip	195 msec	320 msec
Max. message rate/link	5/sec	3/sec

rate per link, assuming the negligible queueing delay of a lightly loaded net. In this table, "minimum" delay represents a short hop between two nearby IMPs, and "maximum" delay represents a cross-country path involving five IMPs. In all cases the delays are well within the desired half-second goal.

In a lightly-loaded network with a mixture of nearby and distant destinations, an example of heavy Host traffic into its IMP might be that of 20 links carrying ten single-word messages per second and four more links, each carrying one eight-packet message per second.

Computational Load

In general, a line fully loaded with short packets will require more computation than a line with all long packets; therefore the IMP can handle more lines in the latter case. In Fig. 11, we show a curve of the computational utilization of the IMP as a function of message length for fully-loaded communication lines. For example, a 50-kilobit line fully loaded in both directions with one-word messages requires slightly over 13 percent of the available IMP

time. Since a line will typically carry a variety of different length packets, and each line will be less than fully loaded, the computational load per line will actually be much less.

Throughput is defined to be the maximum number of Host data bits that may traverse an IMP each second. The actual number of bits entering the IMP per second is somewhat larger than the throughput because of such overhead as headers, RFNMs, and acknowledgments. The number of bits on the lines is still larger because of additional line overhead such as framing and error control characters. (Each packet on the phone line contains seventeen characters of overhead, nine of which are removed before the packet enters an IMP.)

The computational limit on the IMP throughput is approximately 700,000 bits per second. Figure 12 shows maximum throughput as a function of message length. The difference between the throughput curve and the line traffic curve represents overhead.

Discussion

In this section we state some of our conclusions about the design and implementation of the ARPA Network and comment on possible future directions.

We are convinced that use of an IMP-like device is a more sensible way to design networks than is use of direct Host-to-Host connection. First, for the subnet to serve a store-and-forward role, its functions must be independent of Host computers, which may often be down for extended periods. Second, the IMP program is very complex and is highly tailored to the I/O structure of the DDP-516; building such complex functions into special I/O units

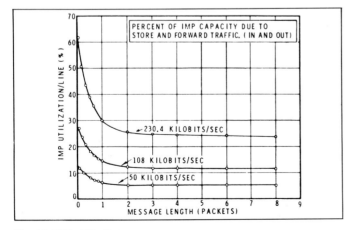

Fig. 11. IMP utilization.

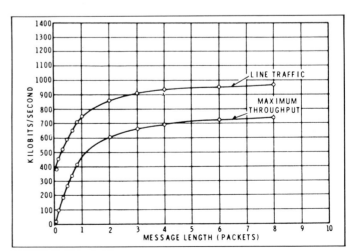

Fig. 12. IMP throughput.

of each computer that might need network connection is probably economically inadvisable. Third, because of the desirability of having several Host computers at a given site connect to the network, it is both more convenient and more economic to employ IMPs than to provide all the network functions in each of the Host computers. The whole notion of a network node serving a multiplexing function for complexes of local Hosts and terminals lends further support to this conclusion. Finally, because we were led to a design having *some* inter-IMP dependence, we found it advantageous to have *identical* units at each node, rather than computers of different manufacture.

Considering the multiplexing issue directly, it now seems clear that individual network nodes will be connected to a wide variety of computer and terminal complexes. Even the initial ten-node ARPA Network includes one Host organization that has chosen to submultiplex several computers via a single Host connection to the IMP. We are now studying variants of the IMP design that address this multiplexing issue, and we also expect to cooperate with other groups (such as at the National Physical Laboratory in England) that are studying such multiplexing techniques.

The increasing interest in computer networks will bring with it an expanding interaction between computers and communication circuits. From the outset, we viewed the ARPA Network as a systems engineering problem, including the portion of the system supplied by the common carriers. Although we found the carriers to be properly concerned about circuit performance (the basic circuit performance to date has been quite satisfactory), we found it difficult to work with the carriers *cooperatively* on the technical details, packaging, and implementation of the communication circuit terminal equipment; as a result, the present physical installations of circuit terminal equipment are at best inelegant and inconvenient. In the longer run, for reasons of economy, performance, and reliability, circuit terminal equipment probably should be integrated more closely with computer input/output equipment. If the carriers are unable to participate conveniently in such integrations, we would expect further growth of a competing circuit terminal equipment industry, and more prevalent common carrier provision of bare circuits.

Another aspect of network growth and development is the requirement to connect different rate communication circuits to IMP-like devices as a function of the particular application. In our own IMP design, although there are limitations on total throughput, the IMP can be connected to carrier circuits of any bit rate up to about 250 kilobits; similarly, the interface to a Host computer can operate over a wide range of bit rates. We feel that this flexibility is very important because the economics of carrier offerings, as well as the user requirements, are subject to surprisingly rapid change; even within the time period of the present implementation, we have experienced such changes.

At this point, we would like to discuss certain aspects of the implementation effort. This project required the design, development, and installation of a very complex device in a rather short time scale. The difficulty in producing a complex system is highly dependent upon the number of people who are simultaneously involved. Small groups can achieve complex optimizations of timing, storage, and hardware/software interaction, whereas larger groups can seldom achieve such optimizations on a reasonable time scale. We chose to operate with a very small group of highly talented people. For example, all software, including software tools for assembly, editing, debugging, and equipment testing as well as the main operational program, involved effort by no more than four people at any time. Since so many computer system projects involve much larger groups, we feel it is worth calling attention to this approach.

Turning to the future, we plan to work with the ARPA Network project along several technical directions: (1) the experimental operation of the network and any modifications required to tune its performance; (2) experimental operation of the network with higher bandwidth circuits; e.g., 230.4 kilobits; (3) a review of IMP variants that might perform multiplexing functions; (4) consideration of techniques for designing more economical and/or more powerful IMPs; and (5) participation with the Host organizations in the very sizeable problem of developing techniques and protocols for the effective *utilization* of the network.

On a more global level, we anticipate an explosive growth of message switched computer networks, not just for the interactive pooling of resources, but for the simple conveniences and economies to be obtained for many classes of digital data communication. We believe that the capabilities inherent in the design of even the present subnet have broad application to other data communication problems of government and private industry.

References

Baran [1964]; Baran, Boehm, and Smith [1964]; Boehm and Mobley [1966]; BBN Report No. 1763 [1969]; BBN Report No. 1822 [1969]; Brown, Miller, and Keenan [1967]; Carr, Crocker, and Cerf [1970]; Cuadra [1968]; Davies [1968a]; Davies [1968b]; Davies, Bartlett, Scantlebury, and Wilkinson [1967]; EDUCOM *EIN Catalog*; Everett, Zraket, and Benington [1957]; FCC [1966a]; Ford and Fulkerson [1962]; Frank, Frisch, and Chou [1970]; James [1966]; Kaplan [1968]; Kleinrock [1964]; Kleinrock [1969]; Kleinrock [1970]; Marill [1966]; Marill and Roberts [1966]; National Library of Medicine [1968]; *NOC Symp.* [1968]; *NOC Symp.* [1969]; Perry and Plugge [1961]; Roberts [1967]; Roberts [1968]; Roberts [1969]; Roberts and Wessler [1970]; Scantlebury, Wilkinson, and Bartlett [1968]; Steiglitz, Weiner, and Kleitman [1969]; Sung and Woodford [1969]; Teitelman and Kahn [1969].

Chapter 25

ALOHA Packet Broadcasting:
A Retrospect[1]

R. Binder / N. Abramson / F. Kuo / A. Okinaka / D. Wax

Introduction

Packet broadcasting is a technique whereby data is sent from one node in a net to another by attaching address information to the data to form a packet—typically from 30 to 1000 bits in length. The packet is then *broadcast* over a communication channel which is shared by a large number of nodes in the net; as the packet is received by these nodes the address is scanned and the packet is accepted by the proper addressee (or addressees) and ignored by the others. The physical communication channel employed by a packet broadcasting net can be a ground based radio channel, a satellite transponder or a cable.

Packet broadcasting networks can achieve the same efficiencies as packet switched networks [Roberts, 1973b], but in addition they have special advantages for local distribution data networks [Kahn, 1975] and for data networks using satellite channels [Abramson, 1973a]. In this paper we concentrate on those characteristics which are of interest for a local distribution data network. In particular, we discuss the lessons learned in the design and implementation of the ALOHANET, a packet broadcasting radio network in operation at the University of Hawaii since 1970. A number of design issues which arose in the construction of the system are defined, our solutions are explained, and in some cases they are justified. The lessons learned from the ALOHANET are used to indicate how such a radio packet broadcasting system might best be built using the technology available in 1975.

In the next section a brief description of the ALOHANET and its rationale is given. This is followed by a detailed discussion of the major system protocol choices that have evolved, pointing out some related theoretical work where appropriate. Choices concerning the design of the radio communication subsystem are then examined, followed by an evolutionary view of the important impact microcomputer technology has had on the user interface design and resulting system capabilities. The concluding section summarizes our present views with respect to the basic system configuration and properties of packet broadcasting nets.

[1]*Proc. APIPS NCC*, 1975, pp. 203–215.

The ALOHANET

The ALOHANET is the first system which successfully utilized the packet broadcasting concept for on-line access of a central computer via radio. Its primary purpose is to provide inexpensive access to one or more time-sharing systems by a large number of terminal users, typically in the hundreds. However, it also allows user-to-user communication within the net and is evolving toward use in a more generally oriented computer communications environment.

Operation

The present network configuration makes use of a broadcast channel for only one direction of traffic flow. (As we shall see in later sections, the lack of a broadcast capability in the other direction has seriously handicapped the development of effective protocols in certain areas). Two 100 KHz channels are used in the UHF band—a *random access* channel for user-to-computer communication at 407.350 MHz and a *broadcast channel* at 413.475 MHz for computer-to-user messages. The original system was configured as a star network, allowing only a central node to receive transmissions in the random access channel; all users received each transmission made by the central node in the broadcast channel. Recently the addition of ALOHA repeaters has generalized the network structure.

A block diagram of the present operational ALOHANET is shown in Fig. 1. The central communications processor of the net is an HP 2100 minicomputer (32K of core, 16 bit words) called the MENEHUNE [Binder, Lai, and Wilson, 1974] (Hawaiian for IMP) which functions as a message multiplexor/concentrator in much the same way as an ARPANET IMP [Heart et al., 1970]. The MENEHUNE accepts messages from the UH central computer,

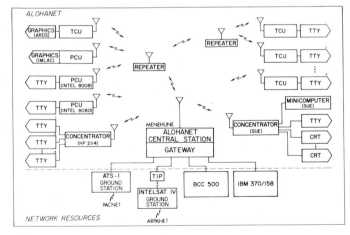

Fig. 1. The ALOHANET.

an IBM System 360/65 running TSO (as of December 1974, a 370/158) or from ALOHA's own time-sharing computer, the BCC 500, or from any ARPANET computer linked to the MENE-HUNE via the ALOHA TIP [Ornstein et al., 1972]. Outgoing messages in the MENEHUNE are converted into packets, the packets are queued on a first-in, first-out basis, and are then broadcast to the remote users at a data rate of 9600 baud.

The packet consists of a header (32 bits) and a header parity check word (16 bits), followed by up to 80 bytes of data and a 16-bit parity check word. The header contains information identifying the particular user so that when the MENEHUNE broadcasts a packet, only the intended user's node will accept it. More will be said about packet formats later.

The random access channel (at 407.35 MHz) for communication between users and the MENEHUNE is designed specifically for the traffic characteristics of interactive computing. In a conventional communication system a user might be assigned a portion of the channel on either an FDMA or TDMA basis. Since it is well known that in time-sharing systems, computer and user data systems are bursty [Jackson and Stubbs, 1969], such fixed assignments are generally wasteful of bandwidth because of the high peak-to-average data rates that characterize the traffic. The multiplexing technique that is utilized by the ALOHANET is a purely random access packet switching method that has come to be known as the *pure ALOHA* technique [Abramson, 1973b]. Under a pure ALOHA mode of operation, packets are sent by the user nodes to the MENEHUNE in a completely unsynchronized manner—when a node is idle it uses none of the channel. Each full packet of 704 bits requires only 73 msecs at a rate of 9600 baud to transmit (neglecting propagation time).

The random or multi-access channel can be regarded as a resource which is shared among a large number of users in much the same way as a multiprocessor's memory is "shared." Each active user node is in contention with all other active users for the user of the MENEHUNE receiver. If two nodes transmit packets at the same time, a collision occurs and both packets are rejected. In the ALOHANET, a positive acknowledgment protocol is used for packets sent on the random-access channel. Whenever a node sends a packet it must receive an acknowledgment message (ACK) from the MENEHUNE within a certain time-out period. If the ACK is not received within this interval the node automatically retransmits the packet after a randomized delay to avoid further collisions. These collisions will limit the number of users and the amount of data which can be transmitted over the channel as loading is increased.

An analysis [Abramson, 1973b] of the random access method of transmitting packets in a pure ALOHA channel shows that the normalized theoretical capacity of such a channel is $1/2e = 0.184$. Thus the average data rate which can be supported is about one sixth the data rate which could be supported if we were able to

synchronize the packets from each user in order to fill up the channel completely. Put another way, this result shows the present 9600 bit/second channel could support between 100 and 500 active teletype users—depending upon the rate at which they generate packets and upon the packet lengths.

ALOHANET Remote Units

The original user interface developed for the system is an all-hardware unit called an ALOHANET Terminal Control Unit (TCU), and is the sole piece of equipment necessary to connect any terminal or minicomputer into the ALOHA channel. As such it takes the place of two dedicated modems for each user, a dial-up connection and a multiplexor port usually used for computer networks. The TCU is composed of a UHF antenna, transceiver, modem, buffer and control unit.

The buffer and control unit functions of the TCU can also be handled by a minicomputer or a microcomputer. In the present system several minicomputers have been connected in this manner in order to act as multiplexors for terminal clusters or as computing stations with network access for resource sharing. A new version of the TCU using an Intel 8080 microcomputer for buffer and control has been built. Since these programmable units allow a high degree of flexibility for packet formats and system protocols, they are referred to as PCU's (Programmable Control Unit). A more detailed discussion of terminal considerations is given in a companion paper in these proceedings [Fralick et al., 1975].

Since the transmission scheme of the ALOHANET is by line-of-sight, the radio range of the transceivers is severely limited by the diversity of terrain (mountains, high rise buildings, heavy foliage) that exists in Hawaii. A recent development has allowed the system to expand its geographical coverage beyond the range of its central transmitting station. Because of the burst nature of the transmissions in the ALOHA channel it is possible to build a simple store-and-forward repeater which accepts a packet within a certain range of ID's and then repeats the packet on the same frequency. Each repeater performs identically and independently for packets directed either to or from the MENEHUNE. Two of the repeaters have been built which extend coverage of the ALOHANET from the island of Oahu to other islands in the Hawaiian chain. These repeaters are discussed in more detail in the following section.

Protocol Choices

Two fundamental choices which have dictated much of the system protocol are the two-channel star configuration of the original network and the use of random accessing for user transmissions. Investigation of the random accessing principle using radio was in fact the original motivation for constructing the ALOHANET, while the two-channel configuration was primarily chosen to allow this investigation without complication from the relatively dense total traffic stream being returned to all users. An additional reason for the star configuration was the desire to centralize as many communication functions as possible at the MENEHUNE, minimizing the cost of the TCU at each user node.

Within this context, a number of protocol issues must be resolved. The more important of these are:

- random access channel control
- broadcast channel queueing
- packet length
- addressing
- error control
- flow control

Many of the original choices in these areas have undergone significant changes as a result of new user resources and user interfaces, or in some instances due to advancements in theoretical knowledge. The addition of repeaters has (potentially) a particularly significant impact on protocol.

We now discuss some of the considerations and resulting choices made in each of the above areas, with the impacts of new factors introduced within the context of each area. The section concludes with a brief discussion of the problem of integrating file traffic into the random access channel, a subject of current concern in the ALOHANET.

Random Access Channel Control

The retransmission strategy used in the random access scheme plays a central role in the scheme's effectiveness. Its determination directly affects the average delay experienced by users for a successful transmission, given a certain number of users accessing the channel, their traffic statistics, and the channel capacity. It can also be used to prevent the occurrence of channel saturation, a situation in which the channel becomes filled with retransmissions and the number of successful packets falls to zero. These topics have only recently been quantified [Metcalfe, 1973a; Lam, 1974] and remain subjects of current investigation.

One approach is to use different constant retransmission intervals at each node, with the intervals equal to integer multiples of the maximum packet transmission time to avoid subsequent conflicts. This results in a priority structure, since nodes assigned the longer intervals will experience a correspondingly longer average delay. As the number of nodes becomes large, however, unacceptably large delays result for the majority of users.

A strategy more appropriate for large user populations is to randomize the retransmission intervals used at each node (note that a priority structure can still be introduced if desired by using larger mean values for lower priority users—in the remaining discussion, equal priorities will be assumed). According to recent results by Lam [1974], the resulting channel behavior appears to be relatively insensitive to the exact nature of the randomization, at least when comparing the use of uniform and geometric distributions. In any event, the cost of implementing a particular distribution at each node is an important design consideration. Based on initial estimates of the expected ALOHANET characteristics, a choice was made to use a uniform distribution. This allowed a relatively simple implementation in both hardware and software user nodes.

A simple technique was used in the original system nodes to achieve short delays when the channel is lightly loaded, while preventing channel saturation from occurring due to peak-hour loading or statistical traffic fluctuations; small retransmission intervals are used (relative to the intervals between new packets), but only for a maximum of three successive retransmission attempts. If the third attempt is unsuccessful, the user is notified of a failure and must manually reinitiate the retransmissions. This in effect introduces a long interval between every three retransmissions, allowing time for retransmissions from other users to succeed. Based on a maximum packet transmission time of 70 milliseconds, the intervals are selected from a range of 0.2 to 1.5 seconds, giving a mean of about 0.7 seconds (ten maximum packet times) per retransmission. The lower bound is chosen to allow sufficient time to receive an ACK from the MENEHUNE if the packet was sent successfully, avoiding unnecessary retransmissions. (This time is based on a direct user-MENEHUNE path; if repeaters form a part of the radio path, the lower limit must be increased accordingly.)

The newer programmable PCU's in the system offer the capability of a more flexible strategy, for example allowing the interval used after each third retransmission to be automatically inserted. The use of different strategies, such as continuously increasing the time range used for selection of successive retransmissions, is also easily implemented by program; these and other strategies are currently under investigation.

Broadcast Channel Queueing

The MENEHUNE acts as a concentrator for the broadcast (F_2) channel, queueing waiting traffic when necessary for sequential transmission to user nodes. Four complicating factors exist, however: a need for priority queueing, fair allocation of the channel, the turnaround delay required by half duplex nodes, and the presence of repeaters.

Priority Queues.   It is important that the F_2 channel data traffic not prevent the prompt return of an ACK to a user node, since this could lead to unnecessary user retransmissions and possible degradation of the random access (F_1) channel. Thus, an integral part of the F_2 channel multiplexing is the priority queueing mechanism maintained by the MENEHUNE, as shown in Fig. 2. Whenever a transmission is completed on the F_2 channel the ACK queue is checked, and if not empty the ACK at the head of the queue is sent. Only when the ACK queue is empty is the data packet queue checked for waiting packets. This guarantees that at most one complete data packet plus any previously queued ACK's will be sent ahead of an ACK just placed on the queue. (Because the average rate of successful arrivals on the F_1 channel is limited to one-sixth the rate of F_2 transmissions by the random access technique, the number of previously queued ACK's will be zero most of the time.)

Fairness. A second problem is the possible hogging of the F_2 channel by one or a few users. This problem is eliminated by the queueing discipline used for the data packet queue. Only one packet per user is allowed on the queue at any time, and the queue is serviced on a first-come-first-served (FIFO) basis. The prevention of more than one packet per user on the queue is handled in conjunction with user flow control, discussed below.

Turnaround Delay. A delay function is used by the MENEHUNE to count off the time required by half-duplex user nodes to switch from a transmit to a receive state. The actual time is determined by the equipment type—the original off-the-shelf equipment required 100 milliseconds due to its use of mechanical relays; approximately 10 milliseconds is counted off for newer equipment now in use.

Repeater Scheduling. The addition of repeaters to the system introduces a number of new problems into the F_2 channel, both because of radio range overlap and the nature of the repeaters themselves. The latter are store-and-forward devices; a packet

which is to be repeated is first received and stored in its entirety, then transmitted on the same frequency on which it was received (preventing reception of a new packet during this time). In order to prevent the loss of a second packet destined to the same repeater, the MENEHUNE must therefore appropriately schedule the packets in its F_2 channel queues.

For efficient scheduling (i.e., to maximize channel utilization), the MENEHUNE must know the repeater routing paths for each user node. This function could thus become quite complicated or even not achievable, depending on the degree of dynamic routing used. Because of the small percentage of traffic currently handled by repeaters in the present ALOHANET, a very simple brute force method is used: whenever a packet is sent which is forwarded by one or more repeaters, the MENEHUNE counts off sufficient time for it to be repeated once before beginning a new transmission to any node (knowledge of which packets are to be repeated is available from the user address, discussed below). This results in wasted channel capacity, but is not significant due to the capacity available in the system at present.

Packet Length

Three factors having an important impact on the system are the use of variable or fixed-length packets, the way packet length or the number of data bytes is indicated, and the maximum packet length allowed. The choices made must take into account the different traffic characteristics generated by line-oriented and character-oriented user-computer interactions.

Line Transmissions. Fixed-length packets were used in the initial system to simplify the design and construction of system hardware. The data packet length for both channels was chosen to allow up to 80 data bytes (640 bits), based on the user delays introduced by the 9600 bps channel data rates, the line length of the terminals in the system, and the line-oriented characteristics of the IBM 360/65 used as the central time-sharing system. An end-of-line (EOL) indicator consisting of eight zero bits was used within the packet to identify the end of actual data, where the latter was restricted to 7-bit ASCII with the eighth (parity) bit set to one. Since it was anticipated that many of the lines typed by users would be less than 40 characters, a second packet type was also defined which contained a 40-byte data field (a "Half-Packet"). This last step proved to be a mistake—the half-packet logic at each end of the link was a significant source of both hardware and software bugs.

The packet formats have since been changed to allow the use of variable-length packets with newer user nodes. An 8-bit count field is used in the packet header to indicate the number of 8-bit data bytes in the packet, with the data parity word immediately following the last data byte. In addition to eliminating the wasted channel capacity of the fixed-length packets, this also removes

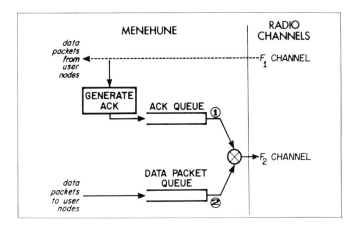

Fig. 2. Broadcast channel multiplexing.

constraints on the data themselves necessitated by unambiguous detection of the EOL indicator within the data stream. The 80 data-byte maximum has been retained for both channels, since it still appears to be a reasonable upper bound with respect to both the multiplexing delays introduced to either channel and node buffering requirements. This should not be construed as an indication that this length is optimal, however; as file-oriented messages are introduced to the total traffic and/or user node storage continues to become cheaper, a larger maximum may be desirable for one or both channels (for a given channel data rate and user response time constraints).

Character-by-Character.   The increased flexibility provided by PCU's has allowed the introduction of a "short" data packet in which a single data byte is sent in the header in place of the byte count, followed only by the header parity word. Although a use for this packet occasionally arises for interactions with line-at-a-time systems, its main use is with the character-oriented ARPANET computers now available to ALOHANET users.

The use of these character-oriented systems can have a considerable impact on the size and frequency of packets sent in the random access channel. This has an important consequence for the buffering strategy and choice of packet-length used at each node: since a new transmission cannot begin until an ACK has been received for the last one, all characters typed by the user during the ACK waiting time should be sent in a single packet. Thus if communication delays tend to overlap inter-character generation times, the affected characters are accumulated at the originating node and sent (more efficiently) in a variable-length packet, without adversely affecting user-' computer interaction.

A logical extension of this last strategy is to buffer all characters typed by the user at his node until one is typed which causes some action to be taken by the computer. If the appropriate set of action characters is known at the user node, this allows an optimum use of both channel capacity and system buffering without degrading the user-computer interaction. A scheme which allows this to be done in conjunction with echoing control is given by Davidson [1972], and is currently being introduced into selected ARPA-NET hosts. Its implementation cost in ALOHANET PCU user nodes appears reasonable, and is anticipated for use as its support by host computers becomes widespread.

Addressing

User Nodes.   User addressing is determined by the radio channel configuration and associated multiplexing technique. Ignoring repeaters for the moment, the two-frequency configuration used in the ALOHANET allows only a single destination in the random access channel (the MENEHUNE), and a single source in the broadcast channel (the MENEHUNE). Thus only the sender's address is required in the random access channel and only the destination address in the broadcast channel, which in both cases is the user address. Concentration of more than one user at a radio node is handled by permanently allocating a block of user addresses to the node, allowing user node multiplexing without introducing another level of addressing complexity to the system. The required address space is determined by the total number of users expected to be supported by the random access channel, and is 2^8 (eight header bits) for the present 9600 bps ALOHANET channel.

Repeaters.   The use of repeaters in the system introduces some significant new factors to be considered in choosing an address scheme. Because of radio range overlap and the store-and-forward nature of the repeaters, problems can arise involving conflicts generated by two or more repeaters repeating simultaneously to the same destination, infinite repeating of the same packet (looping), and weak-signal operation due to multiple (but time-sequential) paths. In addition, the addressing scheme directly affects the MENEHUNE's ability to schedule transmissions in order to maximize broadcast channel utilization, as discussed in a preceding section. The ability to eliminate or minimize these problems depends on the degree of mobility desired for user nodes and/or the repeaters themselves.

Because of the small percentage of user nodes which currently require repeaters in the ALOHANET, a simple scheme is in use based on the hardwired properties of the original repeaters built for the system. A block of user addresses is defined for each repeater, the latter repeating only those addresses in its block. The block assigned to a repeater two hops from the MENEHUNE is a subset of the block assigned to its first hop repeater. User nodes are constrained to operate within the geographic range of their "assigned" repeater by this scheme, but the node's user address is easily changeable if a relocation becomes necessary. Since only one path choice exists between each user node and the MENEHUNE at present, the optimum path is selected by default. As the number of repeaters in use increases and existing units are replaced by programmable devices, a more flexible repeater addressing scheme is expected to be implemented.

Resource Addressing.   This refers to the user's choices regarding which system resource he may communicate with. The system allows users to request a connection to the campus IBM 370/158, the ARPANET, or another ALOHANET user node. This is accomplished by sending special sequences of ASCII characters in the data portion of packets to the MENEHUNE, which may either be typed by a terminal user or automatically generated. If the requested destination is available, its identification is stored in a *Connection Table* entry for the requesting user in the

MENEHUNE, and the user's address stored in a similar entry for the destination. All subsequent packets from the user are passed to the stored destination and conversely, until either end requests that the connection be broken.

Two exceptions exist to this connection table routing of packets. The first are commands intended for the MENEHUNE, such as the "connect" and "disconnect" above. The second is a capability which allows a user to send a single packet to another ALOHA-NET user independently of current connection table entries. The originating user simply types a special two-character ASCII sequence followed by the destination user's address (up to three ASCII digits), followed by the desired text.

Note that in the case of a connection to another ALOHANET node, the latter's address is also the resource address. If the node's resource can service more than one user at a time (such as might be the case for a specialized minicomputer or storage device), the present addressing scheme requires either that a block of addresses be allocated to the receiving node (as in the case of a concentrator for sending), or a sub-address be sent in the text portion of every packet. The block allocation suffers from rigidity in that resource addresses cannot be reused dynamically by different users, and does not appear desirable if many such addresses must be allocated in the system.

Error Control

Random-Access Channel. Two distinct error sources exist at the MENEHUNE receiver, the usual random noise and errors due to packet conflicts. Because of the high probability of errors due to conflicts at full loading of the random access channel, a very reliable error detection mechanism is required. To achieve this it was decided to use two 16-bit cyclic polynomial parity check words in each data packet, one following the header and a second following the data. The separate header parity check forms the basis for a highly reliable packet synchronization method discussed in another part of this paper; it also allows reliable establishment of packet length and other information prior to processing the data portion of a packet. A single header bit is also used in conjunction with the parity check for sequence numbering, allowing the detection of duplicate packets by the MENE-HUNE.

Broadcast Channel. Error control for broadcast channel data packets (MENEHUNE to user nodes) involves some special considerations. For efficient operation, the usual positive acknowledgment scheme in which the ACK's themselves are not acknowledged depends on a high probability of the ACK's being successfully received. However, an ACK sent from user nodes must compete with data traffic in the random access channel. At full channel loading each random access packet must be retrans-

mitted an average of 1.7 times, which means each data packet or ACK must be sent a total of 2.7 times on the average before it is successfully received.[1] But in order to force retransmission of the ACK's, the data packet being acknowledged must also be sent an average of 2.7 times by the MENEHUNE—even though it was received correctly the first time! The problem is compounded by the typically high ratios of computer/user traffic which exist for most interactive systems, resulting in many more ACK's than data packets in the random access channel. This problem was "resolved" for the initial implementation by simply not sending ACK's from user nodes. Because of the high received signal strengths at the nodes, a very low error rate was anticipated; considering also that user nodes consisted only of human terminal users, it was decided that a simple error detection/user notification scheme would be sufficient.

However, this is in general not adequate when more sophisticated data transfer functions take place or significant error rates exist at user nodes. An example of the first case is the loading of programs into core storage of a minicomputer node, where manually initiated error recovery usually requires restarting the loading from the beginning of the file. In the second case, error rates can become appreciable when user nodes are located in weak signal areas caused by distance, multipath interference, or line-of-sight blocking, or in strong signal areas in which strong local noise sources also exist. To allow for these situations, an option which allows user nodes to send positive acknowledgments has been implemented. The scheme works identically to that for the random access channel, but is only used selectively with newer programmable nodes when required (it can be turned on or off by a command from the user node to the MENEHUNE.) Its effectiveness is based on the relatively light existing channel loading of the system and its use by only a few of the nodes.

One solution to this problem when all traffic to user nodes must be acknowledged in a loaded random access channel is to use sequence numbering with a large modulus, sending an ACK only when the maximum sequence number is received. This approach suffers from the unpredictable nature of interactive user-computer traffic, however; if the last computer output prior to new user input is missed by the node, a potential deadlock situation is created until the user decides something is wrong and takes manual action. An additional mechanism can be used to circumvent this, such as using automatic timeouts at the user node or sending dummy traffic to the node to "flush out" missed packets. However, the sequence numbers succeed only in reducing the number of ACK's sent in the random access channel—to eliminate the unnecessary repetitions of data packets from the MENE-

---

[1]This assumes ACK's and data packets are the same length; although the ACK's are in fact shorter, the resulting error rate is still very high compared to a typical conflict-free channel.

HUNE, it is also necessary to acknowledge the ACK. That is, the ACK sent by a user node is timed out and retransmitted until an acknowledgment for it is received, just as for data packets. If another packet is waiting for transmission to the node at this time, its transmission with the next sequence number constitutes the ACK to the ACK; otherwise, a short ACK-ACK packet is sent by the MENEHUNE. This can be easily shown to result in significantly less total channel overhead, at the expense of more complication in the node implementation.

Repeaters. We have so far ignored the effects of repeaters in this discussion on both random access and broadcast channel error control. The repeaters currently in use in the ALOHANET do not generate acknowledgments in either direction, resulting in only end-to-end acknowledgments between the MENEHUNE and user nodes as above (but with longer minimum retransmission timeouts). This choice was made for initial repeater simplicity; it has been shown analytically, however, that a hop-by-hop acknowledgment scheme is in general superior to an end-to-end scheme, at least in contexts such as ARPANET [Metcalfe, 1973a] and the ARPA Packet Radio effort [Frank, Van Slyke, and Gitman, 1975]. Thus we expect to convert to a hop-by-hop scheme when the existing repeaters are replaced by programmable units and/or repeater traffic error rates require it; this area remains a relatively unexplored problem domain within the present ALOHANET implementation.

Single-Channel Configurations. Finally, we note that the problems discussed above concerning ACK's sent by user nodes in the random access channel are effectively non-existent if a single-frequency channel configuration is used (and propagation times are less than the shortest packet transmission times). If all nodes can hear the transmission of all other nodes, it is only necessary that nodes refrain from sending for an ACK packet time following the transmission of a data packet by any node, except for the intended receiver who sends an ACK (if appropriate) during this time. Thus ACK's are sent conflict-free, allowing a simple positive acknowledgment scheme to be used for all traffic. Note that packets sent by the MENEHUNE are treated exactly the same as packets sent by user nodes with respect to ACK's, thus also eliminating any effects due to asymmetric computer-user traffic ratios.

Flow Control

The Initial System. In the initial system environment of a single half-duplex time-sharing system, model 33 Teletypes, and hardwired user nodes which buffered only the line being displayed, flow control was a relatively simple matter. A user always received at least one output line from the time-sharing system (IBM's TSO running on a 360/65) for each input line, and a prompt character when it was ready for more input. The bandwidth between the MENEHUNE and 360 and the latter's I/O response times are such that one or two MENEHUNE buffers are normally sufficient to support transfers of packets received from the random access channel; in the unlikely event that no buffers are available when a packet arrives, the channel protocol guarantees its retransmission. Thus no explicit flow control was provided to prevent new packets from being sent by a user node. If the user sends one before the 360 is ready, the packet is discarded and a "WAIT" message returned to the user by the MENEHUNE (the status of each 360 connection is known in the MENEHUNE by information routinely passed from the 360).

Broadcast channel flow control was necessary, however, since each line (packet) sent to a (hardwired) user node must be completely displayed before a new line can be received. This was accomplished by the scheme shown in Fig. 3, in which the control for each user node is centralized at the MENEHUNE. The latter counts off the required display time following transmission of each packet to a user, inhibiting further transmissions to that user until the time is up. To prevent 360 output from tying up MENEHUNE buffers while packets are being displayed, a handshaking flow control is used; the 360 sends only one line of output for each user, then waits for a *go-ahead* (GA) message with that user's address. The GA is sent by the MENEHUNE whenever a user's display time is up, resulting in at most one buffer required for each user (the MENEHUNE can also hold up acceptance of any packet from the 360 indefinitely until it has buffer space available). Note that this strategy also prevents any user from hogging the broadcast channel, since it allows only one packet per user in the channel queue.

Some Terminal Complications. The introduction of high speed CRT and hardcopy terminals to the system required an expansion of the MENEHUNE's flow control mechanism for the broadcast channel. A set of display rates was added, with the rate used at each user node stored in a permanent table in the MENEHUNE;

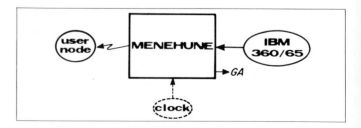

Fig. 3. Broadcast channel flow control (original system).

a user can change the stored value for his node by typing a special command to the MENEHUNE at any time. The CRT terminals require an additional flow control mechanism to suspend output when the CRT screen has filled, allowing the user to signal when he is ready to proceed. Thus a screensize command was created which allows users to specify a screensize of between one and 99 lines (or an infinite screensize); this value is also stored in MENEHUNE tables for each user node. A counter is maintained for each user with a finite screensize specification and is updated for each line sent to the terminal; when the maximum is reached, the MENEHUNE suspends generation of the GA message until the user inputs a carriage return.

Satellite Complications. The next complication to MENE-HUNE flow control processing was caused by the connection of the ALOHANET to the ARPANET. The latter involves a 50 Kbps INTELSAT IV satellite path connecting Hawaii to California; because of its long propagation time (approximately 0.25 seconds) and ARPANET flow control protocol, a large amount of buffering is required at the receive end of the link to support continuous display at higher speed terminals—in particular, a 9600 bps terminal requires approximately a 1000-byte buffer. (Since in general CRT terminal users do not require continuous output at this rate, a smaller amount of buffering is in fact used.) This required a substantial increase in the size of the MENEHUNE buffer pool and a more complicated queueing structure to support the broadcast channel, since now more than one packet per user must in general be stored in the MENEHUNE during display at the user node. To maintain the single-packet-per-user policy for the channel queue, a separate queue was created for each user to hold additional packets. The resulting flow control scheme is shown in Fig. 4, where the GA's sent to the 360 in Fig. 3 are now sent to the internal ARPANET protocol module. The maximum allowed size of each user queue is determined by the user's

terminal rate and the available MENEHUNE buffer pool, and in turn defines the parameters used in the ARPANET flow control protocol.

Multiple-Line Packets. A second complication resulting from the ARPANET connection concerns the extra time required by some higher speed displays for certain characters such as carriage return (CR) and/or line feed (LF). Output from the 360 in the initial system contained such characters only at the end of a line (packet), allowing the transmission time and other inter-packet delays to provide any extra time required. However, many ARPANET computers are character-oriented, at times generating many CR and LF characters within a single packet. Thus it was necessary to provide a padding function in the MENEHUNE which inserts dummy characters or otherwise adds a display time delay after each CR or LF occurrence within packets destined for a higher speed (greater than 110 bps) terminal. This necessitates the splitting of packets whenever the maximum 80-byte packet length is exceeded, and in general involves a significant amount of additional processing per packet.

Full Duplex Interaction. A third complication arising from many ARPANET computers is their full duplex user interaction. Unlike the 360, users do not necessarily receive output in response to each input or an indication of when the computer is waiting for more input. Since no explicit flow control is provided for input from user nodes to the MENEHUNE, users are forced to either interact in a half duplex fashion (guessing as to when the computer has finished its output) or suffer occasional losses of input data and subsequent retyping. The latter can occur frequently with the hardwired TCU's, since they contain a single buffer which is used for both keyboard input and display; if computer output arrives while the user is typing, the typed characters are overwritten in the buffer by the received packet. The newer programmable user nodes now in the system provide full duplex buffering for the terminal, allowing a packet to be received and displayed without disturbing the keyboard buffer.

However, even if user nodes are completely full duplex a flow control problem exists for packets sent to the MENEHUNE. Unlike the case for the 360, users of full duplex hosts may generate successive input packets without receiving responses from the host computer. If the ARPANET or host computer or both slow down, an excessive number of buffers can become queued in the MENEHUNE on behalf of the user. Thus, to prevent user hogging of the buffer pool a count of the number of input buffers queued for each user is now maintained; when equal to the maximum allowed, arriving packets are discarded and a discard notification returned to the user.

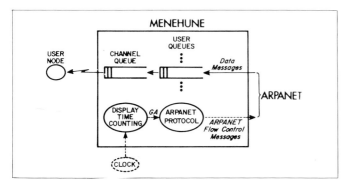

Fig. 4. Broadcast channel/ARPANET flow control.

File Traffic

The original ALOHANET design was based on a homogeneous population of terminal users generating bursty traffic into the random access channel. However, the connection of minicomputers and other terminals with memory has introduced at least two sources of non-bursty, or "file," traffic. The first case occurs when users desire to transfer data from a paper tape or other storage media to a host computer. The second occurs when it is desired to transfer program-generated output from a minicomputer at a user node to a display device at a second user node (users can connect to other user nodes through the MENEHUNE in the same way as to the 360 or ARPANET). In either case the resulting traffic must be prevented from hogging or degrading the random access channel, and must also be constrained to the destination's acceptance rate.

The random access technique itself implicitly provides an anti-hogging mechanism, since retransmission timeouts can be used to decrease the user's average rate if conflicts occur. This does not provide for destination flow control, however, and is not necessarily an optimal solution for the random access channel. A second approach is the use of explicit flow control in the form of GA's sent by the MENEHUNE to the sending user node. This provides a solution to both problems at the expense of a small percentage of broadcast channel capacity. Since the MENE-HUNE receives GA's from the user's destination, either explicitly from the 360 or ARPANET module or from its display time counting for another ALOHANET node, it can simply relay them to the sending node in a short control packet. This approach also allows centralized optimization of traffic in the random access channel by the MENEHUNE, and is the subject of current investigation.

Radio Subsystem Choices

The design of the ALOHANET radio communication system required the balancing of a number of performance goals against various system constraints which are peculiar to the use of radio frequencies for data communication channels. These trade-off studies resulted in the selection of our RF channels and modulation method. The determination of operating ranges and the choice of a data synchronization method resulted from the basic channel and modulation selection decisions. In this section we will describe the primary issues related to RF channel selection, modulation design, radio range determination, and data synchronization design.

RF Channels and Modulation

The choice of radio channels for any communication system is a complex task, requiring the trade-off of many factors such as desired bandwidth, area coverage, spectrum availability, potential interference and noise sources, regulatory requirements, and equipment costs. In the case of the ALOHANET, a wide channel bandwidth was considered desirable for the random access channel since user nodes are required to send messages to the MENEHUNE, at high peak data rates compared to their average data rate. Wide bandwidth was also deemed advisable for the broadcast channel due to the expected high traffic density from the MENEHUNE. The use of wide channel bandwidth tends to force the use of higher frequencies where spectrum crowding is less severe and the availability of bandwidth is greater. Crowded radio bands are undesirable not only from the standpoint of interference to other users but also because of potential interference from them. Another disadvantage of lower frequencies is the higher probability of interference from man-made noise sources, particularly in an urban area where the ALOHANET has most of its terminals.

From the above considerations it can be seen that the system's communication requirements tend to emphasize the use of higher radio frequencies. The primary constraint on moving to even higher ferequencies is equipment cost and radio range. Above 500 MHz equipment costs tend to escalate rapidly. Area coverage also becomes more difficult due to more pronounced shadowing effects of the radio waves by buildings and hilly terrain. (Above 30 MHz radio propagation tends to be limited to line-of-sight paths.)

Therefore, the 400 to 500 MHz UHF band was selected as the optimum for the ALOHANET radio frequencies. Reasonably priced commercial radio equipment was found to be available in this frequency region and radio band crowding was not severe in Hawaii. Initially, assignments in the 450 to 470 MHz mobile radio band were requested but were rejected by the FCC because of our wide channel bandwidth requirements. (The mobile radio channels are specified at about 15 KHz bandwidth, whereas we were requesting 100 KHz.) We were fortunate enough to receive assignments as an experimental service in the government UHF band of 406 to 420 MHz, where spectrum space was available.

Since most radio equipments available in the UHF bands use frequency modulation (FM), this type of modulation was selected for the RF channels. A slight variation was incorporated in the hardware design to minimize the interface problems between the radios and the data modems. This variation was the use of a subcarrier tone to carry the actual data modulation. This tone is phase-shift-keyed by the data and the resultant signal is used to modulate the FM transmitter. This modulated tone is recovered from the FM receiver and fed to the demodulator of the modem. This modulation system is referred to as FM/DPSK to indicate frequency modulation by a differentially phase-shift-keyed subcarrier. (Differential phase-shift-keying is used to resolve the problem of received phase ambiguity.) The resultant configuration is shown in Fig. 5.

Radio Range

The maximum operating distance between any terminal of the ALOHANET and the MENEHUNE (or a repeater) is specified as the system's radio range. This distance is primarily a function of a transmitter's radiated power, the receiver's sensitivity, and the attenuation of radio signal power for the given distance. Local noise conditions at the receiver location can also affect this distance, but for system planning purposes, range is usually calculated on the basis of some given propagation model. For line-of-sight paths, which exist at VHF, UHF, and higher frequencies, two different models are used depending upon local topographical conditions. In an urban area these paths are partially obstructed and suffer from multipath effects. A power loss proportional to $1/R^4$ is usually assumed for these conditions [Okumura et al., 1968]. Where paths are unobstructed and well clear of the local terrain, a spreading loss proportional to $1/R^2$ can be assumed. Receiver threshold sensitivity in the ALOHANET is defined as that receiver input power level which causes an average bit error rate of 10^{-5}. This bit error rate should provide a packet throughput reliability better than 99 percent for full-length ALOHA packets.

Assuming a transmitter equivalent radiated power of 10 watts, a simple whip antenna at a user terminal, an elevated antenna at the MENEHUNE or repeater and a 3 microvolt receiver sensitivity, the radio range works out to about 17 miles in the urban area for the ALOHANET frequencies. Between repeaters and the MENEHUNE terminal, which have well-elevated antennae and good path clearances, the assumed $1/R^2$ model gives a maximum range of 290 miles. The use of high-gain omnidirectional antenna arrays at repeater sites extends these ranges. Tests conducted on a 100 mile path between two ALOHANET repeaters confirmed the $1/R^2$

spreading-loss assumption and indicated a fade margin of 30 db existed (due to the 10 db gain antennae used for the test.)

Data Synchronization

Because of the burst nature of radio transmission of ALOHANET packets, special synchronization techniques must be employed in the modem and data terminal equipment. Since the phase-shift-keying used in the ALOHANET modem design is a bit-synchronous technique, bit synchronization must first be performed in the demodulator before packet synchronization can be attempted. Bit-sync is performed by a phase-locking circuit, and a lock-indication signal is passed to the data equipment when bit-sync has been attained. The bit-sync detection circuit is so designed to provide a very low false detection probability (less than 10^{-6}) and a high probability of packet detection. The narrow bandwidth of the phase-lock circuit presently designed into the ALOHANET modem requires a bit-sync preamble of 90 bits to ensure reliable bit-sync. Studies have indicated that this preamble can be reduced to about 10 bits by use of a redesigned wide-band phase-lock circuit. In fact, we are presently contemplating doing away with the bit-sync preamble entirely, further reducing packet overhead. The unique characteristics of the ALOHA modem design make such an approach feasible.

Packet synchronization is accomplished in the ALOHANET data terminal buffer by means of the 16-bit parity word contained in the packet header. When the parity check routine accepts the header, the packet is assumed to be synchronized. Since the parity check routine is initiated by the first bit of the header, packets can be missed due to detection of an early error bit before the header. This miss probability is presently controlled by the modem at about 10^{-3} or less, providing a packet detection probability of 99.9 percent or better. The false detection probability of this circuit is $\sim 1.5 \times 10^{-5}$, which is independent of that of the modem. Thus, the overall probability of false detection is less than 1.5×10^{-11}. Therefore, less than one out of a thousand packets will be lost due to packet sync errors and packet sync false alarms occur with extreme rarity.

User Interface Choices

The development of the ALOHANET user interface has been an evolutionary process, as is typical of most research developments. Since there were expected to be many user nodes (as compared to the single MENEHUNE node), the primary design goals were initially set as simplicity of design and low cost. This led to the design of a hardwired control unit with limited data storage capability coupled to a modem and radio transceiver. This initial design was termed a Terminal Control Unit (TCU). As experience

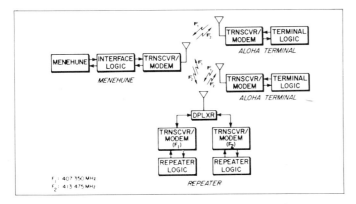

Fig. 5. ALOHA system UHF radio communication system.

developed with operation of the net, other functions became evident as being desirable in a TCU. At about this time the first microprocessor chips and low-cost semiconductor memory chips were becoming available in the marketplace. It was decided that a new TCU design should be initiated using these new devices since much greater flexibility and additional functions could be readily incorporated in a unit having a capability of being programmed. It was also noted that the cost of these new devices was such that a unit could be built for the same cost or less than that of the original design. Thus, the Programmable Control Unit (PCU) was developed, and there are now several operating units in the system. We will now discuss some of the issues involved in designing a terminal control unit for use on the ALOHANET. These issues lie in the general areas of interface considerations, and the technology of microprocessors.

The Original TCU

The ALOHANET was originally envisioned as a terminal network, with the TCU's interfacing human users to a half duplex, line-oriented time-sharing system. At the time of the first TCU design effort memory was relatively expensive, so in order to minimize cost a single buffer was chosen for use with both the terminal keyboard and display. (As noted earlier in this paper, when full duplex computer interactions were available in the system the single buffer was found to be quite a disadvantage.) The buffer was designed for a full line length of 80 characters, which allowed handling of both the 40 and 80 character fixed-length packets defined for the system.

Additional basic functions performed by the TCU's were generation of a cyclic-parity-check code vector and decoding of received parity code words for error-detection purposes, and generation of packet retransmissions using a simple random interval generator. If an acknowledgment was not received from the computer after the prescribed number of retransmissions, a flashing light was used as an indicator to the human user. Since the TCU's did not send acknowledgments to the MENEHUNE, a steady warning light was displayed to the human user when an error was detected in a received packet. Thus it can be seen that considerable simplification was incorporated into the initial design of the TCU, making use of the fact that it was interfacing a human user into the network.

Other functions hardwired into the TCU were the obvious requirements of checking for and generating its address, packet sequence numbering, checking to see if a received packet is an ACK packet or a data packet, and generating and checking for half- or full-packet conditions. (The control bits for these functions all reside in the header portion of the packet.)

The final consideration was the choice of standard interface signals between the TCU and the user's equipment. This was a relatively simple choice, since most equipment is designed to meet the EIA standard RS 232C interface specification. Therefore, the TCU was designed to meet this standard, which allows direct connection of most terminals in use today.

Minicomputer Nodes

As the ALOHANET developed, some minicomputers were interfaced into the network as concentrators for a number of terminals. Many of the logical functions performed in a TCU were now incorporated into the mini's software, with error detection and parity word generation performed in a special hardware interface unit imposed between the minicomputer and an ALOHA modem. (This unit was very much like the encoder/decoder unit used at the MENEHUNE to interface that minicomputer to the channel.) Parallel-to-serial and serial-to-parallel conversion was also performed in this interface unit.

However, a minicomputer is an expensive device to use for these simple functions, and it requires considerable amounts of power and space. If it already exists for the purpose of performing various user-oriented tasks, then it is cost-effective to incorporate the software interface and a minimal amount of hardware for use on the ALOHANET.

The advent of the microprocessor chip changed all this. The relatively low-cost processing power demonstrated by these units made it apparent that many system options we had previously considered and discarded because of hardware complexity and cost limitations in the TCU, were now viable in a PCU. Some of these options—file transfer, remote user ACK's, single frequency operation, character-by-character transmission—were discussed in previous sections. This trend toward programmable and more powerful TCU's has thus led to the development of the ALOHA PCU, using a microprocessor to handle the TCU buffering and control functions, in addition to more complex and sophisticated functions.

Microprocessor Technology

The development from the hardwired TCU concept to the fully-programmable PCU has closely followed the rapidly changing technology of microprocessors. The availability of lower-cost semiconductor memory has allowed the evolution from half-duplex to full-duplex operation in the PCU, with the beneficial side-effect of decreased logical complexity due to separation of the input and output functions. However, the first PCU developed had a hardware complexity level comparable to the TCU due to the relatively primitive structure of early microprocessor designs. This first PCU, designed with the Intel 8008 CPU, required a considerable amount of circuitry for buffering and multiplexing functions needed with this early microprocessor chip. Because of the slow speed of the chip, bit-by-bit processing was not possible and additional buffering was also necessary. But, much greater flexibility was introduced into the scope of functions which could be performed, due to its programmability.

Later microprocessor designs, such as the Intel 8080 and National IMP-16, have introduced much greater sophistication into the processor chips accompanied by significant processing speed improvements. A newer PCU design, incorporating an Intel 8080 chip, has demonstrated a considerable reduction in hardware complexity accompanied by an even greater degree of processing flexibility. For example, parity generation and checking are done in software with this prototype design.

Buffering has progressed from the simple shift-register storage devices of the TCU to the use of semiconductor RAM devices used in the microprocessor's random-access memory. All of the micro-instructions for the Intel 8080 microprocessor PCU design reside on four PROM chips, providing 1024 bytes of microcode. The randon-access memory consists of 2048 bytes of RAM.

Recent product introductions such as Intel's 3000 series bi-polar chips promise even greater reductions in chip counts and increases in processing power and speed. With machines such as these, bit-by-bit processing can be readily incorporated into software, thus further eliminating the need for external interfacing hardware and simultaneously providing greater flexibility in the implementation of additional functions. A more detailed discussion of communications microprocessors is given in a companion paper in these proceedings [Fralick et al., 1975].

Size and Power

In the earlier versions of the TCU smaller size and power drain of the unit were not considered major design objectives. The first units were designed for ease of access and hardware modifications to these TCU's were made on a fairly casual basis. As more and more of the ALOHANET came into use, however, small size, portability and lower power drain became desirable.

Of particular interest is the possibility of designing low power battery operated portable PCU's for mobile units in the ALO-HANET. Since the transmitter power need only be on for a short burst corresponding to the period of the data burst, the average power of the transmitter can be a small percentage of the peak power. Since low power and small size were not original design objectives, it appears that the construction of low power portable PCU's will involve redesign of several subsections of the PCU and some new design efforts. Of particular importance is selection of a microprocessor unit which provides a minimum power-drain computer architecture consistent with functional requirements. The modem should be redesigned to use MOS devices to minimize power drain, and the transceiver designed for minimum complexity.

Conclusions

As the system has been modified during the past several years it has become apparent that packet broadcasting architecture is remarkably flexible in its tolerance of hardware, system and protocol modifications. This flexibility follows from the packet verification algorithms which lie at the basis of packet broadcasting. The only packets accepted by a remote unit or by the MENEHUNE are packets which meet all the tests expected by the potential acceptor, and the only system resource consumed by an unaccepted packet is the capacity of the channel during the short burst of the packet duration. Thus it is perfectly feasible in a packet broadcasting network to introduce a new form of packet (new in format, new in packet length, or even new in modulation technique) without disturbing any unit operating with the existing scheme. Only the units designed to look for the new packets will accept these packets and all other units will simply discard them.

We plan to employ this property of packet switched channels to switch the polynomial used for error control in the present packet format. The new polynomial is available in a single IC chip and will allow the possibility of error correction as well as error detection in some cases. As remote units with new packet formats are put into operation we can continue to operate the existing remote units without modification as long as we have a single unit capable of accepting the new packet format at the MENEHUNE. As a side benefit of the introduction of this modification we also note that we have effectively doubled the number of user addresses in the system. An address in use with the old packet format may be reused with the new, since each is effectively invisible to the other.

Another result of our ALOHANET experience, current technology, and recent theoretical work on ALOHA channels, is that a *single-channel* network configuration appears preferable to the two channels used in our present system. The major reason why this is so has to do with the broadcast property of the single-channel system, in which all nodes can (for a given geographic range) hear the transmission of all other nodes in the net.

A number of desirable properties result from this broadcast feature. First, each node can determine if the channel is free before transmitting, greatly reducing the number of packet conflicts—Kleinrock and Tobagi [1976] have shown analytically that this can increase the throughput of a random access channel by a factor of three to five for reasonable user delays, depending on the propagation times between nodes. Second, the problem of sending acknowledgments from user nodes is resolved in a simple manner. Third, system bandwidth can be optimally allocated to both directions of traffic by simple time-sharing of the channel. Fourth, single channel repeaters require only half the radio hardware of two-channel repeaters, and, in fact, the radio transceivers at all nodes need be only half duplex. Finally, a single-channel system constitutes a fully-connected network allowing direct communication between all nodes. A star configuration can still be imposed by protocol to direct all user traffic through a central node, but is no longer required.

It is important to note that many of the above properties are made feasible by the availability of PCU's at a reasonable cost through microcomputer technology. This raises a related issue: the desirability of distributing presently centralized protocol functions such as flow control among the user nodes. Since we have just begun to gain experience with PCU's in a packet broadcast network, we must leave this as an open question.

References

Abramson [1973a]; Abramson [1973b]; Binder, Lai, and Wilson [1974]; Davidson [1972]; Fralick, Brandin, Kuo, and Harrison [1975]; Frank, Van Slyke, and Gitman [1975]; Heart, Kahn, Ornstein, Crowther, and Walden [1970]; Jackson and Stubbs [1969]; Kahn [1975]; Kleinrock and Tobagi [1976]; Lam [1974]; Metcalfe [1973a]; Okumura, Ohmori, Kawano, and Fukuda [1968]; Ornstein, Heart, Crowther, Rising, Russell, and Michel [1972]; Roberts [1973].

Chapter 26

Ethernet: Distributed Packet Switching for Local Computer Networks[1]

Robert M. Metcalfe / David R. Boggs

Summary Ethernet is a branching broadcast communication system for carrying digital data packets among locally distributed computing stations. The packet transport mechanism provided by Ethernet has been used to build systems which can be viewed as either local computer networks or loosely coupled multiprocessors. An Ethernet's shared communication facility, its Ether, is a passive broadcast medium with no central control. Coordination of access to the Ether for packet broadcasts is distributed among the contending transmitting stations using controlled statistical arbitration. Switching of packets to their destinations on the Ether is distributed among the receiving stations using packet address recognition. Design principles and implementations are described, based on experience with an operating Ethernet of 100 nodes along a kilometer of coaxial cable. A model for estimating performance under heavy loads and a packet protocol for error controlled communication are included for completeness.

1. Background

One can characterize distributed computing as a spectrum of activities varying in their degree of decentralization, with one extreme being remote computer networking and the other extreme being multiprocessing. Remote computer networking is the loose interconnection of previously isolated, widely separated, and rather large computing systems. Multiprocessing is the construction of previously monolithic and serial computing systems from increasingly numerous and smaller pieces computing in parallel. Near the middle of this spectrum is local networking, the interconnection of computers to gain the resource sharing of computer networking and the parallelism of multiprocessing.

The separation between computers and the associated bit rate of their communication can be used to divide the distributed computing spectrum into broad activities. The product of separation and bit rate, now about 1 gigabit-meter per second (1

Gbmps), is an indication of the limit of current communication technology and can be expected to increase with time:

Activity	Separation	Bit rate
Remote networks	> 10 km	< .1 Mbps
Local networks	10–.1 km	.1–10 Mbps
Multiprocessors	< .1 km	> 10 Mbps

1.1 Remote Computer Networking

Computer networking evolved from telecommunications *terminal-computer* communication, where the object was to connect remote terminals to a central computing facility. As the need for *computer-computer* interconnection grew, computers themselves were used to provide communication [Abramson and Kuo, 1973; Baran, 1964; Rustin, 1970]. Communication *using* computers as packet switches [Heart et al., 1970; Heart et al., 1972; Kahn, 1975; Metcalfe, 1972a; Metcalfe, 1972b; Metcalfe, 1973a; Metcalfe, 1973b; Roberts and Wessler, 1970] and communications *among* computers for resource sharing [Crocker et al., 1972; Thomas, 1973] were both advanced by the development of the Arpa Computer Network.

The Aloha Network at the University of Hawaii was originally developed to apply packet radio techniques for communication between a central computer and its terminals scattered among the Hawaiian Islands [Abramson, 1970; Abramson and Kuo, 1973]. Many of the terminals are now minicomputers communicating among themselves using the Aloha Network's Menehune as a packet switch. The Menehune and an Arpanet Imp are now connected, providing terminals on the Aloha Network access to computing resources on the U.S. mainland.

Just as computer networks have grown across continents and oceans to interconnect major computing facilities around the world, they are now growing down corridors and between buildings to interconnect minicomputers in offices and laboratories [Ashenhurst and Vonderohe, 1975; Farber et al., 1973; Farber, 1975; Fraser, 1975; Willard, 1973].

1.2 Multiprocessing

Multiprocessing first took the form of connecting an I/O controller to a large central computer; IBM's Asp is a classic example [Rustin, 1970]. Next, multiple central processors were connected to a common memory to provide more power for compute-bound applications [Thorton, 1970]. For certain of these applications, more exotic multiprocessor architectures such as Illiac IV were introduced [Barnes et al., 1968].

More recently minicomputers have been connected in multiprocessor configurations for economy, reliability, and increased

[1]*Comm. ACM*, vol. 19, no. 7, July 1976, pp. 395–404.

system modularity [Ornstein et al., 1975; Wulf and Bell, 1972]. The trend has been toward decentralization for reliability; loosely coupled multiprocessor systems depend less on shared central memory and more on *thin wires* for interprocess communication with increased component isolation [Metcalfe, 1972a; Roberts and Wessler, 1970]. With the continued thinning of interprocessor communication for reliability and the development of distributable applications, multiprocessing is gradually approaching a local form of distributed computing.

1.3 Local Computer Networking

Ethernet shares many objectives with other local networks such as Mitre's Mitrix, Bell Telephone Laboratory's Spider, and U.C. Irvine's Distributed Computing System (DCS) [Farber et al., 1973; Farber, 1975; Fraser, 1975; Willard, 1973]. Prototypes of all four local networking schemes operate at bit rates between one and three megabits per second. Mitrix and Spider have a central minicomputer for switching and bandwidth allocation, while DCS and Ethernet use distributed control. Spider and DCS use a ring communication path, Mitrix uses off-the-shelf CATV technology to implement two one-way busses, and our experimental Ethernet uses a branching two-way passive bus. Differences among these systems are due to differences among their intended applications, differences among the cost constraints under which trade-offs were made, and differences of opinion among researchers.

Before going into a detailed description of Ethernet, we offer the following overview (see Fig. 1).

2. System Summary

Ethernet is a system for local communication among computing stations. Our experimental Ethernet uses tapped coaxial cables to carry variable length digital data packets among, for example, personal minicomputers, printing facilities, large file storage devices, magnetic tape backup stations, larger central computers, and longer-haul communication equipment.

The shared communication facility, a branching Ether, is passive. A station's Ethernet interface connects bit-serially through an interface cable to a transceiver which in turn taps into the passing Ether. A packet is broadcast onto the Ether, is heard by all stations, and is copied from the Ether by destinations which select it according to the packet's leading address bits. This is broadcast packet switching and should be distinguished from store-and-forward packet switching, in which routing is performed by intermediate processing elements. To handle the demands of growth, an Ethernet can be extended using packet repeaters for signal regeneration, packet filters for traffic localization, and packet gateways for internetwork address extension.

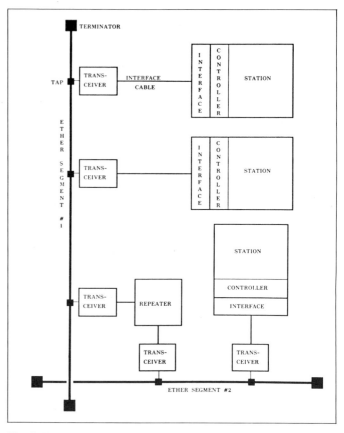

Fig. 1. A two-segment Ethernet.

Control is completely distributed among stations, with packet transmissions coordinated through statistical arbitration. Transmissions initiated by a station defer to any which may already be in progress. Once started, if interference with other packets is detected, a transmission is aborted and rescheduled by its source station. After a certain period of interference-free transmission, a packet is heard by all stations and will run to completion without interference. Ethernet controllers in colliding stations each generate random retransmission intervals to avoid repeated collisions. The mean of a packet's retransmission intervals is adjusted as a function of collision history to keep Ether utilization near the optimum with changing network load.

Even when transmitted without source-detected interference, a packet may still not reach its destination without error; thus, packets are delivered *only with high probability*. Stations requiring a residual error rate lower than that provided by the bare Ethernet packet transport mechanism must follow mutually agreed upon packet protocols.

3. Design Principles

Our object is to design a communication system which can grow smoothly to accommodate several buildings full of personal computers and the facilities needed for their support.

Like the computing stations to be connected, the communication system must be inexpensive. We choose to distribute control of the communications facility among the communicating computers to eliminate the reliability problems of an active central controller, to avoid creating a bottleneck in a system rich in parallelism, and to reduce the fixed costs which make small systems uneconomical.

Ethernet design started with the basic idea of packet collision and retransmission developed in the Aloha Network [Abramson, 1970]. We expected that, like the Aloha Network, Ethernets would carry bursty traffic so that conventional synchronous time-division multiplexing (STDM) would be inefficient [Abramson, 1970; Abramson and Kuo, 1973; Metcalfe, 1973a; Roberts and Wessler, 1970]. We saw promise in the Aloha approach to distributed control of radio channel multiplexing and hoped that it could be applied effectively with media suited to local computer communication. With several innovations of our own, the promise is realized.

Ethernet is named for the historical *luminiferous ether* through which electromagnetic radiations were once alleged to propagate. Like an Aloha radio transmitter, an Ethernet transmitter broadcasts completely-addressed transmitter-synchronous bit sequences called packets onto the Ether and hopes that they are heard by the intended receivers. The Ether is a logically passive medium for the propagation of digital signals and can be constructed using any number of media including coaxial cables, twisted pairs, and optical fibers.

3.1 Topology

We cannot afford the redundant connections and dynamic routing of store-and-forward packet switching to assure reliable communication, so we choose to achieve reliability through simplicity. We choose to make the shared communication facility passive so that the failure of an active element will tend to affect the communications of only a single station. The layout and changing needs of office and laboratory buildings leads us to pick a network topology with the potential for convenient incremental extention and reconfiguration with minimal service disruption.

The topology of the Ethernet is that of an unrooted tree. It is a *tree* so that the Ether can branch at the entrance to a building's corridor, yet avoid multipath interference. There must be only one path through the Ether between any source and destination; if more than one path were to exist, a transmission would interfere with itself, repeatedly arriving at its intended destination having travelled by paths of different length. The Ether is *unrooted* because it can be extended from any of its points in any direction. Any station wishing to join an Ethernet taps into the Ether at the nearest convenient point.

Looking at the relationship of interconnection and control, we see that Ethernet is the dual of a star network. Rather than *distributed* interconnection through many separate links and *central* control in a switching node, as in a star network, the Ethernet has *central* interconnection through the Ether and *distributed* control among its stations.

Unlike an Aloha Network, which is a star network with an outgoing broadcast channel and an incoming multi-access channel, an Ethernet supports many-to-many communication with a single broadcast multi-access channel.

3.2 Control

Sharing of the Ether is controlled in such a way that it is not only possible but probable that two or more stations will attempt to transmit a packet at roughly the same time. Packets which overlap in time on the Ether are said to *collide*; they interfere so as to be unrecognizable by a receiver. A station recovers from a detected collision by abandoning the attempt and retransmitting the packet after some dynamically chosen random time period. Arbitration of conflicting transmission demands is both distributed and statistical.

When the Ether is largely unused, a station transmits its packets at will, the packets are received without error, and all is well. As more stations begin to transmit, the rate of packet interference increases. Ethernet controllers in each station are built to adjust the mean retransmission interval in proportion to the frequency of collisions; sharing of the Ether among competing station-station transmissions is thereby kept near the optimum [Metcalfe, 1973a; Metcalfe, 1973b].

A degree of cooperation among the stations is required to share the Ether equitably. In demanding applications certain stations might usefully take transmission priority through some systematic violation of equity rules. A station could usurp the Ether by not adjusting its retransmission interval with increasing traffic or by sending very large packets. Both practices are now prohibited by low-level software in each station.

3.3 Addressing

Each packet has a source and destination, both of which are identified in the packet's header. A packet placed on the Ether eventually propagates to all stations. Any station can copy a packet from the Ether into its local memory, but normally only an active destination station matching its address in the packet's header will do so as the packet passes. By convention, a zero destination address is a wildcard and matches all addresses; a packet with a destination of zero is called a *broadcast packet*.

3.4 Reliability

An Ethernet is probabilistic. Packets may be lost due to interference with other packets, impulse noise on the Ether, an inactive receiver at a packet's intended destination, or purposeful discard. Protocols used to communicate through an Ethernet must assume that packets will be received correctly at intended destinations *only with high probability*.

An Ethernet gives its *best efforts* to transmit packets successfully, but it is the responsibility of processes in the source and destination stations to take the precautions necessary to assure reliable communication of the quality they themselves desire [Metcalfe, 1972a; Metcalfe, 1973b]. Recognizing the costliness and dangers of promising "error-free" communication, we refrain from guaranteeing reliable delivery of any single packet to get both economy of transmission and high reliability averaged over many packets [Metcalfe, 1973b]. Removing the responsibility for reliable communication from the packet transport mechanism allows us to tailor reliability to the application and to place error recovery where it will do the most good. This policy becomes more important as Ethernets are interconnected in a hierarchy of networks through which packets must travel farther and suffer greater risks.

3.5 Mechanisms

A station connects to the Ether with a *tap* and a *transceiver*. A tap is a device for physically connecting to the Ether while disturbing its transmission characteristics as little as possible. The design of the transceiver must be an exercise in paranoia. Precautions must be taken to insure that likely failures in the transceiver or station do not result in pollution of the Ether. In particular, removing power from the transceiver should cause it to disconnect from the Ether.

Five mechanisms are provided in our experimental Ethernet for reducing the probability and cost of losing a packet. These are (1) carrier detection, (2) interference detection, (3) packet error detection, (4) truncated packet filtering, and (5) collision consensus enforcement.

3.5.1 Carrier Detection.   As a packet's bits are placed on the Ether by a station; they are phase encoded (like bits on a magnetic tape), which guarantees that there is at least one transition on the Ether during each bit time. The passing of a packet on the Ether can therefore be detected by listening for its transitions. To use a radio analogy, we speak of the presence of *carrier* as a packet passes a transceiver. Because a station can sense the carrier of a passing packet, it can delay sending one of its own until the detected packet passes safely. The Aloha Network does not have carrier detection and consequently suffers a substantially higher collision rate. Without carrier detection, efficient use of the Ether would decrease with increasing packet length. In Sec. 6 below, we show that with carrier detection, Ether efficiency increases with increasing packet length.

With carrier detection we are able to implement *deference*: no station will start transmitting while hearing carrier. With deference comes *acquisition*: once a packet transmission has been in progress for an Ether end-to-end propagation time, all stations are hearing carrier and are deferring; the Ether has been acquired and the transmission will complete without an interfering collision.

With carrier detection, collisions should occur only when two or more stations find the Ether silent and begin transmitting simultaneously within an Ether end-to-end propagation time. This will almost always happen immediately after a packet transmission during which two or more stations were deferring. Because stations do not now randomize after deferring, when the transmission terminates, the waiting stations pile on together, collide, randomize, and retransmit.

3.5.2 Interference Detection.   Each transceiver has an interference detector. Interference is indicated when the transceiver notices a difference between the value of the bit it is receiving from the Ether and the value of the bit it is attempting to transmit.

Interference detection has three advantages. First, a station detecting a collision knows that its packet has been damaged. The packet can be scheduled for retransmission immediately, avoiding a long acknowledgment timeout. Second, interference periods on the Ether are limited to a maximum of one round trip time. Colliding packets in the Aloha Network run to completion, but the truncated packets resulting from Ethernet collisions waste only a small fraction of a packet time on the Ether. Third, the frequency of detected interference is used to estimate Ether traffic for adjusting retransmission intervals and optimizing channel efficiency.

3.5.3 Packet Error Detection.   As a packet is placed on the Ether, a checksum is computed and appended. As the packet is read from the Ether, the checksum is recomputed. Packets which do not carry a consistent checksum are discarded. In this way transmission errors, impulse noise errors, and errors due to undetected interference are caught at a packet's destination.

3.5.4 Truncated Packet Filtering.   Interference detection and deference cause most collisions to result in *truncated packets* of only a few bits; colliding stations detect interference and abort transmission within an Ether round trip time. To reduce the processing load that the rejection of such obviously damaged packets would place on listening station software, truncated packets are filtered out in hardware.

3.5.5 Collision Consensus Enforcement.

When a station determines that its transmission is experiencing interference, it momentarily jams the Ether to insure that all other participants in the collision will detect interference and, because of deference, will be forced to abort. Without this *collision consensus enforcement* mechanism, it is possible that the transmitting station which would otherwise be the last to detect a collision might not do so as the other interfering transmissions successively abort and stop interfering. Although the packet may look good to that last transmitter, different path lengths between the colliding transmitters and the intended receiver will cause the packet to arrive damaged.

4. Implementation

Our choices of 1 kilometer, 3 megabits per second, and 256 stations for the parameters of an experimental Ethernet were based on characteristics of the locally distributed computer communication environment and our assessments of what would be marginally achievable; they were certainly not hard restrictions essential to the Ethernet concept.

We expect that a reasonable maximum network size would be on the order of 1 kilometer of cable. We used this working number to choose among Ethers of varying signal attenuation and to design transceivers with appropriate power and sensitivity.

The dominannt station on our experimental Ethernet is a minicomputer for which 3 megabits per second is a convenient data transfer rate. By keeping the peak rate well below that of the computer's path to main memory, we reduce the need for expensive special-purpose packet buffering in our Ethernet interfaces. By keeping the peak rates as high as is convenient, we provide for larger numbers of stations and more ambitious multiprocessing communications applications.

To expedite low-level packet handling among 256 stations, we allocate the first 8-bit byte of the packet to be the destination address field and the second byte to be the source address field (see Fig. 2). 256 is a number small enough to allow each station to get an adequate share of the available bandwidth and approaches the limit of what we can achieve with current techniques for tapping cables. 256 is only a convenient number for the lowest level of protocol; higher levels can accomodate extended address spaces with additional fields inside the packet and software to interpret them.

Our experimental Ethernet implementation has four major

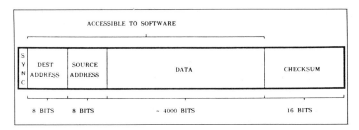

Fig. 2. Ethernet packet layout.

parts: the Ether, transceivers, interfaces, and controllers. (See Fig. 1.)

4.1 Ether

We chose to implement our experimental Ether using low-loss coaxial cable with off-the-shelf CATV taps and connectors. It is possible to mix Ethers on a single Ethernet; we use a smaller-diameter coax for convenient connection within station clusters and a larger-diameter coax for low-loss runs between clusters. The cost of coaxial cable Ether is insignificant relative to the cost of the distributed computing systems supported by Ethernet.

4.2 Transceivers

Our experimental transceivers can drive a kilometer of coaxial cable Ether tapped by 256 stations transmitting at 3 megabits per second. The transceivers can *endure* (i.e. work after) sustained direct shorting, improper termination of the Ether, and simultaneous drive by all 256 stations; they can *tolerate* (i.e. work during) ground differentials and everyday electrical noise, from typewriters or electric drills, encountered when stations are separated by as much as a kilometer.

An Ethernet transceiver attaches directly to the Ether which passes by in the ceiling or under the floor. It is powered and controlled through five twisted pairs in an interface cable carrying transmit data, receive data, interference detect, and power supply voltages. When unpowered, the transceiver disconnects itself electrically from the Ether. Here is where our fight for reliability is won or lost; a broken transceiver can, but should not, bring down an entire Ethernet. A watchdog timer circuit in each transceiver attempts to prevent pollution of the Ether by shutting down the output stage if it acts suspiciously. For transceiver simplicity we use the Ether's base frequency band, but an Ethernet could be built to use any suitably sized band of a frequency division multiplexed Ether.

Even though our experimental transceivers are very simple and can tolerate only limited signal attenuation, they have proven quite adequate and reliable. A more sophisticated transceiver design might permit passive branching of the Ether and wider station separation.

4.3 Interface

An Ethernet interface serializes and deserializes the parallel data used by its station. There are a number of different stations on our Ethernet; an interface must be built for each kind.

Each interface is equipped with the hardware necessary to compute a 16-bit cyclic redundancy checksum (CRC) on serial data as it is transmitted and received. This checksum protects only against errors in the Ether and specifically not against errors in the parallel portions of the interface hardware or station. Higher-level software checksums are recommended for applications in which a higher degree of reliability is required.

A transmitting interface uses a packet buffer address and word count to serialize and phase encode a variable number of 16-bit words which are taken from the station's memory and passed to the transceiver, preceded by a start bit (called SYNC in Fig. 2) and followed by the CRC. A receiving interface uses the appearance of carrier to detect the start of a packet and uses the SYNC bit to acquire bit phase. As long as carrier stays on, the interface decodes and deserializes the incoming bit stream depositing 16-bit words in a packet buffer in the station's main memory. When carrier goes away, the interface checks that an integral number of 16-bit words has been received and that the CRC is correct. The last word received is assumed to be the CRC and is not copied into the packet buffer.

These interfaces ordinarily include hardware for accepting only those packets with appropriate addresses in their headers. Hardware address filtering helps a station avoid burdensome software packet processing when the Ether is very busy carrying traffic intended for other stations.

4.4 Controller

An Ethernet controller is the station-specific low-level firmware or software for getting packets onto and out of the Ether. When a source-detected collision occurs, it is the source controller's responsibility to generate a new random retransmission interval based on the updated collision count. We have studied a number of algorithms for controlling retransmission rates in stations to maintain Ether efficiency [Metcalfe, 1973a; Metcalfe, 1974]. The most practical of these algorithms estimate traffic load using recent collision history.

Retransmission intervals are multiples of a *slot*, the maximum time between starting a transmission and detecting a collision, one end-to-end round trip delay. An Ethernet controller begins transmission of each new packet with a mean retransmission interval of one slot. Each time a transmission attempt ends in collision, the controller delays for an interval of random length with a mean twice that of the previous interval, defers to any

passing packet, and then attempts retransmission. This heuristic approximates an algorithm we have called Binary Exponential Backoff (see Fig. 3) [Metcalfe, 1974].

When the network is unloaded and collisions are rare, the mean seldom departs from one and retransmissions are prompt. As the traffic load increases, more collisions are experienced, a backlog of packets builds up in the stations, retransmission intervals increase, and retransmission traffic backs off to sustain channel efficiency.

5. Growth

5.1 Signal Cover

One can expand an Ethernet just so far by adding transceivers and Ether. At some point, the transceivers and Ether will be unable to carry the required signals. The *signal cover* can be extended with a simple unbuffered *packet repeater*. In our experimental Ethernet, where because of transceiver simplicity the Ether cannot be branched passively, a simple repeater may join any number of

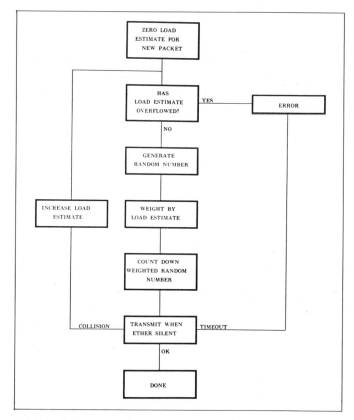

Fig. 3. Collision control algorithm.

Ether *segments* to enrich the topology while extending the signal cover.

We operate an experimental two-segment packet repeater, but hope to avoid relying on them. In branching the Ether and extending its signal cover, there is a trade-off between using sophisticated transceivers and using repeaters. With increased power and sensitivity, transreceivers become more expensive and less reliable. The introduction of repeaters into an Ethernet makes the centrally interconnecting Ether active. The failure of a transceiver will sever the communications of its owner; the failure of a repeater partitions the Ether severing many communications.

5.2 Traffic Cover

One can expand an Ethernet just so far by adding Ether and packet repeaters. At some point the Ether will be so busy that additional stations will just divide more finely the already inadequate bandwidth. The *traffic cover* can be extended with an unbuffered traffic-filtering repeater or *packet filter,* which passes packets from one Ether segment to another only if the destination station is located on the new segment. A packet filter also extends the signal cover.

5.3 Address Cover

One can expand an Ethernet just so far by adding Ether, repeaters, and traffic filters. At some point there will be too many stations to be addressed with the Ethernet's 8-bit addresses. The *address cover* can be extended with *packet gateways* and the software addressing conventions they implement [Cerf and Kahn, 1974]. Addresses can be expanded in two directons: *down* into the station by adding fields to identify destination ports or processes within a station, and *up* into the internetwork by adding fields to identify destination stations on remote networks. A gateway also extends the traffic and signal covers.

There can be only one repeater or packet filter connecting two Ether segments; a packet repeated onto a segment by multiple repeaters would interfere with itself. However, there is no limit to the number of gateways connecting two segments; a gateway only repeats packets addressed to iteself as an intermediary. Failure of the single repeater connecting two segments partitions the network; failure of a gateway need not partition the net if there are paths through other gateways between the segments.

6.   Performance

We present here a simple set of formulas with which to characterize the performance expected of an Ethernet when it is heavily loaded. More elaborate analyses and several detailed simulations have been done, but the following simple model has proven very useful in understanding the Ethernet's distributed contention scheme, even when it is loaded beyond expectations [Abramson, 1970; Metcalfe, 1973a; Metcalfe, 1973b; Metcalfe, 1974; Murthy, 1975; Roberts, 1973b].

We develop a simple model of the performance of a loaded Ethernet by examining alternating Ether time periods. The first, called a *transmission inteval,* is that during which the Ether has been acquired for a successful packet transmission. The second, called a *contention interval,* is that composed of the retransmission slots of Sec. 4.4, during which stations attempt to acquire control of the Ether. Because the model's Ethernets are loaded and because stations defer to passing packets before starting transmission, the slots are synchronized by the tail of the preceding acquisition interval. A slot will be empty when no station chooses to attempt transmission in it and it will contain a collision if more than one station attempts to transmit. When a slot contains only one attempted transmission, then the Ether has been acquired for the duration of a packet, the contention interval ends, and a transmission interval begins.

Let P be the number of bits in an Ethernet *packet*. Let C be the peak *capacity* in bits per second, carried on the Ether. Let T be the *time* in seconds of a slot, the number of seconds it takes to detect a collision after starting a transmission. Let us assume that there are Q stations continuously *queued* to transmit a packet; either the acquiring station has a new packet immediately after a successful acquisition or another station comes ready. Note that Q also happens to give the total *offered load* on the network which for this anaysis is always 1 or greater. We assume that a queued station attempts to transmit in the current slot with probability $1/Q$, or delays with probability $1 - (1/Q)$; this is known to be the optimum statistical decision rule, approximated in Ethernet stations by means of our load-estimating retransmission control algorithms [Metcalfe, 1973a; Metcalfe, 1973b].

6.1 Acquisition Probability

We now compute A, the probability that exactly one station attempts a transmission in a slot and therefore *acquires* the Ether. A is $Q*(1/Q)*((1 - (1/Q))**(Q - 1)$; there are Q ways in which one station can choose to transmit (with probability $(1/Q)$) while $Q - 1$ stations choose to wait (with probability $1 - (1/Q)$). Simplifying,

$$A = (1 - (1/Q))^{(Q-1)}$$

6.2 Waiting Time

We now compute W, the mean number of slots of *waiting* in a contention interval before a successful acquisition of the Ether by a station's transmission. The probability of waiting no time at all is just A, the probability that one and only one station chooses to transmit in the first slot following a transmission. The probability of waiting 1 slot is $A*(1 - A)$; the probability of waiting i slots is $A*((1 - A)**i)$. The mean of this geometric distribution is

$$W = (1 - A)/A$$

6.3 Efficiency

We now compute E, that fraction of time the Ether is carrying good packets, the *efficiency*. The Ether's time is divided between transmission intervals and contention intervals. A packet transmission takes P/C seconds. The mean time to acquisition is $W*T$. Therefore, by our simple model,

$$E = (P/C)/((P/C) + (W*T))$$

Table 1 presents representative performance figures (i.e. E) for our experimental Ethernet with the indicated packet sizes and number of *continuously queued* stations. The efficiency figures given do not account for inevitable reductions due to headers and control packets nor for losses due to imprecise control of the retransmission parameter $1/Q$; the former is straightforwardly protocol-dependent and the latter requires analysis beyond the scope of this paper. Again, we feel that all of the Ethernets in the table are overloaded; normally loaded Ethernets will usually have a Q much less than 1 and exhibit behavior not covered by this model.

For our calculations we use a C of 3 megabits per second and a T of 16 microseconds. The slot duration T must be long enough to allow a collision to be detected or at least twice the Ether's round trip time. We limit in software the maximum length of our packets to be near 4000 bits to keep the latency of network access down and to permit efficient use of station packet buffer storage.

For packets whose size is about 4000 bits, the efficiency of our experimental Ethernet stays well above 95 percent. For packets with a size approximating that of a slot, Ethernet efficiency

Table 1   Ethernet Efficiency

Q	P = 4096	P = 1024	P = 512	P = 48
1	1.0000	1.0000	1.0000	1.0000
2	0.9884	0.9552	0.9143	0.5000
3	0.9857	0.9447	0.8951	0.4444
4	0.9842	0.9396	0.8862	0.4219
5	0.9834	0.9367	0.8810	0.4096
10	0.9818	0.9310	0.8709	0.3874
32	0.9807	0.9272	0.8642	0.3737
64	0.9805	0.9263	0.8627	0.3708
128	0.9804	0.9259	0.8620	0.3693
256	0.9803	0.9257	0.8616	0.3686

approachs $1/e$, the asymptotic efficiency of a slotted Aloha Network [Roberts, 1973b].

7.   Protocol

There is more to the construction of a viable packet communication system than simply providing the mechanisms for packet transport. Methods for error correction, flow control, process naming, security, and accounting must also be provided through higher-level protocols implemented on top of the Ether control protocol described in Sections 3 and 4 above [Cerf and Kahn, 1974; Crocker et al., 1972; Farber et al., 1973; Metcalfe, 1973b; Rowe, 1975; Walden, 1972]. Ether control includes packet framing, error detection, addressing, and multi-access control; like other line control procedures, Ethernet is used to support numerous network and multiprocessor architectures [IBM, 1974; IBM, 1975a].

Here is a brief description of one simple error-controlling packet protocol. The EFTP (Ethernet File Transfer Protocol) is of interest both because it is relatively easy to understand and implement correctly and because it has dutifully carried many valuable files during the development of more general and efficient protocols.

7.1. General Terminology

In discussing packet protocols, we use the following generally useful terminology. A packet is said to have a *source* and a *destination*. A flow of data is said to have a *sender* and a *receiver*, recognizing that to support a flow of data some packets (typically acknowledgments) will be sourced at the receiver and destined for the sender. A connection is said to have a *listener* and an *initiator* and a service is said to have a *server* and a *user*. It is very useful to treat these as orthogonal descriptors of the participants in a communication. Of course, a server is usually a listener and the source of data-bearing packets is usually the sender.

7.2 EFTP

The first 16 bits of all Ethernet packets contain its interface-interpretable destination and source station addresses, a byte each, in that order (see Fig. 2). By software convention, the second 16 bits of all Ethernet packets contain the packet type. Different protocols use disjoint sets of packet types. The EFTP uses 5 packet types: data, ack, abort, end, and endreply. Following the 16-bit type word of an EFTP packet are 16 bits of sequence number, 16 bits of length, optionally some 16-bit data words, and finally a 16-bit software checksum word (see Fig. 4). The ethernet's hardware checksum is present only on the Ether and is not counted at this level of protocol.

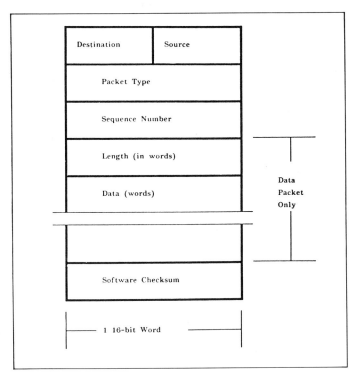

Fig. 4. EFTP packet layout.

It should be obvious that little care has been taken to cram certain fields into just the right number of bits. The emphasis here is on simplicity and ease of programming. Despite this disclaimer, we do feel that it is more advisable to err on the side of spacious fields; try as you may, one field or another will always turn out to be too small.

The software checksum word is used to lower the probability of an undetected error. It serves not only as a backup for the experimental Ethernet's serial hardware 16-bit cyclic redundancy checksum (in Fig. 2), but also for protection against failures in parallel data paths within stations which are not checked by the CRC. The checksum used by the EFTP is a 1's complement add and cycle over the entire packet, including header and content data. The checksum can be ignored at the user's peril at either end; the sender may put all 1's (an impossible value) into the checksum word to indicate to the receiver that no checksum was computed.

7.2.1 Data Transfer. The 16-bit words of a file are carried from sending station to receiving station in data packets consecutively numbered from 0. Each data packet is retransmitted periodically

by the sender until an ack packet with a matching sequence number is returned from the receiver. The receiver ignores all damaged packets, packets from a station other than the sender, and packets whose sequence number does not match either the expected one or the one preceding. When a packet has the expected sequence number, the packet is acked, its data is accepted as part of the file, and the sequence number is incremented. When a packet arrives with a sequence number one less than that expected, it is acknowledged and discarded; the presumption is that its ack was lost and needs retransmission [Metcalfe, 1973b].

7.2.2 End. When all the data has been transmitted, an end packet is sent with the next consecutive sequence number and then the sender waits for a matching endreply. Having accepted an end packet in sequence, the data receiver responds with a matching endreply and then *dallys* for some reasonably long period of time (10 seconds). Upon getting the endreply, the sending station transmits an echoing endreply and is free to go off with the assurance that the file has been transferred successfully. The dallying receiver then gets the echoed endreply and it too goes off assured.

The comparatively complex end-dally sequence is intended to make it practically certain that the sender and receiver of a file will agree on whether the file has been transmitted correctly. If the end packet is lost, the data sender simply retransmits it as it would any packet with an overdue acknowledgement. If the endreply from the data receiver is lost, the data sender will time out in the same way and retransmit the end packet which will in turn be acknowledged by the dallying receiver. If the echoed endreply is lost, the dallying receiver will be inconvenienced having to wait for it, but when it has timed out, the receiver can nevertheless be assured of successful transfer of the file because the end packet has been received.

At any time during all of this, either side is free to decide communication has failed and just give up; it is considered polite to send an abort packet to end the communication promptly in the event of, say, a user-initiated abort or a file system error.

7.2.3 EFTP Shortcomings. The EFTP has been very useful, but its shortcomings are many. First, the protocol provides only for file transfer from station to station in a single network and specifically not from process to process within stations either on the same network or through a gateway. Second, process rendezvous is degenerate in that there are no mechanisms for finding processes by name or for convenient handling of multiple users by a single server. Third, there is no real flow control. If data arrives at a receiver unable to accept it into its buffers, the data can simply be thrown away with complete assurance that it will be retransmitted eventually. There is no way for a receiver to quench the flow of such wasted transmissions or to expedite retransmission. Fourth, data is transmitted in integral numbers of 16-bit words belonging to unnamed files and thus the EFTP is either terribly restrictive or demands some nested file transfer formats internal to its data words. And fifth, functional generality is lost because the receiver is also the listener and server.

8. Conclusion

Our experience with an operating Ethernet leads us to conclude that our emphasis on distributed control was well placed. By keeping the shared components of the communication system to a minimum and passive, we have achieved a very high level of reliability. Installation and maintenance of our experimental Ethernet has been more than satisfactory. The flexibility of station interconnection provided by broadcast packet switching has

encouraged the development of numerous computer networking and multiprocessing applications.

References

Abramson [1970]; Abramson and Kuo [1973]; Ashenhurst and Vonderohe [1975]; Baran [1964]; Barnes, Brown, Kato, Kuck, Slotnick, and Stokes [1968]; Binder, Abramson, Kuo, Okinaka, and Wax [1975]; Cerf and Kahn [1974]; Computer [1974a]; Computer [1974b]; Crocker, Heafner, Metcalfe, and Postel [1972]; Crowther, Heart, McKenzie, McQuillian, and Walden [1975]; Farber, et al. [1973]; Farber [1975]; Fraser [1975]; Heart, Kahn, Ornstein, Crowther, and Walden [1970]; Heart, Ornstein, Crowther, and Barker [1972]; Kahn [1975]; Metcalfe [1972a]; Metcalfe [1972b]; Metcalfe [1973a]; Metcalfe [1973b]; Metcalfe [1974]; Murthy [1975]; Ornstein, Crowther, Kraley, Bressler, Michel, and Heart [1975]; Retz [1975]; Roberts and Wessler [1970]; Roberts [1973b]; Rowe [1975]; Rustin [1970]; IBM [1974]; IBM [1975a]; Thomas [1973]; Thornton [1970]; Walden [1972]; Willard [1973]; Wulf and Bell [1972].

Section 6

Fault-Tolerant Systems

Historically, fault-tolerant computers were limited to military, aerospace, and telephone switching applications, where the consequence of computer failures could be significant economic impact or loss of life. Because of several recent trends, fault-tolerant techniques have become of increasing importance to computers in general. A few of these trends are as follows:

- Critical applications. Computers are being applied in more situations where a computer malfunction could have catastrophic results. Examples include the space shuttle, airliners, hospital patient monitors, and power system control.

- Harsher environments. With the advent of microprocessors, computers have left the clean environments of computer rooms to rest next to arcing motors, ignition coils, and other sources of electromagnetic disturbance. Toleration of transient faults is even more important than in the past.

- Novice users. As computer applications spread, their users are less knowledgeable. Thus the system design has to be more robust not only to run reliably and longer but also to withstand inadvertent user abuse.

- Repair costs. With microprocessor cost coming down and labor costs going up, a user cannot afford to have field service technicians visit too often. In four hours, including transit time, the charge for field service might be one-fourth the total system cost! Users would be better off buying spare computers they can replace themselves or postponing service visits by using fault-tolerant computers.

- Larger systems. As systems become larger there are more components that can fail.

The increased interest in fault tolerance has already had an impact on the industrial world. Large mainframe manufacturers like IBM, UNIVAC, and Amdahl use redundancy both for improving user reliability and for assisting field service personnel in fault isolation. Minicomputer manufacturers have also been incorporating fault-tolerant features (e.g., Hamming error-correcting code on memory), and special LSI chips have been introduced (e.g., cyclic redundancy code encoder/decoders). With low-cost microprocessors, one is tempted to replicate them and "vote" on their outputs; such a system could be built for less than $2,000. The trend has gone so far that companies are being formed to build fault-tolerant computers.

Fault-tolerant computing can be loosely defined as the correct execution of a specified algorithm in the presence of defects. The effect of defects can be overcome through the use of temporal redundancy (repeated calculations) or spatial redundancy (extra hardware or software).

As in all system design, the system goals and specifications constrain the design space and consequently the design techniques that may be used. At the highest level of specification, fault-tolerant systems are categorized as either highly available or highly reliable.

- Availability $A(t)$. The availability of a system as a function of time is the probability that the system is operational at any instant of time t. The limiting availability is the expected proportion of the time that the system is available to run useful computations. Activities such as preventive maintenance and repair reduce the time the system is available to the user. Availability is typically used as a figure of merit in systems where service can be delayed or denied for short periods of time without serious consequence (e.g., batch or time-shared computer systems; telephone and communication systems).

- Reliability $R(t)$. The reliability of a system as a function of time is the conditional probability that the system has survived the interval $[0, t]$, given that it was operational at time $t = 0$. Reliability is used to describe systems in which (1) repair cannot take place or is too costly (e.g., a satellite computer); or (2) the computer is serving a critical function and cannot be lost even for the duration of a repair (e.g., a flight computer on board an aircraft, or the control of a power distribution network). In general it is more difficult to build a highly reliable system than a highly available system because of the more stringent requirements of the reliability definition.

An even more stringent goal than $R(t)$ is sometimes used in aerospace applications: the minimum number of failures anywhere in the system that the system can tolerant while still functioning correctly.

There are three distinct functions a fault-tolerant system can perform: detection, diagnosis, and correction. A highly available system need only worry about fault detection. Diagnosis (fault location) and correction (fault repair) can be done manually. For an ultrareliable system, diagnosis and correction must also be done automatically. Incorporating such features can lead to a significant increase in system cost. Current architectural trends in highly reliable systems are focusing on complete and early detection supported by software and/or firmware (microcode) diagnosis. Repair may be through reconfiguration or spare switching.

Several definitions have become standard in the fault-tolerant literature:

Failure   Physical damage.
Fault   An event in which a logical value differs from the

designed value. Faults may be permanent (caused by a physical failure), intermittent (recurring, probably because a component is on its way to a permanent failure), or transient (induced by something in the outside environment, such as electromagnetic noise).

Error   The first noticeable manifestation of a fault.

Since fault-tolerant computers have usually been custom-designed and are one of a kind, there are not yet enough examples to densely populate a design space. Hence Table 1 is sparsely populated and deals primarily with the desired attributes of the final design. Any fault-tolerant design is heavily influenced by the assumed failure model (i.e., fault type and extent) and the system goal. There are two major redundancy techniques: spatial for surviving permanent faults and temporal for cost-effectively surviving transient faults.

Rather than attempt a concise description of the fault-tolerant space, we shall present a brief description of fault-tolerant techniques. These techniques will be introduced with respect to the three functions: detection, diagnosis, and isolation and corrective action.

Various techniques exist for each activity, their use depending upon the allowable period between error generation and error detection. The longer an error, and hence a physical fault, goes undetected, the more data structures in the system may be polluted. The situation is even more critical in a multiprocessor, where memory and data structures are shared by several concurrently executing processes. Errors can be multiplied by nonfailed components that make incorrect decisions or initiate incorrect operations based on the erroneous information. The longer an error goes undetected, the more difficult the recovery is; eventually recovery becomes impossible. Thus the techniques are aimed at detecting errors at well-defined conceptual boundaries. Generally, smaller boundaries are most costly in terms of hardware or time but allow for more complete recovery. Consider the following conceptual boundaries:

- Hardware subsystem. Typical subsystems may range in size from an arithmetic unit to processors, memories, and buses. Error detection is performed by hardware, and

Table 1   Fault-Tolerant Dimensions

Fault type	System measures
Permanent	Availability
Intermittent	Reliability
Transient	Data integrity
Fault extent	Redundancy type
Single	Spatial
Multiple	Replication
Local	Coding
Distributed	Temporal

recovery is by retry. The goal is to effect recovery without program intervention.

- Task. A dynamic program environment spread across several hardware subsystems. Error detection can be performed at task boundaries by software. Intermediate data may be incorrect, but data passed between task boundaries is correct.

- System. The total hardware/software environment. At this level, application-dependent characteristics are used to simplify the detection/recovery functions. (The previous two levels were application-independent). Here the focus is on continuous service, as opposed to having totally correct data crossing the system boundary. An example might be a sonar signal processor and display. Data arrive continuously, but errors can be detected on a millisecond basis and recovery can be a cold restart.

The next three subsections will briefly discuss detection, diagnosis, and isolation and corrective action at each of three conceptual boundaries. For a more thorough discussion of techniques the reader should consult Neumann [1973] and Avižienis [1975].

Detection

The percentage of faults detected is the single most important factor in successful recovery. An undetected error usually has the result that incorrect information crosses conceptual boundaries and ultimately leads to a system failure.[1] Detection techniques can be continuous (online) or periodic (offline).

- Hardware subsystem. Detection techniques include replication (duplication and comparison [Downing, Nowak, and Tuomenoksa, 1964; Vance, 1957]) and coding for data transmission/storage (parity; arithmetic codes [Rao, 1974; Avižienis, 1971]); self-checking checkers [Anderson and Metze, 1973; Carter et al., 1971; Carter and Schneider, 1969]; cyclic redundancy codes [Peterson and Weldon, 1972]; and hardware processor checks (generated by the hardware subsystem level [IBM, 1972a]).

- Task. Detection techniques include audit programs (checking the integrity of data structures); checksums; memory violations, in which the task attempts to access a memory which does not exist or which it has no right to access [Schroeder and Saltzer, 1972] or is attempting an incorrect

[1]While there is a certain class of applications that rely on statistical properties of data and can function at an acceptable level with internally incorrect data (e.g., speech understanding systems frequently depend on the redundancy in natural speech), those properties have not been applied to computer organization in general and will not be considered here.

access type [Cosserat, 1972; Swan, Fuller, and Siewiorek, 1976]; repeating tasks and comparing; comparing results of two different algorithms and encoding for the same task; and reasonability checks on input/output data.

- System. The detection techniques for the task level also apply at the system level. In addition, a sanity or watchdog timer [Downing, Nowak, and Tuomenoksa, 1964] can be used to detect whether a processor is still executing code in a reasonable sequence.

Diagnosis

Location of a failure can be achieved by analysis of the state of the system when the error is detected. The activity of the error-associated components should be stopped and their intermediate state frozen. A mechanism should be provided to notify some other components in the system of the stoppage. Some unaffected intelligence can then examine state, exercise the components, and initiate a recovery. Thus at each conceptual boundary the object should be controllable and observable. If the fault cannot be resolved by the existing state, a diagnostic sequence can be initiated.

- Hardware subsystem. Control, input, and output signals should be made available to at least one other subsystem. Classical combinational and sequential circuit-testing theory can be used for the diagnostics. Note that the diagnostic resoltuion need only be to the smallest replaceable unit (the chip, the printed circuit board, or even the hardware subsystem itself).

- Task. Each subsystem should be controllable (by halt, start, continue, interrupt, and reinitialize [Wulf and Bell, 1972]) and its internal state (status such as running or disconnected, general-purpose registers, program counter, and error status register) should be observable by at least one external subsystem. Diagnostic programs consist of the functional and implementation-dependent diagnostics typical of any stand-alone computer. Diagnostics for special hardware (e.g., error-detection circuits, controllability and observability logic, and memory protection logic) must also be written. The diagnostics are loaded, initiated, and run by the subsystem that has been notified by an error signal. These autodiagnostics should also be run periodically as a regularly scheduled task or as an idle task.

- System. Same as for task.

Isolation and Corrective Action

The simplest form of isolation is achieved by disconnection or power switching. In either case careful design should ensure that electrical continuity of shared control signals is maintained. For example, most buses have daisy-chained signals, so that disconnecting a module from the bus breaks the daisy chain and denies bus signals to modules downstream from the disconnection.

It should be noted that certain techniques encompass all three steps (detection, diagnosis, and corrective action) in one activity (i.e., massive redundancy techniques, such as triplication and voting [Von Neumann, 1956]). Typically, corrective action takes one of two forms: retry (which is useful for transient-error correction and permanent-failure detection) and standby sparing/graceful degradation. In the latter case, the computation is moved to another part of the system and restarted; enough information must be retained that the restart can be executed cleanly without interference from the side effects of the partially completed first instantiation.

Generally retry is cheaper (as one does not have to keep information for restart) and more effective (the information does not have to be regenerated after negation of side effects). Consider the ARPANET [Heart et al., 1970], where geographically distributed minicomputers form the backbone of a computer communication network (see Chap. 24). All information is buffered by a minicomputer until it receives a positive acknowledgment. Thus a minicomputer can have a transient failure, go through a cold restart by throwing away its memory state, and still have enough information buffered in the rest of the network to pick up with its activities. Even in the case of a permanent failure, the network can reroute the buffered messages without having to regenerate the information.

- Hardware subsystem. Corrective action includes switching in of standby spares (which is effective for combination logic) and transmission retry of buffered information.

- Task. Corrective action includes checkpointing the task and moving to nonfailed hardware subsystems [Avižienis et al., 1971] and instruction retry [IBM, 1972a]. It should be noted that care in design of the processor's instruction set can greatly simplify the retry. For example, PDP-11 instructions can generate up to seven addresses, any of which may cause an error. Certain addressing modes (such as autoincrement) have side effects. Thus it is not enough to know the start of the instruction; it is also necessary to know how far it has progressed so that side effects can be undone prior to instruction retry.

- System. Many timesharing systems have developed techniques that allow retry and graceful degradation. For user programs, the operating system checkpoints the initialization information and buffers the output information until task completion. Thus when an error occurs the task can be restarted. For large tasks the user may decide to issue commands to the operating system that save intermediate states so that computations can restart at the latest intermediate state. Certain user programs that process continuous data (sonar signal processing and speech recognition, for example) or transform data (sorting) can be restarted without any checkpoint information. The operating system must be able to dynamically handle failed resources (memories, disk blocks, and processors, for example) by reassignment. Errors during the execution of the operating system are more serious, since critical systems tables may be affected or pending interrupts lost. Both cases should be guarded against by redundancy and buffering.

There are several examples of fault-tolerant computers described in this book.

STAR

The Self-Test and Repair (STAR) experimental computer developed by the Jet Propulsion Laboratory (JPL) is a milestone in fault-tolerant system design. The STAR was intended to be a prototype for real time satellite-control computer targeted for a 10-year mission[1] to the outer planets of the solar system. For such a purpose, the fault-tolerant emphasis was on a high probability of computer and system program survival through a 10-year mission in an unattended environment. Data collection and telemetry integrity was of less concern, given the natural redundancy in data and the long time frame involved. Certain system status information had to be reliably remembered and certain control functions had to be unerringly carried out.

Chapter 27 presents the architecture of this unique computer. STAR primarily used hardware-subsystem fault-tolerant techniques such as functional-unit redundancy, voting, power switching of spares, coding, and self-checks. Task-level rollback was also blended into this design, which represented the leading edge of fault-tolerant techniques in the 1960s.

Pluribus

As discussed earlier (Part 2, Sec. 4), Pluribus was conceived as a modular, highly available multiprocessor for the ARPANET IMP task. Chapter 23 described the architecture as well as the fault-tolerant techniques employed.

Most of the Pluribus fault tolerance is achieved at the software task level. A relatively long period between fault occurrence and fault detection is acceptable because of the nature of the IMP task. The several levels of protocol in the ARPANET (See Part 2, Sec.

---

[1]The "Grand Tour" mission was to take advantage of the alignment of the five outer planets of the solar system in the early 1980s. A spacecraft launched from earth could use the planetary alignment for a gravitational boost in traveling from one planet to the next. The Grand Tour was replaced in NASA's budget by a series of cheaper Pioneer probes that visited different sets of planets.

5), each with its own error detection and recovery, mean that the Pluribus need not concentrate on data integrity. If a failure in a Pluribus occurs, all the in-progress messages are buffered at other ARPANET nodes until positively acknowledged. These messages are eventually rerouted past the failed Pluribus. Even if the subnet protocol fails to reliably complete the message transmission, the Host-to-Host protocol will retry the entire message transmission.

Thus the application requires only that the Pluribus recover gracefully from a failure. This goal can be achieved by quick system reinitialization with omission of questionable components.

The Pluribus IMP software utilizes:

- Periodic software checks including diagnostics
- Redundancy in data structures
- Watchdog timers that must constantly be reset by software

The multiprocessor structure allows for maximum performance when there are no failures (i.e., the periodic checks are estimated to degrade performance by only 1 percent) and maximum assistance when there are failures (i.e., by focusing all resources on reaching a consensus on a failure-free configuration).

The network structure allows for remote diagnosis from the Network Control Center (NCC). Even in the case of total destruction of memory contents, the Pluribus can request that the code be transmitted from the NCC or other Pluribuses in the network. Any transitory messages lost will be restored via the retransmission mechanism in the various levels of protocol.

It is well known that the best system diagnostic is the normal execution of programs. Frequently, normal execution will stress the system in ways not reproduced by diagnostics (this is especially true for I/O or timing-sensitive problems). The "friendly" environment provided by the IMP application allows the Pluribus to rotate hardware into use. Any problematic hardware will appear only as a transient to the system, since the offender will be quickly configured out.

The Pluribus represents a cost-effective fault-tolerant architecture that takes fullest advantage of the characteristics of its application environment (i.e., real time applications where data loss and brief outages are tolerable). The Pluribus is operational in the ARPANET and has achieved a measured factor of 5 improvement in unavailability (0.32 percent) over the previous-generation IMPs (1.64 percent) [Kleinrock and Naylor, 1974].

ESS Processors

The Electronic Switching Systems (ESS) developed by Bell Laboratories over the last two decades are the most numerous fault-tolerant digital systems. The ESS systems handle the routing of telephone calls through central offices. They have a severe availability goal, only 2 hours' downtime in 40 years (i.e., 3 min/yr).

Telephone switching has many properties in common with the ARPANET IMP's real time routing of information. There is some natural redundancy in the network and in the data (telephone users will re-dial if they get a wrong number or are disconnected). However, there is a user aggravation level that must be avoided: users will re-dial so long as it does not happen too frequently. Note, moreover, that the thresholds are different for failure to establish a call (moderately high) and disconnection of an established call (very low). Thus a staged recovery from failures is followed as depicted in Table 2.

A substantial portion of the complexity of an ESS system is in the peripheral hardware. Since the telephone switching application leads to a substantially different PMS structure from others studied so far, the following abstract has been included to briefly describe the hardware of the No. 4 ESS system.[1]

Figure 1 contains an overall system diagram of a No. 4 ESS office, broken down by major functional blocks. Essentially it consists of a digital time division network which switches digitally encoded 4-wire long distance telephone traffic. This is controlled by a stored-program processor abetted by a group of autonomous

[1] The remainder of the subsection on ESS processors, including Fig. 1, is abstracted from J. J. Kulzer, "Systems Reliability: A Case Study of No. 4 ESS," in *System Security and Reliability. Infotech State of the Art Report,* 1977, pp. 186–188.

Table 2   ESS Stages

Phase	Recovery action	Effect
1	Initialize specific transient memory.	Affects temporary storage. No calls lost.
2	Reconfigure peripheral hardware. Initialize all transient memory.	Calls in process of being established lost. Calls in progress not lost.
3	Verify memory operation, establish a workable processor configuration, verify program, configure peripheral hardware, initialize all transient memory.	Calls in process of being established lost. Calls in progress not lost.
4	Establish a workable processor configuration, configure peripheral hardware, initialize all memory.	All calls lost.

signalling units (signal processors and terminals). The major functional blocks of Fig. 1 can be further segregated into four major areas: 1A Processor, network, signal processors, and transmission interface.

Each area is reviewed below with a brief functional description of its component subsystems.

1A Processor

- Central Control (CC): Main processor performing logic and data manipulation associated with call processing, administrative tasks, and a recovery task.

- Program Store (PS): Memory complex storing executable instructions.

- Call Store (CS): Memory complex storing transient information related to the processing of telephone calls as well as data describing office equipment and routing (referred to as translations).

- File Store (FS): Disk system used to store backup program copies, seldom used maintenance programs, and other miscellaneous types of data.

- Auxiliary Units (AU): Additional units used to reference magnetic tape storage media which retain basic restart programs, new input data, and support maintenance. Also possible future use for data link features.

- Input/Output (I/O): Interface hardware used to reference input and output terminal devices.

- Bus Systems (AU, PS, CS, PU): Bus systems used to interconnect the various functional units with the Central Control.

- Master Control Console (MCC): Control and display console to permit limited manual control of system and provide performance information.

Network

Time Slot Interchange (TSI): First and fourth stage of the 4-stage time-shared switching network. Performs time division of the time-space-time switching function (described in later paragraphs).

- Time Multiplexed Switch (TMS): Provides second and third stage of 4-stage switching (time-shared space portion).

- Network Clock (NC): Provides very accurate timing signals for the switching network.

- Peripheral Unit Bus Interface (PUBI): Provides interface between 1A Processor and the peripheral units.

Transmission Interface

- Voiceband Interface Frame (VIF): Interfaces analogue transmission facilities with the network of converting analogue

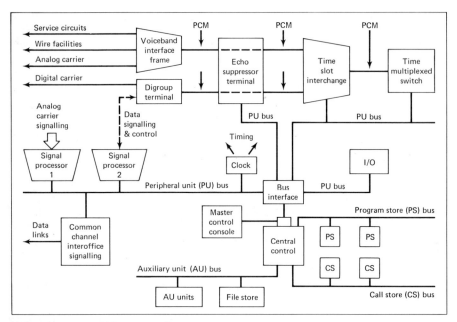

Fig. 1. The No. 4 ESS system diagram.

voiceband channels into digitally encoded Pulse-Code Modulated (PCM) signals.

- Digroup Terminal (DT): Interfaces digital transmission facilities with the network. Provides signalling interfaces with these facilities.

- Echo Suppressor Terminal (EST): Provides digital 4-wire Echo Suppression capability for long distance trunks, both analogue and digital.

Signal Processors

- Signal Processor 1 (SP1): provides scanning and signal distributing functions for analogue carrier, metallic trunk and service circuits. Also can provide miscellaneous control points for other peripheral units.

- Signal Processor 2 (SP2): Performs scanning and signal distributing functions for digital carrier trunks terminated on DTs. Can also provide miscellaneous scan and signal distribution functions similar to the SP1.

- Common Channel Interoffice Signalling (CCIS) Terminal. Terminates the Interoffice CCIS data links serving as the interface between these data links and the signal processors and 1A Processor.

Briefly, No. 4 ESS operates in the following manner. Various types of transmission channels, analogue and digital carriers, and

both 2-wire and 4-wire metallic trunks are connected to voice-frequency terminal units. The 4-wire outputs are connected to subunits (VIUs) of the Voiceband Interface Frame (VIF). These VIUs sample, multiplex, and digitally encode analogue signals in one direction, reversing the process for the other. The digital output, a 128 time-slot digital bus, carries 8-bit Pulse-Code Modulated (PCM) signals in each time slot to the Time Slot Interchange (TSI). The TSI, among other functions, provides a stage of switching PCM signals to different time slots on the bus. The output of the TSI goes to the Time Multiplexed Switch (TMS), which permits switching of the PCM signals during a particular time slot from any bus to any other. The output of the TMS goes to the TSI where PCM signals may be interchanged to another time slot and back to a VIU for reconversion to analogue space-divided signals. The VIU does no switching. A similar scenario exists for digital lines (T1 carrier) which terminate on subunits of the Digroup Terminals, called DTUs. However, the DTU also handles synchronization and signal extraction/insertion for these facilities, eliminating any need for conventional scan and signal distribution interfaces to channel banks in the transmission area.

Four-wire echo suppression can be provided optionally by the Echo Suppressor Terminal (EST) which can be placed between the VIF and TSI or DT and TSI depending on facility needs.

The EST has subunits, ESUs which reside on the digital bus between the VIF/DT and the TSI. These subunits process the digital PCM signals passing in both directions of each 4-wire trunk and digitally suppress detected echos. Coordinated timing for all of the above functions is critical and is provided by the network clock. The wired logic Signal Processor (SP) is used to provide scanning and signal distribution functions, relieving the central processor of any need to perform these duties. Similar functions are provided for digital trunks by the SP2. The Common Channel Interoffice Signalling (CCIS) terminal provides a separate data link for signalling as an alternative to in-band signalling over trunk facilities. The separate signalling system handles digital signals in a special format over a 2-way data channel between switching machines. This system handles both supervisory and address signals for a group of trunks. The CCIS terminal interfaces to the system processor over the peripheral bus.

The entire complement of peripheral hardware described above is controlled by the 1A Processor using parallel ac-coupled buses. The processor interfaces with the periphery through the Peripheral Unit Bus Interface and has been designed to be separable for use in other applications such as No. 1A ESS.

The 1A Processor provides overall system control, administration and call processing support. Complete self-contained system maintenance is also provided through the 1A Processor. Elements of this include automatic isolation of faulty units, defensive software strategies, and system supported rapid repair.

Chapter 28 sketches the family history of ESS processors as summarized in Table 3.

Tandem

Tandem Computers Inc. was founded in 1974 for the purpose of building high-availability computer systems for commercial transaction processing. The Tandem 16 is the first commercially available, modular expandable system designed specifically for high availability. Design objectives for the system included

- "NonStop"[1] operation wherein failures are detected, components reconfigured out of service, and repaired components configured back into the system without stopping the other system components

- Preventing any single hardware failure from compromising the data integrity of the system

- Modular system expansion through adding more processing power, memory, and peripherals without impacting applications software

The Tandem 16 architecture and performance are depicted in Figs. 2 and 3. It is composed of up to 16 computers interconnected by two message-oriented Dynabuses. A loosely coupled architecture was selected over a tightly coupled shared memory architecture, since it was felt that the former allowed for more complete fault containment. Built-in hardware error detection includes

- Checksums on Dynabus messages

- Parity on data paths

- Error-correcting code memory

- Watchdog timers

All I/O device controllers are dual-ported so that they can be accessed by an alternate path in case of Pc or Pio failure. Upon this hardware structure, the software builds a process-oriented system with all communications handled as messages. This abstraction allows the blurring of the physical boundaries between processors and peripherals. Any I/O device or resource in the system can be accessed by a process, no matter where the resource and process reside.

Data integrity is maintained through the mechanism of I/O

[1]NonStop is a trademark of Tandem Computers Inc.

Table 3

System	Number of lines	Year introduced	Processor	Number installed	Comments
EES-1	5,000–65,000	1965	No.1	1,000	First processor with separate control and data memories.
ESS-2	1,000–10,000	1969	No. 2	500	
ESS-1A	>10,000	1976	No. 1A		Four to eight times faster than No. 1 processor.
ESS-2B	1,000-20,000	1975	No. 3	500	Combined control and data store.
ESS-3	500-5,000	1976	No. 3		Microcoded, emulates No. 2 processor.

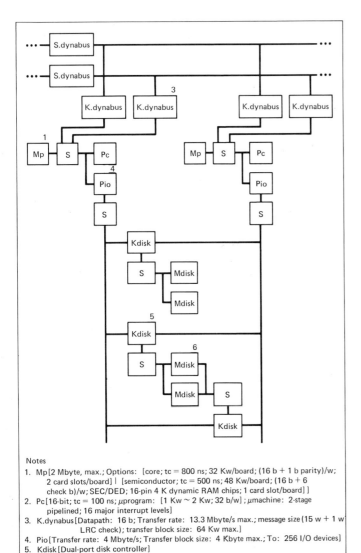

Notes

1. Mp[2 Mbyte, max.; Options: [core; tc = 800 ns; 32 Kw/board; (16 b + 1 b parity)/w; 2 card slots/board] │ [semiconductor; tc = 500 ns; 48 Kw/board; (16 b + 6 check b)/w; SEC/DED; 16-pin 4 K dynamic RAM chips; 1 card slot/board]]

2. Pc[16-bit; tc = 100 ns; μprogram: [1 Kw ~ 2 Kw; 32 b/w]; μmachine: 2-stage pipelined; 16 major interrupt levels]

3. K.dynabus[Datapath: 16 b; Transfer rate: 13.3 Mbyte/s max.; message size (15 w + 1 w LRC check); transfer block size: 64 Kw max.]

4. Pio[Transfer rate: 4 Mbyte/s; Transfer block size: 4 Kbyte max.; To: 256 I/O devices]

5. Kdisk [Dual-port disk controller]

6. Mdisk [Dual-port disk drive]

Fig. 2. Tandem PMS diagram.

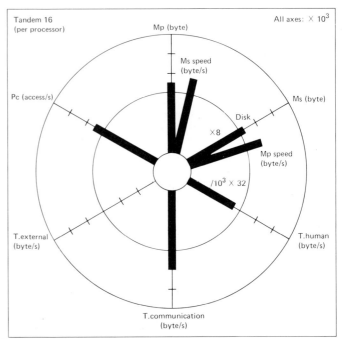

Fig. 3. Tandem 16 (per processor) Kiviat graph.

"process-pairs." One I/O process is designated as primary, the other as backup. All file modification messages are delivered to the primary I/O process. The primary sends a message with checkpoint information to the backup so that it can take over if the primary's processor or access path to the I/O device fails. Files can also be duplicated on physically distinct devices controlled by an I/O process-pair on physically distinct processors. All file modification messages are delivered to both I/O processes. Thus, in the case of physical failure or isolation of the primary, the backup file is up to date and available.

User applications can also use the process-pair mechanism. Consider a NonStop application program A. Program A starts up a backup process A1 in another processor. There are also duplicate file images, one designated primary and the other backup. Program A periodically (at user-specified points) sends checkpoint information to A1. A1 is the same program as A, but it knows that it is a backup program. A1 reads checkpoint messages to update its data area, file status, and program counter. A1 loads and executes if the system reports A's processor is down (i.e., if an error message is sent from A's operating system image or if A's processor fails to respond to a periodic "I'm alive" message). All file activity by A is performed on both the primary and backup file copies. When A1 starts to execute from the last checkpoint, it may attempt to repeat I/O operations successfully completed by A. The system file handler will recognize this situation and send A1 a successfully completed I/O message. A1 periodically asks the operating system whether a backup process exists. Since one no longer does, it can request the creation and initialization of a copy of both the process and file structure. More information on the operating system and the programming of NonStop applications can be found in Bartlett [1977].

Software exists so that up to 255 geographically dispersed Tandem systems can be interconnected in a distributed data processing network. Tandem applications have included order entry, hospital records, bank transactions, and library transactions. As of fall 1978, 109 systems incorporating 257 processors had been installed. The smallest systems employed two processors, and the largest, ten processors.

Chapter 51 discusses Reliability, Availability, and Serviceability (RAS) features in the System/370 line of general-purpose commercial computers.

References

Anderson and Metze [1973]; Avižienis, Mathur, Rennels, and Rohr [1971]; Avižienis [1975]; Bartlett [1977]; Carter, Jessup, Schneider, Wadia, and Bouricius [1971]; Carter and Schneider [1969]; Cosserat [1972]; Downing, Nowak, and Tuomenoksa [1964]; Heart, Kahn, Ornstein, Crowther, and Walden [1970]; IBM [1972a]; Kleinrock and Naylor [1974]; Neumann [1973]; Peterson and Weldon [1972]; Rao [1974]; Schroeder and Saltzer [1972]; Swan, Fuller, and Siewiorek [1976]; Vance, Dooley, and Diss [1957]; Von Neumann [1956]; Wulf and Bell [1972].

Chapter 27

The STAR (Self-Testing And Repairing) Computer:
An Investigation of the Theory and Practice of Fault-Tolerant Computer Design[1]

*Algirdas Avižienis / George C. Gilley /
Francis P. Mathur / David A. Rennels /
John A. Rohr / David K. Rubin*

Summary This paper presents the results obtained in a continuing investigation of fault-tolerant computing which is being conducted at the Jet Propulsion Laboratory. Initial studies led to the decision to design and construct an experimental computer with dynamic (standby) redundancy, including replaceable subsystems and a program rollback provision to eliminate transient errors. This system, called the STAR computer, began operation in 1969. The following aspects of the STAR system are described: architecture, reliability analysis, software, automatic maintenance of peripheral systems, and adaptation to serve as the central computer of an outerplanet exploration spacecraft.

Introduction: Chronology and Rationale

This paper presents a summary of the theoretical results and design experience obtained in an investigation of fault-tolerant computing which is being conducted at the Jet Propulsion Laboratory (JPL). Initial studies (1961–1965) led to the conclusion that dynamic (also called standby) redundancy offered the greatest promise in the design of fault-tolerant digital computer systems [Avižienis, 1967a]. The *dynamic* redundancy [Short, 1968] approach requires a two-step procedure for the elimination of a fault: first, the presence of a fault is determined; second, a corrective action is taken (e.g., replacement of failed unit, repetition of program, reconfiguration of systems, etc.). The alternative to the dynamic approach is *static* (masking) redundancy [Short, 1968], which was already being utilized in existing component-redundant [Lewis, 1963; Kuehn, 1969] and triple-modular-redundant (TMR) [Kuehn, 1969; Anderson and Macri, 1967; Lyons and Vanderkulk, 1962] computers. Early analytic studies of dynamic redundancy with idealized series-parallel system models indicated that mean life gains of an order of magnitude and more

[1]*IEEE Trans. on Computers*, vol. C-20, no. 11, November 1971, pp. 1,312–1,321

over a nonredundant system could be expected from dynamically redundant systems with standby spares replacing failed units [Reed and Brimley, 1962; Kruus, 1963; Flehinger, 1958; Griesmer, Miller, and Roth, 1962]. This gain compared favorably with the mean life gain of less than two in the typical TMR systems. Other qualitative advantages of the dynamic over the static redundancy were: (1) greater isolation of catastrophic (non-independent) faults which is especially important for densely packed microelectronic circuitry; (2) survival of system until all spares of one type are exhausted; (3) ability to eliminate errors which are caused by transient faults by the use of program rollback; (4) ready adjustability of the number and type of spare units; (5) utilization of the potentially lower failure rate of unpowered components in spare units; (6) avoidance of the circuit-related problems of static redundancy: increases in fan-out, fan-in, power requirements, and the need for isolation and synchronization of separate channels; and (7) facilitation of the check out of spare units by means of standard diagnostic programs.

The attainment of the apparent advantages of a dynamically redundant system had been shown to depend very strongly on the successful execution of the detection and replacement operations [Flehinger, 1958; Griesmer, Miller, and Roth, 1962]; these observations have since been formalized as the concept of "coverage" [Bouricius, Carter, and Schneider, 1969].

The second phase of the investigation (1965–1970) was focused on the identification and solution of the problems involved in the design of a general-purpose digital computer possessing the properties attributed to the abstract model of a dynamically redundant computing system. Three major areas of investigation were: (1) an investigation of fault-detection methods; (2) a study of computer architecture with emphasis on partitioning into subsystems with minimal interconnection requirements; and (3) a study of the "hard-core" problem, i.e., the alternate technologies and logic organizations for implementing the detection and switching functions. The choices among feasible alternatives in all three areas are strongly affected by assumptions on the available component technology and on the computing tasks to be required of the computer. In order to retain contact with the practice of computer design, it was decided to design and construct an experimental general-purpose digital computer which would incorporate dynamic redundancy (i.e., fault detection and replacement of failed subsystems) as integral parts of its structure. The design objectives have been carried out and the system, called the STAR (self-testing and repairing) computer, began operation in 1969. The modular nature of the STAR computer has allowed systematic expansion and modifications that are still being continued.

The first objective of the design is to study the class of problems which are encountered in transforming the theoretical model of a self-repairing system into a working computer. State-of-the-art integrated circuit and memory technology was employed in the design. The STAR computer characteristics were chosen to satisfy all predictable requirements of a spacecraft guidance, control, and data acquisition computer which would be used in the very long (ten years and more) unmanned missions exploring the outer planets of the solar system [Long, 1969]. The second objective was to provide a tool for laboratory studies of fault-tolerant computing, including the injection of transient as well as permanent faults of catastrophic nature. Very extensive displays of registers, manually controlled clocking, and provisions for convenient modification of subsystems were incorporated into the experimental STAR computer breadboard (Fig. 1).

The STAR computer employs a balanced mixture of coding, monitoring, standby redundancy, replication with voting, component redundancy, and repetition in order to attain hardware-controlled self-repair and protection against transient faults. The principal goal of the design is to attain fault tolerance for a variety of faults: transient, permanent, random, and catastrophic. The actual construction (rather than simulation) of the STAR breadboard has two significant advantages. First, the design process has uncovered interesting new hardware-related problems and led to numerous improvements. Second, the computer serves as a vehicle for further experimentation and refinement of the recovery techniques.

Fig. 1. The STAR computer.

During the studies of fault-tolerant architecture and the design of the STAR computer, concurrent investigations were being conducted in other closely related areas of fault-tolerant computing, including studies of software, reliability prediction, and extension of dynamic redundancy to peripheral devices [Avižienis et al., 1969]. A complete redesign of the STAR computer is being performed to match the exact requirements of a control computer for the thermoelectric outer planet spacecraft (TOPS) [Astronaut., 1970]. This effort led to the evaluation of additional fault-recovery techniques. The results of the efforts described above are summarized in the following sections of this paper.

Architecture of the STAR Computer

Methods of Fault Tolerance

The STAR computer is a replacement system that provides one standard configuration of functional subsystems with the required computing capacity. The standard computer is supplemented with one or more spares of each subsystem. The spares are unpowered and are used to replace operating units when permanent faults are discovered. The principal methods of error detection and recovery are the following.

1 All machine words (data and instructions) are encoded in error-detecting codes and fault detection occurs concurrently with the execution of the programs.

2 The computer is divided into a set of replaceable functional units containing their own instruction decoders and sequence generators. This decentralization allows simple fault location procedures and simplifies system interfaces.

3 Fault-detection, recovery, and replacement are carried out by special-purpose hardware. In the case of memory damage, software augments the recovery hardware.

4 Transient faults are identified and their effects are corrected by the repetition of a segment of the current program; permanent faults are eliminated by the replacement of faulty functional units.

5 The replacement is implemented by power switching: units are removed by turning power off and connected by turning power on. The information lines of all units are permanently connected to the buses through isolating circuits; unpowered units produce only logic "zero" outputs.

6 The error-detecting codes are supplemented by monitoring circuits which serve to verify the proper synchronization and internal operation of the functional units.

7 The "hard core" test and repair processor (TARP) is protected by triplication and replacement of failed members of the triplet.

Hardware System Organization

The block diagram of the STAR computer is shown in Fig. 2. Communication between the units is carried out on two four-wire buses: the memory-out (M-O) bus, and the memory-in (M-I) bus. The abbreviations designate the following units.

COP   Control processor, contains the location counter and index registers and performs modification of instruction addresses before execution.

LOP   Logic processor, performs logical operations on data words (two copies are powered).

MAP   Main arithmetic processor, performs arithmetic operations on data words.

ROM   READ-ONLY memory, 16,384 permanently stored words.

RWM   READ-WRITE memory unit with 4096 words of storage (at least two copies powered; 12 units are directly addressable).

IOP   Input/output processor, contains I/O buffer registers.

IRP   Interrupt processor, handles interrupt requests.

TARP Test and repair processor, monitors the operation of the computer and implements recovery (three copies are powered).

The functional units (processors and memories) of the STAR computer communicate by means of the M-I and M-O (four-wire) information buses. The 32-bit words are transmitted on these two buses as eight bytes of four bits each. Three control signals are sent from the TARP on the three-wire control bus to synchronize the operations of the functional units and to initiate recovery. Otherwise the functional units operate autonomously. Unless otherwise noted, one copy of each unit is powered at a given time. The decentralized organization allows a standard interface between each unit and the remainder of the computer. Each STAR unit interfaces with the computer by the means of 14 signal lines. Eleven lines, both in active and spare units, are permanently connected to the computer system buses, and three are connected

to the TARP array. An unpowered unit cannot produce logic one outputs. The external connections of a STAR unit are shown in Fig. 3.

The four input and four output lines are connected to the data M-I and M-O buses. They receive and send coded machine words in four-bit bytes. The power switch control input causes power to be applied to the unit. The three control bus input signals are: CLOCK, a basic timing input: SYNC, a periodic synchronization signal; and RESET, a signal that forces the unit into a standard initial state. Two unit status lines send information on the internal operation of the unit to the TARP. These lines carry multiplexed information which will be discussed in a following section. Each functional unit is autonomous and contains its own sequence generator as well as storage for the current operation code, operands, and results. The internal design of a unit may be altered without affecting other units as long as the interface specifications are observed.

It is to be noted that the IOP and IRP units are shown combined in Fig. 2.

Standard Operation

The STAR computer has two modes of operation: the standard mode and the recovery mode (under TARP control). During the *standard mode* the stored programs are carried out. The TARP processor issues the principal CLOCK signal and SYNC signal which occurs when a new step is initiated in the execution of an instruction. Ten CLOCK periods form the basic time unit (cycle) of the computer. During the first period, a four-bit "step-code" (in 2-out-of-4 encoding) is issued by the TARP to the M-O bus. The next eight periods are employed to transmit or manipulate one eight-byte machine word. During the tenth period a four-bit "condition-code" byte may be broadcast by one of the functional units. The ten-period cycle is needed because of the series-parallel organization of the computer.

One instruction is executed in two or three steps. In the first step, the address of the instruction is sent from the location

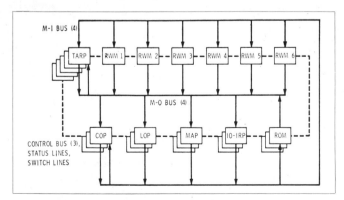

Fig. 2. STAR computer organization.

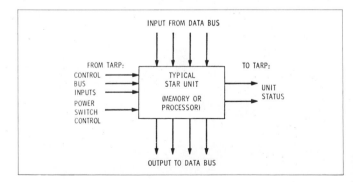

Fig. 3. Functional unit of STAR computer.

counter in the COP to the memory (ROM and RWM) units. In the second step, the addressed memory unit broadcasts on the M-O bus the operation code and address of the instruction to all functional units. The address is indexed in the COP which transmits it to the M-I bus if necessary. The appropriate units recognize the operation code, store the address, and initiate execution. In the third step the instruction is executed: an operand is placed on the appropriate bus and accepted by the destination unit. The first two steps require one cycle each; the duration of the third step depends on the instruction and requires 0, 1, or more cycles. Program interrupts begin without the first step. During the second step an instruction is broadcast by the interrupting unit (IO-IRP or TARP).

The instruction set consists of 180 single-address instructions, about one-third of which are indexable. It includes fixed-point arithmetic, maskable logic, and shift operations. Loop-facilitating and subroutine link register instructions are provided. There are 28 interrupts which can be masked out and tested under program control. A special class of instructions aids in fault tolerance. They include diagnostic instructions which exercise unit status messages and the fault-location logic in the TARP. Others perform updating of the "rollback" register in TARP units, name assignment and cancellation of RWM units, power control of spare units, duplexing of ROMs and processors, and absolute read or write operations in RWM units.

Computer Words: Formats and Encoding

There are two possible effects of logic faults upon the operation of a digital computer. First, a data word or an instruction word may be altered during storage, transmission, or processing. The effect is a *word error*. Second, during the execution of an instruction a processor or a memory module may act incorrectly, act out of turn, or fail to act at all. The effect is a *control error*. Both classes of errors are detected in the STAR computer. The present section considers coding techniques for word error detection; control errors are considered later.

Complete duplication offers the simplest word-error detection at the highest cost. Low-cost arithmetic error-detecting codes [Avižienis, 1967b] are attractive because they are preserved during arithmetic processing and mandatory duplication of an arithmetic processor is avoided. An intensive study of error codes led to the choice of modulo 15 arithmetic checking which is especially effective for a byte-organized computer with four-bit bytes [Avižienis, 1971].

All words in the STAR computer are encoded as shown in Fig. 4. The 32-bit numeric operand word [Fig. 4b] consists of the 28-bit binary number b, and a 4-bit check byte $c(b)$. The check byte is a binary number which has the value

$$c(b) = 15 - |b|_{15}$$

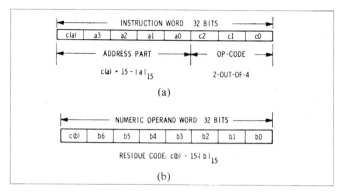

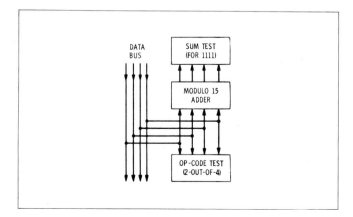

Fig. 4. (a) STAR instruction word format. **(b)** STAR operand word format.

where $|b|_{15}$ means "the modulo 15 residue of b." This check byte causes the 32-bit word to be a multiple of 15. The checking algorithm casts out 15s, that is, it computes the modulo 15 residue of the entire coded word. A zero residue, represented by 1111, indicates a correct word; all other values of the residue indicate a fault. The casting out 15s is implemented with a four-bit "end-around carry" adder and takes place concurrently with the transmission of a word on the bus.

The 32-bit instruction word [Fig. 4a] consists of a 12-bit operation code and a 20-bit residue-coded address part. The 16-bit address is encoded in the same residue code as the operands, and the same checking algorithm is used. The operation code is divided into three bytes, and each byte is encoded in a 2-out-of-4 code. This code permits each byte to be checked individually. There are six valid forms of each byte, giving a total of 216 valid op-code variants. The structure of a bus checker circuit which performs word checking is shown in Fig. 5. The single step-code and condition-code bytes also use the 2-out-of-4 code and are checked by the bus checker.

Fig. 5. The bus checker circuit.

The initial choice of error codes in the STAR computer emphasized variety for the purpose of comparison and evaluation, and the arithmetic product (or AN) code was used for operands [Avižienis, 1967b]. Two reasons for the change to the present encoding of operands were: (1) the residue code is separable and allows the use of the more efficient two's complement algorithms for binary arithmetic, and (2) multiple precision and floating-point arithmetic is much more readily implemented with residue encoding. Residue encoding is also suitable for operation codes in STAR instructions. Its advantage is that an identical checking algorithm is applied to instructions and operands; an explicit identification is not required for checking, and loading of programs is facilitated. The drawback is that the bytes of the op-code cannot be checked individually as in the 2-out-of-4 coding.

Control Error Detection

It has been observed that a large number of faults which cause control errors also cause word errors and are detectable by the use of error codes. Some critical control errors, however, do not fall into this category and require other methods of detection.

The principal method of control fault detection in the STAR computer is the validation that every unit is active at the proper time and that the proper algorithm is carried out within the unit. The initial design [Avižienis, 1968] used a four-wire status line for every replaceable unit to transmit one of six possible "2-out-of-4" coded status messages. Experience has shown that the diagnostic logic in the TARP is significantly simplified when status messages are conveyed to the TARP at predetermined clock times within each ten-unit cycle of operation. In the revised design, each status message is conveyed on two wires (in 1-out-of-2 encoding) and each message covers the time interval between two messages of the same type. The status-message originating circuits are duplicated in each unit to allow the detection of a fault in the status message.

The "output active" message indicates that the unit has produced a nonzero output to the bus in the preceding time interval. It serves to identify improperly active units which otherwise would destroy the information being transmitted on a bus, and make it impossible to locate the source of error. The absence of an expected active message is also a fault condition, since the all-zero word is not a validly coded operand or instruction. The checking of output activity is the most critical of all status monitoring functions.

The other status messages are multiplexed and sent over the same pair of wires as the output active messages because the activity information is not required continuously in the byte-serial machine structure. The status messages which are listed below aid in increasing the probability of immediate detection of incorrect operation.

The "disagree with bus" message is needed for duplex opera-

tion (discussed in the next section). Two identical units produce outputs to a bus which acts as an OR gate. Each unit compares the bus word to its internally held output word and records a disagree message if a mismatch occurs. The message is conveyed to the TARP at a specified time. The bus checker result together with disagree message permits a rapid identification of a faulty unit. In simplex operation this message helps to identify improper activity of another unit.

The "complete" message is essential for functional units which have variable-duration algorithms. Memory units issue "write complete" and "read complete" messages which are essential for immediate detection of incorrect storage events.

The "internal fault" message is produced by internal monitoring circuits within each unit. Its function is to indicate incorrect internal algorithms detected by duplication of critical signals, special test circuits, and "inverse microprogramming" in which an operation is deduced from active gating signals.

In addition to the above listed four types of messages, time is provided for a "special" status message which varies for different units. For example, the IO/IRP uses it to report to the TARP the arrival of an external interrupt request.

Properties of Functional Units

The main arithmetic processor (MAP) input consists of an operation code followed by a coded operand, and the output is a coded result followed by a condition-code byte, indicating either one of three singularities (sum overflow, quotient overflow, zero divisor) or the type of a good result (positive, zero, negative). The control processor (COP) stores the condition code and uses it to implement conditional branches instructions. The COP also contains the location counter LC, two index registers, and a four-bit adder to implement indexing of residue-coded addresses and incrementing the LC. The logic processor (LOP) performs the bit-by-bit logic operations and code conversions on input words. The arithmetic coding is removed from the operand before the operation, since error codes are not preserved during logic operations, and the final result is again encoded. The LOP operation is checked by operating two copies which issue disagree status messages when their outputs differ. The IO/interrupt processor (IO/IRP) receives external interrupt requests, initiates allowable interrupts, and carries out input/output buffering functions.

The READ-ONLY memory (ROM) contains the permanent programs and the associated constants. The present machine uses a "braid" assembly of transformers and wires for the permanent storage of 16,384 words. Complete replicas of the ROM are used as replacements. Each 4096 word READ-WRITE memory (RWM) unit has two modes of operation. In the *absolute* mode a RWM unit recognizes its own wired-in absolute name. In the *relocated* mode a RWM unit responds to an assigned name. All relocated units with the same assigned name store and read out the same locations simultaneously. In case of a disagreement with the word on the M-O bus, the RWM unit sends a disagree status message to the TARP. The relocated mode provides duplicate or triplicate storage for critical programs and data. When a RWM unit fails, its replacement unit can be assigned the same name, avoiding a discontinuity in addresses. Assignment and cancellation of assigned names is performed under program control; this provision allows selective redundancy of storage. A record of RWM name assignments is retained (in nonvolatile storage) in all active TARP units. The accessing of storage locations within a RWM unit is checked by permanently storing the 4-bit check byte of its 12-bit internal address in every location. This byte is read out and checked against the contents of the address register during every read and write operation.

In the STAR computer only the logic processor and the RWM memory unit containing critical system programs are duplexed for normal operation. For experimentation, complete provisions have been made for optional duplex operation of all memory and processor units under program control. The combination of duplication and coding offers detection of all errors as well as a fast identification of one faulty unit. In order to permit duplex operation of processor and ROM units, active TARP units hold a record of units which are operating in duplex.

The Test and Repair Processor (TARP) and Recovery Mode

The "hard core" monitor of the STAR system is designated as TARP (test and repair processor) in Fig. 2. The TARP monitors the operation of the STAR computer by two methods: (1) testing every word sent over the two data buses for validity of its code; and (2) checking the status messages from the functional units for predicted responses. An incorrect word or a deviation from predicted response causes an interruption of normal computing and an entry into the recovery mode of operation. The block diagram of one TARP is shown in Fig. 6. It is functionally divided into two sections. One section provides standard mode machine

control and fault location, and the other controls the recovery mode operation and effects the switching of replaceable units.

The Control and Test (CAT). This section contains the standard mode control logic consisting of an op-code decoder, a clock, and a counter which generates the step-code signals for standard mode operation. The machine-state prediction logic uses the current instruction and step-code to predict which status messages should be received from each powered functional unit. It also predicts the information source and the type of encoding expected on each bus. The fault location logic compares the status and bus checker (Fig. 5) results to the prediction. In most cases, it can localize an error to a particular functional unit. Upon detecting an error, the CAT section stops the machine and transfers its error information to the recovery control section.

Recovery Control (REC). This section of the TARP contains a "rollback point" address register which specifies the location of the instruction at which normal operation is to be resumed after a recovery. This register is updated under program control. Before every updating, the contents of all processor registers needed for recovery are stored in duplexed memory units. Upon receipt of an error message from the CAT section, the REC section issues the "reset" signal, which causes all powered units to be set to an initial state, and then broadcasts an unconditional jump instruction, which causes the program to be resumed at the "rollback" address. A repeated fault indication in the same unit leads to its replacement. The number of repetitions before replacement can be specified in the experimental TARP. To replace, power is turned off in the unit, a spare is turned on, and another reset (and jump) is issued. For cases of temporary power loss and other fault conditions which cannot be resolved by the fault location logic, the REC section contains a wired-in "disaster restart" procedure.

The TARP is the hard core of the system. Three fully powered copies of the TARP are operated at all times together with n standby spares ($n=2$ in the present design). The outputs of the TARPs are decided by a 2-out-of-$(n+3)$ threshold vote. When one powered TARP disagrees with the other two, the recovery mode is entered and an attempt is made to set the internal state of the disagreeing unit to match the other two units. If this TARP rollback attempt fails, the disagreeing unit is returned to the standby condition and one of the standby units receives power, goes through the TARP rollback, and joins the powered triplet. The computer is now restarted, a rollback performed, and standard operation continues. Because of the three unit requirement, design effort has been concentrated on reducing the TARP to the least possible complexity. Experience with the present model has led to several refinements of the design.

The replacement of faulty functional units is commanded by the TARP vote and is implemented by power switching. It offers several advantages over the switching of information lines which

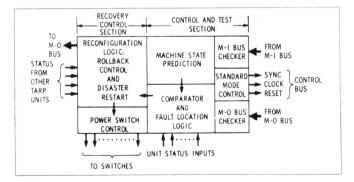

Fig. 6. Test and repair processor (TARP) organization.

connect the units to the bus. The number of switches is reduced to one per unit, power is conserved, and strong isolation is provided for catastrophic failures. Magnetic power switches have been developed which are part of each unit's power supply and are designed to open for most internal failures. The threshold function is inherent in the control windings of the switch. The information lines of each unit are permanently connected to the buses through component-redundant isolation circuits. The signal on a bus is the logic OR of all inputs from the units, and unpowered units produce only logic zero outputs. The power switch and the buses utilize component redundancy for protection against fatal "shorting" failures.

Comparative Reliability Analysis

This section considers the reliability (with respect to permanent failures) which can be expected for the STAR computer. The approach is to estimate the relative reliability with respect to an existing reference system. An absolute reliability prediction is not made because the failure rates for components which are being developed for a flight model are not yet adequately established.

The reference computer for reliability estimation is the nonredundant Mariner Mars 1969 (MM'69) computer, which was the on-board computer for the successful Mariner 6 and 7 missions to Mars. It was chosen because a detailed description and extensive failure rate data are readily available. With respect to computing performance it must be noted that the MM'69 computer is a bit-serial machine with a bit rate of 2.4 kHz and an instruction set of 16 op-codes, whereas the STAR is a byte-serial machine with a 0.5 MHz clock and an instruction set of 130 op-codes. This gain in performance is not used as a factor in reliability estimation.

Reliability models (1) the MM'69 computer, (2) a simplex computer equivalent in performance to the STAR, and (3) the STAR computer are shown in Fig. 7. The MM'69 computer [Fig. 7a] is assigned a complexity of unity. It is assumed that the simplex computer [Fig. 7b] consisting of eight functional units is $8 \times CF$ times as complex as the MM'69 computer. The relative complexity factor CF is defined as the ratio of complexity (component count) of a single STAR unit to the complexity of the entire MM'69 computer. The value CF=1/3 was established by

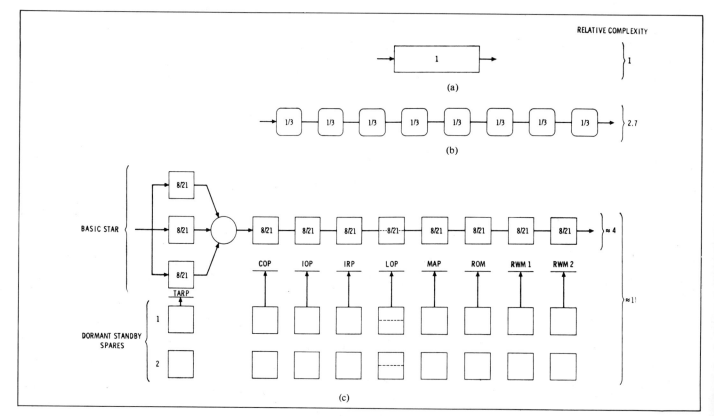

Fig. 7. Reliability models. *(a)* Mariner Mars 1969 computer, *(b)* Simplex computer, *(c)* STAR computer.

detailed comparison and is used in the subsequent analysis. The comparison is made with respect to MM'69 technology, i.e., it is assumed that the simplex and the STAR computers employ the same components and packaging techniques as the MM'69 computer.

The STAR model [Fig. 7c] consists of eight functional units plus the test and repair processor (TARP) array in series reliability. All units are considered to be of similar complexity and are allocated an equal number of spares. Results for S=2 and S=3 are presented. The reliability model applied to all units except the TARP is the standby-replacement redundancy model with dormant spares [Bouricius, Carter, and Schneider, 1969; Mathur, 1971a]. The TARP was modeled as a hybrid-redundant H(3, S) system [Mathur and Avižienis, 1970]. Details of the reliability models and measures are presented in [Mathur, 1971a]. The logic processor LOP is assumed to have an internal duplication of the circuits which are not protected by the error-detecting codes. Two sets of three RWM units each are shown; this is a pessimistic assumption, since the computer can function with only one of the six RWM units surviving.

The fault coverage factor [Bouricius, Carter, and Schneider, 1969] in the STAR model is taken into account in two ways: (1) by including the fault detector and recovery initiator as a separate processor (the TARP), and (2) by applying a self-testing factor (STF) to the relative complexities of the units. Note that the simplex computer [Fig. 7b] does not contain a processor corresponding to the TARP in the STAR computer since the simplex computer is a computationally equivalent nonredundant machine without "test and repair" capabilities. Since 4 bits of the 32-bit STAR word serve for error detection, a STF equal to 8/7 was chosen. The STF expresses the overhead due to the self-testing and repairing features within each STAR unit, that is, a STAR unit has 8/7 of the complexity of the same unit in the "simplex" computer. Applying CF = 1/3 and STF = 8/7 a STAR unit has the relative complexity of 8/21 with respect to the entire MM'69 computer.

Examples of reliability predictions based on the MM'69 data are shown in Tables 1 and 2 and Figs. 8 and 9. The *lower bound* ($K = 1$) assumes equal failure rates of powered and spare units (K is the failure rate ratio). The *upper bound* ($K = \infty$) assumes a zero failure rate of spare units. Two-spare ($S=2$) and three-spare ($S=3$) STAR systems are considered. Table 1 and Fig. 8 show the predicted reliability as a function of time. Table 2 shows the time (in years) for which the reliability remains above a specified value. Figure 9 presents the predicted reliability gain, defined as the ratio STAR reliability/MM'69 reliability.

The computing operations for the foregoing analysis, the generation of tables, and the plotting of graphs was done with the aid of the computer-aided reliability estimation (CARE) program [Mathur, 1971b], which was developed as a design tool during the reliability study. CARE is a software package developed on the Univac 1108 computer system at JPL. CARE may be interactively accessed by a designer from a teletype console to calculate his reliability estimates. The input is in the form of a system

Table 1   Reliability versus Time for Various Configuration (CF = 1/3)

Mission time (h)	MM'69 computer	Simplex computer	STAR computer with S spares Upper bound ($K = \infty$) S = 3	S = 2	Lower bound ($K = 1$) S = 3	S = 2
4368 ($\approx$ 6 months)	0.928	0.82	0.9999998	0.99997	0.999995	0.99982
43 680 ($\approx$ 5 years)	0.475	0.14	0.997	0.97	0.966	0.87
87 360 ($\approx$ 10 years)	0.225	0.019	0.96	0.79	0.71	0.45

Table 2   Mission Duration for Specified Reliability (CF = 1/3)

Desired mission reliability	MM'69 computer	Simplex computer	STAR computer with S spares Upper bound S = 3	S = 2	Lower bound S = 3	S = 2
			Mission duration in years			
0.9	0.7	0.3	12.5	7.5	6.7	4.5
0.8	1.5	0.6	16.0	9.7	8.5	6.0
0.7	2.4	0.9	18.5	11.7	10.0	7.0
0.6	3.5	1.3	20.5	13.5	11.3	8.3

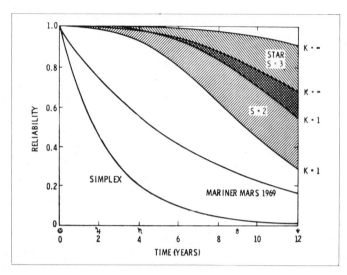

Fig. 8. Reliability versus mission time MM'69, simplex, and STAR computers.

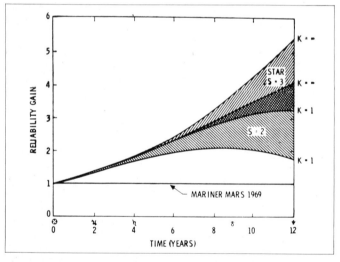

Fig. 9. Reliability gain of STAR computer with respect to the MM'69 computer.

configuration description followed by queries on the various reliability parameters of interest and their behavior with respect to mission time, fault coverage, failure rates, dormancy factors, allocated spares, and partitioning. The CARE program is extensible, and it may be updated to incorporate new reliability models as they become available.

STAR Computer Software System

Early in the design of the STAR computer it became evident that the fault-tolerant architecture would impose unconventional constraints on its software. The development of the software system for the STAR computer was initiated in 1968 and closely followed the hardware development. It is partitioned into two subsystems. The programming subsystem consists of three modules: an assembler, a loader, and a functional simulator. An executive program facilitates coordinated use of these modules. The operating subsystem consists of two modules: the resident executive module and the applications programs module. The programming subsystem has been implemented on the Univac 1108 computer of the Scientific Computing Facility at JPL. The first version of a resident executive for the STAR computer is nearing completion.

SCAP (the star computer assembly program) is the first module of STAR software. Programs for the STAR computer are written in the assembly language SCAL. SCAP is a traditional two-pass assembler incorporating machine instructions, pseudo-operations, and macrofacilities. A unique feature of SCAP is the encoding of instruction and data words as required by the STAR computer. SCAP calculates the code required and generates the encoded value of the word. Another feature of SCAP is the COMPILE pseudo-operation which implements automatic compilation of simple arithmetic statements by the assembler.

The second module LOAD (the loader) reads the program into the simulated STAR computer memory. After all decks have been read, a COMMON area is allocated, relocation is completed, and external linkage is accomplished. A map and cross-reference table are printed to aid in debugging and documenting the program. The third module of STAR software is the functional simulator, which is modular in nature and follows the latest STAR hardware configuration. Two special features are incorporated in the simulator. The first is the facility to simulate hardware errors in order to test the software aspects of error recovery. The second feature provides STAR register and memory dumps. An executive program facilitates the coordinated use of the assembler, loader, and simulator.

The modules of the operating subsystem of the STAR computer software system consist of the resident executive module and the applications programs module. The STAR resident executive augments the self-testing and repairing features of the hardware in addition to its normal functions. The standard features include interrupt control, input/output processing, and job scheduling. Novel features incorporated due to the fault-tolerance architecture of the STAR computer include a "cold start" capability, reconfiguration processing, rollback assistance, and diagnosis of faulty units. The cold start capability resets the hardware and software after a disaster restart as well as prior to an initial load.

Reconfiguration processing is required for memory replacement, since software assistance is required to load a newly activated memory unit. All programs running on the STAR computer require rollback (recovery) points. The resident executive provides rollback status storage and controls events which are nonrepeatable i.e., they may not occur more than once even if a rollback takes place. Finally, it implements diagnosis for faulty units to determine the cause and extent of failures for possible partial reuse. The present application programs module includes floating-point arithmetic subroutines, and test and demonstration programs. The applications programs which will be required for space missions are a part of the TOPS control computer subsystem project discussed later in this paper.

Extension of STAR Techniques to Peripheral Systems

The STAR techniques of fault tolerance can be systematically extended beyond the boundaries of the computer to effect automatic maintenance of various peripheral systems that communicate with the computer. The case which was investigated in connection with the STAR computer development is the implementation of automatic maintenance for a simplified model of the JPL thermoelectric outer planet spacecraft (TOPS) which is being proposed for the exploration of the outer planets [Astronaut., 1970]. The potentially lower failure rates of unpowered spare units and the constant power demand of a replacement system are exceptionally important in missions requiring a ten year survival of the spacecraft under very strict power constraints.

The methodology of extending the STAR techniques consists of several steps: (1) identification of the replaceable peripheral units; (2) selection of internal error detection functions which are economically feasible within the units themselves; (3) identification of possible functional redundancy, in which either another type of peripheral unit or the computer itself can take over the function of a failed unit; (4) algorithmic description of the monitoring and recovery procedures to be performed for each unit by the computer; (5) development of fault-tolerant communication between the peripheral units and the I/O and interrupt processors of the computer; (6) translation of the monitoring and recovery procedures which have been assigned to the computer into computational requirements: speed, instruction set, storage size, input/output and interrupt system complexity; and (7) estimation of reliability and mean life attainable for each peripheral unit. Several iterations of the design process lead to a system for which a balanced gain in reliability has been attained by means of computer-controlled automatic maintenance. A detailed case study of the application of these techniques is presented in Gilley [1970].

The investigation has identified and quantized the computing capability required from the STAR computer in order to effect the automatic maintenance of the TOPS spacecraft. Furthermore, the results have shown that: (1) the fully automatic maintenance of a complex long-life spacecraft is feasible through a systematic extension of STAR techniques, and (2) the automatic maintenance requirements of the spacecraft systems can be algorithmically described to the detail required to produce computer programs for their implementation. The results of the investigation have systematically extended dynamic redundancy to various peripheral subsystems of an information processing system. Beyond the specific example of a spacecraft, the methodology is applicable to computer-controlled automatic maintenance of other complex data processing, communication, and control systems.

Design of the TOPS Control Computer

The most recent step in the development of the STAR computer concept has been the design of a control computer subsystem (CCS) for the thermoelectric outer planet spacecraft (TOPS) [Astronaut., 1970]. After the TOPS requirements were quantified as described in the preceding section, the CCS design had still to meet four major externally-imposed constraints: (1) the weight of the subsystem was not to exceed 40 lb; (2) power consumption was not to be greater than 40 W; (3) probability of successfully completing a 100,000 h mission was to be equal to or greater than 0.95 (using TOPS approved part failure rates, and (4) it could not, as a consequence of any single internal fault, result in a failure mode catastrophic to the mission.

Because of these constraints, it was not possible merely to "shrink" the STAR computer into a flight package. The STAR design was simplified by retaining only the capabilities needed to meet the TOPS functional requirements. The entire self-test and repair ability of the larger machine has been retained; in fact, the TOPS CCS has expanded failure detection and recovery capability. A variety of advances arising from the years of work on the STAR computer that preceded the TOPS effort have been incorporated into its design.

The CCS operates at a clock frequency of 500 kHz. The CCS word is the same length as the STAR word, 32 bits. The word-processing cycle, ten byte-times long in the STAR computer, has been reduced to nine in the CCS: eight for processing or transferring information and one (two in STAR) for the messages and decision making between words. The execution (including fetch) of an instruction requires one to three cycles. The STAR instruction set with over 200 variants has been reduced to less than 100. To detect word errors, the CCS uses the same residue code as the STAR computer. Unlike the STAR, however, the CCS employs the residue encoding also for operation codes of instructions. In addition to these failure detection measures, the CCS incorporates dual control logic and clocking, memory address checking simultaneous with all memory accesses, and a nondestructive read-after-write option on all store instructions.

The CCS consists of the seven STAR computer functional units designated the COP, LOP, IOP, IRP, ROM, RWM, and TARP (Fig. 2). The IO/IRP has been split into independent IOP and IRP units in order to improve failure detection and isolation in a completely unattended environment. The MAP is deleted because software multiplication and division are sufficient, while addition and subtraction are done in the LOP. Simplifications in the instruction set have resulted in reduced hardware in the COP, LOP, IOP, and IRP. Conversely, there is increased hardware in the RWM and TARP for added failure detection. A 4096-word ROM and two 4096 word RWM units constitute the program storage capability of the CCS. In addition, another 4096-word RWM (designated SHM) is shared (by use of two independent ports) by the CCS and measurement processor subsystem (MPS). All the CCS RWM units are identical; any one of them can be assigned either as a CCS internal memory or as the SHM. The SHM contains the MPS operating program and the most recent samples of spacecraft variables gathered by the MPS. Because the SHM is available to the CCS as part of its own memory, these samples are conveniently available to it for fault diagnosis and monitoring of spacecraft activity [Gilley, 1970].

Current Research

The research and development program which led to the STAR computer is continuing in several directions. The design of several improved second generation STAR functional units is under way, including a new arithmetic processor, a control processor for medium-scale integrated-circuit implementation, and the shared

READ-WRITE memory unit for the storage of automatic maintenance information from the spacecraft telemetry system. Analysis of automatic maintenance algorithms and design of a command/data bus for their implementation are under intensive study. Other current investigations are concerned with the following areas: (1) hardware-software interaction in a fault-tolerant system with recovery, especially the interaction of the TARP and the operating system; (2) studies of advanced recovery techniques, i.e., post-catastrophic restart, TARP replacement schemes, recovery from massive interference, partial utilization of failed units; (3) advanced component technology, especially methods to attain bus and power switch (i.e., hard core) immunity to faults; (4) heuristic studies of fault tolerance by interpretation of extensive experiments with the STAR breadboard as the instrument; (5) design of a second-generation STAR-type computer with universal processor and storage modules, and their implementation by large-scale integration; (6) Computational utilization of the spare units for supplemental tasks in a multiprocessing mode.

At the present time it is evident that the STAR computer design and construction effort has led to valuable new insights into the problem of fault-tolerant computing; further results in this field are expected from the research program in the future.

References

Anderson and Macri [1967]; Astronaut [1970]; Avižienis [1967a]; Avižienis [1967b]; Avižienis [1968]; Avižienis [1971]; Avižienis, Mathur, Rennels, and Rohr [1969]; Bouricius, Carter, and Schneider [1969]; Flehinger [1958]; Gilley [1970]; Griesmer, Miller, and Roth [1962]; Kruus [1963]; Kuehn [1969]; Lewis [1963]; Long [1969]; Lyons and Vanderkulk [1962]; Mathur and Avižienis [1970]; Mathur [1971a]; Mathur [1971b]; Reed and Brimley [1962]; Short [1968].

Chapter 28

Fault-Tolerant Design of Local ESS Processors[1]

W. N. Toy

Overview The stored program control of Bell System Electronic Switching Systems (ESS) has been under development since 1953. During this period, the No. 1 ESS, the No. 2 ESS, and the No. 3 ESS have been developed and used extensively by Bell System operating companies to provide commercial telephone service. These systems serve all types of telephone offices: The large-capacity No. 1 ESS serves metropolitan offices, the medium-capacity No. 2 ESS was designed for suburban offices, and the No. 3 ESS can be found in many small rural offices. The fault-tolerant design of ESS processors provides the same highly dependable telephone service established by the previous electromechanical systems. Pertinent process architecture features used to achieve ESS reliability objectives are discussed.

Introduction

Next to computer systems used in space-borne vehicles and U.S. defense installations, no other application has a higher availability requirement than a Bell System Electronic Switching System (ESS). These systems have been designed to be out of service no more than few minutes per year. Furthermore, design objectives permit no more than 0.01 percent of the telephone calls to be processed incorrectly [Downing, Nowak, and Tuomenoksa, 1964]. For example, when a fault occurs in a system, few calls in progress may be handled incorrectly during the recovery process.

At the core of every ESS is a single high-speed central processor [Harr, Taylor, and Ulrich, 1969; Browne et al., 1969; Staehler, 1977]. To establish an ultrareliable switching environment, redundancy of system components and duplication of the processor itself has been the approach taken to compensate for potential machine faults. Without this redundancy, a single component failure in the processor might cause a complete failure of the entire system. With duplication, a standby processor takes over control and provides continuous telephone service.

When the system fails, the fault must be quickly detected and isolated. Meanwhile, a rapid recovery of the call processing functions (by the redundant component(s) and/or processor) is necessary to maintain the system's high availability. Next, the

[1]*Subsetted from Proc. IEEE*, vol. 66, no. 10, October 1978, pp. 1,126–1,145.

fault must be diagnosed and the defective unit repaired or replaced. The failure rate and repair time must be such that the probability is very small for a failure to occur in the duplicated unit before the first one is repaired.

Allocation and Causes of System Downtime

The outage of a telephone (switching) office can be caused by facilities other than the processor. While a hardware fault in one of the peripheral units generally results in only a partial loss of service, it *is* possible for a fault in this area to bring the system down. By design, the processor has been allocated two-thirds of the system downtime. The other one-third is allocated to the remaining equipment in the system.

Field experience indicates that system outages due to the processor may be assigned to one of four categories shown in Fig. 1 [Staehler and Watters, 1976]. The percentages in this figure represent the fraction of total downtime attributable to each cause. The four categories are as follows.

Hardware Reliability

Before the accumulation of large amounts of field data, total system downtime was usually assigned to hardware. We now know that the situation is more complex. Processor hardware actually accounts for only 20 percent of the downtime. With growing use of stored program control, it has become increasingly important to make such systems more reliable. Redundancy is designed into all subsystems so that the system can go down *only* when hardware failures occur simultaneously in duplicated units. However, the data now show that good diagnostic and trouble location programs are very critical parts of the total system reliability performance.

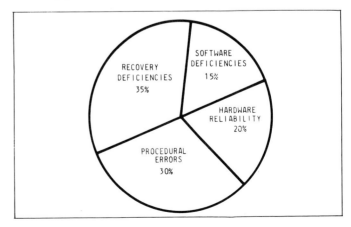

Fig. 1. System outage allocation.

Software Deficiencies

Software deficiencies include all software errors that cause memory mutilation, and program loops that can only be cleared by major reinitialization. Software faults are the result of improper translation or implementation of the original algorithm. In some cases, the original algorithm may have been incorrectly specified. Program changes and feature additions are continuously incorporated into working offices. Software accounts for 15 percent of the downtime.

Recovery Deficiencies

Recovery is the system's most complex and difficult function. Deficiencies may include the shortcomings of either hardware or software design to detect faults when they occur. When faults go undetected, the system remains extensively impaired until the trouble is recognized. Another kind of recovery problem can occur if the system is unable to properly isolate a faulty subsystem and configure a working system around it.

The many possible system states which may arise under trouble conditions make recovery a complicated process. Besides those already mentioned, unforeseen difficulties may be encountered in the field, and lead to inadequate recovery. Because of the large number of variables involved and because the recovery function is so strongly related to all other components of maintenance, recovery deficiencies account for 35 percent of the downtime.

Procedural Errors

Human error on the part of maintenance personnel or office administrators can also cause the system to go down. For example, someone in maintenance may mistakenly pull a circuit pack from the on-line processor while repairing a defective standby processor. Inadequate and incorrect documentation (e.g., users' manuals) may also be classified as human error. Obviously, the number of manual operations must be reduced if procedural errors are to be minimized. Procedural errors account for about 30 percent of the downtime.

The shortcomings and deficiencies of current systems are being continually corrected to improve system reliability.

Duplex Architecture

When a fault occurs in a nonredundant single processor, the system will remain down until the processor is repaired. In order to meet the ESS reliability requirement, *redundancy* is included in the system design; continuous and correct operation is maintained by duplicating all functional units within the processor. If one of the units fails, the duplicated unit is switched in, maintaining continuous operation. Meanwhile, the defective unit is repaired. Should a fault occur in the duplicated unit during the repair interval, the system will, of course, go down. If the repair interval is relatively short, the probability of simultaneous faults occurring in two identical units is quite small. This technique of redundancy has been used throughout each ESS.

The first-generation ESS processor structure consists of two store communities: program store (PS) and call store (CS). The program store is a read-only memory (ROM) containing the call processing, maintenance, and administration programs; it also contains long-term translation and system parameters. The call store contains the transient data related to telephone calls in progress. The memory is electrically alterable to allow its data to be changed frequently. In one particular arrangement, shown in Fig. 2, the complete processor is treated as a single functional block and is duplicated. This type of single-unit duplex system has two possible configurations: Either Processor 0 or Processor 1 can

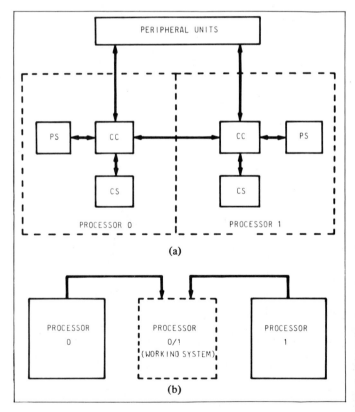

Fig. 2. Single-unit duplex configuration. *(a)* **Processor structure.** *(b)* **Two possible configurations.**

be assigned as the on-line working system, while the other unit serves as standby backup. The mean-time-to-failure (MTTF), a measure of reliability, is given by the following expression [Smith, 1972]:

$$\text{MTTF} = \frac{\mu}{2\lambda^2}$$

where μ is the repair rate (reciprocal of the repair time), and λ is the failure rate.

The failure rate (λ) of one unit is the summation of failure rates of all components within the unit. For medium and small ESS processors, Fig. 2 shows a system structure containing several functional units which are treated as a single entity, with λ still sufficiently small to meet the reliability requirement. The single-unit duplex configuration has the merit of being very simple in terms of the number of switching blocks in the system. This configuration simplifies not only the recovery program but also the hardware interconnection. It does this by eliminating the additional access required to make each duplicated block capable of switching independently into the on-line system configuration.

In the large No. 1 ESS, which contains many components, the MTTF becomes too low to meet the reliability requirement. In order to increase the value of the MTTF, either the number of components (failure rate) or the repair time must be reduced. Alternatively, the single-unit duplex configuration can be partitioned into a multiunit duplex configuration as shown in Fig. 3. In this arrangement, each subunit contains a smaller number of components and is able to be switched into a working system. The system will fail only if a fault occurs in the redundant subunit while the original is being repaired. Since each subunit contains fewer components, the probability of two simultaneous faults occurring in a duplicated pair of subunits is reduced. The MTTF of the multiunit duplex configuration can be computed by taking into consideration the conditional probability of a subunit failing during the repair time of the original subunit.

An example of a multiunit duplex configuration is shown in Fig. 3. A working system is configured with a fault-free CCx-CSx-CSBx-PSx-PSBx-PUBx arrangement, where x is either Subunit 0 or Subunit 1. This means there are 2^6, or 64 possible combinations of system configurations. The MTTF is given by the following expression:

$$\text{MTTF} = \frac{r\mu}{2\lambda^2}$$

where $r =$

$$\frac{1}{(\lambda_{\text{CC}}/\lambda)^2 + (\lambda_{\text{CS}}/\lambda)^2 + (\lambda_{\text{CSB}}/\lambda)^2 + (\lambda_{\text{PS}}/\lambda)^2 + (\lambda_{\text{PSB}}/\lambda)^2 + (\lambda_{\text{PUB}}/\lambda)^2}$$

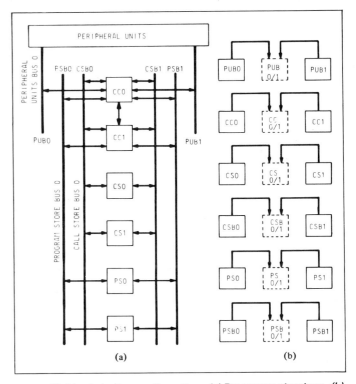

Fig. 3. Multiunit duplex configuration. (a) Processor structure. (b) Sixty-four possible configurations.

The factor r is at a maximum when the failure rate (λ_i) for each subunit is the same. In this case

$$\lambda_{\text{CC}} = \lambda_{\text{CS}} = \lambda_{\text{CSB}} = \lambda_{\text{PS}} = \lambda_{\text{PSB}} = \lambda_{\text{PUB}} = \lambda_i$$

or

$$\lambda_i = \frac{\lambda}{s}$$

where

$s = $ number of subunits, $s = 6$, and $r = s$

At best, the MTTF is improved by a factor corresponding to the number of partitioned subunits. This improvement is not fully realized since equipment must be added to provide additional access and to select subunits. The partitioning of the subsystem into subunits as shown in Fig. 3 results in subunits of different sizes. Again, the failure rate for each individual subunit will not be the same; hence, the r-factor will be smaller than 6. Because of the relatively large number of components used in implementing the No. 1 ESS, the system is arranged in the multiunit duplex configuration in order to meet the reliability requirement.

Reliability calculation is a process of predicting, from available failure rate data, the achieveable reliability of a system and the probability of meeting the reliability objectives for ESS applications. These calculations are most useful and beneficial during the early stages of design in order to assess various types of redundancy and determine the system's organization. In the small and medium ESS's, the calculations have supported the use of single-unit duplex structures. For large ESS's, it was necessary to partition the system into a multiunit duplex configuration.

Fault Simulation Techniques

One of the more difficult tasks of maintenance design is fault diagnosis. Its effectiveness in diagnostic resolution can be determined by simulation of the system's behavior in the presence of a specific fault. By means of simulation, design deficiencies can be identified and corrected prior to any system being deployed in the field. It is necessary to evaluate the system's ability to detect faults, to recover automatically back into a working system, and to provide diagnostic information where the fault is within a few replaceable circuit packs. Fault simulation, therefore, is an important aspect of maintenance design.

There are essentially two techniques used for simulating faults of digital systems: physical simulation or digital simulation. Physical simulation is a process of inserting faults into a physical working model. This method produces more realistic behavior under fault conditions. A wider class of faults can be applied to the system, such as a blown fuse or shorted backplane interconnection. However, fault simulation cannot begin until the design has been completed and the equipment is fully operational. Also, it is not possible to insert faults interior to an integrated circuit.

Digital fault simulation is a means of predicting the behavior under failure of a processor modeled in a computer program. The computer used to execute the program (the host) is generally different from the processor being simulated (the object). Digital fault simulation gives a high degree of automation and excellent access to interior points of logic to monitor the signal flow. It allows diagnostic test development and evaluation to proceed well in advance of unit fabrication. The cost of computer simulation can be quite high for a large, complex system.

The physical fault simulation method was first employed to generate diagnostic data for the Morris Electronic Switching System [Tsiang and Ulrich, 1962]. Over 50 000 known faults were purposely introduced into the central control to be diagnosed by its diagnostic program. Test results associated with each fault were recorded. They were then sorted and printed in dictionary format to formulate a trouble locating manual (TLM). Under trouble conditions, by consulting the TLM, it was possible to determine a set of several suspected circuit packs which might contain the defective component. Using the dictionary technique at the Morris system, the average repair time was kept low and maintenance was made much easier.

The experience gained in the physical fault simulation was applied and extended in the No. 1 ESS development [Downing, Nowak, and Tuomenoksa, 1964]. Each plug-in circuit pack was replaced by a fault simulator which introduced every possible type of single fault on the replaced package one at a time and then recorded the system reaction on magnetic tape. This was done for all circuit packs in the system. In addition to diagnostic data for dictionaries, additional data were collected to determine the adequacy of hardware and software in fault detection and system recovery. Deficiencies were corrected to improve the overall maintenance of the system.

A digital logic simulator called LAMP [Chang, Smith, and Walford, 1974] was developed for the No. 1A ESS development. It played an important role in the hardware and diagnostic development of the No. 1A Processor. The simulator is capable of simulating subsystem with as many as 65 000 logic gates. All classical faults for standard logic gates are simulatable with logic nodes stuck at "0" or stuck at "1." Before physical units are available, digital simulation can be very effective in verifying the design, evaluating diagnostic access, and developing diagnostic tests. Physical fault simulation has been demonstrated in the No. 1 ESS to give a very realistic behavior under fault conditions. The integration of both techniques was employed in the development of the No. 1A Processor to take advantages of both processes. The use of complementary simulation allows faults to be simulated physically (in the system laboratory) and logically (on a computer). Most of the deficiencies of one simulation process are compensated for by the other. The complementary method provided both a convenient method for validating the results and more extensive fault simulation data than would have been normally if either process were used individually. Fig. 4 shows the complementary process of fault simulation used in the No. 1A Processor development [Bowman et al., 1977; Goetz, 1974]. Maximum diagnostic performance was achieved from an integrated use of both simulation methods.

First Generation ESS Processors

The world's first ESS provided commerical telephone service at Morris, IL, in 1959 for about a year on a field trial basis [Keister, Ketchledge, and Lovell, 1960]. The system demonstrated the use of stored program control and the basic maintenance philosophy

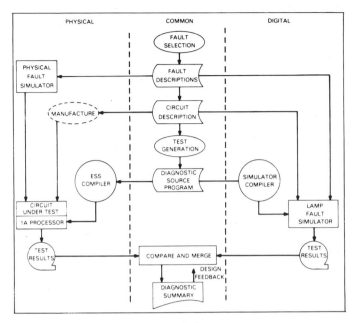

Fig. 4. Complementary fault-simulation system.

clock timing signals be in close tolerance so that every operation in both halves is performed in step, and key outputs are compared for error detection. The synchronization of duplicated units is accomplished by having the on-line oscillator output drive both clock circuits. There are two match circuits in each central control (CC). Each matcher compares 24 bits within one machine cycle of 5.5 μs. Fig. 5 shows that each matcher has access to six sets of internal nodes (24 bits per node). In the routine match mode, the points matched in each cycle are dependent upon the instruction being executed. The selected match points are those most pertinent to the data processing steps occurring during a given machine cycle. The two matchers in each CC compare the same sets of selected test points. The capability of each CC to compare a number of internal nodes provides a highly effective means of detecting hardware errors.

If a mismatch occurs, an interrupt is generated, which causes the fault-recognition program to run. The basic function of this program is to determine which half of the system is faulty. The

No. 1 ESS Processor

The No. 1 ESS was designed to serve large metropolitan telephone offices, ranging from several thousand to 65 000 lines [Keister, Ketchledge, and Vaughan, 1964]. As in most large switching systems, the processor represents only a small percentage of the total system cost. Therefore, performance and reliability were of primary importance in the design of the No. 1 Processor; cost was secondary. In order to meet the reliability standards established by electromechanical systems, all units essential to proper operation of the office are duplicated (see Fig. 3). The multiunit duplex configuration was necessary to increase the MTTF of the processor because of the large number of components in each of the functional blocks.

Even with duplication, troubles must be found and corrected quickly to minimize exposure to system failure due to multiple troubles. All units are monitored continually so that troubles in the standby units are found just as quickly as those in the on-line units. This is accomplished by running the on-line and standby units in the synchronous and match mode of operation [Downing, Nowak, and Tuomenoksa, 1964]. Synchronization requires that

of providing continuous and reliable telephone service. The trial established valuable guides for designing a successor, the No. 1 ESS.

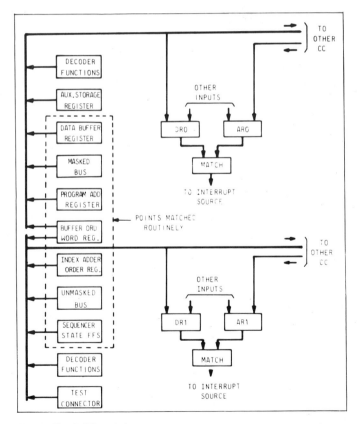

Fig. 5. No. 1 CC match access.

suspected unit is removed from service and the appropriate diagnostic program is run to pinpoint the defective circuit pack.

The No. 1 ESS was designed during the discrete component era (early 1960's) using individual components to implement logic gates [Cagle et al., 1964]. The CC contains approximately 12 000 logic gates. Although this number appears small when compared to large-scale integration (LSI) technology, the No. 1 Processor was a physically large machine for its time.

The match circuits capable of comparing internal nodes are the primary tools incorporated into the CC for diagnosing as well as detecting troubles. Specified information can be sampled by the matchers and retained in the match registers for examination. This mode of operation obtains critical data during the execution of diagnostic programs.

The early program store used permanent magnet twister (PMT) modules as basic storage elements [Ault et al., 1964]. They are a form of ROM in which system failures cannot alter the information content. Experience gained from the Morris field test system, which used the less reliable flying spot store, indicated that Hamming correction code was highly effective in providing continuous operation. At the time of development, it was felt that PMT modules might not be reliable enough. Consequently, the program store word included additional check bits for single-bit error correction (Hamming code). In addition, an overall parity check bit which covers both the data and their address is included in the word. The word size consists of 37 bits of information and seven check bits. When an error is corrected during normal operation, it is logged in an error counter. The maintenance program has access to this counter. Also, detection of a single error in the address or a double error in the word will cause an automatic retry.

The call store is the temporary read and write memory for storing transient data associated with call processing. Ferrite sheet memory modules are the basic storage elements used in implementing the call store in the No. 1 ESS [Genke, Harding, and Staehler, 1964]. The call store used in most No. 1 offices is smaller than the program store. (At the time of design, the cost per bit of call store was considerably higher than that of program store.) Also, ferrite sheet memory modules were considered to be very reliable devices. Consequently, single-bit error detection rather than Hamming correction code was provided in the call store.

There are two parity check bits: one over both the address and data, and the other over the address only. Again, as in the program store, automatic retry is performed whenever an error is detected, and the event is logged in an error counter for diagnostic use.

Troubles are normally detected by fault-detection circuits, and error-free system operation is recovered by fault recognition programs [Downing, Nowak, and Tuomenoksa, 1964]. This requires the on-line processor to be capable of making a proper

decision. If this is not possible, an emergency action timer will "time out" and activate special circuits to establish various combinations of subsystems into a system configuration. A special program which is used to determine whether or not the assembled processor is sane takes the processor through a series of tests arranged in a maze. Only one correct path through the maze exists. If the processor passes through successfully, the timer will be reset, and recovery is successful. If recovery is unsuccessful, the timer will time out again, and the rearrangement of subsystems will be tried one at a time (e.g., combinations of CC, program store, and program store bus systems). For each selected combination, the special sanity program is started and the sanity timer is activated. This procedure is repeated until a working configuration is found. The sanity program and sanity timer determine if the on-line CC is functioning properly. The active CC includes the program store and the program store bus.

Operational Results of No. 1 ESS

The No. 1 ESS has been in commercial operation since 1965. Over 1000 systems are providing telephone service to more than 15 million subscribers. The performance of the No. 1 ESS has continually improved over a decade of continued effort to improve all phases of software and hardware.

Fig. 6 shows the result of field data accumulated over many machine operating hours. This curve was derived from data in a paper [Fleckenstein, 1974] presented at the 1974 International Switching Symposium in Munich, Germany, and data supplied by W. C. Jones of Bell Laboratories.

When the No. 1 ESS was first put into commercial service, many outages occurred because of software and hardware inadequacies that could only be weeded out with field experience. The

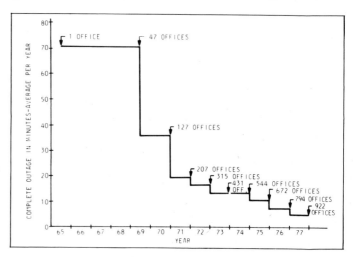

Fig. 6. No. 1 ESS service performance.

inexperience of maintenance personnel also contributed heavily towards system outages. Most hardware and software bugs were corrected during the early years of operation. However, deficiencies still exist, and designs are continually upgraded in working systems. Continual improvements include better diagnostic access, more complete fault recognition and isolation programs, and more effective system recovery.

Improved diagnostic capability reduces repair time and human errors by decreasing the amount of human interaction required by the machine. Better maintenance procedures and more experienced craftpersonnel also contribute to improved system performance. The curve in Fig. 6 shows that the outage rate improved as machine design and operating personnel matured.

No. 2 ESS Processor

The No. 2 ESS was developed during the mid-1960's [Spencer and Vigilante, 1969]. This system was designed for medium-size offices ranging from 1000 to 10 000 lines. The processor's design was derived from experience with the common stored program control of a private branch exchange (PBX), the No. 101 ESS [Seley and Vigilante, 1964]. Since the capacity requirement of the No. 2 ESS was to be less than that of the No. 1 ESS, cost became one of the more important design considerations. (Reliability is equally important in all systems.) The No. 2 ESS contains much less hardware than the No. 1 ESS. Understandably, its component failure rate is also substantially less. Its CC contains approximately 5000 gates (discrete components). To reduce cost and increase reliability, resistor-transistor logic (RTL) gates were chosen for the No. 2's processor since resistors are less expensive and more reliable than diodes [the No. 1 Processor used diode-transistor logic (DTL)].

Because the No 2's CC, program store, and call store are smaller, they are grouped together as a single switchable block in the single-unit duplex configuration shown in Fig. 2. Calculations indicate that its MTTF is approximately the same as the No. 1 multiunit duplex structure, with each of the functional blocks and associated store buses grouped together as a switchable block. The use of only two system configurations reduces considerably the amount of hardware needed to provide gating paths and control for each functional unit. Moreover, the recovery program is simplified, and the reliability of the system is improved.

The No. 2 Processor runs in the synchronous and match mode of operation [Beuscher et al., 1969]. The on-line oscillator output drives both clock circuits in order to keep the timing synchronized. The match operation is not as extensive as it is in the No. 1 ESS. For simplicity, there is only one matcher in the No. 2 ESS; it is located in the nonduplicated maintenance center (see Fig. 7). The matcher always compares the call store input registers in the two CC's when call store operations are performed synchronous-

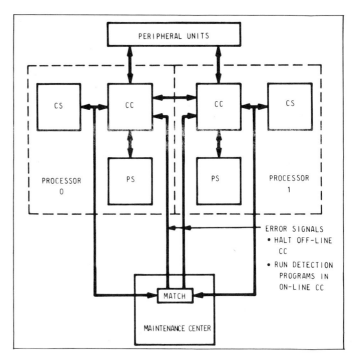

Fig. 7. No. 2 CC match access.

ly. A fault in almost any part of either CC quickly results in a call store input register mismatch. This occurs because almost all data manipulation performed in both the program control and the input-output (I/O) control involves processed data returning to the call store. The call store input is the central point whereby data eventually funnel through to the call store. By matching the call store inputs, an effective check of the system equipment is provided. Compared to the more complex matching of the No. 1 Processor, error detection in the No. 2 Processor may not be as instantaneous since only one crucial node in the processor is matched. Certain faults in the No. 2 Processor will go undetected until the errors propagate into the call store. This interval is probably no more than tens or hundreds of microseconds. During such a short interval, the fault would affect only a single call.

The No. 2 ESS matcher is not used as a diagnostic tool as is the matcher in the No. 1 Processor. Therefore, additional detection hardware is designed into the No. 2 Processor to help diagnose as well as detect faults.

When a mismatch occurs, the detection program is run in the on-line CC to determine if it contains the fault. This is done while the standby processor is disabled. If a solid fault in the on-line processor is detected by the mismatch detection program, the control is automatically passed to the standby processor, causing it to become the on-line processor. The faulty processor is disabled and diagnostic tests are called in to pinpoint the defective circuit pack.

The program store also uses PMT modules as basic storage elements, with a word size of 22 bits, half the width of the No. 1's word size. Experience gained in the design and operation of the No. 101 ESS (PBX) showed that PMT stores were very reliable. The additional protection provided in the No. 1 Processor against memory faults by error correction was not considered to be as essential in the No. 2 Processor. This and the need to keep the cost down led to the choice of error detection *only* instead of the more sophisticated Hamming correction code.

Error detection works as follows: one of the 22 bits in a word is allocated as a parity check bit. The program store contains both program and translation data. Additional protection is provided by using odd parity for program words and even parity for translation data. This detects the possibility of accessing the translation data area of memory as instruction words. For example, a software error may cause the program to branch into the data section of the memory and execute the data words as instruction words. The parity check would detect this problem immediately. The program store includes checking circuits to detect multiple-word access. Under program control, the sense amplifier threshold voltage can be varied in two discrete amounts from its nominal value to obtain a measure of the operating margin. The use of parity check was the proper choice for the No. 2 ESS in view of the high reliability of these memory devices.

The No. 2 Processor call store uses the same ferrite sheet memory modules as the No. 1 Processor. However, the No. 2's data word is 16 bits wide instead of 24. Fault detection depends heavily upon the matching of the call store inputs when the duplex processors run in the synchronous mode. Within the call store circuit, the access circuitry is checked to see that access currents flow in the right direction at the correct time and that only two access switches are selected in any store operation. This ensures that only one word is accessed in the memory operation. Similarly, threshold voltages of the sense amplifiers may be varied under program control to evaluate the operating margins of the store. No parity check bit is provided in the call store.

Each processor contains a program timer which is designed to back up other detection methods. Normally, the on-line processor clears the timer in both processors at prescribed intervals if the basic call processing program cycles correctly. If, however, a hardware or software trouble condition exists (e.g., a program may go astray or a long program loop may prevent the timer from being cleared), the timer will time out and automatically produce a switch. The new on-line processor is automatically forced to run an initialization restart program which attempts to establish a working system. System recovery is simplified by using two possible system configurations rather than the multiunit duplex system.

Second Generation of ESS Processors

The advent of silicon integrated circuits (IC's) in the mid-1960's provided the technological climate for dramatic miniaturization, improved performance, and cost-reduced hardware. "1A technology" refers to the standard set of (IC) devices, apparatus, and design tools that were used to design the No. 1A Processor and the No. 3A Processor [Becker et al., 1977]. The choice of technology and the scale of integration level was dictated by the technological advances made between 1968 and 1970. Small-scale integration (SSI), made possible by bipolar technology, was capable of high yield production. Because of the processor cycle time, high-speed logic gates with propagation delays from 5 to 10 ns were designed and developed concurrent with the No. 1A Processor.

No. 1A Processor

The No. 1A Processor, successor to the No. 1 Processor, was designed primarily for the control of large local and toll ESS with high processing capabilities (the No. 1A ESS and No. 4 ESS, respectively) [Budlong et al., 1977]. An important objective in developing the No. 1A ESS was to maintain commonality with the No. 1 ESS. High capacity was achieved by implementing the new No. 1A integrated technology and a newly designed system structure. These changes made possible an instruction execution rate that is four to eight times faster than the No. 1 Processor. Compatability with the No. 1 ESS also allows the No. 1A Processor to be retrofitted into an in-service No. 1 ESS, replacing the No. 1 Processor when additional capacity is needed. The first 1A Processor was put into service in January 1976, as control for a No. 4 ESS in Chicago. Less than one year later, the first No. 1A ESS was put into commercial operation. By 1980, several hundred will be in service [Nowak, 1976].

The No. 1A Processor architecture is similar to its predecessor in that all of its subsystems have redundant units and are connected to the basic CC via redundant bus systems [Bowman et al., 1977]. One of the No. 1A Processor's major architectural differences is its program store [Ault et al., 1977]. It has a writable random-access memory (RAM) instead of PMT ROM. By combining disk memory and RAM, the system has the same amount of memory as a system with PMT, but at a lower cost. Backup copy of program and translation data is kept on disk. Other programs (e.g., diagnostics) are brought to RAM as needed; the same RAM spare is shared among different programs. More important is the system's ability to change the content of the store quickly and automatically. This simplifies considerably the administration and updating of program and translation information in working offices.

The additional disk (file store) subsystem adds flexibility to the

No. 1A Processor [Ault et al., 1977], but it also increases the complexity of system recovery. Fig. 8 shows the multiunit duplex 1A Processor. This configuration is similar to the No. 1 Processor arrangement (see Fig. 3) with a duplicated file store included. The file store communicates with the program store or call store via the CC and the auxiliary unit bus. This allows direct memory access between the file store and the program store or the call store. The disk file and the auxiliary unit bus are grouped together as a switchable entity.

Error detection is achieved by the duplicated and matched synchronous mode of operation, as in the No. 1 Processor. Both CC's operate in step and perform identical operations. The matching is done more extensively in the 1A to obtain as complete a check as possible. There are two match circuits in each processor. Each matcher has the ability to compare 24 internal bits to 24 bits in its mate once every machine cycle. (A machine

cycle is 700 ns.) Any one of 16 different 24-bit internal nodes can be selected for comparison. The choice is determined by the type of instruction being executed. Rather than compare the same nodes in both CC's, the on-line and the standby CC's are arranged to match different sets of data. Four distinct internal groups are matched in the same machine cycle. This ensures the correct execution of any instruction.

The No. 1A Processor design is an improvement of the No. 1 Processor design. The No. 1A Processor incorporates much more checking hardware throughout various functional units in addition to matching hardware. Checking hardware speeds up fault detection and also aids the fault recovery process by providing indications that help isolate the faulty unit. The matching is used in various modes for maintenance purposes. This capability provides powerful diagnostic tools in isolating faults.

The program store and call store use the same hardware technology. The CC contains approximately 50 000 logic gates. While the initial design of the stores called for core memories, they have been replaced with semiconductor dynamic MOS memories. The word size is 26 bits: 24 data bits and two parity check bits. In the No. 1 Processor, the program store and the call store are fully duplicated. Because of their size, duplication requires a considerable amount of hardware, resulting in higher cost and increased component failures. To reduce the amount of hardware in the No. 1A Processor's store community, the memory is partitioned into blocks of 64K words, as shown in Fig. 9. Two additional store blocks are provided as roving spares. If one of the program stores fails, a roving program store spare is substituted and a copy of the program in the file store is transferred to the program store replacement. This type of redundancy has been made possible by the ability to regenerate data stored in a failing unit. Since a program store can be reloaded from the file store in less than a second, a roving spare redundancy plan is sufficient to meet the reliability requirement. As a result, Hamming correction code was not adopted in the No. 1A program store. However, it is essential that an error be detected quickly. Two parity check bits are generated over a partially overlapped, interleaved set of

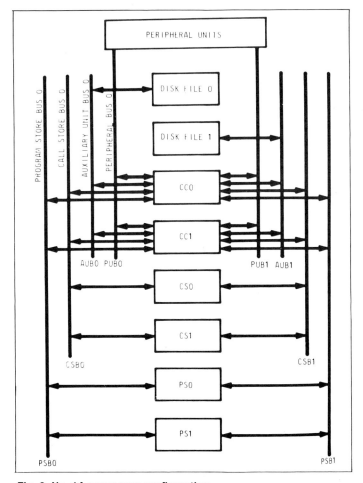

Fig. 8. No. 1A processor configuration.

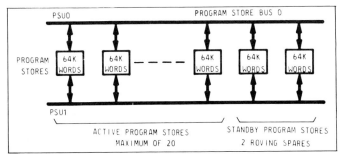

Fig. 9. No. 1A program store structure.

data bits and address. This overlapping is arranged to cope with particular memory circuit failures which may affect more than one bit of a word.

The 1A call stores contain both translation data backed up on the file stores and call-related transient data which are difficult to regenerate. The roving spare concept is expanded for the call stores to include sufficient spares to provide full duplication of transient data. If a fault occurs in a store that contains translation data, one of the duplicated stores containing transient call data is preempted and loaded with the necessary translation data from the duplicated copy in the file store. A parity check is done in the same manner as in the program store, using· two check bits.

The combination of writable program store and file store provides a very effective and flexible system architecture for administrating and implementing a wide variety of features which are difficult to obtain in the No. 1 ESS. However, this architecture also complicates the process of fault recognition and recovery. Reconfiguration into a working system under trouble conditions is an extensive task, depending on the severity of the fault. (For example, it is possible for the processor to lose its sanity or ability to make proper decisions.) An autonomous hardware processor configuration (PC) circuit is provided in each CC to assist in assembling a working system. The PC circuit consists of various timers which ensure that the operational, fault recovery, and configuration programs are successfully executed. If these programs *are not* executed, the PC circuit controls the CC-to-program memory configuration, reloading program memory from file store when required, and isolating various subsystems from the CC until a working system is obtained.

No. 3A Processor

The No. 3A Processor was designed to control the small No. 3 ESS [Irland and Stagg, 1974], which can handle from 500 to 5000 lines. One of the major concerns in the design of this ESS was the cost of its processor. The low cost and high speed of integrated logic circuitry made it possible to design a cost-effective processor that performed better than its discrete component predecessor, the No. 2 Processor. The No. 3A project was started in early 1971. The first system cut into commercial service in late 1975.

Because the number of components in the No. 3A Processor is considerably less than in the No. 1A Processor, all subsystems are fully duplicated, including the main store. The CC, the store bus, and the store are treated as a single switchable entity rather than individual switchable units as in the No. 1A Processor. The system structure is similar to the No. 2 ESS. Experience gained in the design and operation of the No. 2 provided valuable input for the No. 3 Processor design.

The 3A's design makes one major departure from previous ESS

processor designs: it operates in the nonmatched mode of duplex operation. The primary purpose of matching is to detect errors. A mismatch, however, does not indicate *where* (which one of the processors) the fault has occurred. A diagnostic fault-location program must be run to localize the trouble so that the defective unit can be taken off-line. For this reason, the No. 3A Processor was designed to be self-checking, with detection circuitry incorporated as an integral part of the processor. Faults occurring during normal operation are discovered quickly by detecting hardware. This eliminates the need to run the standby system in the synchronous and match mode of operation, or the need to run the fault recognition program to identify the defective unit when a mismatch occurs.

The synchronous and match mode arrangement of the No. 1 Processor and the No. 2 ESS provides excellent detection and coverage of faults. However, there are many instances (e.g., periodic diagnostics, adminstration changes, recent change updates, etc.) when the system is not run in the normal match mode. Consequently, during these periods, the system is vulnerable to faults which may go undetected. The rapid advances in integrated circuit technology make possible the implementation of self-checking circuits in a cost-effective manner. This eliminates the need for the synchronous and match mode of operation. Self-checking design is covered in more detail in Toy [1978].

Another new feature in ESS processor design is the application of microprogram technique in the No. 3A [Storey, 1976]. This technique provides a regular procedure of implementing the control logic. Standard error detection is made part of the hardware to achieve a high degree of checkability. Sequential logic, which is difficult to check, is easily implemented as a sequence of microprogram steps. Microprogramming offers many attractive features: it is simple, flexible, easy to maintain, and easy to expand.

The No. 3A Processor paralleled the design of the No. 1A Processor in its use of an electrically alterable (writable) memory. However, great strides in semiconductor memory technology after the No. 1A became operational permitted the use of semiconductor memory in the 3A rather than core memory.

The 3A's call store and program store are consolidated into a single store system. This reduces cost by eliminating buses, drivers, registers, and controls. A single store system no longer allows concurrent access of call store and program store. However, this disadvantage is more than compensated for by the much faster semiconductor memory. Its access time is 1 μs (the earlier PMT stores had an access time of 6 μs).

Normal operation requires the on-line processor to run and process calls while the standby processor is in the halt state, with its memory updated for each write operation. For the read operation, only the on-line memory is read, *except* when a parity error occurs during a memory read. This results in a microprogram interrupt, which reads the word from the standby store in an attempt to bypass the error.

As discussed previously, the No. 2 Processor (first generation) is used in the No. 2 ESS for medium-size offices. It covers approximately 4000 to 12 000 lines, with a call handling capability of 19 000 busy-hour calls. (The number of calls is related to the calling rate of lines during the busy hour.) The microprogram technique used in the No. 3A Processor design allows the No. 2 Processor's instruction set to be emulated. This enables programs written in the No. 2 assembly language to be directly portable to the No. 3A Processor. The ability to preserve the call processing programs permits the No. 2 ESS to be updated with the No. 3A Processor without having to undergo a complete, new program development.

The combination of the No. 3A Processor and the peripheral equipment of the No. 2 ESS is designated as the No. 2B ESS. It is capable of handling 38 000 busy-hour calls, twice the capability of the No. 2 ESS [Mandigo, 1976]. The No. 2B ESS can be expanded to cover about 20 000 lines. Furthermore, when an existing No. 2 ESS system in the field exceeds its real-time capacity, the No. 2 Processor can be taken out and replaced with the No. 3A Processor. The retrofit operation has been carried out successfully in working offices without disturbing telephone service.

Summary

In order to achieve the reliability requirements, all ESS subsystem units are duplicated. When a hardware failure occurs in any of the subunits, the processor is reconfigured into a working system around the defective unit. The partitioning of subsystem units into switching blocks varies with the size of the ESS processors. For the medium- or small-size processors such as the No. 2 or the No. 3, the central control, the main memory, the bulk memory, and the store bus are grouped as a single switchable entity. A failure in one of the subunits is considered a failure in the switchable block. Since the number of components within a switchable block is sufficiently small, this type of single-unit duplex configuration meets the reliability requirement. For larger processors such as the No. 1 or the No. 1A, the central control, the program store, the call store, the store buses, and the bulk file store are treated individually as switchable blocks. This multiunit duplex configuration allows a considerable number of combinations in which a working system can be assembled. The system is down only when two simultaneous failures occur, one in the subunit and the other in the duplicated subunit. A greater fault tolerance is possible with this configuration. This type of configuration is necessary for the large processor because each subunit contains a larger number of components.

The first generation of ESS processors, which includes the No. 1 and the No. 2, have provided commerical service since 1965 and 1969, respectively. The No. 1 ESS serves large telephone offices (metropolitan); the No. 2 is used in medium-size offices (suburban). Their reliability requirements are the same. Both processors depend on integrated maintenance software, with the hardware that must (1) quickly detect a system failure condition, (2) isolate and configure a working system around the faulty subunit, (3) diagnose the faulty unit, and (4) assist the maintenance personnel in repairing the unit. The primary detection technique is the synchronous and match mode of operation of both central controls. Matching is done more extensively in the No. 1 than in the No. 2 since cost is one of major considerations in the design of the No. 2 Processor. In addition to matching, coding techniques, diagnostic access, and other check logic have been incorporated into the basic design of these processors to realize the reliability objectives.

The widespread acceptance of the No. 1 ESS and the No. 2 ESS has created the need for a second generation of ESS processors: the No. 1A and the No. 3A. They offer greater capability and are also more cost-effective. Both processors use the same integrated technology. The 1A Processor extends its performance range by a factor of four to eight times over the No. 1 Processor by using faster logic and faster memory. The 1A design takes advantage of the experience gained in the design and operation of the No. 1 ESS. The No. 1A Processor provides considerably more hardware for error detection and more extensive matching of a large number of internal nodes within the central control. The design of the No. 3A Processor had benefited by the experience gained from the No. 2 ESS. A major departure in the design of the 3A Processor from the design of other ESS processors is the nonsynchronous and the nonmatch mode of operation. The No. 3A Processor uses self-checking as primary means of error detection. Another departure is in the design of the No. 3A Processor's control section; it is microprogrammed. The No. 3A Processor's flexibility permits emulation of the No. 2 Processor quite easily.

References

Ault et al. [1977]; Ault, Gallaher, Greenwood, and Koehler [1964]; Becker et al. [1977]; Beuscher et al. [1969]; Bowman et al. [1977]; Browne, Quinn, Toy, and Yates [1969]; Budlong et al. [1977]; Cagle et al. [1964]; Chang, Smith, and Walford [1974]; Downing, Nowak, and Tuomenoksa [1964]; Fleckenstein [1974]; Genke, Harding, and Staehler [1964]; Goetz [1974]; Harr, Taylor, and Ulrich [1969]; Irland and Stagg [1974]; Keister, Ketchledge, and Lovell [1960]; Keister, Ketchledge, and Vaughan [1964]; Mandigo [1976]; Nowak [1976]; Seley and Vigilante [1964]; Smith [1972]; Spencer and Vigilante [1969]; Staehler [1977]; Staehler and Watters [1976]; Storey [1976]; Toy [1978]; Tsiang and Ulrich [1962].

Chapter 29

The Tandem 16:
A Fault-Tolerant Computing System[1]

James A. Katzman

Summary A fault-tolerant computer architecture is examined that is commercially available today and installed in many industries. The hardware is examined in this paper and the software is examined in the companion paper.

Introduction

The increasing need for businesses to go on-line is stimulating a requirement for cost effective computer systems having continuous availability [Katzman, 1977; Tandem, 1976]. Certain applications such as automatic toll billing for telephone systems lose money each minute the system is down, and the losses are irrecoverable. Systems commercially available today have met a necessary requirement of multiprocessing but not the sufficient conditions for fault-tolerant computing.

The greatest dollar volumes spent on systems needing these fault-tolerant capabilities are in the commercial on-line, data base transaction, and terminal oriented applications. The design of the Tandem 16 NonStop[2] system was directed toward offering the commercial market an off-the-shelf, general purpose system with at least an order of magnitude better availability than existing off-the-shelf systems without charging a premium. This was accomplished by using a top down system design approach, thus avoiding the shortcomings of the systems currently addressing the fault-tolerant market.

Except for some very expensive special systems developed by the military, universities, and some computer manufacturers in limited quantities, no commercially available systems have been designed for continous availability. Some systems such as the ones designed by ROLM have been designed for high MTBF by "ruggedizing," but typically computers have been designed to be in a monolithic, single processor environment. As certain applications demanded continuous availability, manufacturers recognized that a multiprocessor system was necessary to meet the demands for availability. In order to preserve previous development effort and compatibility, manufacturers invented awkward devices such as I/O channel switches and interprocessor communication adapters to retrofit existing hardware. The basic flaw in this effort is that only multiprocessing was achieved. While that is necessary for continuously available systems, it is far from sufficient.

Single points of failure flourish in these past architectures (Fig. 1). A power supply failure in the I/O bus switch or a single integrated circuit (IC) package failure in any I/O controller on the I/O channel emanating from the I/O bus switch will cause the entire system to fail. Other architectures have used a common memory for interprocessor communications, creating another single point of failure. Typically such systems have not even approached the problem of on-line maintenance, redundant cooling, or a power distribution system that allows for brownout conditions. In today's marketplace, many of the applications of fault-tolerant systems do not allow any down time for repair.

Expansion of a system such as the one in Fig. 1 is prohibitively expensive. A three processor system, strongly connected in a redundant fashion, would require twelve interprocessor links on the I/O channels; five processors would need forty links; for n processors, $2n(n-1)$ links are required. These links often consist of 100–200 IC packages and require entire circuit boards priced between $6,000 and $10,000 each. Using the I/O channel in this manner limits the I/O capabilities as a further undesirable side effect. The resulting hardware changes for expansion, if undertaken, are typically dwarfed in magnitude by the software changes

[1]© 1977. Reprinted with the express permission of Tandem Computers Inc., Cupertino, Calif.
[2]NonStop is a trademark of Tandem Computers.

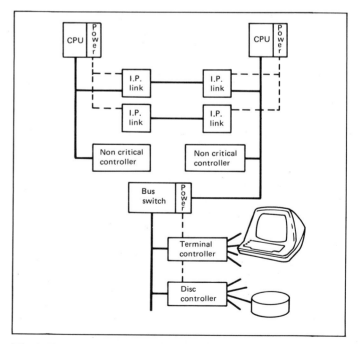

Fig. 1. Example of previous fault-tolerant systems.

needed when applications are to be geographically changed or expanded.

This paper describes the Tandem 16 architecture at the lowest level (the hardware). Section 1 deals with the overall system organization and packaging. Section 2 explains the processor module organization and its attachment to the interprocessor communications system. Section 3 discusses the I/O system organization. Section 4 discusses power, packaging, and on-line maintenance aspects that are not covered elsewhere in the paper.

1. System Organization

The Tandem 16 NonStop system is organized around three basic elements: the processor module, dual-ported I/O controllers, and the DC power distribution system (Figs. 2 and 3). The processors are interconnected by a dual-interprocessor bus system: the Dynabus; the I/O controllers are each connected with two independent I/O channels, one to each port; and the power distribution system is integrated with the modular packaging of the system.

The system design goal is two-fold: (1) to continue operation of the system through any single failure, and (2) to be able to repair

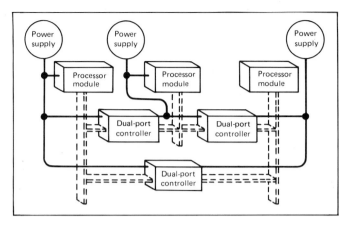

Fig. 3. Power distribution.

that failure without affecting the rest of the system. The on-line maintenance aspects were a key factor in the design of the physical packaging and the power-distribution of the system.

System Packaging

The cabinet (Fig. 4) is divided into 4 sections: the upper card cage, the lower card cage, cooling, and power supplies. The upper card cage contains up to 4 processors, each with up to 512K bytes of independent main memory. The lower card cage contains up to 32 I/O Controller printed circuit (PC) cards, where each controller consists of one to three PC cards. The cooling section consists of 4 fans and a plenum chamber that forces laminar air flow through the card cages. The power supply section contains up to 4 power supply modules. Multiple cabinets may be bolted together, and the system has the capability to accommodate a maximum of 16 processors.

Each processor module, consisting of CPU, memory, Dynabus control and I/O channel, is powered by an associated power

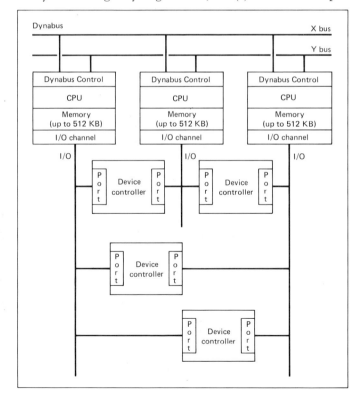

Fig. 2. Tandem 16 system architecture.

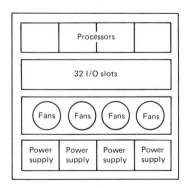

Fig. 4. Tandem 16 physical cabinet.

supply. If a failed module is to be replaced in this section its associated power supply is shut off, the module is replaced, and the power supply is turned on. Each card cage slot in the I/O card cage is powered by two different power supplies. Each of the I/O controllers is connected via its dual-port arrangement to two processors. Each of those processors has its own power supply; usually, but not necessarily, those two supplies are the ones that power the I/O controller (Fig. 3). Each slot in the I/O card cage can be powered down by a corresponding switch disconnecting power from the slot from both supplies without affecting power to the remainder of the system. Therefore, if a power supply fails, or if one is shut down to repair a processor, no I/O controllers are affected.

The dual-power sourcing to the I/O controllers was originally designed using relay switching. This plan was abandoned for several reasons: (a) to contend with relay failure modes is difficult; (b) the number of contact bounces on a switch-over is neither uniform nor predictable, making it difficult for the operating system to handle power-on interrupts from the I/O controllers; and (c) during the switch-over, controllers do lose power, and while most controllers are software-restartable, communications controllers hang up their communications lines. We therefore devised a diode current sharing scheme whereby I/O controllers are constantly drawing current from two supplies simultaneously. If a power supply fails, all the current for a given controller is supplied by the second power supply. There is also circuitry to provide for a controlled ramping of current draw on turn-on and turn-off so there are no instantaneous power demands from a given supply causing a potential momentary dip in supply voltage.

Both fans and power supplies are electrically connected using quick disconnect connectors to speed replacement upon failure. No tools are required to replace a power supply. A screwdriver is all that is needed to replace a fan. Both replacements take less than 5 minutes.

Interconnections

Physical interconnection is done both using front edge connectors and back-planes. Communication within a processor module (e.g., between the CPU and main memory) takes place over four 50 pin front edge connectors using flat ribbon cable. Interprocessor communication takes place over the Dynabus on the back-plane also utilizing ribbon cable. The I/O controllers use etch trace on the back-plane for communication among PC cards of a multicard controller. The I/O channels are back-plane ribbon cable connections between the processors and the I/O controllers.

Peripheral I/O devices are connected via shielded round cable either to a bulk-head patch panel or directly to the front edge connectors of the I/O controllers. If a patch panel is used, then there is a connection using round cables between the patch panel and the front edge connectors of the I/O controllers.

Power is distributed using a DC power distribution scheme. Physically, AC is brought in through a filtering and phase splitting distribution box. Pigtails connect the AC distribution box to one of the input connectors of a power supply. The DC power from the supply is routed through a cable harness to a laminated bus bar arrangement which distributes power on the back-planes to both processors and I/O controllers.

2. Processor Module Organization

The processor (Fig. 5) includes a 16 bit CPU, main memory, the Dynabus interface control and an I/O channel. Physically the CPU, I/O channel and Dynabus control consists of two PC boards 16 inches by 18 inches, each containing approximately 300 IC packages. Schottky TTL circuitry is used. Up to 512K bytes of main memory is available utilizing core or semiconductor technology. Core memory boards hold 32K 17-bit words, and each occupies two card slots because of the height of the core stack. Semiconductor memory is currently implemented utilizing 16 pin, 4K dynamic RAMs. These memory boards contain 48K 22-bit words per board and occupy only one card slot and are therefore three times denser than core.

The processor module is viewed by the user as a 16-bit, stack-oriented processor, with a demand paging, virtual memory system capable of supporting multiprogramming.

The CPU

The CPU is a microprogrammed processor consisting of a bank of 8 registers which can be used as general purpose registers, as a LIFO register stack, or for indexing; an ALU; a shifter; two memory stack management registers; program control registers

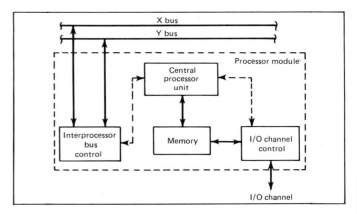

Fig. 5. Tandem 16 processor organization.

(e.g., program counter, instruction register, environment or status register, and a next instruction register for instruction prefetching); scratch pad registers available only to the microprogrammer; and several other miscellaneous flags and counters for the microprogrammer.

The microprogram is stored in read-only memory and is organized in 512-word sectors of 32-bit words. The microinstruction has different formats for branching, sequential functions, and immediate operand operations. The Tandem 16 instruction set occupies 512 words with the decimal arithmetic option occupying another 512 words. The address space for the microprogram is 2K words.

The microprocessor has a 100 ns cycle time and is a two stage pipelined microprocessor; i.e., all microinstructions take two cycles to execute but one completes each cycle. In the first stage of the pipeline any two operands are selected by two source fields in the microinstruction for loading into the ALU input registers. In the second stage of the pipeline the ALU performs a primitive operation on the operands placed in the ALU input registers during the previous cycle and performs a shift operation on the results. In parallel, a miscellaneous operation such as a condition code setting or a counter increment can be done, the result can be stored in any CPU register or dispatched to the memory system or I/O channel, and a condition test made on the results. Each of these parallel operations is controlled by a separate control field in the microinstruction.

The basic set of 123 machine instructions includes arithmetic operations (add, subtract, etc.), logical operations (and, or, exclusive or), bit deposit, block (multiple element) moves/compares/scans, procedure calls and exits, interprocessor SENDs, and I/O operations. All instructions are 16 bits in length. The decimal instruction set provides an additional 20 instructions dealing with four-word operands.

The interrupt system has 16 major interrupt levels which include interprocessor bus data received, I/O transfer completion, memory error, interval timer, page fault, privileged instruction violation, etc.

Provision is made for several events to cause microinterrupts. They are entirely handled by the CPU's microprocessor without causing an interrupt to the operating system. One event, for example, is the receipt of a 16 word packet over the Dynabus. A packet is the primitive unit of data which is transferred over the Dynabus for interprocessor communication. The microprocessor puts the information in a predetermined area of memory and does not cause a system interrupt until the entire message is received.

The register stack is used for most arithmetic operations and for holding parameters for block instructions (moves/compares/scans) which need the parameters updated dynamically so that the instructions may be interruptable and restarted. The 8-register

stack is a "wraparound" stack and is not logically connected to the memory stack.

Main Memory

Main memory is organized in physical pages of 1K words of 16 bits/word. Up to 256K words of memory may be attached to a processor. In the core memory systems there is a parity bit for single error detection, and in semiconductor memory systems there are 6 check bits/word to provide single error correction and double error detection. Due to the relative reliability of these two technologies, we have found that semiconductor memory, without error correction, is much less reliable than core, and that with error correction, it is somewhat more reliable than core. Battery backup provides short term non-volatility to the semiconductor memory system for utility power outage considerations.

It might be noted that there are some memory systems using a 21 bit error correction scheme (5 check bits on a 16 bit data word instead of 6). While 5 bits are enough to correct all single bit errors, it does not detect approximately $\frac{1}{3}$ of the possible double bit error combinations. In these conditions, this 5 check bit scheme will incorrectly deduce that some bit (neither of the bits actually in error) is incorrect and correctable. The scheme will then correct this bit (actually causing 3 bits to be in error), and deliver it to the system as "good" reporting a correctable memory error.

Memory is logically divided into 4 address spaces (Fig. 6). These are the virtual address spaces of the machine; both the system and the user have a code space and a data space. The code space is unmodifiable and the data space can be viewed either as a stack or a random access memory, depending on the addresssing mode used. Each of these virtual address spaces is 64K words long, and is addressed by a 16 bit virtual address.

The physical memory address is 18 bits with conversion from the virtual address to physical address accomplished through a mapping scheme. Four maps are provided, one for each logical address space; each map consists of 64 entries one for each page in the virtual address space. The maps are implemented in 50 ns access bipolar static RAM. The map access and main memory error correction is included in the 500 ns cycle time for semiconductor memory systems.

The unmodifiable code area provides reentrant, recursive, and sharable code. The data space (Fig. 7) can be referenced relative to address 0 (global data or G+ addressing), or relative to the memory stack management registers in the CPU.

The lowest level language provided on the Tandem 16 system is T/TAL, a high-level, block-structured, ALGOL-like language which provides structures to get at the more efficient machine instructions. The basic program unit in T/TAL is the PROCEDURE. Unlike ALGOL, there is no outer block, but rather a main

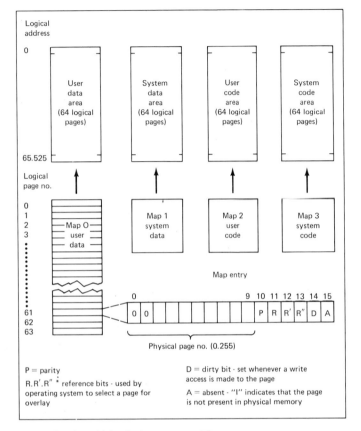

P = parity

R.R'.R" : reference bits - used by operating system to select a page for overlay

D = dirty bit - set whenever a write access is made to the page

A = absent - "I" indicates that the page is not present in physical memory

Fig. 6. Tandem 16 logical memory address spaces.

PROCEDURE. T/TAL has the ability to declare certain variables as global. PROCEDURES cannot be nested in T/TAL, but a SUBPROCEDURE can be nested in a PROCEDURE and only in a PROCEDURE. A SUBPROCEDURE is limited in local variable access capabilities.

The memory stack, defined by two registers in the CPU, is used for efficient linkage to and from procedures, parameter passing, and dynamic storage allocation and deallocation for variables local to the procedure.

The L register (Local variables) points to the last stack marker placed on the stack. This marker contains return information about the caller such as the return address and the previous location of the L register. The contents of the L register are primarily changed by the procedure call and exit instructions.

Addressing relative to the L register provides access to parameters passed to a procedure (L−) and local variables of the procedure (L+). Parameters may be passed either by value (using direct addressing) or by reference (using indirect addressing).

The S register (stack top pointer) points to the last element placed on the stack. It is used for a SUBPROCEDURE's sublocal data area when S relative addressing (S−) is used.

There is a special mode of addressing used by the operating system, called System Global (SG+) addressing. It is used by the operating system while it is working in a user's virtual data space (on his behalf) and needs to address the system data space. The system data space contains many resource tables and buffers and the need to access them quickly justifies the existence of this addressing mode.

There are three tables known to the operating system, the microprogram and the hardware: the system interrupt vector (SIV), the I/O Control (IOC) table, and the Bus Receive Table (BRT). These tables will be explained in later sections as appropriate.

The Dynabus

The Dynabus is a set of two independent interprocessor buses. Bus access is determined by two independent interprocessor bus controllers. Each of these controllers is dual-powered, in the same manner as an I/O controller. The Dynabus controllers are very small, approximately 30 IC packages, and are not associated with, nor physically a part of, any processor. Each bus has a two byte data path and control lines associated with it. There are two sets of radial connections from each interprocessor bus controller to each processor module. They distribute clocks for synchronous transmission over the bus and for transmission enable. Therefore, no failed processor can independently dominate Dynabus utilization upon failure since in order to electrically transmit onto the bus, the bus controller must agree that a given processor has the right to transmit. Each bus has a clock associated with it, running independently of the processor clocks and located on the associated bus controller. The clock rate is 150 ns on two to eight processor systems. The clock does need to be slowed down for the longer interprocessor buses of greater than eight processors. Therefore each bus on small systems transfers at the rate of 13.3M bytes/second and on the larger systems at 10M bytes/second. Performance measurements have shown that under worst case test conditions the Dynabus is only 15% utilized in a ten processor system.

Each processor in the system attaches to both interprocessor buses. The Dynabus interface control section (Fig. 8) consists of 3 high speed caches: an incoming queue associated with each interprocessor bus, and a single outgoing queue that can be switched to either of the buses. All caches are 16 words in length and all bus transfers are cache to cache. All components that attach to either of the buses are kept physically distinct, so that no single component failure can contaminate both buses simultaneously. Also in this section are clock synchronization and interlock circuitry. All processors communicate in a point to point manner

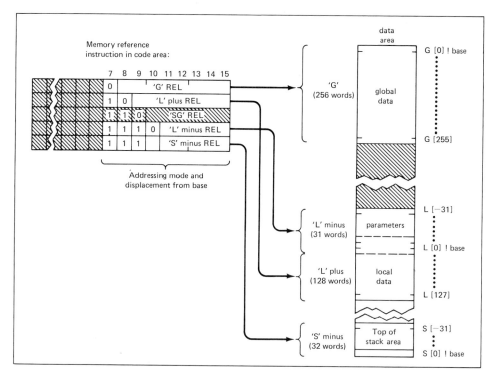

Fig. 7. Tandem 16 data space.

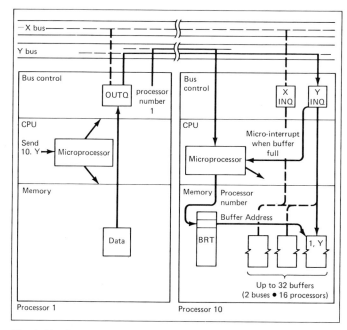

Fig. 8. Tandem 16 dynabus interface and control.

using this redundant direct shared bus (DSB) configuration [Anderson and Jensen, 1975].

For any given interprocessor data transfer, one processor is the sender and the other the receiver. Before a processor can receive data over an interprocessor bus, the operating system must configure an entry in a table (Fig. 9) known as the Bus Receive Table (BRT). Each BRT entry contains the address where the incoming data is to be stored and the number of words expected. To transfer data over a bus, a SEND instruction is executed in the sending processor, which specifies the bus to be used, the intended receiver, and the number of words to be sent. The sending processor's CPU stays in the SEND instruction until the data transfer is completed. Up to 65,535 words can be sent in a single SEND instruction. While the sending processor is executing the SEND instruction, the Dynabus interface control logic in the receiving processor is storing the data away according to the appropriate BRT entry. In the receiving processor this occurs simultaneously with program execution.

The message is divided into packets of 15 information words and an LRC check word. The sending processor first fills its outgoing queue with these packets, requests a bus transfer, and transmits upon grant of the bus by the interprocessor bus controller. The receiving processor fills the incoming queue associated with the

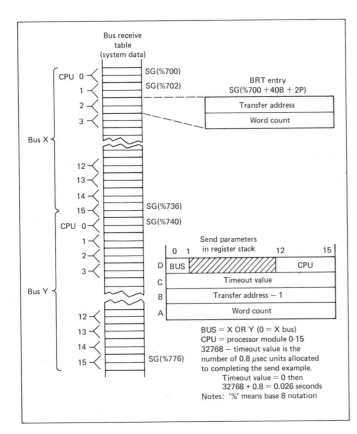

Fig. 9. Bus receive table.

bus over which the packet is received, and issues a microinterrupt to its own CPU. The microprocessor of the CPU checks the BRT entry, stores the packet away, verifies the LRC check word, and updates the BRT entry accordingly. If the count is exhausted the currently executing program is interrupted; otherwise program execution continues.

The BRT entries are two words that include a transfer count and buffer address. The SEND instruction has as parameters the designation of the bus to be used, the intended receiver, the data buffer address in the system data space, the word count to be transferred, and a timeout value. Error recovery action is to be taken in case the transfer is not completed within the timeout interval. These parameters are placed on the register stack and are dynamically updated so that the SEND instruction is interruptible on packet boundaries.

There are several levels of protocol, beyond the scope of this paper, dealing with the interprocessor bus that exist in software [Bartlett, 1978], to assure that valid data is transferred. The philosophy for the hardware/software partitioning was to leave the more esoteric decisions to the software, e.g., alternate path

routing, and error recovery procedures, with fault detection and reporting implemented in the hardware. Fault detection was designed in those areas having the highest anticipated probability of error.

The Input/Output Channel

The heart of the Tandem 16 I/O System is the I/O channel. All I/O is done on a direct memory access (DMA) basis. The channel is a microprogrammed, block multiplexed channel with the block size determined by the individual controllers. All the controllers are buffered to some degree so that all transfers over the I/O channel are at memory speed (4M bytes/second) and never wait for mechanical motion since the transfers always come from a buffer in the controller rather than from the actual I/O device.

There exists a table in the system data space of each processor called the IOC (I/O Control) table that contains a two word entry (Fig. 10) for each of the 256 possible I/O devices attached to the I/O channel. These entries contain a byte count and virtual address in the system data space for data transfers from the I/O system.

The I/O channel moves the IOC entry to active registers during connection of an I/O controller and restores the updated values to the IOC upon a disconnection. The I/O channel alerts the I/O controller when that count has been exhausted and that causes the controller to interrupt the processor.

The channel does not execute channel programs as on many systems but it does do data transfer in parallel with program execution. The memory system priority always permits I/O accesses to be handled before CPU or Dynabus accesses (in an on-line, transaction oriented environment, it is rare that a system is not I/O bound). The maximum I/O transfer is 4K bytes.

3. I/O System Organization

The I/O system had a design goal of being very efficient in a transaction, on-line oriented environment. This environment has constraints different from those of a batch environment. The figure of merit in an on-line system is the number of transactions/second/dollar that can be handled by the system. We also wanted an I/O system that had low overhead, fast transfer rates, no overruns, and no interrupts to the system until a logical entity of work was completed (i.e., no character by character interrupts from the terminals). The resulting design satisfied these goals by implementing an I/O system that was extremely simple.

I/O controllers reconnect to the channel when their buffers are stressed past a configurable threshold, transfer data in a burst mode until their buffer stress is zero (buffer empty on input operations, full on output operations), and disconnect from the channel. When the transfer terminates, the I/O controller interrupts the processor. Controllers may interrupt for other reasons

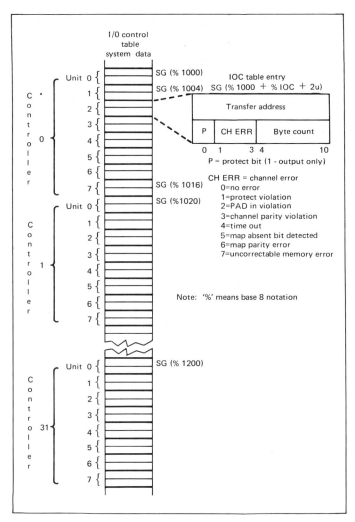

I/O control table system data

Transfer address

P | CH ERR | Byte count

0   1   3 4   10

P = protect bit (1 - output only)

IOC table entry
SG (% 1000 + % IOC + 2u)

Unit 0 { SG (% 1000)
1 { SG (% 1004)
2 {
3 {
4 {
5 {
6 {
7 { SG (% 1016)
Unit 0 { SG (%1020)
1 {
2 {
3 {
4 {
5 {
6 {
7 {

Controller 0

Controller 1

CH ERR = channel error
0=no error
1=protect violation
2=PAD in violation
3=channel parity violation
4=time out
5=map absent bit detected
6=map parity error
7=uncorrectable memory error

Note: '%' means base 8 notation

Unit 0 { SG (% 1200)
1 {
2 {
3 {
4 {
5 {
6 {
7 {

Controller 31

Fig. 10. I/O control table.

than an exhausted byte count, e.g., a terminal controller receiving an end-of-page character from a page mode terminal, or I/O channel error condition, or a disc pack being mounted.

Dual-Port Controllers

The dual-ported I/O device controllers provide the interface between the Tandem 16 standard I/O channel and a variety of peripheral devices using distinct interfaces. While the I/O controllers are vastly different, there is a commonality among them that folds them into the Tandem 16 NonStop architecture.

Each controller contains two independent I/O channel ports implemented by IC packages which are physically separate from each other so that no interface chip can simultaneously cause

failure of both ports. Each port of each controller has a 5-bit configurable controller number, and interrupt priority setting. These settings can be different on each port. The only requirement is that each port attached to an I/O channel must be assigned a controller number and priority distinct from controller numbers and priorities of other ports attached to the same I/O channel.

Each controller has a PON (power-on) circuit which clamps its output to ground whenever the controller's DC supply voltage is not within regulation. The PON circuit has hysteresis in it so that it will not oscillate if the power should hover near the limit of regulation. When the power is within regulation, the output of the PON circuit is at a TTL "1" level. A power-on condition causes a controller reset and also gives an interrupt to one of the two processors to which it is attached. The output of the PON circuit is also used to enable all the I/O channel bus transceivers so that a controller being powered down will not cause interference on the I/O channels during the power transient. This is possible because the PON circuit operates with the supply voltage as low as .2 volts and special transceivers are used which correctly stay in a high impedance state as long as the control enable is at a logical "0."

Logically only one of the two ports of an I/O controller is active and the other port is utilized only in the event of a path failure to the primary port. There is an "ownership" bit (Fig. 11) indicating to each port if it is the primary port or the alternate. Ownership is changed only by the operating system issuing a TAKE OWNERSHIP I/O command. Executing this special command causes the I/O controller to swap its primary and alternate port designation and to do a controller reset. Any attempt to use a controller which is not owned by a given processor will result in an ownership violation. If a processor determines that a given controller is malfunctioning on its I/O channel, it can issue a DISABLE PORT command that logically disconnects the port from that I/O controller. This does not affect the ownership status. That way, if the problem is within the port, the alternate path can be used, but if the problem is in the common portion of the controller, ownership is not forced upon the other processor.

A controller signals an interrupt on the I/O channel if the channel has indicated an exhausted transfer count, if the controller terminates the transfer prematurely, or for attention purposes.

When simultaneous interrupts occur on an I/O channel, a priority scheme determines which interrupt is handled first. There are two levels of priorities, designated "rank 0" and "rank 1." Each rank has up to 16 controllers assigned to it. Jumper wires on each controller determine the rank and position within the rank (positions 0 to 15). The I/O channel issues a rank 0 interrupt poll cycle and each controller assigned to rank 0 can place an interrupt request, if it needs service, on a dedicated data bit of the I/O channel determined by the jumper wires. If there are no controllers on rank 0 requiring service, the I/O channel issues the interrupt poll cycle for rank 1. Note, only 32 controllers can be assigned to a given channel and each one has a unique rank and

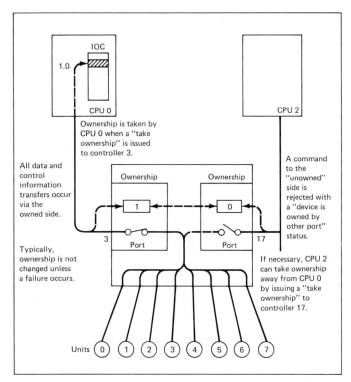

Fig. 11. Ownership circuitry.

position designation. The highest priority controller is granted access to the interrupt system. Thus a radial polling technique allows the processor to resolve 32 different controller priorities in just two poll cycles. Each port of a controller has a separate set of configuration jumpers so that a controller can have different priorities on its primary and alternate path.

Controller Buffer Considerations

In the design of the Tandem 16 I/O system, a lot of attention was paid to the overrun problem. While overruns are possible on this system, they have been made a rare occurrence. Each I/O controller has 3 configurable settings: the I/O controller number, the interrupt priority, and buffer stress threshold reconnect setting.

Each I/O controller is buffered to some extent. The asynchronous terminal controller has 2 bytes of buffering, while the disc controller has 4K bytes of buffering. Considerations of device transfer rate, channel transfer rate, the individual controller's buffer depth, the controller's reconnect priority, and a given channel's I/O complement can be used to determine the buffer's depth (stress threshold) at which a reconnect request should be made to the channel to minimize the chance of overrun. Each

controller with significant buffering (more than 32 bytes) has a configurable stress threshold. Buffer stress is defined as the number of cells full on an input operation, and the number of cells empty on output operations. In general, the I/O channel relieves stress while the I/O device generates more stress. Therefore the higher the stress, the more the buffer needs relief from the I/O channel, regardless of the direction of data transfer.

Tandem has developed a program which takes a system configuration and determines the appropriate stress threshold settings needed to guarantee no data overruns. Since reconnect overhead time is known, and all transfers on the I/O bus take place at memory speed, and the upper bound of the block length is known for each type of controller, it is a deterministic function as to whether or not an overrun is possible. If it is impossible to generate a no-overrun configuration, the program will output a minimum-overrun threshold setting. Most times, however, it is possible to iterate on the configuration until threshold settings can be determined that prevent overruns.

Disc Controller Considerations

The greatest fear that an on-line system user has is that "the data base is down" [Dolotta et al., 1976]. Many of these users are willing to pay the premium of having duplicated or "mirrored" data bases in case a disc drive fails. To meet this requirement, Tandem provides automatic mirroring of data bases.

A disc volume is a set of data contained on one spindle or one removable disc pack. A user may declare any of the disc volumes as mirrored pairs at system generation time (Fig. 12). The system then maintains these pairs so they always contain identical data. Thus protection is achieved for a single drive failure. Each disc drive in the system may be dual-ported. Each port of a disc drive is connected to an independent disc controller. Each of the disc controllers is also dual-ported and connected between two processors. A string of up to 8 drives (4 mirrored pairs) can be supported by a pair of controllers in this manner.

Note that in this configuration there are many paths to any given data and that data can be retrieved regardless of any single disc drive failure, disc controller failure, power supply failure, processor failure, or I/O channel failure.

The disc controller is buffered for a maximum length record which provides several features important in an on-line system. First, the disc controller is absolutely immune to overruns. Second, data to be written on two drives need be transferred over the I/O channel only once. The data may then be posted twice from the controller's internal buffer. Thus the channel's data transfer capacity is little impaired by mirrored volumes.

This disc controller uses a Fire code [Peterson, 1961] for burst error correction and detection. It can correct 11 bit bursts in the controller's buffer before transmission to the channel. Since overlapped seeks are allowed by the controller, when data is to be

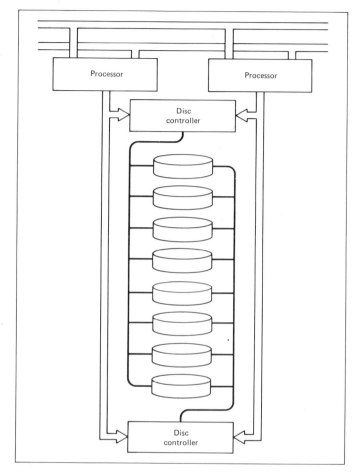

Fig. 12. Tandem 16 disc subsystem organization.

read from a mirrored pair it can be read from the drive which has its arm closest to the data cylinder. It is interesting to note that since the majority of transactions in an on-line system are reads, mirrored volumes actually can increase performance.

NonStop I/O System Considerations

The I/O channel interface consists of a two byte data bus and control signals. All data transferred over the bus is parity checked in both directions, and errors are reported via the interrupt system. A watchdog timer in the I/O channel detects if a non-existent I/O controller has been addressed, or if a controller stops responding during an I/O sequence.

The data transfer byte count word in the IOC entry contains four status bits including a protect bit. When this bit is set to "1" only output transfers are permitted to this device.

Because I/O controllers are connected between two indepen-

dent I/O channels, it is very important that word count, buffer address, and direction of transfer are controlled by the processor instead of within the controller. If that information were to be kept in the controller, a single failure could cause both processors to which it was attached to fail. Consider what would happen if a byte count register was located in the controller and was stuck in such a situation that the count could not decrement to zero on an input transfer. It would be possible to overwrite the buffer and cause system tables to become meaningless. The error would propagate to the other processor upon discovery that the first processor was no longer operating.

Other error conditions that the channel checks for are violations of I/O protocol, attempts to transfer to absent pages (it is the operating system's responsibility to "tack down" the virtual pages used for I/O buffering), uncorrectable memory errors, and map parity errors.

4.   Power, Packaging, On-Line Maintenance

The Tandem 16 power supply has 3 sections: a 5 volt interruptible section, a 5 volt uninterruptible section, and a 12–15 volt uninterruptible section. The interruptible section will stop supplying DC power when AC is lost while the uninterruptible sections will continue to supply DC power. The interruptible section powers I/O controllers and that portion of a processor which is not related to memory refresh operation. The uninterruptible sections provide power for the memory array and refresh circuitry. The 5 volt sections are switching regulated supplies while the 12–15 volt section is linearly regulated. The uninterruptible sections have a provision for a battery attachment so that in case of utility power failure, memory contents are kept for 1.5 to 4 hours, depending on the amount of memory attached to the supply.

The power supply accepts AC input of 110 or 220 volts ±20% to provide brownout insensitivity. At nominal line conditions, over 30 msec of ridethrough is provided by storage capacitors. A power-fail warning signal is provided when there is at least 5 msec of regulated power remaining so that the processor can go through an orderly shut down. Some users must remain operational through utility power failure and have generator systems which provide continuous AC power for the entire system, including peripheral devices.

The power-fail warning scheme in the Tandem 16 power supply monitors charge in the storage capacitors rather than monitoring loss of AC peaks as is conventionally done. This has the advantage that the 5 msec to do a power shutdown sequence in the processor is guaranteed even if it occurs after a brownout period.

The power supply provides all other prudent features required in a computer system, such as over voltage and over current protection, and over temperature protection.

The power-up sequencing on disc drives has been implemented with independent rather than daisy chained circuits. In the daisy chained approach, one bad sequencer circuit can cause the remaining drives in the chain not to sequence up after a power failure.

Further Packaging and On-Line Maintenance Considerations

Modularity is a key concept in the Tandem 16 system. The maintenance philosophy is to make all repairs by module replacement at the user site without making the system unavailable to the user. Therefore the back-planes, power supplies, fans, and I/O channels, as well as the PC cards, are modular and easily replaceable. Thumb screws are used when they can be so that a minimum of tools are needed for repair. The package is designed so that there is easy access to all modules.

Processors and I/O controllers not only can be replaced on-line, but added on-line without system interruption if expansion is planned, all without application software being changed.

Conclusion

The contribution of the Tandem 16 system lies in the synthesis of a system to directly address the need of the NonStop application marketplace. By avoiding the "onus of compatibility" to any previous system, an architecture could be designed from "scratch" that was "clean" and efficient.

The system goals have been met to a large degree. Systems have been shipped containing two to ten processors. Many application programs are on-line and running. They recover from failures, and stay up continuously.

References

Anderson and Jensen [1975]; Bartlett [1978]; Dolotta et al. [1976]; Katzman [1977]; Locks [1973]; Mil 217 [1965]; Peterson [1961]; Tandem [1976].

The Tandem 16:
A "NonStop" Operating System[1]

Joel F. Bartlett

Summary The Tandem/16 computer system is an attempt at providing a general-purpose, multiple-computer system which is at least one order of magnitude more reliable than conventional commercial offerings. Through software abstractions a multiple-computer structure, desirable for failure tolerance, is transformed into something approaching a symmetric multiprocessor, desirable for programming ease. Section 1 of this paper provides an overview of the hardware structure. In Sec. 2 are found the design goals for the operating system, "Guardian." Section 3 provides a bottom-up view of Guardian.

1. Introduction

1.1 Background

On-line computer processing has become a way of life for many businesses. As they make the transition from manual or batch methods to on-line systems, they become increasingly vulnerable

[1]Reprinted with the express permission of Tandem Computers Inc. "NonStop" is a trademark of Tandem Computers Inc.

to computer failures. Whereas in a batch system the direct costs of a failure might simply be increased overtime for the operations staff, a failure of an on-line system results in immediate business losses.

1.2 System Overview

The Tandem/16 [Katzman, 1977; Tandem, 1976] was designed to provide a system for on-line applications that would be significantly more reliable than currently available commercial computer systems. The hardware structure consists of multiple processor modules interconnected by redundant interprocessor buses. A PMS [Bell and Newell, 1971] definition of the hardware is found in Fig. 1.

Each processor has its own power supply, memory, and I/O channel and is connected to all other processors by redundant interprocessor buses. Each I/O controller is redundantly powered and connected to two different I/O channels. As a result, any interprocessor bus failure does not affect the ability of a processor to communicate with any other processor. The failure of an I/O channel or of a processor does not cause the loss of an I/O device. Likewise, the failure of a module (processor or I/O controller) does not disable any other module or disable any inter-module communication. Finally, certain I/O devices such as disc drives may be connected to two different I/O controllers, and disc drives may in turn be duplicated such that the failure of an I/O controller or disc drive will not result in loss of data.

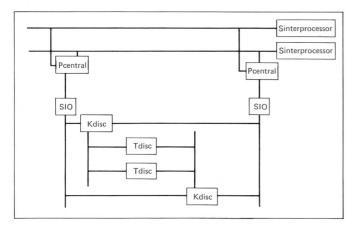

Fig. 1. Hardware structure.

The system is not a true multiprocessor [Enslow, 1977], but rather a "multiple computer" system. The multiple computer approach is preferable for several reasons. First, since no module is shared by the entire system, it increases the system's reliability. Second, a multiple computer system does not require the complex hardware needed to handle multiple access paths to a common memory. In smaller systems, the cost of such a multiported memory is undesirable; and in larger systems, performance suffers because of memory access interference.

On-line repair is as necessary as reliability in assuring system availability. The modular structure of the Tandem/16 system allows processors, I/O controllers, or buses to be repaired or replaced while the rest of the system continues to operate. Once repaired, they may then be reintegrated into the system.

The system structure allows a wide range of system sizes to be supported. As many as sixteen processors, each with up to 512K bytes of memory, may be connected into one system. Each processor may also have up to 256 I/O devices connected to it. This provides for tremendous growth of application programs and processing loads without the requirement that the application be reimplemented on a larger system with a different architecture.

Finally, the system is meant to provide a general solution to the problem of providing a failure-tolerant, on-line environment suitable for commercial use. As such, the system supports conventional programming languages and peripherals and is oriented toward providing large numbers of terminals with access to large data bases.

2.   System Design Goals

2.1 Integrated Hardware/Software Design

The Tandem/16 system was designed to solve a specific problem. This problem was not stated in terms of hardware and software

requirements, but rather in terms of system requirements. The hardware and software designs then proceeded in tandem to provide a unified solution. The hardware design concerned itself with the contents of each module, their interconnections to the common buses, and error detection and correction within modules and on the communication paths. The software design was given the problem of control; that is, selection of which modules to use and which buses to use to communicate with them. Furthermore, as errors are detected, it was the responsibility of the software to control recovery actions.

2.2 Operating System Design Goals

The first and foremost goal of the operating system, Guardian, was to provide a failure-tolerant system. This translated into the following design "axioms":

- The operating system should be able to remain operational after any single detected module or bus failure.

- The operating system should allow any module or bus to be repaired on-line and then reintegrated into the system.

- The operating system should be implemented in a reliable manner. Increased reliability provided by the hardware architecture must not be negated by software problems.

A second set of requirements came from the great numbers and sizes of hardware configurations that are possible:

- The operating system should support all possible hardware configurations, ranging from a two-processor, discless system through a sixteen-processor system with billions of bytes of disc storage.

- The operating system should hide the physical configuration as much as possible so that applications can be written to run on a great variety of system configurations.

3.   Operating System Structure

To satisfy these requirements, the operating system was designed to have the appearance of a true multiprocessor at the user level. The design of the system was strongly influenced by Dijkstra's work on the "THE" system [Dijkstra, 1968a], and Brinch Hansen's implementation of an operating system nucleus for a single-processor system [Brinch Hansen, 1970]. The primary abstractions are processes, which do work, and messages, which allow interprocess communication.

3.1 Processes

At the lowest level of the system is the basic hardware as earlier described. It provides the capability for redundant modules, i.e.,

I/O controllers, I/O devices, and processor modules consisting of a processor, memory, and a power supply. These redundant modules are in turn interconnected by redundant buses. Error detection is provided on all communication paths and error correction is provided within each processor's memory. The hardware does not concern itself with the selection of communication paths or the assignment of tasks to specific modules.

The first abstraction provided is that of the process. Each processor module may have one or more processes residing in it. A process is initially created in a specific processor and may not execute in another processor. Each process has an execution priority assigned to it. Processor time is allocated on a strict priority basis to the highest priority ready process.

Process synchronization primitives include "counting semaphores" and process local "event" flags. Semaphore operations are performed via the functions PSEM and VSEM, corresponding to Dijkstra's P and V operations. Semaphores may only be used for synchronization between processes within the same processor. They are typically used to control access to resources such as resident memory buffers, message control blocks, and I/O controllers.

When certain low-level actions such as device interrupts, processor power-on, message completion or message arrival occur, they result in "event" flags being set for the appropriate process. A process may wait for one or more events to occur via the function WAIT. The process is activated as soon as the first WAITed for event occurs. Events are signaled via the function AWAKE. Event signals are queued using a "wake up waiting" mechanism so that they are not lost if the event is signaled when the process is not waiting on it. Like semaphores, event signals may not be passed between processors. Event flags are predefined for eight different events and may not be redefined.

When a process blocks itself to wait for some event to occur or for a semaphore to be allocated to it, it may specify a maximum time to block. If the time limit expires and the event has not occurred or the resource has not been obtained, then the process will continue execution but an error condition will be returned to it. This timeout allows "watch dog" timers to be easily placed on device interrupts or on resource allocations where a failure may occur.

Each process in the system has a unique identifier or "processid" in the form: <cpu#,process #>, which allows it to be referenced on a system-wide basis. This leads to the next abstraction, the message system, which provides a processor-independent, failure-tolerant method for interprocess communication.

3.2 Messages

The message system provides five primitive operations which can be illustrated in the context of a process making a request to some server process (Fig. 2). The process' request for service will send a message to the appropriate server process via the procedure LINK. The message will consist of parameters denoting the type of request and any needed data. The message will be queued for the server process, setting an event flag, and then the requestor process may continue executing.

When the server process wishes to check for any messages, it calls LISTEN. LISTEN returns the first message queued or an indication that no messages are queued. The server process will then obtain a copy of the requestor's data by calling the procedure READLINK.

Next, the server process will process the request. The status of the operation and any result will then be returned by the WRITELINK procedure, which will signal the requestor process via another event flag. Finally, the requestor process will complete its end of the transaction by calling BREAKLINK.

A communications protocol was defined for the interprocessor buses that would tolerate any single bus error during the execution of any message system primitive. This design assures that a communications failure will occur if and only if the sender or receiver processes or their processors fail. Any bus errors which occur during a message system operation will be automatically corrected in a manner transparent to the communicating processes and logged on the system console. The interprocessor buses are not used for communication between processes in the same processor, which can be done faster in memory. However, the processes involved in the message transfer are unable to detect this difference.

The message system is designed such that resources needed for message transmission (control blocks) are obtained at the start of a message transfer request. Once LINK has been successfully completed, both processes are assured that sufficient resources are in hand to be able to complete the message transfer. Furthermore, a process may reserve control blocks to guarantee that it will always be able to send messages to process a request

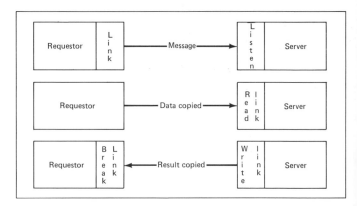

Fig. 2. Message system primitive operations.

that it picks up from its message queue. Such resource controls assure that deadlocks can be prevented in complex producer/consumer interactions, if the programmer correctly analyzes and anticipates potential deadlocks within the application.

3.3 Process-Pairs

With the implementation of processes and messages, the system is no longer seen as separate modules. Instead, the system can be viewed as a set of processes which may interact via messages in any arbitrary manner, as shown in Fig. 3.

By defining messages as the only legitimate method for process-to-process interaction, interprocess communication is not limited by the multiple-computer organization of the system. The system then starts to take on the appearance of a true multiprocessor. Processor boundaries have been blurred, but I/O devices are still not accessible to all processes.

System-wide access to I/O devices is provided by the mechanism of "process-pairs." An I/O process-pair consists of two cooperating processes located in two different processors that control a particular I/O device. One of the processes will be considered the "primary" and one will be considered the "backup." The primary process handles requests sent to it and controls the I/O device. When a request for an operation such as a file open or close occurs, the primary will send this information to the backup process via the message system. These "checkpoints" assure that the backup process will have all information needed to take over control of the device in the event of an I/O channel error or a failure of the primary process' processor. A process-pair for a redundantly-recorded disc volume is illustrated in Fig. 4.

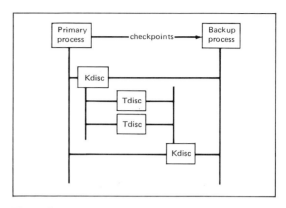

Fig. 4. Process-pair for a redundantly recorded disc volume.

Because of the distributed nature of the system, it is not possible to provide a block of "driver" code that could be called directly to access the device. While potentially more efficient, such an approach would preclude access to every device in the system by every process in the system.

The I/O process-pair and associated I/O device(s) are known by a logical device name such as "$DISC1" or by a logical device number rather than by the processid of either process. I/O device names are mapped to the appropriate processes via the logical device table (LDT) in every processor, which supplies two processids for each device. A message request made on the basis of a device name or number results in the message being sent to the first process in the table. If the message cannot be sent or if the message is sent to the backup process, an error indication will be returned. The processid entries in the LDT will then be reversed and the message resent. Note two things: first, the error recovery can be done in an automatic manner; and second, the requestor is not concerned with what process actually handled the request. Error recovery cannot always be done automatically. For example, the primary process of a pair controlling a line printer fails while handling a request to print a line on a check. The application process would prefer to see the process failure as an error rather than have the request automatically retried, which might result in two checks being printed.

The two primitives, processes and messages, blur the boundaries between processors and provide a failure-tolerant method for interprocess communication. By defining a method of grouping processes (process-pairs), a mechanism for uniform access to an I/O device or other system-wide resource is provided. This access method is independent of the functions performed within the processes, their locations, or their implementations. Within the process-pair, the message system is used to checkpoint state changes so that the backup process may take over in the event of a failure. This checkpoint mechanism is in turn independent of all other processes and messages in the system.

The system structure can be summarized as follows. Guardian is

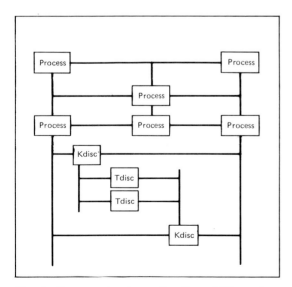

Fig. 3. System structure after the addition of processes and messages.

constructed of processes which communicate using messages. Fault tolerance is provided by duplication of components in both the hardware and the software. Access to I/O devices is provided by process-pairs consisting of a primary process and a backup process. The primary process must checkpoint state information to the backup process so that the backup may take over on a failure. Requests to these devices are routed using the logical device name or number so that the request is always routed to the current primary process. The result is a set of primitives and protocols which allow recovery and continued processing in spite of bus, processor, I/O controller, or I/O device failures. Furthermore, these primitives provide access to all system resources from every process in the system.

3.4 System Processes

The next step in structuring the system comes in assigning functions to processes. As previously shown, I/O devices are controlled by process-pairs. Another process-pair known as the "operator" is present in the system. This pair is responsible for formatting and printing error messages on the system console. Here is an example of where Guardian has not followed a strict level structure. The operator makes requests to a terminal process to print the messages, yet the terminal process wishes to send messages to the operator to report I/O channel errors. An infinite cycle is prevented by having the terminal process not send messages for errors on the operator terminal and having I/O processes never wait for message completions when sending errors to the operator. While it may be preferable to prevent cycles of any type in system design, they have been allowed in Guardian when it can be shown that they will terminate. The ability to reserve message control blocks assures that no cycle will be blocked because of resource problems.

Each processor has a "system monitor" process which handles such functions as process creation and deletion, setting time of day, and processor failure and reload cleanup operations.

A memory management process is also resident in each processor. This process is responsible for allocating a page of physical memory and then sending messages to the appropriate disc processes to do the actual disc I/O. Pages are brought in on a demand basis and pages to overlay are selected on a "least recently used" basis over the entire memory of the processor.

The choice of relatively unsophisticated algorithms for scheduling and memory management was a result of the fact that the system was not intended to be a general-purpose timeshare system. Rather, it was to be a system which supported multiple processes and terminals in an extremely flexible manner.

3.5 Application Process Interface

Above the process and communication structure there exists a library of procedures which are used to access system resources.

These procedures run in the calling process' environment and may or may not send messages to other processes in the system. For example, the file system procedures do not do the actual I/O operations. Instead, they check the caller's parameters, and if all is in order a message is sent to the appropriate I/O process-pair. Likewise, process creation is seen as a procedure call to NEWPROCESS, which does nothing but check the caller's parameters and then send a message to the system monitor process in the processor where the process is to be created. On the other hand, a procedure such as TIME which returns the current time of day does not send any messages. In either case, the access to system resources appears simply as procedure calls, effectively hiding the process structure, message system, hardware organization, and associated failure recovery mechanisms.

3.6 Initialization and Processor Reload

System initialization starts with one processor being cold loaded from some disc on the system. The load file contains a memory image of the operating system resident code and data, with all system processes in existence and at their initial states. The system monitor process then creates a command interpreter process.

Guardian may be brought up even though a processor or peripheral device is down. This is possible because operating system disc images may be kept on multiple disc drives, I/O controllers may be accessed by two different processors, and the terminal that has the initial command interpreter on it is selected by using the processor's switch register.

After a cold load, the system logically consists of one processor and any peripherals attached to it. More processors and peripherals may be added to the system via the command interpreter command:

:RELOAD 1,$DISC

This command will read the disc image for processor 1 from the disc $DISC and send it over either interprocessor bus to processor 1. Once it is loaded, all processes residing in other processors in the system will be notified that processor 1 is up.

This command is also used to reload a processor after it has been repaired. Guardian does not differentiate between an initial load of a processor and a later reload. In each case, resources are being logically added to the system and processes must be notified so that they may make use of them.

The previous example of a reload message being sent to all processes is an example of how functions are split in Guardian. A mechanism is provided for informing a process of a system status change. It may then take some unspecified action (including doing nothing). Similarly, a system power-on simply sets the PON event flag for all processes. The operating system kernel must only insure that the process structure and message system are correctly saved and restored. It is then the responsibility of individual processes to do such things as reinitialize their I/O controllers.

3.7 Operating System Error Detection

Besides the hardware-provided single error detection and correction on memory, and single error detection on the interprocessor and I/O buses, additional software error checks are provided. The first of these is the detection of a down processor. Every second, each processor in the system sends a special "I'm alive" message over each bus to all processors in the system. Every two seconds, each processor checks to see that it has received one of these messages from each processor. If a message has not been received, then it assumes that that processor is down.

Additionally, the operating system makes checks on the correctness of data structures such as linked lists when operations are done on them. Any processor detecting such an error will halt.

All I/O interrupts are bracketed by a "watch dog" timer such that the system will not hang up if an I/O operation does not complete with the expected interrupt. If an I/O bus error occurs then the backup process will take over control of the device using the second I/O bus.

As previously noted, the interprocessor bus protocol is designed to correct single bus errors. In addition to this, extensive checks are made on the control information received over the buses to verify that it is consistent with the state of the receiving processor.

Power-fail/automatic restart is provided within each processor. A power-failure is detected independently by each processor module and as a result is not a system-wide, synchronous event. The system was designed to recover from either a complete system power-fail, or a transient which will cause some of the processors to power-fail and then immediately restart.

4. Conclusions

The innovative aspects of Guardian lie not in any new concepts introduced, but rather in the synthesis of pre-existing ideas. Of particular note are the low-level abstractions, process and message. By using these, all processor boundaries can be hidden from both the application programs and most of the operating system. These initial abstractions are the key to the system's ability to tolerate failures. They also provide the configuration independence that is necessary in order for the system and applications to run over a wide range of system sizes.

Guardian provides the application programmer with extremely general approaches to process structuring, interprocess communication, and failure tolerance. Much has been said about structuring programs using multiple communicating processes, but few operating systems are able to support such structures.

Finally, the design goals of the system have been met to a large degree. Systems, with between two and ten processors, have been installed and are running on-line applications. They are recovering from failures and failures are being repaired on-line.

References

Bell and Newell [1971]; Brinch Hansen [1970]; Dijkstra [1968a]; Enslow [1977]; Katzman [1977]; Tandem [1976].

Section 7

Language-Based Computers

A system designer can place the architectural boundary (i.e., the boundary of the machine as seen by the programmer) at any number of places in the digital system's hierarchy described in Chap. 2. Placing the architectural boundary higher up (as for higher-level–language machines) provides flexibility in exploiting new technology but may constrain the languages or generality of the computer. On the other hand, placing the architectural boundary lower (as for microcoded machines) yields greater flexibility in supporting new languages and programming styles but may restrict the use of new technology. Traditionally, the architectural boundary has been placed at the ISP level. This section explores computer structures that have moved the boundary up to the high-level–language interface, where the programmer is provided with a single high-level-language environment.

Machines that directly execute higher-level languages have been proposed for over 15 years, and several have been implemented. When functions are implemented in hardware to support higher-level languages, intermediate levels of abstraction (e.g., the machine-code and perhaps even the microcode levels) can be eliminated. Elimination of levels of abstraction implies a potential performance improvement, since no time is lost interpreting the intermediate levels.

Early attempts at high-level–language machines used microprogramming to bypass the machine-code level of abstraction. Microprogrammed operators directly manipulate complex data structures (e.g., symbol tables and reverse Polish strings). One example is the implementation of an interpreter for an ALGOL-like language, EULER [Wirth and Weber, 1966a, b], for the IBM System/360 Model 30 [Weber, 1967].

Some general-purpose machines that have writable control stores have added special instructions that assist or boost the performance of specific language constructs. Yet another approach is to provide machine language instructions that map one for one to high-level–language constructs. These instructions can be added to the ISP of general-purpose machines once the most frequently used constructs among the compiler languages have been identified (e.g., three-address operations for common arithmetic statements and the case and loop instructions in the VAX-11/780, Chap. 42).

Chu and Cannont [1976] proposed a taxonomy of high-level–language systems (Table 1) based on user-perceived functionality. Type 1(a) represents the traditional compiler-based systems typified by creation of a source program with an interactive editor, syntax checking via compilation, linking of object programs for

Table 1 Types of High-Level–Language Systems

Interactive compilation systems	
Type 1(a)	Editing, compiling, executing the entire source code
Type 1(b)	Editing, syntax checking, compiling, and executing the entire source code
Type 1(c)	Editing/syntax checking each line, compiling and executing the entire source code
Interactive interpretation systems	
Type 2(a)	Editing, syntax checking, and interpreting the entire source code
Type 2(b)	Editing, syntax checking, and interpreting each line of source code
Interactive direct-execution systems	
Type 3	Editing, syntax checking, and executing each symbol of source code

execution, and debugging by iterating the editing/compiling/linking/execution cycle. Type 1(b) separates the syntax checking and compiling phases in order to speed up program development. Type 1(c) provides incremental syntax checking in dedicated language systems such as interactive BASIC.

Type 2 systems interpret source code directly by bypassing the machine-code level of abstraction (the levels usually bridged by compilers). Type 2(b) systems differ by being incremental interpreters.

Type 3 systems operate on a symbol-by-symbol basis.

This section contains three examples of machines based on, and dedicated to, a single high-level language, SYMBOL, the HP 9845A, and the IBM System/38. It is interesting to note that all three machines are implemented from multiple processors where each processor is personalized to a set of subtasks (e.g., text editing, language translation, or I/O).

SYMBOL

SYMBOL was an experimental machine that provided hardware support for Type 1(a) interactive compilation. SYMBOL was built by Fairchild during the 1964–1970 period. The SYMBOL language [Rice and Smith, 1971] featured decimal arithmetic, dynamically variable fields, and string manipulation and formatting.

SYMBOL consists of eight dedicated processors. One processor translates the input string into an internal form to be executed by another processor. The fundamental unit of memory is a variable-length string maintained via linked lists in the memory controller. Scheduling and I/O algorithms are also hardwired.

The SYMBOL paper (Chap. 30) concludes with a performance and cost analysis, including an informative cost breakdown of operating expenses for a large, central computer.

The HP 9845A

Desk-top calculators have evolved over the years from "function per key" systems with limited I/O to desk-top computers with a general-purpose programming language and extensive I/O (see Chaps. 48 and 49 and Part 4, Sec. 3). The HP 9845A is a sophisticated single-language, single-user computing system (see Figs. 1 and 2) that supports Type 2(b) interactive interpretation.

Since the user environment is well defined, it is possible to customize techniques found in more open-ended computer structures such as timesharing systems.

The HP 9845A has three levels of abstraction. The highest level is a BASIC machine which deals with abstractions such as processes, run queues, symbol tables, and internal forms for language statements. These internal forms allow for more efficient execution than source language interpreters, since the statement

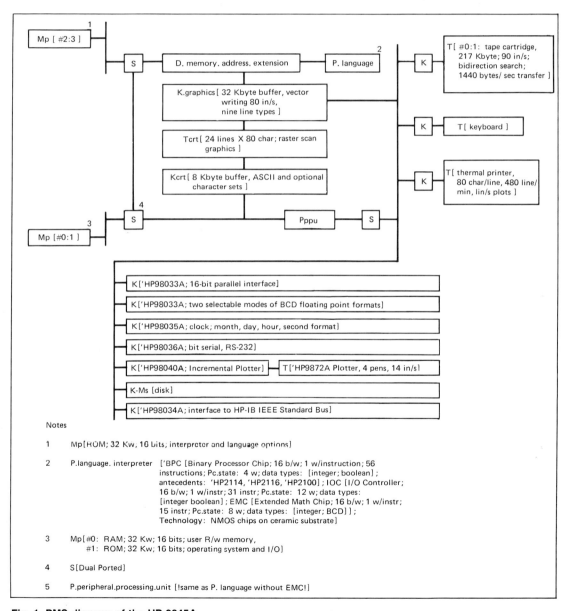

Notes

1   Mp[ROM; 32 Kw, 16 bits; interpreter and language options]

2   P.language. interpreter   ['BPC [Binary Processor Chip; 16 b/w; 1 w/instruction; 56
                                instructions; Pc.state: 4 w; data types: [integer; boolean] ;
                                antecedents: 'HP2114, 'HP2116, 'HP2100] ; IOC [I/O Controller;
                                16 b/w; 1 w/instr; 31 instr; Pc.state: 12 w; data types:
                                [integer boolean] ; EMC [Extended Math Chip; 16 b/w; 1 w/instr;
                                15 instr; Pc.state: 8 w; data types: [integer; BCD]] ;
                                Technology: NMOS chips on ceramic substrate]

3   Mp[#0: RAM; 32 Kw, 16 bits; user R/w memory,
     #1: ROM; 32 Kw, 16 bits; operating system and I/O]

4   S[Dual Ported]

5   P.peripheral.processing.unit [!same as P. language without EMC!]

Fig. 1. PMS diagram of the HP 9845A.

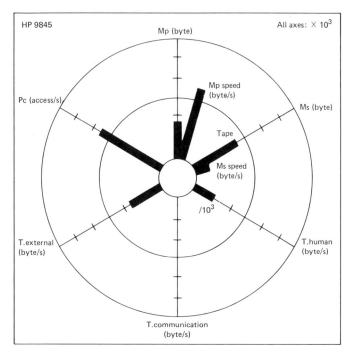

Fig. 2. Kiviat graph of the HP 9845.

information has been transformed into a data structure that is easier to manipulate than source language. The internal form also contains enough information to recreate the original source language statement.

The BASIC machine is implemented by ROM programs for a dual-processor system. Each processor executes a minicomputer instruction set (similar to that of the HP 2116 minicomputer) that is implemented entirely with LSI technology. Special-purpose processors for I/O and BCD arithmetic act as extensions to the main processors.

The final level of abstraction is the microcoded machine that implements an HP 2116–like instruction set. Chapter 31 describes the top two levels of abstraction in detail.

This paper is included for several reasons. It characterizes the desk-top computing (or personal computing) environment as it differs from other environments, such as that of minicomputers. It contains the details of another minicomputer instruction set as well as instruction sets for special-purpose processors (e.g., processors for I/O and BCD arithmetic). Finally, since the HP 9845A is a dedicated, single-user machine, performance is

secondary to ease of use. Without strict performance requirements, the BASIC language machine can be implemented in software ROM on top of a minicomputer ISP.

IBM System/38

The IBM System/38 is a business-oriented data processing system introduced in late 1978. The System/38 standardizes the hardware interface between the traditional ISP level and a higher-level language. Instructions have been implemented whose functionality has traditionally been reserved for operating-system software. Examples of this functionality include queue-driven task management, record-level data management, process management, and object-oriented memory management. Although the first release of the System/38 software only provided RPG and Interactive Data Base Utilities, the Control Program Facility provides a uniform interface to the system hardware upon which other language environments can be built.

While the System/38 is essentially a Type 1(a) system, it deserves special note for several reasons:

- It provides hardware support for high-level–language concepts and may be a harbinger of future ISPs designed to support multiple high-level languages.

- It is the only example in this book of an object-oriented memory management system fully supported in hardware (see Part 2, Sec. 2). Since the access path to objects is machine-controlled, effective authority enforcement and automatic serialization of concurrent operations on the same object are achieved.

- The concept of architecture has been pushed up into the software levels, paving the way for future migration of even more functionality into microcode and hardware.

- A large, 48-bit virtual address is efficiently supported by a hash table lookup into a physical page directory.

- Programs are translated into microcode before execution.

- Program-variable attributes allow automatic data-type conversions.

References

Chu and Cannont [1976]; Rice and Smith [1971]; Weber [1967]; Wirth and Weber [1966a,b].

Chapter 30

The SYMBOL Computer
SYMBOL:
A Large Experimental System Exploring Major Hardware Replacement of Software[1]

William R. Smith / Rex Rice /
Gilman D. Chesley / Theodore A. Laliotis /
Stephen F. Lundstrom / Myron A. Calhoun /
Lawrence D. Gerould / Thomas G. Cook

Introduction

The SYMBOL system is the result of a major developmental effort to increase the functional capability of hardware. Part of the charter of the broad based project was to reexamine the traditional division between hardware and software, to reexamine the respective roles of program instruction and data storage, and to reduce the overall complexity and cost of computing [Rice and Smith, 1971]. In order to adequately evaluate the concepts that had been developed it was concluded that an experimental, usable, real system must be built. The SYMBOL system, now operational, is the embodiment of this effort.

The system was developed in an environment with hardware and software design considered in common. Virtually no one associated with the project could refer to himself as a hardware or software specialist exclusively. As an example, the logic design of the field process units was done by an individual with a basic programming background [Mazor, 1968]. The wire routing automation was developed by an engineer who was formerly a pure logic design specialist.

Even before the system became operational much had been learned about the practical aspects of building highly capable hardware. No claim is made that SYMBOL represents an optimum general purpose, time-sharing, multiprocessing system. In contrast, numerous simplifying assumptions were made in the system where they did not serve the goals of the project. Certain modularity restrictions are examples of this. It is claimed that SYMBOL represents a significant advance in systems technology and provides the foundation for a significant reduction in the cost of computing. As the system moves into an intensive evaluation phase it should prove to be a real asset for advanced systems research.

This paper represents an overview of the SYMBOL organization. An attempt is made to give simplified examples of various key features in contrast to a broad brush treatment of many topics.

Gross Organization

The system has eight specialized processors that operate as autonomous units. Each functional unit is linked to the system by the Main Bus. See Fig. 1. Consider some of the features of the system and their relationship to the gross processor organization as outlined in the following sections.

Dynamic Memory Management

Direct hardware memory management is perhaps the most unique feature of the SYMBOL system. The memory management centers around a special purpose processor called the Memory Controller (MC). The MC effectively isolates the main memory from the main bus and the other processors and in turn provides a more sophisticated storage function for the various processors. In contrast to simple read/write memory operations the MC has a set of fifteen operations that are available to the

[1]*AFIPS SJCC*, 1971, pp. 601–616.

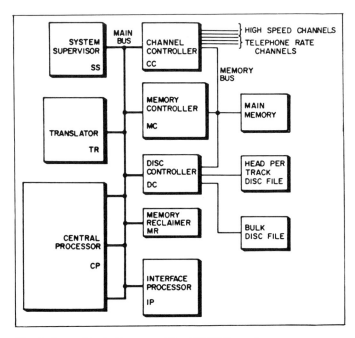

Fig. 1. Gross block diagram of the SYMBOL system.

other processors of the system. The MC is a special purpose processor that allocates memory space on demand, performs address arithmetic, and manages the associative memory needed for paging. The Memory Reclaimer (MR) supports the MC by reprocessing used space to make it available for subsequent reuse. It is a separate unit to allow the task to be performed using a low priority access to the memory.

Direct Compilation

The Translator (TR) accepts the high level SYMBOL language [Chesley and Smith, 1971] as input and produces a reverse Polish object string and name table suitable for processing by the Central Processor (CP). The TR performs the direct hardware compilation using only a small table of about 100 words stored in main memory.

Dynamic Variable Field Length

Within the Central Processor all field processing is done with dynamically variable field lengths. All alphanumeric string processing is done by the Format Processor (FP) while all numeric processing is done by the Arithmetic Processor (AP). The resources of the MC are used extensively by the CP in handling the storage of data.

Dynamically Variable Data Structures

Complete variability of data structures is allowed. They can change size, shape, and depth during processing. Within the CP the Reference Processor (RP) manages the storage and referencing of all data arrays and structure. The MC functions are used extensively by the RP.

Time-Sharing Supervision

The System Supervisor (SS) is the task scheduler for the system. All transitions from one processing mode to another are handled by the SS. Queues are maintained for all of the time-shared processors. The SS executes two important hardware algorithms, job task scheduling and paging management. A real-time clock is used in the process of rationing out critical resources such as central processor time. The SS also performs key information transfers needed to tie hardware algorithms into software system management procedures.

Direct Text Editing

The Interface Processor (IP) and Channel Controller (CC) perform the input/output tasks of the system. The IP has ability to handle general text editing in support of interactive communication via a special terminal. Input/output and text editing do not use the CP resources.

Virtual Memory Management

When the MC detects that a page is not in main memory it notifies the requesting processor and the system supervisor. The SS then utilizes a paging algorithm to supply the appropriate disk transfer commands to the Disk Controller (DC). Each user of memory must, upon receiving a page-out response, be able to shut down and save its current state and status and restart after paging is complete.

System Configuration

The system has a small complement of peripheral and storage equipment associated with the main frame. This complement of equipment has proven sufficient for the experimental purposes of the system. The main memory is an 8K word × 64 bit/word core memory with a cycle time of 2.5 microsec. It is organized into 32 pages with 256 words/page. The main paging memory is a small Burroughs head-per-track disk divided into 800 pages. The bulk paging memory is a Data Products Disk-file organized into 50,000 pages.

The Channel Controller is designed to handle up to 31 channels. This low limit was deemed sufficient for evaluation of the experimental system. As of this writing one high speed (100,000 bits/sec. effective data rate) channel and three phone line (up to 2400 baud) channels have been implemented. More can be added during the evaluation phase.

The main frame contains about 18,000 dual in-line CTμL components. Its physical properties are described in other papers [Cowart, Rice, and Lundstrom, 1971; Smith, 1968]. In order to get a relative measure of the size of the various autonomous processors a chart is given in Fig. 2.

System Communication

The main bus of the system is a time-shared, global communication path. It uses the special properties of the CTμL family in its implementation [Cowart, Rice, and Lundstrom, 1971; Smith, 1968]. The bus contains 111 parallel lines. They are distributed as follows:

Data Bus	64
Address Bus	24
Operation Code Bus	6
Terminal Identification Bus	5
Priority Bus	10
System Clock	1
System Clear	1

Four types of bus usage are available. They are:

Processor to MC transfers

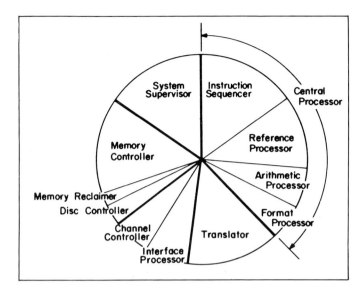

Fig. 2. Breakdown of the SYMBOL hardware showing the relative sizes of the various processors.

MC to Processor transfers

Processor to Processor transfers

Control exchange cycles

The basic information transfers are priority sequenced. The priority bus indicates the desired bus usage for the following cycle; if a unit desires to use the bus it raises its priority line and then checks the priority bus to see if there are any higher priority requests. If not it uses the bus on the following cycle.

Control exchange cycles are used to communicate control information between the SS and the various processors over the data and address buses. See Fig. 3. During a control cycle the data and address bus lines have preassigned uses. Certain lines are used to start the CP. Others indicate the completion mode for the TR. During a given cycle any combination of the paths can be used. The SS has autonomous interface control functions that are used to communicate with the processors during control cycles so that more than one control signal can be transmitted during a given cycle.

Memory Organization

Virtual Memory

The SYMBOL memory is organized as a simple two-level, fixed page size virtual memory [Kilburn et al., 1962]. The page has 256 words with each word having 64 bits. Virtual memory is accessed by a 24 bit address with 16 bits used to select the page and 8 bits to select a particular word within a page. See Fig. 4.

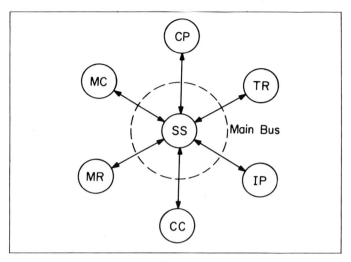

Fig. 3. Use of the main bus for control exchange cycles.

The main memory for the experimental system is logically divided into 32 pages. The relative portion of the address is used directly while the page number accesses an associative memory which in turn supplies the current page address in main memory.

The associative memory has one cell for each page in the main memory. By providing an associative memory tied to the main memory the individual processors need not be concerned with the location association process. This provides a significant reduction in the logical complexity of the processors even though it may lead to slightly more overall electronics.

The paging disk memory has fixed assignment of page locations.

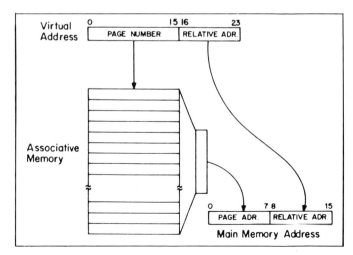

Fig. 4. The simple two level addressing structure for the virtual memory.

See Fig. 5. A page is brought into an available location in main memory upon demand. When it is purged back to disk it is transferred back to the same location on disk. (The return transfer is omitted if the page was not changed in main memory.)

The main memory organization is shown in Fig. 6. The first page is used for system tables. This includes a reserved word table for the translator, a software call table, and the control words for memory allocation and queuing. The next set of pages are used for storing the control words of the various terminals or users on the system. Each active terminal has 24 words of control information in low core. Much of the control information could have been placed in virtual memory as would certainly be required for a system with a larger channel capacity. As a simplifying restriction for SYMBOL all channel tables were placed in main memory.

The input/output buffers for the various active channels are also held in core. The buffers require 16 words per active channel. Variable buffer sizes although possible were not implemented.

The remainder of main memory is available for virtual memory buffering. Paging is managed by the hardware with the page selection for purging under the control of the system supervisor. The algorithm is a very flexible parameterized process that allows most of the conventional paging algorithms to be executed. The parameters are maintained for each terminal so that the paging dynamics can be tailored on a terminal by terminal basis.

The virtual memory organization is quite simple for SYMBOL in contrast to the more common segmentation schemes [Glaser, Couleur, and Oliver, 1965; Corbato and Vyssotsky, 1965]. The

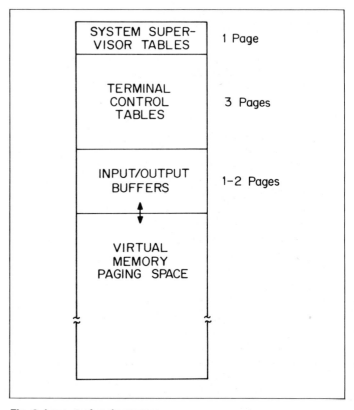

Fig. 6. Layout of main memory.

primary difference that allows the simplified approach to be taken in SYMBOL is that contiguous addressing above the page level is not needed. All users and channels share the same virtual memory space. The 24 bit address space is thoroughly used. With space allocated only upon demand and with no restriction on a scrambled assignment of pages to users it is anticipated that 24 bits will be sufficient for many more than the 31 possible terminals. If file space is needed beyond the 24 bits of address space it can be addressed via special block input/output transfers.

Page Lists

Pages are associated together with the use of linked page lists. Pages available for assignment are maintained on an available page list. As each user needs space a user page list is started by transferring a page from the available page list to the particular user. A control word is established at this time as a focal point for all future page list management for the user. As more space is needed pages are added to form a variable length storage area for general purpose usage. See Fig. 7.

A given user may have more than one page list. Typical page list usage for a terminal would be one page list for program source

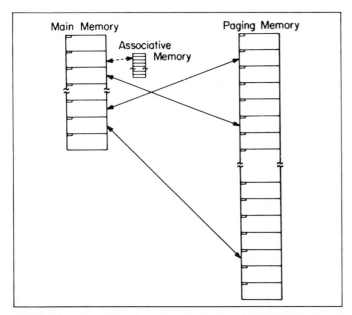

Fig. 5. Virtual memory organization showing the fixed location of pages in the paging memory.

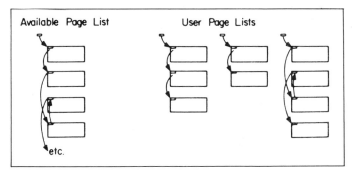

Fig. 7. Simplified page list structure within the virtual memory.

text, another for the compiled object program, and a third for data variable storage. Other page lists are used for long or short term file storage.

Page lists grow monotonically as space is needed. When an entire list is no longer needed it is given back to the system by returning it to the available page list.

Page Organization

In order to handle non-contiguous address space a certain amount of the storage space must be devoted to linking or association data overhead. In SYMBOL about 11 percent of the storage space is for overhead bookkeeping.

Pages have three distinct information regions as shown in Fig. 8. The first region called the page header is used to maintain the page lists and manage the space within the page. The second region is a set of 28 words. The third region is a set of 28 groups

with each group containing eight words. Each group has a corresponding group link word associated by a simple address mapping. Consider in Fig. 8 word 5 and the corresponding group 5. Data is stored in words 28 through 2F. This eight word group is the fundamental quantum of space allocation. It is the smallest amount of memory space that is assignable to a given purpose.

When data is needed for some purpose groups are assigned. For example, if six words were needed to store a data vector one group would be assigned. If space for a vector of 14 one word items were needed two groups would be assigned. Variable length information areas are developed by chaining together these basic units of storage.

Information Strings

Variable length lists of storage locations are used for general information storage in SYMBOL. They are logically contiguous memory cells but not necessarily physically contiguous cells.

Consider a typical variable length information string in Fig. 9. Data space for 24 words of information is tied together by way of the associated group link words. If access to the start of the string is known it is possible to follow the entire string by accessing the corresponding group link word each time the end of a group is encountered. It is also possible to traverse the string backwards by using the back links also stored in the group link word.

Each processor uses the variable length storage service of the memory controller (MC) without cognizance of the address sequence that is involved. For example, when a processor needs space to store a vector of data fields an Assign Group (AG) command is sent to the MC along with a tag specifying a page list with which the string is to be associated. The MC then selects an available group from the page list and returns the address of the first word of the group to the requesting processor. When the

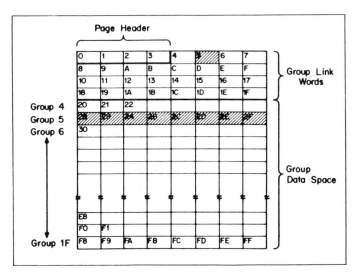

Fig. 8. Page organization showing group and link word layout where addresses are given in HEX notation.

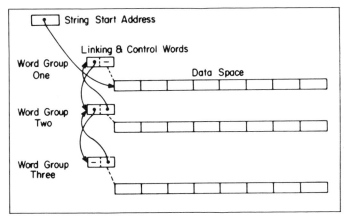

Fig. 9. Structure of a variable length string.

processor is ready to store a word it transmits the data and the address previously assigned to the MC along with the command Store and Assign (SA). The MC stores the word and generates the address of the next available word. When the end of the group or string is encountered the MC assigns another group and links it into the string.

In the string storing process the requesting processor receives addresses from the MC and resubmits them to the MC at a later time for future extension of the string. All address arithmetic is done by the MC. Consider the example in Table 1. The first five commands result in the words A, B, C, and D being stored in a string beginning with word A.

To reaccess the string the original start address A is submitted to the MC with the Fetch and Follow (FF) command. The data in cell A is returned along with the next address in the logical sequence. When the string is no longer needed a Delete String (DS) command along with the string starting address is submitted to the MC. The entire string is then placed on a space reclamation list. The Memory Reclaimer processor scans the space reclamation lists of the various page lists during idle memory time and makes the groups of the deleted strings reassignable.

The basic memory usage process deals with variations of the AG, SA, FF, and DS operations. Eleven other memory commands are available to give a full memory service complement.

Space utilization efficiency was an important aspect of the SYMBOL memory design. Studies have been made into the optimum size of the space allocation group [Smith, 1963]. The trade-offs center on balancing the linking overhead cost and the unused group fragments cost. The overhead cost is compensated by the allocation on demand approach. In most machines, fixed size data arrays are allocated to their maximum needed size. When the average array usage is considered a substantial amount of demand allocation overhead can be afforded before approaching the normal excess fixed allocation space usage.

Information Forms

Data Fields

Two basic data types are defined in the system, namely string and numeric fields. The string field is characterized by a special String Start (SS) character followed by a variable length set of ASCII alphanumeric characters terminated by a special String End (SE) character. This illustrates perhaps the most significant aspect of all SYMBOL data representations. The type and length of the datum is carried with the datum. The instruction code is independent of the dynamic attributes of the data.

The second data type is a variable length, packed decimal, floating point number. The numeric form also carries a designator of the class of precision. Numbers may be *exact* with an infinite number of trailing zeros implied or they may be *empirical* implying that all following digits are unknown and cannot be assumed present for calculation purposes. Like the string field all attributes of the datum are carried by the datum itself.

As a simplifying hardware design decision other forms of data fields were not implemented. It is straightforward to extend the SYMBOL concepts to packed variable-length binary strings, fixed length binary numerics, variable length binary numerics, etc. In any of these cases the datum must carry a type designator and an explicit or implicit designation of field length.

Source Programs

Source programs are special forms of string fields. They are variable length ASCII character strings with delimiters defining length and type. They can be treated as data fields during preparation and then later used as program source for compilation. Source procedures may be assembled into libraries of various forms as long as they retain the string field attributes for compilation purposes.

Data Structures

Data structures are defined as a variable length group of items where an item may be a string field, a numeric field, or another group of items. With this recursive definition a structure could be a vector, a matrix, or an irregular array. There is no limit to the depth or size of an array providing a field or a group does not exceed the size of main memory during execution.

Consider the example of a simple vector shown in Fig. 10. The special graphics <,|, and> have been introduced for representing field boundaries and groupings of fields. They are used to define the extent of variable length fields and referred to as left group marks, field marks, and right group marks, respectively. In memory the string fields are delimited by String Start (SS) and String End (SE) characters. Another special character called the End Vector (EV) code terminates a group of fields. The storage

Table 1 Simplified Example of a Memory Usage Sequence

Mnemonic	Operation	Address to MC	Return address	Data to MC	Return data
AG	Assign Group	....	a	....	-
SA	Store & Assign	a	b	A	-
SA	Store & Assign	b	c	B	-
SA	Store & Assign	c	d	C	-
SA	Store & Assign	d	e	D	-
FF	Fetch & Follow	a	b	-	A
FF	Fetch & Follow	b	c	-	B
FF	Fetch & Follow	c	d	-	C
FF	Fetch & Follow	d	....	-	D
DS	Delete String	a	....	-	-

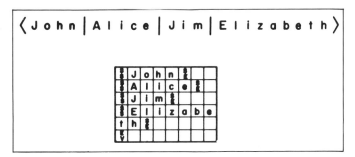

Fig. 10. A vector of string fields and the corresponding representation of the data in memory.

representation in Fig. 10 shows a series of string fields followed by a special End Vector (EV) code which again is a length indicator with the data. The string fields are aligned to start on machine word boundaries. In the case of Elizabeth two machine words are needed to store the field.

In Fig. 11 the matrix representation is similar to the vector example except that two levels of vectors exist. The definition of a structure could be restated as a variable length group of items where an item may be a string field, a numeric field, or an address link to another group.

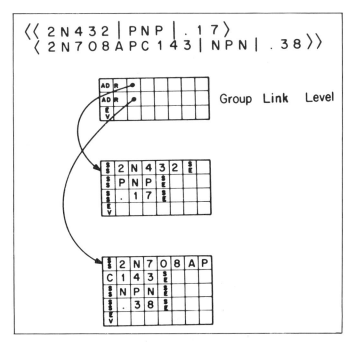

Fig. 11. A simple two dimensional array and the corresponding three variable length memory strings that are used.

Object String and Name Tables

When a program is compiled the translator creates a reverse Polish string with postfix operator notation and a structured name table. The Polish string, called the object string, and the name table are the basic information forms used during program execution by the central processor. The use of a separate name table during execution is perhaps one of the most distinctive departures from traditional processing forms. Where in most systems the program string to be executed contains address references to the data space to be utilized, with the SYMBOL system the object string contains references to entries in the name table which act as a centralized point where all information about a given identifier is kept. It is this feature that gives the system its extreme execution time dynamicism. Whenever the nature of an identifier is modified in any way—location, size, type; etc.—only the name table entry need be changed since all references in the object string to an identifier must go through this entry.

The source form of a simple assignment statement and the corresponding object string and name table are shown in Fig. 12.

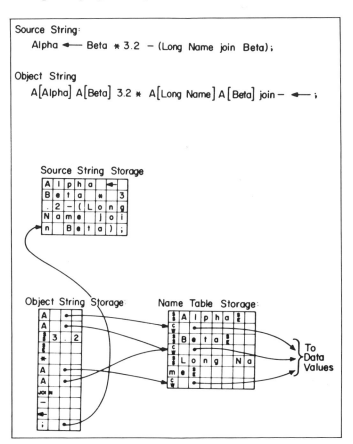

Fig. 12. Information structure for a simple assignment statement.

The identifiers are isolated and added to the name table when not already there. Note that the identifiers can be variable length and have more than one word. Associated with each identifier is a control word. All references in the object string involving the identifier will point to the corresponding control word. The object string is composed of name table addresses, literal data (the value 3.2), operators in postfix representation, and correspondence links back to the source string. The correspondence links are for simple error diagnosis and are therefore ignored during normal execution. The object string and name table are totally independent of the future size and data type of the variable.

Now consider the name table after execution has begun and assume that the data variables have current values. In Fig. 13 the variables Beta and Gamma are simple fields. Gamma is a multiword string and therefore it is stored in a memory string with a link address placed in the corresponding control word. Beta is a short field such that it can be stored in one word directly in the name table. Alpha is an irregular structure. The name table for Alpha contains a link to the first group which in turn contains two string fields, two link addresses, and an end vector mark. The link addresses point to two groups, one containing two fields and one containing three fields. As execution progresses the attributes and storage representation of the variables may change. In any event, the name table and the data itself will contain all the attributes of the variables.

Basic Information Flow

In order to observe how the various processors of SYMBOL are used to serve the end users problem temporarily ignore the multiprocessing aspects of the system. A user at a terminal operates in various modes; program loading, program compilation, and program execution are the fundamental usage modes. Consider the state diagram in Fig. 14. A user would start in the OFF-LINE mode and by some transitional control means he would initialize his tasks into the ON-LINE IDLE mode. From here he can go into the LOAD mode to develop a program. When he is ready to execute his program and assuming he is a perfect programmer, he would have his program compiled and executed. At the end of execution he can restart and rerun his program or he can return to the LOAD mode and modify his program.

The following sections deal with examples of the information flow for the basic operational modes of a terminal. A more detailed system block diagram in Fig. 15 will be used to support the description. Visualize the time sequence of the terminal operational states of Fig. 14 in conjunction with the static hardware diagram of Fig. 15.

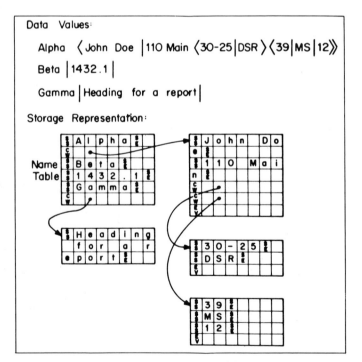

Fig. 13. Examples of a structure and two fields and how they are stored into memory along with the name table.

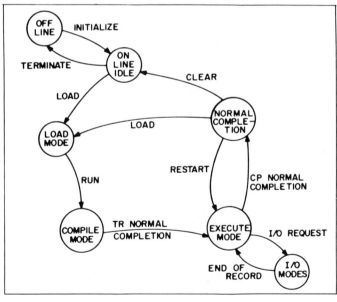

Fig. 14. Idealized task flow for one terminal.

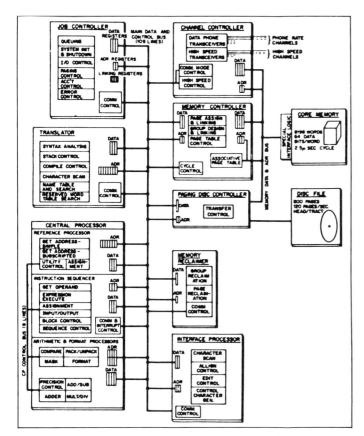

Fig. 15. A more detailed block diagram of the SYMBOL system showing register configuration and major functions within each processor.

Load Mode

The LOAD mode is an input/output text editing mode. Its primary purpose is for program source loading. In the normal case a separate page list is used to store the text string. This area is called the Transient Working Area (TWA).

Three processors work together to perform the text editing tasks. The Channel Controller (CC) transfers data characters to and from I/O devices from and to the I/O Buffers in main memory respectively. When the CC detects control characters in the I/O stream, it communicates the control information directly to the SS by way of a control exchange cycle. The CC is a character oriented processor which services up to 32 processors in a commutating manner. The CC also has a high speed (block) operating mode which is priority driven to allow servicing of disk and high speed tape devices. The block mode is not used in the LOAD or normal I/O mode.

The Interface Processor (IP) operating on a burst basis empties

or fills I/O buffers and transfers appropriate characters to and from the virtual memory. The IP works with a current text pointer while performing its functions. The IP functions include basic text insertion, searching, displaying designated text portions, deletion of designated text portions, and moving the current pointer. In Fig. 16 the basic information flow during the LOAD mode is summarized.

Part of the justification for implementing editing functions in hardware came from the desire to eliminate the CP from many of the system overhead tasks. In addition, response times would be unacceptable if the CC were to communicate directly with virtual memory. The IP was developed to make the basic transfers between small buffers and paging memory. Once a special processor was developed it was found that many editing tasks and double buffering could be handled using essentially the same data transfer hardware.

This IP/CC/SS process is available for both LOAD mode data preparation and program execution I/O. The full text editing facilities are available for any program input statement.

Compile Mode

Program compilation and address linkage editing functions are performed by the Translator (TR). The TR accepts the language source string from the TWA or some other source text area in virtual memory. The high level language is converted into a reverse Polish string and a structured name (identifier) table. The Polish string, called the Object String, and the Name Table may be stored in Virtual Memory on separate page lists or on a common page list. The gross flow of information in the Translation mode is shown in Fig. 17.

The TR performs a one pass compilation generating the object

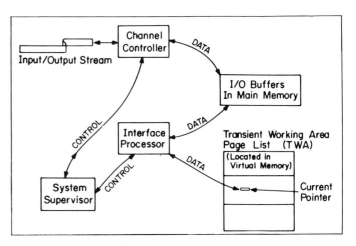

Fig. 16. Information flow in the LOAD mode.

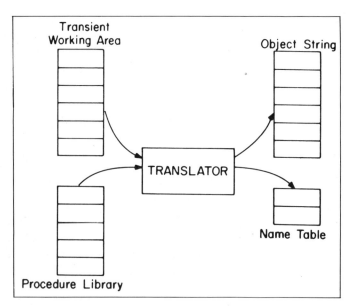

Fig. 17. Information flow in the COMPILE mode.

string as it scans the source string. It also builds the name table during this scan on a program block-by-block basis. At the end of the source pass the TR processes the name table and resolves all global references by creating appropriate indirect links. External procedure references are resolved during the name table pass and they are compiled and included with the object string as needed.

The TR includes external procedures by accessing procedure source libraries and compiling needed procedures into the object string. The procedure libraries are organized into two sets, namely privileged and non-privileged procedures. Privileged programs differ from normal programs in that they can contain privileged statements for direct memory manipulation using the MC operations. Storage protection is obtained by controlling the privileged status of user programs and the programs that they can reference. Non-privileged programs have a high degree of storage protection both from other programs and from themselves due to the hardware storage management and central processor algorithms. Programs using privileged statements lose some of the protection. By controlling the access to privileged programs and the manner in which they are used the overall storage protection in the system is quite satisfactory for multiterminal operation.

Execution Mode

The Central Processor (CP) is the execution unit for the translated language receiving the translated source string along with the nested name table blocks as input. Because the CP operates on a high order language—actually a Polish string, postfixed operator

object string—the CP uses a push-down stack for its operands. That is, the data reference is generated with all indirections traced out until a memory reference point is reached, and then this reference is pushed into the stack. This process continues until the postfixed operators are encountered in the object string. Each operator causes the top one or two (monadic or dyadic operator) stack entries to be pulled up, processing to take place, and the result to replace the operand(s) on the stack.

Substructure referencing, also known as subscripting, is a much more formidable task in SYMBOL than with conventional systems. This is due to the extremely dynamic flexibility of these structures. With conventional, systems, accessing an element of a vector is a simple matter of assigning a base along with an index register for the subscript variable and at execution time merely doing an address calculation to find the desired element. With SYMBOL there can be no possibility of a base address or an address calculation both because of the dynamic nature of space allocation as well as the fact that logically contiguous data need not be physically contiguous in memory. The Reference Processor (RP) has the charter for finding substructure points, basically through a scanning technique along with several speed-ups.

Another novel aspect of the CP is that all processing operations are done on variable length data. The string operations can be of any length, the only limitation being that they must fit into the main memory. The numeric operations are limited to a 99 digit fractional length (numbers are represented internally as normalized floating-point decimal numbers). Furthermore, the length of numeric processing is controlled by the limit register. Also, a precision mode exists whereby numbers tagged with EM (empirical) will limit processing precision to the number of fractional digits they contain, unless the limit register is set to a smaller value.

The information flow for the CP is summarized in Fig. 18. The CP has four distinct sections, namely the Instruction Sequencer (IS), the Reference Processor (RP), the Arithmetic Processor (AP), and the Format and String Processor (FP). As shown in Fig. 15 the CP has a common control bus that is used to control the various processors during program execution. The following four sections describe the functions of each of the processors in the CP.

Instruction Sequencer

The IS portion of the CP is the master controller and switching unit of the CP. It has the task of scanning the object string, and accumulating items in the stack for the various units it supplies. For example, operands are accumulated for the process units and any type conversion required is sensed and requested of the FP by the IS, as appropriate. Similarly, a structure reference and all of its subscripts are computed and placed into the stack which is then turned over to the RP for access.

The IS also prepares data for assignment by the RP or output by

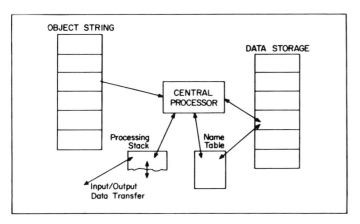

Fig. 18. Information flow during program execution.

the I/O unit. It does this in the former case by stacking both the assignment reference and the data and in the latter case by stacking the data and turning control back to the system.

Another major task performed by the IS is that of dynamically creating nested languaged blocks. Reference should be made to the companion paper on the SYMBOL language [Chesley and Smith, 1971] if the concept is new to the reader. In quick review, blocks are language constructs consisting of program segments contained between the reserved words BLOCK and END (PROCEDURE and ON also establish blocks). Within a block, all uses of an identifier are local to that block, unless contained within a GLOBAL statement, and thus a different name table is constructed for each block. The overall structure of name tables has a static aspect determined by the way the program is written and a dynamic aspect determined by the sequence in which these blocks are executed. It is this latter characteristic that we are concerned with in this discussion. Whenever a new block is encountered by the IS, processing on the old block is suspended by pushing down all information about that block that must be retained (sometimes called the activation record) into the stack, and starting a new stack and activation record for the new block on top of the old stack. Of course, the new record must contain a link to the old record so that when the new block is completed, the old block with its status information can be reestablished.

A further complexity occurs with procedure blocks because of the need to correlate actual and formal parameters (again, see the language paper) [Chesley and Smith, 1971]. The IS transfers the links to the actual parameters from the object string to the stack, accesses the name table for the new block where the formal parameters occur as the first entries of this name table. The actual parameter links are then placed one-by-one into the formal parameter entries of the name table. Parameter linking completed, the remainder of the normal block action for the procedure is

accomplished. Whenever the IS encounters a name table entry tagged as a formal parameter, it indirectly accesses the actual parameter in its place, which may not be a statement, but may be a variable, constant, label, literal, procedure, or expression. This indirection mechanism is also handled in the IS stack. A push down of a limited set of status information takes place, mostly consisting of the address where execution of the object string was temporarily discontinued. Then the new object string of the actual parameter is executed, using the stack until the return operator is encountered indicating the end of the actual parameter string. This causes the previous status to be recovered from the stack and execution of the object string recommences with the results of the execution of the actual parameter remaining in the top of the stack.

Reference Processor

The basic task of the RP is to deal with structures. As a simple added duty, it accesses the address of an item from the name table for the IS. That is, the IS receives an address from the object string and turns it over to the RP with a request to "get simple address." The RP performs several actions depending on the nature of the identifier. If it is an existing data item it provides the address of the data along with a code indicating its nature. If it is an uninitialized data item, it first assigns space before supplying the data address. In a similar manner it provides links to labels and procedures and if any identifiers are global, it first traces out the global indirection before returning the link. Any anomalies in the name table cause an error return.

The structure handling task may be broken down into two subtasks: creation of structures and substructure and the referencing of substructure points. Recall that structures are dynamically variable in all aspects. Thus, there are two further subsets under the creation of structures: creation of basic structures and the reconfiguration of substructures. As a subset task to the referencing of substructures the language contains a character subscripting capability where the final subscript may be a "bound-pair" of subscripts which refer to the starting point and extent of a character subfield with the previous subscripts pointing to the field.

The RP receives a linear representation of the structure to be created in the IS stack. The RP must store this structure in memory, replacing its linear form with a hierarchical form with links to lower or deeper elements occurring at the next higher level. Refer to Figs. 10, 11, and 13. It achieves this by assigning a new memory group each time it encounters a new left group mark, creating a line to the new group in the higher group and filling that group with elements maintaining a link back to the higher group in its own group link stack. Whenever a right group mark is encountered in the IS stack, the current memory group is closed with an "end vector" tag and the next higher memory group continuation point is accessed from the group link stack. This process continues until the structure in the IS stack is exhausted and results in a linked, hierarchical structure.

A similar process takes place when a new structure is assigned to an existing substructure point. The old structure is deleted (for later recovery by the memory reclaimer) and the new linear structure in the stack is structured and linked into the proper substructure point. All combinations of replacement are allowed: structure by a structure, field by a field, structure by a field, field by a structure. The second situation of a field replacing a field can be a problem in the case where the new field is larger than the old field because vector expansion must take place (in the opposite situation, nulls are inserted). The simple solution of providing a non-hierarchical link out of a new space is inadequate for the situation where successive words of a large vector are sequentially expanded. The solution is to link in a new memory group only after checking if there is no space remaining in the present group or the next one, and then rewriting the remainder of the present group adjacent to the new field. In this way, expansion of many fields of a vector makes use of the newly created space.

The general algorithm for structure referencing is for the RP to scan back through the IS stack to find the structured link, and then to proceed upward a subscript at a time, accessing each vector using special speed-up techniques as appropriate, until the final subscript is reached. At this point the RP replaces the subscripted reference in the IS stack with a link to a substructure or a link to a field if the data level was reached. At any point in structure referencing, the structure previously stored may not extend to the referenced point (oversubscripting). The language rule in this situation is that new space should be created as required to expand the structure to the subscripted reference point (fields filled with nulls) and the RP is responsible for accomplishing this task.

If after structure referencing to the field level, a bound pair of subscripts appear in the IS stack, the RP scans and counts across the field, selecting the requisite characters and placing the result in the IS stack. An error is called if the bound pair is encountered before the field level is reached.

Arithmetic Processor

The AP is a serial process unit operating on variable length data consisting of floating-point, normalized, decimal numbers. These operations are done from high-to-low order to simplify data handling by allowing the register operations for both string and numeric processing to be similar. Also, comparisons are faster because a mismatch is immediately known. Two other important features are included in the processing hardware: a limit register, loaded by the IS under command of the language, which causes processing to terminate at the precision specified, and a precision controlling mode whereby each operand can be specified to be accurate to its existing precision and thus control the precision of the result.

The operations add, subtract, multiply, and divide are performed. For add and subtract, one or the other operand is streamed through the unit (high-to-low) until the exponents are aligned, at which time both operands start to stream through. Since the number representation is magnitude plus sign, a positive result is desired so that the signs of the operands and the sign of the operator are combined to control which, if either, of the operands is streamed through in complemented form. High-to-low order arithmetic requires a nine's counter [Mullery, Schauer, and Rice, 1963] to delay output over an intervening string of nines until a carry/no carry decision is reached. Eventually, either an empirical end of an operand is reached, or the limit counter value is reached, or both exact numbers are ended. At this point, arithmetic is finished and control is turned back to the IS.

Multiply is accomplished by successive additions or subtractions followed by a shift until all of the multiplier digits are exhausted. Only after the full trapezoid of the partial product is produced is a rounding pass applied to achieve the precision requirements. The speed-up of adding one to the previous multiplier digit and subtracting from the partial product if the multiplier digit is larger than four is used. Of course, with multiply (and divide) exponents are added (subtracted) so that no shift of the fractional portions of the operands are required. Division is accomplished by a gradual non-restoring reduction of the partial dividend until the precision of the result is equal to the least precise of the two operands or the limit counter.

Since processing in this system is accomplished serially in a decimal mode with few speed-ups, the speed of processing is sharply dependent on the size of the operands. When the limit counter is set to a small value, say 5, processing can be quite fast but 99 digit divides can be extremely slow. It is therefore important that the user selects only as much precision as he really needs.

The numeric comparisons are performed by the AP as a subtract operation but terminate immediately upon a mismatch and return a zero result rather than a one. The IS has the task of combining the result returned by the AP with the desired comparison operation to generate the overall result in the IS stack.

Format Processor

The FP unit performs the string JOIN operation, the binary string operations AND, OR, NOT, the string comparison operations BEFORE, SAME, AFTER, the FORMAT and MASK operations, and the automatic type conversion on operands requested by the IS: numeric to string, string to numeric, and numeric to integer (used primarily for subscripts). These operations are also performed serially.

The JOIN operation is performed in the obvious manner of streaming the second operand onto the tail of the first operand, forming a single result operand.

The binary operations are performed character-by-character, performing the required operation by producing 0/1 result characters, filling in the shorter operand with zeros.

The string comparisons are also performed character-by-character, comparing successive characters until a mismatch is found accor•ing to the built-in ASCII collate sequence and returning a 0/1 result.

The FORMAT and MASK operators provide a powerful string manipulation capability for a wide variety of applications from payroll and banking forms preparation to system software character manipulation. FORMAT is a packed-numeric-to-string operator that allows the user to describe the format of the result with a pictorial like character string. The operation is performed in a serial manner as dictated by the operands. The standard default conversion from packed numeric form to string is a subset of the FORMAT operation. MASK is a string-to-string operator similar to FORMAT. MASK can be used for character insertion, deletion, and spacing control. It is often used to control or measure the length of the fields. MASK is also processed in a serial-by-character manner.

System Supervision

The Load, Compile, Execution, and I/O comprise the basic processing modes for the system. Three additional modes are defined for a terminal, off-line, on-line idle, and normal completion. They are all passive modes and differ only in the allowed transitions that can take place upon an interrupt stimulus. For example, the normal completion state is the only state from which the RESTART execution command can be honored. RESTART is only allowed if the object string were left in a reusable state.

The diagram in Fig. 14 shows a few of the terminal state transitions. These transitions are significant in that they are all supported by hardware algorithms. When the control code corresponding to RUN is received by the SS the transition from the Load mode to the compile mode can be processed without software intervention. Many other transitions can occur but they generally require some system software assistance. The transition from the Load mode to the Compile mode involves the following steps. If the IP is active it must be allowed to complete in such a way that the source string is intact. The task is then removed from the queue for the IP and added to the queue for the TR. In addition, the control tables in main memory are initialized for the TR making available the address of the start of the source string and the address of the procedure libraries to be used.

A typical task queue is illustrated in Fig. 19. It is comprised of a linked list of entries (control words). The queue has a pointer to

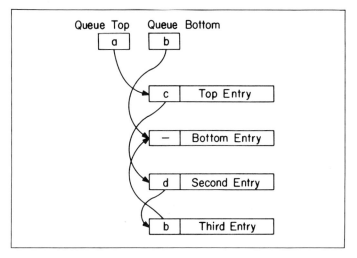

Fig. 19. Typical task queue structure.

the top entry and another pointer to the bottom entry. By maintaining both the top and bottom pointers it is easy to add an entry to either the top or the bottom of the queue.

Each time a control transition occurs the SS updates the queues by performing appropriate add or delete actions to each of the processor queues involved. This is part of first phase of any SS task processing. The second phase of SS processing involves assigning work to free processors that have assignable tasks on their queues.

The multiprocessing algorithm is centered around manipulation and use of queues for the CP, TR, IP, MR, and DC. The SS has a general purpose queue processor that allows an item to be added to the top, added to the bottom, or deleted from any queue. The algorithm has a default mode which is completely hardware controlled. Various parameters can be set by software that bias the operating dynamics. For example, two time values are maintained for each entry in the CP queue. One measures the accumulated processing time and the other measures the actual time that the task is on the top of a queue. The values are preset to parameter values when a task enters the queue. When the values have been counted down to zero an SS task is generated to modify the queues. In most cases this is used to move the task from a high priority position near the top of a queue to a low priority position near the bottom of a queue.

The processing flow in Fig. 14 is greatly oversimplified for general purpose system supervision. In Fig. 20, the control commands to and from the central processor are illustrated. The SS can command the CP to start on a task or to quit working on a task. The CP can terminate processing on a given task for one of six basic reasons. Consider the I/O completion. In most cases for most terminals the hardware algorithm for controlling I/O would be sufficient. If on the other hand, a batch processing terminal

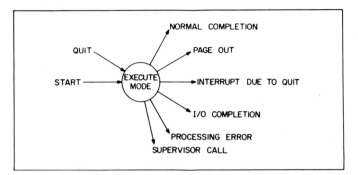

Fig. 20. Mode transitions affecting the central processor.

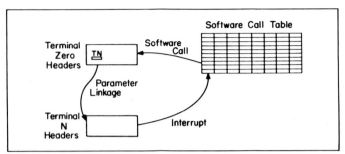

Fig. 21. Mechanism for handling a software call caused by a transition interrupt.

with spooled I/O were desired, it would be necessary to alter the control process for I/O with a system software procedure. To cause software to be called for a specific terminal upon an I/O service request, a specific control bit must be set in the terminal control word for that channel. This causes an automatic software call to be generated by the SS.

The software call is handled in SYMBOL by starting a pseudo terminal operating with the requesting channel number as a parameter. In this manner the control header tables for the requesting channel can be operated upon as data. This is illustrated in Fig. 21 where an interrupt of a specific class causes the corresponding program specified in a software call table to be selected and control transferred to the pseudo terminal with the

parameter TN. Each different class of interrupt maps into a different control word in the software control table. In this manner only the software procedure desired will be accessed in virtual memory. In SYMBOL over 80 different software interrupts are controlled via the software control table located in the lower part of main memory. This represents the principal interface between hardware and system software.

References

Chesley and Smith [1971]; Corbato and Vyssotsky [1965]; Cowart, Rice, and Lundstrom [1971]; Glaser, Couleur, and Oliver [1965]; Kilburn et al. [1962]; Mazor [1968]; Mullery, Schauer, and Rice [1963]; Rice and Smith [1971]; Smith [1963, 1968].

The SYMBOL Computer
SYMBOL:
A Major Departure from Classic Software Dominated von Neumann Computing Systems[1]

R. Rice / W. R. Smith

SYMBOL from a Performance Viewpoint

The evaluation phase of SYMBOL IIR is just beginning with the hardware near completion. In order to obtain a preview of the

[1]From *AFIPS SJCC*, 1971, pp. 575–587.

performance a set of measurements has been made on the hardware.

Basic Operation Rates

The clock period on SYMBOL IIR now stands at 320 nsec and may be later reduced to about 200 nsec. All measurements were taken at the 320 nsec period. The basic clock period in SYMBOL IIR contains long logic chains allowing relatively complex tasks to be performed. Many of the key logic chains contain 20 to 25 levels of AND-OR logic. The system uses Fairchild CTµL, type I throughout. The core memory is a 1964 model with a basic 2.5 µsec cycle. Due to a semi-serial interface on the core memory it has an effective cycle of 4 µsec.

An improved system (referred to as SYMBOL II) has been studied and has been partially specified. This system is based on the technology of the experimental system, SYMBOL IIR, but has been considerably optimized. SYMBOL II is also specified to use the latest cost orientated hardware technology. Conservative performance estimates of SYMBOL II will be made to give a comparison of how the SYMBOL algorithms would stand up in a contemporary hardware technology design. They will be based on a clock period of 100 nsec using a circuit family such as CTμL, type II and an LSI memory with a 200 nsec period. One should keep in mind that the following comparisons are between SYMBOL, which is a VFL machine running in a very dynamic execution time environment, and a more conventional fixed field machine running a language with the data boundaries determined at translate time. The former places more demands on the hardware while the latter shifts the burden of data management to the user.

For the purposes of comparison SYMBOL IIR will be referred to as SIIR and SYMBOL II as SII.

Field Processing Operations

SIIR performs all field operations in a VFL serial-by-character mode. It was always assumed that after system evaluation and bottle-neck analysis, if warranted, certain operators such as those shown below would be executed in a more parallel mode by using additional hardware. SII estimates are based on serial processing and known algorithm improvements that reduce or do not materially increase the hardware required.

The following table gives processing times measured on SIIR and estimated for SII. The execution time values are specified in microseconds and do not include the instruction fetch time or single word operand fetching and storing.

SYMBOL IIR Measured Execution Times in μsec

Operation	SIIR	SII
1234+4321	5.6	1.2
12345678−87654321	10.0	1.6
50 digits + 50 digits	45.0	5.0
Convert to floating point 1234	5.2	1.2
Convert to floating point 12345678	12.5	1.8
Convert to floating point 50 digits	120.0	18.0
Compare 12345678,87654321	4.0	1.0
Compare 12345678,12345670	6.5	1.2
|abc|join|def|	4.5	1.2
|12345678|join|12345678|	60.0	12.0
1234 format |ZZZ.DD|	9.0	3.0
1234 format |ZBZBV|	8.0	2.6
12345.6789 format|·$·*C***C***.DD|	76.0	15.0

Compilation

Several programs were compiled on SIIR and the overall times and space usage measured. The SIIR results are as follows:

SYMBOL IIR Measured Compile Times in μsec

	No. statements	Bytes of source	Bytes of object code	Average time per statement
Program A	195	8330	7315	820
Program B	70	3528	5112	1280
Program C	157	7560	6025	760

This represents about 75,000 statements compiled per minute on SIIR.

A comparative table for SII assuming added flexibility on SII for handling various other languages in addition to the SYMBOL language is given below. The data is based on a sampled study of object code and projected execution times of several recently developed algorithms.

SYMBOL Estimated Compile Times in μsec

	Statements	Bytes of source code	Bytes of object code	Average time per statement
Program A	195	8330	2350	185
Program B	70	3528	1735	220
Program C	157	7560	2110	185

This would give a compilation rate of 300,000 statements per minute.

Paging Overhead

SYMBOL has very low overhead for paging. The algorithms are based on direct hardware execution using parameters set up by software. A count of worst case paging overhead for SIIR in terms of memory cycles for a CP page out is given below.

SYMBOL IIR Paging Overhead in Memory Cycles

Item	Worst case	Average
CP Shut Down	7	7
SS Queuing and Push Selection	50	30
SS Disc Servicing	8	6
CP Start Up	6	6
Total memory cycles	71	49

Assuming an average of 5 μsec per memory cycle counting internal cycles this gives 355 μsec worst case. In SII using an improved algorithm the overhead would be less than 20 μsec.

Input/Output

The overhead for I/O for a time-sharing system becomes an important factor in providing adequate terminal response time. To illustrate the effect of the hidden software overhead an operation trace of a IBM 360/44 during FORTRAN IV output was performed. A similar operation was performed on SIIR. The equivalent output statements in both languages are shown in the table below.

SYMBOL vs. FORTRAN Output Statement Traces in Memory Cycles

Language	Statement	Traced	Est. overhead not traced
SYMBOL	OUTPUT 12345.56 FORMAT |D.DDD$_{10}$DD|;	130	0
FORTRAN	10 WRITE (6,10)× FORMAT (1×,E9.3)	3466	1000

The trace of the FORTRAN statement indicated 1,753 instructions being executed. Each instruction requires an average of two memory cycles. The trace program does not trace any of the supervisor or channel operations so that well over 3,000 and more likely near 4,500 memory cycles were used in executing the FORTRAN statement.

Task Control Overhead

In order to measure the overhead for compilation and execution a program consisting of one CONTINUE statement was executed on SIIR. This causes a null program to be entered, translated, and executed and thus places a large demand on any system resources required, isolating overhead from "useful" actions. All memory cycles were traced with the following distribution:

Processor used	Memory cycles
SS	41
TR	20
CP	18
Total	79

This could be compared with any contemporary system where the entire compiler would have been paged in and much of the supervisor would have been executed to establish many resources that would not have been needed.

Subscripting

It would seem that VFL data structures imply slow data referencing. However, the SYMBOL project demonstrated that efficient handling of dynamically varying data can be achieved with sophisticated list processing techniques. SYMBOL IIR established the foundation and the algorithms have now been developed to be competitive with conventional fixed field indexing while retaining the VFL features. A few references and their

equivalent memory cycles for SIIR are given below. The subscript Fetch cycles are not counted.

Reference	Typical memory cycles required
A[4,9]	4–6
A[16,32,6]	8–10
A[3]	2–3
A[70]	9–12
A	2

A substantial improvement has been obtained for SYMBOL II promising to make it as fast or in some cases faster than conventional indexing.

SYMBOL from a Cost Viewpoint

A study of a modern computer installation and its users as a total "system" reveals where and how the computing dollar is divided. Consultants from Iowa State University made available all the necessary data for such a study early in the program [Rice, 1967]. Figure 1 illustrates the I.S.U. IBM 360/50 installation in 1966 at the time the study was made. This "pie" has since been compared with many other business and scientific installations of varying sizes with different computer systems. There is general agreement that the minor variations in the size of the slices for different installations do not materially affect the picture. This applies to most modern "classic software-dominated systems."

The objective of data processing is to solve problems where the

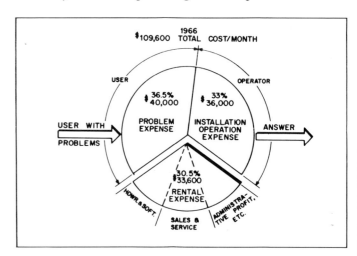

Fig. 1. The computing pie illustrated for Iowa State University 360/50 installation.

"user with a PROBLEM" is the input and the "ANSWER" is the output. It is assumed that the user has his problem well defined and has the data available but the data is not yet programmed. The conversion of his problem to a computable language and the debugging necessary for correct execution is included in the total cost of operating an installation.

I.S.U. calculated the total system operation on this basis as approximately $109,600 per month. The rate and labor costs were adjusted to normal commercial standards for the calculations. Both commercial and scientific problems were run in the problem mix. The following sections discuss the breakdown of the overall cost.

About 37 percent or $40,000 is used by the problem originator and/or the professional programmer to convert the problem to a debugged, high-level language and to obtain answers.

Thirty three percent or $36,000 is required for operating personnel, keypunch operators, file clerks, systems programmers, administration, space, power, etc.

Thirty percent of the total pie or $33,000 goes for machine rental. It is estimated that about one third of the rental expense goes for direct development of hardware and system software (perhaps half and half), one third for sales, service, and application support, and one third for administrative costs, overhead, and profit.

The choice of a hardware configuration and its machine language is the tail wagging the dog. Inexpensive hardware and a good, easy-to-use programming system can reduce the size (i.e., total cost) of the pie but in conventional systems will not materially alter the relative size of the slices.

In the following text the computing pie is used to illustrate SYMBOL concepts from a cost point of view. Each major slice will be further subdivided into its own percentage parts (i.e., each major slice will be 100 percent of the portion under consideration and will be divided into its constituent parts).

Figure 2 shows the potential problem expense saving to be obtained from any good conversation-mode, high-level language, time-sharing system. It has been estimated that approximately 50 percent of the problem expense slice can be saved in reduced user learning time, increased throughput, less professional programming support required, etc. We estimate the SYMBOL system will further reduce these costs with its "clean" and "concise" directly implemented high-level language and simplified operating system [Chesley and Smith, 1971].

The savings in the operation of an installation comes from four sources. This is illustrated in Fig. 3. First: A good time-sharing system will reduce the administrative help such as file clerks, keypunch operators, etc. It is estimated that this saving can be ten to fifteen percent of the installation operating expense exclusive of system rental. The SYMBOL system with conversation-mode multiprocessing and multiprogramming will also share in this saving. Second: The "system software" support required in a conventional installation is a very significant portion of the expense. Here SYMBOL shows a definite added saving. What system software remains can be written in the high-level, general-purpose language and will be easier to write, debug, and understand later. This will reduce the number of professional personnel required. Third: The SYMBOL language is directly implemented in hardware and thus uses less main memory for "system software." For example, a resident compiler is not required. In addition, much less program swapping occurs and thus less virtual memory transfer time is needed. Hardware execution of algorithms is also faster and results in enhanced instruction execution speed. These features will require less programming attention and also provide more throughput per installation dollar spent. Fourth: The SYMBOL hardware is designed with modern integrated circuits and large two-layer printed circuit boards. The total system hardware package is compact and does not need raised floors, special air conditioning, or vast amounts of floor space. It is estimated that these SYMBOL features will reduce installation operating expense by an additional 20–35 percent or a total of 30–50 percent.

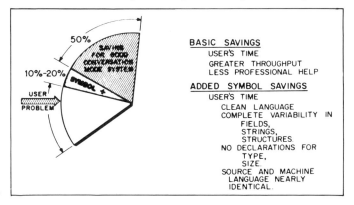

Fig. 2. Savings in problem expense.

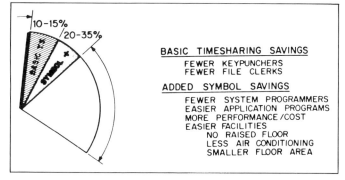

Fig. 3. Savings in installation operation expense.

The slice of the computing pie representing the computer manufacturer's hardware contribution is illustrated in Fig. 4; approximately seventeen percent of this slice is attributable to hardware. For large systems the peripheral equipment and the bulk files can approximate about one half of the total cost. The main storage is another quarter and the CPU logic is another quarter. Naturally some variation in these amounts will occur from installation to installation and for different system types.

The SYMBOL approach saves costs in several ways: The first area of savings is in the use of large two-layer printed circuit boards and two-layer printed circuit bases with cam-operated contacts for *all* system interconnections.

Except for cables to peripherals and wires used for correction of design errors and for logical extensions no wire exists in the system. It is estimated as much as a 50 percent saving will be achieved over small board, wire-wrap back panel, multi-cabinet conventional systems. This same technique reduces costs in terminal equipment but not to such a large degree. We estimate that three percent of the manufacturer's slice of the pie can be saved by this functionally-factored, bus-oriented, large printed circuit board design philosophy. The second way savings are obtained is in the hardware efficiency gained by the SYMBOL system. Since most of the normal system software is hard wired, very little resident main memory is used, thus providing much larger percentages of main memory for application programs. The execution of system instructions is done at "clock speeds" in a "macro" rather than a "micro" manner. This provides much faster high-powered instruction execution. Finally, more of the system hardware is simultaneously operating due to the system organization which allows multiple jobs to be in the main frame for

overlapped execution. We estimate that an additional 2 percent of the manufacturer's slice of the pie is saved here.

The largest and most important single saving for SYMBOL is in the "System Software." Figure 5 illustrates this point. Irrespective of whether the system manufacturer or someone else produces the software for a conventional computer this large expense is real. The SYMBOL features directly implemented in logic (i.e., hard wired) make unnecessary at least 80 percent of the conventional system software used in large time-sharing machines. This represents an estimated 16 percent saving in the system manufacturer's slice of the computing pie.

The field support of the system software is a major expense. The sheer volume of paper and record keeping to keep current with the latest changes is a major problem. In the design of the SYMBOL system this problem was given great attention. In studying the software delivered with large systems using a relatively static high-level language, we note that most (if not all) of the changes made were on the programmed implementation or were due to programming errors. Many levels of machine and assembly language programs and machine runs were between the hardware language and the programmers' source language. This quite naturally introduces confusion (and errors) either in original programming or in understanding the hidden rules when using the system.

It may also be noted that as more and more applications are programmed in a language it automatically becomes more rigid. We believe that the "clean," high-level, general-purpose SYMBOL language is excellent for most uses. Since direct hardware implementation requires little field support in the software sense,

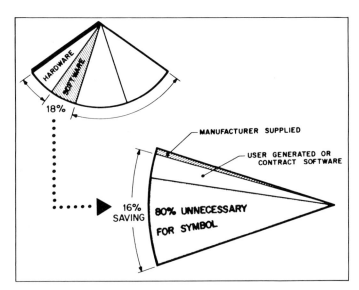

Fig. 4. Manufacturer's direct hardware expense.   **Fig. 5. Manufacturer's system software expense.**

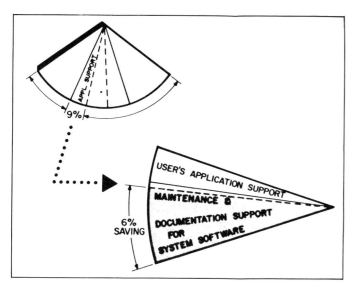

Fig. 6. Manufacturer's software application expense.

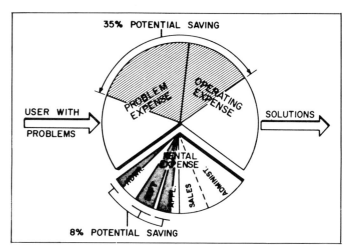

Fig. 7. Potential savings with a good conversation mode hardware/software system.

we estimate approximately a six percent saving in the manufacturer's support expense. This is illustrated in Fig. 6.

Good service is a must in a large system. The SYMBOL hardware has been engineered for good reliability and at the same time easy maintenance. We do not anticipate any added expense for SYMBOL hardware maintenance over conventional systems with equivalent storage and logic circuit counts. Our experience on the SYMBOL model has verified this belief.

The previous material has split the computing dollar up in parts and has described how major savings can be realized with a "total systems" approach. The SYMBOL techniques described herein together with good time-sharing, conversation mode practice can reduce computing costs up to 50 percent. Referring to Fig. 7, one may visualize how the savings in the whole computing pie add up.

Conclusion[1]

The traditional boundary between hardware and software has been weakened during the past ten years and is due for a significant shift beyond the token improvements. It is believed that in SYMBOL a major step towards significantly more capable hardware has been attained.

The SYMBOL system is now entering an extensive evaluation phase where the system's strengths and weaknesses will become more apparent through actual day to day usage. The developers of

[1]This conclusion is taken from the paper by Smith et al. that makes up the first part of this chapter.

the system have gained much insight into the merits of each of the approaches taken. The overall approach to memory management is considered a breakthrough. The moving of data attributes from instructions to the data is considered fundamental.

No claim is made that the SYMBOL system has been balanced for optimum performance and use of hardware. Certain critical areas of memory management and system supervision are felt to be 10 to 100 times more efficient than conventional means. Certain aspects of structure referencing are a major advance over software list processors but fall short of being competitive for some types of large array referencing. Many of the weaknesses in this first SYMBOL model were solved by the designers too late to be factored into the actual hardware. Many other aspects of the system such as the paging and system supervisor algorithms can be evaluated after significant usage experience.

The computing professionals have debated for many years the questions: Can a compiler be developed in hardware? Can the heart of system supervision be committed to hardware? Can data space management be taken over by hardware? Can hardware be designed to take over major software functions? Can complex hardware be debugged? These and many other questions have been positively answered with the running SYMBOL system. The most significant part of the entire project is that the concepts were reduced to full scale, operating hardware.

References

Chesley and Smith [1971]; Rice [1967].

Chapter 31

A Dual-Processor Desk-Top Computer: The HP 9845A

William D. Eads / Jack M. Walden / Edward L. Miller

I. Introduction

What differentiates a desk-top computer, as described in this paper, from a minicomputer? Questions of this type are dangerous and difficult to answer because of the nonspecific usage of the terms and the wide variety of understandings of their meanings on the part of readers. Nevertheless, some useful generalizations can be extracted from common usage, even if they do not apply to all minicomputers or desk-top computers, or to all users.

First, a desk-top computer, unlike a minicomputer, is a complete system that necessarily has a high degree of physical integration of its elements. It has an input device (a keyboard), a display device (a CRT or a single-line display), a mass storage device (mag card, cassette, or floppy disk, for example), a processor, memory, connectors for external I/O devices, and power supplies built into an integrated package which can literally fit on the top of a desk. This high degree of integration is made possible by the large-scale integration of the key components of the computer, including processor, memory, and control logic for internal peripherals.

Second, the typical minicomputer is not ready for operation when it is received by the user, or even when all I/O devices are connected and it is initially powered up. System software, including the operating system, compilers, loaders, interpreters, editors, etc., must first be loaded into memory. The system must be told which I/O devices are (or may be) in the system at each I/O port, and which software module (driver) controls each device; this process is called I/O configuration. Only now is the system available for use. In contrast, the desk-top computer arrives with all system software in ROM already inside the machine, or in packages of optional ROMs that the user can easily install, generally in less than a minute. When I/O devices are attached, the computer can then generally determine for itself the device at each port and which driver is to be used. Users simply connect the external peripherals they plan to use, turn on the equipment, and begin using it. Therefore, desk-top machines incorporate a large degree of *logical* integration.

A third distinction is in the method of use of the two machines. Whereas a mini may have several languages available for the user, and an editor which allows programs to be written in any of these languages, a desk-top machine typically has a single language, with a built-in program editor which understands the syntactic restrictions of that language, and which does not allow a line with syntax errors to be entered into the user's program. Since there is but one language and one user at a time, the operating system for a desk-top machine can accomplish a task with fewer explicit directions from the user. There is no need to use a job control language to specify the language subsystem, any linkage editor, the memory requirements, or what peripherals are to be allocated during program execution. The user simply enters the program or loads it from the built-in mass storage, edits if necessary, and runs it by pressing a single key called RUN.

A similar distinguishing feature is that a desk-top computer can be used as a simple calculator as it stands, at any time during the entry or execution of a program. On most minis, the operating system doesn't understand such constructs as SIN (15) unless the user has entered some interpretive language subsystem, such as BASIC. Even then they don't necessarily have keyboard operation—but may *require* a program to be run.

The desk-top computer which will now be described is Hewlett-Packard System 45, shown in Fig. 1. It contains a typewriter-like keyboard, two cartridge drives for user program and data storage, a 24-line × 80-column CRT, and a built-in 480 line/min 80-column thermal printer, which can make a dot-for-dot copy of any CRT image. The internal thermal printer can also be used as a plotter with 560 by indefinitely many independently addressable dots. This machine has up to 64 Kbyte of user read/write memory (R/W), plus a separate 98-Kbyte operating system including an editor, a BASIC interpreter, and a sophisticated I/O scheduler.

The system is presented in a top-down manner. Section II

Fig. 1. The 9845A desk-top computer.

discusses the user environment and presents the internal storage format for user programs. The system organization, including process and processor synchronization, control, and communication, is outlined in Sec. III. Some details of each LSI component are provided in Sec. IV. Section V focuses on interprocessor communication and memory address sharing. The paper concludes with some considerations about the primary I/O device, the CRT display.

II. The User Language and Internal Form of Programs

The language of the System 45 is ANSI BASIC, enhanced to include string and matrix operations, subprograms, program linking, tracing, formatted output, mass storage files, and graphics. To aid in readability, variable names have been extended from a single letter or a single letter followed by a single digit to include zero to fourteen lowercase letters, digits, and/or underscores following a single uppercase letter. Major design goals in implementation of the BASIC interpreter were:

1　Expandability, to allow additional language features to be added to the system by use of plug-in ROMs

2　Interactive operation, to allow the user to interrogate and change the values of program variables, even as the program proceeds

3　Maximizing speed of execution within the constraint of interactive operation

4　Allowing program lines to be parsed to a form from which they can be reconstructed, in a form similar to that in which they were originally entered

An understanding of how these goals were achieved may best be found in an illustrative example. As shown in Fig. 2, the first operation in the use of the System 45 involves the keying of a program line into the computer. Completion of the line is signaled by depression of the STORE key. At this time the ASCII characters constituting the program line are placed in the *line buffer*, used for syntax analysis and listing. The system control supervisor calls the syntax supervisor, whose task is to convert the ASCII keystrokes into *internal form*, that is, into the format of program lines as stored in user read/write memory. Beginning at the left side of the source line, the syntax supervisor determines the line number and creates the first word of internal form in the *internal form buffer* (see Fig. 3). Next, the syntax supervisor attempts to match the statement name internal form (IF) with one within a linked list of statement keywords, a segment of which is shown in Fig. 4. In order to allow expandability there are actually as many as three linked lists which the syntax supervisor must scan in searching for a match with the statement name. First, an area of user read/write memory may contain binary programs, the

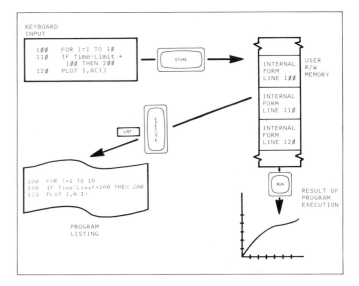

Fig. 2. The programming process.

most flexible way of adding language capability. Second, optional ROMs, increasing language capability, may be plugged into an option ROM port. And finally, the fundamental machine capability which exists within every System 45 includes a fixed set of keywords. Tables of keywords associated with the above three mechanisms are searched in the sequence above (allowing an optional capability to override the capability of the basic machine). When a match is found, the character position of the keyword in the source line is placed in the upper half of the second word of the internal form buffer (Fig. 3), and a pointer, associated with the element of the linked list for which a match was found, is placed in the third word. This pointer actually points to the fourth word down from the end of the keyword (see Fig. 4), at which location the ROM code for execution of that statement is located. Two words up from the execution routine is a pointer to the routine which performs syntax analysis of the rest of the statement. The syntax supervisor uses this address to pass control to the next statement syntax routine.

The statement syntax routine shown in Fig. 4 for the IF statement immediately passes control to the expression syntax routine, which determines the order in which operations will be performed and which operands are used by each operation. The expression syntaxer creates an internal form for expressions which contains a set of operations that will be sequentially executed at run time; the present activity is still part of storing the line. Each operation consists of an operator pointer followed by zero or more operand pointers. For example, the computation of A * B + C * D involves the multiplication of A and B, followed by the multiplication of C and D, followed finally by the sum of these two products, and consists of the three operations, as illustrated in Fig. 5.

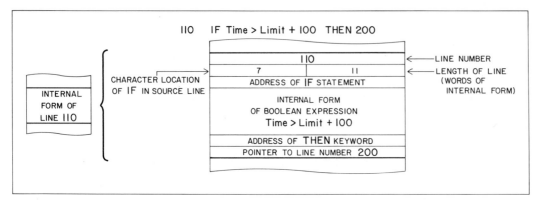

Fig. 3. The internal form of a typical statement.

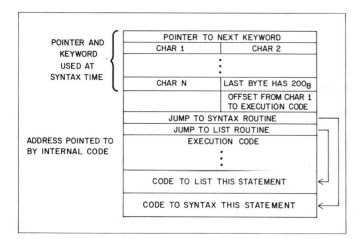

Fig. 4. An entry in the linked list of statement keywords.

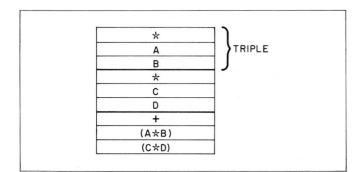

Fig. 5. Internal form for the expression A∗B+C∗D.

The operator-operand-operand entities in Fig. 5 are called *triples*, as are all other operations involving two operands (dyadic operations). Operations involving a single operand (monadic),

such as negation or square root, result in two-word entities called *doubles*. The concept of doubles and triples is extended to *n-tuples*, consisting of an operator pointer followed by $n-1$ generalized operands. Thus the MAX function, which allows N operands, can be written as the $(N+2)$-*tuple* shown in Fig. 6.

The contents of the first triple of Fig. 5 are three sequential 2-byte words: the first is called the operator execution pointer and is a pointer to the first word of an execution routine (in system ROM) which fetches and multiplies two numeric quantities; the second and third entries are pointers into R/W memory to the symbol table entries of variables A and B respectively. The form of symbol table entries for variables is shown in Fig. 7.

Within an expression, the result of each *n*-tuple is placed in a unique 8-byte scratch-pad register. Forty of these registers are

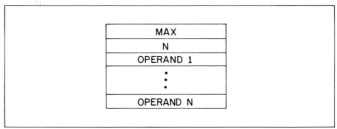

Fig. 6. Internal form for the MAX function.

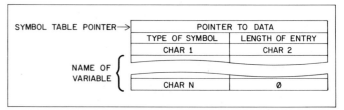

Fig. 7. Format of a symbol table entry.

available in contiguous memory, so that any single expression can have no more than 40 operators. The first operator executed causes the first scratch-pad register, called TEMP 1, to be filled; the second operator fills TEMP 2, and so forth through the expression. Therefore the expression syntax analyzer actually creates the third triple of A * B + C * D (see Fig. 5) as +, TEMP 1, TEMP 2. TEMP 1 is the address of the temporary which will contain A * B, and TEMP 2 is the address of the temporary for C*D. The TEMP pointers are distinguishable from symbol table pointers by the fact that the sign bit (most significant address bit) is 1 for symbol table pointers and 0 for all other machine pointers, including TEMP pointers.

When the expression syntax analyzer recognizes the keyword THEN in the example of Fig. 3, it places a word in the internal form buffer corresponding to the THEN part of the statement. Control is returned to the statement syntax monitor, which recognizes a line number of 200 and places into the internal form buffer a pointer to the symbol table entry for that line; only those lines which are referenced in the program are located in the symbol table. Statement syntaxing is now complete, and control is returned to the syntax monitor. At this time the length of line 110 is known, so that the syntax monitor can place the length of the line, in words of internal form, in the lower half of the second word of the internal form buffer. The final task of the statement syntax analyzer is the placement of the new line in its proper position, ordered by line number, in the user's program area in R/W memory.

The execution of a program as shown in Fig. 2 is most easily understood as a sequence of operations caused by the internal form of the program. The execution of a program in the System 45 may be viewed as sequential execution of each program statement, under control of the operating system. We may therefore use line 110, shown in Fig. 3, as an example. Execution of line 110 within a program would proceed as follows. (The internal code pointer, ICPTR, points initially to the first word of the internal form of the line.)

1 The operating system increments ICPTR by 2.

2 The operating system transfers control to code at the address given by the word pointed to by ICPTR (IF statement code).

3 The IF statement increments ICPTR and transfers control to the expression executor.

4 The expression executor transfers control to the subroutine, which adds two operands.

5 The add subroutine, using ICPTR, fetches Limit and 100 and adds them, placing the result in TEMP 1 and leaving ICPTR pointing to the internal code for the "greater than" operator; it then returns to the expression executor.

6 The expression executor transfers control to the subrou-

tine, which checks for the "greater than" relation of two operands.

7 The "greater than" subroutine computes Time > (Limit + 100). If true, it returns 1; if false, it returns 0. It then returns to the expression executor.

8 The expression executor transfers control to the THEN subroutine, which returns immediately to the expression executor, which in turn returns to the IF statement executor.

9 If the value returned is nonzero, ICPTR is set, using the symbol table pointer for line 200, to the beginning of that line. If not, ICPTR points to the beginning of the next line following 110.

10 Control is returned to the operating system.

Because of the convenient form of the internal representation of the program line, overhead time for running the above sequence is quite small compared to the run time required to interpret the statement type, determine the sequence of the expression execution, and search through the program for a destination line number.

Listing of program lines, using the internal form of statements (Fig. 3) and the linked list of keywords in ROM (Fig. 4), occurs in a process converse to that of syntax analysis. Using the first word of the internal form, the line number is formed in the *source line buffer*, followed by enough spaces (at least one) to begin the keyword in the column position given by the upper half of the second word of the internal form. From the third word of internal form (the statement execution address) the list routine subtracts 3. From Fig. 4, it can be seen that this is the address of the word whose lower byte is the offset of the statement keyword from the first word of execution code. This offset is then subtracted from the statement execution address to give a pointer to the ACSII representation of the keyword, which is located at the beginning of that section of the linked list of keywords, and follows the pointer to the next keyword. These characters are transferred to the source line buffer one by one until a byte is found whose most significant bit is set, indicating the end of the keyword. Next, the address of the beginning of the execution code is decremented by 1 to determine the location of the routine which lists the rest of the internal form for that statement.

Any statement lister may call the expression lister, which determines the location of the operators and operands associated with that expression. Associated with the ROM execution code is the information necessary to list that operator and its operands— including the ASCII representation of the operator and the number of operands (and how they are arranged syntactically with respect to the operator)—as well as the precedence of the operator. The operator precedence, together with the sequence of operator execution in the internal code, furnishes the expression list monitor with sufficient information to list the expression with the same sequence of operands and operators as was entered originally, along with required parentheses. The only differences between the entered and listed lines involve extraneous or missing spaces and redundant parentheses.

In the example of Fig. 3, control passes from the statement lister to the expression lister after 110 IF is listed, and it produces Time > Limit + 100. Note that no parentheses are listed (even if they were placed around Limit + 100 when it was keyed in). The statement lister then adds THEN from a keyword association with its associated execution address and finally adds 200 from the symbol table reference. Control is then transferred back to the operating system to output or display the now complete line in the source line buffer.

The final feature of the language system to be discussed is that of the user's ability to interact with the program as it is executing, a capability which is called having a *live keyboard*. Since all variables are accessible through a symbol table, since the program execution monitor has control of the processor at the end of the execution of each line, and since the system was built to allow the addition of variables and the addition or deletion of program lines at any time (even between executions of program lines), the capability of interacting with an executing program is extensive. Users can interrogate or change variables as the program runs; they can compute complex expressions; they can even delete, add, or modify program lines as the program executes. While these capabilities may be dangerous for a production program, they are certainly convenient during the development and debugging of new programs, and they can be removed during a program run by the execution of the command SUSPEND INTERACTIVE.

The next section provides an overview of the multiprocessor system used to implement the user program environment just described.

III. System Organization and Control

Examination of Fig. 8 reveals that all communication with the outside word is via the Peripheral Processing Unit (PPU). *All* peripherals—keyboard, CRT, printer, etc.—are tied to the PPU's I/O bus. The Language Processing Unit (LPU) has *no* peripherals attached to it, and it can communicate only with the PPU.

The PPU is responsible for managing all the system resources except block 0 random-access memory (RAM), which is managed by the LPU. The resources managed by the PPU are block 1 RAM, all I/O devices, and the LPU.

Interprocessor Communications

Communication between the processors is solely through the use of shared RAM. There are no dedicated signal lines or interrupts between processors. One mode of communication is via messages stored in buffers. Each processor has a fixed buffer of seven words for sending a message to the other processor. These buffers are guarded and controlled through flags. The second mode of communication is quite diverse. Certain words throughout RAM are allocated as convenient for the processes needing them. They are used as flags, semaphores, tables, etc., to synchronize and control the two processors in ways that are specific to the particular task.

In this control/communication mechanism, there are several cases where a processor must have exclusive access to a table, counter, or buffer area; i.e., while one processor is using this area, the other processor must *not* be allowed access into it. This kind of *exclusive access* can be rigorously controlled by the use of a two-flag exclusion algorithm first proposed by T. Dekker [Shaw, 1974]. This algorithm is implemented (in a somewhat simplified form) in the HP 9845A to control LPU/PPU access to critical constructs. For example, the LPU alone can create buffers; once created, a buffer can be filled by either the PPU or the LPU. Both the LPU and PPU may have occasion to read from or modify a given buffer. Buffers may be destroyed by either the PPU or LPU. Clearly, such cooperative use of buffers requires controlled access.

The simplified two-flag algorithm of Fig. 9, implemented in the HP 9845A, does not include the case of *mutual exclusion*, which, in the general case, could lead to endless *synchronized deadlock* if not accounted for. In the HP 9845A this cannot occur, because the "failure" paths for the LPU and PPU are different; the LPU "waits," whereas the PPU "gives up" and returns to process scheduler.

This exclusive access problem is quite fundamental in all multiprocessor systems—which usually implies large systems. It may surprise some to find it occurring in a desk-top machine.

I/O Process Handling

The PPU establishes and controls the keyboard entry protocol. When the user makes a complete keyboard-record entry (terminated by STORE, EXECUTE, or CONTINUE), the keyboard is disabled until the system interprets the record; i.e., the system examines the line and determines what it should do. As soon as the record is interpreted, the keyboard is reenabled while the actual execution takes place. This sequencing allows concurrent execution of a number of commands but prevents the user from submitting a new record before the system is able to accept it. The PPU allows concurrent execution of keyboard commands, and also execution of keyboard commands concurrent with program execution if there is no resource conflict involved. An example of a conflict would be a GET command to load a program from a tape cartridge, followed immediately by a REWIND of the cartridge

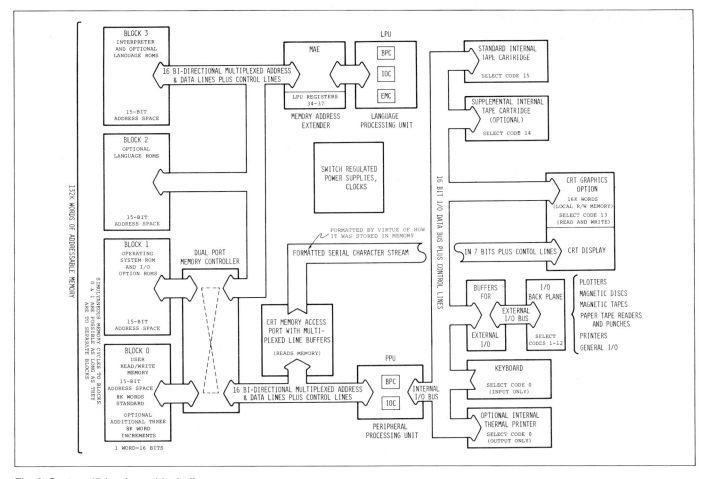

Fig. 8. System 45 hardware block diagram.

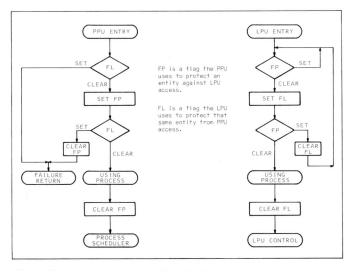

Fig. 9. The two-flag method of exclusive access.

before the GET is completed. When concurrent operations cannot be allowed, a SYSTEM BUSY message is given. Since all peripherals are attached to the PPU, the PPU must perform all transfers of data and programs between the desk-top computer and peripheral devices.

I/O processes can be initiated by the program being executed by the LPU, or by the user via keyboard entry commands. Most such commands can also be stored as a part of a program. The LPU syntaxes, stores, and executes all programs; thus it must be able to interpret and cause execution of most commands. Therefore most commands, although processed by the PPU during keyboard entry, are "handed over" to the LPU for interpretation.

Thus, each I/O activity is *initiated* by the LPU but is turned over to the PPU to be carried out. Each task involves both processors carrying out specific subtasks. These subtasks include communication between processors concerning the state of the subtasks, as well as monitoring, synchronizing, and terminating the overall task. To explain this, each processor and its role will be described.

PPU Process Definition

Except for initialization (power on, SCRATCH ALL) and the Process Scheduler (which is the "idle loop"), all PPU work is carried out by *processes*. When a process is needed it is invoked by "creating" it. A user process and a keyboard process are created during initialization. All other processes are created dynamically at the beginnings of the various individual tasks and are destroyed upon their individual completions.

A process is represented by at least one Process Control Block (PCB). The PCB is a 10-word R/W memory entity used to contain (either directly or indirectly) all the information necessary for the PPU to execute the associated process. Figure 10 shows the structure of a PCB.

PCBs are taken from block 1 RAM by the PPU memory allocator, which maintains a PCB Free List. They are linked to the Process Tree during their active life, and are linked back to the Free List when the process is completed. The Free List is linked through the first word of each PCB.

Some processes need more temporary *process control* storage than the 10 words of a PCB. Those 10 words are strictly allocated in use as per Fig. 10. Additional 10-word entities called *data blocks* may be obtained from the Free List; they are linked to the PCB via the ninth word, Data Block Link (DBL).

Active PCBs are linked together in various ways through the Brother Link (BL), Father Link (FL), and Son Link (SL), labeled in Fig. 10. All processes invoked by the user through execution of a program are represented and controlled by a tree of PCBs linked to the user process (which was created at initialization and is never destroyed). The hierarchy of processes is implemented via the SL BL, and FL links, to create an orderly control structure. In general, the creation of a process, communication between

processes, and the removal of a process take place between processes no more than one level apart in this control structure. In this hierarchical structure, the SL points to a process at a lower level, the FL points back up to the higher-level process, and the BL points to associated processes at the same level.

A process tree which might arise during the execution of a program is illustrated in Fig. 11. The Brother Links (BLs) represent the existence of more than one *incomplete* I/O operation invoked by the execution of the program. This can only occur when the system is running in the OVERLAP mode, which allows concurrent, overlapped I/O operations (discussed later).

In addition to the process tree linking with SL, FL, and BL illustrated in Fig. 11, the PCBs are linked together into other important lists through the tenth word, i.e., the Queue Link.

Each peripheral is attached to the machine via an interface which has a peripheral address (select code) in the range 0 to 15. Each I/O operation invoked by a program statement specifies (explicitly, or implicity by system default) the peripheral address of the device to which it is directed. When the LPU passes to the PPU the I/O process to be handled, the PPU creates a PCB to represent the process and links it into the Process Tree. In addition to this process control mechanism (which is independent of particular devices or select codes) it must also maintain knowledge of the specific device. And if other operations to that device exist (in the Process Tree), it must also see that the chronological sequence is preserved. This is accomplished by also linking the PCBs into queues—one for each peripheral address. These queues are headed (pointed to) by a table with an entry for each peripheral address. In addition to the actual hardware peripheral addresses 0 to 15, there are pseudoaddresses 16, 17, and 18, which represent various areas of the CRT: those for PRINT, DISP ("display" command) and implied DISP.

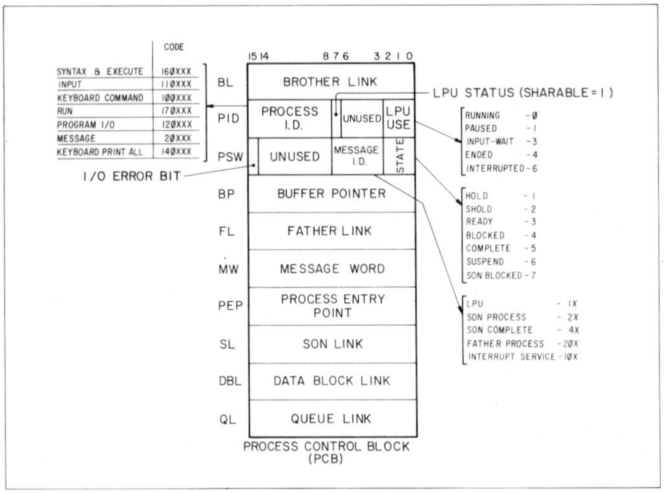

Fig. 10. Format of a process control block (PCB).

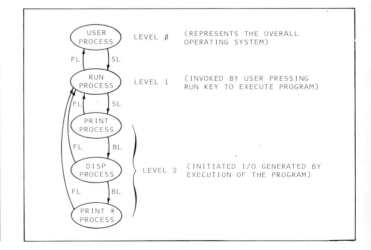

Fig. 11. A typical process tree linking several PCBs.

In addition to the queue of operations for the peripheral address, there is always an associated device buffer. The same table which heads the peripheral address queues also contains pointers to those buffers. This total construct—pointers to PCBs in device queues, and pointers to device buffers—is called the QTABLE.

QTABLE plays an important role in the overall process scheduling. It was mentioned earlier that the Process Scheduler is the PPU idle loop. What the Process Scheduler does to find processes which can be "worked on" is to scan QTABLE for peripheral addresses with active queues attached. If such a queue exists, the top PCB on the queue is examined to see if that process is in a state where anything can be done. If not, the scan continues to the next peripheral address. If something can be done, depending on the state of the process, it is done.

In the System 45, the normal mode of I/O transfers is "interrupt-by-the-character," with all transfers to the peripheral carried out in an Interrupt Service Routine (ISR). The PPU has vectored interrupt as part of its structure (implemented in the Input/Output Chip, IOC in Fig. 8). The overall process of carrying out such tranfers occurs in three stages:

1 Queueing up of the process, obtaining the resources required (buffers, etc.), and activation of the ISR (setting interrupt vector table entry, etc.), *followed by* return of the PPU to the idle loop or other tasks

2 Character-by-character transfer as interrupts occur and watching for the last transfer, when interrupt transfers are terminated

3 Final termination of the process—release of buffers, dequeuing of PCBs, etc.

As indicated in Fig. 10, the third word of the PCB is a Process Status Word (PSW) in which the state of the process is recorded. During its lifetime, a process may go through a number of states to accomplish the three stages of I/O transfer activity previously mentioned. Figure 12 shows the state transitions possible in the life of a PCB. The device transfers in the ISR occur during the BLOCKED state.

Formatting Output

Formatting from internal stored form to external form (such as ASCII character streams) is carried out in the act of transfer from the block 0 (of memory) data buffer to the block 1 (of memory) device buffer. This is performed by the PPU, and so it is interesting to see how this is done within the control structure that has been described.

To see the process involved, refer to Fig. 13. Suppose that the LPU, in executing a program, has encountered a PRINT statement with n expressions (items) in its list whose output is to be directed to an external printer at peripheral address 8. The LPU obtains a data buffer adequate to hold the n items (the size needed is determined when the PRINT statement is syntaxed and stored) from the block 0 memory manager. It sends a Start I/O message to the PPU with three items of information—the peripheral address, the block 0 data buffer address, and the starting address for the PPU PRINT routine.

The LPU now begins (without further concern for the PPU) to

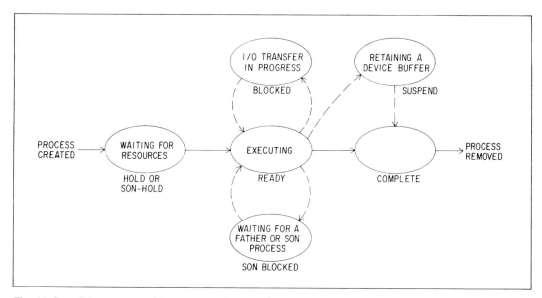

Fig. 12. Possible state transitions in the life of a PCB.

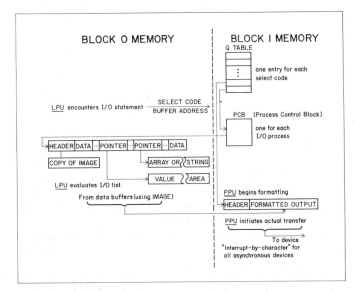

Fig. 13. LPU/PPU interaction during output.

evaluate the output list expressions. As each is evaluated, it is put in the next storage cell of the data buffer, followed by a WAIT item. Simultaneously, the PPU responds to the Start I/O message by obtaining a PCB, filling it with the buffer pointer (BP) and starting address (PEP), and setting it up in the Process Tree, and, we will assume, getting it queued at the head of the appropriate peripheral address queue. The process is in the HOLD state, but the PPU immediately attempts to allocate resources and activate the process. Assuming that a device buffer is available, the PPU will immediately allocate it and set the PCB READY. The Process Scheduler will see the READY and begin execution through the PEP.

The routine at PEP begins the formatting. It will obtain items from the data buffer, formatting each into the device buffer. Three obvious possibilities exist:

1   The formatting catches up with the LPU, by encountering the WAIT item in the buffer. The PPU will change PEP to a "continue formatting" routine, leave the PCB READY, and return to the Process Scheduler. This allows the PPU to work on other processes.

2   The formatting has finished all items when it finds a "done" item in the buffer. The PPU will set the interrupt return vector, initiate the interrupt output, set PEP to a "clear up" routine, BLOCK the PCB, and return to the Process Scheduler. The PPU works on other I/O and on this I/O by interrupt until transfer is done, then marks PCB complete.

3   The formatting generates enough data to fill the device buffer, and so the PPU initiates I/O, sets PEP to a "record gone, resume formatting" routine, sets PCB BLOCKED,

and returns to the Process Scheduler. When the final interrupt occurs, the process is made READY, and formatting resumes.

In case 1 above, the Process Scheduler, finding the PCB READY, will execute the routine at PEP. This routine will check whether the WAIT item is still next, or whether it has been replaced by the LPU with data. If WAIT is there, it just returns; thus each scan of the queues causes a recheck. Notice that there is concurrency present in this process. The LPU is evaluating expressions and filling the buffer while the PPU follows it (as processor time is available) item by item in the formatting.

Device Conflicts

One additional task that is extremely important in the correct handling of I/O is the management of possible device conflicts and the allocation of resources. These conflicts are handled in the Process Scheduler routines which switch a process in the HOLD state to READY.

Some obvious things are involved in resource allocation; for example, device buffers from the pool at block 1 R/W memory. One item not so obvious is the DMA channel. There is only one DMA channel available. However, DMA transfers may be desired for several processes on different peripheral addresses. Thus, the resource allocator must keep track of DMA channel utilization and sequentially allocate it to processes needing it.

Another area of device conflict is the relationship between synchronous and asynchronous devices. Synchronous devices, such as tape transports, require service at intervals dictated by the device. If service is not rendered when required, data are lost or erroneous data written. A synchronous device on a low-priority interrupt might have the processor taken away by a higher-priority interrupt, causing it to miss an essential transfer.

If a synchronous device is protected from this by being allowed only on high-priority interrupt levels, DMA transfers may still cause trouble. The DMA, if activated, may "steal" so many memory cycles that the interrupt service routine response may be slowed to a fraction of its normal speed. Again, an essential transfer may be missed.

These conflicts can be resolved by delaying the transfer from HOLD to READY for processes that would create these conditions.

Overlapped and Serial I/O Processing

The Process Tree and PCB linkage shown in Fig. 11 show the existence of PCBs (and therefore active I/O processes) at the head of three device queues: the printer for the PRINT process; the CRT for the DISP process; and a mass storage device for the PRINT # process. Since I/O transfers are, in general, interrupt-by-character (or DMA for the mass storage device), a number of processes at the heads of different queues could have the I/O transfers initiated and be in the BLOCKED state. Transfers would occur randomly from one process to another as interrupts occurred for the various devices. This is *buffered* and *overlapped* I/O. It is the mode for which the System 45 I/O Process Handling was designed. The LPU is allowed to "forge ahead," sending new Start I/O messages and filling new data buffers as long as memory is available for data buffers, PCBs, and device buffers.

However, there are times when all of this overlapped activity is not desired. For example, it disconnects the LPU execution of a PRINT statement from the PPU outputting of the data. This can be very confusing, particularly during program testing and debugging.

At the end of each program line, the LPU examines a flag which serves to control this overlapping of I/O. If the flag is in the SERIAL mode, the LPU waits for the PPU to send it a message that the output associated with that line is finished. It will then start the next line. If the flag is in the OVERLAP mode, the LPU does not wait for the message, but proceeds on to the next line.

The PPU does not normally send a message to the LPU upon the completion of every I/O operation, so how does it know to do so when the mode is SERIAL? In the discussion of formatting, it was mentioned that the PPU knew it was at the last item of a PRINT list when it encountered a "done" item. This item is placed there by the LPU when it has evaluated the last item on the list—if the mode is OVERLAP. If the mode is SERIAL, it places a "reply" item instead of "done." The PPU knows, when it sees "reply," that this is the end of the list and that it should send a message to the LPU that the I/O process is done.

IV. The Hardware Architecture of the 9845A

The internal architecture of the 9845A hardware is illustrated in the block diagram of Fig. 8. The major elements of the diagram are the two processors called the Language Processor Unit (LPU) and the Peripheral Processor Unit (PPU), and the Memory Address Extender (MAE) with its associated four 32-kiloword blocks of memory (block 0 through block 3). Associated with the memory are the Dual Port Memory Controller and the CRT Memory Access Port.

The main purpose of the LPU is to execute the user's program. To do this it executes a BASIC interpreter encoded in ROM located in blocks 2 and 3 of memory. The user's program is stored in block 0 of R/W memory. The main function of the PPU is to perform I/O and certain other activities. A communications protocol involving shared memory is the basis of LPU/PPU communication.

The LPU and PPU are both processors that, in isolation, can command 16-bit memory address spaces. The PPU does in fact have access to such a 64-kiloword portion of memory, i.e., block 0

and block 1. Assembly language coding for the PPU can, in fact, ignore the memory address extension scheme altogether and simply consider the designations of block 0 and block 1 as an artificial distinction between the two halves of its address space. For the LPU, however, the 64-kiloword address space is split into parts of equal size (32 kilowords) and logically distributed among blocks of memory, the sum of whose memory space is far in excess of the address space of the processor. In the scheme embodied by the MAE the LPU can also access the same memory that the PPU does. This gives rise to the need for the Dual Port Memory Controller, whose function is to resolve conflicts arising when the LPU and PPU try simultaneously to access the same block of memory.

The CRT Memory Access Port accesses memory on behalf of the CRT to provide ongoing access to the information stored in the system-managed CRT buffer in block 0. The alphanumeric (i.e., nongraphic-mode) display is formed on the basis of that information, which must be reread each time the CRT screen is to be refreshed.

Neither the LPU nor the PPU is a homogeneous, monolithic entity. Each is composed of smaller functional units which are LSI chips. Among these units are a Binary Processor Chip (BPC), Input-Output Controller (IOC), and, for LPU only, an Extended Math Chip (EMC). The BPCs used in the LPU and PPU are of identical design, as are the IOCs. The main functions of a BPC are to fetch instructions from memory, execute most instructions that reference memory, execute various instructions that perform bit manipulation, and accomplish program branching. Thus, the BPCs are relatively general-purpose devices, and each serves more or less the same general function in the LPU and PPU. The main functions of the IOC are to provide I/O and instructions for manipulating firmware stacks. The reason the PPU has an IOC is to obtain both those capabilities. The LPU, however, does not do I/O; it contains an IOC merely to obtain the use of the stack instructions. The main function of the EMC is to perform BCD arithmetic. This is strictly an LPU activity; therefore the PPU is not equipped with an EMC.

Also shown in Fig. 8 is the PPU-managed I/O Data Bus and the various peripherals that are normally permanently connected to it. The manner in which I/O is accomplished is discussed in conjunction with the IOC. The notion of a select code as the address of a peripheral will be fully explained at that time. At this point, however, it is appropriate to point out that, in general, two peripherals cannot have the same select code. But the keyboard and the internal thermal printer both have select code 0. This is a special case that doesn't cause any problems, because the keyboard is strictly an input device and the printer is strictly an output device.

There now follows a description of the LPU hardware. Since the hardware description of the PPU is a subset of the LPU hardware description, the PPU will not be described separately.

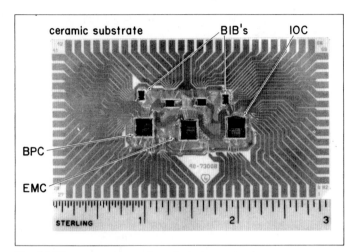

Fig. 14. The processor on its substrate.

Hardware Description of the LPU

The LPU consists of seven integrated circuits mounted on a ceramic substrate (see Fig. 14). Of these, the BPC, IOC, and EMC are N-channel MOS LSI chips. The remaining four chips

(Bi-Directional Interface Buffers, or BIBs) are entirely bipolar and serve as buffers to connect the LSI circuitry to circuitry external to the substrate.

Figure 15 is a block diagram of the LPU and PPU. All of the processing capability of the processor resides in the three LSI chips; except for inversion of the IDA Bus the four BIBs are logically powerless. The three LSI chips communicate among themselves, and also with the outside world, via a collection of control signals and a 16-bit bus called the IDA Bus (IDA stands for *instruction/data/address*). The processor uses 16-bit addressing for memory and implements a single level of indirect addressing.[1]

Memory Conventions

Most of the traffic on the IDA Bus has to do with memory. Both the address of memory locations and the contents of those locations (data and machine instructions) are transmitted over the IDA Bus. Further, memory can be physically distributed along the bus. Each of the three chips in the processor contains registers which are addressable, and of course, addressable memory also exists external to the processor.

[1]Except during interrupt, when a two-level indirect is forced. This is explained in connection with interrupts.

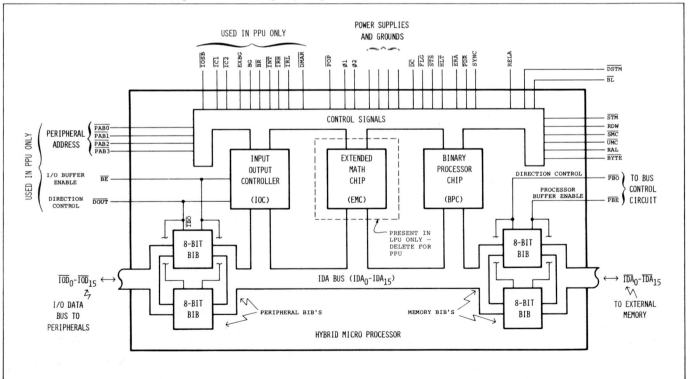

Fig. 15. Processor block diagram.

The first 32 addresses of the address space do not refer to external memory. Instead, these addresses ($0-37_8$) are reserved to designate addressable registers within the microprocessor. Figure 16 lists these registers. There are also a number of nonaddressable internal-use registers in the processor. Registers range in size from 1 to 16 bits; most are 16-bit registers.

A memory cycle involves some control lines as well as the IDA Bus. Start Memory ($\overline{STM}$) is used to initiate a memory cycle by identifying the contents of the IDA Bus as an address. Either of two memory complete signals is used to identify the conclusion of a memory cycle. These are Unsynchronized Memory Complete ($\overline{UMC}$) and Synchronized Memory Complete ($\overline{SMC}$). A line called Read/Write ($\overline{RWD}$) specifies the direction of data movement. Each element in the system decodes the addresses for which it contains addressable memory. To initiate a memory cycle, an element in the system puts the address of the desired location on the IDA Bus, sets the Read/Write line, and gives Start Memory. It is part of the system definition that whatever is on the IDA Bus when a Start Memory is given is an address of a memory (or register) location. Then, elsewhere in the system the address is decoded and recognized, and that agency begins to function as memory.

Among the several service functions performed by the BPC, for the IOC and EMC, is the generation of a signal called RAL (Register Access Line). This occurs whenever an address on the IDA Bus is within the range reserved for register designation ($0-37_8$). RAL is used by the external memory to prevent its response to any memory cycle having such an address.

General Description of the BPC

The BPC has two main functions. The first is to fetch machine instructions from memory for itself, the IOC, and the EMC. A fetched instruction may pertain to one or more of those chips. A chip that is not associated with a fetched instruction simply ignores that instruction. The second main function of the BPC is to execute the 56 instructions in its own repertoire. A condensed description of these instructions is shown in their assembly language format in Fig. 17. These instructions include general-purpose register and memory reference instructions, branching instructions, bit manipulation instructions, and some binary arithmetic instructions. Most of the BPC's instructions involve one of the two accumulator registers, A and B.

There are four addressable registers within the BPC, and they have the following functions: the A and B registers are used as accumulator registers for arithmetic operations, and also as source or destination locations for most BPC machine instructions referencing memory. The R register is an indirect pointer into an area of Read/Write memory designated to store return addresses associated with nests of subroutines encountered during program execution. The P register contains the program counter; its value is the address of the memory location from which the next machine instruction will be fetched.

Upon the completion of each instruction the program counter (P register) has been incremented by 1, except for the instructions JMP, JSM, and RET, and for SKIP instructions whose SKIP condition has been met. For those instructions the value of P will depend on the activity of the particular instruction.

Indirect Addressing Indirect addressing is a technique in which an instruction that references memory treats the first one or more references as an intermediate step in referencing the final destination. An intermediate reference yields the address of the next location to be referenced. When an intermediate location can point to yet another intermediate location, such addressing is termed *multilevel* indirect addressing. The BPC implements single-level indirect addressing for all memory references except those of a single special case. That special case involves two levels and occurs during an interrupt. Indirect addressing is *not* a property of the memory; it is a property of the chips that use the memory. Any chip that is to implement instructions employing indirect addressing must contain special "gear works" for that purpose.

To indicate indirect addressing for a memory-reference instruction, bit 15 of that particular instruction will be set. During

Octal Address	Name	Location	Description (# of Bits)
0	A	BPC	Arithmetic Accumulator (16)
1	B	BPC	Arithmetic Accumulator (16)
2	P	BPC	Program Location Counter (16)
3	R	BPC	Return Stack Pointer (16)
4	R4	IOC	Peripheral Activity Designator (—)
5	R5	IOC	Peripheral Activity Designation (—)
6	R6	IOC	Peripheral Activity Designator (—)
7	R7	IOC	Peripheral Activity Designator (—)
10	IV	IOC	Interrupt Vector (upper 12 of 16)
11	PA	IOC	Peripheral Address Register (least 4 of 16)
12	W	IOC	Working Register (16)
13	DMAPA	IOC	2 MSB = CB & DB; 4 LSB = DMA Periph. Add. Reg.
14	DMAMA	IOC	DMA Memory Address & Direction Register (16)
15	DMAC	IOC	DMA Count Register (16)
16	C	IOC	Stack Pointer (16)
17	D	IOC	Stack Pointer (16)
20-23	AR2	EMC	BCD Arithmetic Accumulator (4 × 16)
24	SE	EMC	Shift Extend Register (least 4 of 16)
25-27	X	EMC	Internal Arithmetic Register (3 X 16)
30-37	UNASSIGNED		
77770/177770	AR1	R/W	BCD Arithmetic Register (4 × 16)

* Not available for general use. Part of processes internal to a chip.

† Read register 13_8 produces:

CB and DB are actually discrete registers, and while they can only be read by reading R13, storing into R13 will not alter their values. Use the CBL, CBU, DBL and DBU machine instructions for that purpose.

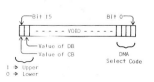

Fig. 16. The processor registers.

```
                                                                          [...] = OPTIONAL SPECIFIERS
                                                                          /  INDICATES CHOICE OF SPECIFIERS

  MEMORY REFERENCE              VALUE OF N MAY RANGE FROM -32 TO 31,
  (M IS AN ASSEMBLY LANGUAGE LABEL, OR  INCLUSIVE.  AT THE CONCLUSION OF THE
  EXPLICIT ADDRESS)             RET R IS DECREMENTED BY ONE.              RL% *±N/M [,S/,C]
  ([,I] IS THE INDIRECT SPECIFIER)                                          SKIP IF THE LEAST SIGNIFICANT
  LD% M [,I]                    EXE O ≤ M ≤ 37₈ [,I]                         BIT OF A (OR B) IS NON-ZERO.
                                 EXECUTE REGISTER M.  THE CON-
    LOAD A (OR B) FROM M.        TENTS OF ANY REGISTER CAN BE             S%P *±N/M [,S/,C]
                                 TREATED AS THE CURRENT INSTRUC-            SKIP IF A (OR B) IS POSITIVE.
  CP% M [,I]                     TION, AND EXECUTED IN THE NORMAL
                                 MANNER.  THE NEXT INSTRUCTION            S%M *±N/M [,S/,C]
    COMPARE THE CONTENTS OF M WITH   EXECUTED WILL BE THE ONE FOLLOW-       SKIP IF A (OR B) IS MINUS.
    THE CONTENTS OF A (OR B); SKIP   ING THE EXE M, UNLESS THE CODE IN
    IF UNEQUAL.                  M CAUSES A BRANCH.                       SO% *±N/M [,S/,C]
                                                                           SKIP IF OVERFLOW SET (OR CLEAR).
  AD% M [,I]                    SKIP
                                (-32<N<31, M WITHIN N OF *, * = CUR-      SE% *±N/M [,S/,C]
    ADD THE CONTENTS OF M TO A (OR B).  RENT VALUE OF P)                    SKIP IF EXTEND IS CLEAR (OR SET).
                                RZ% *±N/M      i.e., (* ± N)/(M), NOT *±(N/M)
  ST% M [,I]
                                  SKIP IF A (OR B) IS NOT ZERO.           COMPLEMENT
    STORE THE CONTENTS OF A (OR B) IN                                     TC%
    M.                          RI% *±N/M                                   TWO'S COMPLEMENT A (OR B).

  JSM M [,I]                      SKIP IF A (OR B) IS NOT ZERO, THEN      CM%
                                  INCREMENT A (OR B).
    JUMP TO SUBROUTINE.  THE CONTENTS                                       COMPLEMENT A (OR B).  THE A (OR B)
    OF THE RETURN STACK REGISTER (R)  SZ% *±N/M                             REGISTER IS REPLACED BY ITS ONE'S
    ARE INCREMENTED BY ONE AND THE                                          COMPLEMENT.
    CONTENTS OF P STORED IN R,I.    SKIP IF A (OR B) IS ZERO.
    PROGRAM EXECUTION RESUMES AT M.                                       SHIFT-ROTATE
                                SI% *±N/M                                 (-32<N<31)
  ISZ M [,I]
                                  SKIP IF A (OR B) IS ZERO, THEN          A%R N
    INCREMENT M; SKIP IF M THEN    INCREMENT A (OR B).
    EQUALS ZERO.                                                           ARITHMETIC RIGHT SHIFT OF A (OR B).  A
                                SF% *±N/M                                   (OR B) IS SHIFTED RIGHT N PLACES WITH
  AND M [,I]                                                               THE SIGN BIT (BIT 15) FILLING ALL
                                  SKIP IF FLAG LINE SET (OR CLEAR).        VACATED BIT POSITIONS.
    LOGICAL "AND" OF A AND M; THE
    RESULT IS LEFT IN A.        SD% *±N/M                                 S%R N

  DSZ M [,I]                      SKIP IF DECIMAL SET (OR CLEAR).           SHIFT A (OR B) RIGHT.  A (OR B) IS
                                                                           SHIFTED RIGHT N PLACES WITH ALL
    DECREMENT M; SKIP IF M THEN  SS% *±N/M                                  VACATED BIT POSITIONS VACATED.
    EQUALS ZERO.
                                  SKIP IF STATUS LINE SET (OR CLEAR).     S%L N
  IOR M [,I]
                                SH% *±N/M                                   SHIFT A (OR B) LEFT.  A (OR B) IS
    INCLUSIVE "OR" OF A AND M;                                             SHIFTED LEFT N PLACES WITH ALL
    THE RESULT IS LEFT IN A.       SKIP IF HALT LINE SET (OR CLEAR).       VACATED BIT POSITIONS CLEARED.

  JMP M [,I]                    ALTER                                     R%R N
                                (IF EITHER S OR C IS PRESENT THE
    JUMP TO M.  PROGRAM EXECUTION  TESTED BIT IS SET OR CLEARED AFTER       ROTATE A (OR B) RIGHT.  A (OR B) IS
    CONTINUES AT LOCATION M.     THE TEST)                                  ROTATED RIGHT N PLACES, WITH BIT 0
                                SL% *±N/M [,S/,C]                           ROTATING INTO BIT 15.
  RET N [,P]
                                  SKIP IF THE LEAST SIGNIFICANT
    RETURN.  A READ R,I OCCURS.  THAT   BIT OF A (OR B) IS ZERO.
    PRODUCES THE ADDRESS (<P>) OF THE
    LATEST JSM THAT OCCURRED.  THE BPC
    THEN JUMPS TO ADDRESS <P> + N.  THE
```

Fig. 17. BPC machine-instructions.

execution, the contents of the referenced location will be read and its entire 16-bit contents treated as the address of the final destination to be read from or written into.

Memory Reference Instructions and Page Addressing   Machine instructions fetched from memory are 16-bit instructions. Some of those bits represent the particular type to which that instruction belongs. Other bits differentiate the instruction from others of the same type. If a BPC machine instruction is one that involves reading from, storing into, or otherwise manipulating the contents of a memory location, it is said to be a memory reference instruction. *Load into A* (LDA) and *store from B* (STB) are examples. Each memory reference instruction contains 10 bits to represent the address of the location that is to be referenced by the instruction. Those 10 bits represent one of $1,024_{10}$ locations on either the *base page* or the *current page* of memory; an additional bit (the B/C bit) in the machine instruction indicates which. As far

as the processor is concerned, its base page is always a particular, nonchanging range of addresses that is exactly $1,024_{10}$ in number. A memory-reference machine instruction fetched from any location in memory (i.e., from any value of the program counter) may reference directly (i.e., without using indirect addressing) any location on the base page. The base-page addresses are 000000_8–000777_8 and 177000_8–177777_8.

The reason the base page was split was to provide a convenient means to ensure that half of it would be in ROM and half in R/W memory, without resorting to special decoding circuits. By separating the base page as described the desired division comes for free, simply by putting the right kind of memory at the right addresses.

What goes in a machine instruction's 10-bit address field is a displacement from some reference location, as an actual complete address has too many bits in it to fit in the instruction. Also, it is the responsibility of the assembler to control the B/C bit at the time the machine instruction is assembled. It does this easily enough by determining whether the address of the operand (or its "value") of an instruction is in the range 177000_8 through 177777_8 or 0 through 777_8.

For base-page references the 10-bit field is sufficient to indicate completely which of the 1,024 locations on the base page is to be referenced. The 32 register addresses are considered a part of the base page.

Current-page addressing refers to memory-reference instructions which reference a location which is not on the base page. Since there are more than 1,024 locations that are not the base page, the 10-bit field by itself is not enough to completely specify the exact location involved. Also, there are two types of current pages. Each type is also $1,024_{10}$ consecutive words in length. The value of P determines the particular collection of addresses that are the current page at any given time. This is done in one of two distinct ways, as determined by the signal called RELA. Depending upon RELA, the BPC is said to address memory in the *relative* mode or in the *absolute* mode. Both the BPC in the LPU and the BPC in the PPU operate in the relative addressing mode.

In the absolute mode of addressing the memory address space is divided into a base page and 64 possible current pages. The possible current pages are the consecutive $1,024_{10}$ word groups beginning with 000000_8. The possible current pages can be numbered 0 through 63_{10}. Thus, the "zero page" is addresses 000000_8–001777_8. Note that the base page is *not* the same as the zero page; the base page overlaps pages 0 and 63.

In relative addressing there are as many possible current pages as there are values of the program counter. In the relative addressing mode a current page is the 512_{10} consecutive locations prior to (that is, having lower-valued addresses than) the current location (value of P), and the 511_{10} consecutive locations following the current location.

During the execution of each memory-reference machine instruction referencing the current page, the BPC uses the value of the P register to form a full 16-bit address based on the 10 bits of address contained within the instruction. How the supplied 10 bits are manipulated before becoming part of the actual address, and how the remaining 6 bits are supplied, depends upon whether the addressing mode is relative or absolute. Base-page addressing requires different manipulation but is the same in either mode.

Subroutines The processor implements subroutines in the following way. The *Jump Subroutine* (JSM) instruction is used to cause a jump (change in value of P) to the start of the subroutine. The BPC saves the value of P that corresponds to the word of programming that is the JSM. That value is saved in a section of Read/Write memory called the *return stack*.

The return stack is a group of contiguous locations whose starting address less 1 was initially stored in the R register (in the BPC). Thus, R is an indirect pointer. What a JSM does is to increment the value in R and then use that new value as the address at which to store the value of P. Once this activity is complete, P is actually set to the address of the first word of the subroutine and its execution commences.

A subroutine is terminated with a RET n instruction. The essence of this instruction is to read the location that R points to, set P to that value plus n, and then decrement R. The most common return is a RET 1. Different values of n permit different returns corresponding to error or other special conditions. For instance, interrupt service routines are generally terminated with a RET 0.

Subroutines can be nested as deep as the size of the return stack will allow. The subroutines themselves can be in either ROM or Read/Write memory.

Flags The BPC is capable of branching based on the condition of each of four signals externally supplied to the chip. These signals are Decimal Carry (DC), Halt (HLT), Flag (FLG), and Status (STS). In the LPU the EMC acts as a source for Decimal Carry, which represents an overflow condition during certain arithmetic operations performed by the EMC. There is no EMC in the PPU, and the DC signal in the PPU is controlled by the CRT. It is used to indicate the duration of CRT retrace.

Bus Requests and Interrupts

Bus Request and Interrupt are two protocols that involve interchip communication. Bus Request ($\overline{BR}$) provides a way for a chip in the processor, or even a device external to the processor (such as the CRT), to request unfettered use of the IDA Bus. A signal called the Bus Grant (BG) is generated if all chips and any other interested entities agree to allow it. The requesting agency can use the IDA Bus for whatever purpose it wants (typically to do memory cycles). During the time that Bus Grant is in effect all chips suspend their activity. Bus Grant can be given even in the middle of the execution of an instruction. Because of this, the chips do not grant a Bus Request indiscriminately. Furthermore, a Bus Grant not requested by the IOC is used by the IOC to create Extended Bus Grant (EXBG), which is routed from chip to chip in a definite order; chips or other entities not at the top of the chain can exercise the right not to pass along the signal. This allows a Bus Request from the IOC to have a higher priority than any entity farther down the chain. Even if both are requesting the Bus, the IOC can "steal" EXBG by not passing it along. Farther down the chain from the IOC, BG serves to indicate only that the IDA Bus is being granted to somebody; a particular requesting device must wait until it sees EXBG before it can use the bus.

An entity on the Bus may ground BG as long as BG is not already being given. This allows any entity anywhere on the chain to protect its own access to the Bus against all agencies. Further, the BPC itself refuses to issue a BG as long as any memory cycle is in progress.

During an instruction fetch a line called *interrupt* ($\overline{\text{INT}}$) can signal the other chips to which the IOC has agreed to allow an interrupt requested by a peripheral. The management of this decision is complicated, but once the decision is made, the IOC signals the BPC with $\overline{\text{INT}}$. This has to occur during a certain period of time ending with the end of the instruction fetch. (A signal called SYNC identifies the instruction fetch.)

What the chips in the system must do when an interrupt occurs is to abort the execution of the instruction just fetched (it will be fetched again, later). The $\overline{\text{INT}}$ causes the BPC to execute the instruction JSM 10_8-indirect in place of the fetched instruction. Register address 10_8 is located in the IOC, and is the Interrupt Vector register (IV). That register is a pointer into a stack of indirect addresses for the starting locations for the various interrupt service routines. These routines handle the traffic needed by the interrupting peripheral. A special mechanism in the IOC sets the bottom four bits of IV to correspond to the select code or peripheral address of the particular peripheral that requested the interrupt. Thus IV points to different service routines, according to which peripheral has interrupted.

The JSM 10_8-indirect causes the value of P for the aborted instruction to be saved on the return stack. A RET 0 at the end of the service routine results in that very instruction's being fetched over again, at the conclusion of the service routine.

General Description of the IOC

The IOC has two main functions. One is to manage the transfer of information between the processor and peripheral devices. This is done by providing capabilities classified as Standard I/O, Interrupt, and Direct Memory Access (DMA). The second main function is to provide machine instructions allowing software management of stacks in Read/Write memory. Figure 18 is a condensed description of the machine instructions in the IOC's repertoire.

```
                                    [...] = OPTIONAL SPECIFIERS
                                    / INDICATES CHOICE OF SPECIFIERS

DMA GROUP                           P%% REG. 0-7 [,I/,D]
SDO                                   PLACE THE ENTIRE WORD (W) OR THE RIGHT
  SET DMA OUTWARDS.                   HALF (B) OF REG. INTO THE STACK POINTED
                                      AT BY C OR D.
SDI
  SET DMA INWARDS.                  W%% REG. 0-7 [,I/,D]
                                      WITHDRAW AN ENTIRE WORD (W) OR A BYTE
DMA                                   (B) FROM THE STACK POINTED AT BY C OR
  ENABLE THE DMA MODE, CANCELS PCM    D AND PUT IT INTO REG.  A BYTE WILL BE
  AND DDR.                            PLACED INTO THE RIGHT HALF OF REG.

PCM                                 CBL
  ENABLE THE PULSE COUNT MODE, CANCELS  C BLOCK LOWER.  CLEARS THE CB
  DMA AND DDR.                        REGISTER.

DDR                                 CBU
  DISABLE DATA REQUEST, CANCELS DMA   C BLOCK UPPER.  SETS THE CB REGISTER.
  AND PCM.
                                    DBL
INTERRUPT                             D BLOCK LOWER.  CLEARS THE DB
EIR                                   REGISTER.
  ENABLE THE INTERRUPT SYSTEM, CANCELS
  DIR.                              DBU
                                      D BLOCK UPPER.  SETS THE DB REGISTER.
DIR
  DISABLE THE INTERRUPT SYSTEM,     I/O
  CANCEL EIR.                       MEM. REF. INST. REG. 4-7 [,I]
                                      INITIATE AN I/O BUS CYCLE.
STACK
   I = INCREMENT STACK POINTER      STACK INST. REG. 4-7 [,I/,D]
   D = DECREMENT STACK POINTER        INITIATE AN I/O BUS CYCLE.
```

Fig. 18. IOC machine-instructions.

General Information about I/O The IOC allows up to 16 peripheral devices to be present at one time. Each peripheral device is connected to the I/O Data (IOD) Bus, Peripheral Address Bus, and the various control signals necessary for that particular device's operation. Individual I/O operations (exchanges of single words) occur between the processor and one peripheral at a time, although interrupt and DMA modes of operation can cause automatic interleaving of individual operations. A select code transmitted by the Peripheral Address Bus ($\overline{\text{PAB0}}$–$\overline{\text{PAB3}}$) identifies which of the 16 devices is the object of an individual I/O operation.

In addition, the peripheral interface is the source of the Flag and Status bits for the BPC instructions SFS, SFC, SSS, and SSC. Since there can be many interfaces, but only one each of Flag and Status, only the interface addressed by the select code is allowed to ground these lines. Their logic is such that if the addressed peripheral is not present on the I/O Bus, Status and Flag are logically false.

$\overline{\text{IC1}}$ and $\overline{\text{IC2}}$ are two control lines that are sent to each peripheral interface by the IOC. The state of these two lines during the non-DMA transfer of information can be decoded to mean something by the interface. Just what "something" will be is subject to agreement between the firmware designer and the interface designer; it can be anything they want, and it might not be the same for different interfaces.

I/O Bus Cycles The IOC's repertoire contains no machine instructions dedicated to I/O operations. That is, there is no specific "output instruction," and no specific "input instruction." Existing machine instructions cause I/O by referencing certain register addresses that cause I/O *bus cycles*. An I/O bus cycle is an exchange of a word between the IDA Bus and IOD Bus, via the Peripheral BIBs. The peripheral involved is specified by the contents of the 4-bit PA register, which controls the peripheral address lines. I/O bus cycles are termed read or write I/O bus cycles, depending upon whether information is being read from or written into a peripheral. Each of the three modes of I/O operation (Standard I/O, Interrupt, and DMA) utilizes I/O bus cycles. The explanation of the various modes of I/O amounts to showing different ways to initiate I/O bus cycles.

I/O bus cycles *do not* involve handshake. It is the responsibility of the firmware not to initiate an I/O bus cycle involving a device that is not ready. To do so will result in lost data, and there will be no warning that this has happened.

Standard I/O   Standard I/O is I/O that has been explicitly programmed by the system programmer, using explicit assembly language coding. Standard I/O involves three activities:

1   Setting the peripheral address (in the PA register)
2   Investigating the status of the peripheral
3   Initiating an I/O Bus Cycle

During standard I/O operation, an I/O bus cycle is initiated by any machine instruction that incorporates a reference to one of addresses R4 through R7 ("in" the IOC). One way that can be done is with a BPC memory-reference instruction: for instance, STA R4 (for a write cycle), or LDA R4 (for a read cycle). However, there are no addresses R4 through R7. The use of addresses 4–7 is just a signal to the IOC to initiate an I/O bus cycle. Each different address produces a different combination of $\overline{IC1}$ and $\overline{IC2}$.

The Interrupt System   When the processor grants an interrupt, the program segment currently being executed is automatically suspended, and there is an automatic JSM to an *interrupt service (sub)routine* that corresponds to the device that has interrupted. The service routine uses Standard I/O to accomplish its task.

The IOC allows two levels of interrupt, and has an accompanying two levels of priority. Priority is determined by select code: select codes $0–7_8$ are the lower level (priority level 1), and select codes $10_8–17_8$ are the higher level (priority level 2). Within a priority level all devices are of "equal" priority, and operation is on a first-come–first-served basis; a level-1 device cannot be interrupted by another level-1 device, but only by a level-2 device. However, priorities are not equal in the case of simultaneous requests by two or more devices on the same level. In such an instance the device with the higher-numbered select code has priority. With no interrupt service routine in progress, any interrupt will be granted.

Devices request an interrupt by grounding one of two interrupt request lines ($\overline{IRL}$ and $\overline{IRH}$—one for each priority level). The IOC determines the requesting select code by means of an interrupt poll. If the IOC grants the interrupt, it saves on an internal stack the existing select code located in PA, puts the interrupting select code in PA, and does a JSM-Indirect through an interrupt table to get to the interrupt service routine. [The top of this stack *is* the Peripheral Address register (PA-11_8).] The stack is deep enough to hold the select code in use prior to any interrupts, plus the select codes for two levels of interrupt.

It is the responsibility of the firmware to maintain an *interrupt table* of 16 consecutive words, starting at some Read/Write Memory address whose four least significant bits are 0s. The words in the interrupt table are set to the starting addresses of the various interrupt service routines for use with the 16 different select codes. When a peripheral is allowed to interrupt, its select code is used to determine which interrupt service routine to jump to. The interrupt service routine then handles the I/O operations needed by the interrupting device.

The firmware must also store the address of the first word of the interrupt table in the IV register (Interrupt Vector register, address 10, located in the IOC). Those contents will merge with the interrupting select code to produce the address of the appropriate table entry. A two-level indirect jump is used to arrive at the interrupt service routine. This happens automatically, because the BPC aborts its instruction fetch and generates a JSM IV, 1 as part of what it does during an interrupt, and because the IOC forces the BPC to do two consecutive "first-level" indirect accesses.

It is difficult to say specific things about interrupt service routines in general; much depends upon the particulars of the host software system. The next few paragraphs examine some generalities relating to interrupt service routines.

The first observation is on the number of service routines. In general, there is not a single service routine for each select code, or even for each type of peripheral. The usual case is collections of routines that perform related functions within the needs of a certain class of peripheral activity; each class of activity has its own collection.

For instance, it is unlikely that there will be a single interrupt service routine for a disk. On the customer's level there are many commands in the disk's operating system. On the firmware level there are a series of routines that perform "fundamental units" of activity, where each fundamental unit involves some amount of I/O. Most commands in the user's disk operating system are made up of a series of these fundamental units of activity. Fundamental units of activity for the disk are things like moving the head to a given track, reading a given sector from a track into such and such a buffer, and writing from such and such a buffer into a given sector.

Assume a fairly involved user's command for a disk is to be performed, one that requires reading the directory on the disk to determine the location of a certain file on the disk and then loading that file into memory. The series of routines here include moving the head to the start of the directory, reading through the information in the directory sector by sector until the information about the desired file is found, moving the head to the file's location, reading its header, reading its first sector, etc.

Each service routine is told or already knows which service routine follows it for the particular high-level task at hand, and if it has a choice based on the way events turn out (error conditions etc.), it knows how to handle that, too. As each new step in the sequence requiring a different interrupt service routine is reached, the concluding routine changes the appropriate entry of the interrupt table to the starting address of the next service routine. In this way a versatile collection of interrupt service routines can serve many purposes.

The computer can be almost anywhere in its internal coding when an interrupt is granted. Since the code is suspended, with JSM, it is obvious that the way to get back to the right spot is with a RET 0,P. (The ,P instructs the IOC to return to the select code in use prior to the interrupt.) But it will do no good to come back if the items in memory related to the routine are not the same. *The interrupt service routine must save and later restore any memory location that will be directly or indirectly disturbed by the activity of the service routine.* This could include the extend and overflow registers of the BPC, decimal carry and shift-extend of the EMC, and possibly CB and DB of the IOC.

The entire interrupt system can be turned off by a DIR machine instruction. After this instruction is given the IOC will refuse to grant any interrupts whatsoever until the interrupt system is turned back on with EIR. While the IOC will not grant any interrupts, the RET 0,P works as usual so that interrupt service routines may be safely terminated, even while the interrupt system is turned off.

Direct Memory Access   Direct memory access is a means to exchange entire collections of data between memory and peripherals. Such a collection must be a series of consecutive memory locations. Once started, the process is automatic; it is done under control of hardware in the IOC, and regulated by the interface.

The DMA process can transfer data in two ways: single words are transferred one at a time, on a cycle-steal basis; or strings of words are transferred consecutively in a burst mode. In either instance data are transferred one word at a time. To transfer a word, a peripheral signals the IOC, which then requests control of the IDA Bus with $\overline{BR}$. That results in an external halt in all other system activity on the bus for the duration of the peripheral's request for DMA service. Herein lies the difference between burst mode and cycle-steal operation: in cycle-steal operation the peripheral ceases to request service after one word is transferred, and requests service again when ready, while in the burst mode the request is held to allow a series of high-speed consecutive transfers to occur.

During a DMA transfer of a collection of data, the IOC knows the next memory location involved, whether to input or output, which select code to use, and (possibly) whether or not the transfer of the entire collection is complete. This information is in registers in the IOC, which are set up by the firmware before the peripheral is told to begin DMA activity. After that, actual transfers are initiated at the request of the interface.

The DMA process is altogether independent of the operation of standard I/O and of the interrupt system and, except for theft of the IDA Bus for memory cycles, does not interfere with them in any way.

The four least significant bits of DMAPA specify the select code which is to be the peripheral side of the DMA activity. During an

Name	Address	Meaning
DMAPA	(=13)	DMA peripheral address
DMAMA	(=14)	DMA memory address
DMAC	(=15)	DMA count
DMAD	......	DMA direction

I/O bus cycle given in response to a DMA data request, the content of the PAB Lines will be determined by the four least significant bits of DMAPA rather than by the PA register.

DMAMA is set to the address of the first word in the block to be transferred. This is the lowest-numbered address; after each transfer DMAMA is automatically incremented by the IOC. A separate one-bit register (DMAD) exists to specify the direction of the transfer; DMAD is controlled by its own set and clear machine instructions and is not addressable.

DMAC can, if desired, be set to $n - 1$, where n is the number of words to be transferred. During each transfer the count in DMAC is decremented. During the last transfer DMAC goes negative and the IOC automatically generates signals which the interface can use to recognize the last transfer. In the case of a transfer of unknown size, DMAC should be set to a very large count, to thwart the automatic termination mechanism. In such cases it is up to the peripheral to identify the last transfer.

Once the control registers are set up, a "start DMA" command is given to the interface through standard programmed I/O. The "start DMA" command is an output I/O bus cycle with a particular combination of $\overline{IC1}$, $\overline{IC2}$, and (perhaps) a particular bit pattern in the transmitted word. The patterns themselves are subject to agreement between the firmware designer and the interface designer. Sophisticated peripherals using DMA in both directions will have two start commands, one for input and one for output. It is also possible that other information can be encoded in the start command (the number of words to be transferred, for instance).

Stack Operations   A stack that is implemented in firmware is simply a series of consecutive memory locations accessed indirectly through a pointer. The entries in the stack do not change their physical locations in the memory during additions and deletions. Instead, the value of the pointer is incremented or decremented.

The IOC implements some firmware stack-manipulation machine instructions. Two registers are provided as stack pointers: C and D. There are eight place and withdraw instructions for putting things into stacks and getting them out. Furthermore, the place and withdraw instructions can handle full 16-bit words, or pack 8-bit bytes in words of a stack. And last, there are provisions for automatic incrementing and decrementing of the stack pointer registers, C and D.

The mnemonics for the place and withdraw instructions are easy to decipher. All place instructions begin with P, and all withdraw instructions begin with W. The next character is a W or

B, for word or byte. The next character is either a C or D, depending upon which stack pointer is to be used. There are eight combinations, and each is a legitimate instruction.

The place and withdraw instructions outwardly resemble the memory reference instructions of the BPC: a mnemonic followed by an operand that is understood as an address, followed by an optional, I or, D. The range of values that the operand may have is restricted, however. The value of the operand must be between 0 and 7, inclusive. Thus, the place and withdraw instructions can place from, or withdraw into, the first eight registers. These are A, B, P, R, *and R4 through R7*. Therefore, the place and withdraw instructions can initiate I/O bus cycles; *they can do I/O.*

Regardless of which of ,I (increment) or ,D (decrement) is specified, a place instruction will do the increment or decrement of the pointer prior to the actual place operation. Withdraw instructions do the increment or decrement after actual withdraw operation. The reason for this is that it always leaves the stack with the pointer pointing at the new "top of the stack," and allows intermixing of place and withdraw instructions without adjustment of the pointer.

Because the stack in memory is composed of words rather than bytes, some means is required to extend the addressing of the pointer registers to include designation of bytes within the addressed word.

Left-right indication of bytes is accomplished with a signal called $\overline{BL}$. $\overline{BL}$ (Byte Left Not) is in turn controlled by bit 0 of either the C or D register. Sixteen-bit addressing is maintained by providing an additional 1-bit register for use with each stack pointer register. The nonaddressable registers are called CB (C Block) and DB (D Block). They are designated *block* because, as the most significant bit of the word pointer value, they divide the address space into two halves, or blocks. It is unfortunate that this terminology was chosen (it was done before the MAE was developed). Do not confuse those blocks with block 0 through block 3 of the Memory Address Extension scheme.

During the automatic increment or decrement to the pointer register, CB and DB function as most significant seventeenth bits of their respective registers. An advantage of having the bit that designates the byte be the least significant bit is that it simplifies the process of arithmetic computation upon byte addresses.

The CB and DB registers can be set to their initial values by machine instructions for setting and clearing each register. For instance, DBU (D Block Upper) sets the DB register; CBL (C Block Lower) clears the CB register.

General Description of the EMC

The Extended Math Chip (EMC) provides 15 instructions. Eleven of these operate on BCD-coded 3-word mantissa data. Two operate on blocks of data of from 1 to 16 words. One is a binary multiply and one clears the Decimal Carry (DC) register. A condensed description of these machine instructions is shown in Fig. 19.

Unless specified otherwise, the contents of registers A, B, SE, and DC are not changed by the execution of any of the EMC's instructions.

AR1 is the label of the 4-word arithmetic register located in R/W memory, locations 177770_8 through 177773_8. The assembler predefines the symbol AR1 as address 177770_8.

AR2 is the label of a 4-word arithmetic accumulator register located within the EMC, and occupying register addresses 20_8 through 23_8. The assembler predefines the symbol AR2 as address 20_8.

SE is the label for the 4-bit shift-extended register, located within the EMC. Although SE is addressable and can be read from and stored into, its primary use is as internal intermediate storage during those EMC instructions that read something from, or put something into, A0–A3. The assembler predefines SE as 24_8.

DC is the mnemonic for the 1-bit decimal-carry register located within the EMC. DC is set by the carry output of the decimal adder. Sometimes DC is part of the actual computation, as well as being a repository for overflow. In such cases the initial value of DC affects the result. However, DC will usually be zero at the beginning of such an instruction. The firmware sees to that by various means. DC does not have a register address. Instead, it is the object of the BPC instructions SDS and SDC (Skip if Decimal Carry Set and Skip if Decimal Carry Clear) and the EMC instruction CDC (Clear Decimal Carry).

It takes a special mechanism to handle BCD numbers. Done in firmware alone, such a mechanism would be slow and cumbersome. The EMC supplies some useful operations on portions of BCD floating-point numbers. This trims the mechanism in size and speeds it up significantly.

The EMC can perform operations on 12-digit BCD-encoded floating-point numbers. Such numbers occupy 4 words of memory, and the various parts of a number are put into specific portions of the 4 words, as shown in Fig. 20. The exponent and mantissa signs (E_s and M_s, respectively) are encoded as 0 and 1 for positive and negative, respectively. All the digits D_1 through D_{12} are encoded in BCD, while the exponent is a 10-bit signed 2's complement number. D_1 is the most significant digit, and D_{12} is the least significant digit. A decimal point is assumed to exist between D_1 and D_2.

Except for intermediate results within the individual arithmetic operations, D_1 will never be 0 unless the entire number is 0. Sometimes, after each individual arithmetic operation the answer needs to be normalized; that is, the digits of the answer need to be shifted toward D_1 until D_1 is no longer 0. The exponent then needs to be adjusted to reflect the change.

An important consideration concerning BCD arithmetic, as implemented by the processor, is that mantissas are represented

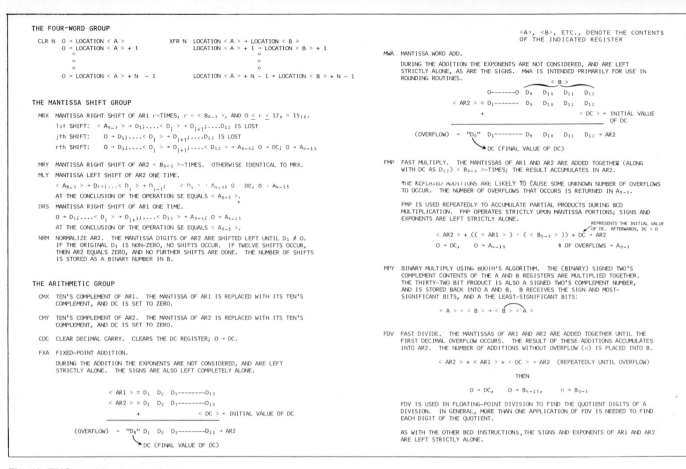

Fig. 19. EMC machine-instructions.

FLOATING-POINT DATA FORMAT.

ADDRESS	15	14	13	12	11	10	9	8	7	6	5	4	3	2	1	0
M	E_s	TWO'S COMPLEMENT EXPONENT									EMPTY					M_s
M + 1	D_1				D_2				D_3				D_4			
M + 2	D_5				D_6				D_7				D_8			
M + 3	D_9				D_{10}				D_{11}				D_{12}			

THE INTERNAL FLOATING POINT REPRESENTATION OF
.003587219 (= 3.587219×10^{-3}).

ADDRESS	15	14	13	12	11	10	9	8	7	6	5	4	3	2	1	0
M	1	1	1	1	1	1	1	1	0	1	0	0	0	0	0	0
M + 1	0011				0101				1000				0111			
M + 2	0010				0001				1001				0000			
M + 3	0000				0000				0000				0000			

Fig. 20. Floating-point data format.

in a sign/magnitude format. Ten's complements are used by the firmware in the computational processes, but only as an intermediate step. Furthermore, it is done in such a way that the automatic generation of the correct sign of a sum does not occur. There is also the frequent need to recomplement an answer.

AR2 frequently functions as an accumulator for EMC operations on BCD numbers, much as the A and B registers are accumulators for the instructions ADA and ADB.

V. Memory Address Extension

General Considerations

The essence of a memory address extention scheme is the concatenation of additional upper address bits to the addresses sent to memory by the processor. A variety of schemes have been devised, and many are not unlike the one to be described. In particular, the use of registers to specify the values of the additional bits is very common. Simple schemes simply always use the contents of such a register to expand the address. More flexibility than this was needed for the 9845A.

It was recognized that certain kinds of memory contents would always be grouped together. That is, the main operating system (whose code is in ROM), the various user's programs (in R/W), operating system data, user's data, and option ROM coding are all occupants of groups of memory disparate but contiguous within themselves. Furthermore, these separate collections frequently need access to each other. The occasions when operating-system code wishes to access the user's program, or when the user's program wishes to access the user's data, are occasions when it would be desirable to have some sort of automatic mechanism for changing the values of the additional address bits. Not only would this save a lot of code (and execution time) otherwise used for manipulating the contents of the address extension registers, but it can also provide an external structure useful in organizing the architecture of the internal software system.

The key features of the memory address extension scheme explained below are these. First, there are several registers used to determine the values of the additional address bits. There is a means to identify the purpose for which a memory cycle is being performed: instruction fetch, indirect reference, base-page reference, etc. Each such purpose can invoke different registers, each providing different and previously determined additional address bits. Note that this is not done simply on a machine instruction–to–machine instruction basis. The process is automatic on a memory cycle–by–memory cycle basis. This is a very important distinction because it allows programmers to let the MAE hardware do the work for them as their program runs, freeing them from constantly giving machine language instructions to a less automatic address extension device.

Second, the MAE hardware is responsive to the most significant bit of the address produced by the processor. By controlling the value of this bit (at programming and assembly time for direct references and at run time via programmer algorithms for indirect accesses), the programmer can signal the MAE hardware whether the additional address bits are to be selected according to the various registers mentioned above, or are to be selected from among fixed and predetermined values. (It could as easily have been from a second collection of additional registers, but this added level of flexibility was deemed unnecessary for the 9845A.) In this way, code executing at addresses in one-half the processor's address space can easily access data in the other half—but the two halves of the processor's address space are represented by a preselected range of memory addresses, on the one hand, and by an arbitrary range of memory address anywhere in memory, on the other. This is of great utility in an operating system whose controlling programming has to be able to quickly access memory anywhere in the system, or in a system where code to be executed can be located anywhere in memory.

As shown in Fig. 8, the computer has a memory with 128 kilowords, yet each processor has the inherent ability to address only 64 kilowords. On the surface it might seem that each

processor handles half the memory, but that is not so. Instead, the memory is divided into four 32-kiloword blocks.

The LPU's 64-kiloword address space is split into two 32-kiloword blocks, as shown in Fig. 21. The Memory Address Extender (MAE) embodies a set of conventions to dynamically determine which blocks make up the two halves of the processor's address space. These conventions involve the processor's most significant addresses bit, the type of memory cycle (i.e., for what purpose—instruction fetch, indirect reference, etc.), and the contents of some additional registers in the MAE. Those registers are R34, R35, and R37 (each is named for its octal address). These each have two bits. The size of the registers is related to the number of blocks managed by the MAE; in principle those registers could be 16 bits each, allowing a possible 64K blocks of 32 kilowords each.

System programmers have exclusive control of the contents of R34–R37. In this way they can control what particular blocks are accessed as the MAE implements its conventions.

The memory address extension scheme is performed for the LPU only. The address space for the PPU is exactly 64K. It just so happens that the bottom half of that address space is the same physical memory that the LPU calls block 1, and that the upper half is the same as what the LPU calls block 0. This arrangement is somewhat arbitrary and was chosen for convenience in coordinating LPU and PPU activities. Bear in mind that the PPU has no connection with the MAE. The function of the MAE is, in principle, altogether separate from the notion of having the processors share memory. If the computer had only the LPU, it would still (presumably) have the MAE. Also, the problems

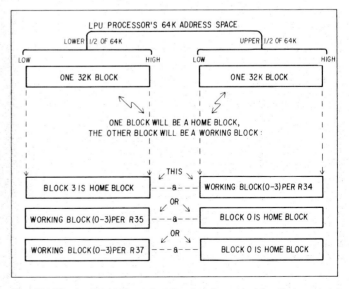

Fig. 21. Block addressing structure implemented by the memory address extender (MAE).

arising from both processors' trying, at the same time, to access block 0 or block 1, and the subsequent need for a dual-port memory controller, are not related to memory address extension.

Basic Principles

The LPU's processor, in terms of its internal architecture and operation, knows absolutely nothing of the memory address extension scheme. Regardless of how many blocks are implemented by the MAE, the LPU understands only a single 64K address space. Yet it is typical for a memory-reference machine instruction for the BPC (refer to Fig. 17) to be fetched from (i.e., located in) one block while its operand (the location in memory referenced) is in a different block. Such an instance requires automatic block switching by the MAE during the execution of the memory-reference instruction. Figure 22 illustrates the various conditions under which the various blocks are accessed.

An understanding of Fig. 22 requires the notion of home blocks and working blocks. A home block is a block that is always the accessed block whenever some particular condition is met. The various home block designations are fixed and cannot be changed. (The foregoing does not mean that certain blocks are always home blocks. Rather, particular circumstances always access certain blocks as home blocks. But any block can also be accessed as a working block, too.) A working block is one that is designated according to the contents of R34–R37. The circumstances which determine which block is the home block also determines which of R34 through R37 is used to identify the working block.

As an example, block 3 is the home block for instruction fetches, while R34 designates the working block for instruction fetches. In other words, the programmer can execute code in block 3 by accessing it as home block, or, execute code out of any other block by setting R34 to its block number and accessing that code as working-block code.

Figure 22 shows that there are three different categories of memory cycles: instruction fetches etc.; IOC and EMC memory references etc.; and bus grants. The MAE listens to the nature of the traffic on the IDA Bus and constantly classifies it according to these categories. Each category can result in an access to either the permanently associated home block or the programmer-designated working block. The most significant bit of the address determines which. That address bit was programmer-controllable at the time the code being executed was assembled.

Some Special Considerations

Observe that, by its address, the upper half of the LPU's base page has the form of a working-block reference. It would appear that there could be four different upper halves, one for each setting of R34. However, in this operating system it is inconvenient to have multiple instances of the upper half of the base page. Accordingly, the MAE automatically routes all references to the upper half of the base page (which it recognizes by its very high addresses) onto block 0. The PPU, of course, has its own base page. See Fig. 23.

Whenever any part of the system addresses a location whose address falls within the range 0–37_8, inclusive, the BPC generates a signal called RAL. This line is used by the bulk memory to prevent itself from responding; this allows the physical location of those addresses to be distributed throughout the system. This causes no problem with R34-type block allocations, as in these cases the addressing space occupied by the registers maps into the home block; and for any block allocation there is only ever one home block. But for register references via indirect addressing, or by the IOC or EMC, some wasted physical memory locations result because it is the working block that has the address space of the registers. So those locations, *in each block*, cannot be accessed. A similar condition exists for R37-type block allocations. These and other details of MAE operation are shown in Fig. 23.

These facts summarize MAE operation in the absence of a bus grant:

1 The MAE knows which memory cycles are instruction fetches.

2 If an instruction is not a BPC memory-reference instruction, its associated memory accesses are done thus:
   a Home block is block 0.
   b Working block is determined by R35.
   c Bit 15 equal to 1 implies home block; bit 15 equal to 0 implies working block.

3 If an instruction is a BPC memory-reference instruction, its associated memory accesses are done thus:

THESE CONDITIONS PREVAIL: FOR THESE TYPES OF MEMORY CYCLES:	THE MAE LISTENS TO THE NATURE OF THE MEMORY CYCLE TRAFFIC AND IMPLEMENTS THESE BLOCK ALLOCATIONS:		
	HOME BLOCK IS DESIGNATED BY:	HOME BLOCK IS:	WORKING BLOCK IS DESIGNATED BY:
ALL INSTRUCTION FETCHES, ALL LINK-POINTER FETCHES FOR INDIRECT REFERENCES, AND ALL BPC DIRECT REFERENCES	ADDRESS BIT 15=0	3 / LOWER 1/2 BASE PAGE IN BLOCK 3	UPPER 1/2 BASE PAGE AUTOMATICALLY IN BLOCK 0 / R34
IOC AND EMC MEMORY REFERENCES, AND BPC INDIRECT FINAL DESTINATION FETCHES	ADDRESS BIT 15=1	0	R35
BUS GRANT (TESTER)	ADDRESS BIT 15=1	0	R37

Fig. 22. Table of simplified MAE operation.

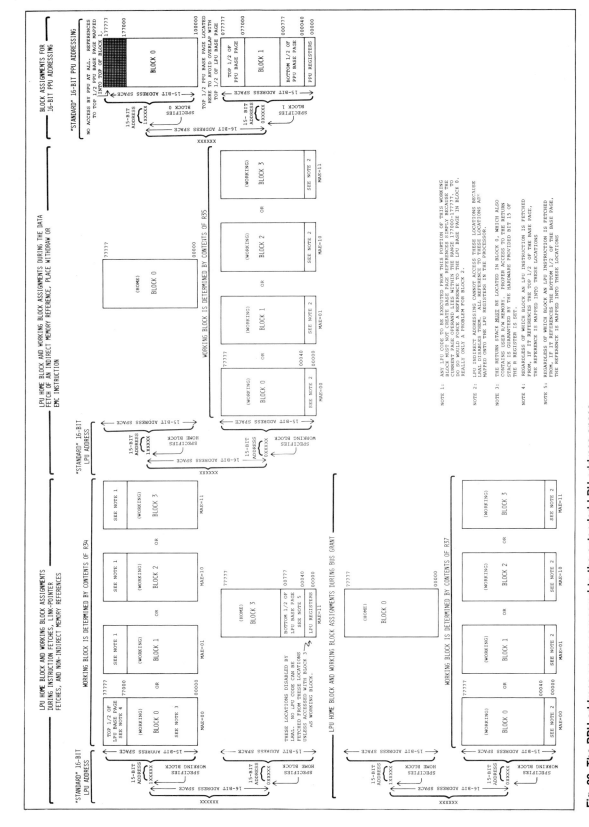

Fig. 23. The PPU address space compared to the extended LPU address space.

529

a   Current-page nonindirect references are almost always made to the same block the instruction was fetched from.

b   Base-page nonindirect references are made to the particular part of the base page specified.

c   Block 3 contains the lower half of the base page and block 0 has the upper half, regardless of which working block is specified.

d   For indirect references the link pointer is accessed according to whether it is on the current page or on the base page, as described above, but the access to the final destination location is made according to the block allocation rules for IOC and EMC instructions.

These facts summarize memory access during a bus grant:

1   The MAE remembers which block allocation scheme was suspended in order to do the bus grant and will correctly restore the suspended mode when that activity is completed.

2   During a bus grant:
   a   Home block is block 0.
   b   Working block is determined by R37.
   c   Bit 15 equal to 1 implies home block; bit 15 equal to 0 implies working block.

VI.   Description of the Display System

General Description

The display is a dual raster-scan CRT display. A 12-in, high-resolution, magnetic-deflection CRT is used to provide adequate viewing area for high-quality alphanumeric and graphic information. In the alphanumeric mode, up to 25 lines of 80 characters can be displayed at one time from a standard 128-character ASCII character set. A foreign character set can be added, as an option, to allow the user to display either French, Spanish, German, or Katakana. Other languages are also possible. Three methods of highlighting information are available to the user: inverse video, underlining, and blinking. Each of these functions can be independently changed on a character-by-character basis. The viewing area for 25 lines of 80 characters, called the alpha raster, is approximately 9.3-in. by 4.8-in. This permits a matrix of 720×375 dots to be displayed. Characters are formed from 7 by 9 dot matrices located in 9 by 15 dot fields.

High-resolution raster graphics can be added to the display as an option. In the graphics mode of operation, the viewing area, called the graphics raster, is approximately 7.9 in by 6.5 in. This permits a matrix of 560×455 dots to be displayed. The graphics raster is a separate, independent raster that is switched into operation when the display is in the graphics mode. The dual raster-scan capability allows the size and aspect ratio of each raster to be chosen to optimize the quality and capability of the display for the function the user wishes to perform, and to achieve compatibility with the internal thermal printer/plotter.

Display Quality

A considerable emphasis was placed on optimizing the design to achieve a high-quality display. To achieve high quality in a CRT display requires the optimization of many parameters. Some of the most important include character size and legibility, brightness, resolution, contrast, glare, focus, position distortion, and stability. Display quality was one of the major reasons for adding the dual raster-scan capability. The alpha raster is tailored to display 80 adequately spaced characters per line, while using the maximum width possible without introducing excessive distortion due to nonuniformity in the CRT screen. A 7 by 9 character font in a 9 by 15 cell was chosen because this matrix is sufficient to generate aesthetically pleasing characters. The extra rows in the cell are used for spaces, ascenders that are needed for some of the European characters, and descenders that are used in some of the lowercase Roman characters.

The graphics raster displays the same high-quality characters but is limited to 62 per line. The graphics raster increases the resolution in the vertical dimension to maximize the proportion of screen area that can be used.

Uniform character size over the entire screen is difficult to achieve in CRT displays. Nonlinear current drives must be supplied to the yoke because the faceplate is not spherical. To achieve a more accurate current waveform, an active correction technique was employed in the display. The yoke current is compared to a reference current generated by a diode function generator and is corrected when a difference occurs. With this scheme, an improvement factor greater than 2 was achieved in the position distortion.

Since visible motion on a display is quite annoying, it was decided to refresh the display at 60 Hz even when the line frequency is 50 Hz to minimize flicker. Sufficient magnetic shielding has been added to eliminate interference due to internal sources within the mainframe itself, as well as from reasonable external magnetic fields.

In the graphics mode of operation the CRT is treated as a genuine peripheral with a select code and driven via the IOD Bus. This capability is briefly considered at the end of this section.

In contrast, the alphanumeric interface is a dedicated mechanism that automatically generates the CRT's display according to the contents of memory. It is connected to the PPU's IDA Bus and performs its own accesses to memory. Thus, to generate a display, the PPU needs only to format and manage the contents of a CRT display buffer in block 1 memory. The alphanumeric interface uses bus requests to interrogate that buffer, and responds to certain conventions regarding control bytes that are placed into the buffer amid the data by the controlling firmware.

The control bytes and their associated conventions amount to a command set for the alphanumeric display. Their employment allows efficient use of the memory allocated to the CRT display buffer. Rather than structuring the buffer to be a character-for-character image of the display, the buffer contains a compacted version of the data. For instance, the blanks to the right of a line are supplied automatically by the display itself, following an end-of-line (EOL) control character. Other control bytes instruct the alphanumeric interface where in the buffer to begin the display; control the location of the cursor; and specify underlining or blinking.

The size chosen for the display buffer is large enough to contain enough characters to fill an entire display. But because of efficient allocation of memory (e.g., suppression of trailing blanks by EOL control characters) the buffer is rarely full and can be loaded with more lines of information than the CRT can display at one time. The display buffer can hold four pages of average BASIC statements. The controlling firmware can cause the display to scroll through the data in the buffer in response to the operator's pressing various control keys on the keyboard. Scrolling requires only the manipulation of a few control bytes, not the wholesale rearrangement of data in the display buffer.

Alpha Display Control Logic

The Control Logic is the alphanumeric interface between the mainframe and the display. It reads memory via DMA, processes the data, and holds them in a format that the display can use. Each byte of a data word represents either a combination of features to be set or cleared, an ASCII character, or a control code for the display. Figure 24 shows the functions that can be interpreted from each byte.

Data bytes consist of a 7-bit ASCII code and a high-order 0, and they will be interpreted as the corresponding ASCII code unless the foreign character set has previously been chosen. If the high-order bit is set, the five low-order feature bits are latched and held until another feature byte occurs to change the state.

The EOL command fills the remainder of the current line buffer (one of two local buffers within the CRT) with blanks. The next data byte will be the first character of the next line of displayed characters.

During normal operation, the Control Logic will read the data at address 70000_8, complement them, and use that as the address for the first character to be displayed. From that point on the address will be incremented by 1 for each new data word. The NWA command indicates that the contents of the next address are to be interpreted as the complement of the address for the next data word. The address will then be incremented from the new point.

In addition to being the pointer of the first word of a page, 70000_8 is also used to choose between the alpha mode and the graphics mode. If the high-order bit is a 0 and the graphics hardware is installed, then the display will be the graphics mode.

An example of an alpha mode data pattern is shown in Fig. 25.

As each data byte is processed, the data are placed into a 12-bit word. The first 7 bits contain the ASCII code for the displayed character. The last 5 bits indicate whether any ongoing highlighting should be applied to this character. These feature bits were previously specified by a control code, whereupon they were latched by the Control Logic and were applied to every character until the latches were changed or cleared. These 12-bit words are stored in groups of 80 in one of two local line buffers within the

BIT # WITHIN BYTE								MEANING
7	6	5	4	3	2	1	0	
0	X	X	X	X	X	X	X	DATA
1	0	0	0	0	0	0	0	CLEAR ALL FEATURE LATCHES
1	0	X	X	X	X	X	0/1	CLEAR/SET THE CURSOR LATCH
1	0	X	X	X	X	0/1	X	CLEAR/SET THE INVERSE VIDEO LATCH
1	0	X	X	X	0/1	X	X	CLEAR/SET THE BLINKING LATCH
1	0	X	X	0/1	X	X	X	CLEAR/SET THE UNDERLINE LATCH
1	0	X	0/1	X	X	X	X	CLEAR/SET THE FOREIGN CHAR. SET LATCH
1	1	X	X	X	X	X	1	END OF LINE COMMAND (EOL)
1	1	X	X	X	X	X	0	NEW WORD ADDRESS COMMAND (NWA)

Fig. 24. The alphanumeric mode control bytes.

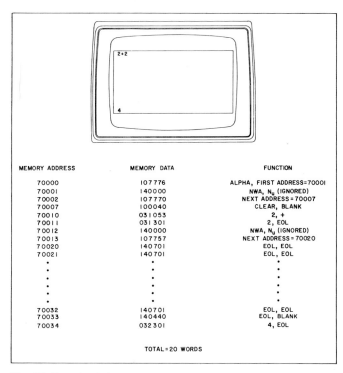

MEMORY ADDRESS	MEMORY DATA	FUNCTION
70000	107776	ALPHA, FIRST ADDRESS=70001
70001	140000	NWA, N_u (IGNORED)
70002	107770	NEXT ADDRESS=70007
70007	100040	CLEAR, BLANK
70010	031053	2, +
70011	031301	2, EOL
70012	140000	NWA, N_u (IGNORED)
70013	107757	NEXT ADDRESS=70020
70020	140701	EOL, EOL
70021	140701	EOL, EOL
•	•	•
•	•	•
•	•	•
•	•	•
70032	140701	EOL, EOL
70033	140440	EOL, BLANK
70034	032301	4, EOL

TOTAL=20 WORDS

Fig. 25. Sample alphanumeric data pattern.

CRT. The purpose of having two line buffers is to provide the Display Logic with one full line of characters to display while the Control Logic is loading the next line of 80 characters into the other buffer. This means that the Control Logic is actually one line ahead of the display. When the Control Logic has entered 80 characters into a line buffer, it waits for the Display Logic to indicate that it is ready for a new line. The Control Logic provides the Display Logic with the newly filled Line Buffer and starts to refill the used Line Buffer with new data. This occurs for each character line on the display. As the Control Logic completes each line it signals the Display Logic that there is a full Line Buffer. The Display Logic cannot wait for a new line once one has been requested, or the data will not be displayed in the correct position on the screen. So if a new full Line Buffer is not available when the Display Logic indicates that it is ready for a new line, the Display Logic will blank the video for the remainder of the page. This is done because the Control Logic and Display Logic will not be synchronized until the beginning of the new page. The Line Buffer must be filled in 637 μs. This figure comes from the time it takes to display the 15 scans that make up the dot matrix of a line of characters. For each scan all 80 words in the buffer are read 15 times before the buffer is refilled.

The Display's Effect on the Mainframe

On account of the nature of the display's mode of data retrieval, there is a definite effect on the performance of the mainframe. Since it is necessary for the display to access memory on a regular basis, it uses memory cycles which might have been used by the PPU for other operations. This will inevitably slow down the PPU. The PPU can execute about 1 million memory cycles per second. The display must read at least one word for every two lines of characters (two blank lines) but doesn't need to read more than 82 words per line of characters (a feature byte and a character byte in every word with a new word address). If a character line is 40 words in length (80 characters or partial lines with features), the display will require 40 memory cycles/line $\times$ 25 lines/page $\times$ 60 pages/s, or 60,000 memory cycles per second. This would reduce the PPU to the use of 940,000 memory cycles per second, or a 6.0 percent increase in execution time. These memory cycles may also indirectly slow the LPU by temporarily holding the Dual Port Memory Controller in an inconvenient position, but that result is probably negligible.

Over a short term (less than 637 μs) the display will be accessing memory to fill a single line of characters. This rate is 158,000 memory cycles per second, which increases PPU execution time by 23 percent (PPU will be allowed 763,000 memory cycles per second). However, as soon as the line is complete, memory access drops to zero until the next line needs to be refreshed.

A conflict occurs when some peripheral device, such as a disk, attempts a burst-mode DMA and where the efficiency of the device depends upon a data transfer rate close to the maximum. The problem arises when the display requires a sufficient number of memory cycles to complete a character line in less than 637 μs while at the same time a disk requires data at a rate determined by the rotating speed of the disk. If the display is allowed memory cycles in such a DMA burst, a disk location might be past the head when the data finally arrive. Similarly, if the display is deprived of memory cycles during the burst, the analog scanning of the display might have started displaying a line before the digital circuitry has completely acquired and processed the next line from memory. To avoid this and allow for efficient use of disk systems the following convention has been adopted. If the display is deprived of enough memory cycles that it cannot fill a character line by the time that line starts to be scanned on the display, then the remainder of the video output for that page will be blanked. Video will be resumed at the beginning of the next instance of displaying that page. Therefore, it is possible for the display to be blank for about 0.3 s if a DMA occurs which reads 64 Kbyte of memory at once. A longer blanked period can occur if smaller DMAs occur regularly after the start of each refresh cycle.

Graphics Overview

Graphics-mode operations allows the generation of entirely arbitrary patterns on the CRT screen through the use of a separate graphics raster. The screen appears as a field 560 dots wide by 455 dots high. The CRT is equipped with an additional interface (select code 13) and a 16-kiloword cache memory. A correspondence between the bits in the cache memory and the dots on the screen is established. The user's software, with help from extra BASIC language constructs supplied by a GRAPHICS option ROM, can generate an image on the CRT by manipulating the contents of the cache memory.

The graphics mode of operation has its own cursors, including one for digitizing information presented on the screen. Also, the CRT need not be in the graphics mode for manipulation of the graphics memory to occur. The CRT display can be switched between the graphics image and the regular alphanumeric format at will.

An additional feature is the CRT–Thermal Printer dump. This was made possible by providing the ability to use the contents of the 16K cache memory as a source of data to drive the internal thermal printer. That printer has a thermal printhead with 560 uniformly spaced print resistors. The Graphics Dump produces a dot-for-dot image of the CRT's graphics-mode display on the printer.

References

Shaw [1974]

Chapter 32

The IBM System/38:
A High-Level Machine[1]

S. H. Dahlby / G. G. Henry / D. N. Reynolds /
P. T. Taylor

One of the primary characteristics of the IBM System/38 that identifies it as an advanced computer system is its high-level machine instruction interface, which incorporates new architectural structures and provides a much higher level of function than traditional machine architectures, such as the IBM System/3. The function and architectural structures are more similar to those of high-level languages than to conventional machines. The purpose of this article is to describe the advantages and salient architectural features provided by the System/38 instruction interface, and how they are realized in the specifics of the System/38 machine.

Relevant system objectives

Many factors influence the choice of the architectural characteristics [Henry, 1978] of a new system. In System/38 the primary influences, such as anticipated user requirements and hardware technology trends, led to the adoption of some major objectives for the total system. Briefly, these were:

- Programming independence from machine implementation and configuration details

- High levels of integrity and authorization capability with minimal overhead

- Efficient support in the machine for commonly used operations in control programming, compilers, and utilities

- Efficient support in the machine for key system functional objectives, such as data base and dynamic multiprogramming.

The following sections highlight the major System/38 instruction interface concepts and features that address these objectives.

Independence from Machine Implementation
and Configuration

In previous systems, the ability for users to take advantage of new technology and implement new function was limited by depen-

[1]*IBM System/38: Technical Developments*, pp. 47–50. © 1978 by International Business Machines Corporation. Reprinted by permission.

dence on a specific low-level instruction interface; for example, dependence upon the hardware-implemented address size. One of the major goals of System/38 architecture was to enable users to be as independent as possible of hardware and device characteristics.

In System/38, hardware dependencies have been absorbed by internal microcode functions that provide an instruction interface, which is largely independent of hardware details. Users of the instruction interface, therefore, need not be concerned with hardware addressing [Berstis, Trutal, and Ranweiler, 1978], auxiliary storage allocation and addressing [French, Collins, and Loen, 1978], internal data structures and relationships [Pinnow, Ranweiler, and Miller, 1978], channel and I/O interface details, and internal microprogramming details [Hoffman and Soltis, 1978].

This hardware independence characteristic of the System/38 instruction interface is due in large measure to the use of an object-oriented interface [Pinnow, Ranweiler, and Miller, 1978] instead of the more conventional byte-oriented interface. An *object* is a System/38 instruction interface construct that contains a specific type of information and can be used only in a specific manner. A number of different types of objects are defined in the interface, and various object-specific instructions are provided to operate upon each object type. An example of a System/38 instruction interface object is a data space (file), which has associated instructions for operations such as the adding and deleting of records [Watson and Aberle, 1978].

Each object is created by a System/38 interface instruction that uses a user-specified data structure to define the object's characteristics and initial values. Once the object is created, its internal stored format is not apparent to the user (with the one exception discussed below). The status and values of the object may be retrieved or changed by using interface instructions, but the internal format of the object cannot be directly viewed or modified. That is, objects can be operated upon functionally, but not as a byte string. This approach prevents dependence on the internal format of the object and enables applications to remain independent of evolving internal implementations of the machine.

There is one specific exception to this shielding of the internal format of an object. A *space object* is a construct that can be used by a program for storage of and operation upon byte-oriented operands such as character strings and numeric values.

In addition to this object orientation, main storage and auxiliary storage addresses are not directly apparent in the System/38 instruction interface [Berstis, Truxal, and Ranweiler, 1978; Pinnow, Ranweiler, and Miller, 1978]. All interface addressing of objects is accomplished by resolving symbolic names (supplied by the user) to a pointer. A *pointer* is an object that is used only for addressing and does not permit examination or manipulation of the implied physical address. A *system pointer* gives a user the ability to address objects; for example, to create or destroy an object or to examine or directly modify its content through associated specific instructions. A *space pointer* allows the direct addressability of bytes within a space object. Both of these pointer types can be contained within a space object, but they can be used for addressing only when operated on by pointer manipulation instructions. Pointers are assured of validity via tagged storage in both main and secondary storage. Direct modification of a pointer area via a "computational" instruction results in the tag becoming invalid and causes the pointer to no longer be usable for addressing purposes.

Similarly, users are not concerned with the addressing structures of either main storage or auxiliary storage [French, Collins, and Loen, 1978], or even necessarily that there are multiple levels of storage, since all storage used for all objects in the system is allocated and managed by the machine. That is, there is no differentiation in the System/38 instruction interface as to where an object or portions of an object reside. The total address space of System/38 thus consists of an unconstrained number of objects, uniformly addressable by pointers.

Similar constructs shield the System/38 instruction interface user from dependencies upon channel and I/O device addresses and low-level communication protocols.

Figure 1 illustrates this basic object-oriented, high-level interface approach.

Integrity and Authorization

A natural consequence of the object-oriented approach is improved system integrity and authorization mechanisms [Berstis, Truxal, and Ranweiler, 1978]. All user information is stored in System/38 instruction interface objects. Access to that information is through System/38 instructions that ensure the structural integrity of the manipulated objects. An attempt to misuse an object is thus detected and causes the instruction execution to be terminated and an exception condition to be raised. An example is the attempt to directly change a byte within a program object.

Authorization capabilities are likewise facilitated by the System/38 instruction-interface object-oriented structure. Each user of the machine is identified by a user profile, which is itself an object. Each object in the system is owned by a user profile, and the owner may delegate to other user profiles various types of authority to operate on the objects. Processes (tasks) execute under a specific user profile (in the name of a user), and functions executed within a process verify that the objects referenced have been properly authorized to that user.

Figure 2 illustrates this approach to providing integrity and authorization capability.

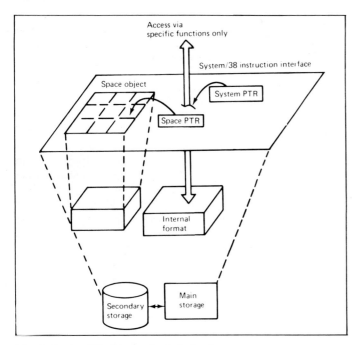

Fig. 1. System/38 object-oriented structure.

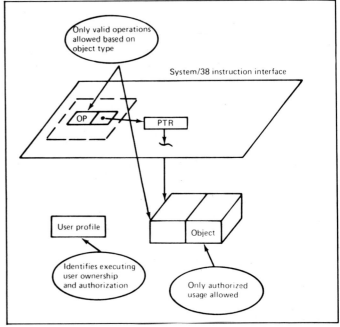

Fig. 2. System/38 instruction interface integrity and authorization scheme.

Support for Common Programming Functions

The System/38 instruction interface is designed to provide direct support for a wide variety of functions common to control programming, compilers, and utilities. This increased level of machine function eliminates the need to implement these common functions in multiple programming components, increases consistency across all programming components, and supports programming approaches conducive to providing integrity and reliability.

There are two basic modes of addressing in the System/38 interface. The first is *pointers*, which allow varying addressability to all objects and bytes within space objects. The second, *dictionary addressing*, deals with program references to values within a space object.

Operands referenced in program instructions are defined in a dictionary portion of the program separate from the instructions themselves. Instruction operands are index references to these dictionary entries which define operand characteristics such as data type and length. Binary, zoned decimal, packed decimal, character, and pointer data types are examples of operand characteristics that may be defined. The dictionary entries do not contain the operand values; the specific location of the operands is not apparent to or required by programs. However, the user can control the general type of location characteristics: for example, relative to the area addressed by a pointer or relative to the storage area allocated for program variables within the executing process.

This approach of having instructions reference dictionary entries describing the operand characteristics allows additional capability over low-level instruction interfaces. For example, the following high-level capabilities are provided:

- Computational instructions are generic with respect to data type and length. For example, there is only one numeric add instruction in the System/38 instruction interface: it operates on whatever data is defined in the operand definition dictionary. This enables the use of source and receiver operands of varying type, length, and decimal positioning with all conversions and scaling being performed by the machine.

- Arrays may be defined in the interface and instruction operands support array indexing to locate specific elements of the array.

- Since applications often allow operations on multiple formats of data, some instructions (for example, the copy instructions) support late-binding of data definition where the data (type, length, and decimal positioning) need not be defined until the instruction is executed.

In addition to these types of high-level data operations, the System/38 instruction interface provides and, in some cases, requires functions intended to support programming constructs more directly than in traditional machines. For example, programs are invoked through call/return functions defined in the interface. Argument/parameter functions provide communications from one program to another. Allocation and initialization of storage for program variables within a process is performed by the System/38 machine. Additional examples are found in [Watson and Aberle, 1978] and [Howard and Borgendale, 1978].

Figure 3 illustrates this System/38 program structure and the general relationship between a high-level language program and the corresponding System/38 constructs.

Support for Key System Functions

The System/38 machine was designed to support a usage environment characterized by a dynamically changing application load consisting of a wide variety of application types—all utilizing advanced functions such as data base. For example, batch, interactive, and transaction processing, along with program development activities, may all be executing concurrently with dynamically changing workloads and priorities. One of the key requirements for the System/38 instruction interface was to provide efficient support in this type of environment for application requirements such as multiprogramming and data base operations. This centralization of function in the machine simplifies the user programming task and reduces overhead in a dynamic multi-user environment.

Two examples of this system function support will be described here—multiprogramming and data base. Similar high levels of

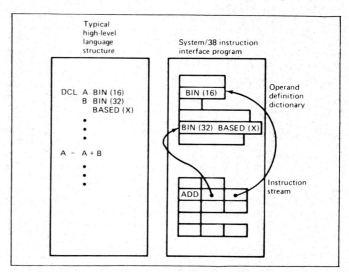

Fig. 3. System/38 instruction interface program structure.

machine capability exist in other major functional areas such as I/O.

System/38 supports multiprogramming through the concept of processes. A "process" is similar to a task in other systems and is the basis for managing work in the machine. The user of the System/38 instruction interface controls the number of processes currently initiated, the priority of each process, and the relationship of one process to another, that is, with respect to processor utilization and storage utilization. The machine then allocates the processor and storage resources based on these parameters as well as on the current status of the process, for example, waiting or dispatchable.

This level of multiprogramming support in the System/38 machine offers advantages like these:

- A single resource management mechanism is applied to processing across all system activities. This reduces overhead and results in better management of resources in a complex and dynamic environment.

- Other efficient resource management mechanisms can be used to take advantage of hardware characteristics without programming dependencies.

Similarly, the System/38 machine provides the basic functional building blocks for a high-function integrated data base. Data base objects include a comprehensive set of functions supporting different access mechanisms, file sharing, record format definition and mapping, efficient record retrieval, update, add, and delete. This allows, for example, a data base file structure to be defined that maps a single physical file into records with multiple formats and content. In addition, a single physical data base file may have multiple indexes (access paths) defined over it, all of which are concurrently updated when the file is changed. Each user of the file may view the data in the form suitable to a particular application.

Overhead Considerations

One of the major problems inherent in the implementation of a high-level instruction interface such as that provided for the System/38 is overhead. In order to reduce the potential overhead, and also to facilitate future extensions, the System/38 instruction interface definition does not require a directly executable implementation of the instruction interface. The instructions and the operand definition dictionary are presented to the instruction interface and are translated into an executable microcode structure called a program object. The internal microcode format is not apparent at the interface. Figure 4, System/38 executable program creation, illustrates this process.

Having an executable program creation step allows the system to have the advantage of both a high-level instruction interface and reduced overhead at execution time.

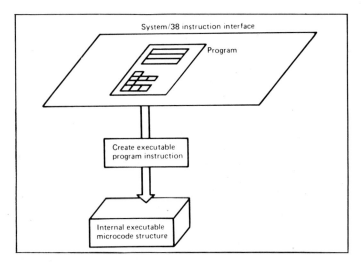

Fig. 4. System/38 executable program creation.

In addition, direct support of high-use functions in the System/38 instruction interface, as previously described, is itself an approach toward reducing *system* overhead. A single implementation of a complex function that can be applied system-wide reduces overhead.

Also, by implementing these functions in the machine, hardware facilities can reduce the overhead that is associated with the higher level implementation typically required in programming.

Summary

The IBM System/38 provides a new type of machine instruction interface that comprises a high level of function together with structures similar to high level language structures and includes computation, addressing, and such traditional programming functions as process (task) management, resource management (storage and processor), data base management, and device handling. This new machine was designed to satisfy major design objectives for the entire system—hardware, microprogramming, and program products. The concept of a high-level machine has been discussed in the literature and has been experimented with in both industrial and research environments; however, System/38 is the first IBM system to bring the advantages of a high-level machine to the business user.

References

Berstis, Truxal, and Ranweiler [1978]; French, Collins, and Loen [1978]; Henry [1978]; Hoffman and Soltis [1978]; Howard and Borgendale [1978]; Pinnow, Ranweiler, and Miller [1978]; Watson and Aberle [1978].

The IBM System/38: Object-Oriented Architecture[1]

K. W. Pinnow / J. G. Ranweiler / J. F. Miller

System/38 provides a range of capability not previously available in low-cost data processing systems. This capability is made possible by the use of a number of technical innovations. One of these is the *object*. This article discusses objects—the means through which information is stored and processed on System/38. Included are the concepts, purpose, and characteristics of System/38 machine objects and their use by the Control Program Facility (CPF).

Object Concepts

Previous machine instruction sets have provided bit- and byte-string manipulation capabilities. The machine instruction set in System/38 provides similar functions and also provides machine instructions that operate on complex data structures to accomplish high-level functions.

Some of the data structures are similar to such things as programs and data files in conventional systems. Some are unique to System/38. The data structures that appear in the instruction interface are collectively categorized as objects.

An object is brought into existence through execution of a create instruction. The user controls the creation of the object through a template [Allsen, 1978] that provides a set of attributes and values that are to apply to the new object. The new object also has operational characteristics that define the set of functions that may be accomplished through it. Examples of object attributes and operations are shown in Fig. 1.

The three examples of attributes illustrated in Fig. 1 are (1) a *name* that permits symbolic reference to the object, (2) an *existence* that specifies whether implicit destruction is *allowed*, and (3) *ownership* that identifies who, if anyone, owns the object.

The set of instructions that are operationally meaningful to an object consist of *generic* operations that apply to all types of objects and *unique* operations that apply to a specific type object. The generic operations are primarily *authorization*-, *addressing*-, and *resource*-related [Berstis, Truxal, and Ranweiler, 1978]. The unique operations include a *destroy* that removes the object from the system, some form of *materialize* that identifies the object's attributes or content, and sometimes a *modify* that changes the attributes of the object. Many other unique operations exist that are not identified in Fig. 1.

[1]*IBM System/38: Technical Developments*, pp. 51–54. © 1978 by International Business Machines Corporation. Reprinted by permission.

Object			
	Attributes	Name	
		Ownership	
		Existence	
	Generic operations	Explicit functions	Authorization
			Addressing
			Resource
		Implicit functions	Atomicity
			Lock enforcement
			Authorization enforcement
	Unique operations	Explicit functions	Materialization
			Modification
			Destruction
		Implicit functions	Atomicity
			Lock enforcement
			Authorization enforcement

Fig. 1. Some examples of object attributes and operations in System/38.

Each operation, whether generic or unique, also provides significant implicit functions. The implicit functions are *authorization*, *lock enforcement*, and *atomic* (exclusive) *operation*.

Object Purpose

The concept of an object gives a common attribute to a group of data structures and enables the definition of an interface that produces a number of benefits.

The existence of objects allows systematic manipulation of structures. Their presence permits the definition of an instruction interface that is consistent across a wide range of supervisor and computational instructions.

Objects exist to make users independent of specific implementation techniques used in the machine. Since it is necessary that users control the data used in supervisor functions, object management capability is provided. When a request for a high-level machine function is made, a specific instruction operator (operation code), optionally an attribute template, and an object are specified. System/38 uses the object to accumulate results of operations, to store them in such a way that they are safe from inadvertent modification, and to assure that they are available for subsequent operations.

Objects exist to make the user independent of the addressing structure actually used in the hardware. Although main storage and auxiliary storage exist in System/38, users are shielded from the mechanics of actually addressing that storage. In other words, objects remove the traditional responsibility of mapping data onto physical storage.

Object Characteristics

For an object like a program, creation establishes the essential content of the object, and subsequent instructions use it operationally. For other objects, the creation is primarily a space allocation mechanism for which succeeding operations establish the content. For example, once a data space has been created, records may be inserted into it. Management of the size of an object and changes to that size are generally transparent to the System/38 user.

All System/38 machine objects are *encapsulated*. Encapsulation is the process of accepting a definition of an object through a create instruction and using this definition to produce an object whose internal structure is only accessible to the machine. Objects are encapsulated to maintain the integrity of the internal structure and to permit different implementations of the machine instruction interface without impact to its users.

It is possible to associate an unencapsulated (byte string) area with each object. This byte-string area is referred to as a *space* and is up to 16 megabytes of virtual storage into which the machine user can build control blocks of other control information or data. As a degenerate case of an object, one with essentially no encapsulated portion, a space exists as an independent object. Whether it is an object itself or is associated with another object, a space has its size modified through explicit instructions by the machine user.

System/38 Machine Objects

The following lists and briefly describes the objects of the System/38 machine-instruction set.

Access group. An object that permits the physical grouping of other objects to achieve more efficient movement of the objects between main storage and auxiliary storage.

Context. An object that contains the *type*, *subtype*, and *name* of other objects to allow addressability.

Controller description. An object that represents an I/O controller for a cluster of I/O devices or a station that attaches groups of communication devices over the same data communication link.

Cursor. An object used to provide addressability into a data space.

Data space. An object used to store data base records of one format.

Data space index. An object used to provide a logical ordering of records stored in a data space.

Index. An object used to store and automatically order data.

Logical unit description. An object that represents a physical I/O device.

Network description. An object that represents a network port of the system.

Process control space. An object used to contain process execution.

Program. An object for uniquely selecting and ordering machine interface instructions.

Queue. An object used to communicate between processes, and between a process and a device.

Space. An object used for storing pointers and scalars.

User profile. An object used to identify a valid user of the machine interface.

CPF Use of Machine Objects

The CPF extends the object-oriented approach of the machine and provides its users with a high-level, object-oriented interface [Harvey and Conway, 1978]. All data stored on the system by CPF users is stored in object form and is processable in terms of control language commands and high-level languages. To the user of CPF, objects are named collections of data, and the functions associated with objects provide the vehicle for processing this data and obtaining work from the system. The 19 objects presented to the user at the CPF interface include conventional constructs, such as files and programs, as well as constructs that are unique to System/38, such as job descriptions and message queues [Demers, 1978].

The functions that CPF provides for its objects include some that are object-type specific and some that are generic with respect to object type. The object-type specific functions define and limit the way in which an object can be used while the generic functions provide for authorization, locking, saving, restoring, dumping, moving, and renaming objects. Through the generic functions, the user has a way of managing objects once they exist.

Objects are brought into existence through the specification of a create command that defines the name, attributes, and initial value of the object to be created. Each object is assigned a type and subtype as a part of the creation process. The object's type is determined by the kind of machine object created to support the object that the CPF user wishes to create; the object's subtype designates the use that CPF intends for the machine object. Each unique use that the CPF makes of a machine object is assigned a unique subtype identifier. This aspect of the design is important because it is through the use of unique types and subtypes that the system can ensure that each type of object is always used in the way it was intended. After an object has been created, it remains on the system until it is explicitly deleted via a delete command. At the time an object is created, CPF places the name of the object into a machine object known as a *context*.

Contexts are presented to the user as libraries. Because the functions associated with contexts are capable of finding an object based on its name, type, and subtype, libraries can be considered as a catalog or container for the user-created objects. Whenever an object is to be found, CPF initiates a search for the object either in a single library or through an ordered list of libraries that the CPF maintains with each executing job. When the list of libraries is used to find an object, each successive library in the list is searched until the object is found. Using the list of libraries to find the objects to be processed is advantageous because the same commands or program can perform functions on different objects merely by changing the order of the libraries in the library list.

CPF maintains descriptive information for all objects and provides functions for the retrieval and display of this data. The descriptive information records who the object owner is, when the object was created, where the object has most recently been saved, and text information provided by the user to further describe the object.

An important feature of CPF object architecture is the manner in which CPF objects are constructed. CPF uses machine objects as building blocks to produce the objects that CPF users see. Figure 2 shows an example of how one kind of Control Program Facility object is constructed.

In this example, four types of machine objects (a data space, a data space index, a cursor, and a space) are combined to produce the higher level CPF object known to the user as a *data base file*. CPF manages the individual pieces of a file in a way that allows the user to perceive the file as a single entity. For example, the separate pieces of the file come into existence when a single create-file command is processed and remain in existence until the file is explicitly deleted. Thus, the user is relieved of the complexity and organizational details of the data and can process it as a logical entity. When lower level objects are put together to form a higher level object, the higher level object is known as a composite object. CPF object architecture permits any type of System/38 machine or CPF object to be combined to produce a new type of object. In fact, CPF-provided functions for managing objects are table-driven, based on unique object type and subtype combinations. This aspect of the design means that the object-oriented approach can be quickly and easily extended. It also permits new kinds of objects to be compatibly introduced later on in the life of the system.

The key advantages of the System/38 building block architecture, however, is that the implicit functions provided by the

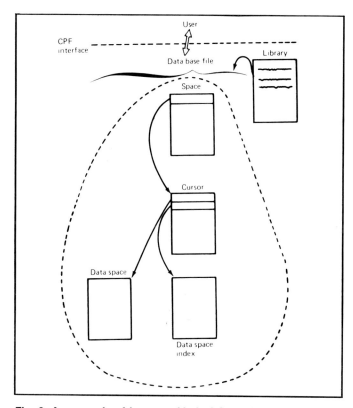

Fig. 2. An example of how one kind of Control Program Facility object is constructed.

machine for its objects are made directly available to the end user in a consistent manner. For example, implicit in all CPF objects are the machine-provided functions of security, lock enforcement, and object resolution by name. The benefits of this architecture are readily apparent when one contrasts the approach of System/38 with that of other systems having different addressing structures for different collections of data, added-on security functions, and user interfaces that require knowledge of the physical aspect of data organization.

Summary

The object orientation of the System/38 machine and CPF interfaces permits common provision of function at each interface. With machine-interface objects, the hardware addressing mechanism and the internal format and organization of data are transparent to the user; serialization and authorization functions are implicit in the objects. The key characteristic that makes this possible is encapsulation of objects in the machine-instruction interface. Since CPF uses the objects of the System/38 instruction interface as building blocks, its objects possess all the function of the machine objects.

References

Allsen [1978]; Berstis, Truxal, and Ranweiler [1978]; Demers [1978]; Harvey and Conway [1978].

The IBM System/38: Addressing and Authorization[1]

V. Berstis / C. D. Truxal / J. G. Ranweiler

The high-level machine interface of System/38 achieves user independence from the internal machine implementation primarily through the use of an object-oriented architecture. Objects representing storage for constructs such as programs, processes, and data base files are accessed through a consistent, integrated addressing structure. Because authority enforcement and control of shared objects are critical in multiprogramming environments, these functions have been incorporated into the addressing path. This article describes some of the key features of the addressing design of System/38 and how they are presented to the user through the Control Program Facility (CPF), which is described by Harvey and Conway [1978].

Objects and Spaces

Before addressing can be described, it is necessary to define what is accessed. Everything stored in the system is an *object* (see Fig. 1), which consists of a functional portion and an associated space (see Pinnow et al. [1978]). The functional part of an object is used to implement a particular construct. For example, the functional part of a program object is created by the translation of System/38 machine instructions into microcode. The program is said to be *encapsulated* because there is no direct access to the storage used to support it. Instead, the object is manipulated at a high level through the System/38 instruction set. In this way, encapsulation ensures the functional integrity of all objects.

The *associated space* portion of an object is a region of bytes that can be directly manipulated by the machine user. The space is associated with the functional part of the object and provides a

convenient way of storing additional (user-defined) data pertinent to that object's usage. One type of object, called a *space object*, has no functional part. Its associated space is used to provide storage for control blocks, buffers, pointers, and other data.

Pointers

There are four different types of pointers. *System pointers* address objects; *space pointers* and *data pointers* address specific byte locations within the space portion of an object; and *instruction pointers* control execution flow. This article covers object addressing through system pointers.

A *system pointer*, used to address an object, contains both the location of the object in storage and object usage rights, as will be discussed later. Only specific System/38 instructions can create pointers. Although pointers can be copied, the user cannot construct pointers by bit manipulation. As a result of these properties, System/38 has the basic elements of *capability based addressing* [Linden, 1976].

Name Resolution

A system pointer exists in one of two states: resolved or unresolved. In the *unresolved state*, the pointer specifies the name of an object and not its location. When the pointer is first referenced (see Fig. 2), the machine searches for an object having the specified name. Once found, the resulting object location is stored in the pointer, thereby eliminating subsequent searches. The pointer is then said to be in the *resolved state*.

The search performed during pointer resolution involves the use of objects called *contexts*, containing object names and locations. Various execution environments are obtained by specifying an ordered list of contexts to be searched. For example, the production and test versions of files can be located through different contexts. Therefore, by simply exchanging the contexts searched, either programming environment can be achieved.

[1]*IBM System/38: Technical Developments*, pp. 55–58. © 1978 by International Business Machines Corporation. Reprinted by permission.

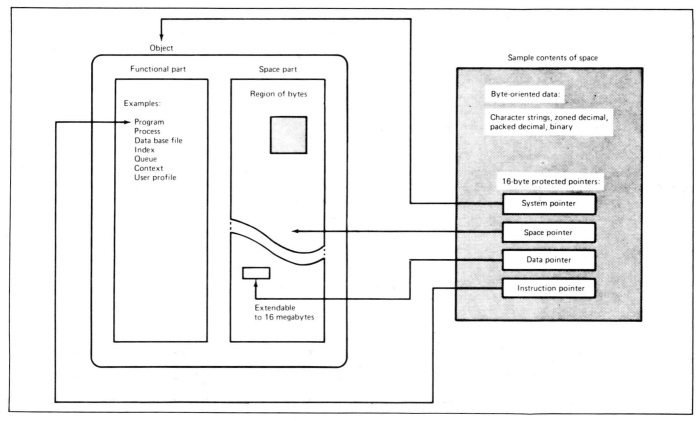

Fig. 1. System/38 objects and pointers.

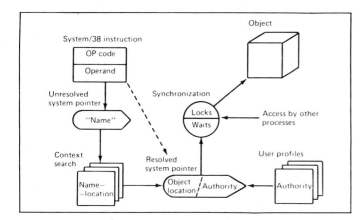

Fig. 2. The object access path.

Authorization

The ability to control pointer resolution in the machine is not sufficient to effectively control the users' access to objects because it is an "all or nothing" type of control. The System/38 object authorization mechanism provides the fineness (granularity) of control needed for the wide range of operations performed on objects.

Every reference to an object requires that the user have the appropriate authority for the operation to be performed; otherwise, the operation is suppressed and the attempted violation is recorded. The authority checking function is uniformly applied to all types of objects. Separate authorities (retrieve or update, for example) can be granted to individual users or to all users (the public). Therefore, a user's authority can be limited to what is exactly necessary for an application. For example, a user might be authorized to retrieve data from a data base file but not to update or destroy the file.

Sources of Authority

A prerequisite for authority verification is the identification of the user. This prerequisite is satisfied through the use of an object called the *user profile*, which identifies the user and the user's authority. Every process is initiated with a specified user profile as the primary source of authority. Object authorities can be granted to or revoked from a user profile, thus providing control over the authority available to the process. Objects can also be publicly authorized, thereby eliminating the need to explicitly authorize every user profile.

In some applications, subprograms require a different amount of authority than that available to the calling program. To accomplish this, programs can *adopt* a user profile (Fig. 3). The adopted user profile adds its authority to what is already present in a process. When the program calls other programs, the adopted user profile authorities can be optionally propagated to the called program. This provides considerable flexibility in controlling the security environment.

Once authority to an object has been established, it can be optionally stored in the pointer to that object. This provides faster authority verification than with unauthorized pointers.

Other Authorizations

One type of authority not related to objects is the *privileged instruction authority*. Such authorization is used for process initiation, user profile creation, machine reconfiguration, etc. Other *special authorities* range over many machine functions rather than specific instructions. For example, *all object* special authority permits unlimited use of all objects in the system. The control of storage resources is another wide-range authority. The storage occupied by objects is charged against the *storage limit* of

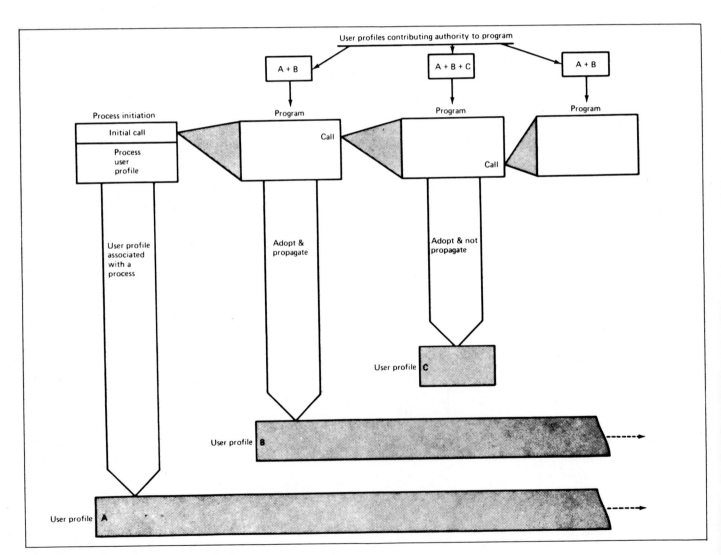

Fig. 3. User profiles as sources of authority.

the user profile (the owner) under which they were treated. Owners have implied object authority to the objects they own.

Locking and Synchronization

The authority mechanism of System/38 ensures that an application accesses only objects within its intended rights. When multiple applications attempt to reference the same objects concurrently, additional controls are provided to prevent interference. System/38 incorporates implicit synchronization functions into the object access implementation to accomplish this. For example, if one process is updating an object while another process is attempting to access the same object, the operations are automatically serialized. On the other hand, if both processes are retrieving data from the same object, the operations are allowed to proceed simultaneously. Therefore, contention is reduced and integrity of the object is ensured.

Explicit synchronization is available to the users in the form of *locks*. By locking an object, the user can control the access of other users to the object. Entire sequences of operations can be serialized when required to maintain data integrity. In addition, record level locks in data base files reduce much of the contention that would be present if the entire file were locked.

Synchronization functions complete the machine addressing path, which starts with the object name and continues through pointer resolution and authority verification.

Addressing Path Usage

The Control Program Facility (CPF) is an IBM program product providing the user a high-function, ease-of-use interface to the machine [Harvey and Conway, 1978]. With the high-level machine facilities available in the System/38, the CPF addressing and authorization function uses both capability-based and symbolic object addressing with authority validation at execution time.

CPF uses machine pointer resolution, authorization management, and locking to implement internal CPF security and synchronization. It provides these facilities to the user through CPF interfaces.

Within CPF, the work management component isolates and protects its critical resource control and scheduling functions by executing them under the system user profile. The remaining CPF modules execute under the user's profile. Thus, the machine authorization management directly validates the user's authority to perform every requested function on any specified object. Everything in CPF is an object. I/O devices and Control Language commands are objects, as are more typically files,

programs, and libraries. Because of this, an installation can control system resources to the extent desired.

Installation Authorization

This control of an installation's resources has led to the concept of one specific user as an installation's *security administrator*. This user is entrusted with authorities allowing system-wide control of all users and their resources. A set of IBM-supplied user profiles is delivered with CPF, including one for the security officer. This profile has all-object authority, as well as authority to create and modify user profiles. Therefore, the security officer can enroll users on the system and control their use of system resources. When a user profile is created or modified, special authorities, resource allocation parameters, and a user password can be specified. The user password is for verification of user identity at sign-on and for determining the user profile associated with a process.

Once the user is executing, functions are performed by executing programs or commands. These functions reference objects (such as files) by name, and CPF locates the object through the use of the machine-addressing facilities. This is easily implemented because contexts (objects that contain names of other objects [Pinnow, Ranweiler, and Miller, 1978]) are used by CPF as system and user libraries. When an object such as a program or file is created, it is placed in a library. Subsequent referencing of the object initiates pointer resolution, and the machine not only locates the object, but validates the current user's authority to the object and determines whether serialization of an operation is necessary. To expedite authority checking, CPF requests that the authority be set in the pointer for future use.

CPF Object Authorities

When a user creates an object, it can be declared "public" or "private." Subsequently, any of the object's authorities can be granted or revoked to individual users or the public. Display commands are also available to report object authority.

Summary

The System/38 is based on an object-oriented architecture in which everything in the system is an object. An object can be referenced by its name, which is used in a pointer resolution process that includes authorization and synchronization functions. The resulting resolved pointer can contain object location and authority to avoid subsequent searches. The machine enforces authority requirements on every object referenced, verifying the authority from the pointer or user profile(s). The user profile is an object that identifies a user in the system and contains all of that user's authorities. The CPF uses the machine addressing, authorization, and synchronization facilities, and provides their function to the user.

The System/38 thus delivers the flexibility of named object addressing and the integrity of machine-enforced authorization and synchronization of those objects.

References

Harvey and Conway [1978]; Linden [1978]; Pinnow, Ranweiler, and Miller [1978].

The IBM System/38:
Hardware Organization of the
System/38[1]

R. L. Hoffman / F. G. Soltis

The IBM System/38 hardware is designed to efficiently support its high-level machine architecture. An engineering design objective was to take advantage of new technologies such that certain high-level functions would be implemented in hardware and microcode. As a result, functions such as task dispatching, queue handling, virtual storage translation, stack manipulation, and object sharing became a basic part of the hardware control structure. A further objective was to provide for sufficient extendability to permit future implementation trade-offs.

Figure 1 shows the hardware configuration of the System/38. This article describes the hardware organization and the functions used by the hardware control structure.

Hardware Organization

System/38 hardware consists of a processor communicating over a high-speed channel to independently functioning I/O units. The processor and the I/O units have access to a main storage array. The System/38 processor, which is implemented in a new, high-performance large-scale integration (LSI) technology [Curtis, 1978], fetches 32-bit micro instructions from the random access memory (RAM) control store shown in Fig. 1 (8K words for both the 5381 Model 3 and Model 5). One micro instruction is executed for each processor cycle. The processor cycle times are

400 to 500 ns for the 5381 Model 3 (200 or 300 ns for the 5381 Model 5), depending on the micro instruction operation. In a single cycle, either one- or two-byte arithmetic operations may be performed on signed binary, unsigned binary, or packed format decimal data.

A new, high-density metal oxide semiconductor field effect transistor (MOSFET) technology main storage [Donofrio, Flur, and Schnadt, 1978] is available at two performance levels: 1100 ns fetch cycle time for the 5381 Model 3 and 600 ns fetch cycle for the 5381 Model 5. Data path width is four bytes to either memory. Available memory capacities are 512K, 768K, 1024K, 1280K, and 1536K bytes for either the Model 3 or 5. In addition, the Model 5 may have memory capacities of 1792K and 2048K bytes. Error correction circuitry (ECC) is used in both models.

Direct memory access for I/O units as well as for the processor is provided by the virtual address translation (VAT) hardware which converts 6-byte segmented virtual addresses to main storage addresses. Address translation tables in main storage and a translation lookaside buffer in hardware provide mapping from virtual to real main storage addresses, as discussed by Houdek and Mitchell [1978]. Virtual addresses are used in I/O operations, and page faults are allowed during data transmissions with low-speed devices.

Page faults are resolved by data transfer from secondary storage. Data is moved to main storage in 512-byte page units from disk storage via the channel.

Each I/O device is connected to a controller which is connected to the channel. Magnetic media controllers (MMC) [Froemke, Heise, and Pertzborn, 1978] are used for high data-rate devices such as disks, while microprogrammed I/O controllers (IOC) [Dumstorff, 1978] handle a multiplicity of lower data-rate devices.

Each system also includes a system control adapter (SCA) which shares an IOC with the keyboard display console. The SCA performs the system maintenance functions, including testing the hardware logic circuitry as described by Berglund [1978].

---

[1]*IBM System/38: Technical Developments*, pp. 19–21. © 1978 by International Business Machines Corporation. Reprinted by permission.

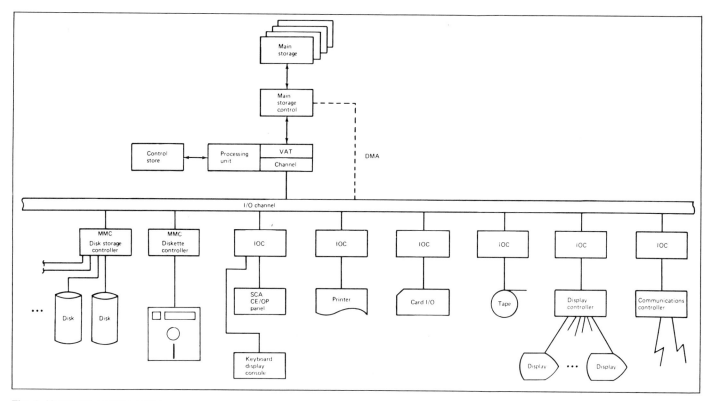

Fig. 1. Hardware configuration.

Control Structure

System/38 manipulates a unit of execution called the "task." All computer systems need to control execution and, in multiprogrammed systems like System/38, switch between units of execution, i.e., tasks. Traditionally, an interrupt structure with a fixed number of interrupt levels or classes, built on the hardware, is transformed by a software supervisor into a multilevel, interrupt-driven system to bridge the gap between the actual hardware and the abstract concepts of multiprogramming. The System/38 replaces this interrupt structure with a single tasking mechanism which is used to control all processing.

A multilevel, queue-driven task control structure is implemented in microcode and hardware on the System/38. A task dispatcher implemented in microcode allocates processor resources to prioritized tasks. I/O and program processing tasks are integrated in a common dispatching structure, with their priorities adjusted for system balance. I/O processing takes place when system resources are available, not when an I/O interrupt occurs.

I/O and program processing requests are stacked in main storage on a linked list called the task dispatching queue (TDQ).

The task dispatcher selects the highest priority request from the TDQ and gives it control of the processor. Instructions associated with this task, known as the active-task, are executed until control is passed to another task.

A set of system control operations (SEND and RECEIVE) are used to communicate between tasks and to pass control between tasks via the task dispatcher. If the active task is to communicate with another task, it does so by sending a message to a queue in main storage known to both tasks. If the active task is to obtain a message from a queue, it executes a RECEIVE operation. If the message is available on the queue, the message is passed to the active task and processing continues. If the message is not available (e.g., it has not yet been sent), the active task is made inactive and the task waits for the message. The task dispatcher is then invoked to select the new active task from the TDQ. The task dispatcher is also invoked on a SEND operation if a task of higher priority than the active task is waiting for the message. If the waiting task is of lower priority than the active task, the task dispatcher is not invoked, but the processing request for the waiting task is placed on the TDQ.

I/O in System/38 is implemented with a queue-driven command structure using the SEND/RECEIVE mechanism to pass information across the I/O interface, which is described by Lewis, Reed, and Robinson [1978]. To a task, a device looks like another task. Commands to devices and responses from devices are exchanged in the same way that messages are communicated between any two tasks in the system. The messages sent to the devices are specially formatted and contain the device commands. In addition to individual commands, a complete channel program can be sent as a single message. Because a queue structure is used, command stacking is automatic. In a similar manner, the device sends response and status information back to a task via a main storage queue. Note that only commands and responses use the queueing structure; data transfers between devices and main storage are direct.

High-level call/return functions are directly supported by another set of system control operations which provide the linkage mechanism between routines executing within the same task. The performance of programs written using structured programming techniques is enhanced by the use of this mechanism. The same linkage mechanism is used by the hardware to report program exceptions. With this mechanism, exceptions for any task (including such things as page faults) execute at the same priority level as the task itself. A low priority task incurring an exception will not interfere with the execution of higher priority tasks.

Summary

The hardware implementation of System/38 provides the foundation on which the high-level machine architecture is built. Through the use of advanced LSI technologies, System/38 achieves a high level of processor performance and reliability. The use of intelligent controllers for I/O device attachments distributes the I/O workload throughout the system.

A unique aspect of the System/38 hardware and microcode is the incorporation of very powerful control functions. These functions provide a single mechanism which is used to control all processing in the system. Other high-level functions implemented in the microcode further enhance the flexibility and performance of the system.

References

Berglund [1978]; Curtis [1978]; Donofrio, Flur, and Schnadt [1978]; Dumstorff [1978]; Froemke, Heise, and Pertzborn [1978]; Houdek and Mitchell [1978]; Lewis, Reed, and Robinson [1978].

Section 8

Personal Computing Systems

In the mid-1970s, spurred by the availability of single-chip microprocessors, personal computing was born. While it is too early to make projections or draw conclusions, some general comments can nevertheless be made. By *personal computing* we mean a low-cost computer structure that is dedicated to a single user. The computing environment usually consists of a Pc, Mp, Mdisk, keyboard, cathode-ray tube (CRT) display with graphics and/or color, and a standard software complement. Entry-level systems (with Pc, Mp, keyboard, CRT, and ROM-based software) are frequently priced as low as $400, while systems with a full set of options may be priced up to $10,000.

Personal computers are often targeted at a particular application area, such as scientific calculation, education, business, or entertainment. As of mid-1979 over 80 companies offered one or more personal computing systems. The following three paragraphs give examples of these systems and their capabilities. Table 1 describes examples of other personal computers available during the latter part of 1978. We can expect functionality to increase and prices to decrease.

TRS-80

In the first 20 months they were available, Radio Shack is reported to have sold in excess of 100,000 TRS-80 systems with Pc, Mp, keyboard, CRT, and ROM-resident BASIC for less than $800. The TRS-80 Model II has a Z-80 Pc (see Part 3, Sec. 2) operating at 4 MHz, 64 Kbyte of RAM, 1.5 Mbyte of floppy disk Ms, keyboard, CRT, and printer for less than $8,000. Available business software includes general ledger, accounts receivable, inventory control, mailing lists, and payroll.

TI 99/4

Based on Texas Instruments' TI 9900 (see Part 3, Secs. 1 and 2) with 16 Kbyte of RAM, the TI 99/4 features a keyboard, color CRT, extended graphics, sound and speech synthesis, the BASIC programming language, and a software library distributed in ROMs. Software is available for entertainment, education, and financial applications.

C8PDF

Ohio Scientific's C8PDF is aimed at the home computing market. The C8PDF can answer or place telephone calls via an acoustic coupler. It can take telephone messages by decoding Touch-Tone inputs. In the case of a problem at home, the C8PDF can dial a number and explain the situation using a built-in phonetic speech synthesizer. The computer can interface with home security systems that incorporate sensors for smoke, fire, intrusion, and AC power outages. Lights and appliances (e.g., furnace, air conditioner, and microwave oven) can also be placed under program control.

Personal computing is a subdimension of the computer function

Table 1 Examples of Personal Computers Using the Basic Programming Language (Late 1978) [Mennie, 1978]

	Apple II	Commodore PET 2001	Exidy Sorcerer	Intelligent Systems Compucolor II	Ohio Scientific Challenger C2-8P	Radio Shack TRS-80
Microprocessor	6502	6502	Zilog Z80	Intel 8080	6502	Z80
ROM (bytes)	8K	14K	12K	16K	9K	Level I: 4K Level II: 12K
RAM (bytes)	4K–48K	8K–32K	8K–32K	8K	4K	Level I: 4K Level II: 16K
Video display	Color or black-and-white TV 40 char/24 lines	Black-and-white monitor 40 char/25 lines	Black-and-white TV or monitor 64 char/30 lines	Color monitor 64 char/32 lines	Black-and-white TV or monitor 32 or 64 char/ 32 lines	Black-and-white monitor 64 char/16 lines
Keyboard style	Typewriter	Calculator	Typewriter	Typewriter	Typewriter	Typewriter
Mass storage	Cassette tape (1,500 bit/s) Floppy disk (116 Kbyte)	Cassette tape Floppy disk	Cassette tape	Minidisk (51 Kbyte)	Cassette tape Floppy disk	Cassette tape Floppy disk (80 Kbyte)
System cost	$900–$1,200	$800	$900–$1,400	$800–$2,400	$600–$2,000	$600–$1,800

dimension. Most of the performance and structure dimensions for general-purpose computers will apply to the Personal computing function. However, certain techniques may be emphasized on account of the requirement for a low price (e.g., time multiplexing of Pc between computation and I/O, as discussed in Chap. 33 on the Alto). Several examples of personal computers can be found in this book.

TMS 1000

Chapter 34 describes a monolithic microcomputer designed for hand-held calculators. These calculators were the first example of widespread low-priced, dedicated computing systems.

HP 9100A, HP 9810/20/30, HP 9845

Chapters 48, 49, and 31 trace the evolution of the Hewlett-Packard scientific calculators from function per key (HP 9100A) to simple algebraic programmable languages (HP 9820), then to BASIC (HP 9830), and finally to a sophisticated single-user computer (HP 9845).

Alto

The Xerox Palo Alto Research Center (PARC) Alto is a high-performance personal computer with sophisticated I/O, including a raster-scanned display for characters, curves, and halftone and gray scale pictures. The high-performance Pc is multiplexed between computation, input (e.g., keyboard and "mouse" pointing device), output (e.g., raster-scanned display), Ms (disk), and network interfaces. This multiplexing reduced cost while allowing high maximum throughput for several devices (e.g., Pc, Mdisk, and Tdisplay). Hardware multiplexing between the Pc and Pio has been used for several years in general-purpose computers such as the IBM System/360 and System/370 implementations (see Part 4, Sec. 5).

References

Mennie [1978]

Chapter 33

Alto: A Personal Computer[1]

C. P. Thacker / E. M. McCreight /
B. W. Lampson / R. F. Sproull / D. R. Boggs

Summary The Alto is a small computer system designed in early 1973 as an experiment in personal computing. Its principal characteristics, some of the design choices that led to the implementation, and some of the applications for which the Alto has been used are discussed.

1. Introduction

During early 1973, the Xerox Palo Alto Research Center designed the Alto computer system ("Alto") as an experiment in personal computing, to study how a small, low-cost machine could be used to replace facilities then provided only by much larger, shared systems. During the succeeding six years, the original Alto underwent several engineering enhancements to increase its memory capacity and reduce its cost, but the basic capabilities of the system have remained essentially unchanged. There are now (early 1979) several hundred Altos in regular use by computer science researchers, engineers, and secretaries.

The primary goal in the design of the Alto was to provide sufficient computing power, local storage, and input-output capability to satisfy the computational needs of a single user. The standard system includes:

- An 875-line raster-scanned display
- A keyboard, a "mouse" pointing device with three buttons, and a five-finger keyset
- A 2.5-Mbyte cartridge disk file
- An interface to the Ethernet system ("Ethernet"), a 3-Mbit/sec communication facility
- A microprogrammed processor that controls input-output devices and supports emulators for a number of instruction sets
- 64K 16-bit words of semiconductor memory, expandable to 256K words

All of these components with the exception of the user terminal are packaged in a small cabinet which is an unobtrusive addition to a normal office. The terminal, keyboard, and pointing device are packaged for desktop use (Fig. 1).

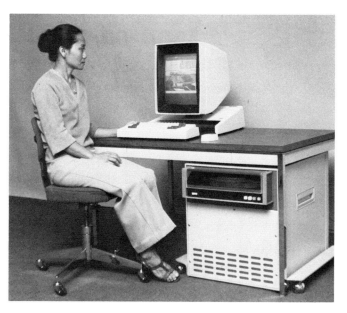

Fig. 1. The Alto personal computer, showing a user at work with the display, mouse, and keyset.

The Alto has led to an entirely new computing environment. Many applications devote the entire machine to interacting with a user and satisfying his needs; examples are document production and illustration, interactive programming, animation, simulation, and playing music. These individual applications are supplemented by a large number of services available via communications; examples are printing service, mailbox services for delivering electronic mail, and bulk file storage services. The Ethernet has also given rise to applications that use several Altos concurrently to furnish additional computing power or to allow several people at their machines to interact with one another.

The principal characteristics of the Alto processor are described in Sec. 2 of this chapter. Sections 3 to 6 describe input-output controllers for the display, disk, Ethernet, and printer. Section 7 surveys the environment and applications that grew up for the Alto. Section 8 offers a brief retrospective look at the design.

2. The Alto Processor

The major applications envisioned for the Alto were interaction text editing for document and program preparation, support for the program development process, experimenting with real-time animation and music generation, and operation of a number of experimental office information systems. The hardware design was strongly affected by this view of the applications. The design is biased toward interaction with the user, and away from significant numerical processing; there are extensive user input-output facilities, but no hardware for arithmetic other than 16-bit integer addition and subtraction.

The processor is microcoded, which permitted the machine to start out with rather powerful facilities, and also allows easy expansion as new capabilities are required. The amount of control store provided has evolved over time as shown in Fig. 2. Initially, the machine contained only 1K words, implemented with PROM. The most recent version provides 4K words, of which 1K is implemented with PROM and 3K is RAM.

The micromachine is shared by sixteen fixed-priority *tasks*. The emulator, which interprets instructions of the user's program, is the lowest-priority task; the remaining tasks are used for the microcoded portions of input-output controllers and for house-keeping functions. Control of the micromachine typically switches from one task to another every few microseconds, in response to *wakeup requests* generated by the I/O controllers. The emulator task requests a wakeup at all times, and runs if no higher-priority task requires the processor. There is usually no overhead associated with a task switch, since the microprogram counters (MPCs) for all tasks are stored in a special high-speed RAM, the MPC RAM. The main memory is synchronous with the processor, which controls all memory requests.

The task-switching mechanism provides a way of multiplexing all the system resources, both processor and memory cycles, among the consumers of these resources. In most small systems with single-ported memories, the *memory* is multiplexed among the I/O controllers and the CPU, and when an I/O controller is accessing the memory, the CPU is idle. In the Alto, the *processor* is multiplexed, and multiplexing of the memory is a natural consequence. By sharing the hardware in this way, it has been possible to provide more capable logical interfaces to the I/O devices than are usually found in small machines, since the I/O

controllers have the full processing capability and temporary storage of the micromachine at their disposal.

The standard Alto contains controllers for the disk, the display, and the Ethernet. The disk controller uses two tasks, the display and the cursor use a total of four tasks, and the Ethernet uses one task. In addition to the emulator task, there is a *timed task* that is awakened every 38 μs, and a *fault task* that is awaked whenever a memory error occurs and is responsible for logging the error and generating an interrupt. The timed task refreshes the main memory, and maintains the real-time clock and an interval timer accessible from the emulator.

The main memory size of the Alto was initially 64K words, implemented with 1K bit semiconductor RAM chips. As semiconductor technology improved, the memory size was increased, as shown in Fig. 2. The initial version of the machine provided parity checking; later configurations employ single error correction and double error detection. Memory access time is 850 ns (five microinstruction cycles), and either one or two words can be transferred during a single memory cycle. In machines with more than 64K, access to extended memory is provided via *bank registers* accessible to the micromachine, and the standard instruction set and I/O controller microcode make use of the additional memory only in limited ways. The reason for this clumsy arrangement is that the lifetime of the Alto has been longer than originally anticipated, and the additional memory was an unplanned addition.

Because the machine was intended for personal use, protection and virtual memory facilities normally included to support sharing were omitted from the Alto.

The multitasking structure of the processor led to an extremely simple implementation. The processor is contained on five printed circuit boards, each of which contains approximately seventy small- and medium-scale TTL integrated circuits. Each of the three standard I/O controllers occupies a board with about 70 ICs. The main memory uses 312 chips.

Year	Main Memory		Control Memory		Processor Memory	
	Size	Technology	Size	Technology	Size	Technology
1973	64K Parity	1K x 1 Dynamic Metal gate PMOS	1K PROM	256 x 4 Schottky bipolar	32 R registers	16 x 4 Schottky bipolar
1974			1K PROM 1K RAM	PROM as above 1K x 1 RAMs Schottky bipolar	32 R registers 32 S registers	16 x 4 Schottky bipolar
1975	64K Error Correction	4K x 1 Dynamic Si gate NMOS				
1976			2K PROM 1K RAM	1K x 4 PROMs Schottky bipolar RAM as above		
1977	256K Error Correction	16K x 1 Dynamic Si gate NMOS				
1979			1K PROM 3K RAM	PROM as above 4K x 1 RAMs Static NMOS	32 R registers 8 x 32 S registers	R registers as above 256 x 4 Schottky bipolar

Fig. 2. Sizes and technologies used for the principal memories in the Alto.

2.1 Emulators

There are emulators for several instruction sets, including BCPL [Richards, 1969], Smalltalk [Kay, 1977; Ingalls, 1978], Lisp [Deutsch, 1979], and Mesa [Mitchell, Maybury, and Sweet, 1979]. The BCPL emulator is contained in the PROM microstore, while the others are loaded into RAM as needed. The BCPL instruction set was chosen because it is straightforward to implement and because we had previously developed a BCPL compiler for a similar instruction set. BCPL is a typeless implementation language; it has much in common with its well-known descendant, C [Ritchie et al., 1978]. The language was used extensively to build Alto software; very little assembly language code has been written for the Alto.

The BCPL instruction set and the virtual machine it provides are summarized in Fig. 3. Instructions are divided into four groups:

M-Group instructions transfer 16-bit words between memory

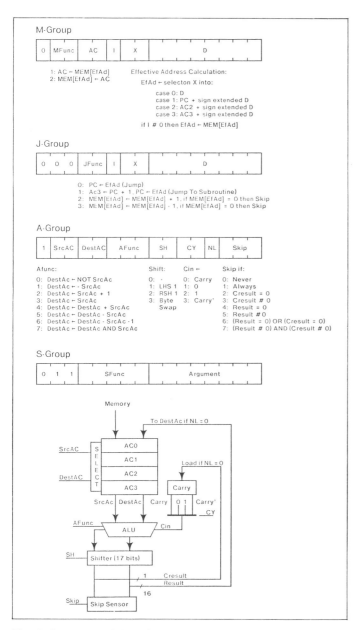

Fig. 3. Summary of the BCPL instruction set and the processor model implemented by that instruction set.

and one of the four accumulators AC0–AC3. These instructions provide four indexing modes, and one level of indirection is allowed. The effective address is a 16-bit quantity, allowing access to a 64K word address space.

J-Group instructions include unconditional and subroutine jumps, and two instructions that increment and decrement a memory location and test the resulting value for zero. The effective address for these operations is calculated in the same way as for the M-Group.

A-Group instructions provide register-to-register arithmetic operations, shifts by one or eight places, and conditional skips based on the result of the operation.

S-Group instructions provide a number of functions that do not fit within the framework of the first three groups. Instructions are provided for loading, reading, and transferring control to special microcode in the writable microstore, operating the real-time clock and interval timers, optimizing BCPL procedure calls, accessing the extended memory, and maintaining specialized data structures used by the display.

The BCPL emulator provides a vectored interrupt system with 16 interrupt channels. There is no hardware support for interrupts; they are implemented entirely in microcode. (Note that the interrupt system is completely separate from the task-switching mechanism; the latter multiplexes the micromachine, while the former multiplexes the emulator.) When the microcode associated with an I/O controller wishes to cause an interrupt, it ORs one or more bits into a micromachine register, NIW (New Interrupts Waiting). If the i-th bit of NIW is set, an interrupt on channel i is requested. At the start of every macroinstruction, NIW is tested; if it is nonzero, and if the corresponding channel is active, the emulator's macroprogram counter is saved in a fixed location in main memory and control is transferred to a location taken from a sixteen-word table that starts at a fixed location. Individual channels are made active by setting bits in another fixed location. There are S-group instructions to enable and disable the entire interrupt system, and to return control from an interrupt routine.

2.2 Input-Output

I/O devices may be connected to the Alto in one of three ways, depending on the bandwidth required by the device and on the degree to which the controller is supported by specialized microcode. The three methods of connection and the level of the machine used to interface the hardware are summarized in the matrix of Fig. 4.

Device controllers that require significant bandwidth, or exploit the computational facilities of the micromachine, are connected directly to the processor bus, and use one or more of the sixteen microcode tasks. The disk, display, and Ethernet controllers, which are part of the standard Alto, are interfaced in

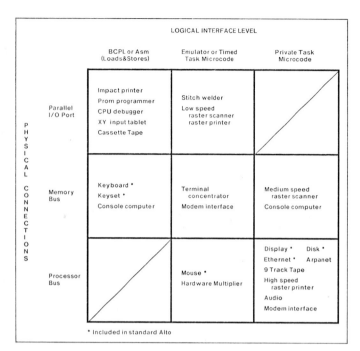

LOGICAL INTERFACE LEVEL

		BCPL or Asm (Loads&Stores)	Emulator or Timed Task Microcode	Private Task Microcode
P H Y S I C A L C O N N E C T I O N S	Parallel I/O Port	Impact printer Prom programmer CPU debugger XY input tablet Cassette Tape	Stitch welder Low speed raster scanner raster printer	
	Memory Bus	Keyboard * Keyset * Console computer	Terminal concentrator Modem interface	Medium speed raster scanner Console computer
	Processor Bus		Mouse * Hardware Multiplier	Display * Disk * Ethernet * Arpanet 9 Track Tape High speed raster printer Audio Modem interface

* Included in standard Alto

Fig. 4. Schematic illustration of input-output attachments used on the Alto.

this way. The controller for a high-speed raster-scanned printer is an example of a non-standard I/O controller interfaced directly to the processor bus. These devices are described in detail in later sections.

Processor bus devices have one or more dedicated tasks that provide processing and initiate all memory references for the device controller; the tasks communicate with programs through fixed locations and data structures in main memory, and through interrupts. By convention, the second page of the address space is reserved for communication with devices of this type. Since there is only one processor, data structures shared between I/O controllers and programs can be interlocked by simply not allowing task switches in critical sections of device-control microcode.

The amount of data buffering in a device controller, its task priority, and the bandwidth of the device trade off much as they do in systems which have DMA controllers competing for memory access. The controller must have enough buffering so that the wakeup latency introduced by higher-priority devices will not cause the buffer to over- or underrun before it can obtain service. The disk, for example, has only one word of buffering (10 μs at 1.5 Mbits/sec), and is therefore the highest-priority task. The Ethernet requires more bandwidth, but since it has a 16-word buffer, it can tolerate much greater latency than the disk (87 μs at 3 Mbits/sec), and hence runs at low priority. The display requires

the highest bandwidth but it also has a 16-word buffer, so it can tolerate slightly more latency than the disk (12.8 μs at 20 Mbits/sec), and is therefore between the disk and Ethernet in priority.

It is also possible to connect a device directly to the processor bus without using a separate task. The microcode of the timed task, normally used to refresh the memory, may be modified to operate devices that require periodic service. When this is done, the timed task microcode is run in the writable microstore. The mouse, a pointing device that provides relative positioning information by being rolled over a work surface, is operated by the timed task. At 38-μs intervals, the mouse is interrogated for changes in position, and two memory locations corresponding to the mouse x and y coordinates are incremented or decremented when a change occurs. Specialized devices may also be operated directly by the emulator microcode; a hardware multiplier is an example of this type of device. An S-group instruction is added in the writable microstore that loads the registers of the multiplier from the ACs, initiates the desired operation, and copies the results back into ACs when the operation terminates.

Devices with less demanding bandwidth requirements, or with computational requirements that can be satisfied by an emulator program rather than by a microprogram, are interfaced to the memory bus of the Alto. The advantage of this method is that no special microcode is needed. Communication between the hardware and a program is done using ordinary memory reference instructions, as in the PDP-11. The device controller decodes the memory address lines and delivers or accepts data under control of a read/write signal generated by the processor. The last two 256-word pages of the address space are reserved by the hardware for this purpose. Since a memory access requires five microinstruction cycles, these devices cannot transfer data as rapidly as those connected directly to the processor bus, where the transfer is controlled by the microinstruction and requires only one cycle. In the standard Alto, the keyboard and keyset are examples of devices handled in this way.

It is also possible to provide special microcode for devices that interface to the memory bus. A network gateway that connects 64 300-baud communication lines to the Ethernet has been implemented in this way. The scanner hardware consists of a single bit of buffering for the output lines and level conversion for the input lines. Serialization and deserialization of eight-bit characters is done by microcode that is a part of the timed task; characters are passed to a macroprogram via queues maintained in main memory by this microcode. The macroprogram implements the higher-level communication protocols.

The standard Alto provides a third method of connecting simple devices, the *parallel I/O port*. This is a memory bus device, and consists of a single 16-bit register that can be loaded by a *store* instruction, and a set of 16 input lines that can be read by a *load* instruction. The device controller does not occupy a card slot in the backplane, but is external to the machine and attaches via a cable to a standard connector on the back of the machine, which in turn is wired to the memory control board. A large number of devices have been connected to the Alto through this simple interface, including low-speed impact printers, a PROM programmer, a stitchwelding machine for the fabrication of circuit boards, and several types of low-speed raster printers. Most devices that use speed-insensitive handshake protocols can be interfaced via the parallel I/O port; such devices require neither specialized hardware nor microcode.

2.3 Details of the Micromachine—Control

The microinstruction format of the Alto is shown in Fig. 5, and the principal data paths and registers of the micromachine are shown in Fig. 6. Each microinstruction specifies:

- The source of processor bus data (BS)
- The operation to be performed by the ALU (ALUF)
- Two special functions controlled by the F1 and F2 fields
- Optional loading of the T and L registers (LT, LL)
- The address of the next microinstruction (NEXT)

All microinstructions require one clock cycle (170 ns) for their execution. If a microinstruction specifies that one or more registers are to be loaded, this happens at the end of the cycle.

The Alto does not have an incrementing microprogram counter. Instead, each microinstruction specifies the least significant ten bits of the address of its successor using the NEXT field in the instruction. This successor address may be modified by the branch logic or by the I/O controllers. There are special functions to switch banks in the microstore, allowing access to the entire 4K address space. The address of the next microinstruction to be

executed by each of the 16 tasks supported by the micromachine is contained in the 16-word MPC RAM. This RAM is addressed by the NTASK register, which contains the number of the task that will have control of the processor in the next cycle. The MPC RAM value for the current task is updated every microinstruction cycle.

Execution of a microinstruction begins when the instruction is loaded into the Microinstruction Register (MIR) from the control store outputs. At this time, the information on the NEXT bus is written into the MPC RAM at the location addressed by the NTASK register. This value is the address of the next instruction; within a short time, it appears at the output of the MPC RAM, the next instruction is fetched from the control store, and the cycle repeats.

Conditional branches are implemented by ORing one or more bits with the NEXT address value supplied by the control store. The source of the data to be ORed is usually specified by the F2 field; it may be a single bit—for example, the result of the BUS=0 test—or it may be several bits supplied on the NEXT bus by an I/O controller or by specialized logic. When the value consists of an n-bit field, a 2^n-way branch, or *dispatch*, is done. Because the next instruction is already being fetched while the instruction is being executed, conditional branches and dispatches affect not the address of an instruction's immediate successor, but the instruction following that one. It is possible to execute branches in successive instructions, providing this pipelining is taken into account by the microprogrammer. This branching scheme constrains the placement of instructions in the microstore, but the constraints are satisfied semi-automatically by the microprogram assembler.

Task switching in the Alto is done by changing the value in the NTASK register. As long as the value in this register does not change, a task will remain in control of the processor. A task gives up control of the processor by executing a microinstruction

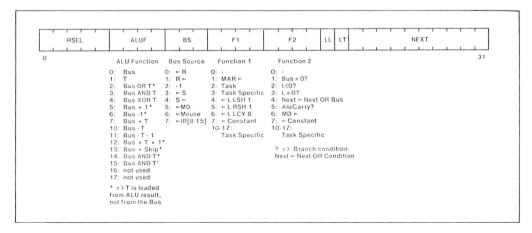

Fig. 5. Alto microinstruction format.

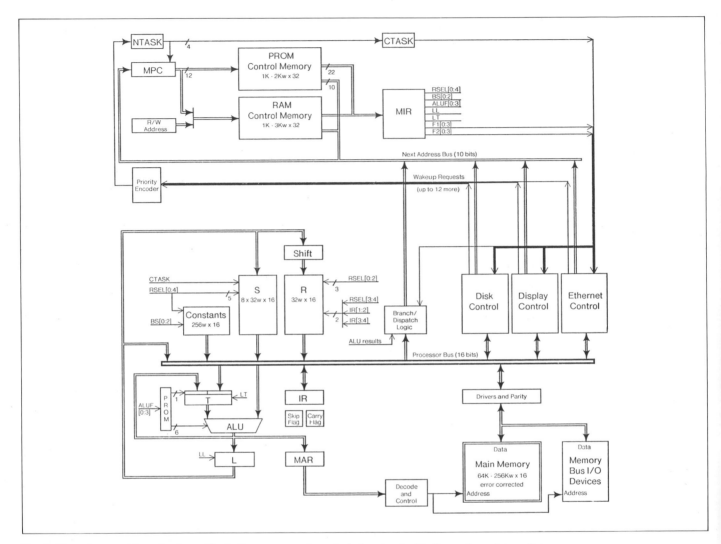

Fig. 6. Alto micromachine structure. Single lines represent control signals, double lines show data paths.

containing F1=TASK. This function loads the NTASK register from the output of a priority encoder whose inputs are the 16 *wakeup request* lines, one per task. An I/O controller indicates its need for service from the processor by asserting the request line associated with its task. If it is the highest-priority requester when the running microprogram executes the TASK function, NTASK will be loaded with its task number; after a one-instruction delay, the new task will acquire the processor. In the microinstruction following a TASK, a microprogram may not execute a conditional branch, and it must not allow a task switch when it has state in the L or T register, since none of the state of a task other than the MPC value is saved across a task switch. With these exceptions, there is no overhead associated with task switching.

The conditions that cause I/O controllers to request wakeups are determined by the controller hardware, and are usually simple—an empty buffer requires data, or a sector pulse has been received by the disk controller, for example. When the microcode associated with the controller has processed the request and commanded the controller to remove the wakeup request, the microprogram then TASKs, relinquishing control of the processor.

By convention, eight of the possible values of the F1 and F2 fields of the microinstruction are *task-specific*; that is, they have different meanings depending on which task is running. Each I/O controller can determine when its associated task has control of the processor by decoding the NTASK lines. When the task associated with a controller is running, the controller decodes the

F1 and F2 lines and uses them to control data transfers, to specify branch conditions, or for other device-specific purposes. This encoding reduces the size of the microinstruction.

The intimate coupling between the micromachine and the I/O controllers has proven to be one of the most powerful features of the Alto. When a new I/O device is added, the controller not only has at its disposal the basic arithmetic and control facilities of the micromachine, but it can also implement specialized functions controlled by the task-specific function fields of the microinstruction. This has led to extremely simple hardware in the I/O controllers. Most controllers consist of a small amount of buffering to absorb wakeup latency, registers and interface logic to implement the electrical protocols of the device, and a small amount of logic to decode the F1 and F2 lines, generate wakeups, and do whatever high-speed housekeeping is required by the device. Since the processor makes all the memory requests, controllers never manipulate memory addresses, and the usual DMA hardware found in most minicomputers is eliminated.

It might appear that sharing the processor in this way would result in a significant degradation in performance, particularly for low-priority tasks such as the emulator. This is in fact not the case; *the major bottleneck in the system is the memory*. Since most computation can be overlapped with memory operation, the performance of the Alto compares favorably with other systems employing single-ported, non-interleaved memory at comparable I/O bandwidths.

2.4 Details of the Micromachine—Arithmetic

The arithmetic section of the Alto contains the following components:

A 16-bit processor bus, used to transmit data between the subsections of the processor, the memory, and the I/O controllers. The source of bus data is controlled by the BS and the F1 fields of the instruction.

A bank of 32 16-bit *R registers*, and eight banks of 32 16-bit *S registers*. These registers have slightly different properties, and together constitute the high-speed storage of the processor. As better integrated-circuit technology has become available, the number of S registers has been increased as shown in Fig. 2. R and S are addressed by the RSEL field of the instruction; either R or S (but not both) can be used during a single instruction. Reading and loading of R and S are controlled by the BS field of the instruction.

A 16-bit T register. T is loaded when the LT bit is set in the microinstruction. The source of T data is determined by the ALU function being executed; it is usually the bus, but may be the output of the ALU. T is one of the inputs of the ALU.

A 16-bit Arithmetic/Logic Unit (ALU). The ALU is implemented with four SN74S181 ICs. These devices can provide 64 arithmetic and logical functions, most of which are useless. The

fourteen most useful functions are selected by the four-bit ALUF field of the microinstruction, which is mapped by a PROM into the control signals required by the chips.

A 16-bit L register. L is loaded from the ALU output when the LL bit is set in the microinstruction.

A shifter capable of shifting the data from L left or right by one bit position and exchanging the two halves of a word. Simple shifts are controlled by the F1 field of the instruction (F1=4, 5,6). In the emulator task, these functions may be augmented by the F2 field to do specialized shifts required by the BCPL instruction set, and to do double-length shifts for microcoded multiply and divide.

A 16-bit Memory Address Register (MAR), described later.

A 256-word by 16-bit constant memory, implemented with PROMS. This memory is addressed by the concatenation of the RSEL and BS fields of the instruction; when F1 or F2=CONSTANT, the normal actions evoked by RSEL and BS are suppressed, and the selected constant is placed on the bus. Approximately 200 of the 256 available constants have been used.

An Instruction Register (IR) that holds the current macroinstruction being executed by the BCPL emulator.

The main memory is synchronous with the processor, which initiates all memory references by loading MAR with the 16-bit address of a location. During a memory reference, data may be transferred between the memory and any register connected to the bus, including registers in the I/O controllers. The memory can transfer a doubleword quantity during two successive instruction cycles, as part of a single memory cycle. Using this access method, which was provided to support high-performance peripherals such as the display, the peak memory bandwidth is 32 bits/(6 * 170 ns) = 31.3 Mbits/sec.

The arithmetic section of the Alto contains a small amount of hardware to support the emulator for the BCPL instruction set. There are special paths to supply part of the R address from the SrcAC and DestAC fields of IR, logic to dispatch on several fields in IR, and hardware to control the shifter and maintain the CARRY and SKIP flags. The total amount of specialized hardware is less than ten ICs.

No special hardware has been added to support emulators for other instruction sets. These usually specify the operation to be performed with a single eight-bit byte, followed by one or two bytes that supply additional parameters for some of the operations. The standard dispatching mechanism is used to do an initial 256-way dispatch to the microcode that emulates each macroinstruction.

The dispatching mechanism has been used for other applications. Although the micromachine does not support subroutine linkage in the hardware, it has been possible to achieve the same effect with only a small performance penalty. The calling microcode supplies a small constant as a *return index* (typically in T) which is saved and used as a dispatch value to return to the caller when the subroutine has completed its work. The Mesa emulator implements an eight word operand stack by dispatching on the value of the stack pointer into several tables of eight microinstructions, each of which reads or writes a particular R-register.

The parallelism available in the microinstruction format encourages the use of complex control structures which are often substituted for specialized data-handling capabilities; it is usually possible to do an arithmetic operation, a branch or dispatch, and at least one special function in each instruction.

3.   User Input-Output

The main goals in the design of the Alto's user input-output were generality of the facilities and simplicity of the hardware. We also attached a high value to modeling the capabilities of existing manual media; after all, these have evolved over many hundreds of years. There are good reasons for most of their characteristics, and much has been learned about how to use them effectively. The manual media we chose as models were paper and ink (the display), pointing devices (the mouse and cursor), and keyboard devices ranging from typewriters to pianos and organs.

3.1 The Display

The most important characteristic of paper and ink is that the ink can be arranged in arbitrarily chosen patterns on the paper; there are almost no constraints on the size, shape, or position of the ink marks. This flexibility is used in a number of ways:

Characters of many shapes and styles not only represent words, but convey much important information by variations in size and appearance (italics, boldface, a variety of styles).

Straight lines and *curves* make up line drawings ranging in complexity from a simple business form to an engineering drawing of an automatic transmission.

Textures and shades of gray, and *color*, are used to organize and highlight information, and to add a third to the two dimensions of spatial arrangement.

Halftones make it possible to represent natural images which have continuous tones.

Fine-grained *positioning* in two dimensions produces effects ranging from the simple (superscripts, marginal notes, multiple columns) to the complex (mathematical formulas, legends in figures).

The *high resolution* of ink, combined with the absence of positioning constraints, means that a large amount of information can be presented on a single page.

In addition to imaging flexibility, paper and ink have several other important properties:

Large sizes of paper can present the spatial relationships of many thousands of objects.

Many sheets of paper can be *spread out*, so that many pages can be wholly or partially visible.

Many sheets of paper can be *bound together*, so that one item from a very large collection of information can be examined within a small number of seconds.

Only one technique is known for approximating *all* these properties of paper in a computer-generated medium: a raster display in which the value of each picture element is independently stored as an element in a two-dimensional array called a *bitmap* or *frame buffer*. If the size of a picture element is small enough, such a display can approximate the first five properties extremely well; about 500–1000 binary (black or white) elements per inch are needed for high quality, or 25–100 million bits for a standard 8.5 by 11-inch page. Another approach (which we did not pursue) is to exploit the fact that unlike paper and ink, the display can provide true gray. If each picture element can assume one of 256 intensity values (or a triple of such values for color), almost all images which are made on paper can be reproduced with many fewer picture elements than are needed if the elements are binary; about 100–150 elements per inch are now sufficient, or 8–18 million bits for a page.

Even eight million bits of bitmap was more than we could afford in 1973. Furthermore, the computer display cannot hope to match paper in size, or in the number of pages which can be visible simultaneously. To make up for this deficiency, and to model page turning, it is necessary to alter the image on the screen very rapidly, so that changes in the single-screen image can substitute for changes in where the eye is looking and for the physical motion of paper. As the number of bits representing the image grows, more processing bandwidth is required to compose it at acceptable speeds.

Fortunately, surprisingly good images can be made with many fewer bits, if we settle for images which preserve the recognizable characteristics of paper and ink, rather than insisting on all the details of image quality. Characters 10 points or larger (these are printer's points, 72 per inch, and the characters in this sentence are 9-point) in several distinguishable styles and in boldface or italic, almost arbitrary line drawings, and dozens of textures are quite comfortable to read when represented by about 70 binary elements per inch; this resolution is also sufficient for crude but recognizable characters down to 7 points, and for halftones of similar quality. One page at this resolution is about half a million bits, or half of the Alto's one-megabit memory.

The display is an interlaced 875-line monitor running at 30

frames/second. There are 808 visible scan lines, and 608 picture elements per line. It is oriented with the long dimension vertical, and the screen area is almost exactly the same size as a standard sheet of paper (Fig. 7). Refreshing the display demands an *average* of 15 Mbits/sec of memory bandwidth. Since the average includes considerable time for horizontal and vertical retrace, the peak bandwidth is 20 Mbits/sec. The 30-Hz refresh rate results in flicker which most people do not find objectionable, provided the image does not contain large amounts of detail which appears in only one of the two interlaced fields. Flicker is reduced by the use of P40 phosphor in the CRT, rather than the faster P4 often used; the greater persistence of images which are being moved has not proved to be a problem.

3.2 Bitmap Representation

A bitmap which can be painted on the display is represented in storage by a contiguous block of words. A bitmap on the Alto represents a rectangular image, w picture elements wide and h elements high. For simplicity, w must be a multiple of 16, and one row of w picture elements corresponds to $w/16$ contiguous words in the bitmap. As a consequence, two vertically adjacent elements correspond to the same bit in two words which are $w/16$ words apart in storage (Fig. 8).

The display microcode interprets a chain of *display control blocks* stored in memory, with its head at a fixed location. Each block specifies its successor, the number of scan lines it controls,

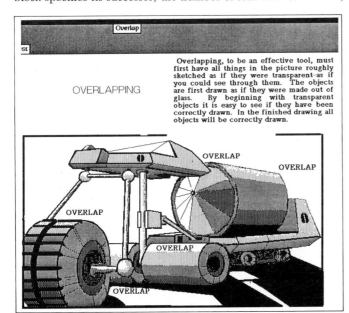

Fig. 7. An example of text and graphics filling an Alto display screen.

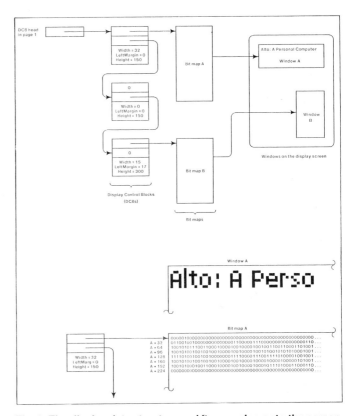

Fig. 8. The display data structure and its mapping onto the screen. The top part of the figure illustrates several control blocks and the corresponding screen windows they control. The lower part shows the relation between a bitmap in memory and the image on the screen. Note that the pattern of 1's in the bitmap corresponds to the pattern of black dots on the screen.

the left margin (in 16-element units) of the screen area to be painted from the bitmap in storage, the address and width of the bitmap array, and the *polarity*, which determines whether zeros in memory are displayed as white (the normal case) or black. The left and right margins not painted from the bitmap are filled with zeros. This scheme allows the screen to be divided into horizontal strips, each with its own bitmap; its advantages and drawbacks are discussed below.

To simulate an 8.5 by 11-inch page we use a single control block which covers all 808 visible scan lines, has no left margin, and is 608 bits (38 words) wide. This is a *full screen* bitmap; it consumes about half the main storage of the standard machine, and displaying it consumes about 60% of the cycles. In return, it can display nearly any image which can appear on a standard sheet of paper. More restricted images, however, can be displayed more economically. An ordinary text page like this one, for example, can be divided into horizontal strips. The white space in the margins, in indentations, and to the right of the last line in each paragraph need not appear in the bitmap. The leading between the lines and the margins at top and bottom, can be represented by control blocks specifying a width of zero. For a typical text page these tricks reduce the size of the bitmap to about 70% of its full size; pages of program listing are reduced by much more. Furthermore, lines can be inserted or deleted simply by splicing pointers in the control block chain, and parts of the image can be scrolled up or down by adjusting the number of scan lines covered by one of the zero-width control blocks, without moving anything in storage.

Unfortunately, these techniques rule out anything except a single column of text in the image, since various parts of the image no longer have any supporting bitmap. Multiple columns (unless the lines are perfectly aligned), marginal notes, long vertical lines, and windows which do not fill the screen horizontally are not possible. We have used multiple control blocks heavily in the Alto's standard text editor, which includes extensive facilities for using multiple fonts, controlling margins and leading, justification, etc. The editor continuously displays the text in its final formatted form, so that no separate operations are required to view the final document. In this context the control block tricks have made it possible to fit the editor into the machine, which we could not have done using a full-screen bitmap. All the other interesting uses of the display, however, have adopted the full-screen bitmap so that they could support more general images, and we are convinced that the cost of memory is no longer high enough to justify giving up this generality.

3.3 Composing the Image

Because many bits are needed to display an image, we have found the machine's ordinary data manipulation instructions inadequate for handling images. It is important to have fast ways of building up the most common kinds of images and making certain common changes (e.g., moving or scrolling a window). For this purpose the Alto has one major microcoded operation called BitBlt (for bit boundary block transfer), with a surprising number of uses. It works on *rectangles* within bitmaps; such a rectangle is defined by the width of the bitmap (which determines the spacing in storage of vertically adjacent elements), the address of the bit which corresponds to the upper left corner of the rectangle, and the height and width of the rectangle (in bits). BitBlt takes two such rectangles, called the *source* and the *destination*, and does

$$destination \leftarrow F \ (destination, \ source)$$

where $F \ (d, s)$ can be s (move), d OR s (paint), d XOR s (invert) or d AND s (erase), or any of these with s complemented. It is also possible to supply a 16×4 rectangle for the source and have it

used repetitively; this is useful for producing uniform textures. The properties of BitBlt, which was designed by Dan Ingalls, are discussed in more detail in Newmann and Sproull [1979], where it goes under the name *RasterOp*.

BitBlt has a large number of applications, among them

> Painting characters from a *font*, which is simply another bitmap, held somewhere in storage, that contains images of the characters. It is interesting to note that "characters" can also be used to represent various specialized kinds of graphics, such as the symbols in hardware logic drawings.

> Drawing horizontal and vertical lines (which are just narrow rectangles).

> Filling in rectangular areas with textured patterns.

> Scrolling an image across a fixed rectangular window on the screen, or moving such a window around on the screen.

> Moving an image onto the screen from a copy elsewhere in storage.

> Saving part of the image in memory that is not part of the display bitmap. Later, the saved image can be copied back to cause it to reappear on the screen.

The Alto also has a specialized operation for painting characters; it is considerably less flexible than BitBlt, but easier to invoke and more efficient.

Sometimes one would also like fast operations for painting arbitrary lines and curves, and for filling solid areas bounded by such shapes, but so far we have not found the need for these to be great. Instead, these requirements are adequately met by the Alto's ordinary memory reference instructions, which can be used to randomly access and update the display with complete flexibility. We have found this to be quite important, and believe that it is a significant advantage of the Alto architecture over conventional frame-buffer organizations. The ability to reuse part or all of the bitmap memory for other purposes when a full-screen display is not required has also been very important; with the decreasing cost of memory this is no longer such a significant consideration.

3.4 Display Hardware

This display is supported by three microcode tasks and some very simple hardware (Fig. 9). Serial video data is clocked by a 50-ns bit clock; everything else is clocked by the machine's 170-ns main clock, which is chosen to be an integral submultiple (224) of the display's line rate $(875 * 30 = 26.25 \ kHz)$. A 16-word RAM and a one-word register implement a FIFO buffer and synchronizer between the processor bus and the shift register which serializes data for the display. There is a sync generator with a counter and PROM for horizontal sync and one for vertical sync, and logic to

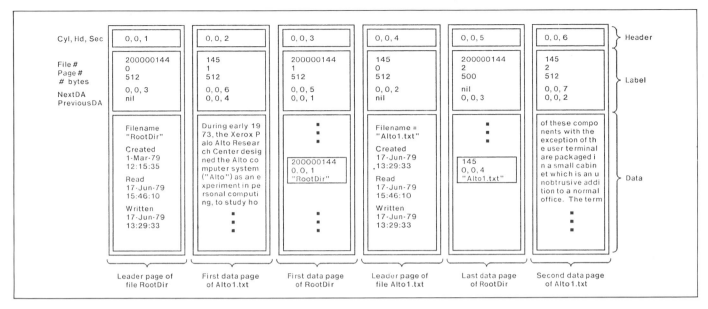

Cyl, Hd, Sec	0, 0, 1	0, 0, 2	0, 0, 3	0, 0, 4	0, 0, 5	0, 0, 6	Header
File # Page # # bytes	200000144 0 512	145 1 512	200000144 1 512	145 0 512	200000144 2 500	145 2 512	Label
NextDA PreviousDA	0, 0, 3 nil	0, 0, 6 0, 0, 4	0, 0, 5 0, 0, 1	0, 0, 2 nil	nil 0, 0, 3	0, 0, 7 0, 0, 2	

Fig. 9. The display controller.

wake up the *data task* whenever the FIFO is not full, the *line task* when horizontal blanking starts, and the *field task* when vertical blanking starts. There is also some logic to support the cursor described in Sec. 3.5.

The field task runs 60 times a second, and is responsible for initializing the line task at the head of the chain of control blocks. It also generates a 60-Hz interrupt. The link task runs every 38 μs; it initializes the left margin width, bitmap address and bitmap width for the data task, and advances to the next control block if the current one is exhausted. When no control blocks remain, it goes to sleep until reawakened by the field task. The data task outputs zeros until the left margin is exhausted, then fetches doublewords from storage and delivers them to the FIFO until the bitmap width is exhausted, after which it goes to sleep until reawakened by the line task. A doubleword fetch takes six cycles or 1.05 μs, and the 32 bits are consumed in 1.6 μs, so the data task consumes two thirds of the machine while data is being displayed (which is 73% of the time, the rest being spent in retracing).

3.5 Pointing

A user working interactively with images frequently points at parts of the image, to identify the spot where something should be done, to select a menu item, to indicate the corners of a region, etc. For this purpose the Alto has a device called a *mouse*, which fits comfortably under a hand and can be rolled around on the work surface [English, Englebart, and Berman, 1967]. The mouse is supported on three ball bearings, and the x and y rotations of

one of these bearings are sensed by the Alto. The hardware senses motion by ±1 increments in each direction (one unit is roughly 1/200 inch), and microcode running in the timed task uses this information to update a pair of *mouse coordinates* in storage. Often it is also nice to be able to draw, and the mouse can do this, too, albeit somewhat clumsily. When drawing is important, a tablet is used, but this device interferes with the keyboard that it is not generally popular.

It is essential to have visual feedback which indicates the mouse position, since there is no direct visual or tactile connection between the mouse position and anything in the image on the screen. This feedback is provided by the *cursor*, which is a special 16×16 bitmap stored at a fixed place in memory, together with x and y coordinates that control where it is displayed. The cursor has its own microcode task, which runs after the display's line task and loads two hardware registers with the proper cursor data for the current scan line, and the x coordinate at which its first element should be displayed. The hardware starts shifting out the data when the display reaches the specified picture element, and it is ORed with the main display data. The connection between the mouse and the cursor coordinates is established entirely by software, which may, for example, restrict the cursor to some region of the screen, force it to move on a grid to facilitate lining things up, or make it "snap" onto sensitive points when it approaches close to them. Much use is made of the fact that the cursor image, though small (about ¼ sq. inch), is programmable. This turns out to be extremely valuable, because the user is much more likely to be looking at the cursor than anywhere else on the screen. A remarkable variety of shapes can be represented on those 256 bits, and a great deal of important information easily and unintrusively conveyed.

Another important property of the mouse is the three buttons on its top surface. These allow the user to specify a number of commands using the same hand with which he is pointing, especially when the meanings of the buttons are modified by shift keys on the keyboard, or by taking account of the duration or frequency of clicks. The current state of each button (up or down) appears as three bits in a special memory location, so that the program is free to attach meaning to any detail of the user's interaction with the buttons.

3.6 Keyboard

The Alto has a standard office typewriter keyboard, augmented with a small number (8) of extra keys. The keyboard appears to the program as four words of memory; each of the bits in these words reflects the current state of one key (up or down). This allows any key to be used as a shift key, and as with the mouse, it permits a variety of non-standard interpretations of the keys to be programmed, ranging from repeating keys to a digital electronic organ manual.

4.   Local Storage

The Alto has a reasonably powerful and very reliable disk file system. This file system is implemented on a 2.5 Mbyte moving-head removable-media rigid disk drive with which every Alto is equipped. All Alto software can read and write disk files, which are the usual interface among Alto software subsystems.

The disk controller consists of one board of special-purpose hardware and a share of the Alto micromachine. The disk controller and the file system were designed together, so that the functions of the controller match the functions of the file system. Thus, certain file system functions are performed entirely by the disk controller to insure speed or reliability. These functions are easily implemented because the full power of the Alto processor is available to the controller.

4.1 File System

An Alto disk pack contains a set of disk files. A disk file is a sequence of bytes, identified by a serial number unique within the disk pack. The disk controller and the file system software together implement a set of operations to create, extend, truncate, or delete files, and to read or write sequences of bytes within a file. A file is implemented as a non-contiguous sequence of fixed-length pages recorded on the disk pack. Each page of a file except the last is completely full of data (Fig. 10).

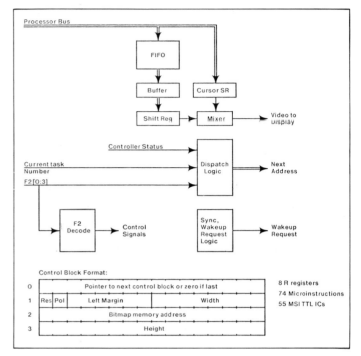

Fig. 10. The Alto file system structure.

The Alto file system is designed to be reliable. Many file systems have the property that bad data on a single page may create such confusion that the good data on the rest of the disk is practically useless. To control the global damage that could result from localized errors, the Alto file system distributes structural information to each page on the disk. Each page contains a special record called the *label*, different from the data record, that says, for example, "I am now serving as page 17 of file number 34152." Page 0 of a file, the *leader page*, holds information about the file: its alphanumeric name, the date of last modification, and so on; actual data begins in page 1. The distributed structural information recorded in the label (serial number, page number, length) and in the leader page (name) is the basic file system data structure.

The basic data structure is supplemented by a set of *hints*, performance-improving assertions whose truth can easily be verified. Because it is inefficient to scan the entire disk to find the leader page of a given file, a *directory* file maintains hints about file locations. If the directory file says that page 0 of file number 3456 is located at disk address 7890, then before doing anything irreversible at disk address 7890, the disk controller checks whether the label record at that address admits to being page 0 of file 3456. To allow rapid access to a sequence of pages, each label records as hints the disk addresses of the immediately preceding and following pages of the file (Fig. 10). If hints of any sort are found to be erroneous, they can be reconstructed from the distributed structural information. In fact, one of the most important programs on the Alto is the hint-reconstructing *Scavenger*.

The disk controller makes it easy to use hints properly and to do other common file-system operations. A disk operation is invoked with a *command block*, a group of words in main memory that specify a disk address, a page buffer address in main memory, and the transfer operation to be performed (Fig. 11). The disk controller is activated by putting the address of a command block into a particular main memory location. The controller performs the requested operation, writes the final status in the command block, and (if all went well) automatically proceeds to the next command block in a chain of blocks, linked by pointers. Disk command blocks are designed to be included in more complex operating system data structures describing pending disk transfers.

File system damage results as often from errant software as from errant hardware. The file system/disk controller design attempts to minimize damage in two ways. First, each disk command block is required to contain the *seal*, a certain exact bit pattern. The disk controller will stop immediately if it encounters an improper seal. Thus if the disk controller is accidentally activated on a block of memory that is not a legal disk command block, its seal would probably be improper, and file system damage would be avoided.

The second way to assure file system integrity is to check the label record before reading or writing, as mentioned earlier. Many disk controllers in other systems implement a header record for each page, separate from the data record, that is checked before reading or writing the data record. This strategy provides protection from failures of seeking or sector counting hardware, but not from software failures. An Alto disk sector incorporates separate header, label, and data records. The disk controller checks the header record to be sure the access hardware works, and then checks the label record to be sure that the file system software works, before reading or writing a data record.

4.2 Disk Interface

The disk controller consists of two micromachine tasks, four R registers, about 150 microinstructions, and a modest amount (about 55 MSI TTL ICs) of hardware (Fig. 11). The hardware is modest because it takes advantage of the computational power available in the micromachine. The hardware does only what the micromachine cannot do, either because of performance limitations or because remote sensing or control is involved: cable driving and receiving, data buffering, data serialization, and de-serialization, data encoding, sync pattern detection, and micromachine communication. With the particular disk drive used on the Alto (Diablo Model 31), the disk controller is responsible for encoding data into a self-clocking Manchester code during a write operation, but during a read operation the disk drive itself performs data-clock separation.

Various applications eventually led us to interface a much higher performance disk (CalComp Trident) as an option. The differences between the two disk controllers are almost entirely in areas where the micromachine has sufficient performance to handle some function for the slower disk, but not for the faster one. For example, although the Alto has sufficient main memory bandwidth to handle the Trident (9 Mbits/sec vs. 1.7 Mbits/sec for the Diablo), task wakeup latency (the time from when a wakeup is requested to when the task gets control of the micromachine) can be up to 2 μs, so multi-word buffering hardware is required in the faster controller.

4.2.1 Disk Sector Task. One micromachine task, called the sector task, is invoked whenever a sector notch on the rotating disk pack passes a reference location on the disk drive. There are 12 such notches around the disk, and one of them passes the reference location every 3 ms. The sector task can run at low priority because its needs for micromachine computation (about 12 μs) can be satisfied at any time in a 100-μs interval. When the sector task is invoked, it records the final status of the just-

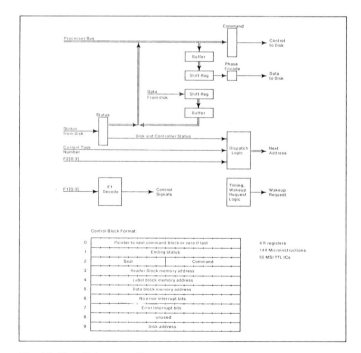

Fig. 11. The disk controller.

completed transfer operation (if there was one) in that operation's disk command block, records any requested interrupts in NIW, and checks to see if another command block requires processing. If there is no work to do, the sector task goes to sleep. This permits lower-priority tasks to run until another sector notch is encountered.

If there is new work, the sector task decides whether the disk access machinery is positioned at the correct cylinder and sector. If the cylinder is incorrect, a seek operation is initiated, using the controller hardware. If both sector and cylinder positions are correct, the data transfer is enabled by leaving the necessary state information in R registers and commanding the controller to generate disk data task wakeup requests. Finally, the sector task sleeps.

4.2.2 Disk Data Task. The other task, called the disk data task, is invoked at a very high priority during reading (or writing) whenever the one-word data buffer in the controller needs emptying (or filling, respectively). This task is awakened about every 10 μs and transfers a single word in at most 1.7 μs (unlike the display task, which transfers two words per wakeup in 1 μs). Thus during disk transfers up to 20% of the micromachine's time is devoted to servicing the disk controller.

The disk data task is expected to read, check, or write each of three records in a sector: the header, the label, and the data. Each record consists of a preamble area written as all 0 bits, a synchronization pattern consisting of a single 1 bit, a number of information words, and a checksum word. The preamble and synchronization bits allow a tolerance for mechanical and electrical misalignment between writing and reading.

In a typical operation the data task might check the header and label records of a sector, and then write its data record. To read or check a record, the Alto waits until the disk head is over the preamble to that record, then reads until the sync pattern is recognized, then gets words from the disk and writes them into memory or compares them with words fetched from main memory, and finally compares the computed checksum against the one read from the disk. To write a record, it must write a certain amount of preamble, then a sync pattern, then the data fetched from main memory, and finally the computed checksum.

A small piece of actual microcode for the disk data task will make the preceding description concrete. In the microassembly language below, all the clauses between a pair of semicolons (; xxx ← yyy, zzz, ...;) assemble into one microinstruction (see Fig. 5). For example, in the first line,

```
;
InPreambleWait:
     L ← MinusPreambleRemaining+1, Block;
```

MinusPreambleRemaining is an R register (say, 16), so RSEL = **MinusPreambleRemaining** (16), ALUF = BUS+1 (5), BS = ←R (0), F1 = BLOCK [task specific] (3), F2 = NULL (0), LL = Yes (1), LT = No (0), and the NEXT field is assigned by the microassembler to point to the next microinstruction in sequence. The label **InPreambleWait** is defined to be the microinstruction address chosen for this microinstruction by the microassembler.

One further general point is that conditional jumps and dispatches are implemented by ORing a computed value (usually just 0 or 1, but not always) with the NEXT address being fetched as part of the next microinstruction. Conditional clauses are identified by a trailing ?. For example,

```
...,L<0?,...;
...,GoTo[0:PreambleDone, 1:InPreambleWait],...;
```

The **L<0?** clause in the first microinstruction will cause a 1 to be ORed with the NEXT field of the next microinstruction, if and only if the previous value of the L register is negative. The second microinstruction includes a NEXT field pointing to **Preamble-Done,** and in addition it tells the assembler to locate **Preamble-Done** at an even address and **InPreambleWait** at the next successive odd address, so that **PreambleDone OR 1 = InPreambleWait.**

The microcode fragment given below uses several functions to communicate with the hardware interface. All of them are task-specific.

Block (F1) tells the controller hardware that the microcode task has run, and the wakeup request should be removed.

DiskBufferWord← (F1) loads the one-word output buffer in the disk controller hardware from the bus.

←Data BufferWord (BS) puts the contents of the one-word input buffer in the disk controller onto the bus.

DiskCommandRegister←(F1) loads the command register in the controller from the bus. The bits in that register then fan out to control several independent conditions in the controller hardware. One bit (**UseReadClock**) determines whether the controller bit clock is being generated from a crystal oscillator in the controller, or whether it is inferred from the data being read from the disk. Another bit (**WaitForSyncPattern**) determines whether the controller should suspend wakeup requests until the arrival of the sync pattern from the disk.

ReadWriteOrCheck? (F2) causes a 2-bit dispatch based on whether the record is to be read, written, or checked (compared with memory data). The two bits have earlier been placed by the microcode into a special register in the disk controller.

The code begins with a description of the R registers used. The code uses four R registers, although for clarity five names are used:

MinusPreambleRemaining: a negative count of the number of words of preamble remaining.

RecordWordCount: the number of words in the record being read or written (e.g., the data record is 256 words long).

BufferBottom: the address of the first word in main memory of the buffer for this record.

OneBeyondNextBufferWord: a pointer into the main memory buffer where the next word should be placed. The pointer is always "one beyond" where the actual store will be done.

Checksum: a register to accumulate the exclusive OR of all data words read or written in the record.

As we join the story, the data task has begun "spacing" into a disk record in preparation for reading, writing, or checking it. If reading or checking, this means marking time until good data is known to be under the read head. If writing, this means writing preamble.

In this loop the microcode counts through the preamble, one count per data task wakeup. Although no data is being transferred, the disk controller is waking up the data task each time the 16-bit buffer is full, so that it can count preamble bits. Between wakeups, the data task's micro-program counter rests pointing at either **InPreambleWait** or **PreambleDone.**

```
;
InPreambleWait:
   L ← MinusPreambleRemaining+1, Block;
   MinusPreambleRemaining ← L, L<0?, Task;
   DiskBufferWord ← PreambleConstant,
     GoTo[0: PreambleDone, 1:InPreambleWait];
   (Send more preamble if writing.)
```

Now the preamble waiting is over. If reading, this means that the head is known to be over a good preamble area before the sync pattern. If writing, this means we should now write a sync pattern.

```
PreambleDone:
   T ← RecordWordCount;
   L ← BufferBottom+T, ReadWriteOrCheck?;
   OneBeyondNextBufferWord ← L, Block,
   (Set up pointer into buffer.)
     GoTo[0:SetupRead, 1:SetupWrite, 2:SetupCheck];

SetupCheck:
```

Adjust by 1 to make transfer loop exit test more efficient:

```
   L ← BufferBottom−1;
   BufferBottom ← L;

SetupRead:
   DiskCommandRegister
        ← UseReadClockAndWaitForSyncPattern,
   GoTo[SetupChecksum];

SetupWrite:
   DataBufferWord ← SyncPatternConstant;

SetupChecksum:
   L ← StartingChecksumConstant, Task;
   (Initialize Checksum register.)

ModifyChecksum:
   Checksum ← L;
```

The data task's micro-program counter rests here between transferring words. If we are reading, and if this is the first word of the record, then the data task will wait here until a word has been read following the deserializer's recognition of a sync pattern. Note that the transfer loop transfers data from high to low addresses; this simplifies the exit test.

```
TransferLoop:
   MAR ← L ← T ← OneBeyondNextBufferWord−1;
   (Start main memory interface by suppling address to
   MAR.)

   OneBeyondNextBufferWord ← L,
        ReadWriteOrCheck?;
   L ← BufferBottom−T,
   (Compute number of words remaining to transfer.)

   GoTo[0:ReadLoop, 1:WriteLoop, 2:CheckLoop];
   (Dispatch.)

ReadLoop:
   T ← Checksum, Block, L=0?;
   (Check L: Enough words transferred?)

   L ← (MD ← DataBufferWord) XOR T, Task,
   GoTo[0:ModifyChecksum, 1:TransferFinished];
   (Move data word from disk controller to memory, mod-
   ify checksum.)

WriteLoop:
   T ← Checksum, Block;
   (Recall L contains number of words to transfer.)
```

L ← (DataBufferWord ← MD) XOR T, L=0?;
(Move data word from memory to disk controller, modify checksum. Check L: enough words transferred?)

Task, GoTo[0:ModifyChecksum, 1:TransferFinished];
.

.

TransferFinished:
  Checksum ← L;

The task's program counter rests here after sending the last data word to the controller or reading the last data word from the controller. Now we must either send the computed checksum to the controller or compare the computed checksum with that read from the controller.

T ← DataBufferWord
      ← Checksum, ReadWriteOrCheck?;
      (Only writes into outgoing buffer word.)

L ← DataBufferWord−T, Block,
    GoTo[0:CheckChecksum, 1:FinishRecord,
      2:CheckChecksum];
      (This uses the incoming buffer word.)

Now if we are reading or checking, we test for correct checksum by checking whether L is 0, etc.
.

.

In the main reading loop, all but one of the microinstructions are executed concurrently with the main memory transfer (i.e., between MAR← and MD←, which are as close together as they can be). This is usually true as well for other high-bandwidth controller microcode loops in the machine. Thus the main speed bottleneck in the Alto is shared access to a single memory interface. The additional degradation resulting from also sharing a single processor is minimal because so much processing is overlapped with memory references.

ReadWriteOrCheck? is a good example of trading off controller hardware against shared processor time, register space, and microcode space. Obviously the same effect could have been obtained by dispatching on the value in an R register in the micromachine, or by having completely separate micromachine routines for reading, writing, and checking. Usually the decision was made to minimize controller hardware. But in this case by introducing a small amount of extra hardware (about two ICs) in the controller, one R register or about 30 microinstructions were saved. It was economical in 1973, but might not be today.

5. Communication

A personal computer provides substantial, predictable service to a single user. Much of the service he wants, however, cannot be provided by his machine alone, either because sharing is essential to the service or because of cost. Communication with other computers and other users is therefore needed. The communication system expands the service available to an individual, by allowing several users to share resources.

Such sharing is advantageous for two reasons. First, it allows several users to access the same data. For example, a person who composes a memorandum using text-editing facilities contained entirely in his Alto may wish to distribute copies to several other people. He transmits the data representing the memorandum to the Altos of the recipients; each of the recipients can then read it on his Alto display. The use of communication is analogous to the use of the telephone or U.S. mail.

Communication can also be used to share resources for economic reasons. Although it is too costly to provide a hard-copy raster-scan printer for each Alto, a group of users may share a printer, transmitting to the printer the data and control information necessary to print a document. Sharing is also economical for high-capacity file storage or for special-purpose processors too expensive to replicate for each person.

At the time the Alto was designed, several computer communication networks such as the ARPA network [Kahn, 1972] had demonstrated the value of packet-switched networks for sharing resources and providing personal communication among research collaborators. A design suited for personal computers, however, has objectives rather different from those of a remote computer network such as the ARPANET:

The transmission *speed* should be high enough that most users will not notice the presence of the network. If network bandwidth approximately matches local disk bandwidth, the user may not know or care whether a file is retrieved from a local disk or from a remote disk.

The *size* of a network linking personal computers must not be limited. It is not unreasonable to imagine networks linking thousands of personal computers. At the same time, just two or three computers can constitute a reasonable network.

The *reliability* of the network is extremely important when essential services such as printing depend on communication. If a user's personal computer malfunctions, he can take his disk cartridge to another one, but a network malfunction severs his access to essential services. In addition, many users are inconvenienced when the network fails, but only one when a machine fails.

Personal computers tend to be near to each other and to the services they need, thus permitting a *local* network transmission technique for clusters of machines.

A design for a communication system must anticipate the need for *standard communication protocols* in addition to standards for the physical transmission media. The protocols control the flow, routing, and interpretation of data in the network. Just as the design of the Alto disk controller addresses the needs of a file system, so must the design of a network address the needs of communications protocols. However, the Alto was designed at a time when experience with protocols was limited: many lessons had been learned from the ARPA protocols, but newer designs such as TCP [Cerf and Kahn, 1974] had yet to emerge. The Alto therefore provides a general packet transport system, which has been used for a number of protocol experiments and evolutionary designs.

5.1 The Ethernet
Local Network

The Ethernet communication system [Metcalfe and Boggs, 1976, Chap. 26 of this book, pp. 429 through 438] is the principal means of communication between an Alto and other computers. An Ethernet is a broadcast, packet-switched digital network that can connect up to 256 computers, separated by as much as a kilometer, with a 3-Mbit/sec channel. Control of the Ether is distributed among the communicating computers to eliminate the reliability problems of an active central controller and to reduce the fixed costs which can make small, centralized networks uneconomical.

A standard Alto includes an Ethernet controller and transceiver. As soon as there are two Altos within a kilometer of each other, connecting the transceivers together with a coaxial cable establishes an Ethernet. Additional Altos and other computers can be connected simply by tapping into the cable as it passes by, above a false ceiling or beneath a raised floor. Connections can be made and power turned on and off without disturbing network communication.

An Ethernet is an efficient low-level packet transport mechanism which gives its best efforts to delivering packets, but it is not error-free. Even when transmitted without an error detected by the sender, a packet may not reach its destination without error; thus, packets are delivered only with high probability. A hierarchy of layered communication protocols is used to achieve reliable transmission on the Ethernet, by requiring receiving processes to acknowledge receipt of correct packets and sending processes to retransmit packets whose correct receipt is not acknowledged.

5.2 The Internetwork

Although the physical size and addressing of the Ethernet are limited, many local networks may be connected together into an *internal network* [Boggs et al., 1980]. The internetwork is implemented by building *gateway* computers (usually Altos) that connect two or more networks, often using long-haul digital communication to connect with gateways on distant local networks. The gateway is responsible for routing packets in the internetwork: it receives a packet from a local network, interprets a destination address in the packet, and then transmits the packet into another network which will get it closer to its ultimate destination. Sometimes packets are forwarded through several gateways before they arrive at the proper local network. As of summer 1979, the Xerox internet provided service to several hundred computers on 25 networks interconnected by 20 gateways.

5.3 Implementation

The Alto Ethernet controller (Fig. 12) contains about 75 MSI TTL ICs—it is slightly larger than the disk and display controllers. The transceiver, on the other hand, is much smaller and less expensive than either the disk drive or the display monitor. The controller hardware consists of the following functions: phase decoder, receiver shift register, FIFO buffer and synchronizing register, transmitter shift register, phase encoder, and micromachine

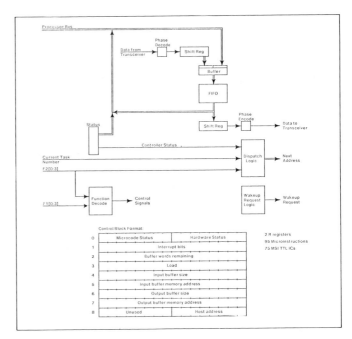

Fig. 12. The Ethernet controller.

interface. The FIFO buffer is shared by the transmitter and receiver, so the interface is half-duplex: it can either be transmitting or receiving but not both simultaneoulsy. This is not a severe limitation, since the Ether itself is half-duplex. It does make hardware checkout more difficult, however, because the controller cannot be looped back on itself; also, the software must make a special check for packets that it sends to itself. Up to three Ethernet interfaces can be attached to an Alto. Unfortunately the tasks cannot share a single copy of the microcode, since the micromachine cannot make indexed R-register references.

The microcode uses one medium-priority task, two R registers, and about 100 microinstructions. The task consumes 16% of the machine in the data transfer loops, since it runs for five cycles (one memory reference) every 5.44 μs (one Ethernet word time), doing all of its bookkeeping while waiting for the memory. To reject a packet the address filter requires 13 cycles (2.21 μs), which consumes as much as 20% of the machine in the improbable case of minimum-length (2-word) back-to-back packets. The rest of the microcode is executed once per packet accepted or transmitted, and so consumes a negligible number of cycles.

The Ethernet task communicates with a program much as the disk and display tasks do. The program builds a command block describing the operation to be done. When the Ethernet task wakes up, it carries out the operation, and then posts status in the command block and causes an interrupt by ORing a word from the command block into NIW. One difference is in the way the task is awakened. The disk and display have periodically occurring events (sector notches and scan line retrace) which cause their tasks to wake up and check for commands from the software, but there is no such periodic event for an Ethernet. Instead, there is an S-group instruction which the program executes to set a flip-flop in the Ethernet hardware; this flip-flop wakes up the Ethernet task to act on the command block. Another difference is that disk and display commands complete after a finite time, but an Ethernet receiver can be started and not receive a packet for days. Hence programs always use interrupts to recognize completion of an operation, rather than busy-waiting as many disk drivers do. Finally, Ethernet command blocks are not chained, partly because of a shortage of microcode space in the early implementations, and partly because it was not then clear how to make use of chaining.

Packet address filtering is done by the microcode. When the hardware has accumulated the first word of a packet, it wakes up the microcode to check the destination address byte. The microcode accepts the packet and copies it into memory if any one of the following conditions is met:

The destination address in the packet matches the *host address* field in the command block.

The host address is zero (in this case the machine is said to be *promiscuous*, and receives all packets).

The destination address is zero (in this case the packet is a *broadcast* packet, and is received by all machines).

Otherwise the microcode tells the hardware to ignore the rest of the current packet and go to sleep until the beginning of the next packet. The address filter takes about 20 microinstructions; done in hardware it would take about 8 ICs.

The flexibility afforded by this filtering scheme has many applications. Any machine can substitute for another by using the other machine's address in the host address field. Promiscuity is invaluable for debugging protocols, since a machine can peek at all of the packets flowing between two others. It is also easy to study the performance of the net by monitoring all the traffic. Broadcasts are used to locate resources and to distribute globally useful information. A less desirable consequence is that the Ethernet itself provides no security; applications which need secure communication must use encryption.

The choice of an eight-bit address has proved to be unfortunate, since it means that a machine cannot have a unique hard-wired serial number which is normally used as its host address. Instead, each Alto has a station address specified by jumpers on the backplane, which is unique only among the machines on the particular Ethernets it happens to be on.

Two or more Ethernet transmitters *collide* when they simultaneously decide that the Ether is free and begin transmitting. When a transmitter detects collision, it aborts transmission and waits a random time interval before trying again, so as not to collide repeatedly. As the load on the net increases, a transmitter retries less vigorously, by doubling the mean of its random interval each time it participates in a collision. This *exponential backoff* algorithm is done by the microcode and a small amount of hardware. The software zeros the LOAD location in the Ethernet command block each time it issues an output command, and the microcode shifts a one bit into it each time a collision happens. The microcode generates a random retransmission interval by masking the LOAD location with the real-time clock R register maintained by the timed task, and then waiting for that interval by telling the hardware to wake it up each time the timed task wakes up, and decrementing the interval register at each wakeup. When the register goes to zero, the microcode again tries to transmit. After 16 consecutive collisions the LOAD location overflows, and the microcode gives up and posts a failure code in the command block. This algorithm takes about 20 microinstructions; done in hardware it would require about 10 ICs.

6. A Controller for a Raster-Scanned Printer

The Alto is predominantly a versatile I/O controller: the design emphasizes the needs of high-bandwidth I/O for personal computing and relegates instruction interpretation to secondary importance. One of the objectives of the design is to provide a convenient framework in which to build experimental or special-purpose I/O controllers, in addition to those for the standard display, keyboard, mouse, disk, and Ethernet. This section illustrates how the resources of the Alto are harnessed to a complex task: an interface to a high-speed raster-scanned page printer. The design shows how the page-generation algorithm is first analyzed and then divided into parts that are implemented in software, microcode, and hardware.

The objectives of a printer are very similar to those of the Alto display: several thousand characters may appear in arbitrary sizes, rotations, font styles, and positions on the page; text may be proportionally spaced; characters may overlap one another (e.g., overstrikes); non-text imagery such as lines and curves may appear. Printing quality generally exceeds that of a display by using higher resolution—a typical device might print in one second an 8.5- by 11-inch page defined with 350 dots/inch (roughly 4000 horizontal scan lines of 3000 dots each).

These observations suggest that the same techniques used to generate a digital video signal for the Alto display be used to drive a printer. The modest average data rate of 12 Mbits/sec means that an image of the page could be buffered in Alto memory and read out to generate video, using the same sort of controller as the Alto display. The image of the printed page can be created the same way as that for a display: using a *character table* that gives the x and y position and character code for each character that appears in the image, and a *font table* that defines a rectangular bitmap pattern for each character, BitBlt is used to OR each character's pattern into the bitmap buffer at the proper coordinate position. Unfortunately, this simple approach fails for two reasons: the Alto does not have enough memory to buffer a full-page image (12 million bits), and the processor cannot execute BitBlt fast enough to generate a bitmap for a moderately complex page in one second. These two problems force changes in the image-generation algorithm. After describing the new algorithm, we sketch its Alto implementation.

Because buffering the entire page is impractical, an *incremental algorithm* must be used to generate portions of the image in sequence, using a smaller buffer. The image is divided into *bands* of 16 scan lines each, and the entire page image is generated by creating the image for each band in turn. This scheme requires two buffers, each capable of holding the bitmap for a single band: while one buffer is being converted into a video signal and sent to the printer, the image of the next band is being prepared in the other buffer.

The incremental approach requires modifications to the image-generation algorithm described for a full-page buffer. The problem is to identify those characters that lie wholly or partly in the band being generated. Although the entire character table can be scanned to compute, for each entry, whether the character lies in the band, it is more efficient to sort the table by the band number

in which the character begins (i.e., by y coordinate of the topmost scan line). The sorted table allows easy identification of "new characters," those that start within the band being generated.

Breaking the page image into bands inevitably causes some characters to span two or more bands, either because they are more than 16 scan lines high, or because their image on the page happens to cross a band boundary. For these characters, the image-generation process is not completed when a band is generated; instead, a portion of the character is *left over* and must be continued in the succeeding band (Fig. 13). The image-generation algorithm records left-over characters in a list that contains sufficient information to continue image generation (BitBlt) in the next band. The companion data structures for new and left-over characters are characteristic of many incremental image-generation algorithms, such as those for solid polygons and hidden-surface images [Newman and Sproull, 1979]. The algorithm to generate the image of a band is:

1 Clear the band buffer to zero.

2 For each character in the character table for this band:
   a Use the character code extracted from the character

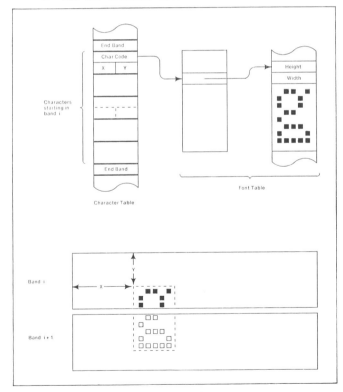

Fig. 13. Schematic diagram of the image-generation process for printing a page. The band buffers show a character that does not completely fit in band *i*. It has a "left-over" part extending into the next band.

table to enter the font table and find a character bitmap, together with a width and height.

b OR into the band buffer the image of the character, at the specified position.

c If the character's image does not terminate in this band, save a left-over entry, specifying the x position of the character, its width, its height (now reduced), and a pointer to the beginning of the next scan line of character bitmap information in the font table.

3 For each character in the left-over table formed when generating the previous band:

a Same as step 2b.

b Same as step 2c.

4 The image in the band buffer is now ready to be converted into a video signal and sent to the printer.

The algorithm was analyzed carefully to design an implementation for the Alto. Table 1 gives several properties required of the memories used in the algorithm, obtained by software simulations of the printing of typical pages. These simulations lead to a number of design decisions for the algorithm and controller. Consider the size of a band: 16 scan lines. The greater the number of scan lines in a band, the larger the band buffers, and hence the expense. The smaller the number of scan lines, the more frequently the left-over tables must be read and written while generating a page. The table shows that a band size of 16 scan lines yields both modest left-over bandwidths and inexpensive band buffers. It also shows that the memories required divide into two classes: small and fast (band buffers) and large but slow (font, character and left-over tables). This division leads to an implementation strategy for the Alto: the main memory will hold the font, character, and left-over tables, and the controller will hold the band buffers, together with some image-generation aids. Such a division is feasible only because the Alto micromachine can intimately control the image-generation hardware, using character parameters and pattern information read from main memory.

6.1 Implementation

The organization of the printer controller is shown in Fig. 14. It is logically divided into two parts that operate concurrently, the *video generator* and the *image generator*. The video generator reads data from one of the two band buffers, converts it into a video signal, and transmits the signal to the printer. As each 16-bit word is read from the buffer, zeros are written back to clear the buffer for subsequent image-generation. When the video generator has emptied a buffer, it switches buffers and begins emptying the other one.

The image generator portion of the controller composes the image in the buffer that is not being sent to the printer, under control of microcode in the *printing task*. The micromachine sets several parameter registers that describe the dimensions and position of a character to be added to the band buffer (*width, height, x* and *y*). Then it enters a tight loop, reading the character's bitmap pattern from the font table, and passing two 16-bit words to the controller every microsecond. This pattern passes through a FIFO and is shifted to align it with the word boundaries of the band buffer. After masking to account for the ends of a character, these 16 values are used to enable writing new data values into selected bits of a particular band buffer word. An "ink" memory provides the data to be written at these positions. Thus the character pattern, shifter, and mask determine *where* a character appears in the band, while the ink memory determines the *video data* values, and thus allows characters to appear to have texture or halftone patterns. When the interface signals to the processor that it is finished processing the current character, the microcode reads the controller status, including the height register, to determine whether the character was completed, or whether a left-over entry must be made, and records the left-over entry in Alto memory if necessary. The microcode repeats this process for all the characters that appear in the band. When the image for the band is completed, the printing task sleeps until the video generator switches buffers, indicating that the task must begin generating the image of the next band.

The design of the printer controller is extremely economical, because it takes maximum advantage of the facilities already available in the standard Alto: substantial memory and a versatile micromachine. This approach retains the flexibility to change easily the sizes, formats, and contents of important structures: the font and character tables. The special hardware helps implement a general mechanism for composing page images (BitBlt), a mechanism that places no restrictions on the size, position, or content of characters, nor on the number of different character shapes that can appear on a page. Indeed, the controller will generate arbitrary video patterns, including lines, curves, and halftones. The performance of the system is limited by two constraints: (1) the font and character tables must not exceed the size of Alto main memory; and (2) the time available to generate a band dictates the number of micromachine cycles available to read character patterns from memory and pass them to the controller.

Each of several dozen printers in the Xerox research environment is driven by a printer controller, plugged into a standard

Table 1

	Size (bits * 10^3)	Bandwidth (bits * 10^6/page)
Band buffers	30	
Clear buffer		12.3
Generate image		6+
Output video		12.3
Font table	368+	2.4+
Character table	80+	.08+
Left-over list	6.4+	.5+

Numbers ending in "+" increase roughly linearly with page complexity.

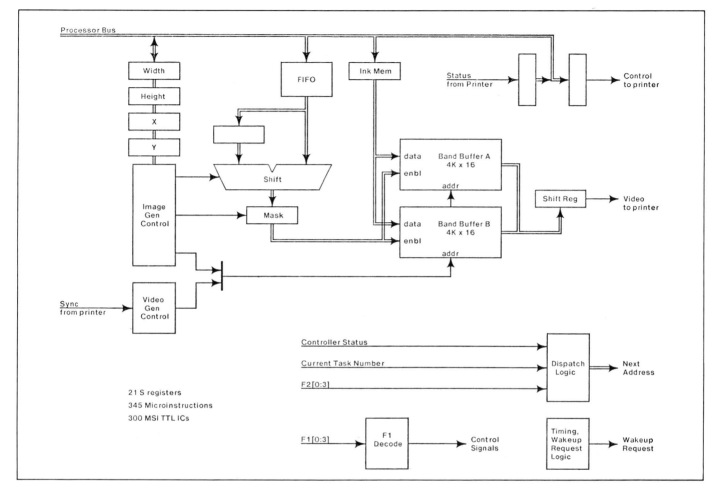

Fig. 14. The printer controller.

Alto. Although the page-printing task is complex, the special hardware is not large (about 300 ICs) because of extensive use of microcode and memory resources in the standard Alto. The design illustrates how a page-generation algorithm was analyzed and then implemented using appropriate facilities: macroinstruction programs for y sorting, microcode for left-over table management and font table references, and special hardware for the "inner loops" of image and video generation.

7. Applications

A successful personal computing environment depends not only on economical hardware and devices for communicating with humans, but also on software constructed to meet personal computing needs. This section surveys the major software systems

that have been built, and discusses the impact of the local network on the Alto computing environment.

7.1 Programming Environments

Two kinds of programming environments have developed on the Alto: conventional compiler-based systems and fully interactive environments. The first conventional environment to be constructed is implemented almost exclusively in the BCPL programming language, and includes common tools: a compiler, an assembler, a linker, a debugger, an "open" operating system [Lampson and Sproull, 1979], a command processor, file-manipulation utilities, etc. Subsequently, the Mesa programming language was designed and implemented on the Alto [Geschke, Morris, and Satterthwaite, 1977; Mitchell, Maybury, and Sweet, 1979]. Both of these environments have been used extensively to build applications.

Interactive programming environments emerged to take advantage of the personal nature of the Alto. The Smalltalk environment turned the Alto into an "interim Dynabook," a prototype for a personal dynamic medium that emphasizes visual and audio communication [Kay and Goldberg, 1977; Kay, 1977; Kay, 1978; Ingalls, 1978]. Smalltalk has been used to interact with documents containing text and graphics, to build visual animations [Baecker, 1976], to synthesize music, and to build a variety of simulations of personal interest.

An implementation of Interlisp [Teitelman, 1978] explored the problem of providing a large interactive environment on the Alto [Deutsch, 1979]. Although the Alto micromachine was successfully adapted to interpret byte-coded Interlisp instructions at reasonably high speeds, the small main memory of most Altos at the time (64K) proved to be a crippling performance limitation.

The various programming environments used on the Alto coexist gracefully by sharing only files stored on the local disk, and network protocols for communication among computers. No other facilities of the Alto are standardized. This policy allows each environment and each application to exploit the hardware in novel ways; for example, it fosters different strategies for using the display and interacting with the user. It also allows a language or application to use special-purpose microcode to interpret instructions or perform application-specific calculations. The policy has a few drawbacks: failure to standardize the use of the display, for example, makes it essentially impossible for one Alto to be used as a remote terminal to another one.

7.2 Personal Applications

Some applications use the Alto as a stand-alone computer, usually making extensive use of the display, mouse, and keyboard for interaction. The most commonly used applications of the Alto today are the various programs developed for document production: a text editor that supports a wide range of formatting styles and text fonts, and a set of "illustrators" to prepare diagrams using geometrical figures such as lines, circles, and curves, or raster images obtained by scanning existing documents or by free-hand drawing. Many of the display techniques used are described in Newman and Sproull [1979]; camera-ready copy for that book was produced with Alto document-production software.

Some uses of the Alto support research in computer science within Xerox. The best example is a design automation system used to aid designers of digital hardware. Logic drawings are prepared with an illustrator, and are then analyzed by a program to determine what integrated circuits are pictured in the diagram and how they are connected. Other software then checks loading rules, makes wire lists, and drives semi-automatic wiring equipment. The Alto also serves as a console computer to simplify debugging or diagnosis of experimental hardware. An umbilical cord connects the Alto to the hardware so that it can load registers and memories, issue control commands such as "single step," and

read back important internal state. An Alto program presents this information on the display, accompanied by symbolic names of the registers or signals in the experimental hardware. The display also presents menus of operations, such as "step," that are invoked by pointing with the mouse and cursor. In this way, the Alto is used to provide a comfortable user interface for an engineer, technician, or system programmer working on the hardware.

7.3 Communication in Applications

No Alto users depend only on the resources available within a single Alto; all use communication to extend these services. Even the user of document-production application requires communication to obtain hardcopy output at a shared printer or to distribute a document file to other users. Alto applications and users depend on a wide variety of services implemented on *server machines* throughout the network:

- *Printing.* An application program running in any Alto may transmit to the *printing server* a description of a document to be printed. The printing server is an Alto that queues requests, and later prints the files using the raster printer controller described in Sec. 6 of this chapter.

- *File storage.* File services are provided both to allow sharing of files among users and to escape the limitations of the local storage available on the standard Alto. The service machines have one or more high-performance disks attached and offer several different styles of file access. Some provide a "page level" access [Swinehart, McDaniel, and Boggs, 1979], some a "file transfer" access patterned after the ARPA network file transfer facilities [Crocker et al., 1972], and some a "transaction access" suitable for implementing a file service that is distributed over several machines [Israel, Mitchell, and Sturgis, 1978].

- *Mailboxes.* A popular application of the Alto is an electronic mail service. The personal machine is used to prepare messages for transmission to other Alto users, and to display and retain on the disk messages that have been received. A network mailbox service is provided to hold messages for a user until he wishes to receive them with the mail program. The mailbox service is often implemented within the same computer that provides network file storage [Levin and Schroeder, 1979].

- *Timesharing.* The Alto can be used as a terminal on the MAXC timesharing system [Fiala, 1978]. For simple applications, the Alto simulates a conventional video character display. More ambitious applications use a "display protocol" to format text and graphics carefully on the screen [Sproull, 1979]. DLISP, which provides display-oriented access to the Interlisp programming environment, is the primary user of the display protocol [Teitelman, 1977].

- *Time of day.* A simple but necessary service is to inform Altos of the correct time. A time serve is conveniently located in the same computer as a communication gateway.

- *Error logging.* This service records a log of error information sent to it, and is usually operated by hardware and software maintenance groups. Altos that are not in use run a diagnostic program that periodically sends error summaries to the logger. The maintenance organization examines the log to schedule service calls.

- *Bootstrap.* Alto microcode allows the computer to be bootstrap-loaded from either the local disk or the Ethernet. An Ethernet bootstrap service accepts a request for an Alto program, reads it from a local disk, and sends it over the network to the computer making the request. This service was first used to bootstrap the Scavenger program, which repairs a damaged disk file structure. Many programs are now distributed in this way, reducing the demands on local disk storage. The ability to bootstrap diagnostic programs over the Ethernet is especially useful to the maintenance staff.

The services outlined above are implemented on various server machines spread throughout the internetwork. Servers can be added or removed straightforwardly as needs grow or shrink. All application programs access the services using standardized protocols, which in effect define the services that are offered. Standardization is necessary to allow sharing; applications that share a file must obey the protocol standards of the service used to store the file. Thus the protocols constitute a standardized interface, analogous to the file system on the disk, which is observed by all programs in the environment [Boggs et al., 1980].

In addition to standard services, individual applications use the network in special ways. For example, the debugger may communicate with an identical debugger running elsewhere in the network, essentially passing the user's commands to the remote machine and returning information to be displayed. Thus a programmer in California can examine and fix a bug on a machine in New York. The Ethernet is used as a performance-analysis tool: the program to be analyzed transmits packets that summarize system status or that record the occurrence of a particular event. An analysis program running elsewhere in the network records and displays the information [McDaniel, 1977]. The network is also used to couple programs together so that two people can cooperatively edit and illustrate documents in real time, sending digitized voice as well as keystrokes and mouse movements through the network.

8.   Conclusions

As an experiment in personal computing, the Alto has been very successful. The number of Altos in use exceeds the original expectations of its designers by more than an order of magnitude.

The Alto has led to an entirely new kind of computing environment, because it puts computing power near the user, and makes it possible for him to do most of his work without relying on a centralized facility. The Alto environment provides a high-bandwidth, comfortable user interface, is extremely reliable because of its distributed nature, and provides performance that scales linearly with cost. One of the Alto's most attractive features is that it does not run faster at night [Morris, personal communication].

A few aspects of the Alto design did not work out well. The limitations on the size of the address space and on the amount of real memory have been serious. Although some programming systems have been able to take advantage of the extended memory banks, not all Altos have this extension, and a great deal of time has been spent fitting standard software that must run on all machines into the limited space available. To a great extent, the memory size limitation is due to the fact that the system's life has been longer than planned.

The facilities of the micromachine are not well suited for emulating existing architectures with structured opcodes. Fortunately, the virtual machines for which new emulators have been built use simple instruction encodings that fit well with the micromachine's dispatch mechanism. The emulator for the Mesa machine interprets instructions just as fast as the emulator for BCPL, even though the latter has some hardware assistance for decoding, and the former does not.

The sharing of the micromachine among I/O activities and emulation has been extremely successful. The micromachine allows these activities to interact by sharing memory, and provides the high memory bandwidth necessary to support the high-speed I/O requirements of the personal computer. Today, hardware costs are low enough that it is possible to replicate the processor in every I/O controller, but if this is done without taking additional steps such as using cache memories to decouple the processors from the memory, or using more complex multi-ported memories, shared memory access will still limit the system's performance. Since both these alternatives add cost, while the multitasking is very inexpensive, we feel that this architecture is still viable today.

Some of the early decisions in the design of the Alto computing environment worked out very well. The arrangement by which all software is standardized at the level of disk files and network messages has made it possible to build a wide variety of cooperating software subsystems. The disk file system has proven to be extremely reliable, primarily due to the distributed redundancy. Although the hardware and software have both had bugs, the reliability *as perceived by users* has been exceptionally high, since files are almost never irretrievably lost.

The high-bandwidth communication provided by the Ethernet has been more valuable than anticipated, since we underestimated the importance of servers. The network and network services have been the mainstays of the environment, and we feel that a facility with an order of magnitude lower bandwidth would have had a qualitatively different effect.

References

Baecker [1976]; Boggs, Shoch, Taft, and Metcalfe [1980]; Cerf and Kahn [1974]; Crocker, Heafner, Metcalfe, and Postel [1972]; Deutsch [1979]; English, Englebart, and Berman [1967]; Fiala [1978]; Geschke, Morris, and Satterthwaite [1977]; Ingalls [1978]; Israel, Mitchell, and Sturgis [1978]; Kahn [1972]; Kay [1977]; Kay [1978]; Kay and Goldberg [1977]; Lampson and Sproull [1979]; Levin and Schroeder [1979]; McDaniel [1977]; Metcalfe and Boggs [1976]; Mitchell, Maybury, and Sweet [1979]; Morris [personal communication]; Newman and Sproull [1979]; Richards [1969]; Ritchie, Johnson, Lesk, and Kernighan [1978]; Shoch and Hupp [1977]; Shoch [1979]; Sproull [1979]; Swinehart, McDaniel, and Boggs [1979]; Teitelman [1977]; Teitelman [1978].

Part 3

Computer Classes

Introduction

This part of the book examines sets of computer architectures grouped by size from the smallest single-chip hand-held calculator systems to the largest high-performance computer systems. Each set of architectures is selected not only to cover the major approaches in each size category but also to provide comparisons and contrasts between systems.

Since each example is a complete system, each system will have a value for each computer space dimension and subdimension discussed in Part 2. The reader is encouraged to both observe the values of the dimensions and question the relationship between the values of the dimensions. Why did the system designer select those particular values?

Part 3 also provides the most detailed systems information in the book. There is the heaviest concentration not only of ISPs but also of implementation details. The ISPs are provided so that the reader can practice programming the machines. Implementation details are given for the smaller machines so that the reader can apply these techniques to understand and/or design portions of the larger systems, which, by necessity, are presented at higher levels of abstraction. The reader is encouraged to partake in design exercises utilizing, say, microprocessor and microprogramming information to design a vector pipeline; for design tradeoffs and interactions are only appreciated after studying *and* practicing design. Design is an act of synthesizing and creating. Analysis of the designs of others only takes the reader so far. To fully appreciate design, one must partake of the art.

Classes

There are four major sections in Part 3, covering monolithic microcomputers, microcomputers, minicomputers, and maxicomputers. What are the definitions of these computer classes, and how does one assign a system to a class?

There is no precise definition of a class, since the concept of class attempts to group points in the computer space that are, in some sense, neighbors. These groupings are difficult to make, since there needs to be a sense of closeness not only on an individual dimension but also between dimensions. Furthermore, the expectations of a class member grow with time; i.e., a 1980-vintage minicomputer is expected to have substantially more capacity and capability than a 1965-vintage minicomputer. This introduction to Part 3 will elaborate the discussion presented in Chap. 1 on computer classes by considering cost and size of address space.

Computer Classes from an Economic Viewpoint[1]

The economic viewpoint is so strongly influenced by technology that the four generations of computers have been named after the technology of their components (see Chap. 5): vacuum tubes, transistors, integrated circuits (multiple transistors packaged together), and LSI circuits (large-scale integration). Every electronic technology has its own set of characteristics (e.g., cost, speed, heat dissipation, packing density, reliability), all of which the designer must balance. These factors combine to limit the applicability of any one technology; typically, one technology is used until a limit is reached or another technology supersedes it.

When an improved basic technology becomes available to a computer designer, there are four paths the designs can take to incorporate the technology:

1   Use the newer technology to build a lower-cost system with the same performance.

2   Hold the cost constant and use the technological improvement to get an increase in performance.

3   Push the design to the limits of the new technology, thereby increasing both performance and cost.

4   Find a drastically new structure using the computer as a basic archetype (e.g., calculators) so that the design can be considered off the evolutionary path.

Figure 1 shows the trajectory of the first three of the design alternatives. In general, the design alternatives occur in an evolutionary fashion as in Fig. 2, with a first (base) design and subsequent designs evolving from the base.

In the first design style, the performance is held constant and the improved technology is used to build lower-cost machines which attract new applications. This design style has as its most important consequence the concept of the "minimal computer." The minimal computer has traditionally been the vehicle for entering new applications, since it is the smallest computer that can be constructed with a given technology. Each year, as the price of the minimal computer declines, new applications become economically feasible.

[1]This viewpoint is expressed in "Seven Views of Computer Systems," Chap. 1 in Bell, Mudge, and McNamara [1978], pp. 9–13.

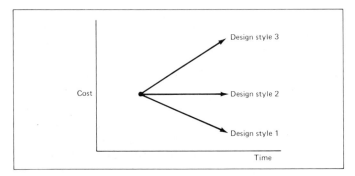

Fig. 1. Three design styles on the evolutionary path.

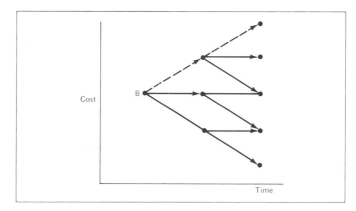

Fig. 2. Evolutions from the base design B.

The second, constant-cost alternative uses the improved technology to get better performance, and will usually yield the best increase in total system cost and effectiveness. This approach provides a growth in performance and quality at a constant price and is probably the best for the majority of existing users.

The third alternative is to use the new technology to build the most powerful machine possible. New designs using this alternative often solve previously unsolved problems and, in doing so, advance the state of the art. The design alternative must be used cautiously, since going too far in cost or performance (i.e., building beyond the technology) is dangerous and can lead to a zero-performance, high-cost product. There are usually two motivations for operating at this leading edge: preliminary research motivated by the knowledge that the technology will catch up; and national defense, where an essentially infinite amount of money is available because the benefit—avoiding annihilation—is infinite. Figure 3 depicts the selling price of several computers described in this book. The stratification of the price range is clearly evident.

Table 1 shows the effect of pursuing the two design strategies of (1) constant performance at decreased cost and (2) constant cost at increased performance. The first column gives the base case at a given time t. Because this is the base case, the cost, performance, and cost/performance ratio of the computer are all 1. As the computer is applied to a particular environment, operational overhead is added at a cost of 2 to 4 times the original cost of the computer; the total cost to operate the computer becomes 3 to 5, and the performance/total cost ratio is reduced to between 0.33 and 0.2 (depending on the total cost).

Now assume the same operating environment, with the same fixed (overhead) costs to operate, at a new generation time, $t + 1$, when technology has "improved" by a factor 2. Two alternative designs are carried out; one is at constant cost and higher performance and the other is at constant performance and lower cost (columns 2 and 3). The application is constant in three cases (columns 1–3), and a new base application is discovered for the fourth case (column 4). Both the constant-cost and constant-performance designs give the same basic performance/cost improvement—when only the cost of the computer is considered. However, when one considers the high fixed overhead costs associated with a base application (columns 1–3), there is a

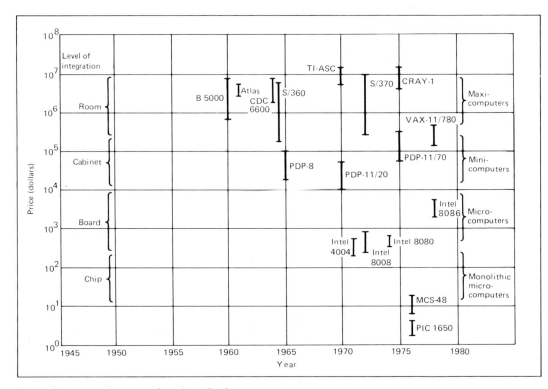

Fig. 3. Computer class as a function of price.

Table 1   Using New Technology for Constant Cost and Constant Performance Designs

Introduction time (generation)	t	$t+1$	$t+1$	$t+1$
Design style	Base case	Constant cost, increased performance	Constant performance, decreased cost	Constant performance, decreased cost
Application	Base	Base	Base	New base
Computer cost	1	1	0.5	0.5
Operating costs (range)	2–4	2–4	2–4	1–2
Total cost	3–5	3–5	2.5–4.5	1.5–3
Performance (and improvement)	1	2	1	1
Improvement (in total cost)	1	1	0.83–0.9	0.5–0.6
Performance/cost (computer only and improvement)	1	2	2	2
Performance/ total-cost	0.33–0.2	0.66–0.4	0.4–0.22	0.66–0.4
Improvement (in perf./total cost)	1	2	1.21–1.1	2

relatively small improvement in performance/cost, although there is a cost savings of 10 to 17 percent with the minimal design. The greatest gains come in applying the computer with greater performance and getting the attendant factor of 2 gain in performance and in performance/cost ratio.

To summarize, the constant cost–increased-performance design style gives a better gain because operating costs remain the same. Its gain can only be equaled by the constant-performance design style when operating costs are halved upon its application. This only occurs when a new application is found, as shown in column 4.

Applying the three design styles shown in Fig. 1 over several generations produces the plot given in Fig. 4. These figures lead to an economic view that computer classes can be distinguished by *cost* and named as follows: monolithic micro, micro, mini, and maxi. The class maxi is sometimes referred to by the single, nondescriptive name *mainframe*.

When one distinguishes computer classes by cost, a new range of costs can be made possible by new technology and can create a new class. The new class appears at the low end of the cost scale, where the minimal computer is introduced at a significantly lower cost level than existing computers.

The measure used to define a new class is cost, whereas the measure defining an established class is performance. This is because once a new class has become established in the marketplace, the users become familiar with what computers and what class can be used for their applications, and tend to characterize that class on a performance basis. The characterization of existing classes on a performance basis is important to this discussion, because at each new technology time, performance

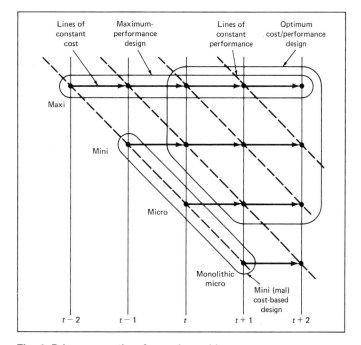

Fig. 4. Price versus time for each machine.

increases by one category, and mini performance becomes available on a micro, for example.

The effect of technology upon computer classes can be summarized in the following thesis: Continual application of technology via the two major design styles results in

1   Cost declines which create new classes of computers

2   New classes becoming established classes

3   Established classes becoming encroached upon

Computer Classes from an Address Space Viewpoint

Another viewpoint of computer classes is based on capacity and functionality. We have selected the one dimension *bytes of virtual address* to capture this viewpoint. Several computer space dimensions are roughly correlated with the number of bytes in the virtual address. A larger virtual address usually means:

- Wider instruction words to hold larger virtual addresses. These wider words imply wider memories and data paths, higher Pc-Mp bandwidth, and larger instruction sets.

- Usually, more functionality in ISP, represented by an ability to support more data-types in hardware.

- Higher cost due to wider everything.

- Higher performance to gain economies of scale (see Chap. 5).

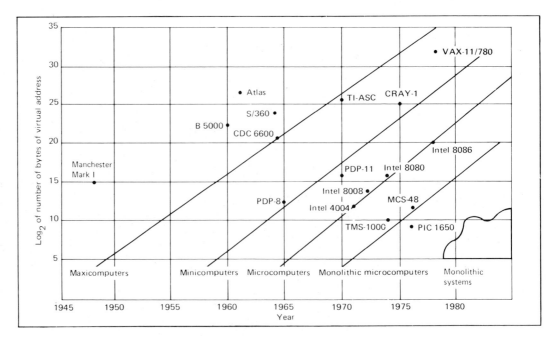

Fig. 5. Computer classes as a function of virtual address space.

Figure 5 plots the number of bytes in the virtual address versus the year for machines found in this book. Four classes are distinguishable: monolithic microcomputer, microcomputer, minicomputer, and maxicomputer. Note that as time progresses, the size of the virtual address in each class grows. The rate of growth is approximately doubling every year, which coincides with the doubling in semiconductor memory chip density every 1 to 2 years. For the purposes of Part 3 we will introduce the machines in order of size, smallest class first, according to the four classes depicted in Fig. 5.

References

Bell, Mudge, and McNamara [1978].

Section 1

Monolithic Microcomputers

As technology has evolved, the fundamental building blocks of computer systems have become more complex. Standard building blocks have evolved from circuit-level components (e.g., discrete transistors and diodes), to gates and flip-flops (SSI, or small-scale integration), to register-transfer–level chip sets (MSI, or medium-scale integration), to PMS-level chip sets (LSI, or large-scale integration). When semiconductor technology had evolved to the point that a whole processor or a whole computer could be implemented on a single chip, a conceptual barrier was breached. No longer were computers expensive and to be used in a centralized facility requiring constant attention. Rather, computers could be used to replace random logic in dedicated applications. Not only would these single-chip processors provide more logical power, but they were also cheaper and easier to use than random logic.

Thus the microprocessor[1] recreated the evolution of computer architectures that had previously been blazed by mainframe computers. The architecture evolution occurred over a shorter time frame, since the experiences of the mainframe manufacturers were available to study and technology was evolving rapidly, allowing new machine generations every 2 years. The availability of low-cost processing power has allowed increased functionality in existing products (e.g., computer peripheral controllers, intelligent terminals, electronic scales, traffic control, and instruments) and has opened entirely new application areas (e.g., calculators, video games, appliance controllers, home computers, word processors, point-of-sale terminals). Indeed, the point has been reached where a semiconductor vendor can sell more processors in a single month than even the most successful minicomputer and/or mainframe manufacturer has been able to sell in the lifetime of a computer.

Sections 1 and 2 of Part 3 explore the two smallest classes of computer systems: monolithic microcomputers and microcomputers. Monolithic microcomputers are single-chip systems incorporating the processor, program ROM, variable RAM, and perhaps dedicated I/O. The intended market is low-cost and high-volume applications such as hand-held calculators, watches, video games, automobiles, and appliances. These architectures may be specialized and limited to the functional characteristics of the application. Microcomputers, on the other hand, are single-chip processors (or processors with a small number of chips) requiring external RAM and ROM chips. These are usually faster and more

[1]*Micro-* here means physically small and does not necessarily imply that the processor is microprogrammed.

powerful than monolithic microcomputer systems, since the off-chip placement of memory and I/O frees gates for more complex instructions and wider data paths. As time passes and technology allows more gates per chip, microcomputer architectures evolve into the monolithic microcomputer class.

This section will illustrate the monolithic microcomputer class via the Texas Instruments TMS 1000, intended for hand-held calculator applications, and the General Instruments PIC1650, intended for control applications. Finally, the selection closes with a brief discussion of program-compatible monolithic microcomputer families. Heretofore the family concept was reserved for only the largest computer classes.

Texas Instruments TMS1000

Because of their limited requirements, hand-held calculators were one of the first consumer-oriented products to take advantage of the emerging LSI technology. After the initial, ad hoc designs, calculators have been implemented as stored-program computers. Today, most calculators consist of a single LSI computer chip plus a display. And the adoption of LSI technology was very rapid. For example, the TI-2500 calculator introduced in 1974, had 119 parts, of which 82 were electronic in nature. By 1976, the TI-1200 consisted of only 22 parts, of which only the calculator chip (a complete computer with programs) and display were electronic.

This single-chip integration is made possible by the tightly specified user environment. Input (e.g., keyboard or magnetic card) and output (e.g., LED display, printer, or magnetic card) options are limited. Further, the input language (i.e., function per key) is also fixed.

Chapter 34 details the LSI MOS chip used in the Texas Instruments SR-16 calculator. The chip contains a microcomputer complete with a program ROM having 1,024 eight-bit words; a temporary storage RAM: input (from keypad); output (to control keypad scan and LED display); and an oscillator (clock).

The TMS1000 chip was designed to span a range of hand-held calculator products (from four-function up through simple memory calculators). Since the chip had to be customized with the ROM program appropriate to a product, other programmable features were included to improve the chip's flexibility. This programmability was provided by two programmable logic arrays (PLAs).

The output PLA converts five bits into twenty 8-bit output patterns in order to conserve program space. These patterns are specified by the calculator designer and represent different output patterns on a seven-segment display.

The second PLA is for instruction decoding. The chip provides 16 microinstructions, such as "gate register Y to ALU." Twelve of these microinstructions form the fixed instruction set. The remaining instructions can be formed by combining any of the 16 microinstructions (a feature found in early minicomputers like the

Table 1　Single-Chip Calculators

Chip Series	TMS1000	TMS1070	TMS1040	TMS0970	TMS1100	TMS1270
Technology	PMOS	PMOS	PMOS	PMOS	PMOS	PMOS
Number of pins per package	28	28	28	28	28	40
Data operation size	4 bits	4 bits	4 bits	4 bits	4 bits	4 bits
Instruction ROM size	1024× 8 bits	1024× 8 bits	1024× 8 bits	1024× 8 bits	2048× 8 bits	1024× 8 bits
Data storage RAM size	64× 4 bits	64× 4 bits	64× 4 bits	64× 4 bits	64× 8 bits	64× 4 bits
No. fixed instructions	11	11	11	11	12	11
No. microprogrammable instructions	32	32	32	32	42	2
Display drive	VLED†	VF	VF	VLED	VLED†	VF
Product, function, and introduction date	SR-16 4-function 11/74	TI-5100 4-function 1/76	2550 II 7-function 10/75	TI-1200 4-function 6/75 TI-1250 4-function 6/75 Little Professor Mathematical drills 6/76	505OM 4-function printing 6/76 5015 4-function printing 1/77	TI-5200 4-function 1/77

VLED = visible-light-emitting diode
VF = vacuum flourescent
LC = liquid crystal
†Will not drive display directly; requires buffer chip.

PDP-8). Thus the ISP can be specialized to improve ROM efficiency and execution speed for a particular application.

Several special features of the microcomputer are aimed at the calculator application. The data paths are 4 bits wide to allow serial processing of binary-coded decimal (BCD) digits. The arithmetic functions assume 2's complement integers, but special instructions can be formed to facilitate BCD arithmetic (e.g., add six to accumulator for adjustment to legal BCD digits).

Another BCD-oriented feature is the RAM addressing, which provides for four words of sixteen 4-bit fields. While the SR-16 only displays eight digits, the extras can be used as "guard" digits to maintain numerical precision or as expansion space for future products with larger displays or exponent displays. (Note that the BCD digit-serial data path allows for this expansion by increasing the loop count on variable-length-dependent operations.) The TMS1000 applicability is primarily limited by ROM (program),

RAM (user-accessible internals and temporaries), speed, and number of I/O pins.

All the calculator functions are done by program. Two time-consuming functions are display refreshing and keypad scanning. The monolithic microcomputer must serially refresh the digits of the current display value at a sufficiently high frequency to achieve "persistency." The monolithic microcomputer must also serially examine keypad rows to see if any keys have been depressed. Even simple functions, such as Add, can take several instructions to execute, since BCD digits are addressed sequentially (see the examples at the end of Chap. 34).

Due to limitations on the LSI chip density, certain architectural features add to programming complexity:

• RAM addressing. Since instruction size is limited to 8 bits, there is not enough room to specify an address in the

Table 1 *(Continued)*

TMS0980	*TMS1980*	*TMS0920*	*TMS1990*	*TMS1500*	*TP0310*	*TP0320*
PMOS	PMOS	PMOS	PMOS	PMOS	CMOS	CMOS
28	28	28	28	28	28	28
4 bits	4 bits	40 bits serially	4 bits	64 bits serially	40 bits serially	4 bits
2048× 9 bits	2048× 9 bits	511× 9 bits	1024× 8 bits	2048× 13 bits	511× 9 bits	2048× 9 bits
64× 9 bits	64× 9 bits	40× 5 bits	64× 4 bits	64× 20 bits	40× 5 bits	64× 13 bits
9	10	30	12	165	30	11
46	47	......	31	......	......	46
VLED	VF	VF	VLED	VLED	LC	LC
TI-30 Slide Rule Business, analytical, financial 6/76 Programmers Number base conversion 8/77	Dataman Mathematical drills 6/77 TI-1050 5-function 6/77	TI-1025 4-function 6/77 TI-1050 5-function 6/77	TI-1000 4-function 6/77	TI-57 Scientific programmable 4/77 MBA Financial, statistical 8/77 TI-55 Scientific programmable 1/78	TI-1030 4-function 6/78	TI-50 Scientific 6/78 BAII Financial 6/78

instruction. Thus, a preloaded register pair (x,y) is assumed to contain the currently valid address when executing the memory-reference instruction. The register can be updated by using instructions with immediate operands or by incrementing. (Note that the x and y registers are physically separated so that a carry from the y register does not change x. x would have to be changed under programmed control.) This mechanism has also been used on microcomputers (e.g., Intel 8008 and 8080).

• Program Counter (PC) incrementing. In order to save a separate incrementer for the PC or trips through the ALU for updating, the PC update is implemented by a pseudo-random sequence to go through all 64 states produced by a feedback shift register such as is used in cyclic redundancy codes. Thus only a shifter and several logic gates are required. Figure 1 gives the logic implementation for the feedback shift counter.

• Instructions with side effects. Certain instruction op codes have been selected so that they can apply appropriate constants to the ALU and RAM. While this saves ROM space for frequently used constants, it seems to make op code selection difficult and add nonsymmetry to the instruction format.

The TMS1000 was introduced in 1974 and used in the SR-16 calculator. Table 1 summarizes the 13 different chips used in TI single-chip calculators. These chips vary in implementation technology, number of I/O lines, display drive, amount of ROM (up to 26.6 Kbit) and amount of RAM (up to 1280 bits). Calculator applications range from simple four-function calculators to the 50-step programmable TI-57. As of mid 1979, over 35 million TMS1000 chips were used in both calculator and noncalculator applications, establishing the TMS1000 as the computer

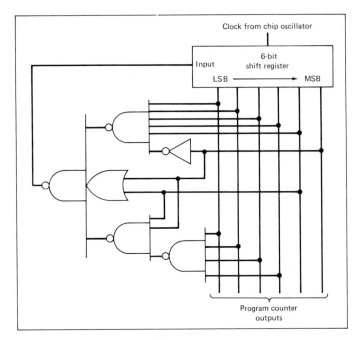

Fig. 1. TMS1000 feedback shift counter.

architecture with the largest installed base. The internal clock rate varies from 200 to 450 KHz, depending on technology.

A follow-on to the TMS1000 is the TMS7000 series announced in 1981 [Hayn, McDonogh, and Bellay, 1981]. The TMS7000 is an 8-bit monolithic microcomputer with 2 or 4 Kbyte a user-definable instruction set. The first two chips, the 7020 and 7040, have 2 or 4 Kbyte of use ROM respectively, and 128 bytes of RAM in a 40-pin package. Up to 60 Kbyte of external memory can be added. A complete family of monolithic microcomputers is planned.

PIC1650

In 1978, General Instrument Corporation (GI) introduced a single-chip computer called the PIC1650 (Programmable Intelligent Controller). Five variations have been produced varying in number of pins (18 to 40), amount of ROM (256 to 1,024 twelve-bit words), amount of RAM (24 to 64 eight-bit bytes), and operational voltage range. The large majority (67 to 80 percent) of the pins are devoted to program-controlled I/O.

GI sought an easy-to-program, general-purpose microcontroller. Thus the PIC1650 differs from the TMS1000 in several significant areas:

- Fixed rather than user-PLA–defined instruction set. In order to increase instruction-set power, symmetry, and understandability, the PIC instruction word was specified to be larger than the internal data path (i.e., 12 bits as opposed to 8 bits). This is in direct contrast to the more conventional practice of making instruction and data words of equal length.

- Focus on 8-bit integer and boolean data-types rather than a 4-bit BCD data-type. Typical control applications are better suited to 8-bit integer data-types for sensing and controlling the magnitude of variables and to boolean data-types for sensing and controlling on/off conditions.

- Program-controlled rather than PLA-controlled output codes. A special literal output instruction allows users to define code conversion tables in memory, adding to display flexibility and variety.

Adherence to the single-word instruction format (which simplifies the implementation of the 1650) poses serious problems for expansion when technology allows more ROM to be implemented on a chip and control applications require more than the 256 to 1,024 words of program in the current PIC architecture. The small-address-space problem has been encountered in all classes of computers; hence there is a wide range of solutions that have historically been tried. The following is a list ordered from smallest to greatest impact on existing user code:

- Increasing the instruction word width by adding more bits to the address field.

- Bank registers: one or more registers, loadable by a special instruction, that are concatenated with the program counter. The user must explicitly manage addressability and be concerned about the absolute value of addresses for various code segments. This scheme has been used in the PDP-8 and Data General Nova minicomputers.

- Address translation: a set of address translation registers placed between the Pc and Mp. The registers supply more bits of physical address than are contained in the instruction word. This scheme has been used in several minicomputers, such as the PDP-11.

- Addressing modes: Adding new addressing modes to the ISP that combine the contents of new, wider, architecture registers with the address supplied by the instruction. An example of this is the base/displacement addressing in the IBM System/360-System/370.

The PIC1650 has been used in electronic toys (by Ideal Toy and Coleco), electronic scales (Detecto), and cameras (Bosch).

Table 2   Intel MCS-48 Microcomputers

	8021	8022	8035	8039	8041	8048	8049	8741	8748
Number of pins per package	28	40	40	40	40	40	40	40	40
On-chip instruction ROM size (bytes)	1K	2K	....	....	1K	1K	2K	1K	1K
Maximum addressable instruction memory (bytes)	1K	2K	4K	4K	1K	4K	4K	1K	4K
On-chip data storage RAM memory (bytes)	64	64	64	128	64	64	128	64	64
Maximum addressable data storage memory (bytes)	64	64	320	384	64	320	384	64	320
I/O bits	21	23	27	27	18	27	27	18	27
Maximum clock frequency (MHz)	3	3	3, 6	6, 11	6	3, 6	11	6	3, 6

Table 3   The TI-9900 Family

	TMS9900	TMS9900-40	SBP9900A	TMS9980/ TMS9981	TMS9985	TMS9940
Technology	NMOS	NMOS	I²L	NMOS	NMOS	NMOS
Number of pins per package	64	64	64	40	40	40
Clock rate (MHz)	3.3	4	3	10	5	1–5
Clock	Off chip	Off chip	Off chip	On chip	On chip	On chip
Relative throughput	1	1.3	0.9	0.6	0.65–0.8	1.2
Maximum memory size (bytes)	65K	65K	65K	16K	65K	2.2K
On-chip memory	....	....	....	....	256 RAM	2K ERAM 128 RAM
Number of address bus lines	15	15	15	14	16	....
Number of data bus lines	16	16	16	8	8	....
Addressable I/O bits	8K	8K	8K	4K	32K	32
Number of interrupt levels	16	16	16	5	5	4

Monolithic Microcomputer Families

The Intel MCS-48 is a family of microcontrollers. Introduced in 1976, the Intel 8048 contains an 8-bit microprocessor, program ROM, data RAM, and program controllable I/O lines. Table 2 lists the MCS-48 family members as of late 1978. More details can be found in Gregoretti [1978] and Wakerly [1979].

The family evolved as the amount of on-chip ROM/RAM was increased, as off-chip RAM/I/O expansion capability was added, and as transducers were integrated (e.g., the 8-bit A/D converters on the 8022). As in the Texas Instruments TMS series, there is a large number of chips with varying capability. Although the range of variability appears small, the family is supported by the marketplace. Consider a mass-produced product that employs electronic control, such as an automobile. With production in the millions per year, substantial savings can be realized by using the smallest microcontroller chip with enough capacity for the application. In such products a small saving (e.g., 50 cents to $1) might be due to a smaller chip package (e.g., because the application requires a small number of I/O lines leading to a cheaper package and less board area) or to a smaller program storage (e.g., because the application requires only a small control program leading to less ROM and a higher chip-fabrication yield).

Another approach to microcomputer families is to take an existing ISP and implement it in as few chips as possible. Future technology growth will eventually allow the total system to be placed on a single chip. This approach simplifies software development, since the existing software is directly usable. Care must be taken, however, that at least some members of the family have expansion capability to handle growth of the larger applications.

The Texas Instruments TMS9900 series is an example of a family in transition (see Table 3). Based on the TI-990 minicomputer ISP, the family offers three microcomputers with varying speed. The TMS9980A is a reduced-complexity chip. The TMS9985 offers a small amount of on-chip memory. Finally the TMS9940 is a single-chip computer system with on-chip RAM/ROM and 32 programmable I/O lines instead of the traditional I/O bus for memory and peripherals.

Conclusion

The monolithic microcomputer class is already well populated with examples. This computer class will increase in importance as technology makes more complex systems feasible.

References

Gregoretti [1978]; Hayn, McDonogh, and Bellay [1981]; Simpson et al. [1978]; Wakerly [1979].

Chapter 34

TMS1000/1200: Chip Architecture and Operation[1]

Introduction

The TMS1000/1200 functional block diagram (Fig. 1) shows all major logic blocks and major data paths in the TMS1000/1200 architecture. The ROM, ROM addressing, and instruction decode are on the left side of the diagram. On the right side of the diagram are the adder/comparator, the RAM, the registers for addressing the RAM, and the accumulator, which is the main working register. The major logic blocks are interconnected to the adder with four-bit parallel data paths. The various portions of the architecture will be discussed in the following paragraphs.

Mp State

The ROM has 8,192 possible matrix points (1,024 eight-bit words) where MOS transistors are placed to define the bit patterns of the machine language code. The ROM is organized into 16 pages of 64 words.

There are four RAM files, each containing 16 four-bit words in the RAM's 256-bit matrix (shown in the upper right of Fig. 1).

There are two modes of RAM access (read and write) during the instruction cycle:

1 Data may be read out of the RAM for the purpose of addition, subtraction, or transfer to the other registers.

2 Data is stored in the RAM via the write bus.

Two sources of information are written into the RAM; these sources are selected by the write multiplexer (shown on the right side of the function diagram, Fig. 1). In one mode the multiplexer selects the accumulator information to be written into the RAM (uses the STO microinstruction). The accumulator data is transferred to memory after data is read from the RAM but before the ALU results are stored into the accumulator. In the second mode, the constant and K-input logic is written into the RAM (by the CKM microinstruction). The constants from the ROM instruction bus are transferred to the RAM directly, and an optional data path from K1, K2, K4, and K8 exists although not selected in the standard instruction set. Four RAM bits are carried on the read bus to either the P-multiplexer or the N-multiplexer and then to the adder/comparator.

[1]Abstracted from *TMS1000 Programmer's Reference Manual*, Texas Instruments, Inc., 1975.

Pc State

a PA<0:3>\Page.Address.Register. Contains the number of the page within the ROM being addressed.

b PB<0:3>\Page.Buffer.Register. The PB is loaded with a new page address which is then shifted into the PA for a successful branch or call. The PB is changed by the load page (LDP) instruction.

c PC<0:5>\Program.Counter. Contains the current location of the word (within the page) being addressed.

d SR<0:5>\Subroutine.Return.Register. Contains the return word address in the call subroutine mode.

e X<0:1>. Designates which of four RAM files are being accessed.

f Y<0:3>. Designates which of 16 four-bit words are being accessed in the specified RAM file.

g R<0:12>. Output register to control external devices.

h O<0:4>. Output register for display.

i K<0:3>. Input register.

j A<0:3>\Accumulator.

k Status.Logic<>. One-bit flag containing the status of previously executed instructions.

On powerup, the program counter is reset to location zero, and the PA is set to 15. Then the program counter counts to the next ROM address in a pseudorandom sequence. The sequence of addresses in the program counter can be altered by a branch instruction or a call instruction. A new branch address (W) can be stored into the program counter upon the completion of a successful branch or call instruction. If the branch instruction is not successful, then the program counter goes to the next ROM location within the current page.

In a successful call or branch execution the page address register (PA) receives its next page address from the buffer register (PB). The contents of the PB are changed by the load page instruction (LDP), which can be executed prior to the branch or call. Execution always continues on the same page unless PB is explicitly changed.

When the branch is executed successfully and when the processor is not in the call mode (CL = 0), the page buffer register is loaded into the page address register. If the contents of the page buffer register have been modified prior to the branch instruction, then this instruction is called a *long branch instruction*, since it may branch anywhere in the ROM (a long branch, BL, directive in the source program generates two instructions—LDP, load page buffer, and BR, branch). In the call mode (CL = 1), only "short" branches are possible, those staying within a given page.

Note that the normal state of the status logic is ONE. Several instructions can alter this state to a ZERO; however, the ZERO

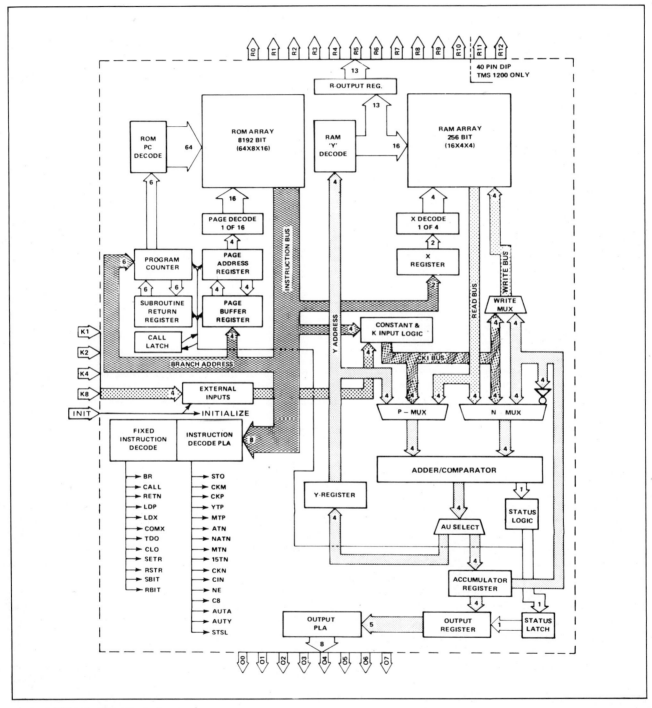

Fig. 1. TMS1000/1200 block diagram.

state lasts for only one subsequent instruction cycle (which could be during a branch or call); then the status logic will normally revert back to its ONE state (unless the following instruction resets it to ZERO).

Like branch instructions, call instructions are conditional. One level of subroutine is permitted, and a call within a call does not execute properly. In the case of a successful call when status logic equals ONE:

1   The call latch (CL) is set to ONE.

2   The contents of the page buffer register (PB) and the page address (PA) register are exchanged simultaneously.

3   The return address is stored in SR and PB. The SR address is one address ahead of the program counter when the call instruction is executed. The return address is saved for a future return instruction.

4   The branch address field of the instruction word writes into the program counter.

When a return instruction occurs:

1   The subroutine return register (containing the call instruction address plus one) is always transferred to the program counter.

2   The contents of the page buffer register (containing the page at call) is always transferred to the page address register.

3   The call mode is reset (CL = 0).

If a call instruction is executed within a previous call (no return has occurred and the call latch is still a ONE and status is a ONE), there is no transfer of the page buffer register to the page address register; instead contents of the page address register transfer to the page buffer register, although the branch address (W) loads into the program counter.

Thus a call within a call to another page will cause the return page to change, losing the correct return page address.

An X and Y address selects one four-bit RAM character, M(X,Y), this address being the storage location in the RAM matrix. The X-register can be set to a constant equal to 0 through 3 (LDX instruction), or X can be complemented (COMX instruction) to flip the address of X to the $\overline{X}$ file (e.g., 00 to 11, or 01 to 10).

The Y-register has three purposes.

1   The Y-register addresses the RAM in conjunction with the X-register for RAM character select.

2   The Y-register is a working register. The Y-register may be set to any constant between 0 and 15 (by the TCY instruction), loaded from memory (TMY instruction), loaded from the accumulator (TAY instruction), decremented (DYN), and incremented (IYC). Note that in the functional block diagram (Fig. 1), the Y-register has no inverted adder input. Thus, the Y-register cannot be subtracted from the accumulator or memory.

3   The Y-register addresses the R-output register for setting and resetting individual latches. Whenever a particular R-output needs to be set, the constant bus inputs the R's address (0 through 12) to Y (TCY instruction), and then a set R-output (SETR) instruction is executed.

The TMS1000 has two outputs:

- R-outputs used for control
- O-outputs used to transmit data

The purpose of the R-outputs is to control the following:

- External devices
- Display scans
- Input encoding
- Dedicated status logic outputs (such as overflow)

Each R-output has a latch that stores a ONE or ZERO, and each latch may be set (ONE) or reset (ZERO) individually by the set R (SETR) or reset R (RSTR) instruction. The Y-register points to which R-output is set by these instructions.

The R-output can be strobed by the ROM program to scan a key matrix (K-input). Figure 2 represents the maximum key matrix possible without external logic. A simple short from an R line to a K-input can be detected by the ROM program and interpreted as any function or data entry. Expanding the matrix is possible by external logic such as using a 4-line to 16-line decoder.

The status latch and the accumulator data are loaded into the O-output register (bottom right of Fig. 1) by a fixed instruction from the ROM (TDO) when the programmer decides to change output data. A separate instruction clears the O-output register. This instruction (CLO) causes all five output register bits to be reset to ZERO. The five bits from the O register are converted to a parallel eight-bit code by the O PLA.

The accumulator is a four-bit register that interacts with the adder, the RAM, and the output registers. The accumulator is the main working register for addition and subtraction. It is the only register which is inverted before its contents are sent to the adder for subtraction. Subtraction is accomplished by two's complement arithmetic. It is a storage register for inputs from the constant and K-input logic as well as the Y-register.

Variable data from the K-inputs is also stored via the accumula-

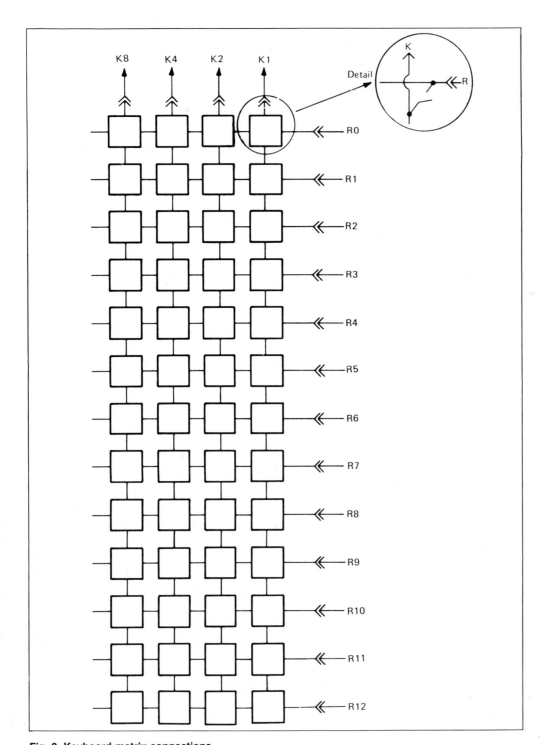

Fig. 2. Keyboard matrix connections.

tor into the RAM array. Therefore, any variable data input from the K-inputs or from the adder output must pass through the accumulator to the RAM array for storage. Likewise, any data to the O-outputs must come through the accumulator. Four accumulator register bits may be latched by the O-output register (where the status latch information is also latched) for decode by the O-output decoder.

There are 18 instructions that affect status logic, either setting it (to ONE) or resetting it (to ZERO). In turn, the status logic will permit the successful execution of a branch or call instruction (if status logic = ONE) or prevent successful execution of these instructions (if reset to ZERO). Status logic will remain at a ZERO level only for the following instruction cycle and then automatically be set to the normal ONE state (unless reset to ZERO by the next instruction).

There are two microinstructions (NE and C8) that are used by instructions affecting status. If the microinstruction C8 is used and a carry occurs in the addition of two four-bit words, the carry goes from the MSB sum to status, setting status logic to a ONE. If no carry occurs, status logic is ZERO. In a logic compare instruction (using microinstruction NE), status logic is set to ONE if the four-bit words at the N and P adder/comparator inputs are not equal; conversely, status logic is ZERO if the inputs are equal.

The status latch buffers the status-logic bit to the O-output register for decode by the O-output PLA. Status-logic output is selectively loaded into the status latch by special microinstruction STSL (used in a logical-compare test instruction that causes the status logic to output a ONE or ZERO). For example, if the test instruction YNEA (in the standard instruction set) causes status to be a ONE (if Y-register is not equal to A), then the ONE writes into the status latch. If a ZERO is output by that instruction from status logic, then the ZERO writes into the status latch.

The status latch transfers to the O-register with the accumulator bits when TDO, transfer data out, is executed.

Instruction Set

Table 1 summarizes the standard instruction set, composed of the 12 "fixed" instructions and the 31 standard microprogrammed instructions. These standard instructions are available as a default to the user if he does not choose to redefine them by specifying a different PLA pattern.

Instruction Formats

The machine instructions have been divided into four instruction formats. A format subdivides the eight bits of each instruction into fields. These fields contain the operation code and operands.

Instruction Format I:

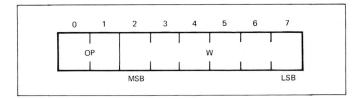

This format has a two-bit operation-code field, and the operand is a six-bit ROM-word address field. This format is used for program control by branch and call instructions. The operand, the branch address, has a value of 0 to 63.

Instruction Format II:

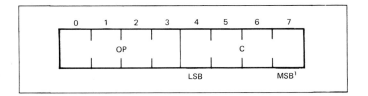

This format has a four-bit operation-code field; the operand is a four-bit constant field. This format is used for instructions that contain an immediate value that loads RAM memory or a register with a constant.

Instruction Format III:

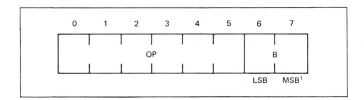

This format has a six-bit operation code, and the operand is a two-bit RAM bit address field. This format is used for addressing a bit in a RAM word. Also, B describes the two-bit X-address operand for the LDX command.

Instruction Format IV:

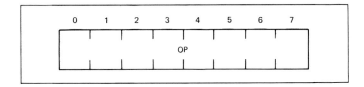

[1]The constant values are reversed in this field. The assembler converts values into proper machine code format.

Table 1   TMS1000/1200 Standard Instruction Set

| Function | Mnemonic | Status† effect | | Description | Instruction format |
		C8	NE		
Register to register	TAY	...	...	Transfer accumulator to Y-register.	IV
	TYA	...	...	Transfer Y-register to accumulator.	IV
	CLA	...	...	Clear accumulator.	IV
Transfer register to memory	TAM	...	...	Transfer accumulator to memory.	IV
	TAMIY	...	...	Transfer accumulator to memory and increment Y-register.	IV
	TAMZA	...	...	Transfer accumulator to memory and zero accumulator.	IV
Memory to register	TMY	...	...	Transfer memory to Y-register.	IV
	TMA	...	...	Transfer memory to accumulator.	IV
	XMA	...	...	Exchange memory and accumulator.	IV
Arithmetic	AMAAC	Y	...	Add memory to accumulator, results to accumulator. If carry, one to status.	IV
	SAMAN	Y	...	Subtract accumulator from memory, results to accumulator. If no borrow, one to status.	IV IV
	IMAC‡	Y	...	Increment memory and load into accumulator. If carry, one to status.	IV
	DMAN‡	Y	...	Decrement memory and load into accumulator. If no borrow, one to status.	IV
	IA	...	...	Increment accumulator, no status effect.	IV
	IYC	Y	...	Increment Y-register. If carry, one to status.	IV
	DAN	Y	...	Decrement accumulator. If no borrow, one to status.	IV
	DYN	Y	...	Decrement Y-register. If no borrow, one to status.	IV
	A8AAC	Y	...	Add 8 to accumulator, results to accumulator. If carry, one to status.	IV
	A10AAC	Y	...	Add 10 to accumulator, results to accumulator. If carry, one to status.	IV
	A6AAC	Y	...	Add 6 to accumulator, results to accumulator. If carry, one to status.	IV
	CPAIZ	Y	...	Complement accumulator and increment. If then zero, one to status.	IV
Arithmetic compare	ALEM	Y	...	If accumulator less than or equal to memory, one to status.	IV
	ALEC	Y	...	If accumulator less than or equal to a constant, one to status.	II
Logical compare	MNEZ	...	Y	If memory not equal to zero, one to status.	IV
	YNEA	...	Y	If Y-register not equal to accumulator, one to status and status latch.	IV
	YNEC	...	Y	If Y-register not equal to a constant, one to status.	II
Bits in memory	SBIT	...	...	Set memory bit.	III
	RBIT	...	...	Reset memory bit.	III
	TBIT1	...	Y	Test memory bit. If equal to one, one to status.	III
Constants	TCY	...	...	Transfer constant to Y-register.	II
	TCMIY	...	...	Transfer constant to memory and increment Y.	II
Input	KNEZ	...	Y	If K-inputs not equal to zero, one to status.	IV
	TKA	...	...	Transfer K-inputs to accumulator.	IV
Output	SETR	...	...	Set R-output addressed by Y.	IV
	RSTR	...	...	Reset R-output addressed by Y.	IV
	TDO	...	...	Transfer data from accumulator and status latch to O-outputs.	IV
	CLO	...	...	Clear O-output register.	IV
RAM X addressing	LDX	...	...	Load X with a constant.	III
	COMX	...	...	Complement X.	IV
ROM addressing	BR	...	...	Branch on status = one.	I
	CALL	...	...	Call subroutine on status = one.	I
	RETN	...	...	Return from subroutine.	IV
	LDP	...	...	Load page buffer with constant.	II

†C8 (microinstruction C8 is used) — Y (Yes) means that if there is a carry out of the MSB, status output goes to the ONE state. If no carry is generated, status output goes to the ZERO state.

NE (microinstruction NE is used) — Y (Yes) means that if the bits compared are not equal, status output goes to the ONE state. If the bits are equal, status output goes to the ZERO state.

A ZERO in status remains through the next instruction cycle only. If the next instruction is a branch or call and status is a ZERO, then the branch or call is not executed.

‡Execution of the DMAN or IMAC instruction does not change (increment or decrement) the content of the addressed memory cell.

This format defines an eight-bit operation code field only. Instructions of this format have no constant operands. The instruction always performs the same action, for example, transferring the accumulator to the Y-register.

Eighteen instructions conditionally affect the machine status logic. The mnemonics for these instructions contain a one- or two-character descriptor to indicate how status logic is affected. Each descriptor (shown in Table 2) indicates the condition where status will remain set (logic ONE). The conditional instructions, branch and call, are successful only if status is set. The mnemonic descriptor therefore indicates the conditions under which an immediately following branch or call will be performed. If the instruction results do not meet the descriptor's condition, then status is reset (logic ZERO) and any immediately following branch or call will not be performed. [Status logic in the reset (ZERO) state affects only branches or calls in the next instruction cycle before returning to the normal (logic ONE) state.]

The way in which the instruction depends upon status or sets status is defined as follows:

- Set: The instruction unconditionally forces status to ONE and is not conditional upon status.

- Carry into Status: The value of the carry from the adder is transferred to status. In the subtraction instructions, carry = $\overline{\text{borrow}}$.

- Comparison Result into Status: The logical comparison value from the ALU is transferred to status (equal: ZERO to status; unequal: ONE to status).

- Conditional on Status: The instruction's execution results are conditional upon the state of the status. After the instruction is executed, status is unconditionally equal to ONE.

Implementation

The instruction timing is fixed and each instruction requires six clock cycles to execute. Each of the 43 basic instructions is defined to enable one or more microinstructions that activate control lines during one instruction cycle. These microinstructions explain the firmware bridge between software instructions and the individual logic block capabilities. A hardwired logic decoder that cannot be modified decodes 12 "fixed" basic instruction codes into 12 fixed microinstructions for output instructions, branching, subroutines, RAM X-addressing, reset and set bit instructions. The remaining 31 basic instructions activate a combination of 16 programmable microinstructions that are encoded by the instruction PLA. The concept of fixed and programmable microinstructions is used as a tool for understanding the software on the machine level and is used to increase the power of the instruction set to fit more applications (microprogramming the instruction set).

The purpose of the CKI logic (Fig. 1) is to select either the K-inputs or the four-bit constants from ROM (the C field of the instruction word) or a bit mask to go out to the CKI data bus. The constant and K-input logic is used whenever microinstructions CKP, CKN, or CKM are selected by an instruction. The data going out on the CKI bus changes for predetermined instruction values, however, and this section details what the data is and the versatility of CKI microinstructions. Since the constant and K-input logic is not changeable, it is important to understand the four separate functions CKI controls before learning how CKI microinstructions are performed. Table 3 shows the binary-decoded groupings of the instruction word and the particular output enabled by the CKI logic.

1   First, for eight hexidecimal instruction values (08 to $0F_{16}$ as listed in Table 3), the K-inputs are active. That is, the constants from the ROM are shut off, and the four-bit external-input bus (center left of Fig. 1) is made available to either the adder/comparator or the RAM. The instruction decoder determines how the available data is used.

2   The second main function is to channel constant data from the instruction bus (from ROM) to the CKI bus output (instruction values 00 to 07 and 40_{16} to $7F_{16}$ as listed in Table 3). The CKI bus is available to the P adder input, the N adder input, or the write multiplexer for the RAM as shown in Fig. 1. The constant data from the ROM can be selected by 72 possible machine instruction values, although the standard instructions use only 68 of these.

3   The constant logic is disabled (output at ZERO for values 20_{16} to $2F_{16}$).

4   A bit mask is active. For example, the bit mask as used in the test bit instruction (TBIT1) determines if a bit from the RAM is a ONE by comparing it with ZERO. The bit mask has only one ZERO in the four-bit CKI output, as determined by the B field of the instruction word (see TBIT1 in Table 3). The B field is two bits and points to the selected opening (ZERO) in the mask. Thus, if the least significant bit is to be tested, then the bit mask outputs the binary word 1110 to the CKI output. Then the CKI bus output goes into both sides of the adder/comparator, and the word at M(X,Y) is input simultaneously (logically ORed) with the

Table 2   Descriptor Action

Descriptor		Cause/result that transfers ONE to status
Last	C	Carry out during addition or increment instructions
character	N	No borrow during subtraction or decrement instructions
in	Z	Zero result from 2's complement
mnemonic	1	Tested memory bit is a logic ONE
Middle of	-LE-	Is less than or equal to
mnemonic	-NE-	Is not equal to

Table 3 Constant and K-Input Logic Truth Table

I	(0)	(1)	(2)	(3)	(4)	(5)	(6)	(7)	Op code (hex)		Mnemonic (standard instructions)	C KI out	C KI logic and other constant operations	Comment
0	0	0	0	0	0	0	0	0	0	0	COMX			
0	0	0	0	0	0	0	1	0	1	A8AAC	Y		
0	0	0	0	0	0	1	0	0	2	YNEA			
0	0	0	0	0	0	1	1	0	3	TAM		$I(7-4) \rightarrow$ CKI bus	$I_{(7)}$ = MSB
0	0	0	0	0	1	0	0	0	4	TAMZA	Y		$I_{(4)}$ = LSB
0	0	0	0	0	1	0	1	0	5	A10AAC	Y		
0	0	0	0	0	1	1	0	0	6	A6AAC	Y		
0	0	0	0	0	1	1	1	0	7	DAN	Y		
0	0	0	0	1	0	0	0	0	8	TKA	Y		
0	0	0	0	1	0	0	1	0	9	KNEZ	Y		
0	0	0	0	1	0	1	0	0	A	TDO			
0	0	0	0	1	0	1	1	0	B	CLO		$K_{1, 2, 4, 8} \rightarrow$ CKI bus	K_8 = MSB
0	0	0	0	1	1	0	0	0	C	RSTR			
0	0	0	0	1	1	0	1	0	D	SETR			
0	0	0	0	1	1	1	0	0	E	IA			
0	0	0	0	1	1	1	1	0	F	RETN			
0	0	0	1	C				1	...		LDP		$I(7-4) \rightarrow$ PB	No effect on CKI; only affect PB
0	0	1	0	0	0	0	0	2	0	TAMIY			
0	0	1	0	0	0	0	1	2	1	TMA			
0	0	1	0	0	0	1	0	2	2	TMY			
0	0	1	0	0	0	1	1	2	3	TYA			
0	0	1	0	0	1	0	0	2	4	TAY			
0	0	1	0	0	1	0	1	2	5	AMAAC			
0	0	1	0	0	1	1	0	2	6	MNEZ			
0	0	1	0	0	1	1	1	2	7	SAMAN		$0 \rightarrow$ CKI BUS	
0	0	1	0	1	0	0	0	2	8	IMAC			
0	0	1	0	1	0	0	1	2	9	ALEM			
0	0	1	0	1	0	1	0	2	A	DMAN			
0	0	1	0	1	0	1	1	2	B	IYC			
0	0	1	0	1	1	0	0	2	C	DYN			
0	0	1	0	1	1	0	1	2	D	CPAIZ			
0	0	1	0	1	1	1	0	2	E	XMA			
0	0	1	0	1	1	1	1	2	F	CLA			
0	0	1	1	0	0		B	3	...		SBIT		Bit mask $\rightarrow$ CKI bus	B = 0 CKI − 1110
0	0	1	1	0	1		B	3	...		RBIT			1 1101
0	0	1	1	1	0		B	3	...		TBIT 1	Y		2 1011
														3 0111
0	0	1	1	1	1		B	3	...		LDX		$I(7-6) \rightarrow$ X	No effect on CKI.
0	1	0	0	C				4	...		TCY	y	$I(7-4) \rightarrow$ CKI bus	$I(7)$ = MSB
0	1	0	1	C				5	...		YNEC	Y		$I(4)$ = LSB
0	1	1	0	C				6	...		TCMIY	Y		
0	1	1	1	C				7	...		ALEC	Y		$C \rightarrow$ CKI bus; C = 0 to 15
1	0	W									BR			Not used
1	1	W									CALL			

Note: I = Instruction (op code), C = Constant, W = Branch Address, Y = Yes (CKP, CKN, or CKM microinstruction is used). PB = Page Buffer Register (ROM)

CKI bus into the P side of the adder/comparator. The compare feature of the adder/comparator is activated, and then the state of the tested bit transfers directly to status logic. The bit mask also selects RAM bits to be set or reset. For the set bit (SBIT) and reset bit (RBIT) instructions, the ZERO in the bit mask field (Table 3) also acts as a pointer to one of the four bits (identified by X- and Y-register contents) in a RAM character.

There are two PLA's in the TMS1000 series:

- The O-output PLA
- The instruction decoder PLA

In a PLA, a matrix of gates first decodes a number of binary logic inputs into a set of output lines (also called "terms"). Each term can select a combination of output lines from a second matrix of gates (see Fig. 3). Both matrices are implemented by programmable-input NAND gates (Fig. 4). Since we are concerned only with the input-to-output code conversion, positive-logic AND and OR functions are used herein.

Figure 4 shows two AND matrix terms, F_0 and F_1, which are encoding two output OR matrix terms, Q_0 and Q_1. The simplified method of presenting the same circuit is shown in Fig. 5. Each

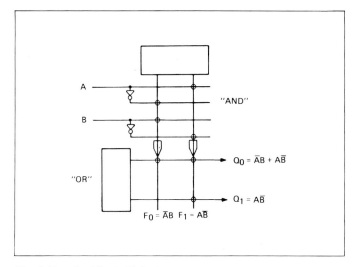

Fig. 4. Standard logic PLA circuit schematic.

circle in the diagram represents a MOSFET which selects a gate input to a matrix term.

User programming of these PLA's requires inputs to the TSM1000 simulator for O-output PLA programming and to the assembler and simulator for instruction PLA programming.

The O-output PLA determines the parallel output definition for each TMS1000 series program. Thus, a user understanding the capabilities can define an efficient output organization before designing an algorithm. The organization of the outputs is a necessary starting point for new system designs.

The O-output register sends five bits to the O-output PLA (bottom of Fig. 1). Figure 6 shows the five corresponding

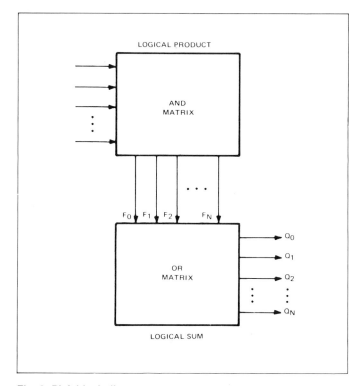

Fig. 3. PLA block diagram.

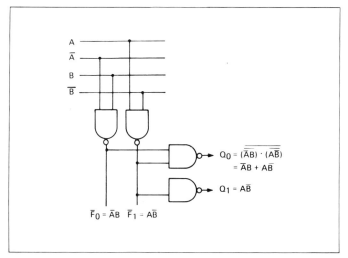

Fig. 5. Array logic equivalent schematic.

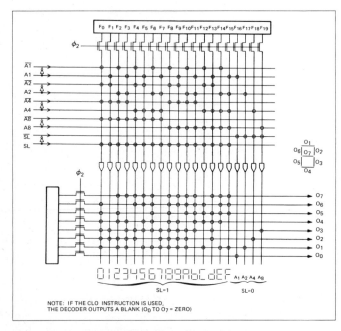

Fig. 6. Typical coding example of O-output PLA.

to the OR matrix. The pattern is stored in the matrix by placing MOS transistors (gates) to select inputs and not placing a gate where an input is not desired.

Each AND matrix term may decode a subset of the following Boolean equation:

$$F_N = (A1 \cdot \overline{A1}) \cdot (A2 \cdot \overline{A2}) \cdot (A4 \cdot \overline{A4}) \cdot (A8 \cdot \overline{A8}) \cdot (SL \cdot \overline{SL})$$

Either the true or the complement (not both) or neither (don't care) of the two inputs enclosed in parentheses can be selected. The AND matrix may decode up to 20 of these Boolean equations.

Each OR matrix line determines the O-output pattern for each AND term used. If an AND term is true, the output selection (represented by a circle) is a subset of the following expression:

$$O \text{ output} = O_0 + O_1 + O_2 + O_3 + O_4 + O_5 + O_6 + O_7$$

If any two or more AND term equations are satisfied, then their ORed output functions are logically ORed together.

The example coding shown in Fig. 6 shows an output classified into seven-segment information and binary information. If the status latch bit is ZERO, then the PLA sends binary information out. If the status latch bit is ONE, then the PLA encodes seven-segment display information. Note that there are 20 input terms to the OR matrix; four terms encode the binary value of the accumulator bits, 16 terms encode the characters 0 to F.

The TDO instruction latches the status latch and the accumula-

O-register bits (from accumulator and status latch) going into the AND matrix in true and complemented form. The AND matrix has 20 terms available for decoding a prescribed pattern of inputs

Table 4   TMS1000 Series Programmable Microinstructions

Execution sequence	Mnemonic	Logic affected	Function
1	CKP	P-MUX	CKI to P-adder input.
	YTP	P-MUX	Y-Reg to P-adder input.
	MTP	P-MUX	Memory (X, Y) to P-adder input.
1	ATN	N-MUX	Accumulator to N-adder input.
	NATN	N-MUX	$\overline{\text{Accumulator}}$ to N-adder input.
	MTN	N-MUX	Memory (X, Y) to N-adder input.
	15TN	N-MUX	F_{16} to N-adder input.
	CKN	N-MUX	CKI to N-adder input.
1	CIN	Adder	One is added to sum of P plus N inputs (P+N+1).
	NE	Adder/status	Adder compares P and N inputs. If they are identical, status is set to zero.
	C8	Adder/status	Carry is sent to status (MSB only).
2	STO	Write MUX	Accumulator data to memory.
	CKM	Write MUX	CKI to memory.
3	AUTA	AU select	Adder result stored into accumulator.
	AUTY	AU select	Adder result stored into Y-Reg.
	STSL	Status latch	Status is stored into status latch.

tor bits in the O register. In the case of term zero (F_0), a ONE from the status latch and ZERO from the accumulator encode the seven-segment character for zero.

Two logic blocks decode the eight-bit instructions into the various microinstructions:

- Fixed instruction decoder
- Programmable instruction PLA

The fixed instruction decoder cannot be modified and enables 12 fixed controls affecting ROM addressing, RAM X-register, output control, set bit and reset bit instructions. Every program must use these instructions with their corresponding fixed microinstructions.

The remaining 31 basic instructions in the standard set (43 basic instructions—we fixed basic instructions equal to 31 programmable instructions) have their operations determined by combining one or more microinstructions as determined by the instruction PLA.

The programmable instructions are defined to the assembler and simulator programs by default definition when the standard instructions are used. When one or more instructions are redefined, the user specifies the entire set of instruction mnemonics to the assembler, and the new PLA implementation is defined to the simulator.

Table 4 defines the operation of the programmable microinstructions, and the logic block controlled by each. In one instruction cycle the sequence of microinstruction execution is as follows:

1 Read RAM, select the inputs to the adder/comparator.
   Microinstructions: CIN, MTP, MTN, CKP, CKN, YTP, ATN, 15TN, NATAN, C8, NE

2 Write accumulator contents or CKI bus information into the RAM.
   Microinstructions: CKM, STO

3 Add or compare, then store results into the Y-register, accumulator, status logic, or status latch.
   Microinstructions: AUTY, AUTA, STSL

Thus the MTP (RAM memory contents to P-adder input) microinstruction is executed before STO (store accumulator data into RAM). The adder can perform one operation per instruction cycle. If two input buses are selected for the same side of the adder, the inputs are logically ORed together.

The programmable microinstructions are an aid to learning how instructions work. For example, the IA instruction (increment accumulator) enables three microinstructions, ATN, CIN, and AUTA:

1 ATN transfers the accumulator data to the N-adder input ($P = 0$).

2 CIN causes 1 to be added to the P- and N-adder inputs.

3 AUTA causes the result of the addition to be stored in the accumulator.

Knowing the hardware and how Texas Instruments combined the microinstructions explains all 31 programmable instructions. For example, the YNEC instruction activates three microinstructions.

1 CKN causes the constant from ROM (immediate operand) to go into the N-input.

2 YTP enables Y to the P-input.

3 NE sends the comparison to status.

Therefore, if Y is logically compared to a constant operand and is *not equal* to the CKI data, status equals ONE.

Figure 7 illustrates the PLA implementation designed by Texas

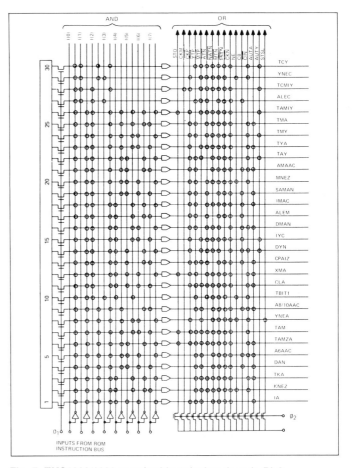

Fig. 7. TMS1000/1200 standard instruction decode PLA.

Instruments for the standard instruction set. The 31 instructions are translated by 30 PLA terms into a combination of the 16 microinstructions possible (the A8AAC and the A10AAC are combined on a single PLA line).

The instruction PLA can be reprogrammed in cases where timing or other requirements dictate an instruction redefinition. Microprogramming this PLA should be considered only when the standard definition is insufficient to accomplish the program objectives.

Addition Instruction

The following example illustrates the addition arithmetic instructions. This example shows adding a word to a BCD draft in memory. BCD correction is performed to keep the digit in the range 0 to 9. Upon exit from this routine the accumulator contains a ONE if a carry has resulted or a ZERO if no carry has resulted.

Label	Op code	Operand	Comment
	AMMAC		ADD CURRENT DIGIT TO A
	BR	FIXUP	BRANCH IF CARRY (SUM > 15)
	TAM		TRANSFER A TO MEMORY
	A6AAC		ADD 6, TEST FOR DIGIT 10 TO 15
	BR	CORRECT	BRANCH IF CARRY
	CLA		CLEAR ACCUMULATOR
CONTU			EXIT
	.		
	.		
	.		
FIXUP	A6AAC		ADD 6 TO CORRECT TO BCD
CORRECT	TAMZA		TRANSFER A TO MEMORY, CLEAR A
	IA		INCREMENT ACCUMULATOR
	BR	CONTU	EXIT
	.		
	.		
	.		

Input

The following example illustrates the input instructions. This example handles input from a keyboard. The keys must be sampled one row at a time. The particular row selected is determined by which R-output line is set on. This example shows sampling on row five only, and determines which of four keys on row five are depressed. If all four K-inputs are zero, no key is currently depressed. For simplicity no key-debounce logic has been included.

Label	Op code	Operand	Comment
	TCY	5	SET ROW 5
	SETR		ENABLE ROW 5
	KNEZ		TEST K INPUTS FOR NON-ZERO
	BR	INPUT	YES, GO TO INPUT
*			

*NO DATA PRESENT ON INPUT LINES

Label	Op code	Operand	Comment
*			
	RSTR		DISABLE ROW 5
	BR	CONTU	EXIT
*			

*NOW STORE THE DATA FROM THE K LINES.

Label	Op code	Operand	Comment
*			
INPUT	TKA		INPUT K LINES TO A
	RSTR		DISABLE ROW 5
*			
*			

*NOW FIND WHICH KEY ON ROW 5.

Label	Op code	Operand	Comment
*			
	ALEC	1	KEY 1?
	BR	ONK1	YES
	ALEC	2	KEY 2?
	BR	ONK2	YES
	ALEC	4	KEY 4?
	BR	ONK4	YES
	BR	ONK8	MUST BE ON K8.

TMS1000 Display Scan

The TMS1000 is a *digit-scan* calculator chip. The displayed information is turned on one digit at a time. The segment lines for each digit are connected in parallel. The correct segment lines for a particular digit are turned on by the TMS1000 O lines and then the correct digit line (R line) is turned on to enable the illumination of that single digit. This process is continued for each digit to complete one display scan cycle, and then the entire cycle is repeated. The display is scanned as rapidly as possible to avoid flicker problems or display "breakup" when the calculator is moved. This rate is typically in the range of 150 to 300 Hz for the TMS1000.

Output

The following example illustrates the various output instructions. Four data words from memory, M(0,3), go to the O-output register. The R-outputs are used to signal which word is presented. The O-register is cleared after each word has been presented. The example assumes that a previous YNEA instruction set the status latch to ZERO.

Label	Op code	Operand	Comment
	.		
	.		
	TCY	3	SET INDEX AND COUNTER
LOOP	SETR		SET R(Y) OUTPUT STROBE
	TMA		LOAD DIGIT INTO A
	TDO		LOAD OUTPUT FROM A AND SL
	RSTR		RESET R(Y) OUTPUT STROBE
	CLO		CLEAR O OUTPUT REGISTER
	DYN		DECREMENT Y REGISTER
	BR	LOOP	LOOP UNIT Y BORROWS
	.		
	.		

Program Control

The following example illustrates the usage of the program control instructions BR, CALL, RETN and LDP.

This example illustrates using a control loop that calls a subroutine to perform a specific function. The control loop continues to call the subroutine until certain conditions are met; then control is passed to another portion of the main program in a different ROM page. This particular example calls a "shift left" routine to shift a five-word string left one word address at a time. The shift routine is called until a non-zero word is found in position M(0,3). Because the subroutine is in another page, a long call is performed by setting a new page address in the page buffer (PB) before the call.

Label	Op code	Operand	Comment
	LDX	0	SET RAM ADDRESS
LOOP	TCY	3	to M(0,3)
	MNEZ		M(0,3) ≠ 0;
	BR	DONE	BRANCH IF NOT EQUAL, DONE
*			
*SET UP TO CALL SHIFT LEFT ROUTINE			
*			
	LDP	5	SLRTN IS IN PAGE 5
	CALL	SLRTN	CALL SLRTN
	BR	LOOP	RETURN HERE, BRANCH TO LOOP
*			
DONE	LDP	4	GO TO PAGE 4
	BR	MORE	PERFORM LONG BRANCH
*			
*COMMON SUBROUTINE, SLRTN, SHIFT LEFT.			
*			
SLRTN	TCY	0	CLEAR Y INDEX
	CLA		CLEAR A
SWITCH	XMA		EXCHANGE MEMORY & ACCUMULATOR
	IYC		INCREMENT Y INDEX
	YNEC	4	Y = 4? (END OF STRING)
	BR	SWITCH	CONTINUE IF NOT EQUAL
	RETN		RETURN TO CALL

APPENDIX 1   ISP of the TMS1000

```
TMS1200 :=
    begin

! Texas Instruments TMS 1000 Series MOS/LSI one chip microcomputer.

! References: TMS 1000 Software User's Guide
!             TMS 1000 Programmer's Reference Manual
!             The Engineering Staff of Texas Instruments Incorporated,
!             Semiconductor Group,
!             Texas Instruments Incorporated
!             P.O. Box 1443,
!             Houston, Texas 77001

! Note that the "INIT" line must be set to "1" before starting a
! simulation of the ISP.  This "feature" is a result of the
! TI "INIT" implementation.

! The Output PLA and the Instruction PLA may be redefined for
! simulation.  The internal initializations should be overlayed
! by files read into the simulator after completion of
! "init.out.pla".  I.E. set ABREAK init.out.pla before starting
! the simulation.  At the break: READ yourdefinition.SIM.

**MP.State**

    ROM[0:1023]<0:7>,                    ! ROM for instruction storage.
    RAM[0:63]<0:3>,                      ! RAM
        ram.bit[0:255]<> := RAM[0:63]<0:3>   ! RAM bit map

**PC.State**

    PA<0:3>,                             ! Page address register
    PB<0:3>,                             ! Page buffer register
    PC<0:5>,                             ! Program counter
    SR<0:5>,                             ! Subroutine return address
    CL<>,                                ! Call latch
    R[0:10]<>,                           ! R output register
    X<0:1>,                              !
    Y<0:3>,                              ! Pointer/storage register
    S<>,                                 ! Logic status
    SL<>,                                ! Conditional branch status
    A<0:3>,                              ! Accumulator
    O<0:4>,                              ! Output buffer
    CKI.BUS<0:3>

**External.State**

    INIT<>,                              ! Init line
    K<0:3>                               ! External inputs

**Implementation.Declarations**

    N.MUX<0:3>,                          ! Multiplexer to adder
    P.MUX<0:3>,                          ! Multiplexer to adder
    ADDER<0:4>,                          ! The adder/ALU
    temp<0:3>,                           ! Temporary register
    s.trace<>,                           ! Status trace
    rom.address<0:9>,                    ! Instruction ROM address reg.
    OUT.PLA[0:31]<0:7>,                  ! Simulation of output pla

    INSTR.PLA[0:255]<0:15>,              ! Simulation of instruction PLA.
    b.rev<0:1>,                          ! Reverse bit b field.
    c.rev<0:3>                           ! Reverse bit c field.

**Instruction.Format**

    I.BUS\Instruction.Bus<0:7>,          ! Doubles as instruction register

                                         ! Format I instructions
    op.I<0:1>    := I.BUS<0:1>,          ! Opcode
    w<0:5>       := I.BUS<2:7>,          ! New branch address

                                         ! Format II instructions
    op.II<0:3>   := I.BUS<0:3>,          ! Opcode
    c<0:3>       := I.BUS<4:7>,          ! Constant (note bit reversal)

                                         ! Format III instructions
    op.III<0:5>  := I.BUS<0:5>,          ! Opcode field
    b<0:1>       := I.BUS<6:7>,          !

                                         ! Format IV instructions
    op.IV<0:7>   := I.BUS<0:7>,          ! Opcode

                                         ! Format V (1000/1300 only)
    op.V<0:4>    := I.BUS<0:4>,          ! Opcode
    f<0:2>       := I.BUS<5:7>,          ! Data for LDX

**PLA.Initialization**{us}

    ! The output Programmable Logic Array (PLA) translates the
    ! contents of the O register into a user defined code on the
    ! O-output lines.  The PLA initialization defined below
    ! provides encoding for driving seven segment LED displays
    ! with the characters:
    !   0, 1, 2, 3, 4, 5, 6, 7, 8, 9, A, b, C, d, E, F.
```

```
! Additionally, BCD output can be selected under program control.

init.out.pla :=
    begin
    OUT.PLA[ 0]  = '00000000;   OUT.PLA[16] = '01111110;
    OUT.PLA[ 1]  = '00000001;   OUT.PLA[17] = '00110000;
    OUT.PLA[ 2]  = '00000010;   OUT.PLA[18] = '01101101;
    OUT.PLA[ 3]  = '00000011;   OUT.PLA[19] = '01111001;
    OUT.PLA[ 4]  = '00000100;   OUT.PLA[20] = '00110011;
    OUT.PLA[ 5]  = '00000101;   OUT.PLA[21] = '01011011;
    OUT.PLA[ 6]  = '00000110;   OUT.PLA[22] = '01011111;
    OUT.PLA[ 7]  = '00000111;   OUT.PLA[23] = '01110000;
    OUT.PLA[ 8]  = '00001000;   OUT.PLA[24] = '01111111;
    OUT.PLA[ 9]  = '00001001;   OUT.PLA[25] = '01111011;
    OUT.PLA[10]  = '00001010;   OUT.PLA[26] = '01110111;
    OUT.PLA[11]  = '00001011;   OUT.PLA[27] = '00011111;
    OUT.PLA[12]  = '00001100;   OUT.PLA[28] = '01001110;
    OUT.PLA[13]  = '00001101;   OUT.PLA[29] = '00111101;
    OUT.PLA[14]  = '00001110;   OUT.PLA[30] = '01001111;
    OUT.PLA[15]  = '00001111;   OUT.PLA[31] = '01000111
    end.
! The Instruction PLA defined below encodes the standard TI 1200
! (micro)programmable instruction set.  The encoding was derived
! from figure 2-17.2 on page 2-27 of the Programmer's Reference
! Manual.

init.instr.pla :=
    begin
    INSTR.PLA["01"] = '0001101111011100;   ! A8AAC
    INSTR.PLA["02"] = '0010101111101001;   ! YNEA
    INSTR.PLA["03"] = '1011111111001000;   ! TAM
    INSTR.PLA["04"] = '1011111111001100;   ! TAMZA
    INSTR.PLA["05"] = '0001101111011100;   ! A10AAC
    INSTR.PLA["06"] = '0001101111011100;   ! A6AAC
    INSTR.PLA["07"] = '0001101111011100;   ! DAN
    INSTR.PLA["08"] = '0001111111001100;   ! TKA
    INSTR.PLA["09"] = '0001111111101100;   ! KNEZ
    INSTR.PLA["0E"] = '0011101111000100;   ! IA
    INSTR.PLA["20"] = '1010111111001000;   ! TAMIY
    INSTR.PLA["21"] = '0011011111001100;   ! TMA
    INSTR.PLA["22"] = '0011011111001100;   ! TMY
    INSTR.PLA["23"] = '0010111111001100;   ! TYA
    INSTR.PLA["24"] = '0011101110111010;   ! TAY
    INSTR.PLA["25"] = '0011001111011100;   ! AMAAC
    INSTR.PLA["26"] = '0011011111101100;   ! MNEZ
    INSTR.PLA["27"] = '0011010111010100;   ! SAMAN
    INSTR.PLA["28"] = '0011011111101000;   ! IMAC
    INSTR.PLA["29"] = '0011010111010000;   ! ALEM
    INSTR.PLA["2A"] = '0011011101011100;   ! DMAN
    INSTR.PLA["2B"] = '0010111111010010;   ! IYC
    INSTR.PLA["2C"] = '0010111101011010;   ! DYN
    INSTR.PLA["2D"] = '0011110111101000;   ! CPIAZ
    INSTR.PLA["2E"] = '1011101111001100;   ! XMA
    INSTR.PLA["2F"] = '0011111111001100;   ! CLA
    INSTR.PLA["38"] = '0001011110101000;   ! TBIT1
    INSTR.PLA["39"] = '0001011110101000;   ! TBIT1
    INSTR.PLA["3A"] = '0001011110101000;   ! TBIT1
    INSTR.PLA["3B"] = '0001011110101000;   ! TBIT1
    temp = 0 next
init.loop :=
    begin
    INSTR.PLA["40 + temp"] = '0001111111001010;   ! TCY
    INSTR.PLA["50 + temp"] = '0010111110101000;   ! YNEC
    INSTR.PLA["60 + temp"] = '0110111111000010;   ! TCMIY
    INSTR.PLA["70 + temp"] = '0001110111010000 next   ! ALEC
    temp = temp + 1 next
    IF temp NEQ 0 => RESTART init.loop
    end
    end
**Service.Routines**{us}

    ! Access routine to translate the O register through the Output PLA.

    activate.out.pla(O<0:4>)<0:7> := (activate.out.pla = OUT.PLA[O]),

    ! Access routine to translate instructions through the instruction PLA.

    activate.instr.pla(I.BUS<0:7>)<0:15> :=
                            (activate.instr.pla = INSTR.PLA[I.BUS])

**Instruction.Interpretation**{us}

    start{main} :=                          ! Main control loop
        begin
        IF init =>                          ! Initialization sequence
            begin
            init.instr.pla(); init.out.pla();
            PC = O = R = CL = 0; PA = PB = '1111;
            S = 1; INIT = 0
            end next
        s.trace = 0;
        rom.address =
            PA@(PC<2:5>@(PC<1> eqv PC<5>)@(PC<0> xor PC<1> eqv PC<5>)) next
        I.BUS = ROM[rom.address] next
        b.rev = b<1>@b<0>;
        c.rev = c<3>@c<2>@c<1>@c<0>;
        PC = PC<1:5> @ ((PC<0> eqv PC<1>) xor (PC<1:5> eql '11111)) next
```

APPENDIX 1 (cont'd.)

```
        DECODE I.BUS =>                         ! CKI.BUS determination
            begin
            "00":"07 := CKI.BUS = c.rev,         ! Load from instruction.
            "08":"0F := CKI.BUS = K,             ! Input from external lines.
            "20":"2F := CKI.BUS = 0,             ! Zero.
            "30":"3B := CKI.BUS = ('1110 SLR b.rev),
            "40":"7F := CKI.BUS = c.rev,         ! Load from instruction.
          otherwise := no.op()
            end next
        DECODE I.BUS =>                         ! Fixed instruction decode
            begin
            "00 := COMX(),                      ! Complement X
            "0A := TDO(),                       ! Transfer: O = A
            "0B := CLO(),                       ! Clear O-output
            "0C := RSTR(),                      ! Reset R[Y]
            "0D := SETR(),                      ! Set   R[Y]
            "0F := RETN(),                      ! Subroutine Return
          "10":"1F := LDP(),                    ! Load Page Buffer (constant)
          "30":"33 := SBIT(),                   ! Set memory bit
          "34":"37 := RBIT(),                   ! Reset memory bit
          "3C":"3F := LDX(),                    ! Load X (constant)
          "80":"BF := BR(),                     ! Branch on status = 1
          "C0":"FF := CALL(),                   ! Call subroutine (status = 1)
        otherwise := microexecution()
            end next
        IF s.trace => RESTART start next
        S = 1 next
        RESTART start
    end
**Instruction.Execution**{us}

    BR :=                                       ! Branch on status = 1
        begin
        DECODE S =>
            begin
            0 := S = 1,
            1 := (IF CL eql '0 => PA = PB; PC = w)
            end
        end,

    CALL :=                                     ! Call subroutine,
        begin                                   ! conditional on status
        DECODE S@CL =>
            begin
            '10 := (SR = PC; temp = PA next
                    PA = PB next
                    PB = temp; PC = w; CL = 1),
            '11 := (PC = w; PB = PA),
        otherwise := S = 1
            end
        end,

    RETN :=                                      ! Return from subroutine
        begin
        IF CL => PC = SR next
        PA = PB; CL = 0
        end,

    LDP  := (PB = c.rev),                        ! Load page buffer
    LDX  := (X = b.rev),                         ! Load x with constant
    COMX := (X = not X),                         ! Complement x
    TDO  := (activate.out.pla(SL@A)),            ! Transfer to output
    CLO  := (activate.out.pla(0)),               ! Clear output register
    SETR := (IF Y leq 10 => R[Y] = 1),           ! Set R[Y] to 1
    RSTR := (IF Y leq 10 => R[Y] = 0),           ! Set R[Y] to 0
    SBIT := (ram.bit[X@Y@b.rev] = 1),            ! Set memory bit
    RBIT := (ram.bit[x@y@b.rev] = 0)             ! Reset memory bit

**Microinstruction.Execution**{us}

    microexecution :=
        begin
        activate.instr.pla(I.BUS); P.MUX = 0; N.MUX = 0 next
        IF     activate.instr.pla<0>  => STO  := RAM[X@Y] = A;
        IF     activate.instr.pla<1>  => CKM  := RAM[X@Y] = CKI.BUS next
        IF not activate.instr.pla<2>  => CKP  := P.MUX = CKI.BUS;
        IF not activate.instr.pla<3>  => YTP  := P.MUX = Y;
        IF not activate.instr.pla<4>  => MTP  := P.MUX = RAM[X@Y];
        IF not activate.instr.pla<5>  => ATN  := N.MUX = A;
        IF not activate.instr.pla<6>  => NATN := N.MUX = not A;
        IF not activate.instr.pla<7>  => MTN  := N.MUX = RAM[X@Y];
        IF not activate.instr.pla<8>  => TN15 := N.MUX = "F;
        IF not activate.instr.pla<9>  => CKN  := N.MUX = CKI.BUS next
        ADDER = P.MUX + N.MUX next
        IF     activate.instr.pla<10> => NE   := (S = (P.MUX neq N.MUX);
                                                  s.trace = 1);
        IF not activate.instr.pla<12> => CIN  := ADDER = P.MUX + N.MUX + 1 next
        IF     activate.instr.pla<11> => C8   := (S = ADDER<0>;
                                                  s.trace = 1) next
        IF     activate.instr.pla<13> => AUTA := A = ADDER<1:4>;
        IF     activate.instr.pla<14> => AUTY := Y = ADDER<1:4>;
        IF     activate.instr.pla<15> => STSL := SL = S
        end
    end         ! End of TMS1000
```

Chapter 35

PIC1650: Chip Architecture and Operation

Frank M. Gruppuso

I. Introduction and Design Goals

The PIC1650 is an MOS/LSI circuit array containing RAM, I/O, a central processing unit, and a customer-defined ROM on a single chip. General Instrument (GI) architectured the PIC (Programmable Intelligent Controller) in 1976 to satisfy the need for a low-level, easy-to-use microcontroller. The only other microcomputer available at the time was the calculator-based design TMS1000, and it was felt that a much more powerful machine could be built around a general-purpose–register, minicomputer-like architecture. Thus was laid the groundwork for the PIC1650.

The PIC is fabricated in an N-channel MOS–process technology that permits fabrication of both enhancement- and depletion-mode transistors. Depletion-mode transistors allow low-voltage (5-volt) operation and, when used as internal load resistors, offer much better speed-power performance than enhancement-mode transistors used in a similar fashion.

As a controller, the PIC chip was designed to emphasize bit, byte, and register-transfer operations. Its main objectives would be to perform logical processing, basic code converting, and formatting, and to generate fundamental timing and control signals for various subservient I/O devices [PIC 1979a,b]. The emphasis was placed on the ability to provide control and interface functions rather than computing functions. The PIC was seen as a key element to providing so-called intelligence to long-established non-computer, small-system designs which, as it turned out, were mostly electromechanical in nature. Some of the initial proposals were for applications in vending machines, small dot-matrix impact printers, and metered mailing systems.

The following are several key issues which motivated the architecture and logic design.

- Wide instruction word. It was felt that a 12-bit-wide instruction word that was wider than the 8-bit data word afforded both simplicity (and thus compactness) of chip design and ease of user-programmability. All instructions were therefore designed to be one word long; this kept the control logic simple since no multiple fetches had to be made from program memory to execute even the most complex instructions. Also, a 12-bit instruction word allows every register to be directly addressed by the program. It

further permits literals in program ROM to be accessed at the same time as the instruction op code. For example, in a machine with an 8-bit-wide instruction word, a load immediate instruction would normally take two 8-bit ROM words fetched and executed in two instruction cycles. In the PIC1650, the equivalent instruction only occupies one 12-bit ROM word in memory and executes in one cycle.

- General-register architecture. Another aspect of the design that was considered important was the general-purpose nature of the register array: the program counter (PC), every I/O register, and most other specialized registers occupy an address in the register array address space. This permits every instruction that can operate on a general-purpose register to operate, say on an I/O file register or the PC. In the case of the program counter, for example, the instruction MOVW F2 (move the contents of the working register to the PC) is actually a computed GOTO instruction.

- Minimal parts count. It was envisioned that the PIC would be applied in areas that would be cost-sensitive from a systems viewpoint. Thus, efforts were taken to minimize the amount of external outboard circuitry. A single-pin oscillator whose frequency of operation was determinable by a single resistor and capacitor was designed. A second power supply, V_{XX} was added to drive the output buffers of the processor. It was expected that TTL gates would not be the only loads that the microcomputer I/O lines were ever going to see. Discrete switching transistors, coils, and large LED displays represent only a few of the different kinds of external circuits it was felt the PIC chip had to be capable of interfacing with. If V_{XX} is varied externally from 5 V to, say, 9 V, the output buffer transistors behave as voltage-controlled resistors. This allows any interface between the PIC chip and the outside world to be more effectively matched. Section VI of this chapter describes an application using this pin.

- Direct Bit Set/Clear/Test instructions. In view of the PIC's overall architectural goal of being a controller, it was highly desirable for the processor to be able to directly set, clear, and test individual bits in any register without forcing the user to program the usual "mask with a literal" coding sequences. Instead, the chip performs these functions internally. Thus, to execute the Bit Set instruction on bit 2 of a particular register, for example, the processor internally sets up the mask B'00000100' and performs a logical OR between this mask and the register.

- Wide operating-voltage range. Soon after the release of the PIC1650 to the marketplace, it became apparent that a number of applications were found which required battery operation (e.g., electronic hand-held games and digital scales) or, more generally, a wide operating-voltage range. A wide operating-voltage–range chip could tolerate a less critical and, hence, less costly external power supply. Thus,

GI initiated a design effort that generated the "A" series of PIC chips—PIC1650A, PIC1655A—that are identical to the original except that the operating voltage range was increased from 4.75–5.25 V to 4.5–7 V. As four C cell batteries fully charged produce 6.8 V in series, 7 V was chosen as the upper limit.

Several versions of the PIC1650 have been architectured which, among other things, vary according to number of I/O lines, RAM size, and ROM size. These are enumerated in Table 1.

Applications using the PIC series have centered around those where a single-chip microcomputer could perform systems functions at a lower cost than non-computer solutions presently available or, alternatively, provide extra features which heretofore would have been prohibitively expensive without a microcomputer. Present applications that use the PIC chip include:

- Digital-readout weight scale. In this application, weight is converted to a digital pulse train via a front-end transducer circuit. The pulses are applied to the RTCC (Real Time Clock Counter) input. The ROM program computes the difference between the frequency with the weight applied and the no-weight frequency (thereby providing for auto-zero correction) and converts the difference to a 4-digit BCD number which is subsequently displayed. To save multiplexing costs, all thirty-two I/O lines drive the display directly.

- Auto-dialer telephone system. This system is capable of storing and retrieving sixteen 10-digit telephone numbers. Here, the PIC chip processes command codes, which are entered through the keyboard, and drives outboard CMOS RAM, which stores the actual digits.

- Motor control. In this application, the PIC chip serves as a feedback element in a constant-speed motor control system. The microcomputer senses the present speed of the motor and adjusts the firing pulse to an external SCR, which, in turn, drives the motor. The high instruction rate permits precise control over a wide range of speeds. Typical applications of this system are found in industrial drill presses and hand drills.

- Consumer electronics. In the consumer arena, the PIC has been programmed into a variety of electronic games. The PIC is quite efficient in the area of sound generation: the high instruction rate permits higher-frequency sounds and thus more complex sounds than would be possible with a slower processor. Other areas of consumer electronics use the aforementioned motor control technique in household mixers, blenders, and food processors. The PIC has also been designed into appliances requiring time controlling, such as microwave oven timing.

Figure 1 shows a functional block diagram of the PIC1650. All data elements—arithmetic logic unit, register file array, I/O registers—are connected via an internal 8-bit bidirectional bus.

Table 1 Family of PIC Architectures

	PIC1650A	PIC1655A	PIC1670	PIC1645	PIC1656
Technology	NMOS	NMOS	NMOS	NMOS	NMOS
Number of pins per package	40	28	40	18	28
Cycle time (μsec)	4	4	4	4	4
Data path width (bits)	8	8	8	8	8
Instruction word width (bits)	12	12	12	12	12
Program ROM size (12-bit bytes)	512	512	1024	256	512
Number of fixed instructions	30	30	33	31	31
Data storage RAM size (8-bit bytes)	32	32	64	24	32
Operating-voltage supply range (volts)	4.5–7.0	4.5–7.0	4.5–7.0	4.5–7.0	4.5–7.0
Interrupt capability	No	No	Yes	Yes	Yes
Levels of pushdown stack	2	2	4	3	3
I/O configuration (registers)					
Input/output	4 8-bit	1 8-bit	4 8-bit	1 4-bit	1 8-bit
Input only		1 4-bit		1 4-bit	1 4-bit
Output only		1 8-bit		1 4-bit	1 8-bit
Date of introduction	1978	1978	Planned 1979	Planned 1979	1979

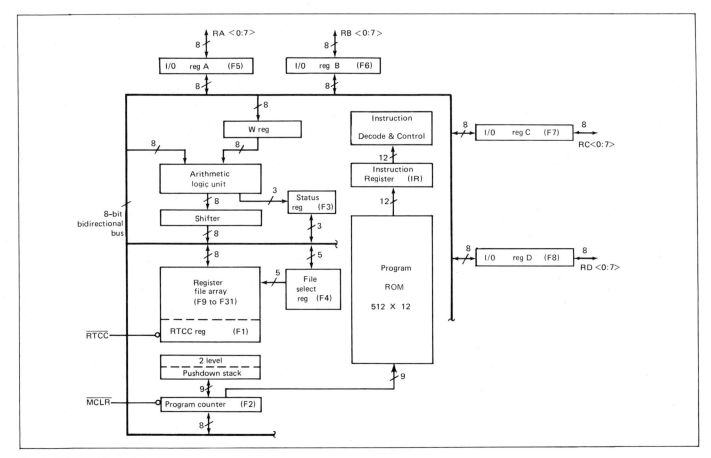

Fig. 1. PIC1650 block diagram.

Descriptions of these various elements appear in the following sections.

II. Mp State

The Program ROM contains 6144 bits organized as 512 twelve-bit words. RAM storage consists of 32 eight-bit registers, all of which are addressable by instructions contained in the program ROM. These registers are divided into two functional groups: operational registers and general-purpose registers. The general registers are addressed as F9 to F31 and contain data and control information. These registers are all located in a contiguous block labeled "Register File Array" in Fig. 1. The operational registers, F0 to F8, are scattered throughout the chip, and not only are they addressable by the program, but they also perform special functions described in Sec. III of this chapter.

III. Pc State

The register file arrangement is delineated as follows:

a   F0. F0 is not a physically implemented register. Rather, it is used as an indirect register-select mechanism; when F0 is specified in the register file field of an instruction, the PIC will use the contents of F4 to select the register to be used in that instruction.

b   F1<7:0>\Real.Time.Clock.Counter.Register. This register counts external events by incrementing on the falling edge of the RTCC pin. This register can also be loaded and read under program control.

c   F2<8:0>\Program.Counter (PC). The program counter points to the next instruction to be executed in memory. This register is 9 bits wide to address the 512-word ROM, but only the low-order 8 bits can be written to or read from by the program. The ninth bit can be considered a page bit and can only be altered by a GOTO instruction. The PC is initialized to 777_8 upon a low-to-high transition of the MCLR input pin. It increments normally thereafter except as modified by the program via the use of the CALL, RETURN or other, similar instructions.

d F3<2:0>\Status.Word.Register. This register contains status bits which are modified as a result of arithmetic operations.

> C<>\ Carry.bit:= F3 <0>. Stores the carry out of the most significant bit of the resultant of an arithmetic operation. This bit is also used as a link for rotate instructions.

> DC<>\ Digit.Carry := F3<1>. Stores the carry out of the fourth low-order bit (bit 3) of the resultant of an arithmetic operation. The bit is useful in processing decimal data.

> Z<>\Zero := F3 <2>. This bit is set if the resultant of an arithmetic operation is zero and cleared if the resultant is not zero.

Since these bits constitute a file register, they can also be modified under program control. However, to avoid a conflict between altering the status flags under program control and altering the status flags as a result of arithmetic operations, F3 can only be modified under program control by either the BIT SET or BIT CLEAR instruction.

e F4<7:0>\ File.Select.Register (FSR). Only the low-order 5 bits are used in this register. The FSR is used in generating effective file register addresses under program control. When this register is directly addressed as a file, all 5 bits can be written to and read from. The upper 3 bits read as a logic "1."

f F5<7:0>\ Input.Output.Register A.

g F6<7:0>\ Input.Output.Register.B.

h F7<7:0>\ Input.Output.Register.C.

i F8<7:0>\ Input.Output.Register.D.

j F9<7:0>–F31<7:0>. Twenty-three general-purpose registers.

k W<7:0>\ Working.Register. The accumulator.

l Stack [1:0]<8:0>. Two registers that store return addresses for use in CALL and RETURN instructions.

m IR<11:0>\ Instruction.Register. A 12-bit register that stores the instruction currently being executed by the PIC.

Note that neither register of the pushdown stack can be directly accessed by the program. When a CALL instruction is executed,

the contents of the program counter (which is·already pointing to the next instruction after the CALL) are pushed into the top register of the pushdown stack. The top register's former contents are pushed onto the second register in the stack. Any prior data in this second register is lost, thereby limiting the amount of subroutine nesting to two. The RETURN instruction (mnemonic RETLW) functions in reverse fashion: the top register of the stack replaces the current PC while the second register of the stack replaces the stack top. The contents of the second register remain unchanged.

IV. Instruction Set

Table 2 summarizes the PIC1650 instruction set. Each instruction is a 12-bit word divided into an op code field which specifies the instruction type and one or more fields which select the operand data source and destination. The instruction set is broken into three different formats: general file register operations, bit-level file register operations, and literal and control operations.

Instruction Format I: General File Register Operations

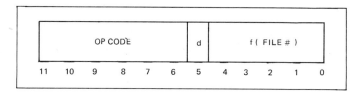

This format has a 6-bit op code field, a 5-bit register select field, and a single-bit destination field. The 5-bit register select field can directly access any one of the 32 file registers (F0 through F31). Instructions in this format will specify either a single source operand—a file register—or two source operands—a file register and the W register.

Two-source operand instructions include SUBTRACT, Inclusive OR, AND, Exclusive OR, ADD, and MOVE. Single-source operand instructions include CLEAR, DECrement, COMplement, INCrement, Rotate Right, Rotate Left, and SWAP. For all instructions in this format, however, the destination bit (bit 5) will specify where the result of the operation will be placed. If the destination bit equals 1, the result will be placed in the file register originally specified as the source; if the destination bit equals 0, the result will be placed in the W register.

Two other instructions in this format permit compact coding in the case of software timing loops. *Decrement file, skip if zero* (DECFSZ) decrements the source file, and if the result of the decrement operation is zero, then the next instruction after

Table 2 PIC 1650 Instruction-Set Summary

In the following PIC instruction descriptions "k" represents an eight-bit constant or literal value, "f" represents a file register designator and "d" represents a destination designator. The file register designator specifies which one of the 32 PIC file registers is to be utilized by the instruction. The destination designator specifies where the result of the operation performed by the instruction is to be placed. If "d" is zero, the result is placed in the PIC W register. If "d" is one, the result is returned to the file register specified in the instruction. If the "d" operand is omitted, the f register is assumed as the destination. "f" and "d" may be numbers, characters, or symbols as described in the PIC Assembler and PIC Simulator instructions. A "b" field specifies the bit number within an 8-bit register, "C" represents the carry bit, "Z" represents the zero bit, and "DC" represents the digit carry bit.

General file register operations

(6–11)	(5)	(0–4)
OP CODE	d	f (FILE #)

for d = 0, f→W
d = 1, f→f

Instruction (octal)				Name	Syntax		Operation	Status affected
000000	0	00000	(0000)	No Operation	NOP	. . .	. . . . .	None
000000	1	fffff	(0040)	Move W to f†	MOVWF	f	W→f	None
000001	0	fffff	(0100)	Clear W	CLRW	–	O→W	Z
000001	1	fffff	(0140)	Clear f	CLRF	f	O→f	Z
000010	d	fffff	(0200)	Subtract W from f	SUBWF	f, d	f−W→d	C, DC, Z
000011	d	fffff	(0300)	Decrement f	DECF	f, d	f−1→d	Z
000100	d	fffff	(0400)	Inclusive OR W and f	IORWF	f, d	W∨f→d	Z
000101	d	fffff	(0500)	AND W and f	ANDWF	f, d	W∧f→d	Z
000110	d	fffff	(0600)	Exclusive OR W and f	XORWF	f, d	W⊽f→d	Z
000111	d	fffff	(0700)	Add W and f	ADDWF	f, d	W+f→d	C, DC, Z
001000	d	fffff	(1000)	Move f	MOVF	f, d	f→d	Z
001001	d	fffff	(1100)	Complement f	COMF	f, d	f̄→d	Z
001010	d	fffff	(1200)	Increment f	INCF	f, d	f+1→d	Z
001011	d	fffff	(1300)	Decrement f, Skip if Zero	DECFSZ	f, d	f−1→d, skip if Zero	None
001100	d	fffff	(1400)	Rotate Right f	RRF	f, d	f(n)→d(n−1), f(0)→C, C→d(7)	C
001101	d	fffff	(1500)	Rotate Left f	RLF	f, d	f(n)→d(n+1), f(7)→C, C→d(0)	C
001110	d	fffff	(1600)	Swap halves f	SWAPF	f, d	f(0−3)⇄f(4−7)→d	None
001111	d	fffff	(1700)	Increment f, Skip if Zero	INCFSZ	f, d	f+1→d, skip if zero	None

BIT-level file register operations

(8–11)	(5–7)	(0–4)
OP CODE	b (BIT #)	f (FILE #)

Instruction (octal)			Name	Syntax		Operation	Status
0100	bbb	fffff	(2000)	Bit Clear f	BCF	f, b	0→f(b)	None
0101	bbb	fffff	(2400)	Bit Set f	BSF	f, b	1→f(b)	None
0110	bbb	fffff	(3000)	Bit Test f, Skip if Clear	BTFSC	f, b	Bit Test f(b); skip if clear	None
0111	bbb	fffff	(3400)	Bit Test f, Skip if Set	BTFSS	f, b	Bit Test f(b); skip if set	None

Literal and control operations

(8–11)	(0–7)
OP CODE	I (LITERAL)

Instruction (octal)			Name	Syntax		Operation	Status
1000	00000000	(4000)	Return	RET	–	0→W, RAR→PC	None
1000	kkkkkkkk	(4000)	Return and place Literal in W	RETLW	k	k→W, RAR→PC	None
1001	kkkkkkkk	(4400)	Call subroutine†	CALL	k	PC+1→RAR, k→PC	None
101x	kkkkkkkk	(5X00)‡	Go To address	GOTO	k	k→PC	None
1100	kkkkkkkk	(6000)	Move Literal to W	MOVLW	k	k→W	None
1101	kkkkkkkk	(6400)	Inclusive OR Literal and W	IORLW	k	k∨W→W	Z
1110	kkkkkkkk	(7000)	AND Literal and W	ANDLW	k	k∧W→W	Z
1111	kkkkkkkk	(7400)	Exclusive OR Literal and W	XORLW	k	k⊽W→W	Z

†The 9th bit of the program counter in the PIC1650 is zero for a CALL and a MOVWF F2. Therefore, subroutines must be located in page 0. However, subroutines can be called from page 0 or page 1 since the RAR is 9 bits wide (Page 0: 0–255. Page 1: 256–511).

‡If x = 0, the address is in page 0; if x = 1, the address is in page 1. The PIC assembler takes care of assigning the correct op codes.

DECFSZ is skipped; if the reslt is not zero, then the next instruction is executed. *Increment file, skip if zero* (INCFSZ) operates in a similar fashion.

Instruction Format II: Bit-Level Register Operations

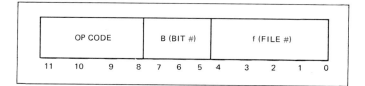

This format has a 5-bit register select field, a 3-bit bit select field and a 4-bit op code field. There are only four instructions in this category: two instructions that set or clear individual bits in a particular register, and the other two instructions that test a bit for a one or zero and skip accordingly. Again, the register select field (bits 0–4) can directly address one of 32 file registers while the bit select field (bits 5–7) selects one of eight bits in that register to be either set or cleared. The other seven bits in the register remain unchanged. None of the status bits are altered by any of the instructions in this category.

Any instruction in the above two classes may specify F0 in the register select field. In that case, as an example, say the PIC is to execute DECF F0, W and the contents of F4 at the time of execution are 14_8. Then register 14_8 is decremented and its results placed in the W register.

Instruction Format III: Literal and Control Operations

This format has a 4-bit op code and an 8-bit constant field. Instructions using this format fall into two sub-groups: one group treats constants located in program ROM as data, while the other treats them as addresses. As an example of the first, IORLW Inclusive ORs an 8-bit constant with the present contents of the W register and places the result in the W register.

The CALL instruction and the GOTO instruction treat the literal field as an address. Although one GOTO mnemonic appears in Table 2 there are really two GOTO instructions. The program counter is 9 bits wide to address 512 words, while the literal field is only 8 bits wide. Thus, bit 8 of the GOTO instruction specifies the ninth bit of the program counter. The op code field is limited,

however, and therefore this same technique cannot be applied to the CALL instruction. Thus, when a CALL instruction is executed, the ninth bit of the PC is forced to a zero. This requires all subroutines to be located in the low 256-word ROM memory space. Similarly, when the PC is also changed by the use of the MOVW F2 instruction, the ninth bit is also forced to a zero. Since the pushdown stack is 9 bits wide, though, subroutines can be called from anywhere in the 512-word ROM space.

The Return and Place Literal in W instruction (RETLW) is a little unusual in that it is two instructions in one. The op code specifies that the top element of the pushdown stack (indicated as RAR for Return Address Register in Table 2) replace the program counter. Simultaneously, the constant contained in the literal field is loaded into the W register. This instruction provides a very convenient facility for table look-up.

V. Implementation

Timing

The basic instruction cycle timing for the PIC is generated from an on-chip ring oscillator. The only external components required to support oscillation are a resistor and a capacitor. The oscillator runs at four times the internal clock frequency; thus, to support a 4-μs instruction cycle, the oscillator must operate at 1 MHz.

An internal two-phase, non-overlapping clocking scheme is central to the microcomputer's internal operation. This is shown in Fig. 2. To keep the control logic simple, a pipelined instruction fetch/instruction execute system was used. Thus, while the PC is accessing the current instruction in ROM memory, the ALU and register array data sections are executing the instruction accessed in the previous cycle. This requires the use of a separate incrementer for the PC as there is no time for the ALU to perform the incrementation. The program counter increments on the

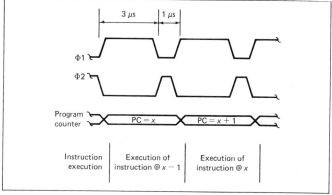

Fig. 2. Instruction cycle timing.

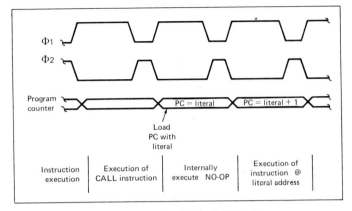

Fig. 3. Modified cycle timing for CALL, GOTO, etc.

rising edge of every $\Phi 1$ clock. At the same time, a master slave flip-flop located at the output of the ROM latches the instruction fetched in the previous cycle. This prevents the new instruction fetch from potentially corrupting the previous fetch. This pipelining scheme keeps the instruction throughput high.

For those instructions that modify the contents of the program counter, this scheme does not work. Opportunity must be given for the ROM to access the instruction at the new address. Thus the PIC must wait an additonal cycle before accessing the next instruction after CALL or similar instructions (Fig. 3).

Input/Output Registers

Thirty-two pins of the PIC1650 (housed in a 40-pin dual in-line package) constitute the input/output pins. They are segregated into four groups of eight pins each. Each group of eight represents a register that occupies an address in the address space of the register file array. Pins RA<0:7> are the I/O pins that constitute F5 (Fig. 1). Similarly, RB<0:7>:= F6<7:0>,RC<0:7>:= F7<7:0>, and RD<0:7>:= F8<7:0>. A circuit diagram of the I/O register interfacing to a TTL gate is shown in Fig. 4.

Each I/O bit contains a latch which will be written into if its I/O file is specified as the destination register in an instruction. If we consider the I/O bit as part of an output file, then the logic value attained by the pin will be the logic value in the latch. If a "1" is stored in the latch, transistor Q_1 will still be on, bit transistor Q_2 will attain an impedance of approximately 200 Ω and drive the pin to a low level.

An auxiliary power supply, V_{xx}, provides the voltage required to turn on transistor Q_2. The higher this supply, the lower the impedance Q_2 attains when it is on. Typically, increasing the V_{xx} supply from 5 V to 10 V will roughly halve the impedance of Q_2 from 200 Ω to 100 Ω. In driving large-segment LED displays, for example, a typical system configuration would call for V_{CC} (primary chip supply) to be 5 V and V_{xx} to be 10 V. This provides the large current-sinking capability necessary to drive the displays without the need for any interfacing bipolar transistors.

Now consider the use of the I/O bit as part of an input file. When an I/O file is used as a source register, an internal READ signal gates the data on the I/O pin into the internal data bus. In this configuration, Q_2 should be kept off by presetting the register to 1 (allowing Q_1 to be conveniently used as a pull-up transistor). If Q_2 is on, an impedance conflict will occur if an external device is attempting to drive the pin to a logic "1" level. For purposes of logic definition, then, it can be said that the I/O bit and the external device form a logical AND when the I/O register is used as an input file.

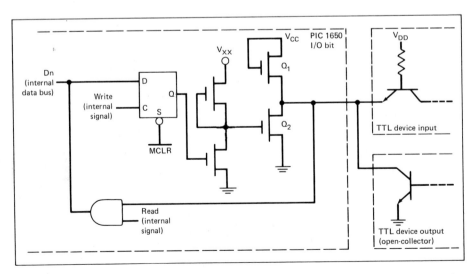

Fig. 4. I/O register circuit diagram.

VI. Program Examples

Use of Indirect Addressing

This example illustrates the use of the File Select Register (F4) and the indirect addressing mode using F0. This program clears files F5 to F31.

Label	Op code	Operand	Comment
	MOVLW	5	Move literal 5 to W REG.
	MOVWF	4	Move W to F4. (F4 = 5).
Loop	CLRF	0	Clear the contents of the file pointed to by F4.
	INCFSZ	4, F	Increment F4. The PC will skip after F31 is cleared.
	GOTO	Loop	Repeat the steps beginning at Loop to clear the next file.
	END		Files F5 and F31 are cleared.

BCD Number Display

This example converts a BCD number held in the four least significant bits of F20 (the 4 MSB's are assumed zero) to a 7-segment code. The 7-segment code is output via I/O port F5,

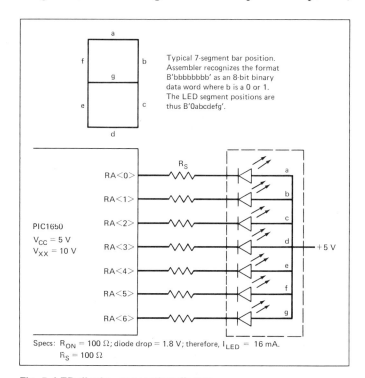

Typical 7-segment bar position. Assembler recognizes the format B'bbbbbbbb' as an 8-bit binary data word where b is a 0 or 1. The LED segment positions are thus B'0abcdefg'.

PIC1650
$V_{CC} = 5$ V
$V_{XX} = 10$ V

Specs: $R_{ON} = 100\ \Omega$; diode drop = 1.8 V; therefore, $I_{LED} = 16$ mA.
$R_S = 100\ \Omega$

Fig. 5. LED display connection diagram.

Label	Op code	Operand	Comment
	MOVLW	TBLSTR	Starting address of table.
	ADDWF	20, W	Add BCD number as offset to Table start.
	CALL	CONVRT	Call the conversion subroutine.
	MOVWF	5	Output the 7-segment code to I/O F5. The 7-segment
	END		will now show the BCD number and this output will remain stable until F5 is set to a new value.
CONVRT:	MOVWF	2	Move the computed address into the PC. Because the ninth bit of the PC is set to zero by a MOVWF 2, the TBLSTR routine must be located in the low 256-word ROM memory area.
TBLSTR:	RETLW	B'00000001	Complement of 0 in 7-segment code.
	RETLW	B'01001111	Complement of 1 in 7-segment code.
	RETLW	B'00010010	Complement of 2 in 7-segment code.
	RETLW	B'00000110	Complement of 3 in 7-segment code.
	RETLW	B'01001100	Complement of 4 in 7-segment code.
	RETLW	B'00100100	Complement of 5 in 7-segment code.
	RETLW	B'01100000	Complement of 6 in 7-segment code.
	RETLW	B'00001111	Complement of 7 in 7-segment code.
	RETLW	B'00000000	Complement of 8 in 7-segment code.
	RETLW	B'00001100	Complement of 9 in 7-segment code.

which is directly tied through current-limiting resistors to a 7-segment LED display. This program illustrates the use of the computed GOTO instruction. Figure 5 shows the external component connections.

The RETLW instruction loads the W register with the specified literal value and returns to the instruction following the CALL instruction (MOVWF 5). The complement of the 7-segment code is used because the LED display unit is common-anode; a segment is activated when the output is set low.

References

PIC [1979a]; PIC [1979b].

Section 2

Microcomputers

Historically, the semiconductor industry had focused its efforts on increasing the number of memory bits per chip. Controllers were built from SSI and MSI. Only when random-logic densities were great enough to fabricate several hundred gates per chip did LSI control elements become available. The first microcomputer chip set was introduced by Intel as the MCS-4 in 1971. The MCS-4 consisted of four different elements, all in 16-pin packages:

- The Intel 4004 four-bit processor with 45 instructions typically requiring 12.5 μs each to execute
- The Intel 4001 2-Kbit ROM for program storage
- The Intel 4002 320-bit RAM for data storage
- The Intel 4003 I/O expander

The processor consisted of about 2,200 transistors, or approximately 750 gates.

On account of the limited number of gates available, these early microcomputers exhibited a number of architectural anomalies: a limitation on the number of op codes, data-types, and addressing modes; limited data-path width; only partial support of some data-types; and limited interrupt capability, if any. An interesting performance anomaly was the relatively slow speed of the processor with respect to the memory and processor-memory bus technology. A single memory could support two to three processors concurrently without showing any degradation, whereas in most computer systems, memory performance is the chief limiting factor on processor performance. As the number of gates per chip has continued to rise, the architecture of microprocessors has become closer to that of larger mainframe computers. Chapter 36 extrapolates from technology trends in order to predict speed-power products, RAM and random-logic densities, and RAM and random-logic costs. Faggin (Chap. 36) also discusses the impact of these technology trends on microcomputer implementation, architecture, and software.

The microcomputer class has been very active with tens of architectures implemented in the first 6 years. Table 1 summarizes the characteristics of some of the more important microcomputers. As time has passed, these architectures have grown to 40-pin packages, 8- to 16-bit data paths, 64-Kbyte to 1-Mbyte address space, large instruction sets, sophisticated addressing modes, and more capable interrupt structures. Chapter 37 traces this evolution for one major manufacturer: Intel. The Intel 8086, which is described in detail, is an architecture exhibiting many of the properties of mainframe computers, including memory management, instruction and data address spaces, support for complex data-types including strings, instruction prefixes as instruction modifiers, and interlocks for multiple-processor systems.

The Intel 8086 control is implemented as a microprogrammed sequencer executing 21-bit microinstructions from a 504-word microstore [McKevitt, 1979]. The microword is kept narrow through the use of instruction register contents to specify ALU data length (e.g., 8 or 16 bits), ALU function, and operand location

Table 1 Microprocessors

	Intel 4004	Intel 8008	National IMP 8	Motorola 6800	Intel 8080	RCA COSMAC	Fairchild F-8	Zilog Z-80	Intel 8086	Motorola MC 68000	Zilog Z-8000
Technology	PMOS	PMOS	PMOS	NMOS	NMOS	CMOS	NMOS	NMOS	HMOS	HMOS	NMOS
Number of pins per package	16	18	24	40	40	28, 40	40	40	40	64	48
Instruction time (μs)	12.5	7.5	4.2	2	2	6	2	1	0.25	0.25	0.75
Data-path width (bits)	4	8	2×4	8	8	8	8	8	8	16	16
Maximum memory size (bytes)	4K	16K	64K	64K	64K	64K	64K	64K	1M	16M	8M
Register file size	16	7	4	3	7	16	72	7 (2 sets)	16	16	16
Stack size	3	7	16	In RAM	In RAM	. . .	. . .	In RAM	In RAM	In RAM	In RAM
Instruction size (bytes)	1–2	1–3	1–2	1–3	1–3	1	1	1–3	1–4	2–6	2–10
Basic instruction-set size	45	66	38	72	111	48	101	89	133	59	110
Number of addressing modes	4	4	Many	7	5	2	3	10	24	10	8
Data-types	Integer, decimal	Integer	Integer	Integer, decimal	Integer, decimal	Integer	Integer, decimal	Integer, decimal	Integer, decimal	Integer, decimal	Integer, decimal, string
Interrupt	None	8 levels	1 level	1 level	8 levels	1 level	2 levels	128 vectored	256 levels	8 levels 256 vec.	3 levels vectored
Year introduced	1971	1972	1973	1974	1974	1975	1975	1975	1978	1980	1979

Table 2 Microcomputers Based on Minicomputers

	Intersil 6100	LSI-11	LSI-11/23	TI TMS9900	Micro Nova MN601	Fairchild 9400
Technology	CMOS	NMOS	NMOS	NMOS	NMOS	I²L
Number of chips	1	4	2	1	4	1
Number of pins per package	40	40	40†	64	40	40
Cycle time (μs)	5	0.4	0.29	0.25	?	0.1
Register move time (μs)	N.A.	3.5	1.7	4.7	2.4	1.5
Data-path width (bits)	12	8	16	16	16	4
Maximum memory size (bytes)	32K	64K	256K	64K	32K	64K
Microcode size	...	1,024 × 22	522 × 25	...	...	...
Register file size	1	26	16	16 (In memory)	4	4
Stack size	...	In RAM	In RAM	...	In RAM	...
Instruction set emulated	PDP-8	PDP-11/40	PDP-11/34	TI-990	Data General Nova	Data General Nova
Year introduced	1975	1975	1979	1976	1976	1978

†Two chips per 40-pin chip carrier.

(e.g., register file or memory buffer registers). See Part 2, Sec. 1. Microprogram sequencing is provided by incrementing a 4-bit microprogram counter, which is concatenated to an 8-bit ROM address register. Sequencing can be modified by a short jump (jamming a 4-bit microword subfield into the microprogram counter) or a long jump (by having 4 bits specify one of sixteen 12-bit addresses stored in an auxiliary ROM).

The 8086 has a two-stage pipeline composed of instruction fetch and execution. A 6-byte buffer allows prefetching of instructions during long–execution-time instructions and supplying instructions with no memory latency following short–execution-time instructions. The instruction execution stage of the pipeline also allows for partial overlap of current instruction execution with next instruction decoding.

Microcomputers Based on Minicomputers

Rather than evolve new instruction sets, some of the simpler existing instruction sets with large software bases could be implemented. Table 2 is a small sample of this growing class of microcomputer systems which are based on minicomputers. It is interesting to note that the PDP-8 was a very early, if not the first, minicomputer, and it was also implemented early as a one-chip processor. Chapters 49 and 31 describe microcomputer implementations of an HP 2116–like ISP. The HP 2116 is a 16-bit minicomputer with a close kinship to the PDP-8 ISP.

References

Adams [1978]; Holt [1974]; McKevitt [1979].

Chapter 36

Trends in Microcomputers[1]

F. Faggin

Technology Trends

Fueling the microcomputer product and market expansion is a rapid technological evolution. Today, the microcomputer market is fundamentally technology-driven, and it is expected to remain in this condition for at least 10 more years. To characterize market trends, it is, therefore, essential to examine first the LSI technology trends and then assess the potential market impact.

The following projections will be limited to the MOS technology, since it represents the fastest-moving and most promising technology for high-performance and large-complexity VLSI circuits.

Each technology is characterized by figures of merit that relate to performance and cost. The most common figures of merit are:

- Propagation delay, i.e., the time delay of a signal through a logic gate driving 10 identical gates. Propagation delay is usually measured in nanoseconds.

- Speed-power product, i.e., the product of the propagation delay of a gate and its power dissipation, usually measured in picojoules.

- Gate density and bit density measured in gates per square millimeter and bits per square millimeter.

- Cost per bit and cost per gate, measured in cents per bit and cents per gate for a product that has reached high-volume production levels.

Figure 1 shows past and expected future trends of speed-power product and propagation delay (tpd) for the major generations of state-of-the-art noncomplementary MOS technologies used for LSI production.

Figure 2 shows past and expected future trends of bit density for major generations of dynamic RAMs. The future also shows expected chip size and the expected first year of production for each major new RAM generation.

Figure 3 shows trends of random-logic gate density and how this translates into practical gate complexity and circuit size for major generations of random-logic circuits.

Underscoring these trends are the following considerations and developments. Optical photolithography limits will be reached by

[1]Adapted from keynote address to ACM Sigarch Workshop on Future Directions in Computer Architecture, November 1977, Austin, Texas.

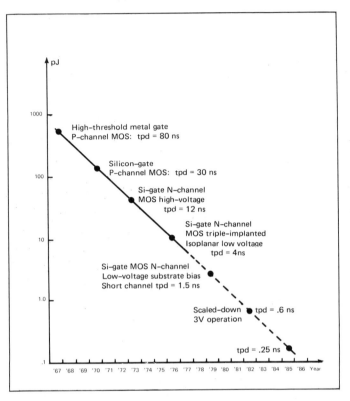

Fig. 1. Speed-power product for MOS noncomplementary technologies.

the late seventies and further progress will be made possible by the application to large-scale production of electron beam lithography now under development. Electron beam lithography will make possible the scaling down of structures to micron and submicron sizes with consequent increase in density. The actual physical limitations to a continuing increase in complexity and performance are not expected to result from line-width limitations but rather from breakdown phenomena in semiconductors and from total power dissipation. Breakdown phenomena are usually proportional to electric field strengths; therefore, as the geometry is scaled down, the supply voltage must be reduced. Ultimately, thermal phenomena will limit this voltage to a multiple of KT/q.

A gross estimate of a practical limit for MOS technology is a circuit using complementary MOS technology, operating at a supply voltage of 400 mV, having minimum line width of ¼ μm, dissipating 1 W at 100 MHz of operating frequency, having a size of about 5 cm by 5 cm, and having the complexity of about 100 million gates! This shows that the trends shown in Fig. 1, Fig. 2, and Fig. 3 are still very far from a practical limit and that technological acceleration will continue well beyond the next decade.

I should also point out that an important assumption contained

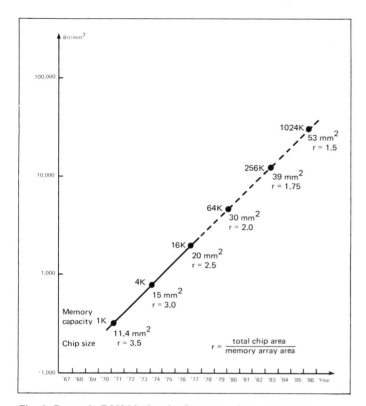

Fig. 2. Dynamic RAM bit density for state-of-the-art RAMs.

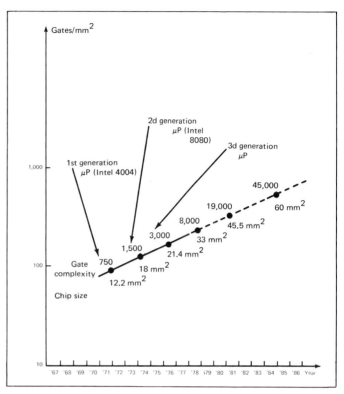

Fig. 3. Random logic gate density for state-of-the-art μPs.

in the previous data is that the data is valid for state-of-the-art, high-volume products or technologies and not for R and D projects.

Finally, Fig. 4 shows the cost-equivalent die size as a function of time for state-of-the-art, high-volume–production products. The increase in die size for a given cost is made possible by the use in production of larger-diameter wafers, as shown, and the continuing improvement and control of yield-limiting factors, such as mask quality, fabrication-equipment sophistication, and cleanroom facilities. I should stress that only mature products follow the curve of Fig. 4, i.e., products in high-volume production with similar production volume history. For a product of a given chip size, the cost (not the price) is found to follow a 70 percent learning curve; i.e., the cost becomes 70 percent of the original every time the cumulative volume produced doubles.

Microcomputer Trends

The data given only shows the inherent capabilities of technology. The products suggested in the curves are only indicative of the increased complexity possible in relationship to and in conformity

with today's products. However, the real impact of such technology potential is in creating the breeding ground for a new revolutionary development of which the microcomputer is the forerunner. To better clarify this concept, let's examine the influence semiconductor technology has had on the evolution of the basic constituents of a computer:

- *Memory.* This function was the first to be integrated, and over a period of 6 years, semiconductor memories have practically replaced the magnetic core memory. Much of the technological development motivation in the seventies was due to the existence and the demands of the memory market.

- *CPU.* As soon as memory technology reached a sufficient level of maturity, the function of a simple CPU could be integrated—the microprocessor was born. Microprocessors still use memory technology for their implementation and have borrowed architectural concepts from the well-developed area of computer architecture. I need to stress here that since computer architecture has evolved under the economic and technological reality of small-scale and medium-scale integration, it is predictable that LSI and

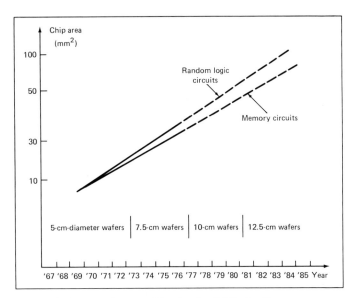

Fig. 4 (a). Cost-equivalent chip size for MOS circuits.

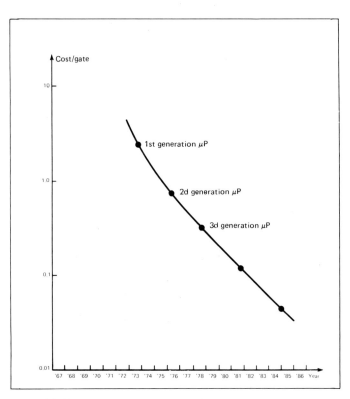

Fig. 4 (c). Microprocessor cost per gate.

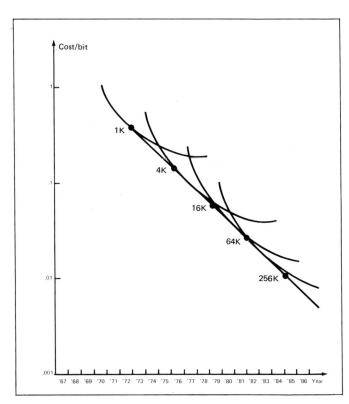

Fig. 4 (b). Dynamic memory cost per bit.

VLSI will have a profound influence on computer and system architecture in general.

• *Input/output*. This function, because of the multiplicity of requirements, was the last to be integrated, and this process is still in its infancy. To solve the I/O problem, our industry has introduced a novel idea, i.e., input/output devices whose hardware configuration and timing requirements are software-programmable. This way, the same circuit can be adapted to a variety of different uses within the same class: parallel interface, serial interface, or specific peripheral controllers.

• *Software*. So far, software technology has only been marginally affected by the existence of microcomputers. Areas of influence are, for example, in diagnostic tools, such as software-development systems and specialized logic analyzers and hardware emulation tools. Under the pressure of an expanding market, however, microcomputer software, is rapidly maturing to the level of sophistication found in minicomputer and megacomputer software. High-level languages specifically designed for microcomputers are now being developed, and the trend will continue by incorporating features into the microcomputer architecture that will make high-level programming very efficient.

Chapter 37

Intel Microprocessors: 8008 to 8086[1]

*Stephen P. Morse / Bruce W. Ravenel /
Stanley Mazor / William B. Pohlman*

I. Introduction

"In the beginning Intel created the 4004 and the 8008."

A. The Prophecy

Intel introduced the microprocessor in November 1971 with the advertisement, "Announcing a New Era in Integrated Electronics." The fulfillment of this prophecy has already occurred with the delivery of the 8008 in 1972, the 8080 in 1974, the 8085 in 1976, and the 8086 in 1978. During this time, throughput has improved 100-fold, the price of a CPU chip has declined from $300 to $3, and microcomputers have revolutionized design concepts in countless applications. They are now entering our homes and cars.

Each successive product implementation depended on semiconductor process innovation, improved architecture, better circuit design, and more sophisticated software, yet upward compatibility not envisioned by the first designers was maintained. This paper provides an insight into the evolutionary process that transformed the 8008 into the 8086, and gives descriptions of the various processors, with emphasis on the 8086.

B. Historical Setting

In the late 1960s it became clear that the practical use of large-scale integrated circuits (LSI) depended on defining chips having

- High gate-to-pin ratio
- Regular cell structure
- Large standard-part markets

In 1968, Intel Corporation was founded to exploit the semiconductor memory market, which uniquely fulfilled these criteria. Early semiconductor RAMs, ROMs, and shift registers were welcomed wherever small memories were needed, especially in calculators and CRT terminals. In 1969, Intel engineers began to study ways of integrating and partitioning the control logic functions of these systems into LSI chips.

At this time other companies (notably Texas Instruments) were exploring ways to reduce the design time to develop custom integrated circuits usable in a customer's application. Computer-aided design of custom ICs was a hot issue then. Custom ICs are making a comeback today, this time in high-volume applications which typify the low end of the microprocessor market.

An alternate approach was to think of a customer's application as a computer system requiring a control program, I/O monitoring, and arithmetic routines, rather than as a collection of special-purpose logic chips. Focusing on its strength in memory, Intel partitioned systems into RAM, ROM, and a single controller chip, the central processor unit (CPU).

Intel embarked on the design of two customer-sponsored microprocessors, the 4004 for a calculator and the 8008 for a CRT terminal. The 4004, in particular, replaced what would otherwise have been six customized chips, usable by only one customer. Because the first microcomputer applications were known, tangible, and easy to understand, instruction sets and architectures were defined in a matter of weeks. Since they were programmable computers, their uses could be extended indefinitely.

Both of these first microprocessors were complete CPUs-on-a-chip and had similar characteristics. But because the 4004 was designed for serial BCD arithmetic while the 8008 was made for 8-bit character handling, their instruction sets were quite different.

The succeeding years saw the evolutionary process that eventually led to the 8086. Table 1 summarizes the progression of features that took place during these years.

II. 8008 Objectives and Constraints

Late in 1969 Intel Corporation was contracted by Computer Terminal Corporation (today called Datapoint) to do a pushdown stack chip for a processor to be used in a CRT terminal. Datapoint had intended to build a bit-serial processor in TTL logic using shift-register memory. Intel counterproposed to implement the entire processor on one chip, which was to become the 8008. This processor, along with the 4004, was to be fabricated using the then-current memory fabrication technology, *p*-MOS. Due to the long lead time required by Intel, Computer Terminal proceeded to market the serial processor and thus compatibility constraints were imposed on the 8008.

Most of the instruction-set and register organization was specified by Computer Terminal. Intel modified the instruction set so the processor would fit on one chip and added instructions to make it more general-purpose. For although Intel was developing the 8008 for one particular customer, it wanted to have the option of selling it to others. Intel was using only 16- and 18-pin packages in those days, and rather than require a new package for what was believed to be a low-volume chip, they chose to use 18 pins for the 8008.

Table 1   Feature Comparison

	8008	*8080*	*8085*	*8086*
Number of instructions	66	111	113	133
Number of flags	4	5	5	9
Maximum memory size	16K bytes	64K bytes	64K bytes	1M bytes
I/O ports	8 input 24 output	256 input 256 output	256 input 256 output	64K input 64K output
Number of pins	18	40	40	40
Address bus width	8†	16	16	16†
Data bus width	8†	8	8	16†
Data types	8-bit unsigned	8-bit unsigned 16-bit unsigned (limited)	8-bit unsigned 16-bit unsigned (limited)	8-bit unsigned 8-bit signed 16-bit unsigned 16-bit signed
		Packed BCD (limited)	Packed BCD (limited)	Packed BCD Unpacked BCD
Addressing modes	Register‡ Immediate	Memory direct (limited) Memory indirect (limited) Register‡ Immediate	Memory direct (limited) Memory indirect (limited) Register‡ Immediate	Memory direct Memory indirect Register Immediate Indexing
Introduction date	1972	1974	1976	1978

† Address and data bus multiplexed.

‡ Memory can be addressed as a special case by using register M.

III.   8008 Instruction-Set Processor

The 8008 processor architecture is quite simple compared to modern-day microprocessors. The data-handling facilities provide for byte data only. The memory space is limited to 16K bytes, and the stack is on the chip and limited to a depth of 8. The instruction set is small but symmetrical, with only a few operand-addressing modes available. An interrupt mechanism is provided, but there is no way to disable interrupts.

A. Memory and I/O Structure

The 8008 addressable memory space consists of 16K bytes. That seemed like a lot back in 1970, when memories were expensive and LSI devices were slow. It was inconceivable in those days that anybody would want to put more than 16K of this precious resource on anything as slow as a microprocessor.

The memory size limitation was imposed by the lack of available pins. Addresses are sent out in two consecutive clock cycles over an 8-bit address bus. Two control signals, which would have been on dedicated pins if these had been available, are sent out together with every address, thereby limiting addresses to 14 bits.

The 8008 provides eight 8-bit input ports and twenty-four 8-bit output ports. Each of these ports is directly addressable by the instruction set. It was felt that output ports were more important than input ports because input ports can always be multiplexed by external hardware under control of additional output ports.

One of the interesting things about that era was that, for the first time, the users were given access to the memory bus and could define their own memory structure; they were not confined to what the vendors offered, as they had been in the minicomputer era. As an example, the user had the option of putting I/O ports inside the memory address space instead of in a separate I/O space.

B. Register Structure

The 8008 processor contains two register files and four 1-bit flags. The register files are referred to as the *scratchpad* and the *address stack*.

1. Scratchpad. The scratchpad file contains an 8-bit accumulator called A and six additional 8-bit registers called B,C,D,E,H, and L. All arithmetic operations use the accumulator as one of the operands and store the result back in the accumulator. All seven registers can be used interchangeably for on-chip temporary storage.

There is one pseudo-register, M, which can be used interchangeably with the scratchpad registers. M is, in effect, that particular byte in memory whose address is currently contained in H and L (L contains the eight low-order bits of the address and H contains the six high-order bits). Thus M is a byte in memory and not a register; although instructions address M as if it were a register, accesses to M actually involve memory references. The M register is the only mechanism by which data in memory can be accessed.

2. Address Stack. The address stack contains a 3-bit stack pointer and eight 14-bit address registers providing storage for eight addresses. These registers are not directly accessible by the programmer; rather they are manipulated with control-transfer instructions.

Any one of the eight address registers in the address stack can serve as the program counter; the current program counter is specified by the stack pointer. The other seven address registers permit storage for nesting of subroutines up to seven levels deep. The execution of a call instruction causes the next address register in turn to become the current program counter, and the return instruction causes the address register that last served as the program counter to again become the program counter. The stack will wrap around if subroutines are nested more than seven levels deep.

3. Flags. The four flags in the 8008 are CARRY, ZERO, SIGN, and PARITY. They are used to reflect the status of the latest arithmetic or logical operation. Any of the flags can be used to alter program flow through the use of the conditional jump, call, or return instructions. There is no direct mechanism for saving or restoring flags, which places a severe burden on interrupt processing (see Appendix 1 for details).

The CARRY flag indicates if a carry-out or borrow-in was generated, thereby providing the ability to perform multiple-precision binary arithmetic.

The ZERO flag indicates whether or not the result is zero. This provides the ability to compare the two values for equality.

The SIGN flag reflects the setting of the leftmost bit of the result. The presence of this flag creates the illusion that the 8008 is able to handle signed numbers. However, there is no facility for detecting signed overflow on additions and subtractions. Furthermore, comparing signed numbers by subtracting them and then testing the SIGN flag will not give the correct result if the subtraction resulted in signed overflow. This oversight was not corrected until the 8086.

The PARITY flag indicates if the result is even or odd parity. This permits testing for transmission errors, an obviously useful function for a CRT terminal.

C. Instruction Set

The 8008 instructions are designed for moving or modifying 8-bit operands. Operands are either contained in the instruction itself (immediate operand), contained in a scratchpad register (register operand), or contained in the M register (memory operand). Since the M register can be used interchangeably with the scratchpad registers, there are only two distinct operand-addressing modes—immediate and register. Typical instruction formats for these modes are shown in Fig. 1. A summary of the 8008 instructions appears in Fig. 2.

The instruction set consists of scratchpad-register instructions, accumulator-specific instructions, transfer-of-control instructions, input/output instructions, and processor-control instructions.

The scratchpad-register instructions modify the contents of the M register or any scratchpad register. This can consist of moving data between any two registers, moving immediate data into a register, or incrementing or decrementing the contents of a register. The incrementing and decrementing instructions were not in Computer Terminal's specified instruction set; they were added by Intel to provide for loop control, thereby making the processor more general-purpose.

Most of the accumulator specific instructions perform operations between the accumulator and a specified operand. The operand can be any one of the scratchpad registers, including M, or it can be immediate data. The operations are add, add-with-carry, subtract, subtract-with-borrow, logical AND, logical OR, logical exclusive-OR, and compare. Furthermore, there are four unit-rotate instructions that operate on the accumulator. These instructions perform either an 8- or 9-bit rotate (the CARRY flag acts as a ninth bit) in either the left or right direction.

Transfer-of-control instructions consist of jumps, calls, and returns. Any of the transfers can be unconditional, or can be conditional based on the setting of any one of the four flags. Making calls and returns conditional was done to preserve the symmetry with jumps and for no other reason. A short one-byte form of call is also provided, which will be discussed later under interrupts.

Each of the jump and call instructions (with the exception of the one-byte call) specifies an absolute code address in the second and

```
no operands
-----------

+-+-+-+-+-+-+-+-+
|    opcode     |
+-+-+-+-+-+-+-+-+


one operand
-----------

+-+-+-+-+-+-+-+-+
| opcode | reg |    operand in register
+-+-+-+-+-+-+-+-+

+-+-+-+-+-+-+-+-+
|opc| reg |opcod|   operand in register
+-+-+-+-+-+-+-+-+

+-+-+-+-+-+-+-+-+
|opc| rp| opcode|   operand in register pair (8080 only)
+-+-+-+-+-+-+-+-+

+-+-+-+-+-+-+-+-+
|opc| rp| opcode|   indirect addressing (8080 only)
+-+-+-+-+-+-+-+-+

+-+-+-+-+-+-+-+-+  +-+-+-+-+-+-+-+-+
|    opcode     |  |     data      |   immediate operand
+-+-+-+-+-+-+-+-+  +-+-+-+-+-+-+-+-+

+-+-+-+-+-+-+-+-+  +-+-+-+-+-+-+-+-+  +-+-+-+-+-+-+-+-+   direct
|    opcode     |  |    addr-lo    |  |    addr-hi    |   addressing
+-+-+-+-+-+-+-+-+  +-+-+-+-+-+-+-+-+  +-+-+-+-+-+-+-+-+   (8080
                                                         only)

two operands
------------

+-+-+-+-+-+-+-+-+
|opc| reg | reg |   both operands in register
+-+-+-+-+-+-+-+-+

+-+-+-+-+-+-+-+-+  +-+-+-+-+-+-+-+-+  one operand in register,
|opc| reg | opc |  |     data      |   other is immediate operand
+-+-+-+-+-+-+-+-+  +-+-+-+-+-+-+-+-+
                                       one operand
+-+-+-+-+-+-+-+-+  +-+-+-+-+-+-+-+-+  +-+-+-+-+-+-+-+-+  in register
|opc| rp| opcode|  |    addr-lo    |  |    addr-hi    |  pair, other
+-+-+-+-+-+-+-+-+  +-+-+-+-+-+-+-+-+  +-+-+-+-+-+-+-+-+  is immediate
                                                        operand
                                                        (8080 only)
input/output
------------

+-+-+-+-+-+-+-+-+
|opc| port  |o|   (8008 only)
+-+-+-+-+-+-+-+-+

+-+-+-+-+-+-+-+-+  +-+-+-+-+-+-+-+-+
|    opcode     |  |    port       |   (8080 only)
+-+-+-+-+-+-+-+-+  +-+-+-+-+-+-+-+-+


jumps and calls
---------------

+-+-+-+-+-+-+-+-+  +-+-+-+-+-+-+-+-+  +-+-+-+-+-+-+-+-+
|    opcode     |  |    addr-lo    |  |////| addr-hi  |   (8008 only)
+-+-+-+-+-+-+-+-+  +-+-+-+-+-+-+-+-+  +-+-+-+-+-+-+-+-+

+-+-+-+-+-+-+-+-+  +-+-+-+-+-+-+-+-+  +-+-+-+-+-+-+-+-+
|    opcode     |  |    addr-lo    |  |    addr-hi    |   (8080 only)
+-+-+-+-+-+-+-+-+  +-+-+-+-+-+-+-+-+  +-+-+-+-+-+-+-+-+


        8008           8080
        -----          -----
        000:A          000:B          8080
        001:B          001:C          -----
        010:C          010:D          00:BC
  reg = 011:D    reg = 011:E    pair = 01:DE
        100:E          100:H          10:HL
        101:H          101:L          11:SP
        110:L          110:M
        111:M          111:A
```

Fig. 1. Typical 8008 and 8080 instruction formats.

third byte of the instruction. The third byte contains the six high-order bits of the address, and the second byte contains the eight low-order bits. This inverted storage, which was to haunt all processors evolved from the 8008, was a result of compatibility with the Datapoint bit-serial processor, which processes addresses from low bit to high bit. This inverted storage did have a virtue in those early days when 256 by 8 memory chips were popular: it allowed all memory chips to select a byte and latch it for output while waiting for the six high-order bits which selected the chip. This speeded up memory access.

There are eight input instructions and 24 output instructions, which altogether use up 32 opcodes. Each of these instructions transfers a byte of data between the accumulator and a designated I/O port.

The processor-control instructions are halt and no-op. Halt puts the processor into a waiting state. The processor will remain in that state until an interrupt occurs. No-op is actually one of the move instructions; specifically, it moves the contents of the accumulator into the accumulator, thereby having no net effect (move instructions do not alter flag settings).

D. Interrupts

Interrupt processing was not a requirement of the 8008. Hence only the most primitive mechanism conceivable—not incrementing the program counter—was provided. Such a mechanism permits an interrupting device to jam an instruction into the processor's instruction stream. This is accomplished by having the interrupting device, instead of memory, respond to the instruction fetch; since the program counter isn't incremented, the instruction in memory that doesn't get fetched won't be skipped. The instruction typically supplied by the interrupting device is a call, so that an interrupt service routine can be entered and then the main program can be resumed after interrupt processing is complete (a jump instruction would result in the loss of the main program return address). To simplify the interrupting device's task of generating an instruction, the 8008 instruction set provides eight one-byte subroutine calls, each to a fixed location in memory.

There are no instructions provided for disabling the interrupt mechanism, and so this function must be realized with external hardware. More important, there are no instructions for conveniently saving the registers and flags when an interrupt occurs.

IV. Objectives and Constraints of the 8080

By 1973 the technology had advanced from p-MOS to n-MOS for memory fabrication. As an engineering exercise it was decided to use the 8008 layout masks with the n-MOS process to obtain a faster 8008. After a short study, it was determined that a new layout was required, so it was decided to enhance the processor at the same time, and to utilize the new 40-pin package made practical by high-volume calculator chips. The result was the 8080 processor.

The 8080 was the first processor designed specifically for the microprocessor market. It was constrained to include all the 8008

Fig. 2. Instruction set of 8008.

Index Register Instructions

The load instructions do not affect all the flag flip-flops. The increment and decrement instructions affect all flip-flops except the carry.

MNEMONIC	D7	D6	D5	D4	D3	D2	D1	D0	DESCRIPTION OF OPERATION
(1) MOV r1,r2	1	1	D	D	D	S	S	S	Load index register r1 with the content of index register r2.
(2) MOV r,M	1	1	D	D	D	1	1	1	Load index register r with the content of memory register M.
MOV M,r	1	1	1	1	1	S	S	S	Load memory register M with the content of index register r.
(3) MVI r	0	0	D	D	D	1	1	0	Load index register r with data B...B.
	B	B	B	B	B	B	B	B	
MVI M	0	0	1	1	1	1	1	0	Load memory register M with data B...B.
	B	B	B	B	B	B	B	B	
INR r	0	0	D	D	D	0	0	0	Increment the content of index register r (r≠A).
DCR r	0	0	D	D	D	0	0	1	Decrement the content of index register r (r≠A).

Accumulator Group Instructions

The result of the ALU instructions affect all of the flag flip-flops. The rotate instructions affect only the carry flip-flop.

MNEMONIC	D7	D6	D5	D4	D3	D2	D1	D0	DESCRIPTION OF OPERATION
ADD r	1	0	0	0	0	S	S	S	Add the content of index register r, memory register M, or data
ADD M	1	0	0	0	0	1	1	1	B...B to the accumulator. An overflow (carry) sets the carry
ADI	0	0	0	0	0	1	0	0	flip-flop.
	B	B	B	B	B	B	B	B	
ADC r	1	0	0	0	1	S	S	S	Add the content of index register r, memory register M, or data
ADC M	1	0	0	0	1	1	1	1	B...B from the accumulator with carry. An overflow (carry) sets
ACI	0	0	0	0	1	1	0	0	the carry flip-flop.
	B	B	B	B	B	B	B	B	
SUB r	1	0	0	1	0	S	S	S	Subtract the content of index register r, memory register M, or
SUB M	1	0	0	1	0	1	1	1	data B...B from the accumulator. An underflow (borrow) sets
SUI	0	0	0	1	0	1	0	0	the carry flip-flop.
	B	B	B	B	B	B	B	B	
SBB r	1	0	0	1	1	S	S	S	Subtract the content of index register r, memory register M, or data
SBB M	1	0	0	1	1	1	1	1	B...B from the accumulator with borrow. An underflow (borrow)
SBI	0	0	0	1	1	1	0	0	sets the carry flip-flop.
	B	B	B	B	B	B	B	B	
ANA r	1	0	1	0	0	S	S	S	Compute the logical AND of the content of index register r, memory
ANA M	1	0	1	0	0	1	1	1	register M, or data B...B with the accumulator.
ANI	0	0	1	0	0	1	0	0	
	B	B	B	B	B	B	B	B	
XRA r	1	0	1	0	1	S	S	S	Compute the EXCLUSIVE OR of the content of index register r,
XRA M	1	0	1	0	1	1	1	1	memory register M, or data B...B with the accumulator.
XRI	0	0	1	0	1	1	0	0	
	B	B	B	B	B	B	B	B	
ORA r	1	0	1	1	0	S	S	S	Compute the INCLUSIVE OR of the content of index register r,
ORA M	1	0	1	1	0	1	1	1	memory register M, or data B...B with the accumulator.
ORI	0	0	1	1	0	1	0	0	
	B	B	B	B	B	B	B	B	
CMP r	1	0	1	1	1	S	S	S	Compare the content of index register r, memory register M, or data
CMP M	1	0	1	1	1	1	1	1	B...B with the accumulator. The content of the accumulator is
CPI	0	0	1	1	1	1	0	0	unchanged.
	B	B	B	B	B	B	B	B	
RLC	0	0	0	0	0	0	1	0	Rotate the content of the accumulator left.
RRC	0	0	0	0	1	0	1	0	Rotate the content of the accumulator right.
RAL	0	0	0	1	0	0	1	0	Rotate the content of the accumulator left through the carry.
RAR	0	0	0	1	1	0	1	0	Rotate the content of the accumulator right through the carry.

Program Counter and Stack Control Instructions

MNEMONIC	D7	D6	D5	D4	D3	D2	D1	D0	DESCRIPTION OF OPERATION
(4) JMP	0	1	X	X	X	1	0	0	Unconditionally jump to memory address B3...B3B2...B2.
	B2	B2	B2	B2	B2	B2	B2	B2	
	B3	B3	B3	B3	B3	B3	B3	B3	
(5) JNC,JNZ, JP,JPO	0	1	0	C4	C3	0	0	0	Jump to memory address B3...B3B2...B2 if the condition flip-flop is false. Otherwise execute the next instruction in sequence.
	B2	B2	B2	B2	B2	B2	B2	B2	
	B3	B3	B3	B3	B3	B3	B3	B3	
JC,JZ JM,JPE	0	1	1	C4	C3	0	0	0	Jump to memory address B3...B3B2...B2 if the condition flip-flop is true. Otherwise, execute the next instruction in sequence.
	B2	B2	B2	B2	B2	B2	B2	B2	
	B3	B3	B3	B3	B3	B3	B3	B3	
CALL	0	1	X	X	X	1	1	0	Unconditionally call the subroutine at memory address B3... B3B2...B2.
	B2	B2	B2	B2	B2	B2	B2	B2	
	B3	B3	B3	B3	B3	B3	B3	B3	
CNC,CNZ, CP,CPO	0	1	0	C4	C3	0	1	0	Call the subroutine at memory address B3...B3B2...B2 if the condition flip-flop is false, and move the current address (up one level in the stack.) Otherwise, execute the next instruction in sequence.
	B2	B2	B2	B2	B2	B2	B2	B2	
	B3	B3	B3	B3	B3	B3	B3	B3	
CC,CZ, CM,CPE	0	1	1	C4	C3	0	1	0	Call the subroutine at memory address B3...B3B2...B2 if the condition flip-flop is true, and save the current address (up one level in the stack). Otherwise, execute the next instruction in sequence.
	B2	B2	B2	B2	B2	B2	B2	B2	
	B3	B3	B3	B3	B3	B3	B3	B3	
RET	0	0	X	X	X	1	1	1	Unconditionally return (down one level in the stack).
RNC,RNZ, RP,RPO	0	0	0	C4	C3	0	1	1	Return (down one level in the stack) if the condition flip-flop is false. Otherwise, execute the next instruction in sequence.
RC,RZ RM,RPE	0	0	1	C4	C3	0	1	1	Return (down one level in the stack) if the condition flip-flop is true. Otherwise, execute the next instruction in sequence.
RST	0	0	A	A	A	1	0	1	Call the subroutine at memory address AAA000 (up one level in the stack).

Input/Output Instructions

MNEMONIC	D7	D6	D5	D4	D3	D2	D1	D0	DESCRIPTION OF OPERATION
IN	0	1	0	0	M	M	M	1	Read the content of the selected input port (MMM) into the accumulator.
OUT	0	1	R	R	M	M	M	1	Write the content of the accumulator into the selected output port (RRMMM,RR≠00).

Machine Instruction

MNEMONIC	D7	D6	D5	D4	D3	D2	D1	D0	DESCRIPTION OF OPERATION
HLT	0	0	0	0	0	0	0	X	Enter the STOPPED state and remain there until interrupted.
	1	1	1	1	1	1	1	1	

NOTES:

(1) SSS = Source Index Register. DDD = Destination Index Register. These registers, r, are designated A(accumulator—000), B(001), C(010), D(011), E(100), H(101), L(110).

(2) Memory registers are addressed by the contents of registers H & L.

(3) Additional bytes of instruction are designated by BBBBBBBB.

(4) X = "Don't Care".

(5) Flag flip-flops are defined by C4C3 carry (00-overflow or underflow), zero (01-result is zero), sign (10MSB of result is "1"), parity (11-parity is even).

instructions but not necessarily with the same encodings. This meant that user's software would be portable but the actual ROM chips containing the programs would have to be replaced. The main objective of the 8080 was to obtain a 10:1 improvement in throughput, eliminate many of the 8008 shortcomings that had by then become apparent, and provide new processing capabilities not found in the 8008. These included a commitment to 16-bit data types mainly for address computations, BCD arithmetic, enhanced operand-addressing modes, and improved interrupt capabilities. Now that memory costs had come down and processing speed was approaching TTL, larger memory spaces were appearing more practical. Hence another goal was to be able to address directly more than 16K bytes. Symmetry was not a goal, because the benefits to be gained from making the extensions symmetric would not justify the resulting increase in chip size and opcode space.

V.   The 8080 Instruction-Set Processor

The 8080 architecture is an unsymmetrical extension of the 8008. The byte-handling facilities have been augmented with a limited number of 16-bit facilities. The memory space grew to 64K bytes and the stack was made virtually unlimited.

Various alternatives for the 8080 were considered. The simplest involved merely adding a memory stack and stack instructions to the 8008. An intermediate position was to augment the above with 16-bit arithmetic facilities that can be used for explicit address manipulations as well as 16-bit data manipulations. The most difficult alternative was a symmetric extension which replaced the one-byte M-register instructions with three-byte generalized memory-access instructions. The last two bytes of these instructions contained two address-mode bits specifying indirect addressing and indexing (using HL as an index register) and a 14-bit displacement. Although this would have been a more versatile addressing mechanism, it would have resulted in significant code expansion on existing 8008 programs. Furthermore, the logic necessary to implement this solution would have precluded the ability to implement 16-bit arithmetic; such arithmetic would not be needed for address manipulations under this enhanced addressing facility but would still be desirable for data manipulations. For these reasons, the intermediate position was finally taken.

A. Memory and I/O Structure

The 8080 can address up to 64K bytes of memory, a fourfold increase over the 8008 (the 14-bit address stack of the 8008 was eliminated). The address bus of the 8080 is 16 bits wide, in contrast to eight bits for the 8008, so an entire address can be sent down the bus in one memory cycle. Although the data handling

facilities of the 8080 are primarily byte-oriented (the 8008 was exclusively byte-oriented), certain operations permit two consecutive bytes of memory to be treated as a single data item. The two bytes are called a word. The data bus of the 8080 is only eight bits wide, and hence word accesses require an extra memory cycle.

The most significant eight bits of a word are located at the higher memory address. This results in the same kind of inverted storage already noted in transfer instructions of the 8008.

The 8080 extends the 32-port capacity of the 8008 to 256 input ports and 256 output ports. In this instance, the 8080 is actually more symmetrical than the 8008. Like the 8008, all of the ports are directly addressable by the instruction set.

B. Register Structure

The 8080 processor contains a file of seven 8-bit general registers, a 16-bit program counter (PC) and stack pointer (SP), and five 1-bit flags. A comparison between the 8008 and 8080 register sets is shown in Fig. 3.

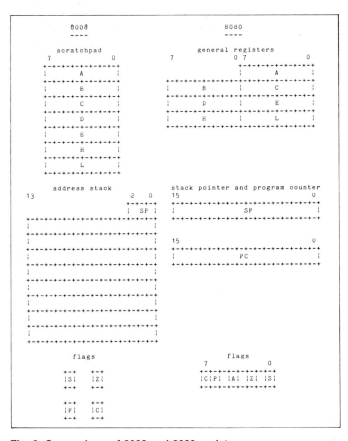

Fig. 3. Comparison of 8008 and 8080 registers.

1. General Registers. The 8080 registers are the same seven 8-bit registers that were in the 8008 scratchpad—namely A,B,C, D,E,H, and L. In order to incorporate 16-bit data facilities in the 8080, certain instructions operate on the register pairs BC, DE, and HL.

The seven registers can be used interchangeably for on-chip temporary storage. The three register pairs are used for address manipulations, but their roles are not interchangeable; there is an 8080 instruction that allows operations on DE and not BC, and there are address modes that access memory indirectly through BC or DE but not HL.

As in the 8008, the A register has a unique role in arithmetic and logical operations: it serves as one of the operands and is the receptacle for the result. The HL register again has its special role of pointing to the pseudo-register M.

2. Stack Pointer and Program Counter. The 8080 has a single program counter instead of the floating program counter of the 8008. The program counter is 16 bits (two bits more than the 8008's program counter), thereby permitting an address space of 64K.

The stack is contained in memory instead of on the chip, which removes the restriction of only seven levels of nested subroutines. The entries on the stack are 16 bits wide. The 16-bit stack pointer is used to locate the stack in memory. The execution of a call instruction causes the contents of the program counter to be pushed onto the stack, and the return instruction causes the last stack entry to be popped into the program counter. The stack pointer was chosen to run "downhill" (with the stack advancing toward lower memory) to simplify indexing into the stack from the user's program (positive indexing) and to simplify displaying the contents of the stack from a front panel.

Unlike the 8008, the stack pointer is directly accessible to the programmer. Furthermore, the stack itself is directly accessible, and instructions are provided that permit the programmer to push and pop his own 16-bit items onto the stack.

3. Flags. A fifth flag, AUXILIARY CARRY, augments the 8008 flag set to form the flag set of the 8080. The AUXILIARY CARRY flag indicates if a carry was generated out of the four low-order bits. This flag, in conjunction with a decimal-adjust instruction, provides the ability to perform packed BCD addition (see Appendix 2 for details). This facility can be traced back to the 4004 processor. The AUXILIARY CARRY flag has no purpose other than for BCD arithmetic, and hence the conditional transfer instructions were not expanded to include tests on the AUXILIA-RY CARRY flag.

It was proposed too late in the design that the PARITY flag should double as an OVERFLOW flag. Although this feature didn't make it into the 8080, it did show up two years later in Zilog's Z-80.

C. Instruction Set

The 8080 includes the entire 8008 instruction set as a subset. The added instructions provide some new operand-addressing modes and some facilities for manipulating 16-bit data. These extensions have introduced a good deal of asymmetry. Typical instruction formats are shown in Fig. 1. A summary of the 8080 instructions appears in Fig. 4.

The only means that the 8008 had for accessing operands in memory was via the M register. The 8080 has certain instructions that access memory by specifying the memory address (direct addressing) and also certain instructions that access memory by specifying a pair of general registers in which the memory address is contained (indirect addressing). In addition, the 8080 includes the register and immediate operand-addressing modes of the 8008. A 16-bit immediate mode is also included.

The added instructions can be classified as load/store instructions, register-pair instructions, HL-specific instructions, accumulator-adjust instructions, carry instructions, expanded I/O instructions, and interrupt instructions.

The load/store instructions load and store the accumulator register and the HL register pair using the direct and indirect addressing mode. Both modes can be used for the accumulator, but due to chip size constraints, only the direct mode was implemented for HL.

The register-pair instructions provide for the manipulation of 16-bit data items. Specifically, register pairs can be loaded with 16-bit immediate data, incremented, decremented, added to HL, pushed on the stack, or popped off the stack. Furthermore, the flag settings themselves can be pushed and popped, thereby simplifying saving the environment when interrupts occur (this was not possible in the 8008).

The HL-specific instructions include facilities for transferring HL to the program counter or to the stack pointer, and exchanging HL with DE or with the top entry on the stack. The last of these instructions was included to provide a mechanism for (1) removing a subroutine return address from the stack so that passed parameters can be discarded or (2) burying a result-to-be-returned under the return address. This became the longest instruction in the 8080 (5 memory cycles); its implementation precluded the inclusion of several other instructions that were already proposed for the processor.

Two accumulator-adjust instructions are provided. One complements each bit in the accumulator and the other modifies the accumulator so that it contains the correct decimal result after a packed BCD addition is performed.

The carry instructions provide for setting or complementing the CARRY flag. No instruction is provided for clearing the CARRY flag. Because of the way the CARRY flag semantics are defined, the CARRY flag can be cleared simply by ORing or ANDing the accumulator with itself.

MOVE, LOAD, AND STORE

Mnemonic	Description	D_7	D_6	D_5	D_4	D_3	D_2	D_1	D_0
MOV r1r2	Move register to register	0	1	D	D	D	S	S	S
MOV M r	Move register to memory	0	1	1	1	0	S	S	S
MOV r M	Move memory to register	0	1	D	D	D	1	1	0
MVI r	Move immediate register	0	0	D	D	D	1	1	0
MVI M	Move immediate memory	0	0	1	1	0	1	1	0
LXI B	Load immediate register Pair B & C	0	0	0	0	0	0	0	1
LXI D	Load immediate register Pair D & E	0	0	0	1	0	0	0	1
LXI H	Load immediate register Pair H & L	0	0	1	0	0	0	0	1
LXI SP	Load immediate stack pointer	0	0	1	1	0	0	0	1
STAX B	Store A indirect	0	0	0	0	0	0	1	0
STAX D	Store A indirect	0	0	0	1	0	0	1	0
LDAX C	Load A indirect	0	0	0	0	1	0	1	0
LDAX D	Load A indirect	0	0	0	1	1	0	1	0
STA	Store A direct	0	0	1	1	0	0	1	0
LDA	Load A direct	0	0	1	1	1	0	1	0
SHLD	Store H & L direct	0	0	1	0	0	0	1	0
LHLD	Load H & L direct	0	0	1	0	1	0	1	0
XCHG	Exchange D & E H & L Registers	1	1	1	0	1	0	1	1

STACK OPS

Mnemonic	Description	D_7	D_6	D_5	D_4	D_3	D_2	D_1	D_0
PUSH B	Push register Pair B & C on stack	1	1	0	0	0	1	0	1
PUSH D	Push register Pair D & E on stack	1	1	0	1	0	1	0	1
PUSH H	Push register Pair H & L on stack	1	1	1	0	0	1	0	1
PUSH PSW	Push A and Flags on stack	1	1	1	1	0	1	0	1
POP B	Pop register Pair B & C off stack	1	1	0	0	0	0	0	1
POP D	Pop register Pair D & E off stack	1	1	0	1	0	0	0	1
POP H	Pop register Pair H & L off stack	1	1	1	0	0	0	0	1
POP PSW	Pop A and Flags off stack	1	1	1	1	0	0	0	1
XTHL	Exchange top of stack H & L	1	1	1	0	0	0	1	1
SPHL	H & L to stack pointer	1	1	1	1	1	0	0	1

JUMP

Mnemonic	Description	D_7	D_6	D_5	D_4	D_3	D_2	D_1	D_0
JMP	Jump unconditional	1	1	0	0	0	0	1	1
JC	Jump on carry	1	1	0	1	1	0	1	0
JNC	Jump on no carry	1	1	0	1	0	0	1	0
JZ	Jump on zero	1	1	0	0	1	0	1	0
JNZ	Jump on no zero	1	1	0	0	0	0	1	0
JP	Jump on positive	1	1	1	1	0	0	1	0
JM	Jump on minus	1	1	1	1	1	0	1	0
JPE	Jump on parity even	1	1	1	0	1	0	1	0
JPO	Jump on parity odd	1	1	1	0	0	0	1	0
PCHL	H & L to program counter	1	1	1	0	1	0	0	1

CALL

Mnemonic	Description	D_7	D_6	D_5	D_4	D_3	D_2	D_1	D_0
CALL	Call unconditional	1	1	0	0	1	1	0	1
CC	Call on carry	1	1	0	1	1	1	0	0
CNC	Call on no carry	1	1	0	1	0	1	0	0
CZ	Call on zero	1	1	0	0	1	1	0	0
CNZ	Call on no zero	1	1	0	0	0	1	0	0
CP	Call on positive	1	1	1	1	0	1	0	0
CM	Call on minus	1	1	1	1	1	1	0	0
CPE	Call on partly even	1	1	1	0	1	1	0	0
CPO	Call on partly odd	1	1	1	0	0	1	0	0

RETURN

Mnemonic	Description	D_7	D_6	D_5	D_4	D_3	D_2	D_1	D_0
RET	Return	1	1	0	0	1	0	0	1
RC	Return on carry	1	1	0	1	1	0	0	0
RNC	Return on no carry	1	1	0	1	0	0	0	0
RZ	Return on zero	1	1	0	0	1	0	0	0
RNZ	Return on no zero	1	1	0	0	0	0	0	0
RP	Return on positive	1	1	1	1	0	0	0	0
RM	Return on minus	1	1	1	1	1	0	0	0
RPE	Return on parity even	1	1	1	0	1	0	0	0
RPO	Return on parity odd	1	1	1	0	0	0	0	0

RESTART

Mnemonic	Description	D_7	D_6	D_5	D_4	D_3	D_2	D_1	D_0
RST	Restart	1	1	A	A	A	1	1	1

INPUT/OUTPUT

Mnemonic	Description	D_7	D_6	D_5	D_4	D_3	D_2	D_1	D_0
IN	Input	1	1	0	1	1	0	1	1
OUT	Output	1	1	0	1	0	0	1	1

INCREMENT AND DECREMENT

Mnemonic	Description	D_7	D_6	D_5	D_4	D_3	D_2	D_1	D_0
INR r	Increment register	0	0	D	D	D	1	0	0
DCR r	Decrement register	0	0	D	D	D	1	0	1
INR M	Increment memory	0	0	1	1	0	1	0	0
DCR M	Decrement	0	0	1	1	0	1	0	1
INX B	Increment B & C registers	0	0	0	0	0	0	1	1
INX D	Increment D & E registers	0	0	0	1	0	0	1	1
INX H	Increment H & L registers	0	0	1	0	0	0	1	1
INX SP	Increment stack pointer	0	0	1	1	0	0	1	1
DCX B	Decrement B & C	0	0	0	0	1	0	1	1
DCX D	Decrement D & E	0	0	0	1	1	0	1	1
DCX H	Decrement H & L	0	0	1	0	1	0	1	1
DCX SP	Decrement stack pointer	0	0	1	1	1	0	1	1

ADD

Mnemonic	Description	D_7	D_6	D_5	D_4	D_3	D_2	D_1	D_0
ADD r	Add register to A	1	0	0	0	0	S	S	S
ADC r	Add register to A with carry	1	0	0	0	1	S	S	S
ADD M	Add memory to A	1	0	0	0	0	1	1	0
ADC M	Add memory to A with carry	1	0	0	0	1	1	1	0
ADI	Add immediate to A	1	1	0	0	0	1	1	0
ACI	Add immediate to A with carry	1	1	0	0	1	1	1	0
DAD B	Add B & C to H & L	0	0	0	0	1	0	0	1
DAD D	Add D & E to H & L	0	0	0	1	1	0	0	1
DAD H	Add H & L to H & L	0	0	1	0	1	0	0	1
DAD SP	Add stack pointer to H & L	0	0	1	1	1	0	0	1

SUBTRACT

Mnemonic	Description	D_7	D_6	D_5	D_4	D_3	D_2	D_1	D_0
SUB r	Subtract register from A	1	0	0	1	0	S	S	S
SBB r	Subtract register from A with borrow	1	0	0	1	1	S	S	S
SUB M	Subtract memory from A	1	0	0	1	0	1	1	0
SBB M	Subtract memory from A with borrow	1	0	0	1	1	1	1	0
SUI	Subtract immediate from A	1	1	0	1	0	1	1	0
SBI	Subtract immediate from A with borrow	1	1	0	1	1	1	1	0

LOGICAL

Mnemonic	Description	D_7	D_6	D_5	D_4	D_3	D_2	D_1	D_0
ANA r	And register with A	1	0	1	0	0	S	S	S
XRA r	Exclusive Or register with A	1	0	1	0	1	S	S	S
ORA r	Or register with A	1	0	1	1	0	S	S	S
CMP r	Compare register with A	1	0	1	1	1	S	S	S
ANA M	And memory with A	1	0	1	0	0	1	1	0
XRA M	Exclusive Or memory with A	1	0	1	0	1	1	1	0
ORA M	Or memory with A	1	0	1	1	0	1	1	0
CMP M	Compare memory with A	1	0	1	1	1	1	1	0
ANI	And immediate with A	1	1	1	0	0	1	1	0
XRI	Exclusive Or with A	1	1	1	0	1	1	1	0
ORI	Or immediate with A	1	1	1	1	0	1	1	0
CPI	Compare immediate with A	1	1	1	1	1	1	1	0

ROTATE

Mnemonic	Description	D_7	D_6	D_5	D_4	D_3	D_2	D_1	D_0
RLC	Rotate A left	0	0	0	0	0	1	1	1
RRC	Rotate A right	0	0	0	0	1	1	1	1
RAL	Rotate A left through carry	0	0	0	1	0	1	1	1
RAR	Rotate A right through carry	0	0	0	1	1	1	1	1

SPECIALS

Mnemonic	Description	D_7	D_6	D_5	D_4	D_3	D_2	D_1	D_0
CMA	Complement A	0	0	1	0	1	1	1	1
STC	Set carry	0	0	1	1	0	1	1	1
CMC	Complement carry	0	0	1	1	1	1	1	1
DAA	Decimal adjust A	0	0	1	0	0	1	1	1

CONTROL

Mnemonic	Description	D_7	D_6	D_5	D_4	D_3	D_2	D_1	D_0
EI	Enable Interrupts	1	1	1	1	1	0	1	1
DI	Disable Interrupt	1	1	1	1	0	0	1	1
NOP	No operation	0	0	0	0	0	0	0	0
HLT	Halt	0	1	1	1	0	1	1	0

NEW 8085A INSTRUCTIONS

Mnemonic	Description	D_7	D_6	D_5	D_4	D_3	D_2	D_1	D_0
RIM	Read Interrupt Mask	0	0	1	0	0	0	0	0
SIM	Set Interrupt Mask	0	0	1	1	0	0	0	0

[1] All mnemonics copyright Intel Corporation 1977.

Fig. 4. Instruction set of 8080/8085.

The expanded I/O instructions permit transferring the contents of any one of 256 8-bit ports either to or from the accumulator. The port number is explicitly contained in the instruction; hence, the instruction is two bytes long. The equivalent 8008 instruction is only one byte long. This is the only instance in which an 8080 instruction requires a different number of bytes than its 8008 counterpart. The motivation for doing this was more to free up 32 opcodes than to increase the number of I/O ports.

The 8080 has the identical interrupt mechanism the 8008 has, but in addition, it has instructions for enabling or disabling the interrupt mechanism. This feature, along with the ability to push and pop the processor flags, made the interrupt mechanism practical.

VI. 8085 Objectives and Constraints

In 1976, technology advances allowed Intel to consider enhancing its 8080. The objective was to come out with a processor set utilizing a single power supply and requiring fewer chips (the 8080 required a separate oscillator chip and system controller chip to make it usable). The new processor, called the 8085, was constrained to be compatible with the 8080 at the machine-code level. This meant that the only extension to the instruction set could be in the twelve unused opcodes of the 8080.

The 8085 turned out to be architecturally not much more than a repackaging of the 8080. The major differences were in such areas as an on-chip oscillator, power-on reset, vectored interrupts, decoded control lines, a serial I/O port, and a single power supply. Two new instructions were added to handle the serial port and interrupt mask. These instructions (RIM and SIM) appear in Fig. 4. Several other instructions that had been contemplated were not made available because of the software ramifications and the compatibility constraints they would place on the forthcoming 8086.

VII. Objectives and Constraints of 8086

The new Intel 8086 microprocessor was designed to provide an order of magnitude increase in processing throughput over the older 8080. The processor was to be assembly-language-level–compatible with the 8080 so that existing 8080 software could be reassembled and correctly executed on the 8086. To allow for this, the 8080 register set and instruction set appear as logical subsets of the 8086 registers and instructions. By utilizing a general-register structure architecture, Intel could capitalize on its experience with the 8080 to obtain a processor with a higher degree of sophistication. Strict 8080 compatibility, however, was not attempted, especially in areas where it would compromise the final design.

The goals of the 8086 architectural design were to provide symmetric extensions of existing 8080 features, and to add processing capabilities not found in the 8080. These features included 16-bit arithmetic, signed 8- and 16-bit arithmetic (including multiply and divide), efficient interruptible byte-string operations, improved bit-manipulation facilities, and mechanisms to provide for re-entrant code, position-independent code, and dynamically relocatable programs.

By now memory had become very inexpensive and micro-processors were being used in applications that required large amounts of code and/or data. Thus another design goal was to be able to address directly more than 64K bytes and support multiprocessor configurations.

VIII. The 8086 Instruction-Set Processor

The 8086 processor architecture is described in terms of its memory structure, register structure, instruction set, and external interface. The 8086 memory structure includes up to one megabyte of memory space and up to 64K input/output ports. The register structure includes three files of registers. Four 16-bit general registers can participate interchangeably in arithmetic and logic operations, two 16-bit pointer and two 16-bit index registers are used for address calculations, and four 16-bit segment registers allow extended addressing capabilities. Nine flags record the processor state and control its operation.

The instruction set supports a wide range of addressing modes and provides operations for data transfer, signed and unsigned 8- and 16-bit arithmetic, logicals, string manipulations, control transfer, and processor control. The external interface includes a reset sequence, interrupts, and a multiprocessor-synchronization and resource-sharing facility.

A. Memory and I/O Structure

The 8086 memory structure consists of two components—the memory space and the input/output space. All instruction code and operands reside in the memory space. Peripheral and I/O devices ordinarily reside in the I/O space, except in the case of memory-mapped devices.

1. Memory Space. The 8086 memory is a sequence of up to 1 million 8-bit bytes, a considerable increase over the 64K bytes in the 8080. Any two consecutive bytes may be paired together to form a 16-bit word. Such words may be located at odd or even byte addresses. The data bus of the 8086 is 16 bits wide, so, unlike the 8080, a word can be accessed in one memory cycle (however, words located at odd byte addresses still require two memory cycles). As in the 8080, the most significant 8 bits of a word are located in the byte with the higher memory address.

Since the 8086 processor performs 16-bit arithmetic, the address objects it manipulates are 16 bits in length. Since a 16-bit quantity can address only 64K bytes, additional mechanisms are required to build addresses in a megabyte memory space. The 8086 memory may be conceived of as an arbitrary number of segments, each at most 64K bytes in size. Each segment begins at an address which is evenly divisible by 16 (i.e., the low-order 4 bits of a segment's address are zero). At any given moment the contents of four of these segments are immediately addressable. These four segments, called the *current code* segment, the *current data* segment, the *current stack* segment, and the *current extra* segment, need not be unique and may overlap. The high-order 16 bits of the address of each current segment are held in a dedicated 16-bit segment register. In the degenerate case where all four segments start at the same address, namely address 0, we have an 8080 memory structure.

Bytes or words within a segment are addressed by using 16-bit offset addresses within the 64K byte segment. A 20-bit physical address is constructed by adding the 16-bit offset address to the contents of a 16-bit segment register with 4 low-order zero bits appended, as illustrated in Fig. 5.

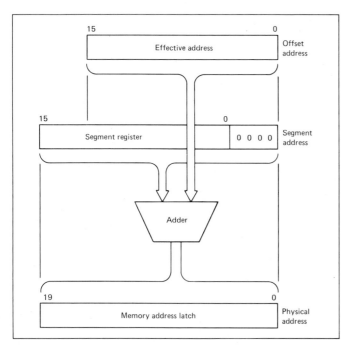

Fig. 5. To address 1 million bytes requires a 20-bit memory address. This 20-bit address is constructed by offsetting the effective address 4 bits to the right of the segment address, filling in the 4 low-order bits of the segment address with zeros, and adding the two.

Various alternatives for extending the 8080 address space were considered. One such alternative consisted of appending 8 rather than 4 low-order zero bits to the contents of a segment register, thereby providing a 24-bit physical address capable of addressing up to 16 megabytes of memory. This was rejected for the following reasons:

- Segments would be forced to start on 256-byte boundaries, resulting in excessive memory fragmentation.

- The 4 additional pins that would be required on the chip were not available.

- It was felt that a 1-megabyte address space was sufficient.

2. Input/Output Space. In contrast to the 256 I/O ports in the 8080, the 8086 provides 64K addressable input or output ports. Unlike the memory, the I/O space is addressed as if it were a single segment, without the use of segment registers. Input/output physical addresses are in fact 20 bits in length, but the high-order 4 bits are always zero. The first 256 ports are directly addressable (address in the instruction), whereas all 64K ports are

indirectly addressable (address in register). Such indirect addressing was provided to permit consecutive ports to be accessed in a program loop. Ports may be 8 or 16 bits in size, and 16-bit ports may be located at odd or even addresses.

B. Register Structure

The 8086 processor contains three files of four 16-bit registers and a file of nine 1-bit flags. The three files of registers are the general-register file, the pointer- and index-register file, and the segment-register file. There is a 16-bit instruction pointer (called the program counter in the earlier processors) which is not directly accessible to the programmer; rather, it is manipulated with control transfer instructions. The 8086 register set is a superset of the 8080 registers, as shown in Figs. 6 and 7. Corresponding registers in the 8080 and 8086 do not necessarily have the same names, thereby permitting the 8086 to use a more meaningful set of names.

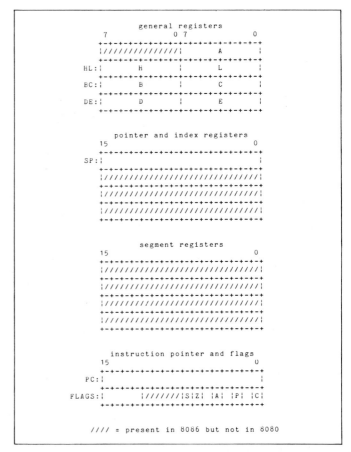

Fig. 6. The 8080 registers as a subset of the 8086 registers.

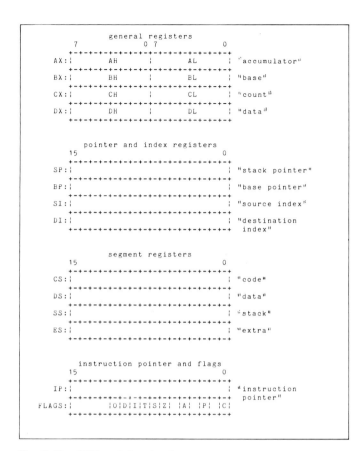

```
            general registers
       7            0 7           0
       +-+-+-+-+-+-+-+-+-+-+-+-+-+-+-+-+
   AX:|      AH      |      AL       |  "accumulator"
       +-+-+-+-+-+-+-+-+-+-+-+-+-+-+-+-+
   BX:|      BH      |      BL       |  "base"
       +-+-+-+-+-+-+-+-+-+-+-+-+-+-+-+-+
   CX:|      CH      |      CL       |  "count"
       +-+-+-+-+-+-+-+-+-+-+-+-+-+-+-+-+
   DX:|      DH      |      DL       |  "data"
       +-+-+-+-+-+-+-+-+-+-+-+-+-+-+-+-+

         pointer and index registers
      15                            0
       +-+-+-+-+-+-+-+-+-+-+-+-+-+-+-+-+
   SP:|                             |  "stack pointer"
       +-+-+-+-+-+-+-+-+-+-+-+-+-+-+-+-+
   BP:|                             |  "base pointer"
       +-+-+-+-+-+-+-+-+-+-+-+-+-+-+-+-+
   SI:|                             |  "source index"
       +-+-+-+-+-+-+-+-+-+-+-+-+-+-+-+-+
   DI:|                             |  "destination
       +-+-+-+-+-+-+-+-+-+-+-+-+-+-+-+-+   index"

             segment registers
      15                            0
       +-+-+-+-+-+-+-+-+-+-+-+-+-+-+-+-+
   CS:|                             |  "code"
       +-+-+-+-+-+-+-+-+-+-+-+-+-+-+-+-+
   DS:|                             |  "data"
       +-+-+-+-+-+-+-+-+-+-+-+-+-+-+-+-+
   SS:|                             |  "stack"
       +-+-+-+-+-+-+-+-+-+-+-+-+-+-+-+-+
   ES:|                             |  "extra"
       +-+-+-+-+-+-+-+-+-+-+-+-+-+-+-+-+

         instruction pointer and flags
      15                            0
       +-+-+-+-+-+-+-+-+-+-+-+-+-+-+-+-+
   IP:|                             |  "instruction
       +-+-+-+-+-+-+-+-+-+-+-+-+-+-+-+-+   pointer"
FLAGS:|       |O|D|I|T|S|Z| |A| |P| |C|
       +-+-+-+-+-+-+-+-+-+-+-+-+-+-+-+-+
```

Fig. 7. The 8086 register structure.

1. General-Register File. The AX-BX-CX-DX register set is called the general-register file, or HL group (for reasons that will be apparent below). The general registers can participate interchangeably in the arithmetic and logical operations of the 8086. Some of the other 8086 operations (such as the string operations) dedicate certain of the general registers to specific uses. These uses are indicated by the mnemonic phrases "accumulator," "base," "count," and "data" in Fig. 7. The general registers have a property that distinguishes them from the other registers—their upper and lower halves are separately addressable. Thus, the general registers can be thought of as two files of four 8-bit registers—the H file and the L file.

2. Pointer- and Index-Register File. The SP-BP-SI-DI register set is called the pointer- and index-register file, or the P and I groups. The registers in this file generally contain offset addresses used for addressing within a segment. Like the general registers, the pointer and index registers can participate interchangeably in

the 16-bit arithmetic and logical operations of the 8086, thereby providing a means to perform address computations. These registers play a major role in effective address computations, as described in Sec. VIII. C. 1. of this chapter.

There is one main difference between the registers in this file, which results in dividing the file into two subfiles, the P or pointer group (SP, BP) and the I or index group (SI, DI). The difference is that the pointers are by default assumed to contain offset addresses within the current stack segment, and the indexes are by default generally assumed to contain offset addresses within the current data segment. The mnemonic phrases "stack pointer," "base pointer," "source index," and "destination index" are mnemonics associated with these registers' names, as shown in Fig. 7.

3. Segment-Register File. The CS-DS-SS-ES register set is called the segment-register file, or S group. The segment registers play an important role in the memory addressing mechanism of the processor. These registers are similar in that they are used in all memory address computations (see Sec. VIII. A. of this chapter). The segment registers names have the associated mnemonic phrases "code," "data," "stack," and "extra," as shown in Fig. 7.

The contents of the CS register define the current code segment. All instruction fetches are taken to be relative to CS, using the instruction pointer (IP) as an offset. The contents of the DS register define the current data segment. Generally, all data references except those involving BP or SP are taken by default to be relative to DS. The contents of the SS register define the current stack segment. All data references which explicitly or implicitly involve SP or BP are taken by default to be relative to SS. This includes all push and pop operations, interrupts, and return operations. The contents of the ES register define the current extra segment. The extra segment has no specific use, although it is usually treated as an additional data segment which can be specified in an instruction by using a special default-segment-override prefix.

In general, the default segment register for the two types of data references (DS and SS) can be overriden. By preceding the instruction with a special one-byte prefix, the reference can be forced to be relative to one of the other three segment registers. This prefix, as well as other prefixes described later, has a unique encoding that permits it to be distinguished from the opcodes.

Programs which do not load or manipulate the segment registers are said to be dynamically relocatable. Such a program may be interrupted, moved in memory to a new location, and restarted with new segment-register values.

At first a set of eight segment registers was proposed along with a field in a program-status word specifying which segment register was currently CS, which was currently DS, and which was currently SS. The other five all served as extra segment registers.

Such a scheme would have resulted in virtually no thrashing of segment register contents; start addresses of all needed segments would be loaded initially into one of the eight segment registers, and the roles of the various segment registers would vary dynamically during program execution. Concern over the size of the resulting processor chip forced the number of segment registers to be reduced to the minimum number necessary, namely four. With this minimum number, each segment register could be dedicated to a particular type of segment (code, data, stack, extra), and the specifying field in the program status word was no longer needed.

4. Flag-Register File. The AF-CF-DF-IF-OF-PF-SF-TF-ZF register set is called the flag-register file or F group. The flags in this group are all one bit in size and are used to record processor status information and to control processor operation. The flag registers' names have the following associated mnemonic phrases:

AF   Auxiliary carry
CF   Carry
DF   Direction
IF   Interrupt enable
OF   Overflow
PF   Parity
SF   Sign
TF   Trap
ZF   Zero

The AF, CF, PF, SF, and ZF flags retain their familiar 8080 semantics, generally reflecting the status of the latest arithmetic or logical operation. The OF flag joins this group, reflecting the signed arithmetic overflow condition. The DF, IF, and TF flags are used to control certain aspects of the processor. The DF flag controls the direction of the string manipulations (auto-incrementing or auto-decrementing). The IF flag enables or disables external interrupts. The TF flag puts the processor into a single-step mode for program debugging. More detail is given on each of these three flags later in the chapter.

C. Instruction Set

The 8086 instruction set—while including most of the 8080 set as a subset—has more ways to address operands and more power in every area. It is designed to implement block-structured languages efficiently. Nearly all instructions operate on either 8- or 16-bit operands. There are four classes of data transfer. All four arithmetic operations are available. An additional logic instruction, test, is included. Also new are byte- and word-string manipulations and intersegment transfers. A summary of the 8086 instructions appears in Fig. 8.

1. Operand Addressing. The 8086 instruction set provides many more ways to address operands than were provided by the 8080. Two-operand operations generally allow either a register or memory to serve as one operand (called the *first operand*), and either a register or a constant within the instruction to serve as the other (called the *second operand*). Typical formats for two-operand operations are shown in Fig. 9 (second operand is a register) and Fig. 10 (second operand is a constant). The result of a two-operand operation may be directed to either of the source operands, with the exception, of course, of in-line immediate constants. Single-operand operations generally allow either a register or a memory to serve as the operand. A typical one-operand format is shown in Fig. 11. Virtually all 8086 operators may specify 8- or 16-bit operands.

Memory operands. An instruction may address an operand residing in memory in one of four ways as determined by the mod and r/m fields in the instruction (see Table 2).

Direct 16-bit offset address

Indirect through a base register (BP or BX), optionally with an 8- or 16-bit displacement

Indirect through an index register (SI or DI), optionally with an 8- or 16-bit displacement

Indirect through the sum of a base register and an index register, optionally with an 8- or 16-bit displacement

The general register, BX, and the pointer register, BP, may serve as base registers. When the base register BX is used without an index register, the operand by default resides in the current data segment. When the base register BP is used without an index register, the operand by default resides in the current stack segment. When both base and index registers are used, the operand by default resides in the segment determined by the base register. When an index register alone is used, the operand by default resides in the current data segment.

Auto-incrementing and auto-decrementing address modes were not included in general, since it was felt that their use is mainly oriented towards string processing. These modes were included on the string primitive instructions.

Register operands. The four 16-bit general registers and the four 16-bit pointer and index registers may serve interchangeably as operands in 16-bit operations. Three exceptions to note are multiply, divide, and the string operations, all of which use the AX register implicitly. The eight 8-bit registers of the HL group may serve interchangeably in 8-bit operations. Again, multiply, divide, and the string operations use AL implicitly. Table 3 shows

Fig. 8. Instruction set of 8086.

DATA TRANSFER

MOV = Move
PUSH = Push
POP = Pop
XCHG = Exchange
IN/INW = Input to AL/AX from
OUT/OUTW = Output from AL/AX to
XLAT = Translate byte to AL
LEA = Load EA to register
LDS = Load pointer to DS
LES = Load pointer to ES
LAHF = Load AH with flags
SAHF = Store AH into flags
PUSHF = Push flags
POPF = Pop flags

ARITHMETIC

ADD = Add
ADC = Add with carry
INC = Increment
AAA = ASCII adjust for add
DAA = Decimal adjust for add
SUB = Subtract
SBB = Subtract with borrow
DEC = Decrement
NEG = Change sign
CMP = Compare
AAS = ASCII adjust for subtract
DAS = Decimal adjust for subtract
MUL = Multiply (unsigned)
IMUL = Integer multiply (signed)
AAM = ASCII adjust for multiply
DIV = Divide (unsigned)
IDIV = Integer divide (signed)
AAD = ASCII adjust for divide
CBW = Convert byte to word
CWD = Convert word to double word

LOGIC

NOT = Invert
SHL/SAL = Shift logical/arithmetic left
SHR = Shift logical right
SAR = Shift arithmetic right
ROL = Rotate left
ROR = Rotate right
RCL = Rotate through carry flag left
RCR = Rotate through carry right
AND = And
TEST = And function to flags, no result
OR = Or
XOR = Exclusive or

STRING MANIPULATION

REP = Repeat
MOVS/MOVW = Move byte/word
CMPS/CMPW = Compare byte/word
SCAS/SCAW = Scan byte/word
LODS/LODW = Load byte/wd to AL/AX
STOS/STOW = Store byte/wd frm AL/A

CONTROL TRANSFER

CALL = Call
JMP = Unconditional Jump
RET = Return from CALL
PROCESSOR CONTROL
CLC = Clear carry
CMC = Complement carry
STC = Set carry
CLD = Clear direction
STD = Set direction
CLI = Clear interrupt
STI = Set interrupt
HLT = Halt
WAIT = Wait
ESC = Escape (to external device)
LOCK = Bus lock prefix

Footnotes:

AL = 8 bit accumulator
AX = 16 bit accumulator
CX = Count register
DS = Data segment
ES = Extra segment
Above/below refers to unsigned value.
Greater = more positive,
Less = less positive (more negative) signed values

SEGMENT OVERRIDE PREFIX

| 0 0 1 reg 1 1 0 |

Segment
00 ES
01 CS
10 SS
11 DS

REG is assigned according to the following table:

16 Bit (w = 1)	8 Bit (w = 0)
000 AX	000 AL
001 CX	001 CL
010 DX	010 DL
011 BX	011 BL
100 SP	100 AH
101 BP	101 CH
110 SI	110 DH
111 DI	111 BH

```
+.+.+.+.+.+.+.+    +-+-+-+-+-+-+-+-+    +-+-+-+-+-+-+-+-+
:    :seg:    :    |  opcode  |d|w|    |mod| reg | r/m |
+.+.+.+.+.+.+.+    +-+-+-+-+-+-+-+-+    +-+-+-+-+-+-+-+-+
 (optional)
                  +.+.+.+.+.+.+.+    +.+.+.+.+.+.+.+.+
                  :   disp-lo   :    :   disp-hi   :
                  +.+.+.+.+.+.+.+    +.+.+.+.+.+.+.+.+
                   (optional)        (optional)

first operand is register or memory specified by seg, mod, r/m,
disp-lo, disp-hi

    mod = 00,01,10: first operand is memory (see Table 2)
         11:        first operand is register (see Table 3)

    seg is overriding segment register


second operand is register specified by reg




    w = 0: operands are 8 bits
        1: operands are 16 bits
    d = 0: destination is first operand
        1: destination is second operand
```

Fig. 9. Typical format of 8086 two-operand operation when second operand is register.

the register selection as determined by the r/m field (first operand) or reg field (second operand) in the instruction.

Immediate operands. All two-operand operations except multiply, divide, and the string operations allow one source operand to appear within the instruction as immediate data represented in 2's complement form. Sixteen-bit immediate operands having a high-order byte which is the sign extension of the low-order byte may be abbreviated to 8 bits.

```
+.+.+.+.+.+.+.+.+    +-+-+-+-+-+-+-+-+    +-+-+-+-+-+-+-+-+
:    :seg:    :    |  opcode  |s|w|    |mod| opc | r/m |
+.+.+.+.+.+.+.+    +-+-+-+-+-+-+-+-+    +-+-+-+-+-+-+-+-+
 (optional)
                  +.+.+.+.+.+.+.+    +.+.+.+.+.+.+.+.+
                  :   disp-lo   :    :   disp-hi   :
                  +.+.+.+.+.+.+.+    +.+.+.+.+.+.+.+.+
                   (optional)        (optional)
                  +-+-+-+-+-+-+-+-+    +.+.+.+.+.+.+.+.+
                  |    data-lo    |    :   data-hi   :
                  +-+-+-+-+-+-+-+-+    +.+.+.+.+.+.+.+.+
                                       (optional)

first operand is register or memory specified by seg, mod, r/m,
disp-lo, disp-hi

    mod = 00,01,10: first operand is memory  (see Table 2)
         11:        first operand is register (see Table 3)

    seg is overriding segment register


second operand is immediate data specified by s, w, data-lo, data-hi

    w = 0: DATA = data-lo (data-hi is absent)
        1: s = 0: DATA = data-hi, data-lo
             1: DATA = data-lo sign extended (data-hi is absent)
```

Fig. 10. Typical format of 8086 two-operand operation when second operand is a constant (immediate data).

```
+.+.+.+.+.+.+.+    +-+-+-+-+-+-+-+-+    +-+-+-+-+-+-+-+-+
:    :seg:    :    |  opcode  |w|    |mod|opcod| r/m |
+.+.+.+.+.+.+.+    +-+-+-+-+-+-+-+-+    +-+-+-+-+-+-+-+-+
 (optional)
                  +.+.+.+.+.+.+.+    +.+.+.+.+.+.+.+.+
                  :   disp-lo   :    :   disp-hi   :
                  +.+.+.+.+.+.+.+    +.+.+.+.+.+.+.+.+
                   (optional)        (optional)

operand is register or memory specified by seg, mod, r/m,
disp-lo, disp-hi

    mod = 00,01,10: operand is memory (see Table 2)
         11;        operand is register (see Table 3)

    seg is overriding segment register




    w = 0: operand is 8 bits
        1: operand is 16 bits
```

Fig. 11. Typical format of 8086 one-operand operation.

Addressing mode usage. The addressing modes permit registers BX and BP to serve as base registers and registers SI and DI as index registers. Possible use of this for language implementation is discussed below.

Simple variables and arrays: A simple variable is accessed with the direct address mode. An array element is accessed with the indirect address mode utilizing the sum of the register SI (where SI contains the index into the array) and displacement (where displacement is the offset of the array in its segment).

Based variables: A based variable is located at a memory address pointed at by some other variable. If the contents of the pointer variable were placed in BX, the indirect addressing mode utilizing BX would access the based variable. If the based variable were an array and the index into the array were placed in SI, the indirect addressing mode utilizing the sum of the register BX and register SI would access elements of the array.

Stack marker: Marking a stack permits efficient implementation of block-structured languages and provides an efficient address mechanism for reentrant procedures. Register BP can be used as a stack marker pointer to the beginning of an activation record in the stack. The indirect address mode utilizing the sums of the base register BP and a displacement (where displacement is the offset of a local variable in the activation record) will access the variable declared in the currently active block. The indirect address mode utilizing the sum of the base register BP, index register SI (where SI contains the index in an array), and displacement (where displacement is the offset of the array in the activation record) will access an element of the array. Register DI can be used in

Table 2 Determining 8086 Offset Address of a Memory Operand
(Use This Table When mod ≠ 11; Otherwise Use Table 3.)

This table applies to the first operand only; the second operand can never be a memory operand.

mod specifies how disp-lo and disp-hi are used to define a displacement as follows:

$$
\text{mod} = \begin{array}{l} 00: \text{DISP=0 (disp-lo and disp-hi are absent)} \\ 01: \text{DISP=disp-lo sign extended (disp-hi is absent)} \\ 10: \text{DISP=disp-hi,disp-lo} \end{array}
$$

r/m specifies which base and index register contents are to be added to the displacement to form the operand offset address as follows:

$$
\text{r/m} = \left.\begin{array}{l} 000: \text{OFFSET=(BX)+(SI)+DISP} \\ 001: \text{OFFSET=(BX)+(DI)+DISP} \\ 010: \text{OFFSET=(BP)+(SI)+DISP} \\ 011: \text{OFFSET=(BP)+(DI)+DISP} \\ 100: \text{OFFSET=\qquad(SI)+DISP} \\ 101: \text{OFFSET=\qquad(DI)+DISP} \\ 110: \text{OFFSET=(BP)\qquad+DISP} \\ 111: \text{OFFSET=(BX)\qquad+DISP} \end{array}\right\} \begin{array}{l}\text{indirect}\\\text{address}\\\text{mode}\end{array}
$$

( ) means "contents of"

The following special case is an exception to the above rules:

$$
\left.\begin{array}{l} \text{if} \quad \text{mod=00} \quad \text{and} \quad \text{r/m=110} \\ \text{then OFFSET=disp-hi, disp-lo} \end{array}\right\} \begin{array}{l}\text{direct}\\\text{address}\\\text{mode}\end{array}
$$

the same manner as SI so that two array elements can be accessed concurrently.

Example: An example of a procedure-calling sequence on the 8086 illustrates the interaction of the addressing modes and activation records.

Table 3 Determining 8086 Register Operand
(Use This Table When mod = 11; Otherwise Use Table 2.)

r/m	*First operand*		reg	*Second operand*	
	8-bit	16-bit		8-bit	16-bit
000:	AL	AX	000:	AL	AX
001:	CL	CX	001:	CL	CX
010:	DL	DX	010:	DL	DX
011:	BL	BX	011:	BL	BX
100:	AH	SP	100:	AH	SP
101:	CH	BP	101:	CH	BP
110:	DH	SI	110:	DH	SI
111:	BH	DI	111:	BH	DI

```
;CALL MYPROC (ALPHA, BETA)
   PUSH ALPHA          ;pass parameters by
   PUSH BETA           ; ...pushing them on
                       ;the stack
   CALL MYPROC         ;call the procedure

;PROCEDURE MYPROC (A, B)
MYPROC:                ;entry point
   PUSH  BP            ;save previous BP value
   MOV   BP,SP         ;make BP point at new
                       ;record
   SUB   SP,LOCALS     ;allocate local storage on
                       ;stack
                       ; ...for reentrant procedur-
                       ;es (stack advances towards
                       ;lower memory)

;body of procedure
   MOV   SP,BP         ;deallocate local storage
   POP   BP            ;restore previous BP
   RET   4            ;return and discard 4 bytes
                       ;of parameters
```

Upon entry to the procedure MYPROC its parameters are addressable with positive offsets from BP (the stack grows towards lower memory addresses). Since usually less than 128 bytes of parameters are passed, only an 8-bit signed displacement from BP is needed. Similarly, local variables to MYPROC are addressable with negative offsets from BP. Again, economy of instruction size is realized by using 8-bit signed displacements. A special return instruction discards the parameters pushed on the stack.

2. Data Transfers. Four classes of data transfer operations may be distinguished: general-purpose, accumulator-specific, address-object transfers, and flag transfers.

The general-purpose data transfer operations are move, push, pop, and exchange. Generally, these operations are available for all types of operands.

The accumulator-specific transfers include input and output and the translate operations. The first 256 ports can be addressed directly, just as they were addressed in the 8080. However, the 8086 also permits ports to be addressed indirectly through a register (DX). This latter facility allows 64K ports to be addressed. Furthermore, the 8086 ports may be 8 or 16 bits wide, whereas the 8080 only permitted 8-bit-wide ports. The translate operation performs a table-lookup byte translation. We will see the useful-ness of this operation below, when it is combined with string operations.

The address-object transfers—load effective address and load pointer—are an 8086 facility not present in the 8080. A pointer is a pair of 16-bit values specifying a segment start address and an offset address; it is used to gain access to the full megabyte of memory. The load pointer operations provide a means of loading a segment start address into a segment register and an offset address into a general or pointer register in a single operation. The load effective address operation provides access to the offset address of an operand, as opposed to the value of the operand itself.

The flag transfers provide access to the collection of flags for such operations as push, pop, load, and store. A similar facility for pushing and popping flags was provided in the 8080; the load and store flags facility is new in the 8086.

It should be noted that the load and store operations involve only those flags that existed in the 8080. This is part of the concessions made for 8080 compatibility (without these operations it would take nine 8086 bytes to perform exactly an 8080 PUSH PSW or POP PSW).

3. Arithmetics. Whereas the 8080 provided for only 8-bit addition and subtraction of unsigned numbers, the 8086 provides all four basic mathematical functions on 8- and 16-bit signed and unsigned numbers. Standard 2's complement representation of signed values is used. Sufficient conditional transfers are provided to allow both signed and unsigned comparisons. The OF flag allows detection of the signed overflow condition.

Consideration was given to providing separate operations for signed addition and subtraction which would automatically trap on signed overflow (signed overflow is an exception condition, whereas unsigned overflow is not). However, lack of room in the opcode space prohibited this. As a compromise, a one-byte trap-on-overflow instruction was included to make testing for signed overflow less painful.

The 8080 provided a correction operation to allow addition to be performed directly on packed binary-coded representations of decimal digits. In the 8086, correction operations are provided to allow arithmetic to be performed directly on unpacked represen-tations of decimal digits (e.g., ASCII) or on packed decimal representations.

Multiply and divide. Both signed and unsigned multiply and divide operations are provided. Multiply produces a double-length product (16 bits for 8-bit multiply, 32 bits for 16-bit multiply), while divide returns a single-length quotient and a single-length remainder from a double-length dividend and single-length divisor. Sign extension operations allow one to construct the double-length dividend needed for signed division.

A quotient overflow (e.g., that caused by dividing by zero) will automatically interrupt the processor.

Decimal instructions. Packed BCD operations are provided in the form of accumulator-adjustment instructions. Two such instructions are provided—one for an adjustment following an addition and one following a subtraction. The addition adjustment is identical to the 8080 DAA instruction; the subtraction adjust-ment is defined similarly. Packed multiply and divide adjustments are not provided, because the cross terms generated make it impossible to recover the decimal result without additional processor facilities (see Appendix 2 for details).

Unpacked BCD operations are also provided in the form of accumulator adjust instructions (ASCII is a special case of unpacked BCD). Four such instructions are provided, one each for adjustments involving addition, subtraction, multiplication, and division. The addition and subtraction adjustments are similar to the corresponding packed BCD adjustments except that the AH register is updated if an adjustment on AL is required. Unlike packed BCD, unpacked BCD byte multiplication does not generate cross terms, so multiplication adjustment consists of converting the binary value in the AL register into BCD digits in AH and AL; the divide adjustment does the reverse. Note that adjustments for addition, subtraction, and multiplication are performed following the arithmetic operation; division adjustment is performed prior to a division operation. See Appendix 2 for more details on unpacked BCD adjustments.

4. Logicals. The standard logical operations AND, OR, XOR, and NOT are carry-overs from the 8080. Additionally, the 8086 provides a logical TEST for specific bits. This consists of a logical AND instruction which sets the flags but does not store the result, thereby not destroying either operand.

The four unit-rotate instructions in the 8080 are augmented with four unit-shift instructions in the 8086. Furthermore, the 8086 provides multi-bit shifts and rotates including an arithmetic right shift.

5. String Manipulation. The 8086 provides a group of 1-byte instructions which perform various primitive operations for the manipulation of byte or word strings (sequences of bytes or words). These primitive operations can be performed repeatedly in hardware by preceding the instruction with a special prefix. The single-operation forms may be combined to form complex string operations in tight software loops with repetition provided by special iteration operations. The 8080 did not provide any string-manipulation facilities.

Hardware operation control. All primitive string operations use the SI register to address the source operands, which are assumed to be in the current data segment. The DI register is used to address the destination operands, which reside in the current extra segment. The operand pointers are incremented or decremented (depending on the setting of the DF flag) after each operation, once for byte operations and twice for word operations.

Any of the primitive string operation instructions may be preceded with a 1-byte prefix indicating that the operation is to be repeated until the operation count in CX is satisfied. The test for completion is made prior to each repetition of the operation. Thus, an initial operation count of zero will cause zero executions of the primitive operation.

The repeat prefix byte also designates a value to compare with the ZF flag. If the primitive operation is one which affects the ZF flag and the ZF flag is unequal to the designated value after any execution of the primitive operation, the repetition is terminated. This permits the scan operation to serve as a scan-while or a scan-until.

During the execution of a repeated primitive operation the operand pointer registers (SI and DI) and the operation count register (CX) are updated after each repetition, whereas the instruction pointer will retain the offset address of the repeat prefix byte (assuming it immediately precedes the string operation instruction). Thus, an interrupted repeated operation will be correctly resumed when control returns from the interrupting task.

Primitive string operations. Five primitive string operations are provided:

- MOVS moves a string element (byte or word) from the source operand to the destination operand. As a repeated operation, this provides for moving a string from one location in memory to another.

- CMPS subtracts the string element at the destination operand from the string element at the source operand and affects the flags but does not return the result. As a repeated operation this provides for comparing two strings. With the appropriate repeat prefix it is possible to compare two strings and determine after which string element the two strings become unequal, thereby establishing an ordering between the strings.

- SCAS subtracts the string element at the destination operand from AL (or AX for word strings) and affects the flags but does not return the result. As a repeated operation this provides for scanning for the occurrence of, or departure from, a given value in the string.

- LODS loads a string element from the source operand into AL (or AX for word strings). This operation ordinarily would not be repeated.

- STOS stores a string element from AL (or AX for word

strings) into the destination operand. As a repeated operation this provides for filling a string with a given value.

Software operation control. The repeat prefix provides for rapid iteration in a hardware-repeated string operation. Iteration-control operations provide this same control for implementing software loops to perform complex string operations. These iteration operations provide the same operation count update, operation completion test, and ZF flag tests that the repeat prefix provides.

The iteration-control transfer operations perform leading- and trailing-decision loop control. The destinations of iteration-control transfers must be within a 256-byte range centered about the instruction.

Four iteration-control transfer operations are provided:

- LOOP decrements the CX ("count") register by 1 and transfers if CX is not 0.

- LOOPE decrements the CX register by 1 and transfers if CX is not 0 and the ZF flag is set (loop while equal).

- LOOPNE decrements the CX register by 1 and transfers if CX is not 0 and the ZF flag is cleared (loop while not equal).

- JCXZ transfers if the CX register is 0. This is used for skipping over a loop when the initial count is 0.

By combining the primitive string operations and iteration-control operations with other operations, it is possible to build sophisticated yet efficient string manipulation routines. One instruction that is particularly useful in this context is the translate operation; it permits a byte fetched from one string to be translated before being stored in a second string, or before being operated upon in some other fashion. The translation is performed by using the value in the AL register to index into a table pointed at by the BX register. The translated value obtained from the table then replaces the value initially in the AL register.

As an example of use of the primitive string operations and iteration-control operations to implement a complex string operation, consider the following application: An input driver must translate a buffer of EBCDIC characters into ASCII and transfer characters until one of several different EBCDIC control characters is encountered. The transferred ASCII string is to be terminated with an EOT character. To accomplish this, SI is initialized to point to the beginning of the EBCDIC buffer, DI is initialized to point to the beginning of the buffer to receive the ASCII characters, BX is made to point to an EBCDIC-to-ASCII translation table, and CX is initialized to contain the length of the EBCDIC buffer (possibly empty). The translation table contains the ASCII equivalent for each EBCDIC character, perhaps with ASCII nulls for illegal characters. The EOT code is placed into those entries in the table corresponding to the desired EBCDIC stop characters. The 8086 instruction sequence to implement this example is the following:

```
        JCXZ      Empty
Next:
        LODS      Ebcbuf      ;fetch next EBCDIC character
        XLAT      Table       ;translate it to ASCII
        CMP       AL,EOT      ;test for the EOT
        STOS      Ascbuf      ;transfer ASCII character
        LOOPNE    Next        ;continue if not EOT
        .
        .
        .

Empty:
```

The body of this loop requires just seven bytes of code.

6. Transfer of Control.   Transfer-of-control instructions (jumps, calls, returns) in the 8086 are of two basic varieties: intrasegment transfers, which transfer control within the current code segment by specifying a new value for IP, and intersegment transfers, which transfer control to an arbitrary code segment by specifying a new value for both CS and IP. Furthermore, both direct and indirect transfers are supported. Direct transfers specify the destination of the transfer (the new value of IP and possibly CS) in the instruction; indirect transfers make use of the standard addressing modes, as described previously, to locate an operand which specifies the destination of the transfer. By contrast, the 8080 provides only direct intrasegment transfers.

Facilities for position-independent code and coding efficiency not found in the 8080 have been introduced in the 8086. Intrasegment direct calls and jumps specify a self-relative direct displacement, thus allowing position-independent code. A shortened jump instruction is available for transfers within a 256-byte range centered about the instruction, thus allowing for code compaction.

Returns may optionally adjust the SP register so as to discard stacked parameters, thereby making parameter passing more efficient. This is a more complete solution to the problem than the 8080 instruction which exchanged the contents of the HL with the top of the stack.

The 8080 provided conditional jumps useful for determining relations between unsigned numbers. The 8086 augments these with conditional jumps for determining relations between signed numbers. Table 4 shows the conditional jumps as a function of flag settings. The seldom-used conditional calls and returns provided by the 8080 have not been incorporated into the 8086.

7. External Interface.   The 8086 processor provides both common and uncommon interfaces to external equipment. The two

Table 4   8086 Conditional Jumps as a Function of Flag Settings

Jump on	Flag settings
EQUAL	ZF = 1
NOT EQUAL	ZF = 0
LESS THAN	(SF xor OF) = 1
GREATER THAN	((SF xor OF) or ZF) = 0
LESS THAN OR EQUAL	((SF xor OF) or ZF) = 1
GREATER THAN OR EQUAL	(SF xor OF) = 0
BELOW	CF = 1
ABOVE	(CF or ZF) = 0
BELOW OR EQUAL	(CF or ZF) = 1
ABOVE OR EQUAL	CF = 0
PARITY EVEN	PF = 1
PARITY ODD	PF = 0
OVERFLOW	OF = 1
NO OVERFLOW	OF = 0
SIGN	SF = 1
NO SIGN	SF = 0

varieties of interrupts, maskable and non-maskable, are not uncommon, nor is single-step diagnostic capability. More unusual is the ability to escape to an external processor to perform specialized operations. Also uncommon is the hardware mechanism to control access to shared resources in a multiple-processor configuration.

Interrupts.   The 8080 interrupt mechanism was general enough to permit the interrupting device to supply any operation to be executed out of sequence when an interrupt occurs. However, the only operation that had any utility for interrupt processing was the 1-byte subroutine call. This byte consists of 5 bits of opcode and 3 bits identifying one of eight interrupt subroutines residing at eight fixed locations in memory. If the unnecessary generalization was removed, the interrupting device would not have to provide the opcode and all 8 bits could be used to identify the interrupt subroutine. Furthermore, if the 8 bits were used to index a table of subroutine addresses, the actual subroutine could reside anywhere in memory. This is the evolutionary process that led to the design of the 8086 interrupt mechanism.

Interrupts result in a transfer of control to a new location in a new code segment. A 256-element table (interrupt transfer vector) containing pointers to these interrupt service code locations resides at the beginning of memory. Each element is four bytes in size, containing an offset address and the high-order 16-bits of the start address of the service code segment. Each element of this table corresponds to an interrupt type, these types being numbered 0 to 255. All interrupts perform a transfer by pushing the current flag setting onto the stack and then performing an indirect call (of the intersegment variety) through the interrupt transfer vector.

The 8086 processor recognizes two varieties of external interrupt—the non-maskable interrupt and the maskable interrupt. A pin is provided for each variety.

Program execution control may be transferred by means of operations similar in effect to that of external interrupts. A generalized 2-byte instruction is provided that generates an interrupt of any type; the type is specified in the second byte. A special 1-byte instruction to generate an interrupt of one particular type is also provided. Such an instruction would be required by a software debugger so that breakpoints can be "planted" on 1-byte instructions without overwriting, even temporarily, the next instruction. And finally, an interrupt return instruction is provided which pops and restores the saved flag settings in addition to performing the normal subroutine return function.

Single step. When the TF flag register is set, the processor generates an interrupt after the execution of each instruction. During interrupt transfer sequences caused by any type of interrupt, the TF flag is cleared after the push-flags step of the interrupt sequence. No instructions are provided for setting or clearing TF directly. Rather, the flag-register file image saved on the stack by a previous interrupt operation must be modified so that the subsequent interrupt return operation restores TF set. This allows a diagnostic task to single-step through a task under test while still executing normally itself.

External-processor synchronization. Instructions are included that permit the 8086 to utilize an external processor to perform any specialized operations (e.g., exponentiation) not implemented on the 8086. Consideration was given to the ability to perform the specialized operations either via the external processor or through software routines, without having to recompile the code.

The external processor would have the ability to monitor the 8086 bus and constantly be aware of the current instruction being executed. In particular, the external processor could detect the special instruction ESCAPE and then perform the necessary actions. In order for the external processor to know the 20-bit address of the operand for the instruction, the 8086 will react to the ESCAPE instruction by performing a read (but ignoring the result) from the operand address specified, thereby placing the address on the bus for the external processor to see. Before doing such a dummy read, the 8086 will have to wait for the external processor to be ready. The "test" pin on the 8086 processor is used to provide this synchronization. The 8086 instruction WAIT accomplishes the wait.

If the external processor is not available, the specialized operations could be performed by software subroutines. To invoke the subroutines, an interrupt-generating instruction would be executed. The subroutine needs to be passed the specific specialized-operation opcode and address of the operand. This

information would be contained in an in-line data byte (or bytes) following the interrupt-generating instruction.

The same number of bytes are required to issue a specialized operation instruction to the external processor or to invoke the software subroutines, as illustrated in Fig. 12. Thus the compiler could generate object code that could be used either way. The actual determination of which way the specialized operations were carried out could be made at load time and the object code modified by the loader accordingly.

Sharing resources with parallel processors. In multiple-processor systems with shared resources it is necessary to provide mechanisms to enforce controlled access to those resources. Such mechanisms, while generally provided through software operating systems, require hardware assistance. A sufficient mechanism for accomplishing this is a locked exchange (also known as test-and-set-lock).

The 8086 provides a special 1-byte prefix which may precede any instruction. This prefix causes the processor to assert its bus-lock signal for the duration of the operation caused by the instruction. It is assumed that external hardware, upon receipt of

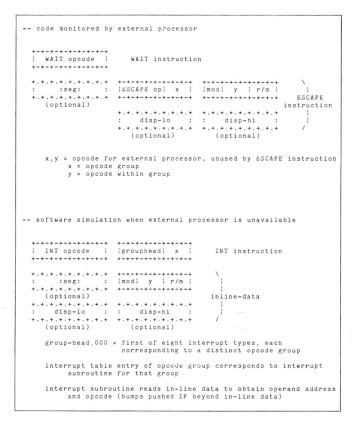

Fig. 12. Example of executing specialized instructions in 8086.

that signal, will prohibit bus access for other bus masters during the period of its assertion.

The instruction most useful in this context is an exchange register with memory. A simple software lock may be implemented with the following code sequences:

```
Check:
    MOV         AL,1        ;set AL to 1 (implies
                            ;locked)
    LOCK XCHG   Sema,AL     ;test and set lock
    TEST        AL,AL       ;set flags based on AL
    JNZ         Check       ;retry if lock already set
    .
    .                       ;critical region
    .
    MOV         Sema,0      ;clear the lock when done
```

IX. Summary and Conclusions

"The 8008 begat the 8080, and the 8080 begat the 8085, and the 8085 begat the 8086."

During the six years in which the 8008 evolved into the 8086, the processor underwent changes in many areas, as depicted by the conceptual diagram of Fig. 13. Figure 14 compares the functional block diagrams of the various processors. Comparisons in performance and technology are shown in Tables 5 and 6.

The era of the 8008 through the 8086 is architecturally notable for its role in exploiting technology and capabilities, thereby lowering computing costs by over three orders of magnitude. By removing a dominant hurdle that has inhibited the computer industry—the necessity to conserve expensive processors—the

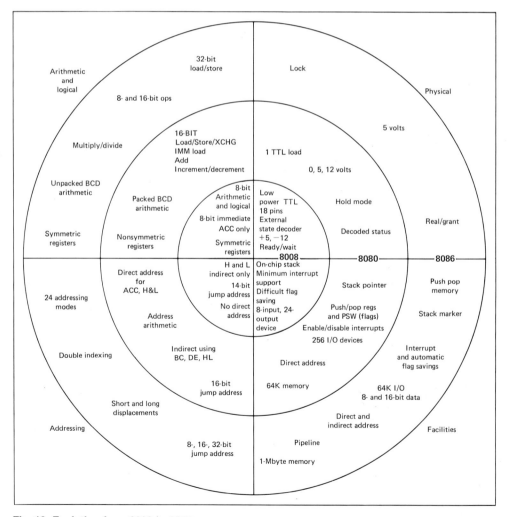

Fig. 13. Evolution from 8008 to 8086.

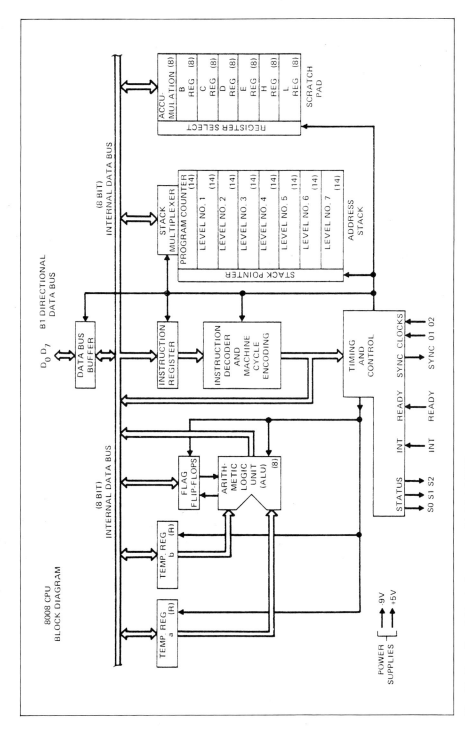

Fig. 14. Functional block diagrams of (a) Intel 8008.

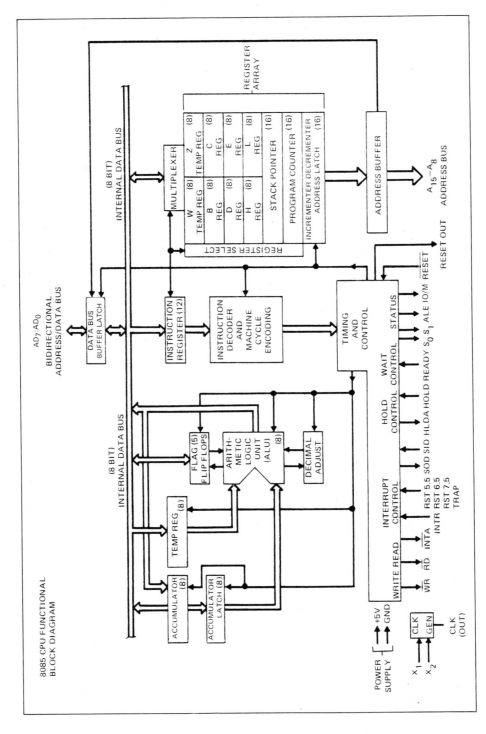

Fig. 14. (cont'd.) (b) Intel 8085.

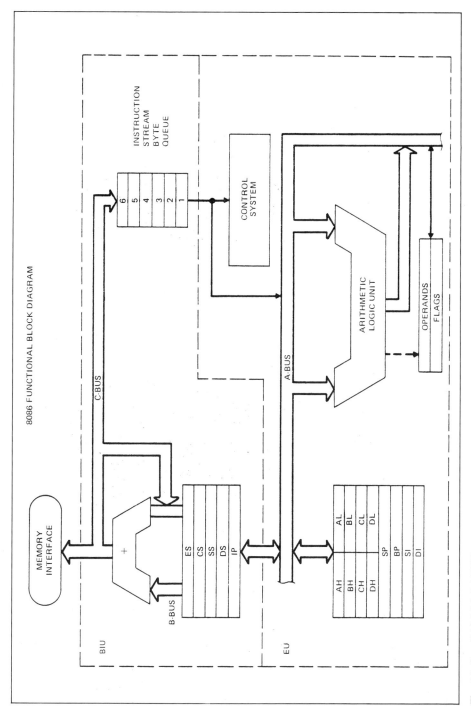

8086 FUNCTIONAL BLOCK DIAGRAM

Fig. 14. (cont'd.) (c) Intel 8086.

Table 5   Performance Comparison

	8008	8080 (2 MHz)	8086 (8 MHz)
register-register transfer	12.5	2	0.25
jump	25	5	0.875
register-immediate operation	20	3.5	0.5
subroutine call	28	9	2.5
increment (16-bit)	50	2.5	0.25
addition (16-bit)	75	5	0.375
transfer (16-bit)	25	2	0.25

All times are given in microseconds.

Table 6   Technology Comparison

	8008	8080	8085	8086
Silicon gate technology	P-channel enhancement load device	N-channel enhancement load device	N-channel depletion load device	Scaled N-channel (HMOS) depletion load device
Clock rate	0.5–0.8 MHz	2–3 MHz	3–5 MHz	5–8 MHz
Min gate delay† F0 = FI = 1	30 ns‡	15 ns‡	5 ns	3 ns
Typical speed-power product	100 pj	40 pj	10 pj	2 pj
Approximate number of transistors¶	2,000	4,500	6,500	20,000§
Average transistor density (mil² per transistor)	8.4	7.5	5.7	2.5

† Fastest inverter function available with worst-case processing.

‡ Linear-mode enhancement load.

§ This is 29,000 transistors if all ROM and PLA available placement sites are counted.

¶ Gate equivalent can be estimates by dividing by 3.

new era has permitted system designers to concentrate on solving the fundamental problems of the applications themselves.

X.   References

Bylinsky [1975]; Faggin et al. [1972]; Hoff [1972]; Intel 8080 Manual [1975]; Intel MCS-8 Manual [1975]; Intel MCS-40 Manual [1976]; Intel MCS-85 Manual [1977]; Intel MCS-86 Manual [1978]; Morse [1980]; Morse, Pohlman, and Ravenel [1978]; Shima, Faggin, and Mazor [1974]; Vadasz et al. [1969].

APPENDIX 1   SAVING AND RESTORING FLAGS IN THE 8008

Interrupt routines must leave all processor flags and registers unaltered so as not to contaminate the processing that was interrupted. This is most simply done by having the interrupt routine save all flags and registers on entry and restore them prior to exiting. The 8008, unlike its successors, has no instruction for directly saving or restoring flags. Thus 8008 interrupt routines that alter flags (practically every routine does) must conditionally test each flag to obtain its value and then save that value. Since there are no instructions for directly setting or clearing flags, the flag values must be restored by executing code that will put the flags in the saved state.

The 8008 flags can be restored very efficiently if they are saved in the following format in a byte in memory.

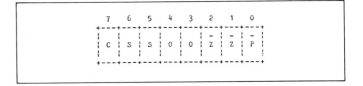

Most significant = bit 7 = original value of CARRY
bit 6 = original value of SIGN
bit 5 = original value of SIGN

bit 4 = 0
bit 3 = 0
bit 2 = complement of original value
of ZERO
bit 1 = complement of original value
of ZERO
bit 0 = complement of original value
of PARITY

With the information saved in the above format in a byte called FLAGS, the following two instructions will restore all the saved flag values:

```
LDA   FLAGS   :load saved flags into accumulator
ADD   A       :add the accumulator to itself
```

This instruction sequence loads the saved flags into the accumulator and then doubles the value, thereby moving each bit one position to the left. This causes each flag to be set to its original value, for the following reasons:

- The original value of the CARRY flag, being in the leftmost bit, will be moved out of the accumulator and wind up in the CARRY flag.

- The original value of the SIGN flag, being in bit 6, will wind up in bit 7 and will become the sign of the result. The new value of the SIGN flag will reflect this sign.

- The complement of the original value of the PARITY flag will wind up in bit 1, and it alone will determine the parity of the result (all other bits in the result are paired up and have no net effect on parity). The new setting of the PARITY flag will be the complement of this bit (the flag denotes even parity) and therefore will take on the original value of the PARITY flag.

- Whenever the ZERO flag is 1, the SIGN flag must be 0 (zero is a positive two's-complement number) and the PARITY flag must be 1 (zero has even parity). Thus an original ZERO flag value of 1 will cause all bits of FLAGS, with the possible exception of bit 7, to be 0. After the ADD instruction is executed, all bits of the result will be 0 and the new value of the ZERO flag will therefore be 1.

- An original ZERO flag value of 0 will cause two bits in FLAGS to be 1 and will wind up in the result as well. The new value of the ZERO flag will therefore be 0.

The above algorithm relies on the fact that flag values are always consistent, i.e., that the SIGN flag cannot be a 1 when the ZERO flag is a 1. This is always true in the 8008, since the flags come up in a consistent state whenever the processor is reset and flags can only be modified by instructions which always leave the flags in a consistent state. The 8080 and its derivatives allow the programmer to modify the flags in an arbitrary manner by popping a value of his choice off the stack and into the flags. Thus the above algorithm will not work on those processors.

A code sequence for saving the flags in the required format is as follows:

```
        MVI   A,0     ; move zero in accumulator
        JNC   L1      ; jump if CARRY not set
        ORA   80H     ; OR accumulator with 80 hex
                      ; (set bit 7)
L1:     JZ    L3      ; jump if ZERO set (and SIGN
                      ; not set and PARITY set)
        ORA   06H     ; OR accumulator with 06 hex
                      ; (set bits 1 and 2)
        JM    L2      ; jump if negative (SIGN set)
        ORA   60H     ; OR accumulator with 60 hex
                      ; (set bits 5 and 6)
L2:     JPE   L3      ; jump if parity even (PARITY
                      ; set)
        ORA   01H     ; OR accumulator with 01 hex
                      ; (set bit 0)
L3:     STA   FLAGS   ; store accumulator in FLAGS
```

APPENDIX 2   DECIMAL ARITHMETIC

A. Packed BCD

1. **Addition.** Numbers can be represented as a sequence of decimal digits by using a 4-bit binary encoding of the digits and packing these encodings two to a byte. Such a representation is called *packed BCD* (unpacked BCD would contain only one digit per byte). In order to preserve this decimal interpretation in performing binary addition on packed BCD numbers, the value 6 must be added to each digit of the sum whenever (1) the resulting digit is greater than 9 or (2) a carry occurs out of this digit as a result of the addition. This is because the 4-bit encoding contains six more combinations than there are decimal digits. Consider the following examples (numbers are written in hexadecimal instead of binary for convenience).

```
Example 1:   81+52
    d2 d1 d0      names of digit positions

        8  1      packed BCD augend
    +   5  2      packed BCD addend
    ──────────
        D  3
    +   6         adjustment because d1 > 9
    ──────────
    1   3  3      packed BCD sum
```

Example 2:   28+19

d2 d1 d0		names of digit positions
	2 8	packed BCD augend
+	1 9	packed BCD addend
	4 1	carry occurs out of d0
+	6	adjustment for carry
	4 7	packed BCD sum

In order to be able to make such adjustments, carries out of either digit position must be recorded during the addition operation. The 4004, 8080, 8085, and 8086 use the CARRY and AUXILIARY CARRY flag to record carries out of the leftmost and rightmost digits respectively. All of these processors provide an instruction for performing the adjustments. Furthermore, they all contain an add-with-carry instruction to facilitate the addition of numbers containing more than two digits.

2. Subtraction.   Subtraction of packed BCD numbers can be performed in a similar manner. However, none of the Intel processors prior to the 8086 provides an instruction for performing decimal adjustment following a subtraction (Zilog's Z-80, introduced two years before the 8086, also has such an instruction). On processors without the subtract adjustment instruction, subtraction of packed BCD numbers can be accomplished by generating the ten's complement of the subtrahend and adding.

3. Multiplication.   Multiplication of packed BCD numbers could also be adjusted to give the correct decimal result if the out-of-digit carries occurring during the multiplication were recorded. The result of multiplying two one-byte operands is two bytes long (four digits), and out-of-digit carries can occur on any of the three low-order digits, all of which would have to be recorded. Furthermore, the carries out of any digit are no longer restricted to unity, and so counters rather than flags would be required to record the carries. This is illustrated in the following example (numbers are written in hexadecimal instead of binary for convenience).

Example 3:   94 * 63

d3 d2 d1 d0		names of digit positions
	9 4	packed BCD multiplicand
*	6 3	packed BCD multiplier
	1 B C	carry occurs out of d1
	3 7 8	carry occurs out of d1, three out of d2
	3 9 3 C	carry occurs out of d1
+	6 6	adjustment for . . .
+	6 6	. . . above six . . .
+	6 6	. . . carries

	4 C 5 C	carry occurs out of d1 and out of d2
+	6 6	adjustment for above two carries
	5 2 B C	carry occurs out of d2
+	6	adjustment for above carry
	5 8 B C	
+	6	adjustment because d0 is greater than 9
	5 8 C 2	
+	6	adjustment because d1 is greater than 9
	5 9 2 2	packed BCD product

The preceding example illustrates two facts. First, packed BCD multiplication adjustments are possible if the necessary out-of-digit carry information is recorded by the multiply instruction. Second, the facilities needed in the processor to record this information and apply the correction are non-trivial.

Another approach to determining the out-of-digit carries is to analyze the multiplication process on a digit-by-digit basis as follows:

Let $x1$ and $x2$ be packed BCD digits in multiplicand.
Let $y1$ and $y2$ be packed BCD digits in multiplier.

Binary value of multiplicand $= 16 * x1 + x2$
Binary value of multiplier $= 16 * y1 + y2$

Binary value of product $= 256 * x1*y1 + 16 * (x1*y2 + x2*y1) + x2 * y2$
$= x1*y1$ in most significant byte, $x2*y2$ in least significant byte, $(x1*y2 + x2*y1)$ straddling both bytes

If there are no cross terms (i.e., either $x1$ or $y2$ is zero and either $x2$ or $y1$ is zero), the number of out-of-digit carries generated by the $x1 * y1$ term is simply the most significant digit in the most significant byte of the product; similarly the number of out-of-digit carries generated by the $x2 * y2$ term is simply the most significant digit in the least significant byte of the product. This is illustrated in the following example (numbers are written in hexadecimal instead of binary for convenience).

Example 4: 90 * 20

d3 d2 d1 d0		names of digit positions
	9 0	packed BCD multiplier
*	2 0	packed BCD multiplier
	0 0 0	
	1 2 0	
	1 2 0 0	

9 * 2   0 * 0

The most significant digit of the most significant byte is 1, indicating that there was one out-of-digit carry from the low-order digit when the 9*2 term was formed. Adjustment is to add 6 to that digit.

```
      1  2  0  0
  +      6
  ─────────────
      1  8  0  0     packed BCD product
```

Thus, in the absence of cross terms, the number of out-of-digit carries that occur during a multiplication can be determined by examining the binary product. The cross terms, when present, overshadow the out-of-digit carry information in the product, thereby making the use of some other mechanism to record the carries essential. None of the Intel processors incorporates such a mechanism. (Prior to the 8086, multiplication itself was not even supported.) Once it was decided not to support packed BCD multiplication in the processors, no attempt was made to even analyze packed BCD division.

B. Unpacked BCD

Unpacked BCD representation of numbers consists of storing the encoded digits in the low-order four bits of consecutive bytes. An ASCII string of digits is a special case of unpacked BCD with the high-order four bits of each byte containing 0110.

Arithmetic operations on numbers represented as unpacked BCD digit strings can be formulated in terms of more primitive BCD operations on single-digit (two digits for dividends and two digits for products) unpacked BCD numbers.

1. Addition and Subtraction. Primitive unpacked additions and subtractions follow the same adjustment procedures as packed additions and subtractions.

2. Multiplication. Primitive unpacked multiplication involves multiplying a one-digit (one-byte) unpacked multiplicand by a one-digit (one-byte) unpacked multiplier to yield a two-digit (two-byte) unpacked product. If the high-order four bits of the multiplicand and multiplier are zeros (instead of don't-cares), each will represent the same value interpreted as a binary number or as a BCD number. A binary multiplication will yield a two-byte product in which the high-order byte is zero. The low-order byte of this product will have the correct value when interpreted as a binary number and can be adjusted to a two-byte BCD number as follows:

High-order byte = (binary product)/10
Low-order byte = binary product modulo 10

This is illustrated in the following example (numbers are written in hexadecimal instead of binary for convenience).

Example 5: 7 * 5
```
  d1 d0          names of digit positions
  ─────
   0  7          unpacked BCD multiplicand
   0  5          unpacked BCD multiplier
  ─────
   2  3          binary product


   2  3          binary product
/  0  A          adjustment for high-order byte (/10)
  ─────
   0  3          unpacked BCD product (high-order byte)


           2  3          binary product
modulo     0  A          adjustment for low-order byte
                         (modulo 10)
          ─────
           0  5          unpacked BCD product (low-order byte)
```

3. Division. Primitive unpacked division involves dividing a two-digit (two-byte) unpacked dividend by a one-digit (one-byte) unpacked divisor to yield a one-digit (one-byte) unpacked quotient and a one-digit (one-byte) unpacked remainder. If the high-order four bits in each byte of the dividend are zeros (instead of don't-cares), the dividend can be adjusted to a one-byte binary number as follows:

Binary dividend = 10 * high-order byte + low-order byte

If the high-order four bits of the divisor are zero, the divisor will represent the same value interpreted as a binary number or as a BCD number. A binary division of the adjusted (binary) dividend and BCD divisor will yield a one-byte quotient and a one-byte remainder, each representing the same value interpreted as a binary number or as a BCD number. This is illustrated in the following example (numbers are written in hexadecimal instead of binary for convenience).

Example 6: 45/6
```
  d1 d0          names of digit positions
  ─────
   0  4          unpacked BCD dividend (high-order byte)
   0  5          unpacked BCD dividend (low-order byte)
  ─────
   2  D          adjusted dividend (4 * 10 + 5)
/  0  6          unpacked BCD divisor
  ─────
   0  7          unpacked BCD quotient
   0  3          unpacked BCD remainder
```

4. Adjustment Instructions. The 8086 processor provides four adjustment instructions for use in performing primitive unpacked BCD arithmetic—one for addition, one for subtraction, one for multiplication, and one for division.

The addition and subtraction adjustments are performed on a

binary sum or difference assumed to be left in the one-byte AL register. To facilitate multi-digit arithmetic, whenever AL is altered by the addition or subtraction adjustments, the adjustments will also do the following:

- set the CARRY flag (this facilitates multi-digit unpacked additions and subtractions)
- consider the one-byte AH register to contain the next most significant digit and increment or decrement it as appropriate (this permits the addition adjustment to be used in a multi-digit unpacked multiplication)

The multiplication adjustment assumes that AL contains a binary product and places the two-digit unpacked BCD equivalent in AH and AL. The division adjustment assumes that AH and AL contain a two-digit unpacked BCD dividend and places the binary equivalent in AH and AL.

The following algorithms show how the adjustment instructions can be used to perform multi-digit unpacked arithmetic.

Addition

    Let augend = a[N] a[N−1] . . . a[2] a[1]
    Let addend = b[N] b[N−1] . . . b[2] b[1]
    Let sum   = c[N] c[N−1] . . . c[2] c[1]

    0 → (CARRY)
    DO i = 1 to N
      (a[i]) → (AL)
      (AL) + (b[i]) → (AL)
        where + denotes add-with-carry
      add-adjust (AL) → (AX)
      (AL) → (c[i])

Subtraction

    Let minuend   = a[N] a[N−1] . . . a[2] a[1]
    Let subtrahend = b[N] b[N−1] . . . b[2] b[1]
    Let difference = c[N] c[N−1] . . . c[2] c[1]

    0 → (CARRY)
    DO i = 1 to N
      (a[i]) → (AL)
      (AL) − (b[i]) → (AL)
        where − denotes subtract-with-borrow
      subtract-adjust (AL) → (AX)
      (AL) → (c[i])

Multiplication

    Let multiplicand = a[N] a[N−1] . . . a[2] a[1]
    Let multiplier   = b
    Let product   = c[N+1] c[N] . . . c[2] c[1]

    (b) AND 0FH → (b)
    0 → (c[1])
    DO i = 1 to N
      (a[i]) AND 0FH → (AL)
      (AL) * (b) → (AX)
      multiply-adjust (AL) → (AX)
      (AL) + (c[i]) → (AL)
      add-adjust (AL) → (AX)
      (AL) → (c[i])
      (AH) → (c[i+1])

Division

    Let dividend = a[N] a[N−1] . . . a[2] a[1]
    Let divisor = b
    Let quotient = c[N] c[N−1] . . . c[2] c[1]

    (b) and 0HF → (b)
    0 → (AH)
    DO i = N to 1
      (a[i]) AND 0FH → (AL)
      divide-adjust (AX) → (AL)
      (AL)／(b) → (AL)
        with remainder going into (AH)
      (AL) → (c[i])

```
I8080:=
    begin

! ISP description of the Intel 8080 microprocessor architecture.

! The following description of the contents are provided to aid
! in reading the ISP.

!           **MP.State**: The primary memory.

!           **PC.State**: Processor registers, status word, and stack
!                    pointer description.

!           **External.State**: Interrupt variables and I/O addresses.

!           **Implementation.Variables**: Registers and temporaries
!                    required by the implementation, but that are
!                    not part of the architecture.

!           **Instruction.Format**: A description of the instruction
!                    register and its fields.

!           **Address.Calculation**: Routines used to access memory
!                    and registers.

!           **Service.Facilities**: Utility routines used to perform
!                    arithmetic, set condition codes, and execute
!                    conditional calls and returns.

!           **Instruction.Interpretation**: The main processor execution
!                    cycle.

!           **Instruction.Execution**: Main instruction decoding.

!           Instruction definitions for execution.


**MP.State**

    m[0:#177777]<7:0>                   ! Primary memory

**PC.State**

    PC<15:0>,                           ! Program counter
    dr[0:3]<15:0>,                      ! Double registers
        r[0:7]<7:0>:=dr[0:3]<15:0>,     ! Registers

! Rename the sequential registers to match INTEL mnemonics

    B<7:0>    := r[0]<7:0>,
    C<7:0>    := r[1]<7:0>,

    D<7:0>    := r[2]<7:0>,
    E<7:0>    := r[3]<7:0>,

    H<7:0>    := r[4]<7:0>,
    L<7:0>    := r[5]<7:0>,

    SP<15:0> := dr[3]<15:0>,            ! Stack pointer is a register pair

    psw<7:0>,                           ! Status word
        S<>    := psw<7>,               ! Sign bit (+  or  -)
        Z<>    := psw<6>,               ! Zero bit
        AC<>   := psw<4>,               ! Auxilliary carry bit
        P<>    := psw<2>,               ! Parity bit
        CY<>   := psw<0>,               ! Carry bit

    A<7:0>                              ! Accumulator

**External.State**

    inte<>,                             ! Interrupt enable bit
    int<>,                              ! Interrupt request bit
    input.device[0:255]<7:0>,
    output.device[0:255]<7:0>

**Implementation.Variables**

    t1<>,                               ! One bit temporary
    temp<8:0>,                          ! Arithmetic temporary
    tempd<16:0>,                        ! Double length arithmetic temporary
    go<>,                               ! Go bit
    dbuf<15:0>,                         ! Memory buffer and temporary register
    buf<7:0> := dbuf<7:0>               ! Lower order byte of double buffer

**Instruction.Format**

    IR<7:0>,                            ! Instruction register
        ebit<>        := IR<3>,
        group<1:0>    := IR<7:6>,       ! Instruction group
        dfield<2:0>   := IR<5:3>,       ! Destination field
        drfield<1:0>  := IR<5:4>,       ! Register pair designator
        sfield<2:0>   := IR<2:0>        ! Source field
```

```
**Address.Calculation**

    source.r(sss<2:0>) :=
        begin
        DECODE sss =>
            begin
            0:5 := buf = r[sss],
            6   := buf = m[H @ L],
            7   := buf = A
            end
        end,

    source.i1 :=
        begin
        buf = m[PC] next
        PC = PC + 1
        end,

    source.i2 :=
        begin
        dbuf = m[PC + 1] @ m[PC] next
        PC = PC + 2
        end,

    source.dr :=
        begin
        dbuf = dr[drfield]
        end,

    dest.r(ddd<2:0>) :=
        begin
        DECODE ddd =>
            begin
            0:5 := r[ddd] = buf,
            6   := m[H @ L] = buf,
            7   := A = buf
            end
        end,

    dest.dr :=
        begin
        dr[drfield] = dbuf
        end,

    dest.load :=
        begin
        DECODE drfield eql '10 =>
            begin
            0 := A = m[dbuf],
            1 := begin
                H = m[dbuf + 1];
                L = m[dbuf]
                end
            end
        end,

    dest.store :=
        begin
        DECODE drfield eql '10 =>
            begin
            0 := m[dbuf] = A,
            1 := begin
                m[dbuf + 1] = H;
                m[dbuf] = L
                end
            end
        end


**Service.Facilities**

! Routines to set condition code bits

    setcc(exp<7:0>, dest4<>) :=
        begin
        S = exp<7>;
        Z = exp<7:0> eql 0<7:0>;
        P = not exp<7> xor exp<6> xor exp<5> xor exp<4>
            xor exp<3> xor exp<2> xor exp<1> xor exp<0>;
        AC = exp<4> xor dest4
        end,

    arith(exp<9:0>, dest4<>)<7:0> :=
        begin
        CY = exp<8>;
        arith = exp<7:0> next
        setcc(arith, dest4)
        end,
```

```
! Routines used for conditional call, return, and jump instructions          1 := DECODE dfield @ sfield EQL #66<5:0> =>
                                                                                          begin
         cond.call(cbit<>) :=                                                               0 := MOV(),                   ! Move
             begin                                                                          1 := HLT()                    ! Halt
             DECODE cbit =>                                                               end,
                 begin
                 0 := PC = PC + 2,
                 1 := begin
                     source.i2() next                                          2 := begin                               ! General arithmetic operations
                     m[SP - 1] = PC<15:8>;                                               source.r(sfield) next
                     m[SP - 2] = PC<7:0> next                                            DECODE dfield =>
                     SP = SP - 2 next                                                       begin
                     PC = dbuf                                                                0 := ADD(),                 ! Add to A
                     end
                 end                                                                          1 := ADC(),                 ! Add to A with carry
             end,                                                                             2 := SUB(),                 ! Subtract from A
         cond.ret(cbit<>):=                                                                   3 := SBB(),                 ! Subtract from A with borrow
             begin                                                                            4 := ANA(),                 ! AND with A
             DECODE cbit =>                                                                   5 := XRA(),                 ! XOR with A
                 begin                                                                        6 := ORA(),                 ! OR with A
                 0 := no.op(),                                                                7 := CMP()                  ! Compare with A
                 1 := begin                                                                 end
                     PC = m[SP + 1] @ m[SP] next                                          end,
                     SP = SP + 2                                                 3 := begin
                     end                                                                   DECODE sfield =>
                 end                                                                        begin
             end,                                                                             0 := begin                  ! Conditional returns
         cond.jump(cbit<>):=                                                                      DECODE dfield =>
             begin                                                                                  begin
             DECODE cbit =>                                                                           0 := RNZ(),           ! Return on no zero
                 begin                                                                                1 := RZ(),            ! Return on zero
                 0 := PC = PC + 2,                                                                    2 := RNC(),           ! Return on no carry
                 1 := begin                                                                           3 := RC(),            ! Return on carry
                     source.i2() next                                                                 4 := RPO(),           ! Return on parity odd
                     PC = dbuf                                                                        5 := RPE(),           ! Return on parity even
                     end                                                                              6 := RP(),            ! Return on positive
                 end                                                                                  7 := RM()             ! Return on minus
             end                                                                                    end,
**Instruction.Interpretation**                                                               1 := begin
                                                                                                 DECODE ebit =>
start{main} :=                                                                                      begin
    begin                                                                                             0 := POP(),           ! Pop register pair
    go = 1 next
    run()                                                                                             1 := begin
    end                                                                                                   DECODE drfield =>
                                                                                                           begin
run\instruction.interpretation :=                                                                            0 := RET(),       ! Return
    begin                                                                                                    1 := no.op(),     ! Undefined instruction
    WAIT(go) next                                                                                             2 := PCHL(),      ! H & L to PC
    IR = m[PC] next                                                                                           3 := SPHL()       ! H & L to SP
    IF not(inte and int) => PC = PC + 1 next    ! Interrupt service                                         end
    exec() next                                                                                          end
    RESTART run                                                                                      end
    end                                                                                          end,
**Instruction.Execution**                                                                    2 := begin                     ! Conditional jumps
                                                                                                 DECODE dfield =>
    Exec:=                                                                                          begin
        begin                                                                                        0 := JNZ(),             ! Jump on no zero
        DECODE group =>                                                                              1 := JZ(),              ! Jump on zero
            begin                                                                                    2 := JNC(),             ! Jump on no carry
            0 := DECODE sfield =>                                                                    3 := JC(),              ! Jump on carry
                begin                                                                                4 := JPO(),             ! Jump on parity odd
                0 := no.op(),                                                                        5 := JPE(),             ! Jump on parity even
                                                                                                    6 := JP(),              ! Jump on positive
                1 := DECODE ebit =>                                                                  7 := JM()               ! Jump on minus
                    begin                                                                           end
                    0 := LXI(),      ! Load immediate register pair                               end,
                    1 := DAD()       ! Double add                                 3 := begin
                    end,                                                                          DECODE dfield =>
                                                                                                   begin
                2 := DECODE drfield<1> @ ebit =>                                                      0 := jmp(),             ! Jump unconditional
                    begin                                                                             1 := no.op(),
                    0 := STAX(),     ! Store A indirect                                               2 := OUT(),             ! Output
                    1 := LDAX(),     ! Load A indirect                                                3 := IN(),              ! Input
                    2 := SHLD.STA(), ! Store H & L direct                                             4 := XTHL(),            ! Exchange top of stack, H&L
                    3 := LHLD.LDA()  ! Load H & L direct                                              5 := XCHG(),            ! Exchange D&E, H&L
                    end,                                                                              6 := DI(),              ! Disable Interrupts
                                                                                                     7 := EI()               ! Enable Interrupts
                3 := DECODE ebit =>                                                                 end
                    begin                                                                         end,
                    0 := INX(),           ! Increment double registers           4 := begin                               ! Conditional calls
                    1 := DCX()            ! Decrement double registers                            DECODE dfield =>
                    end,                                                                            begin
                                                                                                     0 := CNZ(),             ! Call on no zero
                4 := INR(),               ! Increment                                                 1 := CZ(),              ! Call on zero
                5 := DCR(),               ! Decrement                                                 2 := CNC(),             ! Call on no carry
                6 := MVI(),               ! Move immediate                                            3 := CC(),              ! Call on carry
                                                                                                     4 := CPO(),             ! Call on parity odd
                7 := DECODE dfield =>                                                                 5 := CPE(),             ! Call on parity even
                    begin                                                                             6 := CP(),              ! Call on positive
                    0 := RLC(),      ! Rotate A left                                                  7 := CM()               ! Call on minus
                    1 := RRC(),      ! Rotate A right                                               end
                    2 := RAL(),      ! Rotate A left thru carry                                   end,
                    3 := RAR(),      ! Rotate A right thru carry
                    4 := DAA(),      ! Decimal adjust A
                    5 := CMA(),      ! Compliment A
                    6 := STC(),      ! Set carry
                    7 := CMC()       ! Compliment carry
                    end
                end,
```

```
              5 := begin                                        DCR :=                        ! Decrement register
                  DECODE ebit =>                                    begin
                      begin                                            source.r(dfield) next
                      0 := PUSH(),      ! Push double register on stack    t1 = buf<4> next
                                                                          buf = buf - 1 next
                      1 := begin                                          setcc(buf, t1) next
                          DECODE drfield =>                               dest.r(dfield)
                              begin                                   end,
                              0 := CALL(),    ! Call unconditional
                              1:3 := no.op()                    MVI :=                         ! Move immediate
                              end                                   begin
                          end                                         source.i1() next
                      end,                                            dest.r(dfield)
                                                                   end,
              6 := begin      ! Accumulator immediate instructions
                  source.i1() next                              RLC :=                         ! Rotate A left
                  DECODE dfield =>                                  begin
                      begin                                           CY = A<7> next
                      0 := ADI(),      ! Add immediate to A           A = A slr 1
                      1 := ACI(),      ! Add immediate with carry     end,
                      2 := SUI(),      ! Subtract immediate from A
                      3 := SBI(),      ! Subtract Immediate with borrow  RRC :=                  ! Rotate A right
                      4 := ANI(),      ! AND immediate with A          begin
                      5 := XRI(),      ! XOR immediate with A            CY = A<0> next
                      6 := ORI(),      ! OR immediate with A            A = A srr 1
                      7 := CPI()       ! Compare immediate with A       end,
                      end
                  end,                                          RAL :=                         ! Rotate A left thru carry
                                                                   begin
              7 := RST()      ! Restart                             temp = CY @ A slr 1 next
              end                                                   CY = temp<8>; A = temp<7:0>
          end                                                       end,
      end
  end,                                                          RAR :=                         ! Rotate A right thru carry
                                                                   begin
                                                                     temp = CY @ A srr 1 next
! Instruction execution definitions                                  CY = temp<8>; A = temp<7:0>
                                                                     end,
  LXI :=                      ! Load immediate
      begin                                                     DAA :=                         ! Decimal adjust accumulator
      source.i2() next                                             begin{us}
      dest.dr()                                                      IF (A<3:0> gtr 9) or AC => A = arith((A + 6), A<4>) next
      end,                                                           IF (A<7:4> gtr 9) or CY =>
                                                                       begin
  DAD :=                      ! Double add                              temp = A<7:4> + 6 next
      begin                                                             CY = temp<4>; A<7:4> = temp<3:0>
      source.dr() next                                                  end
      tempd = H @ L + dbuf next                                     end,
      CY = tempd<16>; H = tempd<15:8>; L = tempd<7:0>
      end,                                                      CMA := (A = not A),            ! Complement accumulator
                                                                STC := (CY = 1),               ! Set carry
  STAX :=                     ! Store A indirect                CMC := (CY = not CY),          ! Complement carry
      begin
      source.dr() next                                         MOV :=                         ! Move
      dest.store()                                                 begin
      end,                                                          source.r(sfield) next
                                                                    dest.r(dfield)
  LDAX :=                     ! Load A indirect                     end,
      begin
      source.dr() next                                         HLT := (go = 0),               ! Halt
      dest.load()                                              ADD := (A = arith((buf + A), A<4>)),           ! Add to A
      end,                                                     ADC := (A = arith((A + buf +{us}CY),A<4>)),    ! Add to A with carry
                                                                SUB := (A = arith((A - buf), A<4>)),           ! Subtract from A
  SHLD.STA :=                 ! Store H & L direct              SBB := (A = arith((A - buf -{us}CY),A<4>)),    ! Subtract from A with borrow
      begin                                                    ANA := (A = arith((buf and A), A<4>)),         ! AND with A
      source.i2() next                                         XRA := (A = arith((A xor buf), A<4>)),         ! XOR with A
      dest.store()                                             ORA := (A = arith((A or buf), A<4>)),          ! OR with A
      end,
                                                                CMP :=                         ! Compare
  LHLD.LDA :=                 ! Load H & L direct                  begin
      begin                                                         CY = 0 next
      source.i2() next                                              arith((A - buf), A<4>)
      dest.load()                                                   end,
      end,
                                                                RNZ := (cond.ret(not Z)),      ! Return on no zero
  INX :=                      ! Increment register pairs        RZ  := (cond.ret(Z)),          ! Return on zero
      begin                                                     RNC := (cond.ret(not CY)),     ! Return on no carry
      dr[drfield] = dr[drfield] + 1                             RC  := (cond.ret(CY)),         ! Return on carry
      end,                                                      RPO := (cond.ret(not P)),      ! Return on parity odd
                                                                RPE := (cond.ret(P)),          ! Return on parity even
  DCX :=                      ! Decrement register pairs        RP  := (cond.ret(not S)),      ! Return on positive
      begin                                                     RM  := (cond.ret(S)),          ! Return on minus
      dr[drfield] = dr[drfield] - 1
      end,                                                      POP :=                         ! Pop register pair
                                                                   begin
  INR :=                      ! Increment register                 dbuf = m[SP + 1] @ m[SP] next
      begin                                                         SP = SP + 2 NEXT
      source.r(dfield) next                                         DECODE drfield eql '11 =>
      t1 = buf<4> next                                                 begin
      buf = buf + 1 next                                               0 := dest.dr(),
      setcc(buf, t1) next                                             1 := begin
      dest.r(dfield)                                                      A = dbuf<15:8>;
      end,                                                                psw = dbuf<7:0>
                                                                          end
                                                                      end
                                                                   end,
```

APPENDIX 3 *(cont'd.)*

```
RET  := (cond.ret(1)),                    ! Return (unconditional)
PCHL := (PC = H @ L),                     ! H & L to PC
SPHL := (SP = H @ L),                     ! H & L to SP

JNZ := (cond.jump(not Z)),       ! Jump on not zero
JZ  := (cond.jump(Z)),           ! Jump on zero
JNC := (cond.jump(not CY)),      ! Jump on no carry
JC  := (cond.jump(CY)),          ! Jump on carry
JPO := (cond.jump(not P)),       ! Jump on parity odd
JPE := (cond.jump(P)),           ! Jump on parity even
JP  := (cond.jump(not S)),       ! Jump on positive
JM  := (cond.jump(S)),           ! Jump on minus

JMP :=                           ! Jump (unconditional)
    begin
    source.i2() next
    PC = dbuf
    end,

OUT :=                           ! Output (I/O)
    begin
    source.i1() next
    output.device[buf] = A
    end,

IN  :=                           ! Input (I/O)
    begin
    source.i1() next
    A = input.device[buf]
    end,

XTHL :=                          ! Exchange top of stack, H & L
    begin
    tempd = m[SP] @ L   next
    L = tempd<15:8>;
    m[SP] = tempd<7:0> next
    tempd = m[SP + 1] @ H next
    H = tempd<15:8>;
    m[SP + 1] = tempd<7:0>
    end,

XCHG :=                          ! Exchange D@E with H@L
    begin
    temp = H next
    H = D next
    D = temp<7:0> next
    temp = L next
    L = e next
    e = temp<7:0>
    end,

DI  := (inte = 0),                        ! Disable interrupts
EI  := (inte = 1),                        ! Enable interrupts
CNZ := (cond.call(not Z)),                ! Call on no zero
CZ  := (cond.call(Z)),                    ! Call on zero
CNC := (cond.call(not CY)),               ! Call on no carry
CC  := (cond.call(CY)),                   ! Call on carry
CPO := (cond.call(not P)),                ! Call on parity odd
CPE := (cond.call(P)),                    ! Call on parity even
CP  := (cond.call(not S)),                ! Call on positive
CM  := (cond.call(S)),                    ! Call on minus

PUSH :=                                   ! Push double register on stack
    begin
    DECODE drfield eql '11 =>
        begin
        source.dr(),
        dbuf = A @ psw
        end next
    m[SP - 1] = dbuf<15:8>;
    m[SP - 2] = dbuf<7:0> next
    SP = SP - 2
    end,

CALL := (cond.call(1)),                   ! Call (unconditional)
ADI := (A = arith((A + buf), A<4>)),      ! Add immediate to A
ACI := (A = arith((A + buf +(us)CY),A<4>)), ! Add immediate to A with carry
SUI := (A = arith((A - buf), A<4>)),      ! Subtract immediate from A
SBI := (A = arith((A - buf -(us)CY),A<4>)), ! Subtract immediate from A
                                          ! with borrow
ANI := (A = arith((A and buf), A<4>)),    ! AND immediate with A
XRI := (A = arith((A xor buf), A<4>)),    ! XOR immediate with A
ORI := (A = arith((A or buf), A<4>)),     ! OR immediate with A
CPI := (arith((A - buf), A<4>)),          ! Compare immediate with A

RST :=                           ! Restart
    begin
    m[SP - 1] = PC<15:8>;
    m[SP - 2] = PC<7:0> next
    SP = SP - 2   NEXT
    PC = dfield sl0 3
    end,

end        ! end of Intel 8080 description
```

Section 3

Minicomputers

A major attribute of computers below the class of maxi is their use in dedicated applications areas. The minicomputer evolved from a conceptual view of design wherein a programmable controller was perceived to be the cheapest, fastest way to implement a special-purpose function. The minicomputer did not require the generality of larger computers and hence required less software and less overhead. Thus minicomputers were leaner and more responsive than their cousins.

The need for minicomputers evolved from several areas, including control, switching, and data processing. IBM's first minicomputer was the 1401 (c. 1962). As initially conceived, the 1401 was a stored-program replacement for the former hardwired controllers used to interconnect card readers, magnetic tape units, and line printers in an offline batch support system.

The CDC 160, introduced in 1960 at a price of $60,000, was the first high-performance, low-cost, real time computer. Like the 1401 it was designed as a support computer to a larger machine and as a computer to test peripherals. Although it was not intended to be sold as a programmable computer, it was subsequently applied to scientific and commercial computations.

The DEC PDP-5 was introduced in 1964 for real time data collection and control. The PDP-5 had a single 12-bit accumulator, a 1-bit link for overflow and multiple-precision arithmetic, and a 1-bit interrupt enable. The program counter was held in primary memory, and an analog-to-digital converter was built directly into the accumulator.

The immediate successor of the PDP-5, the PDP-8, can be credited with triggering the minicomputer revolution. Its small size (half a cabinet) and cost ($18,000) brought the computer into the region where it was cost-effective in dedicated real time applications, especially since it could be packaged as part of a larger system. By 1980 over 100,000 PDP-8's had been sold since their introduction in 1966.

From these origins, where the minicomputer was considered to be the minimal-complexity computer, the minicomputer has grown in functionality and performance to the point where it rivals the higher-cost, general-purpose computers of a decade ago. This section describes four minicomputers: the PDP-8, the PDP-11, the HP 2116, and the IBM System/38.

The PDP-8

The 12-bit PDP-8 is described in a top-down fashion in Chap. 8. The description is carried from the PMS and ISP levels to register-transfer, gate, and circuit levels, illustrating the hierarchy of design. Since the PDP-8 is conceptually simple, it is possible to provide substantial details of the design in terms of the mid-1960s discrete technology used to implement the original PDP-8. A Kiviat graph for the original PDP-8 is shown in Fig. 1.

Chapter 15 illustrates how the PDP-8 might be implemented by using contemporary bit-sliced microprogrammed chip sets. The design illustrates the use of ISP to describe the hardware building blocks (the Am2901 and 2909) and microcode to emulate other ISPs. PDP-8 programs have been successfully executed by using the ISP simulator on this bit-sliced PDP-8. After Chap. 15, machines are discussed only at the register-transfer level or above. However, the reader should have enough working knowledge about technology at this point to use Am2900 chips and/or ISP in design exercises completing the details in lower-level descriptions of other machines in this book. We encourage the reader to try at least a paper exercise of some other machine.

Finally, Chap. 46 summarizes the evolution of the PDP-8 family of implementations over a decade of technological change ranging from discrete logic to microcomputer implementations.

The PDP-11

The need was felt to increase the functionality of minimal computers, especially by providing a larger address space. This, coupled with a change from 6-bit (e.g., two characters per PDP-8

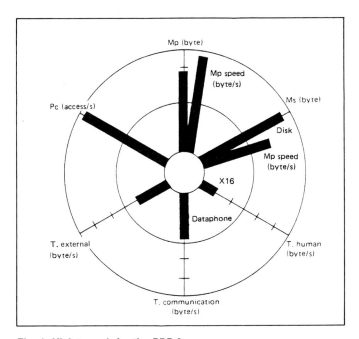

Fig. 1. Kiviat graph for the PDP-8.

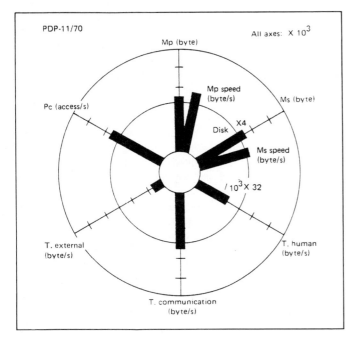

Fig. 2. Kiviat graph for the PDP-11/70.

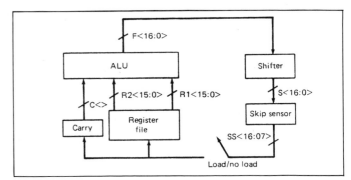

Fig. 3. Data path of the Data General Nova.

12-bit word) to 8-bit character representations lead to a large number of 16-bit machines. The PDP-11, one of the most popular 16-bit minicomputers, is discussed in Chap. 38, which is complete with ISP and PMS descriptions. The performance of one PDP-11 family member, the Model 70, is summarized by the Kiviat graph in Fig. 2. Chapter 39 reviews the major implementation tradeoffs, while Chap. 47 outlines the evolution of the PDP-11 family. A maxicomputer, the VAX-11/780, with strong PDP-11 family ties and PDP-11 compatability, is described in Chap. 42.

A contemporary of the PDP-11 is the data General Nova. Wheras the PDP-11 sought to increase the semantic content of instructions, the Nova designers sought an ISP whose implementations would be simple, provide high performance, and be oriented toward MSI technology. The generic Nova implementation consists of a single fast loop from register file to ALU, to shifter, to condition code sensing, and back to the register file (see Fig. 3). Each instruction can cause one of each type of function to execute on a single cycle throughout the loop. Thus machine-level instructions are microcoded à la the PDP-8 operate group of instructions. The similarity with the PDP-8 is not surprising, since the Nova designers were veteran PDP-8 implementors and users. In order to pay for this rich, easily decoded class of register-to-register instructions, the Nova has a meager (e.g., four-

instruction) memory/register class of instructions. Being simple, the Nova ISP consistently was cheaper and faster on individual instructions than its PDP-11 rival. The Nova ISP was implemented in a single LSI chip in 1976, a feat not yet matched by the PDP-11 as of 1979.

The Nova ISP philosophy represents an interesting tradeoff between ISP power and speed. One way to increase system performance is to increase the semantic content of the ISP so that fewer instructions have to be executed to complete a task. Another way to increase performance is to execute a lot of very simple instructions very fast. In the latter case, an optimizing compiler can provide a higher-level abstract machine so that the user never has to bother with assembly language. One cannot tell from the marketplace which approach is best, since the PDP-11 and the Nova have become the second and third minicomputer ISP, respectively, to surpass 50,000 units sold.

The HP 2116

A contemporary of the PDP-11 resembling a 16-bit stretch of the PDP-8 is the HP 2116. The HP 2116 was also influenced by a PDP-8 alumnus, John Kondek. An instruction set similar to that of the HP 2116 is contained in Chap. 31, where a cousin of the HP 2116 was used to implement a desk-top computer. Another variation of the ISP is found in Chap. 49. Strong family ties with the HP 2116 ISP can be found in the more recent HP 2100 ISP.

The IBM System/38

Chapter 32 describes a business-oriented minicomputer that provides an architectural interface above the traditional ISP level.

Chapter 38

A New Architecture for Mini-Computers: The DEC PDP-11[1]

G. Bell / R. Cady / H. McFarland / B. DeLagi /
J. O'Laughlin / R. Noonan / W. Wulf

Introduction

The mini-computer[2] has a wide variety of uses: communications controller; instrument controller; large-system pre-processor; real-time data acquisition systems . . . ; desk calculator. Historically, Digital Equipment Corporation's PDP-8 Family, with 6,000 installations has been the archetype of these mini-computers.

In some applications current mini-computers have limitations. These limitations show up when the scope of their initial task is increased (e.g., using a higher level language, or processing more variables). Increasing the scope of the task generally requires the use of more comprehensive executives and system control programs, hence larger memories and more processing. This larger system tends to be at the limit of current mini-computer capability, thus the user receives diminishing returns with respect to memory, speed efficiency and program development time. This limitation is not surprising since the basic architectural concepts for current mini-computers were formed in the early 1960's. First, the design was constrained by cost, resulting in rather simple processor logic and register configurations. Second, application experience was not available. For example, the early constraints often created computing designs with what we now consider weaknesses:

1. Limited addressing capability, particularly of larger core sizes

2. Few registers, general registers, accumulators, index registers, base registers

3. No hardware stack facilities

4. Limited priority interrupt structures, and thus slow context switching among multiple programs (tasks)

5. No byte string handling

6. No read only memory facilities

7. Very elementary I/O processing

8. No larger model computer, once a user outgrows a particular model

9. High programming costs because users program in machine language.

In developing a new computer the architecture should at least solve the above problems. Fortunately, in the late 1960's integrated circuit semiconductor technology became available so that newer computers could be designed which solve these problems at low cost. Also, by 1970 application experience was available to influence the design. The new architecture should thus lower programming cost while maintaining the low hardware cost of mini-computers.

The DEC PDP-11, Model 20 is the first computer of a computer family designed to span a range of functions and performance. The Model 20 is specifically discussed, although design guidelines are presented for other members of the family. The Model 20 would nominally be classified as a third generation (integrated circuits), 16-bit word, 1 central processor with eight 16-bit general registers, using two's complement arithmetic and addressing up to 2^{16} eight bit bytes of primary memory (core). Though classified as a general register processor, the operand accessing mechanism allows it to perform equally well as a 0-(stack), 1-(general register) and 2-(memory-to-memory) address computer. The computer's components (processor, memories, controls, terminals) are connected via a single switch, called the Unibus.

[1]*AFIPS Proc. SJCC*, 1970, pp. 657–675.
[2]The PDP-11 design is predicated on being a member of one (or more) of the micro, midi, mini, . . . , maxi (computer name) markets. We will define these names as belonging to computers of the third generation (integrated circuit to medium scale integrated circuit technology), having a core memory with cycle time of .5 ~ 2 microseconds, a clock rate of 5 ~ 10 M *hz* . . . , a single processor with interrupts and usually applied to doing a particular task (e.g., controlling a memory or communications lines, pre-processing for a larger system, process control). The specialized names are defined as follows:

	Maximum addressable primary memory (words)	Processor and memory cost (1970 kilodollars)	Word length (bits)	Processor state (words)	Data types
Micro	8 K	~ 5	8 ~ 12	2	Integers, words, boolean vectors
Mini	32 K	5 ~ 10	12 ~ 16	2–4	Vectors (i.e., indexing)
Midi	65 ~ 128 K	10 ~ 20	16 ~ 24	4–16	Double length floating point (occasionally)

The machine is described using the PMS and ISP notation of Bell and Newell [1971] at different levels. The following descriptive sections correspond to the levels: external design constraints level; the PMS level—the way components are interconnected and allow information to flow; the program level or ISP (Instruction Set Processor)—the abstract machine which interprets programs; and finally, the logical design level. (We omit a discussion of the circuit level—the PDP-11 being constructed from TTL integrated circuits.)

Design Constraints

The principal design objective is yet to be tested; namely, do users like the machine? This will be tested both in the market place and by the features that are emulated in newer machines; it will indirectly be tested by the life span of the PDP-11 and any offspring.

Word Length

The most critical constraint, word length (defined by IBM) was chosen to be a multiple of 8 bits. The memory word length for the Model 20 is 16 bits, although there are 32- and 48-bit instructions and 8- and 16-bit data. Other members of the family might have up to 80 bit instructions with 8-, 16-, 32- and 48-bit data. The internal, and preferred external character set was chosen to be 8-bit ASCII.

Range and Performance

Performance and function range (extendability) were the main design constraints; in fact, they were the main reasons to build a new computer. DEC already has (4) computer families that span a range[1] but are incompatible. In addition to the range, the initial machine was constrained to fall within the small-computer product line, which means to have about the same performance as a PDP-8. The initial machine outperforms the PDP-5, LINC, and PDP-4 based families. Performance, of course, is both a function of the instruction set and the technology. Here, we're fundamentally only concerned with the instruction set performance because faster hardware will always increase performance for any family. Unlike the earlier DEC families, the PDP-11 had to be designed so that new models with significantly more performance can be added to the family.

A rather obvious goal is maximum performance for a given model. Designs were programmed using benchmarks, and the results compared with both DEC and potentially competitive machines. Although the selling price was constrained to lie in the $5,000 to $10,000 range, it was realized that the decreasing cost of logic would allow a more complex organization than earlier DEC computers. A design which could take advantage of medium- and eventually large-scale integration was an important consideration. First, it could make the computer perform well; and second, it would extend the computer family's life. For these reasons, a general registers organization was chosen.

Interrupt Response.   Since the PDP-11 will be used for real time control applications, it is important that devices can communicate with one another quickly (i.e., the response time of a request should be short). A multiple priority level, nested interrupt mechanism was selected; additional priority levels are provided by the physical position of a device on the Unibus. Software polling is unnecessary because each device interrupt corresponds to a unique address.

Software

The total system including software is of course the main objective of the design. Two techniques were used to aid programmability: first benchmarks gave a continuous indication as to how well the machine interpreted programs; second, systems programmers continually evaluated the design. Their evaluation considered: what code the compiler would produce; how would the loader work; ease of program relocability; the use of a debugging program; how the compiler, assembler and editor would be coded—in effect, other benchmarks; how real time monitors would be written to use the various facilities and present a clean interface to the users; finally the ease of coding a program.

Modularity

Structural flexibility (sometimes called modularity) for a particular model was desired. A flexible and straightforward method for interconnecting components had to be used because of varying user needs (among user classes and over time). Users should have the ability to configure an optimum system based on cost, performance and reliability, both by interconnection and, when necessary, constructing new components. Since users build special hardware, a computer should be easily interfaced. As a by-product of modularity, computer components can be produced and stocked, rather than tailor-made on order. The physical structure is almost identical to the PMS structure discussed in the following section; thus, reasonably large building blocks are available to the user.

Microprogramming

A note on microprogramming is in order because of current interest in the "firmware" concept. We believe microprogramming, as we understand it [Wilkes, 1951], can be a worthwhile

---

[1]PDP-4, 7, 9, 15 family; PDP-5, 8, 8/S, 8/I, 8/L family; LINC, PDP-8/LINC, PDP-12 family; and PDP-6, 10 family. The initial PDP-1 did not achieve family status.

technique as it applies to processor design. For example, micro-programming can probably be used in larger computers when floating point data operators are needed. The IBM System/360 has made use of the technique for defining processors that interpret both the System/360 instruction set and earlier family instruction sets (e.g., 1401, 1620, 7090). In the PDP-11 the basic instruction set is quite straightforward and does not necessitate micro-programmed interpretation. The processor-memory connection is asynchronous and therefore memory of any speed can be connected. The instruction set encourages the user to write reentrant programs; thus, read-only memory can be used as part of primary memory to gain the permanency and performance normally attributed to microprogramming. In fact, the Model 10 computer which will not be further discussed has a 1024-word read only memory, and a 128-word read-write memory.

Understandability

Understandability was perhaps the most fundamental constraint (or goal) although it is now somewhat less important to have a machine that can be quickly understood by a novice computer user than it was a few years ago. DEC's early success has been predicated on selling to an intelligent but inexperienced user. Understandability, though hard to measure, is an important goal because all (potential) users must understand the computer. A straightforward design should simplify the systems programming task; in the case of a compiler, it should make translation (particularly code generation) easier.

PDP-11 Structure at the PMS Level[1]

Introduction

PDP-11 has the same organizational structure as nearly all present day computers (Fig. 1). The primitive PMS components are: the primary memory (Mp) which holds the programs while the central processor (Pc) interprets them; io controls (Kio) which manage data transfers between terminals (T) or secondary memories (Ms) to primary memory (Mp); the components outside the computer at periphery (X) either humans (H) or some external process (e.g., another computer); the processor console (T. console) by which humans communicate with the computer and observe its behavior and affect changes in its state; and a switch (S) with its control (K) which allows all the other components to communicate with one another. In the case of PDP-11, the central logical switch structure is implemented using a bus or chained switch (S) called the Unibus, as shown in Fig. 2. Each physical component has a

[1]A descriptive (block-diagram) level [Bell and Newell, 1971] to describe the relationship of the computer components: processors memories, switches, controls, links, terminals and data operators.

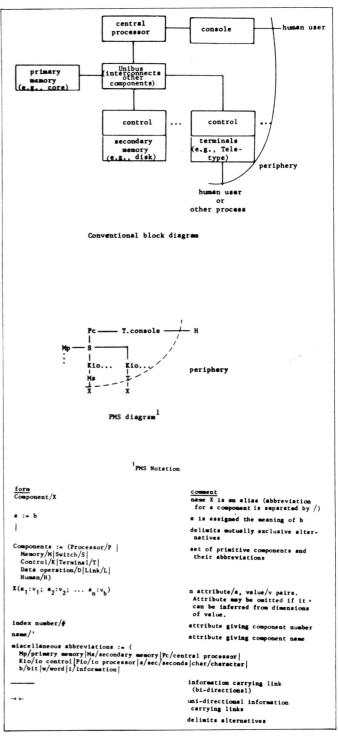

Fig. 1. Conventional block diagram and PMS diagram of PDP-11.

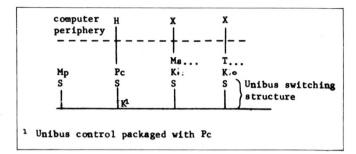

Fig. 2. PDP-11 physical structure PMS diagram.

switch for placing messages on the bus or taking messages off the bus. The central control decides the next component to use the bus for a message (call). The S (Unibus) differs from most switches because any component can communicate with any other component.

The types of messages in the PDP-11 are along the lines of the hierarchical structure common to present day computers. The single bus makes conventional and other structures possible. The message processes in the structure which utilize S (Unibus) are:

1 The central processor (Pc) requests that data be read or written from or to primary memory (Mp) for instructions and data. The processor calls a particular memory module by concurrently specifying the module's address, and the address within the modules. Depending on whether the processor requests reading or writing, data is transmitted either from the memory to the processor or vice versa.

2 The central processor (Pc) controls the initialization of secondary memory (Ms) and terminal (T) activity. The processor sets status bits in the control associated with a particular Ms or T, and the device proceeds with the specified action (e.g., reading a card, or punching a character into paper tape). Since some devices transfer data vectors directly to primary memory, the vector control information (i.e., the memory location and length) is given as initialization information.

3 Controls request the processor's attention in the form of interrupts. An interrupt request to the processor has the effect of changing the state of the processor; thus the processor begins executing a program associated with the interrupting process. Note, the interrupt process is only a signaling method, and when the processor interruption occurs, the interruptee specifies a unique address value to the processor. The address is a starting address for a program.

4 The central processor can control the transmission of data between a control (for T or Ms) and either the processor or a primary memory for program controlled data transfers.

The device signals for attention using the interrupt dialogue and the central processor responds by managing the data transmission in a fashion similar to transmitting initialization information.

5 Some device controls (for T or Ms) transfer data directly to/from primary memory without central processor intervention. In this mode the device behaves similar to a processor; a memory address is specified, and the data is transmitted between the device and primary memory.

6 The transfer of data between two controls, e.g., a secondary memory (disk) and say a terminal/T.display is not precluded, provided the two use compatible message formats.

As we show more detail in the structure there are, of course, more messages (and more simultaneous activity). The above does not describe the shared control and its associated switching which is typical of a magnetic tape and magnetic disk secondary memory systems. A control for a DECtape memory (Fig. 3) has an S(' DECtape bus) for transmitting data between a single tape unit and the DECtape transport. The existence of this kind of structure is based on the relatively high cost of the control relative to the cost of the tape and the value of being able to run concurrently with other tapes. There is also a dialogue at the periphery between X-T and X-Ms which does not use the Unibus. (For example, the removal of a magnetic tape reel from a tape unit or a human user (H) striking a typewriter key are typical dialogues.)

All of these dialogues lead to the hierarchy of present computers (Fig. 4). In this hierarchy we can see the paths by which the above messages are passed (Pc-Mp; Pc-K; K-Pc; Kio-T and Kio-Ms; and Kio-Mp; and, at the periphery, T-X and T-Ms; and T.console-H).

Model 20 Implementation

Figure 5 shows the detailed structure of a uni-processor, Model 20 PDP-11 with its various components (options). In Fig. 5 the Unibus characteristics are suppressed. (The detailed properties of the switch are described in the logical design section.)

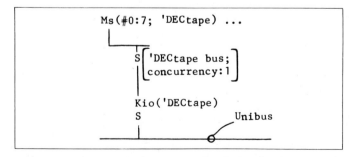

Fig. 3. DECtape control switching PMS diagram.

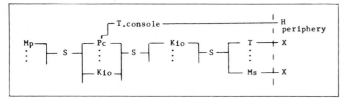

Fig. 4. Conventional hierarchy computer structure.

Extensions to Increase Performance

The reader should note (Fig. 5) that the important limitations of the bus are: a concurrency of one, namely, only one dialogue can occur at a given time, and a maximum transfer rate of one 16-bit word per .75 μsec., giving a transfer rate of 21.3 megabits/second. While the bus is not a limit for a uni-processor structure, it is a limit for multiprocessor structures. The bus also imposes an artificial limit on the system performance when high speed devices (e.g., TV cameras, disks) are transferring data to multiple primary memories. On a larger system with multiple independent memories the supply of memory cycles is 17 megabits/second times the number of modules. Since there is such a large supply of memory cycles/second and since the central processor can only

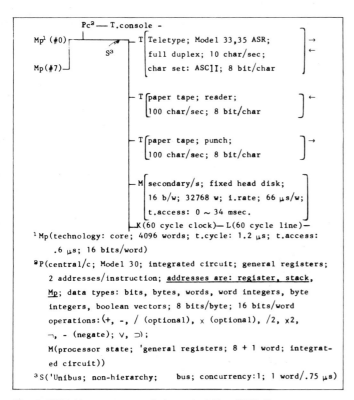

¹Mp(technology: core; 4096 words; t.cycle: 1.2 μs; t.access:
  .6 μs; 16 bits/word)
²P(central/c; Model 30; integrated circuit; general registers;
  2 addresses/instruction; <u>addresses are: register, stack</u>,
  <u>Mp</u>; data types: bits, bytes, words, word integers, byte
  integers, boolean vectors; 8 bits/byte; 16 bits/word
  operations:(+, -, / (optional), x (optional), /2, x2,
  ¬, - (negate); ∨, ⊃);
  M(processor state; 'general registers; 8 + 1 word; integrated circuit))
³S('Unibus; non-hierarchy;   bus; concurrency:1; 1 word/.75 μs)

Fig. 5. PDP-11 structure and characteristics PMS diagram.

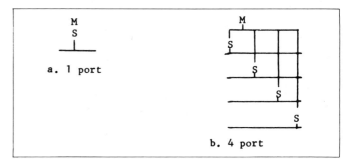

Fig. 6. 1 and 4 port memory modules PMS diagram.

absorb approximately 16 megabits/second, the simple one Unibus structure must be modified to make the memory cycles available. Two changes are necessary: first, each of the memory modules have to be changed so that multiple units can access each module on an independent basis; and second, there must be independent control accessing mechanisms. Figure 6 shows how a single memory is modified to have more access ports (i.e., connect to 4 Unibusses).

Figure 7 shows a system with 3 independent memory modules which are accessed by 2 independent Unibusses. Note that two of the secondary memories and one of the transducers are connected to both Unibusses. It should be noted that devices which can potentially interfere with Pc-Mp accesses are constructed with two ports; for simple systems, the two ports are both connected to the same bus, but for systems with more busses, the second connection is to an independent bus.

Figure 8 shows a multiprocessor system with two central processors and three Unibusses. Two of the Unibus controls are included within the two processors, and the third bus is controlled by an independent control unit. The structure also has a second switch to allow either of two processors (Unibusses) to access common shared devices. The interrupt mechanism allows either processor to respond to an interrupt and similarly either processor may issue initialization information on an anonymous basis. A

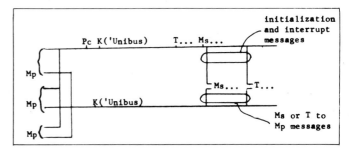

Fig. 7. Three Mp, 2 S('Unibus) structure PMS diagram.

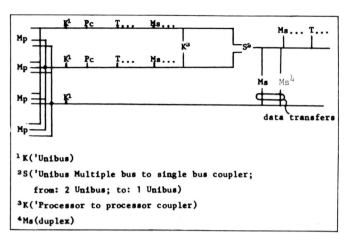

¹K('Unibus)

²S('Unibus Multiple bus to single bus coupler;
    from: 2 Unibus; to: 1 Unibus)

³K('Processor to processor coupler)

⁴Ms(duplex)

Fig. 8. Dual Pc multiprocessor system PMS diagram.

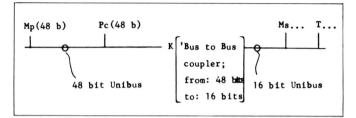

Fig. 9. Computer with 48 bit Pc, Mp with 16 bit Ms, T PMS diagram.

providing multiple busses and defining wider path busses. Finally, and most important, the Unibus is straightforward.

The Instruction Set Processor (ISP) Level-Architecture[1]

Introduction, Background and Design Constraints

The Instruction Set Processor (ISP) is the machine defined by hardware and/or software which interprets programs. As such, an ISP is independent of technology and specific implementations.

The instruction set is one of the least understood aspects of computer design; currently it is an art. There is currently no theory of instruction sets, although there have been attempts to construct them [Maurer, 1966], and there has also been an attempt to have a computer program design an instruction set [Haney, 1968]. We have used the conventional approach in this design: first a basic ISP was adopted and then incremental design modifications were made (based on the results of the benchmarks).[2]

Although the approach to the design was conventional, the

control unit is needed so that two processors can communicate with one another; shared primary memory is normally used to carry the body of the message. A control connected to two Pc's (see Fig. 8) can be used for reliability; either processor or Unibus could fail, and the shared Ms would still be accessible.

Higher Performance Processors

Increasing the bus width has the greatest effect on performance. A single bus limits data transmission to 21.3 megabits/second, and though Model 20 memories are 16 megabits/second, faster (or wider) data path width modules will be limited by the bus. The Model 20 is not restricted, but for higher performance processors operating on double word (fixed point) or triple word (floating point) data two or three accesses are required for a single data type. The direct method to improve the performance is to double or triple the primary memory and central processor data path widths. Thus, the bus data rate is automatically doubled or tripled.

For 32- or 48-bit memories a coupling control unit is needed so that devices of either width appear isomorphic to one another. The coupler maps a data request of a given width into a higher- or lower-width request for the bus being coupled to, as shown in Fig. 9. (The bus is limited to a fixed number of devices for electrical reasons; thus, to extend the bus a bus repeating unit is needed. The bus repeating control unit is almost identical to the bus coupler.) A computer with a 48-bit primary memory and processor and 16-bit secondary memory and terminals (transducers) is shown in Fig. 9.

In summary, the design goal was to have a modular structure providing the final user with freedom and flexibility to match his needs. A secondary goal of the Unibus is open-endedness by

[1]The word architecture has been operationally defined [Amdahl, Blaauw, and Brooks, 1964] as "the attributes of a system as seen by a programmer, i.e., the conceptual structure and functional behavior, as distinct from the organization of the data flow and controls, the logical design and the physical implementation."

[2]A predecessor multiregister computer was proposed which used a similar design process. Benchmark programs were coded on each of 10 "competitive" machines, and the object of the design was to get a machine which gave the best score on the benchmarks. This approach had several fallacies: the machine had no basic character of its own; the machine was difficult to program since the multiple registers were assigned to specific functions and had inherent idiosyncrasies to score well on the benchmarks; the machine did not perform well for programs other than those used in the benchmark test; and finally, compilers which took advantage of the machine appeared to be difficult to write. Since all "competitive machines" had been hand-coded from a common flowchart rather than separate flowcharts for each machine, the apparent high performance may have been due to the flowchart organization.

resulting machine is not. A common classification of processors is as zero-, one-, two-, three-, or three-plus-one-address machines. This scheme has the form:

$$op \; l1, \; l2, \; l3, \; l4$$

where $l1$ specifies the location (address) in which to store the result of the binary operation (op) of the contents of operand locations $l2$ and $l3$, and $l4$ specifies the location of the next instruction.

The action of the instruction is of the form:

$$l1 \leftarrow l2 \; op \; l3; \; goto \; l4$$

The other addressing schemes assume specific values for one or more of these locations. Thus, the one-address von Neumann [Burks, Goldstine, and von Neumann, 1962] machines assumes $l1 = l2 =$ the "accumulator" and $l4$ is the location following that of the current instruction. The two-address machine assumes $l1 = l2$; $l4$ is the next address.

Historically, the trend in machine design has been to move from a 1 or 2 word accumulator structure as in the von Neumann machine towards a machine with accumulator and index register(s).[1] As the number of registers is increased the assignment of the registers to specific functions becomes more undesirable and inflexible; thus, the general-register concept has developed. The use of an array of general registers in the processor was apparently first used in the first-generation, vacuum-tube machine, PEGASUS [Elliott et al., 1956] and appears to be an outgrowth of both 1- and 2-address structures. (Two alternative structures—the early 2- and 3-address per instruction computers may be disregarded, since they tend to always access primary memory for results as well as temporary storage and thus are wasteful of time and memory cycles, and require a long instruction.) The stack concept (zero-address) provides the most efficient access method for specifying algorithms, since very little space, only the access addresses and the operators, needs to be given. In this scheme the operands of an operator are always assumed to be on the "top of the stack." The stack has the additional advantage that arithmetic expression evaluation and compiler statement parsing have been developed to use a stack effectively. The disadvantage of the stack is due in part to the nature of current memory technology. That is, stack memories have to be simulated with random access memories, multiple stacks are usually required, and even though small stack memories exist, as the stack overflows, the primary memory (core) has to be used.

Even though the trend has been toward the general register

concept (which, of course, is similar to a two-address scheme in which one of the addresses is limited to small values), it is important to recognize that any design is a compromise. There are situations for which any of these schemes can be shown to be "best." The IBM System/360 series uses a general register structure, and their designers [Amdahl, Blaauw, and Brooks, 1964] claim the following advantages for the scheme:

1 Registers can be assigned to various functions: base addressing, address calculation, fixed point arithmetic and indexing.

2 Availability of technology makes the general registers structure attractive.

The System/360 designers also claim that a stack organized machine such as the English Electric KDF 9 [Allmark and Lucking, 1962] or the Burroughs B5000 [Lonergan and King, 1961] has the following disadvantages:

1 Performance is derived from fast registers, not the way they are used.

2 Stack organization is too limiting and requires many copy and swap operations.

3 The overall storage of general registers and stack machines are the same, considering point 2.

4 The stack has a bottom, and when placed in slower memory there is a performance loss.

5 Subroutine transparency is not easily realized with one stack.

6 Variable length data is awkward with a stack.

We generally concur with points 1, 2, and 4. Point 5 is an erroneous conclusion, and point 6 is irrelevant (that is, general register machines have the same problem). The general-register scheme also allows processor implementations with a high degree of parallelism since instructions of a local block all can operate on several registers concurrently. A set of truly general purpose registers should also have additional uses. For example, in the DEC PDP-10, general registers are used for address integers, indexing, floating point, boolean vectors (bits), or program flags and stack pointers. The general registers are also addressable as primary memory, and thus, short program loops can reside within them and be interpreted faster. It was observed in operation that PDP-10 stack operations were very powerful and often used (accounting for as many as 20% of the executed instructions, in some programs, e.g., the compilers.)

The basic design decision which sets the PDP-11 apart was based on the observation that by using *truly* general registers and by suitable addressing mechanisms it was possible to consider the

[1] Due in part to needs, but mainly technology which dictates how large the structure can be.

machine as a zero-address (stack), one-address (general register), or two-address (memory-to-memory) computer. Thus, it is possible to use whichever addressing scheme, or mixture of schemes, is most appropriate.

Another important design decision for the instruction set was to have only a few data types in the basic machine, and to have a rather complete set of operations for each data type. (Alternative designs might have more data types with few operations, or few data types with few operations.) In part, this was dictated by the machine size. The conversion between data types must be easily accomplished either automatically or with 1 or 2 instructions. The data types should also be sufficiently primitive to allow other data types to be defined by software (and by hardware in more powerful versions of the machine). The basic data type of the machine is the 16 bit integer which uses the two's complement convention for sign. This data type is also identical to an address.

PDP-11 Model 20 Instruction Set (Basic Instruction Set)

A formal description of the basic instruction set is given in Appendix 1 using the ISP notation [Bell and Newell, 1971]. The remainder of this section will discuss the machine in a conventional manner.

Primary Memory. The primary memory (core) is addressed as either 2^{16} bytes or 2^{15} words using a 16 bit number. The linear address space is also used to access the input-output devices. The device state, data and control registers are read or written like normal memory locations.

General Register. The general registers are named: R[0:7] <15:0>[1]; that is, there are 8 registers each with 16 bits. The naming is done starting at the left with bit 15 (the sign bit) to the least significant bit 0. There are synonyms for R[6] and R[7]:

Stack Pointer/SP<15:0> := R[6]<15:0>. Used to access a special stack which is used to store the state of interrupts, traps and subroutine calls

Program Counter/PC<15:0> := R[7]<15:0>. Points to the current instruction being interpreted. It will be seen that the fact that PC is one of the general registers is crucial to the design.

Any general register, R[0:7], can be used as a stack pointer. The special Stack Pointer (SP) has additional properties that force it to be used for changing processor state interrupts, traps, and subroutine calls (It also can be used to control dynamic temporary storage subroutines.)

---

[1]A definition of the ISP notation used here may be found in Chapter 4.

In addition to the above registers there are 8 bits used (from a possible 16) for processor status, called PS<15:0> register. Four bits are the Condition Codes (CC) associated with arithmetic results; the T-bit controls tracing; and three bits control the priority of running programs Priority <2:0>. Individual bits are mapped in PS as shown in Appendix 1.

Data Types and Primitive Operations. There are two data lengths in the basic machine: bytes and words, which are 8 and 16 bits, respectively. The non-trivial data types are word length integers (w.i.); byte length integers (by.i); word length boolean vectors (w.bv), i.e., 16 independent bits (booleans) in a 1 dimensional array; and byte length boolean vectors (by.bv). The operations on byte and word boolean vectors are identical. Since a common use of a byte is to hold several flag bits (booleans), the operations can be combined to form the complete set of 16 operations. The logical operations are: "clear," "complement," "inclusive or," and "implication" $(x \supset y \text{ or } \neg x \lor y)$.

There is a complete set of arithmetic operations for the word integers in the basic instruction set. The arithmetic operations are: add, subtract, multiply (optional), divide (optional), compare, add one, subtract one, clear, negate, and multiply and divide by powers of two (shift). Since the address integer size is 16 bits, these data types are most important. Byte length integers are operated on as words by moving them to the general registers where they take on the value of word integers. Word length integer operations are carried out and the results are returned to memory (truncated).

The floating point instructions defined by software (not part of the basic instruction set) require the definition of two additional data types (of length two and three), i.e., double word (d.w.) and triple (t.w.) words. Two additional data types, double integer (d.i.) and triple floating point (t.f. or f) are provided for arithmetic. These data types imply certain additional operations and the conversion to the more primitive data types.

Address (Operand) Calculation. The general methods provided for accessing operands are the most interesting (perhaps unique) part of the machine's structure. By defining several access methods to a set of general registers, to memory, or to a stack (controlled by a general register), the computer is able to be a 0, 1 and 2 address machine. The encoding of the instruction Source (S) fields and Destination (D) fields are given in Fig. 10 together with a list of the various access modes that are possible. (Appendix 1 gives a formal description of the effective address calculation process.)

It should be noted from Fig. 10 that all the common access modes are included (direct, indirect, immediate, relative, indexed, and indexed indirect) plus several relatively uncommon ones. Relative (to PC) access is used to simplify program loading,

r = register specification R[r]

d = defer (indirect) address bit

m = mode (00 = R[r]; 01 = R[r]; next R[r] +ai;[1]

    10 = R[r], R[r] -ai, next R[2]

    11 = indexed with next word)

The following access modes can be specified:

0 direct-to a register, R[r]

1 indirect-to a register, R[r] for address of data

2 auto increment via register (pop) - use register as address, then
    increment register

3 auto increment via register (pop) - defer

4 auto decrement via register (push) - decrement register, then use
    register as address

5 auto decrement indirect - decrement register, then use register as the
    address of the address of data

2 immediate data - next full word is the data (r=PC)

3 direct data - next full word is the address of data (r=PC)

6 direct indexed - use next full word indexed with R[r] as address of data

7 direct indexed - indirect - use next full word indexed with R[r] as the
    address of the address of data

6 relative access - next full word plus PC is the address (r=PC)

7 relative indirect access - next full word plus PC is the address of the
    address of data (r=PC)

[1]address increment/ai value is 1 or 2

Fig. 10. Address calculation formats.

Assembler Format	Effect	Description
Two Address Machine format:		
MOVE B,A[1]	A ← B	replace A with contents of B
MOVE #N,A	A ← N	replace A with number, N
MOVE B(RZ), A(RZ)	A[I] ← B[I]	replace element of a connector
MOVE (R$_3$) +, (R$_4$) +	A[I] ← B[I]; I ← I + 1	replace element of a vector, move to next element
General Register Machine format:		
MOVE A,R1	R1 ← A	load register
MOVE R1, A	A ← R1	store register
MOVE @A,R1	R1 ← M[A]	load or store indirect via element A
MOVE R1, R3	R1 ← R3	register to register transfer
MOVE R1, A(RZ)	A[I] ← R1	store indexed (load indexed) (or store)
MOVE @A(R0),R1	R1 ← M[A[I]]	load (or store) indexed indirect
MOVE (R1), R3	R1 ← M[R2]	load indirect via register
MOVE (R1) +, R3	R3 ← M[I]	load (or store) element indirect via register, move to next element
Stack Machine format:		
MOVE #N, -(R0)	S ← N	load stack with literal
MOVE A, -(R0)	S ← A	load stack with contents of A
MOVE @(R0)+, -(R0)	S ← M[S]	load stack with memory specified by top of stack
MOVE (R0)+, A	A ← S	store stack in A
MOVE (R0)+, @(R0)+	M[S$_2$] ← S$_1$	store stack top in memory addressed by stack top -1
MOVE (R0), -(R0)	S ← S	duplicate top of stack

[1]Assembler format:
    () denotes contents of memory addressed by
    - decrement register first
    + increment register after
    @ indirect
    # literal

Fig. 11. Coding for the MOVE instruction to compare with conventional machines.

while immediate mode speeds up execution. The relatively uncommon access modes, auto-increment and auto-decrement, are used for two purposes: access to stack under control of the registers[1] and access to bytes or words organized as strings or vectors. The indirect access mode allows a stack to hold addresses of data (instead of data). This mode is desirable when manipulating longer and variable-length data types (e.g., strings, double fixed and triple floating point). The register auto increment mode may be used to access a byte string; thus, for example, after each access, the register can be made to point to the next data item. This is used for moving data blocks, searching for particular elements of a vector, and byte-string operations (e.g., movement, comparisons, editing).

This addressing structure provides flexibility while retaining the same, or better, coding efficiency than classical machines. As

[1]Note, by convention a stack builds toward register 0, and when the stack crosses 400$_8$, a stack overflow occurs.

an example of the flexibility possible, consider the variations possible with the most trivial word instruction MOVE (see Fig. 11). The MOVE instruction is coded as it would appear in conventional 2-address, 1-address (general register) and 0-address (stack) computers. The two-address format is particularly nice for MOVE, because it provides an efficient encoding for the common operation: A ← B (note, the stack and general registers are not involved). The vector move A[I] ← B(I) is also efficiently encoded. For the general register (and 1-address format), there are about 13 MOVE operations that are commonly used. Six moves can be encoded for the stack (about the same number found in stack machines).

Instruction Formats. There are several instruction decoding formats depending on whether 0, 1, or 2 operands have to be explicitly referenced. When 2 operands are required, they are identified as Source/S and Destination/D and the result is placed at Destination/D. For single operand instructions (unary operators) the instruction action is D ← u D; and for two operand instructions (binary operators) the action is D ← D b S (where u and b are unary and binary operators, e.g., ¬, − and +, −, ×, /, respectively. Instructions are specified by a 16-bit word. The most common binary operator format (that for operations requiring two addresses) is shown below.

$$15 \dots 12; \quad 11 \dots 6; \quad 5 \dots 0$$
$$\text{op} \qquad \quad \text{D} \qquad \quad \text{S}$$

The other instruction formats are given in Fig. 12.

Instruction Interpretation Process. The instruction interpretation process is given in Fig. 13, and follows the common fetch-execute cycle. There are three major states: (1) interrupting—the PC and PS are placed on the stack accessed by the Stack Pointer/SP, and the new state is taken from an address specified by the source requesting the trap or interrupt; (2) trace (controlled by T-bit)—essentially one instruction at a time is executed as a trace trap occurs after each instruction; and (3) normal instruction interpretation. The five (lower) states in the diagram are concerned with instruction fetching, operand fetching, executing the operation specified by the instruction and storing the result. The non-trivial details for fetching and storing the operands are not shown in the diagram but can be constructed from the effective address calculation process (Appendix 1). The state diagram, though simplified, is similar to 2- and 3-address computers, but is distinctly different than a 1 address (1 accumulator) computer.

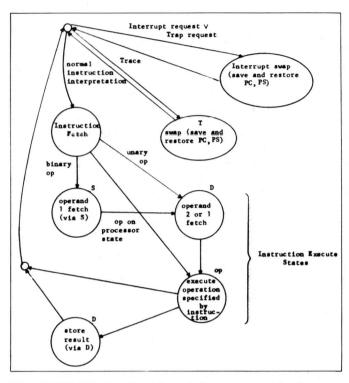

Fig. 13. PDP-11 instruction interpretation process state diagram.

The ISP description (Appendix 1) gives the operation of each of the instructions, and the more conventional diagram (Fig. 12) shows the decoding of instruction classes. The ISP description is somewhat incomplete; for example, the add instruction is defined as: ADD (:= bop = 0010) ← (CC,D ← D + S); *addition* does not exactly describe the changes to the Condition Codes/CC (which means whenever a binary opcode [bop] of 0010_2 occurs the ADD instruction is executed with the above effect). In general, the CC are based on the result, that is, Z is set if the result is zero, N if negative, C if a carry occurs, and V if an overflow was detected as a result of the operation. Conditional branch instructions may thus follow the arithmetic instruction to test the results of the CC bits.

Examples of Addressing Schemes

Use as a Stack (Zero Address) Machine. Figure 14 lists typical zero-address machine instructions together with the PDP-11 instructions which perform the same function. It should be noted that translation (compilation) from normal infix expressions to reverse Polish is a comparatively trivial task. Thus, one of the primary reasons for using stacks is for the evaluation of expressions in reverse Polish form.

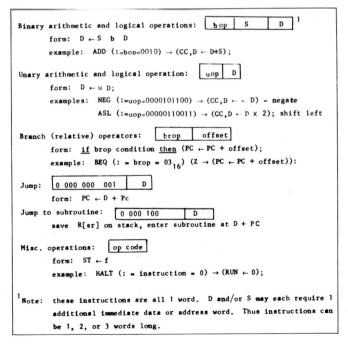

Fig. 12. PDP-11 instruction formats (simplified).

Common stack instruction:	Equivalent PDP-11 instruction:
place address value A on stack	MOVE #A, -(R0) [1]
load stack from memory address specified by stack	MOVE @(R0)+, - (R0)
load stack from memory location A	MOVE A, -(R0)
store stack at memory address specified by stack	MOVE (R0)+, @(R0)+
store stack at memory location A	MOVE (R0)+, A
duplicate top of stack	MOVE (R0), -(R0)
+ , add 2 top data of stack to stack	ADD (R0) +, @R0
-, x, /; subtract, multiply, divide	(see add)
-; negate top data of stack	NEG @R0
clear top data of stack	CLR @R0
v; "inclusive or" 2 top data of stack "and" 2 top data of stack	BSET (R0)+, @R0
¬; complement top of stack	COM @R0
test top of stack (set branch indicators)	TST @R0
branch on indicator	BR (=, ≠, >, ≥, <, ≤)
jump unconditional	JUMP

add addressed location A to top of stack - (not common for stack machine) equivalent to: load stack, add swap top 2 stack data	ADD A, @R0
	 MOVE (R0)+, R1
	 MOVE (R0)+, R2
	 MOVE R1, -(R0)
	 MOVE R2, -(R0)

reset stack location to N	MOVE #N, R0 COM @R0
∧, "and" 2 top stack data	BCLR (R0)+, @R0

[1] Stack pointer has been arbitrarily used as register R0 for this example.

Fig. 14. Stack computer instructions and equivalent PDP-11 instructions.

Consider an assignment statement of the form

$$D \leftarrow A + B/C$$

which has the reverse Polish form

$$DABC/+ \leftarrow$$

and would normally be encoded on a stack machine as follows

> load stack address of D
> load stack A
> load stack B
> load stack C
> /
> +
> store

However, with the PDP-11 there is an address method for improving the program encoding and run time, while not losing the stack concept. An encoding improvement is made by doing an operation to the top of the stack from a direct memory location (while loading). Thus the previous example could be coded as:

> load stack B
> divide stack by C
> add A to stack
> store stack D

Use as a One-Address (General Register) Machine. The PDP-11 is a general register computer and should be judged on that basis. Benchmarks have been coded to compare the PDP-11 with the larger DEC PDP-10. A 16 bit processor performs better than the DEC PDP-10 in terms of bit efficiency, but not with time or memory cycles. A PDP-11 with a 32 bit wide memory would, however, decrease time by nearly a factor of two, making the times essentially comparable.

Use as a Two-Address Machine. Figure 15 lists typical two-address machine instructions together with the equivalent PDP-11 instructions for performing the same operations. The most useful instruction is probably the MOVE instruction because it does not use the stack or general registers. Unary instructions which operate on and test primary memory are also useful and efficient instructions.

Extensions of the Instruction Set for Real (Floating Point) Arithmetic

The most significant factor that affects performance is whether a machine has operators for manipulating data in a particular format. The inherent generality of a stored program computer allows any computer by subroutine to simulate another—given enough time and memory. The biggest and perhaps only factor that separates a small computer from a large computer is whether floating point data is understood by the computer. For example, a small computer with a cycle time of 1.0 microseconds and 16 bit memory width might have the following characteristics for a floating point add, excluding data accesses:

Programmed	250 microseconds
Programmed but (special normalize and differencing of exponent instructions)	75 microseconds
Microprogrammed hardware	25 microseconds
Hardwired	2 microseconds

It should be noted that the ratios between programmed and hardwired interpretation varies by roughly two orders of magnitude. The basic hardwiring scheme and the programmed scheme should allow binary program compatibility, assuming there is an interpretive program for the various operators in the Model 20. For example, consider one scheme which would add eight 48 bit registers which are addressable in the extended instruction set.

Two Address Computer	PDP-11
A ← B; transfer B to A	MOVE B,A
A ← A+B; add	ADD B,A
-, x, /	(see add)
A ← -A; negate	NEG A
A ← A ∨ B; inclusive or	BSETB,A
A ← ¬ A; not	COM
Jump unconditioned	JUMP
Test A, and transfer to B	TST A
	BR (=, ≠, >, ≥, <, ≤) B

Fig. 15. Two address computer instructions and equivalent PDP-11 instructions.

The eight floating registers, F, would be mapped into eight double length (32 bit) registers, D. In order to access the various parts of F or D registers, registers F0 and F1 are mapped onto registers R0 to R2 and R3 to R5.

Since the instruction set operation code is almost completely encoded already for byte and word length data, a new encoding scheme is necessary to specify the proposed additional instructions. This scheme adds two instructions: enter floating point mode and execute one floating point instruction. The instructions for floating point and double word data would be:

binary ops	op	floating point/f	and double word/d
bop' S D	←	FMOVE	DMOVE
	+	FADD	DADD
	−	FSUB	DSUB
	×	FMUL	DMUL
	/	FDIV	DDIV
	compare	FCMP	DCMP
unary ops			
uop' D	−	FNEG	DNEG

Logical Design of S(Unibus) and Pc

The logical design level is concerned with the physical implementation and the constituent combinatorial and sequential logic elements which form the various computer components (e.g., processors, memories, controls). Physically, these components are separate and connected to the Unibus following the lines of the PMS structure.

Unibus Organization

Figure 16 gives a PMS diagram of the Pc and the entering signals from the Unibus. The control unit for the Unibus, housed in Pc for the Model 20, is not shown in the figure.

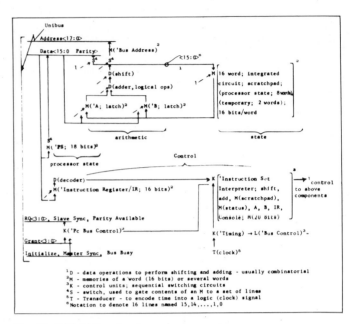

Fig. 16. PDP-11 Pc structure.

The PDP-11 Unibus has 56 bi-directional signals conventionally used for program-controlled data transfers (processor to control), direct-memory data transfers (processor or control to memory) and control-to-processor interrupt. The Unibus is interlocked; thus transactions operate independently of the bus length and response time of the master and slave. Since the bus is bi-directional and is used by all devices, any device can communicate with any other device. The controlling device is the master, and the device to which the master is communicating is the slave. For example, a data transfer from processor (master) to memory (always a slave) uses the Data Out dialogue facility for writing and a transfer from memory to processor uses the Data In dialogue facility for reading.

Bus Control. Most of the time the processor is bus master fetching instructions and operands from memory and storing results in memory. Bus mastership is determined by the current processor priority and the priority line upon which a bus request is made and the physical placement of a requesting device on the linked bus. The assignment of bus mastership is done concurrently with normal communication (dialogues).

Unibus Dialogues

Three types of dialogues use the Unibus. All the dialogues have a common protocol which first consists of obtaining the bus mastership (which is done concurrently with a previous transaction) followed by a data exchange with the requested device. The dialogues are: Interrupt; Data In and Date In Pause; and Data Out and Data Out Byte.

Interrupt. Interrupt can be initiated by a master immediately after receiving bus mastership. An address is transmitted from the master to the slave on Interrupt. Normally, subordinate control devices use this method to transmit an interrupt signal to the processor.

Data In and Data In Pause. These two bus operations transmit slave's data (whose address is specified by the master) to the master. For the Data In Pause operation data is read into the master and the master responds with data which is to be rewritten in the slave.

Data Out and Data Out Byte. These two operations transfer data from the master to the slave at the address specified by the master. For Data Out a word at the address specified by the address lines is transferred from master to slave. Data Out Byte allows a single data byte to be transmitted.

Processor Logical Design

The Pc is designed using TTL logical design components and occupies approximately eight 8″ × 12″ printed circuit boards. The organization of the logic is shown in Fig. 16. The Pc is physically connected to two other components, the console and the Unibus. The control for the Unibus is housed in the Pc and occupies one of the printed circuit boards. The most regular part of the Pc, the arithmetic and state section, is shown at the top of the figure. The 16-word scratch-pad memory and combinatorial logic data operators, D(shift) and D(adder, logical ops), form the most regular part of the processor's structure. The 16-word memory holds most of the 8-word processor state found in the ISP, and the 8 bits that form the Status word are stored in an 8-bit register. The input to the adder-shift network has two latches which are either memories or gates. The output of the adder-shift network can be read to either the data or address parts of the Unibus, or back to the scratch-pad array.

The instruction decoding and arithmetic control are less regular than the above data and state and these are shown in the lower part of the figure. There are two major sections: the instruction fetching and decoding control and the instruction set interpreter (which in effect defines the ISP). The later control section operates on, hence controls, the arithmetic and state parts of the Pc. A final control is concerned with the interface to the Unibus (distinct from the Unibus control that is housed in the Pc).

Conclusions

In this paper we have endeavored to give a complete description of the PDP-11 Model 20 computer at four descriptive levels. These present an unambiguous specification at two levels (the PMS structure and the ISP), and, in addition, specify the constraints for the design at the top level, and give the reader some idea of the implementation at the bottom level logical design. We have also presented guidelines for forming additional models that would belong to the same family.

References

Allmark and Lucking [1962]; Amdahl, Blaauw, and Brooks [1964]; Bell and Newell [1971]; Burks, Goldstine, and Von Neumann [1962]; Elliott, Owen, Devonald, and Maudsley [1956]; Haney [1968]; Lonergan and King [1961]; Maurer [1966]; Rothman [1959]; Wilkes [1951].

APPENDIX 1   PDP-11 ISP

```
PDP11 :=
    begin

! This is a summary description of a PDP-11/70 processor written
! in the ISPS language.

! This summary explicitly defines the instruction fetch and execute
! cycles of the PDP-11/70.

! Most of the actual instruction execution descriptions have been
! eliminated. However, at least one instruction from each of
! the major instruction classes is described in full.

! The memory management description has been eliminated from this summary.

! The register mapping ROM initialization has been eliminated
! from the summary.  If simulations are performed, REGROM[63:0]
! should be initialized by use of an external READ file.

**MP.State**

! Macro definitions to allow easy change of memory configuration.
! The 11/70 allows addressing up to 2M * 2 bytes.  A smaller
! memory is declared for simulator space efficiency.

macro max.byte := |#167777 |,       ! (28k * 2 bytes)

MB[max.byte:0]<7:0>,                         ! The addressing space
MW[max.byte:0]<15:0>{increment:2} := MB[max.byte:0]<7:0>,
MBIO[#17777777:#17760000]<7:0>,     ! The i/o page (4k)
MWIO[#17777777:#17760000]<15:0>{increment:2} := MBIO[#17777777:#17760000]<7:0>,

MAR\Memory.addr.reg<21:0>,

MBR\Memory.buff.reg<15:0>,
    bmbr\byte.mbr<7:0>  := MBR<7:0>,


**PC.State**

R\register[15:0]<15:0>, ! Register file including two sets of general
                        ! registers: R0-R5 (address 0000-0101, 1000-1101).
                        ! One program counter (address 0111), and three
                        ! Stack pointers (address 0110,1110,1111)

PC<15:0>  := R['0111]<15:0>,                 ! Only 1 program counter

macro SP    := |R[cmode<0>@'11@(cmode<1> and cmode<0>)] |, ! Stack pointer (3)
macro link  := |R[rs@'101] |,                ! Two R5's (subroutine link)

PS<15:0>    := MBIO[#17777777:#17777776]<7:0>,   ! Program status word
    cm\current.mode<1:0>  := PS<15:14>,      ! Current address space
                                             ! (kernel/supervisor/user)
    macro kernel    := |(cmode eql '00) |,
    macro super     := |(cmode eql '01) |,
    macro user      := |(cmode eql '11) |,
    pm\previous.mode<1:0>   := PS<13:12>,    ! Previous address space
    p\priority<2:0>         := PS<7:5>,      ! Current process priority
    rs\register.set<>       := PS<11>,
    t\trace<>               := PS<4>,
    cc\condition.codes<3:0> := PS<3:0>,
        N\negative<>    := cc<3>,
        Z\zero<>        := cc<2>,
        V\overflow<>    := cc<1>,
        C\carry<>       := cc<0>,

! External interrupt requests


br7\bus.request.7<>,                     ! External interrupt requests
br6\bus.request.6<>,
br5\bus.request.5<>,
br4\bus.request.4<>,

ERRREG\cpu.error.register<15:0>          := MBIO[#17777767:#17777766]<7:0>,
    illhlt\illegal.halt<>                := ERRREG<7>,
    oddadd\odd.address<>                 := ERRREG<6>,
    nomem\non.existent.memory<>          := ERRREG<5>,
    timeout\unibus.time.out<>            := ERRREG<4>,
    yellow\yellow.zone.limit<>           := ERRREG<3>,
    red\red.zone.stack.limit<>           := ERRREG<2>,

SYSID\system.id<15:0>   := MBIO[#17777765:#17777764]<7:0>, ! Hardwired Sys No.
a\activity<0:1>,

    macro go        := |(a eql '00)|,
    macro WAIT      := |(a eql '01)|,
    macro HALT      := |(a eql '10)|,

! Trap vector addresses:  The associated error conditions cause execution
! to switch to the PC and PS stored in the two words at the trap address.

    macro cpu.errors    := |#004 |,
    macro ill.instr     := |#010 |,
    macro res.instr     := |#010 |,
    macro bpt.trap      := |#014 |,
    macro iot.trap      := |#020 |,
    macro power.fail    := |#024 |,
    macro emt.trap      := |#030 |,
    macro trap.trap     := |#034 |,
```

```
**!implementation.Declarations**
bus.error<>,              ! Bus error detected
byte.access<>,            ! 1 for byte read/write
cmode<1:0>,               ! Temporary for all processing using current mode
busreg<15:0>,             ! Contains trap vector when a trap is set up
dr\destination.reg.addr.in.register.file<3:0>,
iflag<>,                  ! Used with to force I space access
oldval<15:0>,             ! Register value before auto increment/decrement
pc.temp<15:0>,            ! Used during trap routines
pmode<1:0>,               ! Set by mtp and mfp instructions:
                          !       if 0 then normal read/write
                          !       if 1 then use previous instruction space
                          !       if 2 then use previous data space
ps.temp<15:0>,            ! Used during trap routines
regflg<>,                 ! Designates register access to read/write procedures
REGROM\register.mapping.read.only.memory[63:0]<3:0>,
sr\source.reg.addr.in.register.file<3:0>,
state<1:0>,               ! Current state 0 = instruction fetch/decode
                          !               1 = execute
                          !               2 = service
                          !               3 = unused
temp<17:0>,
temp1<3:0>,
trace.flag<>,             ! Trace trap bit temporary
trap.instr<>,             ! Set by emt, trap, bpt, and iot to inhibit
var<21:0>,                ! Virtual address register used in read and write
zeros<63:0>,              ! 64 bits of zeros

**Instruction.Format**

i\instruction<15:0>,
    bop\binary.operation<2:0>   := i<14:12>,

IR\Instruction.register<15:0>   := i<15:0>,

    s\source.field<5:0>         := i<11:6>,   ! Source address information
        sm\source.mode<1:0>         := s<5:4>,
        sd\source.deferred<>        := s<3>,
        srcrag\source.reg<2:0>      := s<2:0>,

! Special handling if register 6 (Stack Pointer) or register 7 (Program
! Counter) is used in autoincrement/autodecrement addressing modes.

    macro sr67  := |(s<2:1> eql '11)|,

    d\destination.field<5:0>    := i<5:0>,    ! Destination address info.
        dm\destination.mode<1:0>    := d<5:4>,
        dd\destination.deferred<>   := d<3>,
        desreg\destination.reg<2:0> := d<2:0>,

    macro dr67  := |(d<2:1> eql '11)|,

! Instruction decoding fields.

    uop\unary.operation<2:0>        := i<8:6>,
    offset<7:0>                     := IR<7:0>,
    rop\register.operation<1:0>     := i<7:6>,
    jetop\jsr.emulator.trap.op<>    := i<15>,
    byop\byte.operation<>           := i<15>,
    etop\emulator.trap.op<>         := i<8>,
    concop\condition.code.op<10:0>  := i<15:5>,
    cpuop\cpu.control.op<2:0>       := i<2:0>,
    contop\cpu.control.class.op<2:0> := i<5:3>,
    brop\branch.op.code<2:0>        := i<10:8>,
    intop\extended.integer.op<2:0>  := i<11:9>,
    typeop\class.op.code.bits<1:0>  := i<10:9>,
    resop\reserve.op<>              := i<11>,
    ccop\condition.code.second.op<> := i<4>,

**Address.Calculation**

! Source loads the value of the source operand into register source.
! Dest loads the address of the destination operand into register dest
! and fetches the operand to the MBR.

    source()<15:0> :=
        begin
        iflag = 0 next
        DECODE sm =>
            begin
            0 := source = R[sr],             ! Register mode: registers
                                             ! are addressed directly.
            1 := begin                       ! Autoincrement mode: use
                iflag = (sr eql {us} #7);    ! the contents of the specified
                MAR = R[sr] next             ! register as an address.
                DECODE (sr67 or sd) =>       ! Increment after use.
                    begin
                    R[sr] = R[sr] + (2 -{us} byte.access),
                    R[sr] = R[sr] + 2
                    end next
                read(byte.access *{us} (1 -{us} sd)) next
                source = MBR; iflag = 0
                end.
            2 := begin                       ! Autodecrement mode:
                DECODE (sr67 or sd) =>       ! decrement contents of the
                    begin                    ! specified register before
                                             ! use.
                    R[sr] = R[sr] - (2 -{us} byte.access),
                    R[sr] = R[sr] - 2
                    end next
```

```
                    MAR = R[sr] next
                    read(byte.access *(us) (1 -(us) sd)) next
                    source = MBR
                    end,
            3 : begin                            ! Index mode: fetch the next
                iflag = 1; MAR = PC next         ! word from memory and add
                PC = PC + 2 next                 ! add it to the contents
                                                 ! of the specified register
                read(0) next iflag = 0;          ! to form the effective address.
                MAR = (MBR + R[sr])<15:0> next   ! The register contents
                                                 ! are unmodified.
                    read(byte.access *(us) (1 -(us) sd)) next
                    source = MBR
                    end
            end next

        IF sd =>                                 ! Correction for all deferred
            begin                                ! mode addresses. Use "source"
            MAR = source next                    ! generated above as an address
            read(byte.access) next               ! to a pointer to the true
            source = MBR                         ! source.
            end
        end,
    dest()<15:0> :=
        begin
        iflag = 0; oldval = R[dr] next
        DECODE dm =>
            begin
            0 := begin                           ! Register mode: registers
                dest = 0; regflg = 1             ! are addressed directly
                end,
            1 := begin                           ! Autoincrement mode: use
                dest = R[dr] next                ! of the specified register
                DECODE (dr67 or dd) =>           ! the contents of the
                    begin                        ! as an address, increment
                                                 ! the register after use.
                    R[dr] = R[dr] + (2 -(us) byte.access),
                    R[dr] = R[dr] + 2
                    end next
                iflag = (dr eql{us} #7)          ! Force I space if using PC
                end,

            2 := begin                           ! Autodecrement mode:
                DECODE (dr67 or dd) =>           ! decrement the register
                    begin                        ! then use the contents
                                                 ! as an address.
                    R[dr] = R[dr] - (2 -(us) byte.access),
                    R[dr] = R[dr] - 2
                    end next
                dest = R[dr]
                end,

            3 := begin                           ! Index mode: fetch the
                iflag = 1; MAR = PC next         ! next word from memory and
                PC = PC + 2 next                 ! add it to the contents
                                                 ! contents of the specified
                read(0) next                     ! register to form the
                iflag = 0; dest = MBR + R[dr]    ! effective address.
                end                              ! Register contents remain
                                                 ! unmodified.
            end next
        MAR = dest next

        IF dd =>                                 ! Correction for all deferred
            begin                                ! mode addresses. Use
            read(0) next                         ! "destination" generated
            iflag = regflg = 0;                  ! above as an address to a
            MAR = MBR                            ! pointer to the true
            end                                  ! destination.
        end,
**Service.Facilities**

    stkref\stack.reference :=
        begin
        regflg = 0;                              ! Stack op cannot go to regs.
        SP = SP - 2
        end,

    odderr\odd.address.error :=
        begin
        oddadd = bus.error = 1 next
        ckstate(1)
        end,

    ckstate(abortt<>) :=                         ! Check state
        begin
        DECODE state =>
            begin
            no.op(),                             ! Ifetch
            LEAVE exec,                          ! Execute
            LEAVE service,                       ! Service
            no.op()                              ! Unused
            end
        end,

    sd.read(byte.acc<>) :=                       ! Source, dest, read
        begin
        source() next
        dest() next
        read(byte.acc)
        end,
```

```
        d.read(byte.acc<>) :=                    ! Dest, read
            begin
            dest() next
            read(byte.acc)
            end,
        read(byte.acc<>) :=
            begin
            IF MAR<0> and not byte.acc => odderr(); var = MAR next
            IF (var<15:13> eql{us} #7) => var<21:6> = #77 next
            DECODE var<21:18> eql{us} #17 =>
                begin
                0 := DECODE regflg =>                        ! Register accessing
                    begin                                    ! check
                    0 := DECODE byte.acc =>                  ! not register
                        begin
                        MBR = MW[var],
                        MBR = MB[var]
                        end,
                    1 := DECODE byte.acc =>                  ! Register
                        begin
                        MBR =    R[dr],
                        MBR = R[dr]<7:0>
                        end
                    end,
                1 := IF var<17:13> eql{us} #37 =>            ! Yes
                    begin
                    DECODE byte.acc =>                       ! IO.page
                        begin
                        MBR = MWIO[var],
                        MBR = MBIO[var]
                        end
                    end
                end
            end,

        write(byte.acc<>) :=
            begin
            IF MAR<0> and not byte.acc => odderr(); var = MAR next
            IF (var<15:13> eql{us} #7) => var<21:16> = #77 next
            DECODE var<21:18> eql{us} #17 =>
                begin
                0 := DECODE regflg =>                        ! Register access
                    begin                                    ! check
                    0 := DECODE byte.acc =>                  ! not register
                        begin
                        MW[var] = MBR,
                        MB[var] = bmbr
                        end,
                    1 := DECODE byte.acc =>                  ! Register
                        begin
                        R[dr] = MBR,
                        R[dr]<7:0> = bmbr
                        end
                    end,
                1 := IF var<17:13> eql{us} #37 =>            ! Yes
                    begin
                    DECODE byte.acc =>                       ! IO.page
                        begin
                        MWIO[var] = MBR,
                        MBIO[var] = bmbr
                        end
                    end
                end
            end,

! Condition code setting and branch operations

    setcc(n.<15:0>, v.<15:0>, z.<15:0>) :=
        begin
        DECODE byte.access =>
            begin
            0 := begin                           ! Word operation
                N = n.<15>;
                V = v.<15:0> eql{us} #100000;
                Z = z.<15:0> eql 0
                end,
            1 := begin                           ! Byte operation
                N = n.<7>;
                V = v.<7:0> eql{us} #200;
                Z = z.<7:0> eql 0
                end
            end
        end,

    branch(condition<>) :=
        begin
        IF condition => PC = PC + (offset sl0 1)
        end,

! Interrupt service routines

    bus.reset := (no.op()),

    intvec\interrupt.trap.vector.setup(vector<8:0>) :=
        begin
        MAR = busreg = vector;
        cmode = byte.access = 0 next            ! Map all traps thru
        read(byte.access) next                  ! kernel space
        pc.temp = MBR next
        MAR = busreg + 2 next
        read(byte.access) next
```

```
            ps.temp = MBR next
            stkref(); MBR = PS next              ! Old PC and PS saved
            MAR = SP next                        ! in new space
            write(byte.access) next
            stkref(); MBR = PC next
            MAR = SP next
            write(byte.access) next
            pm = cm next
            PC = pc.temp; PS = ps.temp
            end,

    instr.trap\instruction.trap(trap.vector<8:0>) :=    ! Reserved and illegal
        begin                                           ! Opcode service
        intvec(trap.vector) next
        IF bus.error => a = 2    ! Halt the processor if bus error occurs here
        end,

! Trap and interrupt service routines.  Service is called after each
! instruction is complete.  The trap pending of the highest priority is
! activated.  If a trap was set by illegal, reserved or trap
! instructions then the PC and PS have already been pushed and the new
! PC and PS are loaded.  An additional trap is permitted.

    grant\bus.grant.processing.routine(type.request<15:0>) :=
        begin
        a = 0 next
        intvec(type.request) next
        LEAVE service
        end,

    service :=
        begin
        IF bus.error =>
            begin
            bus.error = 0 next
            intvec(cpu.errors) next              ! Bus error
            IF bus.error =>
                begin
                a = 2 next
                LEAVE service
                end next
            LEAVE service
            end
        end
**Instruction.Interpretation**

    ! Initialization sequence

    start{main} :=
        begin
        zeros = 0;                    ! Initialize zeros
        ERRREG = 0;                   ! Clear all cpu errors
        a = 0 next                    ! Clear activity
        run()
        end.

    ! Main run cycle of the ISP

    run\instruction.interpretation :=
        begin
        IF go =>
            begin
            state = trap.instr = 0;
            MAR = PC next
            DECODE MAR<0> =>              ! Must be even here
                begin
                0 := begin                   ! Even
                    cmode = cm; regflg = 0 next
                    read(0) next             ! Instruction fetch
                    IR = MBR; PC = PC + 2 next
                    byte.access = byop; trace.flag = t;
                    sr = REGROM[cmode @ rs @ srcreg];
                    dr = REGROM[cmode @ rs @ desreg];
                    state = 1 next
                    exec()
                    end,
                1 := odderr()                ! Call error routine for
                                             ! Odd address error processing
                end
            end next
        IF HALT => STOP() next
        state = 2 next
        service() next
        RESTART run
        end
**!Instruction.Execution**

    exec\instruction.execution :=
        begin
        DECODE bop =>
            begin
            #0 := reserop(),             ! Reserved op code
            #1 := MOV(),                 ! Move instruction
            #2 := CMP := no.op(),        ! Compare instruction
            #3 := BIT := no.op(),        ! Bit test instruction
            #4 := BIC := no.op(),        ! Bit clear instruction
            #5 := BIS := no.op(),        ! Bit set instruction
            #6 := begin                  ! Add and subtract
                DECODE byte.access =>
                    begin
                    '0 := ADD := no.op(),
                    '1 := SUB := no.op()
                    end
                end,
            #7 := no.op()                ! Extended instruction set
            end
        end,

reserop\reserve.op.code :=
    begin
    DECODE resop =>
        begin
        0 := branop(),
        1 := classop()
        end
    end,

branop\branch.op.codes :=
    begin
    DECODE (jetop @ brop)<3:0> =>
        begin
        #00 := regop(),                  ! Register instruction
        #01 := branch('1),               ! Branch (br op #00004)
        #02 := BNE := branch(not Z),     ! Branch if not equal
        #03 := BEQ := branch(Z),         ! Branch if equal
        #04 := BGE := branch(N eqv V),   ! Branch if gtr or equal
        #05 := BLT := branch(N xor V),   ! Branch if less than
        #06 :=                           ! Branch if greater than
            BGT := branch(not (Z or (N xor V))),
        #07 := BLE := branch(Z or (N xor V)),    ! Branch if less or equal
        #10 := BPL := branch(not N),     ! Branch if plus
        #11 := BMI := branch(N),         ! Branch if minus
        #12 := BHI := branch(not (C or Z)),  ! Branch if higher
        #13 := BLOS := branch(C or Z),   ! Branch if lower or same
        #14 := BVC := branch(not V),     ! Branch if overflow clear
        #15 := BVS := branch(V),         ! Branch if overflow set
        #16 := BCC := branch(not C),     ! Branch if carry clear
        #17 := BCS := branch(C)          ! Branch if carry set
        end
    end,

regop\register.operations :=
    begin DECODE rop =>
        begin
        0 := begin
            IF contop eql 0 =>
                begin
                DECODE cpuop =>
                    begin
                    #0 := HLT(),              ! Halt
                    #1 := WAIT. := no.op(),   ! Wait for interrupt
                    #2 := RTI.RTT := no.op(), ! Return from interrupt
                    #3 := BPT := no.op(),     ! Breakpoint trap
                    #4 := IOT := no.op(),     ! Input/output trap
                    #5 := RESET := no.op(),   ! Reset external bus
                    #6 := RTI.RTT := no.op(), ! Return from trap
                    #7 := instr.trap(res.instr) ! Unused opcode
                    end
                end
            end,
        1 := JMP(),                           ! Jump
        2 := begin
            DECODE contop =>
                begin
                #0 := RTS(),                  ! Return from subroutine
                #1:#2 := instr.trap(res.instr),
                #3 := SPL := no.op(),         ! Set priority level
                #4:#7 := cco := no.op()       ! Condition code ops
                end
            end,
        3 := SWAB()                           ! Swap bytes
        end
    end,

classop\secondary.decode.into.classes :=
    begin
    DECODE typeop =>
        begin
        subemt(),                ! Subroutine/emulator trap
        singlop(),               ! Single operand class
        shiftop(),               ! Shift operators
        instr.trap(res.instr)    ! Unused op codes
        end
    end,

subemt\subroutine.emulator.trap.and.trap.instructions :=
    begin
    DECODE jetop =>
        begin
        0 := JSR(),              ! Jump to subroutine
        1 := begin
            DECODE i<8> =>       ! EMT or TRAP
                begin
                0 := EMT(),
                1 := TRAP()
                end
            end
        end
    end,
```

```
        singlop\single.operand.instructions :=
            begin
            DECODE uop =>
                begin
                #0 := CLR(),           ! Clear/byte
                #1 := COM := no.op(),  ! Complement/byte
                #2 := INC := no.op(),  ! Increment/byte
                #3 := DEC := no.op(),  ! Decrement/byte
                #4 := NEG := no.op(),  ! Negate/byte
                #5 := ADC := no.op(),  ! Add carry/byte
                #6 := SBC := no.op(),  ! Subtract carry/byte
                #7 := TEST := no.op()  ! Test/byte
                end
            end,

        shiftop\shift.instructions :=
            begin
            DECODE uop =>
                begin
                #0 := ROR(),           ! Rotate right/byte
                #1 := ROL := no.op(),  ! Rotate left/byte
                #2 := ASR := no.op(),  ! Arithmetic shift right/byte
                #3 := ASL := no.op(),  ! Arithmetic shift left/byte
                #4 := MARK := no.op(), ! Mark
                #5 := MFP := no.op(),  ! Move from previous instruction
                #6 := MTP := no.op(),  ! Move to previous instruction
                #7 := SXT := no.op()   ! Sign extend
                end
            end,

    MOV :=      ! Move and Move Byte
                ! MOV opcode #01, MOVB op code #11
        begin
        source() next
        dest() next
        IF regflg and byte.access =>
            begin
            source <= source<7:0>;
            byte.access = 0
            end next
        MBR = source next
        setcc(MBR, 0, MBR);
        write(byte.access)
        end,

!       . . . .                 ! Indicates instruction descriptions
!       . . . .                 ! not included in this summary

! Subroutine, Emulator Trap, and Trap instruction execution

    JSR :=      ! Jump to subroutine, JMP op code #004
        begin
        DECODE (dm @ dd) eql 0 =>
            begin
            0 := begin                              ! False
                dest() next
                temp = MAR<15:0> next
                stkref() next
                MAR = SP; MBR = R[sr] next
                write(byte.access) next
                R[sr] = PC next
                PC = temp<15:0>
                end,
            1 := instr.trap(ill.instr)              ! True
            end
        end,

    EMT :=      ! Emulator trap op codes, EMT op code #104000:#104377
        begin
        intvec(emt.trap); trap.instr = 1
        end,

    TRAP :=     ! Trap op codes, TRAP op code #104400:#104777
        begin
        intvec(trap.trap); trap.instr = 1
        end,

! Single operand instruction execution

    CLR :=          ! Clear and clear byte,
                    ! CLR op code #0050, CLRB op code #1050
        begin
        cc = '0100 next
        dest() next
        MBR = 0 next
        write(byte.access)
        end,

!       . . . .
!       . . . .
```

```
! Jump, swab execution and register operation decode

    JMP :=                      ! Jump, JUMP op code #0001
        begin
        DECODE (dm @ dd) eql 0 =>
            begin


            0 := (dest() next PC = MAR),            ! False
            1 := instr.trap(ill.instr)              ! True
            end
    end,



    SWAB :=                     ! Swap bytes, SWAB op code #0003
        begin
        d.read(byte.access) next
        MBR = bmbr @ MBR<15:8> next
        C = V = 0; N = MBR<7>; Z = MBR<7:0> eql 0;
        IF d neq #07 => write(byte.access)
        end,

! Shift instruction execution

    ROR :=          ! Rotate right and rotate right byte,
                    ! ROR op code #0060, RORB op code #1060
        begin
        d.read(byte.access) next
        DECODE byte.access =>
            begin
            0 := (temp<16:0> = (c @ MBR) srr 1 next
                    c = temp<16>; MBR = temp<15:0>),
            1 := (temp<8:0> = (c @ bmbr) srr 1 next
                    c = temp<8>; bmbr = temp<7:0>)
            end  next
        setcc(temp, 0, temp) next
        V = N xor C next
        write(byte.access)
        end,

!       . . . .
!       . . . .

! CPU control instruction execution

    HLT :=              ! Halt, HALT op code #000000
        begin
        DECODE kernel =>
            begin
            0 := (illhlt = 1; intvec(cpu.errors)),   ! No
            1 := a = 2                                ! Yes
            end
        end,

    RTS :=              ! Return from subroutine, RTS op code #00020
        begin
        PC = R[dr] next MAR = SP next
        read(byte.access) next
        SP = SP + 2 next
        R[dr] = MBR
        end,

!       . . . .
!       . . . .

end                 ! end of description
```

Chapter 39

Implementation and Performance Evaluation of the PDP-11 Family

Edward A. Snow / Daniel P. Siewiorek

In order that methodologies useful in the design of complex systems may be developed, existing designs must be studied. The DEC PDP-11 was selected for a case study because there are a number of designs (eight are considered here), because the designs span a wide range in basic performance (7 to 1) and component technology (bipolar SSI to MOS LSI), and because the designs represent relatively complex systems.

The goals of the chapter are twofold: (1) to provide actual data about design tradeoffs and (2) to suggest design methodologies based on these data. An archetypical PDP-11 implementation is described.

Two methodologies are presented. A top-down approach uses micro-cycle and memory-read-pause times to account for 90 percent of the variation in processor performance. This approach can be used in initial system planning. A bottom-up approach uses relative frequency of functions to determine the impact of design tradeoffs on performance. This approach can be used in design-space exploration of a single design. Finally, the general cost/performance design tradeoffs used in the PDP-11 are summarized.

1. Introduction

As semiconductor technology has evolved, the digital systems designer has been presented with an ever-increasing set of primitive components from which to construct systems: standard SSI, MSI, and LSI, as well as custom LSI components. This expanding choice makes it more difficult to arrive at a near-optimal cost/performance ratio in a design. In the case of highly complex systems, the situation is even worse, since different primitives may be cost-effective in different subareas of such systems.

Historically, digital system design has been more of an art than a science. Good designs have evolved from a mixture of experience, intuition, and trial and error. Only rarely have design methodologies been developed (among those that have are two-level combinational logic minimization and wire-wrap routing schemes, for example). Effective design methodologies are essential for the cost-effective design of more complex systems. In addition, if the methodologies are sufficiently detailed, they can be applied in high-level design automation systems [Siewiorek and Barbacci, 1976].

Design methodologies may be developed by studying the results of the human design process. There are at least two ways to study this process. The first involves a controlled design experiment where several designers perform the same task. By contrasting the results, the range of design variation and technique can be established [Thomas and Siewiorek, 1977]. However, this approach is limited to fairly small design situations because of the redundant use of the human designers.

The second approach examines a series of existing designs that meet the same functional specification while spanning a wide range of design constraints in terms of cost, performance, etc. This paper considers the second approach and uses the DEC PDP-11[1] minicomputer line as a basis of study. The PDP-11 was selected on account of the large number of implementations (eight are considered here) with designs spanning a wide range in performance (roughly 7 to 1) and component technology (bipolar SSI, MSI, MOS custom LSI). The designs are relatively complex and seem to embody good design tradeoffs as ultimately reflected by their price/performance and commercial success.

Attention here is focused mainly upon the CPU. Memory performance enhancements such as caching are considered only insofar as they impinge upon CPU performance.

This paper is divided into three major parts. The first part (Sec. 2) provides an overview of the PDP-11 functional specification (its architecture) and serves as background for subsequent discussion of design tradeoffs. The second part (Sec. 3) presents an archetypical implementation. The last part (Secs. 4 and 5) presents methodologies for determining the impact of various design parameters on system performance. The magnitude of the impact is quantified for several parameters, and the use of the results in design situations is discussed.

2. Architectural Overview

The PDP-11 family is a set of small- to medium-scale stored-program central processors with compatible instruction sets [Bell et al., 1970]. The family evolution in terms of increased performance, constant cost, and constant performance successors is traced in Fig. 1.[2] Since the 11/45, 11/55, and 11/70 use the same processor, only the 11/45 is treated in this study.

A PDP-11 system consists of three parts: a PDP-11 processor, a collection of memories and peripherals, and a link called the Unibus over which they all communicate (Fig. 2).

A number of features, not otherwise considered here, are available as options on certain processors. These include memory management and floating-point arithmetic. The next three sub-

---

[1]DEC, PDP, LSI-11, Unibus, and Fastbus are registered trademarks of Digital Equipment Corporation.

[2]The original equipment manufacturer (OEM) versions of the 11/10, 11/20, and 11/40 are the 11/05, 11/15, and 11/35 respectively. The OEM machines are electrically identical (or nearly so) to their end-user counterparts, the distinction being made for marketing purposes only.

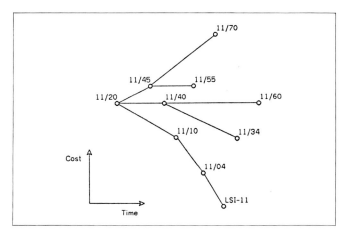

Fig. 1. PDP-11 family tree.

sections summarize the major architectural features of the PDP-11, including memory organization, processor state, addressing modes, instruction set, and Unibus protocol. The references list a number of processor handbooks and other documents which provide a more precise definition of the PDP-11 architecture than is possible here.

2.1 Memory and Processor State

The central processor contains the control logic and data paths for instruction fetching and execution. Processor instructions act upon operands located either in memory or in one of eight general registers. These operands may be either 8-bit bytes or 16-bit words.

Memory is byte- or word-addressable. Word addresses must be even. If N is a word address, then N is the byte address of the low-order byte of the word and N + 1 is the byte address of the high-order byte of the word. The control and data registers of peripheral devices are also accessed through the memory address space, and the top 4 kilowords of the space are reserved for this purpose.

The general registers are 16 bits in length and are referred to as R0 through R7. R6 is used as the system stack pointer (SP) to maintain a push-down list in memory upon which subroutine and

interrupt linkages are kept. R7 is the program counter (PC) and always points to the next instruction to be fetched from memory. With minor exceptions (noted below) the SP and PC are accessible in exactly the same manner as any of the other general registers (R0 through R5).

Data-manipulation instructions fall into two categories: arithmetic instructions (which interpret their operands as 2's complement integers) and logic instructions (which interpret their operands as bit vectors). A set of condition code flags is maintained by the processor and is updated according to the sign and presence of carry/overflow from the result of any data manipulation instruction. The condition codes, processor interrupt priority, and a flag enabling program execution tracing are contained in a processor status word (PS), which is accessible as a word in the memory addressing space.

2.2 Addressing Modes and Instruction Set

The PDP-11 instruction set allows source and destination operands to be referenced via eight different addressing modes. An operand reference consists of a field specifying which of the eight modes is to be used and a second field specifying which of the eight general registers is to be used. The addressing modes are:

Mode 0 *Register.* The operand is contained in the specified register.

Mode 1 *Register deferred.* The contents of the specified register are used to address the memory location containing the operand.

Mode 2 *Autoincrement.* The contents of the specified register are used to address the memory location containing the operand, and the register is then incremented.

Mode 3 *Autoincrement deferred.* The contents of the specified register address a word in memory containing the address of the operand in memory. The specified register is incremented after the reference.

Mode 4 *Autodecrement.* The contents of the specified register are first decremented and then used to address the memory location containing the operand.

Mode 5 *Autodecrement deferred.* The contents of the specified register are first decremented and then used to address a word in memory containing the address of the operand in memory.

Mode 6 *Indexed.* The word following the instruction is fetched and added to the contents of the specified general register to form the address of the memory location containing the operand.

Mode 7 *Indexed deferred.* The word following the instruction is fetched and added to the contents of the specified general register to form the address of a word in memory containing the address of the operand in memory.

The various addressing modes simplify the manipulation of

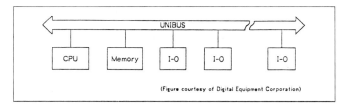

(Figure courtesy of Digital Equipment Corporation)

Fig. 2. Typical PDP-11 configuration.

diverse data structures such as stacks and tables. When used with the program counter these modes enable immediate operands and absolute and PC-relative addressing. The deferred modes permit indirect addressing.

The PDP-11 instruction set is made up of the following types of instructions:

Single-operand instructions. A destination operand is fetched by the CPU, modified in accordance with the instruction, and then restored to the destination.

Double-operand instructions. A source operand is fetched, followed by the destination operand. The appropriate operation is performed on the two operands and the result restored to the destination. In a few double-operand instructions, such as Exclusive OR (XOR), source mode 0 (register addressing) is implicit.

Branch instructions. The condition specified by the instruction is checked, and if it is true, a branch is taken using a field contained in the instruction as a displacement from the current instruction address.

Jumps. Jump instructions allow sequential program flow to be altered either permanently (in a jump) or temporarily (in a jump to subroutine).

Control, trap, and miscellaneous instructions. Various instructions are available for subroutine and interrupt returns, halts, etc.

Floating-point instructions. A floating-point processor is available as an option with several PDP-11 CPUs. Floating-point implementation will not be considered in this paper.

For the purpose of looking at the instruction execution cycle of the various PDP-11 processors, each cycle shall be broken into five distinct phases:[1]

Fetch. This phase consists of fetching the current instruction from memory and interpreting its opcode.

Source. This phase entails fetching the source operand for double-operand instructions from memory or a general register and loading it into the appropriate register in the data paths in preparation for the execute phase.

Destination. This phase is used to get the destination operand for single- and double-operand instructions into the data paths for manipulation in the execute phase. For JMP and JSR instructions the jump address is calculated.

Execute. During this phase the operation specified by the

current instruction is performed and any result rewritten into the destination.

Service. This phase is only entered between execution of the last instruction and fetch of the next to grant a pending bus request, acknowledge an interrupt, or enter console mode after the execution of a HALT instruction or activation of the console halt key.

2.3 The Unibus

All communication among the components of a PDP-11 system takes place on a set of bidirectional lines referred to collectively as the Unibus. The LSI-11 is an exception and uses an adaptation of the Unibus. The Unibus lines carry address, data, and control signals to all memories and peripherals attached to the CPU. Transactions on the Unibus are asynchronous with the processor. At any given time there will be one device which it addresses, the addressed device becoming the bus slave. This communication may consist of data transfers or, in the case where the processor is slave, an interrupt request. The data transfers which may be initiated by the master are:

DATO   Data out—A word is transferred from master to slave.

DATOB   Data out, byte—A byte is transferred from master to slave.

DATI   Data in—A word is transferred from slave to master.

DATIP   Data in, pause—A word is transferred from slave to master and the slave awaits a transfer from master back to slave to replace the information that was read. The Unibus control allows no other data transfer to intervene between the read and the write cycles. This makes possible the reading and alteration of a memory location as an indivisible operation. In addition it permits the use of a read/modify/write cycle with core memories in place of the longer sequence of a read cycle followed by a write cycle.

3. PDP-11 Implementation

The midrange PDP-11's have comparable implementations, yet their performances vary by a factor of 7. This section discusses the features common to these implementations and the variations found between machines which provide the dimensions along which they may be characterized.

3.1 Common Implementation Features

All PDP-11 implementations can be decomposed into a set of data paths and a control unit. The data paths store and operate upon byte and word data and interface to the Unibus, which permits

---

[1]N.B.: The instruction phase names are identical to those used by DEC; however, their application here to a state within a given machine may differ from DEC's since the intent here is to make the discussion consistent over all machines.

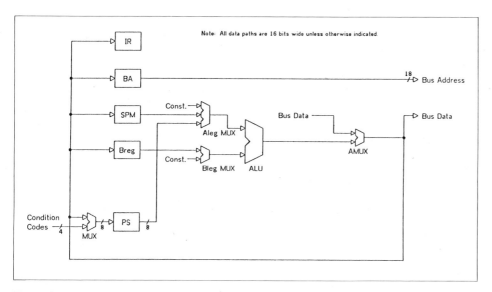

Fig. 3. Archetypical medium-range PDP-11 data paths.

them to read from and write to memory and peripheral devices. The control unit provides all the signals necessary to evoke the appropriate operations in the data paths and Unibus interface. All PDP-11's have comparable data-path and control unit implementations that allow them to be contrasted in a uniform way. In this section a basis for comparing these machines shall be established and used to characterize them.

3.1.1 Data Paths. An archetype may be constructed from which the data paths of all midrange PDP-11's differ but minimally. This archetype is diagrammed in Fig. 3. All major registers and

processing elements, as well as the links and switches which interconnect them, are indicated. The data-path illustrations for individual implementations are shown in Figs. 5 through 7. These figures are laid out in a common format to encourage comparison. Note that with very few exceptions all data paths are 16 bits wide (the PDP-11 word size).

The heart of the data paths is the arithmetic logic unit or ALU, through which all data circulate and where most of the processing actually takes place. Among the operations performed by the ALU are addition, subtraction, 1's and 2's complementation, and logical ANDing and ORing.

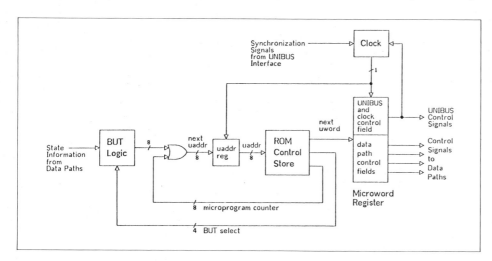

Fig. 4. Archetypical microprogrammed PDP-11 control unit.

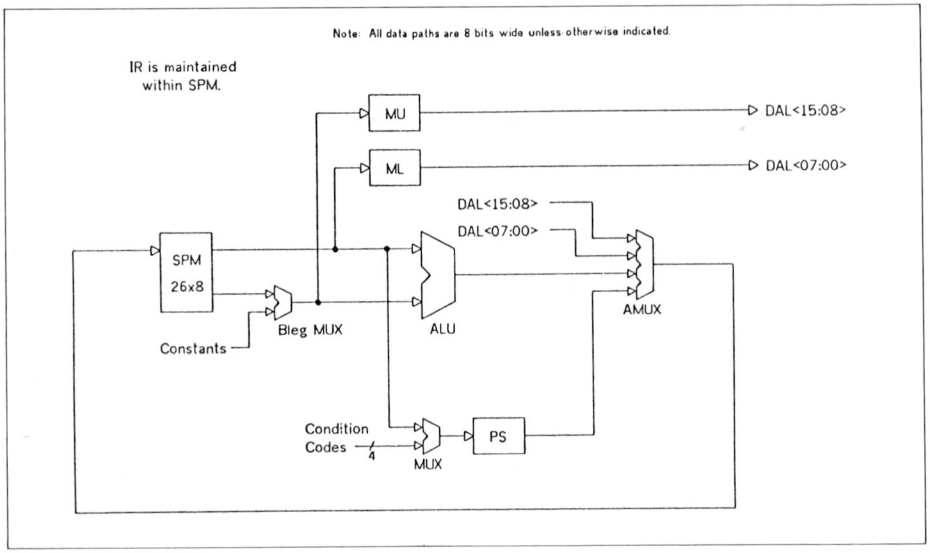

Note: All data paths are 8 bits wide unless otherwise indicated.

Fig. 5. LSI-11 data paths.

The inputs to the ALU are the A leg and the B leg. The A leg is normally fed from a multiplexer (Aleg MUX), which may select from an operand supplied it from the scratch-pad memory (SPM) and possibly from a small set of constants and/or the processor status register (PS). The B leg also is typically fed from its own MUX (Bleg MUX), its selections being among the B register and certain constants. In addition, the Bleg MUX may be configured so that byte selection, sign extension, and other functions may be performed on the operand which it supplies to the ALU.

Following the ALU is a multiplexer (the AMUX) typically used to select between the output of the ALU, the data lines of the Unibus, and certain constants. The output of the AMUX provides

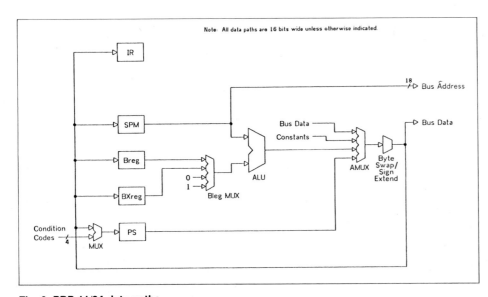

Fig. 6. PDP-11/34 data paths.

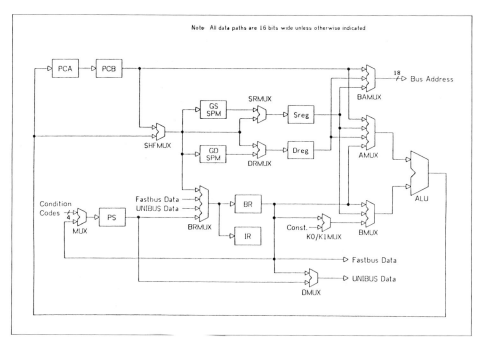

Fig. 7. PDP-11/45 data paths.

the only feedback path in all midrange PDP-11 implementations except the 11/60 and acts as an input to all major processor registers.

The internal registers lie at the beginning of the data paths. The instruction register (IR) contains the current instruction. The bus address register (BA) holds the address placed on the Unibus by the processor. The program status register (PS) contains the processor priority, memory-management-unit modes, condition code flags, and instruction trace-trap enable bit. The scratch-pad memory (SPM) is an array of 16 individually addressable registers which include the general registers (R0 to R7) plus a number of internal registers not accessible to the programmer. The B register (Breg) is used to hold the B leg operand supplied to the ALU.

The variations from this archetype are surprisingly minor. The most frequently used elements (such as the ALU and SPM) are relatively fixed in their position in the data paths from implementation to implementation. Elements which are less frequently used, and hence have less of an impact on performance, can be seen to occupy positions which vary more between implementations. Variations to be encountered include routings for the bus address and processor status register; the point of generation for certain constants; the position of the byte swapper, sign extender, and rotate/shift logic; and the use of certain auxiliary registers present in some designs and not others.

3.1.2 Control Unit. The control unit for all PDP-11 processors (with the exception of the PDP-11/20) is microprogrammed [Wilkes and Stringer, 1953]. The considerations leading to the use of this style of control implementation in the PDP-11 are discussed in O'Loughlin [1975]. The major advantage of microprogramming is flexibility in the derivation of control signals to gate register transfers, to synchronize with Unibus logic, to control microcycle timing, and to evoke changes in control flow. The way in which a microprogrammed control unit accomplishes all of these actions impacts performance.

Figure 4 represents the archetypical PDP-11 microprogrammed control unit. The contents of the microaddress register determine the current control-unit state and are used to access the next microinstruction word from the control store. Pulses from the clock generator strobe the microword and microaddress registers, loading them with the next microword and next microaddress, respectively. Repeated clock pulses thus cause the control unit to sequence through a series of states. The period spent by the control unit in one state is called a *microcycle* (or simply *cycle* when this does not lead to confusion with memory or instruction cycles), and the duration of the state as determined by the clock is known as the *cycle time*. The microword register shortens cycle time by allowing the next microword to be fetched from the control store while the current microword is being used.

Most of the fields of the microword supply signals for conditioning and clocking the data paths. Many of the fields act directly or with a small amount of decoding, supplying their signals to multiplexers and registers to select routings for data and to enable registers to shift, increment, or load on the master clock. Other fields are decoded according to the state of the data paths. An instance of this is the use of auxiliary ALU control logic to generate function-select signals for the ALU as a function of the instruction contained in the IR. Performance as determined by microcycle count is in large measure established by the connectivity of the data paths and the degree to which their functionality can be evoked by the data-path control fields of the microprogram word.

The complexity of the clock logic varies with each implementation. Typically the clock is fixed at a single period and duty cycle; however, processors such as the 11/34 and 11/40 can select from two or three different clock periods for a given cycle depending upon a field in the microword register. This can significantly improve performance in machines where the longer cycles are necessary only infrequently.

The clock logic must provide some means for synchronizing processor and Unibus operation, since the two operate asynchronously with respect to one another. Two alternate approaches are employed in midrange implementations. Interlocked operation, the simpler approach, shuts off the processor clock when a Unibus operation is initiated and turns it back on when the operation is complete. This effectively keeps microprogram flow and Unibus operation in lockstep with no overlap. Overlapped operation is a somewhat more involved approach which continues processor clocking after a DATI or DATIP is initiated. The microinstruction requiring the result of the operation has a function bit set which turns off the processor clock until the result is available. This approach makes it possible for the processor to continue running for several microcycles while a data transfer is being performed, improving performance.

The sequence of states through which the control unit passes would be fixed if it were not for the branch-on-microtest (BUT) logic. This logic generates a modifier based upon the current state of the data paths and Unibus interface (contents of the instruction register, current bus requests, etc.) and a BUT field in the microword currently being accessed from the control store, which selects the condition on which the branch is to be based. The modifier (which will be zero in the case that no branch is selected or that the condition is false) is ORed in with the next microinstruction address so that the next control-unit state is not only a function of the current state but also a function of the state of the data paths. Instruction decoding and addressing mode decoding are two prime examples of the application of BUTs. Certain code points in the BUT field do not select branch conditions, but rather provide control signals to the data paths, Unibus interface, or the control unit itself. These are known as active or working BUTs.

The JAM logic is a part of the microprogram flow-altering mechanism. This logic forces the microaddress register to a known state in the event of an exceptional condition such as a memory access error (bus timeout, stack overflow, parity error, etc.) or power-up by ORing all 1s into the next microaddress through the BUT logic. A microroutine beginning at the address of all 1s handles these trapped conditions. The old microaddress is not saved (an exception to this occurs in the case of the PDP-11/60); consequently, the interrupted microprogram sequence is lost and the microtrap ends by restarting the instruction interpretation cycle with the fetch phase.

The structure of the microprogram is determined largely by the BUTs available to implement it and by the degree to which special cases in the instruction set are exploited by these BUTs. This may have a measurable influence on performance as in the case of instruction decoding. The fetch phase of the instruction cycle is concluded by a BUT that branches to the appropriate point in the microcode based upon the contents of the instruction register. This branch can be quite complex, since it is based upon source mode for double-operand instructions, destination mode for single-operand instructions, and op code for all other types of instructions. Some processors can perform the execute phase of certain instructions (such as set/clear condition code) during the last cycle of the fetch phase; this means that the fetch or service phase for the next instruction might also be entered from BUT IRDECODE. Complicating the situation is the large number of possibilities for each phase. For instance, there are not only eight different destination addressing modes, but also subcases for each that vary for byte and word and for memory-modifying, memory-nonmodifying, MOV, and JMP/JSR instructions.

Some PDP-11 implementations such as the 11/10 make as much use of common microcode as possible to reduce the number of control states. This allows much of the IR decoding to be deferred until some later time into a microroutine which might handle a number of different cases; for instance, byte- and word-operand addressing is done by the same microroutine in a number of PDP-11s. Since the cost of control states has been dropping with the cost of control-store ROM, there has been a trend toward providing separate microroutines optimized for each special case, as in the 11/60. Thus more special cases must be broken out at the BUT IRDECODE, and so the logic to implement this BUT becomes increasingly involved. There is a payoff, though, because there are a smaller number of control states for IR decoding and fewer BUTs. Performance is boosted as well, since frequently occurring special cases such as MOV register to destination can be optimized.

4. Measuring the Effect of Design Tradeoffs on Performance

There are two alternative approaches to the problem of determining just how the particular binding of different design decisions affects the performance of each machine:

1 *Top-down approach.* Attempt to isolate the effect of a particular design tradeoff over the entire space of implementations by fitting the individual performance figures for the whole family of machines to a mathematical model which treats the design parameters as independent variables and performance as the dependent variable.

2 *Bottom-up approach.* Make a detailed sensitivity analysis of a particular tradeoff within a particular machine by comparing the performance of the machine both with and without the design feature while leaving all other design features the same.

Each approach has its assets and liabilities for assessing design tradeoffs. The first method requires no information about the implementation of a machine, but does require a sufficiently large collection of different implementations, a sufficiently small number of independent variables, and an adequate mathematical model in order to explain the variance in the dependent variable to some reasonable level of statistical confidence. The second method, on the other hand, requires a great deal of knowledge about the implementation of the given system and a correspondingly great amount of analysis to isolate the effect of the single design decision on the performance of the complete system. The information that is yielded is quite exact, but applies only to the single point chosen in the design space and may not be generalized to other points in the space unless the assumptions concerning the machine's implementation are similarly generalizable. In the following subsections the first method is used to determine the dominant tradeoffs and the second method is used to estimate the impact of individual implementation tradeoffs.

4.1 Quantifying Performance

Measuring the change in performance of a particular PDP-11 processor model due to design changes presupposes the existence of some performance metric. Average instruction execution time was chosen because of its obvious relationship to instruction-stream throughput. Neglected are such overhead factors as direct memory access, interrupt servicing, and, on the LSI-11, dynamic memory refresh. Average instruction execution times may be obtained by benchmarking or by calculation from instruction frequency and timing data. The latter method was chosen because of its freedom from the extraneous factors noted above and from

the normal clock rate variations found from machine to machine of a given model. This method also allows us to calculate the change in average instruction execution time that would result from some change in the implementation. Such frequency-driven design has already been applied in practice to the PDP-11/60 [Mudge, 1977].

The instruction frequencies are tabulated in Appendix 1 and include the frequencies of the various addressing modes. These figures were calculated from measurements made by Strecker[1] on 7.6 million instruction executions traced in 10 different PDP-11 instruction streams encountered in various applications. While there is a reasonable amount of variation of frequencies from one stream to the next, the figures should be representative.

Instruction times were tabulated for each of the eight PDP-11 implementations and reported in Snow and Siewiorek [1978]. These times were calculated from the engineering documents for each machine. The times differ from those published in the PDP-11 processor handbooks for two reasons. First, in the handbooks, times have been redistributed among phases to ease the process of calculating instruction times. In Snow and Siewiorek the attempt has been made to accurately characterize each phase. Second, there are inaccuracies in the handbooks arising from conservative timing estimates and engineering revisions. The figures included here may be considered more accurate.

A performance figure is arrived at for each machine by weighting its instruction times by frequency. The results, given in Table 1, form the basis of the analyses to follow.

4.2 Analysis of Variance of PDP-11 Performance: Top-Down Approach

The first method of analysis described above will be employed in an attempt to explain most of the variance in PDP-11 performance in terms of two parameters:

1 *Microcycle time.* The microcycle time is used as a measure of processor performance which excludes the effect of the memory subsystem.

2 *Memory-read-pause time.* The memory-read-pause time is defined as the period of time during which the processor clock is suspended during a memory read. For machines with processor/Unibus overlap, the clock is assumed to be turned off by the same microinstruction which initiates the memory access. Memory-read-pause time is used as a measure of the memory subsystem's impact on processor performance. Note that this time is less than the memory access time since all PDP-11 processor clocks will continue to run at least partially concurrently with a memory access.

[1]Private communication.

Table 1   Average PDP-11 Instruction Execution Times in Microseconds

	Fetch	Source	Destination	Execute	Total	Speed relative to LSI-11
LSI-11	2.514	0.689	1.360	1.320	5.883	1.000
PDP-11/04	1.940	0.610	0.811	0.682	4.043	1.455
PDP-11/10	1.500	0.573	0.929	1.094	4.096	1.436
PDP-11/20	1.490	0.468	0.802	0.768	3.529	1.667
PDP-11/34	1.630	0.397	0.538	0.464	3.029	1.942
PDP-11/40	0.958	0.260	0.294	0.575	2.087	2.819
PDP-11/45 (bipolar memory)	0.363	0.101	0.213	0.185	0.863	6.820
PDP-11/60 (87% cache hit ratio)	0.541	0.185	0.218	0.635	1.578	3.727

The choice of these two factors is motivated by their dominant contribution to, and (approximately) linear relationship with, performance. Keeping the number of independent variables low is also important because of the small number of data points being fitted to the model.

The model itself is of the form:

$$t_i = k_1 c_{1i} + k_2 c_{2i}$$

where t_i = the average instruction execution time of machine i from Table 1

c_{1i} = the microcycle time of machine i (for machine with selectable microcycle times, the predominant time is used)

c_{2i} = the memory-read-pause time of machine i

This model is only an approximation, since it assumes k_1 and k_2 will be constant over all machines. In general this will not be the case. k_1 is the number of microcycles expected in a canonical instruction. This number will be a function mainly of data-path connectivity, and strictly speaking, another factor should be included to take that variability into account; however, since the data-path organizations of all PDP-11 implementations considered here (except the 11/03, 11/45, and 11/60) are quite comparable, the simplifying assumption of calling them all identical at the price of explaining somewhat less of the variance shall be made. k_2 is the number of memory accesses expected in a canonical instruction and also exhibits some variability from machine to machine. A small part of this is due to the fact that some PDP-11's actually take more memory cycles to perform a given instruction than do others (this is really only a factor in certain 11/10 instructions, notably JMP and JSR, and the 11/20 MOV instruction). A more important source of variability is the Unibus-processor overlap logic incorporated into some PDP-11 implementations, which effectively reduces the actual contribution of the $k_2 c_{2i}$ term by overlapping more memory access time with processor operation than is excluded from the memory-read-pause time.

Given the model and the dependent and independent data for each machine as given in Table 2, a linear regression was applied to determine the coefficients k_1 and k_2 and to find out how much of the variance is explained by the model.

If the regression is applied over all eight processors, $k_1 = 11.580, k_2 = 1.162$, and $R^2 = 0.904$. R^2 is the amount of variance accounted for by the model, or 90.4 percent. If the regression is applied to just the six midrange processors, $k_1 = 10.896$, $k_2 = 1.194$, and $R^2 = 0.962$. R^2 increases to 96.2 percent partly because fewer data points are being fitted to the model and partly because the LSI-11 and 11/45 can be expected to have different k coefficients from those of the midrange machines and hence do not fit the model as well. Note that if two midrange machines, the 11/04 and the 11/40, are eliminated instead of the LSI-11 and 11/45, then R^2 decreases to 89.3 percent rather than increasing. The k coefficients are close to what should be expected for average microcycle and memory cycle counts. Since k_1 is much larger than

Table 2   Top-Down Model Parameters in Microseconds

	Independent variables		Dependent variable
	Microcycle time	Memory-read-pause-time	Average instruction execution time
LSI-11	0.400	0.400	5.883
PDP-11/04	0.260	0.940	4.043
PDP-11/10	0.300	0.600	4.096
PDP-11/20	0.280	0.370	3.529
PDP-11/34	0.180	0.940	3.029
PDP-11/40	0.140	0.500	2.087
PDP-11/45 (bipolar memory)	0.150	0.000	0.863
PDP-11/60 (87% cache hit ratio)	0.170	0.140	1.578

k_2, average instruction time is more sensitive to microcycle time than to memory-read-pause time by a factor of k_1/k_2 or approximately 10. The implication for the designer is that much more performance can be gained or lost by perturbing the microcycle time than the memory-read-pause time.

Although this method lacks statistical rigor, it is reasonably safe to say that memory and microcycle speed do have by far the largest impact on performance and that the dependency is quantifiable to some degree.

4.3 Measuring Second-Order Effects: Bottom-up Approach

It is a great deal harder to measure the effect of other design tradeoffs on performance. The approximate methods employed in the previous section cannot be used, because the effects being measured tend to be swamped out by first-order effects and often either cancel or reinforce one another, making linear models useless. For these reasons such tradeoffs must be evaluated on a design-by-design basis as explained above. This subsection will evaluate several design tradeoffs in this way.

4.3.1 Effect of Adding a Byte Swapper to the 11/10. The PDP-11/10 uses a sequence of eight shifts to swap bytes and access odd bytes. While saving the cost of a byte swapper, this has a negative effect on performance. In this subsection the performance gained by the addition of a byte swapper either before the B register or as part of the Bleg multiplexer is calculated. Adding a byte swapper would change five different parts of the instruction interpretation process: the source and destination phases where an odd-byte operand is read from memory, the execute phase where a swap byte instruction is executed in destination mode 0 and in destination modes 1 through 7, and the execute phase where an odd-byte address is modified. In each of these cases seven fast shift cycles would be eliminated and the remaining normal-speed shift cycle could be replaced by a byte swap cycle resulting in a saving of seven fast shift cycles or 1.050 μs. None of this time would be overlapped with Unibus operations; hence, all would be saved. This saving is only effected, however, when a byte swap or odd-byte access is actually performed. The frequency with which this occurs is just the sum of the frequencies of the individual cases noted above, or 0.0640. Multiplying by the time saved per occurrence gives a saving of 0.0672 μs or 1.64 percent of the average instruction execution time. The insignificance of this saving can well be used to support the decision for leaving the byte swapper out of the PDP-11/10.

4.3.2 Effect of adding Processor/Unibus Overlap to the 11/04. Processor/Unibus overlap is not a feature of the 11/04 control unit. Adding this feature involves altering the control unit/Unibus synchronization logic so that the processor clock continues to run until a microcycle requiring the Unibus data from a DATI or DATIP is detected. A bus address register must also be added to drive the Unibus lines after the microcycle initiating the DATIP is completed. This alteration allows time to be saved in two ways. First, processor cycles may be overlapped with memory read cycles, as explained in Subsection 3.1.2. Second, since Unibus data are not read into the data paths during the cycle in which the DATIP occurs, the path from the ALU through the AMUX and back to the registers is freed. This permits certain operations to be performed in the same cycle as the DATIP; for example, the microword BA←PC; DATI; PC←PC+2 could be used to start fetching the word pointed to by the PC while simultaneously incrementing the PC to address the next word. The cycle following could then load the Unibus data directly into a scratch-pad register rather than loading the data into the Breg and then into the scratch-pad on the following cycle, as is necessary without overlap logic. A saving of two microcycle times would result.

DATI and DATIP operations are scattered liberally throughout the 11/04 microcode; however, only those cycles in which an overlap would produce a time saving need be considered. An average of 0.730 cycles can be saved or overlapped during each instruction. If all of the overlapped time is actually saved, then 0.190 μs, or 4.70 percent, will be pared from the average instruction execution time. This amounts to a 4.93 percent increase in performance.

4.3.3 Effect of Caching on the 11/60. The PDP-11/60 uses a cache to decrease its effective memory-read-pause time. The degree to which this time is reduced depends upon three factors: the cache-read–hit pause time, the cache-read–miss pause time, and the ratio of cache-read hits to total memory read accesses. A write-through cache is assumed; therefore, the timing of memory write accesses is not affected by caching and only read accesses need be considered. The performance of the 11/60 as measured by average instruction execution time is modeled exactly as a function of the above three parameters by the equation

$$t = k_1 + k_2(k_3 a + k_4[1-a])$$

where t = the average instruction execution time
a = the cache hit ratio
k_1 = the average execution time of a PDP-11/60 instruction excluding memory-read-pause time but including memory-write-pause time (1.339μs)
k_2 = the number of memory reads per average instruction (1.713)
k_3 = the memory-read-pause time for a cache hit (0.000μs)
k_4 = the memory-read-pause time for a cache miss (1.075μs)

The above equation can be rearranged to yield:

$$t = (k_1 + k_2 k_4) - k_2(k_4 - k_3)a$$

The first term and the coefficient of the second term in the equation above are equivalent to 3.181 μs and 1.842 μs respectively with the given k parameter values. This reduces the average instruction time to a function of the cache hit ratio, making it possible to compare the effect of various caching schemes on 11/60 performance in terms of this one parameter.

The effect of various cache organizations on the hit ratio is described for the PDP-11 family in general in Strecker [1976b] and for the PDP-11/60 in particular in Mudge [1977]. If no cache is provided, the hit ratio is effectively 0 and the average instruction execution time reduces to the first term in the model, or 3.181 μs. A set-associative cache with a set size of 1 word and a cache size of 1,024 words has been found through simulation to give a .87 hit ratio. An average instruction time of 1.578 μs results in a 101.52 percent improvement in performance over that without the cache.

The cache organization described above is that actually employed in the 11/60. It has the virtue of being relatively simple to implement and therefore reasonably inexpensive. Set size or cache size can be increased to attain a higher hit ratio at a correspondingly higher cost. One alternative cache organization is a set size of 2 words and a cache size of 2,048 words. This organization boosts the hit ratio to .93, resulting in an instruction time of 1.468 μs, an increase in performance of 7.53 percent. This increased performance must be paid for, however, since twice as many memory chips are needed. Because the performance increment derived from the second cache organization is much smaller than that of the first while the cost increment is approximately the same, the first is more cost-effective.

4.3.4 Design Tradeoffs Affecting the Fetch Phase. The fetch phase holds much potential for performance improvement, since it consists of a single short sequence of microoperations that, as Table 1 clearly shows, involves a sizable fraction of the average instruction time because of the inevitable memory access and possible service operations. In this subsection two approaches to cutting this time are evaluated for four different processors.

The Unibus interface logic of the PDP-11/04 and that of the 11/34 are very similar. Both insert a delay into the initial microcycle of the fetch phase to allow time for bus-grant arbitration circuitry to settle so that a microbranch can be taken if a serviceable condition exists. If the arbitration logic were redesigned to eliminate this delay, the average instruction execution time would drop by 0.220 μs for the 11/04 and 0.150 μs for the 11/34.[1] The resulting increases in performance would be 5.75 percent and 5.21 percent respectively.

[1]These figures are typical. Since the delay is set by an *RC* circuit and Schmitt trigger, the delay may vary considerably from machine to machine of a given model.

Another example of a design feature affecting the fetch phase is the operand–instruction fetch overlap mechanism of the 11/40, 11/45, and 11/60. From the normal fetch times in the appendix and the actual average fetch times given in Table 1, the saving in fetch phase time alone can be calculated to be 0.162 μs for the 11/40, 0.087 μs for the 11/45, and 0.118 μs for the 11/60, or an increase of 7.77 percent, 10.07 percent, and 8.11 percent over what their respective performances would be if fetch phase time were not overlapped.

These examples demonstrate the practicality of optimizing sequences of control states that have a high frequency of occurrence rather than just those which have long durations. The 11/10 byte-swap logic is quite slow, but it is utilized infrequently, so that its impact upon performance is small; while the bus arbitration logic of the 11/34 exacts only a small time penalty but does so each time an instruction is executed and results in a larger performance impact. The usefulness of frequency data should thus be apparent, since the bottlenecks in a design are often not where intuition says they should be.

5. Summary and Use of the Methodologies

The PDP-11 offers an interesting opportunity to examine an architecture with numerous implementations spanning a wide range of price and performance. The implementations appear to fall into three distinct categories: the midrange machines (PDP-11/04/10/20/34/40/60); an inexpensive, relatively low-performance machine (LSI-11); and a comparatively expensive but high-performance machine (PDP-11/45). The midrange machines are all minor variations on a common theme with each implementation introducing much less variability than might be expected. Their differences reside in the presence or absence of certain embellishments rather than in any major structural differences. This common design scheme is still quite recognizable in the LSI-11 and even in the PDP-11/45. The deviations of the LSI-11 arise from limitations imposed by semiconductor technology rather than directly from cost or performance considerations, although the technology decision derives from cost. In the PDP-11/45, on the other hand, the quantum jump in complexity is purely motivated by the desire to squeeze the maximum performance out of the architecture.

From the overall performance model presented in Sec. 4.2 of this chapter, it is evident that instruction-stream processing can be speeded up by improving either the performance of the memory subsystem or the performance of the processor. Memory subsystem performance depends upon the number of memory accesses in a canonical instruction and the effective memory-read-pause time. There is not much that can be done about the first number, since it is a function of the architecture and thus largely fixed. The second number may be improved, however, by the use of faster memory components or techniques such as caching.

The performance of the PDP-11 processor itself can be enhanced in two ways: by cutting the number of processor cycles to perform a given function or by cutting the time used per microcycle. Several approaches to decreasing the effective microcycle count have been demonstrated:

1 *Structure the data paths for maximum parallelism.* The PDP-11/45 can perform much more in a given microcycle than any of the midrange PDP-11's and thus needs fewer microcycles to complete an instruction. To obtain this increased functionality, however, a much more elaborate set of data paths is required in addition to a highly developed control unit to exercise them to maximum potential. Such a change is not an incremental one and involves rethinking the entire implementation.

2 *Structure the microcode to take best advantage of instruction features.* All processors except the 11/10 handle JMP/JSR addressing modes as a special case in the microcode. Most do the same for the destination modes of the MOV instruction because of its high frequency. Varying degrees of sophistication in instruction dispatching from the BUT IRDECODE at the end of every fetch is evident in different machines and results in various performance improvements.

3 *Cut effective microcycle count by overlapping processor and Unibus operation.* The PDP-11/10 demonstrates that a large microcycle count can be effectively reduced by placing cycles in parallel with memory access operations whenever possible.

Increasing microcycle speed is perhaps more generally useful, since it can often be applied without making substantial changes to an entire implementation. Several of the midrange PDP-11's achieve most of their performance improvement by increasing microcycle speed in the following ways:

1 *Make the data paths faster.* The PDP-11/34 demonstrates the improvement in microcycle time that can result from the judicious use of Schottky TTL in such heavily traveled points as the ALU. Replacing the ALU and carry/look-ahead logic alone with Schottky equivalents saves approximately 35 ns in propagation delay. With cycle times running 300 ns and less, this amounts to better than a 10 percent increase in speed.

2 *Make each microcycle take only as long as necessary.* The 11/34 and 11/40 both use selectable microcycle times to speed up cycles that do not entail long data-path propagation delays.

Circuit technology is perhaps the single most important factor in performance. It is only stating the obvious to say that doubling circuit speed will double total performance. Aside from raw speed, circuit technology dictates what it is economically feasible to build, as witnessed by the SSI PDP-11/20, the MSI PDP-11/40, and the LSI-11. Just the limitations of a particular circuit technology at a given point in time may dictate much about the design tradeoffs that can be made, as in the case of the LSI-11.

Turning to the methodologies, the two presented in Sec.4 of this chapter can be used at various times during the design cycle. The top-down approach can be used to estimate the performance of a proposed implementation, or to plan a family of implementations, given only the characteristics of the selected technology and a general estimate of data-path and memory-cycle utilization.

The bottom-up approach can be used to perturb an existing or planned design to determine the performance payoff of a particular design tradeoff. The relative frequencies of each function (e.g., addressing modes and instructions), while required for an accurate prediction, may not be available. There are, however, alternative ways to estimate relative frequencies. Consider the three following situations:

1 *At least one implementation exists.* An analysis of the implementation in typical usage (i.e., benchmark programs for a stored-program computer) can provide the relative frequencies.

2 *No implementation exists, but similar systems exist.* The frequency data may be extrapolated from measurements made on a machine with a similar architecture.

3 *No implementation exists and there are no prior similar systems.* From knowledge of the specifications, a set of most-used functions can be estimated (e.g., instruction fetch, register and relative addressing, move and add instructions for a stored-program computer). The design is then optimized for these functions.

Of course, the relative-frequency data should always be updated to take into account new data.

Our purpose in writing this chapter has been twofold: to provide data about design tradeoffs and to suggest design methodologies based on these data. It is hoped that the design data will stimulate the study of other methodologies while the results of the design methodologies presented here have demonstrated their usefulness to designers.

References

Bell et al. [1970]; Mudge [1977]; O'Loughlin [1975]; Siewiorek and Barbacci [1976]; Snow and Siewiorek [1978]; Strecker [1976b]; Thomas and Siewiorek [1977]; Wilkes and Stringer [1953]. The following Digital Equipment Corporation documents define the architecture and instruction set of the PDP-11 in addition to detailing features peculiar to individual processor implementations: DEC [1971]; DEC [1975]; DEC [1976a–e]; DEC [1977].

APPENDIX 1 INSTRUCTION TIME COMPONENT FREQUENCIES

This appendix tabulates the frequencies of PDP-11 instructions and addressing modes. These data were derived as explained in Subsection 4.1. Frequencies are given for the occurrence of each phase (e.g., source, which occurs only during double-operand instructions), each subcase of each phase (e.g., jump destination, which occurs only during jump or jump to subroutine instructions), and each instance of each phase, such as a particular addressing mode or instruction. The frequency with which the phase is skipped is listed for source and destination phases. Source and destination odd-byte–addressing frequencies are listed as well because of their effect on instruction timing.

	Frequency
Fetch	1.0000
Source Mode	0.4069
0 R	0.1377
1 @R or (R)	0.0338
2 (R)+	0.1587
3 @(R)+	0.0122
4 −(R)	0.0352
5 @−(R)	0.0000
6 X(R)	0.0271
7 @X(R)	0.0022
No Source	0.5931

NOTE: Frequency of odd-byte addressing (SM1–7) = 0.0252.

	Frequency
Destination Mode	0.6872
Data Manipulation Mode	0.6355
0 R	0.3146
1 @R or (R)	0.0599
2 (R)+	0.0854
3 @(R)+	0.0307
4 −(R)	0.0823
5 @−(R)	0.0000
6 X(R)	0.0547
7 @X(R)	0.0080

NOTE: Frequency of odd-byte addressing (DM1–7) = 0.0213.

	Frequency
Jump (JMP/JSR)	0.0517
Operand Mode	
0 R	0.0000 (ILLEGAL)
1 @R or (R)	0.0000
2 (R)+	0.0000
3 @(R)+	0.0079
4 −(R)	0.0000
5 @−(R)	0.0000
6 X(R)	0.0438
7 @X(R)	0.0000
No Destination	0.3128

	Frequency
Execute Instruction	1.0000
Double operand	0.4069
ADD	0.0524
SUB	0.0274
BIC	0.0309
BICB	0.0000
BIS	0.0012
BISB	0.0013
CMP	0.0626
CMPB	0.0212
BIT	0.0041
BITB	0.0014
MOV	0.1517
MOVB	0.0524
XOR	0.0000
Single operand	0.2286
CLR	0.0186
CLRB	0.0018
COM	0.0000
COMB	0.0000
INC	0.0224
INCB	0.0000
DEC	0.0809
DECB	0.0000
NEG	0.0038
NEGB	0.0000
ADC	0.0070
ADCB	0.0000
SBC	0.0000
SBCB	0.0000
ROR	0.0036
RORB	0.0000
ROL	0.0059
ROLB	0.0000
ASR	0.0069
ASRB	0.0000
ASL	0.0298
ASLB	0.0000
TST	0.0329
TSTB	0.0079
SWAB	0.0038
SXT	0.0000
Branch	0.2853
All branches (true)	0.1744
All branches (false)	0.1109
SOB (true)	0.0000
SOB (false)	0.0000

	Frequency
Jump	0.0517
JMP	0.0272
JSR	0.0245
Control, trap and miscellaneous	0.0270
Set/clear condition codes	0.0017
MARK	0.0000
RTS	0.0236
RTI	0.0000
RTT	0.0000
IOT	0.0000
EMT	0.0017
TRAP	0.0000
BPT	0.0000

NOTES: Frequency of destination odd-byte addressing (DM1-7) = 0.0213.

Execution frequencies indicated as 0.0000 have an aggregate frequency < 0.0050.

Section 4

Maxicomputers

Introduction

What distinguishes the maxicomputer class from the classes already presented? As illustrated in Chap. 1, one primary characteristic is price. The maxicomputer tends to be the largest machine that can be built in a given technology at a given time. The typical price for a maxicomputer in 1980 was greater than $1 million. Another characteristic used in Chap. 1 was a large virtual-address space. In 1980 this meant a virtual-address space size in excess of 16 Mbyte.

Maxicomputers usually have a rich set of data-types. Over the years the scientific data-types have progressed from short-word to long-word fixed-point scalars, to floating-point scalars, and finally to vectors and arrays. Commercial data-types have progressed from character-at-a-time to fixed-length instructions using descriptors and on to variable character strings. The PMS structure of maxicomputers has evolved from a single Pc to 1-Pc–n-Pio, then to m-Pc–n-Pio, and on to C–Cio [data-base]–Cio [communication].

Not all maxicomputers satisfy all the characteristics. Several maxicomputers have just basic processing performance as a goal and have only high-performance implementations (as do the TI ASC and the CRAY-1), often with a limited range of peripherals and software. Other maxicomputers have a family of program-compatible implementations spanning a large performance range (as do the System/369-370 Model 91 and Model 195 and the VAX-11). Particular implementations of these families of machines may be high-performance; however, such implementations are constrained by the family ISP, which may not have provision for features related only to high performance. (As an example of such a feature, the TI ASC has a PREPARE TO BRANCH instruction that notifies instruction prefetch logic of an upcoming branch. By prefetching instructions down both possible branch paths this instruction can keep the instruction pipeline filled.)

This section examines five maxicomputers. The System/360 and the VAX-11 represent implementation families, while the CRAY-1 and the TI ASC are explicitly targeted for the very-high-performance market, where the goal is solely performance. The CDC 6600, while designed primarily for the high-performance market, can be assembled into lower-performance models if the high-performance central processor is deleted.

The IBM System/360

The IBM System/360 is the name given to a third-generation series of computers. More recent than the System/360 is the IBM System/370, which has been followed by cost-reduced implementations in the Series 3030 and Series 4300, which constitute the current primary IBM product line. Chapters 40 and 41 focus on the ISP of the original System/360. A discussion of the System/370 and the 3030 and 4300 series plus a comparison of the various models in the System/360, System/370, Series 3030, and Series 4300 is covered in Part 4, Sec. 5.

The following discussion covers only the processor. The instruction set consists of two classes, scientific ISP and data processing ISP, which operate on the different data-types. These data-types correspond roughly to the IBM 7090 and IBM 1401 [Bell and Newell, 1971]. For the scientific ISP there are half- and single-word integers; address integers; single, double, and quadruple (in the Model 85) floating point; and logical words (boolean vectors). For the data processing ISP there are address or single-word integers, multiple-byte strings, and multiple-digit decimal strings. These many data-types give the 360 strength in the minds of its various types of users. However, the many data-types, each performing few operations, may be of questionable utility and may constrain the ISP design in a way that a more complete operation set for a few basic data-types does not.

The ISP uses a general-register organization, as is common in virtually all computers in use during the 1970s. The ISP power can be compared with several similar multiple-register ISP structures, such as those of the UNIVAC 1107 and 1108; the CDC 6600 and 7600; the CRAY-1; the DEC PDP-6, PDP-10, PDP-11, and VAX-11; the Intel 8080 and 8086; the SDS Sigma 5 and Sigma 7; and the early general-register–organized machine Pegasus [Elliott et al., 1956]. Of these machines the System/360 scientific ISP appears to be the weakest in terms of instruction effectiveness and the completeness of its instruction set. As part of the Military Computer Family (MCF) project [Computer, 1977; CFA, 1977], a statistically designed experiment was conducted to compare the effectiveness of the Interdata 8/32, PDP-11, and IBM System/360 ISP. Sixteen programmers implemented test programs from a set of 12 benchmark descriptions. In all, 99 programs were written and measured. The results indicated that the System/360 required 21 percent and 46 percent more memory to store programs than the PDP-11 and the Interdata 8/32, respectively. Further, the System/360 required 37 percent and 49 percent more bytes than the PDP-11 and Interdata 8/32, respectively, to be transferred between primary memory and the processor during execution of the test programs.

In the following discussion, it would be instructive to contrast the System/360 ISP with a more contemporary ISP, such as that of the VAX-11. For example, in the VAX-11/780 (Chap. 42), symmetry is provided in the instruction set. For any binary operation b the following are possible:

GR ← GR b Mp	Memory/register to register
GR ← GR b GR	Register to register
Mp ← GR b Mp	Memory/register to memory
Mp ← Mp b Mp	Memory/memory to memory

The 360 ISP provides only the first two. Additional instructions (or modes) would increase the instruction length.

In the System/360 the only advantage taken of general registers is to make them suitable for use as index registers, base registers, and arithmetic accumulators (for operand storage). Of course, the commitment to extend the general-purpose nature of these general registers would require more operations.

The 360 has a separate set of general registers for floating-point data, whereas the VAX-11/780 uses one register set for all data-types. Data-type–specific register sets provide more processor state and temporary storage but again detract from the general-purpose ability of the existing registers. Special commands are required to manipulate the floating-point registers independently of the other general registers. Unfortunately the floating-point instruction set is not quite complete (e.g., in conversion from fixed to floating point; several instructions are needed to move data between the fixed and floating registers).

When multiple data-types are available, it is desirable to have the ability to convert between them unless the operations are complete in themselves. The VAX-11/780 provides a full set of instructions for converting between data-types. The System/360, on the other hand, might use more data-conversion instructions, for example, between the following:

1 Fixed-precision integers and floating-point data.

2 Address-size integers and any other data.

3 Half-word integers and other data.

4 Decimal and byte string and other data. (Conversion between decimal string and byte string is provided.)

Some of the facilities are redundant and might be handled by better but fewer instructions. For example, decimal strings are not completely variable-length (they are variable up to 31 digits, stored in 16 bytes), and so essentially the same arithmetic results could be obtained by using fixed multiple-length binary integers. This would remove the special decimal arithmetic and still give the same result. If a large quantity of fixed-field decimal or byte

data were processed, then the binary-decimal conversion instructions would be useful.

The communication instructions between Pc and Pio are minimal with the System/360. The Pc must set up Pio program data, but there are inadequate facilities in the Pc for quickly forming Pio instructions (which are actually yet another data-type). There are, in effect, a large number of Pio's, as each device is independent of all others. However, signaling of all Pio's is via a single interrupt channel to the Pc. By contrast, the VAX-11 I/O devices are implemented as a set of registers with addresses in the memory address space. Thus the entire instruction set is usable to directly control the I/O activity. There are no specific I/O instructions.

The Pc state consists of 26 words of 32 bits each:

1 Program state words, including the instruction counter (2 words)

2 Sixteen general registers (16 words)

3 Four 2-word floating-point general registers (8 words)

Many instructions must be executed (taking appreciable time) to preserve the Pc state and establish a new one. A single instruction would be preferable; even better would be an instruction to exchange processor states, as in the CDC 6600 (Chap. 43).

As originally designed in the System/360, the methods used to address data in Mp had some disadvantages. It is impossible to fetch an arbitrary word in Mp in a single instruction, because the address space is limited to a direct address of only 2^{12} bytes. Any Mp access outside the range requires an offset or base address to be placed in a general register. Accesses to several large arrays may take significant time if a base address has to be loaded each time. The reason for using a small direct address is to save space in the instruction. The VAX-11 provides multiple addressing modes, including direct access to 2^{31} bytes, that gives the programmer flexibility in accessing arbitrary operands.

Another difficulty of the 360 addressing is the nonhomogeneity of the address space. Addressing is to the nearest byte, but the system remains organized by words; thus, many addresses are forced to be on word (and even doubleword) boundaries. For example, a double-precision data-type which requires two words of storage must be stored with the first word beginning at a multiple of an 8-byte address. (However, the Model 85, which is a late entry in the series, allows arbitrary alignment of data-types with word boundaries, while the System/370 eliminated this limitation.) When a general register is used as a base or index register, the value in the index register must correspond to the length of the data-type accessed. That is, for the value of a half integer, single integer, single floating (long), and quadruple floating (extended), i must be multiplied by 2, 4, 4, 8, and 16, respectively, to access the proper element. The VAX-11 does not require data-types to be aligned on artificial boundaries.

A single instruction to load or store any string of bits in Mp (as provided in the IBM Stretch) would provide a great deal of generality. Provided the length were up to 64 bits, such an instruction might eliminate the need for the more specialized data-types.

A basic scheme for dynamic multiprogramming through program swapping was nonexistent in the System/360 because of the inadequate relocation hardware. Only a simple method of Mp protection is provided, using protection keys (see Part 2, Sec. 2). This scheme associates a 4-bit number (key) and a 1-bit write protect with each 2-Kbyte block, and each Pc access must have the correct number. Both protection of Mp and assignment of Mp to a particular task (greater than 2^4 tasks) are necessary in a dynamic multiprogramming environment. Although the architects of the System/360 advocate its use for multiprogramming, the operating system does not enforce conventions to enable a program to be moved, once its execution is started. Indeed, the nature of the System/360 addressing is based on absolute binary addresses within a program. The later, experimental Model 67 does, however, have a very nice scheme for protection, relocation, and name assignment to program segments [Arden et al., 1966].

VAX

The VAX-11 (Virtual Address Extension) is a 32-bit successor to the PDP-11 minicomputer (Chap. 38). The VAX-11 ISP bears a strong kinship to the PDP-11 ISP, especially with respect to addressing modes.

While the primary reason for creating an ISP based on 32-bit words was for a 32-bit address space, the extra word width allowed for the addition of new data-types (strings, characters, etc.) and a general cleaning up of the instruction format (e.g., from a variety of op code field lengths of 4, 8, 10, and 16 bits in the PDP-11 to multiples of 8-bit fields). Several of the perceived shortcomings of the System/360 instruction set were fixed, including:

1   ISP symmetry for source and destination operands.

2   A complete set of instructions for each data-type and for converting between data-types.

3   General-register architecture where the registers are used for all data-types. There are no special registers dedicated to a subset of the data-types.

4   I/O handling through the address space, as in the PDP-11. The same set of instructions can be used in either data manipulation or I/O.

5   A virtual-memory system that provides both program protection and memory relocation.

6   Rapid context swap through automatic register saving as determined by a settable bit mask.

7   Addressability of any location in memory by a single instruction.

8   Stacks and stack operators integral to the design, especially for procedure calls.

The VAX-11 ISP represents what the System/360 ISP could have been given 10 years of experience in instruction sets. The evolution of the VAX-11 ISP from the PDP-11 ISP is an interesting study of concern for user-program compatibility on architectures using different word lengths. This evolution is also interesting to compare with that of the System/360 and System/370 (Chap. 51).

Figures 1 and 2 illustrate the PMS diagram and Kiviat graph for the first VAX implementation, the VAX-11/780. An LSI-11 serves as the console processor. The LSI-11 interprets commands typed on the console for machine control. The console teletype replaces the traditional console light and switch panel in performing functions such as HALT, SINGLE STEP, DEPOSIT, and EXAMINE. The console processor also provides for system initiation (booting), diagnosis (through microdiagnostics and the diagnostic control store), and status monitoring. Conceptually, the console terminal could be replaced by a phone line or serial line to another computer for remote monitoring and control.

A set-associative cache provides performance improvement on operand fetching. Because of the elaborate translation from virtual to real address, a translation buffer (or physical address cache) provides speedup to the address translation process.

Any mix of four Unibus or Massbus adaptors provides for attaching to peripheral buses that are not compatible with the VAX-11/780 processor/memory.

The CDC 6600, 7600, and CYBER Series

The CDC 6000 series development began in 1960, using high-speed transistors and discrete components of the second generation. The first 6600 was announced in July 1963 and first delivery was in September 1964. Subsequent, compatible successors included the 6400, in April 1966, which was implemented as a conventional Pc (a single shared arithmetic function unit instead of the 10 D's); the 6500, in October 1967, which uses two 6400 Pc's; and the 6416, in 1966, which has only peripheral and control

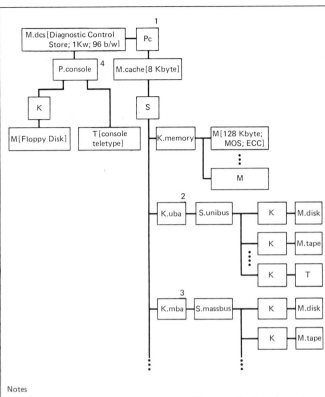

Notes
1. Pc[0-5 addresses/instruction; technology: TTL MSI; options: floating point accelerator]
2. Kuba['Unibus Adaptor; 1.5 Mbyte/s]
3. Kmba['Massbus Adaptor; 2.0 Mbyte/s]
4. Pconsole ['LSI-11; technology: NMOS LSI]

Fig. 1. PMS diagram of VAX-11/780.

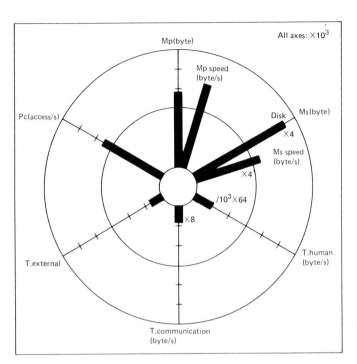

Fig. 2. Kiviat graph for the VAX-11/780.

processors (PCP). The first 7600, which is nearly compatible, was delivered in 1969. The dual-processor 6700, consisting of a 6600 and a 6400 Pc, was introduced in October 1969. Subsequent modifications to the series in 1969 included the extension to 20 peripheral and control processors with 24 channels. CDC also marketed a 6400 with a smaller number of peripheral and control processors (the 6415-7, with seven). Reducing the maximum PCP number to seven also reduced the overall purchase cost by approximately $56,000 per processor.

The computer organization, technology, and construction are described in Chap. 43. ISP descriptions for the Pc are given in Appendix 1 of Chap. 43.

To obtain the very high logic speeds, the components are placed close together. The logic cards use a cordwood-type construction. The logic is direct-coupled–transistor logic, with 5 ns of propaga-

tion time and a clock of 25 ns. The fundamental minor cycle is 100 ns, and the major cycle is 1,000 ns, as is the memory cycle time. Since the component density is high (about 500,000 transistors in the 6600), the logic is cooled by conduction to a plate with Freon circulating through it.

This series is interesting from many aspects. It remained the fastest operational computer for many years, until the advent of the IBM System/360 Model 91 and the follow-on CDC 7600. Its large component count almost implies it cannot exist as an operational entity. Thus it is a tribute to an organization, and the project leader-designer, Seymour Cray, that a large number exist. There are sufficiently high data bandwidths within the system that it remains balanced for most job mixes (an uncommon feature in large C's). It has high-performance Ms.disks and T.displays to avoid bottlenecks. The Pc's ISP is a nice variation of the general-register processor and allows for very efficient encoding of programs. The Pc is multiprogrammed and can be switched from job to job more quickly than any other computer. Ten smaller C's control the main Pc and allow it to spend time on useful (billable) work rather than on its own administration. The independent multiple data operators in the 6600 increase the speed by at least 2½ times over a 6400, which has a shared D. Finally, it realizes the 10 C's in a unique, interesting, and efficient manner. Not many computer systems can claim half as many innovations.

PMS Structure

A simplified PMS structure of the C['6400, '6600] is given in Fig. 3. Here we see the C[io; #1:10], each of which can access the central computer (Cc) primary memory (Mp). Figure 3 shows why we consider the 6600 to be fundamentally a network. Each Cio (actually a general-purpose, 12-bit C) can easily serve the specialized Pio function for Cc. The Mp of Cc is an Ms for a Cio, of course. By having a powerful Cio, more complex input/output tasks can be handled without Cc intervention. These tasks can include data-type conversion and error recovery, among others. The K's which are connected to a Cio can also be less complex. Figure 3 has about the same information as Fig. 1 in Chap. 43.

A detailed PMS diagram for the C['6400, '6416, '6500, and '6600] is given in Fig. 4, accompanied by a Kiviat graph in Fig. 5 that is representative of the CDC 6600 series. The interesting

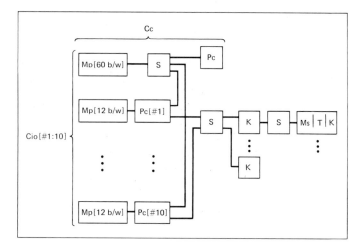

Fig. 3. CDC 6600 PMS diagram (simplified).

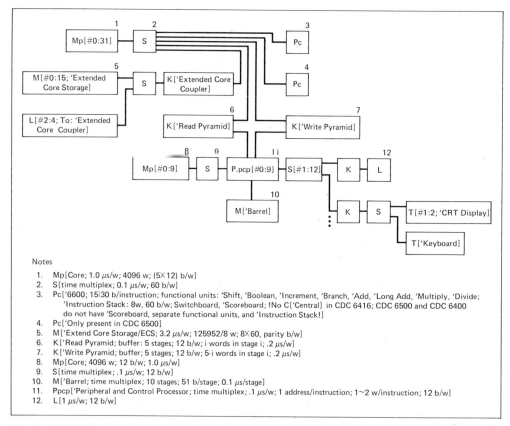

Notes

1. Mp[Core; 1.0 μs/w; 4096 w; (5×12) b/w]
2. S[time multiplex; 0.1 μs/w; 60 b/w]
3. Pc['6600; 15|30 b/instruction; functional units: 'Shift, 'Boolean, 'Increment, 'Branch, 'Add, 'Long Add, 'Multiply, 'Divide; 'Instruction Stack: 8w, 60 b/w; Switchboard, 'Scoreboard; !No C['Central] in CDC 6416; CDC 6500 and CDC 6400 do not have 'Scoreboard, separate functional units, and 'Instruction Stack!]
4. Pc['Only present in CDC 6500]
5. M['Extend Core Storage/ECS; 3.2 μs/w; 125952/8 w; 8×60, parity b/w]
6. K['Read Pyramid; buffer: 5 stages; 12 b/w; i words in stage i; .2 μs/w]
7. K['Write Pyramid; buffer: 5 stages; 12 b/w; 5-i words in stage i; .2 μs/w]
8. Mp[Core; 4096 w; 12 b/w; 1.0 μs/w]
9. S[time multiplex; .1 μs/w; 12 b/w]
10. M['Barrel; time multiplex; 10 stages; 51 b/stage; 0.1 μs/stage]
11. Ppcp['Peripheral and Control Processor; time multiplex; .1 μs/w; 1 address/instruction; 1~2 w/instruction; 12 b/w]
12. L[1 μs/w; 12 b/w]

Fig. 4. CDC 6400, 6416, 6500, and 6600 PMS diagram.

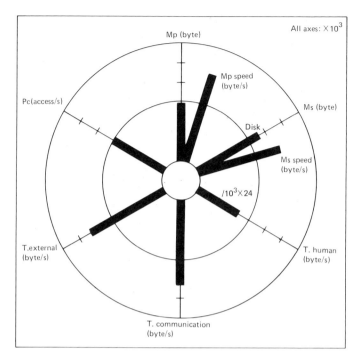

Mp (byte)

All axes: ×10³

Mp speed
(byte/s)

Ms (byte)

Pc(access/s)

Disk

Ms speed
(byte/s)

/10³ × 24

T.external
(byte/s)

T. human
(byte/s)

T. communication
(byte/s)

Fig. 5. Kiviat graph for the CDC 6600.

structural aspects can be seen from Fig. 4. The four configurations, 6400 through 6600, are included just by considering the pertinent parts of the structure. That is, a 6416 has no large Pc; a 6400 has a single, straightforward Pc; a 6500 has two Pc's; and the 6600 has a single, powerful Pc. The 6600 Pc has ten D's, so that several parts of a single instruction stream can be interpreted in parallel. A 6600 Pc also has considerable M.buffer to hold instructions so that Pc need not wait for Mp fetches.

The implementation of the ten Cio's can be seen from the PMS diagram (Fig. 4). Here, only one physical processor is used on a time-shared basis. Each 0.1 μs, a new logical P is processed by the physical P. The ten Mp's are phased so that a new access occurs each 0.1 μs. The ten Mp's are always busy. Thus the i.rate is 10 × 12 bit/μs or 120 Mbit/s. This process of shifting a new Pc state into position each 0.1 μs has been likened to a barrel by CDC. A diagram of the process is shown in Fig. 6.

The T's, K's, and M's are not given, although it should be mentioned that the following units are rather unique: a K for the management of 64 telegraph lines to be connected to a Cio; an Ms(disk) with four simultaneous access ports, each at a data-transfer rate of 1.68 megacharacters per second and a capacity of 168 megacharacters; an Ms[magnetic tape] with a K[#1:4] and S to allow simultaneous transfers to four Ms's; the T[display] for

monitoring the system's operation; K's to other C's and Ms's; and conventional T[card reader, punch, line printer, etc.].

ISP

The ISP description of the Pc is given in Appendix 1 of Chap. 43. The Pc has a very clean, straightforward, scientific-calculation–oriented ISP. We can consider it a variation on the general-register structure because the Pc state has three sets of general registers. Their use is explained both in Chap. 43 and its Appendix 1. This structure assumes that a program consists of several read accesses to a large array (or arrays) and a large number of operations on these accessed elements, followed by occasional write accesses to store results. We would agree that this is a valid assumption for scientific programs (e.g., look at a FORTRAN arithmetic statement), and it is probably valid for most other programs as well.

Cc has provisions for multiprogramming in the form of a protection and relocation address register pair. The mapping is given in the ISP description for both Mp and Ms['Extended Core Storage/ECS].

The 6600 PCP is about the same as the early CDC 160 minicomputer (see Part 3, Sec. 3). The PCP has an 18-bit A register because it has to process addresses for the large Cc.

One interesting aspect of the 6400 which we question is the lack of communication among all components at the ISP (programming) level. When Pc stops, it has no way of explicitly informing any other components. There are no interprocessor interrupts. An I/O device cannot interrupt a Pio, nor can Pio's communicate with one another except by polling. The state switching for Pc is elegant, however, since a Pio can request Pc to stop a job, store Mps, and resume a new task in one instruction. (The t.save + t.restore ~ 2 μs.)

The Operating System

The Cio's functions are data transmission between a peripheral device and the large Cc via the Cio's Mp with some data transformation or conversions; complete task management, including initiation, termination, and error handling; and management of Pc. The Cio's perform in about the same manner as the C['Attached Support Processor] in the System/360 (see Part 4, Sec. 5). The operating-system software is managed by a single fixed Cio. The remaining nine Cio's are free, and as I/O tasks arise in the system, the Cio's assign themselves to particular tasks, carry out the tasks, and then free themselves to take on other tasks. The operating-system software resides in Mp(Pc) (that is, Cc), is accessible to all Cio's, and includes:

1 The variables which determine the state of a particular job, e.g., data pointers to Ms[disk, 'ECS], running time, a list of jobs to do

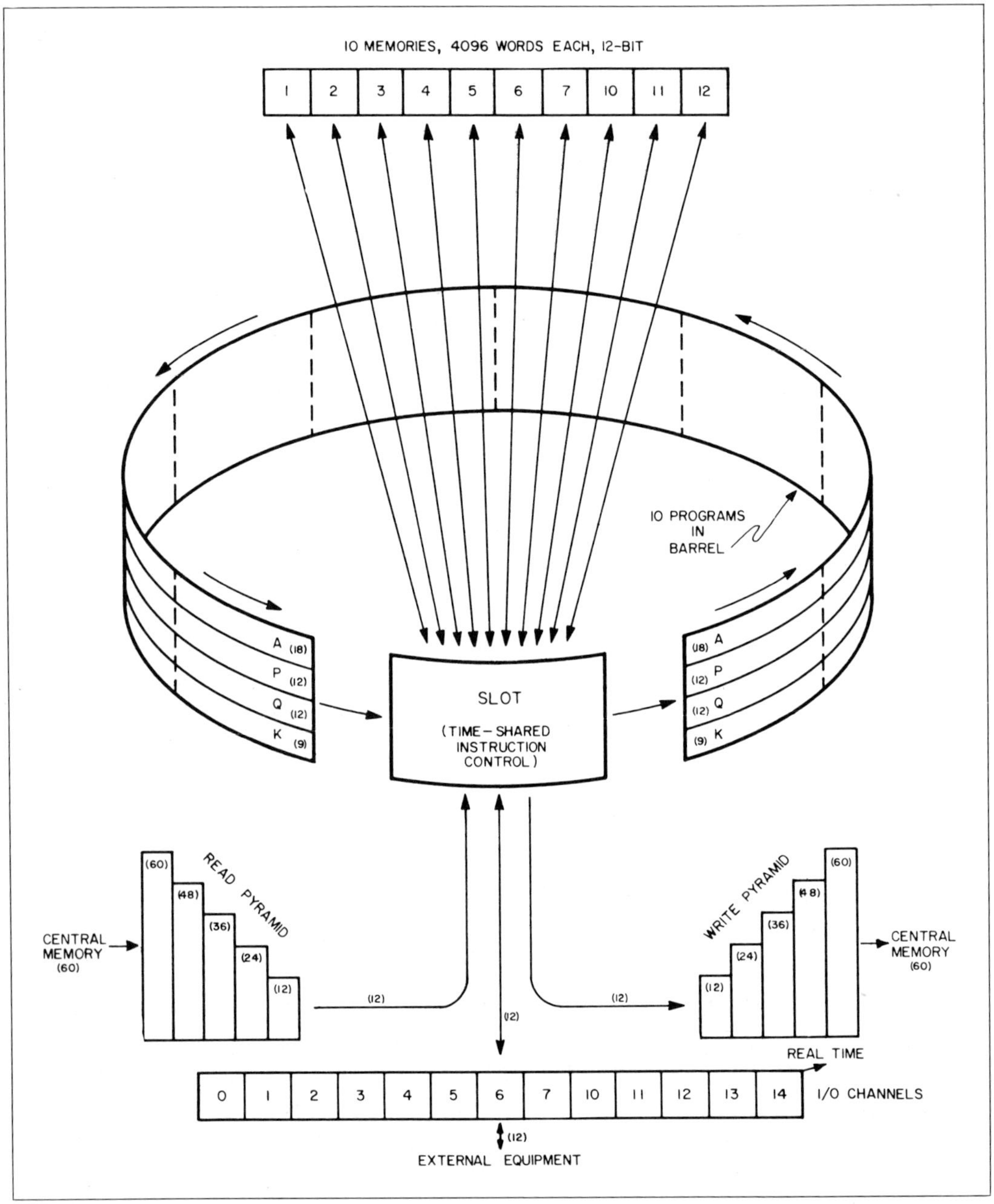

Fig. 6. CDC 6600 peripheral and control processors. *(Courtesy of Control Data Corporation.)*

2 Programs for the Cio's:
  a Parts of the operating system used by the Cio responsible for the system management

  b I/O management programs (or programs to get the task management program from Ms) which Cio's use

In a typical system, one might expect to find the following assignment of PCP's:

1 Operating-system execution, including scheduling and management of Cc and all Cio's

2 Display of job-status data on T[display]

3 Ms[disk] transfer management

4 T[printers, card reader, card punch]

5 L[#1:3; to:C.satellite]

6 Ms[magnetic tape]

7 T[64 Teletypes]

8 Free to be used with Ms[disk] and Ms[magnetic tape]

9 Free

10 Free

The CDC 7600 Series

The CDC 7600 system is an upward-compatible member of the CDC 6000 series. Although the main Pc in the 7600 is compatible with the main Pc of the 6600, instructions have been added for controlling the I/O section and for communicating between Large Core Memories (LCM) and Small Core Memory (SCM). It is expected to compute at an average rate 4 to 6 times that of a C['6600].

The PMS structure (Fig. 7) is substantially different from that of the 6600. The C['7600] Peripheral Processing Unit (PPU), unlike the Peripheral and Control Processors of the C['6600], has a loose coupling with the main C. The PPUs are under control of the main C when transferring words into SCM via K['Input-Output Section]. The fifteen C['PPU]'s have eight input/output channels. These channels, which can run concurrently, provide the link between C['PPU] and peripheral Ms's and T's. Some of the PPUs are located in the same physical space as the Pc.

The 7600 Pc can be interrupted by a clock, the PPUs, and a trap condition within the Pc. A breakpoint address, BPA, can be set up within Pc to initiate a trap when the program reaches BPA. This interruption scheme is in contrast to that of the 6600, which could not be interrupted or trapped. The 7600 interrupt may be a reaction to the lack of intercommunication in the 6600.

The CDC CYBER Series

The CDC CYBER-170's continued the line of computers beginning with the CDC 6600. The CYBER-170 series, manufactured in six models, was announced in 1970. This series extended into timesharing and multimode operations the concept of separate hardware for computation, input/output, and monitoring. The CYBER-170 series, while incorporating refined versions of the architecture and software of its predecessors, offers a broader range of performance levels and applications, as well as cost-effective operation.

The CDC CYBER-170 series of machines features six compatible computer systems in the medium- to large-scale range. All of these high-performance machines share the same basic architec-

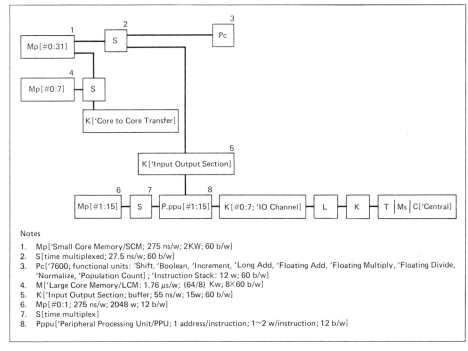

Notes

1. Mp['Small Core Memory/SCM; 275 ns/w; 2KW; 60 b/w]
2. S[time multiplexed; 27.5 ns/w; 60 b/w]
3. Pc['7600; functional units: 'Shift, 'Boolean, 'Increment, 'Long Add, 'Floating Add, 'Floating Multiply, 'Floating Divide, 'Normalize, 'Population Count] ; 'Instruction Stack: 12 w; 60 b/w]
4. M['Large Core Memory/LCM: 1.76 μs/w; (64/8) Kw; 8×60 b/w]
5. K['Input Output Section; buffer; 55 ns/w; 15w; 60 b/w]
6. Mp[#0:1; 275 ns/w; 2048 w; 12 b/w]
7. S[time multiplex]
8. Pppu['Peripheral Processing Unit/PPU; 1 address/instruction; 1~2 w/instruction; 12 b/w]

Fig. 7. CDC 7600 computer PMS diagram.

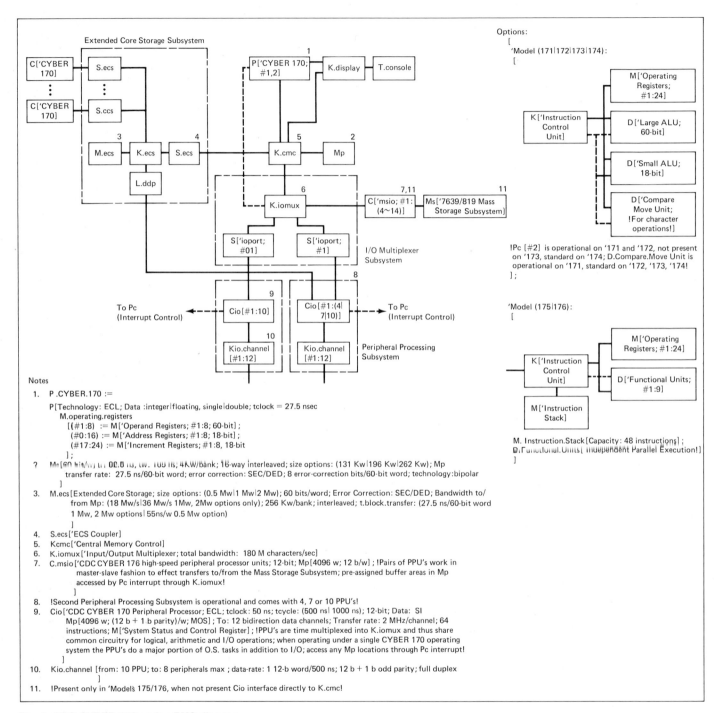

Notes

1. P .CYBER.170 :=

    P[Technology: ECL; Data :integer|floating, single|double; tclock = 27.5 nsec
      M.operating.registers
        [(#1:8) := M['Operand Registers; #1:8; 60-bit] ;
         (#0:16) := M['Address Registers; #1:8, 18-bit] ;
         (#17:24) := M['Increment Registers; #1:8, 18-bit
        ];

2. Mp[60 bit/w; ti: 0₵.5 ns, tw: 100 ns; 4KW/bank; 16-way interleaved; size options: (131 Kw|196 Kw|262 Kw); Mp
      transfer rate: 27.5 ns/60-bit word; error correction: SEC/DED; 8 error-correction bits/60-bit word; technology:bipolar
    ]

3. M.ecs[Extended Core Storage; size options: (0.5 Mw|1 Mw|2 Mw); 60 bits/word; Error Correction: SEC/DED; Bandwidth to/
      from Mp: (18 Mw/s|36 Mw/s 1Mw, 2Mw options only); 256 Kw/bank; interleaved; t.block.transfer: (27.5 ns/60-bit word
      1 Mw, 2 Mw options| 55ns/w 0.5 Mw option)
        ]

4. S.ecs['ECS Coupler]

5. Kcmc['Central Memory Control]

6. K.iomux ['Input/Output Multiplexer; total bandwidth: 180 M characters/sec]

7. C.msio['CDC CYBER 176 high-speed peripheral processor units; 12-bit; Mp[4096 w; 12 b/w] ; !Pairs of PPU's work in
      master-slave fashion to effect transfers to/from the Mass Storage Subsystem; pre-assigned buffer areas in Mp
      accessed by Pc interrupt through K.iomux!
        ]

8. !Second Peripheral Processing Subsystem is operational and comes with 4, 7 or 10 PPU's!

9. Cio['CDC CYBER 170 Peripheral Processor; ECL; tclock: 50 ns; tcycle: (500 ns| 1000 ns); 12-bit; Data: SI
      Mp[4096 w; (12 b + 1 b parity)/w; MOS] ; To: 12 bidirection data channels; Transfer rate: 2 MHz/channel; 64
      instructions; M['System Status and Control Register] ; !PPU's are time multiplexed into K.iomux and thus share
      common circuitry for logical, arithmetic and I/O operations; when operating under a single CYBER 170 operating
      system the PPU's do a major portion of O.S. tasks in addition to I/O; access any Mp locations through Pc interrupt!
        ]

10. Kio.channel [from: 10 PPU; to: 8 peripherals max ; data-rate: 1 12-b word/500 ns; 12 b + 1 b odd parity; full duplex
        ]

11. !Present only in 'Models 175/176, when not present Cio interface directly to K.cmc!

Fig. 8. CDC CYBER-170 series PMS diagram.

ture; which distributes functions among a central processor, for computation, and auxiliary peripheral processors, which perform systems input/output and operating-system functions. (See Fig. 8.) For most of the CYBER-170 models the central processor is field-upgradable, and there is no software conversion necessary throughout the entire line. The six CYBER-170 models (171–176) are built with common components and exhibit a high degree of commonality in their basic configuration, which is composed of the central processor unit, the memory units, and the peripheral processors. All processors in the series are implemented in emitter-coupled logic integrated circuits, and the central memories are implemented in bipolar semiconductor logic. The Kiviat graph (Fig. 9) summarizes the CYBER-170 system performance.

The models 171, 172, 173, and 174 feature a high-speed, unified arithmetic Central Processor Unit, which executes 18-bit and 60-bit operations, and a Compare Move Unit (CMU) to enhance the system's performance when it is working with variable-length character strings.

The base Pc for the CYBER-170 series is the Model 171. A second processor, to increase system performance, is optional. A CMU is also available as an option. The Model 172 has a performance-enhanced Model 171 Pc. Again, one or two Pc's may be configured. The CMU is a standard feature with the Model 172. The Model 173 further enhances the performance level using the same basic Pc as Models 171 and 172; however, only one Pc

may be configured into the system. The CMU is again a standard feature. The Model 174 employs two Model 173 Pc's in a dual-processor configuration with each processor having a CMU.

The Pc's for Models 175 and 176 have nine functional units, which allow concurrent execution of instructions. The Model 175 may have a standard or a performance-enhanced Pc. An instruction stack is also provided to allow fast retrieval of previously executed instructions. The Model 176 is an upgraded version of the Model 175 and in addition has an integrated interrupt system.

The range of capabilities and performance between Models 171 and 176 is significant, and there is total compatibility among the six different processors. The lower-performance models are ideally suited as front-end systems for the more powerful Pc's.

The peripheral processor subsystem consists of 10, 14, 17, or 20 functionally independent, programmable computers (peripheral processing units, or PPUs), each with 4,096 twelve-bit words of MOS memory. These act as system-control computers and peripheral processors. All PPUs communicate with central memory, external equipment, and each other through 12 or 24 independent bidirectional input/output channels. These channels transfer data at the rate of two 12-bit words per microsecond. For the Model 176, optional high-speed PPUs are required to drive high-speed mass-storage devices, such as the CDC 7639/819 units, which transfer data at rates of approximately 40 million bits per second. A minimum of 4 high-speed PPUs are necessary, and a maximum of 13 may be connected to the system.

The central memory options for the CYBER-170 series range in size from 64 to 256 kilowords organized into 8 or 16 interleaved banks of 60-bit words. Depending on the model, the minor cycle transfer rate of the 60-bit words is 50, 27.5, or 25 ns. However, because of interleaving, the memory operates at much higher apparent access rates. The central memory provides orderly data flow between various system elements.

The Central Memory may be supplemented with additional extended memory, which is available in increments ranging from 0.5 to 2 megawords. The extended memory may be used for system storage, data collection, job swapping, or user programs.

The CRAY-1

Chapter 44 introduces the CRAY-1, a direct descendant of the CDC 6600 series. The similarities between the architectures are not surprising, owing to the fact that Seymour Cray was also the chief designer for the CRAY-1.

Points of similarity with the CDC 6600 can be seen in the multiple functional units (address, scalar, vector, floating-point), the instruction buffer, and the field-length/limit registers for memory protection. The most important ISP improvement over the CDC 6600 is the addition of the vector data-type.

A common feature of all the high-performance machines is the

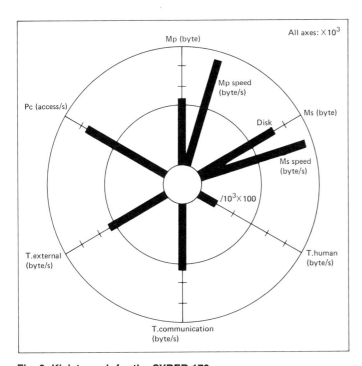

Fig. 9. Kiviat graph for the CYBER 170.

extensive use of buffers to smooth the flow of data and to ensure that the Pc units never have to wait for data. There are buffers to smooth the flow of data to and from memory. There is also an instruction buffer, which provides three functions:

1   The prefetch of instructions in blocks from memory to smooth any mismatch between processor and memory subsystems. The memory boxes are usually *n*-way interleaved, so that *n* words can be fetched at once.

2   An instruction look-ahead past branches, which fetches instructions down both branch paths so that no matter what the outcome of the branch, instructions will be available for execution.

3   If the instruction buffer is large enough, an ability to contain and repeatedly execute whole program segments at instruction buffer speed. Thus the instruction buffer can double in function as a cache.

The arithmetic instructions in the CRAY-1 only operate on the large array of registers:

1   Eight 64-bit scalar registers

2   Eight sets of vector registers, each 64 registers of 64-bits each

These register files are meant to hold intermediate results until computations are completed. They also perform the function of a cache, except that the user or compiler must ensure data locality in the registers.

Figure 10 depicts the PMS structure of the CRAY-1, while Fig. 11 illustrates the internal Pc organization. Each of the 10 functional units is pipelined. Figure 12 shows the mass-storage subsystem, and Fig. 13 summarizes the CRAY-1 performance.

The Pc and memory are implemented in ECL logic. The processor has a 12.5-ns basic clock cycle time, and the memory has an access time of 50 ns. The Pc is capable of accessing a maximum of 1 million 64-bit words. The memory is expandable from 0.25 megaword to a maximum of 1 megaword. There are 12 input channels and 12 output channels in the input/output section. They connect to a Maintenance Control Unit (MCU), a mass-storage subsystem, and a variety of front-end systems or peripheral equipment. The MCU provides for system initialization and for monitoring system performance. The mass-storage subsystem has a maximal configuration that provides storage for 9.7×10^9 eight-bit characters. The CRAY-1 Operating System, COS, is a multiprogramming batch system with up to 63 jobs. As of 1979, two languages were supported: FORTRAN and Assembler. The FORTRAN compiler analyzes the innermost loops of FORTRAN to detect vectorizable sequences and then generates code that takes advantage of the processor organization.

In the fall of 1979, Cray Research introduced the 12 models of the S series computers. Ranging from the S/250 through the S/4400, the models differed in amount of main memory (1/4 megaword to 4 megawords) and I/O configuration. Three models (S/250, S/500, S/1000) have 1/4, 1/2, and 1 megaword of memory each with no I/O subsystem. The nine remaining models have either 1, 2, or 4 megawords of memory with 2, 3, or 4 I/O processors. In the maximal I/O subsystem configuration, there are four I/O processors, 1 megaword of I/O Buffer Memory (maximum transfer rate 2,560 Mbit/s), sixteen Block Multiplexer Channels, and forty-eight 606-Mbyte disks (total storage 2.9×10^9 bytes).

The first customer shipment of a CRAY-1 Computer System was in March 1976 to Los Alamos Scientific Laboratories (LASL). Other customer shipments as of 1979 include the National Center for Atmospheric Research, the Department of Defense (two systems), the National Magnetic Fusion Energy Computer Center, the European Centre for Medium Range Weather Forecasting, and an upgraded version to LASL.

The CRAY-1 processor's performance is 5 times that of a CDC 7600's or 15 times that of an IBM System/370 Model 168.

The TI ASC

The Texas Instruments Advanced Scientific Computer was initially planned for high-speed processing of seismic data. Therefore, vector data-types were also important for the ASC. The ASC shows some strong kinship to the CRAY machines, because it was built on the knowledge of the earlier CDC machines. But it also has some significant differences.

The most important problem was perceived as obtaining a high memory-processor bandwidth. Thus a Memory Control Unit (MCU) that could sustain a transfer rate of 640 megawords per second was designed. The MCU is actually a cross-point switch between eight processor ports and nine memory ports.

The ASC is controlled by eight peripheral processors (PP) executing operating-system code, as in the ten CDC 6600 peripheral processors. The PPs are implemented as virtual processors (VP), as in the CDC 6600. Each VP has its own register set (e.g., program counter, arithmetic, index, base, and instruction registers) sharing ROM, ALU, instruction decoder, and central memory buffers. Also, as in the CDC 6600, the PP's ISP is control-oriented and hence lacks the richer instruction set of the Central Processor (CP).

The CP has dedicated function registers: 16 base, 16 arithmetic, 8 index, and 8 for holding parameters for vector instructions. The CP employs multiple functional units, as do the CDC 6600 and the CRAY-1. However, the units are organized in a rigid order of succession called a *pipeline*. An ASC can support up to four pipelines of eight stations each. The instruction fetch/decode is

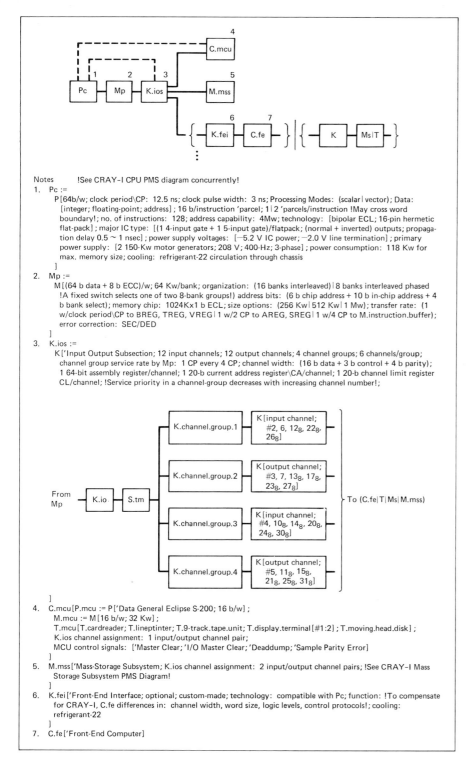

Notes   !See CRAY-I CPU PMS diagram concurrently!
1. Pc :=
    P[64b/w; clock period\CP: 12.5 ns; clock pulse width: 3 ns; Processing Modes: (scalar|vector); Data:
    [integer; floating-point; address]; 16 b/instruction 'parcel; 1|2 'parcels/instruction !May cross word
    boundary!; no. of instructions: 128; address capability: 4Mw; technology: [bipolar ECL; 16-pin hermetic
    flat-pack]; major IC type: [(1 4-input gate + 1 5-input gate)/flatpack; (normal + inverted) outputs; propaga-
    tion delay 0.5 ~ 1 nsec]; power supply voltages: [−5.2 V IC power; −2.0 V line termination]; primary
    power supply: [2 150-Kw motor generators; 208 V; 400-Hz; 3-phase]; power consumption: 118 Kw for
    max. memory size; cooling: refrigerant-22 circulation through chassis
    ]
2. Mp :=
    M[(64 b data + 8 b ECC)/w; 64 Kw/bank; organization: (16 banks interleaved)|8 banks interleaved phased
    !A fixed switch selects one of two 8-bank groups!; address bits: (6 b chip address + 10 b in-chip address + 4
    b bank select); memory chip: 1024Kx1 b ECL; size options: (256 Kw|512 Kw|1 Mw); transfer rate: (1
    w/clock period\CP to BREG, TREG, VREG|1 w/2 CP to AREG, SREG|1 w/4 CP to M.instruction.buffer);
    error correction: SEC/DED
    ]
3. K.ios :=
    K['Input Output Subsection; 12 input channels; 12 output channels; 4 channel groups; 6 channels/group;
    channel group service rate by Mp: 1 CP every 4 CP; channel width: (16 b data + 3 b control + 4 b parity);
    1 64-bit assembly register/channel; 1 20-b current address register\CA/channel; 1 20-b channel limit register
    CL/channel; !Service priority in a channel-group decreases with increasing channel number!;

4. C.mcu[P.mcu := P['Data General Eclipse S-200; 16 b/w];
    M.mcu := M[16 b/w; 32 Kw];
    T.mcu[T.cardreader; T.lineptinter; T.9-track.tape.unit; T.display.terminal[#1:2]; T.moving.head.disk];
    K.ios channel assignment: 1 input/output channel pair;
    MCU control signals: ['Master Clear; 'I/O Master Clear; 'Deaddump; 'Sample Parity Error]
    ]
5. M.mss['Mass-Storage Subsystem; K.ios channel assignment: 2 input/output channel pairs; !See CRAY-I Mass
    Storage Subsystem PMS Diagram!
    ]
6. K.fei['Front-End Interface; optional; custom-made; technology: compatible with Pc; function: !To compensate
    for CRAY-I, C.fe differences in: channel width, word size, logic levels, control protocols!; cooling:
    refrigerant-22
    ]
7. C.fe['Front-End Computer]

Fig. 10. CRAY-1 Computer system PMS diagram.

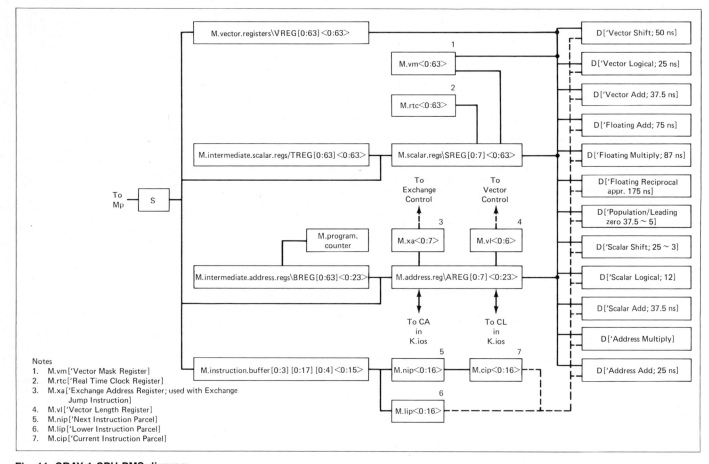

Fig. 11. CRAY-1 CPU PMS diagram.

also pipelined in four stages (fetch, operand decode, effective address calculation, and operand fetch). Thus up to 36 instructions can be in various states of execution at the same time.

The pipeline stages are usually smaller functions than the functions performed by the multiple functional units (e.g., exponent extract versus floating-point multiply). The pipeline also suffers if not all of the stages are to be used for a given instruction. An instruction that utilized stages 1, 2, 3, 5, 6, and 8 (floating add; see Fig. 7 in Chap. 45) would hold up an instruction that utilized only stages 1, 4, 5, and 8 (integer multiply) because of resource conflicts. The multiple functional units are only held up by the unavailability of operands.

The pipeline concept, especially as used in instruction fetch/ decode, is a very effective method to improve processor performance. Since the hardware cost to implement instruction fetch/ decode is small, the method is used almost universally, even appearing on some microprocessors.

The design and control of operand/operator parallelism is much

more complex. Chapter 19 outlines in detail the design of the IBM System/360 Model 91, which employed multiple functional units. The most effective way to gain high-speed parallelism is to have the operands in registers and use register-to-register instructions. The CRAY-1 does this through having only register-to-register arithmetic instructions and forcing the user or compiler to convert the applications program to register form. Since the System/360 Model 91 had to adhere to the System/360 ISP, hardware was added to dynamically convert System/360 instructions into a pseudoregister instruction set.

Chapter 19 also nicely explains the problems faced (and a solution to them) by parallelism in multiple functional units. In particular, the following problems have to be addressed:

1   Condition code dependencies. When a branch instruction is encountered, some strategy must be established on instruction fetching until the instruction setting the condition code is completely executed.

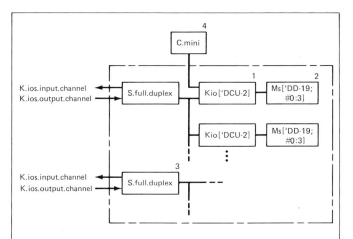

1. Kio['DCU-2 Disk Controller; Technology: [Flatpack ECL; similar to CRAY-I Pc]; upto 4 'DCU-2/'DCC-1 cabinet; to: 4 'DD-19 Disk Drives; Coolant: Refrigerant-22]

2. Ms['DD-19 Disk Storage Unit; Capacity: 2.424 × 10^9 b; 40 recording surfaces; 411 tracks/surface; 18 sectors/track; 32,768 b/sector; 10 head groups; latency: 16.6 ms; access time: 15 ~ 80 ms; transfer rate: 35.4 × 10^6 b/s avg.; max. bit stream length (disk cylinder capacity): 5.9 × 10^6 b; dual-ported drive; !A second independent path may exist to the drive from another 'DCU-2; access arbitration logic is provided!]

3. !A second set of 4 'DCU-2 in a 'DCC-1 cabinet identical to the first set!

4. !Each 'DCU-2 optionally additionally connects to a 16-b minicomputer; access arbitration must be provided in software!

Fig. 12. CRAY-1 mass storage subsystem PMS diagram.

2 Use of results before they are available. Because of the parallelism, several instructions are in partial states of execution at the same time. An instruction requiring the results of a previous instruction has to be held up until the results are available. If the whole instruction stream is held up until the one instruction completes execution, the parallelism in the multiple functional units is lost.

Finally, Dean [1973] states that there are several advantages of TI's PP approach over CDC's:

As has been stated before, the PPU is the unit in which the operating system executes. Other manufacturers have attempted to execute the executive functions in peripheral units with less than satisfactory results. There are some significant differences in the ASC architecture which make this possible, however. First, the PPU can execute code directly from central memory. All of central memory can be addressed by each VP (virtual processor). To change the function of a VP requires only a branch to the new code. This feature greatly enhances the dynamic "balancing" of VP power to meet system requirements. When system programs are written in re-entrant form, one copy of the code suffices for several VP's, thereby reducing the memory requirements for system tasks. Second, a special set of 64 32-bit registers are built

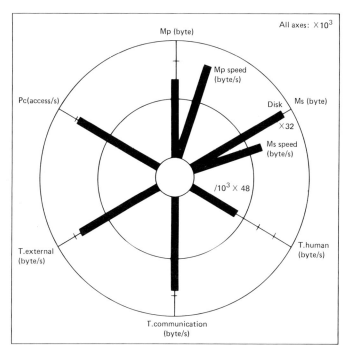

Fig. 13. Kiviat graph for the CRAY-1.

into the PPU. These registers (called communication registers) are literally the nerve center for the entire ASC system. Each VP has the ability to test and set individual bits in these registers in a single clock time. This allows for interprocessor control and communication on a dynamic basis. These registers also serve as control bits for data channels, context switch status, and act as I/O channels for some low bandwidth devices (e.g., the operator's console). Finally, the PPU contains a small execute only memory. Routines stored in the read only memory are accessible to all VP's. The maximum size of this memory is 4096 words. It is used for three purposes. First, it is non-volatile and thus contains the bootstrap routines needed when power is first turned on. Second, it is fast. Being an integral part of the PPU, instructions may be fetched at the clock speed of the PPU. Finally, the ASC is basically a polling oriented system. When a VP is in a polling loop, the instructions can be placed in this memory and not interfere with main memory traffic.

Hardware Technology

The preceding discussion has been concerned with some of the special features and architecture of the ASC system. A final word is in order concerning its physical construction. All of the Central Processor, the Peripheral Processor, and the Memory Control Unit are fabricated of the advanced emitter-coupled logic (ECL) integrated circuits. These circuits are interconnected on 17-layer multilayer circuit board. Further, the back panel wiring found on most large machines has been replaced by multilayer "motherboards" into which the circuit boards are plugged. The entire system is cooled by chilled water and forced air within each logic column and appears to be relatively insensitive to the ambient temperature.

Comparison of Maxicomputers

Bucy and Senne [1978] reported on nonlinear filter design that required the solution of nonlinear partial differential equations. The problem was solved on eight machines, including a general purpose minicomputer (PDP-11/70); a microprogrammed, special purpose auxiliary processor (AP120 B); machines with multiple functional units (CDC 6600, CDC 7600, CRAY 1, IBM S/370-168); machines with pipelines (CDC STAR-100, CRAY 1) and an array processor (Illiac IV). The benchmark consisted of the following floating point computations: 53,341 adds, 28,864 multiplies, one

division, and 32 exponentations. The resultant computation rates and cost per operation are depicted in Table 1. The most cost effective organization from a cost per operation is the functional specialized AP120B. However, when software development costs are considered, systems such as the CRAY 1 with vectorizing FORTRAN compilers may be the best long-term solution.

References

Arden et al. [1966]; Bell and Newell [1971]; Bucy and Senne [1978]; Dean [1973]; Elliott et al. [1956]; Computer [1977]; CFA [1977].

Table 1 Comparative Processor Cost/Performance for Demodulation Problem

Machine	Time per iteration (msec)	Achieved megaflops*	Approx** cost (dollars/flop)	Max theory megaflops	Software develop. time (man-months)
GRAY-1	3.5	23.5	0.33	60-140	0.5
STAR-100	4.9	16.8	0.48	20-40	2.0
Illiac IV	9.0	9.1	1.10	40-80	3.0
AP120B	13.9†	5.9	.03	12	6.0
CDC7600	25.0	3.3	.91	10	1.1
IBM370-168	110.0	0.75	2.67	3	1.0
CDC6600	130.0	0.63	1.59	2	1.0
PDP11-70	870.0	0.09	1.67	0.2	1.2

*Assumes 82.2K Flops per iteration.

**Assumed installation costs of (production) systems:
CRAY-1—$8M, STAR-100—$8M, Illiac-IV—$10M, AP120B—$150K,
CDC7600—$3M, IBM370-168—$2M, CDC6600 $1M, PDP11 70 $130K.

†Does not include PDP11-55 overhead.

Chapter 40

The Structure of SYSTEM/360[1]

Part I—Outline of the Logical Structure

G. A. Blaauw / F. P. Brooks, Jr.

Summary A general introductory description of the logical structure of SYSTEM/360 is given. In addition, the functional units, the principal registers and formats, and the basic addressing and sequencing principles of the system are indicated.

In the SYSTEM/360 logical structure, processing efficiency and versatility are served by multiple accumulators, binary addressing, bit-manipulation operations, automatic indexing, fixed and variable field lengths, decimal and hexadecimal radices, and floating-point as well as fixed-point arithmetic. The provisions for program interruption, storage protection, and flexible CPU states contribute to effective operation. Base-register addressing, the standard interface between channels and input/output control units, and the machine-language compatibility among models contribute to flexible configurations and to orderly system expansion.

SYSTEM/360 is distinguished by a design orientation toward very large memories and a hierarchy of memory speeds, a broad spectrum of manipulative functions, and a uniform treatment of input/output functions that facilitates communication with a diversity of input/output devices. The overall structure lends itself to program-compatible embodiments over a wide range of performance levels.

The system, designed for operation with a supervisory program, has comprehensive facilities for storage protection, program relocation, nonstop operation, and program interruption. Privileged instructions associated with a supervisory operating state are included. The supervisory program schedules and governs the execution of multiple programs, handles exceptional conditions, and coordinates and issues input/output (I/O) instructions. Reliability is heightened by supplementing solid-state components with built-in checking and diagnostic aids. Interconnection facilities permit a wide variety of possibilities for multisystem operation.

The purpose of this discussion is to introduce the functional units of the system, as well as formats, codes, and conventions essential to characterization of the system.

[1]*IBM Sys. J*, vol. 3, no. 2, 1964, pp. 119–135.

Functional Structure

The SYSTEM/360 structure schematically outlined in Fig. 1 has seven announced embodiments. Six of these, namely, Models 30, 40, 50, 60, 62, and 70, will be treated here.[2] Where requisite I/O devices, optional features, and storage capacity are present, these six models are logically identical for valid programs that contain explicit time dependencies only. Hence, even though the allowable channels or storage capacity may vary from model to model (as discussed in Chap. 41), the logical structure can be discussed without reference to specific models.

Input/Output

Direct communication with a large number of low-speed terminals and other I/O devices is provided through a special *multiplexor* channel unit. Communication with high-speed I/O devices is accommodated by the *selector* channel units. Conceptually, the input/output system acts as a set of subchannels that operate concurrently with one another and the processing unit. Each subchannel, instructed by its own control-word sequence, can govern a data transfer operation between storage and a selected I/O device. A multiplexor channel can function either as one or as many subchannels; a selector channel always functions as a single subchannel. The control unit of each I/O device attaches to the channels via a standard mechanical-electrical-programming *interface*.

Processing

The processing unit has sixteen general purpose 32-bit registers used for addressing, indexing, and accumulating. Four 64-bit floating-point accumulators are optionally available. The inclusion of multiple registers permits effective use to be made of small high-speed memories. Four distinct types of processing are provided: logical manipulation of individual bits, character strings and fixed words; decimal arithmetic on digit strings; fixed-point binary arithmetic; and floating-point arithmetic. The processing unit, together with the central control function, will be referred to as the central processing unit (CPU). The basic registers and data paths of the CPU are shown in Fig. 2.

The CPU's of the various models yield a substantial range in performance. Relative to the smallest model (Model 30), the internal performance of the largest (Model 70) is approximately 50:1 for scientific computation and 15:1 for commercial data processing.

[2]A seventh embodiment, the Model 92, is not discussed in this paper. This model does not provide decimal data handling and has a few minor differences arising from its highly concurrent, speed-oriented organization. A paper on Model 92 is planned for future publication in the *IBM Systems Journal*.

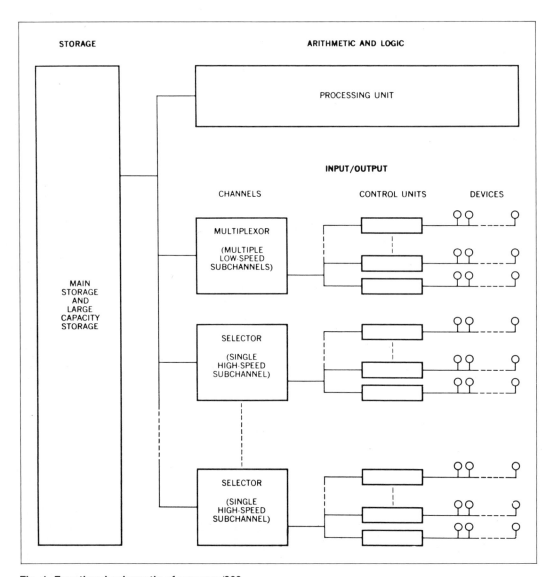

Fig. 1. Functional schematic of SYSTEM/360.

Control

Because of the extensive instruction set, SYSTEM/360 control is more elaborate than in conventional computers. Control functions include internal sequencing of each operation; sequencing from instruction to instruction (with branching and interruption); governing of many I/O transfers; and the monitoring, signaling, timing, and storage protection essential to total system operation. The control equipment is combined with a programmed supervisor, which coordinates and issues all I/O instructions, handles exceptional conditions, loads and relocates programs and data, manages storage, and supervises scheduling and execution of multiple programs. To a problem programmer, the supervisory program and the control equipment are indistinguishable.

The functional structure of SYSTEM/360, like that of most computers, is most concisely described by considering the data formats, the types of manipulations performed on them, and the instruction formats by which these manipulations are specified.

Information Formats

The several SYSTEM/360 data formats are shown in Fig. 3. An 8-bit unit of information is fundamental to most of the formats. A

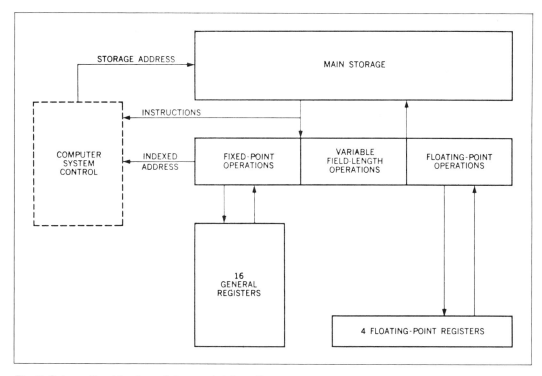

Fig. 2. Schematic of basic registers and data paths.

consecutive group of *n* such units constitutes a *field of length n.* Fixed-length fields of length one, two, four, and eight are termed *bytes, halfwords, words,* and *double words,* respectively. In many instructions, the operation code implies one of these four fields as the length of the operands. On the other hand, the length is explicit in an instruction that refers to operands of variable length.

The location of a stored field is specified by the address of the leftmost byte of the field. Variable-length fields may start on any byte location, but a fixed-length field of two, four, or eight bytes must have an address that is a multiple of 2, 4, or 8, respectively. Some of the various alignment possibilities are apparent from Fig. 3.

Storage addresses are represented by binary integers in the system. Storage capacities are always expressed as numbers of bytes.

Processing Operations

The SYSTEM/360 operations fall into four classes: fixed-point arithmetic, floating-point arithmetic, logical operations, and decimal arithmetic. These classes differ in the data formats used, the registers involved, the operations provided, and the way the field length is stated.

Fixed-Point Arithmetic

The basic arithmetic operand is the 32-bit fixed-point binary word. Halfword operands may be specified in most operations for the sake of improved speed or storage utilization. Some products and all dividends are 64 bits long, using an even-odd register pair.

Because the 32-bit words accommodate the 24-bit address, the entire fixed-point instruction set, including multiplication, division, shifting, and several logical operations, can be used in address computation. A two's complement notation is used for fixed-point operands.

Additions, subtractions, multiplications, divisions, and comparisons take one operand from a register and another from either a register or storage. Multiple-precision arithmetic is made convenient by the two's complement notation and by recognition of the carry from one word to another. A pair of conversion instructions, CONVERT TO BINARY and CONVERT TO DECIMAL, provide transition between decimal and binary radices without the use of tables. Multiple-register loading and storing instructions facilitate subroutine switching.

Floating-Point Arithmetic

Floating-point numbers may occur in either of two fixed-length formats—short or long. These formats differ only in the length of the fractions, as indicated in Fig. 3. The fraction of a floating-point

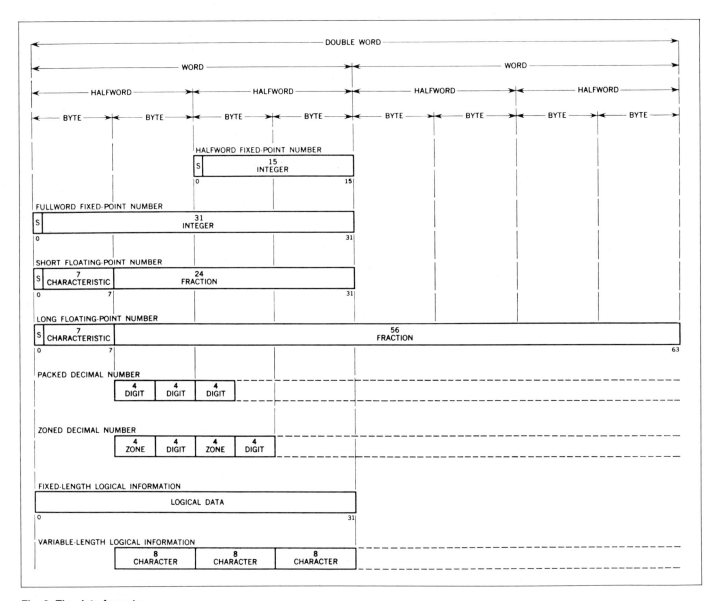

Fig. 3. The data formats.

number is expressed in 4-bit hexadecimal (base 16) digits. In the short format, the fraction has six hexadecimal digits; in the long format, the fraction has 14 hexadecimal digits. The short length is equivalent to seven decimal places of precision. The long length gives up to 17 decimal places of precision, thus eliminating most requirements for double-precision arithmetic.

The radix point of the fraction is assumed to be immediately to the left of the high-order fraction digit. To provide the proper magnitude for the floating-point number, the fraction is consid-

ered to be multiplied by a power of 16. The characteristic portion, bits 1 through 7 of both formats, is used to indicate this power. The characteristic is treated as an excess 64 number with a range from -64 through $+63$, and permits representation of decimal numbers with magnitudes in the range of 10^{-78} to 10^{75}

Bit position 0 in either format is the fraction sign, S. The fraction of negative numbers is carried in true form.

Floating-point operations are performed with one operand from a register and another from either a register or storage. The result, placed in a register, is generally of the same length as the operands.

Logical Operations

Operations for comparison, translation, editing, bit testing, and bit setting are provided for processing logical fields of fixed and variable lengths. Fixed-length logical operands, which consist of one, four, or eight bytes, are processed from the general registers. Logical operations can also be performed on fields of up to 256 bytes, in which case the fields are processed from left to right, one byte at a time. Moreover, two powerful scanning instructions permit byte-by-byte translation and testing via tables. An important special case of variable-length logical operations is the one-byte field, whose individual bits can be tested, set, reset, and inverted as specified by an 8-bit mask in the instruction.

Character Codes

Any 8-bit character set can be processed, although certain restrictions are assumed in the decimal arithmetic and editing operations. However, all character-set-sensitive, I/O equipment assumes either the Extended Binary-Coded-Decimal Interchange Code (EBCDIC) of Fig. 4 or the code of Fig. 5, which is an eight-bit extension of a seven-bit code proposed by the International Standards Organization.

Decimal Arithmetic

Decimal arithmetic can improve performance for processes requiring few computational steps per datum between the source input and the output. In these cases, where radix conversion from decimal to binary and back to decimal is not justified, the use of registers for intermediate results usually yields no advantage over storage-to-storage processing. Hence, decimal arithmetic is pro-

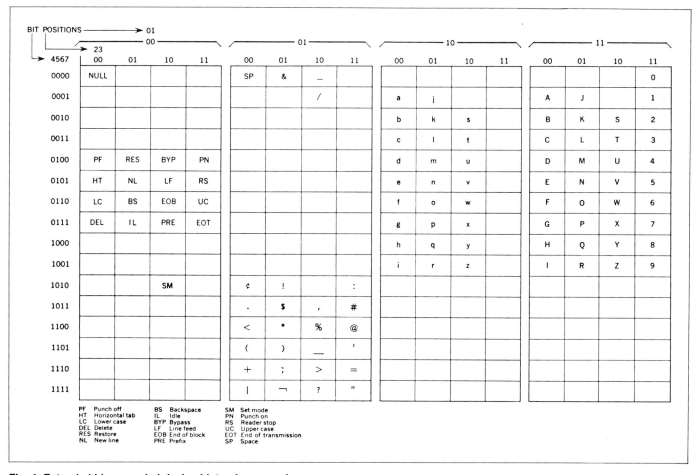

| BIT POSITIONS → 01 | | | | 00 | 01 | | | 10 | | | | 11 | | | |
| 23 → 00 | | | | | | | | | | | | | | | |
4567	00	01	10	11	00	01	10	11	00	01	10	11	00	01	10	11
0000	NULL				SP	&	—									0
0001							/		a	j			A	J		1
0010									b	k	s		B	K	S	2
0011									c	l	t		C	L	T	3
0100	PF	RES	BYP	PN					d	m	u		D	M	U	4
0101	HT	NL	LF	RS					e	n	v		E	N	V	5
0110	LC	BS	EOB	UC					f	o	w		F	O	W	6
0111	DEL	IL	PRE	EOT					g	p	x		G	P	X	7
1000									h	q	y		H	Q	Y	8
1001									i	r	z		I	R	Z	9
1010			SM		¢	!		:								
1011					.	$	,	#								
1100					<	*	%	@								
1101					(	)	_	'								
1110					+	;	>	=								
1111					|	¬	?	"								

PF	Punch off	BS	Backspace
HT	Horizontal tab	IL	Idle
LC	Lower case	BYP	Bypass
DEL	Delete	LF	Line feed
RES	Restore	EOB	End of block
NL	New line	PRE	Prefix

SM	Set mode
PN	Punch on
RS	Reader stop
UC	Upper case
EOT	End of transmission
SP	Space

Fig. 4. Extended binary-coded-decimal interchange code.

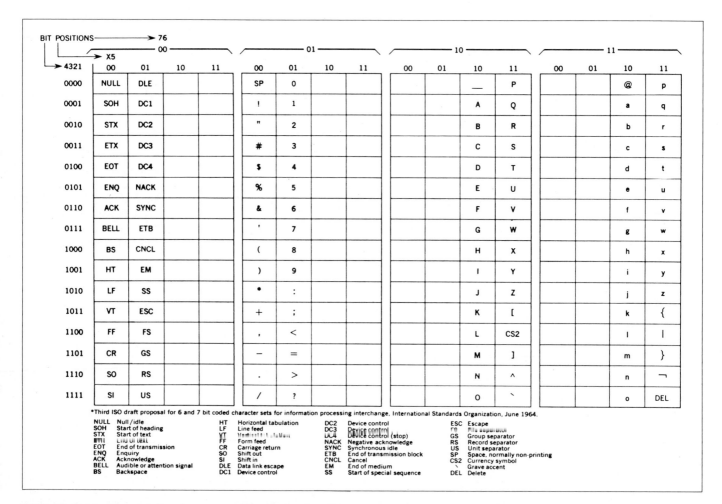

Fig. 5. Eight-bit representation for proposed international code.

vided in SYSTEM/360 with operands as well as results located in storage, as in the IBM 1400 series. Decimal arithmetic includes addition, subtraction, multiplication, division, and comparison.

The decimal digits 0 through 9 are represented in the 4-bit binary-coded-decimal form by 0000 through 1001, respectively. The patterns 1010 through 1111 are not valid as digits and are interpreted as sign codes: 1011 and 1101 represent a minus, the other four a plus. The sign patterns generated in decimal arithmetic depend upon the character set preferred. For EBCDIC, the patterns are 1100 and 1101; for the code of Fig. 5, they are 1010 and 1011. The choice between the two codes is determined by a mode bit.

Decimal digits, packed two to a byte, appear in fields of variable length (from 1 to 16 bytes) and are accompanied by a sign in the rightmost four bits of the low-order byte. Operand fields can be located on any byte boundary, and can have lengths up to 31 digits

and sign. Operands participating in an operation have independent lengths. Negative numbers are carried in true form. Instructions are provided for packing and unpacking decimal numbers. Packing of digits leads to efficient use of storage, increased arithmetic performance, and improved rates of data transmission. For purely decimal fields, for example, a 90,000-byte/second tape drive reads and writes 180,000 digits/second.

Instruction Formats

Instruction formats contain one, two, or three halfwords, depending upon the number of storage addresses necessary for the operation. If no storage address is required of an instruction, one halfword suffices. A two-halfword instruction specifies one address; a three-halfword instruction specifies two addresses. All instructions must be aligned on halfword boundaries.

The five basic instruction formats, denoted by the format

mnemonics RR, RX, RS, SI, and SS are shown in Fig. 6. RR denotes a register-to-register operation, RX a register and indexed-storage operation, RS a register and storage operation, SI a storage and immediate-operand operation, and SS a storage-to-storage operation.

In each format, the first instruction halfword consists of two parts. The first byte contains the operation code. The length and format of an instruction are indicated by the first two bits of the operation code.

The second byte is used either as two 4-bit fields or as a single 8-bit field. This byte is specified from among the following:

Four-bit operand register designator (R)

Four-bit index register designator (X)

Four-bit mask (M)

Four-bit field length specification (L)

Eight-bit field length specification

Eight-bit byte of immediate data (I)

The second and third halfwords each specify a 4-bit base register designator (B), followed by a 12-bit displacement (D).

Addressing

An effective storage address E is a 24-bit binary integer given, in the typical case, by

$$E = B + X + D$$

where B and X are 24-bit integers from general registers

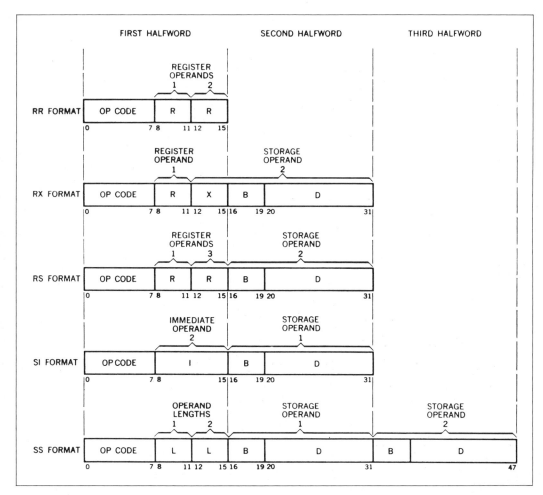

Fig. 6. Five basic instruction formats.

identified by fields B and X, respectively, and the displacement D is a 12-bit integer contained in every instruction that references storage.

The base *B* can be used for static relocation of programs and data. In record processing, the base can identify a record; in array calculations, it can specify the location of an array. The index *X* can provide the relative address of an element within an array. Together, *B* and *X* permit double indexing in array processing.

The displacement provides for relative addressing of up to 4095 bytes beyond the element or base address. In array calculations, the displacement can identify one of many items associated with an element. Thus, multiple arrays whose indices move together are best stored in an interleaved manner. In the processing of records, the displacement can identify items within a record.

In forming an effective address, the base and index are treated as unsigned 24-bit positive binary integers and the displacement as a 12-bit positive binary integer. The three are added as 24-bit binary numbers, ignoring overflow. Since every address is formed with the aid of a base, programs can be readily and generally relocated by changing the contents of base registers.

A zero base or index designator implies that a zero quantity must be used in forming the address, regardless of the contents of general register 0. A displacement of zero has no special significance. Initialization, modification, and testing of bases and indices can be carried out by fixed-point instructions, or by BRANCH AND LINK, BRANCH ON COUNT, or BRANCH ON INDEX instructions. LOAD EFFECTIVE ADDRESS provides not only a convenient housekeeping operation, but also, when the same register is specified for result and operand, an immediate register-incrementing operation.

Sequencing

Normally, the CPU takes instructions in sequence. After an instruction is fetched from a location specified by the instruction counter, the instruction counter is increased by the number of bytes in the instruction.

Conceptually, all halfwords of an instruction are fetched from storage after the preceding operation is completed and before execution of the current operation, even though physical storage word size and overlap of instruction execution with storage access may cause the actual instruction fetching to be different. Thus, an instruction can be modified by the instruction that immediately precedes it in the instruction stream, and cannot effectively modify itself during execution.

Branching

Most branching is accomplished by a single BRANCH ON CONDITION operation that inspects a 2-bit *condition register*. Many of the arithmetic, logical, and I/O operations indicate an outcome by setting the condition register to one of its four possible states. Subsequently a conditional branch can select one of the states as a criterion for branching. For example, the condition code reflects such conditions as non-zero result, first operand high, operands equal, overflow, channel busy, zero, etc. Once set, the condition register remains unchanged until modified by an instruction execution that reflects a different condition code.

The outcome of address arithmetic and counting operations can be tested by a conditional branch to effect loop control. Two instructions, BRANCH ON COUNT and BRANCH ON INDEX, provide for one-instruction execution of the most common arithmetic-test combinations.

Program Status Word

A program status word (PSW), a double word having the format shown in Fig. 7, contains information required for proper execution of a given program. A PSW includes an instruction address, condition code, and several mask and mode fields. The active or controlling PSW is called the *current* PSW. By storing the current PSW during an interruption, the status of the interrupted program is preserved.

Interruption

Five classes of interruption conditions are distinguished: input/output, program, supervisor call, external, and machine check.

For each class, two PSW's, called *old* and *new*, are maintained in the main-storage locations shown in Table 1. An interruption in a given class stores the current PSW as an old PSW and then takes the corresponding new PSW as the current PSW. If, at the conclusion of the interruption routine, old and current PSW's are interchanged, the system can be restored to its prior state and the interrupted routine can be continued.

The system mask, program mask, and machine-check mask bits in the PSW may be used to control certain interruptions. When masked off, some interruptions remain pending while others are merely ignored. The system mask can keep I/O and external interruptions pending, the program mask can cause four of the 15 program interruptions to be ignored, and the machine-check mask can cause machine-check interruptions to be ignored. Other interruptions cannot be masked off.

Appropriate CPU response to a special condition in the channels and I/O units is facilitated by an I/O *interruption*. The addresses of the channel and I/O unit involved are recorded in the old PSW. Related information is preserved in a channel status word that is stored as a result of the interruption.

Unusual conditions encountered in a program create *program interruptions*. Eight of the fifteen possible conditions involve overflows, improper divides, lost significance, and exponent underflow. The remaining seven deal with improper addresses,

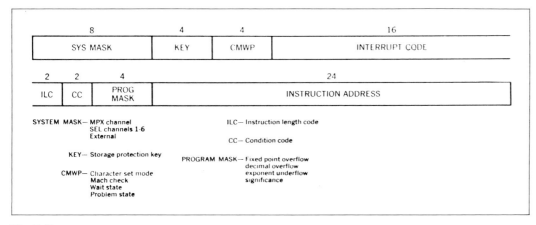

Fig. 7. Program status word format.

attempted execution of privileged instructions, and similar conditions.

A *supervisor-call interruption* results from execution of the instruction SUPERVISOR CALL. Eight bits from the instruction format are placed in the interruption code of the old PSW, permitting a message to be associated with the interruption. SUPERVISOR CALL permits a problem program to switch CPU control back to the supervisor.

Through an *external interruption*, a CPU can respond to signals from the interruption key on the system control panel, the timer, other CPU's, or special devices. The source of the interruption is identified by an interruption code in bits 24 through 31 of the PSW.

The occurrence of a machine check (if not masked off) terminates the current instruction, initiates a diagnostic procedure, and subsequently effects a *machine-check interruption*. A machine check is occasioned only by a hardware malfunction; it cannot be caused by invalid data or instructions.

Interrupt Priority

Interruption requests are honored between instruction executions. When several requests occur during execution of an instruction, they are honored in the following order: (1) machine check, (2) program or supervisor call, (3) external, and (4) input/output. Because the program and supervisor-call interruptions are mutually exclusive, they cannot occur at the same time.

If a machine-check interruption occurs, no other interruptions can be taken until this interruption is fully processed. Otherwise, the execution of the CPU program is delayed while PSW's are appropriately stored and fetched for each interruption. When the last interruption request has been honored, instruction execution is resumed with the PSW last fetched. An interruption subroutine is then serviced for each interruption in the order (1) input/output, (2) external, and (3) program or supervisor call.

Program Status

Overall CPU status is determined by four alternatives: (1) *stopped* versus *operating* state, (2) *running* versus *waiting* state, (3) *masked* versus *interruptable* state, and (4) *supervisor* versus *problem* state.

In the stopped state, which is entered and left by manual procedure, instructions are not executed, interruptions are not accepted, and the timer is not updated. In the operating

Table 1 Permanent Storage Assignments

Address	Byte length	Purpose
0	8	Initial program loading PSW
8	8	Initial program loading CCW 1
16	8	Initial program loading CCW 2
24	8	External old PSW
32	8	Supervisor call old PSW
40	8	Program old PSW
48	8	Machine check old PSW
56	8	Input/output old PSW
64	8	Channel status word
72	4	Channel address word
76	4	Unused
80	4	Timer
84	4	Unused
88	8	External new PSW
96	8	Supervisor call new PSW
104	8	Program new PSW
112	8	Machine check new PSW
120	8	Input/output new PSW
128		Diagnostic scan-out area†

†The size of the diagnostic scan-out area is configuration dependent.

state, the CPU is capable of executing instructions and of being interrupted.

In the running state, instruction fetching and execution proceeds in the normal manner. The wait state is typically entered by the program to await an interruption, for example, an I/O interruption or operator intervention from the console. In the wait state, no instructions are processed, the timer is updated, and I/O and external interruptions are accepted unless masked. Running versus waiting is determined by the setting of a bit in the current PSW.

The CPU may be interruptable or masked for the system, program, and machine interruptions. When the CPU is interruptable for a class of interruptions, these interruptions are accepted. When the CPU is masked, the system interruptions remain pending, but the program and machine-check interruptions are ignored. The interruptable states of the CPU are changed by altering mask bits in the current PSW.

In the problem state, processing instructions are valid, but all I/O instructions and a group of control instructions are invalid. In the supervisor state, all instructions are valid. The choice of problem or supervisor state is determined by a bit in the PSW.

Supervisory Facilities

Timer

A timer word in main storage location 80 is counted down at a rate of 50 or 60 cycles per second, depending on power line frequency. The word is treated as a signed integer according to the rules of fixed-point arithmetic. An external interrupt occurs when the value of the timer word goes from positive to negative. The full cycle time of the timer is 15.5 hours.

As an interval timer, the timer may be used to measure elapsed time over relatively short intervals. The timer can be set by a supervisory-mode program to any value at any time.

Direct Control

Two instructions, READ DIRECT and WRITE DIRECT, provide for the transfer of a single byte of information between an external device and the main storage of the system. These instructions are intended for use in synchronizing CPU's and special external devices.

Storage Protection

For protection purposes, main storage is divided into blocks of 2,048 bytes each. A four-bit *storage key* is associated with each block. When a store operation is attempted by an instruction, the *protection key* of the current PSW is compared with the storage key of the affected block. When storing is specified by a channel operation, a protection key supplied by the channel is used as the comparand. The keys are said to *match* if equal or if either is zero. A storage key is not part of addressable storage, and can be changed only by privileged instructions. The protection key of the CPU program is held in the current PSW. The protection key of a channel is recorded in a status word that is associated with the channel operation.

When a CPU operation causes a protection mismatch, its execution is suppressed or terminated, and the program execution is altered by an interruption. The protected storage location always remains unchanged. Similarly, protection mismatch due to an I/O operation terminates data transmission in such a way that the protected storage location remains unchanged.

Multisystem Operation

Communication between CPU's is made possible by shared control units, interconnected channels, or shared storage. Multisystem operation is supported by provisions for automatic relocation, indication of malfunctions, and CPU initialization.

Automatic relocation applies to the first 4,096 bytes of storage, an area that contains all permanent storage assignments and usually has special significance for supervisory programs. The relocation is accomplished by inserting a 12-bit prefix in each address whose high-order 12 bits are zero. Two manually set prefixes permit the use of an alternate area when storage malfunction occurs; the choice between prefixes is preserved in a trigger that is set during initial program loading.

To alert one CPU to the possible malfunction of another, a machine-check signal from a given CPU can serve as an external interruption to another CPU. By another special provision, initial program loading of a given CPU can be initiated by a signal from another CPU.

Input/Output

Devices and Control Units

Input/output devices include card equipment, magnetic tape units, disk storage, drum storage, typewriter-keyboard devices, printers, teleprocessing devices, and process control equipment. The I/O devices are regulated by control units, which provide the electrical, logical, and buffering capabilities necessary for I/O device operation. From the programming point of view, most control-unit and I/O device functions are indistinguishable. Sometimes the control unit is housed with an I/O device, as in the case of the printer.

A control unit functions only with those I/O devices for which it is designed, but all control units respond to a standard set of signals from the channel. This control-unit-to-channel connection, called the I/O *interface,* enables the CPU to handle all I/O operations with only four instructions.

I/O Instructions

Input/output instructions can be executed only while the CPU is in the supervisor state. The four I/O instructions are START I/O, HALT I/O, TEST CHANNEL, and TEST I/O.

START I/O initiates an I/O operation; its address field specifies a channel and an I/O device. If the channel facilities are free, the instruction is accepted and the CPU continues its program. The channel independently selects the specified I/O device. HALT I/O terminates a channel operation. TEST CHANNEL sets the condition code in the PSW to indicate the state of the channel addressed by the instruction. The code then indicates one of the following conditions: channel available, interruption condition in channel, channel working, or channel not operational. TEST I/O sets the PSW condition code to indicate the state of the addressed channel, subchannel, and I/O device.

Channels

Channels provide the data path and control for I/O devices as they communicate with main storage. In the multiplexor channel, the single data path can be time-shared by several low-speed devices (card readers, punches, printers, terminals, etc.) and the channel has the functional character of many subchannels, each of which services one I/O device at a time. On the other hand, the selector channel, which is designed for high-speed devices, has the functional character of a single subchannel. All subchannels respond to the same I/O instructions. Each can fetch its own control word sequence, govern the transfer of data and control signals, count record lengths, and interrupt the CPU on exceptions.

Two modes of operation, *burst* and *multiplex,* are provided for multiplexor channels. In burst mode, the channel facilities are monopolized for the duration of data transfer to or from a particular I/O device. The selector channel functions only in the burst mode. In multiplex mode, the multiplexor channel sustains several simultaneous I/O operations: bytes of data are interleaved and then routed between selection I/O devices and desired locations in main storage.

At the conclusion of an operation launched by START I/O or TEST I/O, an I/O interruption occurs. At this time a channel status word (CSW) is stored in location 64. Figure 8 shows the CSW format. The CSW provides information about the termination of the I/O operation.

Successful execution of START I/O causes the channel to fetch a channel address word from main-storage location 72. This word specifies the storage-protection key that governs the I/O operation, as well as the location of the first eight bytes of information that the channel fetches from main storage. These 64 bits comprise a channel command word (CCW). Figure 9 shows the CCW format.

Channel Program

One or more CCW's make up the channel program that directs channel operations. Each CCW points to the next one to be fetched, except for the last in the chain which so identifies itself.

Six channel commands are provided: read, write, read backward, sense, transfer in channel, and control. The read command defines an area in main storage and causes a read operation from the selected I/O device. The write command causes data to be written by the selected device. The read-backward command is akin to the read command, but the external medium is moved in the opposite direction and bytes read backward are placed in descending main storage locations.

The control command contains information, called an *order,* that is used to control the selected I/O device. Orders, peculiar to the particular I/O device in use, can specify such functions as rewinding a tape unit, searching for a particular track in disk

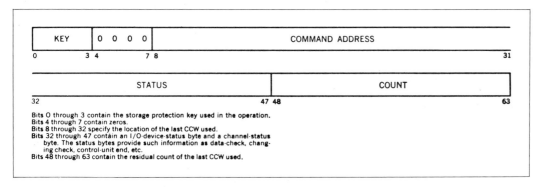

Bits 0 through 3 contain the storage protection key used in the operation.
Bits 4 through 7 contain zeros.
Bits 8 through 32 specify the location of the last CCW used.
Bits 32 through 47 contain an I/O-device-status byte and a channel-status byte. The status bytes provide such information as data-check, changing check, control-unit end, etc.
Bits 48 through 63 contain the residual count of the last CCW used.

Fig. 8. Channel status word format.

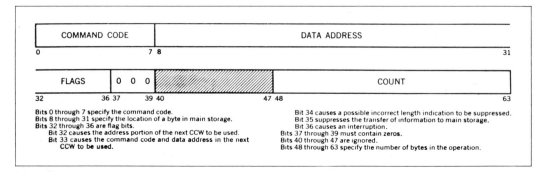

Bits 0 through 7 specify the command code.
Bits 8 through 31 specify the location of a byte in main storage.
Bits 32 through 36 are flag bits.
   Bit 32 causes the address portion of the next CCW to be used.
   Bit 33 causes the command code and data address in the next
   CCW to be used.

Bit 34 causes a possible incorrect length indication to be suppressed.
Bit 35 suppresses the transfer of information to main storage.
Bit 36 causes an interruption.
Bits 37 through 39 must contain zeros.
Bits 40 through 47 are ignored.
Bits 48 through 63 specify the number of bytes in the operation.

Fig. 9. Channel command word format.

storage, or line skipping on a printer. In a functional sense, the CPU executes I/O instructions, the channels execute commands, and the control units and devices execute orders.

The sense command specifies a main storage location and transfers one or more bytes of status information from the selected control unit. It provides details concerning the selected I/O device, such as a stacker-full condition of a card reader or a file-protected condition of a magnetic-tape reel.

A channel program normally obtains CCW's from a consecutive string of storage locations. The string can be broken by a transfer-in-channel command that specifies the location of the next CCW to be used by the channel. External documents, such as punched cards or magnetic tape, may carry CCW's that can be used by the channel to govern the reading of the documents.

The input/output interruptions caused by termination of an I/O operation, or by operator intervention at the I/O device, enable the CPU to provide appropriate programmed response to conditions as they occur in I/O devices or channels. Conditions responsible for I/O interruption requests are preserved in the I/O devices or channels until recognized by the CPU.

During execution of START I/O, a command can be rejected by a busy condition, program check, etc. Rejection is indicated in the condition code of the PSW, and additional detail on the conditions that precluded initiation of the I/O operation is provided in a CSW.

Manual Control

The need for manual control is minimal because of the design of the system and supervisory program. A control panel provides the ability to reset the system; store and display information in main storage, in registers, and in the PSW; and load initial program information. After an input device is selected with the load unit switches, depressing a load key causes a read from the selected input device. The six words of information that are read into main storage provide the PSW and the CCW's required for subsequent operation.

Instruction Set

The SYSTEM/360 instructions, classified by format and function, are displayed in Table 2. Operation codes and mnemonic abbreviations are also shown. With the previously described formats in mind, much of the generality provided by the system is apparent in this listing.

Table 2 (*opposite*) System/360 instructions

RR Format

xxxx	Branching and status switching 0000xxxx		Fixed-point fullword and logical 0001xxxx		Floating-point long 0010xxxx		Floating-point short 0011xxxx	
0000			LPR	LOAD POSITIVE	LPDR	LOAD POSITIVE	LPER	LOAD POSITIVE
0001			LNR	LOAD NEGATIVE	LNDR	LOAD NEGATIVE	LNER	LOAD NEGATIVE
0010			LTR	LOAD AND TEST	LTDR	LOAD AND TEST	LTER	LOAD AND TEST
0011			LCR	LOAD COMPLEMENT	LCDR	LOAD COMPLEMENT	LCER	LOAD COMPLEMENT
0100	SPM	SET PROGRAM MASK	NR	AND	HDR	HALVE	HER	HALVE
0101	BALR	BRANCH AND LINK	CLR	COMPARE LOGICAL				
0110	BCTR	BRANCH ON COUNT	OR	OR				
0111	BCR	BRANCH/CONDITION	XR	EXCLUSIVE OR				
1000	SSK	SET KEY	LR	LOAD	LDR	LOAD	LER	LOAD
1001	ISK	INSERT KEY	CR	COMPARE	CDR	COMPARE	CER	COMPARE
1010	SVC	SUPERVISOR CALL	AR	ADD	ADR	ADD N	ALR	ADD N
1011			SR	SUBTRACT	SDR	SUBTRACT N	SER	SUBTRACT N
1100			MR	MULTIPLY	MDR	MULTIPLY	MER	MULTIPLY
1101			DR	DIVIDE	DDR	DIVIDE	DER	DIVIDE
1110			ALR	ADD LOGICAL	AWR	ADD U	AUR	ADD U
1111			SLR	SUBTRACT LOGICAL	SWR	SUBTRACT U	SUR	SUBTRACT U

RX Format

xxxx	Fixed-point halfword and branching 0100xxxx		Fixed-point fullword and logical 0101xxxx		Floating-point long 0110xxxx		Floating-point short 0111xxxx	
0000	STH	STORE	ST	STORE	STD	STORE	STE	STORE
0001	LA	LOAD ADDRESS						
0010	STC	STORE CHARACTER						
0011	IC	INSERT CHARACTER						
0100	EX	EXECUTE	N	AND				
0101	BAL	BRANCH AND LINK	CL	COMPARE LOGICAL				
0110	BCT	BRANCH ON COUNT	O	OR				
0111	BC	BRANCH/CONDITION	X	EXCLUSIVE OR				
1000	LH	LOAD	L	LOAD	LD	LOAD	LE	LOAD
1001	CH	COMPARE	C	COMPARE	CD	COMPARE	CE	COMPARE
1010	AH	ADD	A	ADD	AD	ADD N	AE	ADD N
1011	SH	SUBTRACT	S	SUBTRACT	SD	SUBTRACT N	SE	SUBTRACT N
1100	MH	MULTIPLY	M	MULTIPLY	MD	MULTIPLY	ME	MULTIPLY
1101			D	DIVIDE	DD	DIVIDE	DE	DIVIDE
1110	CVD	CONVERT-DECIMAL	AL	ADD LOGICAL	AW	ADD U	AU	ADD U
1111	CVB	CONVERT-BINARY	SL	SUBTRACT LOGICAL	SW	SUBTRACT U	SU	SUBTRACT U

RS, SI Format

xxxx	Branching status switching and shifting 1000xxxx		Fixed-point logical and input/output 1001xxxx		1010xxxx	1011xxxx
0000	SSM	SET SYSTEM MASK	STM	STORE MULTIPLE		
0001			TM	TEST UNDER MASK		
0010	LPSW	LOAD PSW	MVI	MOVE		
0011		DIAGNOSE	TS	TEST AND SET		
0100	WRD	WRITE DIRECT	NI	AND		
0101	RDD	READ DIRECT	CLI	COMPARE LOGICAL		
0110	BXH	BRANCH/HIGH	OI	OR		
0111	BXLE	BRANCH/LOW-EQUAL	XI	EXCLUSIVE OR		
1000	SRL	SHIFT RIGHT SL	LM	LOAD MULTIPLE		
1001	SLL	SHIFT LEFT SL				
1010	SRA	SHIFT RIGHT S				
1011	SLA	SHIFT LEFT S				
1100	SRDL	SHIFT RIGHT DL	SIO	START I/O		
1101	SLDL	SHIFT LEFT DL	TIO	TEST I/O		
1110	SRDA	SHIFT RIGHT D	HIO	HALT I/O		
1111	SLDA	SHIFT LEFT D	TCH	TEST CHANNEL		

SS Format

xxxx	1100xxxx	Logical 1101xxxx		1110xxxx	Decimal 1111xxxx	
0000						
0001		MVN	MOVE NUMERIC		MVO	MOVE WITH OFFSET
0010		MVC	MOVE		PACK	PACK
0011		MVZ	MOVE ZONE		UNPK	UNPACK
0100		NC	AND			
0101		CLC	COMPARE LOGICAL			
0110		OC	OR			
0111		XC	EXCLUSIVE OR			
1000					ZAP	ZERO AND ADD
1001					CP	COMPARE
1010					AP	ADD
1011					SP	SUBTRACT
1100		TR	TRANSLATE		MP	MULTIPLY
1101		TRT	TRANSLATE AND TEST		DP	DIVIDE
1110		ED	EDIT			
1111		EDMK	EDIT AND MARK			

NOTE: N = NORMALIZED   DL = DOUBLE LOGICAL   S = SINGLE
SL = SINGLE LOGICAL   U = UNNORMALIZED   D = DOUBLE

APPENDIX 1 IBM System/370 ISP

```
S370 :=                                                    chareg<0:7>,                    ! Channel address register
    BEGIN                                                  devreg<0:7>,                    ! Device register
                                                                                           ! Holds device address (0-255)
! ISP summary description of IBM System/370 architecture.  extreg<0:7>,                    ! External register:
                                                                                           !   Bit 0 = timer interrupt
! This summary gives an overview of the major architectural                                !   Bit 1 = console interrupt
! features of the S370.                                    iodreg<0:7>,                    ! Holds data byte for direct I/O
                                                                                           ! its meaning (command or data)
! Instruction fetch and execution cycles are fully described,                              ! is implementation dependent
! but the actual execution of individual instructions is limited  sigout<0:9>,            ! Signal out for direct I/O
! to one or two examples from each group (RR, RX, RS/SI, and SS).
                                                          **Instruction.Format**
! The summary is fully compatible with the ISPS compiler and simulator.
                                                              IR<0:47>,                    ! Instruction register
    **MP.2.State**                                            irw[0:2]<0:15>  := IR<0:47>, ! 1/2 word address for IR (execute)
                                                                OpCode<0:7>  := IR<0:7>,   ! RR, RX, RS, SI, SS
        macro maxb   := |16383 |,                               R1<0:3>      := IR<8:11>,  ! RR, RX, RS
        macro maxkey :=     |7 |,                               R2<0:3>      := IR<12:15>, ! RR
                                                                X2<0:3>      := IR<12:15>, ! RX
        MB[0:maxb]<0:7>,                    ! Byte memory        B1<0:3>      := IR<16:19>, ! RX, RS, SI, SS
        MH[0:maxb]<0:15>{INCREMENT:2} :=    ! Half word memory   D1<0:11>     := IR<20:31>, ! RX, RS, SI, SS
            MB[0:maxb]<0:7>,                                     R3<0:3>      := IR<12:15>, ! RS
        MW[0:maxb]<0:31>{INCREMENT:4} :=    ! Word memory        M1[0:3]      := IR<8:11>,  ! Mask 1
            MB[0:maxb]<0:7>,                                     I2<0:7>      := IR<8:15>,  ! SI
        MDW[0:maxb]<0:63>{INCREMENT:8} :=   ! Doubleword memory  LFLD<0:7>    := IR<8:15>,  ! SS
            MB[0:maxb]<0:7>,                                     L1<0:3>      := IR<8:11>,  ! SS
                                                                L2<0:3>      := IR<12:15>, ! SS
        MAR<0:23>,                          ! Memory address reg  B2<0:3>     := IR<32:35>, ! SS
        MBR<0:31>,                          ! Memory buffer reg   D2<0:11>    := IR<36:47>  ! SS

        STKEYS[0:maxkey]<0:4>,              ! Storage key array  **Service.Facilities**(us)

    ! Permanent Storage Assignments                        ! Interrupt code 5 implies addressing error
                                                          ! Interrupt code 6 implies specification (alignment error)
        iplpsw<0:63> := MB[0:7]<0:7>,       ! IPL PSW     ! Interrupt code 4 implies protection
        iplcw1<0:63> := MB[8:15]<0:7>,      ! IPL CCW #1  ! The order of setting these codes may be implementation dependent.
        iplcw2<0:63> := MB[16:23]<0:7>,     ! IPL CCW #2  ! Tests on a model 75 show code 6 is first.
        exopsw<0:63> := MB[24:31]<0:7>,     ! External Old PSW
        svcpsw<0:63> := MB[32:39]<0:7>,     ! SVC Old PSW       ckpr :=                        ! Check routine for storage protection
        propsw<0:63> := MB[40:47]<0:7>,     ! Program Old PSW        begin
        mkopsw<0:63> := MB[48:55]<0:7>,     ! Machine check Old PSW    checker(STKEYS[MAR<0:21>]<1:4> neq PROTKY, 4)
        ioopsw<0:63> := MB[56:63]<0:7>,     ! I/O Old PSW            end,
        chstwd<0:63> := MB[64:71]<0:7>,     ! Channel Status Word
        chadwd<0:31> := MB[72:75]<0:7>,     ! Channel Address Word  ckrdpr :=                      ! Check routine for read protection
        timer<0:23>  := MB[80:82]<0:7>,     ! Timer cell             begin
        exnpsw<0:63> := MB[88:95]<0:7>,     ! External New PSW         IF STKEYS[MAR<0:12>]<0> => ckpr()
        svnpsw<0:63> := MB[96:103]<0:7>,    ! SVC New PSW            end,
        prnpsw<0:63> := MB[104:111]<0:7>,   ! Program New PSW                .
        mknpsw<0:63> := MB[112:119]<0:7>,   ! Machine check New PSW keyck :=                       ! Check routine for ssk & isk instructions
        ionpsw<0:63> := MB[120:127]<0:7>,   ! I/O New PSW            begin
        scnout<0:63> := MB[128:135]<0:7>    ! Diagnostic scan out      checker(PROBST, 2) next       ! Privileged state check
    **PC.State**                                                      checker(R[R2]<28:31> neq 0, 6) next
                                                                      checker(R[R2]<8:20> gtr 7, 5)
        R[0:15]<0:31>,                      ! General purpose registers  end,
        PSW<0:63>,                          ! Program Status Word  ckhwad :=                       ! Check 1/2 word address routine
                                                                    begin
        psww[0:3]<0:15>  := PSW<0:63>,      ! Alternate PSW definition checker(MAR<23>, 6) next
            CHAMSK<0:7>  := PSW<0:7>,       ! Channel Mask             checker(MAR<0:22> gtr maxb/2, 5)
            PROTKY<0:3>  := PSW<8:11>,      ! Protection Key         end,
            ASCMSK<>     := PSW<12>,        ! USASCII Mask        ckwdad :=                       ! Check word address routine
            MCHKMK<>     := PSW<13>,        ! Machine check mask     begin
            WAITST<>     := PSW<14>,        ! Wait state              checker(MAR<22:23> neq 0, 6) next
            PROBST<>     := PSW<15>,        ! Problem state           checker(MAR<0:21> gtr maxb/4, 5)
            INTCDE<0:15> := PSW<16:31>,     ! Interrupt code         end,
            ILC<0:1>     := PSW<32:33>,     ! Instruction length code ckdwad :=                    ! Check double word address routine
            CC<0:1>      := PSW<34:35>,     ! Condition code          begin
            FPOPMS<>     := PSW<36>,        ! Fixed point overflow mask checker(MAR<21:23> neq 0, 6) next
            DOFMSK<>     := PSW<37>,        ! Decimal overflow mask     checker(MAR<0:20> gtr maxb/8, 5)
            EXOFMS<>     := PSW<38>,        ! Exponent underflow mask end,
            SIGMSK<>     := PSW<39>,        ! Significance mask
            PC<0:23>     := PSW<40:63>      ! Program counter-24 bits checker(condition<>, intcode<0:15>) :=
                                                                    begin
    **Implementation.Declarations**                                   IF condition =>
                                                                        begin
        amar1<0:23>,                        ! Auxiliary memory address reg.(1)  INTCDE = intcode; intvec<2> = 1 next
        amar2<0:23>,                        ! Auxiliary memory address reg.(2)  LEAVE icycle
        lobyte<0:7>   := MBR<0:7>,          ! Left byte in MBR                end
        hibyte<0:7>   := MBR<24:31>,        ! Right byte in MBR      end,
        laux1<0:7>,                         ! Byte count register 1
        laux2<0:7>,                         ! Byte count register 2 rdbyte :=                       ! Read a byte routine
        exrf<>,                             ! Execute recursion flag   begin
        t2<0:1>,                            ! 2 bit temp               checker(MAR gtr maxb, 5) next  ! Check valid byte address
        t4<0:3>,                            ! 4 bit temp               ckrdpr() next
        t24<0:23>,                          ! 24 bit temp              MBR<24:31> = MB[MAR]
        ovf<>,                              ! Overflow               end,
        stopbit<>,                          ! Stop switch
        intvec<0:4>,                        ! Interrupt vector:     wrbyte :=                       ! Write a byte routine
                                            !   Bit 0 = machine check  begin
                                            !   Bit 1 = svc             checker(MAR gtr maxb, 5) next  ! Check valid byte address
                                            !   Bit 2 = prog check      ckpr() next
                                            !   Bit 3 = timer interrupt MB[MAR] = MBR<24:31>
                                            !   Bit 4 = I/O interrupt end,
        iomsk<0:7>,                         ! Channel mask register
        chrls<>,                            ! Channel release       readhw :=                       ! Read a 1/2 word routine
        chsel<>,                            ! Channel select register  begin
        chancc<0:1>,                        ! Channel condition code   ckhwad() next
        chinst[0:3]<>,                      ! Channel instruction line ckrdpr() next
                                            !   0 => SIO               MBR<16:31> = MH[MAR]
                                            !   1 => TIO             end,
                                            !   2 => HIO
                                            !   3 => TCH
```

```
wrhw :=                        ! Write a 1/2 word routine
      begin
      ckhwad() next
      ckpr() next
      MH[MAR] = MBR<16:31>
      end,

readwd :=                      ! Read a word routine
      begin
      ckwdad() next
      ckrdpr() next
      MBR = MW[MAR]
      end,

wrwd :=                        ! Write a word routine
      begin
      ckwdad() next
      ckpr() next
      MW[MAR] = MBR
      end,

l2fch :=                       ! Fetch of L2 operand if possible or a load
      begin                    ! of zero into the MBR if L2 field is exhausted.
      DECODE laux2 eql 0 =>
            begin
            0 := begin
                 laux2 = laux2 -{tc} 1 next
                 MAR = amar2 + laux2 next
                 rdbyte()
                 end,
            1 := MBR = 0
            end
      end,

adrio :=                       ! Device addressing for I/O instructions
      begin
      chareg = (D1 + R[B1])<15:8>; devreg = (D1 + R[B1])<7:0>
      end,

setfcc :=                      ! Set fixed point condition codes
      begin
      CC = 0 next
      DECODE R[R1]<0> =>
            begin
            0 := IF R[R1] => CC = 2,
            1 := CC = 1
            end next
      IF ovf => CC = 3 next
      checker(ovf and FPOPMS, 8)
      end,

opex := (checker('1, 1)),      ! Illegal op-code
int :=
      begin
      t2 := ILC next           ! Save instruction length

      IF intvec<0> and MCHKMK =>    ! Handle priority (1) interrupts
            begin
            mkopsw = PSW next
            mkopsw<16:31> = 0 next
            scnout = PSW next
            PSW = mknpsw; intvec<0:2> = 0
            end next

      IF intvec<1> =>               ! Handle priority (2) interrupts
            begin
            svcpsw = PSW next
            PSW = svnpsw; intvec<1> = 0
            end next

      IF intvec<2> =>
            begin
            propsw = PSW next
            PSW = prnpsw; intvec<2> = 0
            end next

      IF intvec<3> and CHAMSK =>    ! Handle priority (3) interrupts
            begin
            INTCDE = extreg next
            exopsw = PSW next
            PSW = exnpsw; intvec<3> = 0
            end next

      IF intvec<4> and iomsk =>     ! Handle priority (4) interrupts
            begin
            INTCDE = devreg next
            ioopsw = PSW next
            PSW = ionpsw; intvec<4> = 0
            end next

      INTCDE = 0; ILC = t2          ! Reset ILC & interrupt code
      end
**Instruction.Interpretation**{us}

  start{main} :=
      begin
      stopbit = 0 next
      run()
      end,
```

```
run :=
      begin
      IF not stopbit =>
            begin
            IF not WAITST => icycle() next
            int() next
            RESTART run
            end
      end,

icycle :=                      ! Instruction interpretation cycle
      begin
      ifetch() next
      iexec() next
      IF exrf => (iexec() next exrf = 0)
      end,

ifetch :=                      ! Instruction fetch
      begin
      MAR = PC next
      readhw() next
      IR<0:15> = MBR<16:31>; ILC = (MBR<16> + MBR<17>) + 1;
      PC = PC + ((MBR<16> + MBR<17>) + 1) * 2; ovf = 0 next
      IF ILC gtr 1 =>
            begin
            MAR = MAR + 2 next
            readhw() next
            IR<16:31> = MBR<16:31> next
            IF ILC gtr 2 =>
                  begin
                  MAR = MAR + 2 next
                  readhw() next
                  IR<32:47> = MBR<16:31>
                  end
            end
      end
**Instruction.Execution**{us}

  iexec :=
      begin
      DECODE OpCode<0:1> =>
            begin
            '00 := RR(),
            '01 := RX(),
            '10 := RS.SI(),
            '11 := SS()
            end
      end,
  RR :=            ! RR instruction decode table
      begin
      DECODE OpCode =>
            begin
            "04 := SPM(),             ! Set program mask
            "05 := BALR(),            ! Branch and link

            "06:"3F := no.op(),       ! Opcodes not shown in this summary

       otherwise := opex()
            end
      end,
  RX :=            ! RX instruction decode table
      begin
      MAR = D1 next                   ! Effective address calculation
      IF B1 => MAR = MAR + R[B1] next
      IF X2 => MAR = MAR + R[X2] next

      DECODE OpCode =>                ! Opcode decode for RX
            begin
            "40 := STH(),             ! Store halfword

            "41:"74 := no.op(),       ! Opcodes not shown in this summary

       otherwise := opex()
            end
      end,

  RS.SI :=         ! RS, SI instruction decode table
      begin

      MAR = D1 next                   ! Effective address calculation
      IF B1 => MAR = MAR + R[B1] next

      DECODE OpCode =>                ! Opcode decoding
            begin
            "80 := SSM(),             ! Set system mask

            "81:"9F := no.op(),       ! Opcodes not shown in this summary

       otherwise := opex()
            end
      end,
  SS :=       ! SS instruction decode table
      begin

      amar1 = D1; amar2 = D2 next     ! Effective address calculation
      IF B1 => amar1 = amar1 + R[B1];
      IF B2 => amar2 = amar2 + R[B2] next
```

APPENDIX 1 (Cont'd.)

```
      DECODE OpCode =>                ! Opcode decoding
          begin
           "D1 := MVN(),              ! Move numerics

      "D2:"FD := no.op(),             ! Opcodes not shown in this summary

  otherwise := opex()
          end
      end,
! RR instructions

      SPM :=                ! Set program mask
          begin
          PSW<34:39> = R[R1]<2:7>
          end,

      BALR :=               ! Branch and link register
          begin
          t24 = R[R2]<8:31> next
          R[R1] = PSW<32:63> next
          IF R2 => PC = t24
          end,

!         . . . .                    ! Instruction descriptions not
!         . . . .                    ! included in this summary.

! RX instructions

      STH :=                ! Store halfword
          begin
          MBR = R[R1]<16:31> next
          wrhw()
          end,

!         . . . .
!         . . . .

! RS, SI instructions

      SSM :=                ! Set system mask
          begin
          checker(PROBST, 2) next          ! Privileged state check
          rdbyte() next
          PSW<0:7> = hibyte
          end,

!         . . . .
!         . . . .

! SS instructions

      MVN :=                ! Move numerics
          begin
          laux1 = 0; laux2 = 0 next
          mvn1 := begin
                  MAR = amar2 + laux2 next
                  rdbyte() next
                  MAR = amar1 + laux1; t4 = MBR<28:31> next
                  rdbyte() next
                  MBR<28:31> = t4 next
                  wrbyte() next
                  IF LFLD gtr laux2 =>
                      begin
                      laux1 = laux1 + 1; laux2 = laux2 + 1 next
                      RESTART mvn1
                      end
                  end
          end,

      end

!         . . . .
!         . . . .

! End of S370 summary description
```

Chapter 41

The Structure of SYSTEM/360[1]

Part II—System Implementations

W. Y. Stevens

Summary The performance range desired of SYSTEM/360 is obtained by variations in the storage, processing, control, and channel functions of the several models. The systematic variations in speed, size, and degree of simultaneity that characterize the functional components and elements of each model are discussed.

A primary goal in the SYSTEM/360 design effort was a wide range of processing unit performances coupled with complete program compatibility. In keeping with this goal, the logical structure of the resultant system lends itself to a wide choice of components and techniques in the engineering of models for desired performance levels.

This paper discusses basic choices made in implementing six SYSTEM/360 models spanning a performance range of fifty to one. It should be emphasized that the problems of model implementation were studied throughout the design period, and many of the decisions concerning logical structure were influenced by difficulties anticipated or encountered in implementation.

Performance Adjustment

The choices made in arriving at the desired performances fall into four areas:

Main storage

Central processing unit (CPU) registers and data paths

Sequence control

Input/output (I/O channels)

Each of the adjustable parameters of these areas can be subordinated, for present purposes, to one of three general factors: basic speed, size, and degree of simultaneity.

Main Storage

Storage Speed and Size

The interaction of the general factors is most obvious in the area of main storage. Here the basic speeds vary over a relatively small

[1]*IBM Sys. J*, vol. 3, no. 2, 1964, pp. 136–143.

range: from a 2.5-μsec cycle for the Model 40 to a 1.0-μsec cycle for Models 62 and 70. However, in combination with the other two factors, a 32:1 range in overall storage data rate is obtained, as shown in Table 1.

Most important of the three factors is size. The width of main storage, i.e., the amount of data obtained with one storage access, ranges from one byte for the Model 30, two bytes for the Model 40, and four bytes for the Model 50, to eight bytes for Models 60, 62, and 70.

Another size factor, less direct in its effect, is the total number of bytes in main storage, which can make a large difference in system throughput by reducing the number of references to external storage media. This number ranges from a minimum of 8192 bytes on Model 30 to a maximum of 524,288 bytes on Models 60, 62, and 70. An option of up to eight million more bytes of slower-speed, large-capacity core storage can further increase the throughput in some applications.

Interleaved Storage

Simultaneity in the core storage of Models 60 and 70 is obtained by overlapping the cycles of two storage units. Addresses are staggered in the two units, and a series of requests for successive words activates the two units alternately, thus doubling the maximum rate. For increased system performance, this technique is less effective than doubling the basic speed of a single unit, since the access time to a single word is not improved, and successive references frequently occur to the same unit. This is illustrated by comparing the performances of Models 60 and 62, whose only difference is the choice between two overlapped 2.0-μsec storage units and one single 1.0-μsec storage unit, respectively. The performance of Model 62 is approximately 1.5 times that of Model 60.

CPU Registers and Data Paths

Circuit Speed

SYSTEM/360 has three families of logic circuits, as shown in Table 2, each using the same solid-logic technology. One family, having a nominal delay of 30 nsec per logical stage or level, is used in the data paths of Models 30, 40, and 50. A second and faster family with a nominal delay of 10 nsec per level is used in Models 60 and 62. The fastest family, with a delay of 6 nsec, is used in Model 70.

The fundamental determinant of CPU speed is the time required to take data from the internal registers, process the data through the adder or other logical unit, and return the result to a register. This cycle time is determined by the delay per logical circuit level and the number of levels in the register-to-adder path, the adder, and the adder-to-register return path. The

Table 1 System/360 Main Storage Characteristics

	Model 30	Model 40	Model 50	Model 60	Model 62	Model 70
Cycle time (μsec)	2.0	2.5	2.0	2.0	1.0	1.0
Width (bytes)	1	2	4	8	8	8
Interleaved access	no	no	no	yes	no	yes
Maximum data rate (bytes/μsec)	0.5	0.8	2.0	8.0	8.0	16.0
Minimum storage size (bytes)	8,192	16,384	65,536	131,072	262,144	262,144
Maximum storage size (bytes)	65,536	262,144	262,144	524,288	524,288	524,288
Large capacity storage attachable	no	no	yes	yes	yes	yes

number of levels varies because of the trade-off that can usually be made between the number of circuit modules and the number of logical levels. Thus, the cycle time of the system varies from 1.0 μsec for Model 30 (with 30-nsec circuits, a relatively small number of modules, and more logic levels) and 0.5 μsec for Model 50 (also with 30-nsec circuits, but with more modules and fewer levels) to 0.2 μsec for Model 70 (with 6-nsec circuits).

Local Storage

The speed of the CPU depends also on the speed of the general and floating-point registers. In Model 30, these registers are located in an extension to the main core storage and have a read-write time of 2.0 μsec. In Model 40, the registers are located in a small core-storage unit, called *local storage*, with a read-write time of 1.25 μsec. Here, the operation of the local storage may be overlapped with main storage. In Model 50, the registers are in a local storage with a read-write time of only 0.5 μsec. In Model

60/62, the local storage has the logical characteristics of a core storage with nondestructive read-out; however, it is actually constructed as an array of registers using the 30-nsec family of logic circuits, and has a read-write time of 0.25 μsec. In Model 70, the general and floating-point registers are implemented with 6-nsec logic circuits and communicate directly with the adder and other data paths.

The two principal measures of size in the CPU are the width of the data paths and the number of bytes of high-speed working registers.

Data Path Organization

Model 30 has an 8-bit wide (plus parity) adder path, through which all data transfers are made, and approximately 12 bytes of working registers.

Model 40 also has an 8-bit wide adder path, but has an additional 16-bit wide data transfer path. Approximately 15 bytes

Table 2 System/360 CPU Characteristics

	Model 30	Model 40	Model 50	Model 60/62	Model 70
Circuit family: nominal delay per logic level (nsec)	30	30	30	10	6
Cycle time (μsec)	1.0	0.625	0.5	0.25	0.2
Location of general and floating registers	main core storage	local core storage	local core storage	local transistor storage	transistor registers
Width of general and floating register storage (bytes)	1	2	4	4	4 or 8
Speed of general and floating register storage (μsec)	2.0	1.25	0.5	0.25	
Width of main adder path (bits)	8	8	32	56	64
Width of auxiliary transfer path (bits)		16	8		
Widths of auxiliary adder paths (bits)				8	8, 8, and 24
Approximate number of bytes of register storage	12	15	30	50	100
Approximate number of bytes of working locations in local storage	45 (main storage)	48	60	4	
Relative computing speed	1	3.5	10	21/30	50

of working registers are used, plus about 48 bytes of working locations in the local storage, exclusive of the general and floating-point registers.

Model 50 has a 32-bit wide adder path, an 8-bit wide data path used for handling individual bytes, approximately 30 bytes of working registers, plus about 60 bytes of working locations in the local storage.

Model 60/62 has a 56-bit wide main adder path, an 8-bit wide serial adder path, and approximately 50 bytes of working registers.

Model 70 has a 64-bit wide main adder, an 8-bit wide exponent adder, an 8-bit wide decimal adder, a 24-bit wide addressing adder, and several other data transfer paths, some of which have incrementing ability. The model has about 100 bytes of working registers plus the 96 bytes of floating point and general registers which, in Model 70, are directly associated with the data paths.

The models of SYSTEM/360 differ considerably in the number of relatively independent operations that can occur simultaneously in the CPU. Model 30, for example, operates serially: virtually all data transfers must pass through the adder, one byte at a time. Model 70, however, can have many operations taking place at the same time. The CPU of this model is divided into three units that operate somewhat independently. The instruction preparation unit fetches instructions from storage, prepares them by computing their effective addresses, and initiates the fetching of the required data. The execution unit performs the execution of the instruction prepared by the instruction unit. The third unit is a storage bus control which coordinates the various requests by the other units and by the channels for core-storage cycles. All three units normally operate simultaneously, and together provide a large degree of instruction overlap. Since each of the units contains a number of different data paths, several data transfers may be occurring on the same cycle in a single unit.

The operations of other SYSTEM/360 models fall between those mentioned. Model 50, for example, can have simultaneous data transfers through the main adder, through an auxiliary byte transfer path, and to or from local storage.

Sequence Control

Complex Instruction Sequences

Since the SYSTEM/360 has an extensive instruction set, the CPU's must be capable of executing a large number of different sequences of basic operations. Furthermore, many instructions require sequences that are dependent on the data or addresses used. As shown in Table 3, these sequences of operations can be controlled by two methods; either by a conventional sequential logic circuit that uses the same types of circuit modules as used in the data paths or by a read-only storage device that contains a microprogram specifying the sequences to be performed for the different instructions.

Model 70 makes use of conventional sequential logic control mainly because of the high degree of simultaneity required. Also, a sufficiently fast read-only storage unit was not available at the time of development. The sequences to be performed in each of the Model 70 data paths have a considerable degree of independence. The read-only storage method of control does not easily lend itself to controlling these independent sequences, but is well adapted where the actions in each of the data paths are highly coordinated.

Read-Only Storage Control

The read-only storage method of control is described elsewhere [Peacock, n.d.]. This microprogram control, used in all but the fastest model of SYSTEM/360, is the only method known by which an extensive instruction set may be economically realized in a small system. This was demonstrated during the design of Model 60/62. Conventional logic control was originally planned for this model, but it became evident during the design period that too many circuit modules were required to implement the instruction set, even for this rather large system. Because a sufficiently fast read-only storage became available, it was adopted for sequence control at a substantial cost reduction.

The three factors of speed, size, and simultaneity are applicable

Table 3 System/360 Sequence Control Characteristics

	Model 30	Model 40	Model 50	Model 60/62	Model 70
Type	read-only storage	read-only storage	read-only storage	read-only storage	sequential logic
Cycle time (μsec)	1.0	0.625	0.5	0.25	0.2
Width of read-only storage word (available bits)	60	60	90	100	
Number of read-only storage words available	4096	4096	2816	2816	
Number of gate-control fields in read-only storage word	9	10	15	16	

to the read-only storage controls of the various SYSTEM/360 models. The speed of the read-only storage units corresponds to the cycle time of the CPU, and hence varies from 1.0 μsec per access for Model 30 down to 0.25 μsec for Models 60 and 62.

The size of read-only storage can vary in two ways—in width (number of bits per word) and in number of words. Since the bits of a word are used to control gates in the data paths, the width of storage is indirectly related to the complexity of the data paths. The widths of the read-only storages in SYSTEM/360 range from 60 bits for Models 30 and 40 to 100 bits for Models 60 and 62. The number of words is affected by several factors. First, of course, is the number and complexity of the control sequences to be executed. This is the same for all models except that Model 60/62 read-only storage contains no sequences for channel functions. The number of words tends to be greater for the smaller models, since these models require more cycles to accomplish the same function. Partially offsetting this is the fact that the greater degree of simultaneity in the larger systems often prevents the sharing of microprogram sequences between similar functions.

SYSTEM/360 employs no read-only storage simultaneity in the sense that more than one access is in progress at a given time. However, a single read-only storage word simultaneously controls several independent actions. The number of different gate control fields in a word provides some measure of this simultaneity. Model 30 has 9 such fields. Model 60/62 has 16.

Input/Output Channels

Channel Design

The SYSTEM/360 input/output channels may be considered from two viewpoints: the design of a channel itself, or the relationship of a channel to the whole system.

From the viewpoint of channel design, the raw speed of the components does not vary, since all channels use the 30-nsec family of circuits. However, the different channels do have access to different speeds of main storage and, in the three smaller models, different speeds of local storage.

The channels differ markedly in the amount of hardware devoted exclusively to channel use, as shown in Table 4. In the Model 30 multiplexor channel, this hardware amounts only to three 1-byte wide data paths, 11 latch bits for control, and a simple interface polling circuit. The channel used in Models 60, 62, and 70 contains about 300 bits of register storage, a 24-bit wide adder, and a complete set of sequential control circuits. The

Table 4   System/360 Channel Characteristics

	Model 30	Model 40	Model 50	Model 60/62	Model 70
Selector channels					
Maximum number attachable	0	2	3	6	6
Approximate maximum data rate on one channel in Kbyps†	250	400	800 (1250 on high speed)	1250	1250
Uses CPU data paths for:					
iniation and termination	yes	yes	yes	yes	yes
byte transfers	no	no	no	no	no
storage word transfers	no	low speed only	yes	no	no
chaining	yes	yes	yes	no	no
CPU and I/O overlap possible	yes	yes	regular—yes high speed—no	yes	yes
Multiplexor channels					
Maximum number attachable	1	1	1	0	0
Minimum number of subchannels	32	16	64		
Maximum number of subchannels	96	128	256		
Maximum data rate in byte interleaved mode (Kbyps)	16	30	40		
Maximum data rate in burst mode (Kbyps)	200	200	200		
Uses CPU data paths for all functions	yes	yes	yes		
CPU and I/O overlap possible in byte mode	yes	yes	yes		
CPU and I/O overlap possible in burst mode	no	no	yes		

†Thousand bytes per second.

amount of hardware provided for other channels is somewhere in between these extremes.

The disparity in the amount of channel hardware reflects the extent to which the channels share CPU hardware in accomplishing their functions. Such sharing is done at the expense of increased interference with the CPU, of course. This interference ranges from complete lock-out of CPU operations at high data rates on some of the smaller models, to interference only in essential references to main storage by the channel in the large models.

Channel/System Relationship

When the channels are viewed in their relationship to the whole system, the three factors of speed, size, and simultaneity take on a different aspect. The channel is viewed as a system component, and its effect on system throughput and other system capabilities is of concern. The speeds of the channels vary from a maximum rate of about 16 thousand bytes per second (byte interleaved mode) on the multiplexor channel of Model 30 to a maximum rate of about 1250 thousand bytes per second on the channels of Models 60, 62, and 70. The size of each of the channels is the same, in the sense that each handles an 8-bit byte at a time and each can connect to eight different control units. A slight size difference exists among multiplexor channels in terms of the maximum number of subchannels.

The degree of channel simultaneity differs considerably among the various models of SYSTEM/360. For example, operation of the Model 30 or 40 multiplexor channels in burst mode inhibits all other activity on the system, as does operation of the special high-speed channel on Model 50. At the other extreme, as many as six selector channels can be operating concurrently with the CPU on Models 60, 62, or 70. A second type of simultaneity is present in the multiplexor channels available on Models 30, 40, and 50. When operating in byte interleaved mode, one of these channels can control a number of concurrently operating input/output devices, and the CPU can also continue operation.

Differences in Application Emphasis

The models of SYSTEM/360 differ not only in throughput but also in the relative speeds of the various operations. Some of these relative differences are simply a result of the design choices described in this paper, made to achieve the desired overall performance. The more basic differences in relative performance of the various operations, however, were intentional. These differences in emphasis suit each model to those applications expected to comprise its largest usage.

Thus the smallest system is particularly aimed at traditional commercial data processing applications. These are characterized by extensive input/output operations in relation to the internal processing, and by more character handling than arithmetic. The fast selector channels and character-oriented data paths of Model 30 result from this emphasis. But despite this emphasis, the general-purpose instruction set of SYSTEM/360 results in much better scientific application performance for Model 30 than for its comparable predecessors.

On the other hand, the large systems are expected to find particularly heavy use in scientific computation, where the emphasis is on rapid floating-point arithmetic. Thus Models 60, 62, and 70 contain registers and adders that can handle the full length of a long format floating-point operand, yet do character operations one byte at a time.

No particular emphasis on either commercial or scientific applications characterizes the intermediate models. However, Models 40 and 50 are intended to be particularly suitable for communication-oriented and real-time applications. For example, Model 50 includes a multiplexor channel, storage protection, and a timer as standard features, and also provides the ability to share main storages between two CPU's in a multiprocessing arrangement.

References

Peacock [n.d.].

Chapter 42

VAX-11/780—A Virtual Address Extension to the DEC PDP-11 Family[1]

W. D. Strecker

Introduction

Large Virtual Address Space Minicomputers

Perhaps the most useful definition of a minicomputer system is based on price: depending on one's perspective such systems are typically found in the $20K to $200K range. The twin forces of market pull—as customers build increasingly complex systems on minicomputers—and technology push—as the semiconductor industry provides increasingly lower cost logic and memory elements—have induced minicomputer manufacturers to produce systems of considerable performance and memory capacity. Such systems are typified by the DEC PDP-11/70. From an architectural point of view, the characteristic which most distinguishes many of these systems from larger mainframe computers is the size of the virtual address space: the immediately available address space seen by an individual process. For many purposes the 65K byte virtual address space typically provided on minicomputers (such as the PDP-11) has not been and probably will not continue to be a severe limitation. However, there are some applications whose programming is impractical in a 65K byte virtual address space, and perhaps most importantly, others whose programming is appreciably simplified by having a large virtual address space. Given the relative trends in hardware and software costs, the latter point alone will insure that large virtual address space minicomputers play an increasingly important role in minicomputer product offerings.

In principle, there is no great challenge in designing a large virtual address minicomputer system. For example, many of the large mainframe computers could serve as architectural models for such a system. The real challenge lies in two areas: compatibility—very tangible and important; and simplicity—intangible but nonetheless important.

The first area is preserving the customer's and the computer manufacturer's investment in existing systems. This investment exists at many levels: basic hardware (principally busses and peripherals); systems and applications software; files and data bases; and personnel familiar with the programming, use, and operation of the systems. For example, just recently a major computer manufacturer abandoned a major effort for new computer architectures in favor of evolving its current architectures [McLean, 1977].

The second intangible area is the preservation of those attributes (other than price) which make minicomputer systems attractive. These include approachability, understandability, and ease of use. Preservation of these attributes suggests that simply modelling an extended virtual address minicomputer after a large mainframe computer is not wholly appropriate. It also suggests that during architectural design, tradeoffs must be made between more than just performance, functionality, and cost. Performance or functionality features which are so complex that they appreciably compromise understanding or ease of use must be rejected as inappropriate for minicomputer systems.

VAX-11 Overview

VAX-11 is the **V**irtual **A**ddress e**X**tention of PDP-11 architecture [Bell et al., 1970; Bell and Strecker, 1976]. The most distinctive feature of VAX-11 is the extension of the virtual address from 16 bits as provided on the PDP-11 to 32 bits. With the 8-bit byte the basic addressable unit, the extension provides a virtual address space of about 4.3 gigabytes which, even given rapid improvement in memory technology, should be adequate far into the future.

Since maximal PDP-11 compatibility was a strong goal, early VAX-11 design efforts focused on literally extending the PDP-11: preserving the existing instruction formats and instruction set and fitting the virtual address extension around them. The objective here was to permit, to the extent possible, the running of existing programs in the extended virtual address environment. While realizing this objective was possible (there were three distinct designs), it was felt that the extended architecture designs were overly compromised in the areas of efficiency, functionality, and programming ease.

Consequently, it was decided to drop the constraint of the PDP-11 instruction format in designing the extended virtual address space or *native mode* of the VAX-11 architecture. However, in order to run existing PDP-11 programs, VAX-11 includes a PDP-11 *compatibility mode*. Compatibility mode provides the basic PDP-11 instruction set less only privileged instructions (such as HALT) and floating point instructions (which are optional on most PDP-11 processors and not required by most PDP-11 software).

In addition to compatibility mode, a number of other features to preserve PDP-11 investment have been provided in the VAX-11 architecture, the VAX-11 operating system VAX/VMS, and the VAX-11/780 implementation of the VAX-11 architecture. These features include:

1 The equivalent native mode data types and formats are identical to those on the PDP-11. Also, while extended, the VAX-11 native mode instruction set and addressing modes

[1]*AFIPS Proc. NCC*, 1978, pp. 967–980.

are very close to those on the PDP-11. As a consequence VAX-11 native mode assembly language programming is quite similar to PDP-11 assembly language programming.

2 The VAX-11/780 uses the same peripheral busses (Unibus and Massbus) as the PDP-11 and uses the same peripherals.

3 The VAX/VMS operating system is an evolution of the PDP-11 RSX-11M and IAS operating systems, offers a similar although extended set of system services, and uses the same command languages. Additionally, VAX/VMS supports most of the RSX-11M/IAS system service requests issued by programs executing in compatibility mode.

4 The VAX/VMS file system is the same as used on the RSX-11M/IAS operating systems permitting interchange of files and volumes. The file access methods as implemented by the RMS record manager are also the same.

5 VAX-11 high level language compilers accept the same source languages as the equivalent PDP-11 compilers and execution of compiled programs gives the same results.

The coverage of all these aspects of VAX-11 is well beyond the scope of any single paper. The remainder of this paper discusses the design of the VAX-11 native mode architecture and gives an overview of the VAX-11/780 system.

VAX-11 Native Architecture

Processor State

Like the PDP-11, VAX-11 is organized around a general register processor state. This organization was favored because access to operands stored in general registers is fast (since the registers are internal to the processor and register accesses do not need to pass through a memory management mechanism) and because only a small number of bits in an instruction are needed to designate a register. Perhaps most importantly, the registers are used (as on the PDP-11) in conjunction with a large set of addressing modes which permit unusually flexible operand addressing methods.

Some consideration was given to a pure stack based architecture. However it was rejected because real program data suggests the superiority of two or three operand instruction formats [Myers, 1977b]. Actually VAX-11 is quite stack oriented, and although it is not optimally encoded for the purpose, can easily be used as a pure stack architecture if desired.

VAX-11 has 16 32-bit general registers (denoted R0-R15) which are used for both fixed and floating point operands. This is in contrast to the PDP-11 which has eight 16-bit general registers and six 64-bit floating point registers. The merged set of fixed and floating registers were preferred because it simplifies programming and permits a more effective allocation of the registers.

Four of the registers are assigned special meaning in the VAX-11 architecture:

1 R15 is the *program counter* (PC) which contains the address of the next byte to be interpreted in the instruction stream.

2 R14 is the *stack pointer* (SP) which contains the address of the top of the processor defined stack used for procedure and interrupt linkage.

3 R13 is the *frame pointer* (FP). The VAX-11 procedure calling convention builds a data structure on the stack called a stack frame. FP contains the address of this structure.

4 R12 is the *argument pointer* (AP). The VAX-11 procedure calling convention uses a data structure called an argument list. AP contains the address of this structure.

The remaining element of the user visible processor state (additional processor state seen mainly by privileged procedures is discussed later) is the 16-bit *processor status word* (PSW). The PSW contains the N, Z, V, and C condition codes which indicate respectively whether a previous instruction had a negative result, a zero result, a result which overflowed, or a result which produced a carry (or borrow). Also in the PSW are the IV, DV, and FU bits which enable processor trapping on integer overflow, decimal overflow, and floating underflow conditions respectively. (The trapping on conditions of floating overflow and divide by zero for any data type are always enabled.)

Finally, the PSW contains the T bit which when set forces a trap at the end of each instruction. This trap is useful for program debugging and analysis purposes.

Data Types and Formats

The VAX-11 data types are a superset of the PDP-11 data types. Where the PDP-11 and VAX-11 have equivalent data types the formats (representation in memory) are identical. Data type and data format identity is one of the most compelling forms of compatibility. It permits free interchange of binary data between PDP-11 and VAX-11 programs. It facilitates source level compatibility between equivalent PDP-11 and VAX-11 languages. It also greatly facilitates hardware implementation of and software support of the PDP-11 compatibility mode in the VAX-11 architecture.

The VAX-11 data types divide into five classes:

1 Integer data types are the 8-bit *byte*, the 16-bit *word*, the 32-bit *longword*, and the 64-bit *quadword*. Usually these data types are considered signed with negative values represented in two's complement form. However, for most purposes they can be interpreted as unsigned and the

VAX-11 instruction set provides support for this interpretation.

2 Floating data types are the 32-bit *floating* and the 64-bit *double* floating. These data types are binary normalized, have an 8-bit signed exponent, and have a 25- or 57-bit signed fraction with the redundant most significant fraction bit not represented.

3 The *variable bit field* data type is 0 to 32 bits located arbitrarily with respect to addressable byte boundaries. A bit field is specified by three operands: the address of a byte, the starting bit position P with respect to bit 0 of that byte, and the size S of the field. The VAX-11 instruction set provides for interpreting the field as signed or unsigned.

4 The *character string* data type is 0 to 65535 contiguous bytes. It is specified by two operands: the length and starting address of the string. Although the data type is named "character string," no special interpretation is placed on the values of the bytes in the character string.

5 The *decimal string* data types are 0 to 31 digits. They are specified by two operands: a length (in digits) and a starting address. The primary data type is *packed decimal* with two digits stored in each byte except that the byte containing the least significant digit contains a single digit and the sign. Two ASCII character decimal types are supported: *leading separate* sign and *trailing embedded* sign. The leading separate type is a "+," "−," or "<blank>" (equivalent to "+") ASCII character followed by 0 to 31 ASCII decimal digit characters. A trailing embedded sign decimal string is 0 to 31 bytes which are ASCII decimal digit characters except for the character containing least

significant digit which is an arbitrary encoding of the digit and sign.

All of the data types except field may be stored on arbitrary byte boundaries—there are no alignment constraints. The field data type, of course, can start on an arbitrary bit boundary.

Attributes of and symbolic representations for most of the data types are given in Table 1 and Fig. 1.

Instruction Format and Address Modes

Most architectures provide a small number of relatively fixed instruction formats. Two problems often result. First, not all operands of an instruction have the same specification generality. For example, one operand must come from memory and another from a register; or one must come from the stack and another from memory. Second, only a limited number of operands can be accommodated: typically one or two. For instructions which inherently require more operands (such as field or string instructions), the additional operands are specified in ad hoc ways: small literal fields in instructions, specific registers or stack positions, or packed in fields of a single operand. Both these problems lead to increased programming complexity: they require superfluous move type instructions to get operands to places where they can be used and increase competition for potentially scarce resources such as registers.

To avoid these problems two criteria were used in the design of the VAX-11 instruction format: (1) all instructions should have the "natural" number of operands and (2) all operands should have the same generality in specification. These criteria led to a highly

Table 1 Data Types

Data type	Size	Range (decimal)	
Integer		Signed	Unsigned
Byte	8 bits	−128 to +127	0 to 255
Word	16 bits	−32768 to +32767	0 to 65535
Longword	32 bits	-2^{31} to $+2^{31}-1$	0 to $2^{32}-1$
Quadword	64 bits	-2^{63} to $+2^{63}-1$	0 to $2^{64}-1$
Floating point		$\pm2.9 \times 10^{-37}$ to 1.7×10^{38}	
Floating	32 bits	approximately seven decimal digits precision	
Double Floating	64 bits	approximately sixteen decimal digits precision	
Packed decimal string	0 to 16 bytes (31 digits)	numeric, two digits per byte sign in low half of last byte	
Character string	0 to 65535 bytes	one character per byte	
Variable-length bit field	0 to 32 bits	dependent on interpretation	

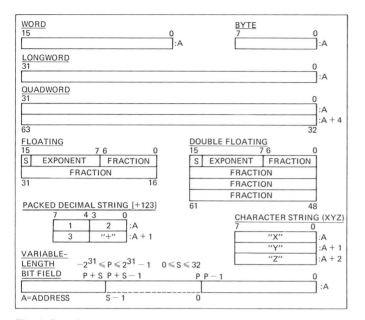

Fig. 1. Data formats.

variable instruction format. An instruction consists of a one or two[1] byte *opcode* followed by the specifications for n operands (n ≥ 0) where n is an implicit property of the opcode. An operand specification is one to 10 bytes in length and consists of a one or two byte *operand specifier* followed by (as required) zero to eight bytes of *specifier extension*. The operand specifier includes the address mode and designation of any registers needed to locate the operand. A specifier extension consists of a displacement, an address, or immediate data.

The VAX-11 address modes are with one exception a superset of the PDP-11 address modes. The PDP-11 address mode auto-decrement deferred was omitted from VAX-11 because it was rarely used.

Most operand specifiers are one byte long and contain two 4-bit fields: the high order field (bits 7:4) contains the address mode designator and the lower field (bits 3:0) contains a general register designator. The address modes include:

1 *Register mode* in which the designated register contains the operand.

2 *Register deferred mode* in which the designated register contains the address of the operand.

3 *Autodecrement mode* in which the contents of the designated register are first decremented by the size (in bytes) of the operand and then used as the address of the operand.

4 *Autoincrement mode* in which the contents of the designated register are first used as the address of the operand and are then incremented by the size of the operand. Note that if the designated register is PC, the operand is located in the instruction stream. This use of autoincrement mode is called *immediate* mode. In immediate mode the one to eight bytes of data are the specifier extension.

Autoincrement mode can be used sequentially to process a vector in one direction and autodecrement mode used to process a vector in the opposite direction. Autoincrement, register deferred, and autodecrement modes can be applied to a single register to implement a stack data structure: autodecrement to "push," autoincrement to "pop," and register deferred to access the top of the stack.

5 *Autoincrement deferred mode* in which the contents of the designated register are used as the address of a longword in memory which contains the address of the operand. After this use, the contents of the register are incremented by four (the size in bytes of the longword address). Note that if PC is the designated register, the absolute address of the operand is located in the instruction stream. This use of autoincrement deferred mode is termed *absolute* mode. In absolute mode the 4-byte address is the specifier extension.

6 *Displacement mode* in which a displacement is added to the contents of the designated register to form the operand address. There are three displacement modes depending on whether a signed byte, word, or longword displacement is the specifier extension. These modes are termed byte, word, and longword displacement respectively. Note that if PC is the designated register, the operand is located relative to PC. For this use the modes are termed byte, word, and longword *relative* mode respectively.

7 *Displacement deferred mode* in which a displacement is added to the designated register to form the address of a longword containing the address of the operand. There are three displacement deferred modes depending on whether a signed byte, word, or longword displacement is the specifier extension. These modes are termed byte, word, and longword displacement respectively. Note that if PC is the designated register, the operand address is located relative to PC. For this use the modes are termed byte, word, and longword *relative deferred* mode respectively.

8 *Literal mode* in which the operand specifier itself contains a 6-bit literal which is the operand. For integer data types the literal encodes the values 0–63; for floating data types the literal includes three exponent and three fraction bits to give 64 common values.

9 *Index mode* which is not really a mode but rather a one byte prefix operator for any other mode which evaluates to a memory address (i.e., all modes except register and literal). The index mode prefix is cascaded with the operand specifier for that mode (called the base operand specifier) to form an aggregate two byte operand specifier. The base

operand specifier is used in the normal way to evaluate a base address. A copy of the contents of the register designated in the index prefix is multiplied by the size (in bytes) of the operand and added to the base address. The sum is the final operand address. There are three advantages to the VAX-11 form of indexing: (a) the index is scaled by the data size and thus the index register maintains a logical rather than a byte offset into an indexed data structure, (b) indexing can be applied to any of the address modes which generate memory addresses and this results in a comprehensive set of indexed addressing methods, and (c) the space required to specify indexing and the index register is paid only when indexing is used.

The VAX-11 assembler syntax for the address modes is given in Fig. 2. The bracketed (||) notation is optional and the programmer rarely needs to be concerned with displacement sizes or whether to choose literal or immediate mode. The programmer writes the simple form and assembler chooses the address mode which produces the shortest instruction length.

In order to give a better feeling for the instruction format and assembler notation, several examples are given in Figs. 3 to 5. In Fig. 3 is an instruction which moves a word from an address which is 56 plus the contents of R5 to an address which is 270 plus the contents of R6. Note, that the displacement 56 is representable in a byte while the displacement 270 requires a word. The instruction occupies 6 bytes. In Fig. 4 is an instruction which adds 1 to a longword in R0 and stores the result at a memory address which is the sum of A and 4 times the contents of R. This instruction occupies 9 bytes. Finally, in Fig. 5 is a return from subroutine instruction. It has no explicit operands and occupies a single byte.

The only significant instance where there is non-general specification of operands is in the specification of targets for

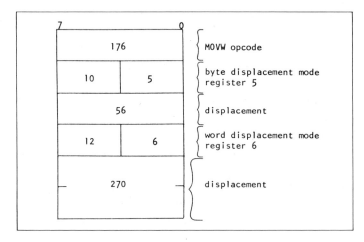

Fig. 3. MOVW 56 (R5), 270 (R6).

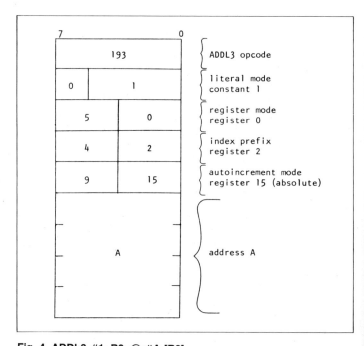

Fig. 4. ADDL3 #1, R0, @ #A [R2].

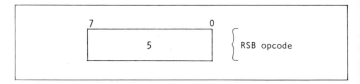

Fig. 5. RSB.

Literal (Immediate)	$\begin{Bmatrix} S\dagger \\ I\dagger \end{Bmatrix}$ # constant	
Register	R*n*	
Register Deferred	(R*n*)	
Autodecrement	– (R*n*)	
Autoincrement	(R*n*) ·	
Autoincrement Deferred	@ (R*n*) ·	Indexed [**R***x*]
(Absolute)	@ # address	
Displacement	$\begin{Bmatrix} B\dagger \\ W\dagger \\ L\dagger \end{Bmatrix}$ displacement (R*n*) address	
Displacement Deferred	@ $\begin{Bmatrix} B\dagger \\ W\dagger \\ L\dagger \end{Bmatrix}$ displacement (R*n*) address	

n = 0 through 15
x = 0 through 14

Fig. 2. Assembler syntax.

branch instructions. Since invariably the target of a branch instruction is a small displacement from the current PC, most branch instructions simply take a one byte PC relative displacement. This is exactly as if byte displacement mode were used with the PC used as the register, except that the operand specifier byte is not needed. Because of the pervasiveness of branch instructions in code, this one byte saving results in a non-trivial reduction in code size. An example of the branch instruction branch on equal is given in Fig. 6.

Instruction Set

A major goal of the VAX-11 instruction set design was to provide for effective compiler generated code. Four decisions helped to realize this goal:

1. A very regular and consistent treatment of operators. Thus, for example, since there is a divide longword instruction, there are also divide word and divide byte instructions.

2. An avoidance of instructions unlikely to be generated by a compiler.

3. Inclusion of several forms of common operators. For example the integer add instructions are included in three forms: (a) one operand where the value one is added to an operand, (b) two operands where one operand is added to a second, and (c) three operands where one operand is added to a second and the result stored in a third. Since the VAX-11 instruction format allows fully general specifications of the operands, VAX-11 programs often have the structure (though not the encoding) of the canonic program form proposed in Flynn [1977].

4. Replacement of common instruction sequences with single instructions. Examples of this include procedure calling, multiway branching, loop control, and array subscript calculation.

The effect of these decisions is reflected in several observations. First, despite the larger virtual address and instruction set support for more data types, compiler (and hand) generated code for VAX-11 is typically smaller than the equivalent PDP-11 code for algorithms operating on data types supported by the PDP-11. Second, of the 243 instructions in the instruction set about 75

percent are generated by the VAX-11 FORTRAN compiler. Of the instructions not generated, most operate on data types not part of the FORTRAN language.

A complete list of the VAX-11 instructions is given in Appendix 1. The following gives an overview of the instruction set.

1. *Integer logic and arithmetic*—Byte, word, and longword are the primary data types. A fairly conventional group of arithmetic and logical instructions is provided. The result generating dyadic arithmetic and logical instructions are provided in two and three operand forms. A number of optimizations are included: clear which is a move of zero; test which is a compare against zero; and increment and decrement which are an optimization of add one and subtract one respectively. A complete set of converts is provided which covers both the integer and the floating data types. In contrast to other architectures only a few shift type instructions are provided: it was felt that shifts are mostly used for field isolation which is much more conveniently done with the field instructions described later. In order to support greater than longword precision integer operations, a few special instructions are provided: extended multiply and divide and add with carry and subtract with carry.

2. *Floating point instructions*—Again a conventional group of instructions are included with result producing dyadic operators in two and three operand forms. Several specialized floating point instructions are included. The extended modulus instruction multiplies two floating operands together and stores the integer and fraction parts of the product in separate result operands. The polynomial instruction computes a polynomial from a table of coefficients in memory. Both these instructions employ greater than normal precision and are useful in high accuracy mathematical routines. A convert rounded instruction is provided which implements the ALGOL rather than FORTRAN conventions for converting from floating point to integer.

3. *Address instructions*—The move address instructions store in the result operand the effective address of the source operand. The push address optimizations push on the stack (defined by SP) the effective address of the source operand. The latter are used extensively in subroutine calling.

4. *Field instructions*—The extract field instructions extract a 0 to 32-bit field, sign- or zero-extend it if it is less than 32 bits, and store it in a longword operand. The compare field instructions compare a (sign- or zero-extended if necessary) field against a longword operand. The find first instructions find the first occurrence of a set or clear bit in a field.

5. *Control instructions*—There is a complete set of conditional branches supporting both a signed and, where appropriate, an unsigned interpretation of the various data types. These branches test the condition codes and take a one byte

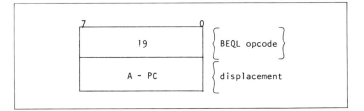

Fig. 6. BEQL A.

PC relative branch displacement. There are three unconditional branch instructions: the first taking a one byte PC relative displacement, the second taking a word PC relative displacement, and the third—called jump—taking a general operand specification. Paralleling these three instructions are three branch to subroutine instructions. These push the current PC on the stack before transferring control. The single byte return from subroutine instruction returns from subroutines called by these instructions. There is a set of branch on bit instructions which branch on the state of a single bit and, depending on the instruction, set, clear, or leave unchanged that bit.

The add compare and branch instructions are used for loop control. A step operand is added to the loop control operand and the sum compared against a limit operand. The result of the comparison determines whether the branch is taken. The sense of the comparison is based on the sign of the step operand. Optimizations of loop control include the add one and branch instructions which assume a step of one and the subtract one and branch instructions which assume a step of minus one and a limit of zero.

The case instructions implement the computed go to in FORTRAN and case statements in other languages. A selector operand is checked to see that it lies in range and is then used to select one of table of PC relative branch displacements following the instruction.

6　*Queue instructions*—The queue representation is a doubly linked circular list. Instructions are provided to insert an item into a queue or to remove an item from a queue.

7　*Character string instructions*—The general move character instruction takes five operands specifying the lengths and starting addresses of the source and destination strings and a fill character to be used if the source string is shorter than the destination string. The instruction functions correctly regardless of string overlap. An optimized move character instruction assumes the string lengths are equal and takes three operands. Paralleling the move instructions are two compare character instructions. The move translated characters instruction is similar to the general move character instruction except that the source string bytes are translated by a translation table specified by the instruction before being moved to destination string. The move translated until escape instruction stops if the result of a translation matches the escape character specified by one of its operands. The locate and skip character instructions find respectively the first occurrence or non-occurrence of a character in a string. The scan and span instructions find respectively the first occurrence or non-occurrence of a character within a specified character set in a string. The match characters instruction finds the first occurrence of a substring within a string which matches a specified pattern string.

8　*Packed decimal instructions*—A conventional set of arithmetic instructions is provided. The arithmetic shift and round instruction provides decimal point scaling and rounding. Converts are provided to and from longword integers, leading separate decimal strings, and trailing embedded decimal strings. A comprehensive edit instruction is included.

VAX-11 Procedure Instructions

A major goal of the VAX-11 design was to have a single system wide procedure calling convention which would apply to all inter-module calls in the various languages, calls for operating system services, and calls to the common run time system. Three VAX-11 instructions support this convention: two call instructions which are indistinguishable as far as the called procedure is concerned and a return instruction.

The call instructions assume that the first word of a procedure is an *entry mask* which specifies which registers are to be used by the procedure and thus need to be saved. (Actually only R0-R11 are controlled by the entry mask and bits 15:12 of the mask are reserved for other purposes.) After pushing the registers to be saved on the stack, the call instruction pushes AP, FP, PC, a longword containing the PSW and the entry mask, and a zero valued longword which is the initial value of a condition handler address. The call instruction then loads FP with the contents of SP and AP with the argument list address. The appearance of the stack frame after the call is shown in the upper part of Fig. 7.

The form of the argument list is shown in the lower part of Fig. 7. It consists of an argument count and list of longword arguments which are typically addresses. The CALLG instruction takes two operands: one specifying the procedure address and the other specifying the address of the argument list assumed arbitrarily located in memory. The CALLS instruction also takes two operands: one the procedure address and the other an argument count. CALLS assumes that the arguments have been pushed on the stack and pushes the argument count immediately prior to saving the registers controlled by the entry mask. It also sets bit 13 of the saved entry mask to indicate a CALLS instruction was used to make the call.

The return instruction uses FP to locate the stack frame. It loads SP with the contents of FP and restores PSW through PC by popping the stack. The saved entry mask controls the popping and restoring of R11 through R0. Finally if the bit indicating CALLS was set, the argument list is removed from the stack.

Memory Management Design Alternatives

Memory management comprises the mechanisms used (1) to map the virtual addresses generated by processes to physical memory addresses, (2) to control access to memory (i.e., to control whether a process has read, write, or no access to various areas of memory), and (3) to allow a process to execute even if all of its virtual address space is not simultaneously mapped to physical memory (i.e., to

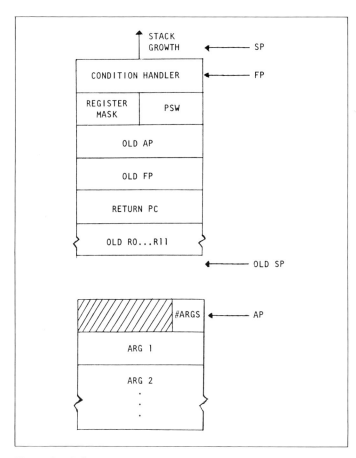

Fig. 7. Stack frame.

provide so called virtual memory facilities). The memory management proved to be the most difficult part of the architecture to design. Three alternatives were pursued and full designs were completed for the first two alternatives and nearly completed for the third. The three alternatives[1] were:

1 A paged form of memory management with access control at the page level and a small number (4) of hierarchical access modes whose use would be dedicated to specific purposes. This represented an evolution of the PDP-11/70 memory management.

2 A paged and segmented form with access control at the segment level and a larger number (8) of hierarchical access

[1]It should not be construed that memory management is independent of the rest of the architecture. The various memory management alternatives required different definitions of the addressing modes and different instruction level support for addressing.

modes which would be used quite generally. Although it differed in a number of ways, the design was motivated by the Multics [Organick, 1972; Schroeder and Saltzer, 1971] architecture and the Honeywell 6180 implementation.

3 A capabilities [Needham, 1972; Needham and Walker, 1977] form with access control provided by the capabilities and the ability to page larger objects described by the capabilities.

The first alternative was finally selected. The second alternative was rejected because it was felt that the real increase in functionality provided inadequately offset the increased architectural complexity. The third alternative appeared to offer functionality advantages that could be useful over the longer term. However, it was unlikely that these advantages could be exploited in the near term. Further it appeared that the complexity of the capabilities design was inappropriate for a minicomputer system.

Memory Mapping

The 4.3 gigabyte virtual address space is divided into four regions as shown in Fig. 8. The first two regions—the *program* and *control* regions—comprise the per process virtual address space which is uniquely mapped for each process. The second two regions—the *system* region and a region reserved for future use—comprise the system virtual address space which is singly mapped for all processes.

Each of the regions serves different purposes. The program region contains user programs and data and the top of the region is a dynamic memory allocation point. The control region contains operating system data structures specific to the process and the user stack. The system region contains procedures which are common to all processes (such as those that comprise the operating system and RMS) and (as will be seen later) page tables.

A virtual address has the structure shown in the upper part of Fig. 9. Bits 8:0 specify a byte within a 512 byte *page* which is the

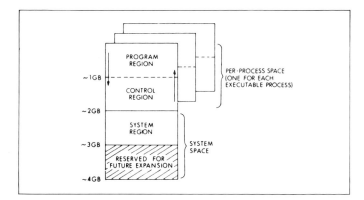

Fig. 8. Virtual address space.

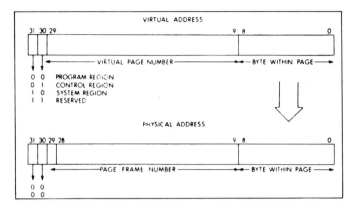

Fig. 9. Virtual and physical addresses.

basic unit of mapping. Bits 29:9 specify a *virtual page number* (VPN). Bits 31:30 select the virtual address region. The mechanism of mapping consists of using the region select bits to select a *page table* which consists of *page table entries* (PTEs). After a check that it is not too large, the VPN is used to index into the page table to select a PTE. The PTE contains either (1) 21-bit physical *page frame number* which is concatenated with the nine low order byte in page bits to form a 30-bit physical address shown in the lower part of Fig. 9, or (2) an indication that the virtual page accessed is not in physical memory. The latter case is called a *page fault.* Instruction execution in the current procedure is suspended and control is transferred to an operating system procedure which will cause the missing virtual page to be brought into physical memory. At this point instruction execution in the suspended procedure can resume transparently.

The page table for the system region is defined by the *system base register* which contains the physical address of the start of the system region page table and the *system length register* which contains the length of the table. Thus the system page table is contiguous in physical memory.

The per process space page tables are defined similarly by the *program* and *control region base registers* and *length registers.* However, the base registers do not contain physical addresses: rather, they contain system region virtual addresses. Thus the per process page tables are contiguous in the system region virtual address space and are not necessarily contiguous in physical memory. This placement of the per process page tables permits them to be paged and avoids what would otherwise be a serious physical memory allocation problem.

Access Control

At a given point in time a process executes in one of four *access modes.* The modes from most privileged to least are called *kernel,*

executive, supervisor and *user.* The use of these modes by VAX/VMS is as follows:

1　Kernel—Interrupt and exception handling, scheduling, paging, physical I/O, etc.

2　Executive—Logical I/O as provided by RMS.

3　Supervisor—The command interpreter.

4　User—User procedures and data.

The accessibility of each page (read, write, or no access) from each access mode is specified in the PTE for that page. Any attempt to improperly access a page is suppressed and control is transferred to an operating system procedure. The accessibility is assumed hierarchically ordered: if a page is writable from any given mode, it is also readable; and if a page is accessible from a less privileged mode, it is accessible from a more privileged mode. Thus, for example, a page can be readable and writable from kernel mode, only readable from executive mode, and inaccessible from supervisor and user modes.

A procedure executing in a less privileged mode often needs to call a procedure which executes in a more privileged mode: e.g., a user program needs an operating system service performed. The access mode is changed to a more privileged mode by executing a change mode instruction which transfers control to a routine executing at the new access mode. A return is made to original access mode by executing a return from exception or interrupt instruction (REI).

The *current access mode* is stored in the *processor status longword* (PSL) whose low order 16 bits comprise the PSW. Also stored in the PSL is the *previous access mode*; i.e., the access mode from which the current access mode was called. The previous mode information is used by the special probe instructions which validate arguments passed in cross access mode calls.

Procedures running at each of the access modes require a separate stack with appropriate accessibility. To facilitate this, each process has four copies of SP which are selected according to the current access mode field in the PSL. A procedure always accesses the correct stack by using R14.

In an earlier section, it was stated that the VAX-11 standard CALL instruction is used for all calls including those for operating system services. Indeed procedures do call the operating system using the CALL instruction. The target of the CALL instruction is the minimal procedure consisting of an entry mask, a change mode instruction, and a return instruction. This access mode changing is transparent to the calling procedure.

Interrupts and Exceptions

Interrupts and exceptions are forced changes in control flow other than that explicitly indicated by the executing program. The distinction between them is that interrupts are normally unrelated to the currently executing program while exceptions are a direct consequence of program execution. Examples of interrupt conditions are status changes in I/O devices while examples of exception conditions are arithmetic overflow or a memory management access control violation.

VAX-11 provides a 31 priority level interrupt system. Sixteen levels (16-31) are provided for hardware while 15 levels (1-15) are provided for software. (Level 0 is used for normal program execution.) The current *interrupt priority level* (IPL) is stored in a field in the PSL. When an interrupt request is made at a level higher than IPL, the current PC and PSL are pushed on the stack and new PC obtained from a vector selected by the interrupt requester (a new PSL is generated by the CPU). Interrupts are serviced by routines executing with kernel mode access control. Since interrupts are appropriately serviced in a system wide rather than a specific process context, the stack used for interrupts is defined by another stack pointer called the *interrupt stack pointer*. (Just as for the multiple stack pointers used in process context, an interrupt routine accesses the interrupt stack using R14.) An interrupt service is terminated by execution of an REI instruction which loads PC and PSL from the top two longwords on the stack.

Exceptions are handled like interrupts except for the following: (1) since exceptions arise in a specific process context, the kernel mode stack for that process is used to store PC and PSL and (2) additional parameters (such as the virtual address causing a page fault) may be pushed on the stack.

Process Context Switching

From the standpoint of the VAX-11 architecture, the process state or context consists of:

1 The 15 general registers R0-R13 and R15.

2 Four copies of R14 (SP): one for each of kernel, executive, supervisor, and user access modes.

3 The PSL.

4 Two base and two limit registers for the program and control region page tables.

This context is gathered together in a data structure called a *process control block* (PCB) which normally resides in memory. While a process is executing, the process context can be considered to reside in processor registers. To switch from one process to another it is required that the process context from the previously executing process be saved in its PCB in memory and the process context for the process about to be executed to be loaded from its PCB in memory. Two VAX-11 instructions support context switching. The save process context instruction saves the complete process context in memory while the load process context instruction loads the complete process context from memory.

I/O

Much like the PDP-11, VAX-11 has no specific I/O instructions. Rather, I/O devices and device controllers are implemented with a set of registers which have addresses in the physical memory address space. The CPU controls I/O devices by writing these registers; the devices return status by writing these registers and the CPU subsequently reading them. The normal memory management mechanism controls access to I/O device registers and a process having a particular device's registers mapped into its address space can control that device using the regular instruction set.

Compatibility Mode

As mentioned in the VAX-11 overview, compatibility mode in the VAX-11 architecture provides the basic PDP-11 instruction set less privileged and floating point instructions. Compatibility mode is intended to support a user as opposed to an operating system environment. Normally a compatibility mode program is combined with a set of native mode procedures whose purpose is to map service requests from some particular PDP-11 operating system environment into VAX/VMS services.

In compatibility mode the 16-bit PDP-11 addresses are zero-extended to 32-bits where standard native mode mapping and access control apply. The eight 16-bit PDP-11 general registers overmap the native mode general registers R0-R6 and R15 and thus the PDP-11 processor state is contained wholly within the native mode processor state.

Compatibility mode is entered by setting the compatibility mode bit in the PSL. Compatibility mode is left by executing a PDP-11 trap instruction (such as used to make operating service requests), and on interrupts and exceptions.

VAX-11/780 Implementation

VAX-11/780

The VAX-11/780 computer system is the first implementation of the VAX-11 architecture. For instructions executed in compatibility mode, the VAX-11/780 has a performance comparable to the PDP-11/70. For instructions executed in native mode, the -11/780 has a performance in excess of the -11/70 and thus represents the new high end of the -11 (LSI-11, PDP-11, VAX-11) family.

A block diagram of the -11/780 system is given in Fig. 10. The system consists of a central processing unit (CPU), the console subsystem, the memory subsystem, and the I/O subsystem. The

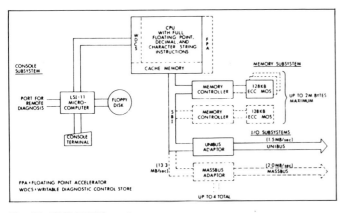

Fig. 10. VAX-11/780 system.

CPU and the memory and I/O subsystems are joined by a high speed synchronous bus called the *Synchronous Backplane Interconnect* (SBI).

CPU

The CPU is a microprogrammed processor which implements the native and compatibility mode instruction sets, the memory management, and the interrupt and exception mechanisms. The CPU has 32-bit main data paths and is built almost entirely of conventional Schottky TTL components.

To reduce effective memory access time the CPU includes an 8K byte write through cache or buffer memory. The cache organization is 2 way associative with an 8-byte block size. To reduce delays due to writes, the CPU includes a write buffer. The CPU issues the write to the buffer and the actual memory write takes place in parallel with other CPU activity.

The CPU contains a 128 entry address translation buffer which is a cache of recent virtual to physical translations. The buffer is divided into two 64 entry sections: one for the per process regions and one for the system region. This division facilitates permitting the system region translations to remain unaffected by a process context switch.

A fourth buffer in the CPU is the 8-byte instruction buffer. It serves two purposes. First, it decomposes the highly variable instruction format into its basic components and, second, it constantly fetches ahead to reduce delays in obtaining the instruction components.

The CPU includes two standard clocks. The programmable real-time clock is used by the operating system for local timing purposes. The time-of-year clock with its own battery backup is the long term time references for the operating system. It is automatically read on system startup to eliminate the need for manual entry of data and time.

The CPU includes 12K bytes of writable diagnostic control store (WDCS) which is used for diagnostic purposes, implementation of certain instructions, and for future microcode changes. As an option for very sophisticated users, another 12K bytes of writable control store is available.

A second option is the floating point accelerator (FPA). Although the basic CPU implements the full floating point instruction set, the FPA provides high speed floating point hardware. It is logically invisible to programs and only affects their running time.

Console Subsystem

The console subsystem is centered around an LSI-11 computer with 16K bytes of RAM and 8K bytes of ROM (used to store the LSI-11 bootstrap, LSI-11 diagnostics, and console routines). Also included are a floppy disk, an interface to the console terminal, and a port for remote diagnostic purposes.

The floppy disk in the console subsystem serves multiple purposes. It stores the main system bootstrap and diagnostics and serves as a medium for distribution of software updates.

SBI

The SBI is the primary control and data transfer path in the VAX-11/780 system. Because the cache and write buffer largely decouple the CPU performance from the memory access time, the SBI design was optimized for bandwidth and reliability rather than the lowest possible access time.

The SBI is a synchronous bus with a cycle time of 200 nsec. The data path width of the SBI is 32 bits. During each 200 nsec cycle either 32 bits of data or a 30-bit physical address can be transferred. Since each 32-bit read or write requires transmission of both address and data, two SBI cycles are used for a complete transaction. The SBI protocol permits 64-bit reads or writes using one address cycle and two data transfer cycles: the CPU and I/O subsystem use this mode whenever possible. For read transactions the bus is reacquired by the memory in order to send the data: thus the bus is not held during the memory access time.

Arbitration of the SBI is distributed: each interface to the SBI has a specific priority and its own bus request line. When an interface wishes to use the bus, it asserts its bus request line. If at the end of a 200 nsec cycle there are no interfaces of higher priority requesting the bus, the interface takes control of the bus.

Extensive checking is done on the SBI. Each transfer is parity checked and confirmed by the receiver. The arbitration process and general observance of the SBI protocol are checked by each SBI interface during each SBI cycle. The processor maintains a running 16-cycle history of the SBI: any SBI error condition causes this history to be locked and preserved for diagnostic purposes.

Memory Subsystem

The memory subsystem consists of one or two memory controllers with up to 1M bytes of memory on each. The memory is organized in 64-bit quadwords with an 8-bit ECC which provides single bit error correction and double bit error detection. The memory is built of 4K MOS RAM components.

The memory controllers have buffers which hold up to four memory requests. These buffers substantially increase the utilization of the SBI and memory by permitting the pipelining of multiple memory requests. If desired, quadword physical addresses can be interleaved across the memory controllers.

As an option, battery backup is available which preserves the contents of memory across short term power failures.

I/O Subsystem

The I/O subsystem consists of buffered interfaces or adapters between the SBI and the two types of peripheral busses used on PDP-11 systems: the Unibus and the Massbus. One Unibus adapter and up to four Massbus adapters can be configured on a VAX-11/780 system.

The Unibus is a medium speed multiplexor bus which is used as a primary memory as well as peripheral bus in many PDP-11 systems. It has an 18-bit physical address space and supports byte and word transfers. In addition to implementing the Unibus protocol and transmitting interrupts to the CPU, the Unibus adapter provides two other functions. The first is mapping 18-bit Unibus addresses to 30-bit SBI physical addresses. This is accomplished in a manner substantially identical to the virtual to physical mapping implemented by the CPU. The Unibus address space is divided into 512 512-byte pages. Each Unibus page has a page table entry (residing in the Unibus adapter) which maps addresses in that page to physical memory addresses. In addition to providing address translation, the mapping permits contiguous transfers on the Unibus which cross page boundaries to be mapped to discontiguous physical memory page frames.

The second function performed by the Unibus adapter is assembling 16-bit Unibus transfers (both reads and writes) into 64-bit SBI transfers. This operation (which is applicable only to block transfers such as from disks) appreciably reduces SBI traffic due to Unibus operations. There are 158-byte buffers in the Unibus adapter permitting 15 simultaneous buffered transactions. Additionally there is an un-buffered path through the Unibus adapter permitting an arbitrary number of simultaneous un-buffered transfers.

The Massbus is a high speed block bus used primarily for disks and tapes. The Massbus adapter provides much the same functionality as the Unibus adapter. The physical addresses into which transfers are made are defined by a page table: again this permits contiguous device transfers into discontiguous physical memory.

Buffering is provided in the Massbus adapter which minimizes the probability of device overruns and assembles data into 64-bit units for transfer over the SBI.

References

Bell and Strecker [1976]; Bell et al. [1970]; Flynn [1977]; Levy and Eckhouse [1980]; McLean [1977]; Myers [1977b]; Needham [1972]; Needham and Walker [1977]; Organick [1972]; Schrocker and Saltzer [1971].

APPENDIX 1 VAX-11 INSTRUCTION SET

Integer and Floating Point Logical Instructions

MOV-	Move(B,W,L,F,D,Q)†
MNEG-	Move Negated(B,W,L,F,D)
MCOM-	Move Complemented(B,W,L)
MOVZ-	Move Zero-Extended(BW,BL,WL)
CLR-	Clear(B,W,L,F,Q,D)
CVT-	Convert(B,W,L,F,D)(B,W,L,F,D)
CVTR-L	Convert Rounded(F,D) to Longword
CMP-	Compare(B,W,L,F,D)
TST-	Test(B,W,L,F,D)
BIS-2	Bit Set(B,W,L)2-Operand
BIS-3	Bit Set(B,W,L)3-Operand
BIC-2	Bit Clear(B,W,L)2-Operand
BIC-3	Bit Clear(B,W,L)3-Operand
BIT-	Bit Test(B,W,L)
XOR-2	Exclusive OR(B,W,L)2-Operand
XOR-3	Exclusive OR(B,W,L)3-Operand
ROTL	Rotate Longword
PUSHL	Push Longword

Integer and Floating Point Arithmetic Instructions

INC-	Increment(B,W,L)
DEC-	Decrement(B,W,L)
ASH-	Arithmetic Shift(L,Q)
ADD-2	Add(B,W,L,F,D)2-Operand
ADD-3	Add(B,W,L,F,D)3-Operand
ADWC	Add with Carry
ADAWI	Add Aligned Word Interlocked

†B = byte, W = word, L = longword, F = floating, D = double floating, Q = quadword, S = set, C = clear.

SUB-2	Subtract(B,W,L,F,D)2-Operand
SUB-3	Subtract(B,W,L,F,D)3-Operand
SBWC	Subtract with Carry
MUL-2	Multiply(B,W,L,F,D)2-Operand
MUL-3	Multiply(B,W,L,F,D)3-Operand
EMUL	Extended Multiply
DIV-2	Divide(B,W,L,F,D)2-Operand
DIV-3	Divide(B,W,L,F,D)3-Operand
EDIV	Extended Divide
EMOD-	Extended Modulus(F,D)
POLY-	Polynomial Evaluation(F,D)

Index Instruction

INDEX	Compute Index

Packed Decimal Instructions

MOVP	Move Packed
CMPP3	Compare Packed 3-Operand
CMPP4	Compare Packed 4-Operand
ASHP	Arithmetic Shift Round and Packed
ADDP4	Add Packed 4-Operand
ADDP6	Add Packed 6-Operand
SUBP4	Subtract Packed 4-Operand
SUBP6	Subtract Packed 6-Operand
MULP	Multiply Packed
DIVP	Divide Packed
CVTLP	Convert Long to Packed
CVTPL	Convert Packed to Long
CVTPT	Convert Packed to Trailing
CVTTP	Convert Trailing to Packed
CVTPS	Convert Packed to Separate
CVTSP	Convert Separate to Packed
EDITPC	Edit Packed to Character String

Character String Instructions

MOVC3	Move Character 3-Operand
MOVC5	Move Character 5-Operand
MOVTC	Move Translated Characters
MOVTUC	Move Translated Unit Character
CMPC3	Compare Characters 3-Operand
CMPC5	Compare Characters 5-Operand
LOCC	Locate Character
SKPC	Skip Character
SCANC	Scan Characters
SPANC	Span Characters
MATCHC	Match Characters

Variable-Length Bit Field Instructions

EXTV	Extract Field
EXTZV	Extract Zero-Extended Field
INSV	Insert Field

CMPV	Compare Field
CMPZV	Compare Zero-Extended Field
FFS	Find First Set
FFC	Find First Clear

Branch on Bit Instructions

BLB-	Branch on Low B(S,Cl)
BB-	Branch on Bit(S,Cl)
BBS-	Branch on Bit Set and(S,Cl)Bit
BBC	Branch on Bit Clear and(Set,Clear)Bit
BBSSI	Branch on Bit Set and Set Bit Interlocked
BBCCI	Branch on Bit Clear and Clear Bit Interlocked

Queue Instructions

INSQUE	Insert Entry in Queue
REMQUE	Remove Entry from Queue

Address Manipulation Instructions

MOVA-	Move Address(B,W,L,F,Q,D)
PUSHA-	Push Address(B,W,L,F,Q,D)on Stack

Processor State Instructions

PUSHR	Push Registers on Stack
POPR	Pop Registers from Stack
MOVPSL	Move from Processor Status Longword
BISPSW	Bit Set Processor Status Word
BICPSW	Bit Clear Processor Status Word

Unconditional Branch and Jump Instructions

BR-	Branch with(B,W)Displacement
JMP	Jump

Branch on Condition Code

BLSS	Less Than
BLSSU	Less Than Unsigned
(BCS)	(Carry Set)
BLEQ	Less Than or Equal
BLEQU	Less Than or Equal Unsigned
BEQL	Equal
(BEQLU)	(Equal Unsigned)
BNEQ	Not Equal
(BNEQU)	(Not Equal Unsigned)
BGTR	Greater Than
BGTRU	Greater Than Unsigned
BGEQ	Greater Than or Equal
BGEQU	Greater Than or Equal Unsigned
(BCC)	(Carry Clear)
BVS	Overflow Set
BVC	Overflow Clear

Loop and Case Branch

ACB-	Add, Compare and Branch(B,W,L,F,D)
AOBLEQ	Add One and Branch Less Than or Equal
AOBLSS	Add One and Branch Less Than
SOBGEQ	Subtract One and Branch Greater Than or Equal
SOBGTR	Subtract One and Branch Greater Than
CASE-	Case on(B,W,L)

Subroutine Call and Return Instructions

BSB-	Branch to Subroutine with(B,W) Displacement
JSB	Jump to Subroutine
RSB	Return from Subroutine

Procedure Call and Return Instructions

CALLG	Call Procedure with General Argument List
CALLS	Call Procedure with Stack Argument List
RET	Return from Procedure

Access Mode Instructions

CHM	Change Mode to (Kernel,Executive,Supervisor, User)

REI	Return from Exception or Interrupt
PROBER	Probe Read
PROBEW	Probe Write

Privileged Processor Register Control Instructions

SVPCTX	Save Process Context
LDPCTX	Load Process Context
MTPR	Move to Process Register
MFPR	Move from Processor Register

Special Function Instructions

CRC	Cyclic Redundancy Check
BPT	Breakpoint Fault
XFC	Extended Function Call
NOP	No Operation
HALT	Halt

Chapter 43
Parallel Operation in the Control Data 6600[1]

James E. Thornton

History

In the summer of 1960, Control Data began a project which culminated October, 1964 in the delivery of the first 6600 Computer. In 1960 it was apparent that brute force circuit performance and parallel operation were the two main approaches to any advanced computer.

This paper presents some of the considerations having to do with the parallel operations in the 6600. A most important and fortunate event coincided with the beginning of the 6600 project. This was the appearance of the high-speed silicon transistor, which survived early difficulties to become the basis for a nice jump in circuit performance.

System Organization

The computing system envisioned in that project, and now called the 6600, paid special attention to two kinds of use, the very large scientific problem and the time sharing of smaller problems. For the large problem, a high-speed floating point central processor with access to a large central memory was obvious. Not so obvious, but important to the 6600 system idea, was the isolation of this central arithmetic from any peripheral activity.

It was from this general line of reasoning that the idea of a multiplicity of peripheral processors was formed (Fig. 1). Ten such peripheral processors have access to the central memory on one side and the peripheral channels on the other. The executive control of the system is always in one of these peripheral processors, with the others operating on assigned peripheral or control tasks. All ten processors have access to twelve input-output channels and may "change hands," monitor channel activity, and perform other related jobs. These processors have access to central memory, and may pursue independent transfers to and from this memory.

Each of the ten peripheral processors contains its own memory for program and buffer areas, thereby isolating and protecting the more critical system control operations in the separate processors.

[1]*AFIPS Proc. FJCC*, pt. 2, vol. 26, 1964, pp. 33–40.

The central processor operates from the central memory with relocating register and file protection for each program in central memory.

Peripheral and Control Processors

The peripheral and control processors are housed in one chassis of the main frame. Each processor contains 4096 memory words of 12 bits length. There are 12- and 24-bit instruction formats to provide for direct, indirect, and relative addressing. Instructions provide logical, addition, subtraction, and conditional branching. Instructions also provide single word or block transfers to and from any of twelve peripheral channels, and single word or block transfers to and from central memory. Central memory words of 60 bits length are assembled from five consecutive peripheral words. Each processor has instructions to interrupt the central processor and to monitor the central program address.

To get this much processing power with reasonable economy and space, a time-sharing design was adopted (Fig. 2). This design contains a register "barrel" around which is moving the dynamic information for all ten processors. Such things as program address, accumulator contents, and other pieces of information totalling 52 bits are shifted around the barrel. Each complete trip around requires one major cycle or one thousand nanoseconds. A "slot" in the barrel contains adders, assembly networks, distribution network, and interconnections to perform one step of any peripheral instruction. The time to perform this step or, in other words, the time through the slot, is one minor cycle or one hundred nanoseconds. Each of the ten processors, therefore, is allowed one minor cycle of every ten to perform one of its steps. A peripheral instruction may require one or more of these steps, depending on the kind of instruction.

In effect, the single arithmetic and the single distribution and assembly network are made to appear as ten. Only the memories are kept truly independent. Incidentally, the memory read-write cycle time is equal to one complete trip around the barrel, or one thousand nanoseconds.

Input-output channels are bi-directional, 12-bit paths. One 12-bit word may move in one direction every major cycle, or 1000 nanoseconds, on each channel. Therefore, a maximum burst rate of 120 million bits per second is possible using all ten peripheral processors. A sustained rate of about 50 million bits per second can be maintained in a practical operating system. Each channel may service several peripheral devices and may interface to other systems, such as satellite computers.

Peripheral and control processors access central memory through an assembly network and a dis-assembly network. Since

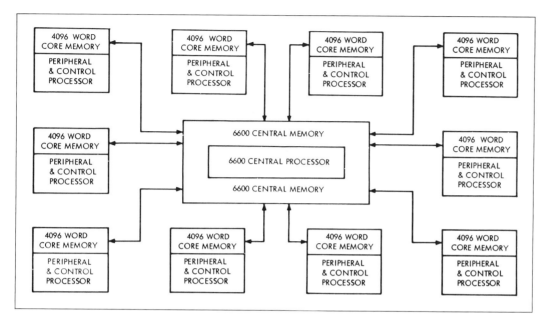

Fig. 1. Control Data 6600.

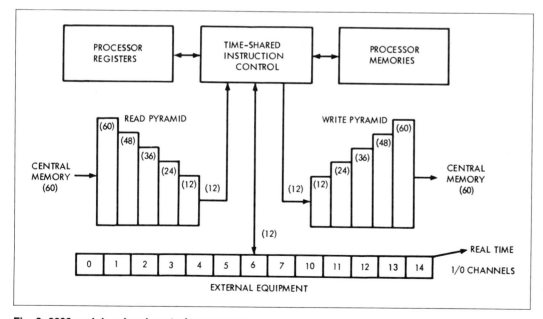

Fig. 2. 6600 peripheral and control processors.

five peripheral memory references are required to make up one central memory word, a natural assembly network of five levels is used. This allows five references to be "nested" in each network during any major cycle. The central memory is organized in independent banks with the ability to transfer central words every minor cycle. The peripheral processors, therefore, introduce at most about 2% interference at the central memory address control.

A single real time clock, continuously running is available to all peripheral processors.

Central Processor

The 6600 central processor may be considered the high-speed arithmetic unit of the system (Fig. 3). Its program, operands, and results are held in the central memory. It has no connection to the peripheral processors except through memory and except for two single controls. These are the exchange jump, which starts or interrupts the central processor from a peripheral processor, and the central program address which can be monitored by a peripheral processor.

A key description of the 6600 central processor, as you will see in later discussion, is "parallel by function." This means that a number of arithmetic functions may be performed concurrently. To this end, there are ten functional units within the central processor. These are the two increment units, floating add unit, fixed add unit, shift unit, two multiply units, divide unit, boolean unit, and branch unit. In a general way, each of these units is a three address unit. As an example, the floating add unit obtains two 60-bit operands from the central registers and produces a 60 bit result which is returned to a register. Information to and from these units is held in the central registers, of which there are twenty-four. Eight of these are considered index registers, are of 18 bits length, and one of which always contains zero. Eight are considered address registers, are of 18 bits length, and serve to address the five read central memory trunks and the two store central memory trunks. Eight are considered floating point

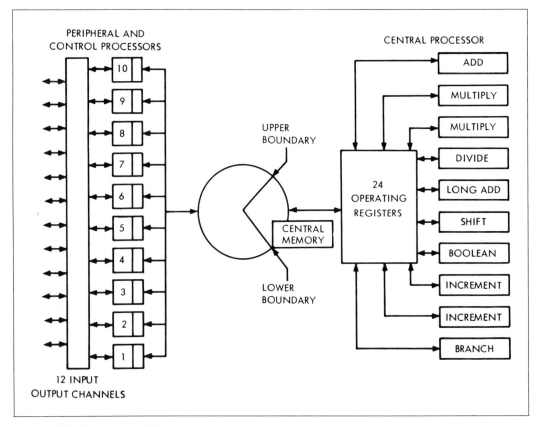

Fig. 3. Block diagram of 6600.

registers, are of 60 bits length, and are the only central registers to access central memory during a central program.

In a sense, just as the whole central processor is hidden behind central memory from the peripheral processors, so, too, the ten functional units are hidden behind the central registers from central memory. As a consequence, a considerable instruction efficiency is obtained and an interesting form of concurrency is feasible and practical. The fact that a small number of bits can give meaningful definition to any function makes it possible to develop forms of operand and unit reservations needed for a general scheme of concurrent arithmetic.

Instructions are organized in two formats, a 15-bit format and a 30-bit format, and may be mixed in an instruction word (Fig. 4). As an example, a 15-bit instruction may call for an ADD, designated by the f and m octal digits, from registers designated by the j and k octal digits, the result going to the register designated by the i octal digit. In this example, the addresses of the three-address, floating add unit are only three bits in length, each address referring to one of the eight floating point registers. The 30-bit format follows this same form but substitutes for the k octal digit an 18-bit constant K which serves as one of the input operands. These two formats provide a highly efficient control of concurrent operations.

As a background, consider the essential difference between a general purpose device and a special device in which high speeds are required. The designer of the special device can generally improve on the traditional general purpose device by introducing some form of concurrency. For example, some activities of a housekeeping nature may be performed separate from the main sequence of operations in separate hardware. The total time to complete a job is then optimized to the main sequence and excludes the housekeeping. The two categories operate concurrently.

It would be, of course, most attractive to provide in a general purpose device some generalized scheme to do the same kind of thing. The organization of the 6600 central processor provides just this kind of scheme. With a multiplicity of functional units, and of operand registers and with a simple and highly efficient addressing system, a generalized queue and reservation scheme is practical. This is called the *scoreboard*.

The scoreboard maintains a running file of each central register, of each functional unit, and of each of the three operand trunks to and from each unit. Typically, the scoreboard file is made up of two-, three-, and four-bit quantities identifying the nature of register and unit usage. As each new instruction is brought up, the conditions at the instant of issuance are set into the scoreboard. A snapshot is taken, so to speak, of the pertinent conditions. If no waiting is required, the execution of the instruction is begun immediately under control of the unit itself. If waiting is required (for example, an input operand may not yet be available in the central registers), the scoreboard controls the delay, and when released, allows the unit to begin its execution. Most important, this activity is accomplished in the scoreboard and the functional unit, and does not necessarily limit later instructions from being brought up and issued.

In this manner, it is possible to issue a series of instructions, some related, some not, until no functional units are left free or until a specific register is to be assigned more than one result. With just those two restrictions on issuing (unit free and no double result), several independent chains of instructions may proceed concurrently. Instructions may issue every minor cycle in the absence of the two restraints. The instruction executions, in comparison, range from three minor cycles for fixed add, 10 minor cycles for floating multiply, to 29 minor cycles for floating divide.

To provide a relatively continuous source of instructions, one buffer register of 60 bits is located at the bottom of an instruction stack capable of holding 32 instructions (Fig. 5). Instruction words from memory enter the bottom register of the stack pushing up the old instruction words. In straight line programs, only the bottom two registers are in use, the bottom being refilled as quickly as memory conflicts allow. In programs which branch back to an instruction in the upper stack registers, no refills are allowed after the branch, thereby holding the program loop completely in the stack. As a result, memory access or memory conflicts are no longer involved, and a considerable speed increase can be had.

Five memory trunks are provided from memory into the central processor to five of the floating point registers (Fig. 6). One address register is assigned to each trunk (and therefore to the

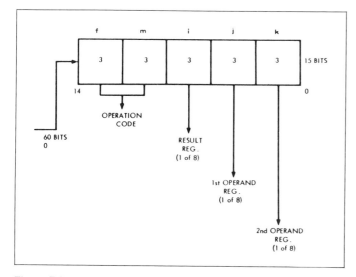

Fig. 4. Fifteen-bit instruction format.

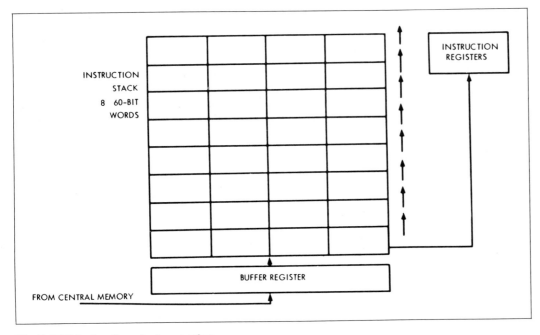

Fig. 5. 6600 instruction stack operation.

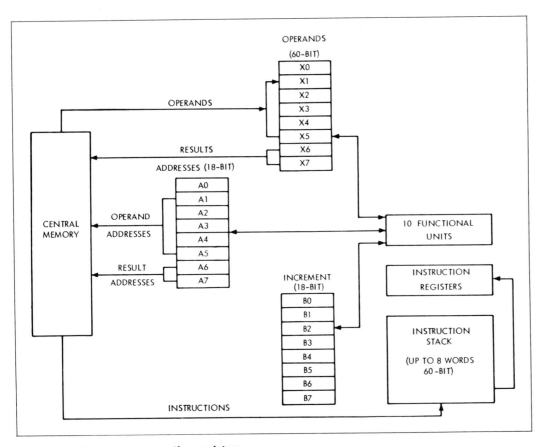

Fig. 6. Central processor operating registers.

floating point register). Any instruction calling for address register result implicitly initiates a memory reference on that trunk. These instructions are handled through the scoreboard and therefore tend to overlap memory access with arithmetic. For example, a new memory word to be loaded in a floating point register can be brought in from memory but may not enter the register until all previous uses of that register are completed. The central registers, therefore, provide all of the data to the ten functional units, and receive all of the unit results. No storage is maintained in any unit.

Central memory is organized in 32 banks of 4096 words. Consecutive addresses call for a different bank; therfore, adjacent addresses in one bank are in reality separated by 32. Addresses may be issued every 100 nanoseconds. A typical central memory information transfer rate is about 250 million bits per second.

As mentioned before, the functional units are hidden behind the registers. Although the units might appear to increase hardware duplication, a pleasant fact emerges from this design. Each unit may be trimmed to perform its function without regard to others. Speed increases are had from this simplified design.

As an example of special functional unit design, the floating multiply accomplishes the coefficient multiplication in nine minor cycles plus one minor cycle to put away the result for a total of 10 minor cycles, or 1000 nanoseconds. The multiply uses layers of carry save adders grouped in two halves. Each half concurrently forms a partial product, and the two partial products finally merge while the long carries propagate. Although this is a fairly large complex of circuits, the resulting device was sufficiently smaller than originally planned to allow two multiply units to be included in the final design.

To sum up the characteristics of the central processor, remember that the broadbrush description is "concurrent operation." In other words, any program operating within the central processor utilizes some of the available concurrency. The program need not be written in a particular way, although certainly some optimization can be done. The specific method of accomplishing this concurrency involves *issuing* as many instructions as possible while handling most of the conflicts during *execution*. Some of the essential requirements for such a scheme include:

1 Many functional units
2 Units with three address properties
3 Many transient registers with many trunks to and from the units
4 A simple and efficient instruction set

Construction

Circuits in the 6600 computing system use all-transistor logic (Fig. 7). The silicon transistor operates in saturation when switched

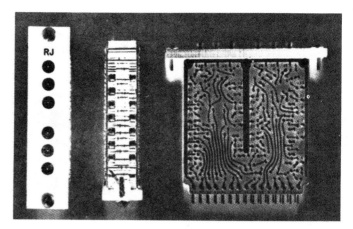

Fig. 7. 6600 printed circuit module.

"on" and averages about five nanoseconds of stage delay. Logic circuits are constructed in a cordwood plug-in module of about 2½ inches by 2½ inches by 0.8 inch. An average of about 50 transistors are contained in these modules.

Memory circuits are constructed in a plug-in module of about six inches by six inches by 2½ inches (Fig. 8). Each memory module contains a coincident current memory of 4096 12-bit

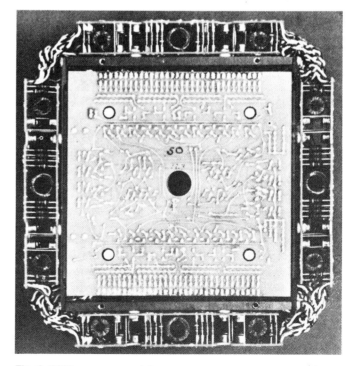

Fig. 8. 6600 memory module.

Fig. 9. 6600 main frame section.

Fig. 10. 6600 display console.

words. All read-write drive circuits and bit drive circuits plus address translation are contained in the module. One such module is used for each peripheral processor, and five modules make up one bank of central memory.

Logic modules and memory modules are held in upright hinged chassis in an X shaped cabinet (Fig. 9). Interconnections between modules on the chassis are made with twisted pair transmission lines. Interconnections between chassis are made with coaxial cables.

Both maintenance and operation are accomplished at a programmed display console (Fig. 10). More than one of these consoles may be included in a system if desired. Dead start facilities bring the ten peripheral processors to a condition which allows information to enter from any chosen peripheral device. Such loads normally bring in an operating system which provides a highly sophisticated capability for multiple users, maintenance, and so on.

The 6600 Computer has taken advantage of certain technology advances, but more particularly, logic organization advances which now appear to be quite successful. Control Data is exploring advances in technology upward within the same compatible structure, and identical technology downward, also within the same compatible structure.

References

Allard, Wolf, and Zemlin [1964]; Clayton, Dorff, and Fagen [1964].

APPENDIX 1   ISP OF CDC 6600 PERIPHERAL AND CONTROL PROCESSOR

```
PC6600{process} :=
    begin

! ISP of the CDC 6600 Peripheral and Control Processor, Barrel distributor,
! and I/O channels. Initial version by Gary Leive (ca. 1978)

! Although the 6600 has 10 identical Peripheral and Control processors, the
! ISP for a single processor is shown.  An identifying parameter is utilized
! to specify which of the ten processors is active during simulation. The CDC
! 6600 Peripheral and Control processors each possess a 4096 word 12 bit local
! memory.  The ISP shows only one 4096 word memory which is used by all the
! "processors".

**Channel.State**

    CHAN[0:11]<11:0>,                    ! I/O channels
    cact[0:11]<>,                        ! Channel active indicator
    cful[0:11]<>,                        ! Channel full indicator

**Barrel.State**

    A[0:9]<17:0>,                        ! Barrel A registers
    P[0:9]<11:0>,                        ! Barrel P registers
    Q[0:9]<11:0>,                        ! Barrel Q registers
    K[0:9]<8:0>,                         ! Barrel K registers

**PCP.Memory.State**

    M.PCP[0:4095]<11:0>,                 ! Only one PCP memory is shown
    read[0:4]<11:0>,                     ! Read pyramid
        c.read<59:0> := read[0:4]<11:0>,
    write[0:4]<11:0>,                    ! Write pyramid
        c.write<59:0> := write[0:4]<11:0>,

**PCP.Instruction.Format**

    pir<23:0>,                           ! PCP Instruction register
        f < 5:0> := pir<23:18>,
        d < 5:0> := pir<17:12>,
        m <11:0> := pir<11:0>,
        dm<17:0> := pir<17:0>,

**Addressing.Calculation**{us}

    index(id<3:0>)<11:0> :=               ! Indexed addressing
        begin
        DECODE d eql 0 =>
            begin
            0 :=   begin
                   index = m + M.PCP[d];
                   P[id] = P[id] + 1
                   end,
            1 :=   index = m
            end
        end,

**Barrel.Execution**

    barrel{main} :=
        begin
        pcp(0) next                      ! Activate processor 0
        pcp(1) next                      ! Activate processor 1
        pcp(2) next                      ! Activate processor 2
        pcp(3) next                      ! Activate processor 3
        pcp(4) next                      ! Activate processor 4
        pcp(5) next                      ! Activate processor 5
        pcp(6) next                      ! Activate processor 6
        pcp(7) next                      ! Activate processor 7
        pcp(8) next                      ! Activate processor 8
        pcp(9) next                      ! Activate processor 9
        RESTART barrel                   ! Do it all again
        end,

**PCP.Execution**{oc}

    pcp(id<3:0>) :=
        begin
        pir<23:12> = M.PCP[P[id]] next
        P[id] = P[id] + 1 next
        m = M.PCP[P[id]];
        K[id]<5:0> = f;
        Q[id] = d next
        DECODE K[id] =>
            begin
            [#00,#24,#25]:= no.op(),                 ! PSN - Pass
            #14 :=  A[id]   = d,                      ! LQN - Load d into a
            #15 :=  A[id]   = #7777@(not d),          ! LCN - Load compliment d
            #30 :=  A[id]   = M.PCP[d],               ! LDD - Load (d)
            #34 :=  M.PCP[d] = A[id],                 ! STD - Store (d)
            #40 :=  A[id]   = M.PCP[M.PCP[d]],        ! LDI - Load ((d))
            #44 :=  M.PCP[M.PCP[d]] = A[id],          ! STI - Store (d))
            #20 :=  begin                             ! LDC - Load dm
                    A[id] = dm; P[id]=P[id]+1
                    end,
            #50 :=  A[id] = M.PCP[index(id)],         ! LDM - Load (m + (d))
            #54 :=  M.PCP[index(id)] = A[id],         ! STM - Store (m + (d))
            #16 :=  A[id] = A[id] +{us} d,            ! ADN - Add d
            #17 :=  A[id] = A[id] -{us} d,            ! SBN - Subtract d
            #31 :=  A[id] = A[id]+{us} M.PCP[d],      ! ADD - Add (d)
            #32 :=  A[id] = A[id]-{us} M.PCP[d],      ! SBD - Subtract (d)
            #41 :=  A[id] = A[id] +{us}               ! ADI - Add ((d))
                        M.PCP[M.PCP[d]],
            #42 :=  A[id] = A[id] -{us}               ! SBI - Subtract ((d))
                        M.PCP[M.PCP[d]],
```

```
            #21 :=  A[id] = A[id] + dm,               ! ADC - Add dm
            #51 :=  A[id] = A[id] +{us}               ! ADM - Add (m + (d))
                        M.PCP[index(id)],
            #52 :=  A[id] = A[id] -{us}               ! SBM - Subtract (m + (d))
                        M.PCP[index(id)],
            #10 :=  DECODE d<5> =>                     ! SHN - Shift d
                        begin
                        0 := A[id] = A[id] slr d,
                        1 := A[id] = A[id] sr0 (not d)
                        end,
            #11 :=  A[id]<5:0> = A[id]<5:0>            ! LMN - Logical difference d
                        xor d,
            #12 :=  A[id] = A[id] and d,               ! LPN - Logical procuct d
            #13 :=  A[id]<5:0> = A[id]<5:0>            ! SCN - Selective clear d
                        and (not d),
            #33 :=  A[id]<11:0>= A[id]<11:0>           ! LMD - Logical difference (d)
                        xor M.PCP[d],
            #43 :=  A[id]<11:0>= A[id]<11:0>           ! LMI - Logical difference ((d))
                        xor M.PCP[M.PCP[d]],
            #22 :=  A[id] = A[id] and dm,              ! LPC - Logical product dm
            #23 :=  A[id] = A[id] xor dm,              ! LMC - Logical difference dm
            #53 :=  A[id]<11:0> =.                     ! LMM - Logical difference
                        A[id]<11:0> xor M.PCP[index(id)],      ! (m +(d))
            #35 :=  M.PCP[d] = A[id] = A[id]           ! RAD - Replace add (d)
                        + M.PCP[d],
            #36 :=  M.PCP[d] = A[id]                   ! AOD - Replace add one (d)
                        = M.PCP[d] + 1,
            #37 :=  M.PCP[d] = A[id]                   ! SOD - Replace subtract one (d)
                        = M.PCP[d] - 1,
            #45 :=  M.PCP[M.PCP[d]] = A[id]            ! RAI - Replace add ((d))
                        = A[id] + M.PCP[M.PCP[d]],
            #46 :=  M.PCP[M.PCP[d]] = A[id]            ! AOI - Replace add one ((d))
                        = M.PCP[M.PCP[d]] + 1,
            #47 :=  M.PCP[M.PCP[d]] = A[id]            ! SOI - Replace subtrace one
                        = M.PCP[M.PCP[d]] - 1, ! ((d))
            #55 :=  M.PCP[index] = A[id]               ! RAM - Replace add (m + (d))
                        = A[id] + M.PCP[index(id)],
            #56 :=  M.PCP[index] = A[id]               ! AOM - Replace add one
                        = M.PCP[index(id)] + 1, ! (m + (d))
            #57 :=  M.PCP[index] = A[id]               ! SOM - Replace subtract one
                        = M.PCP[index(id)] - 1, ! (m + (d))
            #03 :=  P[id] = (P[id] - 1) + d,           ! UJN - Unconditional jump d
            #04 :=  IF A[id] eql{us} 0 =>              ! ZJN - Zero Jump d
                        P[id] = (P[id] - 1) + d,
            #05 :=  IF A[id] neq{us} 0 =>              ! NJN - Nonzero jump d
                        P[id] = (P[id] - 1) + d,
            #06 :=  IF A[id] geq{us} 0 =>              ! PJN - Plus jump d
                        P[id] = (P[id] - 1) + d,
            #07 :=  IF A[id] lss{us} 0 =>.             ! LJN - Minus jump d
                        P[id] = (P[id] - 1) + d,
            #01 :=  P[id] = index(id),                 ! LJM - Long jump to m + (d)
            #02 :=  begin
                    M.PCP[index(id)]=P[id]+2 next! RJM - Return jump to m + (d)
                    P[id] = index + 1
                    end,
            #26 :=  begin
                    WAIT (xjf eqv '0) next             ! EXN - Exchange Jump
                    xja = A[id]; xjf = 1
                    end,
            #27 :=  A[id] = pc,                        ! RPN - Read program address
            #60 :=  begin
                    c.read = MP[A[id]] next            ! CRD - Central read d = (A)
                    M.PCP[d+0] = read[0] next
                    M.PCP[d+1] = read[1] next
                    M.PCP[d+2] = read[2] next
                    M.PCP[d+3] = read[3] next
                    M.PCP[d+4] = read[4]
                    end,
            #61 :=  M.PCP[0] = P[id] + 1 next          ! CRM - Central read (d)
                    P[id] = m; Q[id] = d next !         words from (A) to m
                    CRM0 :=
                        begin
                        c.read = MP[A[id]] next
                        M.PCP[P[id]+0] = read[0] next
                        M.PCP[P[id]+1] = read[1] next
                        M.PCP[P[id]+2] = read[2] next
                        M.PCP[P[id]+3] = read[3] next
                        M.PCP[P[id]+4] = read[4] next
                        P[id] = P[id] + 5;
                        A[id] = A[id] + 1;
                        Q[id] = Q[id] - 1 next
                        IF Q[id] neq 0 => RESTART CRM0
                        end next
                    P[id] = M.PCP[0]
            #62 :=  begin
                    write[0] = M.PCP[d+0] next         ! CWD - Central write (A) = d
                    write[1] = M.PCP[d+1] next
                    write[2] = M.PCP[d+2] next
                    write[3] = M.PCP[d+3] next
                    write[4] = M.PCP[d+4] next
                    MP[A[id]] = c.write
                    end,
            #63 :=  begin
                    M.PCP[0] = P[id] + 1 next          ! CWM - Central write (d)
                    P[id] = m; !                         to (A) from m
                    Q[id] = d next
                    CWM0 :=
                        begin
                        write[0] = M.PCP[P[id]+0] next
                        write[1] = M.PCP[P[id]+1] next
```

APPENDIX 1 (cont'd.)

```
            write[2] = M.PCP[P[id]+1] next                              IF cact[d] =>
            write[3] = M.PCP[P[id]+1] next                                 begin
            write[4] = M.PCP[P[id]+4] next                                    M.PCP[P[id]] = CHAN[d] next ! input
            P[id] = P[id] + 5;                                                P[id] = P[id] + 1;            ! increment address
            A[id] = A[id] + 1;                                                A[id] = A[id] - 1 next        ! decrement count
            Q[id] = Q[id] - 1 next                                            IF A[id] neq 0 => RESTART IAMO
            IF Q[id] neq 0 => RESTART CWMO                                 end
            end next                                                    end next
         P[id] = M.PCP[0]                                            P[id] = M.PCP[0]              ! restore program counter
         end,                                                        end,
#64 := DECODE cact[d] =>          ! AJM - Jump to m if channel   #72 := CHAN[d] = A[id],           ! OAN - Output from A
         begin                    !       d is active                                             !       on channel d
            0 := P[id] = P[id] + 1,                               #73 := begin
            1 := P[id] = m                                                M.PCP[0] = P[id] + 1 next ! OAM - Output (A) words
         end,                                                            P[id] = m next            !       from m on channel d
#65 := DECODE cact[d] =>          ! IJM - Jump to m if channel   OAMO :=
         begin                    !       d is inactive                  begin
            0 := P[id] = m,                                                  IF cact[d] and (A[id] neq 0) =>
            1 := P[id] = P[id] + 1                                              begin
         end,                                                                      CHAN[d] = M.PCP[P[id]] next ! output
#66 := DECODE cful[d] =>          ! FJM - Jump to m if channel                      P[id] = P[id] + 1;          ! increment address
         begin                    !       d is full                                 A[id] = A[id] - 1 next      ! decrement count
            0 := P[id] = P[id] + 1,                                                 RESTART OAMO
            1 := P[id] = m                                                       end next
         end,                                                                P[id] = M.PCP[0]              ! Restore program counter
#67 := DECODE cful[d] =>          ! EJM - Jump to m if channel             end,
         begin                    !       d is empty              #74 := cact[d] = 1,               ! ACN - Activate channel d
            0 := P[id] = m,                                       #75 := cact[d] = 0,               ! DCN - Disconnect channel d
            1 := P[id] = P[id] + 1                                #76 := CHAN[d] = A[id],           ! FAN - Function (A) on CHAN d
         end,                                                    #77 := begin
#70 := A[id] = CHAN[d],           ! IAN - Input A from CHAN d             CHAN[d] = m;              ! FNC - Function m on CHAN d
#71 := begin                                                             P[id] = P[id] + 1
         M.PCP[0] = P[id] + 1 next ! IAM - Input (A) words to m          end
         P[id] = m next           !       from channel d       end
         IAMO :=
            begin                                            end     ! End CDC 6600 Peripheral and Control processor
               IF A[id] neq 0 => M.PCP[P[id]] = 0 next ! clear next
```

APPENDIX 2   ISP OF THE CDC 6600

```
CDC6600{process} :=
    begin

! ISP of the CDC 6600

! Floating point instructions are not described.

! The central processor and central memory are described in this
! ISP.  An auxiliary ISP (PC6600.ISP) describes the peripheral
! processors and control barrel execution.

! The ten functional units are described and allow parallel
! simulation.

! Instructions are processed from an instruction stack.  Instruction
! conflicts are resolved by keeping a "scorecard" containing utilization
! information on all registers and all functional units.
! Reservation control decodes an instruction to determine register
! utilization.  Source and destination registers are allocated
! if they are not being used as destinations of another functional
! unit.  If the required functional unit is free and if both the
! source and destination registers are available, the instruction
! is released to the unit for execution.  If the resources are
! not available, reservation control holds the instruction until
! the resources become available.
! At the completion of execution by a functional unit, the resources
! are released by marking the scorecard.

! The following page by page index of the ISP is provided to aid
! in locating CDC 6600 architectural features.

!         **Central.Memory.State** defines the Central Memory.
!         **Processor.State** defines central processor carriers.
!         **Instruction.Format** defines instruction fields.
!         **Implementation.Declarations** defines ISP related variables.
!         **Reservation.Control.State** defines variables used by
!         reservation control.  These declarations constitute the
!         resource allocation "scorecard".
!              Describe the reservation control execution.
!         **Instruction.Fetch** describes the instruction stack
!         control and instruction fetch processes.
!         **Central.Memory.Access** describes the instruction read
!         and the register associated memory access processes.
!         **Exchange.Jump** is the processor interrupt facility.
!         **Instruction.Cycle** is the main instruction processing
!         cycle.  Instruction execution is initiated by issuing
!         the instructions to the appropriate functional unit.

! The functional units are:

!         Branch Unit.
!         Boolean Unit.
!         Shift Unit.
!         Add Unit.
!         Long Add Unit.
!         Multiply Unit 0.
!         Multiply Unit 1.
!         Divide Unit.
!         Increment Unit 0.
!         Increment Unit 1.

**Central.Memory.State**

    MP[0:4095]<59:0>,              ! Use only 4k of 60 bit memory

**Processor.State**

    xjp[0:15]<59:0>,              ! Exchange Jump Package
    xja<16:0>,                    ! Exchange Jump Address
    xjf<>,                        ! Exchange Jump Flag

    px<19:0>,                     ! Pseudo program counter
        PC<17:0> := px<19:2>,     ! Program counter
        ilc<1:0> := px<1:0>,      ! Instruction length count
        isc<4:0> := px<4:0>,      ! Instruction stack counter
    AREG[0:7]<17:0>,              ! A registers
    BREG[0:7]<17:0>,              ! B registers
    XREG[0:7]<59:0>,              ! X registers
    RACM<17:0>,                   ! Ref Address (central memory)
    FLCM<17:0>,                   ! Field length of program
    RAECS<23:0>,                  ! Reference Address for ECS
    FLECS<23:0>,                  ! Field length for ECS
    EM<17:0>,                     ! Program exit mode
    MA<17:0>,                     ! Monitor exchange

**Instruction.Format**

    I<29:0>,                      ! Instruction register
        i0<14:0> := I<29:15>,     ! Short instruction (15 bit)
        i1<14:0> := I<14:0>,      ! Long instruction extension

        f. <2:0> := I<29:27>,
        m. <2:0> := I<26:24>,
        fm <5:0> := I<29:24>,
        I. <2:0> := i<23:21>,
        j. <2:0> := I<20:18>,
        k. <2:0> := I<17:15>,
        k1<17:0> := I<17:0>,

    is[0:7]<59:0>,                ! Instruction stack
        ism[0:31]<14:0> := is[0:7]<59:0>,
    ishi<17:0>,                   ! High address limit in stack
    islo<17:0>,                   ! Low  address limit in stack
    isa<2:0>,                     ! Stack insert counter

**Implementation.Declarations**

    stop.bit<>,                   ! Stop flag
```

```
    macro not.described := |no.op()|,

**Reservation.Control.State**

    abusy[0:7]<>,                 ! A registers busy bits
    arw  [0:7]<>,                 ! A registers read(0)/write(1)
    bbusy[0:7]<>,                 ! B registers busy bits
    brw  [0:7]<>,                 ! B registers read(0)/write(1)
    xbusy[0:7]<>,                 ! X registers busy bits
    xrw  [0:7]<>,                 ! X registers read(0)/write(1)

    fbusy[0:9]<>,                 ! Functional Unit busy bits

                                  ! The following tables are
                                  ! used to deallocate the
                                  ! resource assignments either
                                  ! in the event of conflict during
                                  ! allocation, or during deallocation
                                  ! at instruction completion.
                                  ! F??U<> indicates usage of the
                                  ! registers by a unit.
                                  ! 1 = used, 0 = not used
    fa [0:9]<2:0>,                ! functional Unit A register
    fau[0:9]<>,                   ! A register usage
    fb [0:9]<2:0>,                ! Functional Unit B register
    fbu[0:9]<>,                   ! B register usage
    fx [0:9]<2:0>,                ! Functional Unit X register
    fxu[0:9]<>,                   ! X register usage

    unit<3:0>,                    ! Temporary for arith unit number

**Reservation.Control**{us}

    source()<> :=                            ! Source register allocation
        begin
        source = 0 next
        DECODE fm =>
            begin
            #01 := IF (i. eql #1) or (i. eql #2) =>
                    (IF fbu[unit] and (fb[unit] eql j.) => source = 1 next
                        fb[unit] = j.; fbu[unit] = 1;
                    IF (not bbusy[j.]) and (not brw[j.]) =>
                        source = bbusy[j.] = 1),
    [#02,#04:#07,#22]:= (IF fbu[unit] and (fb[unit] eql j.) => source = 1 next
                    fb[unit] = i.; fbu[unit] = 1;
                    IF (not bbusy[i.]) and (not brw[i.]) =>
                        source = bbusy[i.] = 1),
    [#04:#07,#23:#27,
    #51,#56:#57,#61,
        #66:#67,#71,
        #76:#77]:= (IF fbu[unit] and (fb[unit] eql j.) => source = 1 next
                    fb[unit] = j.; fbu[unit] = 1;
                    IF (not bbusy[j.]) and (not brw[j.]) =>
                        source = bbusy[j.] = 1),
    [#53:#57,#63:#67]:= (IF fbu[unit] and (fb[unit] eql k.) => source = 1 next
                    fb[unit] = k.; fbu[unit] = 1;
                    IF (not bbusy[k.]) and (not bbusy[k.]) =>
                        source = bbusy[k.] = 1),
    [#50,#54,#55,#60,
    #64,#65,#70,#74,
        #75]:= (IF fau[unit] and (fa[unit] eql j.) => source = 1 next
                    fa[unit] = j.; fau[unit] = 1;
                    IF (not abusy[j.]) and (not arw[j.]) =>
                        source = bbusy[j.] = 1),
    [#03,#10]:= (IF fxu[unit] and (fx[unit] eql i.) => source = 1 next
                    fx[unit] = i.; fxu[unit] = 1;
                    IF (not xbusy[i.]) and (not xrw[i.]) =>
                        source = xbusy[i.] = 1),
    [#11:#13,#15:#17,
    #30:#42,#52:#53,
    #62,#63,#72,#73]:= (IF fxu[unit] and (fx[unit] eql j.) => source = 1 next
                    fx[unit] = j.; fxu[unit] = 1;
                    IF (not xbusy[j.]) and (not xrw[j.]) =>
                        source = xbusy[j.] = 1),
    [#11:#17,#22:#27,
    #30:#42,#44:#45,
        #47]:= (IF fxu[unit] and (fx[unit] eql k.) => source = 1 next
                    fx[unit] = k.; fxu[unit] = 1;
                    IF (not xbusy[k.]) and (not xrw[k.]) =>
                        source = xbusy[k.] = 1),
        otherwise := source = 1
            end
        end,

    dest()<> :=                      ! Destination register allocation
        begin
        dest = 0 next
        DECODE fm =>
            begin
        [#10:#45,
    #47,#70:#77]:= (fx[unit] = i.; fxu[unit] = 1;
                    IF not xbusy[i.] => dest = xbusy[i.] = xrw[i.] = 1),
        #50:#57 := (fa[unit] = i.; fau[unit] = 1;
                    IF not abusy[i.] => dest = abusy[i.] = arw[i.] = 1),
        [#24:#26,
    #60:#67]:= (fb[unit] = i.; fbu[unit] = 1;
                    IF not bbusy[i.] => dest = bbusy[i.] = brw[i.] = 1),
        otherwise := dest = 1
            end
        end,

    mark :=                          ! Mark stack as invalid
        begin
        islo = ishi = PC
        end,

    dealloc(dunit<3:0>){critical} :=    ! Deallocate resources
        begin
```

APPENDIX 2 (cont'd.)

```
            fbusy[dunit] = 0;
            IF fau[dunit] => (fau[dunit] = abusy[fa[dunit]] = arw[fa[dunit]] = 0);
            IF fbu[dunit] => (fbu[dunit] = bbusy[fb[dunit]] = brw[fa[dunit]] = 0);
            IF fxu[dunit] => (fxu[dunit] = xbusy[fx[dunit]] = xrw[fa[dunit]] = 0)
         end.
      reserv :=
         begin
         unit = 15 next                         ! Mark as "no unit"
         DECODE fm =>
            begin
            #00:#07 := unit = 0,                ! Branch Unit
            #10:#17 := unit = 1,                ! Boolean Unit
          [#20:#27,#43]:= unit = 2,             ! Shift Unit
            #30:#35 := unit = 3,                ! Add Unit
            #36:#37 := unit = 4,                ! Long Add Unit
            #40:#42 := DECODE fbusy[5] =>       ! Multiply Units
                          begin
                          0 := unit = 5,
                          1 := IF not fbusy[6] => unit = 6
                          end,
            #44:#47 := unit = 7,                ! Divide Unit
            #50:#77 := DECODE fbusy[8] =>       ! Increment Units
                          begin
                          0 := unit = 8,
                          1 := IF not fbusy[9] => unit = 9
                          end end next
            IF unit neq 15 =>
               begin
               DECODE fbusy[unit] =>
                  begin
                  0 := DECODE (not dest()) or (not source()) =>
                       begin
                       0 := fbusy[unit] = 1,
                       1 := begin
                            dealloc(unit) next
                            RESTART reserv
                            end
                       end,
                  1 := begin
                       WAIT (not fbusy[unit]) next
                       RESTART reserv
                       end
                  end
               end
            end
         end.

**Instruction.Fetch**{us}

! Instruction fetch is always from the instruction stack.  If
! the stack is empty (initial power on or branch out of stack),
! or if there are less than three instruction words left in the
! stack, fetch reloads the stack before obtaining an instruction.
! Instructions may be 15 or 30 bits long and aligned on any 15 bit
! boundry.  Fetch obtains 15 bits of an instruction then determines
! if a second 15 bits are required.

    fetch :=
       begin
       IF (PC lss islo) or (PC gtr ishi) => mark() next
       IF (ishi - PC) leq #2 =>
          begin
          islo = PC + isa next
          sfetch :=
             begin
             is[isa] = rni(PC + isa) next
             ishi = PC + isa next
             isa = isa + 1 next
             IF (ishi - PC) lss #7 => RESTART sfetch
             end
          end next
       i0 = ism[isc] next
       px = px + 1 next
       DECODE fm =>                          ! Check for 30 bit instructions
          begin
        [#00:#01,#04:#07,
         #30:#37,#50:#52,
         #60:#62,#70:#72]:= (i1 = ism[isc] next
                      px = px + 1),
          otherwise := no.op()
          end
       end,

**Central.Memory.Access**{oc}

! Centeral memory is always accessed indirectly by a user program.
! The Read Next Instruction (RNI) routine is used to load the
! instruction stack.  Touching the A registers 1 through 7 causes
! the corresponding X register to be loaded (A[1:5]) from memory
! or stored (A[6:7]) in memory.

    range(rel<17:0>)<> :=                     ! Address range fault check.
       begin
       range = 0 next
       IF rel geq (FLCM - 1) =>
          begin
          range = 1;                          ! Fault
          DECODE EM<12> =>                    ! Address exit select
             begin
             0 := I = MP[0],                  ! Not selected
             1 := begin
                  MP[RACM]<53:48> = MP[RACM]<53:48> or #010000;
                  MP[RACM]<47:30> = rel + 1 next
                  I = MP[RACM]; PC = 0 next
                  STOP()                      ! Stop the processor
                  end
             end
          end
       end,
```

```
    rni(pci<17:0>)<59:0> :=                   ! Read next instruction
       begin
       IF not range(pci) => rni = MP[RACM + pci]
       end,

    aref(reg<2:0>,val<17:0>) :=               ! A register forced
       begin                                  !   memory access
       AREG[reg] = val next
       range(val) next
       DECODE reg =>
          begin
          #0 := no.op(),
          #1:#5 := (IF range => (XREG[reg] = MP[0] next LEAVE aref) next
                       XREG[reg] = MP[AREG[reg] + RACM]),
          #6:#7 := (IF range => LEAVE aref next
                       MP[AREG[reg] + RACM] = XREG[reg])
          end
       end,

**Exchange.Jump**{us}

! Exchange jump is the central processor's interrupt mechanism.
! Exchange jump is initiated by power on or by one of the ten
! peripheral processors.  All of the central processor's state
! (including all registers) is exchanged with 16 words of central
! memory.  The central memory starting address is provided by
! the "interrupting" peripheral processor.  The central memory
! words are formatted such that all of the state can be extracted
! and loaded into the appropriate registers.
! This implementation uses a 16 word holding area (xjp) to format and
! temporarily preserve the old state until the new state is loaded.

    xj :=
       begin
       xjp[00] = PC   @ AREG[0] @ #000000;
       xjp[01] = RACM @ AREG[1] @ BREG[1];
       xjp[02] = FLCM @ AREG[2] @ BREG[2];
       xjp[03] = EM   @ AREG[3] @ BREG[3];
       xjp[04] = RAECS @ AREG[4] @ BREG[4];
       xjp[05] = FLECS @ AREG[5] @ BREG[5];
       xjp[06] = MA   @ AREG[6] @ BREG[6];
       xjp[07] =        AREG[7] @ BREG[7];
       xjp[08] = XREG[0];
       xjp[09] = XREG[1];
       xjp[10] = XREG[2];
       xjp[11] = XREG[3];
       xjp[12] = XREG[4];
       xjp[13] = XREG[5];
       xjp[14] = XREG[6];
       xjp[15] = XREG[7] next
       PC   @ AREG[0]             = MP[xja + 00]<53:18>;
       RACM @ AREG[1] @ BREG[1]   = MP[xja + 01];
       FLCM @ AREG[2] @ BREG[2]   = MP[xja + 02];
       EM   @ AREG[3] @ BREG[3]   = MP[xja + 03];
       RAECS @ AREG[4] @ BREG[4]  = MP[xja + 04];
       FLECS @ AREG[5] @ BREG[5]  = MP[xja + 05];
       MA   @ AREG[6] @ BREG[6]   = MP[xja + 06];
              AREG[7] @ BREG[7]   = MP[xja + 07];
                      XREG[0]     = MP[xja + 08];
                      XREG[1]     = MP[xja + 09];
                      XREG[2]     = MP[xja + 10];
                      XREG[3]     = MP[xja + 11];
                      XREG[4]     = MP[xja + 12];
                      XREG[5]     = MP[xja + 13];
                      XREG[6]     = MP[xja + 14];
                      XREG[7]     = MP[xja + 15] next
       MP[xja + 00] = xjp[00];
       MP[xja + 01] = xjp[01];
       MP[xja + 02] = xjp[02];
       MP[xja + 03] = xjp[03];
       MP[xja + 04] = xjp[04];
       MP[xja + 05] = xjp[05];
       MP[xja + 06] = xjp[06];
       MP[xja + 07] = xjp[07];
       MP[xja + 08] = xjp[08];
       MP[xja + 09] = xjp[09];
       MP[xja + 10] = xjp[10];
       MP[xja + 11] = xjp[11];
       MP[xja + 12] = xjp[12];
       MP[xja + 13] = xjp[13];
       MP[xja + 14] = xjp[14];
       MP[xja + 15] = xjp[15] next
       xjf = 0
       end,

**Instruction.Cycle**

    start{main} :=
       begin
       WAIT (xjf) next                ! Initialization
       stop.bit = 0 next              ! Wait for exchange jump
       mark() next                    ! Clear stop bit
       run :=                         ! Instruction Stack empty
          begin                       ! Main cycle
          IF xjf => xj() next         ! Check for exchange jump
          IF stop.bit => RESTART start next
          IF not range =>
             begin
             fetch() next             ! Get an instruction
             reserv()                 ! Reservation control
             end next                 ! will not return until
          range = 0 next              ! all usage conflicts are
                                      ! resolved.
          exec() next                 ! Issue the instruction
          RESTART run
          end
       end,
```

APPENDIX 2 (cont'd.)

```
exec :=                          ! The instruction is issued
    begin                        ! to the appropiate execution
    DECODE unit =>               ! unit.
        begin
        0 := BRANCH.UNIT(I),
        1 := BOOLEAN.UNIT(I),
        2 := SHIFT.UNIT(I),
        3 := ADD.UNIT(I),
        4 := LONG.ADD.UNIT(I),
        5 := MULTIPLY.UNIT.0(I),
        6 := MULTIPLY.UNIT.1(I),
        7 := DIVIDE.UNIT(I),
        8 := INCREMENT.UNIT.0(I),
        9 := INCREMENT.UNIT.1(I)
        end
    end,

! The remainder of the ISP describes the ten arithmetic processing
! units.  These units will function in parallel much as they do
! in the real CDC 6600.

! Note that floating point instructions are decoded but this ISP
! does not describe their actual execution.

**Branch.Unit**

BRANCH.UNIT(i<29:0>){process; critical} :=
    begin

**Branch.Declarations**

    fm <5:0> := i<29:24>,
    i. <2:0> := i<23:21>,
    j. <2:0> := i<20:18>,
    k. <2:0> := i<17:15>,

    **Branch.Execution**{oc}

    branch{main} :=
        begin
        DECODE fm @ i. =>
            begin
            #00?? := PS  := stop.bit = 1,
            #010 := RJ  := (MP[k1+RACM] = #0400@(PC+1)<17:0>@#0000000000 next
                                     PC = k1 + 1; mark()),
            #02?? := JP  := (PC = k1 + BREG[i.]; mark()),
            #030 := ZR  := IF XREG[j.] eql 0 => PC = k1,
            #031 := NZ  := IF XREG[j.] neq 0 => PC = k1,
            #032 := PL  := IF not XREG[j.]<59> => PC = k1,
            #033 := NG  := IF XREG[j.]<59> => PC = k1,
            #034 := IR  := IF not ((XREG[j.]<59:48> eql{us} #3777) or
                                    (XREG[j.]<59:48> eql{us} #4000)) => PC = k1,
            #035 := OR. := IF     (XREG[j.]<59:48> eql{us} #3777) or
                                    (XREG[j.]<59:48> eql{us} #4000)  => PC = k1,
            #036 := DF  := IF not ((XREG[j.]<59:48> eql{us} #1777) or
                                    (XREG[j.]<59:48> eql{us} #6000)) => PC = k1,
            #037 := ID  := IF     (XREG[j.]<59:48> eql{us} #1777) or
                                    (XREG[j.]<59:48> eql{us} #6000)  => PC = k1,
            #04?? := EQ  := IF BREG[i.] eql{us} BREG[j.] => PC = k1,
            #05?? := NE  := IF BREG[i.] neq{us} BREG[j.] => PC = k1,
            #06?? := GE  := IF BREG[i.] geq{us} BREG[j.] => PC = k1,
            #07?? := LT  := IF BREG[i.] lss{us} BREG[j.] => PC = k1
            end next
        IF (PC lss{us} islo) or (PC gtr{us} ishi) => mark() next
        dealloc(0)
        end
    end,

**Boolean.Unit**

BOOLEAN.UNIT(i<29:0>){process; critical} :=
    begin
**Boolean.Declarations**

    fm <5:0> := i<29:24>,
    i. <2:0> := i<23:21>,
    j. <2:0> := i<20:18>,
    k. <2:0> := i<17:15>,

    **Boolean.Execution**{us}

    boolean{main} :=
        begin
        DECODE fm =>                ! All instructions are "BXi"
            begin
            #10 := XREG[i.] = XREG[j.],
            #11 := XREG[i.] = XREG[j.] and XREG[k.],
            #12 := XREG[i.] = XREG[j.] or  XREG[k.],
            #13 := XREG[i.] = XREG[j.] xor XREG[k.],
            #14 := XREG[i.] = not XREG[k.],
            #15 := XREG[i.] = XREG[j.] and (not XREG[k.]),
            #16 := XREG[i.] = XREG[j.] or  (not XREG[k.]),
            #17 := XREG[i.] = XREG[j.] xor (not XREG[k.])
            end next
        dealloc(1)
        end
    end,
**Shift.Unit**

SHIFT.UNIT(i<29:0>){process; critical} :=
    begin

**Shift.Declarations**

    fm <5:0> := i<29:24>,
    i. <2:0> := i<23:21>,
    j. <2:0> := i<20:18>,
    k. <2:0> := i<17:15>,
    jk <5:0> := i<20:15>,
```

```
**Shift.Execution**{us}

shift{main} :=
    begin
    DECODE fm =>
        begin
        #20 := XREG[i.] = XREG[i.] slr jk,        ! LXi
        #21 := XREG[i.] = XREG[i.] srr jk,        ! AXi
        #22 := DECODE BREG[j.]<17> =>             ! LXi
            begin
            0 := XREG[i.] = XREG[k.] slr BREG[j.]<5:0>,
            1 := DECODE (not BREG[j.]<10:6>) eql '00000 =>
                begin
                0 := XREG[i.] = 0,
                1 := XREG[i.]
                    = XREG[k.] srd (not BREG[j.]<10:0>)
                end
            end,
        #23 := DECODE BREG[j.]<17> =>             ! AXi
            begin
            0 := DECODE BREG[j.]<10:6> eql '00000 =>
                begin
                0 := XREG[i.] = 0,
                1 := XREG[i.] = XREG[k.] srd BREG[j.]
                end,
            1 := XREG[i.] = XREG[k.] slr (not BREG[j.]<5:0>)
            end,
        #24 := not.described,                     ! NXi
        #25 := not.described,                     ! ZXi
        #26 := begin                              ! UXi
            XREG[i.] <= XREG[k.]<59> @ XREG[k.]<47:0>;
            BREG[j.] <= #2000 -{us} XREG[k.]<58:48>
            end,
        #27 := begin                              ! PXi
            XREG[i.]<47:0> = XREG[k.]<47:0>;
            XREG[i.]<59> = XREG[k.]<59>;
            DECODE XREG[k.]<59> =>
                begin
                0 := XREG[i.]<58:48> = not BREG[j.]<10>
                                            @ BREG[j.]<9:0>,
                1 := XREG[i.]<58:48> = BREG[j.]<10>
                                            @ not BREG[j.]<9:0>
                end
            end,
        #43 := begin                              ! MXi
            XREG[i.] = 0 next
            XREG[i.]<59> = (jk neq 0) next
            XREG[i.] = XREG[i.] srd (jk -{us} 1)
            end
        end next
    dealloc(2)
    end
end,
**Add.Unit**

ADD.UNIT(i<29:0>){process; critical} :=
    begin

**Add.Declarations**

    **Add.Execution**{oc}

    add{main} :=
        begin
        DECODE fm =>
            begin
            #30 := not.described,              ! FXi -> (Xj + Xk)
            #31 := not.described,              ! FXi -> (Xj - Xk)
            #32 := not.described,              ! DXi -> (Xj + Xk)
            #33 := not.described,              ! DXi -> (Xj - Xk)
            #34 := not.described,              ! RXi -> (Xj + Xk)
            #35 := not.described               ! RXi -> (Xj - Xk)
            end next
        dealloc(3)
        end
    end,

**Long.Add.Unit**

LONG.ADD.UNIT(i<29:0>){process; critical} :=
    begin

**Long.Add.Declarations**

    fm <5:0> := i<29:24>,
    i. <2:0> := i<23:21>,
    j. <2:0> := i<20:18>,
    k. <2:0> := i<17:15>,

    **Long.Add.Execution**{oc}

    ladd{main} :=
        begin
        DECODE fm =>
            begin
            #36 := XREG[i.] = XREG[j.] + XREG[k.],    ! IXi -> Xj + Xk
            #37 := XREG[i.] = XREG[j.] - XREG[k.],    ! IXi -> Xj - Xk
        otherwise := no.op()
            end next
        dealloc(4)
        end
    end,

**Multiply.Unit.0**

MULTIPLY.UNIT.0(i<29:0>){process; critical} :=
    begin

**Multiply.0.Declarations**
```

APPENDIX 2 (cont'd.)

```
        fm <5:0> := i<29:24>,

    **Multiply.0.Execution**{oc}

    mpy0{main} :=
        begin
        DECODE fm =>
            begin
            #40 := not.described,              ! FXi -> Xj * Xk
            #41 := not.described,              ! RXi -> Xj * Xk
            #42 := not.described               ! DXi -> Xj * Xk
            end next
        dealloc(5)
        end
    end,

**Multiply.Unit.1**

MULTIPLY.UNIT.1(i<29:0>){process; critical} :=
    begin

**Multiply.1.Declarations**

        fm <5:0> := i<29:24>,

    **Multiply.1.Execution**{oc}

    mpy1{main} :=
        begin
        DECODE fm =>
            begin
            #40 := not.described,              ! FXi -> Xj * Xk
            #41 := not.described,              ! RXi -> Xj * Xk
            #42 := not.described               ! DXi -> Xj * Xk
            end next
        dealloc(6)
        end
    end,

**Divide.Unit**

DIVIDE.UNIT(i<29:0>){process; critical} :=
    begin

**Divide.Declarations**

        fm <5:0> := i<29:24>,
        m. <2:0> := i<26:24>,
        i. <2:0> := i<23:21>,
        j. <2:0> := i<20:18>,
        k. <2:0> := i<17:15>,
        k1<17:0> := i<17:0>,
        xcnt<5:0>,                             ! Counter for CXi

    **Divide.Execution**{oc}

    div{main} :=
        begin
        DECODE fm =>
            begin
            #44 := not.described,              ! FXi -> Xi = Xj / Xk
            #45 := not.described,              ! RXi -> Xi = Xj / Xk
            #46 := NO  := no.op(),
            #47 := CXi
                := begin
                    xcnt = 0;
                    XREG[i.] = 0 next
                    CXi. :=
                        begin
                        XREG[i.] = XREG[i.] +{us} XREG[k.]<0> next
                        XREG[k.] = XREG[k.] srr 1;
                        xcnt = xcnt + 1 next
                        IF xcnt lss{us} 60 => RESTART CXi.
                        end
                    end
            end next
        dealloc(7)
        end
    end,

**Increment.Unit.0**

INCREMENT.UNIT.0(i<29:0>){process; critical} :=
    begin

**Increment.0.Declarations**

        fm <5:0> := i<29:24>,
        m. <2:0> := i<26:24>,
        i. <2:0> := i<23:21>,
        j. <2:0> := i<20:18>,
        k. <2:0> := i<17:15>,
        k1<17:0> := i<17:0>,

    **Increment.0.Execution**{oc}

    incr0{main} :=
        begin
        DECODE fm =>
            begin
            #50:#57 := SAi                      ! Increment
                := begin
                    DECODE m. =>
                        begin
                        #0 := aref(i.,AREG[j.] + k1),
                        #1 := aref(i.,BREG[j.] + k1),
                        #2 := aref(i.,XREG[j.]<17:0> + k1),
                        #3 := aref(i.,XREG[j.]<17:0> + BREG[k.]),
                        #4 := aref(i.,AREG[j.] + BREG[k.]),
```

```
                        #5 := aref(i.,AREG[j.] - BREG[k.]),
                        #6 := aref(i.,BREG[j.] + BREG[k.]),
                        #7 := aref(i.,BREG[j.] - BREG[k.])
                        end
                    end,
            #60:#67 := SBi
                := begin
                    DECODE m. =>
                        begin
                        #0 := BREG[i.] = AREG[j.] + k1,
                        #1 := BREG[i.] = BREG[j.] + k1,
                        #2 := BREG[i.] = XREG[j.]<17:0> + k1,
                        #3 := BREG[i.] = XREG[j.]<17:0> + BREG[k.],
                        #4 := BREG[i.] = AREG[j.] + BREG[k.],
                        #5 := BREG[i.] = AREG[j.] - BREG[k.],
                        #6 := BREG[i.] = BREG[j.] + BREG[k.],
                        #7 := BREG[i.] = BREG[j.] - BREG[k.]
                        end
                    end,
            #70:#77 := SXi
                := begin
                    DECODE m. =>
                        begin
                        #0 := XREG[i.] <= AREG[j.] + k1,
                        #1 := XREG[i.] <= BREG[j.] + k1,
                        #2 := XREG[i.] <= XREG[j.]<17:0> + k1,
                        #3 := XREG[i.] <= XREG[j.]<17:0> + BREG[k.],
                        #4 := XREG[i.] <= AREG[j.] + BREG[k.],
                        #5 := XREG[i.] <= AREG[j.] - BREG[k.],
                        #6 := XREG[i.] <= BREG[j.] + BREG[k.],
                        #7 := XREG[i.] <= BREG[j.] - BREG[k.]
                        end
                    end
            end next
        dealloc(8)
        end
    end,

**Increment.Unit.1**

INCREMENT.UNIT.1(i<29:0>){process; critical} :=
    begin

**Increment.1.Declarations**

        fm <5:0> := i<29:24>,
        m. <2:0> := i<26:24>,
        i. <2:0> := i<23:21>,
        j. <2:0> := i<20:18>,
        k. <2:0> := i<17:15>,
        k1<17:0> := i<17:0>,

    **Increment.1.Execution**{oc}

    incr1{main} :=
        begin
        DECODE fm =>
            begin
            #50:#57 := SAi                      ! Increment
                := begin
                    DECODE m. =>
                        begin
                        #0 := aref(i.,AREG[j.] + k1),
                        #1 := aref(i.,BREG[j.] + k1),
                        #2 := aref(i.,XREG[j.]<17:0> + k1),
                        #3 := aref(i.,XREG[j.]<17:0> + BREG[k.]),
                        #4 := aref(i.,AREG[j.] + BREG[k.]),
                        #5 := aref(i.,AREG[j.] - BREG[k.]),
                        #6 := aref(i.,BREG[j.] + BREG[k.]),
                        #7 := aref(i.,BREG[j.] - BREG[k.])
                        end
                    end,
            #60:#67 := SBi
                := begin
                    DECODE m. =>
                        begin
                        #0 := BREG[i.] = AREG[j.] + k1,
                        #1 := BREG[i.] = BREG[j.] + k1,
                        #2 := BREG[i.] = XREG[j.]<17:0> + k1,
                        #3 := BREG[i.] = XREG[j.]<17:0> + BREG[k.],
                        #4 := BREG[i.] = AREG[j.] + BREG[k.],
                        #5 := BREG[i.] = AREG[j.] - BREG[k.],
                        #6 := BREG[i.] = BREG[j.] + BREG[k.],
                        #7 := BREG[i.] = BREG[j.] - BREG[k.]
                        end
                    end,
            #70:#77 := SXi
                := begin
                    DECODE m. =>
                        begin
                        #0 := XREG[i.] <= AREG[j.] + k1,
                        #1 := XREG[i.] <= BREG[j.] + k1,
                        #2 := XREG[i.] <= XREG[j.]<17:0> + k1,
                        #3 := XREG[i.] <= XREG[j.]<17:0> + BREG[k.],
                        #4 := XREG[i.] <= AREG[j.] + BREG[k.],
                        #5 := XREG[i.] <= AREG[j.] - BREG[k.],
                        #6 := XREG[i.] <= BREG[j.] + BREG[k.],
                        #7 := XREG[i.] <= BREG[j.] - BREG[k.]
                        end
                    end
            end next
        dealloc(9)
        end
    end,

REQUIRE.ISP |PC6600.isp|,      ! Peripheral Processor Description

end                 ! End CDC 6600
```

Chapter 44

The CRAY-1 Computer System[1]

Richard M. Russell

This paper describes the CRAY-1, discusses the evolution of its architecture, and gives an account of some of the problems that were overcome during its manufacture.

The CRAY-1 is the only computer to have been built to date that satisfies ERDA's Class VI requirement (a computer capable of processing from 20 to 60 million floating point operations per second) [Keller 1976].

The CRAY-1's Fortran compiler (CFT) is designed to give the scientific user immediate access to the benefits of the CRAY-1's vector processing architecture. An optimizing compiler, CFT, "vectorizes" innermost DO loops. Compatible with the ANSI 1966 Fortran Standard and with many commonly supported Fortran extensions, CFT does not require any source program modifications or the use of additional nonstandard Fortran statements to achieve vectorization. Thus the user's investment of hundreds of man months of effort to develop Fortran programs for other contemporary computers is protected.

Introduction

Vector processors are not yet commonplace machines in the larger-scale computer market. At the time of this writing we know of only 12 non-CRAY-1 vector processor installations worldwide. Of these 12, the most powerful processor is the ILLIAC IV (1 installation), the most populous is the Texas Instruments Advanced Scientific Computer (7 installations) and the most publicized is Control Data's STAR 100 (4 installations). In its report on the CRAY-1, Auerbach Computer Technology Reports published a comparison of the CRAY-1, the ASC, and the STAR 100 [Auerbach, n.d.]. The CRAY-1 is shown to be a more powerful computer than any of its main competitors and is estimated to be the equivalent of five IBM 370/195s.

Independent benchmark studies have shown the CRAY-1 fully capable of supporting computational rates of 138 million floating-point operations per second (MFLOPS) for sustained periods and even higher rates of 250 MFLOPS in short bursts [Calahan, Joy, and Orbits, n.d.; Reeves, 1975]. Such comparatively high performance results from the CRAY-1 internal architecture, which is designed to accommodate the computational needs of carrying out many calculations in discrete steps, with each step producing interim results used in subsequent steps. Through a technique called "chaining," the CRAY-1 vector functional units, in combination with scalar and vector registers, generate interim results and

use them again immediately without additional memory references, which slow down the computational process in other contemporary computer systems.

Other features enhancing the CRAY-1's computational capabilities are: its small size, which reduces distances electrical signals must travel within the computer's framework and allows a 12.5 nanosecond clock period (the CRAY-1 is the world's fastest scalar processor); a one million word semiconductor memory equipped with error detection and correction logic (SECDED); its 64-bit word size; and its optimizing Fortran compiler.

Architecture

The CRAY-1 has been called "the world's most expensive love-seat" [Computer World, 1976]. Certainly, most people's first reaction to the CRAY-1 is that it is so small. But in computer design it is a truism that smaller means faster. The greater the separation of components, the longer the time taken for a signal to pass between them. A cyclindrical shape was chosen for the CRAY-1 in order to keep wiring distances small.

Figure 1 shows the physical dimensions of the machine. The mainframe is composed of 12 wedgelike columns arranged in a 270° arc. This leaves room for a reasonably trim individual to gain access to the interior of the machine. Note that the love-seat disguises the power supplies and some plumbing for the Freon cooling system. The photographs (Figs. 2 and 3) show the interior of a working CRAY-1 and an interior view of a column with one module in place. Figure 4 is a photograph of a single module.

An Analysis of the Architecture

Table 1 details important characteristics of the CRAY-1 Computer System. The CRAY-1 is equipped with 12 i/o channels, 16 memory banks, 12 functional units, and more than 4K bytes of register storage. Access to memory is shared by the i/o channels and high-speed registers. The most striking features of the CRAY-1 are: only four chip types, main memory speed, cooling system, and computation section.

Four Chip Types

Only four chip types are used to build the CRAY-1. These are 16 × 4 bit bipolar register chips (6 nanosecond cycle time), 1024 × 1 bit bipolar memory chips (50 nanosecond cycle time), and bipolar logic chips with subnanosecond propagation times. The logic chips are all simple low- or high-speed gates with both a 5 wide and a 4 wide gate (5/4 NAND). Emitter-coupled logic circuit (ECL) technology is used throughout the CRAY-1.

[1]*Comm. ACM*, vol. 21, no. 1, January 1978, pp. 63–72.

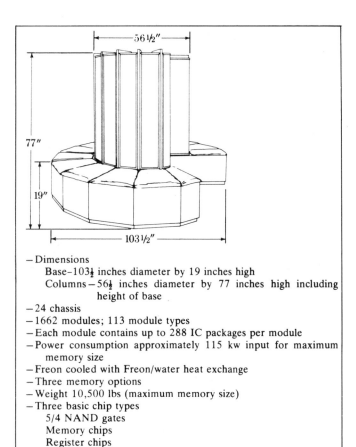

- Dimensions
    Base–$103\frac{1}{2}$ inches diameter by 19 inches high
    Columns–$56\frac{1}{2}$ inches diameter by 77 inches high including
        height of base
- 24 chassis
- 1662 modules; 113 module types
- Each module contains up to 288 IC packages per module
- Power consumption approximately 115 kw input for maximum
    memory size
- Freon cooled with Freon/water heat exchange
- Three memory options
- Weight 10,500 lbs (maximum memory size)
- Three basic chip types
    5/4 NAND gates
    Memory chips
    Register chips

Fig. 1. Physical organization of mainframe.

Fig. 2. The CRAY-1 computer.

The printed circuit board used in the CRAY-1 is a 5-layer board with the two outer surfaces used for signal runs and the three inner layers for −5.2V, −2.0V, and ground power supplies. The boards are six inches wide, 8 inches long, and fit into the chassis, as shown in Fig. 3.

All integrated circuit devices used in the CRAY-1 are packed in 16-pin hermetically sealed flat packs supplied by both Fairchild and Motorola. This type of package was chosen for its reliability and compactness. Compactness is of special importance; as many as 288 packages may be added to a board to fabricate a module (there are 113 module types), and as many as 72 modules may be inserted into a 28-inch-high chassis. Such component densities inevitably lead to a mammoth cooling problem (to be described).

Main Memory Speed

CRAY-1 memory is organized in 16 banks, 72 modules per bank. Each module contributes 1 bit to a 64-bit word. The other 8 bits

Fig. 3. CRAY-1 modules in place.

Table 1   CRAY-1 CPU Characteristics Summary

Computation Section
  Scalar and vector processing modes
  12.5 nanosecond clock period operation
  64-bit word size
  Integer and floating-point arithmetic
  Twelve fully segmented functional units
  Eight 24-bit address *(A)* registers
  Sixty-four 24-bit intermediate address *(B)* registers
  Eight 64-bit scalar *(S)* registers
  Sixty-four 64-bit intermediate scalar *(T)* registers
  Eight 64-element vector *(V)* registers (64-bits per element)
  Vector length and vector mask registers
  One 64-bit real time clock *(RT)* register
  Four instruction buffers of sixty-four 16-bit parcels each
  128 basic instructions
  Prioritized interrupt control
Memory Section
  1,048,576 64-bit words (plus 8 check bits per word)
  16 independent banks of 65,536 words each
  4 clock period bank cycle time
  1 word per clock period transfer rate for *B, T,* and *V* registers
  1 word per 2 clock periods transfer rate for *A* and *S* registers
  4 words per clock period transfer rate to instruction buffers (up to
    16 instructions per clock period)
i/o Section
  24 i/o channels organized into four 6-channel groups
  Each channel group contains either 6 input or 6 output channels
  Each channel group served by memory every 4 clock periods
  Channel priority within each channel group
  16 data bits, 3 control bits per channel, and 4 parity bits
  Maximum channel rate of one 64-bit word every 100 nanoseconds
  Maximum data streaming rate of 500,000 64-bit words/second
  Channel error detection

Fig. 4. A single module.

are used to store an 8-bit check byte required for single-bit error correction, double-bit error detection (SECDED). Data words are stored in 1-bank increments throughout memory. This organization allows 16-way interleaving of memory accesses and prevents bank conflicts except in the case of memory accesses that step through memory with either an 8 or 16-word increment.

Cooling System

The CRAY-1 generates about four times as much heat per cubic inch as the 7600. To cool the CRAY-1 a new cooling technology was developed, also based on Freon, but employing available metal conductors in a new way. Within each chassis vertical aluminum/stainless steel cooling bars line each column wall. The Freon refrigerant is passed through a stainless steel tube within the aluminum casing. When modules are in place, heat is dissipated through the inner copper heat transfer plate in the

module to the column walls and thence into the cooling bars. The modules are mated with the cold bar by using stainless steel pins to pinch the copper plate against the aluminum outer casing of the bar.

To assure component reliability, the cooling system was designed to provide a maximum case temperature of 130°F (54°C). To meet this goal, the following temperature differentials are observed:

Temperature at center of module	130°F(54°C)
Temperature at edge of module	118°F(48°C)
Cold plate temperature at wedge	78°F(25°C)
Cold bar temperature	70°F(21°C)
Refrigerant tube temperature	70°F(21°C)

Functional Units

There are 12 functional units, organized in four groups: address, scalar, vector, and floating point. Each functional unit is pipelined

Table 2 CRAY-1 Functional Units

	Register usage	Functional unit time (clock periods)
Address function units		
address add unit	A	2
address multiply unit	A	6
Scalar functional units		
scalar add unit	S	3
scalar shift unit	S	2 or 3 if double word shift
scalar logical unit	S	1
population/leading zero count unit	S	3
Vector functional units		
vector add unit	V	3
vector shift unit	V	4
vector logical unit	V	2
Floating-point functional units		
floating-point add unit	S and V	6
floating-point multiply unit	S and V	7
reciprocal approximation unit	S and V	14

into single clock segments. Functional unit time is shown in Table 2. Note that all of the functional units can operate concurrently so that in addition to the benefits of pipelining (each functional unit can be driven at a result rate of 1 per clock period) we also have parallelism across the units too. Note the absence of a divide unit in the CRAY-1. In order to have a completely segmented divide operation the CRAY-1 performs floating-point division by the method of reciprocal approximation. This technique has been used before (e.g. IBM System/360 Model 91).

Registers

Figure 5 shows the CRAY-1 registers in relationship to the functional units, instruction buffers, i/o channel control registers, and memory. The basic set of programmable registers is as follows:

  8 24-bit address (A) registers

  64 24-bit address-save (B) registers

  8 64-bit scalar (S) registers

  64 64-bit scalar-save (T) registers

  8 64-word (4096-bit) vector (V) registers

Expressed in 8-bit bytes rather than 64-bit words, that's a total of 4,888 bytes of high-speed (6ns) register storage.

The functional units take input operands from and store result

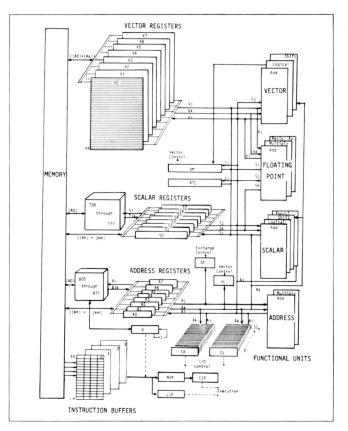

Fig. 5. Block diagram of registers.

operands only to A, S, and V registers. Thus the large amount of register storage is a crucial factor in the CRAY-1's architecture. Chaining could not take place if vector register space were not available for the storage of final or intermediate results. The B and T registers greatly assist scalar performance. Temporary scalar values can be stored from and reloaded to the A and S register in two clock periods. Figure 5 shows the CRAY-1's register paths in detail. The speed of the CFT Fortran IV compiler would be seriously impaired if it were unable to keep the many Pass 1 and Pass 2 tables it needs in register space. Without the register storage provided by the B, T, and V registers, the CRAY-1's bandwidth of only 80 million words/second would be a serious impediment to performance.

Instruction Formats

Instructions are expressed in either one or two 16-bit parcels. Shown is the general form of a CRAY-1 instruction. Two-parcel instructions may overlap memory-word boundaries, as follows:

Fields	g 0-3 (4)	h 4-6 (3)	i 7-9 (3)	j 10-12 (3)	k 13-15 (3)	m 16-31 (16)
Bit posi- tions						
	Parcel 1					Parcel 2

The computation section processes instructions at a maximum rate of one parcel per clock period.

For arithmetic and logical instructions, a 7-bit operation code (gh) is followed by three 3-bit register designators. The first field, i, designates the result register. The j and k fields designate the two operand registers or are combined to designate a B or T register.

The shift and mask instructions consist of a 7-bit operation code (gh) followed by a 3-bit i field and a 6-bit jk field. The i field designates the operand register. The jk combined field specifies a shift or mask count.

Immediate operand, read and store memory, and branch instructions require the two-parcel instruction word format. The immediate operand and the read and store memory instructions combine the j, k, and m fields to define a 22-bit quantity or memory address. In addition, the read and store memory instructions use the h field to specify an operating register for indexing. The branch instructions combine the i, j, k, and m fields into a 24-bit memory address field. This allows branching to any one of the four parcel positions in any 64-bit word, whether in memory or in an instruction buffer.

Operating Registers

Five types of registers—three primary (A, S, and V) and two intermediate (B and T)—are provided in the CRAY-1.

A *registers*—eight 24-bit A registers serve a variety of applications. They are primarily used as address registers for memory references and as index registers, but also are used to provide values for shift counts, loop control, and channel i/o operations. In address applications, they are used to index the base address for scalar memory references and for providing both a base address and an index address for vector memory references.

The 24-bit integer functional units modify values (such as program addresses) by adding, subtracting, and multiplying A register quantities. The results of these operations are returned to A registers.

Data can be transferred directly from memory to A registers or can be placed in B registers as an intermediate step. This allows buffering of the data between A registers and memory. Data can also be transferred between A and S registers and from an A register to the vector length registers. The eight A registers are individually designated by the symbols A0, A1, A2, A3, A4, A5, A6, and A7.

B *registers*—there are sixty-four 24-bit B registers, which are used as auxiliary storage for the A registers. The transfer of an operand between an A and a B register requires only one clock period. Typically, B registers contain addresses and counters that are referenced over a longer period than would permit their being retained in A registers. A block of data in B registers may be transferred to or from memory at the rate of one clock period per register. Thus, it is feasible to store the contents of these registers in memory prior to calling a subroutine requiring their use. The sixty-four B registers are individually designated by the symbols B0, B1, B2, . . . , and B77$_8$.

S *registers*—eight 64-bit S registers are the principal data handling registers for scalar operations. The S registers serve as both source and destination registers for scalar arithmetic and logical instructions. Scalar quantities involved in vector operations are held in S registers. Logical, shift, fixed-point, and floating-point operations may be performed on S register data. The eight S registers are individually designated by the symbols S0, S1, S2, S3, S4, S5, S6, and S7.

T *registers*—sixty-four 64-bit T registers are used as auxiliary storage for the S registers. The transfer of an operand between S and T registers requires one clock period. Typically, T registers contain operands that are referenced over a longer period than would permit their being retained in S registers. T registers allow intermediate results of complex computations to be held in intermediate access storage rather than in memory. A block of data in T registers may be transferred to or from memory at the rate of one word per clock period. The sixty-four T registers are individually designated by the symbols T0, T1, T2, . . . , and T77$_8$.

V *registers*—eight 64-element V registers provide operands to and receive results from the functional units at a one clock period rate. Each element of a V register holds a 64-bit quantity. When associated data is grouped into successive elements of a V register, the register may be considered to contain a vector. Examples of vector quantities are rows and columns of a matrix, or similarly related elements of a table. Computational efficiency is achieved by processing each element of the vector identically. Vector merge and test instructions are provided in the CRAY-1 to allow operations to be performed on individual elements designated by the content of the vector mask (VM) register. The number of vector register elements to be processed is contained in the vector length (VL) register. The eight V registers are individually designated by the symbols V0, V1, V2, V3, V4, V5, V6, and V7.

Supporting Registers

The CPU contains a variety of additional registers that support the control of program execution. These are the vector length (VL) and vector mask (VM) registers, the program counter (P), the base address (BA) and limit address (LA) registers, the exchange address (XA) register, the flag (F) register, and the mode (M) register.

VM *register*—the 64-bit vector mask (VM) register controls vector element designation in vector merge and test instructions. Each bit of the VM register corresponds to a vector register element. In the vector test instruction, the VM register content is defined by testing each element of a V register for a specific condition.

P *register*—the 24-bit P register specifies the memory register parcel address of the current program instruction. The high order 22 bits specify a memory address and the low order two bits indicate a parcel number. This parcel address is advanced by one as each instruction parcel in a nonbranching sequence is executed and is replaced whenever program branching occurs.

BA *registers*—the 18-bit base address (BA) register contains the upper 18 bits of a 22-bit memory address. The lower four bits of this address are considered zeros. Just prior to initial or continued execution of a program, a process known as the "exchange sequence" stores into the BA register the upper 18 bits of the lowest memory address to be referenced during program execution. As the program executes, the address portion of each instruction referencing memory has its content added to that of the BA register. The sum then serves as the absolute address used for the memory reference and ensures that memory addresses lower than the contents of the BA register are not accessed. Programs must, therefore, have all instructions referencing memory do so with their address portions containing relative addresses. This process supports program loading and memory protection operations and does not, in producing an absolute address, affect the content of the instruction buffer, BA, or memory.

LA *register*—the 18-bit limit address (LA) register contains the upper 18 bits of a 22-bit memory address. The lower 4 bits of this address are considered zeros. Just prior to initial or continued execution of a program, the "exchange sequence" process stores into the LA register the upper 18 bits of that absolute address one greater than allowed to be referenced by the program. When program execution begins, each instruction referencing a memory location has the absolute address for that reference (determined by summing its address portion with the BA register contents) checked against the LA register content. If the absolute address equals or exceeds the LA register content, an out-of-range error condition is flagged and program execution terminates. This process supports the memory protection operation.

XA *register*—the 8-bit exchange address (XA) register contains the upper eight bits of a 12-bit memory address. The lower four bits of the address are considered zeros. Because only twelve bits are used, with the lower four bits always being zeros, exchange addresses can reference only every 16th memory address beginning with address 0000 and concluding with address 4080. Each of these addresses designates the first word of a 16-word set. Thus, 256 sets (of 16 memory words each) can be specified. Prior to initiation or continuation of a program's execution, the XA register contains the first memory address of a particular 16-word set or exchange package. The exchange package contains certain operating and support registers' contents as required for operations following an interrupt. The XA register supports the exchange sequence operation and the contents of XA are stored in an exchange package whenever an exchange sequence occurs.

F *register*—the 9-bit F register contains flags that, whenever set, indicate interrupt conditions causing initiation of an exchange sequence. The interrupt conditions are: normal exit, error exit, i/o interrupt, uncorrected memory error, program range error, operand range error, floating-point overflow, real-time clock interrupt, and console interrupt.

M *register*—the M (mode) register is a three-bit register that contains part of the exchange package for a currently active program. The three bits are selectively set during an exchange sequence. Bit 37, the floating-point error mode flag, can be set or cleared during the execution interval for a program through use of the 0021 and 0022 instructions. The other two bits (bits 38 and 39) are not altered during the execution interval for the exchange package and can only be altered when the exchange package is inactive in storage. Bits are assigned as follows in word two of the exchange package.

Bit 37—Floating-point error mode flag. When this bit is set, interrupts on floating-point errors are enabled.

Bit 38—Uncorrectable memory error mode flag. When this bit is set, interrupts on uncorrectable memory parity errors are enabled.

Bit 39—Monitor mode flag. When this bit is set, all interrupts other than parity errors are inhibited.

Integer Arithmetic

All integer arithmetic is performed in 24-bit or 64-bit 2's complement form.

Floating-Point Arithmetic

Floating-point numbers are represented in signed magnitude form. The format is a packed signed binary fraction and a biased binary integer exponent. The fraction is a 49-bit signed magnitude value. The exponent is 15-bit biased. The unbiased exponent range is:

$$2^{-20000_8} \text{ to } 2^{+17777_8}$$

or approximately

$$10^{-2500} \text{ to } 10^{+2500}$$

An exponent equal to or greater than 2^{+20000_8} is recognized by the floating-point functional units as an overflow condition, and causes an interrupt if floating point interrupts are enabled.

Chaining

The chaining technique takes advantage of the parallel operation of functional units. Parallel vector operations may be processed in two ways: (a) using different functional units and V registers, and (b) chaining; that is, using the result stream to one vector register simultaneously as the operand set for another operation in a different functional unit.

Parallel operations on vectors allow the generation of two or more results per clock period. A vector operation either uses two vector registers as sources of operands or uses one scalar register and one vector register as sources of operands. Vectors exceeding 64 elements are processed in 64-element segments.

Basically, chaining is a phenomenon that occurs when results issuing from one functional unit (at a rate of one/clock period) are immediately fed into another functional unit and so on. In other words, intermediate results do not have to be stored to memory and can be used even before the vector operation that created them runs to completion.

Chaining has been compared to the technique of "data forwarding" used in the IBM 360/195. Like data forwarding, chaining takes place automatically. Data forwarding consists of hardware facilities within the 195 floating-point processor communicating automatically by transferring "name tags," or internal codes between themselves [O'Murphy and Wade, 1970]. Unlike the CRAY-1, the user has no access to the 195's data-forwarding buffers. And, of course, the 195 can only forward scalar values, not entire vectors.

Interrupts and Exchange Sequence

Interrupts are handled cleanly by the CRAY-1 hardware. Instruction issue is terminated by the hardware upon detection of an interrupt condition. All memory bank activity is allowed to complete as are any vector instructions that are in execution, and

then an exchange sequence is activated. The Cray Operating System (COS) is always one partner of any exchange sequence. The cause of an interrupt is analyzed during an exchange sequence and all interrupts are processed until none remain.

Only the address and scalar registers are maintained in a program's exchange package (Fig. 6). The user's B, T, and V registers are saved by the operating system in the user's Job Table Area.

The CRAY-1's exchange sequence will be familiar to those who have had experience with the CDC 7600 and Cyber machines. One major benefit of the exchange sequence is the ease with

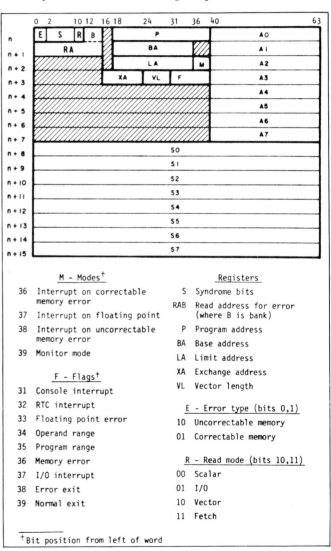

Fig. 6. Exchange package.

which user jobs can be relocated in memory by the operating system. On the CRAY-1, dynamic relocation of a user job is facilitated by a base register that is transparent to the user.

Evolution of the CRAY-1

The CRAY-1 stems from a highly successful line of computers which S. Cray either designed or was associated with. Mr. Cray was one of the founders of Control Data Corporation. While at CDC, Mr. Cray was the principal architect of the CDC 1604, 6600, and 7600 computer systems. While there are many similarities with these earlier machines, two things stand out about the CRAY-1: first it is a vector machine; second it utilizes semiconductor memories and integrated circuits rather than magnetic cores and discrete components. We classify the CRAY-1 as a second generation vector processor. The CDC STAR 100A and the Texas Instruments ASC are first-generation vector processors.

Both the STAR 100 and the ASC are designed to handle long vectors. Because of the startup time associated with data streaming, vector length is of critical importance. Vectors have to be long if the STAR 100 and the ASC vector processors are to be at all competitive with a scalar processor [Calahan, Joy, and Orbits, n.d.]. Another disadvantage of the STAR 100 architecture is that elements of a "vector" are required to be in consecutive addresses.

In contrast with these earlier designs, the CRAY-1 can be termed a short vector machine. Whereas the others require vector lengths of a 100 or more to be competitive with scalar processors, the cross over point between choosing scalar rather than vector mode on the CRAY-1 is between 2 and 4 elements. This is demonstrated by a comparison of scalar/vector timings for some mathematical library routines shown in Fig. 7.[1]

Also, the CRAY-1's addressing scheme allows complete flexibility. When accessing a vector, the user simply specifies the starting location and an increment. Arrays can be accessed by column, row, or diagonal; they can be stepped through with nonunary increments; and, there are no restrictions on addressing, except that the increment must be a constant.

Vector Startup Times

To be efficient at processing short vectors, vector startup times must be small. On the CRAY-1, vector instructions may issue at a rate of one instruction parcel per clock period. All vector

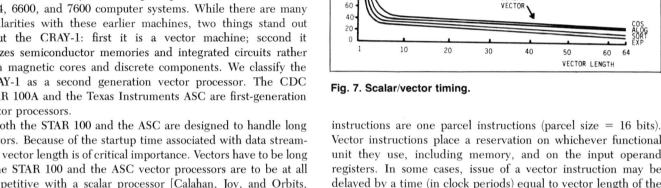

Fig. 7. Scalar/vector timing.

instructions are one parcel instructions (parcel size = 16 bits). Vector instructions place a reservation on whichever functional unit they use, including memory, and on the input operand registers. In some cases, issue of a vector instruction may be delayed by a time (in clock periods) equal to vector length of the preceding vector operation + 4.

Functional unit times are shown in Table 2. Vector operations that depend on the result of a previous vector operation can usually "chain" with them and are delayed for a maximum "chain slot" time in clock periods of functional unit time + 2.

Once issued, a vector instruction produces its first result after a delay in clock periods equal to functional unit time. Subsequent results continue to be produced at a rate of 1 per clock period. Results must be stored in a vector register. A separate instruction is required to store the final result vector to memory. Vector register capacity is 64-elements. Vectors longer than 64 are processed in 64-element segments.

Some sample timings for both scalar and vector are shown in Table 3.[2] Note that there is no vector ASIN routine and so a reference to ASIN within a vectorized loop generates repetitive calls to the scalar ASIN routine. This involves a performance degradation but does allow the rest of the loop to vectorize (in a case where there are more statements than in this example). Simple loops 14, 15, and 16 show the influence of chaining. For a long vector, the number of clock periods per result is approximately the number of memory references + 1. In loop 14, an extra clock period is consumed because the present CFT compiler will load all four operands before doing computation. This problem is

---

[1]Work done by Paul Johnson, Cray Research.

[2]Work done by Richard Hendrickson, Cray Research.

Table 3 Execution Time in Clock Periods per Result for Various Simple DO Loops of the Form

$$DO\ 10\ I = 1,N$$
$$10\ A(I) = B(I)$$

Loop body	N = 1	10	100	1000	1000 Scalar
1. A(I) = 1.	41.0	5.5	2.6	2.5	22.5
2. A(I) = B(I)	44.0	5.8	2.7	2.5	31.0
3. A(I) = B(I) + 10.	55.0	6.9	2.9	2.6	37.0
4. A(I) = B(I) + C(I)	59.0	8.2	3.9	3.7	41.0
5. A(I) = B(I)*10.	56.0	7.0	2.9	2.6	38.0
6. A(I) = B(I)*C(I)	60.0	8.3	4.0	3.7	42.0
7. A(I) = B(I)/10.	94.0	10.8	4.1	3.7	52.0
8. A(I) = B(I)/C(I)	89.0	13.3	7.6	7.2	60.0
9. A(I) = SIN(B(I))	462.0	61.0	33.3	31.4	198.1
10. A(I) = ASIN(B(I))	430.0	209.5	189.5	188.3	169.1
11. A(I) = ABS(B(I))	61.0	7.5	2.9	2.6	
12. A(I) = AMAX1(B(I), C(I))	80.0	11.2	5.2	4.8	
13. { C(I) = A(I) / A(I) = B(I) / B(I) = C(I) }	90.0	12.7	6.3	5.8	47.0
14. A(I) = B(I)*C(I) + D(I)*E(I)	110.0	16.0	7.7	7.1	57.0
15. A(I) = B(I)*C(I) + (D(I)*E(I))	113.0	14.7	6.6	6.0	63.0
16. A(I) = B(I)*C(I) + D(I)	95.0	12.7	5.5	5.0	52.0

overcome in loop 15 by helping the compiler with an extra set of parentheses.

Software

At the time of this writing, first releases of the CRAY Operating System (COS) and CRAY Fortran Compiler (CFT) have been delivered to user sites. COS is a batch operating system capable of supporting up to 63 jobs in a multiprogramming environment. COS is designed to be the recipient of job requests and data files from front-end computers. Output from jobs is normally staged back to the front-ends upon job completion.

CFT is an optimizing Fortran compiler designed to compile ANSI 66 Fortran IV to take best advantage of the CRAY-1's vector processing architecture. In its present form, CFT will not attempt to vectorize certain loops which, due to dependence conditions, appear at first sight, unvectorizable.

However, future versions of CFT will be designed to eliminate as many dependency conditions as possible increasing the amount of vectorizable code. Basically, to be vectorizable, a DO loop should manipulate arrays and store the results of computations in arrays. Loops that contain branches such as GO TO's, IF's, or CALL statements are not currently vectorized. Loops may contain function references if the function is known to the compiler to have a vector version. Most of the mathematical functions in the CRAY library are vectorizable. By using the vector mask and vector merge features of the CRAY-1, future versions of the compiler will be able to vectorize loops containing IF and GO TO statements.

Early experience with CFT has shown that most Fortran loops will not run as fast as optimally hand-coded machine language equivalents. Future versions of CFT will show improved loop timings due mainly to improved instruction scheduling.

Other CRAY-1 software includes Cray Assembler Language (CAL) which is a powerful macro assembler, an overlay loader, a full range of utilities including a text editor, and some debug aids.

Front-End Computer Interface

The CRAY-1 was not designed for stand-alone operation. At the very minimum a minicomputer is required to act as a conduit between the CRAY-1 and the everyday world. Cray Research software development is currently being done using a Data

General Eclipse computer in this category. The Cray Research "A" processor, a 16-bit, 80 MIPS minicomputer is scheduled to replace the Eclipse in early 1978. Front-end computers can be attached to any of the CRAY-1's 12 i/o channels.

The physical connection between a front-end computer and the CRAY-1 is shown in Fig. 8. In this example an IBM 370/168 is assumed in the front-end role. Note that each computer requires a channel adapter between its own channel and a Cray Research phase-modulated long line. The link can only be driven at the speed of its slowest component. In this example it is the IBM block multiplexer channel speed of 3 megabytes/second. The discipline of the link is governed by the Cray Link Interface Protocol.

CRAY-1 Development Problems[1]

Two of the most significant problems encountered on the way to the CRAY-1 were building the first cold bar and designing circuits with a completely balanced dynamic load.

Building the Cold Bar

It took a year and a half of trial and error before the first good cold bar was built. The work was done by a small Minnesota company. A major problem was the discovery, quite early, that aluminum castings are porous. If there is a crack in the stainless steel tubing at the bond between the tubing and the elbow then the Freon leaks through the aluminum casing. The loss of the Freon is not itself a problem, but mixed with the Freon is a little oil, and the oil can cause problems if it is deposited on the modules. Aluminum also tends to get bubbles in it when it is cast, requiring a long process of temperature cycling, preheating of the stainless steel tube, and so on.

[1]This section on CRAY-1 development problems is based on remarks made by Seymour Cray in a speech to prospective CRAY-1 users in 1975.

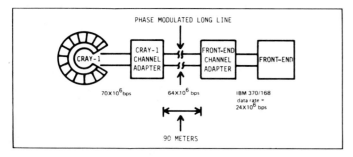

Fig. 8. Front-end system interface.

Designing the Circuits

CRAY-1 modules are 6 inches wide. The distance across the board is about a nanosecond which is just about the edge time of the electrical signals. Unless due precautions are taken, when electric signals run around a board, standing waves can be induced in the ground plane. Part of the solution is to make all signal paths in the machine the same length. This is done by padding out paths with foil runs and integrated circuit packages. All told, between 10 and 20 per cent of the IC packages in the machine are there simply to pad out a signal line. The other part of the solution was to use only simple gates and make sure that both sides of every gate are always terminated. This means that there is no dynamic component presented to the power supply. This is the principal reason why simple gates are used in the CRAY-1. If a more complex integrated circuit package is used, it is impossible to terminate both sides of every gate. So all of the CRAY-1's circuits are perfectly balanced. Five layer boards have one ground layer, two voltage layers, and then the two logic layers on the outside. Twisted pairs which interconnect the modules are balanced and there are equal and opposite signals on both sides of the pairs. The final result is that there is just a purely resistive load to the power supply!

Summary

The design of the CRAY-1 stems from user experience with first generation vector processors and is to some extent, evolved from the 7600 Auerbach [n.d.]. The CRAY-1 is particularly effective at processing short vectors. Its architecture exhibits a balanced approach to both scalar and vector processing. In Keller [1976], the conclusion is drawn that the CRAY-1 in scalar mode is more than twice as fast as the CDC 7600. Such good scalar performance is required in what is often an unvectorizable world.

At the time of this writing, Cray Research has shipped CRAY-1 systems to three customers (Los Alamos Scientific Laboratory, National Center for Atmospheric Research, and the European Center for Medium Range Weather Forecasts) and has contracts to supply three more systems, two to the Department of Defense, and one to United Computing Systems (UCS). Production plans already anticipate shipping one CRAY-1 per quarter. As the population of CRAY-1 computers expands, it will become clear that the CRAY-1 has made a significant step on the way to the general-purpose computers in the future.

References

Auerbach [n.d.]; Calahan, Joy, and Orbits [n.d.]; Computer World [1976]; Keller [1976]; O'Murphy and Wade [1970]; Reeves [1975].

Chapter 45

The TI ASC: A Highly Modular and Flexible Super Computer Architecture[1]

W. J. Watson

Introduction

Early in 1966, a large computer development program was begun by Texas Instruments. The goal for this effort was to provide needed capacity for supporting seismic processing, plus offering a general super computer capability in the support of new markets.

This development has resulted in the Advanced Scientific Computer (ASC)—a highly modular system offering a wide spectrum of computing power and configurability.

Overview of the System

The major subsystems of a typical configuration are shown in Fig. 1: the central memory, the central processor, the peripheral processor, on-line bulk storage, a digital communications interface, plus a selection of standard peripherals.

The peripheral processor has been designed for executing the operating system. The central processor has been designed expressly to provide high computing power for large arrays of data. The central processor operates as a slave to the peripheral processor. This design approach was chosen to maximize the overlapping of system overhead tasks with the execution of user programs. In operation the job stream is analyzed by the peripheral processor. The language processors, plus user object code, are executed by the central processor. System control and I/O tasks are processed by the peripheral processor. I/O is routed through high-speed, head-per-track disc storage. A data communications interface for the common carriers is provided for the support of remote batch and interactive terminals. Standard types of peripherals are also provided. The central memory serves as the common access communications and access storage medium for these subsystems.

Central Memory

The ASC central memory consists of a memory control unit (MCU) and appropriately sized modules of high-speed or

[1]*Proc. AFIPS FICC*, 1972, pp. 221–228. The section on software beginning on p. 759 is excerpted from Dean [1973].

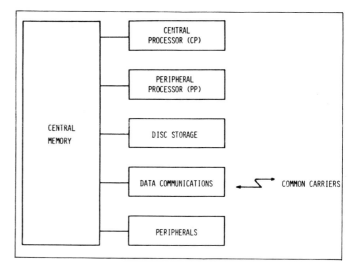

Fig. 1. Major ASC subsystems.

medium-speed central memory. Optionally, a medium-speed central memory extension can be used in conjunction with a high-speed memory.

The MCU is organized as a two-way, 256-bit/channel (8-word) parallel access traffic net between eight independent processor ports having full accessibility to all memories. The nine memory buses are organized to provide eight-way interleaving for the first eight buses with the ninth bus used for the central memory extension. The MCU provides the facilities for controlling access from the eight processor ports to a CM having a 24-bit address space (16 million words). A port expander can be utilized to expand the number of processor ports. Fig. 2 illustrates this structure.

The MCU is designed to operate asynchronously, independent of cable delays, processor clock rates, and memory unit access and cycle times. This capability allows for a great deal of flexibility to accommodate improvements in memory or processor technologies which may be desired. The MCU is capable of handling a maximum data transfer rate of 80 million words per second per port, giving a total transfer capacity of 640M words per second. Therefore, a significant capacity beyond today's memory and processor speeds is available in the MCU.

The semiconductor high-speed central memory modules have a cycle time of 160 ns and a read time of 140 ns. Additionally, all transfers are 256 bits (eight 32-bit words) with a Hamming code providing single-bit error correction and double-bit error detection for each 32-bit word. High-speed central memory is typically divided into eight equal sized modules which permits eight-way interleaving. A patch board within the MCU controls the memory address decoding and sets the interleaving pattern.

The optional central memory extension provides for large

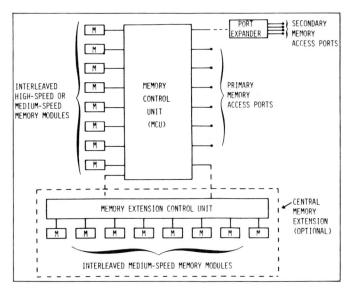

Fig. 2. Modular structure of the ASC central memory.

amounts of relatively economical medium-speed memory to be utilized in support of the high-speed central memory. The memory extension uses 1 μs semiconductor technology and is also accessed in 8-word increments. Single-bit error correction is provided at the 8-word level. The central memory extension is included in the address space of the central memory and, therefore, can be addressed by a processor or channel controller for instructions or operands. It is also possible to effect block transfers of data between high-speed memory and the memory extension. This is possible because both a normal memory bus and a memory access port are provided. Block transfers are initiated by the peripheral processor with the specification of the source starting address, the destination starting address, and the block length. The block transfer proceeds automatically at 40M words per second, and the peripheral processor is notified upon completion.

The central memory size is limited only by the 24-bit address (16 megawords). The proportions of fast memory and memory extension may be varied in order to balance memory capacities to suit the particular system requirements. The present high-speed memory module is modular from 16K to 128K 32-bit words. This permits memories from 128K to one million words to be configured.

Central memory management and access control of memory ports is achieved through the use of two facilities: map registers and protect registers. Each user program has its own unique page address map. Page addresses not required by the program are mapped into absolute page zero which is not accessible to the CP. When a program is loaded into memory, it will likely be loaded

into discontiguous memory pages. During program execution, program developed page addresses are converted, without execution time penalty, to actual page addresses by the map registers. Because a reference to page zero is denied and the relevant processor notified, the map registers provide for inter-user memory protection. Figure 3 shows the mapping scheme. Desired page sizes depend on the amount of central memory and the problem mix of a particular installation. Four different page sizes may be specified for an ASC system, varying from 4K to 256K words. A program may utilize any one of the page sizes available.

The protect registers allow for intra-user protection. These registers consist of three pairs of bounds registers for defining the upper and lower addresses of access for read, write, or execute areas. The five combinations of protection presently used by the system software with the bounds registers are:

- Execute Only
- Read Only
- Execute, Read, No Write
- Read, Write, No Execute
- Read, Write, Execute

An attempt to reference an area out of bounds for a particular control state is denied and the processor notified of the attempted violation.

In large ASC systems, more processors and control units require additional access ports to memory. In these cases memory port expanders are utilized to provide additional ports and are utilized to service the devices not requiring the full bandwidth of a memory port. Each memory access port expander provides a 1:4 expansion with a maximum bandwidth degradation of ten percent;

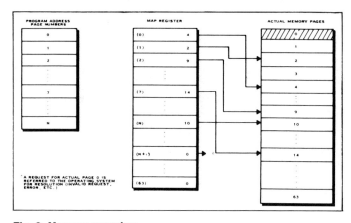

Fig. 3. Memory mapping.

i.e., from 80 million 32-bit words per second to approximately 72 million 32-bit words per second. These expanders can be concatenated to provide further increases in connectivity. Priorities at the single access port interface are resolved on either a fixed or distributed basis. The mode is selected by patch card wiring in the expander hardware.

Central Processor

The central processor (CP) provides both scalar (single operand) and vector (array) instructions at the machine level. The basic instruction size is 32 bits, with 16-, 32-, or 64-bit operands. The single instruction stream, which contains a mixture of scalar and vector instructions, is preprocessed by the instruction processing unit.

The central processor design is such that one, two, three, or four execution units or "pipes" can be provided. These units employ the pipeline concept in both scalar and vector modes. A single execution unit can have up to twelve scalar instructions in process at one time. From one to four vector results can be produced every 60 ns, depending on the number of execution units provided.

The CP has 48 program-addressable registers. This group of 32-bit registers consists of sixteen base address registers, sixteen arithmetic registers, eight index registers, and eight vector parameter registers. This last group is used to extend the instruction format for the complete specification of vector instructions. The basic instruction format is shown as it relates to these register groups in Fig. 4.

The CP scalar instruction repertoire includes an extensive set of Load and Store instructions: halfword, fullword, and doubleword instructions, with immediate, magnitude, and negative operand capabilities. Ability to load and store register files and to load effective addresses is also available. Arithmetic scalars include various adds, subtract, multiply, and divide for halfword (16-bit) and fullword (32-bit) fixed point numbers and fullword and doubleword (64-bit) floating point numbers. Scalar logical instructions are provided as are arithmetic, logical, and circular shifts. Various comparison instructions and combination comparison-logical instructions are provided for halfword, fullword, and doublewords. Many combinations of test and branching instructions with incrementing or decrementing capability are also available. Stacking and modifying arithmetic registers can be done with single instructions. Subroutine linkage is accomplished through Branch and Load instructions. Format conversion for single and doublewords, as well as normalize instructions, are available.

The vector capabilities of the CP are made available through the use of VECTL (vector after loading vector parameter file) and VECT (assumes parameter file is already loaded) instructions. The vector repertoire includes such arithmetic operations as add, subtract, multiply, divide, vector dot product, matrix multiplication, and others for both fixed point and floating point representations. Vector instructions are also available for shifting; logical operations; comparisons; format conversions; normalization; and special operations—such as Merge, Order, Search, Peak Pick, Select and Replace, among others.

One important characteristic of the vector instruction capability is the ability to encompass three dimensions of addressability within a single vector instruction. This is equivalent to a nest of three indexing loops in a conventional machine.

The basic structure of the CP, shown in Fig. 5, has three major components: the instruction processing unit (IPU) for non-arithmetic stages of instruction processing for the CP instruction stream, the memory buffer unit (MBU) to provide operand

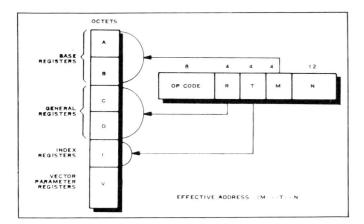

Fig. 4. Instruction format and register groups.

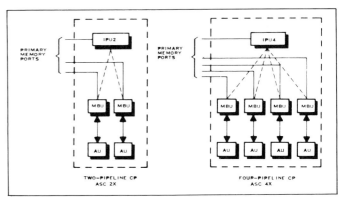

Fig. 5. Basic structure of the CP.

interfacing with the central memory, and an arithmetic unit (AU) to perform the specified arithmetic or logical operations. Figure 5 shows a CP diagram for 2- or 4-pipeline CP's, each with a corresponding number of MBU-AU pairs. Note that a memory port is required for the IPU and, in addition, one memory port for each pipeline (MBU-AU pair) in a CP.

A significant feature of the CP hardware is an operand look-ahead capability which causes memory references to be requested prior to the time of actual need. Double buffering in multiple 8-word (octet) buffers for each pipeline provides a smooth data flow to and from each arithmetic unit. The pipelined AU achieves its highest sustained flow rate in the vector mode, typically a result each 60 ns per AU.

Instruction Processing Unit

The primary function of the instruction processing unit (IPU) is to supply a continuous stream of instructions for execution by the other parts of the CP. One Central Memory port is required to provide the instruction stream. Two 8-word (octet) buffers are utilized to achieve a balanced stream of instructions from memory to the IPU. Instructions are transferred from memory in octets as are all other references to memory for fetching or storing of information.

The following functions are performed by the IPU: (1) instruction fetch, (2) instruction decode, (3) register operand selection, (4) effective address development through indexing and/or indirect addressing, (5) immediate operand development, (6) branch address development, (7) determination of branch condition, (8) storage of AU results into the register file, (9) scalar hazard and register conflict resolution, (10) generation of vector starting addresses, and (11) transmittal of vector parameters to the MBU during vector initialization.

Up to 36 instructions in various stages of execution can be overlapped within the 4-pipe CP. There are twenty positions for instructions in the 2-pipe CP and twelve positions for instructions in the 1-pipe CP. Four levels are contained within the IPU, and eight levels are contained in each arithmetic pipeline (MBU-AU pair). In addition to the previously mentioned functions, the IPU performs routing of instructions to the MBU-AU pairs based on an optimum use of arithmetic unit capability.

Vector processing is altered by software in order to distribute segments of the vector for multiple pipe systems.

Several features are provided to alleviate the potential problems of branches and instruction dependencies in the instruction pipeline. The Prepare-to-Branch instruction, used extensively by the Fortran compiler, increases the execution speed of branches, particularly important in loop iterations. This instruction provides the IPU control hardware with advance address information to facilitate uninterrupted instruction processing. Instruction depen-

dencies are recognized by the hardware. It scans the instruction stream and distributes the independent instructions across MBU-AU pairs to insure proper, yet efficient, execution sequences.

Memory Buffer Unit

The memory buffer unit (MBU) provides an interface between central memory and the arithmetic unit. Its primary function is to supply the arithmetic unit with a continuous stream of operands from memory and to provide for the storing of the results back to memory. Note that all references to memory, whether for fetching or storing, are made in 8-word increments (octets).

The MBU has three double buffers, one octet per buffer, called the "X" and "Y" buffers for input and the "Z" buffers for output. This double buffering is provided so that pipeline processing can be sustained at a high rate with minimal memory access conflicts. These buffers are illustrated in Fig. 6.

During scalar operations, data specified by effective addresses developed in the IPU are fetched or stored as required. The Z buffer can be transferred directly to the X or Y buffers so that memory references are not necessary for scalar operands which reside in the Z buffer.

For most vector operations, two operand data strings are fetched, while a result data string is stored. Addresses for sustaining the vector operations are computed in the MBU using parameters initially specified by the vector parameter file.

Arithmetic Unit

The primary function of a CP arithmetic unit (AU) is to perform the arithmetic operations specified by the operation code of the instruction currently at the AU level. There is one AU per pipeline

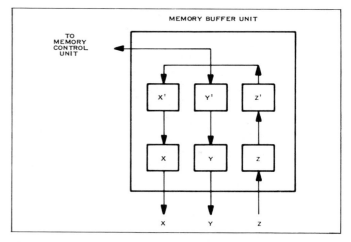

Fig. 6. Multiple operand streams in the memory buffer unit.

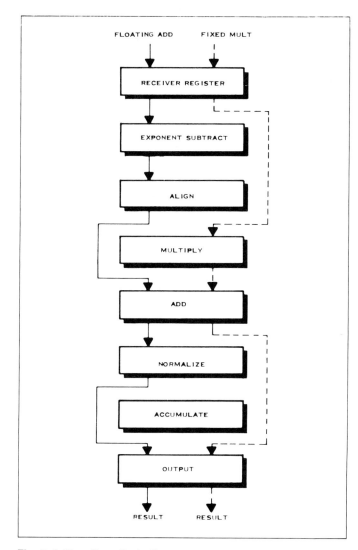

Fig. 7. Arithmetic unit pipeline concept.

in the CP, each having a 60 ns basic cycle time. A distinguishing feature of an AU is the pipeline structure which allows efficient execution of the arithmetic part of all instructions. There are eight exclusive partitions of the AU pipeline involved, each of which can provide an output every 60 ns. These eight sections are (1) receiver register, (2) exponent subtract, (3) align, (4) add, (5) normalize, (6) multiply, (7) accumulate, and (8) output. Figure 7 shows how different sections of the AU are utilized for execution of particular instructions; i.e., floating point addition and fixed point multiplication.

An AU is a 64-bit parallel operating unit for most scalar and vector instructions. Exceptions are double length multiply and all types of division. In these circumstances various combinations of the components of the AU are utilized; and therefore, more than one clock cycle is required to complete these arithmetic operations.

Fixed point negative numbers are represented in two's complement notation, and the floating point representation is hexadecimal with the exponent biased by $40_{(16)}$.

The Peripheral Processor

The peripheral processor (PP) is a powerful multiprocessor designed to perform the control and data management functions of the ASC. Several aspects of the implementation of the peripheral processor concept greatly increase the effectiveness of the ASC system. Figure 8 shows the logical organization of the PP.

The PP is a collection of eight individual processors called virtual processors (VP's). Each VP has its own program counter along with arithmetic, index, base, and instruction registers. The eight VP's share a read only memory, an arithmetic unit, an instruction processing unit, and a central memory buffer. Use of the common units is distributed among the VP's using sixteen single 85 ns cycles. When an equally distributed sequence of time units is used, each of the eight VP's receives two 85 ns cycles every 1.4 μs. The typical PP instruction requires two 85 ns cycles for completion. The distribution of available time units can be dynamically varied to suit particular processing requirements. Figure 9 illustrates two possible distributions.

The read only memory within the PP is utilized for program

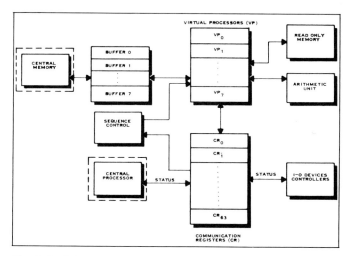

Fig. 8. Peripheral processor.

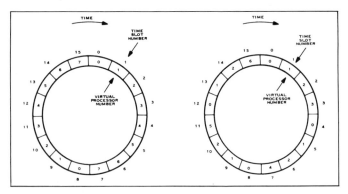

Fig. 9. Two possible VP time slot assignments.

storage and execution of those short routines which are highly utilized by the VP's, such as polling loops. The read only memory consists of up to 4K 32-bit words of non-volatile memory elements with a cycle time of less than 85 ns. It is modular in 256-word increments.

Because the PP is intended to perform control functions rather than execute mathematical algorithms, the instruction set is oriented toward control operations and does not require multiplication, division, or floating point operations. The instruction format is similar to that of the central processor, using a 32-bit word for each instruction. Instructions are provided for bit (1 bit), byte (8 bits), halfword (16 bits), and fullword (32 bits) operations.

Each VP has direct access to the entire central memory for program execution and data storage. Therefore, a single copy of reentrant code can be executed simultaneously by more than one VP.

The communications register (CR) file contains sixty-four 32-bit word registers which are program addressable by the VP's. The CR file serves as the principal storage medium for control information necessary for the coordination of all parts of the ASC system. Synchronization of communications is achieved between all processors (CP, VP's channel controllers, and peripheral unit controllers) from interpretation of status bits received from all devices into the CR file.

Disc Storage

Disc storage is the principal secondary storage system for the ASC system. Disc storage consists of head-per-track (H/T) disc systems supplemented by positioning-arm disc (PAD) systems.

Head-per-Track (H/T) Disc System

The H/T disc system is a high-performance device whose effective performance is further enhanced because the operating system utilizes a shortest-access-time-first (SATF) algorithm [Denning, 1967] for data transfers. This combination of hardware and software provides a very high effective transfer rate. Each H/T disc module has a capacity of 25 million 32-bit words with a transfer rate of approximately 500K words per second. Using the shortest-access-time-first algorithm, access time will average approximately 5 ms which results in an exceptionally fast "effective" transfer rate. The rotational period of the disc is 32 ms. Each H/T disc module has seven discs with fourteen surfaces. Two surfaces of the module are used as alternate storage for inoperative sections. For data ordering purposes, the discs are divided into bands and then further subdivided into sectors of 64 words each.

Positioning-Arm Disc (PAD) System

The PAD system, when utilized to supplement head per track, is available in a variety of configurations. Control of PAD systems is achieved by use of channel interface, disc controller, and disc interface units. From two to eight PAD disc drives may be attached to a set of control devices. The number of controllers and discs per controller will depend upon the storage and retrieval problem requirements.

The PAD system has a transfer rate of 200K words per second and a storage capacity of 25M words per disc drive. Access time is divided into two categories: positioning-arm time which is 30 ms average with a maximum of 55 ms and average rotational latency which is 8.4 ms. Thus, average total access time is approximately 38 ms.

Data Communications

The data communication system is very modular and, thus, externally flexible in the various devices which may be utilized for communication with the ASC. Data communications are controlled by a data concentrator which, in turn, interfaces to the MCU through a channel control device.

Data Concentrator

The data concentrator is a TI-980 minicomputer equipped with special-purpose hardware communication interface units on its direct memory access ports. The TI-980 is a small, general-purpose computer with up to 64K 16-bit words of memory and a one-microsecond cycle time. The data concentrator hardware is under control of a data communications operating system which executes in the TI-980. This operating system provides for the functions of buffering, reformating, routing, protocol handling, error control and recovery procedures, and system control messages. The system services multiple stations concurrently.

The data communications system presently supports communication with three types of stations: high-performance user terminals, other large computers, and remote concentrators. The system can be easily extended to support smaller terminals down to the teletype level. These stations may be either remote or local. When local, the communication link is implemented with multiple conductor cables. Since the transfer is asynchronous by word, the average transfer rate is very dependent upon cable length with a maximum transfer rate of 250,000 words per second for distances less than 500 feet.

Remote Links

Remote links are presently implemented with non-switched, full duplex common carrier data transmission facilities. Data is transferred over these links synchronously at rates determined by the modems and common carrier bandwidths. The data communication system supports transfer rates up to a maximum of 240,000 bits per second. Because the system supports full duplex transmission, this capacity typically translates to the ability to support a 1200 lpm printer simultaneously with a 1000 cpm reader over a 9600 bps transmission facility.

Peripherals

Standard types of magnetic tape drives, card equipment, and printers have been interfaced with the ASC. These interfaces are attached to primary or secondary memory ports through a variety of standard selected and multiplexed data channels.

Summary

Preservation of global system modularity concepts in the design of the ASC has resulted in a capability for configuring systems having a very wide range of cost and capabilities.

In the memory area capacity, performance, connectivity, protection, and mapping are all variable over wide bounds. The central processor can be tailored to provide a wide range of processing power by using one, two, three, or four pipes.

The peripheral processor provides for dynamically matching the execution rates of up to eight independent instruction streams with the task requirements. The highly flexible communication register file provides a matrix of 2048 bits which can be manipulated and sensed by the eight virtual processors. Flexible hardware interfaces are provided for coupling these bits to external I/O signal lines. Finally, the modular read only program memory of the peripheral processor accommodates growth and modifications in read only memory resident operating system code.

An example of a complete system configuration is illustrated in Fig. 10.

Software[1]

At the beginning of the software design effort, several goals were established which have directed the development effort. It was desired that the system support multi-programming, local and remote batch processing, as well as multiple users of the previously mentioned interactive terminals. It was considered important that the powerful central processor be reserved for the scientific computations for which it was designed and that as much as possible of the "overhead" function be performed in the Peripheral Processor Unit. It was determined that the first users of the ASC had a significant investment in Fortran coded programs. Fortran was thus selected as the first high level scientific language and it was important that the compiler produce highly efficient object code with no change in the source. It was required that an extensive file management system be provided with special emphasis on privacy of files. It was desired that the services and facilities of the system—both hardware and software—be made available to the user in a simple and straightforward manner. Simple jobs should require only minimal user descriptions and knowledge of the inner workings of the operating system should not be a requirement for the efficient use of the ASC system. Finally, it was recognized that each installation has somewhat different workload and priority requirements. Anticipating that some of these requirements might be over-looked in the initial design, it was thus considered important that the system be modular and easily modified to meet each installations' particular needs.

In the following paragraphs a description of the ASC Fortran is given.

ASC Fortran

As was mentioned as a design goal, the ASC Fortran was designed to accept previously coded Fortran programs. As such, it contains ANSI Fortran and Fortran IV as a part of its language, but also contains certain extensions. The compiler is designed to optimize the execution of the object code on the ASC. It also performs an extensive diagnostic analysis complete with a set of appropriate output messages.

In the area of extensions, two new features are worthy of special mention. These are the subarray and array cross section. The following example illustrates the concepts using three dimensional

[1]The section from here to the end of this chapter is excerpted from L. C. Dean, "Texas Instructments Advanced Scientific Computer," *Informatie jaargang*, vol. fifteen, no. 4, April 1973, pp. 191–193.

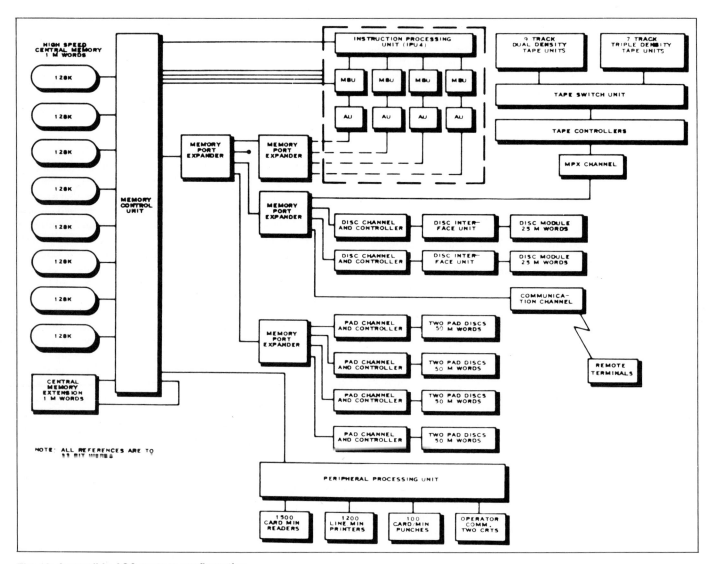

Fig. 10. A possible ASC system configuration.

arrays, although both subarray and array cross section may be applied to arrays up to a dimension of seven.

Dimension A (50, 20, 30)

•

•

– – – – A (∗, ∗, 13) – – –

•

•

Subarray C (4, 5, 8) at A (23, 2, 11)

As shown, the "parent" array, A, is dimensioned as (50, 20, 30). If in an executable statement of the Fortran source code, the array A(∗, ∗, 13) appears, it means the array consisting of all points lying in the 13th "plane" of the array A. Thus the asterisk in a given subscript position means to vary that subscript over its defined range of values in the conventional order. The array cross section may also be used as A (∗, ∗, J) where the array defined depends upon the current value of J.

The subarray statement defines a three-dimensional subset C of A, with dimensions (4, 5, 8), with the point C (1, 1, 1) at A (23, 2, 11). The subarray statement may also be used as: Subarray C(I, J,

K) at A (L, M, N) by (P, Q, R) where the current values of I, J, K determine the size of the array C, where the current values of L, M, N determine the position of C within A, and where P, Q, R determine the increments to be used on the subscripts of A to determine the values in the array C. This latter feature allows the array C to be "less dense" than the parent array A. It has particular utility when iterative procedures are used and larger "grid" spacing is desired at early stages of the iteration.

Both the array cross section and the subarray statement are powerful new tools to the Fortran programmer. They not only allow for more efficient memory utilization and minimize the memory to memory data movement, but they allow the programmer to formulate his array processing problem in a more direct and convenient manner. Both of these extensions are presently under consideration by the X3J3 Standards Committee. They have been approved "in principle" by this committee.

Optimization algorithms within the compiler include such conventional areas as constant propagation, elimination of redundant sub-expressions, reduction in operator strength, register assignment, and removal of loop constant assignment statements and loop constant expressions from DO loops. Further, it includes paired memory fetching techniques, retention of intermediate values, and extensive re-ordering of instructions for optimum "pipe-line" flow.

One of the most powerful procedures in the optimization algorithms is the automatic conversion of scalar source code into vector instructions. The most frequently occurs within DO loops and often results in the complete elimination of software indexing. Figure 11 is an illustration of this process. In Example 1 of this illustration, the source code appears in standard Fortran. In example 2, the array cross-section feature is used. In example 3, pure vector representation is employed. Regardless of the source code, the ASC Compiler will produce a single vector instruction in the object code. In addition to this vectorization, the Compiler uses vector instructions for assignment statements where possible, and provides extensive analysis to optimize memory referencing (e.g., loop reversal and re-ordering).

Figure 12 is an illustration of this type of analysis. The original source code is given in example 1 of that illustration. If no vector instructions or memory optimation were employed, the object code would require approximately 20,000 clocks. Vectorization yields a reduction to 2351 clocks, almost a 10:1 improvement. By reversing the order of the loops and using temporary storage, the execution time can be reduced to 880 clocks even though two passes through memory are employed. In example 3, the loops are reversed and one is inverted, yielding a further reduction and eliminating the need for temporary storage. Finally, in example 4, loops are both inverted and reversed yielding an execution of 437 clocks. Since 400 items are to be moved this result is probably near optimum (only 37 clocks of "overhead"). This example is obviously a simple one involving only the movement of data, but it illustrates the kind of analysis performed by the ASC Compiler in optimizing memory references.

To allow maximum use of mathematical functions within instructions which can or should be vectorized, both scalar and

---

Dimension M(3,3), N(3,3)
Integer K
•
•
•
Example 1.   DO 10 J = 1,3
              DO 10 I = 1,3
          10 N (I, J) = M(I, J)−K
•
Example 2.   DO 10 J = 1,3
          10 N(*,J) = M(*,J)−K
•
Example 3.   N = M−K

Fig. 11

---

1 Basic problem
     Dimension A(25,25)
     DO 10 I = 1,20
     DO 10 J = 1,20
 10 A(I,J+ 1) = A(I+1,J)

2 Reversal of loops
   Reversal of loops introduces fault. This can be circumvented by introduction of temporary vector.
     DO 10 J = 1,20
     DO 10 I = 1,20
 10 T(I,J) = A(I+1,J)
     DO 20 J+1,20
     DO 20 I = 1,20
 20 A(I,J+1) = T(I,J)

3 Loops reversed and inverted
   This removes the fault without introducing temporary vector.
     DO 10 J = 1,20
     DO 10 I = 1,20
 10 A(I,22−J) = A(I+1,21−J)

4 Loops reversed and both inverted
   This has properties of solution 3 but makes better use of memory.
     DO 10 J = 1,20
     DO 10 I = 1,20
 10 A(21−I,22−J) = A(22−I,21−J)

Fig. 12. Vector optimization.

"vector" mathematical subroutines are provided. This allows such functions as "cosine" to have meaning when the argument is an array. For example, COS (A) means: compute the cosine function for every element of A when A is an array.

In general, this will give a performance improvement of between 6:1 and 8:1 (depending on the mathematical function) over repeated calls to the scalar math routines. There is a slightly higher overhead in set up time for the vector math routines, but it appears that the cross-over point is about six elements, i.e., if the number of arguments is greater than six, it is faster to use the vector math pack version.

References

Dean [1973]; Denning [1967].

Part 4

Family Range, Compatibility, and Evolution

The relentless pace of technology has fostered the concept of computer systems that are related through some architectural similarity. Such sets of related computer systems form a family. At least three types of computer families have been historically identified.

- Family by evolution. The most primitive relationship is that of *cultural compatibility*. A computer architecture slowly changes over a number of technological generations. The basic architectural concepts remain (e.g., stack versus general-register) while enhancing the architectural functionality. The PMS organization and even the ISP may change. Machine language programs written for one family member will not execute on another family member. Programs written in high-level languages, with little or no changes, are usually transportable between machines. The Burroughs computers (Part 1, Sec. 3), the CDC 6600/7600, the CRAY-1 (Part 3, Sec. 4), and the Hewlett-Packard calculators (Part 4, Sec. 3) are all examples of families by evolution.

- Family for compatibility. The next strongest family tie is that of program compatibility. Successive generations of family members attempt to capture as much existing software as possible. Assembly language–level programs usually execute directly, since each ISP is a proper superset of its predecessor. The machine languages of family members may differ, thus necessitating a reassembly or recompilation of transported programs. Frequently compatibility is also sought at the PMS level so that peripherals, whose technology changes less rapidly than the Pc technology, can be transported between family members. The Intel 8080/8086 (Part 3, Sec. 2), the PDP-8 (Part 4, Sec. 2), and the IBM System/360-System/370 (Part 4, Sec. 5) are examples of families for compatibility.

- Family for range. A family can be planned so that the various members span a wide cost and performance range. Total compatibility is sought so that software (including machine language) written on any family member can execute unmodified on other family members. Peripherals are also interchangeable. Thus the cost of developmental efforts in software, peripherals, documentation, training, and maintenance is shared among all the family members. The PDP-11 (Part 4, Sec. 2), the IBM System/360 (Part 3, Sec. 4), and the IBM System/370 (Part 4, Sec. 5) are examples of families designed for range.

Part 4 focuses on six families ranging from microcomputers to maxicomputers. Each family grew up under a different set of constraints. The evolution of these families and the decisions on how to utilize technology are traced. The range, compatibility, cost, and cost/performance will be analyzed for each family.

Section 1

Microcomputer Families

The Intel 8080 Family

Chapter 37 traces the evolution of the Intel 8080/8086 microcomputer family. The family was unplanned, and new technology was used to enhance both raw performance and functionality. Because of the limits on single-chip complexity when the microcomputer was launched in 1971, the Intel ISP base represented by the Intel 4004 was in many ways more primitive than the PDP-8. Hence ISP-level family constraints were not imposed until the successors to the Intel 8080 were created. These successors sought either machine code–level or assembly language–level compatibility with the Intel 8080 (i.e., the user's symbolic source code for the Intel 8080 could be reassembled for the Intel 8086).

Section 2

Minicomputer Families

The PDP-8 Family

The PDP-8 was the first minicomputer. As with many early second-generation machines, the popularity and longevity of the basic ISP was greatly underestimated. The first applications of new technology focused on price reduction while maintaining constant performance, although the original PDP-8 had a significant performance increase over its predecessor, the PDP-5. The architecture was also subjected to several painful stretches from 1963 to 1979, including:

- Three changes in the physical I/O bus (from negative-polarity logic to positive-polarity logic, then to a unified bus, and finally to a reduced-width microcomputer bus)
- Memory expansion from 4 kilowords to 32 kilowords, and finally to 128 kilowords

- ISP enhancements, including multiply-divide, and, finally, floating-point instruction sets

The PDP-8 family history (Chap. 46) is an excellent example of the problems with maintaining a family with limited growth potential (primarily due to the simple ISP) through several technological generations.

The PDP-11 and VAX-11 Family

As the System/360 was IBM's follow-on to the 7090 series, the PDP-11 was DEC's follow-on to PDP-8. The PDP-11 also represents a planned family, although one not as tightly controlled as the System/360 (see Chap. 47). The implementation tradeoffs among the PDP-11 models is discussed in Chap. 39, where a simple two-parameter model is developed which relates technology and implementation techniques to performance. The model fits PDP-11 data as well as System/360 and System/370 data.

It is interesting to note that a PDP-11 now fits on a small number of LSI chips (e.g., four) and DEC has developed a semantically richer ISP, the VAX-11/780 ISP (Chap. 42).

Chapter 46

The PDP-8 Family[1]

C. G. Bell / J. E. McNamara

Figure 1 depicts the PDP-8 family tree. The family ancestry began with the Laboratory Instrument Computer (LINC) initially built at the MIT Lincoln Laboratory in 1962, which, incidentally, we believe was the earliest personal computer. DEC began manufacturing LINC's in 1965. Eventually a PDP-8 and LINC were combined in a dual processor called the LINC-8.

In 1962, the need arose to produce a replacement for an analog monitoring system as a front end to a reactor control complex. A 12-bit real time control computer, the PDP-5, was constructed.

[1]Abstracted from C. G. Bell, J. C. Mudge, and J. E. McNamara, *Computer Engineering: A DEC View of Hardware Systems Design*, Digital Press, Maynard, Mass., 1978, pp. 175–208.

The analog nature of the initial application was addressed by building an analog-to-digital converter into the Accumulator. The concept of an I/O bus was introduced instead of the radial I/O structure of previous DEC designs. The I/O Bus permitted equipment options to be added incrementally from a zero base instead of having the pre-allocated space, wiring, and cable drivers that characterized the radial structure. This lowered the entry cost of the system and simplified the later reconfiguring of machines in the field.

Although the design was optimized around the 4-Kword memory, the PDP-5 ultimately evolved to 32-Kword configurations using a memory extension unit. Similarly, although the base machine design did not include built-in multiply and divide functions, these were added later in the form of an Extended Arithmetic Element.

While the PDP-5 had been a reasonably successful computer, it soon became evident that a new machine capable of far greater performance was required. New logic technology promised a substantial speed improvement, and new core memory technology was becoming available that would permit the memory cycle

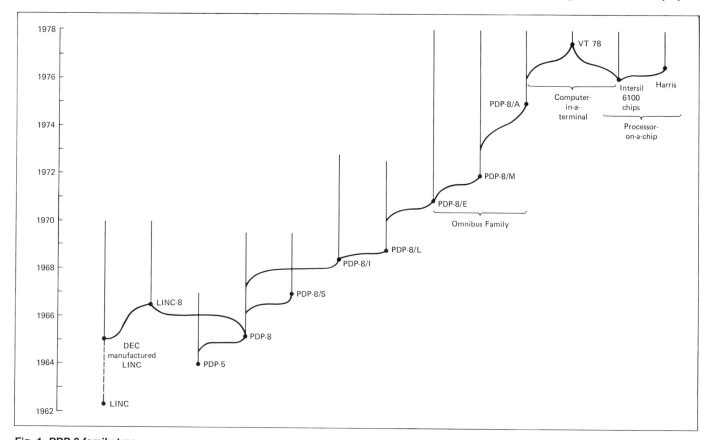

Fig. 1. PDP-8 family tree.

time to be shortened from 6 microseconds in the PDP-5 to 1.6 microseconds in the new machine. In addition, the cost of logic was now low enough so that the program counter could be moved from the memory to a separate register, substantially reducing instruction execution times. The new machine was called the PDP-8.

The new 12-bit machine was only half the size of its predecessor, occupying only half a cabinet. The net small size meant that the PDP-8 was the first true minicomputer. It could be placed on top of a lab bench or built into equipment. It was this latter property that was the most important, as it laid the groundwork for the original equipment manufacturer (OEM) purchase of computers to be integrated into total systems sold by the OEM.

Like its predecessor the PDP-5, the PDP-8 was a single-address 12-bit computer designed for task environments with minimum arithmetic computing and small primary memory requirements. Typical of these environments were process control applications and laboratory applications such as controlling pulse height analyzers and spectrum analyzers.

The PDP-8 was the first of the "8 Family." A subset, called "Omnibus 8" machines, is introduced later when the PDP-8/E, PDP-8/M, and PDP-8/A machines are discussed. Finally, computers which implement the PDP-8 instruction set in a single complementary metal oxide semiconductor (CMOS) chip will be referred to as "CMOS-8" based systems.

The PDP-8, which was first shipped in April 1965, and the other 8 Family machines that followed it achieved a production status formerly reserved for IBM computers with about 50,000 machines produced by 1979, excluding the CMOS-8 based computers. During the 15 years that these machines have been produced, logic cost per function has decreased by orders of magnitude, permitting the cost of entire systems to be reduced by a factor of 10. Thus, the 8 Family offers a rare opportunity to study the effect of technology on implementations of the same instruction set processor from early second generation to late fourth generation.

The PDP-8 was followed in late 1966 by the PDP-8/S, a cost-reduced version. The PDP-8/S was quite small in size, scarcely larger than a file cabinet drawer. It achieved its low cost by implementing the PDP-8 instruction set in serial fashion. This did reduce the cost, but it so radically reduced the performance that the machine was not a good seller.

In 1968, the PDP-8/I was produced, using medium-scale integration (MSI) integrated circuits to implement the PDP-8 instruction set with better performance than the PDP-8, and at two-thirds the price. For those customers wishing a package with less option mounting space but the same performance, the PDP-8/L was introduced later the same year.

The PDP-8/S, PDP-8/I, and PDP-8/L are mentioned only briefly here because their characteristics were basically dictated by the cost and performance improvements made possible by the emerging integrated circuit technology. The cost and performance figures for these machines are examined in greater detail in Figs. 4 to 8 and Table 1.

Shortly after the introduction of the PDP-8/L, it became evident that customers wanted a faster and more expandable machine. The continuing technological trend toward higher-density logic and some new concepts in packaging made it possible to satisfy both of these requirements but to still produce a new machine that would be cheaper than its predecessor. The new machine was the PDP-8/E. The PDP-8/E incorporated an adapter for interconnecting to PDP-8/I and PDP-8/L I/O devices. In addition, signal converters were available for interconnecting to the older PDP-5, PDP-8, and PDP-8/S I/O devices. Thus it was not necessary to design a complete new set of options at the time the machine was introduced, and existing customers could upgrade to the new computer without having to buy new peripherals. The reason for using an adapter to connect to existing I/O devices was that the PDP-8/E featured a new unified-bus I/O Bus implementation called the Omnibus.

The Omnibus, which is still in use in the PDP-8/A, has 144 pins, of which 96 are defined as Omnibus signals. The remainder are power and ground. The large number of signals permit a great number of intraprocessor communications links as well as I/O signals to be accommodated. The Omnibus signals can be grouped as follows:

1   Master timing to all components

2   Processor state information to the console

3   Processor request to memory for instructions and data

4   Processor to I/O device commands and data transfer

5   I/O device to processor, signaling completion (interrupts)

6   I/O Direct Memory Access control for both direct and Three Cycle Data Break transfers

The approximately 30 signals in groups 4 and 5 provide programmed I/O capability. There are about 50 signals in group 6 to provide the Direct Memory Access capability. These 80 signals are nearly equivalent in quantity and function to the preceding PDP-8 I/O Bus design, making the conversion from Omnibus structure to PDP-8/I and PDP-8/L I/O equipment very simple.

The processor for the PDP-8/E occupied three 8- × 10-inch boards; 4 Kwords of core memory took up three more boards; a memory shield board, a terminator board, a teleprinter control board, and the console board completed the minimum system configuration. Thus, a total of ten 8- × 10-inch boards formed a complete system. The three-board PDP-8/E processor, occupying 240 in², was in striking contrast to the 100-board PDP-5 processor, which occupied 2,100 in².

The PDP-8/E implementation was determined by the availability of integrated circuits. Multiplexers, register files, and basic arithmetic logic units performed the basic operations in a straightforward fashion using a simple sequential controller. Microprogrammed control was not feasible because suitable read-only memories were not available. Integrated circuit read-only memories available at that time were too small, holding only about 64 bits.

The PDP-8/E was mounted in a chassis which had space and power to accommodate two blocks of Omnibus slots. Thirty-eight modules could be mounted in the slots, allowing space for the processor and almost 30 peripheral option controllers. Many customers wanted to build the PDP-8/E into small cabinets and have it control only a few things. They found the large chassis and its associated price to be more than they wanted. To reach this market, the PDP-8/M was designed.

THE PDP-8/M was essentially a PDP-8/E cut in half. The cabinet had half the depth of a PDP-8/E, and the power supply was half as big. There were 18 slots available, enough for the basic processor-memory system and about eight options. The processor was the same as that for a PDP-8/E.

By 1975, DEC had been building "hex" size printed circuit boards. The hex boards were 8 × 15 inches, half again as big as the "quad" boards used in the PDP-8/E and PDP-8/M, which were 8 × 10 inches. The dimensional difference was along the contact side of the board. A hex board had six sets of 36 contacts while the quad board had only four sets. Semiconductor memory chips had also become available, so a new machine was designed to utilize the larger boards and new memories to extend the PDP-8/E, PDP-8/M to a new, lower price range. The new machine was the PDP-8/A. The PDP-8/A processor and register transfer diagram is shown in Fig. 2.

The hex modules permitted some of the peripheral controller options that had occupied several boards in the PDP-8/E to fit on a single board in the PDP-8/A. The availability of hex boards and of larger semiconductor read-only memories permitted the PDP-8/A processor to use microprogrammed control and fit onto a single board. It should be noted here that when a logic system occupies more than one board, a lot of space on each board is used by etch runs going to the connectors. This was particularly true of the PDP-8/E and PDP-8/M processor boards, due to the contacts on two edges of the boards. When an option is condensed to a single board, more space becomes available than square inch comparisons would at first indicate because many of the etch lines to the contacts are no longer required.

The first PDP-8/A semiconductor memory took only 48 chips (1 Kbit each) to implement 4 Kwords of memory. Memories of 8 Kwords and 16 Kwords were also offered. In 1977, only 96 16-Kbit chips were needed to form a 128-Kword memory. With greater use of semiconductor memory, especially read-only memory, a scheme was devised and added to the PDP-8/A to permit programs written for read-write memory to be run in read-only memory. The scheme adds a 13th bit to the read-only memory to signify that a particular location is actually a location that is both read and written. When the processor detects the assertion of the 13th bit, the processor uses the other 12 bits to address a location in some read-write memory which holds the variable information. This effectively provides an indirect memory reference.

In 1976, an option to improve the speed of floating-point computation was added to the PDP-8/A. This option is a single accumulator floating-point processor occupying two hex boards. It supports 3- or 6-word floating-point arithmetic (12-bit exponent and 24- or 60-bit fraction) and 2-word double precision 24-bit arithmetic. As a completely independent processor with its own instruction set processor, it has its own program counter and eight index registers. The performance, approximately equal to that of an IBM 360 Model 40, provides what is probably the highest performance/cost ratio of any computer.

More Omnibus 8 computers (PDP-8/E, PDP-8/M, PDP-8/A) have been constructed than any of the previous models. The high demand for this model appears to be due to the basic simplicity of the design, together with the ability of the user to easily build rather arbitrary system configurations.

In 1976, Intersil offered the first PDP-8 processor to occupy a single chip, using CMOS technology. (Here we should note that an internal to DEC processor-on-a-chip effort, the PDP-8/B, yielded a design in 1973.) DEC verified that it was a PDP-8 and began to apply it to a product in the fall of 1976. In the meantime, in additon to Intersil, Harris Semiconductor became a second source of chip supply for DEC.

The CMOS-8 processor block diagram is given in Fig. 3. The block diagram looks very much like a conventional PDP-8/E processor design using medium scale integrated circuits. It has a common data path for manipulating the Program Counter (PC), Memory Address (MA), Multiplier-Quotient (MQ), Accumulator (AC), and Temporary (Temp) registers. The Instruction Register (IR), however, does not share the common arithmetic logic unit (ALU). Register transfers, including those to the "outside world," are controlled by a programmable logic array (PLA), as indicated by the dotted lines in the figure.

While the CMOS-8 is the first DEC processor to be built on a single chip, the most interesting thing about it is the systems configurations that it makes possible. It is not only small in size (a single 40-pin chip), but it also has miniscule power requirements due to its CMOS construction. Thus, some very compact systems can be built using it.

An excellent example of the use of a CMOS-8 as part of a packaged system is the VT78 video terminal. The goals for this terminal were to drastically reduce costs by including the keyboard, cathode ray tube, and processor in a single package the

Table 1   Characteristics of PDP-8 Family Computers

	PDP-5	PDP-8	PDP-8/S	PDP-8/I
Project start, first ship	9/63	4/65	9/66	4/68
Goals	Lowest cost computer, interfaceability	Cost, much greater performance	Cost; tabletop	Better cost, more function than 8
Applications	Process control monitoring; laboratory	+message switch control Lab processing for instruments	Standalone calculator	Remote job entry station, TSS/8
Innovations/improvements	I/O bus; ISP	Wire-wrap; producible; low cost bit-sample communications controller	Serial implementation	Integrated circuits
Processor + 4 Kword memory (K$)	25.8	16.2	8.79	11.6
Same + terminal (K$)	27.0	18.0	9.99	12.8
Price/memory word ($)	1.83	1.83	0.73	1.46
Processor + 8 Kword + terminal + mass storage	51.1	38.8	30.4	28.9
Memory cycle time	6.0	1.6	8.0	1.5
Processor Mwords accessed/s	0.1	0.63	0.04	0.67
Processor bits accessed/s/$	93	466	55	651
Performance/price improvement (over predecessor)	....	5.0	0.12	11.8
Price improvement	....	1.6	1.84	0.76
Performance improvement	....	6.3	0.06	16.75
Product life (years)	3	5	3	3
Programmed I/O bus	49	49	43 + Bus	40
DMA I/O bus	49	49	49	50

size of an ordinary terminal. The CMOS-8 chip and high density RAM chips made this possible. To form a complete, stand-alone computer system that supports five terminals, mass storage was added. Because the mass storage was floppy disks, it was not in the terminal but in a small cabinet. Even without the mass storage, however, the VT78 forms an "intelligent terminal." An intelligent terminal is usually defined to include a computer whose program can be loaded (usually via a communications line) to take on a variety of characteristics—i.e., it can learn. An intelligent terminal can be used either as part of a network or as a stand-alone computer system. In the former case, the application is determined by the network to which the terminal is attached, but in the latter case, the terminal functions as a desk-top computer running various PDP-8 software.

PDP-8/L	PDP-8/E	PDP-8/M	PDP-8/A	VT78
11/68	3/71	6/72	1/75	6/77
Lower cost	Easy to configure; more functions better performance	Lower cost, limited system	Lower cost higher density	Cost; complete system in a terminal
	+Business data processing, testing;		Computer-in-a-desk	Word processing; desk-top computer, terminal
Less package	Omnibus		Semiconductor memory; floating-point processor	Processor-on-a-chip; low power
7.0	4.99	3.69	2.6	NA
8.5	6.49	5.19	4.1	NA
0.98	0.73	0.61	33.0	NA
24.1	15.3	....	....	11.6
1.6	1.3	1.3	1.5	3.6
0.63	0.76	0.76	0.67	0.28
1080	1828	2472	3092	....
1.65	1.69	1.35	1.25	....
1.66	1.4	1.35	1.42	....
0.94	1.23	1.0	0.87	0.42
3	7+	5+	2+	....
30	96	8E	8E	5 connectors
50	....	....	....	....

Technology, Price, and Performance of the 12-Bit Family

The PDP-8 has been re-implemented 10 times with new technology, from early second-generation to late fourth-generation, over a period of 15 years. Its implementations have included a minimal minicomputer and a minimal microcomputer. The performance characteristics of these implementations are given in Fig. 4. New technology can be utilized in the computer industry in three ways: lower cost implementations as constant performance and functionality, higher performance implementations at constant cost, implementation of new basic structures. Of these three ways, the PDP-8 Family has primarily used lower cost implementations of constant performance and functionality.

The points in Fig. 5 are arranged to show the cost trends of

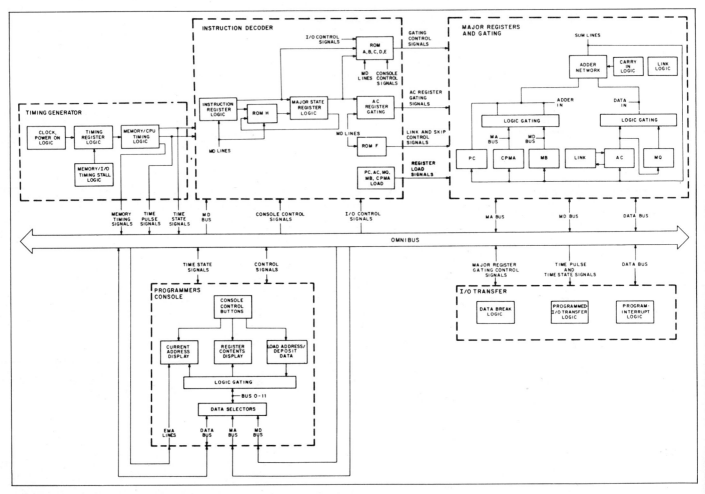

Fig. 2. PDP-8/A processor and register transfer diagram.

three configurations. The first configuration is merely a central processor with 4 Kwords of primary memory. The second configuration adds a console terminal, and the third configuration adds DECtapes or floppy disks for file storage. Note that the basic system represented in the first configuration has declined in price most rapidly: 22 percent per year in the early days and 15 percent per year in recent years. The price of primary memory, on the other hand, has declined at the rate of 19 percent per year, as seen in Fig. 6.

The price and performance trajectories for the PDP-8 family of machines are plotted in Fig. 7, with lines of constant price/performance separated at factors of 2. Note that the early implementations had significantly lower performance than the original PDP-8. Memory performance and instruction execution performance were directly related in all of these machines except the PDP-5 (which kept the Program Counter in primary memory) and the PDP-8/S (which was a serial machine). Thus, with the design emphasis on lowering the cost with each new machine, performance continued to lag behind that of the PDP-8 until higher speed primary memory was available without a cost penalty. Other performance improvements, such as the addition of floating-point hardware or the addition of a cache, are not treated in this comparative analysis.

Figure 8 gives the performance/price ratio for the PDP-8 Family machines. Setting aside the PDP-5 design point, the improvement for the 12-bit machines has been 22 percent per year.

Rather than try to fit a single exponential to the performance/

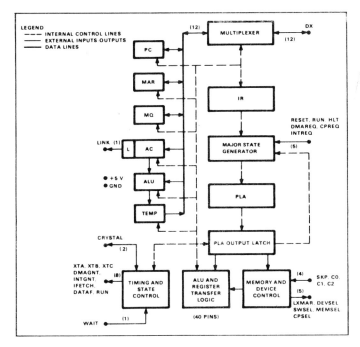

Fig. 3. Block diagram of CMOS-8.

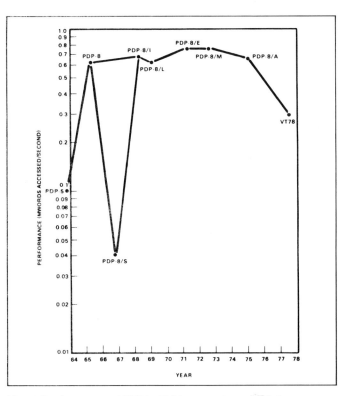

Fig. 4. Performance of DEC's 12-bit computer versus time.

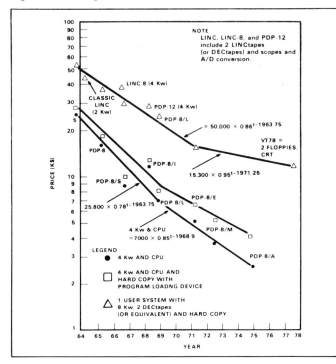

Fig. 5. Price of DEC's 12-bit computers versus time (log).

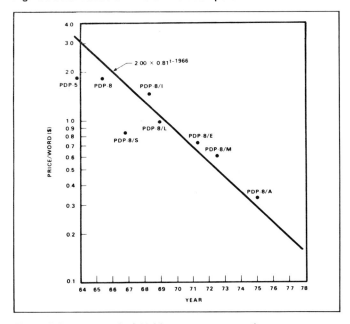

Fig. 6. Price per word of 12-bit memory versus time.

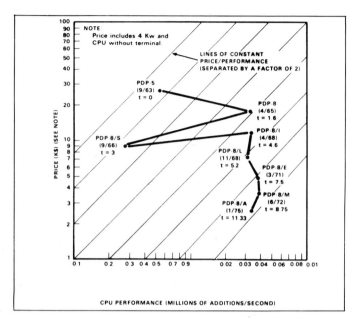

Fig. 7. Price versus performance of DEC's 12-bit computers.

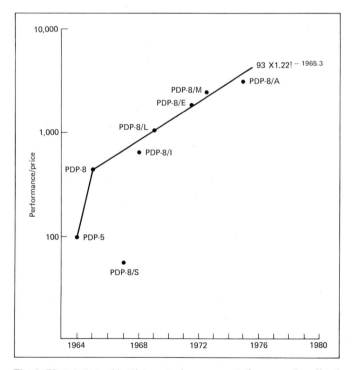

Fig. 8. Bits accessed by the central processor/s/$ versus time (for 4 K word + processor systems).

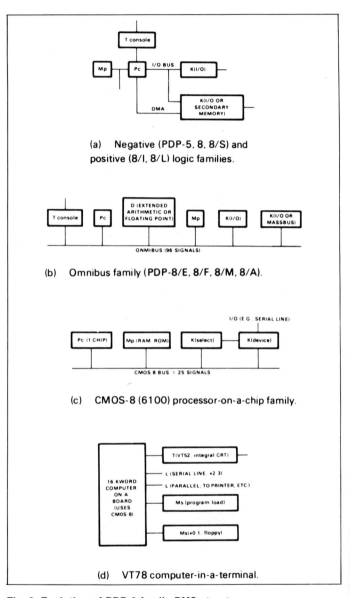

(a)   Negative (PDP-5, 8, 8/S) and positive (8/I, 8/L) logic families.

(b)   Omnibus family (PDP-8/E, 8/F, 8/M, 8/A).

(c)   CMOS-8 (6100) processor-on-a-chip family.

(d)   VT78 computer-in-a-terminal.

Fig. 9. Evolution of PDP-8 family PMS structures.

price data points in Fig. 8, it might be better to try two independent exponentials. The reason for this is that the data points really mark the transition between two generations. The PDP-5 was a mid-second (transistor) generation machine, and the PDP-8 represents a late second generation machine. The PDP-8/I and PDP-8/L were beginning third (integrated circuit) generation designs. These four machines represent a relatively rapid evolution from 1963 to 1968. After the PDP-8/L, the evolution slows somewhat between 1968 and 1977, as medium-scale integrated circuits continued to be the implementation technology, and the cost of packaging and connecting components continued to be controlled by the relatively wide bus structure.

During their evolution, the DEC 12-bit computers have significantly changed in physical structure, as can be seen from the block diagrams in Fig. 9. The machines up through the PDP-8/L had a relatively centralized structure with three buses to interface to memory, program-controlled I/O devices, and Direct Memory Access devices. The Omnibus-8 machines bundled these connections together in a simpler physical structure. The CMOS-8 avoids the wide bus problem by moving the bus to lines on a printed circuit board. The number of interconnection signals on the bus is then reduced by roughly a factor of 4 to about 25 signals which can be brought into and out of the chips within the number of pins available.

Figures 4 and 7 illustrate the oscillating price/performance history of the design evolution summarized below:

1 While the PDP-5 was designed to keep price at a minimum, the PDP-8 had additions to improve the performance while not increasing price significantly over that of a slower speed design. The cost per word was modestly higher with the PDP-8 than with the PDP-5, but the PDP-8 had 6 times the performance of a PDP-5. Thus, the PDP-8 crosses three lines of constant price/performance in Fig. 7.

2 The PDP-8/S was an attempt to achieve a minimum price by using serial logic and a minimum price memory design. However, the performance of the PDP-8/S was low.

3 The market pressures created by PDP-8/S performance probably caused the return to the PDP-8 design, but in an integrated circuit implementation, the PDP-8/I.

4 The PDP-8/I was relatively expensive, so the PDP-8/L was quickly introduced to reduce cost and bring the design into line with market needs and expectations.

5 The PDP-8/E was introduced as a high performance machine that would permit the building of systems larger than those possible with the PDP-8/L.

6 The PDP-8/Mwas a lower cost, smaller cabinet version of the PDP-8/E and was intended to meet the needs of the OEM market.

The design goal of machines subsequent to the PDP-8/M has been primarily one of price reduction. The PDP-8/A was introduced to further reduce cost from the level of the PDP-8/E and PDP-8/M, although some large system configurations are still built with PDP-8/E machines. The CMOS-8 chips represent a substantial cost reduction but also a substantial performance reduction. The CMOS-8 performance is one-third that of a PDP-8/A, so a stand-alone system using a CMOS-8 is less cost-effective than an PDP-8/A when the central processor is used as the only performance criterion. The main reason for using large-scale integration is the reduced cost and smaller package rather than performance. Obviously, the next step is increased performance or more memory, or both more performance and more memory on the same chip.

Chapter 47

The Evolution of the PDP-11[1]

C. G. Bell / J. C. Mudge

In the original 1970 PDP-11 paper (Chap. 38), a set of design goals and constraints were given, beginning with a discussion of the weaknesses frequently found in minicomputers. The designers of the PDP-11 faced each of these known minicomputer weaknesses, and their goals included a solution to each one. This section reviews the original goals, commenting on the success or failure of the PDP-11 in meeting each of them.

The weaknesses of prior designs that were noted were limited addressability, a small number of registers, absence of hardware stack facilities, elementary I/O processing, absence of growth-path family members, and high programming costs.

The first weakness of minicomputers was their limited addressing capability. The biggest (and most common) mistake that can be made in a computer design is that of not providing enough address bits for memory addressing and management. The PDP-11 followed this hallowed tradition of skimping on address bits, but it was saved by the principle that a good design can evolve through at least one major change.

For the PDP-11, the limited address problem was solved for the short run, but not with enough finesse to support a large family of minicomputers. That was indeed a costly oversight, resulting in both redundant development and lost sales. It is extremely embarassing that the PDP-11 had to be redesigned with memory management[2] only two years after writing the paper that outlined the goal of providing increased address space. All earlier DEC designs suffered from the same problem, and only the PDP-10 evolved over a long period (15 years) before a change occurred to increase its address space. In retrospect, it is clear that another address bit is required every two or three years, since memory prices decline about 30 percent yearly, and users tend to buy constant price successor systems.

A second weakness of minicomputers was their tendency to skimp on registers. This was corrected for the PDP-11 by providing eight 16-bit registers. Later, six 64-bit registers were added as the accumulators for floating-point arithmetic. This number seems to be adequate: there are enough registers to allocate two or three registers (beyond those already dedicated to program counter and stack pointer) for program global purposes and still have registers for local statement computation.[3] More registers would increase the context switch time and worsen the register allocation problem for the user.

A third weakness of minicomputers was their lack of hardware stack capability. In the PDP-11, this was solved with the autoincrement/autodecrement addressing mechanism. This solution is unique to the PDP-11, has proved to be exceptionally useful, and has been copied by other designers. The stack limit check, however, has not been widely used by DEC operating systems.

A fourth weakness, limited interrupt capability and slow context switching, was essentially solved by the Unibus interrupt vector design. The basic mechanism is very fast, requiring only four memory cycles from the time an interrupt request is issued until the first instruction of the interrupt routine begins execution. Implementations could go further and save the general registers, for example, in memory or in special registers. This was not specified in the architecture and has not been done in any of the implementations to date. VAX-11 provides explicit load and save process context instructions.

A fifth weakness of earlier minicomputers, inadequate character handling capability, was met in the PDP-11 by providing direct byte addressing capability. String instructions were not provided in the hardware, but the common string operations (move, compare, concatenate) could be programmed with very short loops. Early benchmarks showed that this mechanism was adequate. However, as COBOL compilers have improved and as more understanding of operating systems string handling has been obtained, a need for a string instruction set was felt, and in 1977 such a set was added.

A sixth weakness, the inability to use read-only memories as primary memory, was avoided in the PDP-11. Most code written for the PDP-11 tends to be reentrant without special effort by the programmer, allowing a read-only memory (ROM) to be used directly. Read-only memories are used extensively for bootstrap loaders, program debuggers, and for simple functions. Because large read-only memories were not available at the time of the original design, there are no architectural components designed specifically with large ROMs in mind.

A seventh weakness, one common to many minicomputers, was primitive I/O capabilities. The PDP-11 answers this to a certain extent with its improved interrupt structure, but the completely general solution of I/O computers has not yet been implemented. The I/O processor concept is used extensively in display processors, in communication processors, and in signal processing.

---

[1]Excerpted from C. G. Bell, J. C. Mudge, and J. E. McNamara, *Computer Engineering: A DEC View of Hardware Systems Design*, Digital Press, Maynard, Mass., 1978, pp. 379–408.

[2]The memory management served two other functions besides expanding the 16-bit processor-generated addresses into 18-bit Unibus addresses: program relocation and protection.

[3]Since dedicated registers are used for each Commercial Instruction Set (CIS) instruction, this was no longer true when CIS was added.

Having a single machine instruction that transmits a block of data at the interrupt level would decrease the central processor overhead per character by a factor of 3; it should have been added to the PDP-11 instruction set for implementation on all machines. Provision was made in the 11/60 for invocation of a micro-level interrupt service routine in writable control store (WCS), but the family architecture is yet to be extended in this direction.

Another common minicomputer weakness was the lack of system range. If a user had a system running on a minicomputer and wanted to expand it or produce a cheaper turnkey version, he frequently had no recourse, since there were often no larger and smaller models with the same architecture. The PDP-11 has been very successful in meeting this goal.

A ninth weakness of minicomputers was the high cost of programming caused by programming in lower level languages. Many users programmed in assembly language, without the comfortable environment of high-level languages, editors, file systems, and debuggers available on bigger systems. The PDP-11 does not seem to have overcome this weakness, although it appears that more complex systems are being successfully built with the PDP-11 than with its predecessors, the PDP-8 and the PDP-15. Some systems programming is done using higher level languages; however, the optimizing compiler for BLISS-11 at first ran only on the PDP-10. The use of BLISS has been slowly gaining acceptance. It was first used in implementing the FORTRAN-IV PLUS (optimizing) compiler. Its use in PDP-10 and VAX-11 systems programming has been more widespread.

One design constraint that turned out to be expensive, but worth it in the long run, was the necessity for the word length to be a multiple of eight bits. Previous DEC designs were oriented toward 6-bit characters, and DEC had a large investment 1n 12-, 18-, and 36-bit systems.

Microprogrammability was not an explicit design goal, partially because fast, large, and inexpensive read-only memories were not available at the time of the first implementation. All subsequent machines have been microprogrammed, but with some difficulty because some parts of the instruction set processor, such as condition code setting and instruction register decoding, are not ideally matched to microprogrammed control.

The design goal of understandability seems to have received little attention. The PDP-11 was initially a hard machine to understand and was marketable only to those with extensive computer experience. The first programmers' handbook was not very helpful. It is still unclear whether a user without programming experience can learn the machine solely from the handbook. Fortunately, several computer science textbooks [Gear, 1974; Eckhouse, 1975; Stone and Siewiorek, 1975] and other training books have been written based on the PDP-11.

Structural flexibility (modularity) for hardware configurations was an important goal. This succeeded beyond expectations and is discussed extensively in the Unibus Cost and Performance section.

Evolution of the Instruction Set Processor

Designing the instruction set processor level of a machine—that collection of characteristics such as the set of data operators, addressing modes, trap and interrupt sequences, register organization, and other features visible to a programmer of the bare machine—is an extremely difficult problem. One has to consider the performance (and price) ranges of the machine family as well as the intended applications, and difficult tradeoffs must be made. For example, a wide performance range argues for different encodings over the range; for small systems a byte-oriented approach with small addresses is optimal, whereas larger systems require more operation codes, more registers, and larger addresses. Thus, for larger machines, instruction coding efficiency can be traded for performance.

The PDP-11 was originally conceived as a small machine, but over time its range was gradually extended so that there is now a factor of 500 in price ($500 to $250,000) and memory size (8 Kbytes to 4 Mbytes[1]) between the smallest and largest models. This range compares favorably with the range of the IBM System 360 family (4 Kbytes to 4 Mbytes). Needless to say, a number of problems have arisen as the basic design was extended.

Chronology of the Extensions

A chronology of the extensions is given in Table 1. Two major extensions, the memory management and the floating point, occurred with the 11/45. The most recent extension is the Commercial Instruction Set, which was defined to enhance performance for the character string and decimal arithmetic data-types of the commercial languages (e.g., COBOL). It introduced the following to the PDP-11 architecture:

1 Data-types representing character sets, character strings, packed decimal strings, and zoned decimal strings.

2 Strings of variable length up to 65 Kcharacters.

3 Instructions for processing character strings in each data-type (move, add, subtract, multiply, divide).

4 Instructions for converting among binary integers, packed decimal strings, and zoned decimal strings.

5 Instructions to move the descriptors for the variable length strings.

The initial design did not have enough operation code space to

[1]Although 22 bits are used, only 2 megabytes can be utilized in the 11/70.

Table 1   Chronology of PDP-11 Instruction Set Processor (ISP) Evolution

Model(s)	Evolution
11/20	Base ISP (16-bit virtual address) and PMS (16-bit processor physical memory address) Unibus with 18-bit addressing
11/20	Extended Arithmetic Element (hardware multiply/divide)
11/45 (11/55,11/70, 11/60,11/34)	Floating-point instruction set with 6 additional registers (46 instructions) in the Floating-Point Processor
11/45 (11/55,11/70)	Memory management (KT11C). 3 modes of protection (Kernel, Supervisor, User); 18-bit processor physical addressing; 16-bit virtual addressing in 8 segments for both instruction and data spaces
11/45 (11/55,11/70)	Extensions for second set of general registers and program interrupt request
11/40 (11/03)	Extended Instruction Set for multiply/divide; floating-point instruction set (4 instructions)
11/40 (11/34,11/60)	Memory Management (KT11D), 2 modes of protection (Kernel, User); 18-bit processor physical addressing; 16-bit virtual addressing in 8 segments
11/70	22-bit processor physical addressing; Unibus map for peripheral controller 22-bit addressing
11/70 (11/60)	Error register accessibility for on-line diagnosis and retry (e.g., cache parity error)
11/03 (11/04,11/34)	Program access to processor status register via explicit instruction (versus Unibus address)
11/03	One level program interrupt
11/60	Extended Function Code for invocation of user-written microcode
VAX-11/780	VAX architectural extensions for 32-bit virtual addressing VAX ISP
11/03	Commercial Instruction Set (CIS)
11/70mP	Interprocessor Interrupt and System Timers for multiprocessor

accommodate instructions for new data-types. Ideally, the complete set of operation codes should have been specified at initial design time so that extensions would fit. With this approach, the uninterpreted operation codes could have been used to call the various operation functions, such as a floating-point addition. This would have avoided the proliferation of run-time support systems for the various hardware/software floating-point arithmetic methods (Extended Arithmetic Element, Extended Instruction Set, Floating Instruction Set, Floating-Point Processor). The extracode technique was used in the Atlas and Scientific Data Systems (SDS) designs, but these techniques are overlooked by most computer designers. Because the complete instruction set processor (or at least an extension framework) was unspecified in the initial design, completeness and orthogonality have been sacrificed.

At the time the PDP-11/45 was designed, several operation code extension schemes were examined: an escape mode to add the floating-point operations, bringing the PDP-11 back to being a more conventional general register machine by reducing the number of addressing modes, and finally, typing the data by adding a global mode that could be switched to select floating point instead of byte operations for the same operation codes. The floating-point instruction set, introduced with the 11/45, is a version of the second alternative.

It also became necessary to do something about the small address space of the processor. The Unibus limits the physical memory to the 262,144 bytes addressable by 18-bits. In the PDP-11/70, the physical address was extended to 4 Mbytes by providing a Unibus map so that devices in a 256 Kbyte Unibus space could transfer into the 4-Mbyte space via mapping registers. While the physical address limits are acceptable for both the Unibus and larger systems, the address for a single program is still confined to an instantaneous space of 16 bits, the user virtual address. The main method of dealing with relatively small addresses is via process-oriented operating systems that handle many small tasks. This is a trend in operating systems, especially for process control and transaction processing. It does, however, enforce a structuring discipline in (user) program organization. The RSX-11 series of operating systems for the PDP-11 are organized this way, and the need for large addresses is lessened.

The initial memory management proposal to extend the virtual memory was predicated on dynamic, rather than static, assignment of memory segment registers. In the current memory management scheme, the address registers are usually considered to be static for a task (although some operating systems provide functions to get additional segments dynamically).

With dynamic assignment, a user can address a number of segment names, via a table, and directly load the appropriate segment registers. The segment registers act to concatenate additional address bits in a base address fashion. There have been other schemes proposed that extend the addresses by extending the length of the general registers—of course, extended addresses propagate throughout the design and include double length address variables. In effect, the extended part is loaded with a base address.

With larger machines and process-oriented operating systems, the context switching time becomes an important performance factor. By providing additional registers for more processes, the time (overhead) to switch context from one process (task) to another can be reduced. This option has not been used in the operating system implementations of the PDP-11s to date, although the 11/45 extensions included a second set of general registers. Various alternatives have been suggested, and to accomplish this effectively requires additional operators to handle the many aspects of process scheduling. This extension appears to be relatively unimportant since the range of computers coupled with networks tends to alleviate the need by increasing the real parallelism (as opposed to the apparent parallelism) by having various independent processors work on the separate processes in parallel. The extensions of the PDP-11 for better control of I/O devices is clearly more important in terms of improved performance.

Architecture Management

In retrospect, many of the problems associated with PDP-11 evolution were due to the lack of an ongoing architecture management function. The notion of planned evolution was very strong at the beginning. However, a formal architecture control function was not set up until early in 1974. In some sense this was already too late—the four PDP-11 models designed by that date (11/20, 11/05, 11/40, 11/45) had incompatibilities between them. The architecture control function since then has ensured that no further divergence (except in the LSI-11) took place in subsequent models, and in fact resulted in some convergence. At the time the Commercial Instruction Set was added, an architecture extension framework was adopted. Insufficient encodings existed to provide a large number of additional instructions using the same encoding style (in the same space) as the basic PDP-11, i.e., the operation code and operand specifier addressing mode specifiers within a single 16-bit word. An instruction extension framework was adopted which utilized a full word as the opcode, with operand addressing mode specifiers in succeeding instruction stream words along the lines of VAX-11. This architectural extension permits 512 additional opcodes, and instructions may have an unlimited number of operand addressing mode specifiers. The architecture control function also had to deal with the Unibus address space problem.

With VAX-11, architecture management has been in place since the beginning. A definition of the architecutre was placed under formal change control well before the VAX-11/780 was built, and both hardware and software engineering groups worked with the same document. Another significant difference is that an extension framework was defined in the original architecture.

An Evaluation

The criteria used to decide whether or not to include a particular capability in an instruction set are highly variable and border on the artistic. Critics ask that the machine appear elegant, where elegance is a combined quality of instruction formats relating to mnemonic significance, operator/data-type completeness and orthogonality, and addressing consistency. Having completely general facilities (e.g., registers) which are not context dependent assists in minimizing the number of instruction types and in increasing understandability (and usefulness). The authors feel that the PDP-11 has provided this.

At the time the Unibus was designed, it was felt that allowing 4 Kbytes of the address space for I/O control registers was more than enough. However, so many different devices have been interfaced to the bus over the years that it is no longer possible to assign unique addresses to every device. The architectural group has thus been saddled with the chore of device address bookkeeping. Many solutions have been proposed, but none was soon enough; as a result, they are all so costly that it is cheaper just to live with the problem and the attendant inconvenience.

Techniques for generating code by the human and compiler vary widely and thus affect instruction set processor design. The PDP-11 provides more addressing modes than nearly any other computer. The eight modes for source and destination with dyadic operators provide what amounts to 64 possible ADD instructions. By associating the Program Counter and Stack Pointer registers with the modes, even more data accessing methods are provided. For example, 18 varieties of the MOVE instruction can be distinguished as the machine is used in two-address, general register, and stack machine program forms. (There is a price for this generality—namely, fewer bits could have been used to encode the address modes that are actually used most of the time.)

How the PDP-11 Is Used

In general, the PDP-11 has been used mostly as a general register (i.e., memory to registers) machine. This can be seen by observing the use frequency from Strecker's data (see Appendix 1 in Chap. 39). In one case, it was observed that a user who previously used a one-accumulator computer (e.g., PDP-8), continued to do so. A general register machine provides the greatest performance, and the cost (in terms of bits) is the same as when used as a stack machine. Some compilers, particularly the early ones, are stack oriented since the code production is easier. In principle, and with much care, a fast stack machine could be constructed. However, since most stack machines use primary memory for the stack, there is a loss of performance even if the top of the stack is cached. While a stack is the natural (and necessary) structure to interpret the nested block structure languages, it does not necessarily follow that the interpretation of all statements should occur in the context of the stack. In particular, the predominance of register transfer statements are of the simple 2- and 3-address forms:

$$D \leftarrow S$$

and

$$D1(\text{index } 1) \leftarrow f(S2(\text{index } 2), S3(\text{index } 3))$$

These do not require the stack organization. In effect, appropriate assignment allows a general register machine to be used as a stack machine for most cases of expression evaluation. This has the advantage of providing temporary, random access to common subexpressions, a capability that is usually hard to exploit in stack architectures.

The Evolution of the PMS (Modular) Structure

The end product of the PDP-11 design is the computer itself, and in the evolution of the architecture one can see images of the evolution of ideas. In this section, the architectural evolution is outlined, with a special emphasis on the Unibus.

The Unibus is the architectural component that connects together all of the other major components. It is the vehicle over which data flow between pairs of components takes place.

In general, the Unibus has met all expectations. Several hundred types of memories and peripherals have been interfaced to it; it has become a standard architectural component of systems in the $3K to $100K price range (1975). The Unibus does limit the performance of the fastest machines and penalizes the lower performance machines with a higher cost. Recently it has become clear that the Unibus is adequate for large, high performance systems when a cache structure is used because the cache reduces the traffic between primary memory and the central processor since about one-tenth of the memory references are outside the cache. For still larger systems, supplementary buses were added for central processor to primary memory and primary memory to secondary memory traffic. For very small systems like the LSI-11, a narrower bus was designed.

The Unibus, as a standard, has provided an architectural component for easily configuring systems. Any company, not just DEC, can easily build components that interface to the bus. Good buses make good engineering neighbors, since people can concentrate on structured design. Indeed, the Unibus has created a secondary industry providing alternative sources of supply for memories and peripherals. With the exception of the IBM 360 Multiplexer-Selector Bus, the Unibus is the most widely used computer interconnection standard.

The Unibus has also turned out to be invaluable as an "umbilical cord" for factory diagnostic and checkout procedures. Although such a capability was not part of the original design, the Unibus is almost capable of controlling the system components (e.g., processor and memory) during factory checkout. Ideally, the scheme would let all registers be accessed during full operation. This is possible for all devices except the processor. By having all central processor registers available for reading and writing in the same way that they are available from the console switches, a second system can fully monitor the computer under test.

In most recent PDP-11 models, a serial communications line, called the ASCII Console, is connected to the console, so that a program may remotely examine or change any information that a human operator could examine or change from the front panel, even when the system is not running. In this way computers can be diagnosed from a remote site.

Difficulties with the Design

The Unibus design is not without problems. Although two of the bus bits were set aside in the original design as parity bits, they have not been widely used as such. Memory parity was implemented directly in the memory; this phenomenon is a good example of the sorts of problems encountered in engineering optimization. The trading of bus parity for memory parity exchanged higher hardware cost and decreased performance for decreased service cost and better data integrity. Because engineers are usually judged on how well they achieve production cost goals, parity transmission is an obvious choice to pare from a design, since it increases the cost and decreases the performance. As logic costs decrease and pressure to include warranty costs as part of the product design cost increases, the decision to transmit parity may be reconsidered.

Early attempts to build tightly coupled multiprocessor or multicomputer structures (by mapping the address space of one Unibus onto the memory of another), called Unibus windows, were beset with a logic deadlock problem. The Unibus design does not allow more than one master at a time. Successful multiprocessors required much more sophisticated sharing mechanisms such as shared primary memory.

Unibus Cost and Performance

Although performance is always a design goal, so is low cost; the two goals conflict directly. The Unibus has turned out to be nearly optimum over a wide range of products. It served as an adequate memory-processor interconnect for six of the ten models. However, in the smallest system, DEC introduced the LSI-11 Bus, which uses about half the number of conductors. For the largest systems, a separate 32-bit data path is used between processor and memory, although the Unibus is still used for communication with the majority of the I/O controllers (the slower ones).

The bandwidth of the Unibus is approximately 1.7 megabytes per second or 850 K transfers/second. Only for the largest configurations, using many I/O devices with very high data rates, is this capacity exceeded. For most configurations, the demand put on an I/O bus is limited by the rotational delay and head positioning of disks and the rate at which programs (user and system) issue I/O requests.

An experiment to further the understanding of Unibus capacity and the demand placed against it was carried out. The experiment used a synthetic workload; like all synthetic workloads, it can be challenged as not being representative. However, it was generally agreed that it was a heavy I/O load. The load simulated transaction processing, swapping, and background computing in the configuration shown in Fig. 1. The load was run on five systems, each placing a different demand on the Unibus.

Each run produced two numbers: (1) the time to complete 2,000 transactions, and (2) the number of iterations of a program called HANOI that were completed.

System	Benchmark time (minutes)*	Number of HANOI iterations
11/60 cache on	15	12
11/60 cache off	15	2
11/40	15	3
11/70 MBCBUS	15	23
11/70 Unibus	26	38

*2,000 transactions plus swapping plus HANOI.

The results were interpreted as follows:

1   I/O throughput. For this workload the Unibus bandwidth was adequate. For systems 1 through 4, the I/O activity took the same amount of time.

2   11/70 Unibus. The run on this system (no use was made of the 32-bit wide processor/memory bus) took longer because of the retries caused by data lates (approximately 19,000) on the moving head disk (RP04). The extra time taken for the benchmark allowed more iterations of HANOI to occur. The PDP-11/70 Unibus had a bandwidth of about 1 megabyte. It was less than the usual Unibus (about 1.7 megabyte) because of the map delay (100 nanoseconds), the cache cycle (240 nanoseconds), and the main memory bus redriving and synchronization.

3   11/60 Cache. Systems 1 and 2 clearly show the effectiveness of a cache. Most memory references for HANOI were to the cache and did not involve the Unibus, which was the PDP-11/60s I/O Bus. Systems 2 and 3 were essentially equivalent, as expected. There are two reasons for the 11/40 having slightly more compute bandwidth than an 11/60 with its cache off. First, the 11/40 memory is faster than the 11/60 backing store, and second, the 11/40 processor relinquishes the Unibus for a direct memory access cycle; the 11/60 processor must request the Unibus for a processor cycle.

There are several attributes of a bus that affect its cost and performance. One factor affecting performance is simply the data rate of a single conductor. There is a direct tradeoff involving cost, performance, and reliability. Shannon [1948] gives a relationship between the fundamental signal bandwidth of a link and the error rate (signal-to-noise ratio) and data rate. The performance and cost of a bus are also affected by its length. Longer cables cost proportionately more, since they require more complex circuitry to drive the bus.

Since a single-conductor link has a fixed data rate, the number of conductors affects the net speed of a bus. However, the cost of a bus is directly proportional to the number of conductors. For a given number of wires, time domain multiplexing and data encoding can be used to trade performance and logic complexity. Since logic technology is advancing faster than wiring technology, it seems likely that fewer conductors will be used in all future systems, except where the performance penalty of time domain multiplexing is unacceptably great.

If, during the original design of the Unibus, DEC designers could have foreseen the wide range of applications to which it would be applied, its design would have been different. Individual controllers might have been reduced in complexity by more central control. For the largest and smallest systems, it would have been useful to have a bus that could be contracted or expanded by multiplexing or expanding the number of conductors.

The cost-effectiveness of the Unibus is due in large part to the high correlation between memory size, number of address bits,

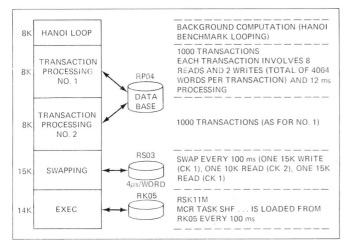

Fig. 1. The synthetic workload used to measure Unibus capacity.

I/O traffic, and processor speed. Gene Amdahl's rule of thumb for IBM computers is that 1 byte of memory and 1 bit/sec of I/O are required for each instruction/sec. For traditional DEC applications, with emphasis in the scientific and control applications, there is more computation required per memory word. Further, the PDP-11 instruction sets do not contain the extensive commercial instructions (character strings) typical of IBM computers, so a large number of instructions must be executed to accomplish the same task. Hence, for DEC computers, it is better to assume 1 byte of memory for each 2 instructions/sec, and that 1 byte/sec of I/O occurs for each instruction/sec.

In the PDP-11, an average instruction accesses 3-5 bytes of memory, so assuming 1 byte of I/O for each instruction/sec, there are 4–6 bytes of memory accessed on the average for each instruction/sec. Therefore, a bus that can support 2 megabytes/sec of traffic permits instruction execution rates of 0.33–0.5 megainstructions/sec. This implies memory sizes of 0.16–0.25 megabytes, which matches well with the maximum allowable memory of 0.064–0.256 megabytes. By using a cache memory on the processor, the effective memory processor rate can be increased to balance the system further. If fast floating-point instructions were added to the instruction set, the balance might approach that used by IBM and thereby require more memory (an effect seen in the PDP-11/70).

The task of I/O is to provide for the transfer of data from peripheral to primary memory where it can be operated on by a program in a processor. The peripherals are generally slow, inherently asynchronous, and more error-prone than the processors to which they are attached.

Historically, I/O transfer mechanisms have evolved through the following four stages:

1 **Direct sequential I/O under central processor control.** An instruction in the processor causes a data transfer to take place with a device. The processor does not resume operation until the transfer is complete. Typically, the device control may share the logic of the processor. The first input/output transfer (IOT) instruction in the PDP-1 is an example: the IOT effects transfer between the Accumulator and a selected device. Direct I/O simplifies programming because every operation is sequential.

2 **Fixed buffer, 1-instruction controllers.** An instruction in the central processor causes a data transfer (of a word or vector), but in this case, it is to a buffer of the simple controller and thus at a speed matching that of the processor. After the high speed transfer has occurred, the processor continues while an asynchronous, slower transfer occurs between the buffer and the device. Communication back to the processor is via the program interrupt mechanism. A single instruction to a simple controller can also cause a complete block (vector) of data to be transmitted between memory and the peripheral. In this case, the

transfer takes place via the direct memory access (DMA) link.

3 **Separate I/O processors—the channel.** An independent I/O processor with a unique ISP controls the flow of data between primary memory and the peripheral. The structure is that of the multiprocessor, and the I/O control program for the device is held in primary memory. The central processor informs the I/O processor about the I/O program location.

4 **I/O computer.** This mechanism is also asynchronous with the central processor, but the I/O computer has a private memory which holds the I/O program. Recently, DEC communications options have been built with embedded control programs. The first example of an I/O computer was in the CDC 6600 (1964).

The authors believe that the single-instruction controller is superior to the I/O processor as embodied in the IBM Channel mainly because the latter concept has not gone far enough. Channels are costly to implement, sufficiently complex to require their own programming environment, and yet not quite powerful enough to assume the processing, such as file management, that one would like to offload from the processor. Although the I/O traffic does require central processor resources, the addition of a second, general purpose central processor is more cost-effective than using a central processor-I/O processor or central processor-multiple I/O processor structure. Future I/O systems will be message-oriented, and the various I/O control functions (including diagnostics and file management) will migrate to the subsystem. When the I/O computer is an exact duplicate of the central processor, not only is there an economy from the reduced number of part types but also the same programming environment can be used for I/O software development and main program development. Notice that the I/O computer must implement precisely the same set of functions as the processor doing direct I/O.

Technology: Components of the Design

Computers are strongly influenced by the basic electronic technology of their components. The PDP-11 Family provides an extensive example of designing with improved technologies. Because design resources have been available to do concurrent implementations spanning a cost/performance range, PDP-11s offer a rich source of examples of the three different design styles: constant cost with increasing functionality, constant functionality with decreasing cost, and growth path.

Memory technology has had a much greater impact on PDP-11 evolution than logic technology. Except for the LSI-11, the one logic family (7400 series TTL) has dominated PDP-11 implementations since the beginning. Except for a small increase after the

Table 2 Characteristics of PDP-11 Models with Techniques Used to Span Cost and Performance Range

| | | Performance | | | Range-spanning techniques | | |
| | | Basic instructions per second (relative to PDP-11/03) | Floating-point arithmetic (whetstone instructions per second) | Memory range (Kbytes) | | | |
Model	First shipment				For high performance	For low cost	Notable attributes
11/03 (LSI-11)	6/75	1	26	8-56		8 bit wide datapath; LSI-11 Bus; tailored PLA control	LSI-4 chips; ODT; Floating-Point (FIS), CIS, WCS mid-life kickers
11/04	9/75	2.8	18	8-56		Standard package; ROM; PLA	Backplane compatible with 11/34 for field upgrade; built-in ASCII console; self-diagnosis
11/05	6/72	2.5	13	8-56		Microprogrammed; ROM	Minimal 11 (2 boards)
11/20	6/70	3.1	20	8-56			ISP; Unibus
11/34	3/76	3.5	204	16-256		Shared use of ALU; PLA; ROM; microprogrammed	Cost-performance balance; 11/34C mid-life kicker; bit-slice FPP
11/34C	5/78	7.3	262	32-256			Classic use of cache
11/40	1/73	3.6	57	16-256	Variable cycle length	Microprogrammed	FIS extension
11/60	6/77	27	592	32-256	Fetch overlap; dual scratch-pads; TTL/S	Heavily microprogrammed	Integral floating-point; WCS for local storage; RAMP
11/45	6/72	Core: 13 MOS: 23 Bipolar: 41	~260 ~335 ~362	8-256	Instruction prefetch; dual scratchpads; Fastbus; autonomous FPP; TTL/S		Pc speed to match 300 ns bipolar; high speed minicomputer FPP; memory management
11/55	6/76	41	725	16-64 (0-192 core)	All bipolar memory		
11/70	3/75	36	671	64-2048	32-bit wide DMA bus; large memory		Cache; multiple buses, RAMP, FP11-C mid-life kicker; remote diagnosis
70mP							Multiprocessor architectural extensions; on-line maintainability; performance; availability
		range: 41-1	range: 56-1	range: 256-1			

PDP-11/20, gate density has not improved markedly. Speed improvement has taken place in the Schottky TTL, and a speed/power improvement has occurred in the low power Schottky (LS) series. Departures from medium-scale integrated transistor-transistor logic, in terms of gate density, have been few, but effective. Examples are the bit-slice in the PDP-11/34 Floating-Point Processor, the use of programmable logic arrays in the PDP-11/04 and PDP-11/34 control units, and the use of emitter-coupled logic in some clock circuitry.

Memory densities and costs have improved rapidly since 1969 and have thus had the most impact. Read-write memory chips have gone from 16 bits to 4,096 bits in density and read-only memories from 16 bits to the 8 or 16 Kbits widely available in 1978.

The memory technology of 1969 imposed several constraints. First, core memory was cost-effective for the primary (program) memory, but a clear trend toward semiconductor primary memory was visible. Second, since the largest high speed read-write memories available were just 16 words, the number of processor registers had to be kept small. Third, there were no large high speed read-only memories that would have permitted a microprogrammed approach to the processor design.

These constraints established four design attitudes toward the PDP-11's architecture. First, it should be asynchronous, and thereby capable of accepting different configurations of memory that operate at different speeds. Second, it should be expandable to take eventual advantage of a larger number of registers, both user registers for new data-types and internal registers for improved context switching, memory mapping, and protected multiprogramming. Third, it could be relatively complex, so that a microcode approach could eventually be used to advantage: new data-types could be added to the instruction set to increase performance, even though they might add complexity. Fourth, the Unibus width should be relatively large, to get as much performance as possible, since the amount of computation possible per memory cycle was relatively small.

As semiconductor memory of varying price and performance became available, it was used to trade cost for performance across a reasonably wide range of PDP-11 models. Different techniques

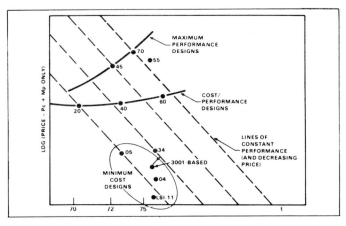

Fig. 2. PDP-11 models price versus time with lines of constant performance.

were used on different models to provide the range. These techniques include: microprogramming for all models except the 11/20 to lower cost and enhance performance with more data-types (for example, faster floating point); use of faster program memories for brute-force speed improvements (e.g., 11/45 with MOS primary memory, 11/55 with bipolar primary memory, and the 11/60 with a large writable control store); use of caches (11/70, 11/60, and 11/34C); and expanded use of fast registers inside the processor (the 11/45 and above). The use of semiconductors versus cores for primary memory is a purely economic consideration.

Table 2 shows characteristics of each of the PDP-11 models along with the techniques used to span a range of cost and performance. (Chapter 39 gives a detailed comparison of the processors.) Figure 2 gives the cost/performance mapping for the various PDP-11 implementations.

References

Bell et al. [1970]; Eckhouse [1975]; Gear [1974]; Shannon [1948]; Stone and Siewiorek [1975].

Section 3

Evolution of HP Calculators

Desk-top calculators present a total computation environment to the user. The syntax and semantics of all the keys are predefined. Individual keystrokes vary widely in power from simple addition to complex I/O operations. Further, support functions such as editing, debugging aids, syntax analyzing, incremental execution, and keyboard monitoring are not only completely defined but also locked into hardware. This is to be contrasted with computer systems whose instruction sets are specified and whose computational environment is defined by ever-evolving multiple layers of software.

This section focuses on the architectures of the Hewlett-Packard series of desk-top calculators, starting with the HP 9100A (c. 1968); its first-generation descendants, the HP 9810/20/30 (c. 1972); and its second-generation descendants, the HP 9815/35/45 (c. 1976). The series span the technology range from discrete components through MSI to LSI in the latest generation. The advances in technology have allowed costs to decrease while allowing functionality to increase. Performance has increased by a factor of 8, operating-system ROM by a factor of 25, and user RAM by a factor of 240. These advances are graphically displayed in Figs. 1 to 4.

These computers represent an unplanned family with no

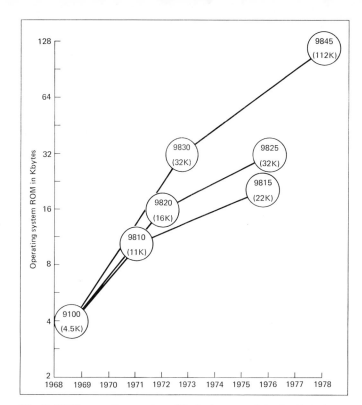

Fig. 2. ROM operating system (Kbytes) versus introduction date.

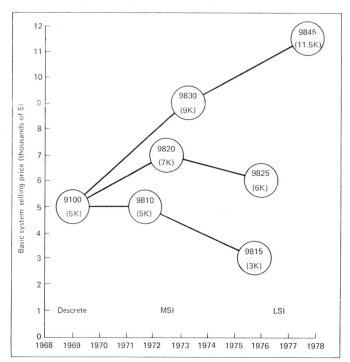

Fig. 1. Selling price (thousands of dollars) versus introduction date.

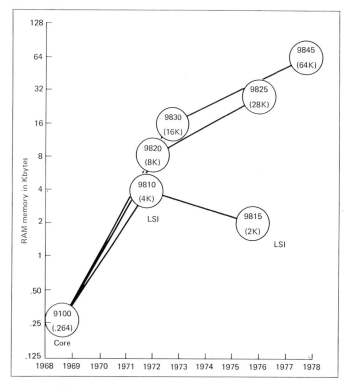

Fig. 3. RAM (minimum configuration) versus introduction date.

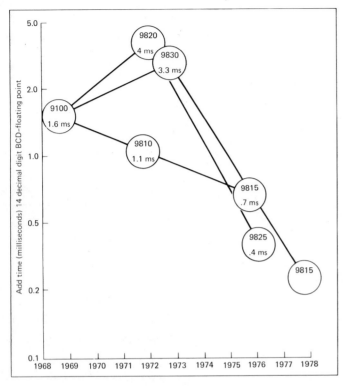

Fig. 4. Floating point add times versus introduction date.

constraint on user compatibility between generations. Chapters 48, 49, and 31 sketch the designs of the three major generations of Hewlett-Packard desk-top calculators. Functionality has increased with each generation and is best exemplified by the programming interface. HP 9100A programs consisted of arithmetic keystroke functions and program control operations (e.g., GO TO and IF). The HP 9800 series ranged from an algebraic language through BASIC, traditionally a computer-based language. The perception is that the HP 9810/20/30 series is matched to user functionality rather than software compatibility. The HP 9845 also supports BASIC. This section concludes, in Chap. 50, with some observations by Tom Osborne, one of the architects of the Hewlett-Packard desk-top series.

Chapter 48

The HP Model 9100A Computing Calculator[1]

Richard E. Monnier / Thomas E. Osborne / David S. Cochran

A New Electronic Calculator with Computerlike Capabilities

Many of the day-to-day computing problems faced by scientists and engineers require complex calculations but involve only a moderate amount of data. Therefore, a machine that is more than a calculator in capability but less than a computer in cost has a great deal to offer. At the same time it must be easy to operate and program so that a minimum amount of effort is required in the solution of typical problems. Reasonable speed is necessary so that the response to individual operations seems nearly instantaneous.

The HP Model 9100A Calculator, Fig. 1, was developed to fill this gap between desk calculators and computers. Easy interaction between the machine and user was one of the most important design considerations during its development and was the prime guide in making many design decisions.

CRT Display

One of the first and most basic problems to be resolved concerned the type of output to be used. Most people want a printed record, but printers are generally slow and noisy. Whatever method is used, if only one register is displayed, it is difficult to follow what is happening during a sequence of calculations where numbers are moved from one register to another. It was therefore decided that a cathode-ray tube displaying the contents of three registers would provide the greatest flexibility and would allow the user to follow problem solutions easily. The ideal situation is to have both a CRT showing more than one register, and a printer which can be attached as an accessory.

Figure 2 is a typical display showing three numbers. The X register displays numbers as they are entered from the keyboard one digit at a time and is called the keyboard register. The Y register is called the accumulator since the results of arithmetic operations on two numbers, one in X and one in Y, appear in the Y register. The Z register is a particularly convenient register to use for temporary storage.

[1]This chapter is a compilation of three articles [Monnier, 1968; Osborne, 1968; Cochran, 1968], reprinted from *Hewlett-Packard Journal*, vol. 20, no. 1, September 1968, pp. 3–9, 10–13, and 14–16.

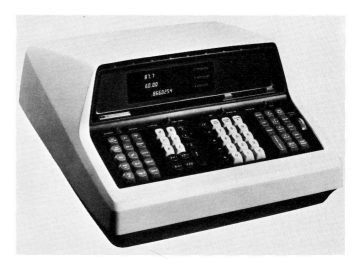

Fig. 1. This new HP Model 9100A calculator is self-contained and is capable of performing functions previously possible only with larger computers.

Numbers

One of the most important features of the Model 9100A is the tremendous range of numbers it can handle without special attention by the operator. It is not necessary to worry about where to place the decimal point to obtain the desired accuracy or to avoid register overflow. This flexibility is obtained because all

Fig. 2. Display in fixed point with the decimal wheel set at 5. The Y register has reverted to floating point because the number is too large to be properly displayed unless the digits called for by the DECIMAL-DIGITS setting are reduced.

numbers are stored in "floating point arithmetic." A floating point number is expressed with the decimal point following the first digit and an exponent representing the number of places the decimal point should be moved—to the right if the exponent is positive, or to the left if the exponent is negative.

$$4.398\ 364\ 291 \times 10^{-3} = .004\ 398\ 364\ 291$$

The operator may choose to display numbers in FLOATING POINT or in FIXED POINT. The FLOATING POINT mode allows numbers, either positive or negative, from 1×10^{-99} to $9.999\ 999 \times 10^{99}$ to be displayed just as they are stored in the machine.

The FIXED POINT mode displays numbers in the way they are most commonly written. The DECIMAL DIGITS wheel allows setting the number of digits displayed to the right of the decimal point anywhere from 0 to 9. Figure 2 shows a display of three numbers with the DECIMAL DIGITS wheel set at 5. The number in the Y register, $5.336\ 845\ 815 \times 10^5 = 533\ 684.5815$, is too big to be displayed in FIXED POINT without reducing the DECIMAL DIGITS setting to 4 or less. If the number is too big for the DECIMAL DIGITS setting, the register involved reverts automatically to floating point to avoid an apparent overflow. In FIXED POINT display, the number displayed is rounded, but full significance is retained in storage for calculations.

To improve readability, 0's before the displayed number and un-entered 0's following the number are blanked. In FLOATING POINT, digits to the right of the decimal are grouped in threes.

Pull-out Instruction Card

A pull-out instruction card, Fig. 3, is located at the front of the calculator under the keyboard. The operation of each key is briefly explained and key codes are listed. Some simple examples are provided to assist those using the machine for the first time or to refresh the memory of an infrequent user. Most questions regarding the operation of the Model 9100A are answered on the card.

Data Entry

The calculator keyboard is shown in Fig. 4. Numbers can be entered into the X register using the digit keys, the π key or the ENTER EXP key. The ENTER EXP key allows powers of 10 to be entered directly which is useful for very large or very small numbers. 6.02×10^{23} is entered 6 · 0 2 [ENTER EXP] 2 3 . If the ENTER EXP key is the first key of a number entry, a 1 is automatically entered into the mantissa. Thus only two keystrokes [ENTER EXP] 6 suffice to enter 1,000,000. The CHG SIGN key changes the sign of either the mantissa or the exponent depending upon which one is presently being addressed. Numbers are entered in the same way, regardless of whether the machine is in FIXED POINT

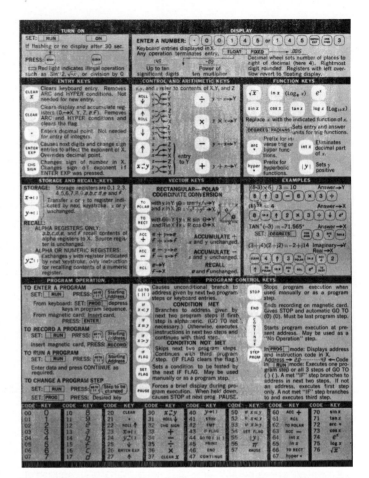

Fig. 3. Pull-out instruction card is permanently attached to the calculator and contains key codes and operating instructions.

or FLOATING POINT. Any key, other than a digit key, decimal point, CHG SIGN or ENTER EXP, terminates an entry; it is not necessary to clear before entering a new number. CLEAR X sets the X register to 0 and can be used when a mistake has been made in a number entry.

Fig. 4. Keys are in four groups on the keyboard, according to their function.

Control and Arithmetic Keys

ADD, SUBTRACT, MULTIPLY, DIVIDE involve two numbers, so the first number must be moved from X to Y before the second is entered into X. After the two numbers have been entered, the appropriate operation can be performed. In the case of a DIVIDE, the dividend is entered into Y and the divisor into X. Then the ÷ key is pressed causing the quotient to appear in Y, leaving the divisor in X.

One way to transfer a number from the X register to the Y register is to use the double sized key, ↑, at the left of the digit keys. This repeats the number in X into Y, leaving X unchanged; the number in Y goes to Z, and the number in Z is lost. Thus, when squaring or cubing a number, it is only necessary to follow ↑ with × or × ×. The ↓ key repeats a number in Z to Y leaving Z unchanged, the number in Y goes to X, and the number in X is lost. The ROLL↑ key rotates the number in the X and Y registers up and the number in Z down into X. ROLL↓ rotates the numbers in Z and Y down and the number in X up into Z. x⇌y interchanges the numbers in X and Y. Using the two ROLL keys and x⇌y, numbers can be placed in any order in the three registers.

Functions Available from the Keyboard

The group of keys at the far left of the keyboard, Fig. 4, gives a good indication of the power of the Model 9100A. Most of the common mathematical functions are available directly from the keyboard. Except for |y| the function keys operate on the number in X replacing it with the function of that argument. The numbers in Y and Z are left unchanged. √x is located with another group of keys for convenience but operates the same way.

The circular functions operate with angles expressed in RADI-ANS or DEGREES as set by the switch above the keyboard. The sine, cosine, or tangent of an angle is taken with a single keystroke. There are no restrictions on direction, quadrant or number of revolutions of the angle. The inverse functions are obtained by using the arc↓ key as a prefix. For instance, two key depressions are necessary to obtain the arc sin x: arc↓ sin x. The angle obtained will be the standard principal value. In radians:

$$-\frac{\pi}{2} \leq \mathrm{Sin}^{-1} x \leq \frac{\pi}{2}$$

$$0 \leq \mathrm{Cos}^{-1} x \leq \pi$$

$$-\frac{\pi}{2} < \mathrm{Tan}^{-1} x < \frac{\pi}{2}$$

The hyperbolic sine, cosine, or tangent is obtained using the hyper↓ key as a prefix. The inverse hyberbolic functions are obtained with three key depressions. $\mathrm{Tanh}^{-1} x$ is obtained by arc↓ hyper↓ TAN x. The arc and hyper keys prefix keys below them in their column.

Log x and ln x obtain the log to the base 10 and the log to the base e respectively. The inverse of the natural log is obtained with the e^x key. These keys are useful when raising numbers to odd powers as shown in one of the examples on the pull-out card, Fig. 3.

Two keys in this group are very useful in programs. int x takes the integer part of the number in the X register which deletes the part of the number to the right of the decimal point. For example $\mathrm{int}(-3.1416) = -3$. |y| forces the number in the Y register positive.

Storage Registers

Sixteen registers, in addition to X, Y, and Z, are available for storage. Fourteen of them, 0, 1, 2, 3, 4, 5, 6, 7, 8, 9, a, b, c, d, can be used to store either one constant or 14 program steps per register. The last registers, e and f, are normally used only for constant storage since the program counter will not cycle into them. Special keys located in a block to the left of the digit keys are used to identify the lettered registers.

To store a number from the X register the key x→( ) is used. The parenthesis indicates that another key depression, representing the storage register, is necessary to complete the transfer. For example, storing a number from the X register into register 8 requires two key depressions: x→( ) 8. The X register remains unchanged. To store a number from Y register the key y→( ) is used.

The contents of the alpha registers are recalled to X simply by pressing the keys a, b, c, d, e, and f. Recalling a number from a numbered register requires the use of the x⇌y key to distinguish the recall procedure from digit entry. This key interchanges the number in the Y register with the number in the register indicated by the following keystroke, alpha or numeric, and is also useful in programs since neither number involved in the transfer is lost.

The CLEAR key sets the X, Y, and Z display registers and the f and e registers are set to zero to initialize them for use with the ACC+ and ACC− keys as will be explained. In addition the CLEAR key clears the FLAG and the ARC and HYPER conditions, which often makes it a very useful first step in a program.

Coordinate Transformation and Complex Numbers

Vectors and complex numbers are easily handled using the keys in the column on the far left of the keyboard. Figure 5 defines the variables involved. Angles can be either in degrees or radians. To convert from rectangular to polar coordinates, with y in Y and x in X, press TO POLAR. Then the display shows θ in Y and R in X. In converting from polar to rectangular coordinates, θ is placed in Y, and R in X. TO RECT is pressed and the display shows y in Y and x in X.

ACC+ and ACC− allow addition or subtraction of vector components in the f and e storage registers. ACC+ adds the contents of the X and Y register to the numbers already stored in f and e respectively; ACC− subtracts them. The RCL key recalls the numbers in the f and e registers to X and Y.

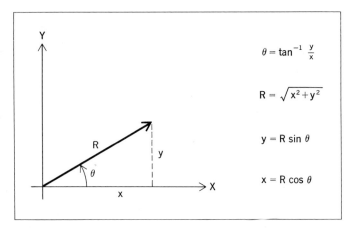

$$\theta = \tan^{-1} \frac{y}{x}$$

$$R = \sqrt{x^2 + y^2}$$

$$y = R \sin \theta$$

$$x = R \cos \theta$$

Fig. 5. Variables involved in conversions between rectangular and polar coordinates.

Illegal Operations

A light to the left of the CRT indicates that an illegal operation has been performed. This can happen either from the keyboard or when running a program. Pressing any key on the keyboard will reset the light. When running a program, execution will continue but the light will remain on as the program is completed. The illegal operations are:

Division by zero

$\sqrt{x}$ where $x < 0$

ln x where $x \leq 0$; log n where $x \leq 0$

$\sin^{-1} x$ where $|x| > 1$; $\cos^{-1} x$ where $|x| > 1$

$\cosh^{-1} x$ where $x < 1$; $\tanh^{-1} x$ where $|x| > 1$

Accuracy

The Model 9100A does all calculations using floating point arithmetic with a twelve digit mantissa and a two digit exponent. The two least significant digits are not displayed and are called guard digits.

The algorithms used to perform the operations and generate the functions were chosen to minimize error and to provide an extended range of the argument. Usually any inaccuracy will be contained within the two guard digits. In certain cases some inaccuracy will appear in the displayed number. One example is where the functions change rapidly for small changes in the argument, as in tan x where x is near 90°. A glaring but insignificant inaccuracy occurs when an answer is known to be a whole number, but the least significant guard digit is one count low: $2.000\ 000\ 000 \simeq 1.999\ 999\ 999$.

Accuracy is discussed further in the "Internal Programming" section in this chapter. But a simple summary is: the answer

resulting from any operation or function will lie within the range of true values produced by a variation of ± 1 count in the tenth digit of the argument.

Programming

Problems that require many keyboard operations are more easily solved with a program. This is particularly true when the same operations must be performed repeatedly or an iterative technique must be used. A program library supplied with the Model 9100A provides a set of representative programs from many different fields. If a program cannot be found in the library to solve a particular problem, a new program can easily be written since no special experience or prior knowledge of a programming language is necessary.

Any key on the keyboard can be remembered by the calculator as a program step except STEP PRGM. This key is used to "debug" a program rather than as an operation in a program. Many individual program steps, such as "sin x" or "to polar" are comparatively powerful, and avoid the need of sub-routines for these functions and the programming space such sub-routines require. Registers 0, 1, 2, 3, 4, 5, 6, 7, 8, 9, a, b, c, d can store 14 program steps each. Steps within the registers are numbered 0 through d just as the registers themselves are numbered. Programs can start at any of the 196 possible addresses. However 0-0 is usually used for the first step. Address d-d is then the last available, after which the program counter cycles back to 0-0.

Registers f and e are normally used for storage of constants only, one constant in each register. As more constant storage is required, it is recommended that registers d, then c, then b, etc., are used starting from the bottom of the list. Lettered registers are used first, for the frequently recalled constants, because constants stored in them are more easily recalled. A register can be used to store one constant or 14 program steps, but not both.

Branching

The bank on the far right of the keyboard, Fig. 4, contains program oriented keys. $\boxed{\text{GO TO}\\(\ )(\ )}$ is used to set the program counter. The two sets of parentheses indicate that this key should be followed by two more key depressions indicating the address of the program step desired. As a program step, "GO TO" is an unconditional branch instruction, which causes the program to branch to the address given by the next two program steps. The "IF" keys in this group are conditional branch instructions. With $\boxed{\text{IF}\\x<y}$ $\boxed{\text{IF}\\x=y}$, and $\boxed{\text{IF}\\x>y}$ the numbers contained in the X and Y registers are compared. The indicated condition is tested and, if met, the next two program steps are executed. If the first is alphameric, the second must be also, and the two steps are interpreted as a branching address. When the condition is not met, the next two steps are skipped and the program continues. $\boxed{\text{IF}\\\text{FLAG}}$ is also a very useful conditional branching instruction which tests a "yes" or "no" condition internally stored in the calculator. This condition is set to "yes" with the SET FLAG from the keyboard when the calculator is in the display mode or from a program as a program step. The flag is set to a "no" condition by either asking IF FLAG in a program or by a CLEAR instruction from the keyboard or from a program.

Data Input and Output

Data can be entered for use in a program when the machine is in the display mode. (The screen is blank while a program is running.) A program can be stopped in several ways. The (stop) key will halt the machine at any time. The operation being performed will be completed before returning to the display mode. As a program step, STOP stops the program so that answers can be displayed or new data entered. END must be the last step in a program listing to signal the magnetic card reader; when encountered as a program step it stops the machine and also sets the program counter to 0-0.

As a program step, PAUSE causes a brief display during program execution. Nine cycles of the power line frequency are counted—the duration of the pause will be about 150 ms for a 60 Hz power line or 180 ms for a 50 Hz power line. More pauses can be used in sequence if a longer display is desired. While a program is running the PAUSE key can be held down to stop the machine when it comes to the next PAUSE in the program. PAUSE provides a particularly useful way for the user and the machine to interact. It might, for instance, be used in a program so that the convergence to a desired result can be observed.

Other means of input and output involve peripheral devices such as an X-Y Plotter or a Printer. The PRINT key activates the printer, causing it to print information from the display register. As a program step, PRINT will interrupt the program long enough for the data to be accepted by the printer and then the program will continue. If no printer is attached, PRINT as a program step will act as a STOP. The FMT key, followed by any other keystroke, provides up to 62 unique commands to peripheral equipment. This flexibility allows the Model 9100A to be used as a controller in small systems.

Sample Program—N!

A simple program to calculate N! demonstrates how the Model 9100A is programmed. Figure 6 (top) shows a flow chart to compute N! and Fig. 6 (bottom) shows the program steps. With this program, 60! takes less than ½ second to compute.

Program Entry and Execution

After a program is written it can be entered into the Model 9100A from the keyboard. The program counter is set to the address of the first program step by using the GO TO ( ) ( ) key. The RUN-PROGRAM switch is then switched from RUN to PRO-

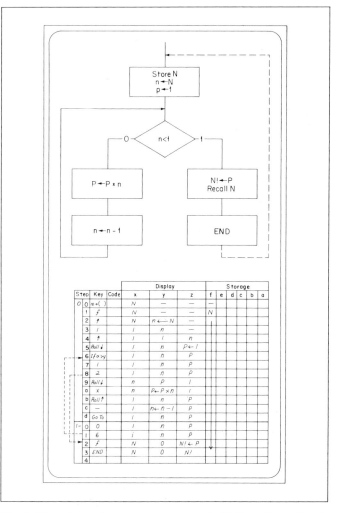

Step		Key	Code	Display			Storage					
				x	y	z	f	e	d	c	b	a
0	0	x→( )		N	—	—	—					
	1	f		N	—	—	N					
	2	↑		N	n←N	—						
	3	/		/	n	—						
	4	↑		/	/	n						
	5	Roll↓		/	n	P←/						
	6	If n>y		/	n	P						
	7	/		/	n	P						
	8	2		/	n	P						
	9	Roll↓		n	P	/						
	a	X		n	P←P×n	/						
	b	Roll↑		/	n	P						
	c	—		/	n←n-/	P						
	d	Go To		/	n	P						
1-	0	0		/	n	P						
	1	6		i	n	P						
	2	f		N	0	N!←P						
	3	END		N	0	N!						
	4											

Fig. 6. Flow chart of a program to compute N! (top). Each step is shown (bottom) and the display for each register. A new value for N can be entered at the end of the program, since END automatically sets the program counter back to 0-0.

GRAM and the program steps entered in sequence by pushing the proper keys. As each step is entered the X register displays the address and key code, as shown in Fig. 7. The keys and their codes are listed at the bottom of the pull-out card, Fig. 3. Once a program has been entered, the steps can be checked using the STEP PRGM key in the PROGRAM mode as explained in Fig. 7. If an error is made in a step, it can be corrected by using the (GO TO 0 0) key without having to re-enter the rest of the program.

To run a program, the program counter must be set to the address of the first step. If the program starts at 0-0 the keys (GO TO 0 0) (0) (0) are depressed, or simply just (END) since this key automatically

Fig. 7. Program step address and code are displayed in the X register as steps are entered. After a program has been entered, each step can be checked using the STEP PRGM key. In this display, set 2-d is 36, the code for multiply.

sets the program counter to 0-0. CONTINUE will start program execution.

Magnetic Card Reader-Recorder

One of the most convenient features of the Model 9100A is the magnetic card reader-recorder, Fig. 8. A program stored in the Model 9100A can be recorded on a magnetic card, Fig. 9, about the size of a credit card. Later when the program is needed again, it can be quickly re-entered using the previously recorded card. Cards are easily duplicated so that programs of common interest can be distributed.

As mentioned earlier, the END statement is a signal to the

Fig. 8. Programs can be entered into the calculator by means of the magnetic program card. The card is inserted into the slot and the ENTER button pressed.

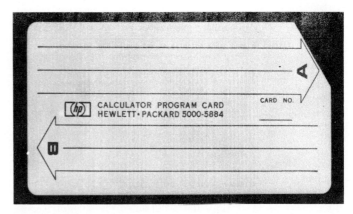

Fig. 9. Magnetic programming card can record two 196-step programs. To prevent accidental recording of a new program over one to be saved, the corner of the card is cut as shown.

reader to stop reading recorded information from the card into the calculator. For this reason END should not be used in the middle of a program. Since most programs start at location 0-0 the reader automatically initializes the program counter to 0-0 after a card is read.

The magnetic card reader makes it possible to handle most programs too long to be held in memory at one time. The first entry of steps can calculate intermediate results which are stored in preparation for the next part of the program. Since the reader stops reading at the END statement, these stored intermediate results are not disturbed when the next set of program steps is entered. The stored results are then retrieved and the program continued. Linking of programs is made more convenient if each part can execute an END when it finishes to set the program counter to 0-0. It is then only necessary to press CONTINUE after each entry of program steps.

Hardware Design of the Model 9100A Calculator

All keyboard functions in the Model 9100A are implemented by the arithmetic processing unit, Figs. 10 and 11. The arithmetic unit operates in discrete time periods called clock cycles. All operations are synchronized by the clock shown at the top center of Fig. 10.

The clock is connected to the control read only memory (ROM) which coordinates the operation of the program read only memory and the coincident current core read/write memory. The former contains information for implementing all of the keyboard operations while the latter stores user data and user programs.

All internal operations are performed in a digit by digit serial

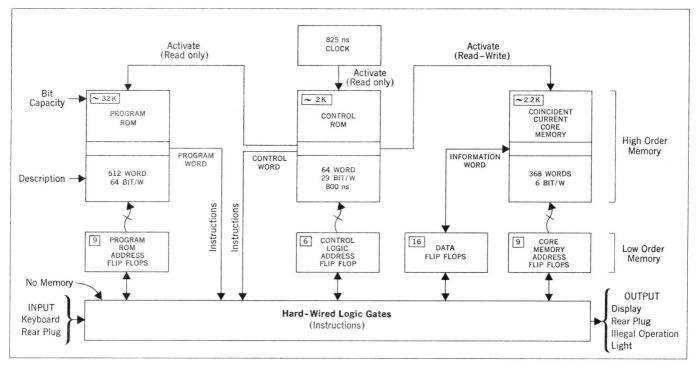

Fig. 10. Arithmetic processing unit block diagram. This system is a marriage of conventional, reliable diode-resistor logic to a 32,000-bit read-only memory and a coincident current core memory.

basis using binary coded decimal digits. An addition, for example, requires that the least significant digits of the addend and augend be extracted from core, then added and their sum replaced in core. This process is repeated one BCD digit at a time until the most significant digits have been processed. There is also a

Fig. 11. Arthmetic unit assembly removed from the calculator.

substantial amount of "housekeeping" to be performed such as aligning decimal points, assigning the proper algebraic sign, and floating point normalization. Although the implementation of a keyboard function may involve thousands of clock cycles, the total elapsed time is in the millisecond region because each clock cycle is only 825 ns long.

The program ROM contains 512 64-bit words. When the program ROM is activated, signals (micro-instructions) corresponding to the bit pattern in the word are sent to the hard wired logic gates shown at the bottom of Fig. 10. The logic gates define the changes to occur in the flip flops at the end of a clock cycle. Some of the micro-instructions act upon the data flip flops while others change the address registers associated with the program ROM, control ROM and coincident current core memory. During the next clock cycle the control ROM may ask for a new set of micro-instructions from the program ROM or ask to be read from or written into the coincident current core memory. The control ROM also has the ability to modify its own address register and to issue micro-instructions to the hard wired logic gates. This flexibility allows the control logic ROM to execute special programs such as the subroutine for unpacking the stored constants required by the keyboard transcendental functions.

Specifications of HP Model 9100*

The HP Model 9100A is a programmable, electronic calculator which performs operations commonly encountered in scientific and engineering problems. Its log, trig and mathematical functions are each performed with a single key stroke, providing fast, convenient solutions to intricate equations. Computer-like memory enables the calculator to store instructions and constants for repetitive or iterative solutions. The easily-readable cathode ray tube instantly displays entries, answers and intermediate results.

Operations

Direct keyboard operations include:

Arithmetic: addition, subtraction, multiplication, division and square-root.

Logarithmic: log x, ln x and e^x.

Trigonometric: sin x, cos x, tan x, $\sin^{-1}x$, $\cos^{-1}x$ and $\tan^{-1}x$ (x in degrees or radians).

Hyperbolic: sinh x, cosh x, tanh x, $\sinh^{-1}x$, $\cosh^{-1}x$, and $\tanh^{-1}x$.

Coordinate transformation: polar-to-rectangular, rectangular-to-polar, cumulative addition and subtraction of vectors.

Miscellaneous: other single-key operations include—taking the absolute value of a number, extracting the integer part of a number, and entering the value of π. Keys are also available for positioning and storage operations.

Programming

The program mode allows entry of program instructions, via the keyboard, into program memory. Programming consists of pressing keys in the proper sequence, and any key on the keyboard is available as a program step. Program capacity is 196 steps. No language or code-conversions are required. A self-contained magnetic card reader/recorder programs from program memory onto wallet-size magnetic cards for storage. It also reads programs from cards into program memory for repetitive use. Two programs of 196 steps each may be recorded on each reusable card. Cards may be cascaded for longer programs.

Speed

Average times for total performance of typical operations, including decimal-point placement:

add, subtract: 2 milleseconds
multiply: 12 milliseconds
divide: 18 milliseconds
square-root: 19 milliseconds
sin, cos, tan: 280 milliseconds
ln x: 50 milliseconds
e^x: 110 milliseconds

These times include core access of 1.6 microseconds.

General

Weight: Net 40 lbs, (18.1 kg.); shipping 65 lbs. (29.5 kg.).
Power: 115 or 230V ± 10%, 50 to 60 Hz, 400 Hz, 70 watts.
Dimensions: 8¼″ high, 16″ wide, 19″ deep.

*Courtesy of Loveland Division.

Control Logic

The control logic uses a wire braid toroidal core read only memory containing 64 29-bit words. Magnetic logic of this type is extremely reliable and pleasingly compact.

The crystal controlled clock source initiates a current pulse having a trapezoidal waveform which is directed through one of 64 word lines. Bit patterns are generated by passing or threading selected toroids with the word lines. Each toroid that is threaded acts as a transformer to turn on a transistor connected to the output winding of the toroid. The signals from these transistors operate the program ROM, coincident current core, and selected micro-instructions.

Coincident Current Core Read/Write Memory

The 2208 (6 × 16 × 23) bit coincident current memory uses wide temperature range lithium cores. In addition, the X, Y, and inhibit drivers have temperature compensated current drive sources to make the core memory insensitive to temperature and power supply variations.

Power Supplies

The arithmetic processing unit operates from a single -15 volt supply. Even though the power supply is highly regulated, all circuits are designed to operate over a voltage range of -13.5 to -16.5

Display

The display is generated on an HP electrostatic cathode ray tube only 11 inches long. The flat rectangular face plate measures $3\frac{1}{4}$ $\times$ $4\frac{13}{16}$ inches. The tube was specifically designed to generate a bright image. High contrast is obtained by using a low transmissivity filter in front of the CRT. Ambient light that usually tends to "wash out" an image is attenuated twice by the filter, while the screen image is only attenuated once.

All the displayed characters are "pieces of eight." Sixteen different symbols are obtained by intensity modulating a figure 8 pattern as shown in Fig. 12. Floating point numbers are partitioned into groups of three digits and the numeral 1 is shifted to improve readability. Zeros to the left of the most significant digit and insignificant zeros to the right of the decimal point are blanked to avoid a confusing display. Fixed point numbers are automatically rounded up according to the decimal wheel setting. A fixed point display will automatically revert to floating point notation if the number is too large to be displayed on the CRT in fixed point.

Multilayer Instruction Logic Board

All of the hard wired logic gates are synthesized on the instruction logic board using time-proven diode-resistor logic. The diodes and resistors are located in separate rows, Fig. 13. All diodes are oriented in the same direction and all resistors are the same value. The maze of interconnections normally associated with the back plane wiring of a computer are located on the six internal layers of the multilayer instruction logic board. Solder bridges and accidental shorts caused by test probes shorting to leads beneath components are all but eliminated by not having interconnections on the two outside surfaces of this multilayer board. The

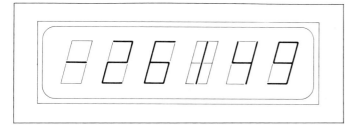

Fig. 12. Displayed characters are generated by modulating these figures. The digit 1 is shifted to the center of the pattern.

instruction logic board also serves as a motherboard for the control logic board, the two coincident core boards and the two flip flop boards, the magnetic card reader, and the keyboard. It also contains a connector, available at the rear of the calculator, for connecting peripherals.

Flip Flops

The Model 9100A contains 40 identical J-K flip flops, each having a threshold noise immunity of 2.5 volts. Worst case design techniques guarantee that the flip flops will operate at 3 MHz even though 1.2 MHz is the maximum operating rate.

Program Read Only Memory

The 32,768 bit read only program memory consists of 512 64-bit words. These words contain all of the operating subroutines, stored constants, character encoders, and CRT modulating patterns. The 512 words are contained in a 16 layer printer-circuit board having drive and sense lines orthogonally located. A drive line consists of a reference line and a data line. Drive pulses are inductively coupled from both the reference line and data line into the sense lines. Signals from the data line either aid or cancel signals from the reference line producing either a 1 or 0 on the output sense lines. The drive and sense lines are arranged to achieve a bit density in the ROM data board of 1000 bits per square inch.

The program ROM decoder/driver circuits are located directly above the ROM data board. Thirty-two combination sense amplifier, gated-latch circuits are located on each side of the ROM data board. The outputs of these circuits control the hard wired logic gates on the instruction logic board.

Side Boards

The program ROM printed circuit board and the instruction logic board are interconnected by the side boards, where preliminary signal processing occurs.

The Keyboard

The keyboard contains 63 molded plastic keys. Their markings will not wear off because the lettering is imbedded into the key body using a double shot injection molding process. The key and switch assembly was specifically designed to obtain a pleasing feel and the proper amount of tactile and aural feedback. Each key operates a single switch having gold alloy contacts. A contact closure activates a matrix which encodes signals on six data lines and generates an initiating signal. This signal is delayed to avoid the effects of contact bounce. An electrical interlock prevents errors caused by pressing more than one key at a time.

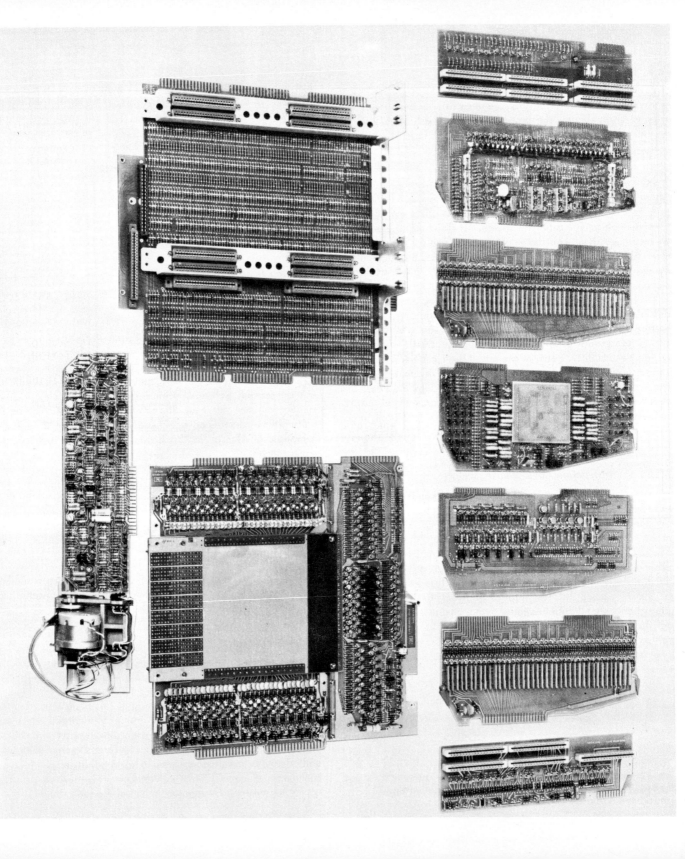

Magnetic Card Reader

Two complete 196 step programs can be recorded on the credit card size magnetic program card. The recording process erases any previous information so that a card may be used over and over again. A program may be protected against accidental erase by clipping off the corner of the card, Fig. 9. The missing corner deactivates the recording circuitry in the magnetic card reader. Program cards are compatible among machines.

Information is recorded in four tracks with a bit density of 200 bits per inch. Each six-bit program step is split into two time-multiplexed, three-bit codes and recorded on three of the four tracks. The fourth track provides the timing strobe.

Information is read from the card and recombined into six bit codes for entry into the core memory. The magnetic card reading circuitry recognizes the "END" program code as a signal to end the reading process. This feature makes it possible to enter subroutines within the body of a main program or to enter numeric constants via the program card. The END code also sets the program counter to location 0-0, the most probable starting location. The latter feature makes the Model 9100A ideally suited to "linking" programs that require more than 196 steps.

Packaging and Servicing

The packaging of the Model 9100A began by giving the HP industrial design group a volume estimate of the electronics package, the CRT display size and the number of keys on the keyboard. Several sketches were drawn and the best one was selected. The electronics sections were then specifically designed to fit in this case. Much time and effort were spent on the packaging of the arithmetic processing unit. The photographs, Figs. 11 and 14, attest to the fact that it was time well spent.

The case covers are die cast aluminum which offers durability, effective RFI shielding, excellent heat transfer characteristics, and convenient mechanical mounts. Removing four screws allows the case to be opened and locked into position, Fig. 14. This procedure exposes all important diagnostic test points and adjustments. The keyboard and arithmetic processing unit may be freed by removing four and seven screws respectively.

Any component failures can be isolated by using a diagnostic routine or a special tester. The fault assembly is then replaced and is sent to a service center for computer assisted diagnosis and repair.

Reliability

Extensive precautions have been taken to insure maximum reliability. Initially, wide electrical operating margins were

Fig. 14. International adjustments of the calculator are easily accessible by removing a few screws and lifting the top.

obtained by using "worst case" design techniques. In production all transistors are aged at 80% of rated power for 96 hours and tested before being used in the Model 9100A. Subassemblies are computer tested and actual operating margins are monitored to detect trends that could lead to failures. These data are analyzed and corrective action is initated to reverse the trend. In addition, each calculator is operated in an environmental chamber at 55°C for 5 days prior to shipment to the customer. Precautions such as these allow Hewlett-Packard to offer a one year warranty in a field where 90 days is an accepted standard.

Internal Programming of the 9100A Calculator

Extensive internal programming has been designed into the HP Model 9100A Calculator to enable the operator to enter data and to perform most arithmetic operations necessary for engineering and scientific calculation with a single key stroke or single program step. Each of the following operations is a hardware subroutine called by a key press or program step:

Fig. 13 (opposite). Printed-circuit boards which make up the arithmetic unit are, left to right at top, side board, control logic, flip flop, core and drivers, core sense amplifiers and inhibit, flip flop, and side board. Large board at the lower left is the multilayer instruction board, and the program ROM is at the right. The magnetic card reader and its associated circuitry are at the bottom.

Basic arithmetic operations
 Addition
 Subtraction
 Multiplication
 Division

Extended arithmetic operations
 Square root
 Exponential—e^x
 Logarithmic—ln x, log x
Vector addition and subtraction

Trigonometric operations
 Sin x, cos x, tan x
 Arcsin x, arccos x, arctan x
 Sinh x, cosh x, tanh x
 Arcsinh x, arccosh x, arctanh x
 Polar to rectangular and rectangular to
  polar coordinate transformation

Miscellaneous
 Enter π
 Absolute value of y
 Integer value of x

In the evolution of internal programming of the Model 9100A Calculator, the first step was the development of flow charts of each function. Digit entry, Fig. 15, seemingly a trivial function, is as complex as most of the mathematical functions. From this functional description, a detailed program can be written which uses the microprograms and incremental instructions of the calculator. Also, each program must be married to all of the other programs which make up the hard-wired software of the Model 9100A. Mathematical functions are similarly programmed defining a step-by-step procedure or algorithm for solving the desired mathematical problem.

The calculator is designed so that lower-order subroutines may be nested to a level of five in higher-order functions. For instance, the "Polar to Rectangular" function uses the sin routine which uses multiply which uses add, etc.

Addition and Subtraction

The most elementary mathematical operation is algebraic addition. But even this is relatively complex—it requires comparing signs and complementing if signs are unlike. Because all numbers in the Model 9100A are processed as true floating point numbers, exponents must be subtracted to determine proper decimal alignment. If one of the numbers is zero, it is represented in the calculator by an all-zero mantissa with zero exponent. The difference between the two exponents determines the offset, and rather than shifting the smaller number to the right, a displaced digit-by-digit addition is performed. It must also be determined if the offset is greater than 12, which is the resolution limit.

Although the display shows 10 significant digits, all calculations

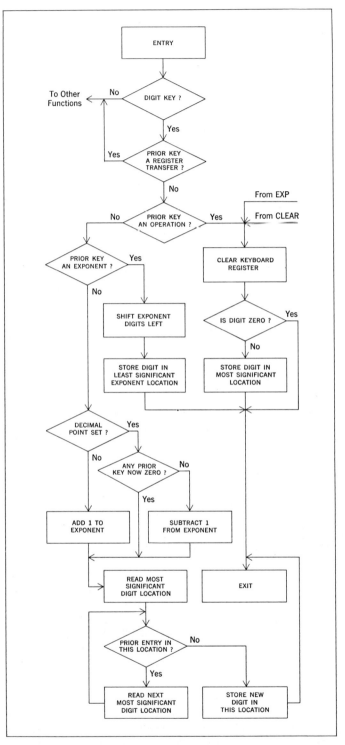

Fig. 15. Flow chart of a simple digit entry. Some of these flow paths are used by other calculator operations for greater hardware efficiency.

are performed to 12 significant digits with the two last significant digits (guard digits) absorbing truncation and round-off errors. All registers are in core memory, eliminating the need for a large number of flip-flop registers. Even with the display in "Fixed Point" mode, every computed result is in storage in 12 digits.

Multiplication

Multiplication is successive addition of the multiplicand as determined by each multiplier digit. Offset in the digit position flip-flops is increased by one after completion of the additions by each multiplier digit. Exponents are added after completion of the product. Then the product is normalized to justify a carry digit which might have occurred.

Division

Division involves repeated subtraction of the divisor from the dividend until an overdraft occurs. At each subtraction without overdraft, the quotient digit is incremented by one at the digit position of iteration. When an overdraft occurs, the dividend is restored by adding the divisor. The division digit position is then incremented and the process continued. Exponents are subtracted after the quotient is formed, and the quotient normalized.

Square Root

Square root, in the Model 9100A, is considered a basic operation and is done by pseudo division. The method used is an extension of the integer relationship.

$$\sum_{i=1}^{n} 2i - 1 = n^2$$

In square root, the divisor digit is incremented at each iteration, and shifted when an overdraft and restore occurs. This is a very fast algorithm for square root and is equal in speed to division.

Circular Routines

The circular routines (sin, cos, tan), the inverse circular routines (arcsin, arccos, arctan) and the polar to rectangular and rectangular to polar conversions are all accomplished by iterating through a transformation which rotates the axes. Any angle may be represented as an angle between 0 and 1 radian plus additional information such as the number of times $\pi/2$ has been added or subtracted, and its sign. The basic algorithm for the forward circular function operates on an angle whose absolute value is less than 1 radian, but prescaling is necessary to indicate quadrant.

To obtain the scaling constants, the argument is divided by 2π, the integer part discarded and the remaining fraction of the circle multiplied by 2π. Then $\pi/2$ is subtracted from the absolute value until the angle is less than 1 radian. The number of times $\pi/2$ is

subtracted, the original sign of the argument, and the sign upon completion of the last subtraction make up the scaling constants. To preserve the quadrant information the scaling constants are stored in the core memory.

The algorithm produces tan θ. Therefore, in the Model 9100A, cos θ is generated as

$$\frac{1}{\sqrt{1 + \tan^2 \theta}}$$

and sin θ as

$$\frac{\tan \theta}{\sqrt{1 + \tan^2 \theta}}$$

Sin θ could be obtained from the relationship $\sin \theta = \sqrt{1 - \cos^2 \theta}$, for example, but the use of the tangent relationship preserves the 12 digit accuracy for very small angles, even in the range of $\theta < 10^{-12}$. The proper signs of the functions are assigned from the scaling constants.

For the polar to rectangular functions, cos θ and sin θ are computed and multiplied by the radius vector to obtain the X and Y coordinates. In performing the rectangular to polar function, the signs of both the X and Y vectors are retained to place the resulting angle in the right quadrant.

Prescaling must also precede the inverse circular functions, since this routine operates on arguments less than or equal to 1. The inverse circular algorithm yields arctangent functions, making it necessary to use the trigonometric identity.

$$\sin^{-1}(x) = \tan^{-1}\frac{x}{\sqrt{1 - x^2}}$$

If $\cos^{-1}(x)$ is desired, the arcsin relationship is used and a scaling constant adds $\pi/2$ after completion of the function. For arguments greater than 1, the arccotangent of the negative reciprocal is found which yields the arctangent when $\pi/2$ is added.

Exponential and Logarithms

The exponential routine uses a compound iteration algorithm which has an argument range of 0 to the natural log of 10 (ln 10). Therefore, to be able to handle any argument within the dynamic range of the calculator, it is necessary to prescale the absolute value of the argument by dividing it by ln 10 and saving the integer part to be used as the exponent of the final answer. The fractional part is multiplied by ln 10 and the exponential found. This number is the mantissa, and with the previously saved integer part as a power of 10 exponent, becomes the final answer.

The exponential answer is reciprocated in case the original argument was negative, and for use in the hyperbolic functions. For these hyperbolic functions, the following identities are used:

$$\sinh x = \frac{e^x - e^{-x}}{2}$$

$$\cosh x = \frac{e^x + e^{-x}}{2}$$

$$\tanh x = \frac{e^x - e^{-x}}{e^x + e^{-x}}$$

Natural Logarithms

The exponential routine in reverse is used as the routine for natural logs, with only the mantissa operated upon. Then the exponent is multiplied by ln 10 and added to the answer. This routine also yields these $\log_{10}$ and are hyperbolic functions:

$$\log_{10} x = \frac{\ln x}{\ln 10}$$

$$\sinh^{-1}(x) = \ln(x + \sqrt{x^2 + 1})$$

$$\cosh^{-1}(x) = \ln(x + \sqrt{x^2 - 1})$$

$$\tanh^{-1}(x) = \ln\sqrt{\frac{1 + x}{1 - x}}$$

The $\sinh^{-1}(x)$ relationship above yields reduced accuracy for negative values of x. Therefore, in the Model 9100A, the absolute value of the argument is operated upon and the correct sign affixed after completion.

Accuracy

It can be seen from the discussion of the algorithms that extreme care has been taken to use routines that have accuracy commensurate with the dynamic range of the calculator. For example; the square root has a maximum possible relative error of 1 part in 10^{10} over the full range of the machine.

There are many algorithms for determining the sine of an angle; most of these have points of high error. The sine routine in the Model 9100A has consistent low error regardless of quadrant. Marrying a full floating decimal calculator with unique mathematical algorithms results in accuracy of better than 10 displayed digits.

Chapter 49

The HP 9810/20/30 Series

A New Series of Programmable Calculators[1]

Richard M. Spangler

In recent years, programmable calculators have taken on a large portion of the computation jobs that were previously handled by computers. Calculators have several advantages that are responsible for this trend. Calculators are small, self-contained, and easily transported—they can be brought directly to the user's desk. They are quiet, and fit easily into a laboratory or office environment. No complicated turn-on procedure is required; the user merely turns on the power switch, and the calculator is ready. The most important advantage is a psychological one—calculators are "friendly." They are interactive, they provide immediate feedback and immediate answers, and they are dedicated to their user.

The 9800 Series is a new line of powerful programmable calculators and an extensive set of calculator peripherals. The series is designed to cover a broad range of applications. Important objectives of the new series are to provide the user with a choice of calculators that are flexible and expandable, and to support those calculators with comprehensive applications software and peripherals.

The new 9800 Series is the successor of the 9100A/B [Hewlett-Packard, September 1968], HP's first programmable calculators. These earlier calculators were as powerful as the limits of technology at the time of their conception would allow them to be. But with technological advances come better calculators, hence the 9800 Series.

Three Models

There are currently three calculators in the 9800 Series. Model 10 is a key-per-function calculator with a keyboard and language that are extensions of the HP 9100A/B. The display is a three-register numeric display like the 9100A/B's, but uses seven-segment light-emitting-diode characters rather than a cathode-ray tube.

Model 20 has a statement-oriented algebraic language. The user doesn't have to position his variables in special registers or keep track of temporary results. He can enter arithmetic expressions in the same order as he would read them, including parentheses. Model 20 even allows implied multiplication, something that's not

[1]*Hewlett-Packard Journal*, vol. 24, December 1972, pp. 2–4.

allowed even in most high-level computer languages. Model 20 has a display of 16 alphanumeric characters that can display a whole statement at a time. The alphanumeric display can be used during program execution to display comments and instructions as well as numeric results. This capability enhances the interactiveness of this model.

Model 30 is even more interactive. The keyboard is alphanumeric, like a typewriter, rather than key-per-function. This complements the 32-character alphanumeric display by making it convenient to enter text and messages. The programming language of the Model 30 is BASIC, a well-known and easy-to-learn computer language that is designed for use in interactive environments.

The electronics of the 9800 Series is general in design and is common to all three calculators. The central processing unit is a microprogrammed, 16 bit serial processor that implements a general computer machine language (see article, p. 820). The three separate keyboard languages and the arithmetic routines are implemented by firmware routines stored in MOS read-only memory (ROM), and the user's programs are stored in MOS read-write memory. The input/output structure is a general purpose system which makes it possible to interface with a wide variety of peripherals (see article, p. 817).

Many Peripherals

Some of the more important peripherals that have been interfaced are:

9860A	Card Reader
9861A	Output Typewriter
9862A	X-Y Plotter
9863A	Mechanical Paper Tape Reader
9864A	Digitizer
9865A	Magnetic Tape Cassette
9866A	Thermal Line Printer
9869A	Hopper Fed Card Reader
2570A	Instrumentation Coupler
2748A	Paper Tape Reader
2895A	Paper Tape Punch

Several general purpose interface cards are also available to interface with other HP instruments, the new HP interface systems [Nelson and Ricci, 1972], and many peripherals from other manufacturers.

Flexible and Expandable

Flexibility and expandability of the keyboard and programming languages of 9800 Series calculators are provided through the use of add-on ROM modules. From the optional ROMs available, the

Comparing 9800 Series Calculators

	9100A/B	9810A	9820A	9830A
Language	Reverse Polish	Reverse Polish	Algebraic	BASIC
Keyboard	Key per function	Key per function	Key per function	Alphanumeric
ROM size (bytes)	4K	5K to 11K	8K to 14K	14K to 31K
RWM size (bytes) Available to user	128(A); 256(B)	908 to 2924	1384 to 3432	3520 to 7616
I/O structure	Special purpose	General	General	General
User definable keys or functions	None	Optional— single key subroutine	Optional— single key subroutine or function with pa- rameters	Standard— subroutine or function with one parameter
Recording device	Magnetic card	Card with cassette optional	Card with cassette optional	Cassette standard
Display	3 register numeric CRT	3 register numeric LED	16 character alphanu- meric LED	32 character alphanumeric LED
Primary Printer	Optional 16 column numeric	Optional 16 column alphanumeric	Standard 16 column alphanumeric	Optional 80 column alphanumeric

user can select the language features that are required by his particular discipline.

In Model 10, three ROM blocks of up to 2048 bytes each may be added to the calculator. The first block is used to define and implement the functions of a set of 15 keys on the keyboard. The second and third blocks are for control of internal and external peripherals.

In Model 20, three blocks may be added, each controlling one of three sets of ten keys on the keyboard.

In Model 30, eight blocks may be added, and since the Model 30 has an alphanumeric keyboard, no special keys are required. The ROMs are accessed through mnemonics which are entered as a sequence of alphabetic characters.

Different Models for Different Users

Each of the three calculators is general purpose, but each has features which make it more appealing to different sets of users. Model 10's advantages are its low cost, and its compatibility with the 9100A/B, which provides the basis for an extensive applications program library. For example, the Surveying and Statistics applications packages that were originally developed for the 9100A/B have been updated and expanded to make use of the new features of Model 10.

Its natural algebraic language and its many programming and editing features, such as program flags and relative addressing, make Model 20 ideal for users who want to do their own programming. These features are particularly appealing to research scientists and engineers. The peripheral control capabilities of the Model 20 also make it attractive for use as a controller in instrumentation systems [Nelson and Ricci, 1972].

Its larger memory, its array-variable capability, and its built-in tape cassette make Model 30 appealing to users with large programs and data bases, such as structural engineers and investment analysts. The alphanumeric keyboard, string-variable capability, and page-width printer appeal to users in fields outside the scientific, such as education and business. The programming language of the Model 30 appeals to a large number of users who already know BASIC as a time-sharing language. With an optional Terminal ROM, time-share users can transform the Model 30 into a versatile terminal with local as well as remote computation and storage capability.

With all three calculators, each user can specify a system of optional ROMs, peripherals, and read-write memory size to meet his own needs. This versatility is enhanced by user-definable keys, optional on the Models 10 and 20 and standard on Model 30. All three machines can also be expanded by the user of special machine language programs that can be loaded into read-write memory from a magnetic card or cassette. This capability can be used, for example, to supply a software driver for a special peripheral.

The special features of each calculator along with the general purpose nature of the hardware are designed so that some combination of 9800 Series instruments will provide a solution to almost any programmable calculator application.

References

Hewlett-Packard [September 1968]; Nelson and Ricci [1972].

Model 10 Maintains Compatibility, Expands Capability[1]

Curtis D. Brown / Jack M. Walden

In keyboard language and appearance, Model 10 of the 9800 Series, or Model 9810A, is closely related to the 9100A/B Calculators, HP's first programmable calculators and the predecessors of the 9800 Series. Most of the 9810A keys are marked the same as the 9100A/B keys, and when used in the same way, perform the same operations. The same "reverse Polish" keyboard language is used. What's more, the keycodes stored in the program memory are the same when the keys are marked the same. This close similarity was maintained wherever possible to provide a useful carryover of the well established 9100A/B keyboard operations and associated programming techniques. However, 9100A/B operations are a *subset* of the 9810A's. Many new capabilities and features have been added in the new calculator.

In hardware implementation the 9810A bears no resemblance to the 9100A/B. Rather, it is similar to the other 9800-Series Calculators, Models 20 and 30. 9800-Series Calculators are all implemented from a common hardware base which is actually a 16-bit-word, general-purpose minicomputer. Individual calculator-model characteristics are obtained by internal ROM-stored machine-language programming. The unique hardware for each model consists primarily of the keyboard and display, which are tailored to the needs of the individual models.

The most important individual characteristics of the 9810A are:

1 A three-register (x, y, and z) light-emitting diode display

2 Separate memories for program and data storage

3 All-decimal addressing of program and data storage

4 Modular internal expansion of program and/or data storage

5 Indirect addressing for any register reference

[1]*Hewlett-Packard Journal*, vol. 24, December 1972, pp. 5–8.

6 Arithmetic operations (all four functions) into or from all data registers

7 Optional function blocks (ROM) to define the operation of the lefthand keyblock and other auxiliary functions, user-installable with ease.

9810A Hardware Features

The three-register LED display is one of the most conspicuous front-of-machine changes noticed by those familiar with the 9100A/B's CRT display. LED display was chosen because it is a bright, highly visible display whose brightness and size of characters are practically uninfluenced by line voltage, it fits in a small space, and its low supply voltages and signal levels interface directly to internal logic levels and supply voltages.

The magnetic card reader has a new feedthrough card path, allowing the use of longer cards than those used in the 9100A/B. The longer cards have greatly increased storage capacity, a necessity for making full use of the larger program and data memories of the 9810A and 9820A Calculators.

The 9810A and 9820A Calculators each have three sockets for plug-in read-only-memory (ROM) modules. These are direct extensions of the internal ROM. They allow expansion of operating features and redefinition of the lefthand keyblock. In the 9810A the lefthand keys may be defined at the user's option to provide standard mathematical functions (almost identical to the 9100A/B), statistical calculations, user-definable (keyboard language) functions, or programming aids.

The optional plotter, cassette, typewriter, and other peripherals are controlled by other plug-in blocks that are accessed by use of the FMT key on the keyboard. This plug-in block concept allows the user to configure and reconfigure the machine and peripheral-control facilities to suit the needs of the moment.

The thermal strip printer, housed within the calculator case, is controlled by internal programming. The basic 9810A provides for the printing of numeric values as they appear in the x register, or the listing of programs as they appear in the program-mode display. An optional plug-in block provides for message printing and the addition of keycode mnemonics (functional abbreviations) to the program listings.

9810A Software Features

While the 9810A has a much larger bit-storage capacity than the 9100A/B, its memory is effectively made still larger by some new step-saving features. A major change from the 9100A/B is the decimal addressing structure for programs and data. The novice programmer adapts more quickly to decimal addressing, but a more important reason for its adoption is that it is necessary for the indirect addressing mode. An indirect reference to register a, say, will result in using the *value* of register a as a new register *address*. For example, the keystroke sequence x→, INDIRECT, a, will store the contents of the calculator's x register in the register whose address is given by the contents of a.

The indirect capability of the calculator can save many steps when a number of data registers are to undergo equivalent operations. One data register can be set aside as a pointer. The value of the pointer register designates one of the data registers to which the operations are to be applied. By incrementing the pointer register, a common subroutine can operate on the desired

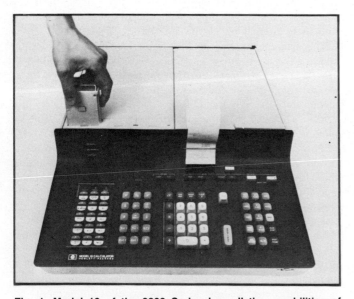

Fig. 1. Model 10 of the 9800 Series has all the capabilities of previous HP programmable calculators, plus many others. New features are the LED display, a larger internally expandable memory, decimal and indirect addressing, arithmetic operations into or from all data registers, and optional plug-in function blocks to define the lefthand keyblock and other auxiliary functions.

data registers in turn, saving many program steps over the direct reference method.

Another important step-saving feature in the 9810A is the register arithmetic capability. Normally, if one wanted to add the x register to register 10, one would recall register 10 to the y register, add the x register, and store the results in register 10. With register arithmetic, however, a mathematical operator may be specified preceding the transfer address in a store or recall operation. One would then say x→, +, 10 to do the above operation.

This capability is bidirectional. Thus x←, +, 10 will add register 10 to the x register. Since any of the four arithmetic operations (+, −, ×, ÷) may be used, each register of the 9810A is in effect a powerful accumulator. This feature greatly increases programming flexibility by reducing the amount of shuffling of the x, y, and z registers.

Indirect addressing may be used with register arithmetic by including the INDIRECT key either before or after the arithmetic operator.

Because of the size of the 9810A memory, an improvement in programming and debugging ease over the 9100A/B was vital. Three new features attack this problem directly: label goto's; alphanumeric key mnemonics; and a printed record of entered keystrokes (keylogging.)

Labeled transfers are most useful during the program creation phase, where actual program step addresses either are not known or may change frequently as debugging progresses. Any step in the calculator program may be assigned a label by entering the LABEL key followed by any other keystroke. Control may later be transferred to that step by executing a GOTO or GOSUB LBL, then the same keystroke. A search is initiated, beginning at program step zero, and continuing through the program area until the label is found. Later, when the program is operating satisfactorily, absolute addresses may be substituted for each labeled GOTO; this gives a speed advantage by eliminating the search. (Model 9820A also has these capabilities.)

Alpha Printing

An alternative to remembering the numerical equivalents of all 64 keys is provided by an optional ROM, which generates three-letter mnemonics during listings on the thermal printer. These are useful for program debugging or documentation. This ROM also allows printing of messages during program execution, using the Format key to change the definition of the calculator keyboard. Two consecutive FMT keystrokes begin the character print mode. Keys that follow are interpreted as characters of the alphabet, rather than as their assigned function, and are printed a line at a time on the strip printer. Another FMT key terminates the character print mode and restores normal calculator operation.

The keylog feature provides a printed record of all calculator keyboard operations. When the keylog mode is selected each key entered from the keyboard is automatically printed. If the calculator is in keyboard mode, the steps in a certain calculation may be verified. In program mode, the result is a full step-by-step listing of the program entered. With the optional plug-in ROM, mnemonics are printed along with the keycode.

Another feature that simplifies the operator's interaction with the 9810A is a backstep key. The backstep key decrements the calculator program step counter. It's helpful in examination of stored programs.

Flexibility through Plug-in ROMs

To one person, his 9810A may be an aid in statistics, to another it may be a purely mathematical or scientific machine, while to a third, it may be a peripheral controller. This changing nature of the 9810A is made possible by the plug-in ROM concept. The implementation of this concept posed a special problem for the machine coding. How can blocks yet to be conceived be slot-independent and still interface readily to the basic calculator?

The solution was to use the Format key to initiate a search through possible ROM block locations. The key following the FMT is compared with a special identifier word in each ROM, and when these codes match, the desired ROM has been found.

Many operations which could not be included in the keyboard directly are also implemented through the FMT key:

1) FMT ↑:	raise the plotter pen and move the coordinates given in the x and y registers.
2) FMT ↓:	lower the plotter pen and move to the coordinates given in the x and y registers.
3) FMT x→ x←	load or record data registers using the magnetic card reader.
4) FMT GOTO	load a magnetic card program at location zero, and begin execution at location zero (useful for chain-loading programs).
5) FMT CONTINUE	start the paper tape reader and prepare the calculator to accept information.

There routines are all contained in the basic 9810A.

Interactive Model 20 Speaks Algebraic Language[1]

Rex L. James / Francis J. Yockey

In Model 20 of the 9800 Series, or Model 9820A, the emphasis is on using the 9800 technology to provide a highly interactive calculator. Like the 9810A, the 9820A is a ROM-driven minicomputer. Its interactive nature stems mainly from its natural algebraic language and its built-in peripherals—keyboard, printer, and display.

Modularity provides another level of interactiveness by allowing the user to configure the 9820A to fit his application.

The display consists of a single register of sixteen alphanumeric characters. Each character is formed by a seven-row, five-column matrix of light-emitting diodes (LEDs). The printer and keyboard

are similar mechanically to those of the 9810A (see box, page 808).

The 9820A's combination of fast LED display and quiet thermal strip printer allows a program to be run in an interactive mode unattainable before. The hard-copy results on the printer aren't cluttered with user instructions, since these appear in the LED display. User instructions appear instantaneously in the display; there's no need to wait for a printout.

When a key is pressed a mnemonic or character appears in the display to give instant visual feedback. The 16 characters are enough so that successive keystrokes can be seen in context. For example, the expression "if the square root of 6 equals A, go to line 17" would require the keystrokes

$$IF \sqrt{6} = A; \; GOTO \; 17$$

and would appear in the display as

$$IF \sqrt{6} = A; \; GTO \; 17$$

[1]*Hewlett-Packard Journal*, vol. 24, December 1972, pp. 8–13.

Natural Algebraic Language

Model 20 uses a powerful but natural instruction set to enable the user to solve complex mathematical problems quickly. The instruction set combines the features of the keyboard with the features of computer languages like ALGOL, FORTRAN, and BASIC. The result is a human-oriented, conversational approach to problem-solving, an approach that follows the structure of algebra in symbols and hierarchy.

A typical program for the 9820A is as follows. The program solves the quadratic equation $(-B \pm \sqrt{(BB-4AC)})/2A$.

```
 0:  ENT "A VALUE",A
 1:  PRT "A=",A
 2:  ENT "B VALUE",B
 3:  PRT "B=",B
 4:  ENT "C VALUE",C
 5:  PRT "C=",C
 6:  IF 4AC>BB;GTO "IMAG"
 7:  PRT "REAL ROOTS";SPC 1
 8:  PRT (-B+√(BB-4AC))/2A;SPC 1
 9:  PRT (-B-√(BB-4AC))/2A;SPC 9;JMP -9
10:  "IMAG"
11:  PRT "COMPLEX ROOTS";SPC 1
12:  PRT "REAL", "IMAGINARY";SPC 2
13:  PRT -B/2A,√(4AC-BB)/2A;SPC 1
14:  PRT -B/2A, -√(4AC-BB)/2A;SPC 9; GTO 0
15:  END
```

Notice in lines 8 and 9 of the program that the answer to the equation is programmed in the same way that the user would write it on paper. There are no artificial machine rules to remember. To maintain the structure of algebra, implied multiplication was implemented to avoid forcing the user to insert "*" between variables to be multiplied. Parentheses can be used and nested to any depth to change the order of evaluation of an algebraic expression.

Lines 0–5 demonstrate the interactiveness of the calculator. First the calculator stops and displays an alpha message of what is to be entered. The user then keys in the desired value. After RUN PROGRAM is pressed the calculator stores the value away and prints the label and the value of the entered data. In this way all three values A, B, and C may be entered. The roots then appear on the printout.

Fig. 2. Model 20 of the 9800 Series has a 16-character alphanumeric LED display that shows several keystrokes or program steps in context. Special features are a natural algebraic language, an interactive mode of operation, and plug-in modules that define the functions of the three lefthand keyblocks.

Editing

Convenient editing features have been included in the 9820A. To edit the above program to change to the absolute form of the GOTO, the user would key in *GOTO 6 RECALL*. Line 6 will be recalled to the display. Hitting the back key 7 times will give the following display:

6:IF 4AC>BB; GTO

To finish the edit, the user keys in *1 0 STORE* to form the new line of program. Since the label is no longer needed in line 10, it can be eliminated by keying in GTO *1 0 RECALL DELETE*.

The new listing is as follows:

```
0:  ENT "A VALUE",A
1:  PRT "A=",A
2:  Ent "B VALUE",B
3:  PRT "B=",B
```

4:   ENT "C VALUE",C

5:   PRT "C=", C

6:   IF 4AC>BB;GTO 10

7:   PRT "REAL ROOTS";SPC 1

8:   PRT (−B+√(BB−4AC))/2A;SPC 1

9:   PRT (−B−√(BB−4AC))/2A;SPC 9;JMP −9

10: PRT "COMPLEX ROOTS";SPC 1

11: PRT "REAL", "IMAGINARY";SPC 2

12: PRT −B/2A,√(4AC−BB)/2A;SPC 1

13: PRT −B/2A, −√(4AC−BB)/2A;SPC 9;GTO 0

14: END

Notice that the label has been deleted and all the lines below it have been moved up and renumbered.

With the editing keys, the user can REPLACE, INSERT, or DELETE any line or character. The user observes all of the changes as they take place, by watching the alphanumeric display.

Machine Language

An algebraic language is easy for humans to understand and use, but is difficult for a machine to understand and execute. Take the example:

$$A*B + C*D \qquad (1)$$

When operators appear between operands as in equation 1, the precedence of the operators becomes important in the sequence of execution. Since multiply is normally assigned a higher precedence than addition, those operations associated with multiplication are performed before addition.

Equation 1 can be rewritten so that operations are executed as they are encountered:

$$A \; B * C \; D * + \qquad (2)$$

This notation is known as "Polish," or more correctly, "reverse Polish" notation.

When equation 2 is executed, operands are passed directly to a stack, which is a temporary holding area organized so that the first item into the stack will be the last item out. When a binary operator is encountered, it is applied to the top two values of the stack. The specified operation is performed and a single result is

returned to the stack. Several forms of Polish notation are widely used by most desk calculators today, including the 9810A. Its main advantages are that it is easy to implement, it has fast execution speed, and it allows compact storage of programs. Its main disadvantage is that it isn't natural to the untrained user.

9820A Has Compiler

To take advantage of both the naturalness of the algebraic language and the speed and compactness of Polish notation, the 9820A's algebraic language is compiled into a machine language similar to the reverse Polish notation shown in equation 2. The compiler flowchart is shown in Fig. 3, along with an example showing the process of compiling the equation.

$$A+B\uparrow(C*D/(D+F)*G)$$

As a string of algebraic codes is input, the compiler forms a string of machine language codes. During the compiling operation a stack is used to hold the operators and establish their order of appearance in the compiled string. All operands are passed directly to the output string while operators are put into the stack.

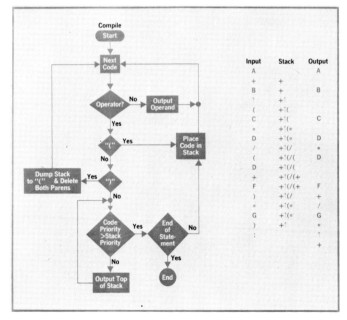

Fig. 3. Model 20 compiles algebraic-language user programs into a faster-executing machine language. Only the compile version is stored.

Printer and Keyboard for Models 10 and 20

The 9810A and 9820A Calculators use the same thermal printer and keyboard design.

The printer (Fig. 1) prints lines of sixteen alphanumeric characters on heat-sensitive paper. A five-by-seven dot matrix is used to form each character. The printer has a row of print elements distributed linearly across its printing head. Each print element is an electrical resistor of the right size and shape to produce a dot on heat-sensitive paper moved at a right angle to the line of print elements. Dots are formed in the conventional manner by exciting a resistor element with a pulse of electrical current, which raises its temperature.

The printer produces each line of print by printing the top row of all sixteen characters, then stepping down to print the second row, and so on until all seven rows are printed. Three blank steps are then added to produce the space between lines.

The printer is quiet and adaptable and has a minimum number of moving parts—all in the paper advance.

The keyboard is a contactless unit made up of an array of printed circuit transformers (Fig. 2). The secondaries of all the coils are tied in series to form the sense line (Fig. 3). The primaries of the coils are arranged in pairs. Each pair is connected in series with opposite polarity. Every pair has a drive and sink line, which is selected and driven by the scanner.

Centered above each coil is a metal disc attached to the end of the key shaft. When a key is pressed the disc moves closer to the coil. The disc acts like a shorted turn, reducing the coupling of the coil and unbalancing the pair. This un-balance is amplified by the comparator when it is greater than the "on" bias. The comparator triggers the one-shot multivibrator, which turns off the scanner and lowers the "on" bias. The scanner remains in the same state, which corresponds to the drive and sink line of the key that was pressed. This state is the keycode of the key pressed.

When the key is released a spring retracts the key and disc. When the unbalance is less than the lowered "on" bias the comparator turns off and the scanner starts again, ready for a new keystroke. The two bias levels give the key mechanical hysteresis.

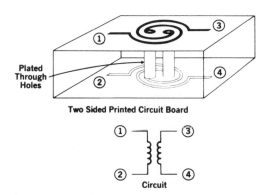

Two Sided Printed Circuit Board

Circuit

Fig. 2. *Printed-circuit transformers, one for each key, are used in the contactless keyboard.*

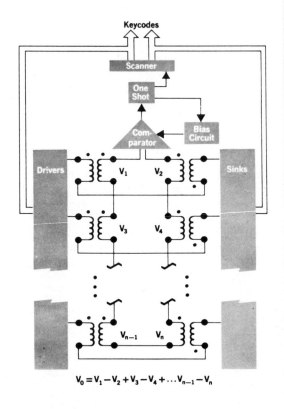

$$V_0 = V_1 - V_2 + V_3 - V_4 + \ldots V_{n-1} - V_n$$

Fig. 3. *Pressing a key unbalances one of the pairs of transformers and causes a keycode to be transmitted by the scanner.*

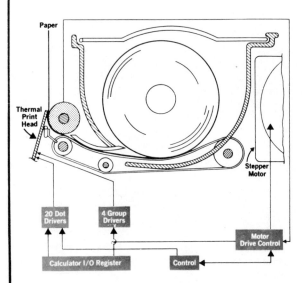

Fig. 1. *Thermal printer has few moving parts.*

Before an operator is placed into the stack, the stack is checked to see that all operators of greater or equal priority are first output.

Parentheses can be used to change the normal order of execution of an algebraic statement. The left parenthesis has the effect of temporarily resetting the compiler for the evaluation of the string of codes found inside the parentheses. The right parenthesis will then cause all operators in the stack to be output until a left parenthesis occurs. However, neither of the two parentheses are needed in the compiled code.

Compilers of this and more complex types have been used for years in computers. When changes to the program have to be made, the source cards or paper tape are changed accordingly and the program is recompiled. With a desk calculator, this operation is too severe a penalty to pay. Also, it isn't possible to store both the source code and the compiled code in the calculator memory at the same time. It's necessary, therefore, to reconstruct the code for editing and program listings.

Uncompiler

The solution to this problem is the concept of the uncompiler (see Fig. 4). With the uncompiler, it's possible to take the compiled code as input and reconstruct the original algebraic form. The code is scanned backwards. Parentheses are inserted where needed in the reconstructed code, and redundant parentheses are omitted. For example,

$$(A*B) + (C*D)$$

will be reconstructed as

$$A*B + C*D$$

after going through the compile/uncompile process.

With the compile/uncompile feature, the 9820A only has to store the compiled form of the code. In the 9820A, a line of program is the basic unit used for the compiler/uncompiler and editing features. As a line of program is entered, it is stored in a buffer area and displayed in its algebraic form. When the STORE key is hit, the line of program is compiled and stored away in the program area.

When the user chooses to edit a line of program, the program line is located in memory, uncompiled into a buffer area, and displayed in its reconstructed form. Now editing can be performed. When the editing is finished, the line is compiled and once again stored in memory. To the user, the compile/uncompile process is transparent except for a slight pause while storing or recalling a line of program.

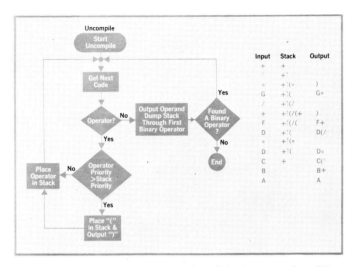

Fig. 4. An uncompiler reconstructs the original program for editing or listing.

Modularity

Another level of interactiveness is brought about by the modularity of the memory structure and the general-purpose minicomputer heart of the calculator. The 9820A can be configured to various applications in three ways: additional keyboard functions by read-only-memory additions, additional read/write memory, and addition of external peripherals.

There are thirty keys, arranged in three blocks of ten, available to the user to be defined for his special needs by means of plug-in ROM. Some plug-in modules provide mathematical functions, others give high-level-language control of external peripheral devices, and another allows users to define subroutines for their own special functions.

Because MOS RWM is used, additional user memory may easily be added to the basic machine. The fully loaded 9820A has 9K (9216) 16-bit words of memory: 7K is ROM and 2K is RWM.

The I/O structure provides four I/O slots on the back of the calculator to accept interface cards for peripheral devices. An I/O expander augments the four I/O slots of the calculator.

Another Program Example

A good example of Model 20's interactive nature is this Butterworth filter design program.

Display: NUMBER OF POLES?
Key in: 3
Display: CENTER FREQUENCY
Key in: 10000000
Display: BAND WIDTH?
Key in: 1000000
Display: RESISTANCE?
Key in: 50
Display: REALIZATION TYPE
Key in: 2

Realization Type 2 specifies the physical configuration of the circuit.

With this input the output shown in Fig. 5 comes from the printer.

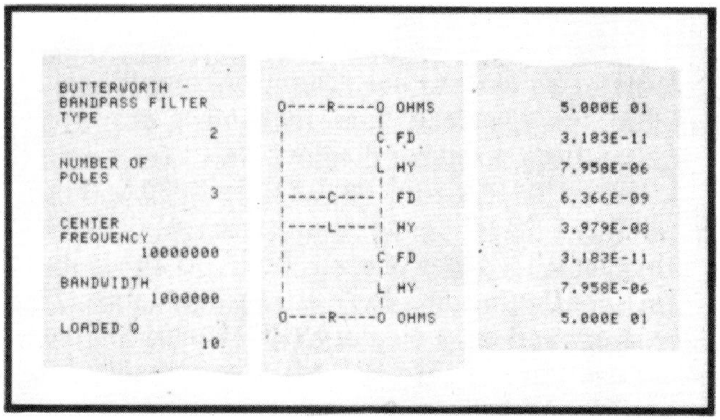

Fig. 5. Butterworth filter design program demonstrated interactiveness of calculator. Printer output is shown here; user instructions appear in display.

BASIC-Language Model 30 Can Be Calculator, Computer, or Terminal[1]

Richard M. Spangler

Model 9830A is the latest and most powerful calculator in the 9800 Series. Its keyboard design, programming language, memory size, I/O capability, and flexibility make the 9830A more like a desktop computer than a calculator. Yet it maintains the convenience and user interaction that makes a programmable calculator so easy to use. The user can still set the machine on his desk, turn the power on, type in 2+2, and see 4 on the display.

Like the 9810A and 9820A, the 9830A (Fig. 6) is a ROM-driven general-purpose minicomputer with specialized peripherals built in. In its minimum configuration, the 9830A contains 7½K words of read-only memory (ROM) and 2K words of read/write memory (RWM). The memory is expandable to 16K words of ROM and, initially, to 4K words of RWM. The display register contains 32 alphanumeric characters, and uses the same 5×7 LED dot matrix as the 9820A.

A built-in tape cassette unit is included in the mainframe in place of the magnetic card reader used in previous HP calculators. The I/O structure of the 9830A is identical to that of the 9810A and 9820A, so all the 9800-Series peripherals operate with the 9830A. The new 9866A page-width thermal line printer (see Fig. 1) is designed to be the primary output peripheral for the 9830A. It fits directly on top of the calculator. It can print 80-column lines at a rate of 250 lines per minute.

[1]*Hewlett-Packard Journal*, vol. 24, December 1972, pp. 14–18.

Fig. 6. Model 30 of the 9800 Series has an alphanumeric keyboard like a teleprinter. Its language is BASIC. It can be used as a desktop computer or a remote computer terminal, yet it maintains the convenience and user interaction of a programmable calculator.

Alphanumeric Keyboard

The keyboard of the 9830A represents its most significant departure from the traditional concept of a programmable calculator. It is not a key-per-function keyboard, but rather an alphanumeric keyboard like that of a typewriter or teleprinter terminal.

Besides the alpha section of the keyboard, there are three groups of special keys that facilitate use of the 9830A. The first group is a calculator section, which contains the digits and the

Fig. 7. Model 9866A Thermal Line Printer is the primary output peripheral for Model 30.

most commonly used arithmetic operators. The second group contains special control keys used in operating, editing, and debugging programs. The keys in the third group are definable by the user.

The use of an alphanumeric keyboard rather than a key-per-function keyboard removes the major restriction to programming language definition and language expandability. It is not necessary to add a new key to the keyboard whenever a new function is added to the language. Rather, a new function is assigned a mnemonic which can be entered as a sequence of alpha characters.

BASIC Language

In the development of the 9830A, it was decided not to define another new and unique programming language. The language of the 9830A is BASIC, which is well known among users of small computer and time-shared systems. All of the changes that have been made in BASIC in the 9830A are additions to standard BASIC, so programs written in versions of BASIC that are close to the standard version will run on the 9830A with little or no modification. This means that a tremendous program library is already available.

Besides being well known and used extensively, BASIC has several other characteristics which make it well suited for a programmable calculator. Since the language was originally designed for use in time-sharing environments, it is interactive and conversational. The 9830A fully exploits these characteristics by communicating through the 32-character alphanumeric display and the thermal line printer.

BASIC is easy to learn because the commands closely resemble English and there are very few tricky syntax rules to memorize. Each statement in a program is given a line number by the programmer, and the BASIC operating system automatically places the statements in order.

Program editing is easily accomplished simply by retyping any incorrect statement or assigning a line number between two existing lines to a statement to be inserted in a program. The 9830A has expanded on this editing capability by providing complete character-by-character editing. The user may recall a line of program to the display, edit the characters within that line, and store the corrected line without retyping the whole line. If an error is made while typing a statement, the incorrect line can be recalled and edited.

BASIC is also well suited for implementation by an interpreter rather than a compiler. With a compiler, the user's program is transformed before execution time into machine-language instructions, which are executed directly by the machine processor. With an interpreter, the user's program remains in memory in source form and an interpreting program examines the source program and calls on the appropriate execution routines. The main advantage of an interpreter in an interactive system like the 9830A is that only one copy of the user's program is needed for program editing and execution. With an interpreter, only minor additions are required to implement calculator functions such as TRACE or single STEP, or execution of statements directly from the keyboard.

Features of BASIC

The BASIC language has several important features which are new to programmable calculators. The most important is the type of variables that are allowed. Simple numeric variables, single- and double-subscripted array variables, and string variables may all be used. Array variables permit the analysis of large numbers of data items. String variables, which are strings of alphanumeric characters, permit such things as names and addresses to be analyzed and stored. Each variable is named by any letter of the alphabet, so the user can use R for resistance, Q for quota and N for the number of elements in an array. The calculator interpreter reserves only enough memory space for the variables currently in use.

Another feature of the BASIC language is user-definable functions. Standard BASIC restricts these functions to single arithmetic expressions, and allows only one parameter.

Like standard BASIC, 9830A BASIC allows only one parameter. However, the definition of the function can consist of more than one statement. For example, a function to evaluate N factorial may be defined as follows:

```
100 DEF FNF (N)
110 N1 = 1
120 FOR N2 = 1 TO N
130 N1 = N1 * N2
140 NEXT N2
150 RETURN N1
```

To assign a function to a user-definable key, the user presses the key labeled FETCH and then presses any of the ten definable keys. This puts the calculator into the key-definition mode. The user then enters his function and presses the END key. Now whenever he presses that particular key, the calculator responds with the name of the function—for example FNF for the factorial function. The user can then enter the argument, 5 for example, followed by the EXECUTE key. The calculator responds with the answer 120. Functions assigned to keys can be called either from the keyboard or from a program.

Single- or multiple-line functions are one of three categories of operations that can be assigned to the user-definable keys. These keys can also be used to store entire programs.

The user may also assign typing aids to his user-definable keys. A typing aid is simply a string of alphanumeric characters. Whenever a typing aid key is pressed, the characters that are assigned to that key are entered into the display just as if those characters had been entered individually from the keyboard. For instance, each of the keys could be assigned a mnemonic such as PRINT, INPUT, READ, and so on. These keys could then be used in typing BASIC programs. These functions of the user-definable keys make the 9830A act more like a calculator.

Output Formatting

A severe limitation of BASIC is its restricted formatting capability. In the 9830A, four new statements have been added to make output formatting more flexible. Two statements, FIXED and FLOAT, allow the user to specify the format for the numeric output in his PRINT or MAT PRINT statements. Two other statements called WRITE and FORMAT give the user formatting capability similar to FORTRAN. Fig. 8 illustrates the 9830A's formatting ability.

A series of tape operating commands has also been added to 9830A BASIC to control the built-in tape cassette. A command called MARK is used to initialize a cassette and set up a structure of fixed length files. These files can then be accessed randomly by file number. Three types of information can be stored and recalled from the cassette: user programs, numeric and string data, and sets of user definable keys. The command structure is simple yet flexible.

```
5 PRINT "   X"TAB10"EXP(X)"TAB22"EXP(-X)"TAB36"SINH(X)"TAB48"COSH(X)","TANH(X)"
6 PRINT
10 FOR X=-1 TO 1 STEP 0.1
20 WRITE (15,130)X,EXPX,EXP(-X),FNSX,FNCX,FNTX
30 DIM Z[51,6],F$[22],L$[22],B$[2],C$[60],B[6,1]
35 FORMAT F12.3
40 NEXT X
50 END
60 FOR J=1 TO 6
70 Z[1,J]=-G(J,1)
80 NEXT J
90 FOR I=1 TO L[2]
100 DEF FNS(X)=(EXPX-EXP(-X))/2
110 DEF FNC(X)=(EXPX+EXP(-X))/2
120 DEF FNT(X)=(EXPX-EXP(-X))/(EXPX+EXP(-X))
130 FORMAT F4.1,2E13.4,3F12.4
```

X	EXP(X)	EXP(-X)	SINH(X)	COSH(X)	TANH(X)
-1.0	3.6788E-01	2.7183E+00	-1.1752	1.5431	-0.7616
-0.9	4.0657E-01	2.4596E+00	-1.0265	1.4331	-0.7163
-0.8	4.4933E-01	2.2255E+00	-0.8881	1.3374	-0.6640
-0.7	4.9659E-01	2.0138E+00	-0.7586	1.2552	-0.6044
-0.6	5.4881E-01	1.8221E+00	-0.6367	1.1855	-0.5370
0.9	2.4596E+00	4.0657E-01	1.0265	1.4331	0.7163
1.0	2.7183E+00	3.6788E-01	1.1752	1.5431	0.7616

Fig. 8. Sample 9886A printout shows the extended formatting capability of the 9830A.

Add-on ROM

The most unique feature in the 9830A BASIC interpreter is its modularity. Each statement or function is accessed through a series of tables in ROM. Tables can be accessed on as many as eight optional add-on ROM modules, or even in the read-write memory. These add-on ROM modules, each containing 1024 words, are available both in small plastic cases and as printed-circuit modules that can be plugged into the 9830A. After a ROM is in place, the calculator can understand the commands implemented by that ROM and the interpreter can jump to the execution routines stored in it.

Five add-on ROMs are now available. The Matrix and String Variable ROMs include commands that are part of many BASIC systems, but are not needed by all BASIC users. The MAT commands on the Matrix ROM allow initialization of an array to all ones, all zeroes, or the identity matrix, or reading of the values for an array from DATA statements. Matrix arithmetic functions—addition, subtraction, multiplication, and multiplication by a scalar—are easily called for, and functions to take the inverse and transpose are also included. This ROM also includes two commands that are not common in BASIC. They are a REDIM statement to redimension an array without changing the values of any elements, and a DET function for taking the determinant of a matrix.

The String Variable ROM allows the BASIC program to handle strings of alphanumeric characters. The program can initialize, change, examine, and test these strings, and it can ask the operator to input character strings through the keyboard. The simplest example of the value of string variables is an operator typing "YES" or "NO" in response to a question posed by the program. This add-on ROM makes the 9830A truly conversational.

The Plotter ROM adds several new statements to the 9830A language and provides the drivers needed to control the 9862A X-Y Plotter. Some of the most significant capabilities added are automatic scaling, convenient axis drawing, absolute and incremental plotting, and plotting relative to any origin. Labeling plots and axes has been made simple by a LABEL statement. This statement allows the user to draw alphanumeric characters of any height and width, at any angle of rotation.

The Extended I/O ROM adds statements and functions which provide convenience and flexibility in controlling input and output peripherals. The two most important features in this block are an ENTER statement that is used to input data from a peripheral in either free field or formatted form, and an automatic code conversion capability which allows the 9830A to communicate with peripherals using character codes other than ASCII. The Extended I/O ROM communicates through the standard interface scheme of the 9800 Series, and uses the standard interface cards.

Terminal Capability

The fifth ROM that is presently available with the 9830A is a Terminal ROM. This ROM gives the 9830A the unusual capability

to act as a computer terminal. It can communicate with a time-sharing service through a modem at any speed from 3 to 300 baud. This optional ROM overrides the standard keyboard input routine and bypasses the syntax routines so that lines of free text can be stored in memory. For example, a FORTRAN program may be entered into the 9830A, edited, and saved on cassette. After a program has been entered and edited, the user can call up his time-sharing service and have the 9830A transmit the program automatically. The user may also have his time-sharing service transmit a program to be saved in the memory of the 9830A. The editing, execution and storage capabilities of the 9830A make it a very powerful computer terminal.

Modular Firmware

Underlying the modularity and expandability of 9830A BASIC is the modular structure of the firmware (machine-language programs) stored in ROM in the 9830A. Fig. 9 is an overall block diagram. Each shaded block can accept optional ROMs to expand its capabilities.

The keyboard input routine and keyboard monitor perform the user interaction and editing functions. The syntax routines, the pre-execution processing routines and the statement execution routines are the essential elements of the BASIC interpreter. There is a separate syntax routine and execution routine for each different statement type.

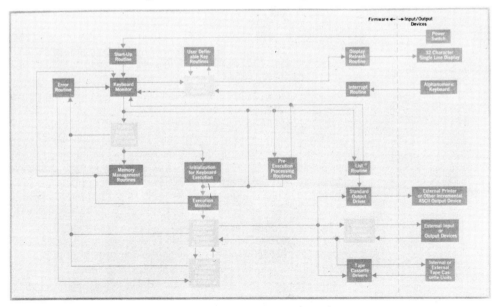

Fig. 9. 9830A BASIC is implemented by firmware routines stored in read-only memory. Modularity makes it easy to expand the language by adding plug-in ROM. The shaded blocks are the expandable modules.

The syntax routines accept an input record from the keyboard routines. This record is a string of the characters that were entered at the keyboard. The syntax routines examine the input record, character by character, checking for proper statement syntax, and transform the string of characters into a series of operation and operand codes that can be more easily used by the execution routines.

The key to the modularity of the syntax firmware is a table search routine which scans a series of name tables on each of the option-block ROMs and the main system ROM. The table search routine searches for a match between the characters in the input record and the characters in the tables in ROM. If a match is found, two codes are stored in the translated format of the input record, a code for the command, and a code for the ROM block where the command is located.

Two codes of information are also stored for each operand, a five-bit code for the letter naming the operand, and a five-bit code for the variable type. The type code is used to distinguish, for example, A, A(1), A1, and A$, which all have the same variable name. During syntax analysis, numeric constants are converted to a floating point format, and line numbers are converted to 16-bit integers. After syntax analysis, control is passed to the memory management routines to store the statement in program memory, or to the initialization routine, which prepares the calculator to execute the statement directly.

The interpreter uses a symbol table to keep track of the variables that are currently in use. It is the job of the pre-execution processing routines to set up this symbol table at the start of program execution. When the RUN command is given, old symbols are deleted, and then the current program is scanned. Any array variable names and their dimensions are saved in the new symbol table.

After the program scan, storage is reserved for each array and a pointer giving the starting memory address for each array is saved in the symbol table. A special key causes the pre-execution processing phase to be performed without the execution phase. This allows the user to set up his symbol table for array variables so they can be used from the keyboard.

Symbol table entries for simple variables and user-defined functions are made during the execution phase. This allows simple variables to be defined by a statement executed directly from the keyboard. The calculator user needn't be aware that a symbol table is being used. Any variable he wants to use is available immediately.

The execution monitor uses the code stored with each statement to locate the proper block of memory and branches to the execution routine for that statement. The execution routines examine the operation and operand codes and call upon subroutines to perform the arithmetic execution. The statement execution routines also call upon driver routines for control of the cassette, printer, display and any external input or output devices.

9800 Processor Incorporates 8-MHz Microprocessor[1]

Henry J. Kohoutek

The processing unit for HP 9800-Series calculators is a micropro-grammed 16-bit serial processor that is capable of executing 75 basic machine-language instructions. The processor

- controls the data flow between memory and working registers,

- performs logical and binary or decimal arithmetic operations on data in the working registers,

- performs logical decisions (branching) based on the states of 16 qualifiers (carry/borrow, operation codes contained in machine-language instructions, etc.),

- controls the internal clock for variable-cycle-time micropro-gram steps, and

- transfers control to the I/O controller for input and output instruction execution.

The processing unit is implemented with MSI bipolar logic circuitry with strong emphasis on read-only memories. Central control of the processor, memory, and I/O unit is nested in microprograms stored in these ROMs in the microprocessor section of the processor (see Fig. 10). The microprocessor executes machine-language instructions in cycles by following these microprograms.

It's important to note that there are two levels of ROM in 9800-Series Calculators. Keystrokes or user program statements initiate sequences of *machine-language instructions*. These sequences are stored in MOS ROMs that are part of the memory system. For each of the 75 machine-language instructions there is a sequence of microinstructions stored in the microprocessor's bipolar ROM. The ROM modules that plug into 9800-Series

[1]*Hewlett-Packard Journal*, vol. 24, December 1972, pp. 19–22.

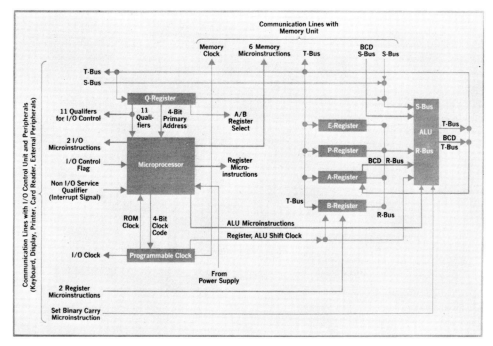

Fig. 10. Processor organization features three buses, five working registers, microprocessor, and arithmetic/logic unit (ALU).

Calculators expand the higher-level MOS ROM, not the microprocessor ROM, which is the same in all models.

The microprocessor ROM, which holds the microprogrammed execution routines for individual machine-language instructions, consists of a block of seven bipolar read-only memories organized in 256 words of 28 bits. Fast routine execution times, based on an internal clock frequency of 8 MHz, help speed up all keyboard functions.

Fig. 11 is a block diagram of the 9800 processor, showing its organization and its relationships with the memory and input/output control unit. The processor has an R-S-T bus configuration. Two buses, R and S, carry data to the arithmetic/logic unit (ALU), and the third bus, T, carries the ALU output.

There are five principal working registers which communicate via the bus system and the ALU, under control of the microprocessor's instruction logic and the number of shift clock pulses that have occurred.

P-register is the calculator's program counter. By going through a step-by-step counting sequence, it causes successive instructions to be read out of the memory. The sequential stepping can be altered by execution of skip or jump instructions, thus causing the program to continue at a different memory address. During

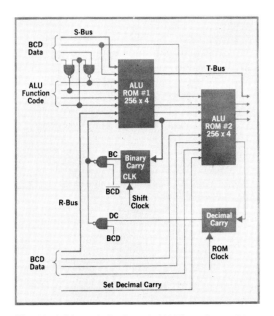

Fig. 11. Arithmetic/logic unit (ALU) performs binary arithmetic and logic operations and binary-coded-decimal operations.

execution of some instructions, the P-register contains a special binary word that is used to simplify digit and word counting.

A-register is one of the calculator's two accumulators. It is capable of accepting results of both binary and decimal arithmetic operations. When a decimal operation is performed, the four-bit result is temporarily received in bits A_3–A_0 of the A register.

B-register is another accumulator. It has the same capabilities as the A-register except for decimal arithmetic.

E-register represents a flexible four-bit extension of all other registers. It's used for left and right shifts with binary-coded-decimal data occupying several memory locations.

Q-register contains the program instruction currently being executed. Its individual bits can be tested as qualifiers to perform microprogram branching according to the instruction code. In the final part of microprogram routines when the instruction code has been fully recognized, the Q register is used for temporary storage of internal processor information.

The programmable clock contains the system clock generator, along with logic which, by decoding the clock field of the microinstruction, causes the correct number of shift pulses to be issued to the working registers and the ALU. This scheme makes it possible to have variable cycle time for each state of the microprogram, and results in a substantial saving in microprocessor ROM. A ROM clock pulse occurs once for each microprogram state and is applied to the ROM address flip-flops.

The binary/BCD arithmetic logic unit (ALU) performs one-bit binary logic and arithmetic operations, as well as four-bit binary-coded-decimal arithmetic operations. Coded results for all logic and arithmetic operations are nested in a form of special look-up table on two bipolar 1024-bit ROM's. Data from working registers and the carry flip-flop, together with the microinstruction to be executed serve as ALU inputs. These inputs define a unique ROM address where the proper result is encoded, and gates are enabled to place this result on the ALU output lines. The states of two ALU carry flip-flops are communicated to the microprocessor where they are recognized as special qualifiers. The ALU organization is shown in Fig. 11.

The processor communicates with the memory unit and the I/O control unit via the T-bus and the S-bus and by special groups of memory and I/O microinstructions. The processor's clock circuitry synchronizes all units by generating memory clock pulses and I/O clock pulses.

Microprocessor

Detailed structure of the microprocessor is shown in Fig. 12.

The primary and secondary address flip-flops form a microprogram counter, which selects the memory location where the microinstruction to be executed is stored. Each microinstruction is 28 bits wide and contains information to control the data flow in

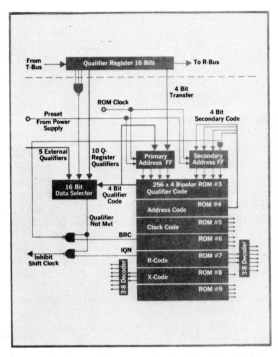

Fig. 12. Microprocessor read-only memories contain sequences of microinstructions that control execution of keyboard instructions.

the system by enabling appropriate gates and generating the proper number of shift clock pulses.

Also included is information to define the ROM address of the next microinstruction. Thus instead of being limited to a fixed address sequence, the microprogram may in effect execute almost a random walk through the ROM addresses.

The microinstruction format is shown in Fig. 13. The four-bit qualifier code in each microinstruction serves a dual purpose. If branching is desired, the microinstruction BRC must be programmed. If the preceding microinstruction is BRC, the four-bit qualifier code selects the proper qualifier to be tested and the primary address of the next microinstruction is the same as the current one. If the preceding microinstruction is not BRC the qualifier code defines the primary address of the next microinstruction.

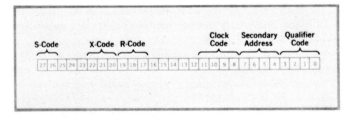

Fig. 13. Microinstruction format.

A single-chip 16-bit data selector permits any one of the 16 qualifiers to be tested according to the qualifier code. If branching is to occur, the microinstruction BRC, along with a signal from the data selector, defines the least significant bit of the secondary address of the next microinstruction, according to the result of the qualifier test.

A special microinstruction, IQN, inhibits all shift clock pulses from the clock decoder in case the selected qualifier condition was not met. This in effect prevents execution of microinstructions in that ROM state.

To minimize the microinstruction width the operation codes for clock decoder, ALU, bus-gate control, and so on, are coded into groups and decoded by hardware into individual signals.

Besides the 75 basic machine-language instructions, the system can also perform indirect memory calls, interrupts, I/O calls, and a simple resident diagnostic of its own performance in start-up conditions.

Testing in Production and Service

The microinstructions that control the calculator's processor and memory define the lowest language that can control the machine hardware. Therefore, for testing 9800 Series Calculators on the production line and in the field, a tester was designed to execute machine diagnostics on the microprocessor level, following a "start-small" strategy.

The tester organization is very similar to that of the microprocessor, but instead of machine-language execution routines, a system of tests is nested in a group of ROM's. Virtually identical organization, hardware, and timing of microprocessor and tester assures similarity between working and testing conditions from a physical and an electrical point of view. This means that the diagnostic information represents a realistic picture of the state of the tested machine.

The tester hardware also contains logic for convenient manual operations, simple aids for troubleshooting in case an error is detected, and circuitry for computer interface.

Test routines are organized in a sequence. There is a pretest, a series of 22 tests, and a posttest to check magnetic-card-reader mechanics. The pretest is a manually controlled resident microdiagnostic routine designed to test the tester's hardware. The start-small strategy is reflected in the test sequence, which begins with very simple tests of binary logic functions of the ALU, and continues through register tests to complex tests of the entire ALU and memory. Each test uses only successfully tested parts of the machine hardware and evaluates only a small new part of the hardware. This makes it easy to locate failures when an error is discovered.

Versatile Input/Output Structure Welcomes Peripheral Variety[1]

Gary L. Egan

The input output structure of 9800-Series Calculators, which links the calculator with its peripherals, is designed to be versatile and easy to use. It is flexible enough so a user can easily interface his calculator with a variety of HP peripherals as well as with many standard units and others of his own design.

I/O Processor

The input/output processor is a self-contained microprocessor composed of commerically available TTL logic circuits which generate the microinstructions necessary to implement the ten input-output instructions. The I/O processor is fully synchronous with the system clock and main processor, receiving starting control from the main processor whenever an input-output instruction is read from memory. While the I/O processor is in control, the main processor remains in a two-state waiting loop until the input-output instruction has been implemented, whereupon control is returned to the main processor. (See Fig. 14.)

The input/output instructions require six to twelve microseconds to execute. There are I/O instructions for setting or clearing flip-flops, for testing the state of flip-flops, and for moving data between registers in the main processor and the input/output register.

I/O Register

The I/O register is a 16-bit universal (parallel in/out, serial in/out) data register that is connected to the main processor by the serial bus system. Data contained in the I/O register is sent bit-serial into the main processor via the S-bus. Conversely, bit-serial data is received from the main processor by the I/O register via the T-bus.

[1]*Hewlett-Packard Journal*, vol. 24, December 1972, pp. 24–27.

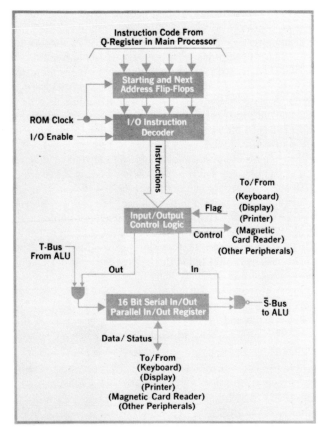

Fig. 14. Input/output processor is a self-contained microprocessor that implements the ten I/0 instructions.

The I/O register's 16 parallel outputs provide the source for an output information bus structure which is common to all connecting peripherals. Parallel input information is received via an input information bus structure terminated by the twelve least significant parallel inputs of the I/O register. Input information may be loaded into the I/O register by interrupt request or upon demand from the calculator.

All data communication between individual peripherals and the calculator makes use of a "handshaking" operation. Data is placed on the bus lines by the transmitter and then a signal indicating data ready is sent. The receiver acknowledges this and returns a signal noting that data has been accepted.

Associated with the I/O register are control circuits that implement this "handshaking" operation. The control circuitry consists of gates and flip-flops which are controlled by the I/O processor.

Internal Peripherals

A group of peripherals which may be contained within the calculator are called internal peripherals and are distinguished from a group called external peripherals by the fact that they are directly addressed as a part of the input/output instruction. This group of internal peripherals includes keyboard, display, magnetic-card storage, thermal printer, and I/O register.

Each internal peripheral has associated with it a driver contained in read-only memory in the basic calculator, plus supporting control hardware. The I/O register is included as an internal peripheral since it is directly addressable from the I/O instruction set and it functions as a holding and passing register for all peripherals. Fig. 15 shows the relationship between the internal peripherals and the I/O structure.

External Peripherals

External peripherals are connected to the calculator by an external signal cable. They are addressed indirectly from the I/O register. In general the driver for any external peripheral is contained in a plug-in ROM which may be unique to a certain peripheral (e.g., a typewriter) or may contain a general-purpose driver which communicates in bit-parallel, character-serial ASCII. Fig. 15 also shows the relationship between external peripherals and the I/O structure.

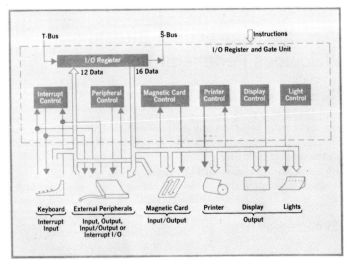

Fig. 15. I/0 structure is designed to accommodate a variety of internal and external peripherals.

Peripheral Communication

All internal peripherals are addressed by the I/O instructions. Therefore, the receiving peripherals have access to the full 16-bit field of the I/O register. In addition each internal peripheral has its own control and flag logic by which "handshaking" takes place.

Communication with an external peripheral requires that a 16-bit word be formed in the processor. This word consists of a four-bit address in the four most significant bit positions, a four-bit status word in the four next-most significant bit positions, and eight data bits in the eight least significant bit positions. This 16-bit word is sent to the I/O register, where the parallel outputs of the I/O register place the word on the bus structure. After this

has been accomplished a control signal is placed on the control line which, with the decoded four-bit address, causes the desired peripheral to take action. A receiving peripheral acknowledges the receipt of data by returning a flag signal. A transmitting peripheral places its data and status on the twelve input lines and sends a data-ready signal to the calculator.

The kinds of external peripherals are unlimited. The addressing scheme of 9800 Series Calculators provides for a maximum of 15 different addresses. Of these, addresses 10 through 15 are fixed and are reserved for unique drivers. Addresses 1 through 9 are variable and may be selected on a peripheral's interface card by means of jumper wires or switches. The bus structure makes the peripheral interfaces slot-independent, that is, they may be

System Information Series 9800 Programmable Calculators

Model 10			Field Installable Option			
Basic Model 10 Calculator, including 51 registers and 500 program steps	9810A	$2475	429 Total Data Registers	11228A	$1490*	
Factory Installed Options			Plug-In Function Blocks			
111 Total Data Registers	Opt. 001	$ 400	Peripheral Control I	11220A	$ 485	
1012 Total Program Steps, or	Opt. 002	$ 500	Mathematics	11221A	$ 485	
2036 Total Program Steps	Opt. 003	$ 850	User Definable	11222A	$ 485	
Printer	Opt. 004	$ 675	Cassette	11223A	$ 225	
Carrying Handle	Opt. 015	$ 25	Peripheral Control II	11224A	$ 485	
Field Installable Options			*Model 30*			
111 Total Data Registers	11216A	$ 440*	Basic Model 30 Calculator, including 3520 Bytes (1760 words) read/write memory	9830A	$5975	
1012 Total Program Steps, or	11217A	$ 540*	Factory Installed Option			
2036 Total Program Steps	11218A	$ 890*	7616 Total Bytes (3808 words) read/write memory	Opt. 275	$1475	
Field Installed Printer	11219A	$ 715*	Plug-In Function Blocks			
Plug-In Function Blocks			Matrix Operations	11270B	$ 485	
Mathematics	11210A	$ 485	Plotter Control	11271B	$ 485	
Printer Alpha	11211A	$ 485	Extended I/O	11272B	$ 485	
Typewriter	11212A	$ 225	String Variables	11274B	$ 485	
User Definable	11213A	$ 485	Terminal I	11277B	$ 485	
Statistics	11214A	$ 485	*9800 Series Peripherals*			
Plotter	11215A	$ 485	Mark-Sense Card Reader	9860A	$ 850	
Plotter/Printer Alpha Comb.	11261A	$ 800	Typewriter Output	9861A	$2250	
Peripheral/Cassette Comb.	11262A	$ 625	Plotter	9862A	$2675	
Peripheral	11264A	$ 485	Paper Tape Reader	9863A	$1470	
Cassette Memory	11265A	$ 225	Digitizer	9864A	$5900	
Peripheral/Printer Alpha Comb.	11266A	$ 800	Tape Cassette	9865A	$1750	
Typewriter/Cassette Comb.	11267A	$ 450	I/O Expander	9868A	$ 975	
Model 20			General I/O Interface	11202A	$ 200	
Basic Model 20 Calculator, including 173 registers	9820A	$4975	BCD Interface	11203A	$ 300	
Factory Installed Option			Thermal Printer	9866A	$2975	
429 Total Registers	Opt. 001	$1250	Hopper-Fed Card Reader	9869A	†	
Carrying Handle	Opt. 015	$ 25				

Hewlett-Packard Manufacturing Division: Calculator Products Division.

*Plus field installation charges

†Not available.

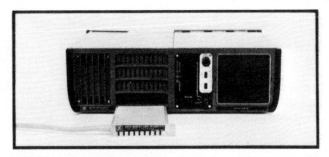

Fig. 16. Basic calculator has four I/0 slots for external peripherals. Expanders add nine more slots each.

connected to any calculator I/O slot (Fig. 16). The basic calculator has 4 slots for peripherals, and this can be expanded to as many as 40 by means of I/O expanders.

Reliability

The I/O system uses time-proven TTL circuits with known good reliability characteristics. Supplementing the hardware reliability, the handshaking operation assures reliable data transmission over cables up to 10 feet long. Although 10 feet is the maximum recommended length, longer cables have been used successfully.

APPENDIX 9800 MICROPROGRAMMED PROCESSOR

Instruction Set of the Central Processor

The instruction set, as alluded to before, is strongly related to the HP 2114 and HP 2116 minicomputer instruction set. There are 75 basic instructions. The memory reference, skip, alter, complement, and shift-rotate classes of instructions are essentially identical to the Binary Processor Chip (BPC) used in the HP 9845 (see Chap. 31). The full set of 28 ROM outputs with their associated microinstructions is shown in Table 1. The list of 16 qualifiers and assigned codes is contained in Table 2.

The 9810/20/30 Series processors did not have separate processors for I/O and extended arithmetic as the HP 9845 does. Thus instructions beyond those in the BPC were required to deal with I/O and decimal arithmetic. These additional instructions are outlined in Table 3.

Table 1   Microinstruction Set—9000 A

Control field	ROM output	Decoded μ-instruction output				Function
	Positive true	*Negative true outputs*				
General	1. IQN					Inhibit shift clock if qualifier not met.
	2. BRC					Branch: inhibits S00 if qualifier not met.
	3. $\overline{TTT}$					T BUS→ T REG
	4. $\overline{TTM}$					T BUS→ M REG
	5. $\overline{XTR}$					A/B REG→ R BUS
				SC1	*SC0*	
S-code	6. SC1	ZTS		0	0	ZERO→ S BUS
	7. SC0	MTS		0	1	M REG→ S BUS
		TTS		1	0	T REG→ S BUS
		UTS		1	1	ONE→ S BUS
			RC2	*RC1*	*RC0*	
R-code	8. RC2	UTR	0	0	0	ONE→ R BUS
	9. RC1	PTR	0	0	1	P REG→ R BUS
	10. RC0	TRE	0	1	0	T REG→ E REG → R BUS
		WTM · ZTR	0	1	1	Store contents T REG → memory
		TQ6 · 2TR	1	0	0	T BUS→ Q REG (bit 6)
		QTR	1	0	1	Q REG→ R BUS
		RDM · ZTR	1	1	0	READ MEMORY <M> → T REG
		ZTR	1	1	1	ZERO→ R BUS

Table 1   *(Cont'd.)*

Control field	ROM output	Decoded μ-instruction output	XC2	XC1	XC0	Function
				Positive true		
				Negative true outputs		
X-code	11. XC2	TTQ	0	0	0	T BUS→ Q REG
	12. XC1	QAB	0	0	1	Q REG (bit 11) → AB flip-flop
	13. XC0	BCD	0	1	0	BCD arithmetic mode of ALU
		TBE	0	1	1	T BUS→ E REG → R BUS
		CAB	1	0	0	Complement the AB flip-flop
		TTP	1	0	1	T BUS→ P REG
		TTX	1	1	0	T BUS→ A/B REG
		NOP	1	1	1	None of the above

Decoded in ALU

Control field	ROM output	Decoded μ-instruction output	AC2	AC1	AC0	Function
ALU	14. AC2	XOR	0	0	0	Exclusive OR .... R⊕S → T BUS
	15. AC1	AND	0	0	1	Logical AND .... R · S → T BUS
	16. AC0	IOR	0	1	0	Inclusive OR .... R + S → T BUS
		ZTT	0	1	1	ZERO→ T BUS
		ZTT · CBC	1	0	0	ZERO→ T BUS, clear binary carry
		IOR · CBC	1	0	1	Inclusive OR, clear binary carry
		IOR · SBC	1	1	0	Inclusive OR, set binary carry
		ADD	1	1	1	Binary add
Clock	17. CC1					This 4-bit code initializes a presettable down counter to generate any number of shift clocks from 1 through 16. Shift is inhibited by IQN if qualifier not met.
	18. CC2					
	19. CC4					
	20. CC8					
Qualifier	21. QC3					This 4-bit code performs *two* functions: (1) addressing the data selector to select one of sixteen qualifier inputs; (2) providing complement code to *primary* flip-flops.
	22. QC2					
	23. QC1					
	24. QC0					
Secondary address	25. S03					This 4-bit code provides complement code to the *secondary* flip-flops. If BRC is given and qualifier is not met, the S00 bit is inhibited
	26. S02					
	27. S01					
	28. S00					

Special microinstructions

TQR = UTR · XTR   transfers Q-Register to primary address as shown

$$Q14 \cdot Q11 \rightarrow P04$$
$$Q12 \rightarrow P05$$
$$Q13 \rightarrow P06$$
$$Q14 \rightarrow P07$$

IOS = PTR · XTR   (a) initiates transfer of control to I/O if Q10 = 1
(b) sets "single service" FF in I/O via $\overline{SRA}$ if Q10 = 0

Special operations

BCD sum → A<0:3> = BCD · $\overline{UTR}$ · ROM CLOCK
Clear decimal carry = QAB · ROM CLOCK
Set decimal carry = UTR · BCD · ROM CLOCK
Decimal add = BCD · ZTT ... T<0:3> + A<0:3> → Q<0:3>
10's complement n/decimal add = BCD · ADD .... $\overline{T<0:3>}$ + A<0:3> → Q<0:3>

Table 2 Qualifier Set—9000A

QC3	QC2	QC1	QC0	Mnemonic	Function

Qualifier code				Mnemonic	Function
QC3	QC2	QC1	QC0		
0	0	0	0	Q00	Shift/skip one bit
0	0	0	1	Q01	Shift/skip two bits
0	0	1	0	Q02	Shift/skip four bits
0	0	1	1	Q03	Shift/skip eight bits
0	1	0	0	Q04	Fast square root qualifier
0	1	0	1	Q05	Set bit in A/S group; FDV qualifier
0	1	1	0	Q06	T-bus qualifier via TQ6
0	1	1	1	QBC	Binary carry from ALU
1	0	0	0	QP0	P Register bit 0, for BCD counting
1	0	0	1	Q15	Indirect address, clear bit in A/S group
1	0	1	0	QMR	Memory reference qualifier
1	0	1	1	Q10	Current page qualifier, FXA qualifier
1	1	0	0	QNR	Non-service request qualifier
1	1	0	1	Q08	FMP qualifier
1	1	1	0	QDC	Decimal carry from ALU
1	1	1	1	QRD*	ROM disable (normally zero)

POP will preset ROM address flip-flops at turn-on.

*QRD may be used with IQN to insure zero shift except when in I/O loop.

Table 3 I/O and Decimal Arithmetic Instructions of the HP9810/20/30 Central Processors

Execute-DMA group

These three special-purpose instructions were chosen to speed up printing and extended memory operations.

EXA/B Execute A. The contents of the A register are treated as the current instruction, and executed in the normal manner.

DMA Direct Memory Access. The DMA control in Extended Memory is enabled.

Input/output group (IOG)

The eleven IOG instructions, when given with a select code, are used for the purpose of checking flags, setting or clearing flag and control flip-flops, and transferring data between the A/B registers and the I/O register.

STF <SC> Set the flag flip-flop of the channel indicated by select code <SC>.

CLF <SC> Clear the flag flip-flop.

SFC <SC> Skip if flag clear.

SFS <SC> H/C Skip if flag set. H/C indicates if the flag flip-flop should be held or cleared after executing SFS.

CLC <SC> H/C Clear control. H/C indicates if the flag flip-flop should be held or cleared after executing CLC.

STC <SC> H/C Set Control. Set the control flip-flop in the channel indicated by <SC>. H/C indicates if the flag flip-flop should be held or cleared after executing STC.

OT* <SC> H/C Output A or B. Sixteen bits from the A/B register are output to the I/O register. H/C allows

Input/output group (IOG)

holding or clearing the flag flop after execution of OT*. The different select codes allow different functions to take place after loading the I/O register.

SC=00 Data from the A or B register is output eight bits at a time for each OT* instruction given. The A or B register is rotated right eight bits.

SC=01 The I/O register is loaded with 16 bits from the A/B registers.

SC=02 Data from the A/B register is output one bit at a time for each OT* instruction for the purpose of giving data to the Magnetic Card Reader. The I/O register is unchanged.

SC=04 The I/O register is loaded with 16 bits from the A/B register and the control flip flop for the printer is then set.

SC=08 The I/O register is loaded with 16 bits from the A/B register and the control flip flop for the display is then set.

SC=16 The I/O register is loaded with 16 bits from the A/B register and then data in the I/O register is transferred to the switch latches.

LI* <01> H/C Load into A or B. Load 16 bits of data into the A/B register from the I/O register. H/C allows

Table 3 *(Cont'd.)*

Input/output group (IOG)

	holding or clearing the flag flop after L1* has been executed.
LI* <00>	The least significant 8 bits of the I/O register are loaded into the most significant locations in the A or B register.
MI* <01> H/C	Merge into A or B. Merge 16 bits of data into the A/B register from the I/O register by "inclusive or." H/C allows holding or clearing the flag flop after MI* has been executed.
MI* <00>	The least significant 8 bits of the I/O register are combined by inclusive OR with the least significant 8 bits of the A or B register, and rotated to the most significant bit locations of the A or B register.

MAC instruction group

A total of 16 MAC instructions are available for operation (a) with the whole floating-point data (transfer, shifts, etc.) or (b) with two floating-point data words to speed up digit and word loops in arithmetic routines.

Note: $A<0:3>$ means: contents of A-register bit 0 to 3.

AR 1   is a mnemonic for arithmetic pseudo-register located in R/W memory on addresses 1744 to 1747 (octal).

AR 2   is a mnemonic for arithmetic pseudo-register located in R/W memory on addresses 1754 to 1757 (octal).

D_i means: mantissas' i-th decimal digit; most significant digit is D1; least significant digit is D12; decimal point is located between D1 and D2.

Every operation with mantissa means BCD-coded decimal operation.

RET	Return
	16-bit number stored at highest occupied address in stack is transferred to the program counter. Stack pointer is decremented by one.
MOV	Move overflow
	The contents of E-register are transferred to $A<0:3>$. Rest of A-register and E-register filled by zeros.
CLR	Clear a floating-point data register in R/W memory on location $<A>$
	ZERO$<A>$, $<A>$+1, $<A>$+2, $<A>$+3

MAC instruction group

XFR	Floating-point data transfer in R/W memory from location $<A>$ to location $<B>$.
MRX	AR1 mantissa is shifted to right n times. Exponent word remains unchanged.
MRY	AR2 mantissa is shifted to right n times.
MLS	AR2 mantissa is shifted to left once. Exponent word remains unchanged.
DRS	AR1 mantissa is shifted to right once. Exponent word remains unchanged.
DLS	AR1 mantissa is shifted to left once. Exponent word remains unchanged.
FXA	Fixed-point addition
	Mantissas in pseudo-registers AR2 and AR1 are added together and result is placed into AR2. Both exponent words remain unchanged. When overflow occurs "0001" is set into E-reg.; in opposite case$<E>$ will be zero.
FMP	Fast multiply
	Mantissas in pseudo-registers AR2 and AR1 are added together $B<0:3>$-times and result is placed into AR2. Total decimal overflow is placed to $A<0:3>$. Both exponent words remain unchanged.
FDV	Fast divide
	Mantissas in pseudo-registers AR2 and AR1 are added together repeatedly until first decimal overflow occurs. Result is placed in AR2. Both exponent words remain unchanged. Each addition without overflow causes +1 increment of $<B>$.
CMX	10's complement of AR1 mantissa is placed back in AR1, and ZERO is set in E-register. Exponent word remains unchanged.
CMY	10's complement of AR2 mantissa.
MDI	Mantissa decimal increment
	Mantissa on location $<A>$ is incremented by decimal ONE on D12 level, result is placed back in the same location, and zero is set in E-reg. Exponent word is unchanged.
NRM	Normalization
	Mantissa is pseudo-register AR2 is rotated to the left to get $D1 \neq 0$. Number of these 4-bit left shifts is stored in $B<0:3>$ binary form ($B<4:15>=0$). Exponent word remains unchanged.

Chapter 50

Hewlett-Packard Calculator Architectures

Thomas E. Osborne

Summary This chapter focues on some of the more important architectural differences between the first Hewlett-Packard electronic calculator, the HP 9100A (c. 1968), and its descendants, the HP 9810/20/30. The architectures of the two generations are so different that the reasons for making the change are, in many ways, as interesting as the differences in the architectures.

Except for using similar components, the early programmable calculators had surprisingly little in common with the concurrent digital computers. Among the many reasons for the differences, none is as large as the fact that very few, if any, of the early calculator designers were defectors from the ranks of computer designers. Contrary to the old adage, anyone engaged in designing computers could see that the grass was *very* green on his side of the fence—so green that few even acknowledged the existence of other pastures.

A quick glance at some of the objectives of the early electronic calculator manufacturers shows that even if there had been defectors from the computer field, precious little technology would have been directly applicable to the calculator environment.

Would a technology that understood megabit core memories designed to operate in a controlled temperature environment have been capable of stretching enough to design inexpensive kilobit memories to operate from 0 to 55°C? Was there any assurance that those who were skilled in the design of microsecond parallel binary adders would find these skills useful in designing inexpensive serial decimal adders? Who knows? The test was never run.

Because the early calculator designers had so little practical exposure to the inner workings and hidden mechanisms of computers, it follows that their designs would not necessarily be an extrapolation from the concurrent computer architectures. Both groups of designers had the same building blocks and shared somewhat similar problems, but in the same way that different life forms sprang from the same primordial soup, early calculator architectures were quite a different species from concurrent computer architectures.

The first Hewlett-Packard programmable calculator, the HP 9100A (c. 1968) [Hewlett-Packard, 1968], was micro-programmed to perform floating-point arithmetic and to evaluate the forward and inverse circular, exponential, and hyperbolic transcendentals. Its I/O was also controlled by its inductive ROM, which contained 512 64-bit words. The ROM's extra-wide micro-words allude to the nonstandard architecture found in the HP 9100A.

Instead of having an arithmetic and logic unit (ALU) connected to various registers by a common bus, the HP 9100A had no ALU per se. Instead, its arithmetic section was distributed throughout the system by assigning small, but specialized, tasks to the various registers within the system. Separate buses then interconnected selected pairs of these registers. As a consequence, several (typically three to seven) micro-instructions were executed simultaneously during each micro-word time. Half of the 64-bit micro-word was used to encode these micro-instructions. The other half of the 64-bit word was used for addressing and to test conditions of both internal registers and asynchronous external signals generated by I/O devices. The results of each test determined the next ROM address and, at the micro-programmer's discretion, whether or not to suppress the action of the micro-instructions in the other half of the ROM micro-word. Figure 1 pictorially demonstrates the syntax of a typical micro-word used in the HP 9100A.

The micro-programmer would interpret Fig. 1 as follows: "When the conditions defined by QX are true, execute the set of micro-instructions (IA, IB, IC, . . .) and go to ROM address 'j' for the next micro-word; when QX is false, inhibit all micro-instructions [symbolically shown by the shaded corner in the right exit of the diamond] and go to address 'k' for the next micro-word." Notice that, unlike what happens in a standard flowchart, in which the instructions within the box precede the test designated by the diamond, both actions occurred simultaneously in the HP 9100A.

The advantages of conditionally inhibiting a set of micro-instructions are many, but one frequent use stands out. In most

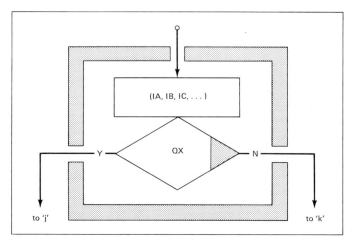

Fig. 1. A typical microword from the HP 9100A.

applications, one tests the exit conditions of an iterative loop (1) to re-enter the loop when the exit conditions are not met or (2) to exit when they are met. When the test occurs at the beginning of a loop and the exit conditions are met, none of the loop instructions are executed. In the HP 9100A, loops of this type frequently consisted of a single micro-word to be repeated until the exit conditions were met, at which time the micro-instructions were inhibited and the exit path selected.

As one would expect, this highly parallel architecture resulted in a very fast system. Contrary to what one might expect, the actual micro-coding was not overly difficult, nor was the multi-bus hardware difficult to lay out on PC boards. Although the "wide word" architecture of the HP 9100A was abandoned for reasons to be discussed later, it seems that it would be worth revisiting. One might find that micro-processor speeds could be enhanced by an order of magnitude without resorting to a higher-speed IC process.

Quantifiers are tested to determine which of the two next micro-address fields should be used. In Fig. 2 a single signal, IQAM, connects the QUALIFIER SELECTION LOGIC to the MAIN CONTROL LOGIC. This signal is actually the output of a comparator whose right inputs come from the QUALIFIER subfield of the ROM and whose left inputs come from an encoder whose inputs are, in turn, all of the individual conditions to be tested. An unobvious, but very beneficial, byproduct of this technique is the fact that the entire system is free from problems resulting from *any* external qualifiers' asynchronously changing state between clock times. The signal IQAM either is effective upon the CONTROL LOGIC or isn't. In either case the CONTROL LOGIC is deterministic in its response to IQAM.

It is interesting to notice that the patents obtained for the HP 9100 did not use the words *micro-program* and *micro-instruction*. We were not aware of either term until after the HP 9100A was introduced, even though it was a micro-programmed machine.

Before discussing some of the aspects of the stack as seen by the HP 9100A user (i.e., the X and Y registers), one must first appreciate the fact that calculator designers and computer designers are in violent disagreement as to the way in which a stack is visualized. Since there are about 100 times as many calculator users visualizing the last entry at the bottom of the stack as there are computer users visualizing the last entry at the top of the stack, we will side with the majority. We justify this position with the attitude that the same person who "inverted" the computer stack was responsible for deciding that "trees" have their "roots" above their "leaves." Regardless of how the minority view came about, the calculator stack is as it is because we wanted the numerator to be above the denominator when a division is performed.

For nontechnical reasons, the HP 9100A presented a unique stack to its users. Prior to the introduction of the HP 9100A, one of the well-established mechanical calculator users introduced an electronic calculator having a classic stack (with its last entry at the bottom). To avert any possible patent infringements, we invented a stack in which a dyadic operator overwrote the first entered operand (the second operand in the stack) and left the bottom of the stack unchanged. (A classic stack could be thought of as performing the same operation but "popping" the stack following the dyadic operator.) In the HP 9100A, an operand that followed any operator simply overwrote the bottom of the stack, with the result that there was no difference between the classic stack and our version in executing a series of dyadic operators. In fact, when an evaluation required multiple uses of the last stack operand, as often occurred, our version was superior to the classic version. Nonetheless, our stack had one shortcoming. When a monadic operator was to be performed upon the result of a dyadic operator, it was necessary to manually "drop" the stack prior to performing the monadic.

We found that the public adapted very well to the concept of a stack. The fact that it was displayed in its entirety on a CRT helped, but the fundamental nature of the concept was even more important. The HP 35 only displayed the bottom of the stack, and it was well received.

Even today, if these were the only choices of stacks, it would be difficult to choose between the two. Fortunately a third choice exists which has the advantages of both. It functions as a classic stack with the feature that the bottom of the stack, which is consumed by an operation, is saved prior to performing the operation and made available for recall as the next operand. Those familiar with any of the later versions of HP hand-held calculators will recognize this feature as the "LAST X" operator and can testify to its usefulness.

As mentioned earlier, the wide-word architecture of the HP 9100A was not used in other HP calculators. No single factor contributed to the demise of the HP 9100A architecture as did the HP 2114 mini-computer. And for good reason. An investigation of its architecture showed that it could be reduced to an MSI

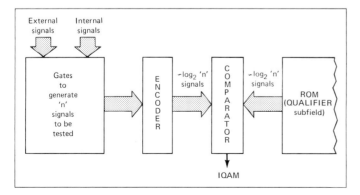

Fig. 2. Next microinstruction address select logic.

micro-processor and that its software could be locked up in ROM. By simulating the calculator on a copy of the HP 2114, an order-of-magnitude increase in performance was realized over the hand-soldered diode-ROM simulator used to develop the HP 9100A. On top of that we thought we could use the software and operating system that had been developed for the HP 2114. As it turned out, little of either was used, but the fact that it existed weighed heavily in the decision to abandon the HP 9100A architecture. Finally, it seemed wise to use the same I/O protocols adopted by the HP 2114.

Shortly after the decision was made to use the HP 2114 architecture, it became evident that portions of the system had to be enhanced to meet the speed required by the three calculators that were to use the 2114 "micro-processor." The MSI version of HP 2114 was enhanced by including a decimal adder in the ALU, and by expanding the instruction set to include an extensive set of macro-instructions whose principal use was to assist floating-point decimal operations.

One of the more interesting consequences of the first generation RAM's was the dramatic impact they had upon scientific desk-top calculators like the HP 9810/20/30 [Hewlett-Packard, 1972]. Most, if not all, of the early RAM's were aimed at replacing large core memories found in digital computers. To achieve this end, the LSI RAM manufacturers were aiming at a price of about two cents per bit. As anyone who has designed a core memory knows, its driving and sensing circuitry is inherently expensive. When this cost is prorated among the few bits found in a small memory like the one used in the HP 9100A, one could easily encounter costs of 20 cents per bit. Fortunately for the calculator designers, the per bit cost of LSI RAM was relatively independent of the ultimate size of the memory. Whereas two cents per bit was a break-even point for the computer environment, it represented an order-of-magnitude improvement for the calculator environment. It was no coincidence that many of the first production orders for RAM's went into programmable desk-top calculators.

Unlike the operating systems of digital computers, which share user RAM, the operating systems of the HP 9810/20/30 were all committed to ROM. As one of the HP engineers recently said, "If you think it takes nerves of steel to release a software operating system, imagine how it feels to release one in firmware."

The firmware of the 9800 Series calculators supports some rather sophisticated features. At the low end of the line, the HP 9810 performed indirect register arithmetic. For example, the sequence

will multiply the contents of the X register by the contents of the register whose address is found in register 50 and place the product in that register.

The HP 9820 was Hewlett-Packard's first algebraic (non-Polish) machine. Instead of running interpretively, it partially compiled its source programs into reverse Polish strings, which accomplished two important objectives. First, the lexical and parsing phases of the compilation were only performed once, but second and more important, a "decompiler" was able to reconstruct the source code from the reverse Polish strings, thereby giving the user unprecedented on-line editing of his source code without storing the source code in user memory.

The HP 9820 firmware also supported recursive functions. For example, one could define a function like MAX and then use it as one of its own arguments. For example, MAX(A, MAX (B,C)) is a valid HP 9820 statement.

At the upper end of the calculator spectrum, the HP 9830 supports BASIC. In its maximum configuration, it offers 16K words of 16 bits to its users. Remember that this is all user memory. The operating system is in ROM. An additional two-and-a-half million words of memory is available in the HP 9880 mass (disc) memory.

Since the introduction of the HP 9830, LSI micro-processor versions of the HP 9810/20/30 have been introduced. As one might expect, they run faster, cost less, and do more than their ancestors. How they achieve these ends will be left to the authors of future research papers.

So far the reader has been told why things are as they are and very little about why they aren't something else. Why, for example, was the HP 9830 not given a CRT? Although one was considered, the designers did not want their product to be confused with the competition of the day, terminals driven from remote computers. It was thought that the combination of a 32-character LED display and an 80-column, 300 line per minute thermal printer would be an adequate solution and at the same time prevent confusion in the minds of potential customers as to what a terminal was and what a stand-alone computing station was. Whether or not this was the best decision remains open. However, one thing is clearly obvious: it was not a bad decision. The HP 9830 is a very successful product.

Negative experiences, though painful, can be helpful in the long run. Such was the case with the HP 9100A I/O. The signals emanating from its I/O connector were fondly referred to as "semi-modulated white lightning." The peripherals that connected to the I/O connector stand as a tribute to engineering. The obstreperous nature of the HP 9100A I/O was a strong contributor to the fact that its descendants have excellent I/O characteristics.

Another disturbing fact of life surrounds the desire to maintain the same fundamental architecture between successive generations so that the software from previous generations can be used in the generation being developed. Unfortunately, two factors team up to defeat this admirable goal. First, it seems that regardless of how carefully the previous software was documented, the (new) personnel who will be responsible for the next generation find the ancestor software's documentation dull and uninspired. Second, the performance objectives of the new generation automatically render much of the ancestral code obsolete. Once Pandora's box is opened, good intentions escape and most of the code is rewritten. The paradoxical result of this process is that an architecture is retained because one wishes to capitalize upon its software when, in fact, very little of the software is actually used. The measurable effect of this logic is that an architecture may persist much longer than it would if its software were removed from the decision process.

It has been more than a decade since the first scientific desk-top calculator was introduced. Since that time the public has had enough time to appraise many systems and use their respective languages. To me it appears that as we add more deep structure to the grammars upon which the languages are based, the users become more confused. In an odd way, the more powerful we make our grammars, the less useful they become to all but a few. The following BASIC statement is an example:

$$1 - 1 \text{ OR NOT } \emptyset \text{ AND } \emptyset = 2 \uparrow \text{SQR } \emptyset * \emptyset$$

Unless you have committed to memory the nine levels of hierarchy involved, there is little chance that you would parse the sentence as:

$$(1 - 1) \text{ OR ((NOT } \emptyset) \text{ AND } (\emptyset = ((2\uparrow (\text{SQR } \emptyset)) * \emptyset)))$$

My point is that while the first sentence is derived from what many consider to be a trivial grammar, the sentence can only be understood if the user has memorized the proper grammatical rules or has access to a manual in which they are described. The entire meaning of what is being said is lost if the rules of the language are forgotten or improperly used.

Based upon my experiences, a language that is easily learned and seldom misused would:

1   Be free from hierarchy, except for parentheses

2   Be left-associative

3   Use the right assignment operator "$\rightarrow$"

In other words, it would be much like APL except that it would execute left to right rather than right to left.

References

Hewlett-Packard [1968]; Hewlett-Packard [1972].

Section 4

Evolution of Burroughs Computers

From the inception of the B 5000, Burroughs' main-line computers have maintained and enhanced the concepts of hardware support for block-structured high-level languages. Part 1, Sec. 3, traces the evolution of the Burroughs B 5000, B 6500/B 7500, and B 6700/7700 machines. The evolution of the virtual to the physical addressing structure is outlined in Part 2, Sec. 2. Finally, Chaps. 9 and 16 discuss individual family members.

Section 5

The System/360 and
System/370 Family

The System/360 was the first planned computer family to cover a range of cost and performance. The System/360 predecessors, the IBM 7090 series and the business models, ran into a number of the same problems of limited growth potential later encountered by the PDP-8. Rather than continuing to tinker with the architecture, IBM opted for a totally new ISP planned right from the start to have growth potential for the future covering both the scientific and business market. Even the initial family plan called for a wide range of cost and performance implementations. Microcode was also extensively used to provide emulation support for prior IBM systems.

Subsequently the System/360 ISP evolved into the System/370. Chapter 51 describes the problems with developing an upward-compatible ISP extension.

Within one generation of technology, the System/360 and System/370 used various implementation techniques (e.g., wider data paths and processor-memory overlap) to provide a performance range. But in the System/370 series, several models have been reimplemented for constant cost and increased performance. The 3030 series and, in 1979, the 4300 series were introduced as lower-cost, constant-performance models of the System/370 ISP. Chapter 52 discusses and analyzes the various family members.

Chapter 51

Architecture of the IBM System/370[1]

Richard P. Case / Andris Padegs

Summary This paper discusses the design considerations for the architectural extensions that distinguish System/370 from System/360. It comments on experiences with the original objectives for System/360 and on the efforts to achieve them, and it describes the reasons and objectives for extending the architecture. It covers virtual storage, program control, data-manipulation instructions, timing facilities, multiprocessing, debugging and monitoring, error handling, and input/output operations. A final section tabulates some of the important parameters of the various IBM machines which implement the architecture.

Introduction

The years since the introduction of System/360 in 1964 have produced very substantial changes in most aspects of the design, manufacture, and use of information-processing systems. The hardware technology for realizing logic functions has evolved from semi-integrated circuit modules with single devices per chip to hundreds or thousands of circuits on a single silicon chip. The technology for high-speed storage has changed from magnetic cores to dense arrays of transistors on silicon chips. The growth in size and function of systems software has surprised even the practitioners. It is not surprising, therefore, to discover that extensions and refinements to the architecture[2] of System/360 were found to be necessary.

This paper reviews the motivation for extending the System/360 architecture and describes the design considerations associated with the extensions adopted for System/370.[3] It comments on some experiences with the original objectives and concepts of System/360. Finally, it summarizes the characteristics of IBM machines implementing the System/360 and the System/370 architectures [Amdahl, Blaauw, and Brooks, 1964; Amdahl, 1964; Blaauw and Brooks, 1964; Blaauw, 1964; Padegs, 1964; and Stevens, 1964].

Experience with System/360

At the time the major decisions were made on the System/370 architecture, a significant amount of experience was available with the initial implementations of System/360. The major conclusions from this experience were:

Compatibility

Compatibility really worked. It was in fact possible to transfer programs routinely from one model to another and expect them to produce the same results. Operational evidence was available that architecture and implementation could be separated; one need not imply the other.

Compatibility also helped reduce development expense. The original plan called for verifying each element of software on each model. Because of the growing confidence that programs which ran on one model would also run on other models, it was possible to significantly reduce the amount of cross-verification to be performed.

Implementation of a whole line of computers according to a common architecture did not take an undue amount of effort. It did, however, require unusual attention to detail and some new procedures, which are described in the Architecture Control Procedure section.

Performance Range

A greater performance range must be planned for. The original System/360 announcement included processors with a performance range of about 25 to 1. Six years later this had increased to about 200 to 1, and plans were being made for even further extensions.

Main Storage

It was obviously necessary to plan for main-storage sizes of more than 2^{24} bytes. The technological improvements in main storage which reduced the relative cost had happened at a rate greater than was expected. The result was that serious thought had to be given to the planned replacement of 24-bit addressing.

The extension of the address size proved to be more difficult than first thought. Our experience in this respect agrees with that of Bell and Strecker [1976], who say: "There is only one mistake . . . that is difficult to recover from—not providing enough address bits. . . ."

The basic addressing mechanism of System/360 had anticipated

[1]*Comm. ACM*, vol. 21, no. 1, January 1978, pp. 73–96.

[2]The term *architecture* is used here to describe the attributes of a system as seen by the programmer, i.e., the conceptual structure and functional behavior, as distinct from the organization of the date flow and controls, the logical design, and the physical implementation.

[3]This chapter is not the definitive reference work for the specification of the features and functions discussed. For the official, and maintained, description, refer to the *IBM System/370 Principles of Operations*, form GA22-7000, which is available through local IBM branch offices.

the eventual need and was well suited to the extension, since it depended on base registers that were already 32 bits wide. The interruption mechanism and the I/O control formats, however, did not have the required extensibility. (We knew in 1962 that this was the case, but the immediate cost and performance consequences outweighed the need to meet the eventual long-term requirements.) More importantly, the operating systems and compiler-produced application programs had used the extra bits in address words for control purposes and hence required extensive modifications.

Operating Systems

Machine architecture must be developed in conjunction with changes and extensions to existing operating systems. Whereas the original System/360 architecture was developed to provide a good basis on which a completely new operating system could be built, extensions to that architecture have to consider the specific usages and capabilities of the available operating systems.

Architecture Control

The design and control of system architecture must be an ongoing function that can never be considered complete. We found ourselves well into the 1970s making changes in the architecture of System/360 to remove ambiguities and, in some cases, to adjust the function provided.

Objectives of System/370

Motivation

The motivation to extend the System/360 architecture for the new series of machines came from two main sources:

1 The experience with the System/360 architecture in writing application programs, in designing and using operating systems, and in debugging and maintaining both software and hardware had identified a number of bottlenecks and limitations in the efficiency of system use and had pointed out areas where additional machine functions were desirable.

2 The general lowering of the cost of technology for main storage and logic circuitry in relation to the overall system cost made it possible economically to include functions that did not appear justified in the original System/360 architecture.

Specific Objectives

The following were the specific objectives of the System/370 architecture:

1 Improving the level of detail, precision, and predictability of the System/360 architecture. These improvements were made primarily in the areas of interruptions, system control, and the order of storage references. They were motivated largely by reliability and serviceability considerations.

2 Adding new instructions to enhance the performance of frequent functions in application programs. A total of 17 new unprivileged instructions were introduced in the System/370 architecture.

3 Extending the architecture to improve system reliability, availability, and serviceability. Extensions were included to assist diagnostics and recovery by software after a hardware failure (machine-check extensions), to assist in debugging software (program-event recording, monitoring, status storing), and to facilitate formation of multiprocessing systems with multiple CPUs sharing common main storage.

4 Adding new facilities to enhance the performance and function of the operating system and to introduce uniform machine-implemented protocols in the system. Dynamic address translation, timing facilities, and a number of privileged instructions were the main extensions provided for this purpose.

Constraints on System/370

The System/370 architecture was developed subject to the following main constraints:

1 Within the limitations described in the *IBM System/370 Principles of Operation*, the architecture must be upward compatible with System/360 architecture as far as user programs are concerned; that is, user programs written for System/360 must run efficiently on System/370 models with no modification to these programs. These limitations are that the systems have the same or equivalent facilities and that the programs have no time dependence, use only model-independent functions defined in the Principles of Operation, and not use unassigned formats and operation codes. These limitations essentially mean that compatibility applies only to valid programs.

2 It must be possible to run certain System/360 operating systems unmodified on System/370 models. Even though such operating systems could not fully benefit from the new functions available in System/370, and new support was planned, the ability to execute them was needed for the transition period.

3 It must be possible to attach and operate most types of System/360 I/O devices on System/370.

4   The System/370 architecture must preserve and extend the open-endedness and generality of design characteristic of the System/360 architecture.

Summary of Architectural Extensions

Table 1 lists the major categories of architectural extension that have been added to the System/360[1] architecture to form the System/370[2] architecture, including those that were originally introduced on the System/360 Model 85. The extensions are grouped in terms of architectural facilities, which are mechanisms provided in the machine for performing a specific function. The table also lists the number of new instructions associated with the facility. Note that many of the new facilities have no new instructions associated with them. Table 2 lists all new instructions, which total 40.

Additionally in a number of areas the System/360 architecture was made more specific and predictable within the freedom permitted by the original definition. The following are two examples:

1   The result of a decimal-arithmetic operation is made predictable when an invalid sign code is encountered. This is a common error in source data, and the change permits correction and resumption of the operation.

2   The priority of recognizing program-interruption conditions is specified to achieve repeatability and to make debugging easier.

Compatibility with System/360

Methods of Achieving Compatibility

Major emphasis in the design of the System/370 architecture was placed on defining all changes and extensions so that a valid System/360 program, executed on a System/370 machine, would

[1]The System/360 Model 20 is not discussed in the referenced papers nor in this paper, as some of its architectural features are so specialized that it is not convenient to discuss them in the same context.

[2]This paper covers only those facilities that are described in *System/370 Principles of Operation*. It does not discuss certain extensions that were made available only on System/360 Models 44 and 67; nor does it describe the following special facilities that are available only on some models: virtual-machine assist (hardware assist for VM/370), extended control-program support (hardware assist for OS/VS1 and for VM/370), APL assist, OS/DOS compatibility, the assist for optical character recognition, emulators for other machines, as well as the System/370 extended facility and recovery extensions first made available on the IBM 3033 Processor Complex.

Table 1   Architectural Extensions Incorporated in System/370

	Instructions	
Facility	Unpriv.	Priv.
Virtual storage		
Dynamic address translation	-	2
Reference and change recording	-	1
Channel indirect data addressing	-	-
Program control and interruptions		
Control registers	-	2
Extended control	-	-
System-mask handling	-	2
PSW-key handling	-	2
Restart interruption	-	-
Extended masking	-	-
Data-manipulation instructions		
General instructions	7	-
Decimal instructions	1	-
Floating-point instructions	7	-
Byte-oriented operands	-	-
Timing facilities		
Time-of-day clock	1	1
Clock comparator	-	2
CPU timer	-	2
Multisystem operation		
Synchronization and serialization	-	-
Prefixing	-	2
Interprocessor signaling	-	2
Debugging and monitoring		
Program-event recording	-	-
Monitoring	1	-
Status storing	-	-
Machine-error handling		
Resets	-	-
Error reporting	-	-
Logout	-	-
Command retry	-	-
Storage validation	-	-
Machine identification	-	2
Input/output		
Block multiplexing	-	-
Control	-	3
Data-rate improvement	-	-
	17	23

obtain the same results as specified in the *IBM System/360 Principles of Operation*. This compatibility was achieved by four devices:

Restriction.   Narrowing System/370 to a more specific operation in areas where the System/360 definition allowed unpredictable

Table 2   New Instructions Incorporated in System/370

Name	Mnemonic	Type		Op code
ADD NORMALIZED (extended)	AXR	RR	Unpriv.	36
CLEAR I/O	CLRIO	S	Priv.	9D01
COMPARE AND SWAP	CS	RS	Unpriv.	BA
COMPARE DOUBLE AND SWAP	CDS	RS	Unpriv.	BB
COMPARE LOGICAL CHARACTERS UNDER MASK	CLM	RS	Unpriv.	BD
COMPARE LOGICAL LONG	CLCL	RR	Unpriv.	0F
HALT DEVICE	HDV	S	Priv.	9E01
INSERT CHARACTERS UNDER MASK	ICM	RS	Unpriv.	BF
INSERT PSW KEY	IPK	S	Priv.	B20B
LOAD CONTROL	LCTL	RS	Priv.	B7
LOAD REAL ADDRESS	LRA	RX	Priv.	B1
LOAD ROUNDED (extended to long)	LRDR	RR	Unpriv.	25
LOAD ROUNDED (long to short)	LRER	RR	Unpriv.	35
MONITOR CALL	MC	SI	Unpriv.	AF
MOVE LONG	MVCL	RR	Unpriv.	0E
MULTIPLY (extended)	MXR	RR	Unpriv.	26
MULTIPLY (long to extended)	MXDR	RR	Unpriv.	27
MULTIPLY (long to extended)	MXD	RX	Unpriv.	67
PURGE TLB	PTLB	S	Priv.	B20D
RESET REFERENCE BIT	RRB	S	Priv.	B213
SET CLOCK	SCK	S	Priv.	B204
SET CLOCK COMPARATOR	SCKC	S	Priv.	B206
SET CPU TIMER	SPT	S	Priv.	B208
SET PREFIX	SPX	S	Priv.	B210
SET PSW KEY FROM ADDRESS	SPKA	S	Priv.	B20A
SHIFT AND ROUND DECIMAL	SRP	SS	Unpriv.	F0
SIGNAL PROCESSOR	SIGP	RS	Priv.	AE
START I/O FAST RELEASE	SIOF	S	Priv.	9C01
STORE CHANNEL ID	STIDC	S	Priv.	B203
STORE CHARACTERS UNDER MASK	STCM	RS	Unpriv.	BE
STORE CLOCK	STCK	S	Unpriv.	B205
STORE CLOCK COMPARATOR	STCKC	S	Priv.	B207
STORE CONTROL	STCTL	RS	Priv.	B6
STORE CPU ADDRESS	STAP	S	Priv.	B212
STORE CPU ID	STIDP	S	Priv.	B202
STORE CPU TIMER	STPT	S	Priv.	B209
STORE PREFIX	STPX	S	Priv.	B211
STORE THEN AND SYSTEM MASK	STNSM	SI	Priv.	AC
STORE THEN OR SYSTEM MASK	STOSM	SI	Priv.	AD
SUBTRACT NORMALIZED (extended)	SXR	RR	Unpriv.	37

results. This approach applied to the extensions in machine-check interruptions, as well as to a number of minor improvements.

Checking.   Allowing new functions to be invoked only by a program that would have been considered invalid in System/360, that is, letting a program observe a change or extension to System/360 operation only when it uses an operation code or specifies a value for a bit ·in the program-status word or in an address that in System/360 is checked for validity and results in a program exception. This device was used for the large majority of extensions, including the byte-oriented-operand feature and virtually all new instructions.

This approach was used also to ensure that all subsequently introduced extensions, such as dynamic address translation and program-event recording, are compatible with the System/370 architecture as initially announced. An exception was that the unused positions in the 16 control registers introduced at the original System/370 announcement were not checked for zeros but instead were reserved for future extensions by an explicit warning in the Principles of Operation. This safeguard was chosen because only privileged programs can load and store control registers, because checking scattered bit positions in the 16 registers is expensive and time-consuming, and because even greater cost would have been required for a predictable ending of an invalid loading operation.

Mode Control.   Defining mode-control and mask bits in control registers such that the reset state specifies an operation compatible with System/360. The external, channel, and machine-check masks, as well as a number of other controls, were defined this way.

Manual Switches.   Introducing a manual switch for setting up a mode where the machine stops on encountering a deviation from System/360 operation. This approach was taken to handle CPU and channel diagnostic logouts. In System/360, the logout area starts with location 128 and, while no limit is set on its size, its extent is smaller than that on a comparable System/370 model. Since such a logout on a System/370 machine may overlay a program or data which assumes System/360 logout, stopping avoids continuation with invalid information. It was assumed that the stop-on-logout mode would be selected only for the rare situations when the machine is operated without the correct error-recovery program.

Incompatibilities

The extensions introduced for System/370 do not meet the compatibility objectives in the following five cases. In each case a program may exist that meets the System/360 validity requirements but does not obtain the same results on System/370. These incompatibilities, however, are confined to programs that are either executed in the supervisor mode or are components of an operating system, and they were deemed justified, considering both the alternative solutions and the likelihood and difficulty of operational problems. The five incompatibilities are reviewed here in some detail to emphasize the kind of careful attention that compatibility requires.

Use of USASCII-8 Bit for Control of EC Model.   System/360 anticipated the adoption of a proposal for a "Decimal ASCII" in punched cards and of a technique for expanding the seven-bit

standard to eight bits. This data representation is referred to as USASCII-8 in the System/360 manuals. Both the card code and the particular expansion technique have since been rejected as a national standard.

System/360 provides for USASCII-8 by a mode under control of PSW bit 12. When bit 12 of the System/360 PSW is one, codes preferred for USASCII-8 are generated for decimal results. When PSW bit 12 is zero, the codes preferred for EBCDIC are generated.

In System/370, the USASCII-8 mode and the associated meaning of PSW bit 12 are removed, and all instructions whose execution in System/360 depends on the setting of PSW bit 12 are executed to yield the EBCDIC codes. PSW bit 12 is used instead to control the format of the PSW and of the information stored on an interruption.

This incompatibility affects only those System/360 programs that specify the USASCII-8 mode. Since the anticipated standard was never adopted, it is highly unlikely that any production programs ever used it. In fact, we are not aware of any instance of its use.

The alternative for System/370 was to assign a control-register bit for controlling the PSW format. Such a definition would not have permitted changing at the same time both the mode and the PSW contents which the mode controls, and it would have precluded program control of the PSW format on initial program loading.

Clearing Storage on Power Off.   In System/360, main storage originally was implemented with magnetic cores, and the architecture specifies that the storage preserve its contents when the power is turned off and on, provided that the CPU is in the stopped state. In System/370, with solid-logic technology, the power-on sequence normally clears storage to zeros. Incompatibility exists to the extent that a program that depends on information stored before power was turned off (in order to dump storage contents, for example) will not operate on System/370.

This change was mandated by the change from core to solid-logic technology, and it had minor impact on compatibility.

A "power warning" interruption is available as a feature on some models of System/370 which, in conjunction with equipment that monitors line voltage, signals when loss of power is imminent. The timing of the signal should be such that the operating system can transfer the contents of main-storage (or at least critical sections) to a permanent medium before the system stops operating. This usually requires some type of stored energy supply.

Operation Code for HALT DEVICE.   The first eight bits of the operation code assigned to the new System/370 instruction HALT DEVICE are the same as those originally assigned to HALT I/O, the distinction between the two being specified by bit 15. In

System/360, bit 15 is ignored, and HALT I/O is performed in both cases. Incompatibility exists to the extent that a HALT I/O instruction of a System/360 program is executed on a System/370 model as HALT DEVICE if bit 15 happens to be one.

This choice of the operation code was made to facilitate the attachment of the IBM 2880 Block Multiplexer Channel, which implements HALT DEVICE, to the Model 85 CPU, the design of which did not initially provide for this new instruction. The likelihood of a problem is minimal, because:

1   Normally bit 15 is zero, since it is set to zero by IBM compilers and assemblers.

2   In many cases the function performed by HALT DEVICE may be substituted for and may even be preferable to that performed by HALT I/O.

3   The occurrence of the HALT I/O instruction is infrequent.

Command Retry.   Most System/370 channels provide the command-retry facility, whereby the channel, in response to a signal from the device, re-executes a channel command. This re-execution is usually invoked when the device or control unit detects a malfunction. The following is a list of some of the effects of command retry:

1   An immediate command specifying no chaining may result in condition code 0 being set rather than condition code 1.

2   Multiple interruptions may be generated for a single channel-command word (CCW) with the program-controlled interruption flag.

3   Since CCWs may be refetched, programs which dynamically modify CCWs may be affected.

4   The residual count in the channel-status word reflects only the last execution of the command and does not necessarily reflect the maximum storage used in previous executions.

These potential difficulties were not deemed to be serious enough to warrant the hardware and software cost of placing command retry under mode control. No problem exists with the compatibility of I/O devices announced prior to System/370, as they do not signal for command retry.

Channel Prefetching.   In System/360, on an output operation the channel may prefetch and buffer as many as 16 bytes; similarly, with data chaining specified, the channel may fetch the new CCW when up to 16 bytes remain to be transferred under control of the current CCW. In System/370, the restriction of 16 bytes is removed.

This incompatibility may affect programs that change data or command words during the execution of the operation. The change was needed for performance reasons and, as with command retry, was not deemed to warrant a mode control.

Extendability and Generality

The compatible evolution of the System/360 architecture into the System/370 architecture was made possible largely by judicious reservation in System/360 of unassigned formats and operation codes. The System/370 architecture maintains and extends the principle of frugal and controlled allocation of architecture resources, so that System/370 can be extended in the future to meet new requirements. The following are some examples where provision is made for future extension:

1   Main-storage-address fields in the new PSW format, control registers, and the permanently allocated storage locations were assigned 32 bit positions, should they be needed for address expansion.

2   The new EC-mode PSW format was defined to provide space for additional control bits.

3   The control registers provide a general method of handling control information that is not contained in the PSW, and provide space for new facilities and for an expansion of the present facilities.

4   The time-of-day clock format contains 12 unassigned low-order bit positions, which could be used for higher resolution.

5   A new instruction format was introduced for instructions that need a single operand address. The unused eight-bit field in this format is made a part of the operation code, thus expanding the number of available operation codes by 255.

Architecture Control Procedure

Beginning with the development of System/360, and continuing to the present day, IBM has gradually adopted a process for the specification and control of architecture. This process has been largely successful in maintaining compatibility among many and varied machines developed in several laboratories around the world. The following are some important attributes of this process.

Specification

There is but one specification of the architecture. It tells IBM machine designers the functions the machine must provide, and it describes to IBM programmers how the machine operates. The same specification, called the Principles of Operation, is made available outside IBM and is the only authoritative specification that describes the architecture.

The architecture specification covers all functions of the machine that are observable by a program. It either specifies the action the machine performs or states that the action is unpredictable. The latter applies to the detailed functions for which neither frequency of occurrence nor usefulness of results warrants identical action in all models or at all times. Normally the specification of unpredictable operation is a considered architectural choice, since the architecture specification must anticipate future implementations and the potential cost of providing specific results of marginal value. Occasionally, it is introduced into the definition because the specific detailed function is overlooked in the initial stages of the architecture resolution process or because the designs of the machines initially implementing the architecture mandate different operations.

All machine implementations are strictly monitored for compliance with the architecture specification. Affirmation of compliance with the architecture is a part of the internal IBM procedure for product-development control, and actual compliance is verified by formal and informal compliance audits and reviews of machine specifications. Deviations from the architecture must be corrected. In the rare cases when the cost to change the design or to retrofit installed machines is excessive in relation to the practical value of the compliance on that machine, deviations are permitted. Any deviation that is likely to affect the execution of a program is published in the IBM System Library manual for the machine.

Most machines have a few deviations, covering such aspects as the precise meaning of the test light on the operator-control panel, the indication of access exceptions for an unused part of an instruction, or the precise instant during execution of the WRITE DIRECT instruction when serialization is performed. A deviation by one implementation does not necessarily lead to a specification of unpredictability, as compliance with the definition may be essential for other applications, and the specific definition better conveys the intended structure, making the architecture simpler and easier to understand.

Development Procedure

The architecture definition starts out with a proposal for extending or improving the function of the machine in a specific area. Extensions to the architecture normally are adopted as part of the development of a new machine or set of machines, and the process includes a number of steps:

1 Preliminary Review: Depending on the scope of the extension, the cost and performance implications of new ideas may be evaluated in various studies and reviews among the architects and the machine and software designers. A number of iterations of such reviews and architecture definitions may take place.

2 Resolution Meetings: After an architecture definition has been produced and reviewed by all interested areas, the adoption of the definition is placed as an item on the agenda of an architecture resolution meeting. These are periodic meetings where all interested and affected groups are represented by people with authority to commit their projects. Depending on the need, the meetings may take place monthly, weekly, or even more frequently. A proposal may be adopted or rejected at the resolution meeting, or concerns may be identified that require further study. A proposal that is adopted at an architecture resolution meeting becomes part of the architecture specification.

3 Resolution Conferences: In order to set the direction for a new product line, stop debate on some issue, or resolve all loose ends, a resolution conference is called. Such conferences may take place a few times during the development of a product. They differ from regular resolution meetings in that participation is wider, higher level of management is involved, and more use is made of executive decision making.

4 Interpretation: The architecture specification occasionally leaves out some aspect of the operation, or the wording may not be quite clear. Implementers are instructed to question the architecture on any doubtful point rather than make assumptions. Most questions are raised and answered by telephone, and the architect then periodically documents the questions and the answers for review by all implementers. These architecture interpretations supplement the original definition and are eventually integrated into the definition. Some questions demand further study or require action at one of the resolution meetings. Although the need for interpretation of the architecture normally diminishes after the initial implementation of the definition, some valid questions are raised and changes in the wording made years later. Continual maintenance and updating of the architecture specification are essential parts of the architecture control procedure.

Responsibility

Although the adoption of the architecture specification and compliance with it are based as much as possible on cost and performance analyses and on consensus among machine and software implementers, final authority for the architecture definition rests with the architecture group. Architecture is recognized within IBM as an autonomous function which analyzes the requirements of users and implementers and, in response, produces the specification of how the machine must appear to the program. It is an ongoing operation, as the definition must be maintained and extended across product cycles.

One person, the chief architect, is responsible for the contents of the Principles of Operation. He must obtain the approval of the managers of each implementation before any change can officially be made, and he calls and chairs architecture resolution meetings. The architect's decisions at these meetings are binding unless and until successfully appealed to high authority.

These procedures, especially the parts that result in less authority or autonomy for implementing engineers, were not accepted lightly or without considerable debate and management leadership. Most of this methodology was developed by Fred Brooks during the early days of the System/360 development, and it has survived to the present. It succeeds in large part because of the high competence and personal professional dedication of the architecture group. They win most of the arguments by being right, not just because they have nominal authority. The process also works because the architecture group has considerable experience and sympathy with the problems of practicing engineers and programmers.

Architecture Extensions

This section describes the main features of the System/370 architecture extensions and provides some discussion of the motivation for them. It includes a brief summary of the architecture, the purpose of the function, the reasons for the architectural decisions, and some of the main alternatives considered.

Virtual Storage

Motivation

The single item that most distinguishes the architecture of System/370 from its predecessor, System/360, is the availability of a dynamic-address-translation facility, which allows programming systems to efficiently implement a group of functions which are collectively known as virtual storage. This sytem incorporates paging from a backing store as introduced in Atlas [Kilburn et al., 1962], and a second level of indirection, segmentation, as suggested by Dennis [1965] and as further detailed by Arden et al. [1966].

The System/370 version of this facility was largely patterned after the System/360 Model 67[Gibson, 1966]. Our experience with that machine and its operating system, TSS, had verified the value of many of the concepts and had given us actual usage data with which to judge design decisions for System/370.

The motivation for virtual storage and some of its value can be understood by considering several somewhat overlapping topics:

1 Roll-in and roll-out

2 Fragmentation of real main storage

3 Application-program development

4 Dynamic size adjustment

5 Compatibility of large and small storage sizes

6 Protection and sharing

7 Virtual-data access

8 Virtual-machine simulation

The following sections discuss each of these items.

Roll-In and Roll-Out. Prior to the introduction of virtual storage, each application program was assigned real main-storage locations at the time it was initiated. Thereafter, the program, as well as its data, might be swapped out of main storage while waiting for terminal or I/O service. When the program was subsequently returned to main storage, it was constrained to occupy the same real locations as it did previously, since relocation to a different set of locations was extremely inconvenient.[1]

This restriction of programs and data to the initially assigned real-storage locations leads to conflicts, such as when a program that is ready for execution is barred from entering main storage by another program residing at the assigned locations, even though contiguous unused space of sufficient size is available at some other address, and even though the CPU may not be fully occupied. The overall result is that system throughput is reduced and response time increased.

With virtual storage, any part of main storage is available for any application, regardless of the locations to which it had initially been assigned. By preventing conflicts for real-storage locations, the performance of the whole system may well be significantly improved.[2]

Fragmentation of Real Main Storage.   If the various application programs are of differing size, the storage-allocation problem is even more difficult. Not only may a program be blocked from its initially assigned locations, but even in batch operations, which run applications to completion after they are initially loaded, only part of the main storage can be utilized at any one time. As jobs are completed at various times, the available storage can be

---

[1]It has been argued that this is not necessarily so. The basic System/360 architecture makes all problem-program main-storage references via a register. With appropriate programming conventions, an operating system might be built to allow the relocation of programs and data on arbitrary boundaries without dynamic-address-translation hardware. In practice, however, such a design would probably become too restrictive in the types of programs allowed, or too complex and too slow to be acceptable for a broad class of applications. It would be particularly inconvenient for programs that store base-register values for later use or for programs which do arithmetic on base-register values, as is often required for the use of SS-format instructions. Finally, because it would introduce new programming conventions, it is very unlikely that such relocation could be applied to existing programs.

[2]This benefit could also be obtained by a system with a simpler relocation mechanism than the one described here.

assigned to new jobs only to the extent to which the waiting jobs can utilize the available contiguous spaces. As a result, relatively long-lived "holes" are formed in main storage which are individually too small for any job, but which collectively are larger than needed for some or all waiting jobs.

Virtual storage allows the efficient collection of fragments of main storage into one contiguous address space without moving or disturbing the programs in process. The result is a more efficient use of main storage and more throughput.

Application-Program Development.   Prior to virtual storage, the size of the installed main storage constrained application-program development. Often the effective upper limit of an application program had to be much less than the installed storage size in order to provide for a resident supervisor and I/O package, and because partitions for other applications were needed to ensure a reasonable level of multiprogramming.

In many cases, a considerable programming effort was expended in planning overlays or phases in processing. This was true even when the application program was such that most of the code was seldom executed, it being present only for unusual or error situations. Furthermore, sometimes modifications to a program which once fitted its allocated partition would cause it to just exceed the available space. Fitting this program into its previous space was likely to require substantial rework for little return.

Virtual storage allows programs to run with an allocation of real main storage which is independent of the size of the application code. It allows many applications to be coded with little regard for absolute space limits. Space in real main storage is not assigned to seldomly executed parts of the program, and programs can continue to be properly executed even if they grow.

It is, of course, misleading to suggest that developers of large or frequently executed applications should remain ignorant of their main-storage requirements or addressing patterns. Poor design can require extensive paging and thus result in poor system performance.

Dynamic Size Adjustment.   In many cases it has been observed that the dynamic allocation of storage to a program can be more effective than the best static allocation by a programmer. Thus, the effective size of an application may well be smaller under dynamic allocation than with preplanned overlays. This allows even more efficient use of main storage and may further increase system throughput. The functions of dynamic location assignment and dynamic size control interact with each other in a favorable way. The "working size" of the application changes with time, and the allocation capability allows more applications to be resident in a fixed memory space. Without dynamic size adjustment, contiguous storage was often reserved to meet the largest storage requirement for the application, part of the storage being unused for most of the execution time.

Compatibility of Large and Small Storage Sizes.   The machine compatibility objectives of System/360 stated that valid programs on one model would also be valid programs on another model, provided (in part) that the second model was configured with at least as much main storage as the program required. On some models it was not possible to install a large enough main storage.

The advent of virtual storage makes this condition obsolete. Since the available virtual storage of all models is now equal, programs written to run under a virtual-storage operating system may be freely transferred to another model, provided that it meets the real storage-size requirements of the operating system. Performance, of course, is significantly degraded on a model that has much less main storage. The ability to run a program on any model, even if at a degraded performance, may prove particularly useful in emergency situations where critical processing must be done when the normal equipment is unavailable.

In addition, virtual storage allows, without reprogramming, an immediate increase in system performance when real main storage is enlarged. This may be important to installations with increasing workload where it is not desired to recode or restructure the application set.

Although usually the contrary is assumed, it is possible to consider systems in which the real main storage is larger than the virtual storage assigned to any one program. Several routines, multiprogrammed, then would reside to utilize the available main storage. Such a system would have the advantage that address constants in problem programs could be smaller. Only the supervisory program would need to have enough total addressability to access the entire main storage.

Protection and Segmentation.   By appropriately managing the contents of the address-translation tables, an operating system may allow one problem program access to only a part of the total data in main storage, or, alternatively, may allow two or more programs to share the same data. This ability to share some but not the entire contents of main storage and to prevent all access to other contents is very useful in maintaining the integrity and security characteristics of an installation.

This method of protection is more flexible and selective than the System/360 key-controlled protection because even routines with key 0 are restrained from accidental access to data that is not assigned to them by translation-table entries. (It may be possible for these routines to modify the tables.) Furthermore, whereas the keys permit up to 15 different concurrently resident programs to be isolated from each other, translation tables permit individual access control for any number of programs. Operating systems may well use a combination of storage keys and translation-table contents for maximum flexibility and control.

Virtual Data Access.   Normally I/O operations are used to transfer data between the data sets on an external storage device and the storage that can be directly addressed by the program. Virtual storage can be used to avoid these explicit I/O operations. This is accomplished by combining the mechanism used to manage virtual storage with that used for managing external files.

Programs which implement virtual storage include tables, related to the address-translation tables, that identify, for pages not currently in main storage, the location of the page on the external storage medium, such as a disk. Analogous tables normally exist for external data files, which map data-set names to locations in external storage. With appropriate design of these tables and data formats, it is possible to "move" data between the virtual-storage area and the data-set area by modifying table entries, thus taking advantage of the paging mechanism to perform the I/O operation.

Such data access improves efficiency, as actual data movement into main storage occurs only when the application program refers to the data; on output, movement may be avoided when the data is already in the external device.

Viewed from another perspective, this approach provides a way of extending the size of the virtual storage to encompass all online data, with the restriction that any one program can have only part of the online data in its own virtual storage at any one time.

This technique was advantageously used in the TSS operating system on System/360 Model 67, where it was known as VIO.

Virtual-Machine Simulation. It has been found useful in many installations to use an operating system to simulate the existence of several machines on a single physical set of hardware. The IBM VM/370 operating system is one example. This technique allows an installation to multiprogram several different operating systems (or different versions of the same operating system) on a single physical machine. The dynamic-address-translation hardware allows such a simulator to be efficient enough to be used, in many cases, in production mode.

Dynamic-Address-Translation Mechanism

Address translation is achieved by treating the addresses supplied by and available to the CPU program as designating locations in virtual storage. The dynamic-address-translation mechanism translates these addresses to real addresses, which designate locations in real main storage.[1]

Translation Procedure

Translation is performed by the use of two stages of tables in main storage. The high-order bits of the virtual address are used to select an entry from the *segment table*. This entry contains the origin of a *page table*, which is indexed by the mid-order bits of

---

[1]The actual reference to main storage may occur only after a further translation known as "prefixing." This is described in the section on multiprocessing.

the address. The low-order bits of the virtual address are concatenated with the real address contained in the page-table entry to form the real main-storage address. The origin of the segment table is designated by the contents of control register 1. The extent of virtual storage accessed through a segment-table entry and a page-table entry is referred to as a *segment* and a *page*, respectively.

Controls are provided in the PSW to turn dynamic address translation on and off and in control register 0 to specify the size of segments and pages. The instruction LOAD REAL ADDRESS allows a program to explicitly determine the current real address corresponding to any virtual address. This is needed in several routines that translate channel programs or allocate and manage real main storage.

The two-stage translation procedure was selected for several reasons:

1 It provides a convenient way for segments to be shared among different programs, using differing virtual addresses, without requiring multiple page tables and multiple table changes when the pages are replaced.

2 It results in less total storage taken by the tables by permitting the tables to be abbreviated when the total possible virtual storage is only sparsely allocated.

3 It limits the size of the largest table to less than a page, thus facilitating the allocation of main storage to the tables.

4 It provides a convenient way for a portion of the tables (the page tables) not to be resident in main storage at all times. The page tables themselves may be paged out, in which case the "invalid" bit in the segment-table entry causes an interruption on an attempt to use the page table for translation.

Translation-Lookaside Buffer. If translation tables in main storage were actually accessed for each storage reference, the number of storage references would be tripled, causing a totally unacceptable performance degradation. In order to avoid such degradation, all implementations in the System/370 line include a hardware facility called the *translation-lookaside buffer* (TLB). The TLB is a group of fast-access registers that contain the results of recent references to translation tables. The access time to information in these registers is a small fraction of the main-storage access time, and they intercept about 99% of all the references to tables in storage. The TLB makes the performance degradation associated with table references minimal.

The instruction PURGE TLB causes the TLB to be cleared of all entries. It provides a way of informing the translation mechanism that the software has changed the contents of the current translation tables in main storage and that the tables must be reaccessed rather than relying on their previous contents as reflected in the buffers.

Segment and Page Sizes. The architecture, as well as its machine implementations, provides for any combination of two different segment sizes (64K bytes and 1M bytes) and two different page sizes (2K bytes and 4K bytes).[1]

These parameters were provided to accommodate the range of expected main-storage sizes and disk characteristics. Small page sizes are needed for efficient use of the smaller main-storage sizes, while large pages are needed to reduce CPU and I/O time in main-storage to disk transfers. Large segment sizes allow convenient handling of large data and program files, while small segment sizes provide for easier storage allocation to translation tables and for more segment names.

Each IBM operating system uses only one combination, the use being as follows:

Segment	Page	System
64K	2K	DOS/VS, OS/VS1
64K	4K	OS/VS2, VM/370
1M	2K	
1M	4K	TSS

Reference and Change Recording

When a reference is made to a page not currently in main storage, the operating system must decide which currently resident page is least likely to be used next and hence should be replaced. For the page that is to be replaced, it must decide if the copy in main storage has been modified and hence needs to be saved or if it can be overlaid because the copy in external storage is still current. Two bits of information about each 2K-byte real-storage block, as well as the instruction RESET REFERENCE BIT, are provided to assist these decision processes.

One bit, called the *reference bit,* is set by the machine to one whenever the block is referred to by the CPU or the channel. It is intended to provide the basis for selecting the page to be replaced. The other bit, called the *change bit,* is set to one whenever storing is performed into the block. This bit may be used by the software to determine if the copy of the page occupying the block must be transferred to external storage prior to reallocation of the block. The page-replacement algorithm may also select unchanged pages in preference to changed pages in order to avoid this transfer.

Translation of Channel Programs

After considerable analysis, it was decided not to include the address-translation capability in the System/370 channels but rather to provide a mechanism to assist software in performing the function. Several considerations were important in reaching this conclusion:

1   The allowable channel data rates were limited in many cases by the main-storage accesses necessary during data chaining or command chaining. On some implementations, the extra storage accesses implied by a translation capability would have reduced the maximum data rates to unacceptably low values.

2   Since the channels operate asynchronously with the CPU, and often on behalf of different tasks, a full channel relocation capability would have implied different translation tables for the CPU and for each of the many subchannels. The resulting constraints on software paging and storage management were felt to be unnecessarily burdensome.

3   The extra channel hardware cost, especially to retrofit some of the existing implementations, would have been significant.

4   The performance penalty, of scanning each newly created channel program at START-I/O time and replacing the virtual addresses with real addresses, was reduced somewhat by the need to scan the same programs anyway to cause the allocated page frames to be fixed (removed from the set eligible for paging) even if the channel were to contain hardware to perform the virtual-to-real translation.

5   The design of new access methods, such as VSAM and VTAM, was expected to eliminate the need for software to translate I/O data addresses in channel programs and hence cause this issue to disappear in the future.

The channel-indirect-data-addressing facility is provided to assist the operating system in the translation of channel programs. It permits a single channel-command word (CCW) to control transfer of data that spans several potentially noncontiguous pages in main storage. When a CCW specifies indirect data addressing, the data-address field of the CCW is not used directly to address data but rather contains the address of a list of indirect-data-address words. A new address word is obtained by the channel whenever a 2K-byte boundary is crossed in main storage. The address words, containing a 32-bit address field, provide also for the eventual extension of the storage address in conformity with the general System/370 objectives.

Program Control

PSW and Control Registers

In System/360, all CPU state information (other than the contents of general and floating-point registers) is arranged in the 64-bit

[1]In this chapter K stands for $2^{10} = 1024$, and M stands for $2^{20} = 1,048,576$.

program-status word (PSW), which provides a convenient way of introducing a new CPU state by an instruction or an interruption, as well as a way of saving the old state on an interruption. The new facilities introduced by System/370 expanded the amount of information relevant to the CPU state, as certain additional control information had to be specified that spans the execution of a sequence of instructions; and, on encountering exceptions, additional status information had to be provided to the program. Since no unused bit positions were available in the PSW, the requirements for the additional control and status information were met by modifying the PSW format, by introducing a set of sixteen 32-bit control registers, and by assigning locations in main storage for control and status purposes.

Additional space in the PSW is obtained by removing the 16-bit interruption code and the two-bit instruction-length code from the System/360 format and by replacing the six channel masks with a single I/O mask. Two new controls are placed in the PSW—one bit to turn program-event recording on and off and one bit to turn dynamic address translation on and off.

All additional control information is placed in the control registers. The control registers are, in effect, an extension to the PSW, except that their contents are not changed by the machine on an interruption. Two instructions, LOAD CONTROL and STORE CONTROL, are provided for loading and inspecting their contents. The control registers are addressed similarly to the 16 general registers, and multiple contiguous registers may be handled by one instruction.

All information that describes the cause of an interruption is placed in specifically assigned main-storage locations. The information is arranged by interruption classes, with additional fields left unassigned for future expansion.

For I/O, a four-byte location is also assigned in main storage that contains an address that specifies the storage area for diagnostic channel logout. Additionally, a four-byte location is assigned in main storage where channel identification is placed on execution of the instruction STORE CHANNEL ID. These I/O related fields are in main storage rather than a control register since they must be accessed or modified by the channel. The channel is, in effect, a separate processor sharing main storage but having otherwise a limited ability to communicate with the CPU.

PSW bit 12 specifies the format of the PSW and the execution of interruptions. When PSW bit 12 is 0, the PSW has the System/360 format, and the CPU is said to operate in the basic-control (BC) mode; when bit 12 is one, the new PSW format and the extended-control (EC) mode are specified. It should be noted that the BC-EC mode distinction pertains only to information appearing in the PSW. Control registers, as well as the facilities associated with control registers (monitoring, machine-check controls, extended external masking, etc.), are operative in both modes, subject to the availability of PSW control bits. Program-event recording is defined to be off in the BC mode, as is implicitly invoked dynamic address translation, but the instruction LOAD REAL ADDRESS with the associated explicit use of the dynamic-address-translation facility is valid in the BC mode.

The following observations guided the architectural decisions:

1 On an interruption, as well as on a programmed transfer of control (LOAD PSW), the machine must indivisibly replace a certain amount of control information, including the instruction address, protection key, problem-supervisor mode specification, and masks to disable further interruptions. For performance reasons, changing of other control information should be optional and can be explicitly performed by the supervisory program. This applies particularly to control information that pertains to system functions and that is changed infrequently (page size, controls for recovery from machine errors, etc.).

2 Certain information in the BC-mode PSW is meaningful only for the determination of the cause of the interruption and is not used to control machine operation. Priority for PSW space should be given to control information. The interruption code and the instruction-length code, which for most interruptions is only a fraction of the total status information provided, can as well be placed with the rest of the status information in main storage.

One alternative for handling the additional control information was to expand the size of the PSW. Such an approach leads to the temptation to define a program status block for the control of the machine containing all information for a dispatchable program unit, including the values of general and floating-point registers, timer values for accounting purposes, etc. This in turn requires some assumptions for operating-system procedures, such as conventions for passing parameters in subroutine linkages. Thus, it leads to further extensions of the control block with information required by the operating system.

Such an approach would have increased the time for simple task switches, already too slow. Additionally, a number of considerations argued against incorporating operating-system structures in the machine architecture. A number of operating systems, with differing requirements, were anticipated for the System/370 line of machines, and no one set of formats and algorithms could satisfy them all. More importantly, the architectural extensions introduced a number of new concepts and facilities that had not yet been implemented in a total system design. As a result, the general design principle was adopted to include in the machine architecture only the essential primitives and elemental tools for performing the needed function.

System-Mask Handling

Normally, on System/360 machines, the OS/360 operating system operated either entirely enabled or entirely disabled for I/O and external interruptions; accordingly, enabling and disabling was accomplished by setting PSW bits 0-7 to a byte of ones or zeros. With the change in the PSW format and the introduction of dynamic address translation, program-event recording, and other potential extensions having control bits in PSW bit positions 0-7, setting all bits to the same value was no longer appropriate, and the operating system had to be modified to treat the system mask accordingly. This required the identification of all places in the program where the mask is changed, including interruptions and execution of LOAD PSW or SET SYSTEM MASK (SSM).

Because of the difficulty of finding all occurrences of SSM and because in the EC-mode PSW bits 0-7 normally are not replaced in their entirety, a mode was introduced where the execution of SSM is suppressed and instead causes a program interruption. The interruption signals where the original program needs to be modified.

The suppression of SSM is useful also for the conversion of the operating system from uniprocessor to multiprocessor operation. In a single-CPU system, the disabling of the CPU is a sufficient means for avoiding use of a serially reusable resource associated with I/O or external interruptions. When two or more CPUs share those routines, such disabling is not adequate, as the use of the resource by the other CPU also must be prohibited. Access to the serially reusable resource must be controlled by other means, and the interruption on encountering SSM aids the conversion by signaling where the semaphore instructions should be placed.

The two new instructions STORE THEN AND SYSTEM MASK and STORE THEN OR SYSTEM MASK provide the means for turning any bit in PSW bit positions 0-7 off or on. Furthermore, these instructions save the original value of the field in main storage so that a service routine making these changes could, on exit, restore the field to its original value. In System/360 the current value of the masks can not be determined without causing an interruption.

PSW-Key Handling

In the original design, most parts of the OS/360 operating system operated with a protection key of zero, thus having access to all parts of main storage. In the design of the OS/VS2 operating system, one step taken to catch programming errors was to use a nonzero protection key for the various components of the control program, thus protecting one component from inadvertent storing by another component.

Two instructions are provided for inspecting and setting the protection key in the PSW: INSERT PSW KEY (IPK) and SET PSW KEY FROM ADDRESS (SPKA). The first one places the protection key into a general register, and the latter replaces the key in the PSW with the four low-order bits of the operand address.

These instructions permit the key in the PSW to be set and subsequently restored when a component is entered with an unknown key and subsequently left, or when a routine must modify data having a different storage key. When a supervisor routine which normally uses a key of zero is called to perform a service that involves storing in a user region, SPKA is also useful for verifying that the requestor is authorized to perform the storing. In this case, the supervisor can use SPKA to set up the user's key for the duration of the operation.

Interruptions

System/370 expands the five System/360 interruption classes (machine check, supervisor call, program, external, and I/O) by introducing a new class—the restart interruption. This interruption occurs in response to the externally initiated restart signal and is intended for the manual debugging of the machine and for intervention by another CPU. In view of the intended purpose, no mask bit is provided for disallowing the interruption.

The control of interruptions is made more flexible by providing mask bits in control registers for each type of external condition, for each I/O channel, and for the different types of machine-check conditions. For any specific source, an interruption can occur only when both the corresponding mask in the control register and the class mask in the PSW allow it.

By means of the masks in the control registers, the supervisory program can disallow interruptions for some sources within a class, such as for machine-check recovery reports. They also allow the enabling for conditions of higher priority after an interruption for a lower-priority condition within the class has occurred, but before other interruptions from the lower-priority condition can be permitted. Thus, the program can simulate an interruption mechanism with a priority hierarchy.

Data-Manipulation Instructions

Well over a hundred instructions were considered for inclusion in System/370 architecture to improve the cost effectiveness of the machine for the applications and data structures that had evolved with the use of System/360 or that were anticipated for System/370.

Out of these, seven general instructions, one decimal instruction, and seven floating-point instructions were adopted for System/370. The floating-point instructions provide for arithmetic on the new extended-precision format, as well as for rounding from extended to long precision and from long to short precision.[1] The extended-precision format has a fraction of 28 hexadecimal digits, and the considerations associated with the design of the architecture are described by Padegs [1968].

The following is a summary of the operation and design considerations for the general and decimal instructions.

Justification Methodology

The value of a new instruction can be expressed in terms of an increase in CPU performance and a reduction in the program size, the performance gain being a function of the gain per occurrence of the instruction and its frequency of use. On the other hand, each instruction has a machine implementation cost that can be expressed in terms of additional circuits and control storage locations. A serious attempt was made to express the cost effectiveness for the more promising proposals in terms of specific value and cost numbers. However, the decision was ultimately based largely on judgment because of the following difficulties:

1 The performance of a new instruction depends on the extent to which it is integrated in the machine. A specific estimate for an addition to the architecture can be made only when the basic design of the machine is already laid out, and such an estimate normally is made assuming the least perturbation of the design, yielding lower performance.

2 An instruction is used depending on its performance, and its performance in a new machine design is a function of its frequency of use. A new instruction without a proven value is likely to be implemented at minimum cost and performance.

3 When the function performed by a new instruction is a concatenation of functions performed by a sequence of more primitive instructions, the cost and performance considerations differ in large and small machines:

> The elimination of the instruction fetching time may yield some performance gain in a medium-speed machine but is likely to be insignificant in a very small serial machine or in a large machine that overlaps phases of execution.

> In a large machine, frequent simple instructions may be performed in their entirety in hardware as part of the instruction decoding phase. If such a simple function is made a part of another more complex instruction, either the execution of the composite function is made slower by implementation in microcode, or additional cost in hardware is incurred.

4 Some instructions, such as those for conversion between fixed- and floating-point formats, are used only in specialized environments, and an average number for their frequency of use is not meaningful. The potential usage of other instructions, such as those for setting and testing bits, is so pervasive that it is not possible to determine a meaningful usage frequency.

5 For some instructions, such as those for moving bit strings or for operations on list structures, justification cannot be based on where the new instructions could be used in programs currently written but rather on what new applications or program structures the instructions would make attractive.

The final choice of the new instructions was strongly moderated by such somewhat subjective attributes as consistency of design, generality of function, and simplicity of use. It was made subject to the rule that a new instruction can be adopted only if it will appear in the object code compiled from a high-level language or if it will be used within a programming system in a significant way.

Movement and Comparison with Long Operands

The two instructions MOVE LONG (MVCL) and COMPARE LOGICAL LONG (CLCL) are enriched versions of the basic byte movement and comparison operations, respectively. They provide for operand sizes of up to 16,777,215 bytes, true length designation, padding, marking the byte of mismatch (for CLCL), and test for destructive overlap (for MVCL).

Many users had asked for "move" and "compare" instructions with long operands, and the padding function in MVCL is valuable for clearing storage to zeros, blanks, or any other code. The specific attributes of these instructions, however, were established largely to permit convenient byte-string manipulation in programs generated by the PL/I compiler. At the time a byte-string operation is compiled, the size and relation of the two operands is not known, the specific parameters being bound in the program only at execution time. Hence, the object code must provide for various special cases of overlap, length mismatch, etc. It was estimated that MVCL could eliminate as many as 1,000 bytes in the PL/I object-code library.

Because the processing of an operand of 16 million bytes would take much longer than the execution time of any other System/370 instruction, execution of MVCL and CLCL was made interruptible, thus avoiding the loss of real-time responsiveness due to the potentially long operands. If a condition is due to cause an interruption, the execution of the instruction is suspended, operand addresses and counts in the general registers are adjusted by the number of bytes processed, and the instruction address is left to point to the MVCL or CLCL instruction. When control is

---

[1]The extended-precision floating-point capability was also available on System/360 Models 85 and 195.

returned to the interrupted program, execution of the interrupted instruction is resumed. To the machine, the initial start and the resumption of execution are identical.

Handling of Bytes in Registers

The three instructions INSERT CHARACTERS UNDER MASK, STORE CHARACTERS UNDER MASK, and COMPARE LOGICAL CHARACTERS UNDER MASK are provided to increase the convenience of manipulating a variable number of bytes between general registers and storage. The instructions select the bytes in the designated register by means of a four-bit mask, with the bits corresponding to the four bytes. The storage operand contains the bytes in a contiguous field. Among other functions, the instructions permit loading and testing 24-bit addresses.

Conditional Swapping

The two instructions COMPARE AND SWAP (CS) and COMPARE DOUBLE AND SWAP (CDS) are intended for use by programs sharing common storage areas in either a multiprogramming or multiprocessing environment. They may be used to add or delete elements in chained lists or to identify the holder or requestor associated with a lock for a serially reusable resource. They are System/370 primitives which can be used to control access to critical regions in a manner similar to Dijkstra's semaphores.

These two instructions designate a storage operand and two register operands. They cause the storage operand to be compared with the first register operand: if they are equal, the storage operand is replaced with the second register operand; if not, the first register operand is replaced with the storage operand. The result is indicated by the condition code. When an equal comparison occurs, no access is permitted to the storage location between the fetching of that operand and its replacement. The two instructions are the same except that for CS the operand comprises one word and for CDS a doubleword.

The following is an example of a procedure using CS, whereby a program can modify the contents of a storage location even though the possibility exists that the program may be interrupted by another program that will update the location or that another CPU may simultaneously update the location.

First, the storage operand is loaded into a general register, which then contains the first register operand. Next, the updated value is made the second register operand. Then CS is executed. If condition code 0 is set, the update has been successful. If condition code 1 is set, the storage location has been found to contain a different value, the update has not been successful, and the first register operand has been replaced by the new current

value of the storage operand. The program in this case can repeat the procedure, bypassing the first step.

Decimal Shifting

The SHIFT AND ROUND DECIMAL instruction is provided for the convenience of decimal shifting, which is common in commercial applications and in the simulation of the decimal floating-point format. To permit "late binding" in the object code generated by a compiler, both left and right shift are included in one instruction. Rounding is accomplished by adding a specific digit specified in the instruction.

Byte-Oriented Operands

System/370 removes the original System/360 requirement that halfword, word, and doubleword operands in storage must be aligned on the natural boundary for the size of the operand. Instead, it permits the operands of virtually all nonprivileged instructions to start on any byte boundary.[1]

This change was made to allow direct processing of all fields obtained from external sources without knowledge of whether they are properly aligned. The primary motivation was to make it easier for users to determine record lengths and to allow compilers to provide a consistent alignment algorithm and therefore to permit convenient data exchange among programs written in different languages. The principal compiler problem occurs when sub-parts of data structures are passed as parameters to separately compiled procedures. In this situation the receiving program cannot assume the starting alignment position, and no universal padding convention can be established to shift the field to its natural boundary. In addition, the change may assist in processing records which are obtained from or destined for equipment not in the System/360-370 families.

The use of operands which are not aligned on natural boundaries will result in considerable performance penalties on some models, especially the faster ones. All machines, however, are designed with the guideline that the performance penalty should be less than the time required to move the operand to an aligned location and then move the result back.

Timing Facilities

Summary

The new timing facilities are introduced as a replacement for the System/360 location-80 interval timer. The 31-bit format of the interval timer provided for a resolution of 13 microseconds and a

[1]The byte-oriented-operand capability was also available on System/360 Models 85 and 195.

period of about 15.5 hours and did not meet some of the more demanding timing requirements. Furthermore, the need to share the single timer for the various timing needs introduced significant software overhead.

System/370 offers three new facilities for measuring time: a time-of-day clock, a clock comparator, and a CPU timer. These facilities jointly provide the time measurements which a program may need. System/370 continues to provide the interval timer at location 80 in main storage, which is included for compatibility with System/360. It meets no requirements not already met by the other three facilities.

The time-of-day (TOD) clock is a binary counter with a period of about 143 years and a resolution, depending on the model, that is on the order of one microsecond. The doubleword format allows for an extension of the resolution to one-quarter nanosecond. Operating in conjunction with the TOD clock, the clock comparator causes an interruption when the TOD clock has advanced to a value greater than that in the clock comparator. The CPU timer is also a binary counter, with a format the same as that of the TOD clock, except that it is considered to have a signed value. The contents of the timer are decremented, and an interruption occurs when the value is negative.

Three "setting" instructions are provided whereby the program can place a specific value in each of these timers, and three "storing" instructions allow for placing the current contents of the timers into main storage for subsequent inspection. The STORE CLOCK instruction is not privileged so that any program can have access to the TOD clock; the other five instructions are made privileged to ensure integrity of the timer values and to permit sharing the clock comparator and CPU timer among programs. Additionally, the SET CLOCK instruction is interlocked with the operation of a console switch, so that the program can alter the clock setting only when such alteration is allowed by the operator. This interlock ensures that the clock value does not get changed accidently because of an error in the operating system, which is helpful for recovering and debugging system operation.

To provide a compatible recording of time among systems, January 1, 1900, 0 am GMT is established as the standard time origin, or epoch, that is the calendar date and time to which a clock value of zero corresponds. This date permits retroactive assignment of TOD clock values to transactions. The enforcing of this convention is the responsibility of the operating system. Local time is calculated when needed by subtracting an offset from the TOD clock value. It is only this offset that needs to be changed for different time zones, daylight-savings time, etc.

Design Considerations

The interaction of several design considerations was involved in the final specification.

Timing Functions.   The new timers are provided to meet four distinct timing functions. Two of these needs related to real time:

The current real-time value, which is needed for labeling events and transactions with the time of their occurrence (time-stamping) and for measuring elapsed real time. Time stamping is needed, for example, to record the time when an exceptional condition is detected or when a transaction request is received. Elapsed real-time measurements, obtained by taking the difference between two real-time values, are needed for such purposes as determining the duration of real-time processes and establishing charges for use of the system's storage media or terminals. This need is met by the TOD clock.

An interruption at a specific real-time instant, which is needed for the control of many real-time processes. Applications may include sampling a sensor, changing traffic light patterns for an approaching rush hour, or polling a terminal. This need is met by the clock comparator.

The time which accrues only when the CPU is actually executing a particular program is referred to as the process time for that program. The following two needs must be met in relation to process time:

The current process time value, which is needed for establishing elapsed process time for performance evaluation and accounting for the use of the CPU, and related functions.

An interruption at a specific process-time instant, which is needed for such functions as checking a program to protect against unending loops and rotating the use of the CPU among different programs, referred to as "time-slicing."

The system must maintain as many accumulators of process time as the number of independent programs that concurrently reside in the system. However, since the CPU executes only one process at a time, only one of these times can be running at one time, and hence only one machine timer is needed. The CPU timer is provided to satisfy both needs associated with the process time.

Long TOD-Clock Period.   In order to permit direct problem program access to the TOD-clock value and to avoid the need for special software procedures for handling of clock overflow, the period should span the lifetime of the environment using the format and algorithm for time measurement. As a minimum, it should cover a number of hardware and operating system generations. A period of 143 years provides this, even with a time origin set to the year 1900.

Unique TOD-Clock Values.   The clock should provide nonrepetitive readings, so that the time-stamp labels provided by the clock can serve as unique serial numbers for the identification and cataloging of system objects. In view of this, the STORE CLOCK instruction is defined such that no two references to the TOD clock of a CPU, or to any of the TOD clocks of a shared-main-storage multiprocessing system, provide the same value. Either the clock has a high enough resolution to be updated between two such instructions, or references to the clock are specifically interlocked to ensure the uniqueness of readings.

Synchronization with External Signals. For the accuracy of the TOD clock's real-time indication to be comparable to its resolution, it must be possible for the program to set the clock to a specific value and then start its operation in response to an external signal. This function is particularly essential for synchronization of the clocks of two CPUs and is provided by the TOD-clock synchronization control, which is included in the multiprocessing feature. When the control bit is one and SET CLOCK is executed, the clock stops. It resumes incrementing only after a synchronizing signal from the other CPU arrives. This signal is generated by a carry into bit position 31 of a running clock, and is defined so that, with zeros in bit positions 32–63 of the stopped clock, the low-order words of the two clocks are subsequently incremented in synchronism. The high-order words of the clocks, approximately corresponding to counts of seconds, can be synchronized by the program.

Format. For interpretation by people, a TOD clock format of such form as year-month-day-hour-minute-second-fraction is most convenient. Such a format, however, was rejected because of the difficulties it would present for arithmetic operations. The specific format was adopted because of the efficiency of binary encoding and by observing that the external formats may have to meet different operating-system or installation requirements and hence should be under software control.

Implementation. In spite of the need for the functions, inclusion of three 64-bit timing facilities would appear rich if each actually required a hardware register. It is possible, however, for a microprogrammed machine to implement the clock comparator and the CPU timer with a small counter and two doublewords of local storage. This is, in fact, the implementation used on most models. Further savings are permissible by implementing most high-order bytes of the TOD clock in local storage.

Multiprocessing

System/370 architecture includes a number of facilities that permit formation of a system where two or more CPUs share common main storage and are controlled by a single copy of the operating system. Such a system has a number of advantages:

1 It offers higher processing power and throughput.

2 It improves reliability by making an alternate CPU available and by increasing the redundancy of other system components.

3 It permits more flexibility in sharing I/O and external storage devices.

4 It provides a larger pool of main storage, channels, and I/O equipment for allocation of these resources in response to demands by various jobs.

This section reviews the facilities included in System/370 for multiprocessing.

A rudimentary form of some multiprocessing facilities was available also on System/360 Models 65 and 67, which offered a shared-main-storage multiprocessing capability. Prefixing on these models was provided using a manually settable prefix. A limited interprocessor signaling capability was made available through the use of the channel-to-channel adapter. Instructions-stream synchronization and serialization were left mostly unspecified by the architecture; the action of the machine was determined by the implementation. In addition, configurations of modified Model 50 CPUs, designated the IBM 9020, were built as part of a special system for the Federal Aviation Administration.

It should be noted that although current implementations offer multiprocessing systems comprised of two CPUs, the architecture allows for a multiplicity of CPUs.

Synchronization and Serialization

In a uniprocessor, the execution of a single instruction, as well as of a disabled routine, can be considered instantaneous in that no other program can observe or change any intermediate result values, and all references to main storage can be considered to occur in the sequence specified by the program.[1] In a multiprocessing system, the results of all communication between CPUs through main storage are based on the actual storage accesses. When these accesses are observed by another processor, they may differ from the expected operation in the following ways:

1 A single instruction may make a number of distinct addresses to main storage, and accesses associated with single instructions may be interleaved by CPUs.

2 The accesses due to a single instruction and due to any two instructions are not necessarily performed in the specified order.

---

[1]This statement is not strictly true with respect to channels which may access an area of storage concurrently with the CPU. The channel may see intermediate or out-of-sequence result values if the CPU changes the contents of the I/O data areas during channel operation.

3 Accesses within a field, such as for an instruction or an operand, may be made piecemeal.

4 Multiple accesses may be made to a storage location for a single use of its contents.

Results become unpredictable, and the conventions of a uniprocessor communications protocol become inadequate when one CPU is changing the contents of a common storage location while the other is observing it, or when both CPUs are updating the contents of the location at the same time.

System/370 architecture includes a number of specific rules and extensions to make a multiprocessor communications protocol more flexible and efficient. Included are constraints on the concurrency, multiplicity, and order of storage accesses. Specific instructions are defined to serialize and synchronize events. A detailed discussion of those considerations is beyond the scope of this paper.

Prefixing

The control and status information associated with a CPU (PSWs, interruption codes, I/O control words, etc.) reside in fixed low-order locations of main storage. When storage is shared by multiple CPUs, each CPU must have a private control and status area. This is accomplished by providing in each CPU a prefix address, which specifies the storage block to which references with addresses 0 to 4,095 are relocated. In order for each processor to have access to all of the attached storage, and for one processor to access another's fixed addresses even if they are prefixed with a value of zero, reverse prefixing is employed: that is, references to the 4K-byte block identified by the prefix address cause access to block 0. Prefixing, as well as reverse prefixing, is applied after dynamic address translation, and it applies to all storage references by the CPU. Two instructions, SET PREFIX and STORE PREFIX, are associated with the facility.

Prefixing is not applied to storage references associated with I/O data transfers. This decision was made to avoid any logical affinity between a channel and a CPU, thus permitting any CPU to start an I/O operation on any channel in a multiprocessing configuration. It also avoids some additional cost for the relocation hardware in standalone channels and for keeping the prefix address in each subchannel.

Interprocessor Signaling

To fully utilize the potential advantages of a multi-CPU system, some explicit ability for programmed communication among the CPUs is necessary. Such communication is needed for initial startup of the operation, to dispatch jobs because of changes in priority or because of an imbalance of I/O equipment, to recover operations after software or hardware failure, and to diagnose a machine or program problem.

All program-initiated CPU-to-CPU communication is performed by means of the SIGNAL PROCESSOR (SIGP) instruction, which designates the addressed CPU and indicates an order specifying an operation to be performed. The instruction can be addressed to the issuing CPU. The orders provide for the following types of functions:

Start; Stop. These two orders are the same as the corresponding operator-console functions.

Stop and Store Status. A sequence of operations is performed comprising the corresponding two operator-console functions.

Restart. A restart interruption is initiated at the addressed CPU, which can be used for initial startup or for dispatching a job.

External Call; Emergency Signal. These two signals cause the corresponding type of external interruption at the addressed CPU, each type of interruption being controlled by a separate mask. They can be used to establish a communications protocol of two priority levels, covering general and unusual conditions.

Sense. The signaling CPU is informed whether the addressed CPU is stopped, still has an external call pending, is in check-stop state, etc.

Reset. Four types of orders are provided for resetting the addressed CPU, permitting a choice in whether channels must be reset and in whether some program-addressable registers must be initialized.

When a CPU enters the check-stop state or loses power, it implicitly generates a malfunction alert. This signal is broadcast to all other CPUs in the system and causes an external interruption in those CPUs that are enabled for it. This mechanism provides for an automatic error alert if and only if programmed communications are no longer possible; at any other time, signaling of all exceptional conditions is under explicit control of the program.

The address assigned to a CPU may be determined by issuing STORE CPU ADDRESS on that CPU. The CPU address may be used to associate with the CPU any facilities that are unique to it, such as an emulator or I/O devices accessible only by it.

Debugging and Monitoring

Two facilities are introduced in System/370 for selectively passing control to a supervisory program on the occurrence of specific events during program execution: *program-event recording* and *monitoring.* Additionally, the *status-storing* facility provides an operator control for recording program status.

Program-Event Recording

The program-event-recording (PER) facility extends and places under program control functions that previously have been available only to the console operator. It is a debugging tool that can be invoked without any preplanning in the design of the program.

The PER facility causes a program interruption on the occurrence of one or more of the following events:

1 Successful execution of a branch instruction

2 Alteration of the contents of designated general registers

3 Fetching of an instruction from a designated main-storage area

4 Alteration of the contents of a designated main-storage area

The information concerning a program event is provided by means of a program interruption, with the cause of the interruption being identified in the interruption code. The occurrence of the event does not affect the execution of the instruction, and the PER interruption is taken after the execution of the instruction responsible for the event. The supervisory program has control over the conditions that are considered events for recording purposes and specifies the registers and the storage area involved.

The PER facility does not affect CPU performance when it is completely disabled by means of the PSW mask, but on most models it reduces performance when the machine is instructed to search for some events. Its primary use is under conditions when the program is suspected of having a bug. In order to reduce the frequency of PER interruptions, the debugging procedure can select events hierarchically, the initial monitoring being only for instruction fetches or storage alteration occurring outside (or within) a designated area. Recording successful branches or base register alterations should be invoked only when the fault is localized to a particular routine.

Monitoring

The monitoring facility causes an interruption when the MONITOR CALL (MC) instruction is encountered. Each MC instruction identifies itself as belonging to one of 16 separately maskable classes and provides a 24-bit code. On a monitor-call interruption, both the class number and the code are stored to identify the condition.

The MC instruction takes very little execution time when the class is not enabled for interruption; it is useful for signaling critical points in a program, such as dispatching, procedure entries, queue access, and page faults. It is expected that potentially useful points will be identified as part of the design of the program, and that the instruction will be a permanent part of many routines. These instructions then could be used to assist in debugging the system, as well as to record frequency and path information for system performance analysis.

Status Storing

The status-storing facility consists of an operator control that causes the contents of the current PSW and of all addressable registers to be stored at preassigned locations in main storage. It provides a means of preserving the essential status information, upon the failure of a program, for subsequent dumping and analysis. This facility makes it possible for a standalone dump program to record the status of the failing program, without the dump program destroying the status that is to be saved.

Machine-Error Handling

System/370 implementations provide extensive checking for equipment malfunction and include a number of steps for automatic recovery by the machine. The architecture includes extensions that permit reporting of error conditions to assist maintenance and repair and to help with programmed recovery. It provides model-independent structure for the initial response and damage assessment and permits passing additional information for model-dependent analysis. This section reviews the architecture extensions and outlines the characteristics of the implementations that motivated the architecture extensions.

Model independence, or compatibility, in the context of machine-check handling has objectives and constraints somewhat different from those applying to the rest of the system. First, the architecture specifies machine actions in the case when the machine is failing, and hence absolute compliance cannot be guaranteed. Second, the architecture has to reflect the physical structure of the machine, and thus has to provide for some model dependence. As a result, the architectural definition permits a set of actions and alternatives, allowing the machine to choose among them and requiring that it indicate the action it has taken. For virtually all error situations, the machine must, however, comply with certain basic rules.

One of the fundamental rules of both System/360 and System/370 architecture is the separation of programming and machine errors. Specifically, it must not be possible either inadvertently or by deliberate programmed action to cause an indication of machine malfunction. (This excludes the use of the instruction DIAGNOSE, which is intended for diagnostic and maintenance functions.) Any condition indicating that the operation of the equipment deviates from that normally expected is brought to the attention of the program either via a machine-check interruption or by turning on the corresponding equipment-error bit in the status word stored by the channel or the SIGNAL PROCESSOR instruction. Conversely, all invalid program situations that are detected by the machine are reported by condition codes, status bits, and interruptions that are distinct from those used for machine errors. In order to ensure that the machine is in a known valid state at the initiation of processing, System/370 architecture defines and introduces a hierarchy of specific reset functions.

The machine-check architecture assumes a rather extensive recording and analysis program as a part of the operating-system facilities. In many cases it is possible to limit the bad effects of a malfunction to just one user, and it should usually be possible to perform an automatic restart so that newly submitted jobs can run. Some solid failures, of course, prevent any useful work from being done. In these cases information must be recorded to expedite diagnosis and repair of the fault.

Recovery Mechanisms

System/370 implementations provide some or all of the following five mechanisms to minimize the destructive effect of machine malfunctions and to ensure integrity of system operation.

Data-Error Detection. Most data and control paths in the CPU, in channels, and on the I/O interface include redundant bits to verify correct transmission and readout of information. The redundancy typically is one bit per byte, or 12.5%. The redundant bit is so chosen as to provide an odd parity for the nine-bit field, thus requiring that at least one bit always have a nonzero value. This organization is capable of detecting any single-bit error.

Data-Error Correction. Main storage for all models except Model 195 is organized into blocks of eight bytes, with eight redundant bits included with the block. The redundant bits form an error-correction code capable of correcting any single-bit error and detecting any double-bit error. When a single-bit error is detected on readout, the error is corrected in the storage array, correct parity is provided to the CPU, and an alert condition is generated. On double-bit errors, an error indication is generated. Error correction may be used also in other parts of the system. Checking and correction is accomplished typically in a fraction of a machine cycle.

CPU Retry. Recovery from transient errors can be accomplished by reexecuting the sequence of steps in which the error occurred. On some models such reexecution, or retry, is invoked automatically by the machine whenever an error is detected, and the steps typically cover the execution of one or a few instructions. CPU retry requires that the machine periodically establish points, referred to as checkpoints, with a known machine-state information. Whenever changes to the machine-state are subsequently made, the previous value for the changed attribute is recorded. In the case of an error, the machine-state is restored to that at the checkpoint, and reexecution is attempted. If the error persists, retry from the same check-point typically may be performed eight times. If the retry is successful, an alert condition is generated; if

not, an error is indicated. The time for CPU state restoration and error analysis may be a millisecond or significantly more.

Unit Deletion. On some models, malfunctions of certain transparent units of the system can be circumvented by discontinuing the use of the unit while still continuing processing. Examples include the disabling of all or a part of the cache, translation lookaside buffer, or the high-speed multiplier. When such automatic reconfiguration has occurred, a special signal indicating degradation of operation is generated.

Command Retry. The command-retry facility, which permits recovery from errors detected by the I/O device, is described in the section "Incompatibilities."

Error Reporting

System/370 architecture groups machine errors by type and severity and provides model-independent means for their identification. All machine-check interruptions are subject to the control of PSW bit 13. Additionally, masks for specific conditions permit control over the causes that are to be reported.

Two major types of machine-check conditions are identified, *repressible* and *exigent*. The indication of repressible conditions can be delayed without affecting the integrity of CPU operation. They include recovery indications, alerts of degradation or imminent power loss, and indications of damage to timing or external facilities.

For exigent machine-check conditions, the execution of the current instruction or interruption cannot safely continue and normally is terminated. If the CPU is disabled for machine-check interruptions, the CPU enters the check-stop state. The machine, however, may choose to proceed with processing when the check-stop-control bit so permits. This option is desirable for some real-time applications.

When a machine-check interruption occurs, extensive model-independent information is provided describing the cause of the error. In addition to the machine-check old PSW and source identification, contents of control registers, general registers, floating-point registers, TOD clock, clock comparator, and CPU timer are stored, and, for storage errors, the address of the suspected location is provided. Such automatic saving avoids the need for programmed storing, which may be impossible because of the error condition. Because of the check-point capability in models with CPU retry, the interruption resulting from an exigent machine-check condition may identify a point in the recovery cycle which is prior to the point of error. For this reason a number of bits are stored to describe the validity of the status information and the relation between the points of error and interruption. Finally, extensive model-dependent logout information may be provided at permanently-assigned locations in main storage or in an area designated by an address in a control register.

Storage Validation

Since the block size for error correction may be larger than the bus width of the system, only part of the checking block may be replaced in any one CPU cycle. In the case of an uncorrectable storage error, such replacement cannot force valid checking-block code on the entire storage block, as no information is available as to which part of the block is invalid. Furthermore, on some models validation of storage contents can be performed only when the entire "cache line" is replaced, which may include a number of checking blocks.

To permit validating storage, that is, replacing storage contents with a valid checking-block code, the instructions MOVE and MOVE LONG are defined to force valid checking-block code on the destination operand when the operand designation meets certain size and alignment requirements.

Machine Identification

The instruction STORE CPU ID provides information that identifies the particular CPU executing the instruction by type, model number, version, and serial number. It also provides the length of the model-dependent status and error-logout fields for this model. The instruction STORE CHANNEL ID provides analogous information for the addressed channel. These instructions make it possible to invoke model-dependent recovery programs and help a general-purpose analysis routine to record essential information about the physical unit for diagnostic and repair purposes.

Input/Output

System/370 architecture adds several facilities and functions in the area of input/output (I/O) operations to improve channel utilization, to make the control of operations more efficient and flexible, and to increase the maximum data rate on the I/O (channel-to-control-unit) interface. This section discusses some of the more important additions.

Utilization of Channel Facilities

The System/360 architecture provided for two channel types, a selector channel capable of operating with relatively high data rates but with only one device at a time, and a byte-multiplexer channel capable of simultaneously operating many devices but at relatively low data rates. System/370 adds the block-multiplexer[1]

[1]The IBM 2880 Block-Multiplexer Channel included most of the System/370 I/O architecture extensions and was available on System/360 Models 85 and 195.

channel with both high-data-rate and multiple-device capabilities [Brown, Gibson, and Thorn, 1972].

The block-multiplexer channel is similar to a byte-multiplexer channel in that both have a number of subchannels, each associated with an I/O device or a group of I/O devices. The subchannel is the logical entity that controls an I/O operation and contains the addresses, count, and control bits associated with the operation. The channel provides the data paths and controls for communicating with the CPU, main storage, and I/O control units and for associating the proper subchannel with each communications sequence. The main difference between the block- and byte-multiplexer channels is in the level of multiplexing: whereas the byte-multiplexer channel can interleave the transfer of individual bytes for different subchannels, the block-multiplexer channel, being designed for high data rates, is limited to interleaving complete blocks of data.

The block-multiplexing capability is particularly advantageous when used in conjunction with rotational position sensing on rotating-storage devices, such as disks and drums. This feature allows the device to disconnect from the channel during the period of rotational delay, thereby releasing the channel for operation with other devices. When the addressed sector is approaching on the track, reconnection is attempted for the transfer of data. In case the channel is so busy that the connection cannot be established by the time the sector is reached, another attempt is made after a delay of one rotation time.

Rotational position sensing is available, for example, on the IBM 2305 fixed head file. The control unit for this file can appear to have 16 devices, each associated with its own subchannel and able to sustain an I/O operation.

In the absence of the block-multiplexing capability, efficient utilization of I/O facilities required separate START I/O instructions to specify the position of the arm on the disk and the subsequent reading or writing. On the block-multiplexer channel, these commands are chained, thus avoiding the interruption of the CPU at the completion of the positioning operation. The number of START I/O instructions is also reduced.

Control

Since the periods when the block-multiplexer channel is busy transferring blocks of data are asynchronous to CPU operation, a new interruption, the channel-available interruption, is provided to indicate when the channel is free to process a CPU instruction. The block-multiplexer channel generates this signal when the busy condition ceases to exist that had previously caused rejection of an I/O instruction.

The new HALT DEVICE instruction also is introduced largely because of the block-multiplexer channel. It is similar to the previously available HALT I/O except that, when the channel is busy, only the operation on the addressed subchannel is affected.

HALT I/O terminates the current burst operation on the channel, ignoring the device address.

The new CLEAR I/O instruction is provided to permit freeing the subchannel associated with the addressed device without such freeing being contingent on the completion of the current I/O operation at the device. This function is useful for situations involving machine errors or reconfiguration of I/O devices and control units.

Finally, an extension is provided to reduce the CPU time to start an I/O operation. When START I/O (SIO) is issued, the channel signals the device as part of SIO execution to ascertain the device's ability to execute the command. This involves a number of signal sequences and the associated propagation delays and logic delays in the channel and the control unit. According to the I/O interface specification [IBM, 1978a], the portion of the total delay introduced by the circuitry in the control unit can be as high as 32 microseconds. Additional delays may be introduced by the channel. On a CPU that can perform a few million average instructions per second, the delay due to the communications with the device can be equivalent to a hundred or more instruction executions.

The new instruction START I/O FAST RELEASE (SIOF) allows the acceptance to be signaled and the CPU to be released as soon as the channel has fetched the channel address word from main storage. The channel subsequently initiates the operation at the device and verifies the validity of the command information. Any exceptions are signaled by means of an interruption. Normally such exceptions are infrequent, and thus, overall, little time is spent processing the interruptions.

Some channels do not currently implement the early release on SIOF and instead execute SIOF as SIO. Such implementations are compatible and permit early conversion of programs to the use of SIOF.

Data Rates

The original System/360 I/O interface specification was adequate for data rates up to about 1M bytes per second. In special cases for disk devices and for very short channel cable lengths, a rate up to 1.25M bytes per second could be supported. With the advent of storage technologies employing higher recording densities, it was necessary to increase this limit. A higher limit was desirable also for certain buffered devices. Changes to System/360 were made in both the width of the interface and in the interface signaling protocols.

The fully interlocked signaling protocol on the System/360 I/O interface allowed one channel cable connection to sustain data transfer at a very wide range of rates, with both the channel and device having complete control over the timing of each byte transfer. It did, however, require an electrical signal to be propagated between the channel and the control unit four times for each byte transferred.

The System/370 channels modify this signaling protocol, with two additional wires in the interface, to provide the same level of transfer interlocks at the expense of only two propagation times per byte transferred. It depends on the control unit if the new facility is used, so that control units implemented to operate with the System/360 protocols can be attached to System/370 channels.

The basic interface bus is one byte wide, comprising eight data bits and a parity bit. On some System/370 models the bus width can be extended optionally to two bytes, thus doubling its data transfer capacity.

As a result of these two additions, the System/370 I/O interface can sustain a data transfer rate of over 1.5M bytes per second in the one-byte version and over 3.0M bytes per second in the two-byte version. Concurrently with the data rate improvement, the allowable cable lengths have been increased.

Implementation

While this chapter is concerned mainly with the logical structure of the system as seen by the programmer, some of the parameters of the realizations are important for practical and efficient use of the equipment and to understand the motivation behind some of the features. This section summarizes some attributes of the System/370 models. For convenience of comparison, it includes also the corresponding values for the models of System/360. Only the most recent characteristics are listed; some of the models were improved after initial announcement.

Central Processing Units

Variation in the cycle time and data-flow width of the central processing unit (CPU) and in the characteristics of its control storage is one important way of obtaining cost and performance differences in a compatible family of machines. Table 3 shows these factors for the various models of System/360, and Table 4 for System/370.[1]

Depending on the CPU, a different amount of "work" is accomplished per CPU cycle. Hence these numbers cannot be used directly as a measure of relative speed. CPU data-flow width is given in bytes and indicates the largest field that can be handled in one cycle time. Instruction fetches and a limited set of operations may be handled by wider paths, as indicated by footnotes.

Control storage, which contains the microprogram, is described in terms of the following attributes: capacity (in K words, where

---

[1]In this chapter, capacities and widths are usually given in bytes. A byte is composed of eight bits. Physical implementations include additional bits for error detection and correction. This redundancy in CPU data flow and in processor storage typically is one bit per byte.

Table 3   System/360 CPU and Control Storage Characteristics

	CPU		Control storage				TLB
Model	Cycle (nsec)	Width (bytes)	Capacity (K words)	Wd size (bits)	Type (RW/RO)	Cycle (nsec)	Entries
22	750	1	4	50 + 5	RO	750	none
25	900	1	8	16 + 2	RW	900	none
30	750	1	4	50 + 5	RO	750	none
40	625	2[a]	4	52 + 2	RO	625	none
44	250	4	none				none
50	500	4	2.75	85 + 3[b]	RO	500	none
65	200	8	2.75	87 + 4[c]	RO	200	none
67	200	8	2.75	87 + 4[c]	RO	200	8
75	195	8	none				none
85	80	8	2	105 + 3[d]	RO	80	none
			0.5	105 + 3[d]	RW	80	
91	60	8	none				none
195	54	8	none				none

[a]Certain registers and paths are 17 or 18 bits wide where a main-storage address is processed in one cycle.

[b]Extended to 90 + 3 for the 1410 emulator, or 92 + 3 for the 7070 emulator.

[c]Extended to 94 + 4 when any emulator is installed.

[d]Extended to 122 + 4 when any emulator is installed.

$K = 2^{10} = 1024$), word size (in bits), and cycle time (in nanoseconds) as used by the processor. The type of storage is also indicated: read-write (RW) or read-only (RO).

A range in the capacity is given for those models where the amount installed depends on the selection of certain optional features. The word size is expressed in terms of two numbers. The number before the plus sign is the number of bits used for logic or control purposes. The number after the plus sign is the number of additional bits used for checking the parity of the control-storage contents.

As explained in the section on virtual storage, the dynamic-address-translation mechanism includes a translation-lookaside buffer (TLB) to improve performance. The number of entries in this buffer is indicated in the last column.

Processor Storage

Another set of key attributes that distinguish various implementations is the size and speed of processor storage. Table 5 shows the options available for the System/360 models, and Table 6 describes System/370. The range of sizes shows the smallest and largest total capacity available on that model. Intermediate values are usually also offered. The width is expressed in terms of two numbers: (basic width) × (interleaving factor). The basic width is the width of the data path from the storage controller to the instruction processor or channels. The interleaving factor indicates the number of accesses to sequential locations that can be made in one cycle. Thus, the storage of the Model 168 is implemented in four sections, each eight bytes wide. Each section contains every fourth doubleword, and their clocks are offset by ¼ of the storage cycle time, so that the total available transfer rate for sequential locations is $8 \times 4 = 32$ bytes per 320-nsec cycle. For the 3033 the effective transfer rate is limited to eight bytes per CPU cycle. The cycle time shown is the minimum time between successive references to the same location.

Some models employ a high-speed buffer, referred to as the cache [Conti, Gibson, and Pitkowsky, 1968; Liptay, 1968], to reduce the average access time to processor storage. The cache contains copies of recently accessed data in processor storage, and its existence is not apparent to the program.[1] The tables list the

[1]This means that the cache does not appear in System/370 architecture, and the operation of the machine is completely described without reference to the cache. Although the cache is not architected, the decision not to do so is a significant architectural conclusion. It means that, except for performance considerations, the program can ignore the existence of the cache. On the other hand, the designer of the machine must ensure that in no case can the existence of the cache affect the logical appearance of the machine.

Table 4   System/370 CPU and Control Storage Characteristics

	CPU		Control storage				TLB
Model	Cycle (nsec)	Width (bytes)	Capacity (K words)	Wd size (bits)	Type (RW/RO)	Cycle (nsec)	Entries
115	480	1	20-28	20 + 2	RW	480	8
115-2	480	2	12-20[a]	19 + 3	RW	480	16
125	480	2	12-20	19 + 3	RW	480	16
125-2	320	2	16-24	19 + 3	RW	320	16
135	$275 - 1485$[b]	2[c]	12-24	16 + 2	RW	275	8
135-3	$275 - 1485$[b]	2[c]	64	16 + 2	RW	275	8
138	$275 - 1430$[b]	2[c]	64	16 + 2	RW	275	8
145	$203 - 315$[b]	4[d]	8-16[e]	32 + 4	RW	203	8
145-3	$180 - 270$[b]	4[d]	32	32 + 4	RW	180	8
148	$180 - 270$[b]	4[d]	32	32 + 4	RW	180	8
155	115	4	6	69 + 3	RO	115	none
155-II	115	4	8	69 + 3	RO	115	128
158	115[f]	4	8	69 + 3	RW	115	128
158-3	115[f]	4	8	69 + 3	RW	115	128
165	80	8	2	105 + 3	RO	80	none
			2	105 + 3[g]	RW	80	
165-II	80	8	4	105 + 3[g]	RO	80	128
			1	105 + 3[g]	RW	80	
168	80	8	4	105 + 3[g]	RO	80	128
			1	105 + 3[g]	RW	80	
168-3	80	8	4	105 + 3[g]	RO	80	128
			2	105 + 3[g]	RW	80	
195	54	8	none				none
3031	115[f]	4	8	69 + 3	RW	115	128
3032	80	8	4	105 + 3	RW	80	128
3033	58	8	4	105 + 3	RW	58	128

[a]The 115-2 contains a separate I/O processing unit for some functions that were executed on the CPU in a 115; hence the smaller CPU control storage capacity.

[b]Variable, depending on the type of operation performed.

[c]A 4-byte wide path is used for instruction fetch and for data access for some instruction types.

[d]An 8-byte wide path is used for instruction fetch.

[e]This capacity is physically a part of the main-storage array. Increments above 8K words subtract from the 145 processor-storage capacities listed in Table 6.

[f]57.5 nsec for the execution of some instructions.

[g]Extended to 122 + 4 when any emulator is installed.

total cache size in K bytes. The two-number notation for the cycle time indicates the minimum time between successive read accesses and the total cache access time. The line-width column gives the number of bytes in the cache which are considered as one unit for addressing and replacement purposes. The first element of the product notation is the minimum transfer unit from processor storage to cache; the second element is the number of such transfer units required to make a line. A CPU instruction

which is waiting for data may proceed as soon as the first unit has been transferred.

Usually, a particular virtual address may be represented in the cache in a subset of the available cache locations. The column labeled "Assoc." shows the number of different locations in the cache that may contain a particular virtual address. The set of virtual addresses that share a group of cache locations is known as an equivalence class. The replacement algorithm (usually LRU or

Table 5 System/360 Processor Storage Characteristics

Model	Processor storage			Cache			
	Size (K bytes)	Width (bytes)	Cycle[a] (nsec)	Size (K bytes)	Cycle (nsec)	Line width (bytes)	Assoc.
22	24-32	1	1500	none			
25	16-48	2	1800	none			
30	16-64	1	1500	none			
40	32-256	2	2500	none			
44	32-256	4	1000	none			
50	128-256	4	2000	none			
65	256-1024	8 × 2	750	none			
67	256-1024	8 × 2	750	none			
75	256-1024	8 × 4	750	none			
85	512-4096	16 × 4	960	16-32	80-160	256 × 4[b]	16
91	2048-6144	8 × 16	780	none			
195	1024-4096	8 × 16	756	32	54-162	8 × 8	4

[a]All models use magnetic-core technology. [b]Blocks of 64 bytes (16 × 4) are fetched from main storage only if referenced.

Table 6 System/370 Processor Storage Characteristics

Model	Processor storage			Cache			
	Size (K bytes)	Width (bytes)	Cycle (nsec)	Size (K bytes)	Cycle (nsec)	Line width (bytes)	Assoc.
115	64-192	2	480	none			
115-2	64-384	2	480	none			
125	96-256	2	480	none			
125-2	96-512	2	480	none			
135	96-512	4	935	none			
135-3	256-512	4	880 R 935 W	none			
138	512-1024	4	880 R 935 W	none			
145	160-2048	8	540 R 608 W	none			
145-3	192-1984	8	405 R 540 W	none			
148	1024-2048	8	405 R 540 W	none			
155	256-2048	8	2070[a]	8	115-230	16	2
155-II	256-2048	8	2070[a]	8	115-230	16	2
158	512-6144	16	920 R 1035 W	8	115-230	16	2
158-3	512-6144	16	920	16	115-230	16 × 2	4
165	512-3072	8 × 4	2000[a]	8-16	80-160	8 × 4	4
165-II	512-3072	8 × 4	2000[a]	8-16	80-160	8 × 4	4
168	1024-8192	8 × 4	320	8-16	80-160	8 × 4	4-8[b]
168-3	1024-8192	8 × 4	320	32	80-160	8 × 4	8
195	1024-4096	8 × 16	756	32	54-162	8 × 8	4
3031	2048-6144	8 × 4	920	32	115-230	8 × 4	8
3032	2048-6144	8 × 4	320	32	80-160	8 × 4	8
3033	4096-8192	8 × 8	290	64	58-116	8 × 8	16

[a]Magnetic core [b]Depends on cache size used.

Table 7 Announcement and Shipment Dates

Model	Announced	First shipped
System/360 dates		
22	71-4	71-7
25	68-1	68-10
30	64-4	65-5
40	64-4	65-4
44	65-8	66-7
50	64-4	65-8
65	65-4	65-11
67	65-8	66-6
75	65-4	66-1
85	68-1	69-8
91	66-1	67-11
195	69-8	71-4
System/370 dates		
115	73-3	74-3
115-2	75-11	76-4
125	72-10	73-4
125-2	75-11	76-2
135	71-3	72-5
135-3	76-6	77-2
138	76-6	76-11
145	70-9	71-8
145-3	76-6	77-4
148	76-6	77-1
155	70-6	71-2
158	72-8	73-4
158-3	75-3	76-9
165	70-6	71-4
168	72-8	73-8
168-3	75-3	76-6
195	71-6	73-5
3031	77-10	
3032	77-10	
3033	77-3	

a close variant) is executed separately for each equivalence class.

Announcement and Shipment Dates

Table 7 lists the year and month when the various models of System/360 and System/370 were announced and first shipped.

References

Amdahl, Blaauw, and Brooks [1964]; Amdahl [1964]; Arden et al. [1966]; Bell and Strecker [1976]; Blaauw and Brooks [1964]; Blaauw [1964]; Brown, Gibson, and Thorn [1972]; Conti, Gibson, and Pitkowsky [1968]; Dennis [1965]; Gibson [1966]; IBM [1978a]; IBM [1978b]; Kilburn et al. [1962]; Liptay [1968]; Padegs [1964]; Padegs [1968]; Stevens [1964].

Chapter 52

The IBM System/360, System/370, 3030, and 4300: A Series of Planned Machines That Span a Wide Performance Range

C. G. Bell / A. Newell / M. Reich / D. Siewiorek

Introduction

In this section, besides making some general comments on the IBM System/360 and System/370 series and System/370 follow-ons, we will attempt an analysis of the performance and costs of the series. Performance is notoriously difficult to measure, as we noted in Chap. 5, and costs are even more so. With respect to the latter, what is publicly available is price data, not manufacturing cost data.

These prices reflect not only marketing policies but also accounting policies within the organization for the attribution of cost to product lines. Nevertheless, the 360 and 370 series provide two things which make a comparative analysis worthwhile. First, the common ISP makes simple performance measures more comparable; second, the common manufacturer makes relative prices more a reflection of relative costs than would otherwise be the case. Neither of these aspects is perfect, as we will note at several points in the discussion. Nevertheless, the 360 and 370 series provide as good an opportunity to attempt cost/performance analysis as we know.

Analyses of the type we attempt here produce only rather crude pictures and are subject to question if all the input data are not very carefully checked. We have not done this, depending instead on published sources. For the purpose of this book, illustration of the style of analysis seems sufficient. In addition, using a performance measure based only on Pc power measurements leaves many questions unanswered because it does not address the soft areas of analysis relating to throughput, task environment, and the operating-system software.

Figure 1 depicts the family tree of IBM computers as a function of introduction date and relative processing power. It can be used as a concise summary and reference for the following discussions. The reader is encouraged to follow the procession of this chapter on Fig. 1.

The IBM System/360 architecture was introduced in Chap. 40. The series has been superseded by the IBM System/370, 3030, and 4300 series. Each series is upward-compatible with the System/360 so far as the user problem state is concerned. The series also share an upward-compatible ISP, as outlined in Chap. 51. The various models differ in interpreter speeds and PMS structure. Many PMS elements are used in common, particularly K's, Ms's, and T's. The 3030 and 4300 series constitutes the currant primary IBM product line.

The System/360, System/370, 3030, and 4300 series are presented both because IBM's market dominance makes it the most prevalent mainframe computer and because its implementations span the largest performance and price range of any series. The various models are compared in Table 1.

This chapter will open with a discussion of the various 360, 370, 3030, and 4300 series models. Finally, the System/360-System/370 series will be evaluated in terms of cost and performance.

The IBM System/360 Family

Figure 2 illustrates the introduction dates of the various System/360 models. Chapters 40, 41, and 12 discuss the logical structure of the System/360, the implementations,[1] and the microprogrammed Model 30, respectively.

A succinct description of the design goals and innovations is given in the abstract of Amdahl, Blaauw, and Brooks [1964]. The architecture[2] of the newly accounted IBM System/360 featured four innovations:

1 An approach to storage which permits and exploits very large capacities, hierarchies of speeds, read-only storage for microprogram control, flexible storage protection, and simple program relocation.

2 An input/output system offering new degrees of concurrent operation; compatible channel operation; data rates approaching 5 million characters per second; integrated design of hardware and software; a new, low-cost, multiple-channel package sharing mainframe hardware; new provisions for device status information; and a standard channel interface between central processing unit and input/output devices.

3 A truly general-purpose machine organization offering new supervisory facilities, powerful logical processing operations, and a wide variety of data formats.

4 Strict upward and downward machine language compatibil-

---

[1]Chapters 40 and 41 are from *IBM Systems Journal*, vol. 3, no. 2, 1964, which was devoted exclusively to the System/360. Other articles, listed in the bibliography at the end of this chapter, are recommended for additional details.

[2]The term *architecture* is used here to describe the attributes of a system as seen by the programmer, i.e., the conceptual structure and functional behavior, as distinct from the organization of the data flow and controls, the logical design, and the physical implementation.

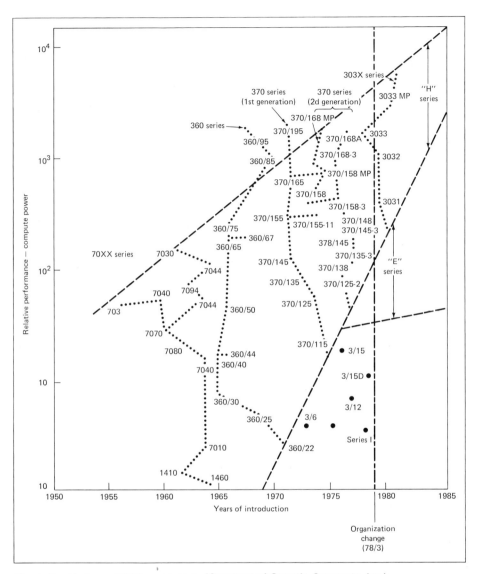

Fig. 1. Family tree of IBM computers. (*Courtesy of Gnostic Concepts, Inc.*)

ity over a line of six models having a performance range factor of 50.

The above four featured innovations are all stated as IBM Corporation design results. It seems better to analyze them in terms of design constraints and implementation results. It appears that the design constraints, from marketing and management directions, were compatibility (item 4 above) and the use of common peripheral equipment (item 2 above). Thus we can measure the 360 design in terms of how well it meets these constraints. With some minor exceptions, all the peripheral

components existed at the time of the design and had been used with other IBM computers; thus a goal was already realized. A difficult and important constraint, though not mentioned above, is the necessity of program compatibility with almost all earlier IBM computers.

It should be noted that, at the outset of the IBM System/360 announcement, another company, RCA, adopted most of the 360 ISP as a design constraint for its own future computer development. Although some price/performance characteristics appear to be better in the RCA series, the implementation scheme is similar. The lower RCA prices do not reflect entirely implementa-

Table 1   Summary of IBM Processor Characteristics

Model	CPU T. cycle (ns)	CPU Width (bytes)	Control store Size (K)	Control store Word size (bits)	Control store Type (RW/RO)	Control store T. cycle (ns)	TLB Number of entries	Technology	Main memory Size (Kbytes) min. tc max.	Main memory T. cycle (ns)	Main memory Number bytes fetched	Interleaving
22	750	1	4	50 + 5	RO	750	None	Core	24–32	1500	1	None
25	900	1	8	16 + 2	RW	900	None	Core	16–48	1800	2	None
30	750	1	4	50 + 5	RO	750	None	Core	16–64	1500	1	None
40	625	2	4	52 + 2	RO	625	None	Core	32–256	2500	2	None
44	250	4	None				None	Core	32–256	1000	4	None
50	500	4	2.75	85 + 3	RO	500	None	Core	128–256	2000	4	None
65	200	8	2.75	87 + 4	RO	200	None	Core	256–1024	750	8	2
67	200	8	2.75	87 + 4	RO	200	8	Core	256–1024	750	8	2
75	195	8	0.5	105 + 3	RW	80	None	Core	256–1024	750	8	4
85	80	8	2	105 + 3	RO	80	None	Core	512–4096	960	16	4
91	60	8	None				None	Core	2048–6144	750	8	16
95	54	8	None				None	Core	1024–4096	756	8	16
115	480	1	20–28	20 + 2	RW	480	8	MOS	64–192	480	2	None
115-2	480	2	12–20	19 + 3	RW	480	16	MOS	64–384	480	2	None
125	480	2	12–20	19 + 3	RW	480	16	MOS	96–256	480	2	None
125-2	320	2	16–24	19 + 3	RW	320	16	MOS	96–512	320–480	2	None
135	275–1485	2	12–24	16 + 2	RW	275	8	BIP	96–512	770 R / 935 W	2 or 4	None
135-3	275–1485	2	64	16 + 2	RW	275	8	BIP	256–512	880 R / 935 W	2 or 4	None
138	275–1430	2	64	16 + 2	RW	275	8	MOS	512–1024	880 R / 935 W	2	None
145	203–315	4	8–16	32 + 4	RW	203	8	BIP	160–2048	540 R / 608 W	4 or 8	None
145-3	180–270	4	32	32 + 4	RW	180	8	BIP	192–1584	405 R / 540 W	4 or 8	None
148	180–270	4	32	32 + 4	RW	180	8	MOS	1024–2048	405 R / 540 W	4	None
155	115	4	6	69 + 3	RO	115	None	Core	256–2048	2070	8	None
155-II	115	4	8	69 + 3	RW	115	128	Core	256–2048	2070	8	None
158	115	4	8	69 + 3	RW	115	128	MOS	512–6144	1035 R / 920 W	8 or 16	None
158-3	115	4	8	69 + 3	RW	115	128	MOS	512–6144	1035 R / 920 W	8 or 16	None
158 MP	115						128			1035 R / 920 W	8 or 16	None
158-3 MP	115						128			1035 R / 920 W	8 or 16	None
165	80	8	2	105 + 3	RO	80	None	Core	512–3072	2000	8	4
165-II	80	8	2	105 + 3	RO	80	128	Core	512–3072	2000	8	4
168	80	8	4	105 + 3	RO	80	128	MOS	1024–8192	320	8	4
168-3	80	8	1	105 + 3	RW	80	128	MOS	1024–8192	320	8	4
168 MP	80		4	105 + 3	RO			MOS	2048–16384		8	4
168-3 MP	80		1	105 + 3	RW			MOS	2048–16384		8	4
195	54	8	None				None	Core	1024–4096	756	8	16
3031	115	4	8	69 + 3	RW	115	128	MOS	2048–6144	345	8	4
3032	80	8	4	105 + 3	RW	80	128	MOS	2048–6144	320	8	4
3033	58	8	4	105 + 3	RW	58	128	MOS	4096–8192	290	8	8
4331	900	4	None		RW	90–1300	None	MOS	512–1024	1300	4	8
4341	150–300	8	64	105 + 3	RW		Yes	MOS	2048–4096	600	8	8

Model	Cache Size (Kbytes)	Cache T. cycle (ns)	Cache Line width (bytes)	Cache assoc.	ISPs implemented in microprogram	Relative performance (COBOL benchmarks)	Relative performance [Phister, 1979]	Relative performance (Data Pro)	Maximum I/O rate (Mbytes/s)
22	None				1401^a	1.0	1.0		
25	None				1401^a|1620	2.0	1.8		
30	None				1401^a|1410^b				
40	None								
44	None								
50	None				1410^b|7070^c	4.5	3.9		
65	None				7070^c|7090^d	10.0	13.7		
67	None				7070^c|7090^d				
75	None					19.3			
85	16–32	80–160	256 × 4	16	7090^d				
91	None								
95	32	54–162	8 × 8	4					
115	None				1401^a		1.0	1.0	0.9
115-2	None				1401^a		1.7	1.4	0.9
125	None				1401^a	1.4	1.95	1.45	0.9
125-2	None				1401^a		2.7	1.8	0.9
135	None				1401^a	1.8	3.9	2.9	2.4
135-3	None				1401^a		5.1	3.8	2.6
138	None				1401^a		5.1	3.9	2.6
145	None				1401^a|1410^b	4.0	7.8	5.45	5.3
145-3	None				1401^a|1410^b			7.1	5.3
148	None				1401^a|1410^b		10.4	7.7	5.0
155	8	115–230	16 × 2	2	1401^a|1410^b|7070^c	10.0	13.5	10.0	5.4
155-II	8	115–230	16 × 2	2	1401^a|1410^b|7070^c			10.0	5.4
158	8	115–230	16 × 2	2	1401^a|1410^b|7070^c	24.2	17.8	15.0	
158-3	16	115–230	16 × 2	4	1401^a|1410^b|7070^c	24.1	19.6	16.4	
158 MP					1401^a|1410^b|7070^c	21.8		27.0	7.5
158-3 MP					1401^a|1410^b|7070^c			29.4	7.5
165	8–16	80–160	8 × 4	4	7070^c|7080|7090^d	31.7	38.7	34.5	8.0
165-II	8–16	80–160	8 × 4	4	7070^c|7090^d			34.5	8.0
168	8–16	80–160	8 × 4	4–8	7070^c|7090^d	51.4	47.4	41.8	16.0
168-3	32	80–160	8 × 4	8	7070^c|7090^d		53.9	45.5	16.0
168 MP					7070^c|7090^d	57.6		75.3	28.0
168-3 MP					7070^c|7090^d	39.9		81.8	28.0
195	32	54–162	8 × 8	8			73.0	86.4	3.0
3031	32	115–230	8 × 4	8			23.5	19.7	
3032	32	80–160	8 × 4	8			53.9	45.1	
3033	64	58–116	8 × 8	16			97.0	77.4	
4331	None				1401^a		4.8	4.0	2.3
4341	8	50–225	8		1401^a		16.1	17.0	9.0

^a C\|IBM 1401\|1440\|1460\|; ^b C\|IBM MP\|7010\|; ^c C\|IBM 7070\|7074\|; ^d IBM \|709\|7040\|7090\|7094\|.

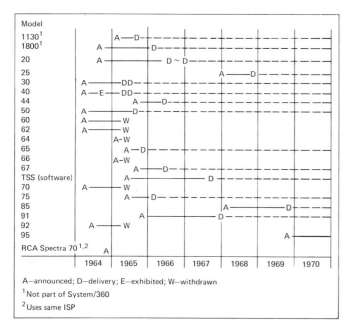

Fig. 2. IBM System/360 model introduction dates.

Most of the above ISPs have a different structure from the 360 ISP. For example, the 1401 series instructions and data [Bell and Newell, 1971] are variable-length character strings; the 1620 has variable-length data strings; the 704 series process fixed- and floating-point data with single-address instructions; and the 7070 is a fixed-word decimal computer. Thus the 360 C's represent the first machines to be two logical processors in the same physical implementation.

The emulated speeds are often better than that of the original hardwired computer. This is not surprising, considering the change in technology; it is a very attractive feature. The 360 Mp performance is often a factor of 5 to 10 times the "emulated" computers; and the M[ROS] data rates are a factor of 25 times the Mp's. For example, the Model 65 emulating a 7090 runs faster than a hardwired 7090. Note, by way of contrast, that the hardwired models 91 and 44 have the lowest cost/performance ratios in the series.

There are minor deviations in the particular models, but all implementations belong to a common ISP subset. The Model 22 and the Model 91, the extremes of the series, deviate most from the standard 360 ISP. The range of models shows the comparative effects of implementation on the actual processing times. For example, the designers of the various C's were constrained by memory bandwidths. Since the core memories have about the same cycle time (0.75 ~ 2.5 μs), variation in bandwidth is obtained by increasing the data-path width from 8 to 64 bits and by increasing the number of independent Mp's. By looking at just Mp bandwidth, for models 30 ~ 65, we obtain a range of 5.3 to 133.5 Mbit/s, corresponding to a performance range of about 1 to 25. By doubling the number of independent memories, this factor can be increased to 50. These models correspond to a Pc performance range of 1 to 50. Although we might expect a narrower range (based on Mp speed), the range can be increased by performance suppression (at the low end). Power range can be increased by lowering the absolute performance of Model 30. This is accomplished by making performance tradeoffs to lower cost.

tion and technology but include RCA marketing and profit strategy. In addition, of course, there should have been lower development costs. RCA's exit from the computer business when it sold its user base to UNIVAC also may be indicative of the fact that the 360 costs were not out of line with the product and service costs.

An interesting aspect of the design is the method used to implement the individual computer models (of the range) and their associated costs. From the standpoint of innovation, the 360 was the first computer series to cover a wide range. The more basic P's (Models 20 ~ 65) were implemented via a microprogrammed processor. This is based on a computer program within an M[read only], i.e., a read-only storage (ROS), to interpret the common ISP. A payoff from this implementation strategy is a solution to the "compatibility design constraint," which is the ability to provide compatibility with the customer's previous (IBM) machine, which, of course, was not a member of the 360 series. This is undoubtedly the most difficult constraint to meet in the P designs, and probably the most significant real innovation. From the marketing viewpoint, it provided the user with a crutch to go from a former IBM computer to the System/360. This is accomplished through "emulation," which (as defined by IBM) means the ability of one C to interpret another's programs *at a reasonable performance level*. These emulations are realized by various microprogrammed P's designed to interpret both the 360 ISP and one or more of IBM 704, 709, 1401, 1410, 1440, 1460, 1620, 7010, 7040, 7044, 7070, 7074, 7090, and 7094.

Logic Technology

The logic of the 360 series is realized in a hybrid technology, composed partly of integrated-circuit techniques and partly of the solid-state techniques standard in second-generation machines. It is a "thick-film" technology, which deposits the circuitry on a ceramic substrate. This is called Solid Logic Technology (SLT) and is used solely by IBM. This production technique allows only for the fabrication of passive circuit elements on the substrate. The semiconductor elements (diodes and transistors) are produced independently, using standard semiconductor production techniques on a wafer. The semiconductors are then cut and bonded to the substrate, and the complete SLT logic unit is encapsulated.

The substrates correspond roughly to logic elements (gates, inverters, flip-flops, etc.). The SLT units are placed on larger printed-circuit boards.

Although SLT differs fundamentally from integrated-circuit technology, the overall size of the final printed-circuit boards is about the same. At the time the decision was made to develop the technology, it was unclear that integrated-circuit technology would reach mass-production state. Thus the SLT program was an intermediate design prior to integrated-circuit technology. The two approaches are about the same from the standpoint of reliability, especially when one considers the soldered printed-circuit mounting. The number of connections to the printed-circuit board are about the same. The production technology of the 360 series is outstanding, perhaps surpassed only by the 360 marketing plan.

PMS Structures and Implementations of the Computer

The PMS structures of the various models in System/360 are basically similar, except for the upper end of the series and for the Model 44 (complete compatibility can be purchased as an option). We take up the main group first and then discuss the others individually.

Models 30, 40, 50, and 65. The PMS structures of Models 30, 40, and 50 are all very similar. Figure 3 shows the tree-structured Mp-Pc of the Model 50.[1] They all use a P.microprogram, although

[1]The structure of the Mp's does not include the local M's used for access control, i.e., the storage protect key mechanism, which it is hoped the student will forget about (forever).

with different ISPs. Some gross characteristics are given in Table 1. The Pc of Model 65 is also microprogrammed, but it has hardwired Pio's. A PMS diagram of Model 65 is given in Fig. 4.

The C structures with M[ROS] use a single physical P.microprogram to realize the Pc, the Pio [Multiplexor Channel], and the Pio [Selector Channel]. This technique of using a single shared physical P.state is the same one that Pio['Multiplexor] uses. The Pio['Multiplexor] is equivalent to multiple Pio's. Within the physical P, interrupts are used to switch among the P's.

The interpretation cycle for the 360 ISP starts by fetching the instruction, proceeds to fetch the operands, executes the instruction, and then returns results to Mp. The instruction-interpretation process takes only a few Mp references for most instructions. The P tests for interrupt requests during instruction fetch. Pending interrupts are serviced by processor microcode. Pio hardware handles data transmission by breaking in (interrupting) for memory service and updating channel information.

A few instructions require a long (or indefinite) interpretation time—e.g., character translate and edit—since the operations are on character strings. Here, the iterative program loop which operates on each character of the string must test the attached K's to detect when the Pio interpreter is to be run for data transfers. The long instructions can take several hundred microseconds and

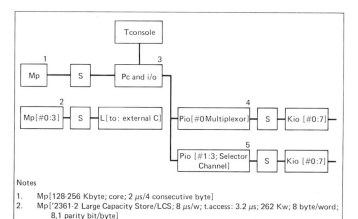

Notes
1. Mp[128-256 Kbyte; core; 2 µs/4 consecutive byte]
2. Mp['2361-2 Large Capacity Store/LCS; 8 µs/w; t.access: 3.2 µs; 262 Kw; 8 byte/word; 8,1 parity bit/byte]
3. Pc[!Time multiplexed between central processing and I/O!]
4. Pio[Byte Multiplexor Channel; to: 8 Kio max; address capability: 192 I/O Devices]
5. Pio[Selector Channel]

Fig. 3. IBM System/360 Model 50 PMS diagram.

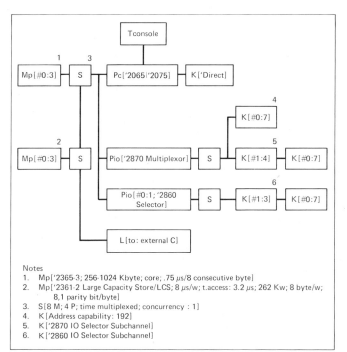

Notes
1. Mp['2365-3; 256-1024 Kbyte; core; .75 µs/8 consecutive byte]
2. Mp['2361-2 Large Capacity Store/LCS; 8 µs/w; t.access: 3.2 µs; 262 Kw; 8 byte/w; 8,1 parity bit/byte]
3. S[8 M; 4 P; time multiplexed; concurrency : 1]
4. K[Address capability: 192]
5. K['2870 IO Selector Subchannel]
6. K['2860 IO Selector Subchannel]

Fig. 4. PMS structure for IBM System/360 Models 65 and 75.

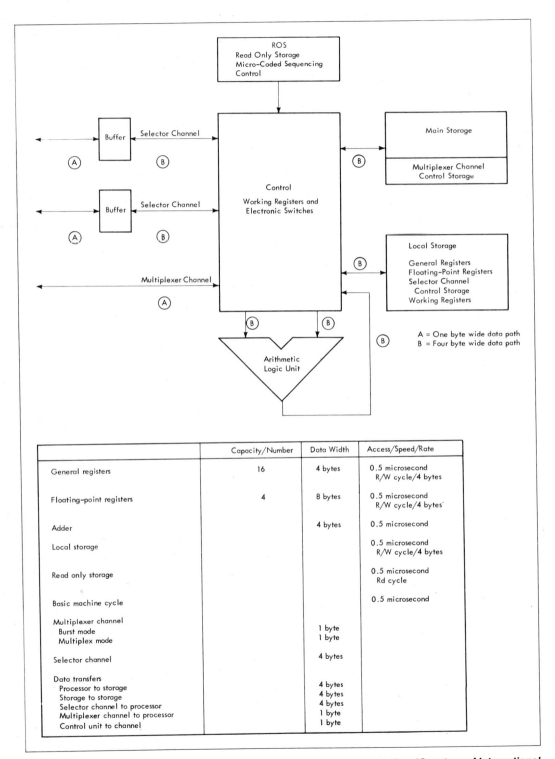

	Capacity/Number	Data Width	Access/Speed/Rate
General registers	16	4 bytes	0.5 microsecond R/W cycle/4 bytes
Floating-point registers	4	8 bytes	0.5 microsecond R/W cycle/4 bytes
Adder		4 bytes	0.5 microsecond
Local storage			0.5 microsecond R/W cycle/4 bytes
Read only storage			0.5 microsecond Rd cycle
Basic machine cycle			0.5 microsecond
Multiplexer channel Burst mode Multiplex mode		1 byte 1 byte	
Selector channel		4 bytes	
Data transfers Processor to storage Storage to storage Selector channel to processor Multiplexer channel to processor Control unit to channel		4 bytes 4 bytes 4 bytes 1 byte 1 byte	

Fig. 5. IBM System/360 Model 50 data-flow diagram and system characteristics. (*Courtesy of International Business Machines Corporation.*)

cannot be interrupted; thus the response time for an interrupt can be very poor. Figure 5 gives a simplified picture of the register organization of a Model 50.

The actual System/360 ISP interpretation program in each of the models is different. In addition, each model has microprograms for interpreting other ISPs through emulation. Tucker [1967] discusses how the models were changed as the emulation constraint was added. Table 1 gives the computers which each of the models can emulate. A register structure of the C['30] and the operation for the P.microprogram ISP are given in Chap. 12. Tables 2 and 3 in Chap. 41 give the additional parameters which influence the instruction interpretation rate of the P.microprogram. The significant parameters for a P.microprogram are the M[ROS] hardware characteristics (speed, size, and information width); the number of fields in the M[ROS] instructions, which gives an indication of the number of control functions performed in parallel; the M[general register] rates and their location in the structure; the Mp data rate; and the characteristics of M[temporary] within P. The activity of transferring data from a K, via the Pio['Selector], is done concurrently with normal instruction interpretation in Models 30, 40, and 50. A program in M[ROS] sets up the data transmission with Mp, and transmission is controlled by an independent hardware control.

Model 25.   The Model 25 is an interesting C. Perhaps some of the interest of the authors is caused by the mystery (to the authors) as to what its ISP is. Its ISP is no doubt described in maintenance manuals. We can make the following observations based on its characteristics taken from its manual of Functional Characteristics. The observations are:

1   It has a very high-performance Mp, namely, Mp[core; .9 μs/w; 16 |24|32|48 kby; 2 by/w]; the Mp power is almost that of a Model 50.

2   There is a relatively straightforward Pc which is microprogrammed. The Pc uses Mp for its memory. The System/360 ISP is defined in conventional M[read, write]. Of the Mp[48Kby] 16 kilobytes are reserved for a microprogram.

3   Its performance is between that of Models 20 and 30, performing a 360 ISP instruction in about 80 μs.

4   The penalty paid (slowdown factor) to interpret the 360 ISP is therefore 80/1.8 $\simeq$ 45.

5   A small 180-ns local store is used for operands.

6   The Pc cost appears to be about the lowest in the series.

We should ask ourselves:

1   Why do we want an intermediate-level P.microprogram

with its own M.read-only, as in the other processors? These P's just seem to waste power.

2   Why should we bother to implement an intermediate-level 360 ISP? We know the final user will write programs in a much higher-level language. Thus two levels of interpretation are required instead of one. It is assumed that to program a given task will take, say, x μs if we are using the 360 ISP. We assume the same task programmed directly in the Pc could take as short a time as $x/45$ μs if the Pc were used directly.

We assume that if the P.microprogram, which is used to define the System/360 ISP, were used to interpret a FORTRAN ISP, the speed for a Model 25 FORTRAN ISP might easily approach that of the Model 50.

Model 44.   Model 44 does not use M[ROS], but its Pc and Pio are hardwired (Models 75 and 91 are also hardwired). The PMS structure of the Model 44 is given in Fig. 6. Model 44 (and Model 91) stand out as having better performance per unit of cost than their nearest neighbors, which are implemented with M[ROS].

It must be noted that Models 44 and 91 are not strictly compatible with the 360 ISP, since they do not process variable-string and variable-decimal-data formats, although Model 44 options can make it completely compatible. (Subroutines will probably perform satisfactorily for most applications.)

The PMS structure of the Model 44 (Fig. 6) is a tree. The C['44] structure indicates 2-Pio['High Speed Multiplexor Channels/HSMPX], which is between a P['Selector] and P['Multiplexor] in power, since a single physical P['HSMPX] with four subchannels

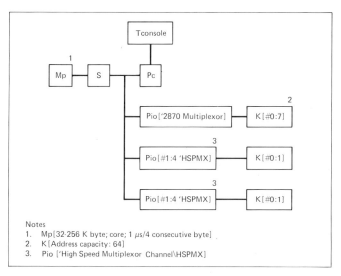

Notes
1.   Mp[32-256 K byte; core; 1 μs/4 consecutive byte]
2.   K[Address capacity: 64]
3.   Pio ['High Speed Multiplexor Channel\HSPMX]

Fig. 6. IBM System/360 Model 44 PMS diagram.

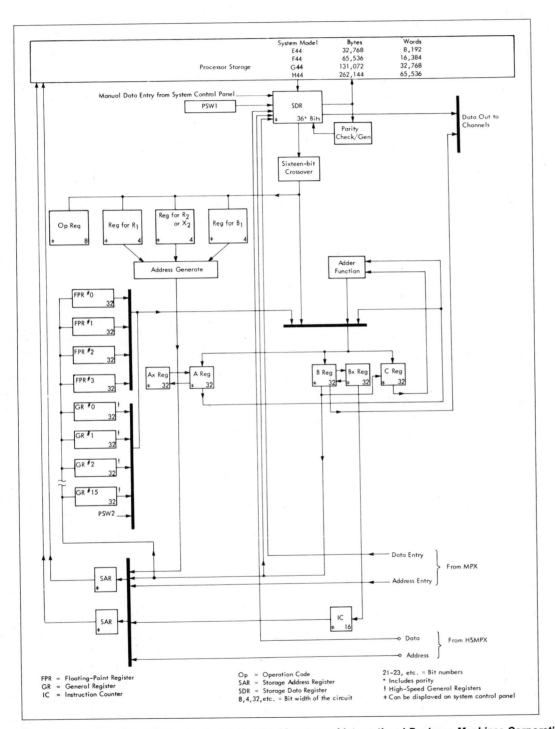

Fig. 7. IBM System/360 data flow in Model 44 CPU. (*Courtesy of International Business Machines Corporation.*)

can behave as four independent Pio's. The organization of the Model 44 Pc registers is given in Fig. 7, which reveals a straightforward implementation. The heavy lines in Fig. 7 indicated an ORing of register outputs to form a single data bus (usually 16 or 32 bits wide). The 16-bit crossover function box allows the right and left halves (16 bits) of the input to be exchanged when output. Almost all the units are registers (except the adders, parity generators, and ORers). The A, Ax, B, and Bx registers are used as the M.working for performing instructions, where the x indicates an extension register used in the 64-bit floating-point operations. The C register is a second operand register used for arithmetic and logical operations.

Model 75. The PMS structure of Model 75 is given in Fig. 4. Models 65, 67, 75, and 91 all use the same basic Mp['2365; core]. The S[n Mp; mP], which switches between the n Mp modules and the m Pc and Pio's, varies with model, however. C['65] and C['75] use a simple time-multiplexed S in Pc, called the S['Bus Control Unit/BCU]. This S makes decisions about which P is to use which Mp, rather than having each Mp arbitrate the P requesting service locally. When the memories are all about the same speed, such an S is all right; however, it has severe limitations when slow-speed (8 μs for the large core store) and high-speed memories (0.75 μs) are intermixed. The principal difference between Models 65 and 75 is that C['75] is hardwired and, depending on the size of the configuration, may have lower cost/performance.

The simplified functional unit diagram of C['75] (Fig. 8) is more abstract than the register interconnection diagram of a C['44](Fig. 7). From this description (Fig. 8) of the logic design, one is able to conjecture what is necessarily within the instruction, execution, variable-field length, and decimal functional units. The diagram is presented at a nonuniform level at both the PMS and register-transfer levels. There is somewhat more detail than in the PMS structure (Fig. 4). The Model 75 is possibly the first System/360 to require an intermedite-level diagram between a PMS structure and a register-transfer diagram. The instruction unit contains the instruction location counter (part of the ISP) and is responsible for obtaining the next instruction and the operands. Since there can be overlap in the instruction fetching process, this unit is responsible for holding a number of instructions and stores up to 128 bits (2 doublewords) of instructions at a time. The execution unit and the variable-field and decimal units carry out operations on data. The execution unit processes floating-point and fixed-point data.

Model 67. The Model 67 was introduced in April 1965 for the purpose of timesharing. The entry was prompted by MIT's project

MULTICS. MIT had ordered a GE 645 for experimental research in timesharing. IBM formed a group for the development of a time-shared computer and responded with the Model 67. The Model 67 is essentially a Pc['65] with adequate S's for multiprocessing and a K between Mp and Pc for multiprogramming and memory mapping. Because of the software uncertainties, the Model 67 ran as a Model 65 in most installations (in 1968). The University of Michigan and MIT's Lincoln Laboratory, the first two customers having considered the MULTICS proposal, were instrumental in outlining the specifications [Arden et al, 1966]. The hardware (Fig. 9) is interesting from several aspects. First, there are adequate facilities for memory mapping and program segmentation. This general scheme is outlined in Fig. 10. In the Model 67 a user's segment and page maps are in Mp, and these maps point to physical Mp blocks of the program. Each time a reference is made, the map is checked for the actual reference. In order to avoid the accesses to Mp for each Mp reference, a K, with an M[content address], is located between Pc and Mp to transform a 24- or 32-bit virtual address in Pc into an actual 19- to 22-bit physical address in Mp. This K is not shown in Fig. 10 because it is not logically necessary. The scheme suggested in Fig. 10 uses control bits in the map to determine legal Mp accesses. In the Model 67 the storage key mechanism holds the information whether a given page can be accessed by a given numbered user (instead of associating the control with the mapping as shown in Fig. 10).

Second, the Model 67 is the first acknowledgment by IBM of multiprocessor computers, since it provides adequate switching to allow multiple Pc's. The C['65] multiprocessing configuration has been introduced based on Model 67 structure. Multiprocessors are necessary for reliability, not solely for performance reasons.

The PMS structure of C['67] in Fig. 9 does not have to use the S['Bus Control Unit/BCU],[1] as in the C['65]. The C['67] can have an S in each Mp, so that four P's can communicate with an Mp, as shown in Fig. 9. Each Mp makes the decision about the P request to be honored next. Thus the problem of having an "all-knowing" S['BCU] is solved by allowing each Mp to do local scheduling, rather than having a dialogue with another component (with time delays). The S['BCU] in a duplex C['67] is still present, but with less power, in the form of the S['2846 Channel Controller]. It is used to arbitrate the Pio accesses to Mp.

Without multiprocessing, the Pc seems very badly mismatched with respect to Mp. Consider, for instance, the data rates on the C['67]. From Fig. 9 its maximum possible Mp data rates are:

[1]A system with only one port at Mp, controlled by BCU, is called a *simplex*. A system with multiport Mp is called a *duplex*.

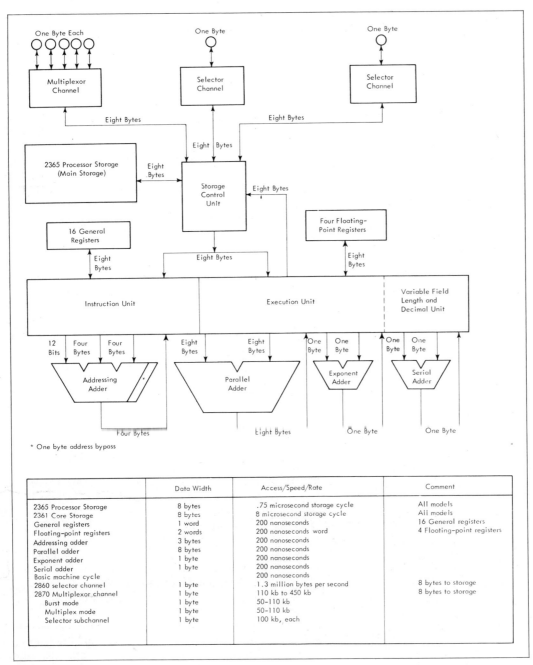

	Data Width	Access/Speed/Rate	Comment
2365 Processor Storage	8 bytes	.75 microsecond storage cycle	All models
2361 Core Storage	8 bytes	8 microsecond storage cycle	All models
General registers	1 word	200 nanoseconds	16 General registers
Floating-point registers	2 words	200 nanoseconds word	4 Floating-point registers
Addressing adder	3 bytes	200 nanoseconds	
Parallel adder	8 bytes	200 nanoseconds	
Exponent adder	1 byte	200 nanoseconds	
Serial adder	1 byte	200 nanoseconds	
Basic machine cycle		200 nanoseconds	
2860 selector channel	1 byte	1.3 million bytes per second	8 bytes to storage
2870 Multiplexor channel	1 byte	110 kb to 450 kb	8 bytes to storage
Burst mode	1 byte	50–110 kb	
Multiplex mode	1 byte	50–110 kb	
Selector subchannel	1 byte	100 kb, each	

Fig. 8. IBM System/360 Model 75 data-flow diagram and system statistics. (*Courtesy of International Business Machines Corporation.*)

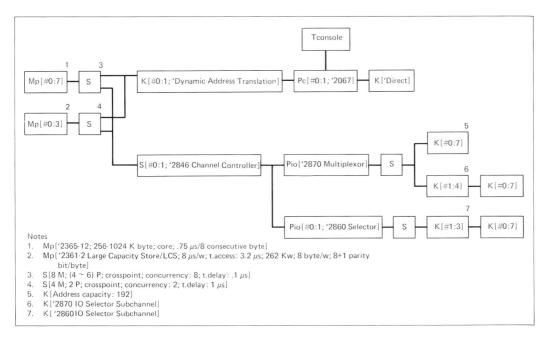

Notes
1. Mp['2365-12; 256-1024 K byte; core; .75 μs/8 consecutive byte]
2. Mp['2361-2 Large Capacity Store/LCS; 8 μs/w; t.access: 3.2 μs; 262 Kw; 8 byte/w; 8+1 parity bit/byte]
3. S[8 M; (4 ~ 6) P; crosspoint; concurrency: 8; t.delay: .1 μs]
4. S[4 M; 2 P; crosspoint; concurrency: 2; t.delay: 1 μs]
5. K[Address capacity: 192]
6. K['2870 IO Selector Subchannel]
7. K['2860 IO Selector Subchannel]

Fig. 9. IBM System/360 Model 67 PMS diagram.

For 1 Mp['2365-12]:

$$\frac{2 \times 64 \text{ bits}}{0.75 \ \mu s} = 171 \text{ Mbit/s}$$

and for 1 Mp['2361 Large Core Store]:

$$\frac{64 \text{ bits}}{8 \ \mu s} = 8 \text{ Mbit/s}$$

Thus the total data rate is

$$171 \times 8 + 8 \times 4 = 1,368 + 32 \text{ Mbit/s}$$
$$= \sim 1,400 \text{ Mbit/s}$$

The processing rate is approximately

$$\frac{64 \text{ bits}}{2.2 \ \mu s} = 29 \text{ Mbit/s}$$

An Ms.drum rate is approximately

$$\frac{8 \text{ bits} \times 1.2}{\mu s} = 10 \text{ Mbit/s}$$

Thus, for the several P's, an effective Mp request rate of 100 Mbit/s might be needed. The data-flow mismatch (between Mp and the P's) occurs because of the P's, the S (the L's connecting P and Mp), the lack of P's, and the fact that t.access = ~ ½ t.cycle. The Pio['2870], used in Model 65 and above, is described at two structural levels in Fig. 4. The Pio includes a large M.working to store the state of each of the logical Pio's. This Pio state includes the instruction location counter, the control state bits (active, running, interpreting an instruction, processing data, etc.), and buffering (one 8-byte word). By having an M.buffer, the demands on Mp from the Pio's are reduced by a factor of 8. Although the expected data rate from many K's does not require the extra M, there are possible times when the uncertainty of the access times for Mp might cause data loss. Since the M.working is necessary to store the Pio state, the additional space for buffering is not expensive. An alternative design might use Mp for this buffering.

The four Pio['2860 Selector Channel]'s are implemented as independent Pio's, using conventional hardwired logic and buffering. However, they are packaged as one unit.

Model 85. The model 85 was announced in February 1968, with the goal of being the highest-performance Model 360 in production. The performance is about 3 to 5 times that of the Model 65 and in some cases outperforms a Model 91 [Conti, Gibson, and Pitkowsky, 1968].

The PMS diagram of the Model 85 is shown in Fig. 11. The Pio, T, Ms structure is identical to that of Models 65 and 75 (Fig. 4). The two interesting aspects of the structure in Fig. 11 are the M[content addressable; 'Buffer Storage; 16|32 page; 1024 by/page] and the Pc. The pages are filled in groups of 64 bytes, as

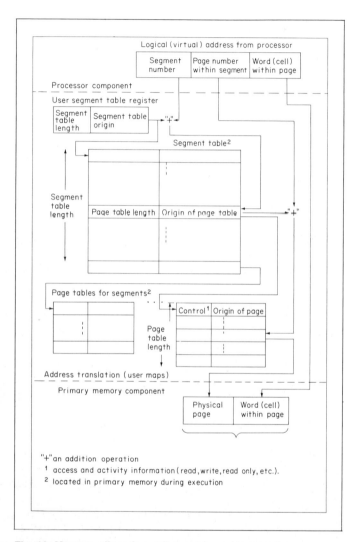

Fig. 10. Memory allocation using pages and segments.

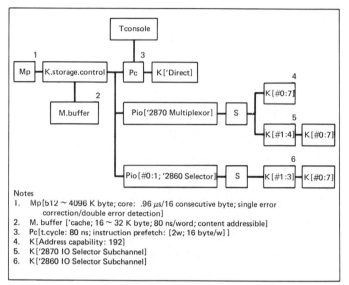

Notes

1.   Mp[512 ~ 4096 K byte; core; .96 μs/16 consecutive byte; single error correction/double error detection]
2.   M. buffer ['cache; 16 ~ 32 K byte; 80 ns/word; content addressible]
3.   Pc[t.cycle: 80 ns; instruction prefetch: [2w; 16 byte/w]]
4.   K[Address capability: 192]
5.   K['2870 IO Selector Subchannel]
6.   K['2860 IO Selector Subchannel]

Fig. 11. IBM System/360 Model 85 PMS diagram.

references to a particular physical block in Mp.core are made. Conti, Gibson, and Pitowsky [1968] give running times for various programs as a function of buffer memory size. Multiprogramming may degrade the performance more than any other case. This process, which has been referred to as *look-aside*, or a *slave memory*, was suggested by Wilkes [1965]. It is completely analogous to the Model 67 M[content.addressable; 8w] which is used to hold the segment-page map for a multiprogrammed timesharing system. It is also analogous to a one-level storage system (Atlas; see Chap. 10) formed from two physical M's whose performance differs significantly. Here, the effect is to try to approximate a computer with a large Mp[80 ns/w] by using a large

Mp[1 μs/w] and a small M[80 ns/w]. The CDC 7600 has a similar structure, but the Mp-Ms migration is under programmed control.

The P.microprogram used for controlling the Pc[K['Execution Unit]] allows for great flexibility in the definition of ISPs. An Mp[500 w] is available for the user; this may be loaded by a program, and it specifies an ISP. One standard option is to emulate the 704-7094 series.

The Model 85 removes the restriction of aligning words at particular boundaries. Thus any logical word, independently of its length, can be located at any physical location addressed in bytes.

The Pc's data operation performance is impressive. A fixed-point multiply is done in 0.4 μs, and a floating-point multiply takes 0.56 μs (not including accesses).

The data-type *extended floating-point number* is used in Model 85. Thus a 24-, 56-, or 112-bit fraction part can be used.

Model 91.   This model has a very low cost/performance ratio. Only about 20 Model 91's were produced before it was withdrawn from the market. It has the highest performance of the series. The Mp is 0.75 μs, but 16 are overlapped to provide a theoretical maximum bandwidth of $16 \times 64/0.75 = 1{,}370$ Mbit/s. About 2.5 mega-instructions per second are executed; thus, a total of 70 Mbit/s of Mp is absorbed by Pc.

There are other interesting models in the '90 series; the Model 92 was a paper machine, and the Model 95 was unannounced but produced, a version of the Model 91 with an Mp[integrated circuit; 60 ns/w; 8 by/w]. The Model 91 is covered in detail in Chaps.

18 and 19. It is similar to other very large computers in that many techniques are employed to obtain parallelism. The January 1967 *IBM Journal of Research* is devoted to design issues of the Model 91.

Models 1130 and 1800. These computers are presented as reference points and have nothing to do with the C['360]. They are implemented outside the System/360 framework but use its technology, and so cost comparisons are still somewhat meaningful. These computers are straightforward, and for a given task which does not use floating-point arithmetic, they should perform as well as any System/360 model. The arguments we use for the intermediate Pc for the Model 25 apply equally well here, too, namely, Why have such a complex ISP when simple ones will do just as well?

The programmed floating-point arithmetic times for 4-μs 1800 and the "hardwired" (microprogrammed) System/360 Model 30 are compared in Table 2. We would expect the 2-μs 1800 to be better by a factor of 2. Note that the times are about the same for Model 30 and the slower 1800. The cost/performance is especially low with the 1130. It is interesting to speculate why the 1130 and 1800 cannot be implemented within the System/360 framework. Are they "loss leaders"? Are they in response to more sophisticated, performance-oriented users?

The PMS Structure of the Controls, Terminals, Secondary Memories, and Special Processors

There are many common components which attach to the C's (Figs. 12 to 17). Most of the components which attach to a Pio are not especially interesting, but they give an idea of the behavior and parameters. For example, the expression T['1403 Model 3; line printer; 1100 line/min; 132 char/line; 8 bits/character; 64 ~ 240 character set] pretty well describes a typical line printer. From the above description one can deduce the data rate of a T[line printer]. It is 132 char/line × 1100 line/min × 1/60 min/s × 8 bits/char = 19.4 Kbit/s.

Table 2   IBM 1800 (4 μs) and IBM System/360 Model 30 Floating-Point Arithmetic Timing

Operation	Operation times (μs)	
	1800 (4 μs)	System/360 Model 30
+ {sf}; + {df}	460; 440	75; 115
× {sf}; {df}	560; 790	320; 1060
÷ {sf}	766	600
√ {f}	4500	2965
sin {f}	3000	3876
exponential {f}	2000	4173

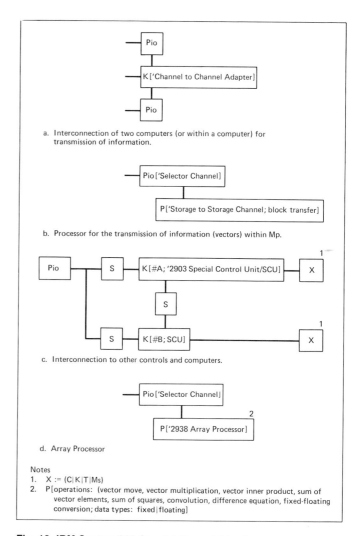

a. Interconnection of two computers (or within a computer) for transmission of information.

b. Processor for the transmission of information (vectors) within Mp.

c. Interconnection to other controls and computers.

d. Array Processor

Notes
1.   X := (C|K|T|Ms)
2.   P[operations: (vector move, vector multiplication, vector inner product, sum of vector elements, sum of squares, convolution, difference equation, fixed-floating conversion; data types: fixed|floating]

Fig. 12. IBM System/360 Special P's and K's diagram.

The Channel-to-Channel Adapter Control. The most interesting group of components (outside the C structures) are the special components shown in Fig. 12. The K['Channel to Channel Adapter] allows two P's, on either the same or a different C, to communicate with one another. This K is used in the construction of a dual C system or the N['Attached Support Processor/ASP]. A C['40|'50] is attached to a C['65|'75]. The C['40|50] is used as a Cio with file processing capabilities. The K has M.buffer. Data can flow in only one direction at a time.

The Special Control Unit. The K['2903 Special Control Unit/ SCU] consists of two independent K's which are physically

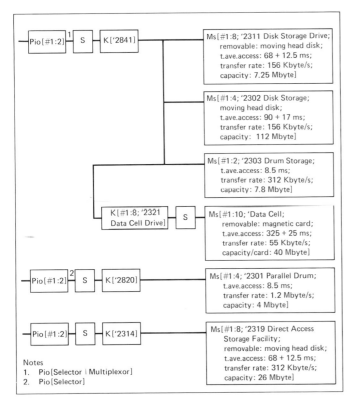

Notes
1. Pio[Selector | Multiplexor]
2. Pio[Selector]

Fig. 13. IBM System/360 Ms [drum; disk; data cell] PMS diagrams.

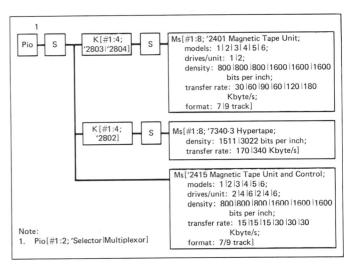

Note:
1.   Pio[#1:2; 'Selector|Multiplexor]

Fig. 14. IBM System/360 Ms [magnetic tape] PMS diagram.

packaged together and allow users to interface with the Pio's. Although it has not been discussed, the actual interconnection with a Pio, via the S[Pio; K]; is via a physical I/O bus which is arranged in a bus (or chained) fashion. Such a single interface to handle a wide range of needs (high and low response and data rates) via a single set of electrical conductors requires a great deal of control information to be passed along the link. Therefore a K must have a great deal of knowledge of the dialogue in order to communicate. The hardware to attach to the I/O bus at a K is costly and must be designed carefully. The K['SCU] provides a rather simplified interface to the Pio. All I/O bus synchronization control, communication protocol control, buffering, and electrical isolation are within K['SCU]. The K['SCU] is fairly flexible, in that devices connected to it can communicate with one another without Pio (see Fig. 12).

Storage-to-Storage-Channel Processor.   The P['Storage to Storage Channel] is a special processor which performs the sole function of transferring data blocks (a word vector) between one location in Mp to another in Mp. It qualifies as a P, since it takes

an instruction from Mp containing the location and length, and once the instruction is executed, another is fetched and executed (if it exists). Thus the component has a well-defined interpretation cycle and set of operations. This P is useful in a multiprogrammed environment requiring programs to be moved.

The 2938 Array Processor.   The P.array['2938] is an extremely interesting special P (Fig. 12). It can be connected to Model 44, 65, or 75. It has a limited instruction repertoire, but the instructions it interprets are more complex than those in the ISP of the Pc. The instructions are algorithms for operating on an array (a vector or a matrix). These instructions include:

1   Vector move, similar to the P['Storage to Storage] described above, with conversion either way between fixed and floating point
2   An element-by-element vector sum
3   An element-by-element vector multiplication
4   A row-by-column vector inner product
5   A convolution multiply
6   The solution to a step in a difference equation

The P.array is microprogrammed, using an M[ROS], which makes it possible to construct complex algorithms in a flexible manner. The hardware logic is capable of doing a combined floating-point multiplication and addition in 200 ns. The impressive results this P achieves in the interpretation of the algorithms are principally

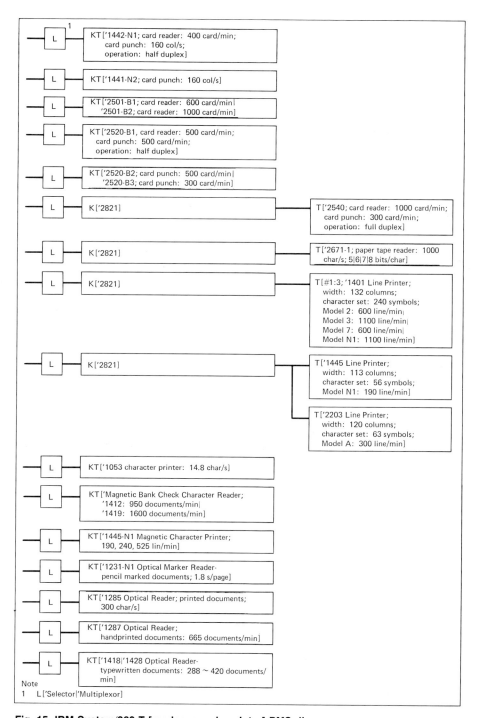

Fig. 15. IBM System/360 T [reader; punch; printer] PMS diagram.

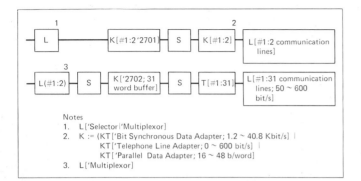

Fig. 16. IBM System/360 communications PMS diagrams.

because the time to access the algorithm has gone to zero. A measure we might apply to a P is the ratio of the time it spends fetching the algorithm's data to the total time it spends executing the algorithm. In a conventional computer Pc we suggest that a ratio of nearly ½ is very good. Two fetches are usually required—one for data, one for the instruction. This P has a ratio near 1, as it is always accessing data (and rarely instructions).

Secondary-Memory Structure.   Figures 13 and 14 present the Ms PMS structures. All the K's have an optional S, which can be placed between the K and the S[P;K] to allow two Pio's to access a common K (from either of two C's or two Pio's of the same C). The K['2841 Storage Control] is interesting only in being able to control a series of quite disparate devices, on a one-at-a-time basis.

Figure 14 presents all the Ms[magnetic tape]'s. The switch is interesting, as it can be used for up to four K's to access simultaneously any of 16 M.tapes. (The vast array of very similar devices is due undoubtedly to marketing rather than production or engineering reasons.) It should be noted that there are two distinct M.tapes: conventional magnetic tape and Hypertape. Hypertape is explicitly addressed and has built-in error-correction coding.

Terminal Structure.   The structure of the vast array of printing devices that can attach to the C['360] is shown in Fig. 15. Some of the devices are interesting, such as the one that reads pencil-marked or typewritten paper. The main parameters of significance to PMS are the rate at which the device reads paper and the kind of paper it reads.

The T and the K's that connect to external processes are given in Fig. 16. The K['2701] and K['2702] are built to transform unsynchronized parallel data from the C into the synchronized serial form required by the telephone line. The K['2701] controls a small number of lines of high data rates; the K['2702] controls a

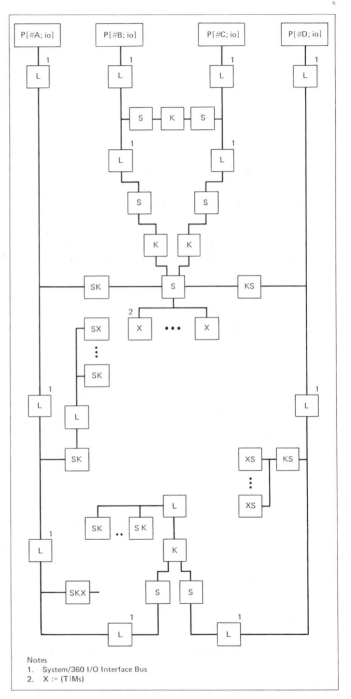

Notes
1.   System/360 I/O Interface Bus
2.   X := (T│Ms)

Fig. 17. IBM System/360 peripheral-switching PMS diagram.

large number of lines at low data rates. The K['2702] is actually an array of up to 31 K's that are time-multiplexed, using an M.core to hold the state of each K.

Peripheral Switching.   For performance, communications, and reliability reasons it is necessary to provide access to K's, M's, or T's from several C's or Pio's. A sample structure of a possible configuration, using the above components, is given in Fig. 17. The PMS diagram also shows the physical structure of S[from:Pc; to:K].

The IBM System/370 Family

The first System/370 model was introduced in the summer of 1970. During a period of 7 years, a total of 23 different processor models were realized. Chapter 51 explains why IBM expanded the System/360 architecture into the System/370 and it also highlights the main differences between the two architectures. Figure 18 illustrates the introduction dates of the various System/ 370 models.

As in the System/360 series, microprogrammed processors were used extensively for processor implementation. In fact, only the System/370 Model 195 is a hardwired implementation. Control store words varied from 16 to 105 bits wide with a capacity of 1 to 64 kilowords. It is interesting to note that the total number of control store bits is relatively constant in all models of the System/370 series. The total number of bits ranges from 380K to 1,024K. If the models with support for OS in microcode are not

considered, the range is only 380 to 560 Kbit, with an average of 476 Kbit. This might indicate a basic complexity for representing the semantics of the System/370 ISP. The basic semantic complexity also holds for the System/360 ISP,[1] where the range of control store size is 128 to 263 Kbit. If the Model 25 and the high-performance Model 85 are ignored, the range is 200 to 240 Kbit, with an average of 220 Kbit. The System/370 implementations require generally twice the number of control store bits required by the System/360. Does this suggest that the semantic content of the System/370 ISP is twice that of the System/360 ISP?

Emulation of prior-generation ISPs is also a major feature of the 370 implementations. Emulators exist in one or more 370 models for the following: IBM 709, 1401, 1410, 1440, 1460, 7010, 7070, 7074, 7080, 7090, and 7094.

CPU cycle time varies from 54 to 480 ns, a 9:1 range. Memory cycle time ranges from 320 to 2,070 ns, a 6:1 range. Performance variations between models are also provided by varying the width of Pc data paths (1 to 8 bytes), the width of Pc-Mp data paths (2 to 16 bytes), the memory interleaving factor (1 to 16), the size of address translation buffers (0 to 128), the size of main memory cache (0 to 32 Kbyte), and the number of Pc functional units. These variations produce a performance range of 40:1 from the System/370 Model 115 (70 K instructions per second) to the System/370 Model 168-3 (2 to 7 MIPS). Inclusion of the 3030 series and multiprocessors pushes the performance range to over 100:1.

Logic Technology

Whereas the System/360 models are implemented in Solid Logic Technology (SLT) as described previously in this chapter, many 370 models are implemented in Monolithic System Technology (MST). An SLT chip usually contains one type of component (e.g., transistors or diodes), with multiple chips and resistors assembled in one package (i.e., a half-inch ceramic substrate with interconnections). MST is similar to SLT but integrates many elementary components (e.g., transistors, diodes, and resistors) on single chips which in turn are mounted several to a package. MST circuits in the System/370 Model 145 are about twice as fast as SLT circuits in the System/360 Model 40. MST logic takes up less space than SLT because of a higher packing density per chip. In the System/370 Model 145, an MST logic chip is about one-sixteenth of an inch square and contains over 100 components. An SLT chip contains only one component. Also, MST logic requires fewer off-chip interconnections than SLT logic and thus is more reliable.

[1]The PDP-11 series implementations ranged from 9,960 bits to 23,424 bits of control store, with an average of 15,942 bits. The VAX-11/780 requires about 390 Kbit.

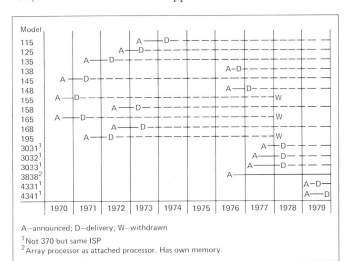

A—announced; D—delivery; W—withdrawn

[1] Not 370 but same ISP
[2] Array processor as attached processor. Has own memory.

Fig. 18. IBM System/370 model introduction dates.

PMS Structures and Implementations of the Computer

The PMS structures of the System/370 family members fall into three main classes. The Models 115 through 125 are low-performance distributed systems. The Models 135 through 158 are medium-performance machines that have the CPU and the channels sharing certain data paths and contending for micropro-gram control. The Models 165 through 195 are high-performance machines that have a great amount of overlap in CPU functions. They also have separately packaged channels. See Fig. 19 for a genealogical System/370 family tree. Each main trunk of the tree will be discussed individually.

Mid-Range Machines: Models 135, 138, 145, 148, 155, and 158. The medium-performance machines are the 135, 138, 145, 148, 155, and 158. These models have similar PMS structures. (See Fig. 20.)

The Models 155 and 165 were introduced in June 1970. These were the first 370 models to appear on the market. The 155 was marketed as a general growth system for System/360 Model 50 and large System/360 Model 40 users. Thus users could upgrade to the better price/performance ratio of the 155 with minimal software changes.

Although the 155 does not incorporate any technological

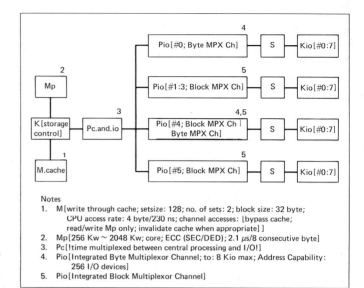

Notes
1. M[write through cache; setsize: 128; no. of sets: 2; block size: 32 byte; CPU access rate: 4 byte/230 ns; channel accesses: [bypass cache; read/write Mp only; invalidate cache when appropriate]]
2. Mp[256 Kw ~ 2048 Kw; core; ECC (SEC/DED); 2.1 μs/8 consecutive byte]
3. Pc[!time multiplexed between central processing and I/O!]
4. Pio[Integrated Byte Multiplexor Channel; to: 8 Kio max; Address Capability: 256 I/O devices]
5. Pio[Integrated Block Multiplexor Channel]

Fig. 20. IBM System/370 Model 155 PMS diagram.

breakthroughs, it is a relatively high-performance machine (see Fig. 21) on account of the following features:

- As do the System/360 Model 85 and the Model 195, the 155 has a cache memory of 8 Kbyte with a cycle time of 115 ns. This 8-Kbyte write-through cache has a set size of 128, an associativity (number of sets) of 2, and a block size of 32 bytes.[1] The channels never access the cache. When a channel writes to Mp in a location which is valid in the cache, the cache data are invalidated.

- The processor-memory data path is 8 bytes wide. Mp is core, with a 2-μs access time.

- When possible, instruction fetch and instruction execution are overlapped. However, operands are not prefetched.

The Pc and the channels share the Pc data paths and contend for microprogram control. The data paths are shared (time-multiplexed) by switching control between the Pc and the channels at well-defined points in the microprograms. When switching (called *break-in*) occurs, the current microprogram is stopped and the new one is given control. For example, once the channel is started, Pc and I/O operations can run concurrently until an I/O storage request occurs. Since the data path from storage is shared, the Pc microprogram stops and gives control to the channel microprogram.

[1]Since the basic Mp fetch is 16 bytes, blocks are loaded 16 bytes at a time. The second 16-byte half block is loaded upon demand, hence the 16×2 notation in Table 1.

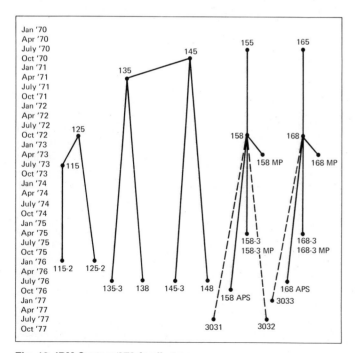

Fig. 19. IBM System/370 family tree.

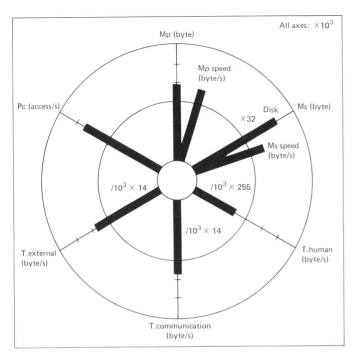

Fig. 21. IBM System/370 Model 155.

As shown in Fig. 22, the three basic data paths in the Pc consist of the following:

- A 4-byte path. This path includes adders, shifters, scratch-pad registers, and Pc and I/O local storage. Fixed-point, floating-point, and enhancement instructions (i.e., those peculiar to the 370 architecture) use this data path.

- A 1-byte data path. This path is used by variable–field-length instructions and single-byte operations. It is also used by certain emulations. Note that the 155 has the capability of emulating the 1401/1440/1460, 1410/7010, and 7070/7074 ISPs.

- An i-fetch path. This path is used for instruction pre-fetching. It includes buffers, counters, incrementers, and backup registers. Every data path in the Pc has byte parity.

The System/370 Model 145 was introduced in September 1970. It was marketed as a growth system for System/360 Model 40 and large System/360 Model 30 users. The medium-performance 145 was the first 370 to use monolithic (bipolar-semiconductor) main memory. This monolithic storage is similar to the monolithic logic previously described. Both 128-bit and 1-Kbit MST chips are used in the 145 memory.

It is interesting to note that a single, writable storage is used for both Mp and Mmicroprogram, the two memories being differentiated by their addresses. Eight bytes can be accessed at a time from Mp (540 ns for read, 608 ns for write) with no interleaving. The basic Pc data paths are 4 bytes wide, although an 8-byte path is used for instruction fetch. The Pc has a variable-length cycle time (203 to 315 ns).

As in the 155, the Pc and the channels share control storage, Pc-Mp data paths, and the Pc's ALU.

The microprogram can emulate the 1401/1440/1460 and 1410/7010 ISPs. The 145 provides for substantial flexibility in channel configuration. The 145-0 and 145-2 differ in their main storage capabilities (2,048K maximum for the Model 2, as opposed to 512K maximum for the Model 0). The Model 3 is an accelerated Model 2, the microcoding of many high-level operating-system functions being a standard feature. The Model 3 has 128 Kbyte of control store as standard, while the Models 0 and 2 have only 32 Kbyte.

The System/370 Model 135, a scaled-down version of the 145, was introduced in 1971. It was marketed as a growth system for 360 Models 20, 22, 25, and 30. Like the 145, the 135 uses monolithic (i.e., bipolar-semiconductor) Mp and Mmicroprogram.

Four bytes (as opposed to 8 bytes for the 145) can be accessed at a time from Mp (770 ns for read) with no interleaving. The basic CPU data paths are 2 bytes wide, although a 4-byte path is used for instruction fetch (no prefetching) and data access for certain instructions. The Pc has a variable-length microcycle time (275 to 1,485 ns). As in the 145 and 155, the Pc and the channels share control storage and some data paths.

The microprogram can emulate the 1401/1440/1460 ISPs. The 135 allows for a flexible I/O configuration, with direct attachment of various disk storage drives via an integrated file adapter, and direct attachment of up to eight communication lines.

The 135 Model 3 is an accelerated Model 0. The acceleration is basically due to larger Mp, larger Mmicroprogram, and certain high-level operating-system functions implemented in microcode.

The 158 and 168 were introduced in August 1972. Although the 158 is similar to the 155, it provides more processing power in smaller cabinets. It has a larger and faster Mp, and has an Integrated Control Storage (ICS) as an option. The ICS provides two data and control paths, each of which can attach to thirty-two IBM 3330, 3340, or 3350 series disk drives. Also, the 158 and 168 were the first System/370 machines to use MOS main memory (the 155 and 165 use core). It is interesting to note that the older 145 and 135 processor used bipolar Mp, the only two models in the 370 family to do so.

However, the main claim to fame and the real *raison d'être* of the 158 (and 168) is "virtual storage." The concept of virtual

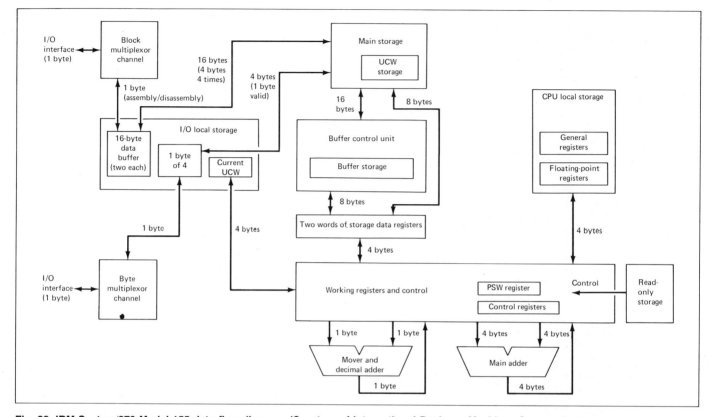

Fig. 22. IBM System/370 Model 155 data-flow diagram. *(Courtesy of International Business Machines Corporation.)*

storage was not implemented in prior processors, including the System/360 Model 67. The 158 and 168 were the first 370 models to incorporate this feature.

At the time of the 158-168 announcement, Dynamic Address Translation (DAT) hardware became available at no charge for the Models 135 and 145. It also became available as an expensive option for purchased Models 155 and 165.

IBM's multiple-processor philosophy is primarily oriented toward increased system throughput (as opposed to decreased time per job) and can be divided into three general categories: tightly coupled, loosely coupled, and peer-coupled. Tightly coupled systems consist of two processors sharing main storage and executing a single operating system. Loosely coupled systems consist of a number of processors coupled via channel-to-channel adapters. Each processor executes its own operating system and shares job queues. One processor is designated the controlling processor. Peer-coupled systems consist of multiple loosely coupled systems.

IBM's tightly coupled systems employ only high-performance processors, presumably to extend the System/370 performance range until the next set of technological advances provides a

higher-performance uniprocessor. One of two general forms is used: (1) multiprocessing (MP) with two Pc's, each with a complete set of I/O options, and (2) attached processors (AP) with two Pc's, one with and one without I/O options. Special instructions have been added for synchronization (e.g., COMPARE AND SWAP, and COMPARE AND DOUBLE SWAP). Also added were serialization (i.e., provisions to allow programs that execute on MP's to have the same storage-reference sequencing they would have if they were executed on a uniprocessor), interprocessor communication (SIGNAL PROCESSOR instruction), redundant time-of-day clocks, and cross-cache invalidation.

February 1973 brought forth the 158 MP. The 158 MP system consists of two 158's or two 158-3's, coupled by a 3058 Multisystem Unit. Channels belong to the Pc to which they are attached, although devices may be shared by using a special "two channel switch" feature. Memory can be configured so that some address space is dedicated to a particular Pc while other space is shared between both processors. Interprocessor communication is via an interrupt capability.

March 1975 saw the announcement of the 158-3. The 158-3 is a 158 with an expanded cache (16 Kbyte as opposed to 8 Kbyte).

Both the 8K and the 16K caches have a set size of 128. However, the 16K cache has an associativity of 4 while the 8K cache has an associativity of 2. Block size is 32 bytes.

In June 1976 the 138 and 148 were introduced. The 138 was announced to have a 29 to 36 percent internal performance increase over the 135, while the 148 was announced to have a 28 to 43 percent internal performance increase over the 145. Data Pro Research Corporation reports that the 138 and 148 cost about 45 percent less for purchase and approximately 22 percent less for rental than the 135 and 145. These machines use MOS Mp, whereas the 135 and 145 use bipolar. However, the MOS memories, created in 1976, of the 138 and 148 are faster than the bipolar memories created in 1971, of the 135 and 145. Also, during June 1976 the 135-3 and 145-3 were announced. They are upgraded versions of the 5-year-old (at that time) 135 and 145 models, and have internal performance equal to the newer 138 and 148, respectively.

Later, in October 1976, the 158 Attached Processor System (APS) was announced. Whereas the 158 MP of 1973 is a tightly coupled system, the 158 AP is even more tightly coupled. The IBM 3052 APU (Attached Processing Unit) and a 158 (or 158-3) are connected to form a dual-processor system, with shared memory and shared I/O. The 3052 APU (with a 115-ns cycle time) is a bare-bones instruction processor with no Mp and no channels. However, it does have a cache. The APU's writable control store (WCS) can execute all of the System/370 instructions, plus the 1401/1440/1460 and 1410/7010 ISPs. Although an AP system is less expensive than an MP system (because it has less hardware), it has lower performance. Contention for memory and I/O results in decreased throughput. The 158 AP yields only from 1.5 to 1.8 times the performance of one 158-3.

High-Range Machines: Models 165, 168, and 195. The high-performance machines consist of the 165, 168, and 195. See Fig. 23 for a PMS diagram of the 165.

The System/370 Model 165, introduced at the same time as the 155 (June 1970), was originally marketed as a high-speed growth system for System/360 Model 65 and 75 users. The 165 is a higher-performance machine than the 155 because of its wider data paths, greater concurrency of operations, and larger and faster memory.

Whereas the 155 has an 8-Kbyte cache, the 165 cache can be extended to 16 Kbyte. The 8K cache of the 165 is set-associative, with a set size of 64 and an associativity of 4. The 16K cache is simply an 8K cache with the set size increased from 64 to 128. Block size is 32 bytes. The channels write into the cache (i.e., cache write-through to Mp) but do not read from it.

An 8-byte data path between Pc and Mp with four-way interleaving yields 32 bytes fetched per Mp reference cycle (as opposed to 16 bytes for the 155).

The 165 has a greater amount of instruction fetch–execute

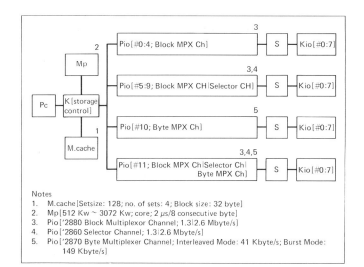

Notes
1. M.cache[Setsize: 128; no. of sets: 4; Block size: 32 byte]
2. Mp[512 Kw ~ 3072 Kw; core; 2 μs/8 consecutive byte]
3. Pio['2880 Block Multiplexor Channel; 1.3|2.6 Mbyte/s]
4. Pio['2860 Selector Channel; 1.3|2.6 Mbyte/s]
5. Pio['2870 Byte Multiplexer Channel; Interleaved Mode: 41 Kbyte/s; Burst Mode: 149 Kbyte/s]

Fig. 23. IBM System/370 Model 165 PMS diagram.

overlap than does the 155 because it uses larger buffers, operand prefetching, and more logic.

The 165 uses separate IBM 2860 Selector Channels, IBM 2870 Byte Multiplexor Channels, and/or IBM 2880 Block Multiplexor Channels (as opposed to having the channels share CPU logic, as in the 155). These channels contain the hardware to control their I/O operations. The 165 extended-channel feature provides a maximum of 12 channels.

The main elements of the Pc are the "Instruction Unit" and the "Execution Unit." (See Fig. 24.) The hardwired Instruction Unit performs fetching, decoding, and buffering of instructions, address calculation, and operand fetching and has partial control of the execution unit. The Instruction Unit contains two 16-byte instruction buffers, a 4-byte instruction register, three instruction-queue registers, a 24-bit, three-input adder, four 24-bit address registers, an incrementer, and a decoder. Two 16-byte instruction buffers are used, so that when a branch instruction is encountered, one buffer continues to prefetch sequential instructions (i.e., assumes the branch will be unsuccessful) while the other buffer prefetches instructions from the branch target location (i.e., assumes the branch will be successful).

The Execution Unit is capable of executing a new instruction each microcycle. It contains two 8-byte buffers for prefetched operands, four 8-byte data registers, and an 8-byte result register. There is a 64-bit parallel adder used for binary and floating-point arithmetic, a 32-bit ALU, a 64-bit shifter, and a 1-byte serial adder, which is used for SS-format instructions, floating-point exponent calculations, and packed decimal arithmetic. The basic data-path width in the execution unit is 8 bytes, with byte parity. While the microprogram controls the Execution Unit most of the

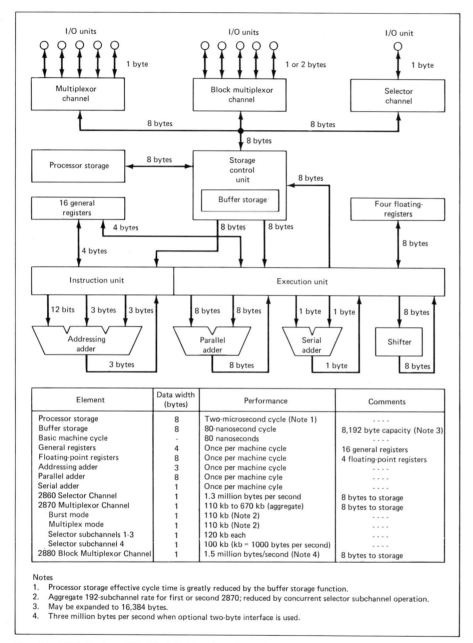

Fig. 24. IBM System/370 Model 165 data-flow diagram and system characteristics. (Courtesy of International Business Machines Corporation.)

time, hardwired control is used when data results determine the execution sequence (e.g., conditional branches).

The Pc can read four general registers and write into a fifth all in one microcycle. This, coupled with Instruction Unit and Execution Unit overlap, yields a great amount of concurrency in CPU operations.

The 80-ns control store contains both read only (ROS) and read/write memory. The WCS is well suited for microdiagnostics and various emulations. The 165 can emulate 7070/7074, 7080, and 709/7090/7094 ISPs.

The year 1971 also saw the introduction of the System/370 Model 195, a slightly upgraded version of the powerful System/360 Model 195. (See Fig. 25.) The 195 contains a 32-Kbyte cache memory with a set size of 128, a block size of 8 doublewords (64 bytes), and an associativity of 4.

A storage control unit (SCU) controls all fetching and storing from Mp, M.cache, and the channels. Sixteen-way memory interleaving, coupled with an 8-byte-wide data path from Mp to SCU, results in 128 bytes accessed per reference cycle. The SCU also contains much of the circuitry for cache control. A processor store always updates Mp, and updates M.cache if the location has previously been valid in the cache. However, I/O fetches and stores completely bypass the cache, invalidating cache data if necessary.

This hardwired machine (which has a 54-ns CPU cycle time) realizes a high degree of concurrency of operations. The central processing element (CPE) consists of the Instruction Processor, the fixed-point/variable–field-length (VFL)/decimal execution element, the floating-point execution element, and the System/370 execution unit.

The Instruction Processor (IP) fetches both instructions and operands, controls the other execution units, handles interrupts, and executes all branch, status-switching, and I/O instructions. (See Fig. 26.) The IP has an 8-doubleword instruction stack (4 times larger than that of the 165), three instruction-control registers, two doublewords of temporary instruction buffer, a decoder, and a three-input adder for effective-address calculation. The fixed-point/VFL/decimal execution element contains the general registers, which the IP uses.

The 8-doubleword instruction stack normally contains the current instruction to be decoded, a few doublewords of instructions already decoded (i.e., instruction history), and a few doublewords of instructions yet to be decoded. Three stack pointers, called the instruction-control registers, keep track of the stack. The instruction register (IR) points to the instruction being decoded. The upperbound register (UB) points to the most recent doubleword brought into the stack, and the lowerbound register (LB) points to the least recent doubleword in the stack.

The 8-doubleword stack allows tight loops to be executed totally within the stack (in what is called the *loop mode*). This is much more efficient than the 2-doubleword buffer of the 165, whose hardware does not provide for the execution of tight loops totally within the buffer.

Conditional mode is entered when a conditional branch is decoded for which the condition code has not yet been evaluated. When this occurs, the IP continues to fetch sequential instructions into the 8-doubleword stack. The sequential instructions prefetched still result in orders to the fixed-point and floating-point execution elements. However, these orders are specially tagged as being conditional, so that they cannot be decoded or

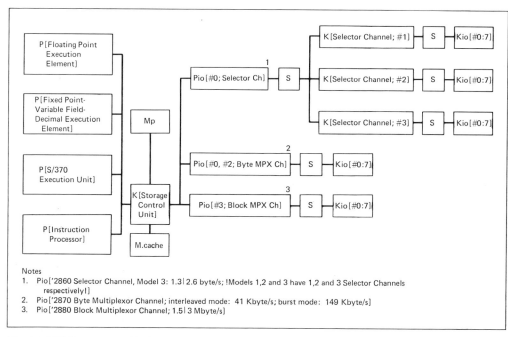

Notes
1. Pio['2860 Selector Channel, Model 3: 1.3|2.6 byte/s; !Models 1,2 and 3 have 1,2 and 3 Selector Channels respectively!]
2. Pio['2870 Byte Multiplexor Channel; interleaved mode: 41 Kbyte/s; burst mode: 149 Kbyte/s]
3. Pio['2880 Block Multiplexor Channel; 1.5|3 Mbyte/s]

Fig. 25. IBM System/370/Model 195 PMS diagram.

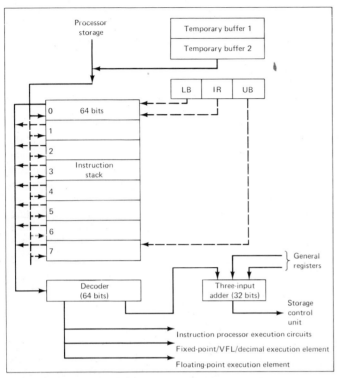

Fig. 26. IBM System/370 Model 195 instruction processor data-flow diagram. *(Courtesy of International Business Machines Corporation.)*

executed until the IP signals to do so. Two doublewords from the branch target location are also prefetched and stored in buffers.

In the highly concurrent 195, the various execution units can simultaneously execute different instructions. Therefore an exceptional condition cannot always be identified with the specific instruction causing it, since the PSW may be pointing to another instruction. This kind of program interruption is called *imprecise*. Imprecise interrupts are identified as such by setting certain bits in the PSW to a known state. Since all instructions decoded prior to the signaling of an imprecise interrupt are executed, more than one exception can occur for a given imprecise interrupt. Also, because instructions may be executing concurrently and out of sequence, the exceptional condition that causes the interrupt may not be the one that should be logically recognized first. In any case, each type of exception that takes place is identified in bits 16 through 27 of the old PSW, with bits 28 to 31 set to zero. There are certain instructions that are executed only after all previously decoded instructions are fully executed. Among these instructions are the six I/O instructions, LOAD PSW, SUPERVISOR CALL, SET STORAGE KEY, DIAGNOSE, STORE CHANNEL ID, LOAD CONTROL, and STORE CONTROL. Also, a special branch on condition (BCR) instruction (usually implemented as a

NOP on other 360 and 370 models) causes all previously decoded instructions in the stack to be executed before the decoding of the next instruction.

See Fig. 27 for a diagram of the fixed-point/VFL/decimal execution element. As its name implies, it executes fixed-point, logical, variable–field-length, and decimal instructions. Operations from the six-position fixed-point operation stack (FXOS) are decoded serially and issued to the appropriate execution units. If the data are available and the execution hardware is free, then the operation can be performed. After completion, the IP is notified that the FXOS position and associated operand buffers are free.

The floating-point execution element is highly efficient because it uses operand and instruction buffering and because it contains multiple execution units linked via a common data bus similar to that of the System/360 Model 91 (Chap. 19). (See Fig. 28.) The floating-point element contains an eight-position operation stack (FLOS), four floating-point registers (FLR), six operand buffers (FLB), and three execution units. The add unit, preceded by three reservation stations, can perform two add operations

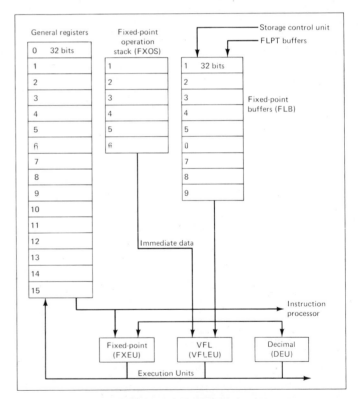

Fig. 27. IBM System/370 Model 195 fixed-point/VFL/decimal execution element data-flow diagram. *(Courtesy of International Business Machines Corporation.)*

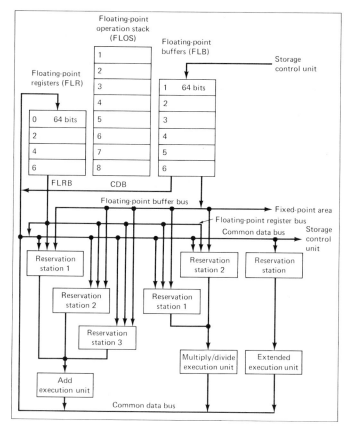

many channels as the Model 168 (22, as opposed to 11) and has a cache twice as large (32K, as opposed to 16K).

February 1973 brought forth the 168 MP. The 168 MP is similar to the 158 MP previously described. Two 168's or 168-3's are connected via a 3068 Multisystem Communication Unit (MCU).

In February 1976, the 168 Attached Processor System (APS) was introduced. Similar to the Model 158's 3052 AP in configuration, the 3062 AP (with an 80-ns cycle time) can execute all System/370 instructions except those involved with the "direct control" facility. The 168 AP yields only from 1.5 to 1.8 times the performance of one 168-3. It is possible that the 168, being a high-performance machine with a great amount of prefetching and buffering, is not well suited for use in a very tightly coupled system.

Low-Range Machines: Models 115 and 125. The low-performance machines consist of the Models 115 and 125.

The 125 was announced in October 1972. It was marketed as a growth system for System/360 Model 20 users. The low-performance 125 is implemented in a distributed fashion. (See the discussion of the Model 115.) Two bytes are fetched at a time from the MOS Mp, with no memory interleaving. Data paths are 2 bytes wide. There is no cache. The 480-ns WCS can emulate the 1401/1440/1460 ISPs.

The System/370 Model 115 was introduced in the spring of 1973. It was marketed as a growth system for users of System/360 Models 20, 22, and 25. It bridged the gap between the IBM System/360 and the higher-performance System/370 machines.

The virtual-storage Model 115, a distributed system, is very similar to the 125. The 115, being the lowest-performance 370, has 1-byte data paths (the 125 has 2-byte paths).

As shown in Fig. 29, the system contains three independent subprocessors. They are the Machine Instruction Processor (MIP), the Input/Output Processor (IOP), and the Service Processor (SVP). Each subprocessor has its own storage, working registers, ALU, and microprogram (MOSFET WCS).

Mp (which is MOS, and requires 480 ns for read/write, and from which 2 bytes are fetched per access, with no interleaving) is controlled by a hardwired Main Storage Controller (MSC). The MSC regularly checks requests for Mp access by the subprocessors, and grants the request with the highest priority. The MSC and the subprocessors communicate via a data bus, a control bus, and direct control lines.

The MIP basically fetches and executes program instructions. The IOP executes I/O commands and supervises the data transfer between the MSC and I/O devices. The interface between the operator and the rest of the system is the SVP. It loads microcode into the subprocessors and boots itself from the console file.

The 115 does not support any block multiplexor or selector channels. However, a byte multiplexor channel can be imple-

Fig. 28. IBM System/370 Model 195 floating-point execution element data-flow diagram. (Courtesy of International Business Machines Corporation.)

concurrently by offsetting them by one cycle. The third reservation station can acquire data while the other two operations are executing. The multiply/divide execution unit has two reservation stations. Only one multiply or divide operation can be executed at a time. The extended execution unit, with one reservation station, handles extended-precision floating-point operands.

The FLOS has its instructions decoded serially. The FLOS issues operations provided that an appropriate reservation station is available. Since several operations may be executing concurrently, dependent operations are sequenced through the use of tagging on the common data bus.

The 168 was introduced in August 1972. It has the same advantages over the 165 that the 158 has over the 155, i.e., more processing power in smaller cabinets, larger and faster Mp (MOS), and an Integrated Storage Controller as an option. At the same time that the virtual-storage 168 was announced, Dynamic Address Translation (DAT) hardware became available as an expensive option for the 165.

In March 1975 the 168-3 was announced. The 168-3 has twice as

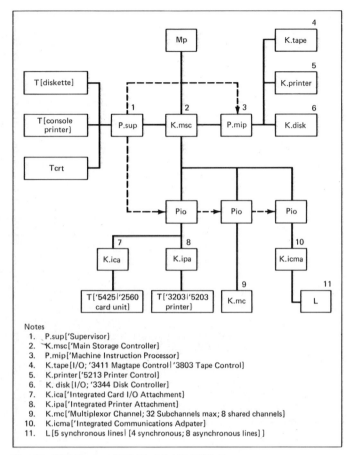

Notes
1. P.sup['Supervisor]
2. K.msc['Main Storage Controller]
3. P.mip['Machine Instruction Processor]
4. K.tape[I/O; '3411 Magtape Control|'3803 Tape Control]
5. K.printer['5213 Printer Control]
6. K. disk[I/O; '3344 Disk Controller]
7. K.ica['Integrated Card I/O Attachment]
8. K.ipa['Integrated Printer Attachment]
9. K.mc['Multiplexor Channel; 32 Subchannels max; 8 shared channels]
10. K.icma['Integrated Communications Adapter]
11. L[5 synchronous lines| [4 synchronous; 8 asynchronous lines]]

Fig. 29. IBM System/370 Model 115 PMS diagram.

mented by using an IOP. Also, some I/O devices can be connected to the MIP with direct attachment features.

The 115-2 and 125-2 were announced in November 1975. The 115-2 split the 115's Machine Instruction Processor into two separate units: a dedicated I/O processor for 3340 disks, and an Instruction Processing Unit.

The 115-2 and 125-2 have higher performance, greater I/O capabilities, and bigger Mp's than the 115 and 125, respectively.

3030 Series Machines

In March 1977, the Model 3033 processor was introduced, and in October of that same year, the Models 3031 and 3032 were announced. The 3030 processors have enhanced price/perform-ance characteristics over their predecessors. High-level operat-ing-system functions are supported in microcode. The 3031 can be configured as an AP system, while the 3033 can be configured as either an MP or an AP system.

The 3031 has a 115-ns Pc microcycle time, a 32-Kbyte cache, and six integrated channels (one byte multiplexor and five block multiplexors). The 3031 yields approximately 1.2 times the performance of a System/370 Model 158-3 [Data Pro, 1978].

The 3032 has an 80-ns Pc microcycle time, a 32-Kbyte cache, and six integrated channels. The system can be extended to include 12 integrated channels. The 3032 yields approximately 2.75 times the performance of a System/370 Model 158-3 [Data Pro, 1978].

The 3033 is a performance-enhanced System/370 Model 168-3 [Connors, Florkowski, and Patton, 1979]. Technology improve-ments reduced gate delays from 1.7 ns to 1 ns, cache access time from 32 ns to 27 ns, Mp access time from 210 ns to 185 ns, and Pc cycle time from 80 to 58 ns. Cache size, block size, and associativity were all doubled, yielding a 92 percent hit ratio. Memory interleaving was increased from four-way to eight way. Instruction prefetch buffer (branch and no branch cases) size was increased from two to four doublewords, operand address and data buffer were increased from two to six doublewords, and a third buffer was added for the situation where a second branch is encountered prior to the resolution of a previously encountered branch. Instruction decoding and address generation was de-creased from two cycles to one. The 3033 provides 12 channels as standard, divided into two groups of six, and four optional channels. Unlike the 168's stand-alone channels, those of the 3033 are accessible by the service processor, and the group concept allows maintenance, including microdiagnostics, to be performed on one group of channels while the other group is being used for customer work. Each byte multiplexor channel is capable of a data rate of from 40 Kbyte to 75 Kbyte per second, while a block multiplexor channel is capable of up to 1.5 Mbyte. The 3033 system requires one-half of the space and 30 percent less power than a similarly configured 168. Performance is 1.8 to 1.9 times that of a 168. Both the 3033 MP and 3033 AP are rated at 1.6 to 1.8 times the performance of a uniprocessor 3033.

4300 Series Machines

In January 1979 the models 4331 and 4341 were announced, thus launching the 4300 series. The series is implemented with IBM's bipolar gate arrays, with up to 704 gates/chip at 3-ns switching speeds and 64-Kbit MOS memory chips. The 4300 series added 12 new instructions to the System/370 ISP.

The 4331 is rated at 0.88 to 0.99 times the performance of, requires 70 percent less power than, and costs approximately 28 percent as much as the System/370 Model 138. The 4331 features a 64K writable control store, dynamic address translation, storage protection, a time-of-day clock, support for remote diagnostics, and a support processor for monitoring and recording environ-mentally caused problems such as power variances. The Pc also requires from 16 to 53 Kbyte of main memory for extra control store capacity. An integrated DASD (Direct Access Storage Device) adapter allows the direct attachment (without controllers or channels) of four strings of disk storage. One byte multiplexor channel and one block multiplexor channel are provided for attachment of a variety of System/360 and System/370 peripherals. The channel data rate for the byte multiplexor channel is 18 Kbytes in byte mode and 500 Kbyte in burst mode. The block multiplexor channel has a 500 Kbyte/s maximum data transfer rate. A Communications Adapter allows for attachment of up to eight communications lines operating from 75 bits/s to 56 Kbit/s. Two of the following line protocols can be supported simultaneously: Synchronous Data Link Control (SDLC), Binary Synchronous Control (BSC), and asynchronous line.

The 4341 has two modes of operation (corresponding to whatever microcode is loaded): (1) System/370-compatible mode with Extended Control Program Support for VM/VS software and (2) Extended Control Program Support: Virtual Storage Extended. The latter mode is unique to the 4341, yet is basically compatible with the System/370. The 4341 is rated at 3.2 times the performance of the System/370 Model 138 while costing 6 percent less. Figure 30 depicts the overall organization of the 4341. A portion of Mp, ranging from 14 to 108 Kbyte, is required for dynamic table storage. A separate support processor controls initialization (initial microcode loading), error analysis and logging, and the display console. The Remote Support Facility (RSF) provides the capability of remotely controlling the 4341 from an IBM service center. Diagnostics can be executed remotely and error information sent back to the service center. RSF, ECC (SEC/DED) Mp, Pc parity checks, instruction retry, channel command retry, and internal-state logout provide a comprehensive reliability/maintainability environment.

The 4341 I/O channels, with a few variations, are identical to those of the System/360 and System/370. One byte multiplexor and up to five block multiplexor channels can be configured. The byte multiplexor channel operating in byte-interleaved mode permits several low-speed devices to operate concurrently at up to 32 Kbyte/s if no block multiplexor channels are operating. It can also operate in burst mode, allowing one high-speed device at a time to function at a maximum rate of 1 Mbyte/s. Two block multiplexor channels are standard and three more are optional. Each block multiplexor is capable of a maximum data rate of 1 Mbyte/s. The total system data rate is limited to 9 Mbyte/s.

The PMS Structure of the System 370 Pio, K, Ms, and T

The System/370 peripheral structure has resulted from a slow evolution of the System/360 peripheral structure. The PMS diagrams for the System/370 have been laid out to allow a quick comparison with the System/360 PMS diagrams. In many cases, the System/370 PMS diagrams are a superset of the System/360 diagrams.[1] Thus while some peripherals have been discontinued, IBM continues to support other System/360 peripherals.

[1]The rate of change of the PMS diagrams is directly related to the rate of change of the major technology composing the PMS structure. Thus, as indicated in Part 1, Sec. 2, the Pc, based on electronic technology, changes fastest. Ms, composed of electronic, magnetic, and mechanical technologies, changes at the next highest rate. Indeed, there is only one carryover between the System/360 and System/370 Ms PMS diagrams. The rate of change of magnetic tape, which has a large component of mechanical technology, is slower still than Ms technology. The slowest rate of change is exhibited by paper-handling peripherals (e.g., paper-tape devices, card reader/punches, and line printers), which are essentially mechanical technologies. Thus technologists seek higher performance by seeking ways to replace mechanical technology by electronic technology (e.g., electrostatic units for printing, charge-coupled devices or magnetic bubbles for Ms).

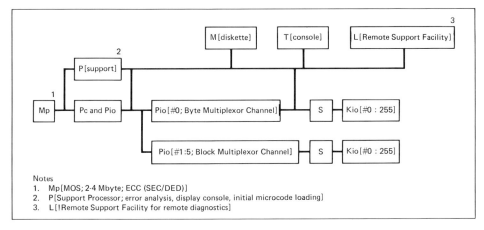

Notes
1. Mp[MOS; 2-4 Mbyte; ECC (SEC/DED)]
2. P[Support Processor; error analysis, display console, initial microcode loading]
3. L[!Remote Support Facility for remote diagnostics]

Fig. 30. IBM 4341 PMS diagram.

The major I/O port for the System/360 processors above the Model 50 was either a 2860 Selector Channel (for high-speed devices) or a 2870 Multiplexor Channel (for low-speed devices). The System/370 added the 2880 Block Multiplexor Channel to support even higher-speed, block-data–oriented peripherals. A major departure from the System/360 I/O architecture is the integration of controller/channels at the high end and adapters at the low end into the Pc cabinet, which eliminates cost and performance penalties of stand-alone cabinets.

Figure 31 depicts secondary storage for System/370 processors. The multipurpose 2841 Storage Control has given way to the 3830. The System/370 utilizes high-speed fixed-head disks for

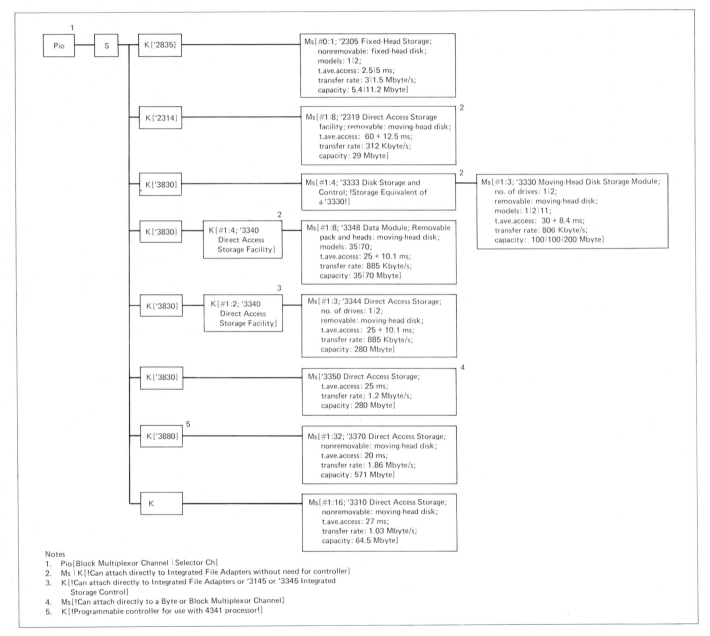

Notes
1. Pio[Block Multiplexor Channel | Selector Ch]
2. Ms | K[!Can attach directly to Integrated File Adapters without need for controller]
3. K[!Can attach directly to Integrated File Adapters or '3145 or '3345 Integrated Storage Control]
4. Ms[!Can attach directly to a Byte or Block Multiplexor Channel]
5. K[!Programmable controller for use with 4341 processor!]

Fig. 31. IBM System/370 Ms [disk] PMS diagrams.

swapping store rather than the high-speed drums used in the System/360. Hence drum storage has been discontinued. The increased storage capacity of disks partially fulfills the requirement for online archival memory as represented by the discontinued System/360 Data Cell magnetic card technology. Disks thus evolved as the dominant MS technology, as graphically indicated by comparing Figs. 31 and 13. New technologies, such as charge-coupled devices or magnetic bubbles, may eventually replace disks as the dominant Ms technology, just as the disks replaced drums. However, disks will remain the dominant Ms technology for at least the next several years.

Figure 32 depicts the growth in magnetic tape peripherals over those of the System/360. The System/360 Hypertape was discontinued.

Figure 33 shows the two card punches, the card reader, and the three card reader/punch units of the System/360, which were augmented for the System/370 by the addition of three reader/punch units. A lower-performance paper-tape reader has been added to the 1000 character per second 2671. A wider range of line printer models (six instead of one) is offered with the System/370, including an electrostatic printer that is 8 times faster than the highest-performance System/360 mechanical line printer. The System/370, like the System/360, offers a range of commercial-document readers, including magnetic character readers, optical readers (for printed, marked, and hand-printed documents), and document-processing units (for semiautomatic document-information input).

Finally, Fig. 34 illustrates that front-end processors have replaced the System/360's simple controllers for communication lines.

Performance and Cost

The IBM System/360 and System/370 series provide a number of data points in the implementation space for a common ISP. Furthermore, being marketed by a single organization, they are probably constrained by a common corporate profit goal. In this section, we will focus on Pc-Mp cost, performance, and cost/performance. Costs vary over time as technology and marketing competition change. However, we can plot cost as a function of time. Performance is more difficult to determine, since it depends on system configuration, software quality, and work load. IBM will announce relative performance ratios for Pc's but will not divulge absolute measures such as mega-instructions per second. Finally, cost/performance is extremely difficult to calibrate because of the many variables impacting both cost and performance.

Price

Figure 35 depicts the price of IBM memory per byte as a function of year. The slope of the line indicates an average decrease in the

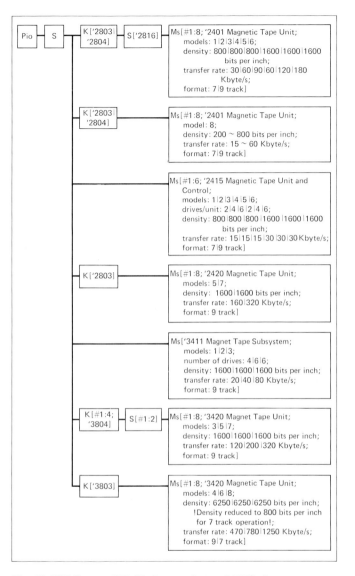

Fig. 32. IBM System/370 Ms [magnetic tape] PMS diagram.

cost of memory per byte of 19 percent per year from the introduction date of the first System/360. Figure 36 plots the price of disk storage, indicating a 21 percent decrease per year in cost.

Unlike memory, where there is essentially one dominant technology at any given time, a plot of processor cost is not very meaningful, because of the wide range in processor performance. Processor evaluation must wait until we discuss performance.

Performance

As indicated, determining the performance of a processor is very difficult because of all the variables that determine performance.

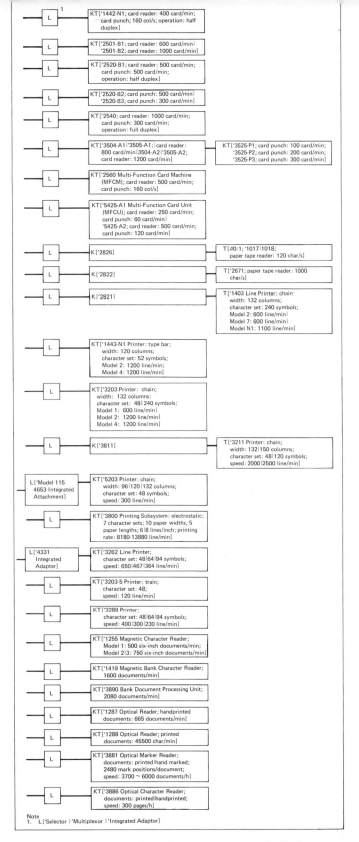

Fig. 33. IBM System/370 T [reader; punch; printer] PMS diagram.

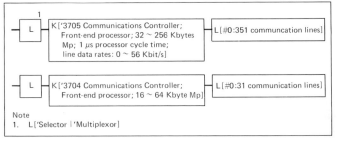

Fig. 34. IBM System/370 communications PMS diagrams.

This is especially true if only one performance number is sought. Table 3 indicates the different results of measuring performance that are quoted in the literature. Both *Electronics* and Dean Witter Reynolds present raw performance ranges in unspecified environments and work loads. Data Pro presents relative processor model performances, again in unspecified situations. *Computer World* (February 5, 1979) provides both raw and relative performance. The COBOL benchmarks represent a synthetic benchmark composed of 11 operations typically found in COBOL application programs. Each test is executed 100,000 times. The COBOL Analysis System (CAS) has been run in 125 different hardware/software environments representing 13 major manufacturers. The first test was run in 1965. Distributed by U.S. Steel, the CAS results allow relative comparisons between various hardware/compiler/operating-system environments on a uniform task. Figure 37 is a compilation of the relative performances of most of the IBM models.

We have attempted to model System/360 and System/370 performance by a simple model relating performance to microcycle time and memory pause time per byte:

$$1/p = k_1 t_1 + k_2 t_2$$

where t_1 is the time for one microcycle and t_2 is the memory pause time per byte. The time for t_2 is the memory access time minus the microcycle time, increased to the next higher multiple of a microcycle and then divided by the number of bytes fetched per memory reference cycle. The same model has been applied to the PDP-11 and resulted in a good fit (see Chap. 39).

Three sources of relatively complete performance data were available: the average instruction time, as used in Bell and Newell [1971] (add up all instruction times and divide by the number of instructions); the relative performance from Data Pro; and the COBOL benchmarks. The average instruction time was not used, since it varied significantly from the more detailed sources (see Table 4).

The data for each machine are given in Tables 5 and 6. The performance is relative to the System/360 Model 30. Where a

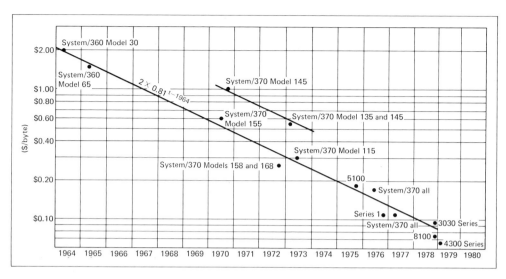

Fig. 35. IBM memory price history. (11 years = factor of 10.)

model is found in both tables, the relative performances agree within a factor of 1.5. A linear regression was applied to both sets of data to determine the coefficients k_1 and k_2 and to find out how much of the variance was explained by the model.

The first question to answer is, Do the System/360 and System/370 constitute one or two families? Figure 37 plots the relative average instruction time versus the microcycle time for both the COBOL benchmark and Data Pro data. It can be seen that the curve through the System/360 processors is substantially displaced with respect to the System/370 curve. The regression analysis upheld this observation.

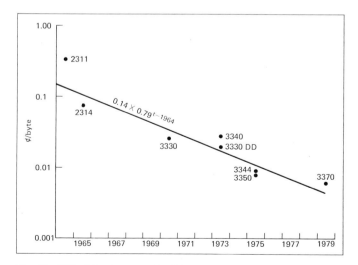

Fig. 36. IBM disk storage price history.

Applying the regression model to the four System/360 processors in Table 5 yielded $k_1 = 8.32 \times 10^{-4}$, $k_2 = 1.19 \times 10^{-4}$, $k_1/k_2 = 7$, and $R^2 = .88$. R^2 is the amount of variance accounted for by the model, or 88 percent. The large ratio of k_1/k_2 indicates that the Pc microcycle time is the dominating factor in determining System/360 performance, almost to the exclusion of memory system performance. Thus System/360 models are processor-bound, or memory subsystems are overdesigned with respect to the processing engine. This mismatch was observed in a different way in the prior discussions on the System/360 Model 67 and the System/360 Model 91.

The regression model was applied to the six System/370 models in Table 5 (the Model 125 was excluded to give a better fit), yielding $k_1 = 4.8 \times 10^{-4}$, $k_2 = 2.1 \times 10^{-3}$, $k_1/k_2 = 0.2285$, and $R^2 = .99$. In the System/370 series the processor is no longer the system bottleneck.

The regression model was also applied to the fifteen System/370 models in Table 6, yielding $k_1 = 7.34 \times 10^{-4}$, $k_2 = 6.51 \times 10^{-4}$, $k_1/k_2 = 1.13$, and $R^2 = .90$. The differences between the two System/370 models represent variation in System/370 performance in different task environments. Indeed, the smaller k_1 (less processor-bound) and larger k_2 (more memory-bound) for the COBOL benchmarks seem to indicate that the System/370 is tuned to the COBOL task. This observation corresponds to the consistently higher relative performance of the COBOL benchmarks in Table 3.

Price/Performance

The System/360 cost is based on dollars per second to rent the equipment. The figures were derived at one point in time from

Table 3   Measures of Performance of System/370 Models

Model number	Electronics performance (mips)[a]	Computer World performance (mips)[b]	Dean Witter Reynolds performance (mips)[c]	Electronics performance relative to Model 135	Data Pro performance relative to Model 135[d]	Computer World performance relative to Model 135	COBOL benchmark performance relative to Model 135[e]
135	0.12–0.16	.18	....	1.0	1.0	1.0	1.0
138	0.15–0.20	.2	....	1.28	1.34	1.11	....
145	0.23–0.3	.3	0.4	2.0	1.87	....	2.29
148	0.33–0.43	.4	0.5	2.86	2.66	2.28	....
158-3	0.7–0.9	....	0.9	5.72	5.65	4.27	13.38
168-3	2.5–2.7	....	2.5	18.57	15.68	....	28.53
3031	....	....	1.1	....	....	5.13	....
3032	....	....	2.5	....	....	....	....
3033	4.5–4.9	....	5.0	33.57	....	21.18	....
4331	....	.2	0.2	....	....	....	....
4341	....	.5	....	....	....	....	....

[a]From A. Durniak, "Soviet Computers: Better than Expected," *Electronics,* Sept. 28, 1978, pp. 85–86.

[b]*Computer World,* Feb. 5, 1979.

[c]Dean Witter Reynolds, Inc., *Random Access Monthly,* June 1978, p. 4.; March 1980, p. 5.

[d]Data Pro [1978].

[e]U.S. Steel [1978].

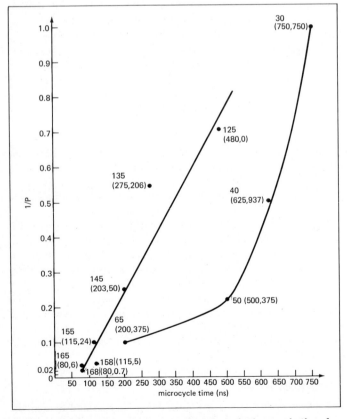

Fig. 37. Relative performance as a function of microcycle time for the IBM System/360 and IBM System/370 series.

the IBM monthly rental prices. The computer prices are based on estimates of minimum, average, and maximum configurations in the *Adams Computer Characteristics Quarterly* [Adams Associates, 1960]. The conversion factors are

$$1 \text{ month} = 1 \text{ month} \times 173.3 \text{ h/month} \times 3{,}600 \text{ s/h}$$
$$= 0.625 \times 10^6 \text{s}$$

The price to buy, in dollars, is approximately

$$\text{Purchase price (\$)} = 45 \times \text{price(\$/month)}†$$
$$= 45 \times 0.625 \times 10^6 \times \text{price(\$/s)}$$
$$= 2.82 \times 10^7 \times \text{price(\$/s)}$$

Three costs are calculated:

Pc(price: ($/s|$)): =   c.Pc: = price of Pc alone

Mp(price.avg): = c.Mp.avg: = price of average-size Mp for a model

C(price.min.): =   c.C.min: = price of minimum-size computer configuration

C(price.avg.): =   c.C.avg: = price of average-size computer configuration

The relative System/360 Pc powers (in instructions per second)

†As of 1977 the purchase/lease ratio on some System/370 systems was as low as 35:1.

Table 4 Relative Performance as Computed from Average Instruction Time and COBOL Benchmarks

	Performance relative to the Model 30	
Model	Bell and Newell [1971]	COBOL benchmarks
30	1	1
40	3	2
50	7.5	4.5
65	31.5	11.5

and prices are given in the graph of Fig. 38. The most significant fact from the graph is that the price/power ratio is roughly constant for each of the Pc's (especially if we ignore Model 44 and Model 50). Figure 38 gives the relative computing power versus price for various configurations.

The performance of C['20] is inaccurately high, since it is a limited subset of the 360 ISP. (C['20] does not have floating-point or fixed-point multiply and divide instructions, and it has only eight 16-bit general registers.) The hardwired Model 44 has a

Table 5 COBOL Benchmarks

Model	p	$1/p$	$t_{\mu c}(ns)$		t_p	
30	1	1	750	[2.4]	750	[3.46]
40	2	0.5	625	[2.0]	937	[9.32]
50	4.5	0.22	500	[1.6]	375	[1.73]
65	10	0.1	200	[0.64]	375	[0.173]
125	1.4	0.71	480	[1.5]	0	
135	1.8	0.55	275	[0.88]	206	[0.949]
145	4	0.25	203	[0.65]	50	[0.23]
155	10	0.1	115	[0.37]	24	[0.11]
158-3	23.7	0.04	115	[0.37]	5	[0.023]
165	31.7	0.03	80	[0.26]	6	[0.028]
168-3	50.5	0.02	80	[0.26]	0.7	[0.003]

$1/p = c_1 t_{\mu c} + c_2 t_p$

Bracketed quantities are normalized wrt average

For $t_{\mu c}, t_p$ normalized:

$\left.\begin{array}{l} c_1 = .40 \\ c_2 = .05 \end{array}\right\}$ 360 & 370 $R^2 = .87$

$\left.\begin{array}{l} c_1 = .31 \\ c_2 = .0038 \end{array}\right\}$ $\begin{array}{l} 360 \ \& \ 370 \quad R^2 = .85 \\ \text{without 125} \end{array}$

$\left.\begin{array}{l} c_1 = .15 \\ c_2 = .46 \end{array}\right\}$ $\begin{array}{l} 370 \quad R^2 = .99 \\ \text{without 125} \end{array}$

$\left.\begin{array}{l} c_1 = .26 \\ c_2 = .026 \end{array}\right\}$ 360 $R^2 = .88$

$t_{\mu c}$ = time for one micro cycle
tp = memory pause time per byte

Table 6 Data Pro Evaluation of the System/370

Model	p	$1/p$	$t_{\mu c}$	t_p
125-2	1.8	0.55	320	160
135	2.9	0.34	275	206
135-3	3.8	0.26	275	206
138	3.9	0.26	275	206
145	5.45	0.18	203	50
145-3	7.1	0.14	180	45
148	7.7	0.13	180	45
155	10	0.1	115	24
155-2	10	0.1	115	24
158	15	0.07	115	5
158-3	16.4	0.06	115	5
165	34.5	0.03	80	6
165-2	34.5	0.03	80	6
168	41.8	0.02	80	0.7
168-3	45.5	0.02	80	0.7

better price/power characteristic than any of the other C's, by any measured criteria (see Fig. 38). In the case of the Model 44, the Pc price also includes Ms.disk. Perhaps the Model 44, designed initially for real time scientific problem solving, is priced more competitively with similar machines (DEC PDP-10 and SDS Sigma 5, 7), whereas the other models compete in a performance-insensitive, competition-free market for general-purpose business data processing. Thus its anomalous position may be due to external market pressures and not manufacturing cost.

The design of the IBM System/360 models is undoubtedly predicated on the basis that performance or computing power is proportional to the price raised to some power g:power = $k \times$ price^g, where $g > 1$.[1] Almost all models follow the above relationship with $g > 1$. When $g > 1$, there is an advantage to having large configurations, since the price/computation will decrease. If $g \le 1$, then an alternative implementation for the 360 C's would simply use multiple C's or Pc's to obtain the same power. Unfortunately, such an approach does not provide for the interconnection of the components to function as a single unit. In many cases, a single task cannot be broken into a number of parallel and independent subtasks. If the performance for the system varied by a factor of 100, then 100 Pc's or C's would be placed together.

The following discussion takes computing power to be measured by instructions per second and Mp [size; t.cycle]. Prices are measured in dollars per second of rental time. The graph (Fig. 39) shows the relationship to computing power p and prices. The power (actually p.Pc) is taken from the measures of instruction

[1]Herb Grosch [Grosch, 1953] first noted this relationship and estimated g to be 2; thus we use g for this exponent. Adams suggested $g = \frac{1}{2}$ [Adams, 1962]. See also Sharpe [1969].

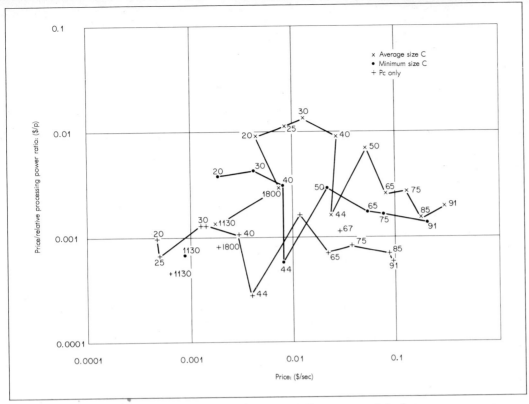

Fig. 38. Graph of IBM System/360 cost/processing power ratio versus rental price.

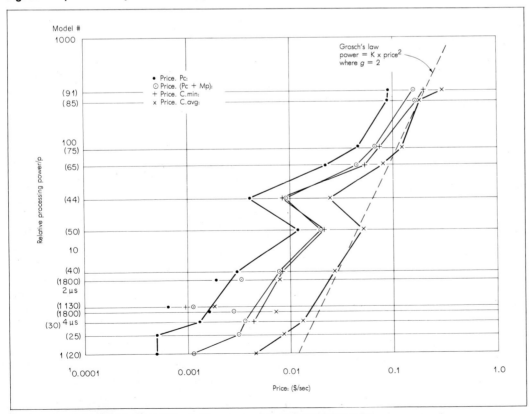

Fig. 39. Graph of IBM System/360 relative processing power versus price.

times for certain fixed work. Solomon [1966] observed Grosch's law to hold for Models 30, 40, 50, 65, and 75. This line is drawn in Fig. 39 for C(price.average). Considering Models 20, 25, 44, 85, and 91, a line with a less steep slope might fit the points better. If we consider C(price.minimum), $g > 2$; considering only Pc, a $g = 1$ might be appropriate (see Fig. 39) for which the Pc power/price is essentially constant with cost.

Pc(price)/Mp(price.avg): = c.Pc/avg.Mp = ~ 1.1, the ratio of processor to memory price

C(price.min)/C(price.avg): = c.min.C/avg.C = ~ 0.47, the ratio of the smallest computer configuration to an average configuration

Pc(price)/C(price.avg): = c.Pc/c.avg.C = ~ 0.23, the ratio of processor to computer price

These are averages over all the series and can be rather misleading. For example, in higher-numbered models the C(price.min)/C(price.avg): = c.min.C/c.avg.C is about 0.6, whereas in lower-numbered models the ratio is 0.3. We might have expected this, since it indicates that a higher proportion of system cost is in Ms and T on lower-number models.

The price for the System/370 series is based on purchase price. Figure 40 gives the relative computing power versus price for a Pc

with average Mp size. Again, the price/power ratio is almost constant with at most a 3:1 variation. The best-performing models seem to be the replacement models (i.e., the 138 for the 135, the 148 for the 145). Presumably, newer technology and packaging yielded an increase in performance. Models 165 and 168 are clear price/performance leaders.

Figure 41 plots the relative performance to purchase price for various processor models and minimum to maximum memory size. Grosch's law is also plotted. It appears that the System/370 series follows a power law with $g \sim 1.6$.

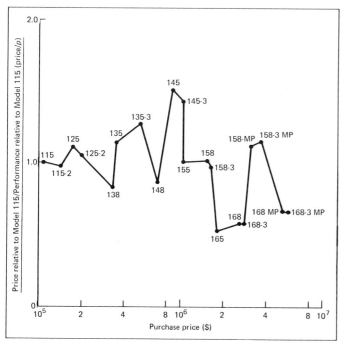

Fig. 40. Graph of IBM System/370 cost/processing power ratio versus purchase price.

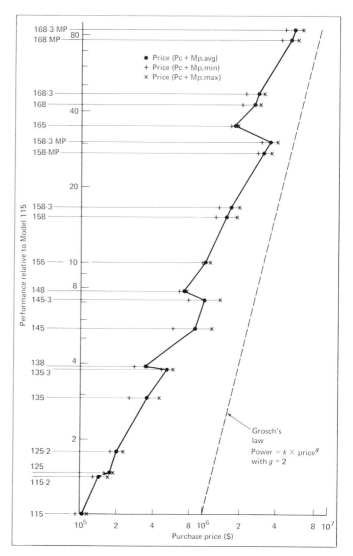

Fig. 41. Graph of IBM System/370 relative processing power versus price.

Conclusions

The IBM System/360 and System/370, by achieving a production record, have fulfilled this principal design objective. The technical goals, however, are of interest to us here. The most interesting aspect of the design is achieving a performance range and a primary memory size range each in excess of 100:1 for both series. Thus a user is given a very large set of configuration alternatives.

There is a vast array of secondary memory and terminal devices to couple with almost any other system. The System/360 is the first computer to make extensive use of microprogramming. Microprogramming is used for the definition of the System/360 instruction-set processor, but more important, microprograms define previous IBM computers so that a user can operate satisfactorily during the interim period when older programs are being updated to use the System/360. Microprogramming also plays a major role in the System/370. There are provisions for multicomputer structures. Within a single computer structure there is adequate means of peripheral switching so that reliable and high-performance structures can be assembled.

References

Adams [1962]; Amdahl, Blaauw, and Brooks [1964]; Arden et al. [1966]; Bell and Newell [1971]; Connors, Florkowski, and Patton [1979]; Conti, Gibson, and Pitkowsky [1968]; Data Pro [1978]; Grosch [1953]; Sharpe [1969]; Solomon [1966]; Tucker [1967]; U.S. Steel [1978]; Wilkes [1965].

Selected Bibliography

Architecture and logical structure: Amdahl, Blaauw, and Brooks [1964]; Blaauw [1964]; Blaauw and Brooks [1964]. General implementations: Amdahl [1964]; Carter et al. [1964]; Padegs [1964]; Stevens [1964]. Microprogramming: Greene, Dean, and Updike [1964]; Tucker [1967]; Weber [1967]. Formal description of Pc: Falkoff, Iverson, and Sussenguth [1964]. Performance and reviews: Hillegass [1966]; Solomon [1966]. Model 40 modifications for multiprogramming: Lindquist, Seeber, and Comeau [1966]. Model 67: Arden et al. [1966]; Fikes, Lauer, and Vareha [1968]; Gibson [1966]; Lauer [1967]. Model 85: Conti [1964]; Liptay [1968]; Padegs [1968]. Model 91 architecture and technology: Anderson, Sparacio, and Tomasulo [1967]; Anderson et al. [1967]; Boland et al. [1967]; Flynn and Low [1967]; Langdon and Van Derveer [1967]; Lloyd [1967]; Sechler, Strube, and Turnbull [1967]. Servicability: Carter et al. [1964]. IBM reference manuals: System/360 and System/370 functional characteristics manuals for each model; System/360 and System/370 configurator (diagram) for each model; System/360 Principles of Operation; System/360 System Summary; processor facts folders for the 4331 and 4341; *Guide to the System/370 Model 135; Guide to the System/370 Model 145*, 6th ed.; *Guide to the System/370 Model 155*, 1st ed.; product announcements for the System/370 Models 135 and 145, System/370 Model 138, System/370 Model 148, and System/370 Model 168; *4341 Processor Functional Characteristics and Processor Complex Configurator.*

Section 6

Evolution of CDC/CRAY Computers

The evolution of the CDC 6600/7600/CYBER series and the CRAY-1 is described in Part 3, Sec. 4. Chapters 43 and 44 discuss the CDC 6600 and CRAY-1, respectively.

Bibliography

Abbreviations

ACM	Association for Computing Machinery
AFIPS	American Federation of Information Processing Societies
Comm.	Communications
Comp.	Computer(s)
Compcon	Computer Conference
Conf.	Conference
Dig.	Digest
EJCC	Eastern Joint Computer Conference
Elect.	Electronic
FJCC	Fall Joint Computer Conference
IEE	Institute of Electrical Engineers, London
IEEE	Institute of Electrical and Electronic Engineers
IFIP	International Federation for Information Processing
IRE	Institute of Radio Engineers
J.	Journal
NBS	National Bureau of Standards
NCC	National Computer Conference
Proc.	Proceedings
Rel.	Reliability
Res. and Dev.	Research and Development
SIGPLAN	Special Interest Group on Programming Languages
SJCC	Sprint Joint Computer Conference
Soft.	Software
Supp.	Supplement
Symp.	Symposium
Tech. Dev.	Technical Developments
Trans.	Transactions
WJCC	Western Joint Computer Conference

Sources

Abramson [1970]: Abramson, N., "The ALOHA System," *Proc. AFIPS FJCC*, vol. 37, 1970, pp. 281–285. Also in Abramson and Kuo [1973].

Abramson [1973]: Abramson, N., "Packet Switching with Satellites," *Proc. AFIPS NCC*, vol. 42, 1973, pp. 695–702.

Abramson and Kuo [1973]: Abramson, N., and F. F. Kuo, *Computer-Communication Networks*, Prentice-Hall, Englewood Cliffs, NJ, 1973.

Adams [1960]: Adams Associates, *Computer Characteristics Quarterly* (summary of the characteristics of computers currently being manufactured), Cambridge, MA. Specific issues used: vol. 6, no.1 (1966); vol. 7,nos. 1, 2, and 4 (1967); vol. 8, no. 1 [(1968) first published in 1960].

Adams [1962]: Adams, C. W., "Grosch's Law Repealed," *Datamation*, vol. 8, no. 7, July 1962, pp. 38–39.

Adams and Smith [1978]: Adams, W. T., and S. M. Smith, "How Bit-Slice Families Compare, Part 1: Evaluation Processor Elements," *Electronics*, August 1978, pp. 91–98.

Alexander and Wortman [1975]: Alexander, W. G., and D. B. Wortman, "Static and Dynamic Characteristics of XPL Programs," *Computer*, November 1975, pp. 41–46.

Allard, Wolf, and Zemlin [1964]: Allard, R. W., K. A. Wolf, and R. A. Zemlin, "Effects of the 6600 Computer on Language Structures," *Comm. ACM*, vol. 7, no. 2, February 1964, pp. 112–119.

Allmark and Lucking [1962]: Allmark, R. H., and J. R. Lucking, "Design of an Arithmetic Unit Incorporating a Nesting Store," *Proc. IFIP Cong.*, 1962, pp. 694–698.

Allsen [1978]: Allsen, J. K., "System/38 Common Code Generation," *IBM System/38 Tech. Dev.*, IBM GS80-0237, 1978, pp. 100–103.

Almes and Robertson [1978]: Almes, G., and G. Robertson, "An Extensible File System for Hydra," *Proc. 3d IEEE Conf. on Software Engineering*, 1978.

Amdahl [1964]: Amdahl, G. M., "The Structure of System/360, Part III: Processing Unit Design Considerations," *IBM Syst. J.*, vol. 3, no. 2, 1964, pp. 144–164.

Amdahl, Blaauw, and Brooks [1964]: Amdahl, G. M., G. A. Blaauw, and F. P. Brooks, Jr., "Architecture of the IBM System/360," *IBM J. Res. and Dev.*, vol. 8, no. 2, April 1964, pp. 87–101.

Anacker [1979]: Anacker, W., "Computing at 4 Degrees Kelvin," *IEEE Spectrum*, vol. 16, no. 5, May 1979, pp. 26–37.

Anderson [1961]: Anderson, J. P., "A Computer for Direct Execution of Algorithmic Languages," *Proc. AFIPS FJCC*, vol. 20, 1961, pp. 184–193.

Anderson et al. [1962]: Anderson, J. P., S. A. Hoffman, J. Shifman, and R. J. Williams, "D825; A Multiple: Computer System for Command and Control," *Proc. AFIPS FJCC*, vol. 22, 1962, pp. 86–96.

Anderson et al. [1967]: Anderson, S. F., J. G. Earle, R. E. Goldschmidt, and D. M. Powers, "The IBM System/360 Model 91 Floating-Point Execution Unit," *IBM J. Res. and Dev.*, vol. 11, no. 1, 1967, p. 34.

Anderson and Jensen [1975]: Anderson, G. A., and E. D. Jensen, "Computer Interconnection Structures: Taxonomy, Characteristics and Examples," *Comp. Surv.*, vol. 7, no. 4, December 1975, pp. 197–213.

Anderson and Macri [1967]: Anderson, J. E., and F. J. Macri, "Multiple Redundancy Applications in a Computer," *Proc. Annual Symp. Rel.*, Washington, 1967, pp. 553–562.

Anderson and Metze [1973]: Anderson, D. A., and G. Metze, "Design of Totally Self-Checking Check Circuits for m-out-of-n Codes," *IEEE Trans. Comp.*, vol. C-22, no. 3, pp. 263–269.

Anderson, Sparacio, and Tomasulo [1967]: Anderson, D. W., F. J. Sparacio, and R. M. Tomasulo, "The IBM System/360 Model 91: Machine Philosophy and Instruction-Handling," *IBM J. Res. and Dev.*, vol. 11, no. 1, 1967, pp. 8–24. Chapter 18 of this book.

Arbuckle [1966]: Arbuckle, R. A., "Computer Analysis and Thruput Evaluation," *Computers and Automation*, January 1966, pp. 12–19.

Arden et al. [1966]: Arden. B. W., B. A. Galler, T. C. O'Brien, and F. H. Westervelt, "Program and Addressing Structure in a Time-Sharing Environment," *J. ACM*, vol. 13, no. 1, January 1966, pp. 1–16.

Ashenhurst and Vonderohe [1975]: Ashenhurst, R. L., and R. H. Vonderohe, "A Hierarchical Network," *Datamation*, vol. 21, no. 2, February 1975, pp. 40–44.

Astronaut. [1970]: "TOPS Outer Planet Spacecraft," Special issue of *Astronaut. Aeronaut.*, vol. 8, September 1970.

Auerbach [n.d.]: Auerbach Computer Technology Report on CRAY-1, Pennsauken, NJ

Ault et al. [1964]: Ault, C. F., L. E. Gallaher, T. S. Greenwood, and D. C. Koehler, "No. 1 ESS Program Store," *Bell Syst. Tech. J.*, September 1964, pp. 2,097–2,146.

Ault et al. [1977]: Ault, C. F., J. H. Brewster, T. S. Greenwood, R. E. Haglund, W. A. Read, and M. W. Rolund, "1A

Processor—Memory Systems," *Bell Syst. Tech. J.*, February 1977.

Aupperle [1973]: Aupperle, E. M., "MERIT Network Re-examined," in *Seventh Annual IEEE Comp. Soc. Int. Conf., Dig. Papers*, 1973, pp. 25–30.

Austing et al [1979]: Austing, R. H., B. H. Barnes, D. T. Bonnette, G. L. Engel, and G. Stokes, "Curriculum '78, Recommendations for the Undergraduate Program in Computer Science: A Report of the ACM Curriculum Committee on Computer Science," *Comm. ACM*, vol. 22, no. 3, 1979, pp. 147–166.

Avižienis [1967a]: Avižienis, A. A., "Design of Fault-Tolerant Computers," *Proc. AFIPS FJCC*, vol. 31, 1967, pp. 733–743.

Avižienis [1967b]: Avižienis, A. A., "Concurrent Diagnosis of Arithmetic Processors," *Digest 1st Annual IEEE Comput. Conf.*, 1967, pp. 34–97.

Avižienis [1968]: Avižienis, A. A., "An Experimental Self-Repairing Computer," *Proc. IFIP Cong.*, vol. 2, 1968, pp. 872–877.

Avižienis [1971]: Avižienis, A. A., "Arithmetic Error Codes: Cost and Effectiveness Studies for Application in Digital System Design," *IEEE Trans. Comp.*, vol. C-20, no. 11, November 1971, pp. 1,322–1,331.

Avižienis [1975]: Avižienis, A. A., "Architecture of Fault-Tolerant Computing Systems," *Int. Symp. Fault-Tolerant Computing*, 1975.

Avižienis [1976]: Avižienis, A. A., "Approaches to Computer Reliability: Then and Now," *Proc. AFIPS NCC*, vol. 45, 1976, pp. 401–411.

Avižienis et al. [1969]: Avižienis, A. A., F. P. Mathur, D. Rennels, and J. Rohr, "Automatic Maintenance of Aerospace Computers and Spacecraft Information and Control Systems," *Proc. AIAA Aerosp. Comp. Syst. Conf.*, 1969, pp. 1–11.

Avižienis et al. [1971]: Avižienis, A. A., G. C. Gilley, F. P. Mathur, D. A. Rennels, J. A. Rohr, and D. K. Rubin, "The STAR (Self-Testing and Repairing) Computer: An Investigation of the Theory and Practice of Fault-Tolerant Computer Design," *IEEE Trans. Comp.*, vol. C-20, no. 11, November 1971, pp. 1,312–1,321. Chapter 27 in this book.

Baecker [1976]: Baecker, R. M., "A Conversational Extensible System for the Animation of Shaded Images," *Computer Graphics*, vol. 10, no. 2, 1976, pp. 32–39.

Baran [1964]: Baran, P., "On Distributed Communication Networks," *IEEE Trans. Comm. Syst.*, vol. CS-12, March 1964.

Baran, Boehm, and Smith [1964]: Baran, P., S. Boehm, and P. Smith, "On Distributed Communications," Rand Corporation Memorandum RM-3420-PR, Santa Monica, Calif., August 1964.

Barnes et al. [1968]: Barnes, G. H., R. M. Brown, M. Kato, D. J. Kuck, D. L. Slotnick, and R. A. Stokes, "The Illiac IV Computer," *IEEE Trans. Comp.*, vol. C-17, no. 8, August 1968, pp. 746–757.

Bartlett [1977]: Bartlett, J. P., "A 'NonStop' Operating System," Tandem Computers, Inc., 1977; also printed in *Proc. Hawaii on System Sciences*, 1978, and in Chap. 29 of this book.

Barton, [1961]: Barton, R. S., "A New Approach to the Functional Design of a Digital Computer," *Proc. WJCC*, 1961, pp. 393–396.

Batcher [1968]: Batcher, K. E., "Sorting Networks and Their Applications," *Proc. AFIPS SJCC*, vol. 32, 1968, pp. 307–314.

Batcher [1974]: Batcher, K. E., "STARAN Parallel Processor System Hardware," *Proc. AFIPS NCC*, 1974, pp. 405–410. In Chap. 21 of this book.

Batcher [1976]: Batcher, K. E., "The FLIP Network in STARAN," *Proc. 1976 Int. Conf. on Parallel Processing*, Waldenwoods, Mich., 1976.

Batcher [1977]: Batcher, K. E., "The Multidimensional Access Memory in STARAN," *IEEE Trans. Comp.*, vol. C-26, no. 2, February 1977, pp. 174–177.

BBN [1969a]: Bolt Beranek and Newman, Inc., *Initial Design for Interface Message Processors for the ARPA Computer Network*, report no. 1763, 1969.

BBN [1969b]: Bolt Beranek and Newman, Inc., *Specifications for the Interconnection of a Host and an IMP*, report no. 1822, 1969.

Becker et al. [1977]: Becker, J. O., J. G. Chevalier, R. K. Eisenhart, J. H. Forster, A. W. Fulton, and W. L. Harrod, "1A Processor: Technology and Physical Design," *Bell Syst. Tech. J.*, February 1977, pp. 207–236.

Belady [1966]: Belady, L. A., "A Study of Replacement Algorithms for Virtual Storage Computers," *IBM Syst. J.*, vol. 5, no. 2, 1966, pp. 78–101.

Bell et al. [1970]: Bell, C. G., R. Cady, H. McFarland, B. Delagi, J. O'Loughlin, R. Noonan, and W. Wulf, "A New Architecture for Mini-computers: The DEC PDP-11," *Proc. AFIPS SJCC*, vol. 36, 1970, pp. 657–675. Chapter 38 in this book.

Bell, Mudge, and McNamara [1978]: Bell, C. G., J. C. Mudge, and J. E. McNamara, *Computer Engineering: A DEC View of Hardware System Design*, Digital Press, Bedford, Mass, 1978.

Bell and Newell [1971]: Bell, C. G., and A. Newell, *Computer Structures: Readings and Examples*, McGraw-Hill Book Company, New York, 1971.

Bell and Strecker [1976]: Bell, C. G., and W. D. Strecker, "Computer Structures: What Have We Learned from the

PDP-11?" in *Proc. 3d Annual Symp. on Computer Architecture*, 1976.

Bellis [1978]: Bellis, H., "AUTOFAIL: Automatic Failure Rate Calculator User Manual," Carnegie-Mellon Univ. Dept. of Computer Science Technical Report, Pittsburgh, May 1978.

Berglund [1978]: Berglund, N. C., "Processor Development in the LSI Environment," *IBM Syst./38 Tech. Dev.* GS80-0237, 1978, pp. 7–10.

Bernwell [1975]: Bernwell, N., ed. *Benchmarking: Computer Evaluation and Measurement*, John Wiley & Sons, Inc., New York, 1975.

Berstis [1978]: Berstis, V., C. D. Truxal, and J. G. Ranweiler, "System/38 Addressing and Authorization," *IBM Syst./38 Tech. Dev.* GS80-0237, 1978, pp. 51–54. In Chap. 32 of this book.

Beuscher et al. [1969]: Beuscher, H. J., G. E. Fessler, D. W. Huffman, P. J. Kennedy, and E. Nussbaum, "Administration and Maintenance Plan," *Bell Syst. Tech. J.*, October 1969.

Bhandarkar [1972]: Bhandarkar, D. P., *Analytic Models for Memory Interference in Multiprocessor Computer Systems*, Ph. D. thesis, Carnegie-Mellon Univ., Pittsburgh, September 1972.

Bhandarkar and Juliussen [1978]: Bhandarkar, D. P., and J. E. Juliussen, "Semiconductor Technology: Trends and Implications," *ACM Comp. Architecture News*, vol. 7, no. 1, 1978, pp. 4–14.

Binder, Lai, and Wilson [1974]: Binder, R., W. S. Lai, and M. Wilson, "The ALOHANET MENEHUNE: Version II," Univ. of Hawaii ALOHA SYSTEM Tech. Rep. B74-6, September 1974.

Binder et al. [1975]: Binder, R., N. Abramson, F. Kuo, A. Okinaka, and D. Wax, "ALOHA Packet Broadcasting: A Retrospect," *Proc. AFIPS NCC*, vol. 44, 1975. Chapter 25 of this book.

Blaauw [1964]: Blaauw, G. A., "The Structure of System/360, Part V: Multi-System Organization," *IBM Syst. J.*, vol. 3, no. 2, 1964, pp. 181–195.

Blaauw and Brooks [1964]: Blaauw, G. A., and F. P. Brooks, Jr., "The Structure of System/360, Part I: Outline of the Logical Structure," *IBM Syst. J.*, vol. 3, no. 2, 1964, pp. 119–135. Chapter 40 of this book.

Blake [1977]: Blake, R. P., "Exploring a Stack Architecture," *Computer*, vol. 10, no. 5, May 1977, pp. 30–39.

Bloch and Galage [1978]: Bloch, E., and D. Galage, "Component Progress: Its Effect on High-Speed Computer Architecture and Machine Organization," *Computer*, April 1978, pp. 64–76.

Bock [1963]: Bock, R. V., "An Interrupt Control for the B5000

Data Processor System," *Proc. AFIPS FJCC*, vol. 24, 1963, pp. 229–241.

Boehm and Mobley [1966]: Boehm, B. W., and R. L. Mobley, "Adaptive Routing Techniques for Distributed Communication Systems," Rand Corporation Memorandum RM-4781-PR, 1966.

Boggs et al. [1980]: Boggs, D. R., J. F. Shoch, E. A. Taft, and R. M. Metcalfe, "Pup: An Internetwork Architecture," *IEEE Trans. Comm.*, vol. COM-28, no. 1, January 1980.

Boland et al. [1967]: Boland, L. J., G. D. Granito, A. U. Marcotte, B. U. Messina, and J. W. Smith, "IBM System/360 Model 91 Storage System," *IBM J. Res. and Dev.*, vol. 11, 1967, p. 54–68.

Bouknight, et al. [1972]: Bouknight, W. J., S. A. Denenberg, D. E. McIntyre, J. M. Randall, A. H. Sameh, and D. L. Slotnick, "The Illiac IV System," *Proc. IEEE*, April 1972, pp. 369–379. Chapter 20 of this book.

Boulis and Faiss [1977]: Boulis, R. L., and R. O. Faiss, "STARAN E Performance and LACIE Algorithms," *Proc. 1977 Int. Conf. on Parallel Processing*, 1977.

Bouricius, Carter, and Schneider [1969]: Bouricius, W. G., W. G. Carter, and P. R. Schneider, "Reliability Modeling Techniques for Self-Repairing Computer Systems," *Proc. 24th ACM Natl. Conf.*, 1969, pp. 295–309.

Boutwell and Hoskinson [1963]: Boutwell, E., Jr., and E. A. Hoskinson, "The Logical Organization of the PB 440 Microprogrammable Computer," *Proc. AFIPS FJCC*, vol. 24, 1963, pp. 201–213.

Bowman et al. [1977]: Bowman, P. W., et al., "1A Processor-Maintenance Software," *Bell Syst. Tech. J.*, February 1977.

Bressler, Kraley, and Michel [1975]: Bressler, R. D., M. F. Kraley, and A. Michel, "Pluribus: A Multiprocessor for Communications Networks," in *14th Ann. ACM/NBS Tech. Symp.: Computing in the Mid-70's: An Assessment*, 1975, pp. 13–19.

Brinch Hansen [1970]: Brinch Hansen, P., "The Nucleus of a Multi-programming system," *Comm. ACM.* vol. 13, April 1970, pp. 238–241.

Brooker [1960]: Brooker, R. A., "Some Techniques for Dealing with Two-Level Storage," *Comp. J.*, vol. 2, 1960, pp. 189–194.

Brown, Gibson, and Thorn [1972]: Brown, D. T., R. L. Gibson, and C. A. Thorn, "Channel and Direct Access Device Architecture," *IBM Syst. J.*, vol. 11, no. 3, 1972, pp. 186–199.

Brown, Miller, and Keenan [1967]: Brown, G. W., J. G. Miller, and T. A. Keenan, *EDUNET Report of the Summer Study on*

Information Networks Conducted by the Interuniversity Communications Council, John Wiley & Sons, Inc., New York, 1967.

Brown and Walden [1972]: Brown, C. D., and J. M. Walden, "Model 10 Maintains Compatibility, Expands Capability," *Hewlett-Packard J.*, vol. 24, December 1972, pp. 5–8. In Chap. 49 of this book.

Browne et al. [1969]: Browne, T. E., T. M. Quinn, W. N. Toy, and J. E. Yates, "No. 2 ESS Control Unit System," *Bell Syst. Tech. J.*, October 1969, pp. 2,619–2,668.

Buchholz and Ballance [1962]: Buchholz W., and R. S. Ballance, *Planning a Computer System*, McGraw-Hill Book Company, New York, 1962.

Bucy and Senne [1978]: Bucy, R. S., and K. D. Senne, "New Frontiers in Nonlinear Filtering," MIT Lincoln Laboratory, Tech. Rep. 1978-16, May 1978.

Budlong et al. [1977]: Budlong, A. H., B. G. DeLugish, S. M. Neville, J. S. Nowak, J. L. Quinn, and F. W. Wenland, "1A Processor: Control System," *Bell Syst. Tech. J.*, February 1977, pp. 135–179.

Burks, Goldstine, and von Neumann [1962]: Burks, A. W., H. H. Goldstine, and J. von Neumann, "Preliminary Discussion of the Logical Design of an Electronic Computing Instrument, Part II," *Datamation*, vol. 8, no. 10, October 1962, pp. 36–41.

Burroughs [1964]: Burroughs Corporation B5500 Information Processing System Reference Manual, 1964.

Burroughs [1965]: *A Narrative Description of the Burroughs' B5500 Disk File Master Control Program*, Burroughs Corporation, 1965.

Buzen and Gagliardi [1973]: Buzen, J. P., and U. O. Gagliardi, "The Evolution of Virtual Machine Architecture," *Proc. AFIPS NCC*, vol. 42, June 1973, pp. 291–299.

Bylinsky [1975]: Bylinsky, G., "Here Comes the Second Computer Revolution," *Fortune*, November 1975.

Cagle et al. [1964]: Cagle, W. B., R. S. Menne, R. S. Skinner, R. E. Staehler, and M. D. Underwood, "No. 1 ESS Logic Circuits and Their Application to the Design of the Central Control," *Bell Syst. Tech. J.*, September 1964, pp. 2,055–2,095.

Calahan, Joy, and Orbits [n.d.]: Calahan, Joy, and Orbits, "Preliminary Report on Results of Matrix Benchmarks on Vector Processors," System Engineering Laboratory, Univ. of Michigan, Ann Arbor, Mich.

Carlson [1963]: Carlson, C. B., "The Mechanization of a Pushdown Stack," *AFIPS Proc. FJCC*, vol. 24, 1963, pp. 243–250.

Carr, Crocker, and Cerf [1970]: Carr, S., S. Crocker, and V. Cerf, "HOST-HOST Communication Protocol in the ARPA Network," *Proc. AFIPS SJCC*, 1970.

Carter et al. [1964]: Carter, W. C., H. C. Montgomery, R. J. Preiss, and H. J. Reinheimer, "Design of Serviceability Features for the IBM System/360," *IBM J. Res. and Dev.*, vol. 8, no. 2, April 1964, pp. 115–125.

Carter et al. [1971]: Carter, W. C., D. C. Jessep, P. R. Schneider, A. B. Wadia, and W. G. Bouricius, "Logic Design for Dynamic and Interactive Recovery," *IEEE Trans. Comp.*, vol. C-30, no. 11, November 1971, pp. 1,300–1,305.

Carter and Schneider [1969]: Carter, W. C., and P. R. Schneider, "Design of Dynamically Checked Computers," *Proc. IFIP Cong.*, vol. 2, North Holland Publishing Company, Amsterdam, 1969, pp. 878–883.

Casale [1962]: Casale, C. T., "Planning the CDC 3600," *Proc. AFIPS FJCC*, vol. 22, 1962, pp. 73–85.

Case and Padegs [1978]: Case, R. P., and A. Padegs, "Architecture of the IBM System/370," *Comm. ACM*, vol. 21, no. 1, January 1978, pp. 73–96. Chapter 51 of this book.

Cerf and Kahn [1974]: Cerf, V. G., and R. E. Kahn, "A Protocol for Packet Network Intercommunication," *IEEE Trans. Comp.*, vol. COM-22, no. 5, May 1974, pp. 637–648.

CFA [1977]: "Selection Methods for a Computer Family Architecture," series of articles, *Proc. AFIPS NCC*, vol. 46, 1977, pp. 131–200.

Chang, Smith, and Walford [1974]: Chang, H. Y., G. W. Smith, and R. B. Walford, "LAMP: System Description," *Bell Syst. Tech. J.*, October 1974, pp. 1,431–1,449.

Chesley and Smith [1971]: Chesley, G. D., and W. R. Smith, "The Hardware-Implemented High-Level Machine Language for SYMBOL," *Proc. AFIPS SJCC*, vol. 38, 1971, pp. 563–573.

Chu and Cannont [1976]: Chu, Y., and E. R. Cannont, "Interactive High-Level Language Direct-Execution Microprocessor System," *IEEE Trans. Soft. Eng.*, vol. SE-2, no. 2, June 1976, pp. 126–134.

Clark [1957]: Clark, W. A., "The Lincoln TX-2 Computer Development," *Proc. WJCC*, 1957, pp. 143–145.

Clayton, Dorff, and Fagen [1964]: Clayton, B. B., E. K. Dorff, and R. E. Fagen, "An Operating System and Programming Systems for the 6600," *Proc. AFIPS FJCC*, vol. 26, pt. 2, 1964, pp. 41–57.

Cleary [1969]: Cleary, J. G., "Process Handling on Burroughs B6500," *Proc. 4th Australian Comp. Conf.*, 1969, pp. 231–239.

Cochran [1968]: Cochran, D. S.: "Internal Programming of the 9100A Calculator," *Hewlett-Packard J.*, vol. 20, no. 1, September 1968, pp. 14–16. In Chap. 48 of this book.

Cohen and Jefferson [1975]: Cohen, E., and D. Jefferson: "Protection in the Hydra Operating System," *Proc. 5th Symp. on Operating Systems Principles*, 1975, pp. 141–160.

Computer [1974a]: "The Shrinking World: Computer Networks and Communications," special issue of *Computer*, vol. 7, no. 2, February 1974.

Computer [1974b]: "Distributed-Function Computer Architectures," Special issue of *Computer*, vol. 7, no. 3, March 1974.

Computer [1976]: *Computer World*, August 1976.

Computer [1977]: "Military Computer Architectures: A Look at the Alternatives," special issue of *Computer*, vol. 10, no. 10, October 1977.

Computer Review [1975]: *Computer Review (formerly Computer Characteristics Review)*, GML Corp., Lexington, Mass., 1975.

Computer Review [1977]: *Computer Review*, vol. 1, GML Corp., Lexington, Mass., 1977.

Connors, Florkowski, and Patton [1979]: Connors, W. D., J. H. Florkowski, and S. K. Patton, "The IBM 3033: An Inside Look," *Datamation*, vol. 25, no. 5, May 1979, pp. 198–218.

Connors, Mercer, and Sorlini [1970]: Connors, W. D., V. S. Mercer, and T. A. Sorlini, "S/360 Instruction Usage Distribution," Rep. IBM-SDS TR 00.2025, May 8, 1970.

Conti [1964]: Conti, C., "System Aspect: System/360 Model 92," *Proc. AFIPS FJCC*, vol. 26, pt. 2, 1964, pp. 81–95.

Conti, Gibson, and Pitkowsky [1968]: Conti, C. J., D. H. Gibson, and S. H. Pitkowsky, "Structural Aspects of the System/360 Model 85, Part 1: General Organization," *IBM Syst. J.*, vol. 7, no. 1, 1968, pp. 2–14.

Corbato and Vyssotsky [1965]: Corbato, F. J., and V. A. Vyssotsky, "Introduction and Overview of the Multics System," *Proc. AFIPS FJCC*, vol. 27, pt. 1, 1965.

Cornyn et al. [1977]: Cornyn, J. J., W. R. Smith, W. R. Svirsky, and A. H. Coleman, "Two Life-Cycle Cost Models for Comparing Computer Architectures," *Proc. AFIPS NCC*, vol. 46, 1977.

Cosserat [1972]: Cosserat, D. C., "A Capability Oriented Multiprocessor System for Real-Time Applications," *Proc. Int. Conf. Comp. Comm.*, 1972.

Cowart, Rice, and Lundstrom [1971]: Cowart, B. E., R. Rice, and S. F. Lundstrom, "The Physical Attributes and Testing Aspects of the SYMBOL System," *Proc. AFIPS SJCC*, vol. 38, 1971, pp. 589–600.

Crocker et al. [1972]: Crocker, S. D., J. F. Heafner, R. M. Metcalfe, and J. B. Postel, "Function-Oriented Protocols for the ARPA Computer Network," *Proc. AFIPS SJCC*, vol. 40, 1972, pp. 271–279.

Crowther et al. [1975]: Crowther, W. R., F. E. Heart, A. A. McKenzie, J. M. McQuillan, and D. C. Walden, "Issues in Packet-Switching Network Design," *Proc. AFIPS NCC*, vol. 44, 1975, pp. 161–175.

Cuadra [1968]: Cuadra, C. A., Chapters 7 and 10, in *Annual Review of Information Science and Technology*, Interscience, 1968.

Curtis [1978]: Curtis, H. W., "Integrated Circuit Design, Production, and Packaging for System/38," *IBM System/38 Tech. Dev.*, IBM GS80-0237, 1978, pp. 11–14.

Dahlby et al. [1978]: Dahlby, S. H., G. G. Henry, D. N. Reynolds, and P. T. Taylor, "System/38: A High Level Machine, *IBM System/38 Tech. Dev.*, IBM GS80-0237, 1978, pp. 47–50. In Chap. 32 of this book.

Data [1978]: Data Pro Research Corp., 1978, pp. 70c-491-04a through 70c-491-05p.

Davidson [1972]: Davidson, J., "An Echoing Strategy for Satellite Links," Stanford Research Institute NIC Document 10599 (RFC 357), June 1972.

Davies [1968a]: Davies, D. W., "The Principles of a Data Communication Network for Computers and Remote Peripherals," *Proc. IFIP Cong.*, vol. 2, 1968.

Davies [1968b]: Davies, D. W., "Communications Networks to Serve Rapid-Response Computers," *Proc. IFIP Cong.*, vol. 2, 1968.

Davies [1972]: Davies, P. M., "Readings in Microprogramming," *IBM Syst. J.*, no. 1, 1972, pp. 16–40.

Davies et al. [1967]: Davies, D. W., K. A. Bartlett, R. A. Scantlebury, and P. T. Wilkinson, "A Digital Communication Network for Computers Giving Rapid Response at Remote Terminals," *Proc. ACM Symp. on Operating Systems Principles*, 1967.

Davis [1960]: Davis, G. M., "The English Electric KDF9 Computer System," *Comp. Bull.*, December 1960, pp. 119–120.

Dean [1973]: Dean, L. C., "Texas Instruments Advanced Scientific Computer," *Informatie Jrg.*, vol. 15, no. 4, April 1973, pp. 191–193. In Chap. 45 of this book.

DEC [1971]: Digital Equipment Corp. PDP-11/20/15/R20 Processor Handbook, 1971.

DEC [1972]: Digital Equipment Corp. KD11-A Processor Maintainence Manual, 1972.

DEC [1973]: Digital Equipment Corp. PDP-11 Peripherals Handbook, 1973.

DEC [1975]: Digital Equipment Corp. LSI-11/PDP-11/03 Programming Reference Card, 1975.

DEC [1976a]: Digital Equipment Corp. PDP-11/04/05/10/35/40/45 Processor Handbook, 1976.

DEC [1976b]: Digital Equipment Corp. PDP-11/04/34/45/55 Processor Handbook, 1976.

DEC [1976c]: Digital Equipment Corp. LSI-11 Microcomputer Handbook, 1976.

DEC [1976d]: Digital Equipment Corp. PDP-11 Peripherals Handbook, 1976.

DEC [1976e]: Digital Equipment Corp. PDP-11 Programming Reference Card, 1976.

DEC [1977]: Digital Equipment Corp. PDP-11/60 Processor Handbook, 1977.

Demers [1978]: Demers, R. A., "The Generalized Message Handler in System/38," *IBM System/38 Tech. Dev.*, IBM GS80-0237, 1978, pp. 97–99.

Denenberg [1971]: Denenberg, S. A., "An Introductory Description of the ILLIAC IV System," Center for Advanced Computation, Univ. of Illinois Tech. Memo Doc. 225, File 850, Urbana, Ill., July 1971.

Denning [1967]: Denning, P. J., "Effects of Scheduling on File Memory Operations," *Proc. AFIPS SJCC*, 1967.

Denning [1970]: Denning, P. J., "Virtual Memory," *Comp. Surv.*, vol. 2, no. 3, September 1970, pp. 153–189.

Dennis [1965]: Dennis, J. B., "Segmentation and the Design of Multiprogrammed Computer Systems," *J. ACM*, vol. 12, no. 4, October 1965, pp. 589–602.

Deutsch [1979]: Deutsch, P., "Experience with a Microprogrammed Interlisp System," *IEEE Trans. Comp.*, vol. C-28, no. 10, October 1979.

Dijkstra [1968a]: Dijkstra, E. W., "Co-operating Sequential Processes," In F. Genuys, ed., *Programming Languages*, p. 43, Academic Press, London, 1968.

Dijkstra [1968b]: Dijkstra, E. W., "The Structure of the 'THE'

Multiprogramming System," *Comm. ACM*, vol. 11, May 1968, pp. 341–346.

"Distributed-Function Architectures" [1974]: "Distributed Function Computer Architectures," special issue of *Computer*, vol. 7, no. 3, March 1974.

Doll [1974]: Doll, D. R., "Telecommunications Turbulence and the Computer Network Evolution," *Computer*, vol. 7, no. 2, February 1974, pp. 13–22.

Dolotta et al. [1976]: Dolotta, T. A., M. I. Bernstein, R. S. Dickson, Jr., N. A. France, B. A. Rosenblatt, D. M. Smith, and T. B. Steel, Jr., *Data Processing in 1980–1985*, John Wiley & Sons, Inc., 1976.

Donofrio, Flur, and Schnadt [1978]: Donofrio, M. N., B. Flur, and R. T. Schnadt, "Memory Design/Technology for System/38," *IBM System/38 Tech. Dev.*, IBM GS80-0237, 1978, pp. 16–19.

Doran [1975]: Doran, R. W., "The ICL 2900 Computer Architecture (Compared with the Burroughs B6700)," *Computer Architecture News*, vol. 4, no. 3, 1975, p. 24.

Dorn [1974]: Dorn, P., "ICL's Brand of 'Me-too-ism,'" *Datamation*, December 1974.

Downing, Nowak, and Tuomenoksa [1964]: Downing, R. W., J. S. Nowak, and L. L. Tuomenoksa, "No. 1 ESS Maintenance Plan," *Bell Syst. Tech. J.*, vol. 43, no. 5, pt. 1, September 1964, pp. 1,961–2,019.

Dumstorff [1978]: Dumstorff, E. F., "Application of a Microprocessor for I/O Control," *IBM System/38 Tech. Dev.*, IBM GS80-0237, 1978, pp. 28–31.

Durniak [1978]: Durniak, A., "Soviet Computers: Better Than Expected," *Electronics*, September 1978, pp. 85–86.

Eckhouse [1975]: Eckhouse, R. H., *Minicomputer Systems: Organization and Programming Inc. (PDP-11)*, Prentice Hall, Englewood Cliffs, N.J., 1975.

EDUCOM [n.d.]: EDUCOM *EIN Software Catalogue*, 100 Charles River Park, Boston.

Edwards, Lanigan, and Kilburn [1960]: Edwards, D. B. G., M. J. Lanigan, and T. Kilburn, "Ferrite-Core Memory systems with Rapid Cycle Times," *Proc. IEE*, vol. 107, pt. B, November 1960, pp. 585–598.

Egan [1972]: Egan, G. L., "Versatile Input/Output Structure Welcomes Peripheral Variety," *Hewlett-Packard J.*, vol. 24, December 1972, pp. 24–27. In Chap. 49 of this book.

Elliott et al. [1956]: Elliott, W. S., C. E. Owen, C. H. Devonald, and B. G. Maudsley, "The Design Philosophy of Pegasus, a Quantity-Production Computer," *Proc. IEEE*, vol. 103, pt. B, supp. 2, 1956, pp. 188–196.

English, Englebart, and Berman [1967]: English, W. K., D. C. Englebart, and M. L. Berman, "Display-Selection Techniques for Text Manipulation," *IEEE Trans. HFE*, vol. HFE-8, no. 1, March 1967, pp. 5–15.

Enslow [1974]: Enslow, P. H., Jr., ed., *Multiprocessors and Parallel Processing*, John Wiley & Sons, Inc., New York, 1974.

Enslow [1977]: Enslow, P. H., Jr., "Multiprocessor Organization: A Survey," *Comp. Surv.*, vol. 9, no. 1, March 1977, pp. 103–129.

Everett, Zraket, and Benington [1957]: Everett, R. R., C. A. Zraket, and H. D. Benington, "SAGE: A Data-Processing System for Air Defense, *Proc. EJCC*, 1957, pp. 148–155.

Fagg et al. [1964]: Fagg, P., J. L. Brown, J. A. Hipp, D. T. Doody, J. W. Fairclough, and J. Greene, "IBM System/360 Engineering," *Proc. AFIPS FJCC*, pt. 1, vol. 26, 1964, pp. 205–231.

Faggin [1977]: Faggin, F., "Trends in Microcomputers" (speech), in *ACM Sigarch Workshop on Future Directions in Computer Architecture*, Austin, Tex., 1977. Chapter 36 of this book.

Faggin et al. [1972]: Faggin, F., M. Shima, M. E. Hoff, Jr., H. Feeney, and S. Mazor, "The MCS-4: An LSI Micro Computer System," *IEEE Region 6 Conf. 1972*, pp. 8–11.

Falk [1976]: Falk, H. "Reaching for a Gigaflop," *IEEE Spectrum*, vol. 13, no. 10, October 1976, pp. 64–69.

Falk and McQuillan [1977]: Falk, G., and J. M. McQuillan, "Alternatives for Data Network Architectures," *Computer*, vol. 10, no. 11, November 1977, pp. 22–29.

Falkoff, Iverson, and Sussenguth [1964]: Falkoff, A. D., K. E. Iverson, and E. H. Sussenguth, "A Formal Description of System/360," *IBM Syst. J.*, vol. 3, no. 3, 1964, pp. 198–261.

Farber [1975]: Farber, D. J., "A Ring Network," *Datamation*, vol. 21, no. 2, February 1975, pp. 44–46.

Farber et al. [1973]: Farber, D. J., et al., "The Distributed Computing System," *Proc. 7th Annual IEEE Comp. Soc. Int. Conf.*, 1973, pp. 31–34.

FCC [1966]: Federal Communications Commission "Policies and Regulatory Procedures Relating to Computer and Communication Services", Notice of Inquiry, Docket No. 16969, 1966.

Feierbach and Stevenson [1979]: Feierbach, G., and D. Stevenson, "The Illiac IV," in *Infotech State of the Art Report on Supercomputers*, Maidenhead, England, 1979.

Feldman [n.d.]: Feldman, J. D., "RADCAP: An Operational Parallel Processing Facility," Goodyear Aerospace Corp.

Ferrari [1978]: Ferrari, D., *Computer Systems Performance Evaluation*, Prentice-Hall, Inc., Englewood Cliffs, N.J., 1978.

Feustal [1973]: Feustal, E. A., "On the Advantages of Tagged Architecture," *IEEE Trans. Comp.*, vol. C-22, no. 7, July 1973, pp. 644–656.

Fiala [1978]: Fiala, E. R., "The MAXC Systems," *Computer*, vol. 11, no. 5, May 1978, pp. 57–67.

Fikes, Lauer, and Vareha [1968]: Fikes, R. E., H. C. Lauer, and A. L. Vareha, Jr., "Steps toward a General-Purpose Time-sharing System Using Large Capacity Core Storage and TSS/360," *Proc. 23d ACM Natl. Conf.*, 1968, pp. 7–18.

Fleckenstein [1974]: Fleckenstein, W. O., "Bell System ESS Family: Present and Future," *ISS Rec.*, Munich, 1974.

Flehinger [1958]: Flehinger, B. J., "Reliability Improvement through Redundancy at Various Systems Levels," *IBM J. Res. and Dev.*, vol. 2, April 1958, pp. 148–158.

Flynn [1966]: Flynn, M. J., "Very High-Speed Computing Systems," *Proc. IEEE*, vol. 54, December 1966, pp. 1,901–1,909.

Flynn [1977]: Flynn, M. J., "The Interpretive Interface: Resources and Program Representation in Computer Organization," in Kuck, Lawrie, and Sameh, eds., *High Speed Computer and Algorithm Organization*, Academic Press, Inc., New York, 1977.

Flynn and Low [1967]: Flynn, M. J., and P. R. Low, "The IBM System/360 Model 91: Some Remarks on System Development," *IBM J. Res. and Dev.*, vol. 11, 1967, pp. 2–7.

Flynn and MacLaren [1967]: Flynn, M. J., and M. D. MacLaren, "Microprogramming Revisited," Argonne National Laboratory, Applied Mathematics Div. Tech. Memorandum 134, Argonne, Ill., 1967.

Ford and Fulkerson [1962]: Ford, L. R., Jr., and D. R. Fulkerson, *Flows in Networks*, Princeton University Press, 1962.

Forrester [1951]: Forrester, J. W., "Digital Information Storage in Three Dimensions Using Magnetic Cores," *J. Appl. Phys.*, vol. 22, January 1951, pp. 44–48.

Fotheringham [1961]: Fotheringham, J., "Dynamic Storage Allocation in the Atlas Computer, Including an Automatic Use of a Backing Store," *Comm. ACM*, vol. 4, no. 10, October 1961, pp. 435–436.

Fralick et al. [1975]: Fralick, S. C., D. H. Brandin, F. F. Kuo, and C. Harrison, "Digital Terminals for Packet Broadcasting," *Proc. AFIPS NCC*, vol. 44, 1975, pp. 253–261.

Frank, Frisch, and Chou [1970]: Frank, H., I. T. Frisch, and W. Chou, "Topological Considerations in the Design of the ARPA Computer Network," *Proc. AFIPS SJCC*, vol. 36, 1970, pp. 581–587.

Frank, Van Slyke, and Gitman [1975]: Frank, H., R. M. Van Slyke, and I. Gitman, "Packet Radio Network Design: System Considerations," *Proc. AFIPS NCC*, vol. 44, 1975, pp. 217–231.

Fraser [1975]: Fraser, A. G., "A Virtual Channel Network," *Datamation*, vol. 21, no. 2, February 1975, pp. 51–53.

French, Collins, and Loen [1978]: French, R. E., R. W. Collins, and L. W. Loen, "System/38 Machine Storage Management," *IBM System/38 Tech. Dev.*, IBM GS80-0237, 1978, pp. 63–66.

Froemke, Heise, and Pertzborn [1978]: Froemke, J. W., N. N. Heise, and J. J. Pertzborn, "System/38 Magnetic Media Controller," *IBM System/38 Tech. Dev.*, IBM GS80-0237, 1978, pp. 41–44.

Fuller et al. [1976]: Fuller, S. H., G. T. Almes, W. H. Broadley, C. L. Forgy, P. L. Karlton, V. R. Lesser, and J. R. Teter, "PDP-11/40E Microprogramming Reference Manual," Carnegie-Mellon Univ. Dept. of Computer Science Tech. Rep., 1976.

Fuller et al. [1977]: Fuller, S. H., P. Shaman, D. Lamb, and W. E. Burr, "Evaluation of Computer Architectures via Test Programs," *Proc. AFIPS NCC*, vol. 46, 1977, pp. 147–160. Originally in "Computer Family Architecture Selection Committee Final Report," Naval Research Laboratory, Washington, December 1976.

Fuller, Stone, and Burr [1977]: Fuller, S. H., H. S. Stone, and W. E. Burr, "Initial Selection and Screening of the CFA Candidate Computer Architectures," *Proc. AFIPS NCC*, vol. 46, 1977, pp. 130–146.

Fuller and Harbison [1978]: Fuller, S. H., and S. P. Harbison, "The C.mmp Multiprocessor," Carnegie-Mellon Univ. Dept. of Computer Science Tech. Rep., October 1978.

Fuller et al. [1978]: Fuller, S. H., J. Ousterhout, L. Raskin, P. Rubinfeld, P. Sindhu, and R. Swan, "Multi-Microprocessors: An Overview and Working Example," *Proc. IEEE*, vol. 66, no. 2, February 1978, pp. 216–228.

Fulmer and Meilander [1970]: Fulmer, L. C., and W. C. Meilander, "A Modular Plated Wire Associative Processor, *Proc. IEEE Comp. Group Conf.*, 1970.

Gear [1974]: Gear, C. W., *Computer Organization and Programming*, 2d ed., McGraw-Hill, New York, 1974.

Genke, Harding, and Staehler [1964]: Genke, R. M., P. A.

Harding, and R. E. Staehler, "No. 1 ESS Call Store: A-A0, 2-Megabit Ferrite Sheet Memory, *Bell Syst. Tech. J.*, September 1964.

Geschke, Morris, and Satterthwaite [1977]: Geschke, C. M., J. H. Morris, Jr., and E. H. Satterthwaite, "Early Experience with Mesa," *Comm. ACM*, vol. 20, no. 8, August 1977, pp. 540–553.

Gibson [1966]: Gibson, C. T., "Time-sharing in the IBM System/360: Model 67, *Proc. AFIPS SJCC*, vol. 28, 1966, pp. 61–78.

Gibson [1970]: Gibson, J. C., "The Gibson Mix," Rep. TR 00.2043, IBM Systems Development Div., Poughkeepsie, N.Y., 1970. Research done in 1959.

Gilley [1970]: Gilley, G. C., "Automatic Maintenance of Spacecraft Systems for Long-Life, Deep-Space Missions," Ph.D. thesis, Univ. of California at Los Angeles, September 1970.

Glaser, Couleur, and Oliver [1965]: Glaser, F. L., J. F. Couleur, and G. A. Oliver, "System Design of a Computer for Time Sharing Applications," *Proc. AFIPS FJCC*, vol. 27, pt. 1, 1965.

Goetz [1974]: Goetz, F. M., "Complementary Fault Simulation," *Proc. 3d Annual Texas Conf. Comp. Sys.*, Austin, Tex., 1974.

Goldberg [1975]: Goldberg, J., "New Problems in Fault-Tolerant Computing," in *Int. Symp. Fault-Tolerant Computing*, 1975, pp. 29–34.

Gonter [1969]: Gonter, R. H., "Comparison of the Gibson Mix with UMASS Mix," Publication No. TN/RCC/004, Univ. of Massachusetts Research Computing Center, 1969.

Green [1966]: Green, J., "Microprogramming, Emulators and Programming Languages," *Comm. ACM*, vol. 9, no. 3, March 1966, pp. 230–231.

Greene, Dean, and Updike [1964]: Greene, J. E., R. F. Dean, and B. M. Updike, "Microprogrammed Implementation of the IBM System/360 Machine Organization," IBM General Products Div., Development Lab., Engineering Publication, Dept. PTP 792, Endicott, N.Y., April 1964.

Greene and Pooch [1977]: Greene, W., and U. W. Pooch: "A Review of Classification Schemes for Computer Communication Networks," *Computer*, vol. 10, no. 11, November 1977, pp. 12–21.

Gregoretti [1978]: Gregoretti, F., "The 8048 Microcomputer Family," *Microscope*, vol. 2, no. 14, November 1978, pp. 6–19.

Gregory and McReynolds [1963]: Gregory, J., and R. McReynolds, "The SOLOMON Computer," *IEEE Trans. Electronic Computers*, vol. EC-12, no. 6, December 1963, pp. 774–781.

Griesmer, Miller, and Roth [1962]: Griesmer, J. E., R. E. Miller, and J. P. Roth, "The Design of Digital Circuits to Eliminate Catastrophic Failures," in *Redundancy Techniques for Computing Systems*, Spartan Press, Washington, 1962, pp. 328–348.

Grosch [1953]: Grosch, H. R. J., "High Speed Arithmetic: The Digital Computer as a Research Tool," *J. Optical Soc. of America*, vol. 4, no. 4, April 1953, pp. 306–310.

Gudz [1977]: Gudz, R. T., "Application of the Pluribus Multiprocessor in a distributed Data Collection and Processing Network," *Conf. Rec. OCEANS 77*, 1977.

Habermann [1972]: Habermann, A. N., "Synchronization of Communicating Processes," *Comm. ACM*, vol. 15, no. 3, March 1972, pp. 171–176.

Hamblin [1962]: Hamblin, C. L., "Translation to and from Polish Notation," *Comp. J.*, vol. 5, October 1962, pp. 210–213.

Haney [1968]: Haney, F. M., "Using a Computer to Design Computer Instruction Sets," Ph.D. thesis, Carnegie-Mellon Univ., May 1968.

Hargraves [1974]: Hargraves, R. F., Jr., "The Dartmouth Time Sharing Network," in N. Abramson and F. F. Kuo, eds., *Computer Communication Networks*, Prentice-Hall, Inc., Englewood Cliffs, N.J., 1974.

Harr, Taylor, and Ulrich [1969]: Harr, J. A., F. F. Taylor, and W. Ulrich, "Organization of the No. 1 ESS Central Processor," *Bell Syst. Tech. J.*, September 1969, pp. 1,845–1,922.

Harrahy [1977]: Harrahy, I. I., "Assessment of Plastic, Commercial Grade IC Failure Rates Achieved in Field Operation," in *IEEE Annual Spring Reliability Seminar*, 1977.

Hartley, Landy, and Needham [1968]: Hartley, D. F., B. Landy, and R. M. Needham, "The Structure of a Multiprogramming Supervisor," *Comp. J.*, vol. 11, no. 3, November 1968, pp. 247–255.

Harvey and Conway [1978]: Harvey, D. G., and A. J. Conway, "Introduction to the System/38 Control Program Facility," *IBM System/38 Tech. Dev.*, IBM GS80-0237, 1978, pp. 74–77.

Hauck and Dent [1968]: Hauck, E. A., and B. A. Dent, "Burroughs' B6500/B7500 Stack Mechanism," *Proc. AFIPS SJCC*, vol. 32, 1968, pp. 245–251. Chapter 16 of this book.

Hayes [1978]: Hayes, J., *Computer Architecture and Organization*, McGraw-Hill, New York, 1978.

Hayn, McDonough, and Bellay [1981]: Hayn, J., K. McDonough, and J. Bellay, "Strip Architecture Fits Microcomputer into Less Silicon," *Electronics*, vol. 54, no. 2, January 27, 1981, pp. 107–111.

Heart [1975]: Heart, F. E., "The ARPA Network," in R. L. Grimsdale and F. F. Kuo, eds., *Proc. of the NATO Advanced Study Institute of September 1973, Sussex, England*, Noordhoff Int. Publ., The Netherlands, 1975, pp. 19–33.

Heart et al. [1970]: Heart, F. E., R. E. Kahn, S. M. Ornstein, W. R. Crowther, and D. C. Walden, "The Interface Message Processor for the ARPA Computer Network," *Proc. AFIPS SJCC*, vol. 36, 1970, pp. 551–567. Reprinted in W. W. Chu, ed., *Advances in Computer Communications*, Artech House, Dedham, Mass., 1974, pp. 300–316; in P. E. Green and R. W. Lucky, eds., *Computer Communications*, IEEE Press, New York, 1975, pp. 375–391; and in R. P. Blanc and P. W. Cotton, eds., *Computer Networking*, IEEE Press, 1976, pp. 60–76. Chapter 24 of this book.

Heart et al. [1973]: Heart, F. E., S. M. Ornstein, W. R. Crowther, and W. B. Barker, "A New Minicomputer-Multiprocessor for the ARPA Network," *Proc. AFIPS SJCC*, vol. 42, 1973, pp. 529–537.

Heart et al. [1976]: Heart, F. E., S. M. Ornstein, W. R. Crowther, W. B. Barker, M. F. Kraley, R. D. Bressler, and A. Michel, "The Pluribus Multiprocessor System," in *Multiprocessor Systems: Infotech State of the Art Report*, pp. 307–330, Infotech International Ltd., Maidenhead, England, 1976.

Henry [1978]: Henry, G. G., "Introduction to IBM System/38 Architecture," *IBM System/38 Tech. Dev.*, IBM GS80-0237, 1978, pp. 3–6.

Herbst, Metropolis, and Wells [1955]: Herbst, E. H., N. Metropolis, and M. B. Wells, "Analysis of Problem Codes on the MANIAC," *MTOCA* 9, January 1955, pp. 14–20.

Hewlett-Packard [1968]: *Hewlett-Packard Journal*, September 1968.

Hewlett-Packard [1972]: *Hewlett-Parkard Journal*, December 1972.

Hillegass [1966]: Hillegass, J. R., "Auerbach on Equipment IBM System 360: The First Two Years," *Data Processing*, vol. 8, no. 5, May 1966, pp. 44–51.

Hoagland [1979]: Hoagland, A. S., "Storage Technology: Capabilities and Limitations," *Computer*, vol. 12, no. 5, May 1979, pp. 12–18.

Hodges [1964]: Hodges, D., "IPL-VC: A Proposal for a Computer System Having the IPS-V Instruction Set," Argonne National Laboratory, Applied Math. Div. Tech. Memo 66, January 1964.

Hoff [1972]: Hoff, M. E., Jr., "The New LSI Components," *6th Annual IEEE Comp. Soc. Int. Conf.*, 1972.

Hoffman and Soltis [1978]: Hoffman, R. L., and F. G. Soltis, "Hardware Organization of the System/38," *IBM System/38 Tech. Dev.*, IBM GS80-0237, 1978, pp. 19–21. In Chap. 32 of this book.

Holt and Lenas [1974]: Holt, R. M., and M. R. Lenas, "Current Microcomputer Architecture," *Computer Design*, February 1974, pp. 65–74.

Hopkins, Smith, and Lala [1978]: Hopkins, A. L., Jr., T. B. Smith, III, and J. H. Lala, "FTMP: A Highly Reliable Fault-Tolerant Multiprocessor for Aircraft," *Proc. IEEE*, vol. 66, no. 10, October 1978, pp. 1,221–1,239.

Houdek and Mitchell [1978]: Houdek, M. E., and G. R. Mitchell, "Translating a Large Virtual Address," *IBM System/38 Tech. Dev.*, IBM GS80-0237, 1978, pp. 22–25.

Howard and Borgendale [1978]: Howard, P. H., and K. W. Borgendale, "System/38 Machine Indexing Support," *IBM System/38 Tech. Dev.*, IBM GS80-0237, 1978, pp. 67–70.

Howarth [1963]: Howarth, D. J., "Experience with the Atlas Scheduling System," *Proc. AFIPS SJCC*, vol. 23, 1963, pp. 59–67.

Howarth, Jones, and Wyld [1962]: Howarth, D. J., P. D. Jones, and M. T. Wyld, "The ATLAS Scheduling System," *Computer*, vol. 5, no. 3, October 1962, pp. 238–244.

Howarth, Payne, and Sumner [1961]: Howarth, D. J., R. B. Payne, and F. H. Sumner, "The Manchester University Atlas Operating System, Part II: User's Description," *Comp. J.*, vol. 4, no. 3, October 1961, pp. 226–229.

Ibbett and Capon [1978]: Ibbett, R., and P. C. Capon, "The Development of the MU5 Computer System," *Comm. ACM*, vol. 21, no. 1, January 1978, pp. 13–24.

IBM [1970a]: IBM Corporation: *IBM System/360 Principles of Operation*, GA22-6821-4, 1970.

IBM [1970b]: IBM Corporation: *IBM System/360 System Summary*, GA22-6810-8, 1970.

IBM [1970c]: IBM Corporation: *IBM System/370 Model 165 Functional Characteristics*, 1st ed., GA22-6935, June 1970.

IBM [1970d]: IBM Corporation: *IBM System/370 Model 165 Functional Characteristics*, 1st ed., GA22-6935-0, 1970.

IBM [1970e]: IBM Corporation: *A Guide to the IBM System/370 Model 155*, 1st ed., GC20-1729-0, 1970.

IBM [1972a]: IBM Corporation Technical Publications Department: *A Guide to the IBM System/370 Model 145*, 3d ed., White Plains, N.Y., 1972.

IBM [1972b]: IBM Corporation: *IBM System/370 Model 155*,

Functional Characteristics, 3d ed., GA22-6942-2, file no. S370-01, 1972.

IBM [1974]: *IBM Synchronous Data Link Control: General Information*, Publication Center, IBM Systems Development Div., Research Triangle Park, N.C., 1974.

IBM [1975a]: *IBM System Network Architecture: General Information*, Publication Center, IBM Systems Development Div., Research Triangle Park, N.C., 1975.

IBM [1975b]: IBM Corporation: *IBM System/360 and System/370 Model 195, Functional Characteristics*, 5th ed., GA22-6943-4, file no. S/360 S/370-01, 1975.

IBM [1975c]: IBM Corporation: *IBM System/370 Model 158, Functional Characteristics*, 4th ed., GA22-7011-3 file no. S/370-01, 1975.

IBM [1976a]: IBM Corporation: *A Guide to the IBM System/370 Model 145*, 6th ed., GC20-1734-5, file no. S370-01, 1976.

IBM [1976b]: IBM Corporation: *IBM System/370 Model 168, Functional Characteristics*, 5th ed., GA22-7010-4 file no. S/370-01, 1976.

IBM [1976c]: IBM Corporation: Data Processing Division: product announcement, "New Accelerated Processors of System/370 Models 135 and 145," June 1976.

IBM [1976d]: IBM Corporation: *A Guide to the IBM System/370 Model 165*, 5th ed., 1976

IBM [1976e]: IBM Corporation: *IBM System/370 Model 115, Functional Characteristics*, GA33-1510, 1976.

IBM [1978a]: *IBM System/360 and System/370 I/O Interface Channel to Control Unit Original Equipment Manufacturer's Information*, IBM Corp., GA22-6974, 1978.

IBM [1978b]: *IBM System/370 Principles of Operation*, IBM Corp., GA22-77000, 1978.

IBM [1979a]: IBM Corporation, Data Processing Division: *IBM 4331 Processor Facts Folder*, G520-3388-0, 1979.

IBM [1979b]: IBM Corporation, Data Processing Division: *IBM 4341 Processor Facts Folder*, G520-3387-0, 1979.

IBM [1979c]: IBM Corporation: *IBM 4341 Processor Functional Characteristics and Processor Complex Configurator*, 1st ed., GA24-3672-0, 1979.

IBM [n.d.a]: IBM Corporation: *A Guide to the IBM System/370 Model 135.*

IBM [n.d.b]: IBM Corporation, Data Processing Division: product announcement, "System 370 Model 168 Attached Processor System."

IBM [n.d.c]: IBM Corporation: product announcement, "System/370 Model 138, A Growth System for Model 125 and Model 135 Users, Offers a New Level of Price/Performance and Function."

IBM [n.d.d]: IBM Corporation: Data Processing Division: product announcement, "System 370 Model 148, Offers Increased Price/Performance and Function to Intermediate System Users."

IBM [n.d.e]: IBM Corporation: *IBM System/360 Functional Characteristics Manuals for each Model.*

IBM [n.d.f]: IBM Corporation: *IBM System/360 Configurator (diagram) for Each Model.*

Ingalls [1978]: Ingalls, D. H. H., "The Smalltalk-76 Programming System: Design and Implementation," in *5th ACM Symp. on Principles of Programming Languages*, 1978, pp. 9–16.

Intel 8080 [1975]: Intel 8080 Microcomputer Systems User's Manual, September 1975.

Intel MCS-8 [1975]: Intel MCS-8 User's Manual, April 1975.

Intel MCS-40 [1976]: Intel MCS-40 User's Manual, 3d ed., March 1976.

Intel MCS-85 [1977]: Intel MCS-85 User's Manual, March 1977.

Intel MCS-86 [1978]: Intel MCS-86 User's Manual, July 1978.

Irland and Stagg [1974]: Irland, E. A., and U. K. Stagg, "New Developments in Suburban and Rural ESS (No. 2 and No. 3 ESS)," in *ISS Rec.*, Munich, 1974.

Israel, Mitchell, and Sturgis [1978]: Israel, J. E., J. G. Mitchell, and H. E. Sturgis, "Separating Data from Function in a Distributed File System," *Proc. 2d Int. Symp. on Operating Systems*, 1978; reprinted in D. Lanciaux, ed., *Operating Systems*, North-Holland Publishing Company, Amsterdam.

Jackson and Stubbs [1969]: Jackson, P. E., and C. D. Stubbs, "A Study of Multiaccess Computer Communications," *Proc. AFIPS SJCC*, vol. 34, 1969, pp. 491–504.

Jain [1978]: Jain, N, "Measurements of KMPS Semaphores," Carnegie-Mellon Univ. Dept. of Comp. Sci. Tech. Rep., 1978.

James [1966]: James, R. T., "The Evolution of Wideband Services in the United States," *IEEE Int. Conv. Rec., Pt. I: Wire and Data Communication*, 1966, pp. 180–185.

James and Yockey [1972]: James, R. L., and F. J. Yockey, "Interactive Model 20 Speaks Algebraic Language," *Hewlett-Packard J.*, vol. 24, December 1972, pp. 8–13. In Chap. 49.

Kahn [1972]: Kahn, R. E., "Resource-Sharing Computer Communication Networks," *Proc. IEEE*, vol. 60, no. 11, November 1972, pp. 1,397–1,407.

Kahn [1975]: Kahn, R. E., "The Organization of Computer Resources into a Packet Radio Network," *Proc. AFIPS NCC*, vol. 44, 1975, pp. 177–186.

Kaplan [1968]: Kaplan, S. J., "The Advancing Communication Technology and Computer Communication Systems," *Proc. AFIPS SJCC*, vol. 32, 1968.

Katsuki et al. [1978]: Katsuki, D., E. S. Elsam, W. F. Mann, E. S. Roberts, J. G. Robinson, F. S. Skowronski, and E. W. Wolf, "Pluribus: An Operational Fault-Tolerant Multiprocessor," *Proc. IEEE*, vol. 66, no. 10, October 1978, pp. 1,146–1,159. Chapter 23 of this book.

Katzan [1971]: Katzan, H., Jr., "Storage Hierarchy Systems," *Proc. AFIPS SJCC*, vol. 38, May 1971, pp. 325–336.

Katzman [1977]: Katzman, J. A., "System Architecture for NonStop Computing," Tandem Computers, Inc., 1977; also printed in *Compcon*, 1977, pp. 77–80. In Chap. 29 of this book.

Kay [1977]: Kay, A., "Microelectronics and the Personal Computer," *Scientific American*, September 1977, pp. 230–244.

Kay [1978]: Kay, A., "Programming Your Own Computer," in *Science Year, The World Book Science Annual, 1979*, World Book-Childcraft International, Inc., Chicago, Ill., 1978.

Kay and Goldberg [1977]: Kay, A., and A. Goldberg, "Personal Dynamic Media," *Computer*, vol. 10, no. 3, March 1977, pp. 31–41.

Keedy [1976]: Keedy, J. L., "The Management and Technological Approach to the Design of System B," in *Proc. 7th Australian Comp. Conf. at Perth*, vol. 2, 1976, p. 997.

Keedy [1977]: Keedy, J. L., "An Outline of the ICL 2900 Series System Architecture," *Australian Comp. J.*, vol. 9, no. 2, July 1977, pp. 53–62. Chapter 17 in this book.

Keister, Ketchledge, and Lovell [1960]: Keister, W., R. W. Ketchledge, and C. A. Lovell: "Morris Electronic Telephone Exchange," in *Proc. IEE*, vol. 107, pt. B suppl., no. 20, 1960.

Keister, Ketchledge, and Vaughan [1964]: Keister, W., R. W. Ketchledge, and H. E. Vaughan, "No. 1 ESS System Organization and Objectives," *Bell Syst. Tech. J.*, September 1964, pp. 1,831–1,844.

Keller [1975]: Keller, R. M., "Look Ahead Processors," *Comp. Surv.*, vol. 7, no. 4, December 1975, pp. 177–195.

Keller [1976.]: Keller, T. W., "CRAY-1 Final Evaluation," Los Alamos Scientific Laboratory Rep. LA-6456-MS, 1976.

Kenney et al. [1979]: Kenney, G. C., D. Y. K. Lou, R. McFarlane, A. Y. Chan, J. S. Nadan, T. R. Kohler, J. G. Wagner,, and F. Zernike, "An Optical Disk Replaces 25 Mag Tapes," *IEEE Spectrum*, February 1979, pp. 33–38.

Kilburn [1948]: Kilburn, T., "A Storage System for Use with Binary Digital Computing Machines," Ph.D. thesis, Univ. of Manchester, England, 1948.

Kilburn et al. [1961]: Kilburn, T., D. J. Howarth, R. B. Payne, and F. H. Sumner, "The Manchester University Atlas Operating System, Part I: Internal Organization," *Comp. J.*, vol. 4, October 1961, pp. 222–225.

Kilburn et al. [1962]: Kilburn, T., D. B. G. Edwards, M. J. Lanigan, and F. H. Sumner, "One-level Storage System," *IRE Trans. Electronic Computers*, vol. EC-11, no. 2, April 1962, pp. 223–235. Chapter 10 of this book.

Kilburn, Edwards, and Aspinall [1960]: Kilburn, T., D. B. G. Edwards, and D. Aspinall, "A Parallel Arithmetic Unit Using a Saturated Transistor Fast-Carry Circuit," *Proc. IEE*, vol. 107, pt. B, November 1960, pp. 573–584.

Kilburn, Edwards, and Thomas [1956]: Kilburn, T., D. B. G. Edwards, and C. E. Thomas, "The Manchester University Mark II Digital Computing Machine," *Proc. IEE*, vol. 103, pt. B, supp. 2, 1956, pp. 247–268.

Kilburn and Grimsdale [1960]: Kilburn, T., and R. L. Grimsdale, "A Digital Computer Store with a Very Short Read Time," *Proc. IEE*, vol. 107, pt. B, November 1960, pp. 567–572.

Klein [1976]: Klein, M. R., "Microcircuit Device Reliability Digital Detailed Data," MDR-4, Reliability Analysis Center, Griffiss Air Force Base, New York, 1976.

Kleinrock [1964]: Kleinrock, L., *Communications Nets-Stochastic Message Flow and Delay*, McGraw-Hill Book Company, New York, 1964.

Kleinrock [1969]: Kleinrock, L., "Models for Computer Networks," *Proc. Int. Comm. Conf.*, 1969.

Kleinrock [1970]: Kleinrock, L., "Optimization of Computer Networks for Various Channel Cost Functions," *Proc. AFIPS SJCC*, 1970.

Kleinrock and Naylor [1974]: Kleinrock, L., and W. E. Naylor, "On Measured Behavior of the ARPA Network," *Proc. AFIPS NCC*, vol. 43, 1974, pp. 767–780.

Kleinrock, Naylor, and Opderbeck [1976]: Kleinrock, L, W. E. Naylor, and H. Opderbeck; "A Study of Line Overhead in the Arpanet," *Comm. ACM*, vol. 19, no. 1, January 1976, pp. 3–13.

Kleinrock and Tobagi [1975]: Kleinrock, L., and F. Tobagi,

"Packet Switching in Radio Channels, Part I: Carrier Sense Multiple-Access Modes and Their Throughput Delay Characteristics," *IEEE Trans. Comm.*, vol. T-COM. 23, no. 12, December 1975, pp. 1,400–1,416.

Knight [1966]: Knight, K. E., "Changes in Computer Performance," *Datamation*, vol. 12, no. 9, September 1966, pp. 40–54.

Knight [1972]: Knight, J. R., "A Case Study: Airline Reservation Systems," *Proc. IEEE*, vol. 60, no. 11, November 1972, pp. 1,423–1,430.

Kohoutek [1972]: Kohoutek, H. J., "9800 Processor Incorporates 8-MHz Microprocessor," *Hewlett-Packard J.*, vol. 24, December 1972, pp. 19–22. In Chap. 49 of this book.

Kolence [1979]: Kolence, K. W., "The Software Physics Handbook," Institute for Software Engineering, Palo Alto, Ca., 1979.

Kruus [1963]: Kruus, J., "Upper Bounds for the Mean Life of Self-Repairing Systems," Coordinated Science Lab., University of Illinois R-172, AD-418 174, Urbana, Ill., July 1963.

Kuck [1968]: Kuck, D. J., "Illiac IV Software and Applications Programming," *IEEE Trans. Comp.*, vol. C-17, no. 8, August 1968, pp. 758–770.

Kuck [1977]: Kuck, D. J., "A Survey of Parallel Machine Organization and Programming," *Comp. Surv.*, vol. 9, no. 1, March 1977, pp. 29–59.

Kuck [1978]: Kuck, D. J., *The Structure of Computers and Computations, Vol. 1*, John Wiley & Sons, Inc., New York, 1978.

Kuehn [1969]: Kuehn, R. E., "Computer Redundancy: Design, Performance and Future," *IEEE Trans. Rel.*, vol. R-18, February 1969, pp. 3–11.

Kulzer [1977]: Kulzer, J. J., "Systems Reliability: A Case Study of No. 4 ESS," in *System Security and Reliability, Infotech State of the Art Report*, 1977, pp. 186–188.

Lam [1974]: Lam, S. S., "Packet Switching in a Multi-access Broadcast Channel with Application to Satellite Communication in a Computer Network," Univ. of California at Los Angeles, Computer Science Dep., UCLA-ENG-7429, April 1974.

Lampson and Sproull [1979]: Lampson, B. W., and R. F. Sproull, "An Open Operating System for a Single-User Machine," *Operating Syst. Rev.*, vol. 13, no. 5, November 1979.

Langdon and Van Derveer [1967]: Langdon, J. L., and E. J. Van Derveer, "Design of a High-Speed Transistor for the ASLT Current Switch," *IBM J. Res. and Dev.*, vol. 11, no. 1, January 1967, pp. 69–73.

Lauer [1967]: Lauer, H. C., "Bulk Core in a 360/67 Time-sharing System," *Proc. AFIPS FJCC*, vol. 31, 1967, pp. 601–609.

Lavington [1975]: Lavington, S., "A History of Manchester Computers," *NCC Publications*, 1975. Excerpted in Chapter 7 of this book.

Lawson and Magenhagen [1975]: Lawson, H. W., Jr., and B. Magenhagen, "Advantages of Structured Hardware," in *Proc. 2nd Annual Symp. on Comp. Arch.*, University of Houston, 1975, pp. 152–158.

Levin et al. [1975]: Levin, R., E. Cohen, W. Corwin, F. Pollack, and W. Wulf: "Policy/Mechanism Separation in Hydra," *Proc. 5th Symp. on Operating Systems Principles*, 1975, pp. 132–140.

Levin and Schroeder [1979]: Levin, R., and M. D. Schroeder, "Transport of Electronic Messages through a Network," Xerox Palo Alto Research Center GSL 79-4, 1979.

Levy and Eckhouse [1960]: Levy, H. M., and R. H. Eckhouse, Jr., *Computer Programming and Architecture, The VAX-11*, Digital Press, Bedford, MA, 1980.

Lewis [1963]: Levis, T. B., "Primary Processor and Data Storage Equipment for Orbiting Astronimical Observatory," *IEEE Trans. Electronic Computers*, vol. EO-12, December 1963, pp. 677–686.

Lewis, Reed, and Robinson [1978]: Lewis, D. O., J. W. Reed, and T. S. Robinson, "System/38 I/O Structure," *IBM System/38 Tech. Dev.*, IBM GS80-0237, 1978, pp. 25–27.

Linden [1976]: Linden, T. A., "Operating System Structures to Support Security and Reliable Software," *Comp. Surv.*, vol. 8, no. 4, 1976, p. 409.

Lindquist, Seeber, and Comeau [1966]: Lindquist, A. B., R. R. Seeber, and L. W. Comeau, "A Time-sharing System Using an Associative Memory," *Proc. IEEE*, vol. 54, no. 12, December 1966, pp. 1,774–1,779.

Liptay [1968]: Liptay, J. S., "Structural Aspects of the System/360 Model 85, Part II: The Cache," *IBM Syst. J.*, vol. 7, no. 1, 1968, pp. 15–21.

Lipton [1973]: Lipton, R. J., "On Synchronization of Primitive Systems," Ph. D. thesis, Carnegie-Mellon Univ., May 1973.

Lloyd [1967]: Lloyd, R. H. F., "ASLT: An Extension of Hybrid Miniaturization Techniques," *IBM J. Res. and Dev.*, vol. 11, no. 1, January 1967, pp. 86–92.

Locks [1973]: Locks, M. O., *Reliability, Maintainability, & Availability Assessment*, Spartan Books/Hayden Book Company, Inc., New York, 1973.

Lonergan and King [1961]: Lonergan, W., and P. King, "Design of the B 5000 System," *Datamation*, vol. 7, no. 5, May 1961, pp. 28–32. Chapter 9 of this book.

Long [1969]: Long, J. E., "To the Outer Planets," *Astronaut. Aeronaut.*, vol. 7, June 1969, pp. 32–47.

Lonsdale and Warburton [1956]: Lonsdale, L., and E. T. Warburton, "Mercury: A High Speed Digital Computer," *Proc. IEE*, vol. 103, pt. B., supp. 2, 1956, pp. 174–183.

Lowerre [1976]: Lowerre, B., "The HARPY Speech Recognition System," Ph.D. thesis, Carnegie-Mellon Univ., 1976.

Lucas [1971]: Lucas, H. C., "Performance Evaluation and Monitoring," *Comp. Surv.*, vol. 3, no. 3, 1971, pp. 79–91.

Lunde [1977]: Lunde, A, "Empirical Evaluation of Some Features of Instruction Set Processor Architecture," *Comm. ACM*, vol. 20, no. 3, 1977, pp. 143–153.

Lyons, and Vanderkulk [1962]: Lyons, R. E., and W. Vanderkulk, "The Use of Triple-Modular Redundancy to Improve Computer Reliability," *IBM J. Res. and Dev.*, vol. 6, April 1962, pp. 200–209.

Maher [1961]: Maher, R. J., "Problems of Storage Allocation in a Multiprocessor Multiprogrammed System," *Comm. ACM*, vol. 4, no. 10, October 1961, pp. 421–422.

Mandigo [1976]: Mandigo, P. D., "No. 2B ESS: New Features for a More Efficient Processor," *Bell Syst. Tech. J.*, February 1976.

Mann, Ornstein, and Kraley [1976]: Mann, W. F., S. M. Ornstein, and M. F. Kraley, "A Network-Oriented Multiprocessor Front-End Handling Many Hosts and Hundreds of Terminals," *Proc. AFIPS NCC*, vol. 45, 1976, pp. 533–540.

Marathe [1977]: Marathe, M. V., *Performance Evaluation at the Hardware Architecture Level and the Operating System Kernal Design Level*, Ph.D. thesis, Carnegie-Mellon Univ., 1977.

Marill [1966]: Marill, T., "Cooperative Networks of Time-shared Computers," Computer Corporation of America preliminary study, 1966. Also private report, Lincoln Laboratory, Massachusetts Institute of Technology, Cambridge, Mass. 1966.

Marill and Roberts [1966]: Marill, T., and L. G. Roberts, "Toward a Cooperative Network of Time-shared Computers," *Proc. AFIPS SJCC*, 1966.

Mathur [1971a]: Mathur, F. P., "On Reliability Modeling and Analysis of Ultra-reliable Fault-Tolerant Digital Systems," *IEEE Trans. Comp.*, vol. C-20, no. 11, November 1971, pp. 1,376–1,382.

Mathur [1971b]: Mathur, F. P., "Reliability Estimation Procedures and CARE: The Computer Aided Reliability Estimation Program," *Jet Propulsion Lab. Quarterly Tech. Rev.*, vol. 1, October 1971.

Mathur and Avižienis [1970]: Mathur, F. P., and A. Avižienis: "Reliability Analysis and Architecture of a Hybrid-Redundant Digital System: Generalized Triple Modular Redundancy with Self-Repair," *Proc. AFIPS SJCC*, vol. 36, 1970, pp. 375–383.

Maurer [1966]: Maurer, W. D., "A Theory of Computer Instructions," *J. ACM*, vol. 13, no. 2, April 1966, pp. 226–235.

Mazor [1968]: Mazor, S., "Programming and/or Logic Design," in *Dig. 1968 Comp. Conf.*, Los Angeles, Calif., 1968.

McCalley and Barrett [1978]: McCalley, R. D., and K. J. Barrett, "Network Design Allows Diverse Gear Access to Host," *Data Comm.*, February 1978.

McDaniel [1977]: McDaniel, G., "METRIC: A Kernel Instrumentation System for Distributed Environments," *Operating Syst. Rev.*, vol. 11, no. 5, November 1977, pp. 93–99.

McGehearty [1980]: McGehearty, P., "Performance Evaluation of a Multiprocessor under an Interative Workload," Ph.D. thesis, Carnegie-Mellon Univ., 1980.

McKenzie et al. [1972]: McKenzie, A. A., B. P. Cosell, J. M. McQuillan, and M. Thrope, "The Network Control Center for the ARPA Network," *Proc. 1st Int. Conf. Comp. Comm.*, 1972, pp. 185–191. Also in R. P. Blanc and I. W. Cotton, eds., *Computer Networking*, IEEE Press, New York, 1976, pp. 319–325.

McKevitt and Bayliss [1979]: McKevitt, J., and J. Bayliss, "New Options from Big Chips," *IEEE Spectrum*, vol. 16, no. 3, March 1979, pp. 28–34.

McLean [1977]: McLean, J., "Univac Disbanding Future Systems Plan," *Electronic News*, December 1977.

McQuillan et al. [1972]: McQuillan, J. M., W. R. Crowther, B. P. Cosell, D. C. Walden, and F. E. Heart, "Improvements in the Design and Performance of the ARPA Network," *Proc. AFIPS FJCC*, vol. 41, pt. 2, 1972, pp. 741–754.

Meade [1970]: Meade, R. M., "On Memory System Design," *Proc. AFIPS FJCC*, vol. 37, November 1970, pp. 33–43.

Mennie [1978]: Mennie, D., "Personal Computers for the Entrepreneur," *IEEE Spectrum*, vol. 15, no. 9, September 1978, pp. 30–35.

Mercer [1957]: Mercer, R. J., "Micro-programming," *J. ACM*, vol. 4, no. 2, 1957, pp. 151–171.

Metcalfe [1972a]: Metcalfe, R. M., "Strategies for Interprocess Communication in a Distributed Computing system," in *Proc. Symp. Comp. Comm. Networks and Teletraffic,* Polytechnic Press, New York, 1972.

Metcalfe [1972b]: Metcalfe, R. M., "Strategies for Operating Systems in Computer Networks," *Proc. ACM Natl. Conf.*, 1972, pp. 278–281.

Metcalfe [1973a]:Metcalfe, R. M., "Packet Communication," Project MAC, MIT MAC TR-114, July 1973.

Metcalfe [1973b]: Metcalfe, R. M., "Steady-State Analysis of a Slotted and Controlled Aloha System with Blocking," *Proc. 6th Hawaii Int. Conf. Sys. Sci.*, 1973, pp. 375–380.

Metcalfe [1974]: Metcalfe, R. M., "Distributed Algorithms for a Broadcast Queue," talk given at Stanford Univ., November 1974, and at Univ. of California at Berkeley, February 1975.

Metcalfe and Boggs [1976]: Metcalfe, R. M., and D. R. Boggs, "Ethernet: Distributed Packet Switching for Local Computer Networks," *Comm. ACM,* vol. 19, no. 7, July 1976, pp. 395–404. Chapter 26 of this book.

Mil 217A [1965]: U.S. Dept. of Defense, Military Standardization Handbook 217A: "Reliability Prediction of Electronic Equipment," 1965.

Mil 217B [1974]: U.S. Dept. of Defense, Military Standardization Handbook 217B: "Reliability Prediction of Electronic Equipment," 1974.

"Military Computer Architectures" [1977]: "Military Computer Architectures: A Look at the Alternatives," special issue of *Computer,* vol. 10, no. 10, October 1977.

Minker [1971]: Minker, J., *A Bibliography of Associative or Content-Addressable Memory System: 1956–1971,* Auerbach Corp., Philadelphia, 1971.

Mitchell, Maybury, and Sweet [1979]: Mitchell, J. G., W. Maybury, and R. E. Sweet, "Mesa Language Manual," Xerox Palo Alto Research Center CSL 79-3, 1979.

Molnar, Ornstein, and Anne [1967]: Molnar, C. E., S. M. Ornstein, and A. Anne, "The CHASM: A Macromodular Computer for Analyzing Neuron Models," *Proc. AFIPS SJCC,* vol. 30, 1967, pp. 393–401.

Monnier [1968]: Monnier, R. E., "A New Electronic Calculator with Computerlike Capabilities," *Hewlett-Packard J.*, vol. 20, no. 1, September 1968, pp. 3–9. In Chap. 48 of this book.

Morris, Sumner, and Wyld [1967]: Morris, D., F. H. Sumner,

and M. T. Wyld, "An Appraisal of the Atlas Supervisor," *Proc. ACM Natl. Meeting,* 1967, pp. 67–75.

Morse, Pohlman, and Ravenel [1978]: Morse, S. P., W. B. Pohlman, and B. W. Ravenel, "The Intel 8086 Micropocessor A 16-Bit Evolution of the 8080," *Computer,* June 1978, pp. 18–27.

Morse [1980]: Morse, S. P: "The 8086 Primer," Hayden Book Co., New York, 1980.

Mudge [1977]: Mudge, J. C., "Design Decisions Achieve Price/Performance Balance in Mid-range Minicomputers," *Computer Design,* vol. 16, no. 3, August 1977, pp. 87–95.

Mullery, Schauer, and Rice [1963]: Mullery, A. P., R. F. Schauer, and R. Rice, "Adam: A Problem-Oriented Symbol Processor," *Proc. AFIPS SJCC,* vol. 23, 1963, pp. 367–380.

Murthy [1975]: Murthy, P., "Analysis of a Carrier-Sense Random-Access System with Random Packet Length," Univ. of Hawaii Aloha System Technical Report B75-17, May 1975.

Myer and Sutherland [1968]: Myer, T. H., and I. E. Sutherland, "On the Design of Display Processors," *Comm. ACM,* vol. 11, no. 6, June 1968, pp. 410–414.

Myers [1977]: Myers, G. J., "The Case against Stack-Oriented Instruction Sets," *Sigarch News,* August 1977.

Myers et al. [1977]: Myers, M. N., et al., "Maintenance Software," *Bell Syst. Tech. J.*, vol. 56, no. 7, September 1977, pp. 1,139–1,167.

National Library of Medicine [1968]: National Library of Medicine, "Biomedical Communications Network," Tech. Dev. Plan, June 1968.

Needham [1972]: Needham, R. M., "Protection Systems and Protection Implementations," *Proc. AFIPS FJCC,* vol. 41, pt. 1, 1972, pp. 571–578.

Needham and Walker [1977]: Needham, R. M., and R. D. H. Walker, "The Cambridge CAP Computer and Its Protection System," *Proc. 6th Symp. on Operating Systems Principles,* 1977.

Nelson and Ricci [1972]: Nelson, G. E., and D. W. Ricci, "A Practical Interface System for Electronic Instruments," *Hewlett-Packard J.*, October 1972.

Neumann, et al. [1973]: Neumann, P. G., K. N. Levitt, J. Goldberg, and J. H. Wensley, "A Study of Fault-Tolerant Computing: Final Report," Stanford Research Institute, July 1973.

Newcomer et al. [1976]: Newcomer, J., E. Cohen, D. Jefferson, T. Lane, R. Levin, F. Pollack, and W. Wulf, "Hydra: Basic Kernel Reference Manual," Carnegie-Mellon Univ. Dept. of Computer Science Technical Report, 1976.

Newman and Sproull [1979]: Newman, W. M., and R. F. Sproull, *Principles of Interactive Computer Graphics*, 2d ed., McGraw-Hill Book Company, New York, 1979.

NOC Symp [1968]: National Security Agency, "Networks of Computers Symposium NOC-68," in *Proc. Invitational Workshop*, Fort Meade, Md., 1969.

NOC Symp [1969]: National Security Agency: "Networks of Computers Symposium NOC-69," in ibid.

Nowak [1976]: Nowak, J. S., "No. 1A ESS: A New High Capacity Switching System," *Int. Switching Symp. Rec.*, Japan, 1976.

Noyce [1977]: Noyce, R. N., "Large-Scale Integration: What Is Yet to Come?," *Science*, vol. 195, no. 4,283, March 1977, pp. 1,102–1,106.

O'Loughlin [1975]; O'Loughlin, J. F., "Microprogramming a Fixed Architecture Machine," in *Infotech State of the Art Report, Microprogramming and Systems Architecture*, pp. 205–224, 1975.

O'Murphy and Wade [1970]: O'Murphy, J., and R. M. Wade, "The IBM 360/195," *Datamation*, April 1970.

Okumura et al. [1968]: Okumura, Y., E. Ohmori, T. Kawano, and K. Fukuda, "Field Strength and Its Variability in UHF and VHF Land-Mobile Radio Service," *Rev. Electrical Comm. Lab.*, vol. 16, nos. 9–10, September–October 1968.

Oleinick [1979]: Oleinick, P. N., "The Implementation and Evaluation of Parallel Algorithms on C.mmp," Ph.D. thesis, Carnegie-Mellon Univ., 1979.

Oleinick and Fuller [1978]: Oleinick, P. N., and S. H. Fuller, "The Implementation and Evaluation of a Parallel Algorithm on C.mmp.," Carnegie-Mellon Univ. Dept. of Computer Science Technical Report, 1978.

Organick [1972]: Organick, E. I., *The Multics System: An Examination of Its Structure*, MIT Press, Cambridge, Mass., 1972.

Organick [1973]: Organick, E. I., *Computer System Organization: The B5700/6700 Series*, Academic Press, Inc., New York, 1973.

Ornstein et al. [1972]: Ornstein, S. M., F. E. Heart, W. R. Crowther, S. B. Russell, H. K. Rising, and A. Michel, "The Terminal IMP for the ARPA Computer Network," *Proc. AFIPS SJCC*, vol. 40, 1972, pp. 243–254. Also in W. W. Chu, ed., *Advances in Computer Communications*, Artech House, Dedham, Mass., 1974, pp. 317–328; and in P. E. Green and R. W. Lucky, eds., *Computer Communications*, IEEE Press, New York, 1975, pp. 354–365.

Ornstein et al. [1975]: Ornstein, S. M., W. R. Crowther, M. F. Kraley, R. D. Bressler, A. Michel, and F. E. Heart: "Pluribus: A Reliable Multiprocessor," *Proc. AFIPS NCC*, vol. 44, 1975, pp. 551–559.

Ornstein and Walden [1975]: Ornstein, S. M., and D. C. Walden, "The Evolution of a High Performance Modular Packet-Switch," *1975 Int. Conf. Comm.*, vol. I, 1975, pp. 6-17 to 6-21.

Osborne [1968]: Osborne, T. E., "Hardware Design of the Model 9100A Calculator," *Hewlett-Packard J.*, vol. 20, no. 1, September 1968, pp. 10–13. In Chap. 48 of this book.

Padegs [1964]: Padegs, A., "The Structure of System/360, Part IV: Channel Design Considerations," *IBM Syst. J.*, vol. 3, no. 2, 1964, pp. 165–180.

Padegs [1968]: Padegs, A., "Structural Aspects of the System/360 Model 85, Part III: Extension to Floating-Point Architecture," *IBM Syst. J.*, vol. 7, no. 1, 1968, pp. 22–29.

Papain [1957]: Papian, W. N., "High-Speed Computer Stores 2.5 Megabits," *Electronics*, vol. 30, no. 10, October 1957, pp. 162–167.

Parnas [1972]: Parnas, D. L., "On the Response to Detected Errors in Hierarchially Structured Systems," Carnegie-Mellon Univ. Dept. of Computer Science Technical Report, 1972.

Patzer and Vandling [1967]: Patzer, William J., and Gilbert C. Vandling, "Systems Implications of Microprogramming," *Computer Design*, vol. 6, no. 12, December 1967, pp. 62–66.

Peacock [19??]: Peacock, A., "Read-Only Memory and Computer Control."[1]

Perry and Plugge [1961]: Perry, M. N., and W. R. Plugge, "American Airlines 'Sabre' Electronic Reservations System," *Proc. AFIPS WJCC*, 1961.

Peterson [1961]: Peterson, W. W., *Error Correcting Codes*, MIT Press, Cambridge, Mass., 1961.

Peterson and Weldon [1972]: Peterson, W. W., and E. J. Weldon, *Error Correcting Codes*, MIT Press, Cambridge, Mass., 1972.

Phister [1979]: Phister, M., Jr., *Data Processing Technology and Economics*, 2d ed., Santa Monica Publishing Co. and Digital Press, Maynard, Mass., 1979.

PIC [1979a]: *PIC Series Microcomputer User's Manual*, General Instrument Corp., Hicksville, N. Y., 1979.

PIC [1979b]: *PIC Cross Assembler User's manual*, General Instrument Corp., Hicksville, N.Y., 1979.

[1]To the authors' knowledge, this article has not been published. However, Tucker covers the material that should be in Peacock.

Pinnow, Ranweiler, and Miller [1978]: Pinnow, K. W., J. G. Ranweiler, and J. F. Miller, "System/38 Object-Oriented Architecture," *IBM System/38 Tech. Dev.*, IBM GS80-0237, 1978, pp. 55–58. In Chap. 32 of this book.

Popek and Goldberg [1974]; Popek, G. J., and R. P. Goldberg, "Formal Requirements for Virtualizable Third Generation Architectures," *Comm. ACM.*, vol. 17., no. 7, July 1974, pp. 412–421.

Presser [1975]: Presser, L., "Multiprogramming Coordination," *Comp. Surv.*, vol. 7, no. 1, March 1975, pp. 21–44.

Queyssac [1979]: Queyssac, D., "Projecting VLSI's Impact of Microprocessors," *IEEE Spectrum*, vol. 16, no. 5, 1979, pp. 38–41.

Raichelson and Collins [1966]: Raichelson, E., and G. A. Collins, "A Method for Comparing the Internal Operating Speeds of Computers," *Comm. ACM*, vol. 7, no. 5, May 1966, pp. 309–310.

Ramamoorthy and Li [1977]; Ramamoorthy, C. V., and H. F. Li, "Pipeline Architecture," *Comp. Surv.*, vol. 9, no. 1, March 1977, pp. 61–102.

Randall and Russell [1964]; Randall, B., and L. J. Russell, *ALGOL 60 Implementation,* Academic Press, Inc., New York, 1964.

Randell and Kuehner [1968]: Randell, B., and C. J. Kuehner, "Dynamic Storage Allocation Systems," *Comm. ACM*, vol. 11, no. 5, May 1968, pp. 297–306.

Rao [1974]: Rao, T. R. N., *Error Coding for Arithmetic Processors*, Academic Press, Inc., New York, 1974.

Reed and Brimley [1962]: Reed, I. S., and D. E. Brimley, "On Increasing the Operating Life of Unattended Machines," RAND Corporation Memorandum RM-3338-PR, November 1962.

Reeves [1975]: Reeves, R. E., "Computer Architecture Issues in Large-Scale Systems," in *9th Asilomar Conference*, Naval Postgraduate School, Monterey, Calif., 1975.

Retz [1975]: Retz, D. L., "Operating System Design Considerations for the Packet Switching Environment," *Proc. AFIPS NCC*, vol. 44, 1975, pp. 155–160.

Reynolds [1978]: Dean Witter Reynolds, Inc., *Random-Access Monthly*, A1 437/20, June 1978, p. 4.

Rice [1967]: Rice, R., "Impact of Arrays on Digital Systems," *IEEE J. Solid-State Circuits*, vol. SC-2, no. 4, December 1967.

Rice and Smith [1971]; Rice, R., and W. R. Smith, "SYMBOL: A Major Departure from Classic Software Dominated von Neumann Computing Systems," *Proc. AFIPS SJCC*, vol. 38, 1971, pp. 575–587. In Chap. 30 of this book.

Richards [1969]: Richards, M., "BCPL: A Tool for Compiler Writing and System Programming," *Proc. AFIPS SJCC*, vol. 35, 1969, pp. 557–566.

Ritchie et al. [1978]: Ritchie, D. M., S. C. Johnson, M. E. Lesk, and B. W. Kernighan, "The C Programming Language," *Bell Syst. Tech. J.*, vol. 57, no. 6, July–August 1978, pp. 1,991–2,019.

Roberts [1967]: Roberts, L. G., "Multiple Computer Networks and Intercomputer Communication," *Proc. ACM Symp. on Operating Systems Principles*, 1967.

Roberts [1968]: Roberts, L. G., "Access Control and File Directories in Computer Networks," in *IEEE Int. Conv.*, 1968.

Roberts [1969]: Roberts, L. G., "Resource Sharing Computer Networks," in *IEEE Int. Conf.*, 1969.

Roberts [1973]: Roberts, L., "Capture Effects on Aloha Channels," *Proc. 6th Hawaii Int. Conf. Sys. Sci.*, 1973.

Roberts and Wessler [1970]: Roberts, L. G., and B. D. Wessler, "Computer Network Development to Achieve Resource Sharing," *Proc. AFIPS SJCC*, vol. 36, 1970, pp. 543–549.

Roberts and Wessler [1973]: Roberts, L. G., and B. Wessler, "The ARPA Computer Network," in Abramson and Kuo, eds., *Computer Communication Networks*, Prentice-Hall, Inc., Englewood Cliffs, N.J., 1973.

Robertson and Ramakrishna [1977]: Robertson, G., and K. Ramakrishna, "ZOG: A Man-Machine Communication Philosophy," Carnegie-Mellon Univ. Dept. of Computer Science Technical Report, August 1977.

Rosen [1969]: Rosen, S., "Electronic Computers: A Historical Survey," *Comp. Surv.*, vol. 1, no. 1, March 1969, pp. 7–36.

Rosin [1969]: Rosin, R. F., "Contemporary Concepts of Microprogramming and Emulation," *Comp. Surv.*, vol. 1, no. 4, December 1969, pp. 197–212.

Rothman [1959]: Rothman, S., "R/W 40 Data Processing System," International Conference on Information Processing and Auto-Math 59, Ramo-Wooldridge (a division of Thompson Ramo Woodridge, Inc.), Los Angeles, Calif., June 1959.

Rowe [1975]: Rowe, L. A., "The Distributed Computing Operating System," Dept. of Information Science, Univ. of California at Irvine, Technical Report 66, June 1975.

Ruben et al. [1976]: Ruben, S., R. Faiss, J. Lyon, and M. Quinn, "Application of a Parallel Processing Computer in LACIE," in *Proc. 1976 Int. Conf. on Parallel Processing*, Waldenwoods, Mich., 1976, pp. 24–32.

Rubin, Guggenheim, and Bihary [1978]; Rubin, S., R. Guggenheim, and D. Bihary, "Graphics Display Processor Users Manual," Carnegie-Mellon Univ. Dept. of Computer Science Technical Report, 1978.

Rudolph [1972]: Rudolph, F. A., "A Production Implementation of an Associative Array Processor: STARAN," *Proc. AFIPS FJCC*, 1972, pp. 229–241. Excerpted in Chap. 21 of this book.

Rudolph, Fulmer, and Meilander [1971]: Rudolph, J. A., L. C. Fulmer, and W. C. Meilander, "The Coming of Age of the Associative Processor," *Electronics*, February 1971, pp. 91–96.

Russell [1978]; Russell, R. M., "The CRAY-1 Computer System," *Comm. ACM*, vol. 21, no. 1, January 1978, pp. 63–72. Chapter 44 of this book.

Rustin [1970]: Rustin, R., ed., *Computer Networks: Courant Computer Science Symposium 3*, Prentice-Hall, Inc., Englewood Cliffs, N. J., 1970.

Scantlebury, Wilkinson, and Bartlett [1968]: Scantlebury, R. A., P. T. Wilkinson, and K. A. Bartlett, "The Design of a Message Switching Centre for a Digital Communication Network," *Proc. IFIP Cong.*, vol. 2, 1968.

Schroeder [1972]: Schroeder, M., Cooperation of Mutually Suspicious Subsystems in a Computer Utility, Ph.D. thesis, Massachusetts Institute of Technology, September 1972.

Schroeder and Saltzer [1972]: Schroeder, M. D., and J. H. Saltzer, "A Hardware Architecture for Implementing Protection Rings," *Comm. ACM*, vol. 15, March 1972, pp. 157–170.

Schwartz [1977]: Schwartz, M., *Computer-Communication Network Design and Analysis*, Prentice-Hall, Inc., Englewood Cliffs, N.J., 1977.

Sechler, Strube, and Turnbull [1967]: Sechler, R. F., A. R. Strube, and J. R. Turnbull, "ASLT Circuit Design," *IBM J. Res. and Dev.*, vol. 11, no. 1, January 1967, pp. 74–85.

Seley and Vigilante [1964]: Seley, E. L., and F. S. Vigilante, "Common Control: For an Electronic Private Branch Exchange," *IEEE Trans. Comm. and Elect.*, July 1964, pp. 321–329.

Shannon [1948]: Shannon, C. E., "A Mathematical Theory of Communication," *Bell Syst. Tech. J.*, 27, 1948, pp. 379–423, 623–656.

Sharpe [1969]: Sharpe, W. F., *The Economics of Computers*, Columbia University Press, New York, 1969.

Shaw [1974]: Shaw, A. C., *The Logical Design of Operating Systems*, Prentice-Hall, Inc., Englewood Cliffs, NJ, 1974, p. 74

Shaw et al. [1958]: Shaw, J. C., A Newell, H. A. Simon, and T. O.

Ellis, "A Command Structure for Complex Information Processing," *Proc. WJCC*, 1958, pp. 119–128.

Shima, Faggin, and Mazor [1974]: Shima, M., F. Faggin, and S. Mazor, "An N-Channel 8-Bit Single Chip Microprocessor," *IEEE Int. Solid-State Circuits Conf.*, February 1974, pp. 56–57.

Shoch [1977]: Shoch, J. F., "An Overview of the Programming Language Smalltalk-72," in *Convention Informatique*, Paris, 1977; and in *SIGPLAN NOT.*, 1979.

Shoch and Hupp [1979]: Shoch, J. F., and J. Hupp, "Performance of an Ethernet Local Network: A Preliminary Report," in *Proc. Local Area Communication Network Symposium, NBS*, Boston, 1979.

Short [1968]; Short, R. A., "The Attainment of Reliable Digital Systems through the Use of Redundancy: A Survey," *IEEE Computing Group News*, vol. 2, March 1968, pp. 2–17.

"Shrinking World" [1974]: "The Shrinking World: Computer Networks and Communications," special issue of *Computer*, vol. 7, no. 2, February 1974.

Shustek [1978]: Shustek, L. J., "Analysis and Performance of Computer Instruction Sets," Stanford Linear Accelerator Center 205, STAN-CS-78-658, Stanford, Calif., May 1978.

Siewiorek and Barbacci [1976]: Siewiorek, D. P., and M. R. Barbacci, "The CMU RT-CAD System: An Innovative Approach to Computer Aided Design," *Proc. AFIPS NCC*, vol. 45, 1976, pp. 643–655.

Siewiorek et al. [1978a]: Siewiorek, D. P., V. Kini, H. Mashburn, S. McConnel, and M. Tsao, " A Case Study of C.mmp, Cm* and C.vmp, Part I: Experiences with Fault Tolerance in Multiprocessor Systems," *Proc. IEEE*, vol. 66, no. 10, October 1978, pp. 1,178–1,199.

Siewiorek et al. [1978b]: Siewiorek, D. P., V. Kini, H. Mashburn, and R. Joobbani, "A Case Study of C.mmp, Cm*, and C.vmp, Part II: Predicting and Calibrating Reliability of Multiprocessor Systems," *Proc. IEEE*, vol. 66, no. 10, 1978, pp. 1,200–1,220.

Simpson et al. [1978]: Simpson, W. D., G. Luecke, D. L. Cannon, and D. H. Clemens, *9900 Family Systems Design and Data Book*, Texas Instruments, Inc., 1978.

Slade and McMahon [1957]: Slade, A. E., and H. O. McMahon, "The Cryotron Catalog Memory System," *Proc. EJCC*, vol. 10, 1957, pp. 115–120.

Slotnick [1967]: Slotnick, D. L., "Unconventional Systems," *Proc. AFIPS SJCC*, 1967, pp. 477–481.

Slotnick [1971]: Slotnick, D. L., "The Fastest Computer," *Scientific American*, February 1971, pp. 76–87.

Slotnick, Borck, and McReynolds [1962]: Slotnick, D. L., W. C. Borck, and R. C. McReynolds, "The SOLOMON Computer," *Proc. AFIPS FJCC*, 1962, pp. 97–107.

Smith [1963]: Smith, W. R., "Associative Memory Techniques for Large Data Processors," Ph.D. thesis, Iowa State Univ., 1963.

Smith [1968]: Smith, W. R., "System Design Based on LSI Constraints: A Case History," in *Dig. 1968 Comp. Group Conf.*, Los Angeles, Calif., 1968.

Smith [1972]: Smith, D. J., *Reliability Engineering*, Barnes & Noble, Inc., New York, 1972.

Smith et al. [1971]: Smith, W. R., R. Rice, G. D. Chesley, T. A. Laliotis, S. F. Lundstrom, M. A. Calhoun, L. D. Gerould, and T. C. Cook, "SYMBOL: A Large Experimental System Exploring Major Hardware Replacement of Software," *Proc. AFIPS SJCC*, 1971, pp. 601–616. In Chap. 30 of this book.

Smith et al. [1977]: Smith, W. R., J. J. Cornyn, A. H. Coleman, W. Svirsky, R. Estell, and P. Sabin, "Life Cycle Cost Models for Comparing Computer Family Architectures," *Proc. AFIPS NCC*, vol. 46, 1977.

Snow and Siewiorek [1978]: Snow, E. A., and D. P. Siewiorek, "Impact of Implementation Design Tradeoffs on Performance: The PDP-11, A Case Study," Carnegie-Mellon Univ. Dept. of Computer Science Technical Report, Pittsburgh, 1978.

Solomon [1966]: Solomon, M. B., Jr., "Economies of Scale and the IBM System/360," *Comm. ACM*, vol. 9, no. 6, June 1966, pp. 435–440.

Spangler [1972a]: Spangler, R. M., "A New Series of Programmable Calculators," *Hewlett-Packard J.*, vol. 24, December 1972, pp. 2–4. In Chap. 49 of this book.

Spangler [1972b]: Spangler, R. M., "BASIC-Language Model 30 Can Be Calculator, Computer, or Terminal," *Hewlett-Packard J.*, vol. 24, December 1972, pp. 14–18. In Chap. 49 of this book.

Spencer and Vigilante [1969]: Spencer, A. E., and F. S. Vigilante, "No 2 ESS: System Organization and Objectives," *Bell Syst. Tech. J.*, October 1969.

Sproull [1979]: Sproull, R. F., "Raster Graphics for Interactive Programming Environments," *Computer Graphics*, summer 1979.

Staehler [1977]: Staehler, R. E., "1A Processor: Organizations and Objectives," *Bell Syst. Tech. J.*, February 1977, pp. 119–134.

Staehler and Watters [1976]: Staehler, R. E., and R. J. Watters, "1A Processor: An Ultra-dependable Common Control," in *Int. Switching Symp. Rec.*, vol. 2, Japan, 1976, pp. 1.1–1.7.

Stieglitz, Weiner, and Kleitman [1969]: Steiglitz, K., P. Weiner, and D. J. Kleitman, "The Design of Minimum Cost Survivable Networks," *IEEE Trans. Circuit Theory*, vol. CT-16, November 1969.

Stevens [1964]: Stevens, W. Y., "The Structure of System/360, Part II: System Implementations," *IBM Syst. J.*, vol. 3, no. 2, 1964, pp. 136–142. Chapter 41 of this book.

Stillman [1972]: Stillman, N. J., "Associative Processing and Computer Graphics: A Feasibility Study," USAF RADC-TR-72-57, April 1972.

Stone [1971]: Stone, H. S., "Parallel Processing with the Perfect Shuffle," *IEEE Trans. Comp.*, vol. C-20, no. 2, February 1971, pp. 153–161.

Stone and Siewiorek [1975]: Stone, H. S., and D. P. Siewiorek, *Introduction to Computer Organization and Data Structures: PDP-11 Edition*, McGraw-Hill, New York, 1975.

Storey [1976]: Storey, T. F., "Design of a Microprogram Control for a Processor in an Electronic Switching System," *Bell Syst. Tech. J.*, February 1976, pp. 183–232.

Strecker [1971]: Strecker, W. D., "An Analysis of the Instruction Execution Rate in Certain Computing Structures," Ph.D. thesis, Carnegie-Mellon Univ., 1971.

Strecker [1976a]: Strecker, W. D., Personal Communication, 1976.

Strecker [1976b]: Strecker, W. D., "Cache Memories for PDP-11 Family Computers," *Proc. 3d Symp. Computer Architecture*, 1976, pp. 155–158.

Strecker [1978]: Strecker, W. D., "VAX-11/780: A Virtual Address Extension to the DEC PDP-11 Family," *Proc. AFIPS NCC*, vol. 47, 1978, pp. 967–980. Chapter 42 in this book.

Sumner, Haley, and Chen [1962]: Sumner, F. H., G. Haley, and E. C. Y. Chen, "The Central Control Unit of the 'Atlas' Computer," *Proc. IFIP Cong.*, 1962, pp. 657–662.

Sung and Woodford [1969]: Sung, R., and J. B. Woodford, "Study of Communication Links for the Biomedical Communication Network," Aerospace Report ATR-69 (7130-06)-1, 1969.

Swan [1976]: Swan, R. J., "K.mon: The C.mmp Hardware Monitor," Carnegie-Mellon Univ. Dept. of Computer Science Technical Report, 1976.

Swan, Fuller, and Siewiorek [1976]: Swan, R. J., S. H. Fuller, and

D. P. Siewiorek, "The Structure and Architectures of Cm*: A Modular, Multi-Microprocessor," in *Computer Science Research Review*, Carnegie-Mellow Univ. Dept. of Computer Science, 1976.

Swan, Fuller, and Siewiorek [1977]: Swan, R. J., S. H. Fuller, and D. P. Siewiorek, "Cm*: A Modular, Multi-Microprocessor," *Proc. AFIPS NCC*, vol. 46, 1977, pp. 637–644.

Swinehart, McDaniel, and Boggs [1979]: Swinehart, D. C., G. McDaniel, and D. R. Boggs, "WFS: A Simple Shared File System for a Distributed Environment," *Operating Syst. Rev.*, vol. 13, no. 5, November 1979.

Tandem [1976]: Tandem Computers, Inc., Tandem/16 System Description, 1976.

Teitelman [1977]: Teitelman, W., "A Display-Oriented Programmer's Assistant," *Proc. 5th Int. Joint Conf. on Artificial Intelligence*, 1977, pp. 905–917.

Teitelman [1978]: Teitelman, W., *Interlisp Reference Manual*, Xerox Palo Alto Research Center, October 1978.

Teitelman and Kahn [1969]: Teitelman, W., and R. E. Kahn, "A Network Simulation and Display Program," *Proc. 3d Annual Princeton Conf. on Information Sciences and Systems*, 1969.

Tennant and Chesley [1965]: Tennant, J. R., and G. D. Chesley, "Design and Layout of Large Integrated Circuit Boards," in *2d Annual Seminar on Integrated Circuits*, 1965.

Thomas [1973]: Thomas, R. H., "A Resource Sharing Executive for the ARPANET," *Proc. AFIPS NCC*, 1973, pp. 155–163.

Thomas and Siewiorek [1977]: Thomas, D. E., and D. P. Siewiorek, "Measuring Designer Performance to Verify Design Automation Systems," *Proc. Design Automation Conf.*, vol. 14, 1977, pp. 411–418.

Thornton [1964]: Thornton, J. E., "Parallel Operation in the Control Data 6600," *Proc. AFIPS FJCC*, vol. 26, pt. 2, 1964, pp. 33–40. Chapter 43 of this book.

Thornton [1970]: Thornton, J. E., "Design of a Computer: The Control Data 6600," Scott, Foresman & Company, Glenview, Ill., 1970.

Thurber and Wald [1975]: Thurber, K. J., and L. D. Wald, "Associative and Parallel Processors," *ACM Comp. Surv.* special issue on computer systems architecture, vol. 7, no. 4, December 1975, pp. 215–255.

TI [1975]: Texas Instruments, Inc., TMS1000 Programmer's Reference Manual, 1975.

Tomasulo [1967]: Tomasulo, R. M., "An Efficient Algorithm for Exploiting Multiple Arithmetic Units," *IBM J. Res. and Dev.*, vol. 11, 1967, pp. 25–33. Chapter 19 of this book.

"TOPS" [1970]: "TOPS Outer Planet Spacecraft," special issue of *Astronaut. Aeronaut.*, vol. 8, September 1970.

Toy [1978]: Toy, W. N., "Fault-Tolerant Design of Local ESS Processors," *Proc. IEEE*, vol. 66, no. 10, October 1978, pp. 1,126–1,145. Excerpted in Chap. 28 of this book.

Tsiang and Ulrich [1962]; Tsiang, S. H., and W. Ulrich, "Automatic Trouble Diagnosis of Complex Logic Circuits," *Bell Syst. Tech. J.*, July 1962, pp. 1,177–1,200.

Tucker [1967]: Tucker, S. G., "Microprogram Control for System/360," *IBM Syst. J.*, vol. 6, no. 4, 1967, pp. 222–241.

Turn [1974]: Turn, R., *Computers in the 1980s*, Columbia University Press, New York, 1974.

U.S. Dept. of Defense [1965]: U.S. Dept. of Defense, *Military Standardization Handbook 217A: Reliability Prediction of Electronic Equipment*, 1965.

U.S. Dept. of Defense [1974]: U.S. Dept. of Defense, *Military Standardization Handbook 217B: Reliability Prediction of Electronic Equipment*, 1974.

U.S. Patent 4,035,766 [1977].

U.S. Steel [1978]: U.S. Steel, *COBOL Analysis System (CAS) Timing Test*, May 1978.

Vadasz et al. [1969]: Vadasz, L. L., A. S. Grove, T. A. Rowe, and G. E. Moore, "Silicon Gate Technology," *IEEE Spectrum*, October 1969, pp. 27–35.

Vance, Dooley, and Diss [1957]: Vance, P. R., L. G. Dooley, and C. E. Diss, "Operation of the SAGE Duplex Computers," *Proc. EJCC*, 1957, pp. 160–163.

Vocar and Faiss [1977]: Vocar, J. M., and R. O. Faiss, "WARP Processing Using STARAN," *Proc. 1977 Picture Data Description and Management Workshop*.

Von Neumann [1956]: Von Neumann, J., "Probabilistic Logics and the Synthesis of Reliable Organisms from Unreliable Components," in C. E. Shannon and J. McCarthy, eds., *Automata Studies*, Princeton University Press, 1956, pp. 43–98.

Wagner et al. [1977]: Wagner, J. B. Lieblein, J. Rodriguez, and H. S. Stone, "Evaluation of the Candidate Architectures for the Military Computer Family," *Proc. AFIPS NCC*, vol. 46, 1977.

Wakerly [1979]: Wakerly, J. F., "The Intel MCS-48 Microcomputer Family: A Critique," *Computer*, vol. 12, no. 2, February 1979, pp. 21–31.

Walden [1972]: Walden, D. C., "A System for Interprocess Communication in a Resource Sharing Computer Network," *Comm. ACM*, vol. 15, no. 4, April 1972, pp. 221–230.

Watson [1972]: Watson, W. J., "The TI ASC: A Highly Modular and Flexible Super Computer Architecture," *Proc. AFIPS FJCC*, vol. 41, pt. 1, 1972, pp. 221–228. In Chap. 45 of this book.

Watson and Aberle [1978]: Watson, C. T., and G. F. Aberle, "System/38 Machine Data Base Support," *IBM System/38 Tech. Dev.*, IBM GS80-0237, 1978, pp. 59–62.

Weber [1967]: Weber, H., "A Microprogrammed Implementation of EULER on IBM System/360 Model 30," *Comm. ACM*, vol. 10, no. 9, September 1967, pp. 549–558. Excerpted in Chapter 12 of this book.

Wensley et al. [1978]: Wensley, J. H., L. Lamport, J. Goldberg, M. W. Green, K. N. Levitt, P. M. Melliar-Smith, R. E. Shotak, and C. B. Weinstock, "SIFT: The Design and Analysis of a Fault-Tolerant Computer for Aircraft Control," *Proc. IEEE*, vol. 66, no. 10, 1978, pp. 1,240–1,255.

Wichmann [1973]: Wichmann, B. A., *Algol 60 Compilation and Assessment*, Anderson Press, New York, 1973.

Wichmann [1976]: Wichmann, B. A., "Ackermann's Function: A Study in the Efficiency of Calling Procedures," *BIT*, vol. 16, 1976, pp. 103–110.

Wilkes [1951]: Wilkes, M. V., "The Best Way to Design an Automatic Calculating Machine," in *Manchester Univ. Comp. Inaugural Conf.*, Ferranti, Ltd., London, 1951.

Wilkes [1958]: Wilkes, M. V., "Microprogramming," *Proc. EJCC*, 1958, pp. 18–20.

Wilkes [1965]: Wilkes, M. V. "Slave Memories and Dynamic Storage Allocation," *IEEE Trans. Elect. Comp.*, Vol. EC-14, no. 2, February 1965, pp. 270–271

Wilkes and Stringer [1953]: Wilkes, M. V., and J. B. Stringer, "Microprogramming and the Design of the Control Circuits in an Electronic Digital Computer," in *Proc. Cambridge Philosophical Society*, vol. 49, 1953, pp. 230–238. Chapter 11 of this book.

Willard [1973]: Willard, D. G., "Mitrix: A Sophisticated Digital Cable Communications System," in *Proc. National Telecommunications Conference*, 1973.

Williams and Kilburn [1948]: Williams, F. C., and T. Kilburn, "Electronic Digital Computers" letter, *Nature*, vol. 162, September 1948, p. 487.

Williams and Kilburn [1949]: Williams, F. C., and T. Kilburn, "A Storage System for Use with Binary Digital Computing Machines," *Proc. IEE*, vol. 96, pt. 2, no. 30, 1949, pp. 183ff.

Williams, Kilburn, and Tootill [1951]: Williams, F. C., T. Kilburn, and G. C. Tootill, "Universal High-Speed Digital Computers: A Small Scale Experimental Machine," *Proc. IEE*, vol. 98, pt. 2, no. 61, February 1951, pp. 13–28.

Wirth and Weber [1966a]: Wirth, N., and H. Weber, "EULER: A Generalization of ALGOL, and Its Formal Definition, Part I," *Comm. ACM*, vol. 9, no. 1, January 1966, pp. 13–25.

Wirth and Weber [1966b]: Wirth, N., and H. Weber, "EULER: A Generalization of ALGOL, and Its Formal Definition, Part II," *Comm. ACM*, vol. 9, no. 2, February 1966, pp. 89–99.

Wolf [1973]: Wolf, E. W., "An Advanced Computer Communication Network," in *AIAA Computer Network Systems Conf. Rec.*, 1973.

Wulf and Bell [1972]: Wulf, W. A., and C. G. Bell, "C.mmp: A Multi-Mini-Processor," *Proc. AFIPS FJCC*, vol. 41, pt. 2, 1972, pp. 765–777.

Wulf et al. [1974]: Wulf, W. A., Cohen, W. Corwin, A. Jones, R. Levin, C. Pierson, and F. Pollack, "Hydra: The Kernel of a Multiprocessor Operating System," *Comm. ACM*, vol. 17, June 1974, pp. 337–345.

Wulf and Harbison [1978]: Wulf, W., and S. P. Harbison, "Reflections in a Pool of Processors: An Experience Report on C.mmp," *Proc. AFIPS NCC*, 1978.

Wulf, Levin, and Harbison [1980]: Wulf, W., R. Levin, and S. Harbison, *Hydra/C.mmp: An Experimental Computer System*, McGraw-Hill Book Company, New York, 1980.

Wulf, Levin, and Pierson [1975]: Wulf, W. A., R. Levin, and C. Pierson, "Overview of the Hydra Operating System Development," *Proc. 5th Symp. on Operating Systems Principles*, 1975, pp. 122–131.

Wulf, Russell, and Habermann [1971]: Wulf, W., D. B. Russell, and A. N. Habermann, "Bliss: A Language for Systems Programming," *Comm. ACM*, vol. 14, December 1971, pp. 780–790.

Yau and Fung [1977]: Yau, S. S., and H. S. Fung, "Associative Processor Architecture: A Survey," *Comp. Surv.*, vol. 9, no. 1, March 1977, pp. 3–27.

Yourdon [1972]: Yourdon, E., *Design of On-line Computer Systems*, Prentice Hall, Inc., Englewood Cliffs, N. J., 1972.

Zadeh and Desoer [1963]: Zadeh, L. A., and C. A. Desoer, *Linear System Theory*, McGraw-Hill Book Company, New York, 1963.

Acknowledgments

Advanced Micro Devices, Inc.: "Am2910 Microprogram Controller," *AMD Technical Data Bulletin*, January 1978, pp. 1–12, copyright 1977 by Advanced Micro Devices, Inc. Reproduced with permission of copyright owner.

Advanced Micro Devices, Inc.: "Am2903 Four-Bit Bipolar Microprocessor Slice," *AMD Technical Data Bulletin*, January 1978, pp. 1–22, copyright 1977 by Advanced Micro Devices, Inc. Reproduced with permission of copyright owner.

D. W. Anderson, F. J. Sparacio, and R. M. Tomasulo: "The IBM System/360 Model 91: Machine Philosophy and Instruction-Handling," *IBM Journal of Research and Development*, January 1967, pp. 8–24, copyright 1967 by and with permission of International Business Machines Corporation.

ARPANet, ARPANet Logical Map, ARPANet Geographic Map: *ARPANet Directory*, December 1978, by permission of ARPANet Project Manager.

A. Avižienis, G. C. Gilley, F. P. Mathur, D. A. Rennels, J. A. Rohr, and D. K. Rubin: "The STAR (Self-Testing And Repairing) Computer: An Investigation of the Theory and Practice of Fault-Tolerant Computer Design," *IEEE Transactions on Computers*, C-20, no. 11, November 1971, pp. 1,312–1,321, copyright 1971 by and with permission of the Institute of Electrical and Electronics Engineers, Inc., and the authors.

M. R. Barbacci: "An ISPS Primer for Instruction Set Processor," by permission of Digital Equipment Corporation, Maynard, Mass., and the author.

J. P. Bartlett: "A 'NonStop' Operating System," Tandem Computers, Inc., copyright by Tandem Computers, Inc., and reprinted with the express permission of Tandem Computers, Inc.

K. E. Batcher: "STARAN Parallel Processor System Hardware," *Proceedings AFIPS NCC*, 1974, pp. 405–410, by permission of AFIPS.

G. Bell, R. Cady, H. McFarland, B. Delagi, J. O'Loughlin, and R. Noonan: "A New Architecture for Mini-Computers: The DEC PDP-11," *Proceedings AFIPS SJCC*, 1970, pp. 657–675, by permission of AFIPS.

C. G. Bell, J. C. Mudge, and J. E. McNamara. The authors acknowledge permission of Digital Press/Digital Equipment Corporation to reprint excerpts of pp. 3–6, 9–13, and 15–17 from Chap. 1; pp. 28–34 from Chap. 2; and pp. 201–202 from Chap. 7; abstractions from Chap. 7, pp. 175–208, and Chap. 16, pp. 379–408; Chap. 8, pp. 209–228; and Appendix 1, pp. 519–535 from *Computer Engineering: A DEC View of Hardware Systems Design* (Bedford, Mass., 1978).

V. Berstis, C. D. Truxal, and J. G. Ranweiler: "System/38 Addressing and Authorization," *IBM System/38 Technical Developments*, 1978, pp. 51–54, copyright 1978 and reprinted with permission of International Business Machines Corporation.

R. Binder, N. Abramson, F. Kuo, A. Okinaka, and D. Wax: "ALOHA Packet Broadcasting: A Retrospect," *Proceedings AFIPS NCC*, 1975, pp. 203–215, by permission of AFIPS.

G. A. Blaauw and F. P. Brooks, Jr.: "The Structure of System/360, Part I: Outline of the Logical Structure," *IBM Systems Journal*, vol. 3, no. 2, 1964, pp. 119–135, copyright 1964 by and reprinted by permission of International Business Machines Corporation.

W. J. Bouknight, S. A. Denenberg, D. E. McIntyre, J. M. Randall, A. H. Sameh and D. L. Slotnick: "The Illiac IV System," *Proceedings of the IEEE*, April 1972, pp. 369–379, copyright 1972 by and printed by permission of the Institute of Electrical and Electronics Engineers, Inc.

C. D. Brown, J. M. Walden: "Model 10 Maintains Compatibility, Expands Capability," *Hewlett-Packard Journal*, no. 24, December 1972, pp. 5–8, by permission of Hewlett-Packard Company.

Burroughs Corporation: *B7700 Information Processing Systems Reference Manual*, Section 1, Chapter III, page 3-2. Copyright 1976 Burroughs Corporation. Reproduced with the permission of Burroughs Corporation.

R. P. Case and A. Padegs: "Architecture of the IBM System/370," *Communications of the ACM*, vol. 21, no. 1, January 1978, pp. 73–96, copyright 1978, Association for Computing Machinery, Inc., reprinted by permission, and by permission of the authors.

S. H. Dahlby, G. G. Henry, D. N. Reynolds, and P. T. Taylor: "System/38: A High-Level Machine," *IBM System/38 Technical Developments*, 1978, pp. 47–50, copyright 1978 by and reprinted with permission of International Business Machines Corporation.

L. C. Dean: "Texas Instruments Advanced Scientific Computer," *Informatie Jrg.*, vol. 15, no. 4, April 1973, pp. 191–193, by permission of *Informatie Jrg.* and the author.

William D. Eads, Jack M. Walden, and Edward L. Miller: "A Dual-Processor Desk-Top Computer: The HP 9845A," Hewlett-

Packard Company, by permission of Hewlett-Packard Company and the authors.

G. E. Eagn: "Versatile Input/Output Structure Welcome Peripheral Variety," *Hewlett-Packard Journal*, no. 24, December 1972, pp. 24–27, by permission of Hewlett-Packard Company.

F. Faggin: "Trends in Microcomputers," Data Show, '77 *International Symposium Proceedings*, October 4, 1977, Tokyo, pp. 51–66, by permission of the author.

S. H. Fuller, P. Shaman, D. Lamb, and W. E. Burr: "Evaluation of Computer Architectures via Test Programs," *AFIPS Conference Proceedings*, vol. 46, 1977, pp. 147–160, by permission of the publisher, AFIPS Press, and the authors.

S. H. Fuller, H. S. Stone, and W. E. Burr: "Initial Selection and Screening of the CFA Candidate Computer Architectures," *AFIPS Conference Proceedings*, vol. 46, 1977, pp. 139–146, by permission of the publisher, AFIPS Press, and the authors.

Goodyear Aerospace Corporation: "STARAN Apple Instruction Set," in *STARAN: A New Class of Computer*, pp. 14–15, by permission of Goodyear Aerospace Corporation. STARAN is a registered trademark of Goodyear Aerospace Corporation.

F. M. Gruppuso: "PIC1650 Chip Architecture and Operation," General Instrument Corporation, March 1979, by permission of the author.

E. A. Hauck and B. A. Dent: "Burroughs' B6500/B7500 Stack Mechanism," *AFIPS Conference Proceedings SJCC*, 1968, pp. 245–251, by permission of AFIPS.

R. L. Hoffman and F. G. Soltis: "Hardware Organization of the System/38," *IBM System/38 Technical Developments*, 1978, pp. 19–21, copyright 1978 by and reprinted with permission of International Business Machines Corporation.

F. E. Heart, R. E. Kahn, S. M. Ornstein, W. R. Crowther, and D. C. Walden: "The Interface Message Processor for the ARPA Computer Network," *AFIPS Proceedings SJCC*, vol. 36, 1970, pp. 551–567, by permission of AFIPS.

IBM: Figure 1, "Model 165 Data Flow and System Statistics," *IBM System/370 Model 165, Functional Characteristics*, first edition, June 1970, p. 6, copyright 1970 by and reprinted with permission of International Business Machines Corporation. In Chap. 52.

IBM: Figure 2, "Model 155 Data Flow," GA22-6942-2, File No.

S/370-01, *IBM System/370 Model 155, Functional Characteristics*, third edition, May 1972, p. 9, copyright 1972 by and reprinted with permission of International Business Machines Corporation. In Chap. 52.

IBM: Figure 7, "Instruction Processor," GA22-6943-4, File No. S/360/370-01, *IBM System/360 and System/370 Model 195, Functional Characteristics*, fifth edition, October 1975, p. 12, copyright 1975 by and reprinted with permission of International Business Machines Corporation. In Chap. 52.

IBM: Figure 10, "Fixed-Point/VFL/Decimal Execution Element," GA22-6943-4, File No. S/360/S/370-01, *IBM System/360 and System/370 Model 195, Functional Characteristics*, fifth edition, October 1975, p. 20, copyright 1975 by and reprinted with permission of International Business Machines Corporation. In Chap. 52.

IBM: Figure 11, "Floating-Point Execution Element," GA22-6943-4, File No. S/360/370-01, *IBM System/360 and System/370 Model 195, Functional Characteristics*, fifth edition, October 1975, p. 22, copyright 1975 by and reprinted with permission of International Business Machines Corporation. In Chap. 52.

R. L. James and F. J. Yockey: "Interactive Model 20 Speaks Algebraic Language," *Hewlett-Packard Journal*, vol. 24, December 1972, pp. 8–13, by permission of Hewlett-Packard Company.

D. Katsuki, E. S. Elsam, W. F. Mann, E. S. Roberts, J. G. Robinson, F. S. Skowronski, and E. W. Wolf: "Pluribus: An Operational Fault-Tolerant Multiprocessor," *Proceedings of the IEEE*, vol. 66, no. 10, October 1978, pp. 1,146–1,159, copyright 1978 by and printed by permission of the Institute of Electrical and Electronics Engineers, Inc., and the authors. The authors are with Bolt, Beranek, and Newman, Inc., Cambridge, Mass. 02138.

J. A. Katzman: "A Fault-Tolerant Computing System," Tandem Computers, Inc., copyright by Tandem Computers, Inc., and reprinted with the express permission of Tandem Computers, Inc.

J. L. Keedy: "An Outline of the ICL 2900 Series System Architecture," *Australian Computer Journal*, vol. 9, no. 2, July 1977, pp. 53–62, by permission of the *Australian Computer Journal*.

T. Kilburn, D. B. G. Edwards, M. J. Lanigan, and F. H. Sumner: "One-Level Storage System," *IRE Transactions*, EC-11, vol. 2, April 1962, pp. 223–235, copyrighted 1962 by and by permission of the Institute of Electrical and Electronics Engineers, Inc., and the authors.

H. J. Kohoutek: "9800 Processor Incorporates 8-MHz Microprocessor," *Hewlett-Packard Journal*, vol. 24, December 1972, pp. 19–22, by permission of Hewlett-Packard Company.

J. J. Kulzer: "Systems Reliability: A Case Study of No. 4 ESS," *Infotech State of the Art Report*, 1977, pp. 186–188, by permission of Infotech International Limited and the author.

S. H. Lavington: *A History of Manchester Computers*, National Computing Centre, Manchester, England, pp. 7–11, 1975, by permission of the author.

W. Lonergan and P. King: "Design of the B 5000 System," *Datamation*, vol. 7, no. 5, May 1961, pp. 28–32. Reprinted with permission of *Datamation* magazine. Copyright by Technical Publishing Company, a division of Dun-Donnelley Publishing Corporation, a Dun and Bradstreet Company, 1978. All rights reserved.

H. H. Mashburn: "The C.mmp/Hydra Project: An Architectural Overview," Department of Computer Science, Carnegie-Mellon University, Pittsburgh, Pa., by permission of the author.

R. M. Metcalfe and D. Boggs: "Ethernet: Distributed Packet Switching for Local Computer Networks," *Communications of the ACM*, vol. 19, no. 7, July 1976, pp. 395–404, copyright 1976, Association for Computing Machinery, Inc., reprinted by permission, and by permission of the authors.

R. E. Monnier, T. E. Osborne, D. S. Cochran: "The HP Model 9100A Computing Calculator," *Hewlett-Packard Journal*, vol. 10, no. 1, September 1968, pp. 3–9, 10–13, and 14–16, by permission of Hewlett-Packard Company.

S. P. Morse, B. W. Ravenel, S. Mazor, and W. B. Pohlman: "Intel Microprocessors: 8008 to 8086," Intel Corporation, copyright 1978 by and printed by permission of Intel Corporation, and the authors.

R. N. Noyce: "Microelectronics," *Scientific American*, September 1977, figure on page 67, by permission of the publisher, W. H. Freeman and Company. Copyright 1977 by Scientific American, Inc. All rights reserved.

T. E. Osborne: "Hewlett-Packard Calculator Architectures," 1978, by permission of the author.

K. W. Pinnow, J. G. Ranweiler, and J. F. Miller: "System/38 Object-Oriented Architecture," *IBM System/38 Technical Developments*, 1978, pp. 55–58, copyright 1978 by and reprinted with permission of International Business Machines Corporation.

R. Rice and W. R. Smith: "SYMBOL: A Major Departure from Classic Software Dominated von Neumann Computing Systems," *Proceedings AFIPS SJCC*, 1971, pp. 575–587, by permission of AFIPS.

J. A. Rudolph: "A Production Implementation of an Associative Array Processor: STARAN," *AFIPS Conference Proceedings FJCC*, 1972, pp. 229–241, by permission of AFIPS.

R. M. Russell: "The CRAY-1 Computer System," *Communications of the ACM*, vol. 21, no. 1, January 1978, pp. 63–72, copyright 1978, Association for Computing Machinery, Inc., reprinted by permission, and by permission of the author.

W. R. Smith, R. Rice, G. D. Chesley, T. A. Laliotis, S. F. Lundstrom, M. A. Calhoun, L. D. Gerould, and T. C. Cook: "SYMBOL: A Large Experimental System Exploring Major Hardware Replacement of Software," *Proceedings AFIPS SJCC*, 1971, pp. 601–616, by permission of AFIPS.

E. A. Snow and D. P. Siewiorek: "Implementation and Performance Evaluation of the PDP-11 Family," by permission of the authors.

R. M. Spangler: "A New Series of Programmable Calculators," *Hewlett-Packard Journal*, vol. 24, December 1972, pp. 2–4, by permission of Hewlett-Packard Company.

R. M. Spangler: "BASIC-Language Model 30 Can Be Calculator, Computer, or Terminal," *Hewlett-Packard Journal*, vol. 24, December 1972, pp. 14–18, by permission of Hewlett-Packard Company.

W. Y. Stevens: "The Structure of System/360, Part II: System Implementations," *IBM Systems Journal*, vol. 3, no. 2, 1964, pp. 136–143, copyright 1964 by and reprinted by permission of International Business Machines Corporation.

W. D. Strecker: "VAX-11/780: A Virtual Address Extension to the DEC PDP-11 Family," *Proceedings AFIPS NCC*, June 1978, pp. 967–980, by permission of AFIPS.

Texas Instruments, Inc.: extractions from "TMS1000/1200 Chip Architecture and Operation," *TMS1000 Programmer's Reference Manual*, 1975, copyright 1975 by and printed by permission of Texas Instruments, Inc.

C. P. Thacker, E. M. McCreight, B. W. Lampson, R. F. Sproull, and D. R. Boggs: "Alto: A Personal Computer," 1979, copyright 1979 by Xerox Corporation and reproduced by permission of Xerox Corporation.

J. E. Thornton: "Parallel Operation in the Control Data 6600," *AFIPS Conference Proceedings FJCC*, part 2, vol. 16, 1964, pp. 33–40, by permission of AFIPS.

R. M. Tomasulo: "An Efficient Algorithm for Exploiting Multiple Arithmetic Units," *IBM Journal of Research and Development*, January 1967, pp. 25–33, copyright by and reprinted with permission of International Business Machines Corporation.

W. N. Toy: "Fault-Tolerant Design of Local ESS Processors," *Proceedings of the IEEE*, vol. 66, no. 10, October 1978, pp. 1,126–1,145, copyright 1978 by and printed by permission of the Institute of Electrical and Electronics Engineers, Inc., and Prentice-Hall, Inc.

M. Tsao: "A PDP-8 Implemented from AMD Bit-Sliced Microprocessors," Department of Electrical Engineering, Carnegie-Mellon University, Pittsburgh, Pa., by permission of the author.

W. J. Watson: "The TI ASC: A Highly Modular and Flexible Super Computer Architecture," *AFIPS Proceedings FJCC*, 1972, pp. 221–228, by permission of AFIPS.

M. V. Wilkes and J. B. Stringer: "Microprogramming and the Design of the Control Circuits in an Electronic Digital Computer," *Proceedings of the Cambridge Philosophical Society*, part 2, vol. 49, April 1953, pp. 230–238, by permission of the publisher, Cambridge University Press.

H. Weber: "A Microprogrammed Implementation of EULER on IBM System/360 Model 30," *Communications of the ACM*, September 1967, vol. 10, no. 9, pp. 551–556, copyright 1967, Association for Computing Machinery, Inc., reprinted by permission, and by permission of the author.

Many of the chapters in this book first appeared in print elsewhere. The following are the acknowledgments that accompanied these chapters when they were originally published.

Chapter 16: Recognition for the stack concepts and operating philosophy of Burroughs' B6500/B7500 system must be extended to many system designers engaged in both the B5500 and B6500/B7500 programs. Among the contributors, special mention should be made for B. A. Creech, Burroughs Corporation, and R. S. Barton, W. M. McKeeman, consultants.

Chapter 17: In addition to indebtedness to the original designers within International Computers Limited, thanks should also be given to International Computers (Australia) Pty. Ltd. for its invaluable assistance in the prepartion of "An Outline of the ICL 2900 Series System Architecture."

Chapter 18: The authors wish to thank Mr. R. J. Litwiller for his interest, suggestions and design effort, and Messrs. J. G. Adler, R. N. Gustafson, P. N. Prentice, and C. Zeitler for their contributions to the design of the instructions units.

Chapter 19: The author wishes to acknowledge the contributions of Messrs. D. W. Anderson and D. M. Powers, who extended the original concept, and Mr. W. D. Silkman, who implemented all of the central control logic discussed in the paper.

Chapter 22: This research was sponsored by the Defense Advanced Research Projects Agency (DOD), ARPA Order No. 3597, monitored by the Air Force Avionics Laboratory under Contract F33615-78-C-1551.
Many people have contributed to the project, and special mention must go to Bill Wulf, Sam Fuller, Roy Levin, Fred Pollack, Bill Corwin, David Jefferson, Ellis Cohen and Chuck Pierson, the original design group; Bill Broadley for designing the hardware, which was built and maintained by Jim Teter, David Babcock, and the CMU Computer Science Department Engineering Lab.; other workers on Hydra: Guy Almes, Rick Gumpertz, Sam Harbison, Tom Lane, Joe Newcomer, Pete Schwarz, Mary Thompson; for providing the measurements and most of the figures: Pete Oleinick, Pat McGehearty, Madhav Marathe, and Navindra Jain.

Chapter 23: Much of the initial development of the Pluribus computer was supported by the Information Processing Techniques Office of the U.S. Defense Advanced Research Projects Agency, under Contract Numbers DAHC15-69-C-0179, F08606-73-C0027, and F08606-75-C-0032, and by the Defense Communications Agency under Contract DCA200-C-616. Additionally, a number of the applications systems were developed under contracts from various branches of the U.S. Government. Many people have contributed to the Pluribus project; Frank Heart has led the effort since its inception.

Chapter 24: The ARPA Network has in large measure been the conception of one man, Dr. L. G. Roberts of the Advanced Research Projects Agency; we gratefully acknowledge his guidance and encouragement. Researchers at many other institutions deserve credit for early interactions with ARPA concerning basic network design; in particular we would like to acknowledge the insight about IMPs provided by W. A. Clark.
At BBN, many persons contributed to the IMP project. We

acknowledge the contributions of H. K. Rising, who participated in the subnet design and acted as associate project manager during various phases of the project; B. P. Cosell, who participated significantly in the software implementation; W. B. Barker and M. J. Thrope, who participated significantly in the hardware implementation; and T. Thatch, J. H. Geisman, and R. C. Satterfield, who assisted with various implementation aspects of the project. We also acknowledge the helpful encouragement of J. I. Elkind and D. G. Bobrow.

Finally, we wish to acknowledge the hardware implementation contribution of the Computer Control Division of Honeywell, where many individuals worked cooperatively with us despite the sometimes abrasive pressures of a difficult schedule.

This work was sponsored by the Advanced Research Projects Agency under Contract No. DAHC 15-69-C-0179.

Chapter 25: Supported by the Advanced Research Projects Agency of the Department of Defense and monitored by NASA Ames Research Center under Contract No. NAS2-8590.

Chapter 26: Our colleagues at the Xerox Palo Alto Research Center, especially Tat C. Lam, Butler W. Lampson, John F. Shoch, and Charles P. Thacker, have contributed in many ways to the evolution of Ethernet ideas and to the construction of the experimental system without which such ideas would be just so much speculation.

Chapter 27: The research and development of the STAR computer has been performed in the Spacecraft Computers Section of the JPL Astrionics Division, and recognition is due to most of the Section's members for support in their respective specialties. The STAR concept of computer architecture is due to A. Aviẑienis, who has directed the overall research effort. The hardware design is directed by D. A. Rennels, the software effort by J. A. Rohr, reliability analysis by F. P. Mathur, and the implementation of peripheral automatic maintenance by G. C. Gilley. Technical contributions to the design have been made by P. H. Sobel and A. D. Weeks, and consultation has been contributed by R. K. Caplette, E. Greenberg, G. R. Hansen, E. H. Imlay, G. R. Kunstmann, J. Nievergelt, J. J. Wedel, and L. J. Zottarelli. The STAR effort has been administered by J. R. Scull, W. F. Scott, and J. J. Wedel. The power switch has been developed by the Stanford Research Institute, Menlo Park, CA., and a fault-tolerant READ-ONLY memory has been designed by the M.I.T. Instrumentation Laboratory, Cambridge, MA, under subcontracts from JPL. Construction of the computer was performed by J. Buchok, J. L. Cline, N. B. Funsten, J. C. Schooler, and B. Stall. The design of the TOPS Control Computer is due to D. K. Rubin, with technical contributions by N. Deo, G. Milligan, and M. Vineberg. A special acknowledgment is due to R. V. Powell of the JPL Research and Advanced Development Program Office, and F. J.

Sullivan, Director, Electronics and Control, J. L. East, J. I. Kanter, T. S. Michaels, and G. A. Vacca of the NASA Office of Advanced Research and Technology, Washington, DC, for their continued support and encouragement of the STAR computer effort.

Chapter 28: The author would like to acknowledge the kind assistance of Pat Loprete, Jr.

Chapter 29, An operating system is the work of many people. In particular I would like to acknowledge the contributions of Dennis McEvoy, Dave Hinders, Jerry Held, and Robert Shaw in its design, implementation, and testing.

Chapter 30: In addition to the authors of this paper, many others contributed to some aspect of the SYMBOL project. Critical to the completion of the system was the team spirit and devotion displayed throughout the project by all members of the staff. The authors wish to acknowledge George Powers, Stanley Mazor, and Rusel Briggs for their contributions to the hardware development and Hamilton Richards and Mrs. Hilma Mortell for their contributions to the early software development.

The authors wish to express their thanks to the Fairchild Camera and Instrument Corporation for the opportunity to do this research.

Special thanks are due to Professor Robert Stewart, Professor Arthur Pohm and Professor Roy Zingg of Iowa State University for their constructive help and support. We are most grateful to the National Science Foundation for the grant which made it possible for the SYMBOL IIR system to be delivered to Iowa State University for evaluation and continuing research on this technology.

Finally, we are deeply indebted to the past and present members of this Digital Systems Research Department at Fairchild. Their hard work and enthusiasm made this research project result in a real and operating system.

Chapter 33: The concept and structure of the Alto are due primarily to Chuck Thacker, Ed McCreight, Butler Lampson, and Alay Kay. The hardware described in this paper was designed by the authors together with Roger Bates, Tat Lam, Bob Metcalfe, and Severo Ornstein. The working environment, network, software, and microcode that grew on the Alto are due to hard work and fine craftsmanship contributed by many members of the Computer Science laboratory and System Science Laboratory of the Xerox Palo Alto Research Center.

Chapter 37: Many people played significant roles in the development of these processors and it is not possible to single out a few to take all the credit. However, if forced to choose those people who played the most significant roles on each, the following names stand out: M. E. (Ted) Hoff was the architect and Federico Faggin the chip designer of the 4004. Stanley Mazor contributed to the 4004 architecture as well as to the architectures of the 8008 and 8080. Hoff, along with Hal Feeney, were the major contributors to the 8008 development. Faggin managed the development of the 8080 and participated in defining the architecture, with Masatoshi Shima doing the logic and circuit design. Roger Swanson defined the new instructions for the 8085 while Peter Stoll and Andrew Volk performed the 8085 logic and circuit design. The 8086 architecture was defined by Stephen Morse and refined by Bruce Ravenel, with James McKevitt and John Bayliss responsible for the logic and circuit design. William Pohlman managed both the 8085 and 8086 activities.

The authors would like to thank Stephen Hanna for reviewing this material and for his many suggestions and comments.

Chapter 38: The authors are grateful to Mr. Nigberg of the technical publication department at DEC and to the reviewers for their helpful criticism. We are especially grateful to Mrs. Dorothy Josephson at Carnegie-Mellon University for typing the notation-laden manuscript.

Chapter 39: This research was supported in part by the National Science Foundation under grant GJ-32758X and by an IBM Fellowship. Engineering documentation was supplied by Digital Equipment Corporation.

Chapter 42: Although the final architecture is the result of several design iterations involving many hardware and software engineers, the author would like to acknowledge the other members of the initial architectural group: Gordon Bell, Peter Conklin, Dave Cutler, Bill Demmer, Tom Hastings, Richy Lary, Dave Rodgers and Steve Rothman. Mary Janes Forbes and Louise Principe deserve special thanks for typing this manuscript.

Chapter 44: Acknowledgments are due to my colleagues at Cray Research, G. Grenander, R. Hendrickson, M. Huber, C. Jewett, P. Johnson, A. LaBounty, and J. Robidoux, without whose contributions this paper could not have been written.

Chapter 45: Although it would not be possible to acknowledge all of the contributors to the ASC program, particular recognition should be given to Messrs. H. G. Cragon, W. D. Kastner, E. H. Husband, D. R. Best, C. M. Stephenson, C. R. Hall, F. A. Galindo, and E. C. Garth, all of whom contributed immeasurably to the architecture of the ASC system. Many other members of the Texas Instruments Equipment Group staff have also made significant contributions in the development of the ASC system.

Index